A TOPICAL GUIDE TO THE SCRIPTURES OF THE CHURCH OF JESUS CHRIST OF LATTER-DAY SAINTS

A TOPICAL GUIDE TO THE SCRIPTURES OF THE CHURCH OF JESUS CHRIST OF LATTER-DAY SAINTS

Deseret Book Company   Salt Lake City, Utah   1977

FOREWORD

The Church of Jesus Christ of Latter-day Saints accepts as sacred scripture four standard works—the Bible, the Book of Mormon, the Doctrine and Covenants, and the Pearl of Great Price. These four sacred works of scripture are encompassed in a fundamental teaching of the Church that states: "We believe all that God has revealed, all that He does now reveal, and we believe that He will yet reveal many great and important things pertaining to the Kingdom of God." (Pearl of Great Price, Article of Faith 9.)

Over the years members of the Church have used various editions of the Bible. Naturally, these have not contained cross references or notes pertaining to material found in the other three standard works. To help readers understand the Bible, the leaders of the Church determined to undertake a project to provide an edition of the Bible with cross references and other scriptural study aids for the Latter-day Saints.

The major study aids included in the project are cross references to all four standard works, excerpts from Joseph Smith's new translation, notes and translation variants on difficult passages, a topical guide to scriptural passages on hundreds of major gospel themes, a revised Bible dictionary, a glossary of archaic and unusual words, a brief concordance, and some maps.

The preparation of these aids has been carried on in all these areas for several years by Latter-day Saint scholars at Brigham Young University. The work has been greatly enhanced and facilitated by modern computer processing of the data.

As the work progressed, it was determined that one of the most useful parts would be the topical guide to scriptural passages on major gospel themes. It was deemed wise to publish this part of the project as a separate publication so that it could be used, tested, and refined before ultimately being placed as a study aid in the new edition of the Bible. This volume represents the first publishing of the topical guide. Listed herein are some 640 gospel subjects with extensive references cited from all four standard works. In many cases, scriptures are cited that have indirect as well as direct relevance to a topic. Each user will need to be selective as he chooses passages having significance for his needs.

The scriptural references to each topic cite one or more verses. A short quoted excerpt from a key verse bearing the concept is provided, and a key word is indicated in **bold-face** type.

The topics are arranged alphabetically by major headings to facilitate use of the work, but a separate index is also provided at the front of the book to help users find information on any subject even though they may not be familiar with the topics available. In many cases, several related topics are suggested under a particular index listing to facilitate scriptural study of other aspects of the subject. Space limitations preclude listing all passages that might have been included. It is hoped, however, that sufficient coverage is provided to satisfy many needs, and to lead the careful student to additional research through the use of complete concordances. The key words in **bold-face** type will provide a starting point for the reader to make use of such concordances in his study.

The Publisher
September 1977

TO THE READER

This publication includes, under one cover, the most extensive Latter-day Saint listing of gospel subjects with scriptural references yet published. It is divided into two sections:

1. An index of 60 pages at the beginning of the document. The topics in the index are listed alphabetically. The numbers following each topic shown in the index refer to the page of the *Topical Guide* where the topic can be found. *See* and *See also* references in the index refer to other titles within the index.

2. A *Topical Guide* of 640 topics on 500 pages. The titles of these topics are listed alphabetically also.

As indicated in the Foreword, the index and the *Topical Guide,* together with other study aids, will eventually be published in the Bible.

Users of this *Topical Guide* are invited to assist in the process of refining and improving this material before it is bound in the Bible. You are invited to send your comments, suggestions, corrections, or additions to:

Bible Aids Project
c/o Correlation Department
50 East North Temple
Salt Lake City, Utah 84150

KEY TO ABBREVIATIONS AND CHANGES OF TITLES IN THE PEARL OF GREAT PRICE

OLD	(Abbreviation)	NEW	(Abbreviation)
The Book of Moses	Moses	Selections from the Book of Moses	Moses
The Book of Abraham	Abraham	The Book of Abraham	Abraham
Writings of Joseph Smith An extract from a translation of the Bible	JS1	Joseph Smith—Matthew Joseph Smith's Translation of Matt. 23:39; 24	JS-M
Writings of Joseph Smith Extracts from the History of Joseph Smith, the Prophet	JS2	Joseph Smith—History Extracts from the History of Joseph Smith, the Prophet	JS-H
		Joseph Smith—Vision of the Celestial Kingdom	JS-V
		Joseph F. Smith—Vision of the Redemption of the Dead	JFS-V
The Articles of Faith of The Church of Jesus Christ of Latter-day Saints	AofF	The Articles of Faith of The Church of Jesus Christ of Latter-day Saints	AofF

INDEX

A TOPICAL
GUIDE
TO THE
SCRIPTURES OF
THE CHURCH
OF JESUS CHRIST
OF LATTER-DAY
SAINTS

ABOMINATION OF DESOLATION

Dan. 9:27	overspreading of **abominations** he shall make it
Dan. 11:31	they shall place the **abomination** that maketh desolate.
Dan. 12:11	the **abomination** that maketh desolate set up, there
Matt. 24:15	see the **abomination** of desolation, spoken of by Daniel
Luke 21:20(20-22)	Jerusalem compassed...the **desolation** thereof is nigh.
D&C 84:117	the desolation of **abomination** in the last days.
D&C 88:85	the desolation of **abomination** which awaits the wicked
JS-M 1:12(4-32)	the abomination of **desolation**, spoken of by Daniel the

ABRAHAMIC COVENANT

Gen. 12:3(1-3)	in thee shall all **families** of the earth be blessed.
Gen. 15:18	in the same day the Lord made a **covenant** with Abram
Gen. 17:2(1-9)	I will make my **covenant** between me and thee, and will
Gen. 17:21(2,21)	but my **covenant** will I establish with Isaac, which
Gen. 18:18(17-19)	all the **nations** of the earth shall be blessed in him
Gen. 21:12	in Isaac shall thy **seed** be called.
Gen. 22:17(15-18)	I will bless thee...I will multiply thy **seed** as the
Gen. 26:4(2-5)	in thy seed shall all the **nations** of the earth be
Gen. 27:29	and **blessed** be he that blesseth thee.
Gen. 28:14(10-15)	in thy seed shall all the **families** of the earth be
Ex. 19:5	if ye will obey my voice indeed, and keep my **covenant**
Deut. 14:2	holy people...**peculiar** people...above all the nations
Judg. 2:1(1-3)	and I said, I will never break my **covenant** with you.
Isa. 49:6	I will also give thee for a **light** to the Gentiles
Isa. 50:1	where is the bill of your mother's **divorcement**, whom
Isa. 54:5	for thy maker is thine **husband**; the Lord of hosts is
Jer. 3:14	for I am **married** unto you: and I will take you one
Jer. 31:31(31-34)	I will make a new **covenant** with the house of Israel
Hosea 2:19(19-20)	and I will **betroth** thee unto me for ever; yea, I will
Luke 3:8(6-11)	begin not to say...we have **Abraham** to our father: for
John 8:33(31-47)	we be **Abraham's** seed, and were never in bondage to any
John 8:39(32-39)	if ye were **Abraham's** children, ye would do the works
Acts 3:25	ye are...children of the prophets, and of the **covenant**
Rom. 9:4(1-9)	Israelites; to whom pertaineth the adoption..**covenants**
Rom. 11:27(26-28)	for this is my **covenant** unto them, when I shall take
Gal. 3:7(1-29)	they which are of faith...are the **children** of Abraham.
Heb. 6:14(13,14)	saying, surely blessing I will **bless** thee, and
Heb. 11:18(17-18)	it was said, that in Isaac shall thy **seed** be called
1 Ne. 15:14(12-20)	they are the **covenant** people of the Lord; and then
1 Ne. 17:40	he **covenanted** with them, yea, even Abraham, Isaac, and
1 Ne. 19:15(14-17)	then will he remember the **covenants** which he made to
1 Ne. 22:9(3-25)	in thy **seed** shall all the kindreds of the earth be
2 Ne. 6:12(6-12)	Lord God will fulfil his **covenants** which he has made
2 Ne. 9:1(1-2)	the **covenants** of the Lord that he has covenanted with
2 Ne. 10:7(7-15)	**covenanted** with their fathers...they shall be restored
2 Ne. 11:5	my soul delighteth in the **covenants** of the Lord which
2 Ne. 29:1	that I may remember my **covenants** which I have made
2 Ne. 29:14	I am God, and that I **covenanted** with Abraham that I
3 Ne. 20:25(25-29)	ye are of the **covenant** which the father made with your
3 Ne. 21:4(1-29)	that the **covenant** of the father may be fulfilled which
Morm. 5:20(14-21)	the Lord remember the **covenant** which he made unto

1

ABRAHAMIC COVENANT cont.

Morm. 5:20	the **covenant** which he made unto Abraham and unto all
Ether 13:11(1-13)	**covenant** which God made with their father, Abraham.
D&C 52:2(1,2)	those who are heirs according to the **covenant**.
D&C 84:34(33-34)	they become...the seed of **Abraham**, and the church and
D&C 84:99	brought to pass by the faith and **covenant** of their
D&C 86:9(8-11)	for ye are lawful **heirs**, according to the flesh, and
D&C 103:17	ye are...of the **seed** of Abraham, and ye must needs be
D&C 110:12	Elias...committed the dispensation...of **Abraham**
D&C 124:58	I said unto **Abraham**...in thee and in thy seed shall
D&C 132:30(29-33)	**Abraham** received promises concerning his seed, and of
Abr. 1:19(18,19)	through thy **ministry** my name shall be known in the
Abr. 2:9(6-11)	thy seed...shall bear this **ministry** and priesthood

ABSTINENCE

Prov. 1:15(10-16)	walk not...with them; **refrain** thy foot from their path
Jer. 14:10	loved...**refrained** their feet, therefore the Lord doth
Acts 15:20	that they **abstain** from pollutions of idols, and from
1 Cor. 8:13(7-13)	if meat make my brother to offend, I will **eat** no flesh
1 Thes. 4:3	that ye should **abstain** from fornication
1 Thes. 5:6(6-8)	but let us watch and be **sober**.
1 Thes. 5:22	**abstain** from all appearance of evil.
1 Tim. 4:3	commanding to **abstain** from meats, which God...created
James 4:7	**resist** the devil, and he will flee from you.
1 Pet. 2:11	I beseech you...**abstain** from fleshly lusts, which war
Alma 38:12(10-12)	see that ye **refrain** from idleness.
Alma 39:12(11-14)	in the fear of God...**refrain** from your iniquities
D&C 49:18	whoso forbiddeth to **abstain** from meats...is not ordain
D&C 59:9	more fully keep thyself **unspotted** from the world, thou
D&C 82:2(2,3)	beware...and **refrain** from sin, lest sore judgments
D&C 88:124(121-124)	**cease** to be idle; cease to be unclean; cease to find
D&C 89:5(1-21)	**drinketh** wine or strong drink...not good, neither
D&C 136:21	**keep** yourselves from evil to take the name of the Lord

ABUNDANT LIFE

2 Chr. 20:20	believe his prophets, so shall ye **prosper**.
Ps. 1:2(1-6)	but his **delight** is in the law of the Lord; and in his
Ps. 19:7(7-11)	the **law** of the Lord is perfect, converting the soul
Ps. 112:3(1-10)	**riches** shall be in his house: and his righteousness
Ps. 144:15	**happy** is that people, that is in such a case: yea
Prov. 3:10(1-10)	so shall thy barns be filled with **plenty**, and thy
Isa. 1:19(16-20)	be willing and obedient...eat the **good** of the land
Isa. 58:11(8-14)	thou shalt be like a...**spring**...whose waters fail not.
Matt. 6:33	all these things shall be **added** unto you.
Matt. 16:25(24-26)	whosoever will lose his life for my sake shall **find**
John 10:10	they might have life, and...have it more **abundantly**.
Gal. 5:13(13-23)	brethren, ye have been called unto **liberty**; only use
Gal. 6:9(7-10)	not be weary in well doing: for...we shall **reap**, if
Titus 2:12(1-12)	we should live soberly, **righteously**, and godly, in
1 Pet. 3:12(1-12)	the **eyes** of the Lord are over the righteous, and his

2 Pet. 1:8(5-10)	if these things be in you, and **abound**..neither be
2 Ne. 4:35(15-35)	I know that God will give **liberally** to him that asketh
Jacob 2:18(17-19)	but before ye seek for riches, **seek** ye for the kingdom
Alma 37:37(35-37)	counsel with the Lord...he will direct thee for **good**
Hel. 13:38(31-39)	ye have sought for **happiness** in doing iniquity, which
D&C 58:28(26-29)	as men do good they shall in nowise lose their **reward**.
D&C 59:16(16-21)	as ye do this, the **fulness** of the earth is yours, the
D&C 64:34(33-35)	willing and obedient shall eat the **good** of the land
D&C 88:32	to enjoy that which they are **willing** to receive
D&C 93:27(26-28)	no man receiveth a **fulness** unless he keepeth his
D&C 121:46(41-46)	the Holy Ghost shall be thy constant **companion**, and

ACCOUNTABILITY

Ex. 20:5(4-6)	the third and fourth generation of them that **hate** me
Ex. 28:38	that Aaron may **bear** the iniquity of the holy things
Ex. 32:33(31-35)	whosoever hath **sinned** against me, him will I blot out
Ex. 34:7(1-10)	visiting the **iniquity** of the fathers upon the children
Lev. 4:2	if a soul shall sin through **ignorance** against any of
Lev. 5:17(1-17)	if a soul...commit any of these things...**bear** his
Lev. 10:17	God hath given it you to **bear** the iniquity of the
Lev. 20:9	his **blood** shall be upon him.
Num. 15:30(30-31)	soul that doeth ought **presumptuously**...shall be cut
Num. 35:33	**cleansed**...blood...by...blood of him that shed it.
Deut. 5:9(9,10)	the third and fourth generation of them that **hate** me
Deut. 24:16	every man shall be put to death for his **own** sin.
Josh. 7:19(16-26)	**tell** me now what thou hast done; hide it not from me.
2 Kgs. 14:6(1-6)	but every man shall be put to death for his **own** sin.
2 Chr. 25:4	every man shall die for his own **sin**.
Isa. 53:11	he shall **bear** their iniquities.
Jer. 31:30	every one shall die for his own **iniquity**: every man
Ezek. 3:18(17-21)	shall die...but his blood will I **require** at thine hand
Ezek. 18:20(1-32)	the son shall not **bear** the iniqity of the father
Ezek. 33:4	his blood shall be upon his **own** head.
Ezek. 33:6(6,8)	but his blood will I **require** at the watchman's hand.
Amos 3:2	therefore I will **punish** you for all your iniquities.
Matt. 7:1(1-2)	judge not, that ye be not **judged**.
Matt. 12:36(36-37)	every idle word...they shall give **account** thereof in
Matt. 18:23	which would take **account** of his servants.
Luke 12:47(47-48)	knew his Lord's will, and **prepared** not himself
Luke 12:48(47,48)	much is given, of him shall be much **required**: and to
Luke 16:2(1-2)	give an **account** of thy stewardship; for thou mayest
John 9:41	now ye say, we **see**; therefore your sin remaineth.
Rom. 2:6(5-11)	who will render to every man **according** to his deeds
Rom. 2:12(12-14)	as many as have sinned without **law** shall also perish
2 Cor. 5:10	**according** to that he hath done, whether it be good or
2 Cor. 9:6	he which **soweth** bountifully shall reap also
Gal. 6:7(7-9)	whatsoever a man **soweth**, that shall he also reap.
1 Pet. 2:24	who his own self **bare** our sins in his own body on the
Jude 1:15(14,15)	to execute **judgment** upon all, and to convince all that
Rev. 20:12	dead were **judged** out of those things which were
2 Ne. 9:25(25-27)	where there is no **law** given there is no punishment

ACCOUNTABILITY cont.

Jacob 1:19	answering the **sins** of the people upon our own heads
Mosiah 2:33	dieth in his **sins**, the same drinketh damnation to his
Mosiah 3:11(11-12)	died not knowing the will of God...**ignorantly** sinned.
Mosiah 3:21(20-27)	none shall be found **blameless**...except...children
Mosiah 15:24(24-26)	died before Christ came, in their **ignorance**, not
Mosiah 26:29(29-30)	whosoever transgresseth...judge **according** to the sins
Alma 12:14	our words...works...thoughts will also **condemn** us; and
Alma 29:5	he that knoweth not good from evil is **blameless**; but
Alma 41:3(2-8)	men should be **judged** according to their works; and
Moro. 8:10(7-23)	teach- repentance and baptism unto those...**accountable**
Moro. 8:22(8-23)	redemption cometh on all them that have **no law**
D&C 10:23(20-23)	but I will **require** this at their hands, and it shall
D&C 20:71	**accountability** before God,and is capable of repentance
D&C 29:47(47-50)	they cannot sin...until they...become **accountable**
D&C 42:32	every man shall be made **accountable** unto me, a steward
D&C 45:54	they that knew no **law** shall have part in the first
D&C 76:72	behold, these are they who died without **law**
D&C 82:3	of him unto whom **much** is given much is required; and
D&C 98:46(39-48)	children's **children** of all them that hate me, unto the
D&C 101:78(77-80)	every man may be **accountable** for his own sins in the
D&C 104:13	the Lord, should make every man **accountable**, as a
D&C 124:50	iniquity...upon the **heads** of those who hindered my
D&C 134:1	he holds men **accountable** for their acts in relation
A of F 1:2	believe that men will be punished for their own **sins**

ADAM

Gen. 1:26(26-28)	and God said, let us make **man** in our image, after our
Gen. 2:7(7-9,15)	and **man** became a living soul.
Gen. 5:2(1-3)	called their name **Adam**, in the day when they were
Gen. 5:4(4-32)	days of **Adam** after he had begotten Seth were eight
1 Chr. 1:1(1-4)	**Adam**, Sheth, Enosh
Dan. 7:9(9-14)	and the **Ancient** of days did sit, whose garment was
Dan. 10:13(13,21)	but, lo, **Michael**, one of the chief princes, came to
Dan. 12:1	**Michael**...the great prince which standeth for the
Luke 3:38(36-38)	**Adam**, which was the son of God.
1 Cor. 15:22(21-22)	for as in **Adam** all die, even so in Christ shall all
1 Cor. 15:45(45-48)	the first man **Adam** was made a living soul; the last
1 Thes. 4:16	with the voice of the **archangel**, and with the trump
Jude 1:9	**Michael** the archangel, when contending with the devil
Rev. 12:7	**Michael** and his angels fought against the dragon; and
1 Ne. 5:11	creation of the world, and also of **Adam** and Eve, who
2 Ne. 2:20(20,23)	brought forth children...**family** of all the earth.
2 Ne. 2:25(18-25)	**Adam** fell that men might be; and men are, that they
2 Ne. 9:21(20,21)	pains of all...who belong to the family of **Adam**.
D&C 27:11	and also with Michael, or **Adam**, the father of all, the
D&C 29:26	**Michael**, mine archangel, shall sound his trump, and
D&C 78:16	who hath appointed **Michael** your prince, and
D&C 84:16	by the hand of his father **Adam**, who was the first
D&C 88:112(111-115)	and **Michael**, the seventh angel, even the archangel
D&C 107:54(41-56)	**Adam**, and called him Michael, the **prince**, the
D&C 116:1	**Adam-ondi-Ahman**...where **Adam** shall...visit his people

ADAM cont.

D&C 117:8	the mountains of Adam-ondi-Ahman...where **Adam** dwelt
D&C 128:21	angels, from Michael or **Adam** down to the present time
Moses 1:34	first man of all men have I called **Adam**, which is many
Moses 3:7	**man** became a living soul, the first flesh upon the ear
Moses 3:23(21-25)	and **Adam** said: this I know now is bone of my bones
Moses 5:59(57-59)	and thus all things were confirmed unto **Adam**, by an
Moses 6:45	and even the first of all we know, even **Adam**.
Moses 6:65(58-68)	he was **baptized**, and the spirit of God descended upon
Abr. 1:3	first man, who is **Adam**, our first father, through the
Abr. 5:20(20-21)	**Adam** called every living creature, that should be the
JS-V 1:5(1-10)	I saw father **Adam** and Abraham; and my father and my
JFS-V 1:38	father **Adam**, the Ancient of Days and father of all

ADMINISTRATIONS TO THE SICK

1 Kgs. 17:21(17-23)	**stretched** himself upon the child three times, and
2 Kgs. 4:34(31-34)	and his **hands** upon his hands: and he stretched himself
2 Kgs. 5:14(10-14)	dipped himself seven times...he was **clean**.
Matt. 9:18(18-19,23-26)	come and lay thy **hand** upon her, and she shall live.
Mark 5:23(22-23,41-42)	come and lay thy **hands** on her, that she may be healed
Mark 6:5(4-6)	he laid his **hands** upon a few sick folk, and healed the
Mark 6:13(12-13)	**anointed** with oil many that were sick, and healed them
Mark 7:32(31-37)	they beseech him to put his **hand** upon him.
Mark 8:23(22-26)	put his **hands** upon him, he asked him if he saw ought.
Mark 16:18(17-18)	they shall lay **hands** on the sick, and they shall
Luke 4:40(38-41)	laid his **hands** on every one of them, and healed them.
Luke 13:13(10-13)	he laid his **hands** on her: and immediately she was made
Acts 9:17(11-18)	Ananias...putting his **hands** on him said, brother Saul
Acts 28:8(7-9)	laid his **hands** on him, and healed him.
James 5:14(14-16)	elders of the church ...pray...**anointing** him with oil
Mosiah 27:23(22-24)	fasted and prayed...Alma received their **strength**, and
Alma 15:8(3-11)	believest...redemption of Christ thou canst be **healed**.
3 Ne. 17:7	afflicted...I will **heal** them, for I have compassion
3 Ne. 17:9(8-10)	he did **heal** them every one as they were brought forth
3 Ne. 26:15	**healed** all their sick, and their lame, and opened the
D&C 24:14(13-14)	not do, except...required...by them who **desire** it
D&C 42:44(43-44,48)	elders...shall pray for and lay their **hands** upon them
D&C 66:9(8-9)	lay your **hands** upon the sick, and they shall recover.

ADULTERY

Gen. 39:9(7-10)	do this great **wickedness**, and sin against God
Ex. 20:14	thou shalt not commit **adultery**.
Lev. 20:10(10-17)	**adulterer** and...adulteress shall...be put to death.
Deut. 5:18	neither shalt thou commit **adultery**.
Deut. 22:22(21-29)	if a man be found lying with a woman **married** to an
Prov. 2:16(16-19)	to deliver thee from the **strange** woman, even from the
Prov. 6:24(24-26)	to keep thee from the **evil** woman, from the flattery
Prov. 6:32(24-32)	whoso committeth **adultery** with a woman lacketh
Jer. 3:8(8-9)	Israel committed **adultery** I had put her away, and
Jer. 5:7(7-9)	fed them to the full, they then committed **adultery**

ADULTERY cont.

Jer. 23:14	they commit **adultery**, and walk in lies: they
Jer. 29:23(22-23)	have committed **adultery** with their neighbours' wives
Ezek. 23:37	they have committed **adultery**, and blood is in their
Hosea 3:1	woman beloved of her friend, yet an **adulteress**
Hosea 4:13(12-14)	and your spouses shall commit **adultery**.
Mal. 3:5	I will be a swift witness...against the **adulterers**
Matt. 5:28(27-32)	looketh on a woman to lust...committed **adultery** with
Matt. 15:19	evil thoughts, murders, **adulteries**, fornications
Matt. 16:4	a wicked and **adulterous** generation seeketh after a
Matt. 19:18(16-22)	thou shalt not commit **adultery**, thou shalt not steal
Mark 7:21(20-23)	evil thoughts, **adulteries**, fornications, murders
John 8:3(3-11)	Pharisees brought unto him a woman taken in **adultery**
Rom. 2:22	thou that sayest a man should not commit **adultery**
Rom. 13:9	thou shalt not commit **adultery**, thou shalt not kill
1 Cor. 6:9(9-11)	unrighteous...fornicators...idolaters...**adulterers**...
Heb. 13:4	but whoremongers and **adulterers** God will judge.
James 2:11	he that said, do not commit **adultery**, said also, do
Rev. 2:22(21-23)	them that commit **adultery** with her into great
Rev. 21:8	**whoremongers**...shall have their part in the lake which
Rev. 22:15	for without are...**whoremongers**, and murderers, and
Mosiah 13:22	thou shalt not commit **adultery**. thou shalt not steal.
Alma 16:18	did preach against...committing **adultery**, and all
Alma 23:3	they ought not to murder...nor to commit **adultery**, nor
Alma 30:10(9-11)	if he committed **adultery** he was also punished; yea
Alma 39:5(3-5)	most **abominable**...save it be the shedding of innocent
3 Ne. 12:28(27-28)	looketh on a woman, to lust...hath committed **adultery**
3 Ne. 12:32(31-32)	marry her who is divorced committeth **adultery**.
3 Ne. 30:2	turn, all ye Gentiles, from your...**whoredoms**, and of
D&C 42:24(22-26)	he that committeth **adultery**, and repenteth not, shall
D&C 42:75(74-77)	have left their companions for the sake of **adultery**
D&C 42:80(80-83)	if any...commit **adultery**, he or she shall be tried
D&C 59:6	not...commit **adultery**...nor do anything like unto it.
D&C 63:16(16-18)	commit **adultery** in their hearts, they shall not have
D&C 66:10	commit not **adultery**- a temptation with which thou hast
D&C 76:103	these are they who are...**adulterers**, and whoremongers
D&C 132:39	in none...did he **sin**...save in the case of Uriah and
D&C 132:41(41-44)	she hath committed **adultery** and shall be destroyed.
D&C 132:61(61-63)	he cannot commit **adultery** with that that belongeth

ADVERSITY

1 Sam. 10:19	God, who himself saved you out of all your **adversities**
2 Chr. 15:4	they in their **trouble** did turn unto the Lord God of
Job 5:7(6-7)	man is born unto **trouble**, as the sparks fly upward.
Job 13:15	though he **slay** me, yet will I trust in him: but I will
Ps. 35:15	in mine **adversity** they rejoiced, and gathered
Ps. 59:16	my defense and refuge in the day of my **trouble**.
Ps. 107:6(1-9)	they cried unto the Lord in their **trouble**, and he
Eccl. 7:14	in the day of **adversity** consider: God also hath set
Isa. 30:20(20,21)	the Lord give you the bread of **adversity**, and the
Hosea 5:15	in their **affliction** they will seek me early.
Matt. 7:25(24-27)	floods came...winds blew, and **beat** upon that house

ADVERSITY cont.

Acts 14:22(21-22)   we must through much **tribulation** enter into the
Rom. 8:18(18,28,35)   **sufferings** of this...time are not worthy to be
Rom. 12:12(9-12)   patient in **tribulation**; continuing instant in prayer
2 Cor. 4:8(8-14)   we are **troubled**...yet not distressed; we are perplexed
2 Cor. 12:10(7-10)   therefore I take pleasure in **infirmities**, in
2 Ne. 2:11(11-13)   needs be, that there is an **opposition** in all things.
Mosiah 24:14(13-16)   Lord God, do visit my people in their **afflictions**.
Alma 7:11(9-12)   he shall go forth, suffering pains and **afflictions** and
Alma 14:11(10-11)   he doth **suffer** that they may do this thing, or that
Alma 32:6(6,13-16)   their **afflictions** had truly humbled them and that they
Alma 62:41   many were softened because of their **afflictions**
Alma 62:50(48-51)   from prisons, and from all manner of **afflictions** and
D&C 50:5   blessed are they who are faithful and **endure**, whether
D&C 58:2   he that is faithful in **tribulation**, the reward of the
D&C 88:6   he **descended** below all things, in that he comprehended
D&C 121:7(7-8)   thine **adversity** and thine afflictions shall be but a
D&C 122:7(4-8)   all these things shall give thee **experience**, and shall
D&C 136:31(30-31)   my people must be **tried** in all things, that they may
JS-H 1:25(23-25)   though I was hated and **persecuted** for saying that I

AFFLICTION

Ex. 3:7(7-10)   I have surely seen the **affliction** of my people which
2 Chr. 20:9(5-9)   cry unto thee in our **affliction**, then thou wilt hear
2 Chr. 33:12(11-13)   when he was in **affliction**, he besought the Lord his
Neh. 9:9(7-10)   didst see the **affliction** of our fathers in Egypt, and
Ps. 34:19   many are the **afflictions** of the righteous: but the Lord
Ps. 88:9(1-18)   mine eye mourneth by reason of **affliction**: Lord, I
Ps. 119:50   this is my comfort in my **affliction**: for thy word hath
Isa. 48:10(9-11)   I have chosen thee in the furnace of **affliction**.
Isa. 53:7   and he was **afflicted**, yet he opened not his mouth: he
Isa. 63:9(8-9)   in all their **affliction** he was afflicted, and the
Hosea 5:15   in their **affliction** they will seek me early.
Jonah 2:2   I cried by reason of mine **affliction** unto the Lord
Matt. 5:10(10-12)   blessed are they which are **persecuted** for
Mark 4:17(16,17)   when **affliction** or persecution ariseth for the word's
Mark 13:19(14-20)   in those days shall be **affliction**, such as was not
John 16:33   ye shall have **tribulation**: but be of good cheer; I
Acts 7:10(9-10)   delivered him out of all his **afflictions**, and gave him
2 Cor. 8:2   that in a great trial of **affliction** the abundance of
1 Thes. 1:6   having received the word in much **affliction**, with joy
1 Thes. 3:7   we were comforted over you in all our **affliction** and
James 1:27   to visit the fatherless and widows in their **affliction**
James 5:13   is any among you **afflicted**? Let him pray. Is any merry
1 Ne. 16:35(34-39)   because of their **afflictions** in the wilderness; and
1 Ne. 20:10   I have chosen thee in the furnace of **affliction**.
2 Ne. 2:2   he shall consecrate thine **afflictions** for thy gain.
2 Ne. 4:20(20-35)   he hath led me through mine **afflictions** in the
Jacob 3:1   he will console you in your **afflictions**, and he will
Mosiah 1:17   smitten with famine and sore **afflictions**, to stir them
Mosiah 24:14(8-25)   the Lord God, do visit my people in their **afflictions**.
Alma 4:13(1-20)   suffering all manner of **afflictions**, for Christ's sake

AFFLICTION cont.

Alma 7:11(5-13) suffering pains and **afflictions** and temptations of Eve
Alma 26:27(27-31) bear with patience thine **afflictions**, and I will give
Alma 31:31(24-38) suffer with patience these **afflictions** which shall
Alma 33:11 cry unto thee in all mine **afflictions**, for in thee
Alma 34:40(39-41) bear with all manner of **afflictions**; that ye do not
Alma 36:3(3,27) trust in God shall be supported in...their **afflictions**
Alma 53:13(10-15) the many **afflictions** and tribulations which the Nephi
Alma 60:13(12-13) suffereth the **righteous** to be slain that his justice
Alma 62:41 and many were softened because of their **afflictions**
Hel. 12:3 the Lord doth chasten his people with many **afflictions**
3 Ne. 6:13(12-14) persecution and all manner of **afflictions**, and would
D&C 24:8 be patient in **afflictions**, for thou shalt have many
D&C 25:5 be...a comfort unto...thy husband, in his **afflictions**
D&C 30:6 be you afflicted in all his **afflictions**, ever lifting
D&C 31:9 be patient in **afflictions**, revile not against those
D&C 64:8 forgave not...for this evil...**afflicted** and sorely
D&C 93:42 not taught your children..the cause of your **affliction**
D&C 98:3 things wherewith you have been **afflicted** shall work
D&C 101:2(1-5) I, the Lord, have suffered the **affliction** to come upon
D&C 121:7(7,8) thine **afflictions** shall be but a small moment
D&C 122:7(5-8) all these things shall give thee **experience**, and shall
JS-H 1:56 father's family met with a great **affliction** by the

AGENCY

Gen. 2:16(16,17) of every tree of the garden thou mayest **freely** eat
Gen. 4:7 if thou **doest** not well, sin lieth at the door. And
Deut. 11:26(26-28) I set before you this day a **blessing** and a curse
Deut. 30:1(1-3) the **blessing** and the curse, which I have set before
Deut. 30:19(15-19) therefore **choose** life, that both thou and thy seed may
Josh. 24:15(14-15) **choose** you this day whom ye will serve; whether the
1 Sam. 8:18(10-22) ye shall cry...because of...king...ye...have **chosen**
1 Kgs. 18:21 if the Lord be God, **follow** him: but if Baal, then
Prov. 1:29(27-31) and did not **choose** the fear of the Lord
Jer. 8:3 and death shall be **chosen** rather than life by all the
Matt. 26:39 nevertheless not as I **will**, but as thou wilt.
Luke 10:42 one thing is needful...Mary hath **chosen** that good part
John 5:30 I seek not mine own **will**, but the will of the father
Gal. 6:7(7-8) whatsoever a man **soweth**, that shall he also reap.
Heb. 5:8(7,8) learned he **obedience** by the things which he suffered
Heb. 12:9 rather be in **subjection** unto the Father of spirits
2 Ne. 2:11(11-13) for it must needs be, that there is an **opposition** in
2 Ne. 2:16(14-16) man could not **act** for himself save...he was enticed
2 Ne. 2:27(17-29) men are free...to **choose**...eternal life...or...death
2 Ne. 10:23 and remember that ye are **free** to act for yourselves-
2 Ne. 26:10(9,10) yield unto the devil and **choose** works of darkness
2 Ne. 31:13(12-14) that ye are **willing** to take upon you the name of
Mosiah 2:21(21,22) that ye may...move and do according to your own **will**
Mosiah 2:33 to **obey** that spirit; for if he listeth to obey him
Mosiah 5:8(7-9) under this head ye are made **free**, and there is no
Alma 3:26(26,27) which they listed to **obey**, whether it be a good spirit
Alma 12:31 in a state to **act** according to their wills and

8

AGENCY cont.

Alma 13:3   in the first place being left to **choose** good or evil
Alma 13:10(10,11)   they **choosing** to repent and work righteousness rather
Alma 29:4(4-5)   he allotteth unto men according to their **wills**
Alma 30:8(6-11)   scripture: **choose** ye this day, whom ye will serve.
Alma 33:23(21-23)   even all this can ye do if ye **will**. Amen.
Alma 41:7(2-9)   they are their own **judges**, whether to do good or do
Alma 42:7(5-7)   they became subjects to follow after their own **will**.
Alma 42:27(24-28)   come and partake of the waters of life **freely**; and who
Hel. 14:30(29-31)   ye are **free**; ye are permitted to act for yourselves
Moro. 7:15(14-19)   it is given unto you to **judge**, that ye may know good
D&C 29:36(35-40)   hosts of heaven turned he...because of their **agency**
D&C 29:39(35-40)   tempt...or they could not be **agents** unto themselves
D&C 37:4(1-4)   let every man **choose** for himself until I come. even
D&C 58:28(27-28)   wherein they are **agents** unto themselves. And inasmuch
D&C 88:86   abide ye in the liberty wherewith ye are made **free**
D&C 93:31(30-31)   here is the **agency** of man, and here is the
D&C 98:5(4-10)   principle of **freedom** in maintaining rights and
D&C 98:8(5-8)   I, the Lord God, make you **free**, therefore ye are free
D&C 101:78(76-95)   moral **agency** which I have given unto him, that every
D&C 104:17(17-18)   unto the children of men to be **agents** unto themselves.
D&C 121:41(41-46)   no **power** or influence can or ought to be maintained
D&C 134:2   secure to each...the **free** exercise of conscience, the
D&C 134:5   governments...holding sacred the **freedom** of conscience
Moses 3:17(16-17)   thou mayest **choose** for thyself, for it is given unto
Moses 4:3(1-4)   sought to destroy the **agency** of man, which I, the Lord
Moses 6:33   say unto this people: **choose** ye this day, to serve the
Moses 6:56   they are **agents** unto themselves, and I have given unto
Moses 7:32(32,33)   in the garden of Eden, gave I unto man his **agency**
Abr. 3:25(24-26)   we will **prove** them herewith, to see if they will do
A of F 1:2   men will be punished for their **own** sins, and not for
A of F 1:11   according to the **dictates** of our own conscience, and
JS-V 1:9(7-10)   according to the **desire** of their hearts.

ALMSGIVING

Ex. 23:11(9-11)   that the **poor** of thy people may eat: and what they
Deut. 15:8(7-11)   but thou shalt open thine **hand** wide unto him, and
Ps. 112:9(5,9)   he hath dispersed, he hath **given** to the poor; his
Prov. 22:9   he giveth of his bread to the **poor**.
Prov. 28:27   he that giveth unto the **poor** shall not lack: but he
Isa. 58:7(6-10)   is it not to deal thy bread to the **hungry**, and that
Matt. 5:42   **give** to him that asketh thee, and from him that would
Matt. 6:1(1-4)   do not your **alms** before men, to be seen of them: other
Matt. 19:21(21,22)   if thou wilt be perfect...**give** to the poor, and thou
Matt. 25:35(34-46)   I was an hungred, and ye **gave** me meat: I was thirsty
Mark 12:43(41-44)   this **poor** widow hath cast more in, than all they which
Luke 11:41   but rather give **alms** of such things as ye have; and
Luke 12:33(31-34)   sell that ye have, and give **alms**; provide yourselves
Acts 3:3(2-11)   who seeing Peter and John...asked an **alms**.
Acts 10:2(1-4)   gave much **alms** to the people, and prayed to God alway
Acts 11:29   determined to send **relief** unto the brethren which
Acts 20:35   it is more blessed to **give** than to receive.

ALMSGIVING cont.

Acts 24:17 — now after many years I came to bring **alms** to my nation
Rom. 15:26(25-28) — make a certain **contribution** for the poor saints which
Jacob 2:17(17-19) — be familiar with all and free with your **substance**
Mosiah 4:26(26-30) — should impart of your substance to the **poor**, every man
Mosiah 18:27(27,28) — if he have more abundantly he should **impart** more
Alma 1:27(26-28) — they did **impart** of their substance...to the poor, and
Alma 4:13(12-14) — imparting their substance to the **poor** and the needy
Alma 34:28 — **impart** of your substance, if ye have, to those who
3 Ne. 13:1(1-4) — do not your **alms** before men to be seen of them
D&C 42:31(30-31) — inasmuch as ye impart of your substance unto the **poor**
D&C 44:6 — ye must visit the poor...and **administer**...relief, that
D&C 56:16 — wo unto you rich men, that will not **give**...to the poor
D&C 88:2 — the **alms** of your prayers have come up into the ears
D&C 105:3(2,3) — **impart** of their substance, as becometh saints, to the
D&C 112:1 — and thine **alms** have come up as a memorial before me

ANGELS

Gen. 16:9(7-16) — and the **angel** of the Lord said unto her, return to thy
Gen. 18:2(1-8) — he lift up his eyes...and, lo, three **men** stood by him
Gen. 19:1 — and there came two **angels** to Sodom at even; and Lot
Gen. 19:15(15,16) — then the **angels** hastened Lot, saying, arise, take thy
Gen. 21:17(17,18) — the **angel** of God called Hagar out of heaven, and said
Gen. 24:7 — he shall send his **angel** before thee, and thou shalt
Gen. 28:12(12-15) — behold a ladder...the **angels** of God ascending and
Gen. 31:11 — and the **angel** of God spake unto me in a dream, saying
Ex. 3:2 — and the **angel** of the Lord appeared unto him in a flame
Ex. 33:2(1-3) — I will send an **angel** before thee; and I will drive out
Num. 20:16 — he heard our voice, and sent an **angel**, and hath
Judg. 6:22(11-22) — because I have seen an **angel** of the Lord face to face.
Judg. 13:6(3-22) — was like the countenance of an **angel** of God, very
1 Sam. 29:9 — thou art good in my sight, as an **angel** of God
1 Kgs. 13:18 — **angel** spake unto me by the word of the Lord, saying
1 Kgs. 19:5 — then an **angel** touched him, and said unto him, arise
2 Kgs. 1:15 — and the **angel** of the Lord said unto Elijah, go down
Ps. 34:7 — the **angel** of the Lord encampeth round about them that
Ps. 78:25 — man did eat **angels'** food: he sent them meat to the
Ps. 91:11 — give his **angels** charge over thee, to keep thee in all
Ps. 104:4 — maketh his **angels** spirits; his ministers a flaming fir
Dan. 3:28 — sent his **angel**, and delivered his servants that
Dan. 6:22 — my God hath sent his **angel**, and hath shut the lions
Dan. 9:21(21-23) — **Gabriel**, whom I had seen in the vision at the
Dan. 10:21(4-21) — none...with me...but **Michael** your prince.
Hosea 12:4 — he had power over the **angel**, and prevailed: he wept
Zech. 1:9(7-21) — the **angel** that talked with me said unto me, I will she
Zech. 3:1 — standing before the **angel** of the Lord, and Satan stand
Matt. 4:11 — behold, **angels** came and ministered unto him.
Matt. 13:41 — the son of man shall send forth his **angels**, and they
Matt. 24:31 — he shall send his **angels** with a great sound of a trump
Matt. 24:36 — no, not the **angels** of heaven, but my father only.
Matt. 28:2 — the **angel** of the Lord descended from heaven, and came
Luke 1:19(11-38) — and the **angel** answering said unto him, I am Gabriel

Luke 12:8(8-9)	son of man also confess before the **angels** of God
Luke 15:10	joy in the presence of the **angels** of God over one
Luke 16:22	was carried by the **angels** into Abraham's bosom: the
Luke 20:36	die any more: for they are equal unto the **angels**; and
Luke 22:43	there appeared an **angel** unto him from heaven, strength
John 12:29	said...it thundered: others...an **angel** spake to him.
John 20:12	and seeth two **angels** in white sitting, the one at the
Acts 5:19(19,20)	but the **angel** of the Lord by night opened the prison
Acts 6:15	his face as it had been the face of an **angel**.
Acts 8:26	and the **angel** of the Lord spake unto Philip, saying
Acts 10:30(30-32)	behold, a **man** stood before me in bright clothing
Acts 12:23(19-25)	the **angel** of the Lord smote him, because he gave not
Acts 27:23	there stood by me this night the **angel** of God, whose
2 Cor. 11:14	Satan himself is transformed into an **angel** of light.
Gal. 1:8	though we, or an **angel** from heaven, preach any other
1 Tim. 5:21	I charge thee before God...and the elect **angels**, that
Heb. 1:14	are they not all **ministering** spirits, sent forth to
Heb. 2:16	verily he took not on him the nature of **angels**; but
Heb. 12:22(22-24)	ye are come...an innumerable company of **angels**
Heb. 13:2	thereby some have entertained **angels** unawares.
1 Pet. 1:12	which things the **angels** desire to look into.
1 Pet. 3:22	**angels** and authorities and powers being made subject
2 Pet. 2:4	God spared not the **angels** that sinned, but cast them
Jude 1:6	and the **angels** which kept not their first estate, but
Jude 1:9	Michael the **archangel**, when contending with the devil
Rev. 12:7(7-9)	Michael and his **angels** fought against the dragon; and
Rev. 14:6(6,7)	I saw another **angel** fly in the midst of heaven, having
Rev. 20:1(1-3)	and I saw an **angel** come down from heaven, having the
Rev. 22:16(8-21)	I Jesus have sent mine **angel** to testify unto you these
1 Ne. 3:29(29-31)	behold, an **angel** of the Lord came and stood before the
2 Ne. 32:3(2-3)	**angels** speak by the power of the Holy Ghost; wherefore
Jacob 7:5	I truly had seen **angels**...wherefore, I could not be
Mosiah 3:2	things which I shall tell you...by an **angel** from God.
Mosiah 27:18(11-18)	beheld an **angel** of the Lord; and his voice was as
Alma 8:14(14-18)	an **angel** of the Lord appeared unto him, saying
3 Ne. 28:30	and they are as the **angels** of God, and if they shall
Moro. 7:29(29-32)	neither have **angels** ceased to minister unto the
D&C 13:1	holds the keys of the ministering of **angels**, and of
D&C 29:37(36-38)	and thus came the devil and his **angels**
D&C 76:67(66-69)	they who have come to an innumerable company of **angels**
D&C 76:88	who are appointed to be **ministering** spirits for them
D&C 84:88	and mine **angels** round about you, to bear you up.
D&C 103:19	mine **angel** shall go up before you, but not my presence
D&C 109:22	and thine **angels** have charge over them
D&C 128:21(20,21)	Michael...Gabriel...and of divers **angels**, from Michael
D&C 129:1(1-9)	**angels**, who are resurrected personages, having bodies
D&C 130:5(4-7)	there are no **angels** who minister to this earth but
Moses 5:6(6-8)	after many days an **angel** of the Lord appeared unto
Moses 7:27	**angels** descending out of heaven, bearing testimony of
JS-H 1:30(30-33,43)	immediately a **personage** appeared at my bedside

ANGER

Gen. 27:45	until thy brother's **anger** turn away from thee, and he
Gen. 49:7	cursed be their **anger**, for it was fierce; and their
Ex. 4:14	and the **anger** of the Lord was kindled against Moses
Ex. 11:8	he went out from Pharaoh in a great **anger**.
Ex. 32:19	Moses' **anger** waxed hot, and he cast the tables out of
Deut. 1:37	Lord was **angry** with me for your sakes, saying, thou
Deut. 4:25(25-29)	do evil in...sight of the Lord...provoke him to **anger**
Deut. 9:18(15-21)	doing wickedly...of the Lord, to provoke him to **anger**.
Judg. 2:12	other Gods...and provoked the Lord to **anger**.
1 Sam. 20:30(27-34)	then Saul's **anger** was kindled against Jonathan, and
1 Kgs. 15:30	he provoked the Lord God of Israel to **anger**.
Neh. 9:17(5-17)	thou art a God...slow to **anger**, and of great kindness
Ps. 37:8	cease from **anger**, and forsake wrath: fret not thyself
Ps. 85:4	turn us, O God...cause thine **anger** toward us to cease.
Ps. 103:8	slow to **anger**, and plenteous in mercy.
Prov. 14:17	he that is soon **angry** dealeth foolishly: and a man of
Prov. 15:18(1,18)	he that is slow to **anger** appeaseth strife.
Prov. 16:32	he that is slow to **anger** is better than the mighty
Prov. 19:11	discretion of a man deferreth his **anger**; and it is his
Prov. 21:14	a gift in secret pacifieth **anger**: and a reward in the
Prov. 22:24	make no friendship with an **angry** man; and with a
Prov. 27:4	wrath is cruel, and **anger** is outrageous; but who is
Eccl. 7:9	for **anger** resteth in the bosom of fools.
Isa. 1:4(2-4)	they have provoked the Holy One of Israel unto **anger**
Isa. 48:9(1-12)	for my name's sake will I defer mine **anger**, and for
Isa. 65:3(1-3)	a people that provoketh me to **anger** continually to my
Jer. 8:19	provoked me to **anger** with their graven images, and wit
Jer. 32:30(30-35)	have only provoked me to **anger** with the work of their
Jonah 4:9(1,9)	Jonah, doest thou well to be **angry** for the gourd? And
Matt. 5:22(21-24)	whosoever is **angry** with his brother without a cause
1 Cor. 13:5(1-13)	seeketh not her own, is not easily **provoked**, thinketh
Eph. 4:26	let not the sun go down upon your **wrath**
Eph. 4:31(31-32)	let all bitterness...and **anger**...be put away from you
Col. 3:8	also put off all these; **anger**, wrath, malice
Col. 3:21	fathers, provoke not your children to **anger**, lest they
Titus 1:7	a bishop...not selfwilled, not soon **angry**, not given
James 1:19(19-20)	let every man be swift to hear...slow to **wrath**
1 Ne. 16:38(36-39)	after this manner...stir up their hearts to **anger**.
2 Ne. 4:13(12-15)	**angry** with me because of the admonitions of the Lord.
2 Ne. 4:29(28-30)	do not **anger** again because of mine enemies. do not
2 Ne. 28:20(19-21)	stir them up to **anger** against that which is good.
2 Ne. 28:28	**angry** because of the truth of God! For behold, he that
3 Ne. 11:30(28-30)	not my doctrine, to stir up...men with **anger**, one
Moro. 9:3(1-6)	continually to **anger** one with another.
D&C 1:13	and the **anger** of the Lord is kindled, and his sword
D&C 5:8	stiffnecked generation- mine **anger** is kindled against
D&C 10:24(24-34)	he stirreth up their hearts to **anger** against this work
D&C 60:2	wo unto such, for mine **anger** is kindled against them.
D&C 63:11	with whom God is **angry** he is not well pleased
D&C 63:32	I, the Lord, am **angry** with the wicked; I am holding
D&C 84:24	for his **anger** was kindled against them, swore that the
Moses 8:15(13-15)	**anger** is kindled...they will not hearken to my voice.

ANOINTING

Ex. 28:41	shalt **anoint** them, and consecrate them, and sanctify
Ex. 30:25(22-25)	oil of holy ointment...shall be an holy **anointing** oil.
Ex. 40:15(12-15)	thou shalt **anoint** them, as thou didst anoint their fat
Lev. 8:10	Moses...**anointed** the tabernacle and all that was there
Lev. 21:12(10-12)	the crown of the **anointing** oil of his God is upon him
Deut. 28:40	thou shalt not **anoint** thyself with the oil; for thine
1 Sam. 9:16(15-17)	thou shalt **anoint** him to be captain over my people
1 Sam. 15:1(1-3)	Lord sent me to **anoint** thee to be king over his people
1 Sam. 24:6(1-10)	seeing he is the **anointed** of the Lord.
2 Sam. 1:14	stretch forth thine hand...destroy the Lord's **anointed**
2 Sam. 12:7(7-9)	I **anointed** thee king over Israel, and I delivered thee
2 Sam. 19:21	because he cursed the Lord's **anointed**
Ps. 2:2	against the Lord, and against his **anointed**, saying
Ps. 23:5	thou **anointest** my head with oil; my cup runneth over.
Isa. 61:1(1-3)	because the Lord hath **anointed** me to preach good
Mark 6:13	they...**anointed** with oil many that were sick, and heal
Luke 4:18(16-21)	because he hath **anointed** me to preach the gospel to
Luke 7:38(37-50)	kissed his feet, and **anointed** them with the ointment.
Acts 4:27(23-30)	thy holy child Jesus, whom thou hast **anointed**, both
Acts 10:38	how God **anointed** Jesus of Nazareth with the Holy Ghost
2 Cor. 1:21(21-22)	he which stablisheth us...and hath **anointed** us, is God
James 5:14(14-15)	pray...**anointing** him with oil in the name of the Lord
1 Jn. 2:27	the same **anointing** teacheth you of all things, and is
Jacob 1:9(9-11)	he **anointed** a man to be a king and a ruler over his
Ether 6:22	people desired...**anoint** one of their sons to be a king
D&C 68:20	descendant of Aaron...must be...**anointed**, and ordained
D&C 109:35(35-36)	let the **anointing** of thy ministers be sealed upon them
D&C 109:80	let these, thine **anointed** ones, be clothed with
D&C 121:16	cursed...those..lift up the heel against mine **anointed**
D&C 124:39	**anointings**..ordained by the ordinance of my holy house
D&C 124:57(57-58)	for this **anointing** have I put upon his head, that his
D&C 132:41	I have not appointed unto her by the holy **anointing**

ANTI-CHRIST

2 Thes. 2:3(3-12)	falling away first...**man** of sin be revealed, the son
1 Jn. 2:18(15-19)	ye have heard that **antichrist** shall come, even now
1 Jn. 2:22(21-23)	he is **antichrist**, that denieth the father and the son
1 Jn. 4:3(1-3)	this is that spirit of **antichrist**, whereof ye have
2 Jn. 1:7(6-8)	this is a deceiver and an **antichrist**.
Rev. 16:13(13,14)	unclean spirits..out of the mouth of the **false** prophet
Rev. 19:20(19,20)	the beast was taken, and with him the **false** prophet
Jacob 7:1(1-23)	a man among the people of Nephi...**Sherem**.
Alma 1:3(2-15)	he had gone about...bearing down **against** the church
Alma 30:12(6-60)	this **Anti-Christ**, whose name was Korihor, (and the law

APATHY

Ps. 142:4(4-6)	refuge failed me; no man **cared** for my soul.
Prov. 6:6(6-9)	go to the ant, thou **sluggard**; consider her ways, and
Prov. 13:4	the soul of the **sluggard** desireth, and hath nothing

13

APATHY cont.

Prov. 20:4 — the **sluggard** will not plow by reason of the cold
Prov. 21:25(25,26) — the desire of the **slothful** killeth him; for his hands
Isa. 51:13(12-13) — and **forgettest** the Lord thy maker, that hath stretched
Luke 10:27(25-37) — love the Lord thy God with all thy **heart**, and with all
Acts 6:1(1-6) — widows were **neglected** in the daily ministration.
Rom. 13:11(11-12) — it is high time to awake out of **sleep**: for now is our
Philip. 2:21(20-21) — for all **seek** their own, not the things which are Jesus
Rev. 3:16(14-17) — because thou art **lukewarm**, and neither cold nor hot
2 Ne. 9:32(31-32) — wo unto the **blind** that will not see; for they shall
2 Ne. 28:21(21-25) — carnal **security**, that they will say: all is well in
Jacob 3:11 — **arouse** the faculties of your soul; shake yourselves
Alma 5:55(55-56) — persist in **turning** your backs upon the poor, and the
Alma 13:27(27-29) — hearken...not **procrastinate** the day of your repentance
Alma 33:21(19-23) — would ye rather harden your hearts...and be **slothful**
Alma 34:28(28-29) — if ye **turn** away the needy, and the naked, and visit
Alma 34:32(31,32) — this life is the day for men to **perform** their labors.
Alma 34:33(30-38) — do not **procrastinate** the day of your repentance until
Alma 37:41(38-46) — they were **slothful**, and forgot to exercise their faith
Alma 60:7(6-14) — upon your thrones in a state of thoughtless **stupor**
Hel. 13:38 — ye have **procrastinated** the day of your salvation
Morm. 8:37(37-39) — love money...more than...the poor and the **needy**, the
D&C 4:2(1-7) — **serve** him with all your heart, might, mind and
D&C 39:9 — **rejected** me...because of...the cares of the world.
D&C 58:26(26-29) — the same is a **slothful** and not a wise servant
D&C 60:13 — thou shalt not **idle** away thy time, neither shalt thou
D&C 68:31(30,31) — seek not **earnestly** the riches of eternity, but their
D&C 76:79 — these are they who are not **valiant** in the testimony
D&C 90:18 — keep **slothfulness** and uncleanness far from you.
D&C 107:100(99,100) — he that is **slothful** shall not be counted worthy to
D&C 131:6 — it is impossible for a man to be saved in **ignorance**.
JS-M 1:43(42-43) — **knew** not until the flood came, and took them all away

APOSTASY, OF INDIVIDUALS

Deut. 29:18(18-25) — whose heart **turneth** away this day from the Lord our
1 Kgs. 11:9(4-13) — angry with Solomon...heart was **turned** from the Lord
Prov. 29:18 — where there is no vision, the people **perish**: but he
Isa. 24:5(4-6) — changed the ordinance, **broken** the everlasting covenant
Jer. 17:5(5-8) — and whose heart **departeth** from the Lord.
Ezek. 18:26(24-26) — when a righteous man **turneth** away from his
Ezek. 33:13(12-13) — if he trust to his own righteousness...commit **iniquity**
Ezek. 33:18 — righteous **turneth** from his righteousness...shall...die
Hosea 13:6 — heart was exalted; therefore have they **forgotten** me.
Matt. 7:27(26,27) — beat upon that house; and it **fell**: and great was the
Matt. 12:45(43-45) — the last **state** of that man is worse than the first.
Matt. 13:21(3-8,18-23) — when tribulation...ariseth...by and by he is **offended**.
Matt. 24:12(9-12) — iniquity shall abound..love of many shall wax **cold**.
Luke 12:10(9-10) — **blasphemeth** against the Holy Ghost...not be forgiven.
Luke 12:47(43-48) — **servant**, which knew his Lord's will, and prepared not
John 6:66(60-69) — many of his **disciples** went back, and walked no more
Acts 20:30(28-30) — speaking perverse things, to **draw** away disciples after
Gal. 1:6(6-9) — I marvel that ye are so soon **removed** from him that

1 Tim. 1:19(19-20)	some...put away concerning faith have made **shipwreck**
2 Tim. 4:10	Demas hath **forsaken** me, having loved this present
Titus 3:10(10,11)	a man that is an **heretick** after the first and second
Heb. 3:12	heart of unbelief, in **departing** from the living God.
Heb. 6:6(4-6)	if they shall **fall** away, to renew them again unto
Heb. 10:26(26-29)	if we **sin** wilfully after...have received the knowledge
Heb. 10:38	but if any man **draw** back, my soul shall have no
2 Pet. 2:15(9-15)	which have **forsaken** the right way, and are gone astray
2 Pet. 2:22(20-22)	the dog is turned to his own **vomit** again; and the sow
Jude 1:18(17-19)	told you there should be **mockers** in the last time, who
1 Ne. 8:23	that they wandered off and were **lost**.
1 Ne. 8:28(26-28)	scoffing at them...they **fell** away into forbidden paths
1 Ne. 12:17(17-19)	the temptations of the devil, which **blindeth** the eyes
1 Ne. 15:10(2-11)	how is it that ye will **perish**, because of the hardness
2 Ne. 9:46(45-47)	devil hath **obtained** me, that I am a prey to his awful
2 Ne. 28:21(19-29)	devil cheateth their souls, and **leadeth** them away care
Mosiah 16:5(2-5)	**rebellion** against God, remaineth in his fallen state
Mosiah 26:32	whosoever will not **repent**...shall not be numbered Amon
Mosiah 27:9(8-9)	a...hinderment..**stealing** away the hearts of the people
Mosiah 27:13	nothing shall overthrow it, save...**transgression** of
Alma 12:11(9-11,13)	know nothing...and...are taken **captive** by the devil
Alma 13:20	scriptures..ye..wrest them..to your own **destruction**.
Alma 24:30	once enlightened...and then have **fallen** away into sin
Alma 31:9(8-11)	they had **fallen** into great errors, for they would not
Alma 32:38(37-39)	if ye **neglect** the tree, and take no thought for its
Alma 41:1	some have wrested the scriptures, and..gone far **astray**
Alma 45:10(8-14)	the Nephites...shall dwindle in **unbelief**.
Alma 47:36	now these **dissenters**, having the same instruction and
Alma 48:24	had **dissented** from their church, and had left them and
Hel. 5:35	the church of God but had **dissented** from them.
Hel. 12:2(2-6)	they do **harden** their hearts, and do forget the Lord
3 Ne. 18:13(12-14)	built upon a sandy foundation...they shall **fall**, and
3 Ne. 18:15(15-18)	watch and pray...lest ye be tempted...led away **captive**
3 Ne. 21:5	**dwindle** in unbelief because of iniquity
4 Ne. 1:27(26-34)	they did **deny** the more parts of his gospel, insomuch
Morm. 8:33(26-41)	**transfigured** the holy word...bring damnation upon your
D&C 1:15(11-17)	strayed...**broken** mine everlasting covenant
D&C 3:9(4-11)	because of transgression, if..not aware thou wilt **fall**
D&C 10:26(22-28)	he **flattereth** them...causeth them to catch themselves
D&C 11:25(24-25)	revelation...prophecy...wo unto him that **denieth** these
D&C 20:32(32-33)	a possibility that man may **fall** from grace and depart
D&C 40:2(1-3)	fear..cares of the world caused him to **reject** the word
D&C 50:44	he that buildeth upon this rock shall never **fall**.
D&C 56:10(8-10)	otherwise he shall...be **cut** off out of my church
D&C 82:3(2-3)	he who **sins** against the greater light...greater
D&C 82:21	soul that...**hardeneth** his heart...buffetings of Satan
D&C 84:41	whoso breaketh this **covenant**...shall not have forgiven
D&C 84:54(49-57)	your minds...have been darkened because of **unbelief**
D&C 85:11	they who...have **apostatized**, or...been cut off from
D&C 112:26(25,26)	**blasphemed** against me in the midst of my house, saith
D&C 114:2	there are those among you who **deny** my name, others
D&C 121:37(34-38)	undertake to **cover** our sins...Amen to the priesthood
JS-H 1:19(18-19)	draw near to me with their lips...**hearts** are far from

APOSTASY, OF ISRAEL

Ex. 32:9	this people...is a **stiffnecked** people
Lev. 18:3	after the **doings** of the land of Egypt, wherein ye
Lev. 18:27(26-28)	all these **abominations** have the men of the land done
Lev. 26:15(14-33)	not do all my commandments, but that ye **break** my
Deut. 7:4(1-4)	for they will **turn** away thy son from following me
Deut. 9:7(7,24)	ye have been **rebellious** against the Lord.
Deut. 29:25(24-27)	because they have **forsaken** the covenant of the Lord
Judg. 3:7(5-7,12)	Israel did **evil** in the sight of the Lord, and forgat
1 Kgs. 11:2(1-11)	surely they will **turn** away your heart after their God
1 Kgs. 11:33(7,8,33)	they have **forsaken** me, and have worshipped Ashtoreth
1 Kgs. 12:32(25-33)	he placed in Bethel the **priests** of the high places
1 Kgs. 13:34	this thing became **sin** unto the house of Jeroboam, even
1 Kgs. 14:22(22-24)	Judah did **evil** in the sight of the Lord, and they
2 Kgs. 17:7(7-18)	Israel had **sinned** against the Lord their God, which
2 Kgs. 21:2(1-9)	he did...evil...after the **abominations** of the heathen
2 Kgs. 23:15	both that **altar** and the high place he brake down, and
2 Chr. 11:15(13-15)	he ordained him **priests** for the high places, and for
2 Chr. 36:16	but they **mocked** the messengers of God, and despised
Ps. 106:36(19,36-39)	they served their **idols**: which were a snare unto them.
Isa. 1:3	Israel doth not **know**, my people doth not consider.
Isa. 1:21(10-21)	how is the faithful city become an **harlot**! It was full
Isa. 1:22(22-25)	thy silver is become **dross**, thy wine mixed with water
Isa. 2:8(6-8)	their land also is full of **idols**; they worship the
Isa. 3:9	declare their **sin** as Sodom, they hide it not. woe
Isa. 5:4(1-7)	my vineyard...wherefore...brought it forth **wild** grapes
Isa. 6:9(9-10)	hear ye indeed, but **understand** not; and see ye indeed
Isa. 24:5(4-6)	changed the ordinance, **broken** the everlasting covenant
Isa. 29:13(13-14)	but have **removed** their heart far from me, and their
Isa. 50:1(1-11)	for your **iniquities** have ye sold yourselves, and for
Isa. 52:3	ye have **sold** yourselves for nought; and ye shall be
Jer. 2:13	my people have committed two **evils**; they have forsaken
Jer. 2:17(14-17)	thou hast **forsaken** the Lord thy God, when he led thee
Jer. 3:25(20-25)	for we have **sinned** against the Lord our God, we and
Jer. 5:19(1-31)	as ye have **forsaken** me, and served strange Gods in you
Jer. 7:11(8-11)	this house...become a den of **robbers** in your eyes
Jer. 7:13(13-16)	I called you, but ye **answered** not
Jer. 7:24	their evil heart, and went **backward**, and not forward.
Jer. 8:5	Jerusalem slidden back by a perpetual **backsliding**?
Jer. 8:9(7-9)	lo, they have **rejected** the word of the Lord; and what
Jer. 11:13(12-14)	have ye set up **altars**...to burn incense unto Baal.
Jer. 14:10(10-12)	he will now remember their **iniquity**...visit their sins
Jer. 16:20(17-21)	shall a man make **gods** unto himself, and they are no
Jer. 23:10(10-12)	for the land is full of **adulterers**; for because of
Jer. 26:9	this city shall be **desolate** without an inhabitant? and
Ezek. 2:3(3-5)	Israel, to a **rebellious** nation that hath rebelled
Ezek. 11:12	have done after the **manners** of the heathen that are
Ezek. 22:18(18-22)	house of Israel is to me become **dross**...dross of
Ezek. 22:26(25-29)	her **priests** have violated my law, and have profaned
Ezek. 34:8(8-10)	**shepherds** fed themselves, and fed not my flock
Hosea 4:6(1-9)	thou hast forgotten the **law** of thy God, I will also
Hosea 4:17(12-19)	Ephraim is joined to **idols**: let him alone.
Amos 5:26	ye have...your **Moloch** and Chiun your images, the star
Amos 8:11(11-13)	I will send a **famine** in the land, not a famine of

16

APOSTASY, OF ISRAEL cont.

Micah 1:5(2-9)	for the **transgression** of Jacob is all this, and for
Micah 3:11(5-11)	the **prophets**...divine for money: yet will they lean
Matt. 13:15(14-16)	for this people's **heart** is waxed gross, and their ears
Matt. 15:9(1-9)	teaching for doctrines the **commandments** of men.
Matt. 23:13(1-33)	woe unto you, scribes and **Pharisees**, hypocrites! For
Mark 7:6(6-13)	this people **honoureth** me with their lips, but their
Acts 7:52(51-53)	which of the prophets have not your fathers **persecuted**
Rom. 9:31(31,32)	**Israel**...hath not attained to the law of righteousness
Rom. 10:3(2-4)	have not **submitted** themselves unto the righteousness
Rom. 10:14(13-15)	how...call on him in whom they have not **believed**? And
Rom. 10:16	they have not all **obeyed** the gospel. for Esaias saith
Rom. 10:21	stretched forth my hands unto a **disobedient** and
Rom. 11:3(1-5)	they have **killed** thy prophets, and digged down thine
Rom. 11:20(7-24)	because of **unbelief** they were broken off, and thou
1 Ne. 1:19(19-20)	the **Jews** did mock him because of the things which he
2 Ne. 7:1(1-3)	for your iniquities have ye **sold** yourselves, and for
2 Ne. 10:5(4-6)	**priestcrafts** and iniquities, they at Jerusalem will
2 Ne. 13:9	their **sin**...even as Sodom, and they cannot hide it.
Jacob 5:3(3-7)	Israel, like...olive-tree...waxed old...began to **decay**
D&C 1:15(11-17)	strayed from mine ordinances...**broken** mine everlasting
D&C 133:71(70-71)	ye **obeyed** not my voice when I called to you out of

APOSTASY, OF THE EARLY CHRISTIAN CHURCH

Isa. 24:5(4-6)	changed the ordinance, **broken** the everlasting covenant
Isa. 29:13(13-24)	this people draw near me with their **mouth**, and with
Isa. 60:2(2-3)	for, behold, the **darkness** shall cover the earth, and
Amos 8:11(11-12)	a **famine**...of hearing the words of the Lord
Matt. 13:25(24-30)	his enemy came and sowed **tares** among the wheat, and
Matt. 24:5(4-5)	saying, I am Christ; and shall **deceive** many.
Matt. 24:11(9-12)	and many **false** prophets shall rise, and shall deceive
Matt. 24:24(23-24)	for there shall arise **false** Christs, and false prophet
John 6:66(59-66)	his disciples went back, and **walked** no more with him.
Acts 20:29(29-30)	shall **grievous** wolves enter in among you, not sparing
Rom. 11:21(17-21)	take heed lest he also **spare** not thee.
1 Cor. 1:11(10-13)	that there are **contentions** among you.
1 Cor. 3:3(1-9)	there is among you envying, and strife, and **divisions**
1 Cor. 4:18	some are **puffed** up, as though I would not come to you.
1 Cor. 11:18(17-20)	there be **divisions** among you; and I partly believe
2 Cor. 2:17	we are not as many, which **corrupt** the word of God: but
Gal. 1:6(6-9)	I marvel that ye are so soon **removed** from him that
Gal. 3:1(1-4)	who hath **bewitched** you, that ye should not obey the
Col. 2:22(20-23)	after the **commandments** and doctrines of men
2 Thes. 2:3(1-12)	shall not come, except there come a **falling** away first
1 Tim. 1:6	some having swerved have **turned** aside unto vain
1 Tim. 1:19	having put away concerning faith have made **shipwreck**
1 Tim. 4:1(1-4)	giving heed to **seducing** spirits, and doctrines of
2 Tim. 1:15	all they which are in Asia be **turned** away from me; of
2 Tim. 2:18	who concerning the truth have **erred**, saying that the
2 Tim. 3:5(1-7)	having a form of godliness, but **denying** the power
2 Tim. 4:4(3-4)	turn away their ears from the truth...unto **fables**.
Titus 1:10(10-11)	many unruly and vain talkers and **deceivers**, specially

Titus 1:16(10-16)   profess that they know God; but in works they **deny** him
James 4:1(1-5)   wars and **fightings** among you? Come they not hence, Eve
2 Pet. 2:1(1-3)   but there were **false** prophets also among the people
2 Pet. 2:22(20-22)   the dog is turned to his own **vomit** again; and the sow
2 Pet. 3:17(15-17)   being led **away** with the error of the wicked, fall from
1 Jn. 2:18(18-24)   now are there many **antichrists**; whereby we know that
1 Jn. 4:1   because many **false** prophets are gone out into the
3 Jn. 1:9   Diotrephes, who loveth..preeminence..**receiveth** us not.
Jude 1:4(3-4)   certain men crept in...**denying** the only Lord God, and
Rev. 2:2   which say they are **apostles**, and are not, and hast
Rev. 2:5   will remove thy **candlestick** out of his place, except
Rev. 3:16(14-19)   thou art **lukewarm**, and neither cold nor hot, I will
Rev. 11:7(6-7)   make war against them, and shall **overcome** them, and
1 Ne. 11:34(34,35)   together to **fight** against the apostles of the Lamb
1 Ne. 13:26(23-28)   the foundation of a great and abominable **church**, which
1 Ne. 13:28(26-28)   plain and precious things taken away from the **book**
2 Ne. 26:20(20-29)   the Gentiles...have **stumbled**, because of the greatness
2 Ne. 27:1(1,25)   Gentiles...will be **drunken** with iniquity and all
Morm. 8:33(26-41)   **transfigured** the holy word of God, that ye might bring
D&C 1:15(11-17)   strayed from mine ordinances...**broken** mine everlasting
D&C 86:3(1-8)   Satan...he soweth the **tares**; wherefore, the tares
D&C 112:23   **darkness** covereth the earth, and gross darkness the
JS-H 1:19(18-19)   they were all **wrong**...their hearts are far from me

APOSTLES

Matt. 4:19(18-22)   follow me, and I will make you **fishers** of men.
Matt. 10:1(1-5)   he had called unto him his **twelve** disciples, he gave
Matt. 16:19(18-19)   I will give unto thee the **keys** of the kingdom of heave
Matt. 18:18   whatsoever ye shall **bind** on earth shall be bound in
Matt. 19:28   ye also shall sit...**judging** the twelve tribes of
Matt. 28:19(19-20)   go ye therefore, and **teach** all nations, baptizing them
Mark 1:17(16-20)   come ye after me, and I will make you...**fishers** of men
Mark 3:14(14-19)   he **ordained** twelve, that they should be with him, and
Mark 6:7(7-11)   **twelve**...and gave them power over unclean spirits
Mark 16:14(14-20)   he appeared unto the **eleven** as they sat at meat, and
Luke 5:11(2-11)   they forsook all, and **followed** him.
Luke 6:13(13-16)   of them he chose **twelve**, whom also he named apostles
Luke 9:1(1-6)   he called his **twelve** disciples together, and gave them
Luke 22:30   sit on thrones **judging** the twelve tribes of Israel.
Luke 24:47(46-48)   repentance...should be **preached**...among all nations
John 1:40(40-48)   two which...**followed** him, was Andrew, Simon Peter's
John 15:16(15-16)   ye have not chosen me, but I have **chosen** you, and
Acts 1:26(21-26)   the Lot fell upon **Matthias**...numbered with the eleven
Acts 14:14   when the **apostles**, Barnabas and Paul, heard of, they
1 Cor. 12:28   God hath set some in the church, first **apostles**
Gal. 1:1   Paul, an **apostle**, (not of men, neither by man, but by
Gal. 1:19(17-19)   other of the **apostles** saw I none, save James the Lord
Eph. 2:20(19,20)   built upon the foundation of the **apostles** and prophets
Eph. 4:11(11-16)   he gave some, **apostles**; and some, prophets; and some
1 Tim. 2:7   whereunto I am ordained a preacher, and an **apostle**
2 Tim. 1:11   whereunto I am appointed a preacher, and an **apostle**

APOSTLES cont.

Titus 1:1	Paul, a servant of God, and an **apostle** of Jesus Christ
1 Ne. 1:10	and he also saw **twelve** others following him, and their
1 Ne. 12:9	shall **judge** the twelve tribes of Israel; wherefore
3 Ne. 12:1(1,2)	heed...the words of these **twelve** whom I have chosen
3 Ne. 13:25(25-34)	looked upon the **twelve** whom he had chosen, and said
4 Ne. 1:14	and there were other **disciples** ordained in their stead
Morm. 3:19(18-19)	they shall be judged by the other **twelve** whom Jesus
Morm. 9:22(22-25)	said Jesus Christ...unto his **disciples** who should
D&C 1:14	give heed to the words of the prophets and **apostles**
D&C 18:27(26-47)	the **twelve** shall be my disciples, and they shall take
D&C 20:2(1-4)	Joseph Smith...called of God...ordained an **apostle** of
D&C 20:38(38-44)	an **apostle** is an elder, and it is his calling to
D&C 21:1	seer, a translator, a prophet, an **apostle** of Jesus
D&C 27:12(12-13)	I have ordained you and confirmed you to be **apostles**
D&C 29:12	mine **apostles**...to judge the whole house of Israel
D&C 52:9	that which the prophets and **apostles** have written, and
D&C 64:39(37-39)	they who are not **apostles** and prophets shall be known.
D&C 84:63(61-64)	for you are mine **apostles**, even God's high priests
D&C 102:30(30-32)	traveling high council composed of the twelve **apostles**
D&C 107:23(23,24)	traveling councilors are...to be the Twelve **Apostles**
D&C 107:33(33-39)	the **Twelve** are a Traveling Presiding High Council, to
D&C 107:35(35-37)	the **Twelve** being sent out, holding the keys, to open
D&C 107:58	it is the duty of the **Twelve**, also, to ordain and set
D&C 112:30(14-32)	unto...**Twelve**...is the power of this priesthood given
D&C 124:128	which **Twelve** hold the keys to open up the authority
D&C 136:3	under the direction of the Twelve **Apostles**.

APPAREL

Gen. 3:7	were naked..sewed fig leaves..made themselves **aprons**.
Gen. 3:21	unto Adam...wife...coats of skins, and **clothed** them.
Lev. 6:10(10-11)	the priest shall put on his linen **garment**, and his
Deut. 22:5	woman shall not **wear** that which pertaineth unto a man
Judg. 17:10(9-10)	I will give thee...a suit of **apparel**, and thy victuals
2 Sam. 1:24	who put on ornaments of gold upon your **apparel**.
2 Sam. 12:20(19-20)	David arose...washed...and changed his **apparel**, and
2 Chr. 5:12	being arrayed in white **linen**, having cymbals and
Ps. 45:13(12-14)	her **clothing** is of wrought gold.
Prov. 31:22(19-24)	coverings of tapestry; her **clothing** is silk and purple
Isa. 3:22(16-26)	the changeable suits of **apparel**, and the mantles, and
Isa. 32:11(9-11)	and gird **sackcloth** upon your loins.
Jer. 6:26	O daughter of my people, gird thee with **sackcloth**, and
Dan. 9:3(3-4)	with fasting, and **sackcloth**, and ashes
Luke 7:25	behold, they which are gorgeously **apparelled**, and live
1 Thes. 5:22	abstain from all **appearance** of evil.
1 Tim. 2:9(9-10)	women adorn themselves in modest **apparel**, with
1 Pet. 3:3	let it not be that outward **adorning** of plaiting the
Rev. 6:11(9-11)	and white **robes** were given unto every one of them; and
Jacob 2:13(13-16)	high heads because of the costliness of your **apparel**
Alma 1:6	he began...to wear very costly **apparel**, yea, and even
Alma 1:27(27-32)	they did not wear costly **apparel**, yet they were neat
Alma 4:6(6-7)	for they began to wear very costly **apparel**.

APPAREL cont.

Alma 32:2(2-3)   cast out...because of the coarseness of their
Morm. 8:36(36-37)   pride of...hearts, unto the wearing of...fine **apparel**
D&C 42:40(38-41)   let all thy **garments** be plain, and their beauty the
Moses 4:13   they sewed fig-leaves together..made themselves **aprons**
Moses 4:27   make coats of skins, and **clothed** them.

ARK OF THE COVENANT

Ex. 25:22(10-22)   I will commune with thee from above the **mercy-seat**
Ex. 37:1(1-9)   and Bezaleel made the **ark** of shittim wood: two cubits
Ex. 40:3(1-3,20-21)   thou shalt put therein the **ark** of the testimony, and
Num. 3:31(27-32)   their charge shall be the **ark**, and the table, and the
Num. 10:33(33-36)   the **ark** of the covenant of the Lord went before them
Deut. 31:26(24-26)   book of the law...put it in...the **ark** of the covenant
Josh. 3:3(3-17)   when ye see the **ark** of the covenant of the Lord your
Josh. 4:7(1-9)   waters of Jordan were cut off before the **ark** of the
Josh. 6:6(4-11)   take up the **ark** of the covenant, and let seven priest
1 Sam. 4:3(1-22)   let us fetch the **ark**...out of Shiloh unto us, that
1 Sam. 6:21   Philistines have brought again the **ark** of the Lord
1 Sam. 7:1(1-2)   fetched up the **ark** of the Lord, and brought it into
2 Sam. 6:12(1-18)   David...brought up the **ark**...into the city of David
1 Kgs. 8:9(1-11)   there was nothing in the **ark** save the two tables of
1 Chr. 13:3(3-13)   let us bring again the **ark** of our God to us: for we
1 Chr. 15:1   prepared a place for the **ark** of God, and pitched for
1 Chr. 16:1(1-6)   brought the **ark** of God, and set it in the midst of the
1 Chr. 22:19(17-19)   build...sanctuary...to bring the **ark** of the covenant
2 Chr. 5:2(2-10)   to bring up the **ark** of the covenant of the Lord out
Jer. 3:16(12-19)   they shall say no more, the **ark** of the covenant of the
Heb. 9:4(1-12)   **ark** of the covenant overlaid round about with gold
Rev. 11:19   there was seen in his temple the **ark** of his testament
D&C 85:8(6-8)   that putteth forth his hand to steady the **ark** of God

ART

Ex. 25:18   thou shalt **make** two cherubims of gold, of beaten work
Ex. 26:36(1-37)   fine twined linen, wrought with **needlework**.
Ex. 28:11(11,39)   the work of an **engraver** in stone, like the engravings
Ex. 31:3(3-11)   with the spirit of God...in all manner of **workmanship**
Ex. 35:35(31-35)   to **work** all manner of work, of the engraver, and of
Ex. 39:29(1-43)   purple, and scarlet, and **needlework**; as the Lord
Num. 21:8(8-9)   the Lord said unto Moses, **make** thee a fiery serpent
1 Kgs. 6:23(23-30)   within the oracle he **made** two cherubims of olive tree
1 Ne. 18:1(1-4)   we did work timbers of curious **workmanship**. And the
2 Ne. 5:15(15-17)   to **work** in all manner of wood, and of iron, and of
2 Ne. 12:8   worship the **work** of their own hands, that which their
Jarom 1:8   in fine **workmanship** of wood, in buildings, and in
Mosiah 10:5   **work** all manner of fine linen, yea, and cloth of ever
Mosiah 11:8(8-11)   he **ornamented** them with fine work of wood, and of all
Hel. 6:13   did **make** all manner of cloth, of fine-twined linen and
Hel. 12:2   prosper...precious things of every kind and **art**
3 Ne. 21:17   thou shalt no more worship the **works** of thy hands

Ether 10:7(6,7)	all manner of fine **workmanship** he did cause to be
Ether 10:23(23-24,27)	and they did work all manner of fine **work**.

ASSEMBLY, FOR WORSHIP

1 Chr. 16:29(28-31)	**worship** the Lord in the beauty of holiness.
1 Chr. 29:20(20-22)	all the **congregation** blessed the Lord God of their
2 Chr. 7:3(1-3)	**worshipped**, and praised the Lord, saying, for he is
2 Chr. 29:28(28-30)	all the **congregation** worshipped, and the singers sang
Ps. 22:25	my praise shall be of thee in the great **congregation**
Ps. 26:12	in the **congregations** will I bless the Lord.
Ps. 111:1(1-10)	I will praise the Lord..in the **assembly** of the upright
John 20:19(19,26)	first day of the week...disciples were **assembled** for
Acts 4:31	they were **assembled** together; and they were all
Acts 11:26	they **assembled** themselves with the church, and taught
Acts 20:7	first day of the week...disciples came **together** to
1 Cor. 11:18(18-20)	when ye come together in the **church**, I hear that there
Heb. 10:25(23-25)	not forsaking the **assembling** of ourselves together
Mosiah 2:1(1,5,6)	people **gathered** themselves together throughout all
Mosiah 18:25	one day in every week...to **assemble** themselves
Alma 32:4	there came a great **multitude** unto him, who were those
3 Ne. 11:1	a great multitude **gathered** together, of the people of
Moro. 6:6	and they did **meet** together oft to partake of bread and
D&C 20:75(55,75)	expedient that the church **meet** together often to
D&C 43:8	when ye are **assembled** together ye shall instruct and
D&C 59:9(9-13)	go to the house of **prayer**...upon my holy day

ASTRONOMY

Gen. 1:1(1-2)	in the beginning God created the **heaven** and the earth.
Gen. 1:14(14-18)	and God said, let there be **lights** in the firmament of
Gen. 1:16(14-18)	two great lights...he made the **stars** also.
Deut. 4:19	when thou seest the sun, and the moon, and the **stars**
Josh. 10:13(12-14)	and the **sun** stood still, and the moon stayed, until
1 Sam. 20:5(4-5)	to morrow is the new **moon**, and I should not fail to
Job 9:9(7-9)	which maketh Arcturus, **Orion**, and Pleiades, and the
Job 38:31(31-33)	canst thou...loose the bands of **Orion**
Ps. 8:3(3,4)	thy heavens...the **moon** and the stars, which thou hast
Ps. 136:8(7-9)	the **sun** to rule by day: for his mercy endureth for eve
Ps. 147:4	he telleth the number of the **stars**...by their names.
Jer. 31:35	the Lord, which giveth the **sun** for a light by day, and
Joel 2:30(28-32)	I will shew wonders in the **heavens** and in the earth
Amos 5:8	seek him that maketh the seven **stars** and Orion, and
Matt. 24:29(27-29)	shall the **sun** be darkened, and the moon shall not
Luke 21:25(7,25,26)	signs in the sun, and in the **moon**, and in the stars
1 Cor. 15:41(40-42)	there is one glory of the **sun**, and another glory of
Heb. 1:2	his son...by whom also he made the **worlds**
Jude 1:13	wandering **stars**, to whom is reserved the blackness
2 Ne. 23:10	the **constellations** thereof shall not give their light
Alma 30:44	all the **planets** which move in their regular form do
Hel. 12:15(12-15)	surely it is the **earth** that moveth and not the sun.

ASTRONOMY cont.

Hel. 14:3(3-6) night before he cometh there shall be no **darkness**
Hel. 14:5(3-6) and behold, there shall a new **star** arise, such an one
D&C 45:42(40-42) the **moon** be turned into blood, and the stars fall fro
D&C 76:24 and of him, the **worlds** are and were created, and the
D&C 88:37(36-38) there is no **space** in the which there is no kingdom
D&C 130:7(4-8) reside in the presence of God, on a **globe** like a sea
Moses 1:33(32-38) and **worlds** without number have I created; and I also
Moses 2:18(14-19) and the **sun** to rule over the day, and the moon to rule
Moses 7:30(29-31) particles of the earth...millions of **earths** like this
Abr. 1:31 a knowledge...also of the **planets**, and of the stars
Abr. 3:3(1-19) the name of the great one is **Kolob**, because it is
Abr. 3:4(1-19) revolution was a **day** unto the Lord, after his manner
Abr. 3:9(1-19) reckoning of the time of one **planet** above another
Abr. 3:13(1-19) Kokaubeam, which signifies **stars**, or all the great
Abr. 5:13 that it was after the Lord's **time**, which was after

AUTHORITY

Ex. 3:12(12-15) token unto thee, that I have **sent** thee: when thou hast
Ex. 4:15(10-17) and I will be with thy **mouth**, and with his mouth, and
Ex. 7:2(1,2) thou shalt speak all that I **command** thee: and Aaron
2 Kgs. 17:13(13-16) Lord testified...by all the **prophets**, and by all the
2 Chr. 24:19(17-22) yet he **sent** prophets to them, to bring them again unto
Neh. 5:15(14-16) their servants bare **rule** over the people: but so did
Prov. 29:2 when the wicked beareth **rule**, the people mourn.
Isa. 6:8 whom shall I **send**, and who will go for us? Then said
Isa. 48:16(16-18) the Lord God, and his spirit, hath **sent** me.
Jer. 7:25 I have even **sent** unto you all my servants the prophets
Jer. 14:15(13-16) prophets that prophesy in my name, and I **sent** them not
Jer. 23:21(21,22) I have not **sent** these prophets, yet they ran: I have
Ezek. 2:7(1-7) thou shalt **speak** my words unto them, whether they will
Dan. 2:39(37-39) which shall bear **rule** over all the earth.
Matt. 8:9 for I am a man under **authority**, having soldiers ur
Matt. 10:1(1-42) twelve disciples, he gave them **power** against uncle
Matt. 21:23(23-27) by what **authority** doest thou these things? And who
Mark 1:22 he taught them as one that had **authority**, and not as
Mark 1:27(21-28) with **authority** commandeth he even the unclean spirits
Mark 13:34(34-37) Son of man is as a man...gave **authority** to his servant
Luke 9:1(1-6) gave them power and **authority** over all devils, and to
Luke 10:1(1-11) the Lord **appointed** other seventy also, and sent them
Luke 19:17 good servant...have thou **authority** over ten cities.
Luke 22:29(29-30) a kingdom, as my Father hath **appointed** unto me
John 5:27(25-29) hath given him **authority** to execute judgment also
John 5:43 I am come in my Father's **name**, and ye receive me not
John 8:28(28-30) I do nothing of myself; but as my **father** hath taught
John 15:16 not chosen me, but I have chosen you, and **ordained** you
John 20:21(19-23) as my Father hath sent me, even so **send** I you.
Acts 13:3(1-3) prayed, and **laid** their hands on them, they sent them
Acts 14:23(21-23) when they had **ordained** them elders in every church
1 Cor. 15:24(24-28) shall have put down all rule and all **authority** and
Eph. 4:11(11-13) he **gave** some, apostles; and some, prophets; and some
Titus 2:15 and rebuke with all **authority**. Let no man despise thee

22

AUTHORITY cont.

1 Pet. 3:22	angels and **authorities** and powers being made subject
1 Pet. 4:11(10-11)	if any man speak, let him speak as the **oracles** of God
1 Ne. 2:22(19-24)	thou shalt be made a **ruler** and a teacher over thy
2 Ne. 5:26	that they should be **priests** and teachers over the land
Mosiah 21:33(33,34)	none in the land that had **authority** from God. And
Mosiah 24:8(8-9)	Amulon began to exercise **authority** over Alma and his
Alma 11:2	the judge executed **authority**, and sent forth officers
Alma 17:3(2,3)	they taught with power and **authority** of God.
Alma 25:5	having usurped the power and **authority** over the
Alma 49:30	**ordained** by the holy order of God, being baptized unto
3 Ne. 18:36(36-39)	he **touched**...disciples whom he had chosen...and spake
Ether 12:10	they of old were **called** after the holy order of God.
D&C 11:15(13-17)	need not suppose..you are **called**..until you are called
D&C 18:26(26-30)	there are others who are **called** to declare my gospel
D&C 20:2(2-3)	Joseph Smith, Jun., who was **called** of God, and
D&C 25:3(1-3)	thou art an elect lady, whom I have **called**.
D&C 27:8	that you might be called and **ordained** even as Aaron
D&C 42:11	except he be ordained by some one who has **authority**
D&C 63:62	use...name of the Lord...in vain, having not **authority**
D&C 68:8(8-19)	acting in the **authority** which I have given you
D&C 84:21	without...the **authority** of the priesthood, the power
D&C 107:8(8,18-36)	Melchizedek priesthood...has power and **authority** over
D&C 110:16(11-16)	the **keys** of this dispensation are committed into your
D&C 112:21(20-21)	twelve, duly recommended and **authorized** by you, shall
D&C 113:8(7-8)	put on the **authority** of the priesthood, which she
D&C 121:39	as they get a little **authority**, as they suppose, they
D&C 128:9	whatsoever those men did in **authority**, in the name of
D&C 134:10	any religious society has **authority** to try men on the
Moses 6:58(57-58)	I give unto you a **commandment**, to teach these things
Moses 8:19	the Lord **ordained** Noah...and commanded him that he
Abr. 1:3(1-4)	it was **conferred** upon me from the fathers; it came
A of F 1:5	called of God...by those who are in **authority** to

BABYLON

Isa. 13:19(1-22)	**Babylon**...shall be as...Sodom and Gomorrah.
Isa. 14:4	shalt take up this proverb against...**Babylon**, and say
Jer. 51:1(1-64)	I will raise up against **Babylon**...a destroying wind
Jer. 51:6(1-60)	flee out of the midst of **Babylon**...be not cut off in
Jer. 51:37(1-64)	**Babylon** shall become...without an inhabitant.
1 Pet. 5:13	the church that is at **Babylon**, elected together with
Rev. 13:4(1-18)	worshipped the dragon which gave power unto the **beast**
Rev. 14:8	**Babylon** is fallen, is fallen, that great city, because
Rev. 16:19	and great **Babylon** came in remembrance before God, to
Rev. 17:5(1-18)	**Babylon** the great, the mother of harlots and
Rev. 18:2(1-24)	**Babylon**...is fallen...become the habitation of devils
Rev. 18:21	with violence shall...**Babylon** be thrown down, and
1 Ne. 1:13(7-15)	many should be carried away captive into **Babylon**.
1 Ne. 10:3(1-3)	many be carried away captive into **Babylon**, according
1 Ne. 20:14(14,20)	and he will do his pleasure on **Babylon**, and his arm
2 Ne. 23:1(1-22)	the burden of **Babylon**, which Isaiah the son of Amoz
2 Ne. 24:4(4-23)	take up this proverb against the king of **Babylon**, and

BABYLON cont.

2 Ne. 25:15(10,15)	and also **Babylon** shall be destroyed; wherefore, the
1:15	Zedekiah...was carried away captive into **Babylon**.
D&C 1:16(14-16)	even **Babylon** the great, which shall fall.
D&C 35:11	desolations upon **Babylon**, the same which has made all
D&C 64:24	I will not spare any that remain in **Babylon**.
D&C 86:3	the apostate, the whore, even **Babylon**, that maketh all
D&C 133:14(5,7,14)	go ye out from..wickedness, which is spiritual **Babylon**

BACKBITING

Ps. 15:3(1-5)	he that **backbiteth** not with his tongue, nor doeth evil
Ps. 101:5(1-8)	whoso...**slandereth** his neighbour, him will I cut off
Prov. 25:23	an angry countenance a **backbiting** tongue.
Matt. 5:11	blessed are ye, when men shall...say...**evil** against
Rom. 1:30	**backbiters**, haters of God, despiteful, proud, boasters
2 Cor. 12:20	envyings, wraths, strifes, **backbitings**, whisperings
Eph. 4:31	let all bitterness, and wrath...and **evil** speaking, be
James 5:9	**grudge** not one against another, brethren, lest ye be
1 Pet. 2:1(1-2)	laying aside all malice...and all evil **speakings**
Alma 5:30(30-32)	one among you that doth make a **mock** of his brother
3 Ne. 29:8	need not any longer hiss, nor **spurn**, nor make game of
Ether 7:24(23-25)	the people did **revile** against the prophets, and did
D&C 20:54	neither lying, **backbiting**, nor evil speaking
D&C 88:124	cease to find **fault** one with another; cease to sleep
D&C 136:23	cease to speak **evil** one of another.

BAPTISM

1 Kgs. 7:23(23-26)	and he made a molten **sea**, ten cubits from the one brim
2 Chr. 4:2(2-5)	also he made a molten **sea** of ten cubits from brim to
Isa. 1:16(16-18)	**wash** you, make you clean; put away the evil of your
Isa. 48:1	are come forth out of the **waters** of Judah, which swear
Jer. 52:20	one **sea**, and twelve brasen bulls...in the house of the
Zech. 13:1	a **fountain** opened to the house of David...for sin and
Matt. 3:16(13-16)	Jesus, when he was **baptized**, went up...out of the
Matt. 28:19	**baptizing** them in the name of the Father, and of the
Mark 1:4(4,5)	preach the **baptism** of repentance for the remission of
Mark 1:9(9-10)	and was **baptized** of John in Jordan.
Mark 16:16(15-16)	he that believeth and is **baptized** shall be saved; but
Luke 3:3	**baptism** of repentance for the remission of sins
John 3:5(3-5)	except a man be born of **water** and of the Spirit, he
John 3:23	because there was much water...they...were **baptized**.
Acts 2:38(37-38)	repent, and be **baptized** every one of you in the name
Acts 8:38(36-39)	they went down both into the water...and he **baptized**
Acts 22:16(14-16)	be **baptized**, and wash away thy sins, calling on the
Rom. 6:4(1-6)	we are buried with him by **baptism** into death: that
1 Cor. 6:11	but ye are **washed**, but ye are sanctified, but ye are
1 Cor. 10:2(1-4)	and were all **baptized** unto Moses in the cloud and in
Gal. 3:27	as many...as have been **baptized**...have put on Christ.
Col. 2:12	buried with him in **baptism**, wherein also ye are risen
1 Pet. 3:21(20-21)	the like figure whereunto even **baptism** doth also now

BAPTISM cont.

1 Ne. 20:1	out of the waters of Judah, or...waters of **baptism**
2 Ne. 31:5(2-13)	if the Lamb of God...have need to be **baptized** by water
2 Ne. 31:17	the gate...is repentance and **baptism** by water; and the
Mosiah 18:10(8-10)	**baptized** in the name of the Lord, as a witness before
Mosiah 21:35(32-35)	**baptized** as a witness...they were willing to serve God
Alma 7:14(14-16)	come and be **baptized** unto repentance, that ye may be
3 Ne. 7:25(24-26)	**baptized**...as a witness...they had repented and
3 Ne. 11:27(24-27)	after this manner shall ye **baptize** in my name; for
3 Ne. 11:34(33-34)	whoso believeth not in me, and is not **baptized**, shall
3 Ne. 12:2(1,2)	blessed are they who shall believe...and be **baptized**
Moro. 8:25(25,26)	the first fruits of repentance is **baptism**; and baptism
D&C 13:1	I confer...the keys...of **baptism** by immersion for the
D&C 19:31	declare repentance...and remission of sins by **baptism**
D&C 20:68(68,69)	the duty of the members after...received by **baptism**.
D&C 68:8(8,9)	go ye into all the world...**baptizing** in the name of
D&C 84:27(25-28)	**baptism**...caused to continue with...Israel until John
Moses 6:59(53-62)	be born again into the kingdom of heaven, of **water**
JS-H 1:69	the keys...of the gospel of repentance, and of **baptism**
JS-H 1:73(68-73)	after...**baptized**, we experienced great and glorious
A of F 1:4	first principles...are...**baptism** by immersion for the
JFS-V 1:33(31-34)	vicarious **baptism** for the remission of sins, the gift

BAPTISM, ESSENTIAL

Matt. 3:15(13-17)	suffer it to be so now...to **fulfil** all righteousness.
Matt. 7:14(13,14)	strait is the **gate**...which leadeth unto life, and few
Matt. 28:19(19-20)	go ye therefore, and teach all nations, **baptizing** them
Mark 1:9(7-12)	Jesus came...and was **baptized** of John in Jordan.
Mark 16:16(15-16)	he that believeth and is **baptized** shall be saved; but
Luke 3:21(21,22)	that Jesus also being **baptized**, and praying, the heave
Luke 7:30(28-30)	rejected the counsel of God...being not **baptized** of
John 3:5(3-5)	except...born of **water**...cannot enter into the kingdom
Acts 2:38(37-38)	repent, and be **baptized** every one of you in the name
Acts 8:12	when they believed...they were **baptized**, both men and
Acts 9:18(1-18)	received sight forthwith, and arose, and was **baptized**.
Acts 10:48(46-48)	he commanded them to be **baptized** in the name of the
Acts 19:5(1-6)	when they heard this, they were **baptized** in the name
Acts 22:16(10-16)	arise, and be **baptized**, and wash away thy sins
1 Cor. 10:2(1-4)	and were all **baptized** unto Moses in the cloud and in
1 Cor. 15:29	else what shall they do which are **baptized** for the
Eph. 4:5	one Lord, one faith, one **baptism**
Titus 3:5	saved us, by the **washing** of regeneration, and renewing
Heb. 6:2(1,2)	of the doctrine of **baptisms**, and of laying on of hands
1 Pet. 3:21	**baptism** doth also now save us (not the putting away
2 Ne. 9:23(23-24)	he commandeth all men that they must...be **baptized** in
2 Ne. 31:5(4-14)	much more need have we, being unholy, to be **baptized**
3 Ne. 11:21(21,22)	power that ye shall **baptize** this people when I am
3 Ne. 11:33(33-35)	whoso believeth in me, and is **baptized**..shall be saved
3 Ne. 27:20(16-22)	this is the commandment: repent...and be **baptized** in
Ether 4:18(18-19)	he that believeth and is **baptized** shall be saved; but
D&C 18:22(21-25)	as many as repent and are **baptized** in my name...and
D&C 22:4(1-4)	enter ye in at the **gate**, as I have commanded, and seek

BAPTISM, ESSENTIAL cont.

D&C 39:20(19-24)	go forth **baptizing** with water, preparing the way
D&C 55:1(1-3)	after...**baptized**...shall have a remission of your sins
D&C 76:51(50-53)	they are they who...were **baptized**...according to the
D&C 84:74(74,75)	they who...are not **baptized**...shall be damned, and
D&C 112:29(28,29)	he that believeth and is **baptized** shall be saved, and
Moses 6:52(51-66)	turn unto me...repent...and be **baptized**, even in water
Moses 6:59(52-62)	ye must be born again...of **water**, and of the spirit
Moses 7:11(10-11)	a commandment that I should **baptize** in the name of the
Moses 8:24(23-24)	believe and repent of your sins and be **baptized** in the
A of F 1:4	first principles and ordinances...third, **baptism** by

BAPTISM, IMMERSION

Matt. 3:16	Jesus, when he was **baptized**, went up straightway out
Mark 1:5(4-5)	all **baptized** of him in the river of Jordan, confessing
Mark 1:10	straightway coming **up** out of the water, he saw the
John 3:23	John also was baptizing...there was much **water** there
Acts 8:38(38-39)	they went down both into the water...he **baptized** him.
Rom. 6:4(3-5)	we are **buried** with him by baptism into death: that
Eph. 4:5	one Lord, one faith, one **baptism**
Col. 2:12	buried with him in **baptism**, wherein also ye are risen
Mosiah 18:14(14-16)	both Alma and Helam were **buried** in the water; and they
3 Ne. 11:26(22-26)	then shall ye **immerse** them in the water, and come
3 Ne. 19:11(11-13)	Nephi went **down** into the water and was baptized.
3 Ne. 19:13(11-13)	had come **up** out of the water, the Holy Ghost did fall
D&C 20:74(72-74)	then shall he **immerse** him or her in the water, and
D&C 76:51	were baptized...being **buried** in the water in his name
D&C 128:12(12-13)	ordinance of baptism by water, to be **immersed** therein
Moses 6:64(64-65)	Adam...was laid under the **water**, and was brought forth
A of F 1:4	baptism by **immersion** for the remission of sins; fourth

BAPTISM, QUALIFICATIONS FOR

Matt. 3:8(5-8)	bring forth therefore fruits meet for **repentance**
Matt. 3:11(7-12)	I indeed baptize you with water unto **repentance**: but
Matt. 28:20(19,20)	teaching them to **observe** all things whatsoever I have
Mark 1:5(4-5)	baptized...in the river of Jordan, **confessing** their
Mark 16:16(15-16)	he that **believeth** and is baptized shall be saved; but
Luke 3:8(7-8)	bring forth therefore **fruits** worthy of repentance, and
Acts 2:38(37-38)	**repent**, and be baptized...in the name of Jesus Christ
Acts 2:41	they that gladly received his **word** were baptized: and
Acts 8:37(35-37)	if thou **believest** with all thine heart, thou mayest.
Acts 16:31(25-34)	**believe** on the Lord Jesus Christ, and thou shalt be
Acts 18:8	many of the Corinthians hearing **believed**, and were
Acts 19:4(1-6)	John verily baptized with the baptism of **repentance**
Rom. 6:4(1-12)	we also should walk in **newness** of life.
Gal. 3:26(26-29)	ye are all the children of God by **faith** in Christ
2 Ne. 9:23	be baptized...having perfect **faith** in the Holy One of
2 Ne. 31:7(6-8)	witnesseth unto the Father that he would be **obedient**
2 Ne. 31:13(10-21)	if ye shall **follow** the Son, with full purpose of heart
Mosiah 18:9(7-11)	yea, and are **willing**...to stand as witnesses of God

BAPTISM, QUALIFICATIONS FOR cont.

Mosiah 18:10(8-14) — as a **witness**...that ye have entered into a covenant
Mosiah 21:35(33-35) — baptized as a witness...**willing** to serve God with all
Mosiah 26:22(21,22) — whosoever is baptized...shall **believe** in my name; and
Alma 6:2 — who **repented** of their sins were baptized unto
Alma 7:14(13-16) — ye must **repent**, and be born again; for the spirit
Alma 9:27 — to redeem those who will be **baptized** unto repentance
Alma 19:35 — as many as did **believe** were baptized; and they became
3 Ne. 7:24(24,25) — none...brought unto **repentance** who were not baptized
3 Ne. 11:23 — whoso repenteth...and **desireth** to be baptized in my
3 Ne. 11:38(37,38) — baptized in my name, and become as a little **child**, or
3 Ne. 27:16(13-20) — whoso repenteth and is baptized in my **name** shall be
Morm. 9:29 — see that ye are not baptized **unworthily**; see that ye
Moro. 6:1(1-4) — not baptized save they brought forth **fruit** meet that
Moro. 6:2(1-4) — receive...unto baptism...broken heart..contrite **spirit**
Moro. 6:3(1-4) — none..received..save..**took** upon them the name of
Moro. 8:8 — little children...whole..not **capable** of committing sin
Moro. 8:11(5-26) — little **children** need no repentance, neither baptism.
Moro. 8:25(25,26) — the first fruits of **repentance** is baptism; and baptism
D&C 19:31 — thou shalt declare repentance and **faith** on the Savior
D&C 20:37 — all those who **humble** themselves...desire to be baptize
D&C 20:71 — unless he has arrived unto the years of **accountability**
D&C 33:11(10-12) — **repent** and be baptized, every one of you, for a
D&C 49:12(12-14) — **believe** on the name of the Lord Jesus, who was on the
D&C 68:27(25-27) — children shall be baptized...when **eight** years old, and
D&C 76:51(50-53) — received the **testimony** of Jesus...believed...baptized
Moses 6:57(51-60) — all men, everywhere, must **repent**, or they can in
Moses 8:24(23-24) — **believe** and repent of your sins and be baptized in the
A of F 1:4 — first principles...are: first, **faith** in the Lord Jesus

BAPTISM FOR THE DEAD

1 Cor. 15:29 — what shall they do which are **baptized** for the dead
D&C 124:29(28-55) — baptismal font..saints, may be **baptized** for those who
D&C 127:5(5-9) — a word in relation to the **baptism** for your dead.
D&C 128:1(1-25) — the subject of the **baptism** for the dead, as that

BARRENNESS

Gen. 11:30 — but Sarai was **barren**; she had no child.
Gen. 18:11(9-14) — **ceased** to be with Sarah after the manner of women.
Gen. 25:21(20-21) — Isaac intreated...wife, because she was **barren**: and
Gen. 29:31 — but Rachel was **barren**.
Gen. 30:23 — God hath taken away my **reproach**
Ex. 23:26(22-26) — there shall nothing...be **barren**, in thy land: the
Deut. 7:14(12-16) — shall not be male or female **barren** among you, or Amon
Judg. 13:3(2-20) — now, thou art **barren**...but thou shalt conceive, and
1 Sam. 1:2(1-8) — he had two wives...but Hannah had **no** children.
1 Sam. 2:5(1-10) — so that the **barren** hath born seven; and she that hath
2 Kgs. 2:21(19,21) — not be from thence any more death or **barren** land.
Ps. 113:9 — the **barren** woman...to be a joyful mother of children.
Isa. 54:1(1-4) — sing, O **barren**, thou that didst not bear; break forth

BARRENNESS cont.

Luke 1:7(7,13,36)	because that Elisabeth was **barren**, and they both were
Luke 1:25	to take away my **reproach** among men.
Gal. 4:27(21-31)	rejoice, thou **barren** that bearest not; break forth and
2 Pet. 1:8	neither be **barren** nor unfruitful in the knowledge of
Alma 32:39	it is because your ground is **barren**, and ye will not
D&C 133:29	and in the **barren** deserts there shall come forth pools
Moses 7:8(7,8)	the **barrenness** thereof shall go forth forever; and the

BEAUTY

Gen. 29:17	Rachel was **beautiful** and well favoured.
Ex. 28:2(2,40)	for Aaron thy brother for glory and for **beauty**.
1 Sam. 16:12	he was ruddy...of a **beautiful** countenance, and goodly
1 Chr. 16:29	worship the Lord in the **beauty** of holiness.
2 Chr. 3:6(4-7)	garnished the house with precious stones for **beauty**
Ezra 7:27	**beautify** the house of the Lord which is in Jerusalem
Ps. 8:3(3-9)	when I **consider** thy heavens, the work of thy fingers
Ps. 27:4	to behold the **beauty** of the Lord, and to inquire in
Ps. 29:2	worship the Lord in the **beauty** of holiness.
Ps. 48:2(1-5)	**beautiful** for situation...is mount Zion, on the sides
Ps. 50:2	out of Zion, the perfection of **beauty**, God hath shined
Ps. 90:17	and let the **beauty** of the Lord our God be upon us: and
Ps. 149:4	he will **beautify** the meek with salvation.
Prov. 4:9(7-9)	give to thine head an **ornament** of grace: a crown of
Prov. 20:29	and the **beauty** of old men is the gray head.
Prov. 31:30	**beauty** is vain: but a woman that feareth the Lord, she
Eccl. 3:11	he hath made every thing **beautiful** in his time: also
Isa. 3:24(16-24)	it shall come to pass...burning instead of **beauty**.
Isa. 4:2(2-4)	branch of the Lord be **beautiful** and glorious, and the
Isa. 33:17(15-17)	thine eyes shall see the king in his **beauty**: they
Isa. 52:1	O Zion; put on thy **beautiful** garments, O Jerusalem
Isa. 52:7	how **beautiful** upon the mountains are the feet of him
Isa. 53:2	no **beauty** that we should desire him.
Isa. 60:13	to **beautify** the place of my sanctuary; and I will make
Isa. 61:3	to give unto them **beauty** for ashes, the oil of joy for
Isa. 64:11(9-12)	our holy and our **beautiful** house, where our fathers
Matt. 23:27	whited sepulchres...appear **beautiful** outward, but are
Philip. 4:8	whatsoever things are **lovely**...think on these things.
1 Pet. 3:4(3,4)	even the **ornament** of a meek and quiet spirit, which
1 Ne. 11:8	beheld a tree...exceeding of all **beauty**; and the white
Mosiah 18:30	forest of Mormon, how **beautiful** are they to the eyes
D&C 42:40	their **beauty** the beauty of the work of thine own hands
D&C 82:14	for Zion must increase in **beauty**, and in holiness; her
JS-H 1:14	on the morning of a **beautiful**, clear day, early in the
A of F 1:13	virtuous, **lovely**, or of good report...we seek after
JS-V 1:2(1-4)	I saw the transcendent **beauty** of the gate through

BENEVOLENCE

Gen. 45:5(1-15)   be not **grieved**..angry with yourselves, that ye sold
Josh. 2:12(1-14)   since I have shewed you **kindness**, that ye will also
1 Sam. 24:10(10,11)   bade me kill thee: but mine eye **spared** thee; and I
1 Sam. 26:23   I would not stretch forth mine hand **against** the Lord's
Isa. 38:5(1-8)   heard thy prayer..will **add** unto thy days fifteen years
Jonah 4:11(4-11)   should not I **spare** Nineveh, that great city, wherein
Matt. 5:44(43-48)   do **good** to them that hate you, and pray for them
Matt. 7:12(7-12)   whatsoever ye would that men should do to you, **do** ye
Matt. 26:10(6-13)   for she hath **wrought** a good work upon me.
Luke 10:33(30-35)   certain Samaritan...had **compassion** on him
Luke 15:20(11-24)   his father saw him, and had **compassion**..and kissed him
Luke 23:34   then said Jesus, Father, **forgive** them; for they know
John 8:11(3-11)   neither do I **condemn** thee: go, and sin no more.
Acts 3:6   such as I have **give** I thee: in the name of Jesus
1 Cor. 7:3   let the husband render unto the wife due **benevolence**
1 Cor. 13:4   charity suffereth long, and is **kind**; charity envieth
Gal. 5:22(22,23)   peace, longsuffering, **gentleness**, goodness, faith
Eph. 4:32(29-32)   and be ye **kind** one to another, tenderhearted
Philip. 2:2(1-5)   that ye be likeminded, having the same **love**, being of
Col. 3:12(12-15)   **kindness**, humbleness of mind, meekness, longsuffering
Heb. 13:1(1-3)   let brotherly **love** continue.
James 1:5   ask of God, that **giveth** to all men liberally, and
James 1:27   pure religion...**visit** the fatherless and widows in the
James 5:16   confess your faults...and **pray** one for another, that
2 Pet. 1:7(5-9)   and to godliness brotherly **kindness**; and to brotherly
2 Ne. 11:5(5-7)   my soul delighteth in his **grace**...in the great...plan
Enos 1:9(9-11)   I began to feel a desire for the **welfare** of my
Mosiah 4:26(16-26)   I would that ye should **impart** of your substance to the
Alma 41:14(14,15)   do **good** continually; and if ye do all these things the
Alma 44:6(5-6)   but we will **spare** your lives, if ye will go your way
3 Ne. 12:44(43-48)   do **good** to them that hate you, and pray for them who
3 Ne. 26:19   and they taught, and did **minister** one to another; and
Ether 4:12(11,12)   whatsoever thing persuadeth men to do **good** is of me
Moro. 7:13(5-17)   which inviteth and enticeth to do **good**, and to love
D&C 4:6   patience, brotherly **kindness**, godliness, charity
D&C 6:33(33,34)   if ye sow **good** ye shall also reap good for your reward
D&C 11:12(12-14)   put your trust in that spirit which leadeth to do **good**
D&C 38:24   let every man **esteem** his brother as himself, and
D&C 64:10(9-10)   you it is required to **forgive** all men.
D&C 64:33   be not weary in **well-doing**, for ye are laying the
D&C 107:30(30,31)   decisions...made in...temperance, **patience**, godliness
D&C 121:45   bowels also be full of **charity** towards all men, and
A of F 1:13   We believe in being...**benevolent**...in doing good to

BIRTH CONTROL

Gen. 1:28   be fruitful, and **multiply**, and replenish the earth
Gen. 49:25(22-26)   bless thee with blessings of heaven...of the **womb**
Ex. 21:22(22-25)   hurt a woman with **child**, so that her fruit depart from
Deut. 7:13(11-13)   he will...**multiply** thee: he will also bless the fruit
Deut. 28:4(1-4)   blessed shall be the **fruit** of thy body, and the fruit
Deut. 28:11(4,11)   Lord shall make thee plenteous...in..**fruit** of thy body

BIRTH CONTROL cont.

Ps. 113:9	the barren woman...to be a joyful **mother** of children.
Ps. 127:3(3-5)	**children** are an heritage of the Lord: and the fruit
Jer. 1:5(4,5)	before thou camest forth out of the womb I **sanctified**
1 Tim. 2:15	she shall be saved in **childbearing**, if they continue
1 Ne. 7:1(1-6)	that they might raise up **seed** unto the Lord in the
2 Ne. 2:23(22-25)	they would have had no **children**...having no joy, for
D&C 83:4	all children have claim upon their **parents** for their
D&C 132:19	which glory shall be...a continuation of the **seeds** for
D&C 132:30(29-32)	Abraham received promises concerning his **seed**, and of
Moses 2:28	be **fruitful**, and multiply, and replenish the earth
Moses 5:11	were it not for our transgression we never...had **seed**

BIRTHRIGHT

Gen. 25:31(31-34)	and Jacob said, sell me this day thy **birthright**.
Gen. 27:36	he took away my **birthright**; and, behold, now he hath
Gen. 43:33	they sat...the firstborn according to his **birthright**
Gen. 48:20(5-20)	he set **Ephraim** before Manasseh.
Ex. 40:15(12-15)	everlasting priesthood throughout their **generations**.
Num. 3:10(5-13)	shalt appoint Aaron and his **sons**, and they shall wait
Num. 18:21(20-24)	for an **inheritance**, for their service which they serve
Num. 25:13(10-13)	and his **seed** after him, even the covenant of an
1 Chr. 5:2(1-2)	but the **birthright** was Joseph's
Jer. 31:9	Ephraim is my **firstborn**.
Rom. 4:13(13-16)	**heir** of the world...through the righteousness of faith
Rom. 8:17(16-18)	heirs of God, and joint-**heirs** with Christ; if so be
Heb. 12:16(16-17)	Esau, who for one morsel of meat sold his **birthright**.
1 Ne. 1:1	**born** of goodly parents, therefore I was taught
2 Ne. 1:28(28,29)	if ye will hearken...I leave unto you a **blessing**, yea
2 Ne. 3:23(22-25)	wherefore, because of this covenant thou art **blessed**
Mosiah 6:7(4-7)	do according to that which his **father** had done in all
Alma 5:3	I, Alma...consecrated by my **father**, Alma, to be a high
Alma 9:8(8-11)	how have ye forgotten the **tradition** of your fathers
Alma 56:47	think more upon the **liberty** of their fathers than they
D&C 86:9(8-11)	ye are lawful **heirs**, according to the flesh, and have
D&C 113:8(5-8)	priesthood, which...Zion, has a **right** to by lineage
Abr. 1:4(1-5)	**appointment**...unto...fathers concerning the seed.
Abr. 2:11(9-11)	this **right** shall continue in thee, and in thy seed

BISHOP

Num. 3:10(9-13)	thou shalt appoint **Aaron** and his sons, and they shall
Neh. 11:16	chief of the Levites, had the **oversight** of the outward
Neh. 11:22	the **overseer** also of the Levites at Jerusalem was Uzzi
Jer. 3:15(14-16)	I will give you **pastors** according to mine heart, which
Jer. 23:4(1-4)	I will set up **shepherds** over them which shall feed the
Acts 20:28	the Holy Ghost hath made you **overseers**, to feed the
Eph. 4:11(11-14)	and he gave some, apostles; and some...**pastors** and
Philip. 1:1	the saints...at Philippi, with the **bishops** and deacons
1 Tim. 3:1(1-7)	if a man desire the office of a **bishop**, he desireth a
Titus 1:7(5-9)	a **bishop** must be blameless, as the steward of God; not

BISHOP cont.

1 Pet. 2:25	returned unto the shepherd and **bishop** of your souls.
D&C 20:67	every...**bishop**...is to be ordained by the direction
D&C 41:9(9-10)	he should be appointed...and ordained a **bishop** unto
D&C 42:31(30-42)	impart of your substance...laid before the **bishop** of
D&C 42:82(80-83)	it is necessary that the **bishop** be present also.
D&C 46:27	**bishop**...to discern all those gifts lest...not of God.
D&C 58:17(17-18)	this mission is appointed to be a **judge** in Israel
D&C 64:40	the **bishop**, who is a judge, and his counselors, if the
D&C 68:14(14-24)	other **bishops** to be set apart unto the church, to
D&C 68:19(19,20)	high priest...may officiate in the office of **bishop**
D&C 72:5(1-6)	elders...account of their stewardship unto the **bishop**
D&C 107:15(13-17)	**bishopric** is the presidency of this priesthood, and
D&C 107:17	high priest...may officiate in the office of **bishop**
D&C 107:68(68-88)	office of a **bishop** is in administering all temporal
A of F 1:6	apostles, prophets, **pastors**, teachers, evangelists

BLASPHEMY

Lev. 24:16(15-16)	he that **blasphemeth** the name of the Lord, he shall
1 Kgs. 21:10(10,13)	thou didst **blaspheme** God and the king. And then carry
Job 2:9	then said his wife unto him...**curse** God, and die.
Isa. 8:21(21,22)	**curse** their king and their God, and look upward.
Isa. 52:5(5-6)	my name continually every day is **blasphemed**.
Ezek. 35:12(11-13)	I have heard all thy **blasphemies** which thou hast
Ezek. 36:20	they **profaned** my holy name, when they said to them
Matt. 12:31(31-32)	but the **blasphemy** against the Holy Ghost shall not be
Matt. 15:19(18-20)	out of the heart proceed evil...**blasphemies**
Matt. 26:65(64-66)	he hath spoken **blasphemy**; what further need have we
Mark 2:7(5-7)	why doth this man thus speak **blasphemies**? Who can
Luke 5:21	who is this which speaketh **blasphemies**? Who can
John 10:33(22-42)	for a good work we stone thee not; but for **blasphemy**
Acts 6:11(11,13)	we have heard him speak **blasphemous** words against
Acts 13:45(44-46)	Jews...spake...contradicting and **blaspheming**.
Rom. 2:24	the name of God is **blasphemed** among the Gentiles
Col. 3:8(4-8)	but now ye also put off...**blasphemy**, filthy
Rev. 2:9(8-10)	I know the **blasphemy** of them which say they are Jews
Rev. 13:5(5,6)	a mouth speaking great things and **blasphemies**; and
Rev. 16:9(9,11,21)	men were scorched...and **blasphemed** the name of God
Jacob 7:7(6,7)	I, Sherem, declare unto you that this is **blasphemy**
Jarom 1:5	they profaned not; neither did they **blaspheme**. and the
Alma 30:30(29-31)	yea, he went on to **blaspheme**.
Alma 49:27(25-27)	he was exceedingly wroth, and he did **curse** God, and
Morm. 2:14(13-15)	but they did **curse** God, and wish to die. Nevertheless
D&C 45:32	wicked, men shall lift up their voices and **curse** God
D&C 132:27	the **blasphemy** against the Holy Ghost, which shall not

BLESSINGS

Gen. 4:7(1-7)	if thou doest well, shalt thou not be **accepted**? And
Gen. 12:3(1-3)	I will **bless** them that bless thee, and curse him that
Gen. 14:19(18-20)	**blessed** be Abram of the most high God, possessor of

BLESSINGS cont.

Gen. 27:29(1-29)	and blessed be he that **blesseth** thee.
Gen. 30:13	Leah said, happy am I...daughters will call me **blessed**
Gen. 30:27	I have learned...the Lord hath **blessed** me for thy sake
Gen. 39:23(20-23)	and that which he did, the Lord made it to **prosper**.
Deut. 9:4	for my **righteousness** the Lord hath brought me in to
Deut. 11:26(26-28)	I set before you this day a **blessing** and a curse
Deut. 28:2(1-14)	all these **blessings** shall come on thee, and overtake
Ps. 2:12	**blessed** are all they that put their trust in him.
Ps. 119:1	**blessed** are the undefiled in the way, who walk in the
Prov. 3:10(7-10)	so shall thy barns be filled with **plenty**, and thy
Mal. 3:10(8-12)	the windows of heaven, and pour you out a **blessing**
Matt. 5:3(3-12)	**blessed** are the poor in spirit: for theirs is the king
Matt. 6:33	first the kingdom...all these **things** shall be added
Matt. 21:22	all **things**...ask in prayer, believing, ye shall
Matt. 25:34	come, ye **blessed** of my Father, inherit the kingdom
Luke 11:28(27,28)	**blessed** are they that hear the word of God, and keep
Luke 14:14(12-14)	and thou shalt be **blessed**; for they cannot recompense
1 Cor. 2:9(9,10)	the things which God hath **prepared** for them that love
1 Cor. 10:16	the cup of **blessing** which we bless, is it not the
Gal. 3:14	that the **blessing** of Abraham might come on the gentile
James 1:12	**blessed** is the man that endureth temptation: for when
1 Pet. 3:9(8,9)	not rendering evil for evil...contrariwise **blessing**
1 Ne. 17:2(1-3)	so great were the **blessings** of the Lord upon us, that
1 Ne. 17:35(33-35)	he that is righteous is **favored** of God. but behold
3 Ne. 10:18(18,19)	great **blessings** poured out upon their heads, insomuch
3 Ne. 12:1(1-11)	**blessed** are ye if ye shall give heed unto the words
3 Ne. 24:10(8-12)	the windows of heaven, and pour you out a **blessing**
Ether 2:7(7-12)	land...which...God had **preserved** for a righteous
D&C 18:8	if...diligent...he shall be **blessed** unto eternal life
D&C 35:24	keep..commandments...cause..heavens to shake for..**good**
D&C 36:1	you are **blessed**, and your sins are forgiven you, and
D&C 41:1	I delight to bless with the greatest of all **blessings**
D&C 58:4(3-4)	for after much tribulation come the **blessings**.
D&C 59:23	righteousness shall receive his **reward**, even peace in
D&C 62:3	ye are **blessed**, for the testimony which ye have borne
D&C 63:50	he that liveth when the Lord shall come...**blessed** is
D&C 82:10(8-10)	Lord...**bound** when ye do...but when...not...no promise.
D&C 130:21(20-21)	when we obtain any **blessing** from God, it is by
Abr. 1:26	**blessings** of the earth, and with the blessings of
Abr. 2:11(10,11)	and I will **bless** them that bless thee, and curse them
JFS-V 1:52(49-52)	partakers of all **blessings** which were held in reserve

BLOOD, EATING OF

Gen. 9:4	flesh with the...**blood** thereof, shall ye not eat.
Lev. 3:17	that ye eat neither fat nor **blood**.
Lev. 17:10	set my face against that soul that eateth **blood**, and
Lev. 17:14(11-14)	eat the **blood** of no manner of flesh..life..is the
Lev. 19:26	ye shall not eat any thing with the **blood**: neither
Deut. 12:23(23-25)	eat not the blood: for the **blood** is the life; and thou
1 Sam. 14:34(33-34)	sin not against the Lord in eating with the **blood**. And
Ezek. 33:25	ye eat with the **blood**, and lift up your eyes toward

BLOOD, EATING OF cont.

Ezek. 44:7	when ye offer my bread, the fat and the **blood**, and the
Acts 15:20(20,29)	abstain...from things strangled, and from **blood**.
Enos 1:20	became wild...ferocious, and a **blood-thirsty** people
Jarom 1:6	loved murder and would drink the **blood** of beasts.
Alma 49:27(25-28)	an oath that he would drink his **blood**; and this

BLOOD, SHEDDING OF

Gen. 9:6(4-6)	whoso **sheddeth** man's blood, by man shall his blood be
Ex. 20:13	thou shalt not **kill**.
Ex. 21:28	if an ox gore...that they **die**...ox shall be surely
2 Kgs. 21:16	Manasseh shed innocent **blood** very much, till he had
Ezek. 7:23	the land is full of **bloody** crimes, and the city is
Ezek. 11:6(6,7)	ye have multiplied your **slain** in this city, and ye
Ezek. 22:3	the city sheddeth **blood** in the midst of it, that her
Ezek. 24:6	woe to the **bloody** city, to the pot whose scum is there
Matt. 5:21(21,22)	thou shalt not **kill**; and whosoever shall kill shall
Matt. 15:19(19,20)	out of the heart proceed evil thoughts, **murders**
Matt. 19:18(16-19)	thou shalt do no **murder**, thou shalt not commit
Matt. 27:4	sinned in that I have betrayed the innocent **blood**. and
Rev. 13:10	he that **killeth** with the sword must be killed with
1 Ne. 4:10(9-18)	never at any time have I shed the **blood** of man. and I
2 Ne. 6:15	they that believe not...destroyed...by **bloodsheds**, and
Mosiah 13:21	thou shalt not **kill**.
Alma 1:13(12-15)	were we to spare thee his **blood** would come upon us for
Alma 34:12(11-12)	the law requireth the **life** of him who hath murdered
Alma 34:13(11-14)	there should be, a stop to the **shedding** of blood; then
Alma 42:19(16-20)	would he be afraid he would **die** if he should murder
Alma 48:14(14-25)	even to the shedding of **blood** if it were necessary
D&C 42:19(18-19)	he that **killeth** shall die.
D&C 42:79	if any...**kill** ...dealt with according...laws of the
D&C 63:31(27-31)	if by blood, as you are forbidden to shed **blood**, lo
D&C 132:19(19,27)	commit no murder whereby to shed innocent **blood**, and
Moses 6:60	and by the **blood** ye are sanctified

BLOOD, SYMBOLISM OF

Ex. 30:10	the **blood** of the sin offering of atonements: once in
Lev. 17:11	it is the **blood** that maketh an atonement for the soul.
John 6:54(53-57)	whoso...drinketh my **blood**, hath eternal life; and I
Rom. 3:25	to be a propitiation through faith in his **blood**, to
Rom. 5:9	being now justified by his **blood**, we shall be saved
Heb. 9:14	how much more shall the **blood** of Christ...purge your
Heb. 9:22(22-28)	and without **shedding** of blood is no remission.
Heb. 13:12	Jesus...sanctify the people with his own **blood**, suffer
1 Jn. 1:7	**blood** of Jesus Christ...cleanseth us from all sin.
1 Jn. 5:8(1-8)	three that bear witness in earth..spirit..water..**blood**
Rev. 1:5	Jesus Christ..washed us from our sins in his own **blood**
Rev. 8:8	and the third part of the sea became **blood**
1 Ne. 12:10	their garments are made white in his **blood**.
Mosiah 3:11	his **blood** atoneth for the sins of those who have

BLOOD, SYMBOLISM OF cont.

Mosiah 4:2(2-3)	and apply the atoning **blood** of Christ that we may
Alma 34:10	not a **sacrifice** of man, neither of beast, neither of
Alma 34:11(11-12)	not any man that can sacrifice his own **blood** which
Alma 34:13(13-14)	a stop to the shedding of **blood**; then shall the law
3 Ne. 18:11	do it in remembrance of my **blood**, which I have shed
3 Ne. 18:29(28-30)	drinketh my...**blood** unworthily..ye shall forbid him.
Moro. 10:33	sanctified...through the shedding of the **blood** of
D&C 27:2	and my **blood** which was shed for the remission of your
D&C 76:69	perfect atonement through...shedding of his own **blood**.
D&C 88:87	not many days...and the moon shall be bathed in **blood**
D&C 135:3	sealed his mission and his works with his own **blood**
Moses 5:7(6-7)	a similitude of the **sacrifice** of the Only Begotten of
Moses 6:60	and by the **blood** ye are sanctified
Moses 6:62	plan of salvation...through the **blood** of mine Only

BOASTING

1 Kgs. 20:11(1-12)	let not him...**boast** himself as he that putteth it off.
Ps. 10:3	the wicked **boasteth** of his heart's desire, and
Prov. 10:19	in the multitude of **words** there wanteth not sin: but
Prov. 20:14	when he is gone his way, then he **boasteth**.
Prov. 25:14	whoso **boasteth** himself of a false gift is like clouds
Prov. 27:1	**boast** not thyself of to morrow; for thou knowest not
Prov. 27:2	let another man **praise** thee, and not thine own mouth
Isa. 10:15(12-15)	shall the axe **boast** itself against him that heweth the
Rom. 1:30(28-32)	backbiters, haters of God, despiteful, proud, **boasters**
Rom. 11:18(16-25)	**boast** not against the branches. But if thou boast
1 Cor. 3:18	if any man among you **seemeth** to be wise in this world
2 Cor. 7:14	even so our **boasting**, which I made before Titus, is
2 Cor. 10:13(12-18)	but we will not **boast** of things without our measure
2 Cor. 10:18	not he that **commendeth** himself is approved, but whom
2 Cor. 11:16	that I may **boast** myself a little.
2 Cor. 12:1(1-11)	it is not expedient for me doubtless to **glory**. I will
2 Cor. 12:5(1-11)	yet of myself I will not **glory**, but in mine
Eph. 2:9(8-10)	not of works, lest any man should **boast**.
James 3:5	tongue is a little member, and **boasteth** great things.
James 4:16(13-16)	but now ye rejoice in your **boastings**: all such
2 Pet. 2:10	**presumptuous** are they, selfwilled, they are not afraid
2 Ne. 20:15(12-15)	shall the ax **boast** itself against him that heweth
Mosiah 2:15(15,16,24)	I have not done these things that I might **boast**
Mosiah 11:19	they did **boast** in their own strength, saying that
Alma 30:31	he did rise up in great **swelling** words before Alma
Alma 38:11	do not **boast** in your own wisdom, nor of your much
Hel. 4:13	because of...their **boastings** in their own strength
Hel. 5:8	that ye may not do these things that ye may **boast**, but
Hel. 12:5(4-23)	how quick to **boast**, and do all manner of that which
Hel. 13:22	swell with great pride, unto **boasting**, and unto great
3 Ne. 6:10	some were lifted up unto pride and **boastings** because
Morm. 3:9(9-10)	they began to **boast** in their own strength, and began
Morm. 4:8	they did again **boast** of their strength; and they went
D&C 3:4(4,13)	if he **boasts** in his own strength, and sets at naught
D&C 50:33	neither with **boasting** nor rejoicing, lest you be

BOASTING cont.

D&C 84:73(64-73)	they shall not **boast** themselves of these things
D&C 105:24	neither **boast** of faith nor of mighty works, but
Moses 5:33	Cain **gloried** in that which he had done, saying: I am

BODY, SANCTITY OF

Gen. 1:31(25,27,31)	God saw every thing...he had made...it was very **good**.
Gen. 9:6	for in the **image** of God made he man.
Lev. 19:28	not make any cuttings in your **flesh** for the dead, nor
Lev. 21:5	nor make any cuttings in their **flesh**.
Deut. 14:1(1-3)	ye shall not **cut** yourselves, nor make any baldness
Matt. 5:28(27-28)	looketh on a **woman** to lust after her hath committed
Rom. 12:1	that ye present your **bodies** a living sacrifice, holy
1 Cor. 3:16(16-17)	know ye not that ye are the **temple** of God, and that
1 Cor. 6:19(9-20)	your **body** is the temple of the Holy Ghost which is in
2 Cor. 6:16	ye are the **temple** of the living God; as God hath said
Eph. 5:29(28-29)	for no man ever yet hated his own **flesh**; but
1 Thes. 4:4(3-5)	to possess his **vessel** in sanctification and honour
2 Tim. 2:21	he shall be a **vessel** unto honour, sanctified, and
2 Ne. 9:4	in our **bodies** we shall see God.
2 Ne. 9:12	the **bodies** and the spirits of men will be restored one
Mosiah 2:37(36-37)	the Lord...dwelleth not in unholy **temples**.
Alma 40:23	soul shall be restored to the **body**, and the body to
Alma 41:2	every part of the **body** should be restored to itself.
3 Ne. 28:39(38-40)	they were sanctified in the **flesh**, that they were holy
Morm. 6:21	must soon become incorruptible **bodies**; and then ye
Ether 3:16	man have I created after the **body** of my spirit; and
Moro. 9:9(8-9)	this great **abomination** of the Lamanites, it doth not
Moro. 10:34	my spirit and **body** shall again reunite, and I am
D&C 38:42	be ye **clean** that bear the vessels of the Lord. Even
D&C 84:33	are sanctified...unto the renewing of their **bodies**.
D&C 88:15	the spirit and the **body** are the soul of man.
D&C 88:28(27,28)	shall receive the same **body** which was a natural body
D&C 89:8(1-21)	tobacco is not for the **body**, neither for the belly
D&C 93:35	yea, man is the tabernacle of God, even **temples**; and
D&C 130:22	the father has a **body** of flesh and bones as tangible
D&C 133:5	be ye **clean** that bear the vessels of the Lord.
D&C 136:27	be diligent in **preserving** what thou hast...it is the

BONDAGE, PHYSICAL

Gen. 27:40(38-40)	that thou shalt break his **yoke** from off thy neck.
Ex. 1:14(7-14)	they made their lives bitter with hard **bondage**, in
Ex. 6:5(5-7)	Israel, whom the Egyptians keep in **bondage**; and I have
Ex. 13:14(14-16)	the Lord brought us out...from the house of **bondage**
Ex. 21:2(1-4)	buy an Hebrew **servant**...in the seventh...go out free
Lev. 25:39(39-42)	thou shalt not compel him to serve as a **bondservant**
Lev. 26:13	have broken the bands of your **yoke**, and made you go
Deut. 28:48	he shall put a **yoke** of iron upon thy neck, until he
1 Kgs. 12:4(1-15)	thy father made our **yoke** grievous: now therfore make
2 Kgs. 8:20(20-22)	in his days Edom revolted from under the **hand** of Judah

BONDAGE, PHYSICAL cont.

Ezra 9:9(8,9)	God hath not forsaken us in our **bondage**, but hath
Isa. 10:27	the **yoke** shall be destroyed because of the anointing.
Isa. 14:25	his **yoke** depart from off them, and his burden depart
Jer. 30:8(4-9)	I will break his **yoke** from off thy neck, and will
Ezek. 34:27(26-28)	broken the bands of their **yoke**, and delivered them out
Nahum 1:13(12,13)	for now will I break his **yoke** from off thee, and will
2 Cor. 11:20(16-20)	for ye suffer, if a man bring you into **bondage**, if a
1 Tim. 6:1(1-3)	servants as are under the **yoke** count their own masters
1 Ne. 17:25(23-26)	ye know that the children of Israel were in **bondage**
Mosiah 7:15(13-15)	our brethren will deliver us out of our **bondage**, or
Mosiah 12:2(2-8)	shall be brought into **bondage**, and shall be smitten
Mosiah 21:13(11-15)	subjecting themselves to the **yoke** of bondage
Mosiah 21:36(35-36)	the study...was to deliver themselves...from **bondage**.
Mosiah 24:17(15-20)	go with thee and deliver this people out of **bondage**.
Alma 44:2	to the **yoke** of bondage. but this is the very cause for
Alma 61:12(10-13)	subject ourselves to the **yoke** of bondage if it were
D&C 19:35	release thyself from **bondage**.
D&C 45:17	absence of your spirits from your bodies...a **bondage**
D&C 101:79(78-80)	it is not right that any man should be in **bondage** one
D&C 103:17(15-18)	be led out of **bondage** by power, and with a
D&C 104:83	shall be delivered this once out of your **bondage**.
D&C 109:47(47,63)	this **yoke** of affliction that has been put upon them.
D&C 123:8(7,8)	it is an iron **yoke**, it is a strong band; they are the

BONDAGE, SPIRITUAL

Isa. 5:13(13-14)	my people are gone into **captivity**...no knowledge: and
Isa. 9:4(1-7)	for thou hast broken the **yoke** of his burden, and the
Isa. 52:2	O Jerusalem: loose thyself from the **bands** of thy neck
Isa. 61:1	proclaim liberty to the **captives**, and the opening of
Jer. 30:8(4-9)	I will break his **yoke** from off thy neck, and will
Ezek. 34:27(26-28)	broken the bands of their **yoke**, and delivered them out
Luke 4:18	deliverance to the **captives**, and recovering of sight
John 8:32(31-34)	know the truth, and the truth shall make you **free**.
John 8:36	if the Son therefore shall make you **free**, ye shall be
Acts 8:23	and in the **bond** of iniquity.
Rom. 6:18(12-18,23)	made free from **sin**, ye became the servants of
Rom. 7:23	bringing me into **captivity** to the law of sin which is
Rom. 8:2	Jesus hath made me **free** from the law of sin and death.
Rom. 8:15(13-16)	ye have not received the spirit of **bondage** again to
Gal. 2:4(3-4)	that they might bring us into **bondage**
Gal. 3:13	Christ hath redeemed us from the **curse** of the law
Gal. 4:3(1-9)	were in **bondage** under the elements of the world
Gal. 5:1	be not entangled again with the yoke of **bondage**.
1 Tim. 3:7	lest he fall into reproach and the **snare** of the devil.
2 Tim. 2:26(24-26)	who are taken **captive** by him at his will.
Heb. 2:15(14-15)	deliver them who...were...subject to **bondage**.
2 Pet. 2:19(19-21)	servants of corruption...brought in **bondage**.
1 Ne. 13:5(4-6)	with a **yoke** of iron, and bringeth them down into
2 Ne. 1:13(12-14)	shake off the awful **chains** by which ye are bound
2 Ne. 2:29(26-29)	will of the flesh...giveth...devil power to **captivate**
2 Ne. 9:12(8-13)	hell must deliver up its **captive** spirits, and the

BONDAGE, SPIRITUAL cont.

2 Ne. 28:22(19-22)	his awful **chains**, from whence there is no deliverance.
Mosiah 16:5	the **devil** hath all power over him. Therefore, he is
Mosiah 23:13(12-13)	also from the **bonds** of iniquity, even so I desire that
Alma 5:7(7-13)	they were encircled about by the **bands** of death, and
Alma 12:11(9-11)	now this is what is meant by the **chains** of hell.
Alma 13:30(29-30)	that ye may not be **bound** down by the chains of hell
Alma 40:13(13-14)	they chose evil works...the **devil** did enter into them
Alma 41:11	in a state of nature...in the **bonds** of iniquity; they
Morm. 8:31(30-32)	gall of bitterness and in the **bonds** of iniquity.
D&C 84:49(49-51)	darkness and under the **bondage** of sin.
D&C 88:86	entangle not yourselves in **sin**, but let your hands
D&C 98:8	I, the Lord God, make you **free**, therefore ye are free
D&C 109:32(29-33)	complete deliverance from under this **yoke**
D&C 109:67(65-67)	be redeemed from **oppression**, and rejoice before thee.
D&C 113:10(9-10)	the **bands** of her neck are the curses of God upon her
D&C 123:8(7-17)	chains, and shackles, and **fetters** of hell.
Moses 4:4(3-4)	to lead them **captive** at his will, even as many as
Moses 5:23(21-25)	Satan desireth to have thee...I will **deliver** thee up
Moses 5:41(34-41)	Cain was **shut** out from the presence of the Lord, and

BOOK OF LIFE

Ex. 32:33(32-33)	whosoever hath sinned...will I blot out of my **book**.
Ezra 2:62(59,62)	sought their **register** among...genealogy, but they were
Ps. 69:28	let them be blotted out of the **book** of the living, and
Dan. 12:1(1-4)	every one that shall be found written in the **book**.
Philip. 4:3	fellowlabourers, whose names are in the **book** of life.
Rev. 3:5	I will not **blot** out his name out of the book of life
Rev. 13:8	names are not written in the **book** of life of the Lamb
Rev. 20:12(12-15)	another book was opened, which is the **book** of life
Rev. 21:27	they which are written in the Lamb's **book** of life.
Rev. 22:19	take away his part out of the **book** of life, and out
2 Ne. 29:11	out of the **books**...I will judge the world, every man
Mosiah 26:36(34-36)	not numbered among..the church..names were **blotted** out
Alma 5:58(57-58)	names of the righteous...written in the **book** of life
Alma 6:3	their names were not **numbered** among those of the right
3 Ne. 24:16(15-18)	a **book** of remembrance was written before him for them
3 Ne. 27:26(25-26)	out of the **books**...shall the world be judged.
Moro. 6:7	their names...not **numbered** among the people of Christ.
D&C 62:3	the testimony...is **recorded** in heaven for the angels
D&C 76:68(67-68)	these are they whose names are **written** in heaven
D&C 85:5(1-5)	names shall not be found...written in the **book** of the
D&C 85:11(11-12)	names are not found written in the **book** of the law
D&C 88:2(1-2)	recorded in the **book** of the names of the sanctified
D&C 127:7(6,7)	that in all your recordings it may be **recorded** in
D&C 128:7(6-7)	the **book** of life is the record which is kept in heaven
D&C 132:19	shall it be written in the Lamb's **Book** of Life, that

BOOK OF MORMON

Gen. 11:9(6-9)	from thence did the Lord **scatter** them abroad upon the
Gen. 49:22(22-26)	Joseph is a fruitful bough...**branches**...over the wall
Deut. 33:13(13-16)	of **Joseph** he said, blessed of the Lord be his land
Ps. 85:11	truth shall spring out of the **earth**; and righteousness
Isa. 29:4(2-4)	voice shall be...familiar spirit, out of the **ground**
Isa. 29:11(9-14)	vision of all...as the words of a **book** that is sealed
Isa. 29:14(13-18)	I will proceed to do a **marvellous** work...and a wonder
Isa. 29:18(17,18)	shall the deaf hear the words of the **book**, and the eye
Isa. 45:8	let the earth open, and let them bring forth **salvation**
Ezek. 37:19(15-20)	**stick** of Joseph...of Judah...shall be one in mine hand
John 10:16(14-16)	and other **sheep** I have, which are not of this fold
2 Cor. 13:1	in the mouth of two or three **witnesses** shall every
2 Tim. 3:16(16-17)	all **scripture** is given by inspiration of God, and is
Rev. 14:6(6-7)	I saw another angel fly..having the everlasting **gospel**
1 Ne. 13:40(38-42)	these last **records** ...shall establish the truth of the
1 Ne. 15:14(12-16)	**remnant** of our seed know that they...are the covenant
2 Ne. 3:12(1-24)	the fruit of thy loins shall **write**; and...of Judah
2 Ne. 3:20(19-20)	they shall cry from the **dust**; yea, even repentance
2 Ne. 10:7(7-15)	I **convenanted** with their fathers...shall be restored
2 Ne. 25:18	the purpose of **convincing** them of the true Messiah
2 Ne. 26:16(14-18)	shall speak unto them out of the **ground**, and their
2 Ne. 27:6(1-35)	God shall bring forth unto you the words of a **book**
2 Ne. 29:3(1-14)	many of the Gentiles shall say: A **Bible**! A Bible! we
2 Ne. 29:8(8-9)	the **testimony** of the two nations shall run together
2 Ne. 33:10(10,11)	believe in these **words**...words of Christ, and he hath
Enos 1:16(13-18)	preserve the **records**...covenanted...bring them forth
3 Ne. 15:21(11-24)	that ye are they of whom I said: other **sheep** I have
Morm. 5:12(12-15)	these things are **written** unto the remnant...of Jacob
Morm. 7:9(8-10)	this is **written**...that ye may believe that; and if ye
Morm. 8:16(12-17)	it shall be brought out of the **earth**, and it shall
Ether 2:11(11,12)	this cometh unto you...Gentiles...that ye may **repent**
Ether 5:4	all this shall stand as a **testimony** against the world
Moro. 10:4(3-5)	ask God...if these things are not **true**; and if ye
Moro. 10:29(27-29)	God shall show..that that which I have written is **true**
D&C 1:29	by the power of God, the **Book** of Mormon.
D&C 3:19(16-20)	for this very purpose are these **plates** preserved
D&C 10:42	I will **confound** those who have altered my words.
D&C 17:6(1-6)	he has translated the **book**...it is true.
D&C 20:9(8-12)	which contains...fulness of the **gospel** of Jesus Christ
D&C 42:12	**Book** of Mormon, in..which is the fulness of the gospel
Moses 7:62(61-62)	**truth** will I send..out of the earth..testimony of mine
JS-H 1:34(29-75)	he said there was a **book** deposited, written upon gold
A of F 1:8	We...believe the **Book** of Mormon to be the word of God.

BOOK OF REMEMBRANCE

Ex. 32:33(32-33)	whosoever hath sinned...will I blot out of my **book**.
Ezra 2:62(59,62)	sought...register among those...reckoned by **genealogy**
Neh. 7:5	I found a register of the **genealogy** of them which came
Ps. 56:8	my wanderings...are they not in thy **book**
Ezek. 13:9	neither shall they be...in the **writing** of the house
Mal. 3:16(16-18)	and a book of **remembrance** was written before him for

Matt. 1:17(1-17)	Babylon unto Christ are fourteen **generations**.
1 Ne. 5:14(14-16)	the plates of brass a **genealogy** of his fathers; where
3 Ne. 24:16(16-18)	a book of **remembrance** was written before him for them
D&C 85:9(7-9)	they who are not found...in the book of **remembrance**
D&C 128:24	a **book** containing the records of our dead, which
Moses 6:5(4-9)	and a book of **remembrance** was kept, in the which was
Moses 6:46(43-46)	for a book of **remembrance** we have written among us
Abr. 1:31	I shall...write...this **record**, for...my posterity that

BORROWING

Ex. 22:14(14,15)	if a man **borrow** ought of his neighbour, and it be hurt
Deut. 15:6	thou shalt lend...but thou shalt not **borrow**; and thou
Deut. 28:12	thou shalt lend unto many nations...not **borrow**.
2 Kgs. 6:5(1-7)	cried, and said, alas, master! For it was **borrowed**.
Neh. 5:4	we have **borrowed** money for the king's tribute, and
Ps. 37:21	the wicked **borroweth**, and payeth not again: but the
Prov. 22:7	the **borrower** is servant to the lender.
Matt. 5:42	him that would **borrow** of thee turn not thou away.
Mosiah 4:28	whosoever..**borroweth** of his neighbor should return
3 Ne. 12:42	from him that would **borrow** of thee turn thou not away.
Ether 14:2	and would not **borrow** neither would he lend; and every
D&C 136:25	if thou **borrowest** of thy neighbor, thou shalt restore

BREAD

Gen. 3:19	in the sweat of thy face shalt thou eat **bread**, till
Gen. 14:18	Melchizedek king of Salem brought forth **bread** and wine
Ex. 16:4	behold, I will rain **bread** from heaven for you; and the
Ex. 16:15(11-36)	manna...this is the **bread** which the Lord hath given
Ex. 23:25	serve the Lord...and he shall bless thy **bread**, and thy
Deut. 8:3	man doth not live by **bread** only, but by every word
Neh. 9:15	and gavest them **bread** from heaven for their hunger
Job 22:7	and thou hast withholden **bread** from the hungry.
Prov. 22:9	for he giveth of his **bread** to the poor.
Prov. 28:21	for for a piece of **bread** that man will transgress.
Eccl. 11:1	cast thy **bread** upon the waters: for thou shalt find
Isa. 55:10	the earth...that it may give...**bread** to the eater
Matt. 4:3	tempter came...command that these stones be made **bread**
Matt. 4:4	it is written, man shall not live by **bread** alone, but
Matt. 6:11	give us this day our daily **bread**.
Matt. 7:9	if his son ask **bread**, will he give him a stone
Matt. 15:36(32-38)	and he took the seven **loaves** and the fishes, and gave
Matt. 26:26	Jesus took **bread**...and said, take, eat; this is my
Luke 14:15	blessed is he that shall eat **bread** in the kingdom of
Acts 2:42	continued stedfastly...in breaking of **bread**, and in
Acts 20:7	when the disciples came together to break **bread**, Paul
2 Thes. 3:12(8-12)	with quietness they work, and eat their own **bread**.
Alma 8:21(21-23)	brought forth **bread** and meat and set before Alma.
3 Ne. 18:6(1-7)	as I have broken **bread** and blessed it and given it
3 Ne. 20:3(1-9)	he brake **bread** again and blessed it, and gave to the

BREAD cont.

3 Ne. 26:13	did break **bread** oft, and bless it, and give it unto
D&C 20:40	to administer **bread** and wine- the emblems of the flesh
D&C 20:75	meet together often to partake of **bread** and wine in
D&C 20:77	bless and sanctify this **bread** to the souls of all
D&C 42:42	idle shall not eat the **bread**...of the laborer.
D&C 88:141	after partaking of **bread** and wine, he is to gird
D&C 89:14(10-17)	all **grain** is ordained for the use of man and of beasts
D&C 124:90	not be forsaken, nor his seed be found begging **bread**.
D&C 136:9	each company prepare houses...fields for raising **grain**
Moses 4:25	by the sweat of thy face shalt thou eat **bread**, until

BREAD, SHEWBREAD

Ex. 25:30	and thou shalt set upon the table **shewbread** before me
Ex. 35:13	the table,...and all his vessels, and the **shewbread**
Ex. 39:36(33-43)	table, and all the vessels thereof, and the **shewbread**
Lev. 24:5(5-9)	take fine flour, and bake twelve **cakes** thereof: two
Num. 4:7	upon the table of **shewbread**...spread a cloth of blue
1 Sam. 21:4(1-6)	no common bread under mine hand, but...hallowed **bread**
2 Chr. 2:4	and for the continual **shewbread**, and for the burnt off
Neh. 10:33(32,33)	for the **shewbread**, and for the continual meat offering
Matt. 12:4(1-8)	did eat the **shewbread**, which was not lawful for him

BREAD, UNLEAVENED

Gen. 19:3	and did bake **unleavened** bread, and they did eat.
Ex. 12:8(5-8)	they shall eat...**unleavened** bread...with bitter herbs
Ex. 12:17(15-20)	ye shall observe the feast of **unleavened** bread; for
Ex. 12:39(30-48)	baked **unleavened** cakes of the dough..brought forth out
Ex. 29:23	basket of the **unleavened** bread that is before the Lord
Lev. 23:6(5,6)	seven days ye must eat **unleavened** bread.
Num. 6:15(13-21)	and a basket of **unleavened** bread, cakes of fine flour
Num. 9:11	eat it with **unleavened** bread and bitter herbs.
Deut. 16:3(1-4)	eat **unleavened** bread therewith, even the bread of
Deut. 16:8(3-8)	six days thou shalt eat **unleavened** bread: and on the
Josh. 5:11(10-11)	they did eat...**unleavened** cakes, and parched corn in
1 Sam. 28:24	and did bake **unleavened** bread thereof
2 Kgs. 23:9	did eat of the **unleavened** bread among their brethren.
2 Chr. 30:13(13-22)	keep the feast of **unleavened** bread in the second
Ezek. 45:21	passover...seven days; **unleavened** bread shall be eaten
Matt. 26:17(17,26)	now the first day of the feast of **unleavened** bread the
Mark 14:22(12-22)	Jesus took **bread**, and blessed, and brake it, and gave
Luke 22:7(7,19)	then came the day of **unleavened** bread, when the
Acts 12:3	then were the days of **unleavened** bread.
1 Cor. 5:7(6-8)	ye may be a new lump, as ye are **unleavened**.

BREAD OF LIFE

Deut. 8:3	man doth not live by **bread** only, but by every word
Matt. 26:26(26-28)	Jesus took **bread**, and blessed it, and brake it, and
John 6:35(30-36)	I am the **bread** of life: he that cometh to me shall
John 6:51(48-58)	the **bread** that I will give is my flesh, which I will
1 Cor. 11:27(17-34)	whosoever shall eat this **bread**...unworthily...guilty
Rev. 2:17	will I give to eat of the hidden **manna**, and will give
2 Ne. 32:3	**feast** upon the words of Christ; for behold, the words
Jacob 3:2(1-3)	and **feast** upon his love; for ye may, if your minds are
Alma 5:34(34-36)	eat and drink of the **bread** and the waters of life free
3 Ne. 18:7(1-12)	this shall ye do in remembrance of my **body**, which I
3 Ne. 18:29(28-32)	whoso eateth and drinketh my **flesh** and blood
3 Ne. 20:8(7-9)	eateth this **bread** eateth of my body to his soul; and
Moro. 4:3(1-3)	to bless and sanctify this **bread** to the souls of all
D&C 20:40(40-46)	administer **bread** and wine- the emblems of the flesh
D&C 20:77(75-77)	to bless and sanctify this **bread** to the souls of all
D&C 46:4	**sacrament**...not partake until he makes reconciliation.

BREATH OF LIFE

Gen. 2:7	and breathed into his nostrils the **breath** of life; and
Gen. 7:22	all in whose nostrils was the **breath** of life...died.
Job 12:10	in whose hand is...the **breath** of all mankind.
Job 33:4	the **breath** of the Almighty hath given me life.
Ps. 104:29(29-30)	thou takest away their **breath**, they die, and return
Ps. 146:4(3-4)	his **breath** goeth forth, he returneth to his earth; in
Isa. 42:5	he that giveth **breath** unto the people upon it, and
Ezek. 37:5(5-10)	I will cause **breath** to enter into you, and ye shall
Ezek. 37:10(9-12)	the **breath** came into them, and they lived, and stood
Acts 17:25	giveth to all life, and **breath**, and all things
Moses 3:7(4-7)	and breathed into his nostrils the **breath** of life; and
Moses 3:19	I, God, breathed into them the **breath** of life, and com

BRIBERY

Ex. 23:8	thou shalt take no **gift**: for the gift blindeth the
1 Sam. 12:3	of whose hand have I received any **bribe** to blind mine
Job 15:34	fire shall consume the tabernacles of **bribery**.
Ps. 26:10(9,10)	and their right hand is full of **bribes**.
Prov. 17:23	wicked man taketh a **gift** out of the bosom to pervert
Isa. 1:23	every one loveth **gifts**, and followeth after rewards
Isa. 33:15	that shaketh his hands from holding of **bribes**, that
Amos 5:12	they afflict the just, they take a **bribe**, and they
Acts 8:20	that the gift of God may be **purchased** with money.
Acts 24:26(24-26)	hoped...**money** should have been given him of Paul, that
2 Ne. 15:23(13-23)	who justify the wicked for **reward**, and take away the
2 Ne. 26:10	they **sell** themselves for naught; for, for the reward
Mosiah 29:40	for that lucre which doth **corrupt** the soul; for he had
Alma 11:22(21-25)	all these will I **give** thee if thou wilt deny the exist
Hel. 7:5	wicked go unpunished because of their **money**; and
Hel. 9:20(19-21)	behold here is **money**; and also we will grant unto thee
Ether 9:11(10,11)	sons of Akish did offer them **money**, by which means the

Moro. 10:30   touch not the evil **gift**, nor the unclean thing.

BROTHERHOOD AND SISTERHOOD

Gen. 4:9	I know not: am I my **brother's** keeper
Deut. 15:7(7-12)	shalt not harden thine heart...from thy poor **brother**
Deut. 22:1(1-4)	see the **brother's** ox or his sheep go astray, and hide
Ruth 1:16(14-18)	Ruth said...thy **people** shall be my people, and thy
1 Kgs. 12:24	nor fight against your **brethren** the children of Israel
Ps. 35:14	as though he had been my friend or **brother**: I bowed
Prov. 17:17	a **brother** is born for adversity.
Prov. 18:19	a **brother** offended is harder to be won than a strong
Prov. 18:24	a friend that sticketh closer than a **brother**.
Amos 1:9	remembered not the **brotherly** covenant
Matt. 12:50(46-50)	the same is my **brother**, and sister, and mother.
Luke 11:8(6-9)	because he is his **friend**, yet because of his
John 15:13	that a man lay down his life for his **friends**.
Acts 15:36	let us go again and visit our **brethren** in every city
Rom. 12:10	affectioned one to another with **brotherly** love; in
1 Thes. 4:9	touching **brotherly** love ye need not that I write unto
2 Thes. 3:15	not as an enemy, but admonish him as a **brother**.
1 Tim. 5:2(1-3)	elder women as mothers; the younger as **sisters**, with
Philem. 1:16	not now as a servant, but...a **brother** beloved, special
Heb. 2:11	he is not ashamed to call them **brethren**
Heb. 13:1	let **brotherly** love continue.
James 2:15(13-16)	if a brother or **sister** be naked, and destitute of
1 Pet. 2:17	love the **brotherhood**. Fear God. Honour the king.
1 Pet. 3:8	compassion one of another, love as **brethren**, be
2 Pet. 1:7	to godliness **brotherly** kindness; and to brotherly kind
1 Jn. 2:10(9-11)	he that loveth his **brother** abideth in the light, and
1 Jn. 3:14(14-15)	we have...life, because we love the **brethren**.
1 Jn. 4:20(20-21)	I love God, and hateth his **brother**, he is a liar: for
1 Ne. 22:6	also all our **brethren** who are of the house of Israel.
Mosiah 2:17	service of your **fellow** beings...service of your God.
Mosiah 5:7	have become his **sons** and his daughters.
Mosiah 18:8(8,9)	to be called his **people**, and are willing to bear one
Alma 5:30	doth make a mock of his **brother**, or that heapeth upon
D&C 4:6	temperance, patience, **brotherly** kindness, godliness
D&C 38:24	esteem his **brother** as himself, and practise virtue and
D&C 42:88(88-92)	if thy **brother** or sister offend thee, thou shalt take
D&C 88:133(132-135)	to be your friend and **brother** through the grace of God

CALLED OF GOD

Ex. 3:10(1-12)	I will **send** thee unto Pharaoh
Ex. 28:1	take thou unto thee **Aaron**...that he may minister unto
Ex. 40:13(13-15)	**anoint** him, and sanctify him; that he may minister
Num. 27:23(18-23)	gave him a **charge**, as the Lord commanded by the hand
1 Sam. 3:20(1-21)	Samuel was **established** to be a prophet of the Lord.
1 Sam. 9:16(15-17)	I will send thee a man...**anoint** him to be captain over
1 Sam. 13:14	Lord hath **sought** him a man after his own heart, and

CALLED OF GOD cont.

1 Sam. 15:17(17-23)	thou wast little...Lord **anointed** thee king over Israel
1 Sam. 16:3(1-13)	thou shalt **anoint** unto me him whom I name unto thee.
1 Kgs. 19:16(15-21)	Elisha...shalt thou **anoint** to be prophet in thy room.
Isa. 6:8(8-10)	voice of the Lord, saying, whom shall I **send**, and who
Jer. 1:5(4-7)	I **ordained** thee a prophet unto the nations.
Ezek. 2:4(2-4)	I do **send** thee unto them; and thou shalt say unto the
Amos 7:15(14-15)	the **Lord** said unto me, go, prophesy unto my people
Matt. 4:21(18-22)	he saw...James...and John...and he **called** them.
Matt. 20:16	first last: for many be **called**, but few chosen.
Luke 6:13(12-16)	called unto him his disciples..of them he **chose** twelve
Luke 9:59(59-62)	and he said unto another, **follow** me. But he said, Lord
Luke 10:1(1,17)	the Lord **appointed** other seventy also, and sent them
John 15:16	I have **chosen** you, and ordained you, that ye should
Acts 1:24(23-26)	thou, Lord...shew whether...thou hast **chosen**
Acts 6:5(1-6)	and they **chose** Stephen, a man full of faith and of the
Acts 9:17(1-18)	the Lord, even Jesus...hath **sent** me, that thou
Acts 13:2(1-2)	the Holy Ghost said...whereunto I have **called** them.
Rom. 10:15(13-17)	how shall they preach, except they be **sent**? As it is
1 Cor. 1:26	not many wise men...not many noble, are **called**
2 Cor. 10:8	our **authority**, which the Lord hath given us for
1 Tim. 2:7	I am **ordained** a preacher, and an apostle, (I speak the
Heb. 5:4(4-10)	no man taketh this honour..but he that is **called** of
1 Jn. 5:19(18-19)	we know that we are of **God**, and the whole world lieth
1 Ne. 2:2	the Lord **commanded** my father, even in a dream, that
Alma 13:3(1-12)	are **called** with a holy calling, yea, with that holy
3 Ne. 12:1	give heed unto...these twelve whom I have **chosen** from
D&C 1:17(17-18)	I the Lord...**called** upon my servant Joseph Smith, Jun.
D&C 4:3	desires to serve God ye are **called** to the work
D&C 9:14	stand fast in the work wherewith I have **called** you
D&C 20:60	**ordained** according to the gifts and callings of God
D&C 42:11	except he be **ordained** by some one who has authority
D&C 90:11	through those who are **ordained** unto this power, by the
D&C 95:5(5-6)	many...ordained among you...few of them are **chosen**.
D&C 105:35	there has been a day of **calling**, but the time has come
D&C 121:34(34-40)	many **called**, but few are chosen. and why are they not
JS-H 1:28	by one who was **called** of God as I had been. but this
A of F 1:5	We believe that a man must be **called** of God, by

CAPITAL PUNISHMENT

Gen. 9:6(5,6)	whoso sheddeth man's blood, by man shall his **blood** be
Gen. 42:22	therefore, behold, also his **blood** is required.
Ex. 21:12	so that he die, shall be surely put to **death**.
Ex. 21:29(28-29)	and his owner also shall be put to **death**.
Ex. 35:2	doeth work therein shall be put to **death**.
Lev. 20:10(10-16)	the adulteress shall surely be put to **death**.
Num. 35:16(16-21)	the murderer shall surely be put to **death**.
Num. 35:27	revenger of blood **kill** the slayer; he shall not be
Num. 35:30(30-34)	the murderer shall be put to **death** by the mouth of wit
Deut. 13:5(1-11)	that prophet...shall be put to **death**; because he hath
Deut. 17:5(1-7)	that man or that woman...stone them...till they **die**.
Deut. 17:6(5-7)	he that is worthy of death be put to **death**; but at the

CAPITAL PUNISHMENT cont.

Deut. 22:21(21-27)   stone her with stones that she **die**: because she hath
Josh. 1:18   whosoever he be that doth rebel..shall be put to **death**
1 Kgs. 2:24   Adonijah shall be put to **death** this day.
Ezra 7:26   let judgment be executed...whether it be unto **death**
Esth. 4:11   there is one law of his to put him to **death**, except
Matt. 15:4(3-6)   curseth father or mother, let him **die** the death.
Acts 26:31(30-32)   doeth nothing worthy of **death** or of bonds.
Rom. 1:32(28-32)   which commit such things are worthy of **death**, not only
2 Ne. 9:35   murderer who deliberately killeth, for he shall **die**.
Alma 1:14   thou art condemned to **die**, according to the law which
Alma 1:18   for he that murdered was punished unto **death**.
Alma 30:10(10-11)   if he murdered he was punished unto **death**; and if he
Alma 34:12(11,12)   law requireth the life of him who hath **murdered**; there
Alma 62:9(9-10)   **executed** according to the law; yea, those men of
Hel. 1:12(8,12)   as many as were found were condemned unto **death**.
D&C 42:19(18-19)   thou shalt not kill; but he that killeth shall **die**.

CARNAL MIND

Job 20:11(4-29)   his bones are full of the **sin** of his youth, which
Ps. 78:18(12-33)   and they tempted God...by asking meat for their **lust**.
Eccl. 11:10(9-10)   put away **evil** from thy flesh: for childhood and youth
Isa. 3:16(16-26)   because the daughters of Zion...walk with..**wanton** eyes
Matt. 5:28(27,28)   whosoever looketh on a woman to **lust** after her hath
Rom. 7:14   the law is spiritual: but I am **carnal**, sold under sin.
Rom. 8:6(4-7)   to be **carnally** minded is death; but to be spiritually
1 Cor. 3:3   for ye are yet **carnal**: for whereas there is among you
2 Ne. 9:39   to be **carnally-minded** is death, and to be spiritually
2 Ne. 28:21   and lull them away into **carnal** security, that they
Mosiah 4:2   viewed themselves in their own **carnal** state, even less
Mosiah 16:5(2-5)   persists in his own **carnal** nature, and goes on in the
Mosiah 27:25   changed from their **carnal** and fallen state, to a state
Alma 30:53   they were pleasing unto the **carnal** mind; and I taught
Alma 36:4   not of the **carnal** mind but of God.
Alma 39:9   repent...and go no more after the **lusts** of your eyes
Alma 41:11   in a **carnal** state, are in the gall of bitterness and
Alma 42:10   as they had become **carnal**, sensual, and devilish, by
3 Ne. 12:28(27-30)   looketh on a woman, to **lust** after her, hath committed
D&C 3:4   dictates of his own will and **carnal** desires, he must
D&C 29:35(34,35)   my commandments are spiritual...neither **carnal** nor Sen
D&C 42:23   he that looketh upon a woman to **lust** after her shall
D&C 67:10(10-12)   not with the **carnal** neither natural mind, but with the
D&C 84:27   and the law of **carnal** commandments, which the Lord in
D&C 88:121   cease...from all your **lustful** desires, from all your
D&C 101:6   and **lustful** and covetous desires among them; therefore
Moses 5:13   men began from that time forth to be **carnal**, sensual
Moses 6:49   men have become **carnal**, sensual, and devilish, and are

CELESTIAL GLORY

Ps. 110:1	sit thou at my right **hand**, until I make thine enemies
Ps. 148:13	his **glory** is above the earth and heaven.
Dan. 12:3(1-3)	they that be wise shall **shine** as the brightness of the
Matt. 13:43	then shall the righteous **shine** forth as the sun in the
Matt. 26:64(59-64)	son of man sitting on the right hand of **power**, and
John 17:5(3-5)	with the **glory** which I had with thee before the world
Rom. 9:23(22-24)	the riches of his **glory** on the vessels of mercy, which
1 Cor. 15:40(35-57)	the glory of the **celestial** is one, and the glory of
2 Cor. 3:18(17-18)	beholding...the **glory** of the Lord, are changed into
2 Cor. 12:2(1-4)	such an one caught up to the **third** heaven.
Heb. 1:3(1-3)	who being the brightness of his **glory**, and the express
Rev. 1:6(4-6)	to him be **glory** and dominion for ever and ever. Amen.
1 Ne. 1:8(5-18)	God sitting upon his **throne**, surrounded with
D&C 59:2(1-2)	they shall receive a **crown** in the mansions of my
D&C 76:6(5-10)	eternal shall be their **glory**.
D&C 76:19(19-20)	the **glory** of the Lord shone round about.
D&C 76:70(50-70)	these are they whose bodies are **celestial**, whose glory
D&C 76:92(92-96)	thus we saw the **glory** of the celestial, which excels
D&C 77:1	earth, in its sanctified, immortal, and **eternal** state.
D&C 78:7(3-7)	a place in the **celestial** world, you must prepare yours
D&C 84:32(31-34)	shall be filled with the **glory** of the Lord, upon mount
D&C 88:18(14-29)	that it may be prepared for the celestial **glory**
D&C 88:22	not...abide the law...cannot abide a **celestial** glory.
D&C 88:67(66-68)	if your eye be single to my **glory**, your whole bodies
D&C 88:107(106-107)	the saints shall be filled with his **glory**, and receive
D&C 93:22(19-23)	partakers of the **glory**...the church of the firstborn.
D&C 101:65(63-66)	be crowned with celestial **glory**, when I shall come in
D&C 130:2(1-2)	same sociality...will be coupled with eternal **glory**
D&C 131:1(1-4)	in the **celestial** glory there are three heavens or
D&C 132:19(18-21)	which **glory** shall be a fulness and a continuation of
Moses 1:5(3-5)	and no man can behold all my **glory**, and afterwards
Moses 6:59(57-61)	eternal life in the world to come, even immortal **glory**
JS-H 1:32(30-32)	but his whole person was **glorious** beyond description
JS-V 1:1(1-10)	I beheld the **celestial** kingdom of God, and the glory

CHARITY

Ex. 23:5(4,5)	him that hateth thee...thou shalt surely **help** with him
Lev. 19:10(9,10)	thou shalt leave them for the **poor** and stranger: I am
Lev. 19:18(17,18)	but thou shalt **love** thy neighbour as thyself: I am the
Isa. 1:17(16-23)	do well...**relieve** the oppressed...plead for the widow.
Isa. 63:9(7-9)	in his **love** and in his pity he redeemed them; and he
Jer. 7:6(5-6)	if ye oppress not the stranger, the **fatherless**, and
Zech. 7:9(9-10)	shew mercy and **compassions** every man to his brother
Mark 10:21	**give** to the poor, and thou shalt have treasure in
Luke 6:35(30-38)	**love** ye your enemies, and do good, and lend, hoping
Luke 10:34(30-35)	brought him to an inn, and took **care** of him.
Luke 11:41	but rather give **alms** of such things as ye have; and
1 Cor. 8:1	knowledge puffeth up, but **charity** edifieth.
1 Cor. 13:4(1-13)	**charity** suffereth long, and is kind; charity envieth
1 Cor. 16:14	let all your things be done with **charity**.
Col. 3:14	above all these things put on **charity**, which is the

CHARITY cont.

1 Tim. 1:5	end of the commandment is **charity** out of a pure heart
James 1:27	pure **religion** and undefiled...to visit the fatherless
1 Pet. 4:8	for **charity** shall cover the multitude of sins.
2 Pet. 1:7(4-10)	brotherly kindness; and to brotherly kindness **charity**.
2 Ne. 26:30	all men should have **charity**, which charity is love.
2 Ne. 33:7(7-9)	I have **charity** for my people, and great faith in
Mosiah 4:16(16-26)	will **succor** those that stand in need of your succor
Alma 7:24	faith, hope, and **charity**, and then ye will always
Alma 34:29(28-29)	if ye do not remember to be **charitable**, ye are as
Ether 12:28(28-37)	faith, hope and **charity** bringeth unto me- the fountain
Moro. 7:47(43-48)	**charity** is the pure love of Christ, and it endureth
Moro. 8:14(13,14)	he hath neither faith, hope, nor **charity**; wherefore
Moro. 8:17(16,17)	I am filled with **charity**, which is everlasting love
Moro. 8:26(25,26)	Comforter filleth with hope and perfect **love**, which
Moro. 10:21(20-23)	except ye have **charity** ye can in nowise be saved in
D&C 4:5	faith, hope, **charity** and love, with an eye single to
D&C 12:8(7-8)	faith, hope, and **charity**, being temperate in all thing
D&C 18:19	if you have not faith, hope, and **charity**, you can do
D&C 42:45	thou shalt live together in **love**, insomuch that thou
D&C 88:125	clothe yourselves with the bond of **charity**, as with a
D&C 112:11	let thy **love** abound unto all men, and unto all who
D&C 121:41	power...by gentleness and meekness...by **love** unfeigned
D&C 121:43	sharpness...afterwards an increase of **love** toward him
D&C 121:45	let thy bowels also be full of **charity** towards all men
D&C 124:116	clothe himself with **charity**; and cease to do evil, and
D&C 133:53(52-59)	in his **love**, and in his pity, he redeemed them, and

CHASTENING

Lev. 26:28	even I, will **chastise** you seven times for your sins.
Deut. 8:5	as a man **chasteneth** his son, so the Lord thy God
Job 5:17	despise not thou the **chastening** of the Almighty
Job 34:31(31,32)	I have borne **chastisement**, I will not offend any more
Ps. 94:12	blessed is the man whom thou **chastenest**, O Lord, and
Ps. 119:71(67,71)	it is good for me that I have been **afflicted**; that I
Prov. 3:11(11-12)	despise not the **chastening** of the Lord; neither be
Prov. 9:8(7-9)	**reprove** not a scorner, lest he hate thee: rebuke a
Prov. 10:17	but he that refuseth **reproof** erreth.
Prov. 12:1	but he that hateth **reproof** is brutish.
Prov. 13:24	he that loveth him **chasteneth** him betimes.
Prov. 19:18	**chasten** thy son while there is hope, and let not thy
Prov. 23:13(13,14)	withhold not **correction** from the child: for if thou
Prov. 25:12	so is a wise **reprover** upon an obedient ear.
Prov. 29:15	the rod and **reproof** give wisdom: but a child left to
Isa. 26:16(8,9,16)	they poured out a prayer when thy **chastening** was upon
Isa. 54:7	for a small moment have I **forsaken** thee; but with
Jer. 2:30	I smitten your children; they received no **correction**
1 Cor. 11:32	we are **chastened** of the Lord, that we should not be
1 Tim. 5:1	**rebuke** not an elder, but intreat him as a father; and
1 Tim. 5:20	them that sin **rebuke** before all, that others also may
2 Tim. 3:16(16,17)	all scripture is given...for **reproof**, for correction
2 Tim. 4:2	**reprove**, rebuke, exhort with all longsuffering and

CHASTENING cont.

Titus 2:15(1-15)	speak, and exhort, and **rebuke** with all authority. let
Heb. 3:13(12,13)	but **exhort** one another daily, while it is called to
Heb. 12:6(5-11)	for whom the Lord loveth he **chasteneth**, and scourgeth
Rev. 3:19	as many as I love, I rebuke and **chasten**: be zealous
1 Ne. 16:2(1-3)	spoken **hard** things against the wicked, according to
1 Ne. 16:25(22-27)	he was truly **chastened** because of his murmuring
1 Ne. 16:39	and did **chasten** them exceedingly; and after they were
Mosiah 23:21(21-22)	the Lord seeth fit to **chasten** his people; yea, he
Hel. 12:3	and thus we see that except the Lord doth **chasten** his
Hel. 13:8(5-39)	I will **withdraw** my spirit from them..suffer them no
Hel. 15:3	hath he **chastened** them; yea, in the days of their
Ether 2:14(14,15)	**chastened** him because he remembered not to call upon
D&C 1:27(24-28)	inasmuch as they sinned they might be **chastened**, that
D&C 42:90(89-92)	offend many, he or she shall be **chastened** before many.
D&C 58:60	until he is sufficiently **chastened** for all his sins
D&C 61:8(7-8)	you were **chastened** for all your sins, that you might
D&C 64:8	they were afflicted and sorely **chastened**.
D&C 75:7(6-8)	the Lord, **chasten** him for the murmurings of his heart
D&C 87:6	to feel the wrath, and indignation, and **chastening**
D&C 90:36	and **chasten** her until she overcomes and is clean
D&C 93:50	hath need to be **chastened**, and set in order his
D&C 95:1(1-2)	whom I love I also **chasten** that their sins may be for
D&C 97:6	there are those that must needs be **chastened**, and
D&C 98:21(21,22)	the Lord, will **chasten** them and will do whatsoever I
D&C 100:13	redeemed, although she is **chastened** for a little
D&C 101:5(4,5)	who will not endure **chastening**, but deny me, cannot
D&C 103:4(3-4)	be **chastened** for a little season with a sore and
D&C 105:6	my people must needs be **chastened** until they learn
D&C 121:43(41-44)	**reproving** betimes with sharpness, when moved upon by
D&C 136:31	he that will not bear **chastisement** is not worthy of

CHASTITY

Gen. 2:24	a man...shall **cleave** unto his wife: and they shall
Gen. 39:12(1-20)	she caught him...and he...**fled**, and got him out.
Ex. 20:14	thou shalt not commit **adultery**.
Ps. 24:4(3-4)	he that hath **clean** hands, and a pure heart; who hath
Prov. 6:25(20-35)	**lust** not after her beauty in thine heart; neither let
Prov. 12:4	a **virtuous** woman is a crown to her husband: but she
Prov. 31:10(10-31)	who can find a **virtuous** woman? for her price is far
Isa. 35:8(3-10)	way of holiness; the **unclean** shall not pass over it
Isa. 52:11	be ye **clean**, that bear the vessels of the Lord.
Matt. 5:8	blessed are the **pure** in heart: for they shall see God.
Matt. 5:28(27-32)	whosoever looketh on a woman to **lust** after her hath
Matt. 15:19(1-20)	out of the **heart** proceed...adulteries, fornications
Rom. 8:6(5-7)	**carnally** minded is death...spiritually minded is life
1 Cor. 6:13(9-11,13)	the body is not for **fornication**, but for the Lord; and
1 Cor. 6:19(15-20)	your **body** is the temple of the Holy Ghost which is in
1 Cor. 7:10(10-11)	let not the **wife** depart from her husband
1 Cor. 9:27	I keep under my **body**, and bring it into subjection
2 Cor. 7:1	**cleanse** ourselves from all filthiness of the flesh and
Gal. 5:16(16-25)	walk in the spirit...not fulful the **lust** of the flesh.

CHASTITY cont.

Eph. 5:3(1-5)	**fornication**...all uncleanness...let it not be...named
Eph. 5:5(1-5)	no **whoremonger**...hath any inheritance in the kingdom
Eph. 6:11(10-17)	put on the whole **armour** of God, that ye may be able
Philip. 4:8	if there be any **virtue**...think on these things.
1 Thes. 4:3(2-7)	will of God...that ye should abstain from **fornication**
1 Tim. 2:9(9-10)	that women adorn themselves in **modest** apparel, with
1 Tim. 4:12	be thou an example of the believers...in **purity**.
2 Tim. 2:22	flee also youthful **lusts**: but follow righteousness
Titus 2:5(4-5)	to be discreet, **chaste**, keepers at home, good
James 1:14(12-17)	man is tempted, when he is drawn away of his own **lust**
James 1:27	to keep himself **unspotted** from the world.
1 Pet. 3:2(1-4)	while they behold your **chaste** conversation coupled wit
2 Pet. 1:5(5-8)	add to your faith **virtue**; and to virtue knowledge
1 Jn. 2:16(15-17)	**lust** of the flesh...not of the Father...of the world.
1 Jn. 3:3(1-3)	every man that hath this hope in him **purifieth** himself
Rev. 21:8(7-8)	**whoremongers**...shall have their part in the lake which
1 Ne. 10:21(17-22)	no **unclean** thing can dwell with God; wherefore, ye
2 Ne. 9:36(27-40)	wo unto them who commit **whoredoms**, for they shall be
2 Ne. 26:32(32-33)	commanded that men...should not commit **whoredoms**; and
Jacob 2:7	feelings are exceedingly tender and **chaste** and
Jacob 2:28(23-35)	for I, the Lord God, delight in the **chastity** of women.
Jacob 3:5(5-12)	there should not be **whoredoms** committed among them.
Mosiah 13:22	thou shalt not commit **adultery**. thou shalt not steal.
Alma 7:21(18-21)	he doth not dwell in **unholy** temples; neither can filth
Alma 23:3(1-3)	convinced that...they ought not...to commit **adultery**
Alma 39:9(3-13)	now my son...go no more after the **lusts** of your eyes
3 Ne. 12:28(27-32)	whosoever looketh on a woman, to **lust** after her, hath
4 Ne. 1:16(15-18)	there were no envyings...nor **whoredoms**...nor any...
Morm. 9:28(27-28)	ask...that ye will yield to no **temptation**, but that
Moro. 9:9(7-10)	precious above all things, which is **chastity** and
D&C 3:4(1-4)	if he...follows...**carnal** desires, he must fall and
D&C 4:6(5-6)	remember faith, **virtue**, knowledge, temperance
D&C 38:42(10,42)	be ye **clean** that bear the vessels of the Lord. even
D&C 42:25(23-83)	he that has committed **adultery** and repents with all
D&C 46:33	practise **virtue** and holiness before me continually.
D&C 59:6	neither commit **adultery**...nor do anything like unto
D&C 63:16(14-19)	if any shall commit **adultery** in their hearts, they
D&C 88:40	**virtue** loveth virtue; light cleaveth unto light; mercy
D&C 88:86	entangle not...in sin, but let your hands be **clean**
D&C 88:121	cease...from all your **lustful** desires, from all your
D&C 97:15(15-21)	build a house unto me...not suffer any **unclean** thing
D&C 121:45(45-46)	let **virtue** garnish thy thoughts unceasingly; then
D&C 132:44(41-66)	give her unto him that hath not committed **adultery** but
Moses 6:57(55-57)	no **unclean** thing can dwell...in his presence; for
A of F 1:13	We believe in being honest, true, **chaste**, benevolent

CHEERFULNESS

Deut. 28:47	with **gladness** of heart, for the abundance of all thing
Ps. 19:8(7-10)	statutes of the Lord are right, **rejoicing** the heart
Ps. 45:7(7,15)	God, hath anointed thee with the oil of **gladness** above
Ps. 100:2(1-5)	serve the Lord with **gladness**: come before his presence

CHEERFULNESS cont.

Ps. 107:22	thanksgiving, and declare his works with **rejoicing**.
Ps. 119:111(111,112)	thy testimonies...are the **rejoicing** of my heart.
Prov. 15:13	a merry heart maketh a **cheerful** countenance: but by
Prov. 17:22	a **merry** heart doeth good like a medicine: but a broken
Eccl. 9:7(7-9)	eat...with joy, and drink...with a **merry** heart; for
Isa. 51:3(1-3,11)	**joy** and gladness shall be found therein, thanksgiving
Matt. 14:27(26-27)	be of good **cheer**; it is I; be not afraid.
Rom. 12:8(5-8)	he that sheweth mercy, with **cheerfulness**.
2 Cor. 9:7	for God loveth a **cheerful** giver.
Philip. 2:29(28-30)	receive him...in the Lord with all **gladness**; and hold
2 Ne. 10:23(23-25)	**cheer** up your hearts, and remember that ye are free
Mosiah 24:15	did submit **cheerfully** and with patience to all the
3 Ne. 1:13(12-14)	lift up your head and be of good **cheer**; for behold
D&C 19:39(29,39)	rejoicing and lifting up thy heart for **gladness**
D&C 59:15(9-21)	with thanksgiving, with **cheerful** hearts and
D&C 61:36	be of good **cheer**, little children; for I am in your
D&C 68:6	be of good **cheer**, and do not fear, for I the Lord am
D&C 78:18	be of good **cheer**, for I will lead you along. The king
D&C 123:17(13-17)	brethren, let us **cheerfully** do all things that lie in
JS-H 1:28	is acquainted with my native **cheery** temperament.

CHERUBIM

Gen. 3:24	placed...**cherubims**, and a flaming sword which turned
Ex. 25:18(18-20,22)	thou shalt make two **cherubims** of gold, of beaten work
Ex. 26:1	make the tabernacle...with **cherubims** of cunning work
Ex. 37:7(6-9)	and he made two **cherubims** of gold, beaten out of one
Num. 7:89	heard the voice...between the two **cherubims**: and he
1 Sam. 4:4	Lord of hosts, which dwelleth between the **cherubims**
2 Sam. 6:2	the Lord of hosts that dwelleth between the **cherubims**.
2 Sam. 22:11	he rode upon a **cherub**, and did fly: and he was seen
1 Kgs. 6:23(23-28)	within the oracle he made two **cherubims** of olive tree
1 Kgs. 8:7(6,7)	the **cherubims** spread forth their two wings over the
2 Chr. 3:10(10-13)	holy house he made two **cherubims** of image work, and
2 Chr. 5:8	the **cherubims** spread forth their wings over the place
Ps. 80:1	thou that dwellest between the **cherubims**, shine forth.
Ps. 99:1	he sitteth between the **cherubims**; let the earth be
Isa. 6:2(1-7)	above it stood the **seraphims**: each one had six wings
Isa. 37:16	God of Israel, that dwellest between the **cherubims**
Ezek. 9:3	glory of the God...was gone up from the **cherub**
Ezek. 10:19(2-22)	the **cherubims** lifted up their wings, and mounted up
Ezek. 28:14	thou art the anointed **cherub** that covereth; and I have
Heb. 9:5	over it the **cherubims** of glory shadowing the mercyseat
Rev. 4:6(6-9)	four **beasts** full of eyes before and behind.
Rev. 6:1(1-7)	one of the four **beasts** saying, come and see.
Rev. 7:11	angels...about the elders and the four **beasts**, and
Rev. 19:4	the four **beasts** fell down and worshipped God that sat
2 Ne. 16:2(2-7)	above it stood the **seraphim**; each one had six wings
Alma 12:21(21-29)	scripture mean...that God placed **cherubim** and a
Alma 42:3(2-3)	the Lord God placed **cherubim** and the flaming sword
D&C 38:1	all the **seraphic** hosts of heaven, before the world
D&C 77:2(2-4)	to understand by the four **beasts**, spoken of in the

CHERUBIM cont.

D&C 109:79	shining **seraphs** around thy throne, with acclamations
Moses 4:31	I placed...**cherubim** and a flaming sword, which turned

CHILDREN

Gen. 1:28	be **fruitful**, and multiply, and replenish the earth
Gen. 3:16	in sorrow thou shalt bring forth **children**; and thy
Gen. 18:19(18-19)	he will command his **children** and his household after
Deut. 4:10	that they may teach their **children**.
Deut. 11:19(19-21)	ye shall teach them your **children**, speaking of them
Josh. 4:6(6-7)	when your **children** ask their fathers in time to come
Josh. 4:22(22-24)	then ye shall let your **children** know, saying, Israel
Ps. 8:2	out of the mouth of **babes**..hast thou ordained strength
Prov. 17:6	glory of **children** are their fathers.
Prov. 22:6	train up a **child** in the way he should go: and when he
Isa. 54:13	all thy **children** shall be taught of the Lord; and
Mal. 4:6	turn...the heart of the **children** to their fathers
Matt. 18:3(1-5)	except ye...become as little **children**, ye shall not
Matt. 18:4(1-4)	whosoever...shall humble himself as this little **child**
Matt. 18:10	despise not one of these **little** ones; for I say unto
Matt. 18:14	these **little** ones should perish.
Matt. 19:14(13-15)	suffer little **children**, and forbid them not, to come
Mark 9:37	whosoever shall receive one of such **children** in my
Eph. 6:1(1-4)	**children**, obey your parents in the Lord: for this is
Col. 3:20(20-21)	**children**, obey your parents in all things: for this
1 Tim. 5:4	**children**...learn first to shew piety at home, and to
1 Tim. 5:14	women marry, bear **children**, guide the house, give none
Mosiah 4:14(14-15)	ye will not suffer your **children** that they go hungry
Mosiah 15:25(24-25)	and little **children** also have eternal life.
3 Ne. 17:11(11-12)	commanded that their little **children** should be brought
3 Ne. 17:21(21-25)	he took their little **children**, one by one, and blessed
3 Ne. 17:24(23-24)	angels descending...and encircled those **little** ones
Moro. 8:11(8-16)	little **children** need no repentance, neither baptism.
D&C 18:42	must repent...**children** who have arrived at the years
D&C 20:70	**children**...bring them unto the elders before the
D&C 29:46(46-48)	**children** are redeemed from the foundation of the world
D&C 45:58(54-58)	**children** shall grow up without sin unto salvation.
D&C 55:4	little **children** also may receive instruction before
D&C 63:51(50-51)	**children** shall grow up until they become old; old men
D&C 68:25(25-28)	parents have **children**...teach them not to understand
D&C 68:31	and their **children** are also growing up in wickedness
D&C 74:7(1-7)	little **children** are holy, being sanctified through the
D&C 83:4(4-5)	**children** have claim upon their parents for their
D&C 93:40(40-44)	commanded...bring up your **children** in light and truth.
D&C 98:47(45-48)	if the **children** shall repent, or the children's
Moses 6:54(54-55)	atoned for original guilt...of the **children**, for they
JS-V 1:10	all **children** who die before they arrive at the years

CHILDREN OF LIGHT

Ps. 112:1(1-10)	blessed...that delighteth greatly in his **commandments**.
Ps. 119:2(1-6)	blessed are they...that **seek** him with the whole heart.
Micah 6:8	love mercy, and to walk **humbly** with thy God
Matt. 5:16(14-16)	let your **light** so shine before men, that they may see
Luke 16:8(1-13)	in their generation wiser than the **children** of light.
John 12:36(32-36)	believe...that ye may be the **children** of light. these
Rom. 13:12(7-14)	and let us put on the armour of **light**.
Eph. 5:8(1-10)	now are ye light in...Lord: walk as **children** of light
1 Thes. 5:5(1-8)	ye are all the **children** of light, and the children of
1 Pet. 2:12	having your conversation **honest** among the Gentiles
Mosiah 5:7(7-9)	because of the covenant..called the **children** of Christ
D&C 4:2(1-7)	ye that embark in the **service** of God, see that ye
D&C 27:15(15-17)	take upon you my whole **armor**, that ye may be able to
D&C 50:24(23-25)	he that receiveth **light**, and continueth...receiveth
D&C 90:24	search diligently, **pray** always, and be believing, and
D&C 93:40(36-44)	bring up your children in **light** and truth.
D&C 103:9	for they were set to be a **light** unto the world, and
D&C 106:5(4-5)	gird up...loins, that you may be...**children** of light
A of F 1:13	We believe in being **honest**, true, chaste, benevolent

CHURCH

Ex. 16:22(2,22)	all the rulers of the **congregation** came and told Moses
Ex. 27:21	in the tabernacle of the **congregation** without the vail
Ex. 40:2	set up the tabernacle of the tent of the **congregation**.
Lev. 4:15(13-15)	the elders of the **congregation** shall lay their hands
Lev. 8:3(1-5)	and gather thou all the **congregation** together unto the
Lev. 16:33(29-34)	atonement for the tabernacle of the **congregation**, and
Num. 3:7(5-10)	charge of the whole **congregation** before the tabernacle
Num. 4:34	Moses and Aaron and the chief of the **congregation**
Josh. 8:35(32-35)	read not before all the **congregation** of Israel, with
Josh. 22:16	thus saith the whole **congregation** of the Lord, what
Judg. 21:5	came not up with the **congregation** unto the Lord? For
2 Chr. 29:28(27-29)	all the **congregation** worshipped, and the singers sang
Ps. 89:5(5,7)	faithfulness also in the **congregation** of the saints.
Ps. 107:32(32-33)	exalt him also in the **congregation** of the people, and
Isa. 40:11	he shall feed his **flock** like a shepherd: he shall
Isa. 63:11	brought..out of the sea with the shepherd of his **flock**
Jer. 13:17	because the Lord's **flock** is carried away captive.
Lam. 1:10	that they should not enter into thy **congregation**.
Matt. 18:17	but if he neglect to hear the **church**, let him be unto
Matt. 18:20	where two or three are **gathered** together in my name
Acts 2:47	Lord added to the **church** daily such as should be saved
Acts 8:1	persecution against the **church** which was at Jerusalem
Acts 20:28(28-29)	unto yourselves, and to all the **flock**, over the which
Acts 20:28	the **church** of God, which he hath purchased with his
Rom. 12:5(4,5)	we, being many, are one **body** in Christ, and every one
1 Cor. 1:10(10-13)	all speak the same thing...no **divisions** among you; but
1 Cor. 11:18	when ye come together...I hear that there be **divisions**
1 Cor. 11:22	houses to eat and to drink in...despise ye the **church**
1 Cor. 12:13(12-27)	for by one spirit are we all baptized into one **body**
1 Cor. 14:33	as in all **churches** of the saints.

CHURCH cont.

Eph. 1:22(22,23)	the head over all things to the **church**
Eph. 4:4(4-6)	there is one **body**, and one spirit, even as ye are call
Eph. 5:23(23-25)	Christ is the head of the **church**: and he is the
1 Tim. 3:15	the **church** of the living God, the pillar and ground
Heb. 3:6(1-6)	Christ as a son over his own **house**; whose house are
1 Pet. 5:2	feed the **flock** of God which is among you, taking the
1 Ne. 4:26	spake of the brethren of the **church**, and that I was
1 Ne. 14:10(9-10)	two **churches** only; the one is the Church of the Lamb
Mosiah 18:17(1-30)	called the church of God, or the **church** of Christ
Mosiah 25:21(18-24)	they did **assemble** themselves together in different
Alma 4:4(3-6)	and they began to establish the **church** more fully; yea
Alma 5:59(59-60)	watch...the wolves enter not and devour his **flock**? And
Alma 46:14(14,15)	believers of Christ, who belonged to the **church** of God
Hel. 11:21	the Nephites...the Lamanites...belong to the **church**
3 Ne. 18:5	the people of my **church**, unto all those who shall
3 Ne. 18:16	so shall ye pray in my **church**, among my people who do
3 Ne. 21:22	if they will repent...I will establish my **church** among
3 Ne. 26:21(19-21)	baptized in the name of Jesus were called the **church**
3 Ne. 27:7(1-10)	ye shall call the **church** in my name; and ye shall call
4 Ne. 1:1	the disciples of Jesus had formed a **church** of Christ
Moro. 4:2(1-3)	and they did kneel down with the **church**, and pray to
Moro. 6:5(5,6)	**church** did meet together oft, to fast and to pray, and
D&C 1:30	the only true and living **church** upon the face of the
D&C 5:14	coming forth of my **church** out of the wilderness- clear
D&C 6:34	fear not, little **flock**; do good; let earth and hell
D&C 10:53(53-55)	I will establish my **church** among them.
D&C 10:67(67-69)	whosoever repenteth and cometh unto me...is my **church**.
D&C 11:16	you shall have my word, my rock, my **church**, and my
D&C 18:5(4-5)	build up my **church**, upon...my gospel and my rock, the
D&C 20:1	**church** of Christ...regularly organized and established
D&C 26:2	all things...done by common consent in the **church**, by
D&C 33:5	this **church**...called forth out of the wilderness.
D&C 35:27	fear not, little **flock**, the kingdom is yours until I
D&C 46:3(2-5)	never...cast any one out from your public **meetings**
D&C 84:110(108-110)	also the body hath need of every **member**, that all may
D&C 88:72	I will take care of your **flocks**, and will raise up
D&C 112:25(24-26)	upon my **house** shall it begin, and from my house shall
D&C 115:4	the **Church** of Jesus Christ of Latter-day Saints.

CHURCH ORGANIZATION

Gen. 14:18	Melchizedek...was the **priest** of the most high God.
Ex. 18:21(12-27)	provide...able men...to be **rulers** of the men of truth
Ex. 24:9(1,9-11)	Moses, and Aaron...and **seventy** of the elders of Israel
Num. 11:16(16-25)	**seventy** men of the elders of Israel, whom thou
Num. 27:17(15-17)	the **congregation** of the Lord be not as sheep which
Num. 27:18(18-23)	take thee Joshua...and **lay** thine hand upon him
Deut. 27:1	Moses with the **elders** of Israel commanded the people
Deut. 34:9	Moses had **laid** his hands upon him: and the children
Josh. 4:4(1-4)	Joshua called the **twelve** men..out of every tribe a man
Matt. 16:18	upon this rock I will build my **church**; and the gates
Luke 6:13(12-16)	he chose twelve, whom also he named **apostles**

CHURCH ORGANIZATION cont.

Luke 10:1(1-3)   the Lord appointed other **seventy** also, and sent them

John 15:16   I have chosen you, and **ordained** you, that ye should

Acts 1:25(21-26)   that he may take part of this ministry and **apostleship**

Acts 6:6(1-8)   when they had prayed, they **laid** their hands on them.

Acts 13:1(1-3)   there were in the church...**prophets**...teachers;

Acts 14:23(21-23)   ordained them **elders** in every church, and had prayed

Acts 15:6(4-6)   **apostles** and elders came together for to consider of

1 Cor. 12:27(27-31)   ye are the body of Christ, and **members** in particular.

Eph. 2:20(19-21)   built upon the foundation of the **apostles** and prophets

Eph. 4:11(11-14)   and he gave some, **apostles**; and some, prophets; and

Philip. 1:1   which are at Philippi, with the **bishops** and deacons

Titus 1:5   ordain **elders** in every city, as I had appointed thee

1 Ne. 4:26(22-27)   supposing that I spake of the brethren of the **church**

Mosiah 18:17(1-30)   called the church of God, or the **church** of Christ, fro

Mosiah 26:8(7-12)   Mosiah had given Alma the authority over the **church**.

Alma 4:7   consecrated to be teachers, and **priests**, and elders

3 Ne. 11:21(18-23)   I give unto you **power** that ye shall baptize this

3 Ne. 12:1(1,2)   the number of them who had been **called**, and received

3 Ne. 13:25(25-34)   ye are they whom I have chosen to **minister** unto this

3 Ne. 15:12(11-13)   ye are my **disciples**; and ye are a light unto this

3 Ne. 18:5(1-12)   shall one be **ordained** among you, and to him will I

3 Ne. 19:20(20-36)   given the Holy Ghost unto these whom I have **chosen**

3 Ne. 27:3(1-12)   the name whereby we shall call this **church**; for there

4 Ne. 1:1(1-6)   disciples of Jesus had formed a **church** of Christ in

Moro. 3:1(1-4)   elders of the church, **ordained** priests and teachers

Moro. 3:4(1-4)   after this manner did they **ordain** priests and teachers

D&C 20:38(38-60)   the **duty** of the elders, priests, teachers, deacons

D&C 21:3(1-6)   which **church** was organized and established in the year

D&C 26:2(1,2)   done by common consent in the **church**, by much prayer

D&C 68:14   bishops to be set apart unto the **church**, to minister

D&C 84:29(29-30)   the **offices** of elder and bishop are necessary

D&C 84:109(106-111)   therefore, let every man stand in his own **office**, and

D&C 124:123(123-145   the **officers** belonging to my priesthood, that ye may

A of F 1:6   We believe in the same **organization** that existed in

CIRCUMCISION

Gen. 17:10(9-14)   my covenant...every man child...shall be **circumcised**.

Gen. 17:23(23-27)   **circumcised** the flesh of their foreskin in the

Gen. 21:4(2-4)   Abraham **circumcised** his son Isaac being eight days old

Gen. 34:15(13-17,22)   be as we be, that every male of you be **circumcised**

Ex. 4:26(24-26)   a bloody husband thou art, because of the **circumcision**

Ex. 12:48(44,48)   when a stranger...keep the passover...be **circumcised**

Lev. 12:3(2-4)   eighth day...flesh of...foreskin shall be **circumcised**.

Deut. 10:16(12-16)   **circumcise** therefore the foreskin of your heart, and

Deut. 30:6   and the Lord thy God will **circumcise** thine heart, and

Josh. 5:2(2-9)   **circumcise** again the children of Israel the second

Jer. 4:4   **circumcise** yourselves to the Lord, and take away the

Jer. 9:25(25-26)   I will punish all them which are **circumcised** with the

Ezek. 44:9(7-9)   no stranger, **uncircumcised**...shall enter..my sanctuary

Luke 1:59   eighth day they came to **circumcise** the child; and they

Luke 2:21   eight days...for the **circumcising** of the child..Jesus

CIRCUMCISION cont.

John 7:22(22,23)	Moses therefore gave unto you **circumcision**; (not
Acts 7:8	he gave him the covenant of **circumcision**: and so
Acts 11:2(1-3)	they that were of the **circumcision** contended with him
Acts 15:1(1-28)	except ye be **circumcised** after the manner of Moses
Acts 16:3(1-3)	Paul...took and **circumcised** him because of the Jews
Acts 21:21	they ought not to **circumcise** their children, neither
Rom. 2:25(25-29)	**circumcision** verily profiteth, if thou keep the law
Rom. 2:29(25-29)	**circumcision** is that of the heart, in the spirit, and
Rom. 3:1(1,2)	or what profit is there of **circumcision**
Rom. 3:30	justify the **circumcision** by faith, and uncircumcision
Rom. 4:11(6-14)	he received the sign of **circumcision**, a seal of the
Rom. 15:8	Christ was a minister of the **circumcision** for the
1 Cor. 7:19(18-19)	**circumcision** is nothing, and uncircumcision is nothing
Gal. 2:3	neither Titus...was compelled to be **circumcised**
Gal. 2:7(7-9)	gospel of the **circumcision** was unto Peter
Gal. 5:6(2-6)	neither **circumcision** availeth anything, nor
Gal. 6:15(12-16)	in Christ Jesus neither **circumcision** availeth anything
Eph. 2:11	Gentiles...who are called **uncircumcision** by that which
Philip. 3:3(3-5)	for we are the **circumcision**, which worship God in the
Col. 2:11(10-15)	circumcised with the **circumcision** made without hands
Col. 3:11	there is neither...**circumcision** nor uncircumcision
Col. 4:11	who are of the **circumcision**. these only are my
Titus 1:10	there are many unruly and vain...of the **circumcision**
Moro. 8:8	the law of **circumcision** is done away in me.
D&C 74:3(1-7)	contention...concerning the law of **circumcision**, for

CITIZENSHIP

Ex. 22:28	not revile the Gods, nor curse the **ruler** of thy people
Deut. 1:16(15-18)	**judge** righteously between every man and his brother
Ps. 82:3(3,4)	do **justice** to the afflicted and needy.
Eccl. 8:2	I counsel thee to keep the **king's** commandment, and
Eccl. 10:20	curse not the **king**, no not in thy thought; and curse
Matt. 7:12	men should **do** to you, do ye even so to them: for this
Matt. 17:27(24-27)	money...that take, and **give** unto them for me and thee.
Matt. 19:19	thou shalt **love** thy neighbour as thyself.
Matt. 22:21(19-22)	**render** therefore unto Caesar the things which are
Luke 19:14	his **citizens** hated him, and sent a message after him
Acts 23:5(1-5)	thou shalt not speak evil of the **ruler** of thy people.
Rom. 13:1(1-14)	let every soul be **subject** unto the higher powers. for
Eph. 2:19(19-20)	no more strangers...**fellowcitizens** with the saints
1 Tim. 2:2(1-3)	for kings..that we may lead a quiet and peaceable **life**
Titus 3:1	be **subject** to principalities and powers, to obey
James 4:11(10-12)	he that..speaketh evil of the **law**, and judgeth the law
1 Pet. 2:13(13-17)	**submit** yourselves to every ordinance...to the king
1 Pet. 2:17(13-17)	honour all men...fear God. Honour the **king**.
Mosiah 2:17(15-18)	in the **service** of your fellow beings...service of your
Mosiah 4:13	**live** peaceably, and to render to every man according
Mosiah 29:25(25-27)	choose you by the **voice** of this people, judges, that
Alma 1:1	people...obliged to abide by the **laws** which he had mad
Alma 1:14	this people must **abide** by the law.
Alma 43:9(9-10)	preserve their **rights** and their privileges, yea, and

CITIZENSHIP cont.

Alma 46:13(11-16)	and he called it the title of **liberty)** and he bowed
Alma 51:6(6,7)	**freeman**...maintain their rights and the privileges of
Alma 51:22(20-22)	subjecting them to peace and **civilization**, and making
D&C 42:27	not speak evil of thy **neighbor**, nor do him any harm.
D&C 58:21(20-22)	let no man break the **laws** of the land, for he that
D&C 98:4(4-11)	the **laws** of the land...people should observe to do all
D&C 98:10(9-10)	good men and wise men ye should observe to **uphold**
D&C 101:77(76-80)	laws and **Constitution**...rights and protection of all
D&C 134:1(1-12)	**governments** were instituted of God for the benefit of
D&C 134:5(5-9)	uphold the respective **governments** in which they reside
D&C 134:6(1-12)	to the laws all men owe **respect** and deference, as with
D&C 134:7(1-12)	laws for the protection of all **citizens** in the free
Moses 7:18(17-19)	called his **people** Zion, because they were of one heart
A of F 1:12	We believe in being **subject** to kings, presidents, rule

CLEANLINESS

Ex. 19:10	sanctify them...and let them **wash** their clothes
2 Sam. 22:21(21-25)	Lord rewarded me according to...**cleanness** of my hands
Ps. 18:24(20-24)	recompensed me..according to the **cleanness** of my hands
Ps. 24:4(3-5)	he that hath **clean** hands, and a pure heart; who hath
Ps. 51:10(7-12)	create in me a **clean** heart, O God; and renew a right
Isa. 1:16(15-19)	make you **clean**; put away the evil of your doings from
Jer. 4:14	O Jerusalem, **wash** thine heart from wickedness, that
Matt. 5:8	blessed are the **pure** in heart: for they shall see God.
Matt. 15:11(11-20)	not that which goeth into the mouth **defileth** a man
Matt. 23:27(25-29)	full of dead men's bones, and of all **uncleanness**.
Luke 11:41(37-41)	behold, all things are **clean** unto you.
Acts 10:15(15-28)	what God hath **cleansed**, that call not thou common.
1 Cor. 3:17(16-17)	if any man **defile** the temple of God, him shall God
2 Cor. 7:1	**cleanse** ourselves from all filthiness of the flesh
1 Ne. 10:21(20-22)	found **unclean** before the judgment-seat of God; and no
1 Ne. 15:34(33-34)	the kingdom of God is not **filthy**, and there cannot any
Alma 5:21(19,21-28)	garments...purified until...**cleansed** from all stain
Alma 7:14	mighty to save and to **cleanse** from all unrighteousness
Alma 7:25(19-25)	having your garments **spotless**...as their garments are
Alma 34:36	Lord...dwelleth not in **unholy** temples, but in the
Alma 60:23(23,24)	the inward vessel shall be **cleansed** first, and then
Hel. 3:35	**purifying** and the sanctification of their hearts
3 Ne. 8:1	save he were **cleansed** every whit from his iniquity
3 Ne. 20:41	be ye **clean** that bear the vessels of the Lord.
Morm. 9:6	having been **cleansed** by the blood of the Lamb, at that
Ether 12:37	thy garments shall be made **clean**. And because thou has
Moro. 6:4(1-4)	wrought upon..**cleansed** by the power of the Holy Ghost
Moro. 7:48	that we may be **purified** even as he is pure. Amen.
D&C 38:10(10-12)	ye are **clean**, but not all; and there is none else with
D&C 38:24	let every man...practise **virtue** and holiness before
D&C 42:41	and let all things be done in **cleanliness** before me.
D&C 88:74(74-75)	purify your hearts, and **cleanse** your hands and your
D&C 88:86	entangle not...in sin, but let your hands be **clean**
D&C 90:36	contend with Zion...chasten her until she...is **clean**
D&C 121:45(45-46)	let **virtue** garnish thy thoughts unceasingly; then

CLEANLINESS cont.

D&C 133:5(4-5)	be ye **clean** that bear the vessels of the Lord.
Moses 6:57	for no **unclean** thing can dwell there, or dwell in his

CLOTHING

Gen. 3:7	sewed fig leaves together, and made themselves **aprons**.
Gen. 3:21	did the Lord God make coats of skins, and **clothed** them
Ex. 28:2(1-3)	and thou shalt make holy **garments** for Aaron thy
Ex. 28:40(39,40)	and for Aaron's sons thou shalt make **coats**, and thou
Deut. 22:5	woman shall not **wear** that which pertaineth unto a man
Dan. 7:9	whose **garment** was white as snow, and the hair of his
Mark 1:6	and John was **clothed** with camel's hair, and with a
Mark 16:5	**clothed** in a long white garment; and they were
Rev. 19:14	the armies...**clothed** in fine linen, white and clean.
1 Ne. 8:5	he was dressed in a white **robe**; and he came and stood
1 Ne. 13:8(7-8)	fine-twined linen, and the precious **clothing**, and the
Mosiah 10:5	**cloth** of every kind, that we might clothe our
Alma 1:29	twined linen, and all manner of good homely **cloth**.
Hel. 6:13	cloth of every kind, to **clothe** their nakedness. And
3 Ne. 11:8	he was **clothed** in a white robe; and he came down and
Ether 10:24	they did work all manner of **cloth**, that they might
D&C 42:40	all thy **garments** be plain...work of thine own hands
D&C 49:19(19-20)	ordained for the use of man for food and for **raiment**
Moses 4:27	the Lord God, make coats of skins, and **clothed** them.
JS-H 1:31(31-32)	he had on a loose **robe** of most exquisite whiteness.

COMFORT

Gen. 24:67	Isaac was **comforted** after his mother's death.
Ps. 18:2(1-3)	the Lord is my **rock**, and my fortress, and my deliverer
Ps. 23:4(1-6)	thy rod and thy staff they **comfort** me.
Ps. 71:21	thou shalt...**comfort** me on every side.
Ps. 119:50(49-52)	this is my **comfort** in my affliction: for thy word hath
Isa. 25:4(4,5)	thou hast been a...**refuge** from the storm, a shadow
Isa. 49:13	for the Lord hath **comforted** his people, and will have
Isa. 51:3	for the Lord shall **comfort** Zion: he will comfort all
Isa. 57:18(15-19)	I will...restore **comforts** unto him and to his mourners
Isa. 61:2(1-3)	to **comfort** all that mourn
Isa. 66:13(10-13)	as...mother comforteth, so will I **comfort** you; and ye
Matt. 5:4	blessed...they that mourn...they shall be **comforted**.
Matt. 11:29(28-30)	ye shall find **rest** unto your souls.
John 14:18(16-26)	I will not leave you **comfortless**: I will come to you.
John 15:26	but when the **Comforter** is come, whom I will send unto
Acts 9:31	and in the **Comfort** of the Holy Ghost, were multiplied.
2 Cor. 1:3(3-6)	father of mercies, and the God of all **comfort**
2 Cor. 7:4	I am filled with **comfort**, I am exceeding joyful in all
2 Cor. 7:7	consolation wherewith he was **comforted** in you, when
Mosiah 18:9(8-10)	**comfort** those that stand in need of comfort, and to
3 Ne. 12:4	blessed...they that mourn...they shall be **comforted**.
Ether 12:29	having heard these words, was **comforted**, and said: O
Ether 15:3	his soul mourned and refused to be **comforted**.

COMFORT cont.

D&C 25:5	thy calling shall be for a **comfort** unto my servant
D&C 36:2	**Comforter**, which shall teach you the peaceable things
D&C 101:14(11-16)	all they who have mourned shall be **comforted**.
D&C 121:7(1-7)	my son, **peace** be unto thy soul; thine adversity and
JFS-V 1:42	anointed to bind up the **broken-hearted**, to proclaim

COMMANDMENTS OF GOD

Gen. 2:16	God **commanded** the man, saying, of every tree of the
Gen. 6:22	thus did Noah; according to all that God **commanded** him
Ex. 20:1(1-17)	and God **spake** all these words, saying
Ex. 20:6	shewing mercy unto...them that...keep my **commandments**.
Ex. 39:32	Israel did according to all...the Lord **commanded** Moses
Deut. 4:13	covenant...commanded you to perform...ten **commandments**
Deut. 5:1(1-21)	hear, O Israel, the **statutes** and judgments which I
Deut. 5:31(29-33)	speak unto thee all the **commandments**, and the statute
Deut. 6:17(1-25)	ye shall diligently keep the **commandments** of the Lord
Deut. 6:24(24-25)	Lord **commanded** us ...for our good always, that he
Deut. 10:13(12-13)	to keep the **commandments** of the Lord...for thy good
Matt. 5:21(21-28)	it was said...thou **shalt** not kill; and whosoever shall
Matt. 22:38(37-40)	this is the first and great **commandment**.
John 14:15(15-31)	if ye love me, keep my **commandments**.
John 15:14	ye are my friends, if ye do whatsoever I **command** you.
1 Jn. 3:23(22-24)	this is his **commandment**, that we should believe on the
1 Ne. 3:7	Lord giveth no **commandments** unto the children of men
1 Ne. 22:31	if ye shall be obedient to the **commandments**, and
Jacob 2:10(10-34)	do according to the strict **commands** of God, and tell
Jarom 1:9	inasmuch as ye...keep my **commandments** ye shall prosper
Mosiah 2:22	keep his **commandments** he doth bless you and prosper
Mosiah 13:11(11-25)	read unto you the remainder of the **commandments** of God
Alma 12:31(31-37)	wherefore, he gave **commandments** unto men, they having
D&C 29:35	my **commandments** are spiritual..not natural nor
D&C 42:15(15-29)	do as I have **commanded** concerning your teaching, until
D&C 43:8	a **commandment**, that...ye shall instruct and edify each
D&C 58:26(26-29)	it is not meet that I should **command** in all things
D&C 61:13	for your good I gave unto you a **commandment** concerning
D&C 89:2(2-21)	showing forth the order and **will** of God...all saints

COMMITMENT

Num. 14:24(22-24)	Caleb..had another spirit...and hath **followed** me fully
Deut. 6:5(5-9)	love the Lord...with all thine **heart**, and with all thy
Deut. 10:12(12-22)	serve the Lord thy God with all thy **heart** and...soul
Deut. 26:16(16,17)	keep and do them with all thine **heart**, and with all
Josh. 22:5(1-7)	and to **serve** him with all your heart and with all your
Josh. 24:15(14-25)	**choose** you this day whom ye will serve; whether the
Ruth 1:18(14-18)	she was **stedfastly** minded to go with her, then she
1 Sam. 12:24(14,20,24)	**serve** him in truth with all your heart: for consider
2 Kgs. 23:3(1-25)	**covenant**...to walk after the Lord...keep his
Ps. 37:5	**commit** thy way unto the Lord; trust also in him; and
Ps. 112:7(6-8)	his **heart** is fixed, trusting in the Lord.

COMMITMENT cont.

Ps. 119:10(2,10,15)	with my whole **heart** have I sought thee: O let me not
Dan. 1:8(8-21)	Daniel **purposed** in his heart that he would not defile
Joel 2:12(12,13)	turn...to me with all your **heart**, and with fasting
Matt. 4:20(18-22)	they straightway left their nets, and with **followed** him.
Matt. 6:33(24-34)	but **seek** ye first the kingdom of God, and his
Matt. 7:24(21-27)	whosoever heareth these sayings...and **doeth** them, I
Matt. 8:22(19-22)	**follow** me; and let the dead bury their dead.
Matt. 19:21(16-21)	if thou wilt be **perfect**, go and sell that thou hast
Mark 12:30(28-34)	love the Lord thy God with all thy **heart**, and with all
Luke 4:8(2-13)	worship...Lord thy God, and him only shalt thou **serve**.
Luke 6:47(46-49)	cometh to me, and heareth my sayings, and **doeth** them
Luke 9:62(57-62)	having put his hand to the **plough**, and looking back
Luke 12:43(41-48)	blessed...servant, whom his Lord...shall find so **doing**
Luke 14:28(27-35)	build a tower...first...counteth the cost...to **finish**
Luke 23:46	Father, into thy hands I **commend** my spirit: and
John 8:31(28-32)	if ye **continue** in my word, then are ye my disciples
John 13:37(36,37)	**follow** thee now? I will lay down my life for thy sake.
John 14:15(15-31)	if ye love me, keep my **commandments**.
Acts 2:42(41-47)	continued **stedfastly** in the apostles' doctrine and
Rom. 1:15(15-17)	I am **ready** to preach the gospel to you...at Rome also.
Rom. 6:17(15-18)	**obeyed** from the heart that form of doctrine which was
Col. 3:23(22-24)	whatsoever ye do, do it **heartily**, as to the Lord, and
James 1:22(22-27)	but be ye **doers** of the word, and not hearers only
James 2:24(14-26)	by **works** a man is justified, and not by faith only.
1 Pet. 2:23(21-23)	but **committed** himself to him that judgeth righteously
1 Pet. 3:13(13-17)	if ye be **followers** of that which is good
1 Ne. 2:3(1-4)	he was **obedient** unto the word of the Lord, wherefore
1 Ne. 3:7(1-31)	I will go and do the things...the Lord...**commanded**
1 Ne. 3:15(2-15)	we will not go down...until we have **accomplished** the
2 Ne. 31:20(15-21)	wherefore, ye must press forward with a **steadfastness**
Jacob 6:11	**continue** in the way which is narrow, until ye shall
1:26	come unto him, and **offer** your whole souls as an
Mosiah 5:5(1-5)	we are willing to enter into a **covenant** with our God
Mosiah 18:10(8-11)	entered into a **covenant** with him, that ye will serve
Alma 1:25	**steadfast** and immovable in keeping the commandments
Alma 5:26(11-42)	if ye have experienced a **change** of heart, and if ye
Alma 5:57(11-57)	you that are desirous to **follow** the voice of the good
Alma 23:6(1-18)	were **converted** unto the Lord, never did fall away.
Alma 38:2(1-15)	have great joy in you, because of your **steadiness** and
Alma 46:21(16-22)	**covenant**, that they would not forsake the Lord their
Alma 46:22(16-22)	we **covenant**..be destroyed..if..fall into transgression
3 Ne. 13:33(19-34)	**seek** ye first the kingdom of God and his righteousness
3 Ne. 18:10(1-11)	ye are **willing** to do that which I have commanded you.
3 Ne. 29:8(1-8)	Lord remembereth his **covenant**...he will do unto them
Morm. 9:27(27-29)	come unto the Lord with all your **heart**, and work out
Moro. 10:32(30-33)	**love** God with all your might, mind and strength, then
D&C 4:2(1-7)	**serve** him with all your heart, might, mind and
D&C 11:20(12-24)	**keep** my commandments, yea, with all your might, mind
D&C 20:37	having a **determination** to serve him to the end, and
D&C 20:77(77-79)	**witness**...they are willing to take upon them the name
D&C 36:7(5-7)	**embrace** it with singleness of heart may be ordained
D&C 42:13(11-15)	**observe** the covenants and church articles to do them
D&C 59:11	nevertheless thy **vows** shall be offered up in righteous

COMMITMENT cont.

D&C 78:7	prepare...by **doing** the things which I have commanded
D&C 88:68(67-69)	sanctify yourselves that your minds become **single** to
D&C 90:24	things shall work...good, if ye...remember...**covenant**
D&C 97:8(8-9)	are willing to observe their covenants by **sacrifice**
Abr. 1:2(2-4)	desiring...to be a greater **follower** of righteousness

COMMON CONSENT

Ex. 24:3(1-4)	all the people answered with one **voice**, and said, all
Num. 27:19(18-23)	**set** him before...the priest, and before all the
1 Sam. 14:45	the **people** said...shall Jonathan die...the people
Neh. 4:6	built we the wall...for the **people** had a mind to work.
Ps. 133:1	for brethren to dwell together in **unity**
Zeph. 3:9(8,9)	call upon...Lord, to serve him with one **consent**.
Matt. 18:19	if two of you shall **agree** on earth...it shall be done
Acts 15:25(24-26)	being assembled with **one** accord, to send chosen men
Mosiah 29:26(23-26)	not common that the **voice** of the people desireth
Mosiah 29:39	to cast in their **voices** concerning who should be their
Alma 2:6(2-6)	to cast in their **voices** concerning the matter; and
D&C 20:65(60-67)	no person is to be ordained...without the **vote** of that
D&C 26:2	all things shall be done by common **consent** in the
D&C 28:13	all things must be done in order...by common **consent**
D&C 38:27	be **one**; and if ye are not one ye are not mine.
D&C 124:144(124-144	fill all these offices and **approve** of those names

COMMUNICATION

Gen. 11:7(6-9)	confound their **language**, that they may not understand
Ex. 33:11	spake unto Moses...as a man **speaketh** unto his friend.
Prov. 8:7	for my mouth shall **speak** truth; and wickedness is an
Prov. 12:13	snared by the transgression of his **lips**: but the just
Prov. 12:14	satisfied with good by the fruit of his **mouth**: and the
Prov. 12:17(17-19)	he that **speaketh** truth sheweth forth righteousness
Prov. 14:23	but the **talk** of the lips tendeth only to penury.
Prov. 15:1	a soft **answer** turneth away wrath: but grievous words
Prov. 15:2	the **tongue** of the wise useth knowledge aright: but the
Prov. 15:7	the **lips** of the wise disperse knowledge: but the heart
Prov. 15:28	the heart of the righteous studieth to **answer**: but the
Prov. 16:13	righteous **lips** are the delight of kings; and they love
Prov. 17:7	excellent **speech** becometh not a fool: much less do
Zeph. 3:9	a pure **language**, that they may all call upon the name
Matt. 5:25(25-26)	**agree** with thine adversary quickly, whiles thou art
Matt. 5:37	let your **communication** be, yea, yea; nay, nay: for
Rom. 8:26(26-27)	but the spirit itself maketh **intercession** for us with
Gal. 6:6	let him that is taught in the word **communicate** unto
Eph. 4:29(29,31,32)	let no corrupt **communication** proceed out of your mouth
Col. 4:6	let your **speech** be alway with grace, seasoned with
1 Thes. 5:18(14-23)	in every thing give **thanks**: for this is the will of
1 Tim. 6:18(17-19)	ready to distribute, willing to **communicate**
Heb. 13:16(15,16)	but to do good and to **communicate** forget not: for with
1 Pet. 3:16(14-22)	that falsely accuse your good **conversation** in Christ.

COMMUNICATION cont.

1 Ne. 17:45	he hath **spoken** unto you in a still small voice, but
2 Ne. 25:4	my soul delighteth in **plainness** unto my people, that
Alma 7:23(22-24)	**asking** for whatsoever things ye stand in need, both
Alma 22:16(15,16)	and **call** on his name in faith, believing that ye
Alma 26:22	and **prayeth** continually without ceasing- unto such it
Alma 37:36	yea, and **cry** unto God for all thy support; yea, let
Alma 37:37	**counsel** with the Lord in all thy doings, and he will
3 Ne. 12:37	but let your **communication** be yea, yea; nay, nay; for
3 Ne. 14:7(7,8)	**ask**, and it shall be given unto you; seek, and ye
Morm. 9:21	whatsoever he shall **ask** the Father in the name of
Ether 1:34(33-37)	not confound us that...not **understand** our words.
Moro. 7:48(45-48)	**pray** unto the Father with all the energy of heart
D&C 9:8(7-9)	must study it out in your mind; then you must **ask** me
D&C 25:12	for my soul delighteth in the **song** of the heart; yea
D&C 29:33	**speaking** unto you that you may naturally understand
D&C 52:16	he that **speaketh**, whose spirit is contrite, whose
D&C 59:7	thou shalt **thank** the Lord thy God in all things.
D&C 88:64(64,65)	whatsoever ye **ask** the Father in my name it shall be
D&C 90:24	search diligently, **pray** always, and be believing, and
D&C 121:41(41-45)	only by **persuasion**, by long-suffering, by gentleness
D&C 136:28	if thou art merry, **praise** the Lord with singing, with
D&C 136:29	if thou art sorrowful, **call** on the Lord thy God with
Moses 1:2(1,2)	and he saw God face to face, and he **talked** with him
JS-H 1:13	would **give** liberally, and not upbraid, I might venture

COMPASSION

Ex. 33:19	and will shew **mercy** on whom I will shew mercy.
Lev. 19:14	thou shalt not curse the **deaf**, nor put a
2 Kgs. 13:23(22-25)	had **compassion** on them...because of his covenant with
Job 6:14(10-14)	to him that is afflicted **pity** should be shewed from
Prov. 19:17(16-19)	he that hath **pity** upon the poor lendeth unto the Lord
Isa. 49:13(13-17)	Lord hath comforted..will have **mercy** upon his
Isa. 53:4(1-12)	surely he hath borne our **griefs**, and carried our
Isa. 61:2(1-3)	to **comfort** all that mourn
Isa. 63:9(8-9)	in all their **affliction** he was afflicted, and the
Lam. 3:32(22-36)	yet will he have **compassion** according to the multitude
Zech. 7:9(8-14)	shew mercy and **compassions** every man to his brother
Matt. 9:36(35-38)	he was moved with **compassion** on them, because they
Matt. 14:14(13,14)	and was moved with **compassion** toward them, and he
Matt. 18:33(23-35)	shouldest not thou also have had **compassion** on thy
Matt. 20:34(30-34)	so Jesus had **compassion** on them, and touched their eye
Mark 1:41(40-42)	and Jesus, moved with **compassion**, put forth his hand
Mark 5:19(18-20)	done for thee, and hath had **compassion** on thee.
Mark 6:34(32-34)	and Jesus...was moved with **compassion** toward them
Mark 9:22(17-29)	if thou canst do any thing, have **compassion** on us, and
Luke 7:13(11-15)	when the Lord saw her, he had **compassion** on her, and
Luke 10:33(25-37)	Samaritan...when he saw him, he had **compassion** on him
Luke 15:20(11-32)	his father saw him, and had **compassion**, and ran, and
Rom. 9:15(14-16)	I will have **compassion** on whom I will have compassion.
Rom. 12:15(12-18)	do rejoice, and **weep** with them that weep.
1 Cor. 12:26(24-26)	one member suffer, all the members **suffer** with it; or

COMPASSION cont.

Gal. 6:2(1-2)	bear ye one another's **burdens**, and so fulfil the law
Heb. 5:2(1-3)	who can have **compassion** on the ignorant, and on them
Heb. 13:3(1-3)	remember...them which **suffer** adversity, as being your
James 5:11(10,11)	that the Lord is very **pitiful**, and of tender mercy.
1 Pet. 3:8(8-9)	be...of one mind, having **compassion** one of another
1 Jn. 3:17(16,17)	shutteth up his bowels of **compassion** from him, how
Jude 1:22(21,22)	and of some have **compassion**, making a difference
2 Ne. 4:26(26,27)	hath visited men in so much **mercy**, why should my heart
2 Ne. 9:53(52,53)	because of his greatness, and his grace and **mercy**, he
Mosiah 15:9(5-9)	being filled with **compassion** towards the children of
Mosiah 18:9(8-9)	**mourn** with those that mourn; yea, and comfort those
Mosiah 20:26(25,26)	they had **compassion** on them and were pacified towards
Mosiah 23:34(33,34)	the Lamanites had **compassion** on Amulon and his
Alma 7:11(11-13)	he will take upon him the **pains** and the sicknesses of
Alma 27:4(1-30)	they were moved with **compassion**, and they said unto
3 Ne. 17:6(1-10)	my bowels are filled with **compassion** towards you.
Ether 1:35(34,35)	the Lord had **compassion** upon Jared; therefore he did
D&C 25:5	thy calling shall be for a **comfort** unto my servant
D&C 52:40	remember...the poor and the **needy**, the sick and the
D&C 64:2(2-4)	I will have **compassion** upon you.
D&C 88:40	mercy hath **compassion** on mercy and claimeth her own
D&C 101:9(1-9)	my bowels are filled with **compassion** towards them. I
D&C 121:3(1-6)	thy bowels be moved with **compassion** toward them
Moses 7:41(28-41)	his heart swelled wide...and his bowels **yearned**; and

CONCEIVED IN SIN

Ps. 51:5(4-5)	and in sin did my mother **conceive** me.
Ps. 58:3	the wicked...go **astray** as soon as they be born
Mosiah 3:16(16-19,21)	little **children**...blood of Christ atoneth for their
Mosiah 3:18(16-19,21)	**infant** perisheth not that dieth in his infancy; but
Ether 3:2	because of the fall our **natures** have become evil
Moro. 8:8(4-21)	**children** are whole...not capable of committing sin
Moro. 8:22(22-26)	**children** are alive in Christ, and also all they that
D&C 29:46(40-46)	little **children** are redeemed from the foundation of
D&C 29:47	cannot sin...not given...to tempt little **children**
D&C 74:1	**children** unclean, but now are they holy.
D&C 74:7(6-7)	but little **children** are holy, being sanctified through
D&C 93:38	man was **innocent** in the beginning; and God having
Moses 6:55(53-56)	children are **conceived** in sin...sin conceiveth in

CONFESSION

Lev. 5:5(1-5)	he shall **confess** that he hath sinned in that thing
Lev. 16:21(21-22)	**confess** over him all the iniquities of...Israel, and
Lev. 26:40(40-42)	if they shall **confess** their iniquity, and the iniquity
Num. 21:7(7-9)	came to Moses, and said, we have **sinned**, for we have
Josh. 7:19(18-21)	make **confession**...tell me now what thou hast done; hid
1 Sam. 15:24(24,25)	Saul said unto Samuel, I have **sinned**: for I have
Ezra 10:1	Ezra had prayed, and when he had **confessed**, weeping
Neh. 1:6(3-7)	I pray...and **confess** the sins of the children of

CONFESSION cont.

Neh. 9:2(1-3)   seed of Israel...stood and **confessed** their sins, and
Ps. 32:5(1-6)   I said, I will **confess** my transgressions unto the Lord
Ps. 38:18   I will **declare** mine iniquity; I will be sorry for my
Ps. 51:3(1-3)   I **acknowledge** my transgressions: and my sin is ever
Prov. 28:13   whoso **confesseth** and forsaketh them shall have mercy.
Jer. 14:20   we **acknowledge**, O Lord, our wickedness, and the
Dan. 9:4(3-15)   I prayed...and made my **confession**, and said, O Lord
Hosea 5:15(14,15)   till they **acknowledge** their offence, and seek my face
Matt. 3:6   and were baptized of him...**confessing** their sins.
Luke 15:18(18-21)   will say unto him, Father, I have **sinned** against heaven
Acts 19:18   and many that believed came, and **confessed**, and shewed
James 5:16   **confess** your faults one to another, and pray one for
1 Jn. 1:9(8-10)   if we **confess** our sins, he...forgive us our sins, and
Mosiah 26:29(29-30)   if he **confess** his sins...him shall ye forgive, and I
Mosiah 26:35   repented of their sins and did **confess** them, them he
Mosiah 26:36   those that would not **confess**...names were blotted out.
Moro. 6:7   **confessed** not, their names were blotted out, and they
D&C 19:20(15-20)   **confess** your sins, lest you suffer these punishments
D&C 42:88(88-93)   and if he or she **confess** thou shalt be reconciled.
D&C 58:43(42-43)   if a man repenteth of his sins...he will **confess** them
D&C 59:12   **confessing** thy sins unto thy brethren, and before the
D&C 61:2   am merciful unto those who **confess** their sins with
D&C 64:7(7-11)   I...forgive sins unto those who **confess** their sins
D&C 64:12   him that repenteth not...and **confesseth** them not, ye

CONSCIENCE

Gen. 3:22   as one of us, to **know** good and evil: and now, lest
Job 32:8   Almighty giveth them **understanding**.
Ps. 73:21(21-24)   my heart was grieved, and I was **pricked** in my reins.
Ps. 73:24(21-24)   thou shalt **guide** me with thy counsel, and afterward
Isa. 32:17   the work of righteousness shall be **peace**; and the
Isa. 57:21(19-21)   there is no **peace**, saith my God, to the wicked.
John 8:9   convicted by their own **conscience**, went out one by one
John 16:13(7-14)   **spirit** of truth...will guide you into all truth: For
Acts 2:37(37-40)   they were **pricked** in their heart, and said unto Peter
Acts 23:1   I have lived in all good **conscience** before God until
Acts 24:16   **conscience** void of offence toward God, and toward men
Rom. 2:15(13-15)   their **conscience** also bearing witness, and their
Rom. 9:1(1-2)   my **conscience** also bearing me witness in the Holy
Rom. 13:5   ye must needs be subject...for **conscience** sake.
1 Cor. 8:7(7-13)   and their **conscience** being weak is defiled.
1 Cor. 10:29(23-33)   why is my liberty judged of another man's **conscience**
2 Cor. 4:2   commending ourselves to every man's **conscience** in the
2 Cor. 5:11(10-11)   I trust also are made manifest in your **consciences**.
Eph. 4:19(17-19)   being past **feeling** have given themselves over unto
1 Tim. 3:9(8-10)   holding the mystery of the faith in a pure **conscience**.
1 Tim. 4:2(1-3)   having their **conscience** seared with a hot iron
2 Tim. 1:3   I serve from my forefathers with pure **conscience**, that
Titus 1:15   but even their mind and **conscience** is defiled.
Heb. 9:14(13-14)   purge your **conscience** from dead works to serve the
Heb. 10:22(19-23)   hearts sprinkled from an evil **conscience**, and our

CONSCIENCE cont.

Heb. 13:18	we have a good **conscience**, in all things willing to
1 Pet. 3:16(15-21)	having a good **conscience**; that, whereas they speak Evi
Mosiah 2:15(15,27)	answer a clear **conscience** before God this day.
Mosiah 4:3	having peace of **conscience**, because of the exceeding
Alma 12:1	tremble under a **consciousness** of his guilt, he opened
Alma 14:6	**consciousness** of his own guilt; yea, he began to be
Alma 29:5	whether he desireth...joy or remorse of **conscience**.
Alma 42:18	brought remorse of **conscience** unto man.
Morm. 9:3(3-4)	your souls are racked with a **consciousness** of guilt
Moro. 7:16(12-19)	**Spirit** of Christ is given to every man, that he may
D&C 1:3	the rebellious shall be **pierced** with much sorrow; for
D&C 84:46(45-46)	spirit giveth **light** to every man that cometh into the
D&C 88:11(3-12)	same light that quickeneth your **understandings**
D&C 93:32(31-32)	man whose spirit receiveth not the **light** is under
D&C 134:2(2-5)	free exercise of **conscience**, the right and control of
D&C 135:4	I have a **conscience** void of offense towards God, and
A of F 1:11	worshiping...according to...our own **conscience**, and

CONSECRATION

Acts 2:44	believed were together, and had all things **common**
Acts 4:32(32-37)	they had all things **common**.
Acts 5:2(1-11)	and kept back **part** of the price, his wife also being
2 Cor. 8:14(13-15)	abundance...a supply...that there may be **equality**
Mosiah 4:21	ye ought to **impart** of the substance that ye have one
Mosiah 18:27(27-29)	people of the church should **impart** of their substance
Alma 1:27	and they did **impart** of their substance, every man
3 Ne. 26:19(19,20)	they had all things **common** among them, every man deal
4 Ne. 1:3	they had all things **common** among them; therefore there
4 Ne. 1:25(24-26)	goods and their substance no more **common** among them.
D&C 42:30(30-42)	remember the poor, and **consecrate** of thy properties
D&C 49:20	not given that one man should **possess**...above another
D&C 51:3(2-15)	every man **equal** according to his family, according
D&C 78:5(3-7)	that you may be **equal** in the bonds of heavenly things
D&C 105:5	Zion...be built up...by the **principles** of the law of
Moses 7:18	righteousness; and there was no **poor** among them.

CONSPIRACY

Gen. 37:18(17-21)	before he came near...they **conspired**...to slay him.
1 Sam. 22:8(7-8)	all of you have **conspired** against me, and there is none
2 Sam. 15:12	the **conspiracy** was strong; for the people increased
2 Kgs. 10:9(8-11)	I **conspired** against my master, and slew him: but who
2 Kgs. 17:4	the king of Assyria found **conspiracy** in Hoshea: for
Jer. 11:9(8-10)	a **conspiracy** is found among the men of Judah, and among
Ezek. 22:25(23-26)	there is a **conspiracy** of her prophets in the midst the
Acts 23:13(12-13)	were more than forty which had made this **conspiracy**.
2 Thes. 2:7(6-12)	**mystery** of iniquity doth already work: only he who now
2 Ne. 27:27	seek deep to hide their **counsel** from the Lord! And the
Alma 37:21(21-32)	or the **secret** works of those people who have been
Alma 47:35(13-35)	Amalickiah...by his **fraud**...obtained the kingdom; yea

CONSPIRACY cont.

Hel. 2:8(1-13)	object...to murder, and to rob, and to gain power, (an
Hel. 6:26(15-40)	those **secret** oaths and covenants did not come forth
Moses 6:15	because of **secret** works, seeking for power.

CONTENTION

Gen. 13:8	let there be no **strife**, I pray thee, between me and
Prov. 10:12	hatred stirreth up **strifes**: but love covereth all sins
Prov. 13:10	only by pride cometh **contention**: but with the well
Prov. 15:18	he that is slow to anger appeaseth **strife**.
Prov. 18:6	a fool's lips enter into **contention**, and his mouth
Prov. 18:19(17-19)	their **contentions** are like the bars of a castle.
Prov. 22:10	cast out the scorner, and **contention** shall go out; yea
Prov. 23:29	who hath **contentions**? Who hath babbling? Who hath
Prov. 26:21(20-28)	as coals...so is a **contentious** man to kindle strife.
Hosea 4:4(1-5)	yet let no man **strive**, nor reprove another: for thy
Acts 11:2(1-4,18)	they that were of the circumcision **contended** with him
Acts 15:39	and the **contention** was so sharp between them, that the
Rom. 2:8(8-9)	but unto them that are **contentious**, and do not obey
1 Cor. 1:11(10-13)	that there are **contentions** among you.
1 Cor. 11:16	if any man seem to be **contentious**, we have no such
2 Tim. 3:2(1-15)	for men shall be...**disobedient** to parents, unthankful
Titus 3:9	avoid foolish questions...and **contentions**, and
James 3:16(1-18)	where envying and **strife** is, there is confusion and
1 Ne. 12:3	after the manner of wars and **contentions** in the land
Jacob 7:26	hated of..brethren, which caused wars and **contentions**
Jarom 1:13	wars, and **contentions**, and dissensions, for the space
Mosiah 2:32(32-33)	beware lest there shall arise **contentions** among you
Mosiah 4:14	and fight and **quarrel** one with another, and serve the
Mosiah 18:21	commanded them that there should be no **contention** one
Mosiah 29:7	I fear there would rise **contentions** among you. and who
Alma 4:9(8-9)	there began to be great **contentions** among the people
Alma 50:25(21-25)	it not been for a **contention** which took place among
Alma 51:9	such **contentions**...again stirred up the hearts of the
3 Ne. 11:29(28-30)	he that hath the spirit of **contention** is not of me
4 Ne. 1:2	there were no **contentions** and disputations among them
4 Ne. 1:15	there was no **contention**...because of the love of God
Ether 11:7	there began to be wars and **contentions** in all the land
D&C 10:63	Satan...stir...hearts of the people to **contention**
D&C 64:8	my disciples, in days of old, sought **occasion** against
D&C 74:3	**contention** among the people concerning the law of
D&C 95:10	**contentions** arose in the school of the prophets
D&C 101:6(6-7)	there were jarrings, and **contentions**, and envyings
D&C 136:23	cease to **contend** one with another; cease to speak evil

CONTENTMENT

Ps. 4:8(6-8)	lay me down in **peace**, and sleep: for thou, Lord, only
Ps. 23:1(1-6)	the Lord is my shepherd; I shall not **want**.
Isa. 26:3(1-4)	thou wilt keep him in perfect **peace**, whose mind is
Jer. 29:7(4-7)	for in the **peace** thereof shall ye have peace.

CONTENTMENT cont.

Matt. 5:9	blessed are the **peacemakers**: for they shall be called
Luke 3:14	and be **content** with your wages.
John 14:27	my **peace** I give unto you: not as the world giveth
Rom. 14:17	the kingdom of God is...righteousness, and **peace**, and
Gal. 5:22	fruit of the spirit is love, joy, **peace**, longsuffering
Philip. 4:11	in whatsoever state I am, therewith to be **content**.
1 Tim. 6:6	but godliness with **contentment** is great gain.
1 Tim. 6:8(6-10)	having food and raiment let us be therewith **content**.
2 Tim. 4:7(6-8)	I have fought a good **fight**, I have finished my course
Heb. 13:5	be **content** with such things as ye have: for he hath
2 Ne. 4:27(26-28)	give way to temptations...destroy my **peace** and afflict
Enos 1:27	then shall I see his face with **pleasure**, and he will
Alma 29:3	for I ought to be **content** with the things which the
Alma 58:11	he did speak **peace** to our souls, and did grant unto
D&C 6:23	did I not speak **peace** to your mind concerning the
D&C 105:25	rest in **peace** and safety, while you are saying unto
JS-H 1:26	I had now got my mind **satisfied** so far as the

CONTRITE HEART

Lev. 26:41(40-42)	if then their uncircumcised hearts be **humbled**, and the
Ps. 10:12(12-17)	O God, lift up thine hand: forget not the **humble**.
Ps. 34:18	and saveth such as be of a **contrite** spirit.
Ps. 51:17(14-17)	the sacrifices of God...a broken and a **contrite** heart
Prov. 16:19(18,19)	better it is to be of an **humble** spirit with the lowly
Isa. 57:15	with him also that is of a **contrite** and humble spirit
Isa. 66:2	him that is poor and of a **contrite** spirit, and tremble
Matt. 5:3(3-5)	blessed are the **poor** in spirit: for theirs is the king
Matt. 11:29(28-30)	for I am meek and **lowly** in heart: and ye shall find
Luke 14:11(7-11)	he that **humbleth** himself shall be exalted.
Luke 15:21(11-32)	and am no more **worthy** to be called thy son.
Luke 18:13(10-14)	saying, God be merciful to me a **sinner**.
Heb. 3:15(14,15)	**harden** not your hearts, as in the provocation.
James 4:10(8-10)	**humble** yourselves in the sight of the Lord, and he
1 Pet. 5:6(5-7)	**humble** yourselves therefore under the mighty hand of
2 Ne. 4:32(31-32)	my **heart** is broken and my spirit is contrite! O Lord
3 Ne. 9:20(19-20)	sacrifice unto me a broken **heart** and a contrite spirit
3 Ne. 12:19(18-20)	come unto me with a broken **heart** and a contrite spirit
Morm. 2:14(13-14)	did not come unto Jesus with broken **hearts** and
Ether 4:15(13-16)	in my name, with a broken **heart** and a contrite spirit
Moro. 6:2(1-4)	save they came forth with a broken **heart** and a
D&C 20:37	come forth with broken hearts and **contrite** spirits
D&C 21:9	for the remission of sins unto the **contrite** heart.
D&C 52:15(14-17)	he that prayeth, whose spirit is **contrite**, the same
D&C 56:18(16-20)	hearts are broken, and whose spirits are **contrite**, for
D&C 59:8	even that of a broken heart and a **contrite** spirit.
D&C 136:33	spirit is sent...to enlighten the humble and **contrite**

CONVERSION

Ruth 1:16   thy people shall be my people, and thy God my **God**
Ps. 19:7(7-9)   law of the Lord is perfect, **converting** the soul: the
Ps. 51:13(11-13)   sinners shall be **converted** unto thee.
Isa. 1:27   Zion shall be redeemed..her **converts** with
Isa. 14:1(1-3)   yet choose Israel..**strangers** shall be joined with them
Isa. 19:22(21-25)   Egypt...shall **return** even to the Lord...shall be
Isa. 44:5(1-5)   one shall say, I am the **Lord's**; and another shall call
Isa. 45:20(20-24)   draw near together, ye that are escaped of the **nations**
Isa. 56:8(3-8)   yet will I gather **others** to him, beside those that are
Isa. 60:3(3-5)   and the **Gentiles** shall come to thy light, and kings
Jer. 31:33   inward parts, and write it in their **hearts**; and will
Jer. 32:39   and I will give them one **heart**, and one way, that they
Ezek. 11:19   and I will give them one **heart**, and I will put a new
Ezek. 18:31   and make you a new **heart** and a new spirit: for why
Ezek. 36:23(23-24)   and the **heathen** shall know that I am the Lord, saith
Ezek. 36:26(26-27)   take away the stony **heart** out of your flesh, and I
Ezek. 38:16(16,23)   that the **heathen** may know me, when I shall be
Ezek. 39:7   the **heathen** shall know that I am the Lord, the holy
Ezek. 39:21   I will set my glory among the **heathen**, and all the
Ezek. 39:23   **heathen** shall know that the house of Israel went into
Hosea 12:6   **turn** thou to thy God: keep mercy and judgment, and
Joel 2:12   **turn** ye even to me with all your heart, and with
Luke 22:32(31,32)   when thou art **converted**, strengthen thy brethren.
John 8:32(31-32)   ye shall **know** the truth, and the truth shall make you
Acts 2:37(37,38)   heard this, they were pricked in their **heart**, and said
Acts 3:19(19-21)   repent ye therefore, and be **converted**, that your sins
Acts 9:6(3-19)   Lord, **what** wilt thou have me to do? And the Lord said
Acts 15:3(2-4)   the **conversion** of the Gentiles: and they caused great
Acts 22:16(6-16)   arise, and be **baptized**, and wash away thy sins
Acts 26:16(13-18)   to make thee a minister and a **witness** both of these
Gal. 3:29(6-9,14-29)   if ye be Christ's, then are ye **Abraham's** seed, and
James 5:20(19,20)   he which **converteth** the sinner from the error of his
Mosiah 18:8(8-10)   as ye are desirous to come into the **fold** of God, and
Mosiah 27:25   all mankind...must be **born** again; yea, born of God
Alma 5:12(12,14)   a mighty **change** wrought in his heart. Behold I say
Alma 22:16   **bow** down before God, and call on his name in faith
Alma 36:23(12-23)   manifest unto the people that I had been **born** of God.
Hel. 15:7   repentance bringeth a **change** of heart unto them
D&C 7:4(1-6)   for he desired of me that he might bring **souls** unto
D&C 15:6   declare repentance...that you may bring **souls** unto me
D&C 18:16(10-16)   your joy if you should bring many **souls** unto me
D&C 44:4(3-5)   and many shall be **converted**, insomuch that ye shall
D&C 45:54   then shall the heathen nations be **redeemed**, and they
D&C 109:65(65-67)   the remnants of Jacob...be **converted** from their wild
D&C 109:70(68-70)   that they may be **converted** and redeemed with Israel
D&C 112:13   they shall be **converted**, and I will heal them.
Abr. 2:15   and the souls that we had **won** in Haran, and came forth

CORNERSTONE

Deut. 32:15(15-31)	lightly esteemed the **rock** of his salvation.
1 Sam. 2:2	neither is there any **rock** like our God.
Job 38:6(4-7)	who laid the **corner** stone thereof
Ps. 11:3	if the **foundations** be destroyed, what can the
Ps. 118:22(22-23)	**stone**...refused is become the head stone of the corner
Isa. 8:14	for a **stone** of stumbling and for a rock of offence to
Isa. 28:16	I lay in Zion for a foundation...a precious **corner**
Matt. 21:42(42-44)	**stone**...builders rejected...head of the corner: this
Mark 12:10	**stone**...rejected is become the head of the corner
Acts 4:11(10-12)	**stone**...set at nought...become the head of the corner.
Rom. 9:33(31-33)	behold, I lay in Sion a **stumblingstone** and rock of off
1 Cor. 3:11(9-13)	for other **foundation** can no man lay than that is laid
1 Cor. 10:4(1-4)	drank of...spiritual **rock**...and that rock was Christ.
Eph. 2:20(19-21)	foundation..Jesus Christ..being the chief **corner** stone
1 Pet. 2:6(6-8)	I lay in Sion a chief **corner** stone, elect, precious
2 Ne. 18:14(14,15)	for a **stone** of stumbling, and for a rock of offense
Jacob 4:15(15-17)	Jews...will reject the **stone** upon which they might
Hel. 5:12(9-12)	the **rock** of our Redeemer, who is Christ, the Son of
D&C 50:44(43-44)	I am...the **stone** of Israel. he that buildeth upon
D&C 124:2	stake...I have planted to be a **corner-stone** of Zion
D&C 124:23(23,60)	and the **corner-stone** I have appointed for Zion.
D&C 124:131	a high council, for the **corner-stone** of Zion
Moses 7:53(52-54)	I am Messiah...the **Rock** of Heaven, which is broad as

COUNCIL IN HEAVEN

Job 38:7(4-7)	when...all the **sons** of God shouted for joy
Isa. 14:13(12-15)	I will exalt my **throne** above the stars of God: I will
Luke 10:18(17-20)	I beheld **Satan** as lightning fall from heaven.
Rev. 12:7(7-9)	**war** in heaven: Michael...fought against the dragon
2 Ne. 2:17(16-18)	an **angel** of God...had fallen from heaven; wherefore
D&C 29:36(36-38)	he **rebelled** against me, saying, give me thine honor
D&C 76:25(25-27)	an angel of God...**rebelled** against the...Son whom the
Moses 4:3(1-4)	Satan **rebelled** against me, and sought to destroy the
Abr. 3:22(22-28)	**intelligences** that were organized before the world was

COUNSEL

Ps. 2:2	the rulers take **counsel** together, against the Lord
Ps. 73:24(23-24)	guide me with thy **counsel**, and afterward receive me
Prov. 1:25(24-33)	set at nought all my **counsel**, and would none of my
Prov. 11:14	where no **counsel** is, the people fall: but in the
Isa. 11:2(1-2)	spirit of the Lord shall rest...the spirit of **counsel**
Isa. 40:14(13-14)	with whom took he **counsel**, and who instructed him, and
Mark 3:6(1-6)	and straightway took **counsel**...against him, how they
John 11:53(51-53)	they took **counsel** together for to put him to death.
Acts 8:6(5-8)	the people...heed...those things which Philip **spake**
Acts 20:27(22-27)	shunned to declare unto you all the **counsel** of God.
1 Cor. 2:16(11-16)	who hath known the mind of the Lord...may **instruct** him
Eph. 6:1(1-9)	children, **obey** your parents in the Lord: for this is
Rev. 3:18(15-21)	I **counsel** thee to buy of me gold tried in the fire

COUNSEL cont.

2 Ne. 9:28(28-29)	hearken not unto the **counsel** of God, for they set it
2 Ne. 9:29(28-29)	be learned is good if...hearken unto...**counsels** of God
2 Ne. 27:27(25-27)	them that seek deep to hide their **counsel** from the lor
2 Ne. 28:9(9-10)	shall seek deep to hide their **counsels** from the Lord
2 Ne. 28:30(30-31)	lend an ear unto my **counsel**, for they shall learn
Jacob 4:10(9,10)	seek not to **counsel** the Lord, but to take counsel from
D&C 3:4(3-14)	sets at naught the **counsels** of God, and follows after
D&C 19:33	misery...receive if thou wilt slight these **counsels**
D&C 56:14	you seek to **counsel** in your own ways.
D&C 78:2(2,13-16)	listen to the **counsel** of him who has ordained you from
D&C 101:8(7-9)	they esteemed lightly my **counsel**; but, in the day of
D&C 103:5(1-8)	hearken...unto the **counsel** which I, the Lord their God
D&C 105:37	follow the **counsel** which they receive, they shall have
D&C 108:1	to receive **counsel** of him whom I have appointed.
D&C 122:2	the wise...noble, and the virtuous, shall seek **counsel**
D&C 124:16	not fail if he receive **counsel**.
D&C 124:89(89-90)	hearken to the **counsel** of my servant Joseph, and with
D&C 136:19	and seeketh not my **counsel**, he shall have no power
Moses 7:35	I am God...Man of **Counsel** is my name; and Endless and
Abr. 4:26	and the Gods took **counsel** among themselves and said
Abr. 5:2(2-3)	end our work, which we have **counseled**; and we will

COUNSELORS

2 Sam. 15:12(10-13)	Ahithophel the Gilonite, David's **counseller**, from his
1 Chr. 27:32(32-34)	Jonathan David's uncle was a **counseller**, a wise man
Ps. 1:1(1,2)	the man that walketh not in the **counsel** of the ungodly
Prov. 11:14	in the multitude of **counsellers** there is safety.
Prov. 12:5(5,6)	but the **counsels** of the wicked are deceit.
Prov. 24:6	in multitude of **counsellers** there is safety.
Isa. 1:26(25-27)	I will restore...thy **counsellers** as at the beginning
Isa. 9:6	his name shall be called Wonderful, **Counseller**, the
Isa. 29:15(13-16)	woe unto them that seek deep to hide their **counsel**
Isa. 30:1(1,2)	rebellious children...that take **counsel**, but not of
Isa. 40:13(12-14)	who...being his **counseller** hath taught him
Mark 15:43(42-47)	Joseph of Arimathaea, and honourable **counseller**, which
Rom. 11:34(33-36)	mind of the Lord? or who hath been his **counseller**
Heb. 6:17(17-20)	shew..heirs of promise the immutability of his **counsel**
2 Ne. 19:6	his name shall be called, wonderful, **counselor**, the
D&C 42:31(30,31)	laid before the bishop of my church and his **counselors**
D&C 58:18(17,18)	judge...by the assistance of his **counselors**, according
D&C 58:25(24-26)	as they shall **counsel** between themselves and me.
D&C 81:1(1-3)	a **counselor** unto my servant Joseph Smith, Jun.
D&C 107:72(64-76)	by the assistance of his **counselors**, whom he has
D&C 107:79(78-84)	even twelve, to assist as **counselors**; and thus the
D&C 112:30(30-32)	your **counselors** and your leaders, is the power of this
D&C 124:126(125,126	I give unto him for **counselors** my servant Sidney
D&C 124:142(142-145	Samuel Rolfe and his **counselors** for priests, and the

COURAGE

Deut. 20:1	be not **afraid**...God is with thee, which brought thee
Deut. 31:6	be strong and of a good **courage**, fear not, nor be
Josh. 1:7(6-7,9)	be thou strong and very **courageous**, that thou mayest
Josh. 23:6(6-8)	be ye therefore very **courageous** to keep and to do all
Ruth 1:18(16-18)	she saw that she was **stedfastly** minded to go with her
1 Sam. 17:32(32-47)	let no man's heart fail..thy servant will go and **fight**
2 Sam. 2:7	your hands be strengthened, and be ye **valiant**: for you
2 Sam. 13:28	I commanded you? be **courageous** and be valiant.
1 Chr. 22:13	be strong, and of good **courage**; dread not, nor be
1 Chr. 28:20	be strong and of good **courage**, and do it: fear not
2 Chr. 19:11	deal **courageously**, and the Lord shall be with the good
Ezra 10:4	be of good **courage**, and do it.
Ps. 27:14	be of good **courage**, and he shall strengthen thine
Ps. 31:24	be of good **courage**, and he shall strengthen your heart
Acts 5:29(17-42)	we ought to **obey** God rather than men.
Acts 28:15	he thanked God, and took **courage**.
Gal. 1:10	if I yet **pleased** men, I should not be the servant of
2 Tim. 1:7(7-8)	God hath not given us the spirit of **fear**; but of power
1 Ne. 4:1(1-3)	let us be **faithful** in keeping the commandments of the
1 Ne. 4:18(10-18)	I did **obey** the voice of the spirit, and took Laban by
Alma 15:4(4-6)	his heart began to take **courage**; and he sent a message
Alma 51:21	and to fight **valiantly** for their freedom from bondage.
Alma 53:20(20-21)	they were exceedingly valiant for **courage**, and also
Alma 56:45	never had I seen so great **courage**, nay, not amongst
D&C 3:7(5-8)	you should not have **feared** man more than God. although
D&C 30:11	open your mouth in my cause, not **fearing** what man can
D&C 38:15(14,15)	be ye **strong** from henceforth; fear not, for the
D&C 128:22	**courage**, brethren; and on, on to the victory! Let
D&C 136:17	go thy way...and **fear** not thine enemies; for they
JS-H 1:25	I had seen a vision...and I could not **deny** it, neither

COURTESY

Gen. 18:2(1-8)	he ran to meet them...and **bowed** himself toward the
Gen. 33:3(1-11)	**bowed** himself to the ground seven times, until he came
Lev. 19:32	thou shalt rise up...and **honour** the face of the old
Matt. 7:12	whatsoever...men should **do** to you, do ye...to them
John 13:14(1-17)	I...have **washed** your feet; ye also ought to wash one
Acts 28:7	received us, and lodged us three days **courteously**.
1 Cor. 13:4(4,5)	**charity** suffereth long, and is kind; charity envieth
Eph. 4:32	be ye **kind** one to another, tenderhearted, forgiving
Eph. 5:33	the wife see that she **reverence** her husband.
1 Pet. 3:8	be pitiful, be **courteous**
3 Ne. 14:12	whatsoever...men should **do** to you, do ye...to them
D&C 4:6	knowledge, temperance, patience, brotherly **kindness**
D&C 121:42	**kindness**...which shall greatly enlarge the soul

COVENANTS

Gen. 9:15(9-17)	and I will remember my **covenant**, which is between me
Gen. 17:10(2-21)	this is my **covenant**, which ye shall keep, between me
Gen. 26:3(1-5)	I will perform the **oath** which I sware unto Abraham thy
Ex. 19:5(5-6)	if ye..keep my **covenant**...shall be a peculiar treasure
Ex. 24:8(1-8)	blood of the **covenant**, which the Lord hath made with
Ex. 31:16(12-16)	keep the sabbath...for a perpetual **covenant**.
Lev. 26:42(42-45)	then will I remember my **covenant** with Jacob, and also
Num. 25:13(12,13)	even the **covenant** of an everlasting priesthood
Deut. 4:13	and he declared unto you his **covenant**, which he
Deut. 4:23(23,31)	lest ye forget the **covenant** of the Lord your God
Deut. 7:8	because he would keep the **oath** which he had sworn unto
Deut. 29:12(12-15)	enter into **covenant** with the Lord thy God, and into
Deut. 29:25(18-29)	they have forsaken the **covenant** of the Lord God of the
Judg. 2:1	I said, I will never break my **covenant** with you.
1 Kgs. 11:11(9-13)	thou hast not kept my **covenant** and my statutes, which
2 Chr. 34:31(29-33)	a **covenant** before the Lord, to walk after the Lord
Ps. 50:5	those that have made a **covenant** with me by sacrifice.
Ps. 105:9(7-11)	which **covenant** he made with Abraham, and his oath unto
Isa. 24:5	ordinance, broken the everlasting **covenant**.
Isa. 61:8(8-9)	I will make an everlasting **covenant** with them.
Jer. 31:31(27-34)	I will make a new **covenant** with the house of Israel
Jer. 31:32(31-34)	not according to the **covenant** that I made with their
Jer. 32:40(37-41)	and I will make an everlasting **covenant** with them
Jer. 50:5	join ourselves to the Lord in a perpetual **covenant**
Ezek. 16:60(59-62)	I will establish unto thee an everlasting **covenant**.
Zech. 9:11(9-11)	by the blood of thy **covenant**...sent forth thy prisoner
Matt. 26:28(26-30)	my blood of the new **testament**...shed for many for the
Luke 1:72(68-74)	to remember his holy **covenant**
Eph. 2:12(11-13)	strangers from the **covenants** of promise, having no
Heb. 6:17	wherein God...confirmed it by an **oath**
Heb. 8:6(6-13)	he is the mediator of a better **covenant**, which was
Heb. 12:24	Jesus the mediator of the new **covenant**, and to the
Heb. 13:20	through the blood of the everlasting **covenant**
1 Ne. 14:14	and upon the **covenant** people of the Lord, who were
1 Ne. 15:18	which **covenant** the Lord made to our father Abraham
2 Ne. 1:5(1-9)	the Lord hath **covenanted** this land unto me, and to my
Mosiah 18:13(8-13)	ye have entered into a **covenant** to serve him until you
Alma 24:18(12-19)	**covenanting**...rather than shed the blood of their
Alma 37:27	retain all their oaths, and their **covenants**, and their
Alma 56:6(6-8)	now ye also know concerning the **covenant** which their
3 Ne. 15:8(8,9)	for behold, the **covenant** which I have made with my
3 Ne. 20:29(19-29)	I have **covenanted** with them that I would gather them
3 Ne. 21:4(4-11,22)	that the **covenant** of the father may be fulfilled which
Morm. 8:23	he will remember the **covenant** which he hath made with
Moro. 10:33	blood of Christ, which is in the **covenant** of the
D&C 1:15	have broken mine everlasting **covenant**
D&C 1:22(15,22)	that mine everlasting **covenant** might be established
D&C 5:3(1-3,23-29)	I have caused...that you should enter into a **covenant**
D&C 22:1(1-4)	this is a new and an everlasting **covenant**, even that
D&C 45:9	I have sent mine everlasting **covenant** into the world
D&C 52:2	those who are heirs according to the **covenant**.
D&C 54:6(1-6)	blessed are they who have kept the **covenant** and
D&C 66:2	mine everlasting **covenant**, even the fulness of my

COVENANTS cont.

D&C 78:11(3-12)	organize yourselves by a bond or everlasting **covenant**
D&C 84:57	remember the new **covenant**, even the Book of Mormon and
D&C 88:133(131-133)	I salute you...in token...of the everlasting **covenant**
D&C 90:24	remember the **covenant**...ye have covenanted one with
D&C 97:8(8,9)	willing to observe their **covenants** by sacrifice- yea
D&C 98:14(13-14)	I will prove...whether you will abide in my **covenant**
D&C 104:52	**covenants** being broken through transgression, by covet
D&C 109:68	how he has **covenanted** with Jehovah, and vowed to thee
D&C 132:4(4,19)	I reveal unto you a new and an everlasting **covenant**
D&C 132:19	man marry a wife...by the new and everlasting **covenant**
D&C 136:4	our **covenant**- that we will walk in all the ordinances
Moses 7:51	he **covenanted** with Enoch, and sware unto him with an

COVETOUSNESS

Gen. 12:14(11-20)	the Egyptians **beheld** the woman that she was very fair.
Ex. 20:17	thou shalt not **covet** thy neighbour's house, thou shalt
Deut. 5:21	neither...**desire**...anything that is thy neighbour's.
2 Sam. 11:2(2-17)	from the roof he **saw** a woman washing herself; and the
Prov. 21:26	he **coveteth** greedily all the day long: but the
Prov. 28:16	he that hateth **covetousness** shall prolong his days.
Isa. 5:8(8-10)	woe unto them that **join** house to house, that lay field
Isa. 56:11	they are **greedy** dogs which can never have enough, and
Jer. 6:13	every one is given to **covetousness**; and from the
Micah 2:2	they **covet** fields, and take them by violence; and
Hab. 2:9	woe to him that **coveteth** an evil covetousness to his
Mark 7:22(21-23)	thefts, **covetousness**, wickedness, deceit
Luke 12:15(15-21)	take heed, and beware of **covetousness**: for a man's
Acts 20:33	I have **coveted** no man's silver, or gold, or apparel.
Rom. 7:7	the law had said, thou shalt not **covet**.
Rom. 13:9	thou shalt not **covet**; and if there be any other
1 Cor. 5:10(10,11)	with the **covetous**, or extortioners, or with idolaters
1 Cor. 12:31	but **covet** earnestly the best gifts: and yet shew I
1 Cor. 14:39	**covet** to prophesy, and forbid not to speak with tongue
Col. 3:5(5,6)	**covetousness**, which is idolatry
1 Thes. 2:5(4-9)	nor a cloke of **covetousness**; God is witness
1 Tim. 6:10(3-10)	money..which while some **coveted** after, they have erred
2 Tim. 3:2(1-5)	for men shall be...**covetous**, boasters, proud
Heb. 13:5	let your conversation be without **covetousness**; and be
1 Ne. 3:25(22-26)	when Laban saw our property ...he did **lust** after it
1 Ne. 22:23	churches which are built up to get **gain**, and all those
Mosiah 13:24	thou shalt not **covet** thy neighbor's house, thou shalt
Alma 39:9	go no more after the **lusts** of your eyes, but cross you
Morm. 9:28	ask not, that ye may consume it on your **lusts**, but ask
D&C 19:25	thou shalt not **covet** thy neighbor's wife; nor seek thy
D&C 19:26	thou shalt not **covet** thine own property, but impart
D&C 25:10	lay aside the **things** of this world, and seek for the
D&C 49:20	not given that one man should **possess**...above another
D&C 56:17(16-17)	eyes are full of **greediness**, and who will not labor
D&C 88:123	cease to be **covetous**; learn to impart one to another
D&C 104:4	broken the covenant through **covetousness**, and with
D&C 104:52	covenants being broken...by **covetousness** and feigned

COVETOUSNESS cont.

D&C 136:20	and **covet** not that which is thy brother's.
Moses 5:33(29-33)	surely the **flocks** of my brother falleth into my hands.
Moses 5:38	Satan **tempted** me because of my brother's flocks. and

CREATION

Gen. 1:1(1-31)	in the beginning God **created** the heaven and the earth.
Gen. 1:26(26,27)	let us **make** man in our image, after our likeness: and
Gen. 2:1(1-25)	thus the heavens and the **earth** were finished, and all
Gen. 2:5(4-6)	every plant of the field before it was in the **earth**
Gen. 2:7	the Lord God formed **man** of the dust of the ground, and
Gen. 2:23(21-23)	bone of my bones, and flesh of my flesh...**woman**
Ex. 31:17	in six days the Lord **made** heaven and earth, and on the
Job 38:4(1-13)	where wast thou when I laid the **foundations** of the
Ps. 102:25(24-28)	thou laid the foundation of the **earth**: and the heavens
Ps. 136:6(5-9)	to him that stretched out the **earth** above the waters
Ps. 148:5(1-6)	the Lord...he commanded, and they were **created**.
Prov. 8:22(22-31)	Lord possessed me in the beginning...before his **works**
Eccl. 11:5	knowest not the works of God who **maketh** all.
Isa. 42:5	he that **created** the heavens, and stretched them out
Isa. 48:13(12,13)	mine hand also hath laid the foundation of the **earth**
Isa. 51:13(12-16)	the Lord...laid the foundations of the **earth**; and hast
Isa. 64:8	O Lord...we all are the **work** of thy hand.
Zech. 12:1	the Lord...layeth the foundation of the **earth**, and for
John 1:3(1-4)	all things were **made** by him; and without him was not
John 1:10	the **world** was made by him, and the world knew him not.
Acts 17:24	God that **made** the world and all things therein, seeing
Eph. 3:9	God, who **created** all things by Jesus Christ
Col. 1:16(16-17)	by him were all things **created**, that are in heaven
Heb. 1:2(2,10)	heir of all things, by whom also he made the **worlds**
Heb. 11:3	the worlds were **framed** by the word of God, so that
2 Pet. 3:5(5-7)	by the word of God the heavens were...and the **earth**
Rev. 3:14	the Amen...the beginning of the **creation** of God
1 Ne. 17:36	behold, the Lord hath **created** the earth that it should
2 Ne. 2:14(14,15)	there is a God, and he hath **created** all things, both
2 Ne. 11:7	if there be no God...there could have been no **creation**
2 Ne. 29:7	I, the Lord your God, have **created** all men, and that
Jacob 2:21	all flesh...hath he **created** them, that they should
Jacob 4:9	which earth was **created** by the power of his word.
Mosiah 2:21(21-25)	ye should serve him who has **created** you from the begin
Mosiah 3:8	Jesus Christ ...the **creator** of all things from the
Mosiah 4:9(2,9,20,21)	he **created** all things, both in heaven and in earth
Mosiah 7:27	man was **created** in the beginning; or in other words
Mosiah 28:17	from that time back until the **creation** of Adam.
Alma 18:28(24-36)	who is God, **created** all things which are in heaven and
Alma 22:10(10-13)	he is that great spirit, and he **created** all things
Hel. 14:12	Christ...the **creator** of all things from the beginning
3 Ne. 9:15	I **created** the heavens and the earth, and all things
Morm. 9:11(11,12,17)	God who **created** the heavens...earth, and all things
Ether 3:15(13-16)	all men were **created** in the beginning after mine own
D&C 14:9	I am Jesus Christ...who **created** the heavens and the
D&C 20:18(17-18)	and that he **created** man, male and female, after his

CREATION cont.

D&C 29:31(30-33)	for by the power of my spirit **created** I them; yea, all
D&C 45:1	by whom all things were **made** which live, and move, and
D&C 49:17(16-17)	man, according to his **creation** before the world was
D&C 76:24(23-24)	by him...the worlds are and were **created**, and the
D&C 77:12	as God **made** the world in six days, and on the seventh
D&C 88:7(5-15)	he is in the sun..and the power...by which it was **made**
D&C 88:19(19,20,25)	after it hath filled the measure of its **creation**, it
D&C 93:10(7-10)	the worlds were **made** by him; men were made by him; all
D&C 93:29(29-33)	intelligence, or the light of truth, was not **created**
D&C 95:7	Lord of Sabaoth...the **creator** of the first day, the
D&C 104:14(14-16)	I, the Lord...**built** the earth, my very handiwork; and
D&C 117:6(6,7)	have I not **made** the earth? Do I not hold the destinies
Moses 1:33(33,38)	**worlds** without number have I created; and I also
Moses 2:1(1-31)	by mine Only Begotten I **created**...heaven, and the
Moses 2:27(26-27)	and I, God, **created** man in mine own image, in the
Moses 3:1(1-25)	thus the **heaven** and the earth were finished, and all
Moses 3:5(4-6)	**created** all things...spiritually, before they were
Moses 3:7	I, the Lord God, formed **man** from the dust of the
Moses 3:19	out of the ground I...formed every **beast** of the field
Moses 3:22(21-23)	the rib which I...had taken from man, made I a **woman**
Moses 6:8(7-9)	God **created** man, in the likeness of God made he him
Moses 7:30(30-36)	number of thy **creations**; and thy curtains are stretch
Abr. 4:1(1-31)	they...the Gods, **organized** and formed the heavens and
Abr. 4:26(26,27)	let us go down and form man in our **image**, after our
Abr. 5:1(1-21)	thus we will **finish** the heavens and the earth, and all
Abr. 5:7	the Gods **formed** man from the dust of the ground, and
Abr. 5:17(15-17)	bone of my bones, and flesh of my flesh...**woman**

CRUELTY

Gen. 49:5(5-7)	brethren; instruments of **cruelty** are in their
Gen. 49:7	cursed be...their wrath, for it was **cruel**: I will
Ex. 6:9	hearkened not unto Moses...and for **cruel** bondage.
1 Chr. 20:3	and he...**cut** them with saws, and with harrows of iron
Job 30:21(20-21)	thou art become **cruel** to me: with thy strong hand thou
Ps. 25:19	enemies...are many; and they hate me with **cruel** hatred
Ps. 27:12	false witnesses are risen...as breathe out **cruelty**.
Ps. 71:4(1-5)	deliver me..my God..out of the hand of the..**cruel** man.
Ps. 74:20	dark places of the earth are full of...**cruelty**.
Prov. 11:17	but he that is **cruel** troubleth his own flesh.
Prov. 12:10	but the tender mercies of the wicked are **cruel**.
Prov. 27:4	wrath is **cruel**, and anger is outrageous; but who is
Song. 8:6(6,7)	jealousy is **cruel** as the grave: the coals thereof are
Jer. 30:14(10-17)	wounded thee...with the chastisement of a **cruel** one
Jer. 50:42	they are **cruel**, and will not shew mercy: their voice
Lam. 4:3(1-6,10)	daughter of my people is become **cruel**, like the
Ezek. 18:18	because he **cruelly** oppressed, spoiled his brother by
Ezek. 34:4	but with force and with **cruelty** have ye ruled them.
Hab. 2:12(8-12)	woe to him that buildeth a town with **blood**, and
Zech. 7:10(8-10)	and **oppress** not the widow, nor the fatherless, the
Matt. 27:26(26-35)	**scourged** Jesus, he delivered him to be crucified.
Mark 3:5(1-5)	being grieved for the **hardness** of their hearts, he

73

CRUELTY cont.

Luke 10:30(30-33)	stripped him...and **wounded** him, and departed, leaving
Acts 16:23(19-24)	when they had laid many **stripes** upon them, they cast
Acts 22:24(24,25)	he should be examined by **scourging**; that he might know
2 Tim. 3:12(10-12)	all that will live godly...shall suffer **persecution**.
Heb. 11:36(35-38)	and others had trial of **cruel** mockings and scourgings
Alma 14:11(10,11)	the **blood** of the innocent shall stand as a witness
Alma 48:24	massacred by the barbarous **cruelty** of those who were
Hel. 4:12	it was because of their **oppression** to the poor
Moro. 9:10	they did murder them in a most **cruel** manner, torturing
D&C 49:21	sheddeth blood or that **wasteth** flesh and hath no need.
D&C 121:3	suffer these wrongs and unlawful **oppressions**, before
D&C 123:7(4-8)	damning hand of murder, tyranny, and **oppression**
D&C 124:8	the portion of the **oppressor** among hypocrites, where
Moses 6:15	a man's hand was against his own **brother**, in

CURSE

Gen. 3:14(13-16)	thou art **cursed** above all cattle, and above every
Gen. 3:17(17-19)	**cursed** is the ground for thy sake; in sorrow shalt
Gen. 4:11(9-15)	now art thou **cursed** from the earth, which hath opened
Gen. 5:29(28-32)	toil..because of the ground which the Lord hath **cursed**
Gen. 8:21(20-22)	I will not...**curse** the ground any more for man's sake
Gen. 9:25(18-27)	**cursed** be Canaan; a servant of servants shall he be
Gen. 12:3	I will...**curse** him that curseth thee: and in thee
Gen. 49:7(5-7)	**cursed** be their anger, for it was fierce; and their
Ex. 21:17	he that **curseth** his father, or his mother, shall
Ex. 22:28	thou shalt not...**curse** the ruler of thy people.
Lev. 19:14	thou shalt not **curse** the deaf, nor put a
Lev. 20:9	every one that **curseth** his father or his mother shall
Lev. 24:15	whosoever **curseth** his God shall bear his sin.
Deut. 11:26(26-29)	I set before you this day a blessing and a **curse**
Deut. 23:5(4-6)	God turned the **curse** into a blessing unto thee
Deut. 27:15(15-25)	**cursed** be the man that maketh any graven or molten
Deut. 27:26(14-26)	**cursed** be he that confirmeth not all the words of this
Deut. 28:15(15-68)	that all these **curses** shall come upon thee, and
Deut. 29:20(10-29)	all the **curses** that are written in this book shall lie
Deut. 30:7(1-10)	God will put all these **curses** upon thine enemies, and
Deut. 30:19(1,19)	set before you life and death, blessing and **cursing**
Josh. 8:34(32-35)	he read...blessings and **cursings**, according to all
2 Kgs. 22:19(15-20)	they should become a desolation and a **curse**, and hast
2 Chr. 34:24(23-25)	bring evil...even all the **curses** that are written in
Neh. 10:29(28-31)	entered into a **curse**, and into an oath, to walk in
Job 1:5(1-5)	my sons have sinned, and **cursed** God in their hearts.
Job 1:11(6-12)	and he will **curse** thee to thy face.
Job 2:5(1-6)	touch his bone and his flesh, and he will **curse** thee
Job 2:9	then said his wife unto him...**curse** God, and die.
Job 3:1(1-26)	after this opened Job his mouth, and **cursed** his day.
Job 31:30(29,30)	suffered my mouth to sin by wishing a **curse** to his
Ps. 10:7	his mouth is full of **cursing** and deceit and fraud
Ps. 37:22(16-22)	they that be **cursed** of him shall be cut off.
Ps. 62:4(1-4)	bless with their mouth, but they **curse** inwardly. Selah
Ps. 109:28(26-31)	let them **curse**, but bless thou: when they arise, let

CURSE cont.

Prov. 3:33(33-35)	the **curse** of the Lord is in the house of the wicked
Prov. 27:14	it shall be counted a **curse** to him.
Isa. 24:6(5,6)	therefore hath the **curse** devoured the earth, and they
Isa. 34:5(1-10)	and upon the people of my **curse**, to judgment.
Jer. 11:3	**cursed** be the man that obeyeth not the words of this
Jer. 17:5(5-8)	**cursed** be the man that trusteth in man, and maketh
Jer. 48:10(7-10)	**cursed** be he that doeth the work of the Lord deceitful
Dan. 9:11(3-15)	transgressed...therefore the **curse** is poured upon us
Zech. 8:13(9-15)	as ye were a **curse** among the heathen, O house of Judah
Mal. 1:14(12-14)	but **cursed** be the deceiver, which hath in his flock a
Mal. 2:2	I will even send a **curse** upon you, and I will curse
Mal. 3:9(8-9)	ye are **cursed** with a curse: for ye have robbed me,
Mal. 4:6(5,6)	lest I come and smite the earth with a **curse**.
Matt. 5:44	love your enemies, bless them that **curse** you, do good
Matt. 25:41	depart from me, ye **cursed**, into everlasting fire
Mark 7:10(10-13)	whoso **curseth** father or mother, let him die the death
John 7:49	but this people who knoweth not the law are **cursed**.
Acts 23:12(11,12,14)	under a **curse**, saying that they would neither eat nor
Rom. 12:14	bless them which persecute you: bless, and **curse** not.
Gal. 3:10	**cursed** is every one that continueth not in all things
Gal. 3:13	Christ hath redeemed us from the **curse** of the law
James 3:9(8-10)	therewith bless we God...therewith **curse** we men, which
Rev. 22:3(3,4)	and there shall be no more **curse**: but the throne of
1 Ne. 2:23	I will **curse** them even with a sore curse, and they
1 Ne. 17:35	the Lord did **curse** the land against them, and bless
1 Ne. 17:38(36-38)	wicked he destroyeth, and **curseth** the land unto them
2 Ne. 1:18(17,18)	a **cursing** should come upon you for the space of many
2 Ne. 1:22(21,22)	that ye may not be **cursed** with a sore cursing; and
2 Ne. 4:6(5-7)	that the **cursing** may be taken from you and be
2 Ne. 4:34	**cursed** is he that putteth his trust in the arm of
2 Ne. 5:21(21-24)	he had caused the **cursing** to come upon them, yea, even
2 Ne. 5:24(21-24)	because of their **cursing** which was upon them they did
2 Ne. 28:31	**cursed** is he that putteth his trust in man, or maketh
2 Ne. 29:5	nay; but ye have **cursed** them, and have hated them, and
Jacob 2:29(28,29)	keep my commandments...or **cursed** be the land for their
Jacob 3:3(2-4)	except ye repent the land is **cursed** for your sakes
Alma 3:19(18-19)	every man..**cursed** bring upon himself his own
Alma 17:15(14-16)	**curse** of God had fallen upon them because of the
Alma 23:18(17,18)	and the **curse** of God did no more follow them.
Alma 30:53(52-57)	I have brought this great **curse** upon me.
Alma 32:19(17-19)	more **cursed** is he that knoweth the will of God and
Alma 45:16(15,16)	this is the **cursing** and the blessing of God upon the
Hel. 13:21(21,23)	ye are **cursed** because of your riches, and also are
D&C 41:1	ye that hear me not will I **curse**, that have professed
D&C 61:14(14-17)	in the last days...I **cursed** the waters.
D&C 61:17	I, the Lord, in the beginning **cursed** the land, even
D&C 121:16	**cursed** are all those that shall lift up the heel again
D&C 124:93	and whoever he **curses** shall be cursed; that whatsoever
D&C 128:18	be smitten with a **curse** unless there is a welding link
Moses 5:25(21-26)	a **cursing** which I will put upon thee, except thou
Moses 5:36(35,36)	be **cursed** from the earth which hath opened her mouth
Moses 5:40(40,41)	and I the Lord set a **mark** upon Cain, lest any finding
Moses 5:52(51,52)	**cursed** Lamech, and his house, and all them that had

CURSE cont.

Moses 8:4	a great famine...the Lord **cursed** the earth with a sore
Moses 8:9(8,9)	toil..because of the ground which the Lord hath **cursed**
Abr. 1:24(21-27)	sprang that race which preserved the **curse** in the land
Abr. 1:26(21-27)	but **cursed** him as pertaining to the Priesthood.
Abr. 2:11(9-11)	bless them that bless thee..**curse** them that curse thee

DAMNATION

2 Sam. 22:6(5-7)	the sorrows of **hell** compassed me about; the snares of
Ps. 16:10(9-11)	for thou wilt not leave my soul in **hell**; neither wilt
Ps. 116:3(3,4)	the pains of **hell** gat hold upon me: I found trouble
Prov. 5:5(3-6)	her feet go down to death; her steps take hold on **hell**
Prov. 7:27(24-27)	her house is the way to **hell**, going down to the
Isa. 14:15(12-17)	yet thou shalt be brought down to **hell**, to the sides
Dan. 12:2(1-3)	shall awake...some to **shame** and everlasting contempt.
Matt. 5:29(29,30)	not that thy whole body should be cast into **hell**.
Matt. 23:14	therefore ye shall receive the greater **damnation**.
Matt. 23:33	vipers, how can ye escape the **damnation** of hell
Matt. 25:46(45,46)	these shall go away into everlasting **punishment**: but
Mark 3:29(28,29)	blaspheme...in danger of eternal **damnation**
Mark 12:40(38-40)	long prayers: these shall receive greater **damnation**.
Mark 16:16(15-16)	he that believeth not shall be **damned**.
John 5:29(28,29)	done evil, unto the resurrection of **damnation**.
John 17:12(12,13)	none of them is lost, but the son of **perdition**; that
Rom. 3:8(8-10)	do evil, that good may come? whose **damnation** is just.
Rom. 13:2(1,2)	that resist shall receive to themselves **damnation**.
1 Cor. 11:29(24-30)	unworthily, eateth and drinketh **damnation** to himself
2 Thes. 1:9(7-9)	punished with everlasting **destruction** from the
2 Thes. 2:12(11,12)	all might be **damned** who believed not the truth, but
1 Tim. 5:12(11,12)	**damnation**, because they...cast off their first faith.
2 Pet. 2:3	their **damnation** slumbereth not.
Rev. 20:14(12-14)	death and **hell** were cast into the lake of fire. this
1 Ne. 14:3(3,4)	lead away the souls of men down to **hell**- yea, that
2 Ne. 1:13(13,14)	awake...even from the sleep of **hell**, and shake off
2 Ne. 9:24(20-24)	if they will not repent...they must be **damned**; for the
2 Ne. 28:21(21-23)	and leadeth them away carefully down to **hell**.
Jacob 6:10(8-10)	lake of fire and brimstone is endless **torment**.
Mosiah 2:33(32,33)	his sins, the same drinketh **damnation** to his own soul
Mosiah 2:39(36-39)	his final doom is to endure a never-ending **torment**.
Mosiah 3:18(18,24,25)	drink **damnation** to their own souls except they humble
Mosiah 16:11(10-12)	resurrection of endless **damnation**, being delivered up
Alma 9:28(27,28)	the **damnation** of their souls, according to the power
Alma 12:17(12-18)	chained down to an everlasting **destruction**, according
Alma 12:32	everlasting **death** as to things pertaining unto
Alma 12:36	the everlasting **destruction** of your souls; therefore
Alma 13:30	by the chains of **hell**...the second death.
Alma 14:14	they shall be cast into a lake of **fire** and brimstone
Alma 14:21(16-29)	saying: how shall we look when we are **damned**
Alma 36:16(6-23)	I racked, even with the pains of a **damned** soul.
Alma 40:13(11-14)	these shall be cast out into outer **darkness**; there
Hel. 6:28(25-31)	dragged the people down to an entire **destruction**, and
Hel. 12:26(23-26)	have done evil shall have everlasting **damnation**. and

76

DAMNATION cont.

3 Ne. 18:29(28-32)	unworthily eateth and drinketh **damnation** to his soul
3 Ne. 26:5(3-5)	if they be evil, to the resurrection of **damnation**
3 Ne. 27:32(30-32)	they are led away **captive** by him even as was the son
Morm. 2:13(12-14)	not unto repentance...sorrowing of the **damned**, because
Morm. 8:33(32,33)	transfigured..word...bring **damnation** upon your souls
Morm. 9:4(3-5)	more miserable..with..God...than...**damned** souls in
Morm. 9:23	he that believeth not shall be **damned**
Ether 4:18	he that believeth not shall be **damned**; and signs shall
D&C 29:44(43-45)	eternal **damnation**; for they cannot be redeemed from
D&C 42:60(59,60)	doeth them not shall be **damned** if he so continue.
D&C 49:5(5,6)	and he that receiveth him not shall be **damned**
D&C 58:29(26-29)	doeth not anything until he is commanded...is **damned**.
D&C 68:9(8-10)	he that believeth not shall be **damned**.
D&C 76:44(31-49)	they shall go away into...eternal **punishment**, to reign
D&C 76:104(103-106)	these are they who suffer the **wrath** of God on earth.
D&C 76:106(103-106)	these are they who are cast down to **hell** and suffer
D&C 88:100(95-102)	to be judged, and are found under **condemnation**
D&C 112:29(28-29)	believeth not, and is not baptized, shall be **damned**.
D&C 132:4(3-6)	abide not that covenant, then are ye **damned**; for no
D&C 132:27	blasphemy against the Holy Ghost...shall be **damned**
Moses 5:15(14,15)	believed not and repented not, should be **damned**; and
Moses 7:39(38-40)	and until that day they shall be in **torment**

DARKNESS, PHYSICAL

Gen. 1:2	and **darkness** was upon the face of the deep. And the
Gen. 1:5	and the **darkness** he called night. And the evening and
Ex. 10:21(21-23)	that there may be **darkness** over the land of Egypt, Eve
Josh. 24:7	he put **darkness** between you and the Egyptians, and
Matt. 27:45(44-45)	from the sixth hour there was **darkness** over all the
Mark 15:33(32-34)	sixth hour was come, there was **darkness** over the whole
Luke 23:44	there was a **darkness** over all the earth until the
Acts 2:20	the sun shall be turned into **darkness**, and the moon
1 Ne. 19:11	Lord God surely shall visit...with...vapor of **darkness**
Hel. 14:3	the night before he cometh there shall be no **darkness**
3 Ne. 1:15	going down of the sun there was no **darkness**; and the
3 Ne. 8:3(3,20-22)	there should be **darkness** for the space of three days
3 Ne. 10:9	and the **darkness** dispersed from off the face of the
D&C 29:14	the sun shall be **darkened**, and the moon shall be turn
Moses 2:2(2-4)	I caused **darkness** to come up upon the face of the deep
Moses 2:18(16-18)	to divide the light from the **darkness**; and I, God, saw
Moses 7:61	the heavens shall be **darkened**, and a veil of darkness
Abr. 4:2(2-4)	and **darkness** reigned upon the face of the deep, and
Abr. 4:17(15-17)	cause to divide the light from the **darkness**.
JS-H 1:15(15-17)	thick **darkness** gathered around me, and it seemed to

DARKNESS, SPIRITUAL

Ps. 107:10(8-10)	such as sit in **darkness** and in the shadow of death
Prov. 4:19	the way of the wicked is as **darkness**: they know not
Eccl. 2:13	wisdom excelleth folly...as light excelleth **darkness**.

Isa. 5:20	woe unto them that...put **darkness** for light, and light
Isa. 5:30	the light is **darkened** in the heavens thereof.
Isa. 8:22(21,22)	look unto the earth; and behold trouble and **darkness**
Isa. 9:2(1,2)	the people that walked in **darkness**...in...the...shadow
Isa. 29:18	eyes of the blind shall see out of **obscurity**, and out
Isa. 50:10	who...feareth the Lord...that walketh in **darkness**, and
Isa. 60:2	**darkness** shall cover..earth..gross **darkness** the people
Jer. 13:16	the shadow of death, and make it gross **darkness**.
Micah 7:8	I sit in **darkness**, the Lord shall be a light unto me.
Matt. 6:23(22-23)	in thee be darkness, how great is that **darkness**
Luke 1:79(78-79)	to give light to them that sit in **darkness** and in the
Luke 11:34(34-36)	thy body also is full of **darkness**.
Luke 22:53(52-53)	this is your hour, and the power of **darkness**.
John 1:5	light shineth in **darkness**; and the darkness comprehend
John 3:19(19-21)	light is come..and men loved **darkness** rather than
John 8:12	he that followeth me shall not walk in **darkness**, but
John 9:4	the **night** cometh, when no man can work.
John 12:35(35,46)	he that walketh in **darkness** knoweth not whither he
Rom. 1:21(21-23)	their foolish heart was **darkened**.
Rom. 13:12(12-14)	cast off the works of **darkness**, and let us put on the
Eph. 5:11(8-11)	have no fellowship with...works of **darkness**, but
Eph. 6:12(11-18)	against the rulers of the **darkness** of this world
1 Jn. 1:5	God is light, and in him is no **darkness** at all.
1 Jn. 2:8(8-11)	**darkness** is past, and the true light now shineth.
Rev. 16:10	his kingdom was full of **darkness**; and they gnawed
1 Ne. 22:12(11-12)	brought out of obscurity and out of **darkness**; and the
2 Ne. 10:15(14-15)	I must needs destroy the secret works of **darkness**, and
2 Ne. 30:6(4-6)	their scales of **darkness** shall begin to fall from
Alma 34:33	then cometh the night of **darkness**...no labor performed
D&C 1:30	to bring it forth out of...**darkness**, the only true and
D&C 6:21	I am the light which shineth in **darkness**, and the dark
D&C 10:21(20-22)	they love **darkness** rather than light, because their
D&C 14:9	Jesus Christ...a light which cannot be hid in **darkness**
D&C 24:1	delivered from the powers of Satan and from **darkness**
D&C 50:23(23-25)	that which doth not edify is not of God...is **darkness**.
D&C 57:10(9-10)	gospel may be preached unto those who sit in **darkness**
D&C 82:5(1-7)	adversary spreadeth his dominions...**darkness** reigneth
D&C 84:49	world...groaneth under **darkness** and...bondage of sin.
D&C 95:6(5-6,12)	they are walking in **darkness** at noon-day.
D&C 112:23(23-24)	**darkness** covereth the earth, and...minds of the people
D&C 133:72(72-73)	and ye were delivered over unto **darkness**.
Moses 5:55	thus the works of **darkness** began to prevail among all
Moses 7:57	reserved in chains of **darkness** until the judgment of
JFS-V 1:22(20-22)	where these were, **darkness** reigned, but among the

DAY OF THE LORD

Isa. 2:12(10-21)	for the **day** of the Lord of hosts shall be upon every
Isa. 13:6(6-13)	howl ye; for the **day** of the Lord is at hand; it shall
Isa. 24:6(1-6)	the inhabitants of the earth are **burned**, and few men
Isa. 24:21(19-23)	in that **day**...the Lord shall punish the host of the
Joel 1:15	for the **day** of the Lord is at hand, and as a

DAY OF THE LORD cont.

Joel 2:1(1-3)	for the **day** of the Lord cometh, for it is nigh at hand
Joel 2:31(30-32)	before the great and the terrible **day** of the Lord come
Zeph. 1:7(7-17)	the **day** of the Lord is at hand: for the Lord hath
Mal. 3:2(2-3)	but who may abide the **day** of his coming? and who shall
Mal. 4:1(1-6)	the **day** cometh, that shall burn as an oven; and all
Matt. 24:29(29-31)	the tribulation of those **days** shall the sun be
Mark 13:32(32-37)	of that **day** and that hour knoweth no man, no, not the
Acts 2:20	that great and notable **day** of the Lord come
1 Thes. 5:2(1-3)	the **day** of the Lord so cometh as a thief in the night.
2 Thes. 1:7(7-10)	when the **Lord** Jesus shall be revealed from heaven with
2 Pet. 3:10	but the **day** of the Lord will come as a thief in the
Rev. 6:17(12-17)	the great **day** of his wrath is come; and who shall be
2 Ne. 12:12(12-16)	the **day** of the Lord of hosts soon cometh upon all
2 Ne. 13:18(17-20)	in that **day** the Lord will take away the bravery of the
2 Ne. 15:30	in that **day** they shall roar against them like the roar
2 Ne. 23:6(6-9)	the **day** of the Lord is at hand; it shall come as a
3 Ne. 25:5	Elijah...before...great and dreadful **day** of the Lord
3 Ne. 26:3	from the beginning until the **time** that he should come
D&C 1:10(9,10,35)	unto the **day** when the Lord shall come to recompense
D&C 29:9(8-14)	for the hour is nigh and the **day** soon at hand when the
D&C 34:8(7-9)	and it shall be a great **day** at the time of my coming
D&C 43:21(17-26)	what will ye say when the **day** cometh when the thunders
D&C 45:39(26,39-44)	looking forth for the great **day** of the Lord to come
D&C 49:7	the hour and the **day** no man knoweth, neither the angel
D&C 50:45	and the **day** cometh that you shall hear my voice and
D&C 112:24(24,25)	behold, **vengeance** cometh speedily upon the inhabitants
D&C 128:24	behold, the great **day** of the Lord is at hand; and who
D&C 133:51(41-56)	this was the **day** of vengeance which was in my heart.
JS-H 1:37	for behold, the **day** cometh that shall burn as an oven
JFS-V 1:46	before the...great and dreadful **day** of the Lord- were

DEACONS

Philip. 1:1	the saints...at Philippi...the bishops and **deacons**
1 Tim. 3:8(8-13)	**deacons** be grave, not doubletongued...not greedy of
D&C 20:57(38-64)	is to be assisted always...by the **deacons**, if occasion
D&C 84:111(30,111)	**deacons**...should be appointed to watch over the church
D&C 107:62(62,63)	in like manner, and also the **deacons**
D&C 107:85	duty of a president over the office of a **deacon** is to
D&C 124:142(142-143	also the president of the **deacons** and his counselors

DEATH

Gen. 2:17	the day that thou eatest thereof thou shalt surely **die**
Gen. 23:4	give me a...buryingplace...that I may bury my **dead** out
Gen. 35:18	as her soul was in departing, (for she **died**) that she
Ex. 12:30	there was not a house where there was not one **dead**.
Num. 16:48	he stood between the **dead** and the living; and the
Num. 23:10	let me die the **death** of the righteous, and let my last
Josh. 23:14	this day I am going the **way** of all the earth: and ye
Job 10:21	the land of darkness and the shadow of **death**

DEATH cont.

Job 16:22	then I shall go the **way** whence I shall not return.
Job 34:15(14-15)	flesh shall perish...man shall turn again unto **dust**.
Ps. 23:4	walk through the valley of the shadow of **death**, I will
Ps. 116:15	precious in..sight of..Lord is..**death** of his saints.
Prov. 8:36	all they that hate me love **death**.
Eccl. 12:7	dust return to the earth...**spirit**...unto God who gave
Matt. 8:22	follow me; and let the **dead** bury their dead.
Matt. 17:9	until the son of man be risen again from the **dead**.
Luke 23:46	and having said thus, he gave up the **ghost**.
John 5:25	when the **dead** shall hear the voice of the son of God
John 11:25	he that believeth in me, though he were **dead**, yet
John 12:24	but if it **die**, it bringeth forth much fruit.
Rom. 5:12	so **death** passed upon all men, for that all have sinned
Rom. 6:23	the wages of sin is **death**; but the gift of God is
Rom. 8:6	for to be carnally minded is **death**; but to be
1 Cor. 15:21(21-22)	for since by man came **death**, by man came also the
1 Cor. 15:52(29,52-55)	the **dead** shall be raised incorruptible, and we shall
James 2:26	for as the body without the spirit is **dead**, so faith
1 Pet. 3:18(18-20)	being put to **death** in the flesh, but quickened by the
Rev. 14:13	blessed are the **dead** which die in the Lord from hence
Rev. 20:12	and I saw the **dead**, small and great, stand before God
2 Ne. 1:14	the cold and silent **grave**...the way of all the earth.
2 Ne. 9:11(6,11)	this death...the temporal...which **death** is the grave.
2 Ne. 9:39	to be carnally-minded is **death**, and to be
Mosiah 15:8(7,8)	God breaketh the bands of **death**, having gained the
Mosiah 16:7(7-8)	that **death** should have no sting, there could have been
Alma 1:18	for he that murdered was punished unto **death**.
Alma 11:42(42,45)	Christ shall loose the bands of this temporal **death**
Alma 12:24(16,24)	**death** comes upon mankind, yea...the temporal death
Alma 42:6(6-9)	it was appointed unto man to **die**- therefore, as they
Morm. 9:13(13,14)	eternal band of **death**, which death is a temporal death
D&C 18:11(11-12)	the Lord your redeemer suffered **death** in the flesh
D&C 29:42(42,43)	should not **die** as to the temporal death, until I, the
D&C 42:46	die in me...not taste of **death** ...sweet unto them
D&C 58:2	keepeth my commandments, whether in life or in **death**
D&C 63:50(49-52)	appointed to him to **die** at the age of man.
D&C 64:7	forgive...those...who have not sinned unto **death**.
D&C 88:116	they shall not any more see **death**.
D&C 135:1(1,5)	Hyrum...fell calmly, exclaiming: I am a **dead** man!
Moses 6:48	by his fall came **death**; and we are made partakers of

DEATH, POWER OVER

1 Kgs. 17:22(17-24)	soul of the child came into him again, and he **revived**.
2 Kgs. 4:35(8-37)	stretched himself upon him...the child **opened** his eyes
Mark 5:41(35-42)	took...by the hand ...damsel, I say unto thee, **arise**.
Luke 7:15(11-16)	and he that was **dead** sat up, and began to speak. and
John 10:18(17-18)	I have **power** to lay it down, and I have power to take
John 11:44(1-44)	he that was **dead** came forth, bound hand and foot with
Acts 9:40(36-41)	Tabitha, **arise**. and she opened her eyes: and when she
Acts 20:12(9-12)	they brought the young man **alive**, and were not a
1 Cor. 15:26(26,54)	the last enemy that shall be **destroyed** is death.

DEATH, POWER OVER cont.

2 Ne. 9:10(6-12)	God, who prepareth a way for our **escape** from...death
2 Ne. 9:26	that they are **delivered** from that awful monster, death
2 Ne. 10:25	may God **raise** you from death by the power of the
Mosiah 3:5	go forth amongst men...**raising** the dead, causing the
Mosiah 15:23	through Christ, who has **broken** the bands of death.
Alma 11:45(42-45)	**raised** to an immortal body, that is from death, even
3 Ne. 7:19	his brother did he **raise** from the dead, after he had
3 Ne. 19:4	his brother whom he had raised from the **dead**, whose
3 Ne. 26:15	and raised a man from the **dead**, and had shown forth
4 Ne. 1:5	they did heal the sick, and **raise** the dead, and cause
D&C 7:2	give unto me **power** over death, that I may live and
D&C 42:48(46-48)	he that...is not appointed unto death, shall be **healed**
D&C 45:2	hearken unto my voice, lest **death** shall overtake you
D&C 101:36(29,36)	fear not even unto **death**...in me your joy is full.
D&C 121:44	faithfulness is stronger than the cords of **death**.
D&C 124:100	he should **raise** the dead, let him not withhold his

DEATH, SPIRITUAL, FIRST

Gen. 2:17(16,17)	in the day...eatest thereof thou shalt surely **die**.
Gen. 3:4	serpent said unto the woman, ye shall not surely **die**
Lev. 22:3	that soul shall be **cut** off from my presence: I am the
Ps. 37:9	for evildoers shall be **cut** off: but those that wait
Ps. 51:11(11,12)	cast me not away from thy **presence**; and take not thy
Prov. 8:36(35,36)	all they that hate me love **death**.
Isa. 14:15(13-15)	yet thou shalt be brought down to **hell**, to the sides
John 8:51	man keep my saying, he shall never see **death**.
Rom. 6:23(16,21,23)	for the wages of sin is **death**; but the gift of God is
Rom. 8:6(4-9)	for to be carnally minded is **death**; but to be
2 Pet. 2:4	**angels** that sinned, but cast them down to hell, and
1 Jn. 3:14	he that loveth not his brother abideth in **death**.
Jude 1:6	and the **angels** which kept not their first estate, but
Rev. 12:8(7-9)	neither was their place found any more in **heaven**.
1 Ne. 10:6	all mankind were in a lost and in a **fallen** state, and
2 Ne. 9:12(10-16)	the spiritual **death**, shall deliver up its dead; which
2 Ne. 9:39	to be carnally-minded is **death**, and to be
Alma 12:16	he shall **die** as to things pertaining unto
Alma 15:17	delivered from Satan, and from **death**, and from
Alma 36:18(18-20)	encircled about by the everlasting chains of **death**.
Alma 41:11	men...in a state of **nature**...without God in the world
Alma 42:9(7-11)	fall had brought upon all mankind a spiritual **death**
Hel. 14:16(15,16)	all mankind, by the fall...are considered as **dead**
D&C 29:41(40,41)	he became spiritually **dead**, which is the first death
D&C 67:12(10-13)	neither can any **natural** man abide the presence of God
Moses 5:9	as thou hast **fallen** thou mayest be redeemed, and all
Moses 6:55	when...begin to grow up, **sin** conceiveth in their heart

DEATH, SPIRITUAL, SECOND

Dan. 12:2(2-3) and some to shame and **everlasting** contempt.
Matt. 12:32(31,32) speaketh against the Holy Ghost...not be **forgiven** him
Luke 12:5(4-5) fear him, which...hath power to cast into **hell**; yea
John 8:51(51-53) if a man keep my saying, he shall never see **death**.
John 17:12 none of them is lost, but the son of **perdition**; that
1 Tim. 6:9(8-11) lusts, which drown men in destruction and **perdition**
Heb. 10:39(38-39) we are not of them who draw back unto **perdition**; but
2 Pet. 3:7 reserved...against the day of judgment and **perdition**
Rev. 2:11 he that overcometh shall not be hurt of...second **death**
Rev. 17:8(5-8,11) beast...shall ascend out of the...pit...into **perdition**
Rev. 20:6 on such the **second** death hath no power, but they shall
Rev. 20:14(12-14) lake of fire. this is the **second** death.
Rev. 21:8(4,8) lake...burneth with fire and brimstone...second **death**.
Jacob 3:11 fire and brimstone which is the second **death**.
Alma 12:16(16-18) a second **death**, which is a spiritual death; then is
Alma 12:32 a second **death**, which was an everlasting death as to
Alma 13:30 repentance...that ye may not suffer the second **death**.
Alma 40:13 spirits of the wicked...cast out into outer **darkness**
Hel. 14:18(16-18) **spiritual** death, yea, a second death, for they are cut
D&C 29:41 same death which is the last **death**, which is spiritual
D&C 29:44(42-45) cannot be redeemed from their spiritual **fall**, because
D&C 63:17(17,18) fire and brimstone, which is the second **death**.
D&C 76:37(30-38) only ones on whom the second **death** shall have any
D&C 132:25(13,25) wide the way that leadeth to the **deaths**; and many
D&C 132:27 not be **forgiven** in the world nor out of the world

DEBT

Ex. 22:25(25-27) if thou **lend** money to any of my people that is poor
Lev. 25:37(35-38) thou shalt not give him thy money upon **usury**, nor lend
Deut. 23:20(19,20) unto thy brother thou shalt not **lend** upon usury: that
2 Kgs. 4:1(1-7) the **creditor** is come to take...my two sons to be
Neh. 5:4(1-13) we have **borrowed** money ...upon our lands and vineyards
Ps. 37:21 the wicked **borroweth**, and payeth not again: but the
Prov. 22:7 the **borrower** is servant to the lender.
Matt. 5:42 from him that would **borrow** of thee turn not thou away.
Matt. 6:12 and forgive us our **debts**, as we forgive our debtors.
Matt. 18:32(23-35) I forgave thee all that **debt**, because thou desiredst
Luke 11:4 for we also forgive every one that is **indebted** to us.
Rom. 13:8(7-8) **owe** no man any thing, but to love one another: for he
Mosiah 2:23(23-24) your lives, for which ye are **indebted** unto him.
Mosiah 2:34 ye are eternally **indebted** to your heavenly Father
Mosiah 4:28 whosoever...**borroweth** of his neighbor should return
3 Ne. 12:42 from him that would **borrow** of thee turn thou not away.
3 Ne. 13:11 and forgive us our **debts**, as we forgive our debtors.
D&C 19:35 pay the **debt**...release thyself from bondage.
D&C 64:27 forbidden, to get in **debt** to thine enemies
D&C 104:78(78-86) it is my will that you shall pay all your **debts**.
D&C 136:25 if thou **borrowest** of thy neighbor, thou shalt restore

DECEIT

Lev. 6:4(1-5)	he shall restore that...which he hath **deceitfully**
Deut. 11:16(16-17)	heed...yourselves, that your heart be not **deceived**
Job 27:4(2-8)	speak wickedness, nor my tongue utter **deceit**.
Job 31:5(5-8)	vanity, or if my foot hath hasted to **deceit**
Ps. 24:4(3-5)	not lifted up..soul unto vanity, nor sworn **deceitfully**
Ps. 36:3(1-4)	the words of his mouth are iniquity and **deceit**: he
Ps. 38:12(12-15)	mischievous things, and imagine **deceits** all the day
Ps. 43:1(1-5)	O deliver me from the **deceitful** and unjust man.
Ps. 50:19(16-21)	mouth to evil, and thy tongue frameth **deceit**.
Ps. 101:7(6-8)	he that worketh **deceit** shall not dwell within my house
Ps. 120:2(1-7)	from lying lips, and from a **deceitful** tongue.
Prov. 11:18	the wicked worketh a **deceitful** work: but to him that
Prov. 12:5(5,17,20)	the counsels of the wicked are **deceit**.
Prov. 14:8	the folly of fools is **deceit**.
Prov. 20:17	**deceit** is sweet to a man; but afterwards his mouth
Prov. 26:24(22-28)	hateth..with his lips, and layeth up **deceit** within him
Prov. 27:6	but the kisses of an enemy are **deceitful**.
Isa. 53:9(7-12)	no violence, neither was any **deceit** in his mouth.
Jer. 14:14(13-15)	thing of nought, and the **deceit** of their heart.
Matt. 13:22(18-23)	care of this world, and the **deceitfulness** of riches
Matt. 24:24	they shall **deceive** the very elect.
Mark 7:22(20-23)	thefts, covetousness, wickedness, **deceit**
Rom. 1:29(18,29-32)	full of envy, murder, debate, **deceit**, malignity
Gal. 6:7	be not **deceived**; God is not mocked: for whatsoever a
Eph. 5:6	let no man **deceive** you with vain words: for because
Col. 2:8	beware lest any man spoil you through...vain **deceit**
2 Jn. 1:7	for many **deceivers** are entered into the world, who
1 Ne. 16:38	tells us these...that he may **deceive** our eyes
2 Ne. 9:41	he cannot be **deceived**, for the Lord God is his name.
2 Ne. 25:18	a false Messiah which should **deceive** the people; for
2 Ne. 31:13	follow the son...acting no hypocrisy and no **deception**
Jacob 7:18(18-19)	deceived by the power of the **devil**. and he spake of
Mosiah 10:18	lying craftiness...**deceived** me, that I have brought
Mosiah 11:7	they were **deceived** by the vain and flattering words
Mosiah 14:9(7-12)	he had done no evil, neither was any **deceit** in his
Mosiah 26:6	they did **deceive** many with their flattering words, who
Alma 16:18(18-20)	preach against all lyings, and **deceivings**, and envying
Alma 30:53(53,59-60)	devil..**deceived** me..appeared..in the form of an angel
Alma 48:7(1-7)	Amalickiah...obtaining power by fraud and **deceit**
3 Ne. 2:2(1-3)	to lead away and **deceive** the hearts of the people; and
3 Ne. 16:10(10-13)	filled with all manner of lyings, and of **deceits**, and
3 Ne. 21:19(14-22)	all lyings, and **deceivings**, and envyings, and strifes
3 Ne. 30:2(1,2)	repent of your evil doings...**deceivings**, and of your
D&C 10:28(25,28)	wo be unto him that lieth to **deceive** because he
D&C 43:6(1-7)	this I give unto you that you may not be **deceived**
D&C 45:57(56-58)	they that...taken the Holy Spirit...not been **deceived**
D&C 46:8(7-9)	that ye may not be **deceived** seek ye earnestly the best
D&C 50:6(2-9)	but wo unto them that are **deceivers** and hypocrites
D&C 129:7	contrary to...heaven for a just man to **deceive**; but
Moses 4:4(3-4)	and he became Satan...to deceive and to blind men, and

DEDICATION

Ex. 32:29	consecrate yourselves to day to the Lord, even every
1 Kgs. 8:63(1-65)	children of Israel dedicated the house of the Lord.
2 Chr. 7:5(1-9)	all the people dedicated the house of God.
2 Chr. 7:16(12-22)	have I chosen and sanctified this house, that my name
Ezra 6:16(14-19)	kept the dedication of this house of God with joy
Ps. 37:5	commit thy way unto the Lord; trust also in him; and
Ps. 119:4(1-7)	thou hast commanded us to keep thy precepts diligently
Prov. 10:4	the hand of the diligent maketh rich.
Matt. 5:33	perform unto the Lord thine oaths
Matt. 6:22(20-25)	if...thine eye be single, thy whole body shall be full
Matt. 6:33(24-33)	but seek ye first the kingdom of God, and his
Matt. 22:37(37-38)	love the Lord thy God with all thy heart...soul...mind
2 Tim. 4:7	I have finished my course, I have kept the faith
2 Pet. 3:14	be diligent that ye may be found of him in peace, with
1 Ne. 3:15(1-15)	we will not go...until we have accomplished the thing
2 Ne. 31:20	press forward with a steadfastness in Christ...endure
Jacob 1:19	our own heads if we did not teach...with all diligence
Mosiah 2:21	if ye should serve him with all your whole souls yet
Mosiah 5:5(5-9)	obedient to his commandments in all things that he
Hel. 10:4	thou hast with unwearyingness declared the word, which
Hel. 10:5	because thou hast done this with such unwearyingness
Hel. 15:6(5-8)	they are striving with unwearied diligence that they
3 Ne. 6:14	immovable, willing with all diligence to keep the Com
3 Ne. 13:22	if...thine eye be single, thy whole body shall be full
Ether 12:3(2-4)	did cry from the morning, even until the going down
Moro. 9:6(1-6)	notwithstanding...hardness, let us labor diligently
Moro. 10:32	love God with all your might, mind and strength, then
D&C 4:2(1-7)	serve him with all your heart, might, mind and
D&C 11:3	let him thrust in his sickle with his might, and reap
D&C 11:20	keep my commandments...with all your might, mind and
D&C 58:27	men should be anxiously engaged in a good cause, and
D&C 58:57	consecrate and dedicate this land, and the spot for
D&C 64:33	be not weary in well-doing, for ye are laying the
D&C 82:24	kingdom...if you fall not from your steadfastness.
D&C 84:61	remain steadfast in your minds in solemnity and the
D&C 88:67(67-68)	if your eye be single to my glory, your whole bodies
D&C 90:24	search diligently, pray always, and be believing, and
D&C 94:7(1-9)	it shall be wholly dedicated unto the Lord for the
D&C 103:36	victory...is brought to pass...through your diligence
D&C 107:99(99-100)	act in the office... he is appointed, in all diligence
D&C 109:78(1-80)	accept the dedication of this house unto thee, the
D&C 110:7	I have accepted this house, and my name shall be here
D&C 110:8	keep my commandments...do not pollute this holy house.
D&C 123:13(12-13)	we should waste and wear out our lives in bringing to
D&C 127:4	diligence...perseverance...and your works be redoubled

DELEGATION OF RESPONSIBILITY

Ex. 18:25(21-25)	Moses chose able men...made them heads over the people
Num. 11:16(16-17)	to be the elders of the people, and officers over them
Num. 27:20(15-23)	thou shalt put some of thine honour upon him, that all
Deut. 1:13(13-15)	take you wise men...and I will make them rulers over

DELEGATION OF RESPONSIBILITY cont.

2 Sam. 23:2(1-3)	the Lord **spake** by me, and his word was in my tongue.
1 Kgs. 4:7	Solomon had twelve **officers** over all Israel, which
Jer. 1:10(7-10)	see, I have this day **set** thee over the nations and
Ezek. 3:17(1-4,17,27)	I have made thee a **watchman** unto the house of Israel
Matt. 10:1(1-7)	when he had **called** unto him his twelve disciples, he
Matt. 16:19(13-20)	and I will **give** unto thee the keys of the kingdom of
John 5:27(19-30)	and hath given him **authority** to execute judgment also
John 8:28(26-28)	as my Father hath **taught** me, I speak these things.
Acts 9:17(17-18)	Jesus...hath **sent** me, that thou mightest receive thy
1 Cor. 4:2(1,2)	moreover it is required in **stewards**, that a man be
Titus 1:7	bishop must be blameless, as the **steward** of God; not
Jacob 1:18(18-19)	had been **consecrated** priests and teachers of this
1:3	I had kept these plates...**conferred** them upon my son
Mosiah 26:8	Mosiah had given Alma the **authority** over the church.
Mosiah 28:20	Mosiah...**conferred** them upon Alma, who was the son of
Mosiah 29:11	let us **appoint** judges, to judge this people according
Mosiah 29:42	Alma..chief judge...father having **conferred** the office
Alma 2:13	and there were **appointed** captains, and higher captains
Alma 63:11	became expedient for Shiblon to **confer** those sacred
3 Ne. 11:25	having **authority** given me of Jesus Christ, I baptize
3 Ne. 12:1	these twelve whom I have **chosen** from among you to
3 Ne. 13:25	they whom I have chosen to **minister** unto this people.
Moro. 8:16	I speak with boldness, having **authority** from God; and
D&C 13:1	upon you my fellow servants...I **confer** the Priesthood
D&C 38:23(23-24)	teach...according to the office...I have **appointed** you
D&C 38:34(34-36)	men...shall be **appointed** by the voice of the church
D&C 42:10	stand in the office whereunto I have **appointed** him.
D&C 84:79(79,87)	I **send** you out to prove the world, and the laborer is
D&C 97:14	keys of which kingdom have been **conferred** upon you.
D&C 107:60(58-63)	there must needs be **presiding** elders to preside over
D&C 124:123	give unto you the **officers** belonging to my priesthood
D&C 134:3	all governments...require civil **officers** and
Abr. 2:6	and to make of thee a **minister** to bear my name in a

DELIVERANCE

Gen. 32:11(9-11)	**deliver** me, I pray thee, from the hand of my brother
Ex. 3:8(7-8)	I am come down to **deliver** them out of the hand of the
Ex. 12:27(26,27)	he smote the Egyptians, and **delivered** our houses. and
Judg. 2:16(11-19)	which **delivered** them out of the hand of those that
Judg. 3:9(7-11)	Lord raised up a **deliverer** to the children of Israel
Judg. 10:13(13-14)	wherefore I will **deliver** you no more.
Judg. 13:5(1-5)	he shall begin to **deliver** Israel out of the hand of
1 Sam. 17:37(34-37)	the Lord that **delivered** me out of the paw of the lion
Job 36:15	he **delivereth** the poor in his affliction, and openeth
Ps. 39:8(7,8)	**deliver** me from all my transgressions: make me not the
Ps. 51:14(10-14)	**deliver** me from bloodguiltiness, O God, thou God of
Ps. 54:7(1-7)	for he hath **delivered** me out of all trouble: and mine
Ps. 116:8(5-13)	for thou hast **delivered** my soul from death, mine eyes
Ps. 140:1(1-8)	**deliver** me, O Lord, from the evil man: preserve me
Eccl. 8:8	neither shall wickedness **deliver** those that are given
Isa. 46:4(3,4)	even I will carry, and will **deliver** you.

DELIVERANCE cont.

Dan. 3:17(8-30)	our God...is able to **deliver** us from the burning fiery
Dan. 6:27(14-27)	who hath **delivered** Daniel from the power of the lions.
Amos 2:14(13-15)	neither shall the mighty **deliver** himself
Obad. 1:17(15-17)	but upon mount Zion shall be **deliverance**, and there
Matt. 6:13(9-13)	lead us not into temptation, but **deliver** us from evil
Matt. 27:43(41-43)	let him **deliver** him now, if he will have him: for he
Luke 4:18(18-22)	to preach **deliverance** to the captives, and recovering
Acts 7:25(23-25)	God by his hand would **deliver** them: but they
Acts 7:35(35-37)	Moses...did God send to be a ruler and a **deliverer** by
Rom. 8:21(18-25)	the creature...shall be **delivered** from the bondage of
2 Cor. 1:10(8-11)	who **delivered** us from so great a death, and doth
1 Thes. 1:10(9,10)	even Jesus, which **delivered** us from the wrath to come.
Heb. 11:35(35,36)	others were tortured, not accepting **deliverance**; that
2 Pet. 2:9(7-9)	Lord knoweth how to **deliver** the godly out of
1 Ne. 1:20(18-20)	mighty even unto the power of **deliverance**.
1 Ne. 4:3(2,3)	let us go up; the Lord is able to **deliver** us, even as
1 Ne. 17:14	I, the Lord, did **deliver** you from destruction; yea
2 Ne. 9:11(10-16)	the way of **deliverance** of our God, the holy one of
2 Ne. 11:5(4-6)	great and eternal plan of **deliverance** from death.
Alma 4:14(11-14)	**deliverance** of Jesus Christ from the bands of death.
Alma 7:13(12-14)	according to the power of his **deliverance**; and now
Alma 9:28(26-28)	according to the power and **deliverance** of Jesus Christ
Alma 14:26	give us strength...unto **deliverance**. And they broke
Alma 15:2(2,3)	related unto them...of their power of **deliverance**.
Alma 46:7	their **deliverance** by the hand of the Lord.
Alma 58:11(10-12)	we should hope for our **deliverance** in him.
D&C 8:4(3,4)	it shall **deliver** you out of the hands of your enemies
D&C 24:1(1-3)	thou hast been **delivered** from the powers of Satan and
D&C 30:6(5,6)	prayer and faith, for his and your **deliverance**; for I
D&C 39:10(7-10)	the days of thy **deliverance** are come, if thou wilt
D&C 56:18(17-20)	coming in power and great glory unto their **deliverance**
D&C 95:1(1,2)	I prepare a way for their **deliverance** in all things
D&C 104:80	I shall send means unto you for your **deliverance**.
D&C 105:8	behold, he will **deliver** them in time of trouble, other
D&C 108:8(5-8)	I am with you to bless you and **deliver** you forever.
D&C 109:32(31-34)	we plead...for a full and complete **deliverance** from
D&C 133:67(66,67)	my arm was not shortened...neither my power to **deliver**
JS-H 1:17	I found myself **delivered** from the enemy which held me
JFS-V 1:15(1-16,23)	joy and gladness...because...**deliverance** was at hand.

DEPENDABILITY

Ps. 118:8	better to trust...Lord than to put **confidence** in man.
Prov. 3:26(21-26)	the Lord shall be thy **confidence**, and shall keep thy
Prov. 31:11(10-12)	the heart of her husband doth safely **trust** in her, so
Luke 12:33	provide yourselves...treasure...that **faileth** not
1 Cor. 13:8(1-8)	charity never **faileth**: but whether there be prophecies
Gal. 5:10	I have **confidence** in you through the Lord, that ye
1 Thes. 4:12(9-12)	that ye may walk **honestly** toward them that are without
2 Thes. 3:4(3-7)	we have **confidence** in the Lord touching you, that ye
Heb. 6:11(10-12)	shew the same **diligence** to the full assurance of hope
1 Ne. 2:10(8-11)	O that thou mightest be...firm and **steadfast**, and

DEPENDABILITY cont.

1 Ne. 3:7(2-31)	I will...do the things which the Lord hath **commanded**
1 Ne. 17:8(8-16,49)	thou shalt **construct** a ship, after the manner which
2 Ne. 4:19(19-23)	nevertheless, I know in whom I have **trusted**.
2 Ne. 4:34	I will **trust** in thee forever. I will not put my trust
2 Ne. 6:2(1,2)	my brother Nephi...on whom ye **depend** for safety
Mosiah 5:15	therefore, I would that ye should be **steadfast** and
Mosiah 7:19(18-20)	and put your **trust** in God, in that God who was the God
Alma 48:13(13,17)	he had **sworn** with an oath to defend his people, his
Alma 53:20(18-21)	**true** at all times in whatsoever thing they were
Hel. 10:4(2-5)	thou hast with **unwearyingness** declared the word, which
D&C 18:3	**rely** upon the things which are written
D&C 70:15(14-15)	this commandment...for a reward of their **diligence** and
D&C 82:24	kingdom is yours..if..fall not from your **steadfastness**
D&C 84:80	fail not to continue **faithful**...shall not be weary in
Abr. 3:26(25,26)	they who **keep** their first estate shall be added upon
JS-H 1:59(59,60)	that I should be **responsible** for them; that if I

DESPAIR

Job 3:3(1-26)	let the day **perish** wherein I was born, and the night
Job 6:2(1-4)	Oh that my **grief** were throughly weighed, and my
Ps. 10:1(1-18)	why standest thou **afar** off, O Lord? why hidest thou
Ps. 13:1(1-6)	how long wilt thou **forget** me, O Lord? for ever? how
Ps. 22:1(1-31)	my God, why hast thou **forsaken** me? why art thou so far
Ps. 32:10(10-11)	many **sorrows** shall be to the wicked: but he that trust
Ps. 69:20(19-21)	reproach hath broken my heart...I am full of **heaviness**
Eccl. 2:20(17-23)	to cause my heart to **despair** of all the labour which
Jer. 9:1(1-9)	that I might **weep** day and night for the slain of the
Jer. 15:10(10-21)	**woe** is me, my mother, that thou hast borne me a man
Jer. 20:7(7-18)	I am in **derision** daily, every one mocketh me.
2 Cor. 1:8	we **despaired** even of life
2 Cor. 4:8(6-10)	we are perplexed, but not in **despair**
1 Thes. 4:13(13,14)	that ye **sorrow** not, even as others which have no hope.
Jacob 7:19(1-20)	I **fear** lest I have committed the unpardonable sin, for
Alma 15:3(3-12)	sins, did **harrow** up his mind until it did become
Alma 26:19(16-20)	justice fall upon us, and doom us to eternal **despair**
Alma 26:27(27-28)	when our hearts were **depressed**...the Lord comforted
Alma 36:12(5-24)	I was racked with eternal **torment**, for my soul was
Morm. 6:16(16-22)	and my soul was rent with **anguish**, because of the
Moro. 10:22(20-22)	**despair** cometh because of iniquity.
D&C 19:20(15-20)	**punishments**...tasted at the time I withdrew my spirit.
D&C 121:6(1-8)	remember thy **suffering** saints, O our God; and thy
D&C 122:7(1-7)	all the elements combine to **hedge** up the way; and
JS-H 1:16(15-17)	sink into **despair** and abandon myself to destruction

DEVIL

Gen. 3:1(1-3)	now the **serpent** was more subtil than any beast of the
Gen. 3:14(14-15)	the Lord God said unto the **serpent**, because thou hast
1 Chr. 21:1	and **Satan** stood up against Israel, and provoked David
Job 1:6(6-9)	and **Satan** came also among them.

DEVIL cont.

Job 2:1(1-4)	and **Satan** came also among them to present himself
Isa. 14:12(12-15)	fallen from heaven, O **Lucifer**, son of the morning! How
Matt. 4:3(3-10)	and when the **tempter** came to him, he said, if thou be
Matt. 4:10	get thee hence, **Satan**: for it is written, thou shalt
Matt. 10:28	fear him which is able to **destroy** both soul and body
Matt. 12:28	but if I cast out **devils** by the Spirit of God, then
Mark 3:15	power to heal sicknesses, and to cast out **devils**
Mark 4:15	**Satan** cometh immediately, and taketh away the word
Luke 4:2(1-13)	being forty days tempted of the **devil**. And in those
Luke 10:18	I beheld **Satan** as lightning fall from heaven.
Luke 12:5	fear him, which...hath power to cast into **hell**; yea
Luke 22:31(31-32)	behold, **Satan** hath desired to have you, that he may
John 8:44	ye are of your father the **devil**, and the lusts of your
John 12:31	now shall the **prince** of this world be cast out.
John 13:27	after the sop **Satan** entered into him. Then said Jesus
John 14:30	for the **prince** of this world cometh, and hath nothing
Rom. 16:20	God of peace shall bruise **Satan** under your feet
1 Cor. 7:5	that **Satan** tempt you not for your incontinency.
2 Cor. 4:4	the **God** of this world hath blinded the minds of them
2 Cor. 11:3	the **serpent** beguiled Eve through his subtilty, so your
2 Cor. 11:14(13-15)	**Satan** himself is transformed into an angel of light.
2 Thes. 2:3(3-4)	**man** of sin be revealed, the son of perdition
Heb. 2:14	him that had the power of death, that is, the **devil**
James 4:7	resist the **devil**, and he will flee from you.
1 Pet. 5:8	your adversary the **devil**, as a roaring lion, walketh
1 Jn. 3:8	that he might destroy the works of the **devil**.
Jude 1:6	the **angels** which kept not their first estate...he hath
Rev. 12:7(7-9)	and the **dragon** fought and his angels
Rev. 12:9(7-9)	the **devil**,...**Satan**, which deceiveth the whole world
Rev. 20:2(1-6)	the dragon, that old serpent...is the **devil**, and Satan
Rev. 20:7(1-10)	when..thousand years are expired, **Satan** shall be loose
1 Ne. 13:6	great and abominable church...**devil**...foundation of
1 Ne. 14:3(3-7)	abominable church...founded by the **devil** and his
1 Ne. 15:24	the fiery darts of the **adversary** overpower them unto
1 Ne. 22:26(15,26)	because of the righteousness...**Satan** has no power
2 Ne. 1:18(17-18)	led according to the will and captivity of the **devil**.
2 Ne. 2:18(17-18)	that old serpent...the **devil**...the father of all lies
2 Ne. 9:8(6-12)	that angel who fell ...and became the **devil**, to rise
2 Ne. 9:16	they who are filthy are the **devil** and his angels; and
2 Ne. 24:12(12-20)	how art thou fallen from heaven, O **Lucifer**, son of the
2 Ne. 26:22	combinations...according to..combinations of the **devil**
2 Ne. 30:18	**Satan** shall have power over...hearts of...men no more
Jacob 7:18	he had been deceived by the power of the **devil**. and
1:25	and that which is evil cometh from the **devil**.
Mosiah 2:32(32-39)	arise contentions..and ye list to obey the **evil** spirit
Mosiah 16:5(4-5)	an enemy to God...also is the **devil** an enemy to God.
Alma 12:5(3-6)	now this was a plan of thine **adversary**, and he hath
Alma 30:60	thus we see that the **devil** will not support his
Alma 34:23	the **devil**, who is an enemy to all righteousness.
3 Ne. 18:18	for **Satan** desireth to have you, that he may sift you
Ether 15:19	**Satan** had full power over the hearts of the people
Moro. 7:12(10-12)	for the **devil** is an enemy unto God, and fighteth again
D&C 1:35	the **devil** shall have power over his own dominion.

DEVIL cont.

D&C 3:8	supported you against...fiery darts of the **adversary**
D&C 10:10(10-12)	**Satan** hath put it into their hearts to alter the words
D&C 10:12	the **devil** has sought to lay a cunning plan, that he
D&C 10:20(20-27)	**Satan**...stirreth them up to iniquity against that
D&C 10:33	**Satan** thinketh to overpower your testimony in this
D&C 10:63(56-63)	**Satan** doth stir up the hearts of the people to content
D&C 20:20	by...transgression...man became sensual and **devilish**
D&C 24:13	require not miracles...except casting out **devils**
D&C 29:28	everlasting fire, prepared for the **devil** and his
D&C 29:36(36-45)	Adam, being tempted of the **devil**...the devil was
D&C 29:37	thrust down, and thus came the **devil** and his angels
D&C 29:39	it must needs be that the **devil** should tempt the
D&C 43:31(30-33)	**Satan** shall be bound, and when he is loosed again he
D&C 45:55	**Satan** shall be bound, that he shall have no place in
D&C 50:3(3,7)	**Satan** hath sought to deceive you, that he might
D&C 50:7(6-9)	deceived some, which has given the **adversary** power
D&C 52:14	**Satan** is abroad in the land, and he goeth forth
D&C 63:28	**Satan** putteth it into their hearts to anger against
D&C 64:17	**Satan** seeketh to destroy his soul; but when these
D&C 76:28(28-36)	we beheld Satan, that old serpent, even the **devil**, who
D&C 76:44(44-47)	to reign with the **devil** and his angels in eternity
D&C 76:85(33,44,85)	they who shall not be redeemed from the **devil** until
D&C 78:10(10-12)	**Satan** seeketh to turn their hearts away from the truth
D&C 82:5(4-6)	the **adversary** spreadeth his dominions, and darkness
D&C 88:110(110-116)	**Satan** shall be bound...for the space of a thousand
D&C 93:39	**wicked** one...taketh away light and truth, through
D&C 104:9(9-10)	ye cannot escape the buffetings of **Satan** until the day
D&C 128:20	detecting the **devil** when he appeared as an angel of
D&C 132:26	shall be delivered unto the buffetings of **Satan** unto
D&C 132:57	for **Satan** seeketh to destroy; for I am the Lord thy
Moses 1:12(12-22)	**Satan** came tempting him, saying: Moses...worship me.
Moses 4:4(1-6)	became Satan...the **devil**...to deceive and to blind men
Moses 4:6(1-7)	**Satan**...knew not the mind of God...sought to destroy
Moses 5:13(13,23-24)	**Satan** came...saying: I am also a son of God; and he
Abr. 3:28(27,28)	the **second** was angry, and kept not his first estate
JS-H 1:20	as though the **adversary** was aware, at a very early

DEVIL, CHURCH OF

Matt. 13:38(38-40)	the **tares** are the children of the wicked one
John 8:44(39-47)	ye are of your father the **devil**, and the lusts of your
1 Pet. 4:3(3-5)	we walked in...**abominable** idolatries
Rev. 12:17(16,17)	**dragon**...went to make war with...her seed, which keep
Rev. 17:1(1-18)	great **whore** that sitteth upon many waters
Rev. 18:21(1-24)	with violence shall...great city **Babylon** be thrown
1 Ne. 13:6(4-29)	I beheld this great and **abominable** church; and I saw
1 Ne. 13:32(32-34)	kept back by that **abominable** church, whose formation
1 Ne. 14:9(9-17)	abominable church...whose foundation is the **devil**.
1 Ne. 14:10(3,9-17)	two churches only...of the Lamb of God...of the **devil**
1 Ne. 22:13(13-18,23)	**abominable** church, which is the whore of all the earth
2 Ne. 6:12	do not unite themselves...great and **abominable** church
2 Ne. 10:16	they are they who are the **whore** of all the earth; for

DEVIL, CHURCH OF cont.

2 Ne. 28:18(3-32)   great and **abominable** church, the whore of all the
Alma 5:39(39-40)   the **devil** is your shepherd, and ye are of his fold
3 Ne. 27:11   not built upon my gospel..upon....works of the **Devil**
Morm. 8:32(26-41)   **churches**..shall say..for your money..forgiven of..sins
D&C 10:56   build up **churches** unto themselves to get gain, yea
D&C 18:20   contend against no church, save...**church** of the devil.
D&C 29:21   **abominable** church...shall be cast down by devouring
D&C 88:94(94-96)   that great **church**, the mother of abominations, that

DILIGENCE

Ex. 15:26   if thou wilt **diligently** hearken to the voice of the
Deut. 6:17(3-17)   ye shall **diligently** keep the commandments of the Lord
Josh. 22:5(4-6)   take **diligent** heed to do the commandment and the law
Ps. 119:4(1-6)   thou hast commanded us to keep thy precepts **diligently**
Prov. 10:4(4,5)   slack hand: but the hand of the **diligent** maketh rich.
Prov. 12:24   the hand of the **diligent** shall bear rule: but the
Prov. 12:27   the substance of a **diligent** man is precious.
Prov. 22:29   a man **diligent** in his business? he shall stand before
Isa. 55:2   hearken **diligently** unto me, and eat ye that which is
2 Cor. 8:7   abound in every thing...in all **diligence**, and in your
Heb. 6:11(9-12)   shew the same **diligence** to the full assurance of hope
Heb. 11:6   he is a rewarder of them that **diligently** seek him.
2 Pet. 1:5(5-10)   beside this, giving all **diligence**, add to your faith
2 Pet. 3:14   be **diligent** that ye may be found of him in peace, with
Mosiah 1:11   this I do because they have been a **diligent** people in
Mosiah 4:27   it is expedient that he should be **diligent**, that
Mosiah 7:33   serve him with all **diligence** of mind, if ye do this
Alma 12:9   impart..word...according to..**diligence** which they give
Alma 17:2   they had searched the scriptures **diligently**, that they
Alma 32:42(41,42)   and because of your **diligence** and your faith and your
Alma 49:30   because of their heed and **diligence** which they gave
3 Ne. 6:14   steadfast...willing with all **diligence** to keep the
Moro. 8:26   love endureth by **diligence** unto prayer, until the end
Moro. 9:6   let us labor **diligently**; for if we should cease to
D&C 4:6   brotherly kindness, godliness...humility, **diligence**.
D&C 6:20   be...**diligent** in keeping the commandments of God, and
D&C 10:4   enable you to translate; but be **diligent** unto the end.
D&C 18:8   if...**diligent**...he shall be blessed unto eternal life
D&C 58:27(26-29)   men should be **anxiously** engaged in a good cause, and
D&C 59:4   shall also be crowned...that are...**diligent** before me.
D&C 70:15(15-18)   for a reward of their **diligence** and for their
D&C 75:3   neither be idle but labor with your **might**
D&C 75:29   let every man be **diligent** in all things. and the idler
D&C 84:43   give **diligent** heed to the words of eternal life.
D&C 90:24   search **diligently**, pray always, and be believing, and
D&C 93:50   see that they are more **diligent** and concerned at home
D&C 103:36   all victory and glory is brought...through...**diligence**
D&C 104:79   obtain this blessing by your **diligence** and humility
D&C 107:99(99-100)   man learn his duty and to act...in all **diligence**.
D&C 124:49   perform that work, and cease not their **diligence**, and
D&C 127:4   let your **diligence**, and your perseverance, and

DILIGENCE cont.

D&C 130:19   gains more knowledge...through...**diligence** and
D&C 136:27   thou shalt be **diligent** in preserving what thou hast

DISCERNMENT, SPIRITUAL

Gen. 3:22   become as one of us, to **know** good and evil: and now
1 Sam. 16:7   man looketh on the outward **appearance**, but the Lord
1 Kgs. 3:9(5-15)   that I may **discern** between good and bad: for who is
Prov. 1:7   fear of the Lord is the beginning of **knowledge**: but
Prov. 4:18(14-19) that **shineth** more and more unto the perfect day.
Isa. 5:20   woe unto them that call evil **good**, and good evil; that
Isa. 11:3   he shall not judge after the **sight** of his eyes
Ezek. 44:23   teach my people the **difference** between the holy and
Matt. 7:16(16-20) ye shall **know** them by their fruits. do men gather
John 1:9(4-9)   true light, which **lighteth** every man that cometh into
John 3:21(19-21) he that doeth truth cometh to the **light**, that his deed
John 7:17   if any man will do his will, he shall **know** of the
John 10:4(1-18)   the sheep follow him: for they **know** his voice.
1 Cor. 2:14(9-16) because they are spiritually **discerned**.
1 Cor. 12:10   to another **discerning** of spirits; to another divers
1 Jn. 4:2(1-2)   hereby **know** ye the Spirit of God: every spirit that
1 Jn. 4:6   hereby **know** we the spirit of truth, and the spirit of
2 Ne. 32:8(8,9)   if ye would hearken unto the **Spirit** which teacheth a
Alma 18:18   beheld that Ammon could **discern** his thoughts; but
Alma 24:30   and thus we can plainly **discern**, that after a people
Alma 26:22(21,22) unto such it is given to **know** the mysteries of God
Alma 29:5   he that knoweth **good** and evil, to him it is given
Alma 32:28(28-33) good seed...it beginneth to **enlighten** my understanding
3 Ne. 11:3(3-7)   a small **voice** it did pierce them that did hear to the
3 Ne. 24:18(15-18) then shall ye return and **discern** between the righteous
Ether 4:12(11,12) whatsoever thing persuadeth men to do **good** is of me
Moro. 7:15(15-19) it is given unto you to **judge**, that ye may know good
Moro. 10:5(3-7)   by the power of the Holy Ghost ye may **know** the truth
D&C 6:22(22,23)   that you might **know** concerning the truth of these
D&C 11:13(11-14) my Spirit, which shall **enlighten** your mind, which
D&C 46:8(7,8,23) that ye may not be **deceived** seek ye...the best gifts
D&C 46:27(10-27) given unto them to **discern** all those gifts lest there
D&C 50:15(1-3,13-35) then received ye **spirits** which ye could not understand
D&C 52:19(14-19) by this pattern ye shall **know** the spirits in all cases
D&C 63:41   he shall be enabled to **discern** by the Spirit those who
D&C 84:46(44-53) the spirit **enlighteneth** every man through the world
D&C 88:67(67,68) body which is filled with light **comprehendeth** all
D&C 93:19(1-40)   that you may **understand** and know how to worship, and
D&C 101:95(92-95) that men may **discern** between the righteous and the
D&C 129:9   three grand **keys** whereby you may know whether any
D&C 131:7(7,8)   spirit is matter...can only be **discerned** by purer eyes
Moses 1:27(27-29) beheld the earth...**discerning** it by the Spirit of God.

DISOBEDIENCE

Deut. 8:20(19-20)	because ye would not be **obedient** unto the voice of the
Deut. 11:28(26-28)	curse, if ye will not **obey** the commandments of the Lord
Deut. 21:18(18-21)	rebellious son...will not **obey** the voice of his father
Deut. 28:62(58-64)	because thou wouldest not **obey** the voice of the Lord
Josh. 5:6	were consumed, because they **obeyed** not the voice of
Judg. 2:2(1,2)	but ye have not **obeyed** my voice: why have ye done this
Judg. 6:10(8-10)	I am...your God...but ye have not **obeyed** my voice.
1 Sam. 8:19(19-22)	the people refused to **obey** the voice of Samuel; and
1 Sam. 12:15(14,15)	but if ye will not **obey** the voice of the Lord, but
1 Sam. 15:23(22-26)	thou hast **rejected** the word of the Lord, he hath also
1 Kgs. 13:21(21,26)	thou hast **disobeyed** the mouth of the Lord, and hast
2 Kgs. 18:12(11,12)	because they **obeyed** not the voice of the Lord their
Neh. 9:26(17,26,27)	they were **disobedient**, and rebelled against thee, and
Job 36:12(11,12)	but if they **obey** not, they shall perish by the sword
Prov. 1:24(24-27)	I have called, and ye **refused**; I have stretched out
Prov. 5:13(11-14)	have not **obeyed** the voice of my teachers, nor inclined
Isa. 24:5	they have **transgressed** the laws, changed the ordinance
Isa. 42:24(24,25)	neither were they **obedient** unto his law.
Jer. 3:13(12,13)	only acknowledge...ye have not **obeyed** my voice, saith
Jer. 8:9(8,9)	they have **rejected** the word of the Lord; and what
Jer. 9:13(13-16)	have not **obeyed** my voice, neither walked therein
Jer. 11:3(3-8)	cursed be the man that **obeyeth** not the words of this
Jer. 12:17(1-17)	but if they will not **obey**, I will utterly pluck up and
Jer. 18:10(9,10)	if it do evil in my sight, that it **obey** not my voice
Jer. 22:21(21,22)	from thy youth, that thou **obeyedst** not my voice.
Jer. 42:21(19-22)	I have...declared it to you; but ye have not **obeyed**
Jer. 44:23(22,23)	ye have sinned...and have not **obeyed** the voice of the
Dan. 9:11(10,11)	Israel...might not **obey** thy voice; therefore the
Dan. 9:14(8-14)	God is righteous in all his works...for we **obeyed** not
Hosea 4:6(1-7)	because thou hast **rejected** knowledge, I will also
Zeph. 3:2(1,2)	she **obeyed** not the voice; she received not correction
Luke 1:17	to turn...the **disobedient** to the wisdom of the just
Luke 6:46(46-49)	call...Lord, Lord, and **do** not the things which I say
Acts 7:39(37-39)	to whom our fathers would not **obey**, but thrust him
Acts 7:53	have received the law...and have not **kept** it.
Acts 26:19(19,20)	I was not **disobedient** unto the heavenly vision
Rom. 1:30(28-32)	despiteful, proud, boasters...**disobedient** to parents
Rom. 2:8(6-11)	them that are contentious, and do not **obey** the truth
Rom. 5:19	as by one man's **disobedience** many were made sinners
Rom. 10:21	stretched forth my hands unto a **disobedient**...people.
2 Cor. 10:6(4-6)	having in a readiness to revenge all **disobedience**
Gal. 5:7(5-9)	who did hinder you that ye should not **obey** the truth
Eph. 2:2(2-3)	spirit that...worketh in the children of **disobedience**
Eph. 5:6(5,6)	wrath of God upon the children of **disobedience**.
Col. 3:6(5,6)	wrath of God cometh on the children of **disobedience**
2 Thes. 1:8(7-9)	taking vengeance on them that...**obey** not the gospel
1 Tim. 1:9(8,9)	the law is...for the lawless and **disobedient**, for the
2 Tim. 3:2(1-5)	boasters, proud, blasphemers, **disobedient** to parents
Titus 1:16(15,16)	they deny him, being abominable, and **disobedient**, and
Titus 3:3(1-3)	we ourselves also were sometimes foolish, **disobedient**
Heb. 2:2(1-2)	every..**disobedience** received a just recompence of
James 4:17	knoweth to do good, and **doeth** it not, to him it is sin
1 Pet. 2:7(6-8)	but unto them which be **disobedient**, the stone which

DISOBEDIENCE cont.

1 Pet. 3:1(1,2)	husbands...if any **obey** not the word, they...may
1 Pet. 3:20(18-20)	which sometime were **disobedient**, when once the
1 Pet. 4:17	what shall the end be of them that **obey** not the gospel
2 Ne. 9:27	has all the commandments...and that **transgresseth** them
Mosiah 1:17(16,17)	as they were **unfaithful** they did not prosper nor
Mosiah 2:36(36-37)	transgress...go **contrary** to that which has been spoken
Mosiah 27:11(10,11)	as they were going about **rebelling** against God, behold
Mosiah 29:26(25-27)	not common...people desireth anything **contrary** to that
Alma 9:23(23-25)	should transgress **contrary** to the light and knowledge
Alma 12:31(30-32)	having first **transgressed** the first commandments as
Alma 36:13(8-13)	I had **rebelled** against my God, and that I had not kept
Alma 42:12(11-15)	man had brought upon himself because of...**disobedience**
Hel. 7:18(17-20)	ye will not **hearken** unto the voice of the good
Hel. 13:21(21-22)	and have not **hearkened** unto the words of him who gave
Hel. 16:12(11,12)	do more...of that which was **contrary** to the
3 Ne. 28:34(34,35)	wo be unto him that will not **hearken** unto the words
D&C 1:14(14-16)	they who will not..give **heed** to..words of the prophets
D&C 56:3(1-4)	he that will not **obey** shall be cut off in mine own due
D&C 58:32(30-32)	I command and men **obey** not; I revoke and they receive
D&C 59:21(18-22)	confess not his hand...and **obey** not his commandments.
D&C 88:35(35-39)	that which **breaketh** a law, and abideth not by law, but
D&C 93:39	taketh away light and truth, through **disobedience**,
D&C 103:4(3-10)	they did not **hearken** altogether unto the precepts and
D&C 133:63(62-74)	upon them that **hearken** not to the voice of the Lord
Moses 4:4(3,4)	captive...as many as would not **hearken** unto my voice.
Moses 5:57(54-57)	would not **hearken** unto his voice, nor believe on his
Moses 8:15(13-17)	men, for they will not **hearken** to my voice.
Moses 8:21(20-24)	they **hearkened** not unto the words of Noah.

DISPENSATIONS

Deut. 4:31(27-32)	neither destroy thee, nor forget the **covenant** of thy
Isa. 2:2(1-4)	the mountain of the Lord's house shall be **established**
Isa. 11:12(1-16)	and he shall set up an **ensign** for the nations, and
Isa. 52:7(1-12)	how beautiful...feet of him that **bringeth** good tidings
Dan. 2:44(44,45)	the God of heaven set up a **kingdom**, which shall never
Joel 2:28(28-31)	I will **pour** out my spirit upon all flesh; and your son
Micah 1:3(1-4)	behold, the Lord **cometh** forth out of his place, and
Micah 4:1(1-11)	mountain of the house of the Lord shall be **established**
Matt. 17:11(9-13)	Elias truly shall first come, and **restore** all things
Mark 9:12(11-13)	Elias verily cometh first, and **restoreth** all things
Acts 1:6(6-9)	wilt thou at this time **restore** again the kingdom to
Acts 2:17(17,18)	last days..I will **pour** out my spirit upon all flesh
Acts 3:21	until the times of **restitution** of all things, which
1 Cor. 9:17	a **dispensation** of the gospel is committed unto me.
Eph. 1:10	in the **dispensation** of the fulness of times he might
Eph. 3:2	heard of the **dispensation** of the grace of God which
Col. 1:25	the **dispensation** of God which is given to me for you
1 Ne. 15:13(13-20)	latter days...**fulness** of the gospel..unto the Gentiles
2 Ne. 3:24(7-24)	much **restoration** unto the house of Israel, and unto
2 Ne. 12:2(2-4)	the mountain of the Lord's house shall be **established**
3 Ne. 21:22(22-25)	I will **establish** my church among them, and they shall

DISPENSATIONS cont.

Ether 13:6(4-7)	a new Jerusalem should be built...unto the remnant of
D&C 27:13	a dispensation of the gospel..for the fulness of times
D&C 110:12(12-16)	the dispensation of the gospel of Abraham, saying that
D&C 110:16(12,16)	the keys of this dispensation are committed into your
D&C 112:30(30-32)	last time...the dispensation of the fulness of times.
D&C 121:31	revealed in....dispensation of the fulness of times
D&C 128:9	whenever the Lord has given a dispensation of the
D&C 128:18	dispensation of the fulness of times...is now
D&C 128:21	all declaring their dispensation, their rights, their
JFS-V 1:48(47,48)	in the dispensation of the fulness of times, for the

DISPUTATIONS

Deut. 17:8	being matters of controversy within thy gates: then
Deut. 19:17	between whom the controversy is, shall stand before
Deut. 25:1	if there be a controversy between men, and they come
Job 23:7	there the righteous might dispute with him; so should
Prov. 6:19(14,19)	speaketh lies, and he that soweth discord among
Matt. 5:25(21-26)	agree with thine adversary quickly, whiles thou art
Mark 9:34(33-34)	they had disputed among themselves, who should be the
Acts 6:9	them of Cilicia and of Asia, disputing with Stephen.
Acts 9:29	disputed against the Grecians: but they went about
Acts 15:2	had no small dissension and disputation with them, the
Acts 15:7	and when there had been much disputing, Peter rose up
Acts 17:17	therefore disputed he in the synagogue with the Jews
Acts 19:8	disputing and persuading the things concerning the
Acts 24:12(11-13)	they neither found me in the temple disputing with any
Rom. 14:1	weak...receive ye, but not to doubtful disputations.
1 Cor. 1:20	where is the disputer of this world? hath not God made
Philip. 2:14(14-15)	do all things without murmurings and disputings
1 Tim. 6:5(4-5)	perverse disputings of men of corrupt minds...withdraw
1 Ne. 15:2	my brethren, and they were disputing one with another
3 Ne. 8:4	began to be great doubtings and disputations among the
3 Ne. 11:22(22-28)	and there shall be no disputations among you.
3 Ne. 11:28(28-30)	there shall be no disputations among you, as there
3 Ne. 18:34	blessed are ye if ye have no disputation among you.
3 Ne. 27:3(2-5)	for there are disputations among the people concerning
4 Ne. 1:2	no contentions and disputations among them, and every
Moro. 8:4(4,5)	grieveth me that there should disputations rise among
D&C 10:63(59-63)	Satan doth stir up...the people to contention
D&C 18:20(18-22)	contend against no church, save it be the church of
D&C 95:10	contentions arose in the school of the prophets
D&C 101:6(1-8)	there were jarrings, and contentions, and envyings
D&C 136:23(23-27)	cease to contend one with another; cease to speak evil

DIVORCE

Gen. 2:24(21-25)	man..cleave unto his wife: and they shall be one flesh
Deut. 24:1(1-4)	a bill of divorcement, and give it in her hand, and
Isa. 50:1	where is the bill of your mother's divorcement, whom
Jer. 3:1	they say, if a man put away his wife, and she go from

DIVORCE cont.

Jer. 3:8	put her away, and given her a bill of **divorce**; yet her
Jer. 3:20	as a wife treacherously **departeth** from her husband
Mal. 2:16(13-16)	the Lord...saith that he hateth **putting** away: for one
Matt. 5:31(31-32)	it hath been said...give her a writing of **divorcement**
Matt. 14:4(3-10)	for John said...it is not **lawful** for thee to have her.
Matt. 19:7(3-9)	Moses then command to give a writing of **divorcement**
Mark 10:9(2-12)	what...God hath joined...let not man put **asunder**.
Luke 16:18	whosoever **putteth** away his wife, and marrieth another
1 Cor. 7:10(10-11)	let not the wife **depart** from her husband
1 Cor. 7:11(10-11)	let not the husband **put** away his wife.
2 Ne. 7:1	where is the bill of your mother's **divorcement**? To who
3 Ne. 12:31(31,32)	hath been written...give her a writing of **divorcement**.
D&C 42:22	thou shalt love thy wife...**cleave** unto her and none
D&C 42:75(75-77)	any..have **left** their companions for the sake of
D&C 132:44(43,44)	take her and **give** her unto him that hath not committed
Moses 3:24(22-25)	and they shall be **one** flesh.
Abr. 5:18(15-19)	and they shall be **one** flesh.

DOUBT

Ex. 4:1(1-17)	behold, they will not **believe** me, nor hearken unto my
Ex. 17:2(1-7)	wherefore do ye **tempt** the Lord
Deut. 1:32(30-35)	ye did not **believe** the Lord your God
Deut. 6:16(16-18)	ye shall not **tempt** the Lord your God, as ye tempted
Deut. 28:66(65-67)	thy life shall hang in **doubt** before thee; and thou
2 Kgs. 17:14(13-18)	they would not hear, but **hardened** their necks, like
Matt. 14:31(22-33)	O thou of little faith, wherefore didst thou **doubt**
Matt. 17:20(14-21)	Jesus said unto them, because of your **unbelief**: for
Matt. 21:21(17-22)	if ye have faith, and **doubt** not, ye shall not only
Matt. 28:17(16-20)	saw him, they worshipped him: but some **doubted**.
Mark 9:24(14-29)	the father...said...I believe; help thou mine **unbelief**
Mark 11:23(22-24)	and shall not **doubt** in his heart, but shall believe
Luke 12:29(16-31)	neither be ye of **doubtful** mind.
John 10:24(22-30)	how long dost thou make us to **doubt**? if thou be the
John 20:27(24-29)	be not **faithless**, but believing.
Rom. 14:1(1-3)	weak...faith receive ye, but not to **doubtful**
Rom. 14:23(1-23)	he that **doubteth** is damned if he eat, because he
1 Tim. 2:8(7-8)	pray every where...without wrath and **doubting**.
James 1:6(5-8)	ask in faith, nothing **wavering**. for he that wavereth
1 Ne. 4:3	wherefore can ye **doubt**? Let us go up; the Lord is able
1 Ne. 10:11	concerning the dwindling of the Jews in **unbelief**. And
2 Ne. 10:2(1-2)	many...shall perish in the flesh because of **unbelief**
2 Ne. 32:7(7-9)	I am left to mourn because of the **unbelief**, and the
Jacob 3:7(5-8)	their **unbelief** and their hatred towards you is because
Mosiah 26:3(1-36)	because of...**unbelief** they could not understand...word
Alma 7:6(3-7)	I trust that ye are not in a state of so much **unbelief**
Alma 19:6(4-6)	the dark veil of **unbelief** was being cast away from his
Alma 32:28(26-34)	if...a good seed...do not cast it out by your **unbelief**
Alma 33:21	would ye rather harden your hearts in **unbelief**, and
Alma 46:29	his people were **doubtful** concerning the justice of the
Alma 56:47(43-56)	if they did not **doubt**, God would deliver them.
Alma 57:26(18-27)	whosoever did not **doubt**, that they should be preserved

DOUBT cont.

Alma 59:11(11,12)   Moroni...was exceeding sorrowful, and began to **doubt**
Hel. 5:49(21-52)   bidden to go forth...neither should they **doubt**.
3 Ne. 1:18   they began to fear because of their...**unbelief**.
3 Ne. 5:1(1-6)   not a living soul...who did **doubt** in the least the
3 Ne. 8:4(3-25)   there began to be great **doubtings** and disputations
3 Ne. 15:18   because of...**unbelief** they understood not my word; the
3 Ne. 16:7(6-7)   because of the **unbelief** of you, O house of Israel, in
3 Ne. 19:35   could not show...miracles, because of their **unbelief**.
Morm. 9:27(15-29)   **doubt** not, but be believing, and begin as in times
Ether 3:19(17-20)   he had faith no longer, for he knew, nothing **doubting**.
Ether 4:13(10-16)   greater things...knowledge...hid...because of **unbelief**
Moro. 7:37(20-48)   miracles...have ceased...because of **unbelief**, and all
Moro. 10:19(8-19)   done away...only according to the **unbelief** of the
Moro. 10:24(23-25)   if...the power and gifts of God...done away...**unbelief**
D&C 3:18(16-20)   who dwindled in **unbelief** because of the iniquity of
D&C 6:36(34-37)   look unto me in every thought; **doubt** not, fear not.
D&C 8:8(1-12)   therefore, **doubt** not, for it is the gift of God; and
D&C 58:15(14-16)   repent not of his sins, which are **unbelief** and
D&C 58:29(26-33)   receiveth a commandment with **doubtful** heart, and
D&C 60:7(6-7)   declare...with loud voices, without wrath or **doubting**
D&C 84:54(54-61)   your minds...have been darkened because of **unbelief**

DREAMS

Gen. 20:3(3-7)   God came to Abimelech in a **dream** by night, and said
Gen. 28:12(11-16)   and he **dreamed**, and behold a ladder set up on the
Gen. 31:24   God came to Laban the Syrian in a **dream** by night, and
Gen. 37:5(5-10)   Joseph dreamed a **dream**, and he told it his brethren
Gen. 40:8(5-18)   we have dreamed a **dream**..there is no interpreter of
Gen. 41:1(1-7)   Pharaoh **dreamed**: and, behold, he stood by the river.
Gen. 41:25(25-32)   Joseph said...God hath **shewed** Pharaoh what he is
Gen. 42:9   Joseph remembered the **dreams** which he dreamed of them
Num. 12:6   I the Lord...will speak unto him in a **dream**.
Deut. 13:1(1-3)   if there arise...a dreamer of **dreams**, and giveth thee
Judg. 7:13(13-14)   behold, I dreamed a **dream**, and, lo, a cake of barley
1 Sam. 28:6(6,15)   Lord answered him not, neither by **dreams** nor by Urim
1 Kgs. 3:5(5-15)   the Lord appeared to Solomon in a **dream** by night: and
Job 33:15(14-15)   in a **dream**, in a vision of the night, when deep sleep
Jer. 23:32(25-32)   I am against them that prophesy false **dreams**, saith
Jer. 29:8(8-9)   neither hearken to your **dreams** which ye cause to be
Dan. 2:1   Nebuchadnezzar dreamed **dreams**, wherewith his spirit
Dan. 2:19(17-19)   secret revealed unto Daniel in a night **vision**. Then
Dan. 2:28(26-30)   God in heaven that revealeth secrets...thy **dream**, and
Dan. 7:1(1,2)   Daniel had a **dream** and visions of his head upon his
Joel 2:28   your old men shall **dream** dreams, your young men shall
Zech. 10:2   diviners have seen a lie, and have told false **dreams**
Matt. 1:20   Lord appeared unto him in a **dream**, saying, Joseph
Matt. 2:12(12-13)   warned of God in a **dream** that they should not return
Matt. 2:19(19-20)   an angel of the Lord appeareth in a **dream** to Joseph
Matt. 2:22   being warned of God in a **dream**, he turned aside into
Matt. 27:19   I have suffered many things..in a **dream** because of him
Acts 2:17   your old men shall **dream** dreams

DREAMS cont.

1 Ne. 1:16   hath written many things which he saw...in **dreams**; and
1 Ne. 2:2(1,2)   the Lord commanded my father, even in a **dream**, that
1 Ne. 3:2   behold I have dreamed a **dream**, in the which the Lord
1 Ne. 8:2(2-36)   I have dreamed a **dream**; or, in other words, I have see
1 Ne. 10:2   made an end of speaking the words of his **dream**, and
1 Ne. 15:21   meaneth this thing which our father saw in a **dream**
2 Ne. 4:23   he hath given me knowledge by **visions** in the nighttime
2 Ne. 27:3   shall be as a **dream** of a night vision; yea, it shall
Jacob 7:26   our lives passed away like as it were unto us a **dream**
Alma 30:28   their **dreams** and their whims and their visions and the
Ether 9:3   the Lord warned Omer in a **dream** that he should depart

DROUGHT

Gen. 31:40   in the day the **drought** consumed me, and the frost by
Gen. 41:54(30,54-57)   the seven years of **dearth** began to come, according as
Deut. 8:15   wilderness, wherein were...scorpions, and **drought**
1 Kgs. 17:1(1-7)   there shall not be dew nor **rain** these years, but
Job 24:19   **drought** and heat consume the snow waters: so doth the
Isa. 50:2   I **dry** up the sea, I make the rivers a wilderness
Isa. 58:11   Lord shall...satisfy thy soul in **drought**, and make fat
Jer. 17:8   shall not be careful in the year of **drought**, neither
Jer. 50:38   a **drought** is upon her waters; and they shall be dried
Hosea 13:5   in the wilderness, in the land of great **drought**.
Hag. 1:11   I called for a **drought** upon the land, and upon the
Matt. 24:7(6-8)   there shall be **famines**, and pestilences, and
Acts 7:11   now there came a **dearth** over all the land of Egypt and
Acts 11:28(27-30)   there should be great **dearth** throughout all the world
James 5:17(17,18)   it **rained** not...by the space of three years and six
2 Ne. 1:18(16-18)   a cursing should come..visited by sword, and by **famine**
2 Ne. 6:15(14-15)   they that believe not...shall be destroyed...by **famine**
Mosiah 1:17(15-17)   smitten with **famine** and sore afflictions, to stir them
Alma 10:22(22-23)   if it were not for the prayers..destruction..by **famine**
Hel. 10:6(5-11)   ye shall have power..shall smite the earth with **famine**
Hel. 11:6(4-18)   the earth was smitten that it was **dry**, and did not
Ether 9:30(28-31)   there began to be a great **dearth** upon the land, and
D&C 43:25(24-27)   by the voice of **famines** and pestilences of every kind
D&C 87:6(4-8)   with **famine**, and plague...and chastening hand of an
D&C 133:68(65-74)   I **dry** up the sea. I make the rivers a wilderness

DRUNKENNESS

Num. 6:3(2-4)   he shall separate himself from **wine** and strong drink
Deut. 29:19(18,19)   mine heart, to add **drunkenness** to thirst
Prov. 20:1   **wine** is a mocker, strong drink is raging: and
Prov. 23:31(29-35)   look not thou upon the **wine** when it is red, when it
Isa. 5:11(11-12)   that continue until night, till **wine** inflame them
Isa. 5:22(22,23)   woe unto them that are mighty to **drink** wine, and men
Rom. 13:13   walk...not in rioting and **drunkenness**, not in
1 Cor. 5:11   not to keep company...**drunkard**, or an extortioner;
1 Cor. 6:10(9-10)   nor **drunkards**...shall inherit the kingdom of God.

DRUNKENNESS cont.

Gal. 5:21(16-21)   drunkenness...such things shall not inherit the
Eph. 5:18   be not **drunk** with wine, wherein is excess; but be
1 Tim. 3:3(1-4)   not given to **wine**, no striker, not greedy of filthy
1 Ne. 4:7   fallen to the earth before me, for he was **drunken** with
2 Ne. 15:11(11-12)   that continue until night, and **wine** inflame them
Mosiah 22:7(6,7)   they will be **drunken**; and we will pass through the
Alma 55:19(16-24)   not fall upon...and destroy them in their **drunkenness**.
D&C 89:5(5-7)   any man drinketh **wine** or strong drink...it is not good
D&C 136:24   cease **drunkenness**; and let your words tend to edifying

DUTY

Deut. 5:32(32-33)   ye shall **observe** to do...as...God hath commanded you
Deut. 7:11   keep the commandments...which I **command** thee this day
Deut. 10:12(12-13)   what doth...God **require** of thee, but to fear the Lord
1 Sam. 15:22(20-22)   behold, to **obey** is better than sacrifice, and to
2 Chr. 8:14   praise and minister...as the **duty** of every day require
Eccl. 12:13   for this is the whole **duty** of man.
Micah 6:8   what doth the Lord **require** of thee, but to do justly
Matt. 7:21(21-23)   not every one...but he that **doeth** the will of my
Luke 12:48   whomsoever...is given, of him shall be much **required**
Luke 17:10(7-10)   have done that which was our **duty** to do.
John 14:15   if ye love me, **keep** my commandments.
Acts 5:29   we ought to **obey** God rather than men.
Rom. 15:27(25-28)   partakers of their spiritual things, their **duty** is
1 Cor. 9:16   **necessity** is laid upon me; yea, woe is unto me, if I
James 1:22(18-27)   but be ye **doers** of the word, and not hearers only
1 Ne. 3:7   I will go and **do** the things which the Lord hath
Jacob 2:2(2,3)   **responsibility**...to God, to magnify mine office with
Mosiah 1:17(15-17)   to stir them up in remembrance of their **duty**.
Mosiah 2:24   he doth **require** that ye should do as he hath commanded
Mosiah 13:30(28-30)   in remembrance of God and their **duty** towards him.
Alma 4:19(3,19)   in remembrance of their **duty**, and that he might pull
Alma 7:22(22-24)   awaken you to a sense of your **duty** to God, that ye may
Alma 43:46(45-47)   doing that which they felt was the **duty** which they owe
Hel. 15:5(4-6)   the more part of them are in the path of their **duty**
Moro. 9:6   we have a **labor** to perform whilst in this tabernacle
D&C 20:19   commandments that they should love and **serve** him, the
D&C 20:38(38-67)   the **duty** of the elders, priests, teachers, deacons
D&C 20:68(68-70)   the **duty** of the members after they are received by
D&C 72:9(9-23)   making known the **duty** of the bishop who has been
D&C 105:10(8-12)   know more perfectly concerning their **duty**, and the
D&C 107:91(85-91)   the **duty** of the president of the office of the high
D&C 107:99(99-100)   now let every man learn his **duty**, and to act in the
D&C 123:7(7-17)   it is an imperative **duty** that we owe to God, to angels

EARTH, CLEANSING OF

Gen. 6:17(17-18)   a flood of **waters** upon the earth, to destroy all flesh
Gen. 7:4(1-24)   **rain** upon the earth forty days...destroy from off the
Gen. 7:23   **Noah** only remained alive, and they that were with him

EARTH, CLEANSING OF cont.

Gen. 8:21	neither will I again **smite** any more every thing living
Gen. 9:11(8-17)	neither shall there...be a flood to **destroy** the earth.
Isa. 13:9(6-13)	he shall **destroy** the sinners thereof out of it.
Isa. 24:6(1-6)	inhabitants of the earth are **burned**, and few men left.
Isa. 54:9(9-10)	sworn...**waters** of Noah should no more go over the
Nahum 1:5	hills melt, and the earth is **burned** at his presence
Mal. 3:2(1-3)	for he is like a refiner's **fire**, and like fullers
Mal. 4:1	day cometh, that shall **burn** as an oven; and all the
Luke 17:26(26-37)	as it was in the days of **Noe**, so shall it be also in
1 Pet. 3:20	longsuffering of God waited in the days of **Noah**
2 Pet. 2:5(4-9)	bringing in the **flood** upon the world of the ungodly
2 Pet. 3:7(6-7)	reserved unto **fire** against the day of judgment and
1 Ne. 22:15(15-28)	the day cometh that they must be **burned**.
2 Ne. 30:10(9-10)	if it so be that...must destroy the wicked by **fire**.
Alma 10:22(22-23)	not be by flood, as...in the days of **Noah**, but it
3 Ne. 22:9	the **waters** of Noah should no more go over the earth
3 Ne. 24:2(2-3)	he is like a **refiner's** fire, and like fuller's soap.
3 Ne. 25:1	shall **burn** as an oven; and all the proud, yea, and all
3 Ne. 26:3	even until the elements should **melt** with fervent heat
D&C 29:9(9,16-23)	shall be as stubble; and I will **burn** them up, saith
D&C 45:50(47-50)	watched for iniquity shall be...cast into the **fire**.
D&C 63:34(32-35)	I...will...consume the wicked with unquenchable **fire**.
D&C 64:24(23-25)	for after today cometh the **burning**- this is speaking
D&C 88:94	that great church...is ready to be **burned**. and he
D&C 101:25(23-25)	that of element shall **melt** with fervent heat...become
D&C 128:24	he is like a **refiner's** fire, and like fuller's soap
D&C 133:41	presence of the Lord..as the **melting** fire that burneth
D&C 133:64	the day cometh that shall **burn** as an oven, and all the
Moses 7:48	when shall I rest, and be **cleansed** from the filthiness
Moses 7:50(43,50-52)	earth might never more be covered by the **floods**.
Moses 8:26	I will **destroy** man whom I have created, from the face
JS-M 1:44(41-46)	in the **last** days...one shall be taken...the other left
JS-H 1:37(36-37)	day cometh that shall **burn** as an oven, and all the
A of F 1:10	We believe...that the earth will be **renewed** and

EARTH, CURSE OF

Gen. 3:17(17-19)	**cursed** is the ground for thy sake; in sorrow shalt
Gen. 5:29(28-30)	because of the ground which the Lord hath **cursed**.
Gen. 8:21	I will not again **curse** the ground any more for man's
Isa. 24:6(3-6)	therefore hath the **curse** devoured the earth, and they
Mal. 4:6(5,6)	lest I come and smite the earth with a **curse**.
Rom. 8:22(20-22)	whole creation **groaneth** and travaileth in pain
Rev. 22:3(1-5)	and there shall be no more **curse**: but the throne of
1 Ne. 17:35(35-38)	the Lord did **curse** the land against them, and bless
2 Ne. 1:7	if iniquity shall abound **cursed** shall be the land for
Jacob 3:3	except ye repent the land is **cursed** for your sakes
Alma 37:31	**cursed** be the land forever and ever unto those workers
Alma 45:16	thus saith the Lord God- **cursed** shall be the land, yea
Hel. 13:18(18,19)	find...no more, because of the great **curse** of the land
Hel. 13:30(27-30)	he hath **cursed** the land because of your iniquity.
D&C 27:9	the whole earth may not be smitten with a **curse**

EARTH, CURSE OF cont.

D&C 38:18(17-20)   upon which there shall be no **curse** when the Lord
D&C 61:17   I, the Lord, in the beginning **cursed** the land, even
D&C 128:18   a **curse** unless there is a welding link of some kind
Moses 4:23(23-25)   **cursed** shall be the ground for thy sake; in sorrow
Moses 5:56(55,56)   God **cursed** the earth with a sore curse, and was angry
Moses 7:8   Lord shall **curse** the land with much heat, and the

EARTH, DESTINY OF

1 Chr. 16:33   because he cometh to judge the **earth**.
Ps. 25:13   his seed shall inherit the **earth**.
Ps. 37:9   those...wait upon the Lord...shall inherit the **earth**.
Ps. 37:11   the meek shall inherit the **earth**; and shall delight
Ps. 37:22   such as be blessed of him shall inherit the **earth**; and
Eccl. 1:4   the **earth** abideth for ever.
Isa. 51:3   wilderness like **Eden**, and her desert like the garden
Isa. 65:17   new heavens and a new **earth**: and the former shall not
Ezek. 34:27(26-27)   the **earth** shall yield her increase, and they shall
Joel 2:10   the **earth** shall quake before them; the heavens shall
Amos 8:9   in that day...I will darken the **earth** in the clear day
Hab. 2:14   **earth** shall be filled with the knowledge of the glory
Zeph. 3:8(8-10)   **earth** shall be devoured with the fire of my jealousy.
Hag. 2:21(21-23)   I will shake the heavens and the **earth**
Mal. 4:6(5-6)   turn the heart...lest I come and smite the **earth** with
Matt. 5:5   the meek: for they shall inherit the **earth**.
2 Pet. 3:10(7-13)   the **earth**...works that are therein shall be burned up.
Rev. 4:6   before the throne...a **sea** of glass like unto crystal
Rev. 15:2   I saw as it were a sea of **glass** mingled with fire: and
Rev. 21:1(1-5)   a new heaven and a new **earth**: for the first heaven and
Rev. 21:21(1-27)   street of the city was pure gold...transparent **glass**.
Rev. 22:5   need no candle...for the Lord God giveth them **light**
3 Ne. 12:5   blessed are the meek, for they shall inherit the **earth**
3 Ne. 26:3(3-4)   **earth** should be wrapt together as a scroll...pass away
Morm. 9:2   **elements** shall melt with fervent heat, yea, in that
Ether 13:9   and there shall be a new heaven and a **new** earth; and
D&C 29:13   all the **earth** shall quake, and they shall come forth
D&C 29:23(22-25)   heaven and the **earth** shall be consumed and pass away
D&C 45:58(57-59)   **earth** shall be given unto them for an inheritance; and
D&C 56:18(18-20)   the fatness of the **earth** shall be theirs.
D&C 63:21   **earth** shall be transfigured, even according to the
D&C 77:1   **earth**, in its sanctified, immortal, and eternal state.
D&C 77:6(6-7)   **earth** during the seven thousand years of its
D&C 84:101   **earth**...is clothed with the glory of her God; for he
D&C 88:17(17-26)   poor and the meek of the **earth** shall inherit it.
D&C 88:19(17-20)   it shall be crowned with **glory**, even...presence of God
D&C 88:25(17-26)   the **earth** abideth the law of a celestial kingdom, for
D&C 88:26   shall be **sanctified**...quickened again, and shall abide
D&C 101:25(24-25)   all things shall become new...upon all the **earth**.
D&C 101:33(32,33)   of the **earth**...the purpose and the end thereof
D&C 103:7(7,8)   until...the **earth** is given unto the saints, to possess
D&C 121:32(26-32)   **world**...reserved unto the finishing and the end
D&C 128:18   **earth** will be smitten...unless there is a welding link

EARTH, DESTINY OF cont.

D&C 130:7(6-9)	a globe like a sea of **glass** and fire, where all things
D&C 130:9(5-9)	**earth**...made like unto crystal...Urim and Thummim to
D&C 133:24(23-25)	**earth** shall be like as it was...before it was divided.
Moses 7:64	for the space of a thousand years the **earth** shall rest

EARTH, DIVIDING OF

Gen. 1:9	let the **waters**...be gathered together unto one place
Gen. 10:25	Peleg...in his days was the earth **divided**; and his
Gen. 11:16(10-26)	and Eber lived four and thirty years, and begat **Peleg**
1 Chr. 1:19	because in his days the earth was **divided**: and his
Isa. 40:15	he taketh up the **isles** as a very little thing.
Ether 13:2	waters had receded ...it became a choice **land** above
D&C 133:24(23-24)	earth shall be like as it was...before it was **divided**.
Moses 1:29(27-29)	many lands; and each land was called **earth**, and there
Moses 2:9	let the **waters**...be gathered together unto one place

EARTH, PURPOSE OF

Gen. 1:28(26-31)	replenish the **earth**, and subdue it: and have dominion
Gen. 2:15(15-17)	put him into the **garden** of Eden to dress it and to
Gen. 3:5	ye shall be as Gods, **knowing** good and evil.
Gen. 3:22(22-24)	the man is become as one of us, to **know** good and evil
Ps. 78:69	like the earth which he hath established for **ever**.
Isa. 45:18(17-18)	created it not in vain, he formed it to be **inhabited**
John 16:33(27-33)	in the **world**...have tribulation: but...I have overcome
John 17:11(6-21)	I am no more in the world, but these are in the **world**
Eph. 3:11(7-12)	according to the eternal **purpose** which he purposed in
2 Pet. 1:4(2-4)	partakers of the **divine** nature, having escaped the
2 Ne. 2:12(11-13)	would have been no **purpose** in the end of its creation.
2 Ne. 2:15(14-30)	to bring about his eternal **purposes** in the end of man
Alma 12:24(23-37)	a **probationary** state; a time to prepare to meet God
Alma 42:4	time granted unto man to repent...a **probationary** time
Alma 42:26	**purposes**...prepared from the foundation of the world.
D&C 2:3(1-3)	if...not so, the whole **earth** would be utterly wasted
D&C 29:43(39-45)	thus did I..appoint unto man the days of his **probation**
D&C 49:16(16-17)	that the **earth** might answer the end of its creation
D&C 59:18(16-21)	all things...made for the **benefit** and the use of man
D&C 88:18(17-18)	it must needs be **sanctified** from all unrighteousness
D&C 88:20(19-20)	bodies who are of the **celestial** kingdom may possess
D&C 88:26(25-26)	it shall die, it shall be **quickened** again, and shall
D&C 101:33(32-34)	things of the earth...the **purpose** and the end
D&C 104:17	the **earth** is full, and there is enough and to spare
D&C 121:32(26-32)	that which was **ordained**...before this world was, that
D&C 130:9(8,9)	this **earth**...will be a Urim and Thummim to the
Moses 1:31(27-35)	for mine own **purpose** have I made these things. here
Moses 1:39(36-39)	to bring to pass the immortality and eternal **life** of
Moses 7:48(48-67)	**earth**...voice from...wo, wo is me, the mother of men
Moses 7:54	when the Son of Man cometh...shall the earth **rest**? I
Moses 7:64	for the space of a thousand years the earth shall **rest**
Abr. 2:7	the **earth** is my footstool; I stretch my hand over the

EARTH, PURPOSE OF cont.

Abr. 3:24(22-25) we will make an earth whereon these may **dwell**
Abr. 3:25(24-26) **prove** them...to see if they will do all things

EARTH, RENEWAL OF

Ps. 67:6(4-7) then shall the earth yield her **increase**; and God, even
Ps. 107:35(35-37) he turneth the **wilderness** into a standing water, and
Isa. 11:9(6-9) **earth** shall be full of the knowledge of the Lord, as
Isa. 13:13 the earth shall **remove** out of her place, in the wrath
Isa. 14:7(5-8) the whole earth is at **rest**, and is quiet: they break
Isa. 24:19(19,20) clean dissolved, the earth is **moved** exceedingly.
Isa. 32:15(15-20) wilderness be a **fruitful** field, and the fruitful
Isa. 35:1(1-10) desert shall rejoice, and **blossom** as the rose.
Isa. 40:4 every **mountain** and hill shall be made low: and the
Isa. 41:18(18-19) I will make the **wilderness** a pool of water, and the
Isa. 43:19(19,20) make a way in the **wilderness**, and rivers in the desert
Isa. 51:3 wilderness like **Eden**, and her desert like the garden
Isa. 54:10 for the **mountains** shall depart, and the hills be
Isa. 55:13(12,13) instead of the thorn shall come up the **fir** tree, and
Isa. 65:17(17-25) behold, I create new heavens and a **new** earth: and the
Isa. 66:22(22-24) for as the **new** heavens and the new earth, which I will
Joel 3:18(17-21) **mountains** shall drop down new wine, and the hills
2 Pet. 3:13(7-13) we...look for new heavens and a **new** earth, wherein
Rev. 21:1(1-27) and I saw a new heaven and a new **earth**: for the first
1 Ne. 21:13 **break** forth into singing, O mountains; for they shall
2 Ne. 8:3 make her wilderness like **Eden**, and her desert like the
2 Ne. 21:10(6-10) his **rest** shall be glorious.
2 Ne. 21:16 there shall be a **highway** for the remnant of his people
2 Ne. 23:13 the earth shall **remove** out of her place, in the wrath
2 Ne. 24:7(3-8) the whole earth is at **rest**, and is quiet; they break
2 Ne. 30:12(8-15) then shall the wolf **dwell** with the lamb; and the
3 Ne. 22:10(10-12) the **mountains** shall depart and the hills be removed
D&C 29:23(22-25) there shall be a new heaven and a **new** earth.
D&C 49:23(23-25) **mountains** to be made low, and for the rough places to
D&C 101:25(23-25) all things shall become **new**, that my knowledge and
D&C 117:7 solitary places to bud and to **blossom**, and to bring
D&C 133:22(22-29) shall break down the **mountains**, and the valleys shall
A of F 1:10 earth will be **renewed** and receive its paradisiacal

EDEN

Gen. 2:8 the Lord God planted a garden eastward in **Eden**; and
Gen. 2:10 a river went out of **Eden** to water the garden; and from
Gen. 2:15 put him into the garden of **Eden** to dress it and to
Gen. 3:23 the Lord God sent him forth from the garden of **Eden**
Gen. 4:16 Cain...dwelt in the land of Nod, on the east of **Eden**.
Isa. 51:3 wilderness like **Eden**, and her desert like the garden
Joel 2:3 the land is as the garden of **Eden** before them, and
2 Ne. 2:19 they were driven out of the garden of **Eden**, to till
2 Ne. 8:3 Lord shall comfort Zion..make her wilderness like **Eden**
Alma 12:21(20-24) flaming sword on the east of the garden of **Eden**, lest

EDEN cont.

Alma 42:2	God sent...parents forth from the garden of **Eden**, to
D&C 29:41	caused that he...be cast out from the garden of **Eden**
D&C 117:8(8-9)	**Adam-ondi-Ahman**...or the land where Adam dwelt, that
Moses 3:8	Lord God, planted a garden eastward in **Eden**, and there
Moses 3:10	Lord God, caused a river to go out of **Eden** to water
Moses 3:15	God, took the man, and put him into the garden of **Eden**
Moses 4:29	send him forth from the garden of **Eden**, to till the
Moses 4:31	I placed at the east of the garden of **Eden**, cherubim
Moses 5:4	voice of the Lord...toward the garden of **Eden**
Abr. 5:8	the Gods planted a garden, eastward in **Eden**, and there
Abr. 5:11	Gods took the man and put him in the garden of **Eden**

EDIFICATION

Deut. 4:36	to hear his voice, that he might **instruct** thee: and
Ps. 18:28	the Lord my God will **enlighten** my darkness.
Ps. 19:8	commandment of the Lord is pure, **enlightening** the eyes
Prov. 1:3(1-3)	to receive the **instruction** of wisdom, justice, and
Prov. 12:1	whoso loveth **instruction** loveth knowledge: but he that
Prov. 19:20	hear counsel, and receive **instruction**, that thou
Acts 9:31	the churches...were **edified**; and walking in the fear
Rom. 14:19	things wherewith one may **edify** another.
Rom. 15:2(1,2)	please his neighbour for his good to **edification**.
1 Cor. 8:1	knowledge puffeth up, but charity **edifieth**.
1 Cor. 10:23	lawful for me, but all things **edify** not.
1 Cor. 14:3(3,4)	he that prophesieth speaketh unto men to **edification**
1 Cor. 14:12	seek that ye may excel to the **edifying** of the church.
2 Cor. 10:8	authority...Lord hath given us for **edification**, and
2 Cor. 12:19	do all things, dearly beloved, for your **edifying**.
Eph. 4:12(11-16,29)	for the **edifying** of the body of Christ
1 Thes. 5:11	**edify** one another, even as also ye do.
1 Tim. 1:4	which minister questions, rather than godly **edifying**
Alma 32:28	yea, it beginneth to **enlighten** my understanding, yea
D&C 43:8(8,9)	ye shall instruct and **edify** each other, that ye may
D&C 50:22(21-22)	understand one another, and both are **edified** and
D&C 50:23	that which doth not **edify** is not of God, and is
D&C 52:16	whose language is meek and **edifieth**, the same is of
D&C 84:106	that he may be **edified** in all meekness, that he may
D&C 84:110(109-110)	that all may be **edified** together, that the system may
D&C 88:122	that all may be **edified** of all, and that every man may
D&C 88:137(136,137)	a tabernacle of the Holy Spirit to your **edification**.
D&C 107:85	to teach them their duty, **edifying** one another, as it
D&C 136:24(23-24)	let your words tend to **edifying** one another.

EDUCATION

Ps. 25:8(8-9)	the Lord...will...**teach** sinners in the way.
Prov. 1:5(5-6)	a wise man will hear, and will increase **learning**; and
Prov. 1:8(7-9)	hear the **instruction** of thy father, and forsake not
Prov. 4:13(5-13)	take fast hold of **instruction**; let her not go: keep
Prov. 22:6	**train** up a child in the way he should go: and when he

EDUCATION cont.

Dan. 1:17(3-6,17)	God gave them knowledge and skill in all **learning** and
Matt. 7:8(7-8)	he that **seeketh** findeth; and to him that knocketh it
John 5:39	**search** the scriptures; for in them ye think ye have
John 8:32(31-32)	know the **truth**, and the truth shall make you free.
Acts 7:22(20-22)	Moses was **learned** in all the wisdom of the Egyptians
Acts 18:25(24-25)	this man was **instructed** in the way of the Lord; and
1 Cor. 2:11(9-14)	for what man **knoweth** the things of a man, save the
1 Cor. 8:2	he knoweth nothing yet as he ought to **know**.
1 Cor. 14:20	in malice be ye children, but in **understanding** be men.
Eph. 1:18(17-19)	the eyes of your understanding being **enlightened**; that
Col. 1:10(9-10,27-28)	increasing in the **knowledge** of God
Col. 2:8	spoil you through philosophy and vain **deceit**, after
2 Tim. 3:16(14-17)	all scripture...for **instruction** in righteousness
1 Ne. 1:1(1-2)	I was **taught** somewhat in all the learning of my father
2 Ne. 9:28(28-29,42)	when they are **learned** they think they are wise, and
2 Ne. 28:30	line upon line, **precept** upon precept, here a little
Mosiah 1:2(1-2)	they should be **taught** in all the language of his
Mosiah 1:5(3-6)	that we might read and **understand** of his mysteries
Mosiah 4:12(11-12)	ye shall grow in the **knowledge** of the glory of him
Alma 10:15(12-15)	lawyers were **learned** in all the arts and cunning of
Alma 17:2(1-2)	they had **searched** the scriptures diligently, that they
Alma 37:8(1-3,8)	brought them to the **knowledge** of their God unto the
Alma 37:35(33-35)	**learn** wisdom in thy youth; yea, learn in thy youth to
Alma 38:9(5-9)	that ye may **learn** of me that there is no other way or
Alma 56:47(45-48)	they had been **taught** by their mothers, that if they
Moro. 10:10(9-10)	**teach** the word of knowledge by the same spirit
D&C 6:7	seek not for riches but for **wisdom**, and behold, the
D&C 11:7	seek not for riches but for **wisdom**; and, behold, the
D&C 11:22(21,22)	**study** my word which shall come forth among the
D&C 19:23	**learn** of me, and listen to my words; walk in the
D&C 42:12(12-15)	teachers...shall **teach** the principles of my gospel
D&C 46:18	to another is given the word of **knowledge**, that all
D&C 55:4(4-5)	selecting and writing books for **schools** in this church
D&C 88:78(70-80)	that you may be **instructed** more perfectly in theory
D&C 88:118(118-119)	seek **learning**, even by study and also by faith.
D&C 88:127(127-141)	**school** of the prophets, established for their
D&C 90:15	**study** and learn, and become acquainted with all good
D&C 93:36	the glory of God is **intelligence**, or...light and truth
D&C 93:53	obtain a **knowledge** of history, and of countries, and
D&C 107:99(99-100)	let every man **learn** his duty, and to act in the office
D&C 130:19(18-19)	if a person gains more **knowledge** and intelligence in
D&C 131:6	it is impossible for a man to be saved in **ignorance**.
D&C 136:32(32-33)	let him that is ignorant **learn** wisdom by humbling
Moses 6:6(1-6)	by them their children were **taught** to read and write
Moses 6:23(21-23)	faith was **taught** unto the children of men.
Moses 6:58(55-62)	a commandment, to **teach** these things freely unto your
Abr. 1:2(1-2)	desiring also to be one who possessed great **knowledge**

ELDERS

Ex. 3:16	go, and gather the **elders** of Israel together, and say
Ex. 24:9(9,10)	then went up Moses...and seventy of the **elders** of
Num. 11:25(24,25)	took...spirit ...gave it unto the seventy **elders**: and
Deut. 31:9	Moses wrote this law...unto all the **elders** of Israel.
2 Sam. 17:4	and all the **elders** of Israel.
Ezek. 8:1	the **elders** of Judah sat before me, that the hand of
Ezek. 20:1	certain of the **elders** of Israel came to inquire of the
Acts 11:30(29-30)	sent it to the **elders** by the hands of Barnabas and
Acts 14:23	when they had ordained them **elders** in every church
Acts 15:6(4-6,23)	apostles and **elders** came together for to consider of
1 Tim. 5:17(17,19)	**elders** that rule well be counted worthy of double
Titus 1:5	ordain **elders** in every city, as I had appointed thee
James 5:14	sick among you? let him call for the **elders** of the
1 Pet. 5:1(1-4)	the **elders** which are among you I exhort, who am also
Alma 4:7(7,16)	Alma had consecrated to be...**elders** over the church
Alma 6:1	he ordained priests and **elders**, by laying on his hands
Moro. 3:1	disciples, who were called the **elders** of the church
Moro. 4:1	manner of their **elders** and priests administering the
Moro. 6:7(1,7)	condemn them before the **elders**, and if they repented
D&C 20:2(2-5)	Joseph Smith, Jun....the first **elder** of this church
D&C 20:38(38-45)	an apostle is an **elder**...his calling to baptize
D&C 20:60	every **elder**...is to be ordained according to the gifts
D&C 42:12(12-14)	and again, the **elders**, priests and teachers of this
D&C 105:11(9-13)	until mine **elders** are endowed with power from on high.
D&C 107:7	the office of an **elder** comes under the priesthood of
D&C 107:12(7,11-12)	the high priest and **elder** are to administer in
D&C 107:89(89-90)	the duty of the president over the office of **elders**
D&C 124:137	which priesthood...preside over the quorum of **elders**
JFS-V 1:57	faithful **elders**...preaching...in...world of the spirit

ELECTION

Gen. 12:3(1-3)	in thee shall all families of the earth be **blessed**.
Ex. 19:6(5-6)	ye shall be unto me a **kingdom** of priests, and an holy
Isa. 42:1(1-4)	mine **elect**, in whom my soul delighteth; I have put my
Isa. 45:4	Israel mine **elect**, I have even called thee by thy name
Isa. 49:6	give thee for a **light** to the Gentiles...my salvation
Isa. 65:9(9,22)	mine **elect** shall inherit it, and my servants shall
Matt. 24:31(22,30-31)	and they shall gather together his **elect** from the four
John 15:16	ye have not chosen me, but I have **chosen** you, and
Rom. 8:17(15-18)	heirs of God, and **joint-heirs** with Christ; if so be
Rom. 9:4(4-33)	Israelites; to whom pertaineth the **adoption**, and the
Rom. 11:5(1-32)	a remnant according to the **election** of grace.
Gal. 4:5(1-7)	that we might receive the **adoption** of sons.
Eph. 1:4(3-5)	**chosen** us in him before the foundation of the world
Col. 3:12(12,13)	put on therefore, as the **elect** of God, holy and
1 Thes. 1:4(3-6)	knowing, brethren beloved, your **election** of God.
2 Thes. 2:13	God hath from the beginning **chosen** you to salvation
Titus 1:1	according to the faith of God's **elect**, and the
1 Pet. 1:2	**elect** according to the foreknowledge of God the father
1 Pet. 2:9(9-10)	but ye are a **chosen** generation, a royal priesthood
2 Pet. 1:10(1-11,19)	give diligence to make your calling and **election** sure

ELECTION cont.

Enos 1:27	he will say unto me...there is a **place** prepared for
Mosiah 5:15	Lord...may **seal** you his, that you may be brought to
Mosiah 26:20(14-20)	thou shalt have **eternal** life; and thou shalt serve me
Alma 13:3(1-9)	**called** and prepared from the foundation of the world
3 Ne. 28:3	ye shall come unto me in my **kingdom**; and with me ye
D&C 29:7	mine **elect** hear my voice and harden not their hearts
D&C 35:20(20,21)	to the salvation of mine own **elect**
D&C 59:23	peace in this world and **eternal** life in the world to
D&C 84:34(33-41)	become...the church and kingdom, and the **elect** of God.
D&C 84:99(98-102)	redeemed his people, Israel, according to the **election**
D&C 95:8(5-8)	build a house...to endow those...I have **chosen** with
D&C 131:5	knowing that he is **sealed** up unto eternal life, by
D&C 132:19(18,19)	to their **exaltation** and glory in all things, as hath
D&C 132:49	I seal upon you your **exaltation**, and prepare a throne
D&C 132:57	I was with Abraham...even unto his **exaltation** and
Abr. 2:11(9-12)	in thee...and in thy **seed**...shall all...be blessed
Abr. 3:23(22-23)	thou wast **chosen** before thou wast born.

ENEMIES

Ex. 23:4(4-5)	meet thine **enemy's** ox or his ass going astray, thou
Ps. 5:8	in thy righteousness because of mine **enemies**; make thy
Ps. 110:1	until I make thine **enemies** thy footstool.
Prov. 24:17(17-18)	rejoice not when thine **enemy** falleth, and let not
Prov. 25:21(21-22)	if thine **enemy** be hungry, give him bread to eat; and
Micah 7:6(5-7)	a man's **enemies** are the men of his own house.
Matt. 5:44	love your **enemies**, bless them that curse you, do good
Acts 13:10	thou **enemy** of all righteousness, wilt thou not cease
Rom. 12:14(14,20)	bless them which **persecute** you: bless, and curse not.
Rom. 12:20	if thine **enemy** hunger, feed him; if he thirst, give
1 Cor. 15:26(23-26)	the last **enemy** that shall be destroyed is death.
1 Thes. 5:15(14-15)	none render evil for evil unto any **man**; but ever
2 Thes. 3:15(14-15)	count him not as an **enemy**, but admonish him as a
James 4:4	a friend of the world is the **enemy** of God.
2 Ne. 4:28(26-31)	give place no more for the **enemy** of my soul.
Mosiah 2:37(36-37)	becometh an **enemy** to all righteousness; therefore
Mosiah 3:19	for the natural man is an **enemy** to God, and has been
Mosiah 4:14	the devil...he being an **enemy** to all righteousness.
Alma 58:10	deliver us out of the hands of our **enemies**, yea, and
3 Ne. 12:44(43-44)	I say unto you, love your **enemies**, bless them that
D&C 38:31	escape the power of the **enemy**, and be gathered unto
D&C 65:6	that thine **enemies** may be subdued; for thine is the
D&C 71:7	confound your **enemies**; call upon them to meet you both
D&C 98:14	be not afraid of your **enemies**, for I have decreed in
D&C 98:39(39-45)	after thine **enemy** has come upon thee the first time
D&C 121:43(41-44)	increase of love...lest he esteem thee to be his **enemy**

ENSIGN

Ps. 74:4	they set up their **ensigns** for signs.
Isa. 5:26	lift up an **ensign** to the nations from far, and will
Isa. 11:10(10-12)	shall stand for an **ensign** of the people; to it shall
Isa. 11:12	and he shall set up an **ensign** for the nations, and
Isa. 13:2	lift ye up a **banner** upon the high mountain, exalt the
Isa. 18:3	lifteth up an **ensign** on the mountains; and when he
Isa. 49:22	I will... set up my **standard** to the people: and they
Isa. 62:10	lift up a **standard** for the people.
Isa. 66:19(18-19)	and I will set a **sign** among them, and I will send
Jer. 4:6(6,21)	set up the **standard** toward Zion: retire, stay not: for
Jer. 51:27	set ye up a **standard** in the land, blow the trumpet
Zech. 9:16(14-16)	lifted up as an **ensign** upon his land.
1 Ne. 21:22(22-23)	I will... set up my **standard** to the people; and they
2 Ne. 6:6	set up my **standard** to the people; and they shall bring
2 Ne. 15:26	he will lift up an **ensign** to the nations from far, and
2 Ne. 21:12(10-12)	shall set up an **ensign** for the nations, and shall
2 Ne. 29:2(1-3)	my words shall hiss forth...for a **standard** unto my
D&C 45:9	a **standard** for my people, and for the Gentiles to seek
D&C 64:42(41-43)	she shall be an **ensign** unto the people, and there
D&C 98:34(33-36)	lift a **standard** of peace unto that people, nation, or
D&C 105:39(38-40)	and lift up an **ensign** of peace, and make a
D&C 113:6(5,6)	for an **ensign**, and for the gathering of my people in
D&C 115:5(4-6)	thy light may be a **standard** for the nations

ENVY

Gen. 30:1	Rachel **envied** her sister; and said unto Jacob, give
Gen. 37:11	and his brethren **envied** him; but his father observed
Ps. 73:3	I was **envious** at the foolish, when I saw the
Ps. 106:16(13-16)	they **envied** Moses also in the camp, and Aaron the
Prov. 14:30	but **envy** the rottenness of the bones.
Prov. 24:1	be not thou **envious** against evil men, neither desire
Isa. 11:13	Ephraim shall not **envy** Judah, and Judah shall not vex
Matt. 27:18(17-18)	for he knew that for **envy** they had delivered him.
Mark 15:10(9-10)	the chief priests had delivered him for **envy**.
Acts 7:9(8-9)	the patriarchs, moved with **envy**, sold Joseph into
Acts 13:45	Jews saw the multitudes, they were filled with **envy**
Rom. 13:13	walk honestly...not in strife and **envying**.
1 Cor. 3:3	whereas there is among you **envying**, and strife, and
1 Cor. 13:4	charity **envieth** not; charity vaunteth not itself, is
Gal. 5:21(19-21)	**envyings**, murders, drunkenness, revellings, and such
1 Tim. 6:4(3-5)	he is proud...whereof cometh **envy**, strife, railings
James 3:16	where **envying** and strife is, there is confusion and
James 4:5	spirit that dwelleth in us lusteth to **envy**
2 Ne. 21:13	Ephraim shall not **envy** Judah, and Judah shall not vex
2 Ne. 26:21	many churches built up which cause **envyings**, and
2 Ne. 26:32	Lord God hath commanded...should not **envy**; that they
Alma 1:32	babblings, and in **envyings** and strife; wearing costly
Alma 4:9	yea, there were **envyings**, and strife, and malice, and
Alma 5:29	there one among you who is not stripped of **envy**? I say
Alma 16:18	did preach against...**envyings**, and strifes, and malice
Hel. 13:22	great swelling, **envyings**, strifes, malice, persecution

ENVY cont.

3 Ne. 21:19	all lyings, and deceivings, and **envyings**, and strifes
3 Ne. 30:2	repent of...your **envyings**, and your strifes, and from
4 Ne. 1:16(15-18)	there were no **envyings**, nor strifes, nor tumults, nor
Morm. 8:28	even to the **envying** of them who belong to their
Morm. 8:36	a few only who do not lift themselves...unto **envying**
Moro. 7:45	and charity...**envieth** not, and is not puffed up
D&C 101:6	jarrings, and contentions, and **envyings**, and strifes
D&C 127:2	the **envy** and wrath of man have been my common lot all

ETERNAL LIFE

Ps. 49:15	but God...shall **receive** me. Selah.
Ps. 73:24(24-26)	and afterward receive me to **glory**.
Isa. 33:14(14-16)	who among us shall dwell with **everlasting** burnings
Isa. 60:20(18-21)	the Lord shall be thine **everlasting** light, and the day
Dan. 12:2	many...that sleep...shall awake...to **everlasting** life
Matt. 25:46	but the righteous into life **eternal**.
John 3:36(16,36)	he that believeth on the son hath **everlasting** life
John 6:40	believeth on him, may have **everlasting** life: and I
John 6:47	he that believeth on me hath **everlasting** life.
John 14:2(1-6)	in my Father's house are many **mansions**: if it were not
John 17:3(2-3)	this is **life** eternal, that they might know thee the
Rom. 5:21	through righteousness unto **eternal** life by Jesus
Rom. 6:23(21-23)	gift of God is **eternal** life through Jesus Christ our
Rom. 8:17(16-18)	heirs of God, and **joint-heirs** with Christ; if so be
2 Cor. 4:17(17-18)	a far more exceeding and **eternal** weight of glory
Gal. 4:7(1-7)	and if a son, then an **heir** of God through Christ.
1 Tim. 6:12	lay hold on **eternal** life, whereunto thou art also
1 Jn. 3:2(2-3)	we shall be **like** him; for we shall see him as he is.
1 Jn. 5:11(11-20)	given to us **eternal** life, and this life is in his Son.
Rev. 21:7(1-7)	he that overcometh shall inherit **all** things; and I
Rev. 22:5(3-5)	and they shall **reign** for ever and ever.
2 Ne. 9:18	their joy shall be full **forever**.
2 Ne. 9:39	to be spiritually--minded is life **eternal**.
2 Ne. 33:4	believe in him...endure to the end...is life **eternal**.
Alma 41:4	raised to **endless** happiness to inherit the kingdom of
Moro. 7:41	life **eternal**, and this because of your faith in him
D&C 14:7	**eternal** life...is the greatest of all the gifts of God
D&C 75:5(1-5)	crowned with honor..glory..immortality..**eternal** life.
D&C 76:62(50-70)	these shall dwell in the **presence** of God and his
D&C 93:33(33-34)	spirit...element...connected, receive a **fulness** of joy
D&C 130:2(1-11)	same sociality...will be coupled with **eternal** glory
D&C 132:24(18-25)	this is **eternal** lives- to know the only wise and true
D&C 132:55(51-56)	crowns of **eternal** lives in the eternal worlds.
Moses 1:39(38-39)	bring to pass the immortality and **eternal** life of man
JFS-V 1:51(49-52)	crowned with immortality and **eternal** life

ETERNITY

Ex. 40:15(13-15)	an **everlasting** priesthood throughout their generation
Deut. 33:27(26-29)	the **eternal** God is thy refuge, and underneath are the
Ps. 90:2(1-4)	even from **everlasting** to everlasting, thou art God.
Ps. 102:27(24-28)	thou art the same, and thy years shall have no **end**.
Prov. 8:23(1-36)	I was set up from **everlasting**, from the beginning, or
Isa. 26:4(1-4)	in the Lord Jehovah is **everlasting** strength
Dan. 7:27(15-27)	an **everlasting** kingdom, and all dominions shall serve
Matt. 19:16(16-21)	that I may have **eternal** life
Mark 3:29(28,29)	but is in danger of **eternal** damnation
2 Cor. 4:18	but the things which are not seen are **eternal**.
2 Thes. 1:9(7-9)	**everlasting** destruction from the presence of the Lord
2 Ne. 1:13(13-25)	carried away captive down to the **eternal** gulf of
2 Ne. 10:25(24,25)	be received into the **eternal** kingdom of God, that ye
Jacob 7:18	and he spake of hell, and of **eternity**, and of eternal
Mosiah 3:5	who was, and is from all **eternity** to all eternity
Alma 3:26	to reap **eternal** happiness or eternal misery, according
Alma 7:20	therefore, his course is one **eternal** round.
Alma 13:7(6-9)	this high priesthood...prepared from **eternity** to all
Alma 34:10(10-34)	but it must be an infinite and **eternal** sacrifice.
Alma 37:44	Christ..will point..a straight course to **eternal** bliss
Alma 42:16	plan of happiness, which was as **eternal** also as the
Moro. 7:47	charity...love of Christ, and it endureth **forever**; and
Moro. 8:18	unchangeable from all **eternity** to all eternity.
D&C 20:17	there is a God in heaven, who is infinite and **eternal**
D&C 38:39	ye shall have the riches of **eternity**; and it must need
D&C 39:1	the voice of him who is from all **eternity** to all
D&C 43:34	let the solemnities of **eternity** rest upon your minds.
D&C 67:2	the riches of **eternity** are mine to give.
D&C 68:31	they also seek not earnestly the riches of **eternity**
D&C 76:8(4-10)	even the wonders of **eternity** shall they know, and
D&C 78:18	the riches of **eternity** are yours.
D&C 93:33	the elements are **eternal**, and spirit and element
D&C 132:7(7,49)	anointed, both as well for time and for all **eternity**
D&C 132:46	sins you remit on earth shall be remitted **eternally**
Moses 6:67	beginning of days or end of years, from all **eternity**
Moses 7:53(29-53)	heaven, which is broad as **eternity**; whoso cometh in
Abr. 2:16	**eternity** was our covering and our rock and our

EVIL

Gen. 3:5(1-24)	and ye shall be as Gods, knowing good and **evil**.
Gen. 3:22	man is become as one of us, to know good and **evil**: and
Gen. 6:5	imagination...thoughts of his heart was only **evil**
Gen. 8:21	imagination...of man's heart is **evil** from his youth
Gen. 50:20	but as for you, ye thought **evil** against me; but God
Deut. 4:25(25-31)	when thou...shall do **evil** in the sight of the Lord thy
Deut. 9:18	ye sinned, in doing **wickedly** in the sight of the Lord
Deut. 30:15(15-19)	I have set...life and good, and death and **evil**
2 Kgs. 17:17(17,18)	sold themselves to do **evil** in the sight of the Lord
Ezra 9:13(13-15)	after all that is come upon us for our **evil** deeds, and
Job 2:10(9-10)	shall we receive good...and...not receive **evil**? in all
Ps. 5:4	neither shall **evil** dwell with thee.

EVIL cont.

Ps. 23:4	I will fear no evil: for thou art with me; thy rod and
Ps. 97:10	ye that love the Lord, hate evil: he preserveth the
Prov. 17:13	evil shall not depart from his house.
Isa. 1:16(13-25)	put away the evil of your doings from before mine eyes
Isa. 5:20(20-25)	woe unto them that call evil good, and good evil; that
Isa. 7:16(14-16)	child shall know to refuse the evil, and choose the
Jer. 6:19(18-30)	bring evil upon this people...fruit of their thoughts
Amos 5:14	seek good, and not evil, that ye may live: and so the
Matt. 5:39(38-42)	that ye resist not evil: but whosoever shall smite the
Matt. 6:13(9-13)	deliver us from evil: for thine is the kingdom, and
Matt. 12:35(34-37)	an evil man...bringeth forth evil things.
John 3:20(19-20)	every one that doeth evil hateth the light, neither
John 7:7	the world...the works thereof are evil.
John 17:15(3-16)	but that thou shouldest keep them from the evil.
Rom. 12:9	abhor that which is evil; cleave to that which is good
Rom. 12:17	recompense to no man evil for evil. Provide things
1 Thes. 5:22(15-23)	abstain from all appearance of evil.
James 1:13(12-15)	God cannot be tempted with evil, neither tempteth he
1 Pet. 3:12(8-13)	face of the Lord is against them that do evil.
1 Ne. 4:13	Lord slayeth the wicked to bring forth his righteous
2 Ne. 2:29	the will of the flesh and the evil which is therein
1:25	and that which is evil cometh from the devil.
Alma 1:33(31-33)	durst not commit any wickedness if it were known
Alma 4:3	judgments of God...because of their wickedness and the
Alma 5:40(40-42)	whatsoever is evil cometh from the devil.
Alma 12:31	act according to their wills...to do evil or to do
Alma 40:13(11-14)	spirits...who are evil...have no part nor portion of
Alma 41:10(10-11)	wickedness never was happiness.
Hel. 12:4	how vain, and how evil...are the children of men; yea
Moro. 7:12(12-19)	evil cometh of the devil; for the devil is an enemy
D&C 10:14(4-14)	not suffer that Satan shall accomplish his evil design
D&C 10:21	love darkness rather than light...their deeds are evil
D&C 20:54	no iniquity in the church...backbiting...evil speaking
D&C 64:8(8-10)	for this evil they were afflicted and sorely chastened
D&C 64:16(16-17)	they sought evil in their hearts, and I, the Lord, wit
D&C 93:37(36-37)	light and truth forsake that evil one.
D&C 98:11	forsake all evil and cleave unto all good, that ye
D&C 136:21	keep yourselves from evil to take the name of the Lord

EXALTATION

Ps. 16:11(10,11)	in thy presence is fulness of joy; at thy right hand
Matt. 19:29(28,29)	and shall inherit everlasting life.
Matt. 25:34(34,35)	inherit the kingdom prepared for you from the
Luke 13:28	Abraham...in the kingdom of God, and you yourselves
John 6:47(47-51)	he that believeth on me hath everlasting life.
Rom. 8:17(13-17)	heirs of God, and joint-heirs with Christ; if so be
Philip. 2:9(5-15)	God also hath highly exalted him, and given him a name
2 Tim. 4:8(7,8)	laid up for me a crown of righteousness, which the Lord
James 1:12	when he is tried, he shall receive the crown of life
1 Pet. 5:4(1-6)	ye shall receive a crown of glory that fadeth not away
Rev. 3:21(19-22)	will I grant to sit with me in my throne, even as I

EXALTATION cont.

Rev. 21:7	he that overcometh shall **inherit** all things; and I
2 Ne. 9:18(18-22)	they shall inherit the **kingdom** of God, which was
Alma 14:11	receiveth them up unto himself, in **glory**; and he doth
Alma 36:28	to dwell with him in **glory**; yea, and I will praise
Alma 41:4(3-7)	endless happiness to **inherit** the kingdom of God, or
3 Ne. 11:33	they who shall **inherit** the kingdom of God.
D&C 14:7(7,8)	you shall have **eternal** life, which gift is the
D&C 20:14(13-16)	shall receive a **crown** of eternal life
D&C 25:15	a **crown** of righteousness thou shalt receive. and
D&C 29:13(10-13)	dead which died in me, to receive a **crown** of
D&C 52:43(42-44)	will **crown** the faithful with joy and with rejoicing.
D&C 58:4(1-4)	after much tribulation...**crowned** with much glory; the
D&C 59:2	they shall receive a **crown** in the mansions of my
D&C 75:5(1-5)	**crowned** with honor, and glory, and immortality, and
D&C 76:58(50-70)	as it is written, they are **Gods**, even the sons of
D&C 78:15(15-22)	come up unto the **crown** prepared for you, and be made
D&C 81:6(4-6)	thou shalt have a **crown** of immortality, and eternal
D&C 84:38(35-40)	receiveth my Father's **kingdom**; therefore all that my
D&C 88:19(17-20)	it shall be **crowned** with glory, even with the presence
D&C 88:107	receive their **inheritance** and be made equal with him.
D&C 101:65(65,66)	and be **crowned** with celestial glory, when I shall come
D&C 109:76	**crowns** of glory upon our heads, and reap eternal joy
D&C 132:20(19-24)	then shall they be **Gods**, because they have no end; the
D&C 132:37(29,37)	they have entered into their **exaltation**, according to
D&C 133:32(30-35)	fall down and be **crowned** with glory, even in Zion, by
D&C 133:56(55-56)	saints shall...stand on the **right** hand of the Lamb
Moses 7:56	saints arose, and were **crowned** at the right hand of
JS-V 1:7(1-10)	who would have received it...shall be **heirs** of the

EXAMPLE

Gen. 39:8(1-23)	but he **refused**, and said unto his master's wife
Josh. 24:15(14-28)	but as for me and my house, we will **serve** the Lord.
Ruth 1:14(1-18)	kissed her mother in law; but Ruth **clave** unto her.
Prov. 4:18	but the path of the just is as the shining **light**, that
Matt. 1:19(18-19)	Joseph...not willing to make her a publick **example**
Matt. 5:16(13-16)	let your **light** so shine before men, that they may see
Mark 10:14(13-16)	suffer the little **children** to come unto me, and forbid
John 13:15	I have given you an **example**...do as I have done to you
John 14:6	Jesus saith unto him, I am the **way**, the truth, and the
Acts 13:47	I have set thee to be a **light** of the Gentiles, that
1 Cor. 10:11(1-11)	all these things happened unto them for **ensamples**: and
Philip. 3:17(17-19)	them which walk so as ye have us for an **ensample**.
1 Thes. 1:7(6-8)	ye were **ensamples** to all that believe in Macedonia and
2 Thes. 3:9(6-15)	we...make ourselves an **ensample** unto you to follow us.
1 Tim. 1:16	in me...Jesus Christ might shew forth...a **pattern** to
1 Tim. 4:12(12-16)	be thou an **example** of the believers, in word, in
James 5:10	take...the prophets...for an **example** of suffering
1 Pet. 2:21(21-22)	Christ...leaving us an **example**, that ye should follow
1 Pet. 5:3(1-4)	neither as...lords...but being **ensamples** to the flock.
Jude 1:7(4-7)	Sodom and Gomorrha...are set forth for an **example**
1 Ne. 3:7	I will go and **do** the things which the Lord hath

EXAMPLE cont.

1 Ne. 7:8(6-22)	how is it...that I...should...set an **example** for you
2 Ne. 31:9(5-9)	he having set the **example** before them.
2 Ne. 31:16(16-18)	endure to the end, in following the **example** of the Son
Jacob 2:35(31-35)	lost...confidence ...because of your bad **examples**
Jacob 3:10	grieved their hearts because of...**example**...ye...set
Alma 4:11(6-12)	**example** of the church...bringing on...destruction of
Alma 17:11(9-12)	show forth good **examples** unto them in me, and I will
Alma 39:1	behold, has he not set a good **example** for thee
Alma 39:11	when they saw your **conduct** they would not believe in
3 Ne. 12:16(13-16)	let your **light** so shine before this people, that they
3 Ne. 15:12	ye are my disciples...ye are a **light** unto this people
3 Ne. 18:16(15-16)	I am the **light**; I have set an **example** for you.
3 Ne. 27:21(13-22)	that which ye have seen me **do** even that shall ye do
D&C 68:3(2-5)	**ensample**...that they shall speak...by the Holy Ghost.
D&C 72:23(9-26)	an **ensample** for all the extensive branches of my
D&C 78:13(3-13)	this is...the **ensample** which I give unto you, whereby
D&C 98:38(32-38)	this is an **ensample** unto all...for justification
D&C 103:9(8-10)	they were set to be a **light** unto the world, and to be
D&C 106:8	if he continue to be a faithful witness and a **light**
D&C 115:5	that thy light may be a **standard** for the nations

EXCOMMUNICATION

Ex. 12:15(11-15)	whosoever eateth leavened bread...shall be **cut** off fro
Lev. 7:21(20-27)	even that soul shall be **cut** off from his people.
Lev. 18:29(6-30)	commit any of these abominations...shall be **cut** off
Lev. 20:6	will **cut** him off from among his people.
Num. 15:30(29-31)	soul that doeth ought presumptuously...shall be **cut**
Num. 19:13(11-13)	whosoever...defileth the tabernacle...shall be **cut** off
Ezra 2:62(61,62)	therefore were they...**put** from the priesthood.
Mal. 2:12(11,12)	the Lord will **cut** off the man that doeth this, the
Gal. 5:12(10-12)	I would they were even **cut** off which trouble you.
2 Thes. 3:6(6,11-15)	**withdraw**...from every brother that walketh disorderly
Mosiah 26:36(10-37)	would not...repent...their names were **blotted** out.
Alma 1:24(21-24)	hearts...were hardened, and...names were **blotted** out
Alma 6:3(3,4)	lifted up in the pride...names were **blotted** out, that
3 Ne. 18:31(28-32)	repent not...shall not be **numbered** among my people
Moro. 6:7(7,8)	confessed not, their names were **blotted** out, and they
D&C 20:80(80-83)	any member...**transgressing**...shall be dealt with as
D&C 41:5(5,6)	receiveth it and doeth it not...shall be **cast** out from
D&C 42:28(18-28)	he that sinneth and repenteth not shall be **cast** out.
D&C 42:75(74-83)	adultery...offenders..shall be **cast** out from among you
D&C 50:8(7-9)	hypocrites shall be detected and shall be **cut** off
D&C 64:35(34-40)	the rebellious shall be **cut** off out of the land of
D&C 68:22(22-24)	no bishop...tried or **condemned** for any crime, save it
D&C 85:11(9-12)	names...not...in the book of the law...been **cut** off
D&C 102:16(12-32)	present the **case**, after the evidence is examined, in
D&C 104:9(4-10)	**cut** off for transgression, ye cannot escape..
D&C 107:72(71-84)	a **judge**...to sit in judgment upon transgressors upon

FAITH

Gen. 15:6(1-6)	he **believed** in the Lord; and he counted it to him for
Ex. 14:31(29-31)	**believed** the Lord, and his servant Moses.
Num. 14:11(11,12)	how long will it be ere they **believe** me, for all the
Deut. 32:20	froward generation, children in whom is no **faith**.
2 Sam. 22:3	in him will I **trust**: he is my shield, and the horn of
2 Kgs. 17:14(13-15)	their fathers, that did not **believe** in the Lord their
2 Chr. 20:20(20,21)	**believe** in the Lord your God, so shall ye be
Job 13:15	though he slay me, yet will I **trust** in him: but I will
Ps. 25:2(1-5)	O my God, I **trust** in thee: let me not be ashamed, let
Ps. 27:14(13,14)	**wait**, I say, on the Lord.
Ps. 28:7(6-8)	my heart **trusted** in him, and I am helped: therefore
Ps. 31:14(14,15)	but I **trusted** in thee, O Lord: I said, thou art my God
Ps. 34:22(21,22)	none of them that **trust** in him shall be desolate.
Ps. 78:22	because they **believed** not in God, and trusted not in
Prov. 3:5(5,6)	**trust** in the Lord with all thine heart; and lean not
Isa. 7:9	if ye will not **believe**, surely ye shall not be
Isa. 43:10	ye may know and **believe** me, and understand that I am
Dan. 6:23	no...hurt was found...because he **believed** in his God.
Nahum 1:7	Lord...knoweth them that **trust** in him.
Hab. 2:4	the just shall live by his **faith**.
Matt. 6:30	shall he not much more clothe you...ye of little **faith**
Matt. 7:7(7,8)	**ask**, and it shall be given you; seek, and ye shall
Matt. 8:10(5-13)	I have not found so great **faith**, no, not in Israel.
Matt. 9:29(27-31)	saying, according to your **faith** be it unto you.
Matt. 17:20(19,20)	if ye have **faith** as a grain of mustard seed, ye shall
Matt. 21:21(21,22)	if ye have **faith**, and doubt not, ye shall not only do
Mark 1:15	God is at hand: repent ye, and **believe** the gospel.
Mark 9:23(14-26)	all things are possible to him that **believeth**.
Mark 11:22(20-24)	Jesus answering saith unto them, have **faith** in God.
Mark 16:16(15-18)	he that **believeth** and is baptized shall be saved; but
John 3:12	ye **believe** not, how shall ye believe, if I tell you
John 3:16(15-18,36)	whosoever **believeth** in him should not perish, but have
John 5:24	heareth my word, and **believeth** on him that sent me
John 6:29	ye **believe** on him whom he hath sent.
John 6:40	**believeth** on him, may have everlasting life: and I
John 6:47	he that **believeth** on me hath everlasting life.
John 8:24	for if ye **believe** not that I am he, ye shall die in
John 10:25(24-27)	I told you, and ye **believed** not: the works that I do
John 10:38(37,38)	though ye believe not me, **believe** the works: that ye
John 11:15	to the intent ye may **believe**; nevertheless let us go
John 11:25(11-44)	resurrection, and the life: he that **believeth** in me
John 12:36	while ye have light, **believe** in the light, that ye may
John 12:44(44-50)	he that **believeth** on me, believeth not on me, but on
John 14:12(10-14)	he that **believeth** on me, the works that I do shall he
John 14:29	when it is come to pass, ye might **believe**.
John 16:27	ye have loved me, and have **believed** that I came out
John 17:8	they have **believed** that thou didst send me.
John 20:29(19-29)	blessed...that have not seen, and yet have **believed**.
John 20:31(30,31)	that ye might **believe** that Jesus is the Christ, the
Acts 3:16	yea, the **faith** which is by him hath given him this
Acts 10:43	whosoever **believeth** in him shall receive remission of
Acts 14:9(8-10)	and perceiving that he had **faith** to be healed
Rom. 1:17(16-17)	the just shall live by **faith**.

FAITH cont.

Rom. 3:28	man is justified by **faith** without the deeds of the law
Rom. 4:3(3-22)	Abraham **believed** God, and it was counted unto him for
Rom. 4:16(12-16)	to that also which is of the **faith** of Abraham; who is
Rom. 5:1(1,2)	being justified by **faith**, we have peace with God
Rom. 10:17	**faith** cometh by hearing, and hearing by the word of
Rom. 12:6	prophesy according to the proportion of **faith**
Rom. 14:23(22,23)	for whatsoever is not of **faith** is sin.
1 Cor. 12:9	to another **faith** by the same spirit; to another the
1 Cor. 13:13	now abideth **faith**, hope, charity, these three; but the
2 Cor. 5:7	(for we walk by **faith**, not by sight
Gal. 2:20	the life...in the flesh I live by the **faith** of the son
Gal. 3:11	the just shall live by **faith**.
Gal. 5:6	but **faith** which worketh by love.
Gal. 5:22	fruit of the spirit is love...goodness, **faith**
Eph. 2:8	for by grace are ye saved through **faith**; and that not
Eph. 6:16	above all, taking the shield of **faith**, wherewith ye
1 Tim. 4:10	saviour of all men, specially of those that **believe**.
Heb. 4:2	not being mixed with **faith** in them that heard it.
Heb. 11:1(1-40)	now **faith** is the substance of things hoped for, the
Heb. 11:6(1-40)	without **faith** it is impossible to please him: for he
James 1:6(5-6)	but let him ask in **faith**, nothing wavering. for he
James 2:18(14-26)	I will shew thee my **faith** by my works.
James 2:20	**faith** without works is dead
James 2:23	Abraham **believed** God, and it was imputed unto him for
James 5:15(14,15)	and the prayer of **faith** shall save the sick, and the
1 Jn. 3:23	commandment...we should **believe** on the name of his Son
1 Jn. 5:10(5-13)	he that **believeth** on the Son of God hath the witness
1 Ne. 3:7	I will **go** and do the things which the Lord hath
1 Ne. 16:28(26-29)	pointers...did work according to the **faith** and
2 Ne. 9:23	having perfect **faith** in the Holy One of Israel, or the
2 Ne. 26:13(8-13)	working...miracles, signs...according to their **faith**.
2 Ne. 31:19(18-21)	by the word of Christ with unshaken **faith** in him, rely
Enos 1:8(1-19)	because of thy **faith** in Christ, whom thou hast never
Enos 1:11(11-12,15)	my **faith** began to be unshaken in the Lord; and I
Jarom 1:4	many as are not stiffnecked and have **faith**, have
Mosiah 3:9(8-12)	salvation might come...through **faith** on his name; and
Mosiah 4:3(1-3)	exceeding **faith** which they had in Jesus Christ who
Mosiah 24:16(8-25)	so great was their **faith** and their patience that the
Mosiah 27:14(8-37)	prayers...might be answered according to their **faith**.
Alma 2:30	Alma...being exercised with much **faith**, cried, saying
Alma 5:48(45-48)	sins of every man who steadfastly **believeth** on his
Alma 11:40	transgressions of those who **believe** on his name; and
Alma 13:3(2-11)	called...on account of their exceeding **faith** and good
Alma 14:26(24-28)	give us strength according to our **faith**...in Christ
Alma 15:10(1-12)	heal him according to his **faith** which is in Christ.
Alma 22:16(12-18)	call on his name in **faith**, believing that ye shall
Alma 24:19(1-30)	Lamanites...brought to **believe**...were firm...unto
Alma 31:38	prayer of Alma; and this because he prayed in **faith**.
Alma 32:21(18-43)	**faith** is not to have a perfect knowledge of things
Alma 34:17(15-17)	may begin to exercise your **faith** unto repentance, that
Alma 57:26(19-27)	spared...because of their exceeding **faith** in that
Hel. 5:41	even until ye shall have **faith** in Christ, who was
Hel. 5:47(44-50)	peace...because of your **faith** in my well beloved, who

FAITH cont.

Hel. 8:15	look upon the Son of God with **faith**...might live, even
3 Ne. 11:35(31-39)	whoso **believeth** in me believeth in the Father also
3 Ne. 19:35(27-36)	so great **faith** have I never seen among all the Jews
3 Ne. 26:9(8-11)	try their **faith**..then..greater things be made manifest
3 Ne. 27:19	washed...garments in my blood, because of their **faith**
Morm. 7:5(5-10)	**believe** in Jesus Christ, that he is the Son of God
Ether 3:15(1-28)	never has man **believed** in me as thou hast. Seest thou
Ether 3:19(19-20)	he had **faith** no longer, for he knew, nothing doubting.
Ether 4:7(6-19)	in that day that they shall exercise **faith** in me
Ether 12:6(1-40)	no witness until after the trial of your **faith**.
Ether 12:13(11-30)	it was the **faith** of Alma and Amulek that caused the
Moro. 7:33	if ye will have **faith** in me ye shall have power to do
Moro. 7:42(1-48)	if a man have **faith** he must needs have hope; for
Moro. 10:4(4-7)	with real intent, having **faith** in Christ, he will
Moro. 10:11	and to another, exceeding great **faith**; and to another
D&C 8:10(10-11)	without **faith** you can do nothing; therefore ask in
D&C 10:47(46-52)	granted...according to their **faith** in their prayers
D&C 11:17(15-22)	even according to your **faith** shall it be done unto
D&C 18:19(18,19)	have not **faith**, hope, and charity, you can do nothing.
D&C 19:31(31-32)	declare repentance and **faith** on the Savior, and
D&C 20:29	endure in **faith** on his name to the end, or they cannot
D&C 35:9(8-11)	whoso shall ask it in my name in **faith**, they shall
D&C 42:48(48-51)	he that hath **faith** in me to be healed, and is not
D&C 45:8	even unto them that **believed** on my name gave I power
D&C 46:19(19-20)	to some it is given to have **faith** to be healed
D&C 63:10(8-11)	signs come by **faith**, not by the will of men, nor as
D&C 67:3	ye endeavored to **believe** that ye should receive the
D&C 84:54	minds...have been darkened because of **unbelief**, and
D&C 88:118(118-119)	as all have not **faith**, seek ye diligently and teach
D&C 98:12	he will give unto the **faithful** line upon line, precept
D&C 104:55	these properties are mine, or else your **faith** is vain
D&C 105:19(19,24)	should be brought thus far for a trial of their **faith**.
Moses 5:15	as many as **believed** in the Son, and repented of their
Moses 6:23(22,23)	and **faith** was taught unto the children of men.
Moses 7:13(13-16)	so great was the **faith** of Enoch, that he led the
Moses 7:47	through **faith** I am in the bosom of the Father, and
A of F 1:4	first principles...are: first, **faith** in the Lord Jesus
JFS-V 1:33(31-35)	these were taught **faith** in God, repentance from sin

FALL OF MAN

Gen. 2:17(15-17)	day that thou eatest thereof thou shalt surely **die**.
Gen. 3:6(4-24)	she took of the fruit thereof, and did **eat**, and gave
Gen. 3:7(1-24)	the eyes of them both were **opened**, and they knew that
Rom. 5:12(11-19)	by one man **sin** entered into the world, and death by
Rom. 8:7(5-9)	the **carnal** mind is enmity against God: for it is not
1 Cor. 15:22(21-22)	for as in **Adam** all die, even so in Christ shall all
2 Cor. 11:3	the serpent **beguiled** Eve through his subtilty, so your
1 Tim. 2:14(14-15)	the woman being **deceived** was in the transgression.
2 Ne. 2:19(14-21)	Adam and Eve had **partaken** of the forbidden fruit they
2 Ne. 2:25(22-26)	Adam **fell** that men might be; and men are, that they
2 Ne. 9:6(6-7)	resurrection must...come...by reason of the **fall**; and

Mosiah 3:11	those who have **fallen** by the transgression of Adam
Mosiah 3:19	from the **fall** of Adam, and will be, forever and ever
Mosiah 4:7(6,7)	atonement...for all mankind...since the **fall** of Adam
Mosiah 16:4(3-8)	redeemed his people from their lost and **fallen** state.
Mosiah 16:12	according to their own **carnal** wills and desires
Alma 12:22(20-37)	Adam did **fall** by the partaking of the forbidden fruit
Alma 22:14	since man had **fallen** he could not merit anything of
Alma 26:21	what **natural** man is there that knoweth these things
Alma 34:9	all are **fallen** and are lost, and must perish except
Alma 41:11	in a **carnal** state, are in the gall of bitterness and
Alma 42:6(1-31)	man became lost forever, yea, they became **fallen** man.
Alma 42:9(2-10)	**fall** had brought...a spiritual death as well as a
Hel. 14:16(16-18)	the **fall** of Adam...cut off from the presence of the
Morm. 9:12	by Adam came the **fall** of man. and because of the fall
Ether 3:2	because of the **fall** our natures have become evil
D&C 29:41(35-41)	he should be **cast** out ...from my presence, because of
D&C 93:38(38-40)	God having redeemed man from the **fall**, men became
Moses 4:12(5-31)	woman...did **eat**, and also gave unto her husband with
Moses 5:9(4-11)	as thou hast **fallen** thou mayest be redeemed, and all
Moses 6:48(45-48)	because that Adam **fell**, we are; and by his fall came
A of F 1:2	their own sins, and not for Adam's **transgression**.
JFS-V 1:19(18,19)	preached...redemption of mankind from the **fall**, and

FALSE CHRISTS

Matt. 24:5(3-5)	come in my name, saying, I am **Christ**; and shall
Matt. 24:24(23-24)	there shall arise false **Christs**, and false prophets
Mark 13:22(19-26)	for **false** Christs and false prophets shall rise, and
Luke 17:23(20-25)	see here; or, **see** there: go not after them, nor follow
2 Ne. 25:16(16-18)	look not forward any more for **another** Messiah, then
2 Ne. 25:18	save it should be a **false** Messiah which should
W of M 1:15(15-18)	after there had been false **Christs**, and their mouths
Moses 1:19(12-22)	**Satan** cried...I am the Only Begotten, worship me.
JS-M 1:6(5-9)	saying- I am **Christ**- and shall deceive many
JS-M 1:22(22-26)	there shall also arise false **Christs**, and false

FALSE DOCTRINE

Deut. 4:2	ye shall not **add** unto the word which I command you
Deut. 12:32	thou shalt not **add** thereto, nor diminish from it.
Deut. 13:5(1-11)	prophet...hath spoken to **turn** you away from the Lord
Job 21:34	in your answers there remaineth **falsehood**
Isa. 30:10(8-11)	speak unto us **smooth** things, prophesy deceits
Jer. 14:14(13-16)	prophets prophesy **lies** in my name: I sent them not
Jer. 23:16(14-32)	a **vision** of their own heart, and not...of the Lord.
Ezek. 13:22(1-23)	with **lies** ye have made the heart of the righteous sad
Acts 20:30(29,30)	shall men arise, speaking **perverse** things, to draw
Gal. 1:9(8,9)	if any man preach any other **gospel** unto you than that
1 Tim. 4:1(1-3)	heed to seducing spirits, and **doctrines** of devils
2 Pet. 2:1	there shall be **false** teachers among you, who privily
Rev. 13:5(4-7)	mouth speaking great things and **blasphemies**; and power

FALSE DOCTRINE cont.

1 Ne. 13:26(24-29)	they have **taken** away from the gospel of the lamb many
2 Ne. 3:12	the confounding of **false** doctrines and laying down of
2 Ne. 28:9(9-15)	shall teach...**false** and vain and foolish doctrines
2 Ne. 28:12	because of false teachers, and **false** doctrine, their
2 Ne. 28:21(20-22)	others will he **pacify**, and lull them away into carnal
Jacob 7:2(1-23)	that he might **overthrow** the doctrine of Christ.
Alma 1:16	and they went forth preaching **false** doctrines; and
Alma 30:6(6-60)	preach unto the people **against** the prophecies which
D&C 10:28(28,29)	wo be unto him that **lieth** to deceive because he
D&C 28:11(11,12)	from that stone are not of me...Satan **deceiveth** him
D&C 43:5(5,6)	receive not the **teachings** of any that shall come
D&C 50:2(2-4)	false spirits...forth in the earth, **deceiving** the
D&C 50:23(22,23)	which doth not **edify** is not of God, and is darkness.
D&C 123:12	who are blinded by the subtle **craftiness** of men, where
JS-H 1:19	professors were all **corrupt**; that: they draw near to

FALSE PRIESTHOODS

Ex. 7:11(10-22)	the **magicians** of Egypt, they also did in like manner
1 Kgs. 12:31	made **priests** of the lowest of the people, which were
2 Kgs. 23:5(4-5,20)	idolatrous **priests**, whom the kings of Judah had
2 Cor. 11:13(13-15)	**false** apostles...transforming themselves into the
2 Thes. 2:9	after the working of Satan with all **power** and signs
2 Pet. 2:1(1-3)	false prophets...**false** teachers...denying the Lord.
Rev. 13:7(4-7)	to overcome them: and **power** was given him over all
Jacob 7:4(1-20)	power of speech, according to the **power** of the devil.
Mosiah 11:5(5-14)	he put down all the **priests**...consecrated new ones in
D&C 33:4	they err...because of **priestcrafts**, all having corrupt
Abr. 1:10(5-11)	a child did the **priest** of Pharaoh offer upon the altar
Abr. 1:12(12-17)	**priests** laid violence upon me, that they might slay

FALSE PROPHETS

Ex. 7:11(10-12)	Pharaoh also called the wise men and the **sorcerers**
Deut. 13:1(1-11)	if there arise among you a **prophet**, or a dreamer of
Deut. 13:3(1-3)	thou shalt not hearken unto the words of that **prophet**
Deut. 18:20(18-22)	but the **prophet**, which shall presume to speak a word
1 Kgs. 18:20(19-40)	Ahab...gathered the **prophets** together unto mount
Isa. 9:15(14-16)	the **prophet** that teacheth lies, he is the tail.
Isa. 28:7(7,8)	the priest and the **prophet** have erred through strong
Jer. 2:8	and the **prophets** prophesied by Baal, and walked after
Jer. 5:31(11-13,31)	the **prophets** prophesy falsely, and the priests bear
Jer. 12:10(10-11)	many **pastors** have destroyed my vineyard, they have
Jer. 14:14(13-16)	the **prophets** prophesy lies in my name: I sent them not
Jer. 23:11(9-40)	both **prophet** and priest are profane; yea, in my house
Jer. 23:16(9-17)	the prophets that **prophesy** unto you: they make you
Jer. 27:15(9-15)	they **prophesy** a lie in my name; that I might drive
Jer. 28:15(1-17)	Hananiah the **prophet** ...the Lord hath not sent thee
Jer. 29:9(8-9)	they **prophesy** falsely unto you in my name: I have not
Lam. 2:14	thy **prophets** have seen vain and foolish things for the
Ezek. 13:2(2-6)	prophesy against the **prophets** of Israel that prophesy

FALSE PROPHETS cont.

Ezek. 22:25(25-28)	there is a conspiracy of her **prophets** in the midst the
Hosea 4:5(4-6)	and the **prophet** also shall fall with thee in the night
Micah 3:5(5-7)	the **prophets** that make my people err, that bite with
Micah 3:11(11-12)	the **prophets** thereof divine for money: yet will they
Matt. 7:15(15-23)	beware of **false** prophets, which come to you in sheep's
Matt. 24:11(4,5,11)	many **false** prophets shall rise, and shall deceive many
Matt. 24:24	there shall arise false Christs, and **false** prophets
Mark 13:22(21-22)	for false Christs and **false** prophets shall rise, and
2 Cor. 11:13(12-14)	for such are **false** apostles, deceitful workers
2 Tim. 4:3(3-4)	they heap to themselves **teachers**, having itching ears
Titus 1:16	they **profess** that they know God; but in works they
2 Pet. 2:1(1-3)	but there were **false** prophets also among the people
1 Jn. 2:18(18-19)	that **antichrist** shall come, even now are there many
1 Jn. 4:1(1-3)	many **false** prophets are gone out into the world.
Rev. 16:13(13,14)	and out of the mouth of the **false** prophet.
Rev. 19:20	beast..with him the **false** prophet that wrought miracle
1 Ne. 14:10(3-17)	two churches only...other is the church of the **devil**
2 Ne. 28:12(3-14)	because of **false** teachers...their churches..corrupted
Jacob 7:1(1-20)	came a man...whose name was **Sherem**.
W of M 1:16(15,16)	after there had been **false** prophets, and false
Alma 1:15(2-16)	and his name was **Nehor**; and they carried him upon the
Alma 30:6(6,12-31)	he was **Anti-Christ**, for he began to preach unto the
Hel. 13:27(25-28)	ye will receive him, and say that he is a **prophet**.
3 Ne. 14:15(15-20)	beware of **false** prophets, who come to you in sheep's
4 Ne. 1:34	many priests and **false** prophets to build up many
D&C 28:2	**no** one shall be appointed to receive commandments and
D&C 33:4	they err in many instances because of **priestcrafts**
D&C 43:3(2-7)	**none** other appointed unto you to receive commandments
D&C 64:39	who are **not** apostles and prophets shall be known.
D&C 123:12	many...among all sects...blinded by...**men**, whereby the
D&C 128:20	the **devil**...appeared as an angel of light! The voice
Moses 5:13(9-13)	**Satan** came among them, saying: I am also a son of God
JS-M 1:9(5-10)	and many **false** prophets shall arise, and shall deceive
JS-H 1:19(18-20)	those **professors** were all corrupt; that: they draw

FAMILY

Gen. 10:5(1-5)	every one...after their **families**, in their nations.
Gen. 12:3	and in thee shall all **families** of the earth be blessed
Gen. 18:19	I know...will command his **children** and his household
Deut. 17:20(18-20)	prolong his days...he, and his **children**, in the midst
Ps. 103:13	like as a father pitieth his **children**, so the Lord
Ps. 113:9(7-9)	keep house, and to be a joyful mother of **children**.
Prov. 20:7	walketh in his integrity: his **children** are blessed
Jer. 31:1	will I be the God of all the **families** of Israel, and
Eph. 3:15(14-15)	of whom the whole **family** in heaven and earth is named
1 Pet. 3:7(1-7)	**husbands**...giving honour unto the wife, as unto the
2 Ne. 2:23(22-25)	and they would have had no **children**; wherefore they
Alma 43:47	ye shall defend your **families** even unto bloodshed.
3 Ne. 18:21	pray in your **families**...that your wives and your child
D&C 19:34(34,36)	impart...property...all save the support of thy **family**
D&C 20:47	attend to all **family** duties.

FAMILY cont.

D&C 23:3(3,6)	thy duty is unto the church...because of thy **family**.
D&C 57:14(14-15)	be planted in the land of Zion...with their **families**
D&C 74:7	little **children** are holy, being sanctified through the
D&C 75:24(24-25)	duty of the church...to support the **families** of those
D&C 75:28	every man who is obliged to provide for his own **family**
D&C 84:103(103-104)	inasmuch as they have **families**, and receive money by
D&C 93:48	your **family** must needs repent and forsake some things
D&C 98:16	seek diligently to turn the hearts of the **children** to
D&C 98:47(39-48)	if the **children** shall repent...then thine indignation
Moses 5:11(5-12)	transgression we never should have had **seed**, and never
Moses 5:12(5-12)	made all things known unto ...**sons** and...daughters.

FAMILY, CHILDREN, DUTIES OF

Ex. 20:12	**honour** thy father and thy mother: that thy days may
Lev. 19:32	thou shalt...**honour** the face of the old man, and fear
Lev. 20:9	every one that curseth his **father** or his mother shall
Prov. 1:8(8,9)	forsake not the law of thy **mother**
Prov. 6:20(20-23)	my son, keep thy **father's** commandment, and forsake not
Prov. 10:1	but a foolish son is the heaviness of his **mother**.
Prov. 17:6	children's children are the **crown** of old men; and the
Prov. 23:22(22-25)	**hearken** unto thy father that begat thee, and despise
Mal. 1:6	a son **honoureth** his father, and a servant his master
Mal. 4:6(5,6)	and the heart of the **children** to their fathers, lest
Matt. 19:19	**honour** thy father and thy mother: and, thou shalt love
Luke 2:51(48-51)	and he...was **subject** unto them: but his mother kept
Rom. 1:30(29-30)	despiteful, proud, boasters...**disobedient** to parents
Eph. 6:1(1-4)	children, **obey** your parents in the Lord: for this is
Col. 3:20	children, **obey** your parents in all things: for this
2 Tim. 3:2(1-4)	men shall be...blasphemers, **disobedient** to parents
1 Ne. 17:55	worship the Lord...and **honor** thy father and thy mother
Mosiah 3:19(19-21)	as a child doth **submit** to his father.
Mosiah 13:20	**honor** thy father and thy mother, that thy days may be
Morm. 1:2	thou art a sober **child**, and...quick to observe
D&C 2:2(1-3)	plant in the hearts of the children the **promises** made
D&C 18:42	repent and be baptized...men...women, and **children** who
D&C 128:18(15-18)	a welding link...between..fathers and..**children**, upon

FAMILY, CHILDREN, RESPONSIBILITIES TOWARD

Gen. 18:19	for I know him, that he will **command** his children and
Deut. 4:9(9-10)	**teach** them thy sons, and thy sons' sons
Deut. 6:7	thou shalt **teach** them diligently unto thy children
Deut. 11:19	ye shall teach them your **children**, speaking of them
Josh. 24:15	as for me and my **house**, we will serve the Lord.
1 Sam. 2:12(12-17)	the **sons** of Eli...knew not the Lord.
1 Sam. 3:13(10-18)	sons made themselves vile, and he **restrained** them not.
Ps. 78:5(4-6)	he commanded...make them known to their **children**
Prov. 13:24	son...he that loveth him **chasteneth** him betimes.
Prov. 22:6	**train** up a child in the way he should go: and when he
Prov. 23:13(13,14)	withhold not **correction** from the child: for if thou

FAMILY, CHILDREN, RESPONSIBILITIES TOWARD cont.

Prov. 29:15	a **child** left to himself bringeth his mother to shame.
Isa. 54:13	and all thy **children** shall be taught of the Lord; and
Mal. 4:6	turn the heart of the fathers to the **children**, and the
Matt. 18:10(9-10)	take heed that ye despise not one of these **little** ones
Eph. 6:4(1-4)	**children**...bring them up in the nurture...of the Lord.
Col. 3:21	**fathers**, provoke not your children to anger, lest they
1 Tim. 3:4(4,12)	**children** in subjection with all gravity
1 Tim. 5:8	if any **provide** not for his own, and specially for
3 Jn. 1:4	joy than to hear that my **children** walk in truth.
1 Ne. 1:1	having been born of goodly parents...was **taught**
1 Ne. 8:37(35-38)	did **exhort**...with all the feeling of a tender parent
2 Ne. 4:5	**brought** up in the way ye should go ye will not depart
2 Ne. 25:26(23,26)	that our **children** may know to what source they may
Jacob 2:35	lost the confidence of your **children**, because of your
Jacob 3:10	remember your **children**...because of the example that
Enos 1:1(1-3)	father...was a just man- for he **taught** me in his
Mosiah 1:4	and teach them to his **children**, that thereby they
Mosiah 4:15(13-16)	**teach** them to walk in the ways of truth and soberness
Alma 43:47(45-47)	ye shall **defend** your families even unto bloodshed. the
3 Ne. 18:21	pray in your families...that...**children** may be blessed
D&C 55:4	children...receive **instruction** before me as is
D&C 68:25(25-31)	parents..that **teach** them not to understand the
D&C 83:4(1-6)	children have claim...parents for their **maintenance**
D&C 93:40(40-44)	commanded you to bring up your **children** in light and
Moses 6:6(5-6)	**children** were taught to read and write, having a
Moses 6:58(57-58)	teach these things freely unto your **children**, saying

FAMILY, ETERNAL

Gen. 2:24(21-24)	and they shall be **one** flesh.
Gen. 25:8	Abraham...died...and was **gathered** to his people.
Gen. 35:29	Isaac...died, and was **gathered** unto his people, being
Gen. 49:33(29,33)	Jacob...yielded...ghost...was **gathered** unto his people
Isa. 51:2	look unto Abraham your **father**, and unto Sarah that
Isa. 65:23(17,19-23)	the blessed of the Lord, and their **offspring** with them
Jer. 31:1	will I be the God of all the **families** of Israel, and
Mal. 4:6(5,6)	turn the heart of the **fathers** to the children, and the
Matt. 19:8(3-12)	put away...**wives**: but from the beginning it was not
Mark 10:9(6-9)	what...God hath **joined** together, let not man put
1 Cor. 11:11	neither is the **man** without the woman...in the Lord.
3 Ne. 25:6(3-6)	turn the heart of the **fathers** to the children, and the
D&C 130:2(1,2)	same **sociality** which exists among us here will exist
D&C 131:2(1-4)	in order to obtain the **highest**, a man must enter into
D&C 132:19(19-24)	a continuation of the **seeds** forever and ever.
D&C 132:55(51-56)	and crowns of eternal **lives** in the eternal worlds.
Moses 3:18(18,20-25)	it was not good that the man should be **alone**
JS-V 1:5(1-10)	my **father** and my mother; my brother Alvin, that has
JFS-V 1:48(47,48)	**sealing** of the children to their parents, lest the

FAMILY, HOME EVENINGS WITH

Deut. 4:9(9-10)	but **teach** them thy sons, and thy sons' sons
Deut. 6:7(3-7)	and thou shalt **teach** them diligently unto thy children
Deut. 11:19(18-21)	ye shall **teach** them your children, speaking of them
Deut. 32:46(45-47)	ye shall command your **children** to observe to do, all
Prov. 4:1(1-7)	hear, ye children, the **instruction** of a father, and
Prov. 22:6	**train** up a child in the way he should go: and when he
Jer. 10:25(24,25)	fury...upon the **families** that call not on thy name
Eph. 6:4(1-4)	children..bring them up in the ..**admonition** of the Lord
Col. 3:20(18-21)	**children**, obey your parents in all things: for this
1 Tim. 3:4(2-6)	having his **children** in subjection with all gravity
2 Ne. 4:5	**brought** up in the way ye should go ye will not depart
2 Ne. 25:26(23-27)	that our **children** may know to what source they may
Mosiah 4:15(14,15)	but we will **teach** them to walk in the ways of truth
Alma 39:16(15,16)	prepare the minds of their **children** to hear the word
Alma 56:47(45-48)	they had been **taught** by their mothers, that if they
3 Ne. 18:21(19-21)	pray in your **families** unto the father, always in my
3 Ne. 22:13	and all thy **children** shall be taught of the Lord; and
D&C 20:47(46,47)	pray vocally...secret and attend to all **family** duties.
D&C 68:25(25-28)	**teach** them not...the sin be upon...the parents.
D&C 93:40(40-44)	commanded you to bring up your **children** in light and
Moses 5:12	they made all things known unto their **sons** and their
Moses 6:1	Adam...called upon his **sons** to repent.
Moses 6:58(54-62)	commandment, to **teach** these things..unto your children

FAMILY, LOVE WITHIN

Gen. 14:16(11-16)	brought again his **brother**...and his goods, and the
Gen. 45:5(4-5)	be not **grieved**...that ye sold me hither: for God did
Gen. 50:21(18-21)	I will **nourish** you, and your little ones. And he
Ex. 20:12	**honour** thy father and thy mother: that thy days may
Deut. 24:5	shall **cheer** up his wife which he hath taken.
Ruth 1:16(1-22)	intreat me not...to return from **following** after thee
Ps. 113:9	he maketh the barren woman...to be a joyful **mother** of
Ps. 127:5(3-5)	**happy** is the man that hath his quiver full of them
Ps. 133:1(1-3)	how pleasant...for **brethren** to dwell together in unity
Prov. 5:18	rejoice with the **wife** of thy youth.
Prov. 17:6	children's **children** are the crown of old men; and the
Eccl. 9:9	live joyfully with the wife whom thou **lovest** all the
Mal. 4:6(5-6)	he shall turn the heart of the **fathers** to the children
Matt. 19:5(3-6)	and shall **cleave** to his wife: and they twain shall
Luke 15:20(10-32)	great way off, his father saw him, and had **compassion**
Luke 15:31(10-32)	son, thou art ever with me...all...I have is thine.
John 13:34(34,35)	that ye also **love** one another.
John 19:27(26-27)	behold thy **mother**! And from that hour that disciple
1 Cor. 7:3	husband render unto the wife due **benevolence**: and like
1 Cor. 7:5(3-5)	**defraud** ye not one the other, except it be with
1 Cor. 7:16(12-16)	knowest thou...whether thou shalt **save** thy husband
Eph. 4:32(29-32)	and be ye **kind** one to another, tenderhearted
Eph. 5:25(19-33)	husbands, **love** your wives, even as Christ also loved
Eph. 6:4(1-4)	and, ye **fathers**, provoke not your children to wrath
Col. 3:20(14-21)	**children**, obey your parents in all things: for this
1 Tim. 3:5(1-13)	if a man know not how to **rule** his own house, how shall

1 Tim. 5:4(1-5)	let them learn first to shew **piety** at home, and to
Titus 2:4(3-6)	teach the young women...to **love** their husbands, to
Heb. 12:9(9-12)	we have had fathers of our flesh which **corrected** us
1 Pet. 3:1(1-11)	likewise, ye **wives**, be in subjection to your own
1 Jn. 2:10(9-11)	he that **loveth** his brother abideth in the light, and
1 Jn. 3:23(13-24)	we should...**love** one another, as he gave us
1 Jn. 4:18	there is no fear in **love**; but perfect love casteth out
1 Jn. 4:20(8-21)	if a man say, I love God, and **hateth** his brother, he
1 Jn. 5:2(1-3)	we **love** the children of God, when we love God, and
2 Jn. 1:6	and this is **love**, that we walk after his commandments.
3 Jn. 1:4	joy than to hear that my **children** walk in truth.
1 Ne. 1:1	born of goodly parents, therefore I was **taught**
1 Ne. 2:16(16-18)	spoken by my father...I did not **rebel** against him like
1 Ne. 3:21	I **persuade** my brethren, that they might be faithful
1 Ne. 7:21(20-21)	I did frankly **forgive** them all that they had done, and
1 Ne. 8:12(2-18)	desirous that my **family** should partake of it also; for
1 Ne. 17:55	**honor** thy father and thy mother, that thy days may be
2 Ne. 1:14	awake...and hear the words of a trembling **parent**
2 Ne. 2:30(28-30)	I have none other object save...everlasting **welfare**
2 Ne. 4:5(5-6)	if ye are **brought** up in the way ye should go ye will
2 Ne. 25:23(23-27)	we labor diligently...to **persuade** our children, and
Jacob 3:7(6-7)	their husbands **love** their wives, and their wives love
Jacob 3:10(10-11)	ye shall remember your **children**, how that ye have
Jacob 4:3(2-3)	they...learn with joy...concerning their first **parents**
Mosiah 4:15(11-21)	ye will teach them to **love** one another, and to serve
Mosiah 27:14	thy father..has **prayed** with much faith concerning thee
Alma 19:23(22-23)	therefore, Mosiah **trusted** him unto the Lord.
Alma 43:47	ye shall **defend** your families even unto bloodshed.
Alma 46:12(11-21)	in memory of...our **wives**, and our children- and he
Alma 48:10	preparing to support..their **wives**, and their children
Alma 56:48	they rehearsed unto me the words of their **mothers**, say
3 Ne. 18:21	pray in your **families** unto the Father, always in my
Moro. 8:10(10-12)	parents..must repent..humble..as their little **children**
Moro. 8:17(16-19)	I **love** little children with a perfect love; and they
D&C 20:70	every member of the church of Christ having **children**
D&C 25:5(4-16)	thy calling shall be for a **comfort** unto my servant
D&C 25:14	let thy soul delight in thy **husband**, and the glory
D&C 31:9	govern your **house** in meekness, and be steadfast.
D&C 38:27(24-28)	be one; and if ye are not **one** ye are not mine.
D&C 42:22(22-23)	thou shalt **love** thy wife with all thy heart, and shalt
D&C 49:16(15-17)	have one wife, and they twain shall be **one** flesh, and
D&C 74:1(1-7)	the unbelieving husband is **sanctified** by the wife, and
D&C 75:28	every man who is obliged to provide for his own **family**
D&C 88:123(123-126)	see that ye **love** one another; cease to be covetous
D&C 110:15(13-16)	to turn the **hearts** of the fathers to the children, and
D&C 121:41(41-46)	no power or influence...by **love** unfeigned
D&C 126:3(1-3)	take especial **care** of your family from this time
D&C 130:2(1-2)	that same **sociality** which exists among us here will
D&C 132:56	let mine **handmaid** forgive my servant Joseph his
D&C 136:11	ye shall be blessed...in your **families**.
Moses 3:24(21-25)	therefore shall a man...cleave unto his **wife**; and they
Moses 6:58(53-62)	teach these things freely unto your **children**, saying
JS-H 1:20	**mother** inquired what the matter was. I replied

FAMILY, LOVE WITHIN cont.

JS-H 1:49(49-50)   commanded me to go to my **father** and tell him of the

FAMILY, MANAGING FINANCES IN

Hag. 1:6(5-7)   he that earneth **wages**...put it into a bag with holes.
Mal. 3:10(8-12)   bring ye all the **tithes**...and prove me now herewith
Matt. 6:19(19-21)   lay not up for yourselves **treasures** upon earth, where
1 Tim. 5:8   if any **provide** not for his own... he hath denied the
D&C 48:4   **save** all the money that ye can, and that ye obtain all
D&C 51:3(3,4)   their **portions**, every man equal according to his
D&C 75:24   **support** the families of those who are called and must
D&C 75:28(28-29)   every man who is obliged to **provide** for his own family
D&C 82:17(17,18)   for the benefit of **managing** the concerns of your
D&C 84:103   have families, and receive **money** by gift..send it unto
D&C 88:119(74,119)   **organize** yourselves; prepare every needful thing; and

FAMILY, PATRIARCHAL

Gen. 2:24(21-24)   man...shall cleave unto his **wife**: and they shall be
Gen. 8:16   thy **wife**, and thy sons, and thy sons' wives with thee.
Gen. 12:3   in thee shall all **families** of the earth be blessed.
Gen. 49:2(1-2)   gather...ye sons...and hearken unto Israel your **father**
Ex. 12:21(21-28)   take you a lamb according to your **families**...passover.
Ex. 20:12   honour thy **father** and thy mother: that thy days may
Lev. 25:10   ye shall return every man unto his **family**.
Num. 1:2   Israel, after..families, by the house of their **fathers**
Josh. 7:14   the **family**...shall come by households; and the
Ps. 127:3(3-5)   lo, **children** are an heritage of the Lord: and the
Prov. 17:6   children's **children** are the crown of old men; and the
Luke 1:73   the oath which he sware to our **father** Abraham
Luke 3:38(23-38)   which was the **son** of Enos, which was the son of Seth
Luke 15:21(11-32)   I...am no more worthy to be called thy **son**.
Acts 13:32   that the promise which was made unto the **fathers**
Rom. 4:16   faith of Abraham; who is the **father** of us all
1 Cor. 7:10   let not the **wife** depart from her husband
Eph. 5:25(22-25)   **husbands**, love your wives, even as Christ also loved
Eph. 6:4(1-4)   **fathers**, provoke not your children to wrath: but bring
1 Tim. 3:4(4-5)   ruleth well his own house...his **children** in subjection
Heb. 1:1   God...spake in..past unto the **fathers** by the prophets
Heb. 7:4   unto whom even the **patriarch** Abraham gave the tenth
2 Ne. 4:5(3-6)   I cannot go...to my grave save I...leave a **blessing**
Jacob 3:7(5-7)   **husbands** love their wives, and their wives love their
Mosiah 2:5   every man according to his **family**, consisting of his
Alma 56:47(47,48)   they had been taught by their **mothers**, that if they
3 Ne. 25:6(5,6)   turn the heart of the **fathers** to the children, and the
D&C 68:25(25-31)   **parents** have children in Zion, or in any of her stakes
D&C 83:2(2-3)   women have claim on their **husbands** for their
D&C 107:41(39-57)   this **order** was instituted in the days of Adam, and
D&C 132:19   a fulness and a continuation of the **seeds** forever and
D&C 132:30(30-31)   Abraham received promises concerning his **seed**, and of

FAMINE

Gen. 12:10	and there was a **famine** in the land: and Abram went
Gen. 26:1	and there was a **famine** in the land, beside the first
Gen. 41:27(25-28)	shall be seven years of **famine**.
Gen. 41:30	and the **famine** shall consume the land
Gen. 41:54	and the seven years of **dearth** began to come, according
Gen. 47:13	for the **famine** was very sore, so that the land of
1 Kgs. 17:1	there shall not be dew nor **rain** these years, but
2 Kgs. 8:1	the Lord hath called for a **famine**; and it shall also
Ps. 105:16	moreover he called for a **famine** upon the land: he
Jer. 14:1(1-5)	word of the Lord...to Jeremiah concerning the **dearth**.
Jer. 52:6	the **famine** was sore in the city...there was no bread
Hag. 1:11	I called for a **drought** upon the land, and upon the
Acts 7:11	there came a **dearth** over all the land of Egypt and
Hel. 11:4	let there be a **famine**...to stir them up in remembrance
Ether 9:30	a great **dearth** upon the land...there was no rain upon
D&C 29:16	hailstorm sent forth to destroy the **crops** of the earth
D&C 43:25(23-26)	by the voice of **famines** and pestilences of every kind
D&C 87:6(4-6)	with **famine**...inhabitants...be made to feel the wrath.
D&C 89:13(12-13)	used, only in times of winter...cold, or **famine**.
Moses 8:4	there came forth a great **famine** into the land, and the
Abr. 1:29(29-30)	that there should be a **famine** in the land.
JS-H 1:45(44-45)	judgments...coming...with great desolations by **famine**

FASTING

Ex. 34:28	forty days...he did neither **eat** bread, nor drink water
2 Sam. 12:16(15-23)	David...besought God for the child; and...**fasted**, and
2 Sam. 12:21	thou didst **fast** and weep for the child, while it was
1 Kgs. 19:8	strength of that meat **forty** days and forty nights unto
1 Kgs. 21:9	proclaim a **fast**, and set Naboth on high among the
2 Chr. 20:3	and proclaimed a **fast** throughout all Judah.
Ezra 8:23(21-23)	so we **fasted** and besought our God for this: and he was
Neh. 1:4	and **fasted**, and prayed before the God of heaven
Neh. 9:1(1-3)	children of Israel were assembled with **fasting**, and
Esth. 4:16(15-17)	and **fast** ye for me, and neither eat nor drink three
Ps. 35:13	I humbled my soul with **fasting**; and my prayer returned
Ps. 69:10	when I wept, and chastened my soul with **fasting**, that
Isa. 58:3(3-14)	in the day of your **fast** ye find pleasure, and exact
Joel 1:14	sanctify ye a **fast**, call a solemn assembly, gather the
Joel 2:12(12-14)	turn ye...to me with all your heart, and with **fasting**
Jonah 3:5(5-10)	people of Nineveh believed God, and proclaimed a **fast**
Zech. 7:5(4-6)	did ye at all **fast** unto me, even to me
Matt. 4:2	when he had **fasted** forty days and forty nights, he was
Matt. 6:18(16-18)	appear not unto men to **fast**, but unto thy Father which
Matt. 9:15(14-15)	bridegroom shall be taken...and then shall they **fast**.
Matt. 17:21	this kind goeth not out but by prayer and **fasting**.
Luke 2:37	served God with **fastings** and prayers night and day.
Acts 10:30	four days ago I was **fasting** until this hour; and at
Acts 13:2	they ministered to the Lord, and **fasted**, the Holy
Acts 14:23	ordained them elders...and had prayed with **fasting**
Acts 27:9	because the **fast** was now already past, Paul
Acts 27:33(32-38)	fourteenth day..continued **fasting**, having taken

FASTING cont.

1:26	continue in **fasting** and praying, and endure to the
Alma 5:46(45,46)	I have **fasted** and prayed many days that I might know
Alma 6:6	join in **fasting**..in behalf of..those who knew not God.
Alma 17:3	much...**fasting**; therefore they had the spirit of
Alma 17:9	they **fasted** much...that the Lord would grant unto them
Hel. 3:35(34,35)	they did **fast**...and did wax stronger...firmer in the
3 Ne. 13:16(16-18)	when ye **fast** be not as the hypocrites, of a sad
3 Ne. 27:1(1-2)	disciples...were united in mighty prayer and **fasting**.
D&C 59:13(13-22)	that thy **fasting** may be perfect, or, in other words
D&C 88:76	ye shall continue in prayer and **fasting** from this time
D&C 88:119	a house of **fasting**, a house of faith, a house of learn
D&C 95:7	your **fastings**...come up into the ears of the Lord of

FEARFULNESS

Gen. 15:1	**fear** not, Abram: I am thy shield, and thy exceeding
Ex. 3:11(10-14)	who am I, that I should go unto **Pharaoh**, and that I
Ex. 20:20(18-21)	Moses said...**fear** not: for God is come to prove you
Ps. 36:1(1-4)	wicked saith...there is no **fear** of God before his eye
Isa. 2:19(10-21)	go into the holes of the rocks...for **fear** of the Lord
Dan. 1:10(8-16)	I **fear** my Lord the king, who hath appointed your meat
Matt. 8:26(23-27)	why are ye **fearful**, O ye of little faith? Then he
Matt. 14:30(22-33)	when he saw the wind boisterous, he was **afraid**; and
Luke 1:30(28-35)	**fear** not, Mary: for thou hast found favour with God.
Luke 19:21(20-26)	I **feared** thee, because thou art an austere man: thou
Acts 2:43(42-43)	and **fear** came upon every soul: and many wonders and
2 Tim. 1:7(7-8)	God hath not given us the spirit of **fear**; but of power
1 Jn. 4:18	there is no **fear** in love; but perfect love casteth out
1 Ne. 8:28(24-28)	they were **ashamed**, because of those that were scoffing
Alma 14:26(26,27)	for the **fear** of destruction had come upon them.
Morm. 6:7	that awful **fear** of death which fills...all the wicked
D&C 3:7(6-10)	you should not have **feared** man more than God. although
D&C 6:33(33-36)	**fear** not to do good, my sons, for whatsoever ye sow
D&C 9:11(10-11)	but you **feared**, and the time is past, and it is not
D&C 10:55(55,56)	whosoever belongeth to my church need not **fear**, for
D&C 38:15(15,30)	be ye strong...**fear** not, for the kingdom is yours.
D&C 45:39(37-42,74)	he that **feareth** me shall be looking forth for the
D&C 60:2(2-3)	hide the talent...because of the **fear** of man. wo unto
D&C 63:6	and let the rebellious **fear** and tremble; and let the
D&C 63:16(16,17)	but shall deny the faith and shall **fear**.
D&C 63:17(16,17)	the **fearful**, and the unbelieving, and all liars, and
D&C 67:3	there were **fears** in your hearts, and verily this is
D&C 67:10	strip yourselves from...**fears**...and you shall see me
D&C 68:6	be of good cheer, and do not **fear**, for I the Lord am
D&C 101:36(35-37)	wherefore, **fear** not even unto death; for in this world
D&C 122:9(5-9)	**fear** not what man can do, for God shall be with you
D&C 136:17(17,30)	**fear** not thine enemies; for they shall not have power
Moses 1:20	it came to pass that Moses began to **fear** exceedingly

FELLOWSHIPING

Lev. 19:18	thou shalt love thy **neighbour** as thyself: I am the Lord
Lev. 19:34(33-34)	**stranger**...love him as thyself; for ye were strangers
Matt. 19:19	thou shalt love thy **neighbour** as thyself.
Luke 22:32	when thou art converted, **strengthen** thy brethren.
John 13:35(34-35)	ye are my disciples, if ye have **love** one to another.
John 21:17(15-17)	Jesus saith unto him, **feed** my sheep.
Acts 2:42(41-47)	continued stedfastly in...doctrine and **fellowship**, and
1 Cor. 1:9	**fellowship** of his Son Jesus Christ our Lord.
2 Cor. 6:14(12-14)	be ye not unequally yoked...**fellowship** hath
Gal. 2:9	gave to me and Barnabas the right hands of **fellowship**
Eph. 2:19	no more strangers and foreigners, but **fellowcitizens**
1 Jn. 1:3	**fellowship** is with the father, and with his Son Jesus
1 Jn. 4:21(20-21)	he who **loveth** God love his brother also.
Mosiah 2:17	service of your **fellow** beings...service of your God.
Alma 17:25(19-25)	unto him: nay, but I will be thy **servant**. Therefore
D&C 38:24(24-25)	and let every man **esteem** his brother as himself, and
D&C 38:27	I say unto you, be **one**; and if ye are not one ye are
D&C 42:52	break not my laws thou shalt **bear** their infirmities.
D&C 59:6	thou shalt love thy **neighbor** as thyself. Thou shalt
D&C 88:133	I receive you to **fellowship**, in a determination that

FILTHINESS

2 Chr. 29:5	carry forth the **filthiness** out of the holy place.
Ezra 6:21(19-22)	separated themselves unto them from the **filthiness** of
Ezra 9:11(10-12)	an unclean land with the **filthiness** of the people of
Job 15:16	how much more abominable and **filthy** is man, which
Ps. 14:3(2-3)	they are all together become **filthy**: there is none
Prov. 30:12	yet is not washed from their **filthiness**.
Isa. 28:8(7-8)	for all tables are full of vomit and **filthiness**, so
Isa. 64:6(6-7)	all our righteousnesses are as **filthy** rags; and we all
Lam. 1:9(8-10)	her **filthiness** is in her skirts; she remembereth not
Ezek. 16:36(35-43)	because thy **filthiness** was poured out, and thy
Ezek. 22:15(13-16)	I ...will consume thy **filthiness** out of thee.
Ezek. 23:17(1-21)	defiled her with their whoredom, and she was **polluted**
Ezek. 24:13(6-13)	in thy **filthiness** is lewdness: because I have purged
Ezek. 36:25(25-38)	ye shall be clean: from all your **filthiness**, and from
Zeph. 3:1(1-7)	woe to her that is **filthy** and polluted, to the
Zech. 3:3(3-4)	now Joshua was clothed with **filthy** garments, and stood
1 Cor. 3:17(16-17)	if any man **defile** the temple of God, him shall God
2 Cor. 7:1	cleanse ourselves from all **filthiness** of the flesh and
Eph. 5:4(1-4)	neither **filthiness**, nor foolish talking, nor jesting
1 Tim. 3:3(3,8)	not greedy of **filthy** lucre; but patient, not a brawler
James 1:21	wherefore lay apart all **filthiness** and superfluity of
1 Pet. 5:2	feed the flock...willingly; not for **filthy** lucre, but
2 Pet. 2:7(4-8)	vexed with the **filthy** conversation of the wicked
Rev. 17:4(1-18)	cup in her hand full of abominations and **filthiness**
Rev. 22:11(8-13)	he which is **filthy**, let him be filthy still: and he
1 Ne. 12:16	behold the fountain of **filthy** water which thy father
1 Ne. 12:23	a dark, and loathsome, and a **filthy** people, full of
1 Ne. 15:27	the water which my father saw was **filthiness**; and so
1 Ne. 15:34(31-36)	a place of **filthiness** prepared for that which is

FILTHINESS cont.

2 Ne. 9:16	they who are **filthy** shall be filthy still; wherefore
Jacob 2:28	**whoredoms** are an abomination before me; thus saith the
Jacob 3:3(3-11)	Lamanites, which are not **filthy** like unto you
Enos 1:20	blood- thirsty people, full of idolatry and **filthiness**
Mosiah 7:30(30-31)	if my people shall sow **filthiness**...reap the chaff the
Alma 5:22(22-25)	garments stained with blood...all manner of **filthiness**
Alma 7:21(19-22)	neither can **filthiness**...be received into the kingdom
Alma 32:3(2-3)	not permitted to enter...being esteemed as **filthiness**
Morm. 5:15	become a dark, a **filthy**, and a loathsome people
Morm. 9:4	under a consciousness of your **filthiness** before him
Morm. 9:14	he that is **filthy** shall be filthy still; and he that
D&C 38:11(10-13)	for all flesh is **corrupted** before me; and the powers
D&C 88:35	therefore, they must remain **filthy** still.
D&C 88:102	even the end, who shall remain **filthy** still.
D&C 101:24	every **corruptible** thing, both of man, or of the beasts
Moses 7:48	be cleansed from the **filthiness**...gone forth out of

FIRSTBORN

Gen. 29:26	to give the younger before the **firstborn**.
Ex. 4:22	Israel is my son, even my **firstborn**
Ex. 12:12(12-13)	will smite all the **firstborn** in the land of Egypt
Ex. 13:2	sanctify unto me all the **firstborn**, whatsoever openeth
Ex. 13:13(11-16)	all the **firstborn** of man...shalt thou redeem
Ex. 22:29	the **firstborn** of thy sons shalt thou give unto me.
Ex. 34:20	all the **firstborn** of thy sons thou shalt redeem. and
Lev. 27:26	the **firstling** of the beasts, which should be the Lord
Num. 3:12(12-13)	taken the Levites...instead of all the **firstborn** that
Num. 8:18(13-19)	taken the Levites for all the **firstborn** of...Israel.
Num. 18:15	the **firstborn** of man shalt thou surely redeem, and the
Deut. 21:17(15-17)	the right of the **firstborn** is his.
Neh. 10:36	the **firstborn** of our sons...bring to...our God, unto
Ps. 78:51	and smote all the **firstborn** in Egypt; the chief of the
Ps. 89:27	I will make him my **firstborn**, higher than the kings
Jer. 31:9	I am a father to Israel, and Ephraim is my **firstborn**.
Micah 6:7	shall I give my **firstborn** for my transgression; the
Matt. 1:25	till she had brought forth her **firstborn** son: and he
Luke 2:7	and she brought forth her **firstborn** son, and wrapped
Col. 1:15(15,18)	the **firstborn** of every creature
Heb. 12:23	to the general assembly and church of the **firstborn**
2 Ne. 4:3	the sons and the daughters of my **first-born**, I would
Mosiah 2:3	took of the **firstlings** of their flocks...offer
D&C 68:16(16-18)	if they are the **firstborn** among the sons of Aaron
Moses 5:5(5,20)	offer the **firstlings** of their flocks, for an offering
Abr. 1:3	even the right of the **firstborn**, on the first man, who

FLATTERY

Job 17:5	he that speaketh **flattery** to his friends, even the eye
Job 32:22(21,22)	not to give **flattering** titles; in so doing my maker
Ps. 5:9(8-10)	they **flatter** with their tongue.

FLATTERY cont.

Ps. 12:3(1-4)   the Lord shall cut off all **flattering** lips, and the
Ps. 78:36(31-41)   they did **flatter** him with their mouth, and they lied
Prov. 20:19   meddle not with him that **flattereth** with his lips.
Prov. 26:28   a **flattering** mouth worketh ruin.
Prov. 28:23   he that **flattereth** with the tongue.
Ezek. 12:24(21-25)   be no more any vain vision nor **flattering** divination
Dan. 11:21   a vile person...obtain the kingdom by **flatteries**.
1 Thes. 2:5(3-6)   neither at any time used we **flattering** words, as ye
2 Ne. 28:22(19-25)   others he **flattereth** away, and telleth them there is
Jacob 7:4(1-4)   he could use much **flattery**, and much power of speech
Mosiah 11:7(7,8)   deceived by the vain and **flattering** words of the king
Mosiah 26:6(5-7)   did deceive many with their **flattering** words, who were
Mosiah 27:8(8-9)   wicked...man of many words...**flattery** to the people
Alma 30:47(4-48)   by thy lying and by thy **flattering** words; therefore
Alma 46:7(6-10)   many in the church who believed in the **flattering** word
Alma 61:4(1-4)   they have used great **flattery**, and they have led away
D&C 10:29(23-29)   he **flattereth** them away to do iniquity, to get thee

FLESH AND BLOOD

Deut. 12:27   burnt offerings, the **flesh** and the blood, upon the
Job 19:26   yet in my **flesh** shall I see God
Ps. 73:26   my **flesh** and my heart faileth: but God is the strength
Ps. 136:25   who giveth food to all **flesh**: for his mercy endureth
Matt. 16:17(13-20)   **flesh** and blood hath not revealed it unto thee, but
John 1:14   the word was made **flesh**, and dwelt among us, (and we
1 Cor. 15:50   **flesh** and blood cannot inherit the kingdom of God
Gal. 1:16(15-17)   I conferred not with **flesh** and blood
Eph. 6:12   we wrestle not against **flesh** and blood, but against
Heb. 2:14(14-15)   children are partakers of **flesh** and blood, he also him
1 Jn. 4:2   confesseth that Jesus Christ is come in the **flesh** is
Enos 1:27   when my **mortal** shall put on immortality, and shall
Mosiah 7:27   take upon him **flesh** and blood, and go forth upon the
Ether 3:9   I shall take upon me **flesh** and blood; and never has
D&C 93:4   made **flesh** my tabernacle, and dwelt among the sons of
D&C 93:11   dwelt in the **flesh**, and dwelt among us.
Moses 8:17   for he shall know that all **flesh** shall die; yet his

FLOOD

Gen. 5:29(25-32)   **Noah**, saying, this same shall comfort us concerning
Gen. 6:17(5-22)   bring a **flood** of waters upon the earth, to destroy all
Gen. 7:10(1-24)   the waters of the **flood** were upon the earth.
Gen. 8:3(1-21)   end of the hundred and fifty days the **waters** were
Gen. 9:11(9-15)   neither...any more be a **flood** to destroy the earth.
Gen. 9:15(9-17)   the waters shall no more become a **flood** to destroy all
Ps. 29:10   the Lord sitteth upon the **flood**; yea, the Lord sitteth
Isa. 54:9   sworn...**waters** of Noah should no more go over the
Luke 17:26(26-27)   as it was in the days of **Noe**, so shall it be also in
1 Pet. 3:20(18-20)   eight souls were saved by **water**.
2 Pet. 2:5   bringing in the **flood** upon the world of the ungodly

FLOOD cont.

2 Pet. 3:6	world...being **overflowed** with water, perished
Alma 10:22	not be by **flood**, as were the people in the days of
3 Ne. 22:9	the **waters** of Noah unto me, for as I have sworn that
Ether 13:2(1-3)	after the **waters** had receded...it became a choice land
Moses 7:34(4,32-43)	I send in the **floods** upon them, for my fierce anger
Moses 7:43(42-45)	upon the...wicked the **floods** came and swallowed them
Moses 7:50(50-52)	earth might never more be covered by the **floods**.
Moses 8:17	if men do not repent, I will send in the **floods** upon
Moses 8:30(22,28-30)	I will **destroy** all flesh from off the earth.
JS-M 1:42(41-43)	as it was in the days...before the **flood**; for until

FOOD

Gen. 1:29	every herb...every tree...to you it shall be for **meat**.
Gen. 2:9	to grow every tree that is ...good for **food**; the tree
Gen. 3:6	woman saw that the tree was good for **food**, and that
Gen. 6:21	it shall be for **food** for thee, and for them.
Gen. 8:20	took of every **clean** beast, and of every clean fowl
Gen. 9:3	every moving thing that liveth shall be **meat** for you
Gen. 41:48	he gathered up all the **food** of the seven years, which
Lev. 11:2(1-47)	the beasts which ye shall **eat** among all the beasts
Deut. 10:18(17-19)	he...loveth the stranger, in giving him **food** and
Deut. 12:15(15-16)	thou mayest kill and eat **flesh** in all thy gates
Mal. 3:10(8-10)	that there may be **meat** in mine house, and prove me
Acts 14:17	filling our hearts with **food** and gladness.
Rom. 14:17(11-23)	kingdom of God is not **meat** and drink; but
1 Cor. 8:8(4-13)	but **meat** commendeth us not to God: for neither, if we
1 Tim. 4:3(3-4)	commanding to abstain from **meats**, which God hath
1 Tim. 6:8(7,8)	and having **food** and raiment let us be therewith
James 2:15(15-16)	if a brother or sister be...destitute of daily **food**
1 Ne. 16:32(18,32)	beheld that I had obtained **food**, how great was their
Mosiah 4:19(17-19)	depend upon the same being, even God...for both **food**
Alma 8:20	I will impart unto thee of my **food**; and I know that
Alma 14:22	mock...withhold **food** from them that they might hunger
Alma 30:56(56,58)	Korihor...from house to house begging for his **food**.
Alma 58:7	we were about to perish for the want of **food**.
Hel. 4:12(12,13)	withholding their **food** from the hungry, withholding
Hel. 5:22	many days without **food**, behold, they went forth into
3 Ne. 4:3	robbers could not exist...for the want of **food**; for
3 Ne. 13:25(25-34)	is not the life more than **meat**, and the body than
Ether 6:4	they had prepared all manner of **food**...commending them
Ether 9:18	animals which were useful for the **food** of man.
D&C 42:43	sick...nourished with...herbs and mild **food**, and that
D&C 49:18(18-19)	and whoso forbiddeth to abstain from **meats**, that man
D&C 49:19(18-19)	beasts...of the earth...ordained for...man for **food**
D&C 49:21(18-21)	wo be unto man that...wasteth **flesh** and hath no need.
D&C 59:19(16-20)	yea, for **food** and for raiment...to strengthen the body
D&C 89:16(1-21)	all grain is...for...**food** of man...fruit of the vine

FOOLISHNESS

Ps. 69:5	O God, thou knowest my **foolishness**; and my sins are
Prov. 12:23	the heart of fools proclaimeth **foolishness**.
Prov. 14:24	the **foolishness** of fools is folly.
Prov. 15:2	the mouth of fools poureth out **foolishness**.
Prov. 15:14	the mouth of fools feedeth on **foolishness**.
Prov. 19:3	the **foolishness** of man perverteth his way: and his
Prov. 24:9	the thought of **foolishness** is sin: and the scorner is
Jer. 4:22	for my people is **foolish**, they have not known me; they
Jer. 5:21	hear now this, O **foolish** people, and without
Matt. 7:26(24-27)	one that heareth...and doeth them not...a **foolish** man
1 Cor. 1:25(18-25)	the **foolishness** of God is wiser than men; and the weak
1 Cor. 2:14(13-14)	natural man receiveth not...spirit...**foolishness** unto
1 Cor. 3:19(18-21)	the wisdom of this world is **foolishness** with God.
2 Ne. 9:28	**foolishness** of men! When...learned they think they are
2 Ne. 26:10	reward of...**foolishness** they shall reap destruction
Alma 37:6(3-8)	suppose..this is **foolishness** in me; but..by small and
Hel. 12:4	how **foolish**...vain...evil...are the children of men
3 Ne. 14:26	one that heareth...doeth them not...a **foolish** man, who
D&C 35:7	Gentiles..their **folly**..abominations shall be made
D&C 45:49(49-50)	they that have laughed shall see their **folly**.
D&C 63:15(14-16)	their **folly** shall be made manifest, and their works
D&C 124:48	judgments upon your own heads, by your **follies**, and
D&C 124:116	let him repent of all his **folly**, and clothe himself
D&C 136:19	and his **folly** shall be made manifest.

FORBEARANCE

Gen. 26:27(12-33)	wherefore come ye to me, seeing ye **hate** me, and have
Ex. 34:6	the Lord God, merciful and gracious, **longsuffering**
Lev. 19:18	thou shalt not **avenge**, nor bear any grudge against the
Neh. 9:30(28-31)	yet many years didst thou **forbear** them, and
Prov. 20:22	say not thou, I will **recompense** evil; but wait on the
Prov. 24:29	say not, I will **do** so to him as he hath done to me: I
Prov. 25:15	by long **forbearing** is a prince persuaded, and a soft
Nahum 1:3	the Lord is **slow** to anger, and great in power, and
Matt. 5:39(38-48)	smite thee on thy right cheek, **turn** to him the other
Matt. 6:14	if ye **forgive**...your heavenly father will also forgive
Matt. 18:21(21-22)	how oft shall my brother sin...and I **forgive** him? Till
Rom. 2:4	riches of his goodness and **forbearance** and
Rom. 3:25	remission of sins...through the **forbearance** of God
Rom. 12:19(17-21)	**avenge** not yourselves...vengeance is mine...saith the
1 Cor. 6:7(6-8)	why do ye not rather **suffer** yourselves to be defrauded
1 Cor. 13:4	charity **suffereth** long, and is kind; charity envieth
2 Cor. 6:6	by pureness, by knowledge, by **longsuffering**, by
Gal. 5:22	fruit of the spirit is love, joy, peace, **longsuffering**
Eph. 4:2(1-3)	with longsuffering, **forbearing** one another in love
Col. 3:13(12-15)	**forbearing** one another, and forgiving one another, if
1 Thes. 5:15	see that none render **evil** for evil unto any man; but
1 Tim. 1:16	in me..Jesus Christ might shew forth all **longsuffering**
1 Pet. 2:20(18-23)	when ye do well, and **suffer** for it, ye take it patient
1 Pet. 3:9	not rendering **evil** for evil, or railing for railing
1 Pet. 3:20	the **longsuffering** of God waited in the days of Noah

FORBEARANCE cont.

2 Pet. 3:9(9,15)	the Lord is...**longsuffering** to us-ward, not willing
2 Pet. 3:15(9,15)	the **longsuffering** of our Lord is salvation; even as
1 Ne. 19:9	suffereth it, because of...his **long-suffering** towards
Alma 7:23	I would that ye should be...full of...**long-suffering**
Alma 13:28	becoming humble...full of love and all **long-suffering**
Alma 14:11	the spirit **constraineth** me that I must not stretch
Alma 17:11	be **patient** in long-suffering and afflictions, that ye
Moro. 9:25	his mercy and **long-suffering**, and the hope of his
D&C 19:30	**reviling** not against revilers.
D&C 31:9	**revile** not against those that revile. Govern your
D&C 64:10(7-11)	but of you it is required to **forgive** all men.
D&C 98:23(23-32)	if men will smite you ...and ye **bear** it patiently and
D&C 107:30(30-31)	decisions of...quorums...to be made in..**long-suffering**
D&C 118:3	preach...in meekness and humility, and **long-suffering**
D&C 121:41(41-46)	influence...of the priesthood...by **long-suffering**, by

FOREORDINATION

Deut. 32:8(7-8)	he set the **bounds** of the people according to the
Isa. 7:14	virgin shall conceive...shall call his name **Immanuel**.
Isa. 40:3	voice...in the wilderness, **prepare** ye the way of the
Isa. 45:1	thus saith the Lord to his **anointed**, to Cyrus, whose
Isa. 46:10(9-10)	**declaring** the end from the beginning, and from ancient
Jer. 1:5(4-5)	before I formed thee in the belly...I **ordained** thee a
Matt. 3:3(1-3)	this is he that was spoken of by the prophet **Esaias**
Matt. 20:16	for many be **called**, but few chosen.
Luke 1:13(13-17)	wife Elisabeth shall bear thee a **son**, and thou shalt
Luke 22:22	the Son of man goeth, as it was **determined**: but woe
Acts 2:23	delivered by the determinate counsel and **foreknowledge**
Acts 3:18	those things, which God before had **shewed** by the mouth
Acts 17:26	determined the times before **appointed**, and the bounds
Rom. 8:29(29-30)	he also did **predestinate** to be conformed to the image
Rom. 9:11(10-12)	the purpose of God according to **election** might stand
Rom. 11:2	God hath not cast away his people which he **foreknew**.
Eph. 1:4(4-14)	he hath **chosen** us in him before the foundation of the
Eph. 1:5(5,11)	having **predestinated** us unto the adoption of children
2 Thes. 2:13	God hath from the beginning **chosen** you to salvation
2 Tim. 1:9	**calling**...given us...before the world began
1 Pet. 1:2	elect according to the **foreknowledge** of God the Father
1 Pet. 1:20(19-20)	who verily was **foreordained** before the foundation of
Rev. 13:8	the Lamb slain from the **foundation** of the world.
1 Ne. 10:7(7-10)	concerning a **prophet** who should come before the
1 Ne. 11:18(18-19)	**virgin** whom thou seest is the mother of the Son of God
1 Ne. 11:29	I also beheld **twelve** others following him. And it came
1 Ne. 13:12	I looked and beheld a **man** among the Gentiles, who was
1 Ne. 14:20(19-29)	behold one of the **twelve** apostles of the Lamb.
2 Ne. 3:3	Joseph...thy **seed** shall not utterly be destroyed.
2 Ne. 3:10	and **Moses** will I raise up, to deliver thy people out
2 Ne. 3:11(11-15)	a **seer** will I raise up out of the fruit of thy loins
Mosiah 3:8	he shall be called **Jesus** Christ...mother...called Mary
Alma 13:3(3-9)	**called** and prepared from the foundation of the world
D&C 29:7	mine **elect** hear my voice and harden not their hearts

FOREORDINATION cont.

D&C 49:17(16,17)   according to his **creation** before the world was made.
D&C 104:17(15-17)   I **prepared** all things...given unto...men to be agents
Moses 4:2(1-4)   my...Son, which was my...**Chosen** from the beginning
Abr. 3:23(22-23)   Abraham...thou wast **chosen** before thou wast born.
Abr. 3:27   and the Lord said: I will send the **first**.
JFS-V 1:55(53-56)   noble and great ones who were **chosen** in the beginning

FORGIVENESS

Gen. 50:17   say unto Joseph, **forgive**, I pray thee now, the
Ex. 34:7   **forgiving** iniquity and transgression and sin, and that
Ex. 34:9   **pardon** our iniquity and our sin, and take us for thine
Lev. 4:20   atonement for them, and it shall be **forgiven** them.
Lev. 19:22   the sin which he hath done shall be **forgiven** him.
Num. 14:18(18-21)   Lord is...of great mercy, **forgiving** iniquity and
Num. 15:25(25-28)   it shall be **forgiven** them; for it is ignorance: and
Neh. 9:17(17-32)   thou art a God ready to **pardon**, gracious and merciful
Ps. 32:5   I acknowledged my sin...and thou **forgavest** the
Ps. 86:5   ready to **forgive**; and plenteous in mercy unto all them
Ps. 103:3(1-5)   who **forgiveth** all thine iniquities; who healeth all
Ps. 130:4(3-4)   but there is **forgiveness** with thee, that thou mayest
Isa. 1:18   **sins** be as scarlet, they shall be as white as snow
Isa. 6:7(5-7)   thine iniquity is **taken** away, and thy sin purged.
Isa. 40:2   speak...to Jerusalem...that her iniquity is **pardoned**
Isa. 43:25   I, even I, am he that **blotteth** out thy transgressions
Jer. 33:8(1-8)   and I will **cleanse** them from all their iniquity, where
Jer. 50:20(17-20)   I will **pardon** them whom I reserve.
Ezek. 18:22(20-24)   all his **transgressions**...shall not be mentioned unto
Ezek. 33:16   none of his **sins**...shall be mentioned unto him: he
Micah 7:18   who is a God like unto thee, that **pardoneth** iniquity
Matt. 1:21   he shall **save** his people from their sins.
Matt. 5:24(23-24)   first be **reconciled** to thy brother, and then come and
Matt. 6:12   forgive us our debts, as we **forgive** our debtors.
Matt. 6:15(14-15)   if ye **forgive** not men their trespasses, neither will
Matt. 9:6(2-8)   know that the Son of man hath power...to **forgive** sins
Matt. 12:32(31,32)   it shall not be **forgiven** him, neither in this world
Matt. 18:35(21-35)   if ye from your hearts **forgive** not every one his
Mark 3:29   blaspheme against the Holy Ghost hath never
Mark 4:12   be converted, and their sins should be **forgiven** them.
Mark 11:25(25-26)   which is in heaven may **forgive** you your trespasses.
Luke 5:20(20-24)   when he saw their faith...thy sins are **forgiven** thee.
Luke 6:37   forgive, and ye shall be **forgiven**
Luke 7:42(41-43)   they had nothing to pay, he frankly **forgave** them both.
Luke 7:47(44-49)   her sins, which are many, are **forgiven**; for she loved
Luke 11:4(1-4)   **forgive** us our sins; for we also forgive every one
Luke 17:3(3-4)   rebuke him; and if he repent, **forgive** him.
Luke 23:34   Father, **forgive** them; for they know not what they do.
Luke 24:47   repentance and **remission** of sins should be preached
Acts 5:31(30-31)   give repentance to Israel, and **forgiveness** of sins.
Acts 13:38   preached unto you the **forgiveness** of sins
Rom. 9:18   therefore hath he **mercy** on whom he will have mercy
Rom. 12:17(17-21)   **recompense** to no man evil for evil. Provide things

FORGIVENESS cont.

2 Cor. 2:7	contrariwise ye ought rather to **forgive** him, and
Eph. 1:7	redemption through his blood, the **forgiveness** of sins
Eph. 4:32	be ye kind one to another...**forgiving** one another
Heb. 8:12	their sins and their iniquities will I **remember** no
James 5:15	if he have committed sins, they shall be **forgiven** him.
1 Jn. 1:9(8-9)	he is faithful and just to **forgive** us our sins, and
1 Jn. 3:5(4,5)	to take away our **sins**; and in him is no sin.
1 Ne. 7:21	did exhort them...pray unto the Lord...for **forgiveness**
Enos 1:5(5-8)	Enos, thy sins are **forgiven** thee, and thou shalt be
Mosiah 4:2(2-3)	blood of Christ that we may receive **forgiveness** of our
Mosiah 26:29(29-30)	confess his sins...and repenteth..I will **forgive** him
Alma 34:36	garments should be made white through the **blood** of the
Alma 36:20(16-21)	my soul was filled with **joy** as exceeding as was my
Alma 39:6	not easy for him to obtain **forgiveness**; yea, I say
3 Ne. 12:24(23-24)	first be **reconciled** to thy brother, and then come unto
3 Ne. 13:14(14-15)	if ye **forgive** men...your heavenly Father will also
Morm. 8:32	for your money you shall be **forgiven** of your sins.
Moro. 6:8	oft as they repented...they were **forgiven**.
D&C 1:32	repents and does the commandments...shall be **forgiven**
D&C 29:3	at this time your sins are **forgiven** you, therefore ye
D&C 31:5	thrust in your sickle...and your sins are **forgiven** you
D&C 36:1	and your sins are **forgiven** you, and you are called to
D&C 42:25(25-26)	he that...repents...and forsaketh...thou shalt **forgive**
D&C 50:36	for your sins are **forgiven** you.
D&C 56:14	your sins have come up unto me, and are not **pardoned**
D&C 58:42(42-43)	he who has repented of his sins, the same is **forgiven**
D&C 60:7	to make you holy, and your sins are **forgiven** you.
D&C 61:2	for I, the Lord, **forgive** sins, and am merciful unto
D&C 64:10	but of you it is required to **forgive** all men.
D&C 64:10(6-14)	I, the Lord, will **forgive** whom I will forgive, but of
D&C 68:24(22-24)	and if he repent he shall be **forgiven**, according to
D&C 76:34(32-34)	there is no **forgiveness** in this world nor in the world
D&C 82:1(1-7)	as you have **forgiven** one another...I, the Lord
D&C 84:61	I will **forgive** you of your sins with this
D&C 95:1(1-2)	chasten that their sins may be **forgiven**, for with the
D&C 98:40(23-48)	thou shalt **forgive** him, until seventy times seven.
D&C 132:27	blasphemy...the Holy Ghost...shall not be **forgiven** in
Moses 6:53(53-55)	I have **forgiven** thee thy transgression in the garden

FORNICATION

Gen. 39:9(7-18)	how then can I do this great **wickedness**, and sin
Ex. 20:14	thou shalt not commit **adultery**.
2 Sam. 13:12(1-19)	do not **force** me; for no such thing ought to be done
Prov. 7:22(5-23)	goeth after her...as an ox goeth to the **slaughter**, or
Prov. 22:14	the mouth of **strange** women is a deep pit: he that is
Matt. 5:28	**lust** after her hath committed adultery with her
Matt. 5:32	put away his wife, saving for the cause of **fornication**
Matt. 15:19	out of the heart proceed evil thoughts...**fornications**
Matt. 19:9	put away his wife, except it be for **fornication**, and
Acts 15:20(20,29)	abstain from...**fornication**, and from things strangled
Acts 21:25	keep themselves from...**fornication**.

FORNICATION cont.

1 Cor. 5:9(1-13)	I wrote unto you...not to company with **fornicators**
1 Cor. 6:9(9,13-20)	not inherit the kingdom...neither **fornicators**, nor
1 Cor. 6:13(9,13-20)	now the body is not for **fornication**, but for the Lord
1 Cor. 7:2	to avoid **fornication**, let every man have his own wife
1 Cor. 10:8	neither let us commit **fornication**, as some of them
Gal. 5:19	works of the flesh...**fornication**, uncleanness
Eph. 5:3(1-4)	but **fornication**...let it not be once named among you
1 Thes. 4:3	the will of God...ye should abstain from **fornication**
Jude 1:7	giving themselves over to **fornication**, and going after
Jacob 3:12	warning them against **fornication** and lasciviousness
Alma 39:5(3-6)	these things are...**abominable** above all sins save it
Hel. 8:26	ripening, because of your murders and your **fornication**
3 Ne. 12:32(31-32)	put away his wife, saving for the cause of **fornication**
D&C 42:74	put away their companions for the cause of **fornication**

FRAUD

Lev. 19:13	thou shalt not **defraud** thy neighbour, neither rob him
1 Sam. 12:3(3,4)	whom have I **defrauded**? whom have I oppressed? or of
Ps. 10:7	his mouth is full of cursing...and **fraud**: under his
Mark 7:22(21,22)	thefts, covetousness, wickedness, **deceit**
Mark 10:19	**defraud** not, honour thy father and mother.
1 Cor. 6:8(7,8)	nay, ye do wrong, and **defraud**, and that your brethren.
1 Cor. 7:5	**defraud** ye not one the other, except it be with
2 Cor. 7:2(1-3)	corrupted no man, we have **defrauded** no man.
Col. 2:8(6-8)	beware lest any man spoil you...vain **deceit**, after the
Alma 47:30(30-35)	Amalickiah, by his **fraud**, gained the hearts of the
D&C 57:8(8-10)	that he may sell goods without **fraud**, that he may

FRIENDSHIP

Ruth 2:13(8-13)	for that thou hast spoken **friendly** unto thine handmaid
1 Sam. 18:1(1-4)	the soul of Jonathan was **knit** with the soul of David
Job 19:21(14-21)	have pity upon me, O ye my **friends**; for the hand of
Job 42:10	when he prayed for his **friends**: also the Lord gave Job
Prov. 17:17(17-18)	a **friend** loveth at all times, and a brother is born
Prov. 18:24	a **friend** that sticketh closer than a brother.
Prov. 22:24(24,25)	make no **friendship** with an angry man; and with a
Prov. 27:6	faithful are the wounds of a **friend**; but the kisses
Prov. 27:17	a man sharpeneth the countenance of his **friend**.
Luke 11:8(5-8)	because he is his **friend**, yet because of his
John 15:13(13-15)	that a man lay down his life for his **friends**.
James 2:23	Abraham...was called the **friend** of God.
2 Ne. 1:30	thou art a true **friend** unto my son, Nephi, forever.
Alma 15:16(16-18)	Amulek...rejected by those who were once his **friends**
Alma 17:2(1-3)	Alma did rejoice exceedingly to see his **brethren**; and
Alma 27:19(16-19)	joy of Alma in meeting his **brethren** was truly great
Morm. 8:5(1-6)	I have not **friends** nor whither to go; and how long the
Ether 1:36(36,37)	that he will turn away his anger from...our **friends**
Ether 2:1(1-5)	and also the **friends** of Jared and his brother and the
Ether 6:16(16-18)	and the **friends** of Jared and his brother were in

GENEALOGY AND TEMPLE WORK

GENEALOGY AND TEMPLE WORK cont.

D&C 128:24	a book containing the **records** of our dead, which shall
D&C 131:2(1-4)	a man must enter into this **order** of the priesthood
D&C 132:6(6-8)	he...receiveth a fulness...must...abide the **law**, or
D&C 132:19(6-22)	if a man **marry** a wife by my word, which is my law, and
D&C 132:46(45,46)	whatsoever you **seal** on earth shall be sealed in heaven
Moses 6:8(5-8)	a **genealogy** was kept of the children of God. And this
Moses 6:46	for a book of **remembrance** we have written among us
Moses 7:57(55-57)	the spirits as were in **prison** came forth, and stood
JS-H 1:39(37-39)	plant in the hearts of the **children** the promises made
JS-V 1:6(5-10)	how it was that he had obtained an **inheritance** in that
JFS-V 1:27(26-60)	his ministry among those who were **dead** was limited to
JFS-V 1:48(47,48)	great work to be done in the **temples** of the Lord in

GENEROSITY

Ex. 35:21(21-29)	willing...brought...**offering** to the work of the
Ex. 36:5(5-7)	the people **bring** much more than enough for the service
Deut. 15:11(7-11)	thou shalt open thine **hand** wide unto...thy poor, and
Ps. 112:9	he hath dispersed, he hath **given** to the poor; his
Prov. 19:17	he that hath **pity** upon the poor lendeth unto the Lord
Mal. 3:10(7-10)	**open** you the windows of heaven, and pour you out a
Matt. 5:42	**give** to him that asketh thee, and from him that would
Matt. 6:1(1-4)	do not your **alms** before men, to be seen of them: other
Matt. 10:8	freely ye have received, freely **give**.
Matt. 25:35(31-46)	for I was an hungred, and ye **gave** me meat: I was
Mark 10:21(17-26)	sell whatsoever thou hast, and **give** to the poor, and
Mark 12:44(41-44)	she of her want did cast in **all** that she had, even all
Luke 3:11(10-11)	he that hath two coats...**impart** to him that hath none
Luke 6:30	**give** to every man that asketh of thee; and of him that
Luke 6:35(34-35)	do good, and **lend**, hoping for nothing again; and your
Luke 6:38	**give**, and it shall be given unto you; good measure
Luke 11:41	**give** alms of such things as ye have; and, behold, all
Luke 14:13(12-14)	when thou makest a feast, call the **poor**, the maimed
Acts 3:6(6,7)	such as I have **give** I thee: in the name of Jesus
Acts 20:35	he said, it is more blessed to **give** than to receive.
1 Cor. 16:3(1-4)	them will I send to bring your **liberality** unto
2 Cor. 8:2(2,3)	poverty abounded unto the riches of their **liberality**.
2 Cor. 9:7(1-14)	so let him give...for God loveth a cheerful **giver**.
1 Tim. 6:18(17-19)	be rich in good works, ready to **distribute**, willing
Jacob 2:17(17-19)	be familiar with all and free with your **substance**
Mosiah 4:16(16-26)	administer of your **substance** unto him...in need; and
Mosiah 18:28(26-28)	should impart of their **substance** of their own free
Alma 1:30(29-31)	they were **liberal** to all, both old and young, both
Alma 34:29(28-29)	if ye do not remember to be **charitable**, ye are as
3 Ne. 12:42	**give** to him that asketh thee, and from him that would
3 Ne. 13:1(1-4)	do not your **alms** before men to be seen of them
Morm. 8:39	why do ye...suffer the **hungry**...to pass by you, and
Moro. 7:8(6-10)	if a man...**giveth** a gift...grudgingly...counted evil
D&C 42:31(30-31)	impart of your **substance** unto the poor...do it unto
D&C 52:40	remember in all things the **poor** and the needy, the
D&C 56:16	wo unto you rich men, that will not **give** your

GENTILES

Gen. 10:5	these were the isles of the **Gentiles** divided in their
Ex. 34:12(12-17)	lest thou make a covenant with the **inhabitants** of the
Neh. 13:25(23-31)	ye shall not give your daughters unto **their** sons, nor
Isa. 11:10	to it shall the **Gentiles** seek: and his rest shall be
Isa. 49:6(6,22-23)	I will also give thee for a light to the **Gentiles**
Isa. 60:3(1-16)	and the **Gentiles** shall come to thy light, and kings
Isa. 66:19(19-21)	they shall declare my glory among the **Gentiles**.
Mal. 1:11	my name shall be great among the **Gentiles**; and in
Luke 21:24	until the times of the **Gentiles** be fulfilled.
Acts 10:45(9-48)	on the **Gentiles** also was poured out the gift of the
Acts 17:26(24-28)	and hath made of one blood **all** nations of men for to
Rom. 3:29(29-30)	the God...yes, of the **Gentiles** also
Rom. 11:25(11-27)	until the fulness of the **Gentiles** be come in.
Gal. 3:28(26-29)	there is neither Jew nor **Greek**...neither bond nor free
Eph. 2:19(11-20)	now therefore ye are no more **strangers** and foreigners
Eph. 3:6(5-6)	that the **Gentiles** should be fellowheirs, and of the
1 Ne. 13:4(1-11)	I saw among...**Gentiles** the foundation of a great
1 Ne. 13:13(12-19)	**Gentiles**...went forth out of captivity, upon the many
1 Ne. 13:25(25-32)	go forth from the Jews in purity unto the **Gentiles**
1 Ne. 14:1(1,2)	if the **Gentiles** shall hearken unto the Lamb of God in
1 Ne. 15:13(13,16-18)	gospel...unto the **Gentiles**..unto..remnant of our
1 Ne. 22:6(6-9)	Lord...hand upon the **Gentiles**...set...for a standard
2 Ne. 29:3(2-13)	many of the **Gentiles** shall say: A Bible! A Bible! we
Jacob 5:10(3-77)	grafted in the branches of the **wild** olive-tree.
3 Ne. 15:22(20-24)	**Gentiles** should be converted through their preaching.
3 Ne. 16:10(4-17)	day when the **Gentiles** shall sin against my gospel
3 Ne. 20:27(15-28)	pouring out of the Holy Ghost...upon the **Gentiles**
3 Ne. 21:14(12-22)	wo be unto the **Gentiles** except they repent; for it
3 Ne. 22:3(2-3)	thy seed shall inherit the **Gentiles** and make the
D&C 18:6	both the **Gentiles** and also the house of Israel.
D&C 35:7(7-11)	great work...among the **Gentiles**, for their folly and
D&C 45:28(24-30)	when the times of the **Gentiles** is come in, a light
D&C 90:9(8-9)	the word may go forth unto...the **Gentiles** first, and
JS-H 1:41	the fulness of the **Gentiles** was soon to come in. he

GLORY

Ex. 24:17(16-18)	the **glory** of the Lord was like devouring fire on the
Deut. 5:24	God hath shewed us his **glory** and his greatness, and
Ps. 19:1	the heavens declare the **glory** of God; and the
Ps. 62:7	in God is my salvation and my **glory**: the rock of my
Ps. 149:5(1-6)	let the saints be joyful in **glory**: let them sing aloud
Prov. 4:9(7-9)	a crown of **glory** shall she deliver to thee.
Prov. 17:6	the **glory** of children are their fathers.
Prov. 19:11	it is his **glory** to pass over a transgression.
Prov. 20:29	the **glory** of young men is their strength: and the
Prov. 25:27	for men to search their own **glory** is not glory.
Matt. 6:13(9-13)	the kingdom, and the power, and the **glory**, for ever.
Matt. 16:27	son of man shall come in the **glory** of his Father with
Luke 9:32	they saw his **glory**, and the two men that stood with
John 1:14	and we beheld his **glory**, the glory as of the Only
John 2:11	and manifested forth his **glory**; and his disciples

GLORY cont.

John 12:41	Esaias, when he saw his **glory**, and spake of him.
1 Cor. 15:41	for one star differeth from another star in **glory**.
Col. 1:11	according to his **glorious** power, unto all patience and
Titus 2:13	the **glorious** appearing of the great God and our
2 Ne. 12:19(17-21)	the **glory** of his majesty shall smite them, when he
Alma 29:9(9,10)	this is my **glory**, that perhaps I may be an instrument
3 Ne. 20:9(9,10)	did cry out with one voice, and gave **glory** to Jesus
3 Ne. 28:7(7,8)	I shall come in my **glory** with the powers of heaven.
D&C 4:5	with an eye single to the **glory** of God, qualify him
D&C 6:30	blessed are ye, for you shall dwell with me in **glory**.
D&C 7:3	tarry until I come in my **glory**, and shalt prophesy
D&C 21:6	heavens to shake for your good, and his name's **glory**.
D&C 25:14	let thy soul delight in thy husband, and the **glory**...
D&C 27:2	do it with an eye single to my **glory**- remembering
D&C 29:12(11-12)	mine apostles...shall stand...in **glory** even as I am
D&C 45:16(16,56)	when I shall come in my **glory** in the clouds of heaven
D&C 45:44(42-45)	clothed with power and great **glory**; with all the holy
D&C 45:59	his **glory** shall be upon them, and he will be their king
D&C 56:18	see the kingdom of God coming in power and great **glory**
D&C 58:3(3-4)	the **glory** which shall follow after much tribulation.
D&C 64:41	the **glory** of the Lord shall be upon her
D&C 65:5(5,6)	clothed in the brightness of his **glory**, to meet the
D&C 66:2	be made partakers of the **glories** which are to be
D&C 75:5	faithful...shall be...crowned with honor, and **glory**
D&C 76:20(20-119)	we beheld the **glory** of the Son, on the right hand of
D&C 76:81	even as the **glory** of the stars differs from that of
D&C 76:98	as one star differs from another star in **glory**, even
D&C 78:8	it is expedient that all things be done unto my **glory**
D&C 82:19	doing all things with an eye single to...**glory** of God.
D&C 84:5	which cloud shall be even the **glory** of the Lord, which
D&C 84:32	sons of Moses...shall be filled with the **glory** of the
D&C 84:101	she is clothed with the **glory** of her God; for he stand
D&C 88:4(4-116)	even the **glory** of the celestial kingdom
D&C 88:119	establish a house...a house of **glory**, a house of order
D&C 93:11(6-22)	I beheld his **glory**, as the glory of the Only Begotten
D&C 93:36	the **glory** of God is intelligence, or, in other words
D&C 94:8(8-9)	my **glory**...and my presence shall be there.
D&C 97:15	build a house unto me...my **glory** shall rest upon it
D&C 98:3	work together for your good, and to my name's **glory**
D&C 101:25	knowledge and **glory** may dwell upon all the earth.
D&C 101:31	caught up, and his rest shall be **glorious**.
D&C 101:65	and be crowned with celestial **glory**, when I shall come
D&C 104:7	I...have promised unto you a crown of **glory** at my
D&C 110:13	another great and **glorious** vision burst upon us; for
D&C 121:31	their **glories**, laws, and set times, shall be revealed
D&C 124:17(17-18)	will crown him with blessings and great **glory**.
D&C 124:39	for the **glory**, honor, and endowment of all her
D&C 128:12(12-23)	herein is **glory** and honor, and immortality and eternal
D&C 131:1	in the celestial **glory** there are three heavens or
D&C 132:6	new and everlasting covenant..instituted for..my **glory**
D&C 132:19(18-19)	shall pass...to their exaltation and **glory** in all
D&C 132:57	I was with Abraham...unto his exaltation and **glory**.
D&C 132:63	work of my father continued, that he may be **glorified**.

GLORY cont.

D&C 133:49	so great shall be the **glory** of his presence that the
D&C 133:57	that men might be made partakers of the **glories** which
Moses 1:2(1-2)	the **glory** of God was upon Moses; therefore Moses could
Moses 1:5(3-6)	all my works, except he behold all my **glory**; and no
Moses 1:9	presence of God withdrew..his **glory** was not upon Moses
Moses 1:11	his **glory** was upon me; and I beheld his face, for I
Moses 1:14(13-14)	not look upon God, except his **glory** should come upon
Moses 1:18	his **glory** has been upon me, wherefore I can judge
Moses 1:20(19-22)	one God only will I worship, which is the God of **glory**
Moses 1:25(24-29)	he beheld his **glory** again, for it was upon him; and
Moses 1:39(36-39)	my **glory**- to bring to pass the immortality and eternal
Moses 4:2	thy will be done, and the **glory** be thine forever.
Moses 6:59	eternal life in the world to come, even immortal **glory**
Moses 6:61(60-61)	the peaceable things of immortal **glory**; the truth of
Moses 7:17	so great was the **glory** of the Lord, which was upon his
Abr. 3:26	keep their second estate shall have **glory** added upon
JS-H 1:32(29-32)	his whole person was **glorious** beyond description, and
A of F 1:10	earth...be renewed and receive its paradisiacal **glory**.

GOD, ACCESS TO

Gen. 5:24	Enoch **walked** with God: and he was not; for God took
Gen. 6:3(3,5)	my spirit shall not always **strive** with man, for that
Gen. 18:22	but Abraham **stood** yet before the Lord.
Gen. 39:2(2-4)	and the Lord was with **Joseph**, and he was a prosperous
Ex. 3:8(4-8)	and I am come **down** to deliver them out of the hand of
Ex. 6:3(2-4)	and I **appeared** unto Abraham, unto Isaac, and unto
Ex. 25:22	there I will **meet** with thee, and I will commune with
Lev. 9:5	all the congregation drew **near** and stood before the
Deut. 4:29(29-31)	if...thou shalt **seek**...Lord thy God, thou shalt find
2 Chr. 15:4(1-4)	when they...**sought** him, he was found of them.
Job 27:9	will God hear his **cry** when trouble cometh upon him
Ps. 82:1	God **standeth** in the congregation of the mighty; he
Prov. 1:28	then shall they **call** upon me, but I will not answer
Isa. 1:15	many **prayers**, I will not hear: your hands are full of
Isa. 5:25(20-25)	he hath **stretched** forth his hand against them, and
Isa. 9:12(12,17,21)	but his hand is **stretched** out still.
Isa. 55:6(6,7)	**seek** ye the Lord while he may be found, call ye upon
Isa. 59:2(2-3)	your iniquities have **separated** between you and your
Jer. 11:11	though they shall **cry** unto me, I will not hearken unto
Jer. 29:13(10-14)	and ye shall **seek** me, and find me, when ye shall
Micah 3:4	then shall they **cry** unto the Lord, but he will not
Zech. 7:13	so they **cried**, and I would not hear, saith the Lord
Matt. 7:7(7-12)	**ask**, and it shall be given you; seek, and ye shall
John 14:6	no man **cometh** unto the Father, but by me.
Acts 17:27(24-27)	that they should **seek** the Lord, if haply they might
Rom. 2:11(10-12)	for there is no **respect** of persons with God.
Rom. 10:12(12-13)	same Lord over all is rich unto all that **call** upon him
Heb. 10:22	let us draw **near** with a true heart in full assurance
2 Ne. 26:13(12,13)	**manifesteth** himself unto all those who believe in him
2 Ne. 26:33	he inviteth them all to **come** unto him and partake of
2 Ne. 28:32(31-32)	if they will repent and **come** unto me; for mine arm is

GOD, ACCESS TO cont.

Alma 34:17(17-27)	begin to **call** upon his holy name, that he would have
3 Ne. 11:20	he arose and **stood** before him.
3 Ne. 18:21(16-21)	**pray** in your families unto the Father, always in my
D&C 29:11	for I will reveal **myself** from heaven with power and
D&C 84:88	I will **be** on your right hand and on your left, and my
D&C 88:63	draw **near** unto me and I will draw near unto you; seek
D&C 93:1	shall see my face and **know** that I am
D&C 97:16(15,16)	yea, and my **presence** shall be there, for I will come
D&C 110:4	I am your **advocate** with the Father.
D&C 112:10	the Lord thy God shall **lead** thee by the hand, and give
D&C 132:12	no man shall **come** unto the Father but by me or by my
D&C 132:49	Lord thy God, and will be **with** thee even unto the end
Moses 7:4	the Lord...**talked** with me...face to face; and he said
Moses 8:17	my Spirit shall not always **strive** with man, for he
Abr. 3:11	I, Abraham, **talked** with the Lord, face to face, as one

GOD, BODY OF (CORPOREAL NATURE)

Gen. 1:27(26-27)	so God created man in his own **image**, in the image of
Gen. 5:1(1-3)	God created man, in the **likeness** of God made he him
Gen. 9:6(6-9)	for in the **image** of God made he man.
Gen. 18:33(1-33)	Lord **went** his way, as soon as he had left communing
Gen. 32:30	I have seen God **face** to face, and my life is preserved
Ex. 24:10(9-11)	they saw the God...there was under his **feet** as it were
Ex. 33:11	the Lord spake unto Moses **face** to face, as a man speak
Ex. 33:23(20-23)	thou shalt see my **back** parts: but my face shall not
Deut. 4:28(27-28)	gods...which neither **see**, nor hear, nor eat, nor smell
Matt. 3:17(13-17)	and lo a **voice** from heaven, saying, this is my beloved
Matt. 4:4(1-11)	every word that proceedeth out of the **mouth** of God.
Matt. 16:16(13-20)	thou art...the Son of the **living** God.
Matt. 17:5(1-10)	and behold a **voice** out of the cloud, which said, this
Matt. 26:63(59-68)	I adjure thee by the **living** God, that thou tell us
Luke 24:39(36-39)	for a spirit hath not **flesh** and bones, as ye see me
John 1:49(47-50)	thou art the **Son** of God; thou art the king of Israel.
John 5:18(17-30)	said also that God was his **Father**, making himself
John 6:69(67-69)	sure that thou art...the **Son** of the living God.
John 8:54(33-59)	Jesus answered...it is my **Father** that honoureth me
John 11:27(20-46)	yea, Lord: I believe that thou art...the **Son** of God
John 14:9(8-11)	he that hath seen me hath seen the **Father**; and how say
Acts 3:26(19-26)	God, having raised up his **Son** Jesus, sent him to bless
Acts 7:56(54-60)	behold, I see...the Son of man...on the right **hand** of
Rom. 8:29	predestinate to be conformed to the **image** of his Son
2 Cor. 4:4	Christ, who is the **image** of God, should shine unto the
Philip. 2:6(5,6)	who, being in the **form** of God, thought it not robbery
Philip. 3:21(20,21)	our vile body...fashioned like unto his glorious **body**
Col. 1:15	who is the **image** of the invisible God, the firstborn
Heb. 1:3(1-3)	who being...the express image of his **person**, and
James 3:9	men...made after the **similitude** of God.
1 Jn. 3:2	when he shall **appear**, we shall be like him; for we
Rev. 22:4	and they shall see his **face**; and his name shall be in
Mosiah 7:27	the **image** after which man was created in the beginning
Ether 3:15(6-16)	men were created in...beginning after mine own **image**.

GOD, BODY OF (CORPOREAL NATURE) cont.

D&C 20:18	he created man, male and female, after his own **image**
D&C 110:3(2-3)	his **eyes** were as a flame of fire; the hair of his head
D&C 130:1	Savior shall appear...see that he is a **man** like
D&C 130:22	the Father has a **body** of flesh and bones as tangible
Moses 1:16	thou art after the **similitude** of mine Only Begotten.
Moses 2:27(26,27)	I, God, created man in mine own **image**, in the image
Moses 6:9(8-9)	in the image of his own **body**...created he them, and
Abr. 3:11	Abraham, talked with the Lord, face to **face**, as one
Abr. 4:27(26,27)	Gods went down to organize man in their own **image**, in

GOD, CREATOR

Gen. 1:1(1-31)	in the beginning God **created** the heaven and the earth.
Eph. 3:9	who **created** all things by Jesus Christ
Heb. 1:2	by whom also he made the **worlds**
Rev. 14:7(6-7)	**him** that made heaven, and earth, and the sea, and the
2 Ne. 2:14	there is a God, and he hath **created** all things, both
2 Ne. 11:7	no God we are not ...there could have been no **creation**
Jacob 4:9(8,9)	which earth was **created** by the power of his word.
Mosiah 4:9(2,9)	believe that he is, and that he **created** all things
D&C 20:18(17-18)	and that he **created** man, male and female, after his
Moses 1:33(28-38)	and worlds without number have I **created**; and I also
Moses 2:1	in the beginning I **created** the heaven, and the earth
Moses 3:5(4-9)	I, the Lord God, **created** all things, of which I have
Moses 6:8	in the day that God **created** man, in the likeness of
Moses 7:36(29-40)	all the **creations** which I have made; and mine eye can
Abr. 4:1	the Gods, **organized** and formed the heavens and the ear

GOD, ETERNAL NATURE OF

Deut. 33:27	the **eternal** God is thy refuge, and underneath are the
Ps. 90:2(1,2)	from **everlasting** to everlasting, thou art God.
Ps. 93:2(1,2)	established of old: thou art from **everlasting**.
Ps. 102:27(26,27)	but thou art the **same**, and thy years shall have no end
Ps. 146:10	the Lord shall reign for **ever**, even thy God, O Zion
Isa. 57:15	lofty one that inhabiteth **eternity**, whose name is holy
Isa. 63:16	thy name is from **everlasting**.
Mal. 3:6	for I am the Lord, I **change** not; therefore ye sons of
Rom. 1:20(19-21)	even his **eternal** power and Godhead; so that they are
1 Tim. 1:17	the king eternal, **immortal**, invisible, the only wise
Heb. 13:8	Jesus Christ the **same** yesterday, and to day, and for
Rev. 22:13	Alpha and Omega...the **first** and the last.
1 Ne. 10:19(18-19)	course of the Lord is one **eternal** round.
Alma 11:44	one **eternal** God, to be judged according to their works
Morm. 9:9	God is the same **yesterday**, today, and forever, and in
Moro. 7:22	God...being from **everlasting** to everlasting, behold
D&C 19:10(9-12)	for, behold, I am **endless**, and the punishment which
D&C 20:17	there is a God in heaven, who is infinite and **eternal**
D&C 35:1	God...whose course is one **eternal** round, the same
D&C 38:1	**Alpha** and Omega, the beginning and the end, the same
D&C 76:4	from **eternity** to eternity he is the same, and his year

GOD, ETERNAL NATURE OF cont.

Moses 1:3   **Endless** is my name...without beginning of days or end

GOD, FATHER

Gen. 14:19	blessed be Abram of the most high **God**, possessor of
Num. 16:22	O God, the **God** of the spirits of all flesh, shall one
Num. 27:16	**God** of the spirits of all flesh, set a man over the
Mal. 2:10	have we not all one **father**? hath not one God created
Matt. 3:17(13-17)	a voice from heaven, saying, this is my beloved **Son**
Matt. 5:48	be ye therefore perfect, even as your **Father** which is
Matt. 6:9(9-13)	our **Father** which art in heaven, hallowed be thy name.
Matt. 16:17(15-19)	flesh and blood hath not revealed it...but my **Father**
Matt. 17:5(1-9)	a voice...which said, this is my beloved **Son**, in whom
Matt. 26:39(36-45)	O my **Father**...let this cup pass from me: nevertheless
Luke 2:49	wist ye not that I must be about my **Father's** business
Luke 11:2(2-4)	our **Father** which art in heaven, hallowed be thy name.
John 3:16	for **God** so loved the world, that he gave his Only
John 8:18(17-18)	the **Father** that sent me beareth witness of me.
John 14:12	because I go unto my **Father**.
John 17:21(20-21)	that they all may be one; as thou, **Father**, art in me
John 20:17	touch me not; for I am not yet ascended to my **Father**
Acts 7:56(55-56)	I see..the Son...standing on the right hand of **God**.
Eph. 4:6	one God and **Father** of all, who is above all, and
Heb. 12:9	subjection unto the **Father** of spirits, and live
1 Ne. 11:21	even the son of the Eternal **Father**! Knowest thou the
3 Ne. 13:9(9-13)	our **Father** who art in heaven, hallowed be thy name.
3 Ne. 18:27	then I must go unto my **Father** that I may fulfil other
D&C 15:6	you may rest with them in the kingdom of my **Father**.
D&C 20:24(24,27)	sit down on the right hand of the **Father**, to reign wit
D&C 63:34	will come down in heaven from...presence of my **Father**
D&C 76:20(20-23)	glory of the Son, on the right hand of the **Father**, and
D&C 93:17	the glory of the **Father** was with him, for he dwelt
D&C 130:22	the **Father** has a body of flesh and bones as tangible
Moses 4:2	**Father**, thy will be done, and the glory be thine
Abr. 3:19(18,19)	I am the Lord thy **God**, I am more intelligent than they
Abr. 3:27	**Lord** said: whom shall I send? And one answered like
JS-H 1:17	I saw two **Personages**, whose brightness and glory defy
A of F 1:1	We believe in **God**, the Eternal Father, and in his Son
JS-V 1:3(1-3)	wheron was seated the **Father** and the Son.
JFS-V 1:14	through the grace of God the **Father** and...Jesus Christ

GOD, FOREKNOWLEDGE OF

Deut. 32:8(7,8)	he set the **bounds** of the people according to the
Isa. 42:9	the **former** things are come to pass, and new things do
Isa. 46:9(9-10)	remember the **former** things of old: for I am God, and
Isa. 48:3(3-7)	I have declared the **former** things from the beginning
Jer. 1:5(4-5)	before I formed thee...I **knew** thee; and before thou
Acts 2:23(22-23)	delivered by the...**foreknowledge** of God, ye have taken
Acts 17:26(22-28)	and hath **determined** the times before appointed, and
Rom. 8:29(28-30)	for whom he did **foreknow**, he also did predestinate to

Rom. 9:11	that the purpose of God according to **election** might
Rom. 11:2	his people which he **foreknew**. Wot ye not what the
1 Pet. 1:2(1-2)	elect according to the **foreknowledge** of God the Father
1 Ne. 9:6(5,6)	but the Lord **knoweth** all things from the beginning
1 Ne. 20:3	I have declared the **former** things from the beginning
2 Ne. 2:24	in the wisdom of him who **knoweth** all things.
2 Ne. 9:20	he **knoweth** all things, and there is not anything save
W of M 1:7	but the Lord **knoweth** all things which are to come
Alma 13:3(2-3)	called...according to the **foreknowledge** of God, on
Alma 13:7	prepared...according to his **foreknowledge** of all
Alma 40:10(4-10)	God **knoweth** all the times which are appointed unto man
Hel. 8:8	he **knoweth** as well all things which shall befall us
Morm. 8:17	nevertheless God **knoweth** all things; therefore, he
Moro. 7:22(22-25)	God **knowing** all things, being from everlasting to ever
D&C 1:17(2-17)	I the Lord, **knowing** the calamity which should come
D&C 38:2(1-3)	all things are **present** before mine eyes
Moses 1:6(6,35)	all things are present with me, for I **know** them all.
Abr. 2:8	I **know** the end from the beginning; therefore my hand

GOD, GIFTS OF

Gen. 17:8	I will **give**...the land wherein thou art a stranger
Gen. 17:16	I will...**give** thee a son also of her: yea, I will
Lev. 26:4	I will **give** you rain in due season, and the land shall
Lev. 26:6	I will **give** peace in the land, and ye shall lie down
Eccl. 3:13(13-15)	of all his labour, it is the **gift** of God.
Eccl. 5:19(18-20)	rejoice in his labour; this is the **gift** of God.
Ezek. 11:19	**give** them one heart, and...a new spirit within you
Ezek. 36:26(25-29)	a new heart also will I **give** you, and a new spirit
Matt. 16:19	I will **give** unto thee the keys of the kingdom of
Matt. 20:28	to **give** his life a ransom for many.
John 3:16	God so loved the world, that he **gave** his Only Begotten
John 4:10	if thou knewest the **gift** of God, and who it is that
John 6:51	my flesh, which I will **give** for the life of the world.
John 11:22	thou wilt ask of God, God will **give** it thee.
Acts 8:20(18-20)	thou hast thought that the **gift** of God may be
Rom. 6:23	the **gift** of God is eternal life through Jesus Christ
1 Cor. 7:7	but every man hath his proper **gift** of God, one after
1 Cor. 12:4(4,8-10)	now there are diversities of **gifts**, but the same
Eph. 2:8(8,9)	for by grace are ye saved...it is the **gift** of God
1 Tim. 4:14(12-16)	neglect not the **gift** that is in thee, which was given
James 1:17	every perfect **gift** is from above, and cometh down from
Rev. 2:10	be...faithful...I will **give** thee a crown of life.
1 Ne. 10:17	Holy Ghost, which is the **gift** of God unto all those
1 Ne. 15:36	greatest of all the **gifts** of God. and thus I spake
1:20	interpret the engravings by the **gift** and power of God.
1:25	in the **gift** of speaking with tongues, and in the gift
Mosiah 8:13(13-16)	translate all records...it is a **gift** from God. And the
Mosiah 21:28	a **gift** from God, whereby he could interpret such
Alma 9:21	also many **gifts**, the gift of speaking with tongues
4 Ne. 1:3	partakers of the heavenly **gift**.
Ether 12:11	**gift** of his Son...God prepared a more excellent way

GOD, GIFTS OF cont.

Moro. 3:4	according to the **gifts** and callings of God unto men
Moro. 10:8(8-16)	deny not the **gifts** of God, for they are many; and the
D&C 6:13	greatest of all the **gifts** of God; for there is no gift
D&C 14:7(6-7)	eternal life...the greatest of all the **gifts** of God.
D&C 46:26(11-26)	all these **gifts** come from God, for the benefit of the
D&C 107:92(91-92)	having all the **gifts** of God which he bestows upon the

GOD, GLORY OF

Ps. 19:1	the heavens declare the **glory** of God; and the
Ezek. 8:4	and, behold, **the** glory of the God of Israel was there
Luke 2:9(9-14)	the **glory** of the Lord shone round about them: and they
Rom. 9:23(21-24)	make known the riches of his **glory** on the vessels of
2 Cor. 4:6	to give the light of the knowledge of the **glory** of God
Heb. 4:1(1,11)	a promise being left us of entering into his **rest**, any
D&C 76:19(19-20)	and the **glory** of the Lord shone round about.
D&C 84:24	rest is the fulness of his **glory**.
D&C 93:36	**glory** of God is intelligence, or, in other words
Moses 1:2(2,11)	saw God face to face...the **glory** of God was upon Moses

GOD, INDIGNATION OF

Deut. 3:26(21-29)	the Lord was **wroth** with me for your sakes, and would
Deut. 4:21	the Lord was **angry** with me for your sakes, and sware
Deut. 6:15(14,15)	lest the **anger** of the Lord thy God be kindled against
Deut. 7:4	so will the **anger** of the Lord be kindled against you
Deut. 29:28	Lord rooted them out...in great **indignation**, and cast
Judg. 2:14	the **anger** of the Lord was hot against Israel, and he
2 Kgs. 13:3	the **anger** of the Lord was kindled against Israel, and
2 Kgs. 17:20(6-23)	the Lord **rejected** all the seed of Israel, and
2 Kgs. 22:13(13-17)	**wrath** of the Lord...kindled...fathers have not
Ps. 7:11	God is **angry** with the wicked every day.
Ps. 103:9(8,9)	neither will he keep his **anger** for ever.
Isa. 5:25	therefore is the **anger** of the Lord kindled against his
Isa. 30:27	the Lord cometh from far, burning with his **anger**, and
Isa. 51:17(17-23)	hast drunk at the hand of the Lord the cup of his **fury**
Isa. 66:14(14-15)	his **indignation** toward his enemies.
Jer. 7:20(19-20)	saith the Lord God; behold, mine **anger** and my fury
Jer. 10:10	nations shall not be able to abide his **indignation**.
Ezek. 21:31	pour out mine **indignation** upon thee, I will blow again
Ezek. 22:24(24,31)	nor rained upon in the day of **indignation**.
Nahum 1:6	who can stand before his **indignation**? and who can
Mark 3:5(1-5)	looked round about on them with **anger**, being grieved
John 3:36(35,36)	believeth not...but the **wrath** of God abideth on him.
Rom. 1:18	the **wrath** of God...against all ungodliness and
Rom. 2:8(1-15)	unto them that are contentious...**indignation** and wrath
Eph. 5:6(1-7)	because of these things cometh the **wrath** of God upon
Col. 3:6(4-7)	for which things' sake the **wrath** of God cometh on the
Heb. 10:27	fearful looking for of judgment and fiery **indignation**
Rev. 14:10(9-11)	wrath of God...poured...into the cup of his
Rev. 16:19(1,17-21)	great Babylon...the fierceness of his **wrath**.

GOD, INDIGNATION OF cont.

2 Ne. 1:17	God should come out in the fulness of his **wrath** upon
Alma 12:36(36-37)	iniquity provoketh him that he sendeth down his **wrath**
Alma 40:14	fearful looking for the fiery **indignation** of the wrath
Ether 2:9(8-9)	his **wrath** shall come upon them. and the fulness of his
Ether 14:25	the Lord did visit them in the fulness of his **wrath**
D&C 1:13	and the **anger** of the Lord is kindled, and his sword
D&C 5:8	stiffnecked generation- mine **anger** is kindled against
D&C 19:20(15-20)	repent, lest I **humble** you with my almighty power; and
D&C 29:17	because of...wickedness...mine **indignation** is full
D&C 59:21	his **wrath** kindled...who confess not his hand in all
D&C 60:2(2-3)	for mine **anger** is kindled against them.
D&C 63:11	with whom God is **angry** he is not well pleased
D&C 63:32	I, the Lord, am **angry** with the wicked; I am holding
D&C 84:24(23-25)	his **anger** was kindled against them, swore that they
D&C 93:47(47-49)	and must needs stand **rebuked** before the Lord
D&C 97:24	the **indignation** of the Lord is kindled against their
D&C 109:52(50-52)	may thine anger be kindled, and thine **indignation** fall

GOD, INTELLIGENCE OF

1 Sam. 2:3(2,3)	for the Lord is a God of **knowledge**, and by him actions
Ps. 139:6(1-24)	such **knowledge** is too wonderful for me; it is high, I
Isa. 46:10(5-13)	**declaring** the end from the beginning, and from ancient
Isa. 55:8(1-13)	for my **thoughts** are not your thoughts, neither are you
Dan. 2:22(19-23)	he **knoweth** what is in the darkness, and the light
Matt. 6:8	for your Father **knoweth** what things ye have need of
Luke 16:15(14,15)	but God **knoweth** your hearts: for that which is highly
John 16:13	Spirit of truth...will guide you into all **truth**: for
Rom. 11:33(33,34)	depth of...**wisdom** and knowledge of God! How
Col. 2:3(2-3)	in whom are hid all the treasures of **wisdom** and
Col. 3:16	word of Christ dwell in you richly in all **wisdom**
James 3:17	**wisdom** that is from above is first pure, then
1 Jn. 3:20	God is greater than our heart, and **knoweth** all things.
1 Ne. 9:6	the Lord **knoweth** all things from the beginning
2 Ne. 2:24	done in the wisdom of him who **knoweth** all things.
2 Ne. 9:20	he **knoweth** all things, and there is not anything save
W of M 1:7	the Lord **knoweth** all things which are to come
Alma 26:35	God...has all power, all **wisdom**, and all understanding
D&C 38:2(1-3)	the same which **knoweth** all things, for all things are
D&C 76:2(1-4)	great is his **wisdom**, marvelous are his ways, and the
D&C 88:41	he **comprehendeth** all things, and all things are before
D&C 93:26(22-26)	I am the Spirit of **truth**, and John bore record of me
D&C 93:29	**intelligence**, or the light of truth, was not created
D&C 93:36	the glory of God is **intelligence**, or, in other words
Moses 1:31(24-35)	here is **wisdom** and it remaineth in me.
Moses 7:32	I gave unto them their **knowledge**, in the day I created
Abr. 3:19(18,19,21)	I am the Lord thy God, I am more **intelligent** than they

GOD, JUSTICE OF

Deut. 32:4	a God of truth and without iniquity, **just** and right
Neh. 9:33(32-33)	howbeit thou art **just** in all that is brought upon us
Job 37:23	in judgment, and in plenty of **justice**: he will not
Ps. 89:14(14-16)	**justice** and judgment are the habitation of thy throne
Isa. 9:7(6,7)	establish it with judgment and with **justice** from hence
Isa. 26:7(4-9)	thou, most **upright**, dost weigh the path of the just.
Isa. 45:21(20-25)	a **just** God and a saviour; there is none beside me.
Jer. 23:5(5,6)	king shall...execute judgment and **justice** in the earth
John 5:30(25-30)	as I hear, I judge: and my judgment is **just**; because
Rom. 3:26(23-26)	that he might be **just**, and the justifier of him which
Heb. 2:2(1-4)	disobedience received a **just** recompence of reward
Heb. 10:30	vengeance belongeth unto me, I will **recompense**, saith
1 Jn. 1:9	if we confess our sins, he is faithful and **just** to for
Rev. 15:3	Lord God Almighty; **just** and true are thy ways, thou
1 Ne. 12:18(16-18)	the word of the **justice** of the eternal God, and the
1 Ne. 15:30(30-36)	**justice** of God...divide the wicked from the righteous
2 Ne. 2:12(5-29)	the power, and the mercy, and the **justice** of God.
2 Ne. 9:17(15-18)	O the greatness and the **justice** of our God! For he
2 Ne. 9:26(23-27)	atonement satisfieth the demands of his **justice** upon
2 Ne. 9:46	that glorious day when **justice** shall be administered
Jacob 6:10(8-10)	for **justice** cannot be denied, ye must go away into
Mosiah 2:38(36-39)	demands of divine **justice** do awaken his immortal soul
Mosiah 15:9(8,9)	standing betwixt them and **justice**; having broken the
Mosiah 15:27(26-27)	for he cannot deny **justice** when it has its claim.
Mosiah 29:12(10-13)	the judgments of God are always **just**, but the judgment
Alma 12:18(16-18)	cannot be redeemed according to God's **justice**; and the
Alma 12:32	for the works of **justice** could not be destroyed
Alma 34:16(14-16)	and thus mercy can satisfy the demands of **justice**, and
Alma 41:3(2-15)	requisite with the **justice** of God...men should be
Alma 42:1(1-31)	the **justice** of God in the punishment of the sinner
3 Ne. 26:5(3-5)	according to the mercy, and the **justice**, and the
3 Ne. 27:17(16-22)	no more return, because of the **justice** of the Father.
Morm. 3:15(9-15)	vengeance is mine, and I will **repay**; and because this
Morm. 6:22(19-22)	doeth with you according to his **justice** and mercy.
Ether 8:22(22-24)	cry unto him from the ground for **vengeance** upon them
D&C 29:17	I will take **vengeance** upon the wicked, for they will
D&C 82:4(1-10)	**justice** and judgment are the penalty which is affixed
D&C 88:35(34-35)	cannot be sanctified by law...mercy, **justice**, nor
D&C 107:84	none...exempted from the **justice** and the laws of God
D&C 109:77	enthroned, with glory...dominion, truth, **justice**
Moses 6:57(56-62)	Jesus Christ, a righteous **judge**, who shall come in the
Moses 7:31(29-34)	naught but peace, **justice**, and truth is the habitation
JS-V 1:9(7-10)	the Lord, will **judge** all men according to their works

GOD, KNOWLEDGE ABOUT

Gen. 32:30	I have **seen** God face to face, and my life is preserved
Ex. 5:2	I **know** not the Lord, neither will I let Israel go.
Ex. 33:23(11-23)	thou shalt **see** my back parts: but my face shall not
Judg. 2:10	which **knew** not the Lord, nor yet the works which he
Isa. 1:3(1-3)	Israel doth not **know**, my people doth not consider.
Isa. 5:13	gone into captivity, because they have no **knowledge**

Isa. 11:9	the earth shall be full of the **knowledge** of the Lord
Jer. 31:34(33,34)	for they shall all **know** me, from the least of them
Ezek. 6:7(1-14)	slain shall fall...ye shall **know** that I am the Lord.
Ezek. 7:4(4-9)	and ye shall **know** that I am the Lord.
Ezek. 7:27	and they shall **know** that I am the Lord.
Ezek. 20:26(20-44)	that they might **know** that I am the Lord.
Ezek. 37:28	and the heathen shall **know** that I the Lord do sanctify
Ezek. 39:7	so will I make my holy name **known** in the midst of my
Hosea 4:1	there is no truth, nor mercy, nor **knowledge** of God in
Hosea 4:6	my people are destroyed for lack of **knowledge**: because
Hab. 2:14	earth shall be filled with the **knowledge** of the glory
Matt. 7:23(21-23)	I profess unto them, I never **knew** you: depart from me
Luke 24:39(36-40)	a spirit hath not flesh and bones, as ye **see** me have.
John 17:3	life eternal...**know** thee the only true God, and Jesus
John 17:25(25-26)	Father, the world hath not **known** thee: but I have
Acts 17:23(22-31)	an altar with this inscription, to the **unknown** God.
1 Cor. 2:14(10-16)	things of the Spirit...neither can he **know** them
1 Cor. 4:1	ministers of Christ...stewards of the **mysteries** of God
2 Pet. 2:21(20-21)	it had been better for them not to have **known** the way
1 Ne. 22:12(11,12)	and they shall **know** that the Lord is their Savior and
2 Ne. 30:15(10-18)	earth shall be full of the **knowledge** of the Lord as
Jacob 4:4(4-8)	that we **knew** of Christ, and we had a hope of his
Jacob 4:8	no man **knoweth** of his ways save it be revealed unto
Alma 12:9(9-11)	it is given unto many to **know** the mysteries of God
Alma 26:22(21,22)	unto such it is given to **know** the mysteries of God
Ether 3:16(6-20)	I **appear** unto thee to be in the spirit will I appear
D&C 84:98(97-102)	until all shall **know** me, who remain, even from the
D&C 93:1(1,2)	every soul who...keepeth my commandments...**know** that
D&C 97:16(15-16)	all the pure in heart that shall come...shall **see** God.
D&C 130:22	the Father has a **body** of flesh and bones as tangible
D&C 132:24(22-25)	eternal lives- to **know** the only wise and true God, and
Moses 7:4(2-4)	I **saw** the Lord; and he stood before my face, and he
Moses 7:41(28-41)	Lord **spake** unto Enoch, and told Enoch all the doings

GOD, LAW OF

Ezra 7:25	judge all the people...as know the **laws** of thy God
Ps. 1:2(1-2)	but his delight is in the **law** of the Lord; and in his
Ps. 19:7	the **law** of the Lord is perfect, converting the soul
Isa. 2:3(2-4)	out of Zion shall go forth the **law**, and the word of
Isa. 51:4	a **law** shall proceed from me, and I will make my
Jer. 31:33	put my **law** in their inward parts, and write it in
Gal. 5:14	all the **law** is fulfilled in one word, even in this
Heb. 8:10	I will put my **laws** into their mind, and write them in
James 1:25	but whoso looketh into the perfect **law** of liberty, and
2 Ne. 2:26	by the punishment of the **law** at the great and last day
2 Ne. 8:4	a **law** shall proceed from me, and I will make my
2 Ne. 9:25	he has given a **law**; and where there is no law given
2 Ne. 9:27	wo unto him that has the **law** given, yea, that has all
D&C 29:34	**law** which was temporal; neither any man, nor the child
D&C 41:3	by the prayer of your faith ye shall receive my **law**
D&C 42:2	hearken and hear and obey the **law** which I shall give

GOD, LAW OF cont.

D&C 42:59	thou shalt take the things...in my scriptures for a
D&C 88:13	which is the **law** by which all things are governed,
D&C 88:21(21-24)	the **law** which I have given unto you, even the law of
D&C 88:38(36-38)	and unto every kingdom is given a **law**; and unto every
D&C 88:42(42-43)	he hath given a **law** unto all things, by which they
D&C 93:53	obtain a knowledge of...**laws** of God and man, and all
D&C 107:84	none shall be exempted from...the **laws** of God, that
D&C 130:21(20-21)	blessing from God, it is by obedience to that **law** upon
D&C 132:5(5-12)	have a blessing...shall abide the **law** which was
D&C 132:21	except ye abide my **law** ye cannot attain to this glory.
D&C 132:32	enter ye into my **law** and ye shall be saved.

GOD, LOVE OF

Deut. 4:37	and because he **loved** thy fathers, therefore he chose
Deut. 5:10(6-21)	shewing mercy unto thousands of them that **love** me and
Deut. 6:5(4-5)	thou shalt **love** the Lord thy God with all thine heart
Deut. 7:8	but because the Lord **loved** you, and because he would
Deut. 7:13	and he will **love** thee, and bless thee, and multiply
Deut. 10:15	Lord had a delight in thy fathers to **love** them, and
Deut. 10:18(15,18)	he...**loveth** the stranger, in giving him food and
Deut. 23:5	because the Lord thy God **loved** thee.
Ps. 31:23	O **love** the Lord, all ye his saints: for the Lord
Jer. 31:3	I have loved thee with an everlasting **love**: therefore
Hosea 11:1	when Israel was a child, then I **loved** him, and called
Mal. 1:2	I have **loved** you, saith the Lord. Yet ye say, wherein
Matt. 22:37	thou shalt **love** the Lord thy God with all thy heart
John 3:16	for God so **loved** the world, that he gave his only
John 5:42	that ye have not the **love** of God in you.
John 10:17	therefore doth my Father **love** me, because I lay down
John 13:1	were in the world, he **loved** them unto the end.
John 13:35	ye are my disciples, if ye have **love** one to another.
John 14:15	if ye **love** me, keep my commandments.
John 14:21	he that loveth me shall be **loved** of my Father, and I
John 14:23(23-24)	my Father will **love** him, and we will come unto him
John 15:9(9,10)	as the Father hath **loved** me, so have I loved you
John 16:27	the Father himself **loveth** you, because ye have loved
John 17:23	that the world may know that thou...hast **loved** them
John 17:26	the **love** wherewith thou hast loved me may be in them
2 Cor. 13:11	live in peace..God of **love** and peace shall be with you
Eph. 3:19	the **love** of Christ, which passeth knowledge, that ye
1 Jn. 3:1	what manner of **love** the Father hath bestowed upon us
1 Jn. 4:7(7-21)	let us love one another: for **love** is of God; and every
1 Ne. 11:22(16-23)	yea, it is the **love** of God, which sheddeth itself
2 Ne. 1:15	I am encircled about eternally in the arms of his **love**
2 Ne. 26:30	all men should have...**love**. And except they should
2 Ne. 31:20(19-21)	and a **love** of God and of all men. Wherefore, if ye
Jacob 7:23(21-23)	peace and the **love** of God was restored again among the
Mosiah 4:12(11-15)	and be filled with the **love** of God, and always retain
Alma 13:29(27-30)	having the **love** of God always in your hearts, that ye
Alma 26:37(36,37)	God is mindful of every **people**, whatsoever land they
4 Ne. 1:15(15-18)	no contention in the land, because of the **love** of God

GOD, LOVE OF cont.

D&C 20:19(19-20)	commandments that they should **love** and serve him, the
D&C 59:5(5,7,21)	thou shalt **love** the Lord thy God with all thy heart
D&C 76:116	Holy Spirit...God bestows on those who **love** him, and
D&C 95:1	whom I **love** I also chasten that their sins may be
D&C 101:9(7-9)	notwithstanding...sins, my bowels...filled...
JFS-V 1:3(1-4)	wonderful **love** made manifest by the Father and the Son

GOD, MANIFESTATIONS OF

Gen. 5:24	and Enoch **walked** with God: and he was not; for God too
Gen. 32:30	I have seen God **face** to face, and my life is preserved
Ex. 16:10	the **glory** of the Lord appeared in the cloud.
Ex. 19:9	Lord said..I come unto thee in a thick **cloud**, that the
Ex. 19:19(18-19)	and God answered him by a **voice**.
Ex. 20:22	ye have seen that I have **talked** with you from heaven.
Ex. 24:10(9-11)	and they **saw** the God of Israel: and there was under
Deut. 4:12	ye heard the **voice** of the words, but saw no similitude
Deut. 4:36(33-36)	upon earth he **shewed** thee his great fire; and thou
Deut. 5:24	we have heard his **voice** out of the midst of the fire
Deut. 9:10	the Lord **spake** with you in the mount out of the midst
1 Kgs. 8:10	that the **cloud** filled the house of the Lord
Isa. 9:6(6,7)	unto us a child is **born**...the mighty God, the
Ezek. 10:4	the house was filled with the **cloud**, and the court was
Ezek. 10:18	then the **glory** of the Lord departed from off the
Zech. 14:4(4,5)	his **feet** shall stand in that day upon the mount of
Matt. 3:17	and lo a **voice** from heaven, saying, this is my beloved
Mark 9:7	a **voice** came out of the cloud, saying, this is my
Mark 12:26	how in the bush God **spake** unto him, saying, I am the
John 1:14(1-4,14)	the Word was made **flesh**, and dwelt among us, (and we
John 6:46	he which is of God, he hath **seen** the Father.
Acts 7:56(55,56)	I see...the Son of man...on the right hand of **God**.
1 Tim. 3:16	God was **manifest** in the flesh, justified in the spirit
Rev. 12:10	and I heard a loud **voice** saying in heaven, now is come
Rev. 19:12(11-16)	his **eyes** were as a flame of fire, and on his head were
1 Ne. 1:8	he thought he **saw** God sitting upon his throne
Mosiah 15:1(1-5)	God himself shall **come** down among the children of men
Alma 19:6	which was the **light** of the glory of God, which was a
Alma 36:22	saw, God sitting upon his **throne**, surrounded with
3 Ne. 7:21	had been **visited** by the power and Spirit of God, which
3 Ne. 11:7(3-7)	**behold** my Beloved Son, in whom I am well pleased, in
Morm. 9:15(1-16)	God has not ceased to be a God of **miracles**.
Ether 3:16(6-17)	this **body**, which ye now behold, is the body of my
D&C 34:7	I shall come in a **cloud** with power and great glory.
D&C 84:5	a cloud shall...be even the **glory** of the Lord, which
D&C 109:37	and let thy house be filled...with thy **glory**.
D&C 110:2(1-3)	we **saw** the Lord standing upon the breastwork of the
D&C 130:22	the Father has a **body** of flesh and bones as tangible
D&C 133:20	he shall **stand** upon the mount of Olivet, and upon the
D&C 133:25	the Lord...shall **stand** in the midst of his people, and
D&C 133:46	who is this that **cometh** down from God in heaven with
Moses 1:2(1-42)	and he saw God **face** to face, and he talked with him
Abr. 2:6(6,7)	the Lord **appeared** unto me, and said unto me: arise

Abr. 3:11	Abraham, **talked** with the Lord, face to face, as one
JS-H 1:17	I saw two **Personages**...standing above me in the air.

GOD, MERCY OF

Ex. 20:6	shewing **mercy** unto thousands of them that love me, and
Ex. 34:6(6-7)	the Lord God, **merciful** and gracious, longsuffering
Deut. 4:31(30-31)	(for the Lord thy God is a **merciful** God;) he will not
Deut. 7:9(8-9)	covenant and **mercy** with them that love him and keep
2 Sam. 14:14	he devise means, that his banished be not **expelled**
2 Sam. 24:14	into...hand of the Lord; for his **mercies** are great
Neh. 9:31(17,31)	for thou art a gracious and **merciful** God.
Ps. 25:6	remember, O Lord, thy tender **mercies** and thy
Ps. 25:16	turn thee unto me, and have **mercy** upon me; for I am
Ps. 69:16(13,16)	according to the multitude of thy tender **mercies**.
Ps. 103:13	father **pitieth** his children, so the Lord pitieth them
Ps. 103:17	but the **mercy** of the Lord is from everlasting to
Ps. 116:5(5-6)	gracious is the Lord...yea, our God is **merciful**.
Ps. 119:132	look thou upon me, and be **merciful** unto me, as thou
Isa. 49:15	yea, they may forget, yet will I not **forget** thee.
Isa. 54:8(7-9)	with everlasting kindness will I have **mercy** on thee
Ezek. 33:11	I have no pleasure in the **death** of the wicked; but
Micah 7:18	God...retaineth not his anger...he delighteth in **mercy**
Luke 1:58	how the Lord had shewed great **mercy** upon her; and they
Luke 6:36(35,36)	therefore merciful, as your Father also is **merciful**.
Rom. 9:16(14-16,18)	but of God that sheweth **mercy**.
Rom. 15:9	might glorify God for his **mercy**; as it is written, for
2 Cor. 1:3(2-5)	the Father of **mercies**, and the God of all comfort
Eph. 2:4(4-9)	God, who is rich in **mercy**, for his great love
1 Tim. 1:16	for this cause I obtained **mercy**, that in me first
2 Tim. 1:18(16-18)	he may find **mercy** of the Lord in that day: and in how
Titus 3:5	but according to his **mercy** he saved us, by the washing
James 3:17	but the wisdom that is from above...full of **mercy** and
James 5:11	Lord is very pitiful, and of tender **mercy**.
1 Pet. 1:3(3-5)	according to his abundant **mercy** hath begotten us
2 Ne. 4:26	the Lord...hath visited men in so much **mercy**, why
2 Ne. 9:8	O the wisdom of God, his **mercy** and grace! For behold
2 Ne. 9:53	because of his greatness, and his grace and **mercy**, he
Mosiah 28:4	the Lord saw fit in his infinite **mercy** to spare them
Alma 9:26	full of patience, **mercy**, and long-suffering, quick to
Alma 12:33(33-34)	then will I have **mercy** upon you, through mine Only
Alma 26:35(35-37)	he is a **merciful** being, even unto salvation, to those
Alma 32:22	God is **merciful** unto all who believe on his name
Alma 42:15(15-21)	a perfect, just God, and a **merciful** God also.
Alma 42:23(22,23)	God ceaseth not to be God, and **mercy** claimeth the
Alma 42:24(24-29)	and also **mercy** claimeth all which is her own; and
Alma 42:30(30,31)	do you let the justice of God, and his **mercy**, and his
3 Ne. 22:8(7-17)	with everlasting kindness will I have **mercy** on thee
Moro. 8:19(19,23)	little children...alive in him because of his **mercy**.
D&C 61:2(2,36-37)	am **merciful** unto those who confess their sins with
D&C 76:5(5-10)	I, the Lord, am **merciful** and gracious unto those who
D&C 84:102	he is full of **mercy**, justice, grace and truth, and

D&C 97:2   I, the Lord, show **mercy** unto all the meek, and upon

GOD, OMNISCIENCE OF

Gen. 6:5	God saw...every imagination of the **thoughts** of his
Gen. 18:19	for I **know** him, that he will command his children and
1 Sam. 2:3	the Lord is a God of **knowledge**, and by him actions are
1 Sam. 16:7	but the Lord **looketh** on the heart.
1 Chr. 28:9	the Lord **searcheth** all hearts, and understandeth all
2 Chr. 6:30	thou only **knowest** the hearts of the children of men
Job 21:22	shall any teach God **knowledge**? seeing he judgeth those
Job 23:10	he **knoweth** the way that I take: when he hath tried me
Ps. 44:21(20-21)	God...**knoweth** the secrets of the heart.
Ps. 94:11	the Lord **knoweth** the thoughts of man, that they are
Ps. 139:3(1-4)	thou...art **acquainted** with all my ways.
Ps. 147:5	great is our Lord...his **understanding** is infinite.
Prov. 15:3(3,11)	the **eyes** of the Lord are in every place, beholding the
Isa. 41:26	who hath **declared** from the beginning, that we may know
Isa. 46:10(9-10)	**declaring** the end from the beginning, and from ancient
Isa. 48:3(3-7)	I have **declared** the former things from the beginning
Isa. 59:1(1-2)	neither his ear heavy, that it cannot **hear**
Isa. 66:18	I **know** their works and their thoughts: it shall come
Jer. 12:3	but thou, O Lord, **knowest** me: thou hast seen me, and
Jer. 17:10	I the Lord search the **heart**, I try the reins, even to
Jer. 33:3	I will...**shew** thee great and mighty things, which thou
Ezek. 11:5	I **know** the things that come into your mind, every one
Dan. 2:28	there is a God in heaven that **revealeth** secrets, and
Matt. 6:6(6,18)	thy Father which **seeth** in secret shall reward thee
Matt. 6:8	your Father **knoweth** what things ye have need of
Matt. 9:4	Jesus **knowing** their thoughts said, wherefore think ye
Matt. 10:29	**sparrows**...not fall on the ground without your Father.
Luke 12:6	not one of them is **forgotten** before God
Luke 16:15	God **knoweth** your hearts: for that which is highly
John 13:3	Jesus **knowing** that the Father had given all things
John 14:26	Comforter...Holy Ghost...shall **teach** you all things
John 16:13	Spirit of truth...will **guide** you into all truth: for
John 16:30	now are we sure that thou **knowest** all things, and
Acts 1:24	thou, Lord, which **knowest** the hearts of all men, shew
Acts 15:8	and God, which **knoweth** the hearts, bare them witness
Acts 15:18	**known** unto God are all his works from the beginning
Acts 17:26	hath **determined** the times before appointed, and the
Rom. 11:33(33-36)	the wisdom and **knowledge** of God! how unsearchable are
1 Cor. 3:20	the Lord **knoweth** the thoughts of the wise, that they
Eph. 1:8	he hath abounded toward us in all **wisdom** and prudence
Col. 2:3	in whom are hid all the treasures of **wisdom** and
Heb. 4:12	word of God...is a **discerner** of the thoughts and
Rev. 2:2(2,19)	I **know** thy works, and thy labour, and thy patience
Rev. 2:23	I am he which **searcheth** the reins and hearts: and I
Rev. 3:1(1,8,15)	I **know** thy works, that thou hast a name that thou live
1 Ne. 9:6	the Lord **knoweth** all things from the beginning
1 Ne. 10:19	**mysteries** of God shall be unfolded unto them, by the
1 Ne. 20:5(3-5)	before it came to pass I **showed** them thee; and I show

GOD, OMNISCIENCE OF cont.

2 Ne. 2:24	the wisdom of him who **knoweth** all things.
2 Ne. 9:20	God...**knoweth** all things...not anything save he knows
2 Ne. 27:10	**reveal** all things from the foundation of the world
2 Ne. 27:27	that I **know** all their works. For shall the work say
Jacob 2:5	by the help of...creator..I can tell...your **thoughts**
Jacob 2:10	under the glance of the **piercing** eye of the Almighty
W of M 1:7	the Lord **knoweth** all things which are to come
Mosiah 27:31	shrink beneath the glance of his **all-searching** eye.
Alma 7:13	the spirit **knoweth** all things; nevertheless the Son
Alma 13:7	according to his **foreknowledge** of all things
Alma 18:18	art thou that Great Spirit, who **knows** all things
Alma 18:32	he **knows** all the thoughts and intents of the heart
Alma 26:35	all wisdom..understanding; he **comprehendeth** all things
Alma 39:8	ye cannot **hide** your crimes from God; and except ye
Alma 40:5	God **knoweth** all these things...a time appointed that
Alma 40:10	God **knoweth** all the times which are appointed unto man
Hel. 9:41	except he was a God he could not **know** of all things.
3 Ne. 13:6(4-6,18)	thy Father, who **seeth** in secret, shall reward thee
3 Ne. 26:3(3-5)	he did **expound** all things, even from the beginning
3 Ne. 28:6	behold, I **know** your thoughts, and ye have desired the
Morm. 8:17	God **knoweth** all things; therefore, he that condemneth
Ether 3:25(25-27)	Lord...**showed**...all the inhabitants of the earth which
Moro. 7:22	God **knowing** all things, being from everlasting to
Moro. 10:5	by the..Holy Ghost ye may **know** the truth of all things
D&C 1:1	whose **eyes** are upon all men; yea, verily I say
D&C 6:16	God...**knowest** thy thoughts and the intents of thy
D&C 6:24	I have **told** you things which no man knoweth have you
D&C 15:3	I will **tell** you that which no man knoweth save me and
D&C 38:2	**knoweth** all things, for all things are present before
D&C 67:1	and whose hearts I **know**, and whose desires have come
D&C 88:6(6-13)	he **comprehended** all things, that he might be in all
D&C 88:41	he **comprehendeth** all things, and all things are before
D&C 121:24	mine eyes see and **know** all their works, and I have in
D&C 127:2	God **knoweth** all these things, whether it be good or
D&C 130:7	all things...**manifest**, past, present, and future, and
Moses 1:6	all things are present with me, for I **know** them all.
Moses 1:35(35-37)	all things are numbered unto me...I **know** them.
Moses 7:4(4-9)	I will **show** unto thee the world for the space of many
Moses 7:36	all the creations...mine **eye** can pierce them also, and
Moses 7:41	Lord...**told** Enoch all the doings of the children of
Moses 7:67	Lord **showed** Enoch all things, even unto the end of the
Abr. 2:8	I **know** the end from the beginning; therefore my hand
Abr. 3:19	I am the Lord...I am more **intelligent** than they all.
Abr. 3:21	my wisdom excelleth...I rule...in all **wisdom** and

GOD, PERFECTION OF

Num. 23:19	God is not a man, that he should lie; neither...**repent**
Deut. 32:4(3-4)	his work is **perfect**...a God...without iniquity, just
1 Sam. 15:29	the Strength of Israel will not **lie** nor repent: for
2 Sam. 22:31(1-51)	as for God, his way is **perfect**; the word of the Lord
Ps. 18:30	for God, his way is **perfect**: the word of the Lord is

GOD, PERFECTION OF cont.

Ps. 71:19	thy **righteousness** also, O God, is very high, who hast
Prov. 30:5	every word of God is **pure**: he is a shield unto them
Mal. 3:6	I am the Lord, I **change** not; therefore ye sons of
Matt. 5:48	even as your Father which is in heaven is **perfect**.
Matt. 19:17(16,17)	there is none **good** but one, that is, God: but if thou
Luke 18:19	none is **good**, save one, that is, God.
John 16:30	now are we sure that thou **knowest** all things, and need
Rom. 9:14	is there **unrighteousness** with God? God forbid.
Eph. 4:13	the Son of God, unto a **perfect** man, unto the measure
2 Tim. 2:13	he abideth faithful: he cannot **deny** himself.
Titus 1:2	which God, that cannot **lie**, promised before the world
Heb. 5:9	being made **perfect**, he became the author of eternal
Heb. 6:10	for God is not **unrighteous** to forget your work and
Heb. 6:18	it was impossible for God to **lie**, we might have a
James 1:13	God cannot be **tempted** with evil, neither tempteth he
James 1:17	Father of lights, with whom is no **variableness**
1 Jn. 1:5	God is **light**, and in him is no darkness at all.
1 Ne. 9:6	the Lord **knoweth** all things from the beginning
1 Ne. 10:18(18,19)	he is the **same** yesterday, to-day, and forever; and the
Mosiah 2:22	he never doth **vary** from that which he hath said
Mosiah 4:9	he has all **wisdom**, and all power, both in heaven and
Alma 7:20	he cannot walk in **crooked** paths; neither doth he vary
Alma 13:7	according to his **foreknowledge** of all things
Alma 26:35	he has all **power**, all wisdom, and all understanding
Alma 42:15(1-26)	that God might be a **perfect**, just God, and a merciful
3 Ne. 12:48	as I, or your Father who is in heaven is **perfect**.
Morm. 9:9(9,10)	in him there is no **variableness** neither shadow of
Morm. 9:19	God...**changeth** not; if so he would cease to be God
Moro. 8:18	he is **unchangeable** from all eternity to all eternity.
Moro. 8:26	Comforter filleth with hope and **perfect** love, which
D&C 3:2(1-3)	God doth not walk in **crooked** paths, neither doth he
D&C 20:17	from everlasting to everlasting the same **unchangeable**
D&C 38:2	**knoweth** all things, for all things are present before
D&C 62:6	I, the Lord, promise the faithful and cannot **lie**.
D&C 76:4	from eternity to eternity he is the **same**, and his year
D&C 76:70	even the glory of God, the **highest** of all, whose glory
D&C 88:41	he **comprehendeth** all things, and all things are before
D&C 127:2	God **knoweth** all these things, whether it be good or
Moses 6:57	no **unclean** thing can dwell there, or dwell in his
Abr. 3:21	I rule...in all **wisdom** and prudence, over all the

GOD, POWER OF

Gen. 17:1	I am the **Almighty** God; walk before me, and be thou
Gen. 18:14	is any thing too **hard** for the Lord? at the time
Gen. 28:3	and God **Almighty** bless thee, and make thee fruitful
Gen. 49:25	and by the **Almighty**, who shall bless thee with
1 Sam. 14:6	there is no **restraint** to the Lord to save by many or
1 Sam. 17:37	he will **deliver** me out of the hand of this Philistine.
1 Sam. 17:46(45-51)	this day will the Lord **deliver** thee into mine hand
2 Sam. 22:33(33-36)	God is my strength and **power**: and he maketh my way
Isa. 14:27(24,27)	Lord of hosts hath **purposed**, and who shall disannul

Isa. 52:10	the Lord hath made bare his holy **arm** in the eyes of
Jer. 32:17	Ah Lord God!...there is nothing too **hard** for thee
Jer. 51:15(15-16)	he hath made the earth by his **power**, he hath establish
Mal. 3:11(2,3,6-11)	I will **rebuke** the devourer for your sakes, and he
Matt. 8:26(24-26)	he arose, and **rebuked** the winds and the sea; and there
Matt. 17:20	nothing shall be **impossible** unto you.
Matt. 19:26	with God all things are **possible**.
Matt. 21:21	ye shall say unto this **mountain**, be thou removed, and
Matt. 22:29(29-32)	not knowing the scriptures, nor the **power** of God.
Matt. 28:18	all **power** is given unto me in heaven and in earth.
Mark 9:23	all things are **possible** to him that believeth.
Mark 10:27	with God all things are **possible**.
Luke 1:37	for with God nothing shall be **impossible**.
Luke 18:27	things...impossible with men are **possible** with God.
John 1:3	all things were **made** by him; and without him was not
John 5:21	the Father raiseth up the dead, and **quickeneth** them
John 10:18	I have **power** to lay it down...to take it again. this
John 11:43(23-44)	he cried with a loud voice, **Lazarus**, come forth.
Rom. 4:17	God, who **quickeneth** the dead, and calleth those things
Rom. 8:11	he that raised up Christ...shall also **quicken** your
1 Cor. 1:24(23-24)	the **power** of God, and the wisdom of God.
2 Cor. 6:18	be my sons and daughters, saith the Lord **Almighty**.
1 Tim. 6:13	God, who **quickeneth** all things, and before Christ
Heb. 1:3	upholding all things by the word of his **power**, when
Rev. 1:8	I am Alpha and Omega...the **Almighty**.
Rev. 4:8	Lord God **Almighty**, which was, and is, and is to come.
Rev. 11:17	O Lord God **Almighty**, which art, and wast, and art to
Rev. 21:22	the Lord God **Almighty** and the Lamb are the temple of
1 Ne. 1:14	Lord God Almighty ...thy **power**, and goodness, and
1 Ne. 4:1	the Lord...is **mightier** than all the earth, then why
1 Ne. 7:12	the Lord is **able** to do all things according to his
1 Ne. 17:48	filled with the **power** of God, even unto the consuming
1 Ne. 17:51(23-51)	if the Lord has such great **power**, and has wrought so
2 Ne. 27:20(15-20)	I am **able** to do mine own work; wherefore thou shalt
Jacob 4:6(6-10)	we truly can **command** in the name of Jesus and the very
Jacob 4:11(8-11)	the **power** of the resurrection which is in Christ, and
W of M 1:17	did speak the word of God with **power** and with
Alma 17:3(2,3)	they taught with **power** and authority of God.
Alma 57:26(24-27)	justly ascribe it to the miraculous **power** of God
Hel. 10:11	thus saith the Lord God, who is the **Almighty**: except
Hel. 12:11(9-21)	by the **power** of his voice doth the whole earth shake
Ether 3:4	thou hast all **power**...for the benefit of man
Ether 12:27(23-28)	my **grace** is sufficient for all men that humble
Ether 12:30	brother of Jared said unto the mountain Zerin
D&C 3:8(1-3,8)	he would have extended his arm and **supported** you again
D&C 6:16	none else save God that **knowest** thy thoughts and the
D&C 11:30	to them will I give **power** to become the sons of God
D&C 45:8	that believed...gave I **power** to obtain eternal life.
D&C 61:1	hearken unto the voice of him who has all **power**, who
D&C 84:96	for I, the **Almighty**, have laid my hands upon the
D&C 84:118	saith the Lord **Almighty**, I will rend their kingdoms
D&C 87:6	feel the...chastening hand of an **Almighty** God, until
D&C 88:106	the fierceness of the wrath of **Almighty** God.

GOD, POWER OF cont.

D&C 93:17	he received all **power**, both in heaven and on earth
D&C 121:4	O Lord God **Almighty**, maker of heaven, earth, and seas
D&C 121:33	hinder the **Almighty** from pouring down knowledge from
D&C 133:3	he shall make bare his holy **arm** in the eyes of all the
Moses 1:4	my **works** are without end, and also my words, for they
Moses 1:20(16-22)	calling upon God, he received **strength**, and he

GOD, PRESENCE OF

Ex. 13:21(21,22)	Lord went before...in a pillar of a **cloud**, to lead the
Ex. 19:17	Moses brought forth the people...to **meet** with God; and
Ex. 19:18(10-25)	mount Sinai...the Lord **descended** upon it in fire: and
Ex. 20:20(18-22)	God is **come** to prove you, and that his fear may be
Ex. 29:45	I will dwell **among** the children of Israel, and will
Num. 14:14	thou Lord art **among** this people, that thou Lord art
Num. 16:3	and the Lord is **among** them: wherefore then lift ye up
Num. 35:34	I the Lord dwell **among** the children of Israel.
Deut. 5:4	the Lord talked with you **face** to face in the mount out
1 Chr. 16:27	glory and honour are in his **presence**; strength and
Ps. 16:11	in thy **presence** is fulness of joy; at thy right hand
Ps. 68:2	let the wicked perish at the **presence** of God.
Ps. 140:13	the upright shall dwell in thy **presence**.
Isa. 4:5(3-6)	upon every dwelling place...a flaming **fire** by night
Isa. 64:1(1-4)	that the mountains might flow down at thy **presence**
Jer. 30:21(18-22)	I will cause him to **draw** near, and he shall approach
Ezek. 20:35	there will I plead with you **face** to face.
Ezek. 37:26(26-28)	and will set my **sanctuary** in the midst of them for
Joel 2:27	ye shall know that I am in the **midst** of Israel, and
Nahum 1:5(5-6)	hills melt, and the earth is burned at his **presence**
Zech. 2:5(2-5)	for I...will be unto her a wall of **fire** round about
Matt. 5:8	blessed are the pure in heart: for they shall **see** God.
John 1:14	and the Word was made flesh, and **dwelt** among us, (and
Acts 3:19(19-21)	refreshing shall come from the **presence** of the Lord
Acts 7:56(55-56)	I **see**...the Son of man standing on the right hand of
2 Cor. 6:16	I will **dwell** in them, and walk in them; and I will be
Heb. 3:11	I sware in my wrath...not enter into my **rest**.
Heb. 10:22(19-22)	let us **draw** near with a true heart in full assurance
James 4:8	**draw** nigh to God, and he will draw nigh to you.
Rev. 7:15(15-17)	he that sitteth on the throne shall **dwell** among them.
Rev. 21:3	God ...will **dwell** with them, and they shall be his
1 Ne. 1:6	there came a pillar of **fire** and dwelt upon a rock
2 Ne. 9:6(6-7)	they were cut off from the **presence** of the Lord.
2 Ne. 14:5	**Lord** will create...smoke by day...fire by night; for
Mosiah 2:38	guilt...cause..to shrink from the **presence** of the Lord
Alma 36:30	not keep the commandments...cut off from his **presence**.
Alma 38:1	not keep the commandments...cast off from his **presence**
Alma 42:7(7-12)	first parents...cut off...from...**presence** of the Lord
Hel. 12:25(25-26)	some...shall be cast off from the **presence** of the Lord
Hel. 14:15(15-18)	men may be brought into the **presence** of the Lord.
Morm. 9:13(12-13)	they are brought back into the **presence** of the Lord
Ether 3:13(13-20)	therefore ye are brought back into my **presence**
D&C 76:62(50-62)	these shall dwell in the **presence** of God and his

GOD, PRESENCE OF cont.

D&C 76:77(71-77)	they who receive of the **presence** of the Son, but not
D&C 76:94(92-94)	they who dwell in his **presence** are the church of the
D&C 76:118(114-119)	they may be able to bear his **presence** in the world of
D&C 84:5	**cloud** shall be even the glory of the Lord, which shall
D&C 84:24(19-26)	hardened...hearts and could not endure his **presence**
D&C 88:63	**draw** near unto me and I will draw near unto you; seek
D&C 93:1	keepeth my commandments, shall **see** my face and know
D&C 94:8(8-9)	my glory...and my **presence** shall be there.
D&C 97:16	yea, and my **presence** shall be there, for I will come
D&C 101:38	seek the face of the **Lord** always, that in patience ye
D&C 107:19(18-19)	enjoy the communion and **presence** of God the Father
D&C 110:8(1-9)	I will **appear** unto my servants, and speak unto them
D&C 121:45	shall thy confidence wax strong in the **presence** of God
D&C 130:7(6-7)	they reside in the **presence** of God, on a globe like a
D&C 133:35	shall be sanctified...to dwell in his **presence** day and
Moses 6:57	no unclean thing can dwell...in his **presence**; for
Moses 7:16	the Lord came and **dwelt** with his people, and they
Moses 7:69	walked with God, and he **dwelt** in the midst of Zion

GOD, PRIVILEGE OF SEEING

Gen. 32:30	for I have **seen** God face to face, and my life is
Ex. 3:6	he was afraid to **look** upon God.
Ex. 19:11(9-11)	Lord will come down in the **sight** of all the people
Ex. 19:21(20-24)	lest they break through unto the Lord to **gaze**, and man
Ex. 20:18(18-21)	when...people **saw** it, they removed, and stood afar off
Ex. 24:11(9-11)	the nobles of the children of Israel...**saw** God, and
Ex. 33:11	the Lord spake unto Moses **face** to face, as a man
Ex. 33:18(13-23)	and he said, I beseech thee, **shew** me thy glory.
Ex. 33:20	not see my face...there shall no man **see** me, and live.
Num. 12:8(5-8)	with him will I **speak** mouth to mouth, even apparently
Deut. 34:10	Moses, whom the Lord knew **face** to face
Judg. 13:22	we shall surely die, because we have **seen** God.
1 Kgs. 11:9	the Lord God of Israel...**appeared** unto him twice
Ps. 27:8	seek ye my **face**; my heart said unto thee, thy face
Ps. 95:11(8-11)	I sware...that they should not enter into my **rest**.
Isa. 6:5(1-5)	mine eyes have **seen** the king, the Lord of hosts.
Ezek. 1:28(26-28)	this was the **appearance** of the likeness of the glory
Matt. 5:8	blessed are the pure in heart: for they shall **see** God.
Matt. 11:27	he to whomsoever the Son will **reveal** him.
John 1:18	no man hath **seen** God at any time; the Only Begotten
John 5:37(36-37)	ye have neither heard his voice...nor **seen** his shape.
John 6:46(45-46)	he which is of God, he hath **seen** the Father.
John 14:18	I will not leave you comfortless: I will **come** to you.
John 14:21(19-23)	I will love him, and will **manifest** myself to him.
Acts 7:56(55-56)	I **see**...the Son of man standing on the right hand of
1 Tim. 6:16(13-16)	no man hath **seen**, nor can see: to whom be honour and
Heb. 3:11(7-11)	I sware in my wrath, they shall not enter into my **rest**
Heb. 12:14	holiness, without which no man shall **see** the Lord
1 Jn. 3:2(2,3)	we shall be like him; for we shall **see** him as he is.
1 Jn. 4:20	how can he love God whom he hath not **seen**
Rev. 1:17(16-17)	when I **saw** him, I fell at his feet as dead. And he

GOD, PRIVILEGE OF SEEING cont.

Rev. 22:4(3,4)	and they shall **see** his face; and his name shall be in
1 Ne. 1:8(7-15)	saw the heavens open, and he thought he **saw** God
2 Ne. 11:3(2,3)	my brother, Jacob, also has **seen** him as I have seen
Alma 19:13	I have **seen** my Redeemer; and he shall come forth, and
Ether 3:13(6-16)	redeemed...therefore...brought back into my **presence**
Ether 3:15(6-16)	never have I **showed** myself unto man whom I have
D&C 35:21	hear my voice, and shall **see** me, and shall not be
D&C 50:45	shall hear my voice and **see** me, and know that I am.
D&C 58:3	ye cannot behold with your natural **eyes**, for the
D&C 67:11(10-14)	no man has **seen** God at any time in the flesh, except
D&C 76:12	by the power of the spirit our **eyes** were opened and
D&C 76:23(19-24)	for we **saw** him, even on the right hand of God; and we
D&C 76:117(116-118)	he grants this privilege of **seeing** and knowing for the
D&C 84:22	without this no man can **see** the face of God, even the
D&C 84:23	sanctify his people...might **behold** the face of God
D&C 84:24(23-24)	not endure...presence...should not enter into his **rest**
D&C 88:68(68,74,75)	sanctify yourselves...that you shall **see** him; for he
D&C 93:1(1-4)	shall see my **face** and know that I am
D&C 97:16	pure in heart that shall come into it shall **see** God.
D&C 107:19	to enjoy the communion and **presence** of God the Father
D&C 110:2(1-10)	we **saw** the Lord standing upon the breastwork of the
D&C 121:45	shall thy confidence wax strong in the **presence** of God
D&C 130:3	**appearing** of the Father and the Son...is a personal
Moses 1:2(2,11)	and he **saw** God face to face, and he talked with him
Moses 1:5	no man can **behold** all my glory, and afterwards remain
Moses 1:11	mine own eyes have **beheld** God...my spiritual eyes, for
Moses 5:10	and again in the flesh I shall **see** God.
Moses 6:39(34-39)	fear came on all them...for he **walked** with God.
Moses 7:4(3,4)	and I **saw** the Lord; and he stood before my face, and
Moses 7:59	and Enoch **beheld** the Son of man ascend up unto the
Abr. 3:11	Abraham, talked with the Lord, **face** to face, as one
Abr. 3:24(22-28)	there stood one among them that was like unto **God**, and
JS-H 1:17(17-20)	I **saw** two Personages, whose brightness and glory defy

GOD, SPIRIT OF

Gen. 1:2	the **Spirit** of God moved upon the face of the waters.
Gen. 6:3	my **spirit** shall not always strive with man, for that
Gen. 41:38	a man in whom the **Spirit** of God is
Ex. 31:3	I have filled him with the **spirit** of God, in wisdom
Num. 27:18	a man in whom is the **spirit**, and lay thine hand upon
Judg. 3:10	the **Spirit** of the Lord came upon him, and he judged
2 Sam. 23:2	the **Spirit** of the Lord spake by me, and his word was
2 Chr. 24:20	and the **Spirit** of God came upon Zechariah the son of
Job 33:4	the **Spirit** of God hath made me, and the breath of the
Ps. 143:10	thou art my God: thy **spirit** is good; lead me into the
Isa. 11:2	the **spirit** of the Lord shall rest upon him, the spirit
Isa. 40:13(7,13-14)	who hath directed the **Spirit** of the Lord, or...taught
Isa. 42:1	I have put my **spirit** upon him: he shall bring forth
Isa. 59:19	the **Spirit** of the Lord shall lift up a standard
Isa. 61:1	the **Spirit** of the Lord God is upon me; because the Lord
Isa. 63:14	the **Spirit** of the Lord caused him to rest: so didst

Ezek. 3:12	then the **spirit** took me up, and I heard behind me a
Ezek. 8:3	and the **spirit** lifted me up between the earth and the
Ezek. 11:1	moreover the **spirit** lifted me up, and brought me unto
Ezek. 11:24	afterwards the **spirit** took me up, and brought me in a
Ezek. 37:1	carried me out in the **spirit** of the Lord, and set me
Ezek. 43:5	so the **spirit** took me up, and brought me into the
Dan. 4:18(8,18)	thou art able; for the **spirit** of the holy gods is in
Dan. 5:11(11,14)	a man...in whom is the **spirit** of the holy gods; and
Dan. 6:3	Daniel was preferred...because an excellent **spirit** was
Joel 2:28(28-29)	I will pour out my **spirit** upon all flesh; and your son
Micah 3:8	full of power by the **spirit** of the Lord, and of
Zech. 4:6	not by might, nor by power, but by my **spirit**, saith
Matt. 3:16(16-17)	he saw the **Spirit** of God descending like a dove, and
Matt. 10:20	it is not ye that speak, but the **Spirit** of your Father
Matt. 12:28	if I cast out devils by the **Spirit** of God, then the
Luke 4:18	the **Spirit** of the Lord is upon me, because he hath
Acts 8:39	the **Spirit** of the Lord caught away Philip, that the
Rom. 8:14(9,14)	led by the **Spirit** of God, they are the sons of God.
Rom. 15:19	signs and wonders, by the power of the **Spirit** of God
1 Cor. 2:14(10-14)	natural man receiveth not the things of the **Spirit** of
1 Cor. 3:16	ye are the temple of God...the **Spirit** of God dwelleth
1 Cor. 6:11	sanctified...justified...by the **Spirit** of our God.
1 Cor. 12:7(1-11)	manifestation of the **Spirit** is given to every man to
2 Cor. 3:17(17,18)	where the **Spirit** of the Lord is, there is liberty.
Eph. 4:30	and grieve not the holy **Spirit** of God, whereby ye are
Philip. 1:19	the supply of the **Spirit** of Jesus Christ
1 Pet. 3:18(18-20)	but quickened by the **Spirit**
1 Jn. 4:2	hereby know ye the **Spirit** of God: every spirit that
1 Ne. 7:14	the **Spirit** of the Lord ceaseth soon to strive with the
1 Ne. 11:1	I was caught away in the **Spirit** of the Lord, yea, into
1 Ne. 17:52(47-55)	so powerful was the **Spirit** of God; and thus it had
1 Ne. 19:12	the sea shall be wrought upon by the **Spirit** of God
1 Ne. 20:16	the Lord God, and his **Spirit**, hath sent me.
1 Ne. 22:2	by the **Spirit** are all things made known unto the
Jacob 7:8	the Lord God poured in his **Spirit** into my soul
Mosiah 4:20	nay; he has poured out his **Spirit** upon you, and has
Mosiah 5:2	know of their surety and truth, because of the **Spirit**
Mosiah 18:13(8-14)	may the **Spirit** of the Lord be poured out upon you; and
Mosiah 25:24	the Lord did pour out his **Spirit** upon them, and they
Alma 5:47	by the manifestation of the **Spirit** of God.
Alma 8:10	in mighty prayer, that he would pour out his **Spirit**
Alma 9:21	having been visited by the **Spirit** of God; having
Alma 11:22	I shall say nothing which is contrary to the **Spirit**
Alma 17:10	the Lord did visit them with his **Spirit**, and said unto
Alma 19:36	thus the Lord did begin to pour out his **Spirit** upon
Alma 22:15	receive his **Spirit**, that I may be filled with joy
Alma 24:30	have been once enlightened by the **Spirit** of God, and
Alma 40:13	they have no part nor portion of the **Spirit** of the Lord
Alma 61:15	the **Spirit** of God, which is also the spirit of freedom
Hel. 5:45(20-52)	the Holy **Spirit** of God did come down from heaven, and
Hel. 6:36	the Lord began to pour out his **Spirit** upon the
3 Ne. 7:21	visited by the power and **Spirit** of God, which was in
3 Ne. 17:24(21-25)	they were encircled about with **fire**; and the angels

3 Ne. 19:14(13-14)	they were encircled about as if it were by **fire**; and
Morm. 5:16	the **Spirit** of the Lord hath already ceased to strive
Ether 2:15(4-15)	my **Spirit** will not always strive with man; wherefore
Ether 15:19	the **Spirit** of the Lord had ceased striving with them
Moro. 4:3	that they may always have his **Spirit** to be with them.
Moro. 7:16	the **Spirit** of Christ is given to every man, that he
Moro. 10:8(8-19)	gifts are...given by the manifestations of the **Spirit**
D&C 1:33	for my **Spirit** shall not always strive with man, saith
D&C 5:16	with the manifestation of my **Spirit**...even of water
D&C 6:15(14-16)	enlightened by the **Spirit** of truth
D&C 8:3(1-3)	behold, this is the **Spirit** of revelation; behold, this
D&C 11:12(12-13,18)	put your trust in that **Spirit** which leadeth to do good
D&C 18:47(2,35,47)	by the power of my **Spirit** have spoken it. Amen.
D&C 19:20(18,20,23)	you have tasted at the time I withdrew my **Spirit**.
D&C 25:7	according as it shall be given thee by my **Spirit**.
D&C 27:18	and the sword of my **Spirit**, which I will pour out upon
D&C 29:30(30-31)	created by...my power...power of my **Spirit**.
D&C 30:2	you have not given heed unto my **Spirit**, and to those
D&C 33:16	the power of my **Spirit** quickeneth all things.
D&C 35:13	to thrash the nations by the power of my **Spirit**
D&C 46:17(11-28)	by the **Spirit** of God, the word of wisdom.
D&C 63:32	I am holding my **Spirit** from the inhabitants of the
D&C 64:16	I, the Lord, withheld my **Spirit**. They condemned for
D&C 68:1	by the **Spirit** of the living God, from people to people
D&C 76:10(1-30,116)	by my **Spirit** will I enlighten them, and by my power
D&C 84:33	sanctified by the **Spirit** unto the renewing of their
D&C 84:45(45-47)	whatsoever is light is **Spirit**, even the Spirit of
D&C 88:7(6-13)	**light** of Christ...power thereof by which it was made.
D&C 88:66	my voice is **Spirit**; my Spirit is truth; truth abideth
D&C 104:81	write...that which shall be dictated by my **Spirit**; and
D&C 105:36	manifest...by the voice of the **Spirit**, those that are
D&C 111:8	power of my **Spirit**, that shall flow unto you.
D&C 112:22	and hearken to the voice of my **Spirit**.
D&C 121:26(26-28)	God shall give unto you knowledge by his Holy **Spirit**
D&C 124:88(88,97)	as he shall be moved upon by my **Spirit**, unto the
D&C 136:33	for my **Spirit** is sent forth into the world to
Moses 1:15	for his **Spirit** hath not altogether withdrawn from me
Moses 1:27(27,28)	did not behold, discerning it by the **Spirit** of God.
Moses 2:2	my **Spirit** moved upon the face of the water; for I am
Moses 6:26	the **Spirit** of God descended out of heaven, and abode
Moses 6:65(64-65)	the **Spirit** of God descended upon him, and thus he was
Moses 8:17	my **Spirit** shall not always strive with man, for he

GOD, THE STANDARD OF RIGHTEOUSNESS

Lev. 19:2(2-37)	ye shall be **holy**: for I the Lord your God am holy.
Job 28:28(12-28)	the fear of the Lord, that is **wisdom**; and to depart
Prov. 12:22	lips...that deal truly are his **delight**.
Isa. 5:20(20-24)	woe unto them that call evil **good**, and good evil; that
Micah 6:8	Lord **require** of thee, but to do justly, and to love
Matt. 5:48	be ye therefore **perfect**, even as your Father which is
Matt. 6:33	seek ye...kingdom of God, and his **righteousness**; and

GOD, THE STANDARD OF RIGHTEOUSNESS cont.

John 5:44	how can ye believe...and seek not the **honour** that come
John 8:49(49-55)	I **honour** my Father, and ye do dishonour me.
John 13:15	I have given you an **example**, that ye should do as I
John 14:15	if ye **love** me, keep my commandments.
Rom. 1:17(16,17)	therein is the **righteousness** of God revealed from
Rom. 3:21(5,21,22)	now the **righteousness** of God without the law is
Rom. 10:3	they being ignorant of God's **righteousness**, and going
Eph. 5:1(1-9)	be ye therefore **followers** of God, as dear children
1 Tim. 6:13	Jesus, who before Pontius Pilate **witnessed** a good
2 Tim. 4:8	there is laid up for me a crown of **righteousness**
2 Pet. 1:1	obtained...faith...through the **righteousness** of God
1 Jn. 5:3(1-13)	this is the **love** of God, that we keep his commandments
2 Ne. 31:12(9-16)	**follow** me, and do the things which ye have seen me
Jacob 2:28(27,28)	I, the Lord God, delight in the **chastity** of women.
Mosiah 2:22(20-24)	all that he **requires** of you is to keep his commandment
Mosiah 18:10(7-10)	that ye will **serve** him and keep his commandments, that
Alma 5:40(38-42)	whatsoever is **good** cometh from God, and whatosever is
3 Ne. 12:48	I would that ye should be **perfect** even as I, or your
3 Ne. 18:16(14-16)	I am the light; I have set an **example** for you.
Morm. 7:10	following the **example** of our Savior, according to
Ether 12:28(28,29)	bringeth unto me- the fountain of all **righteousness**.
D&C 25:12(12-15)	my soul **delighteth** in the song of the heart; yea, the
D&C 76:5(5-10)	I the Lord...delight to **honor** those who serve me in
Moses 4:2	Father, thy **will** be done, and the glory be thine
Abr. 1:2(1,2)	desiring...to be a greater follower of **righteousness**

GOD, WILL OF

1 Sam. 15:22(22,23)	obeying the **voice** of the Lord? Behold, to obey is
Ps. 40:8	I delight to do thy **will**, O my God: yea, thy law is
Ps. 143:10	teach me to do thy **will**; for thou art my God: thy
Isa. 55:8(8-11)	my **thoughts** are not your thoughts, neither are your
Dan. 4:35(34,35)	and he doeth according to his **will** in the army of
Matt. 6:10(9-13)	thy **will** be done in earth, as it is in heaven.
Matt. 7:21	but he that doeth the **will** of my Father which is in
Matt. 12:50	whosoever shall do the **will** of my Father which is in
Matt. 26:42	thy **will** be done.
Luke 22:42	not my **will**, but thine, be done.
John 4:34	my meat is to do the **will** of him that sent me, and to
John 5:30	I seek not mine own will, but the **will** of the Father
John 6:38(38-40)	the **will** of him that sent me.
John 7:17	do his **will**, he shall know...it be of God, or whether
Acts 22:14(12-16)	that thou shouldest know his **will**, and see that just
Rom. 12:2	prove what is that good...**will** of God.
Gal. 1:4	deliver us...according to the **will** of God and our
Eph. 1:9	the mystery of his **will**, according to his good
Eph. 6:6	doing the **will** of God from the heart
Col. 1:9	be filled with the knowledge of his **will** in all wisdom
Heb. 2:4	bearing them witness...according to his own **will**
Heb. 10:36	done the **will** of God, ye might receive the promise.
Heb. 13:21	make you perfect in every good work to do his **will**
1 Pet. 4:19	suffer according to the **will** of God commit the keeping

GOD, WILL OF cont.

1 Jn. 2:17(15-17)	he that doeth the **will** of God abideth for ever.
1 Jn. 5:14	ask any thing according to his **will**, he heareth us
2 Ne. 2:21	days...prolonged, according to the **will** of God, that
2 Ne. 10:24(22-24)	reconcile yourselves to the **will** of God, and not to
W of M 1:7	he worketh in me to do according to his **will**.
Mosiah 3:11(11,12)	died not knowing the **will** of God concerning them, or
Mosiah 15:2(2,7)	subjected the flesh to the **will** of the Father, being
Alma 32:19(18-20)	he that knoweth the **will** of God and doeth it not, than
Hel. 10:5(3-5)	shalt not ask that which is contrary to my **will**.
3 Ne. 1:14	to do the **will**, both of the Father and of the Son- of
3 Ne. 6:18(17,18)	not sin ignorantly...they knew the **will** of God
3 Ne. 11:11	I have suffered the **will** of the Father in all things
D&C 19:24	I came by the **will** of the Father, and I do his will.
D&C 46:30	Spirit asketh according to the **will** of God; wherefore
D&C 58:20	let God rule...according to ...counsel of his own **will**
D&C 63:20	he that endureth...and doeth my **will**...shall overcome
D&C 76:10	I make known unto them the secrets of my **will**- yea
D&C 89:2	**will** of God in the temporal salvation of all saints
D&C 124:5	given you by the Holy Ghost to know my **will** concerning
D&C 124:89	if he will do my **will** let him from henceforth hearken

GOD, WISDOM OF

Ex. 31:3(3-6)	I have filled him with the spirit of God, in **wisdom**
1 Kgs. 4:29	and God gave Solomon **wisdom** and understanding
Job 28:12(12,13,23)	but where shall **wisdom** be found? and where is the
Job 36:5(4-5)	God is mighty...in strength and **wisdom**.
Ps. 136:5	to him that by **wisdom** made the heavens: for his mercy
Prov. 2:6(5-11)	the Lord giveth **wisdom**: out of his mouth cometh
Isa. 55:8(8-9)	my **thoughts** are not your thoughts, neither are your
Matt. 13:54(53,54)	whence hath this man this **wisdom**, and these mighty
Luke 2:52(40,52)	Jesus increased in **wisdom** and stature, and in favour
1 Cor. 3:19	for the **wisdom** of this world is foolishness with God.
Rev. 5:12	worthy is the lamb that was slain to receive...**wisdom**
2 Ne. 9:8(8,9)	O the **wisdom** of God, his mercy and grace! For behold
2 Ne. 27:22(22,23)	until I shall see fit in mine own **wisdom** to reveal
Jacob 4:10	he counseleth in **wisdom**, and in justice, and in great
Alma 26:35	my God...has all power, all **wisdom**, and all
D&C 9:3(3,6)	be patient, my son, for it is **wisdom** in me, and it is
D&C 10:35(35-37)	here is **wisdom**, show it not unto the world- for I said
D&C 10:43	my **wisdom** is greater than the cunning of the devil.
D&C 42:68	he that lacketh **wisdom**, let him ask of me, and I will
D&C 76:2	great is his **wisdom**, marvelous are his ways, and the
D&C 78:2	who shall speak in your ears the words of **wisdom**, that
D&C 88:6	he **comprehended** all things, that he might be in all
D&C 124:1	that I might show forth my **wisdom** through the weak

GOD, WORKS OF

Deut. 10:14(14-15)	heaven...is the Lord's...earth also, with **all** that the
Job 37:14	still, and consider the wondrous **works** of God.
Job 42:2(1,2)	I know that thou canst **do** every thing, and that no
Ps. 8:3(3-9)	thy heavens, the **work** of thy fingers, the moon and the
Ps. 50:12	the **world** is mine, and the fulness thereof.
Ps. 64:9	declare the **work** of God; for they shall wisely
Isa. 29:14	I will proceed to do a marvellous **work** among this
John 5:17(17-20)	my Father **worketh** hitherto, and I work.
John 5:36	the **works** which the Father hath given me to finish
John 9:3	the **works** of God should be made manifest in him.
Rom. 14:20	destroy not the **work** of God. All things indeed are
1 Cor. 10:26	the **earth** is the Lord's, and the fulness thereof.
1 Ne. 14:7	a **work** which shall be everlasting, either on the one
2 Ne. 25:17	a marvelous **work** and a wonder among the children of
2 Ne. 29:1	I shall...do a marvelous **work** among them, that I may
Alma 5:50	**King** of all the earth; and also the King of heaven
3 Ne. 21:9	the Father work a **work**, which shall be a great and a
D&C 3:1(1-7)	the **works**, and the designs, and the purposes of God
D&C 3:16(16,17)	my **work** shall go forth, for inasmuch as the knowledge
D&C 4:3	desires to serve God ye are called to the **work**
D&C 8:8	doubt not, for it is the gift of God...the **work** of God
D&C 10:43	I will not suffer that they shall destroy my **work**; yea
D&C 11:9(1-4,9)	assist to bring forth my **work**, according to my
D&C 17:4	bring about my righteous purposes...in this **work**.
D&C 67:2	**heavens** and the earth are in mine hands, and the rich
D&C 76:114	great and marvelous are the **works** of the Lord, and the
D&C 84:66(66-72)	in my name they shall do many wonderful **works**
D&C 117:6(6,7)	have I not **made** the earth? Do I not hold the destinies
Moses 1:5(3-5)	no man can behold all my **works**, except he behold all
Moses 1:33(27-38)	**worlds** without number have I created; and I also
Moses 1:39	this is my **work** and my glory- to bring to pass the
Moses 2:1(1-31)	in the beginning I **created** the heaven, and the earth

GODHEAD

Gen. 1:26	and God said, let **us** make man in our image, after our
Gen. 3:22	the man is become as one of **us**, to know good and evil
Matt. 3:17(16-17)	this is my beloved **Son**, in whom I am well pleased.
Matt. 17:5	this is my beloved **Son**, in whom I am well pleased
Matt. 20:23(21-23)	not mine to give, but...given...of my **Father**.
Matt. 26:39	not as I will, but as **thou** wilt.
Matt. 28:19	baptizing them in the name of the **Father**, and of the
Luke 1:32(31-32)	shall be called the **Son** of the highest: and the Lord
Luke 3:22(21-22)	the **Holy** Ghost descended in a bodily shape like a dove
John 5:19(19-26)	son can do nothing...but what he seeth the **Father** do
John 8:18(17-18)	the **Father** that sent me beareth witness of me.
John 10:30	I and my Father are **one**.
John 10:38(34-38)	believe the works...that the **Father** is in me, and I
John 12:28(28-29)	came there a **voice** from heaven, saying, I have both
John 14:28	for my **Father** is greater than I.
John 17:3	that they might know thee the only true **God**, and Jesus
John 17:21(20-23)	that they all may be one; as thou, **Father**, art in me

GODHEAD cont.

John 20:17	I ascend unto my **Father**, and your Father; and to my
Acts 2:33(29-36)	therefore being by the **right** hand of God exalted, and
Acts 7:55(55-56)	saw the glory of **God**, and Jesus standing on the right
1 Cor. 8:6(4-6)	but to us there is but one **God**, the Father, of whom
2 Cor. 4:4	Christ...the image of **God**, should shine unto them.
Eph. 3:14	I bow my knees unto the **Father** of our Lord Jesus
Col. 1:15(12-15)	image of the invisible **God**, the firstborn of every
Heb. 1:2(1-3)	hath in these last days spoken unto us by his **Son**, who
1 Jn. 5:7(5-7)	three that bear record in heaven, the **Father**, the Word
2 Ne. 31:21	the **Father**, and of the Son, and of the Holy Ghost
Mosiah 15:4(1-5)	and they are **one** God, yea, the very eternal Father of
Alma 11:44	Christ the Son, and God the **Father**, and the Holy
3 Ne. 11:7	behold my beloved **Son**, in whom I am well pleased, in
3 Ne. 11:25	I baptize you in the name of the **Father**, and of the
3 Ne. 11:36(32-36)	the Father, and I, and the Holy Ghost are **one**.
Morm. 7:7	**Father**, and unto the Son, and unto the Holy Ghost
D&C 20:28(27-28)	which Father, Son, and Holy Ghost are **one** God
D&C 35:2	one in me as I am **one** in the Father, as the Father is
D&C 76:23(22-24)	for we saw him, even on the right hand of **God**; and we
D&C 130:22	the **Father** has a body of flesh and bones as tangible
JS-H 1:17(15-19)	I saw two **Personages**, whose brightness and glory defy
A of F 1:1	We believe in **God**, the Eternal Father, and in his Son
JS-V 1:3(1-3)	whereon was seated the **Father** and the Son.

GODLINESS

Ps. 1:6(1-6)	but the way of the **ungodly** shall perish.
Ps. 4:3(2-4)	the Lord hath set apart him that is **godly** for himself
Ps. 32:6(5-6)	for this shall every one that is **godly** pray unto thee
Mal. 2:15	seek a **godly** seed. therefore take heed to your spirit
Matt. 5:48	be ye therefore **perfect**, even as your Father which is
2 Cor. 7:10(8-11)	for **godly** sorrow worketh repentance to salvation not
1 Tim. 1:9(8,9)	the law is not made for a **righteous** man, but for the
1 Tim. 2:10(9-10)	(which becometh women professing **godliness)** with good
1 Tim. 4:8	**godliness** is profitable unto all things, having
1 Tim. 6:6(1-11)	but **godliness** with contentment is great gain.
2 Tim. 2:16(15-16)	they will increase unto more **ungodliness**.
2 Tim. 3:12(10-12)	all that will live **godly** in Christ Jesus shall suffer
Titus 2:12(11-13)	denying **ungodliness** and worldly lusts, we should live
1 Pet. 4:18(17,18)	righteous scarcely be saved, where shall the **ungodly**
2 Pet. 1:3(2-8)	all things that pertain unto life and **godliness**
2 Pet. 2:9	the Lord knoweth how to deliver the **godly** out of
Jude 1:4(3,4)	**ungodly** men, turning the grace of our God into
3 Ne. 27:27(25-27)	what **manner** of men ought ye to be? Verily I say unto
Moro. 7:30(29-31)	showing themselves...in every form of **godliness**.
D&C 4:6(5-6)	temperance, patience, brotherly kindness, **godliness**
D&C 20:69(68-69)	members shall manifest...by a **godly** walk and
D&C 84:20(19-22)	in the ordinances...the power of **godliness** is manifest
D&C 107:30(30-31)	decisions of...quorums...are to be made in...**godliness**

GOOD WORKS

Gen. 26:5(4-5)	because...Abraham **obeyed** my voice, and kept my...laws.
2 Chr. 15:7	be ye strong...for your **work** shall be rewarded.
Ps. 28:4	give them according to their **deeds**, and according to
Ps. 62:12	for thou renderest to every man according to his **work**.
Eccl. 12:14(13,14)	God shall bring every **work** into judgment, with every
Isa. 1:17(16-17)	learn to do **well**...relieve the oppressed, judge the
Jer. 17:10	to give every man according to his **ways**, and
Jer. 32:19	to give every one according to his **ways**, and according
Micah 6:8	do **justly**, and to love mercy, and to walk humbly with
Matt. 5:6	they which do hunger and thirst after **righteousness**
Matt. 5:16(14-16)	that they may see your good **works**, and glorify your
Matt. 7:12	**whatsoever** ye would that men should do to you, do ye
Matt. 7:16(15-16)	ye shall know them by their **fruits**. Do men gather
Matt. 7:21(21-27)	he that **doeth** the will of my Father which is in heaven
Matt. 13:23	which also beareth **fruit**, and bringeth forth, some an
Matt. 16:27	he shall reward every man according to his **works**.
Matt. 25:40(31-46)	as ye have done it unto one of the **least** of these my
John 3:21(20-21)	he that **doeth** truth cometh to the light, that his deed
John 7:17(16-17)	if any man...**do** his will, he shall know of the
John 8:39(37-40)	Abraham's children, ye would do the **works** of Abraham.
John 9:4	I must work the **works** of him that sent me, while it
John 14:15(15,21)	if ye love me, keep my **commandments**.
Acts 10:35(34-35)	he that...**worketh** righteousness, is accepted with him.
Rom. 2:6(5-11)	who will render to every man according to his **deeds**
Rom. 2:13	but the **doers** of the law shall be justified.
2 Cor. 5:10(9-10)	receive...according to that he hath **done**, whether it
Gal. 6:4	let every man prove his own **work**, and then shall he
Gal. 6:7(7-10)	whatsoever a man **soweth**, that shall he also reap.
Eph. 2:10	created in Christ Jesus unto good **works**, which God
Eph. 5:9	the fruit of the spirit is in all **goodness** and
Philip. 2:12	**work** out your own salvation with fear and trembling.
2 Tim. 3:17(16-17)	perfect, throughly furnished unto all **good** works.
Titus 3:8	be careful to maintain good **works**. these things are
Heb. 13:21	make you perfect in every good **work** to do his will
James 1:22(22-25)	be ye **doers** of the word, and not hearers only
James 1:27(26-27)	pure religion...is this, to **visit** the fatherless and
James 2:22	and by **works** was faith made perfect
James 2:26(14-26)	faith without **works** is dead also.
James 4:17	him that knoweth to do good, and **doeth** it not, to him
1 Pet. 1:17	the father...judgeth according to every man's **work**
2 Pet. 1:5(5-8)	add to your faith **virtue**; and to virtue knowledge
1 Jn. 3:18	let us not love in word...but in **deed** and in truth.
1 Jn. 3:22	we receive...because we keep his **commandments**, and do
Rev. 20:12(12-13)	dead were judged...according to their **works**.
Rev. 22:14	blessed are they that do his **commandments**, that they
1 Ne. 15:32(30-33)	they must be judged of their **works**, yea, even the work
2 Ne. 25:23	by grace that we are saved, after all we can **do**.
Jacob 2:19(18-19)	riches...seek them for the intent to do **good**- to cloth
Mosiah 2:17	when ye are in the **service** of your fellow beings ye
Mosiah 3:24	they shall be judged...according to...**works**, whether
Mosiah 4:26	ye should impart of your substance to the **poor**, every
Mosiah 5:15	always abounding in **good** works, that Christ, the Lord
Alma 5:41(41,42)	if a man bringeth forth **good** works he hearkeneth unto

GOOD WORKS cont.

Alma 7:24(24-27)	then ye will always abound in **good** works.
Alma 9:28(27-28)	all men shall reap a reward of their **works**, according
Alma 13:3(2-7)	called and prepared...exceeding faith and **good** works
Alma 26:22	bringeth forth good **works**, and prayeth continually
Alma 33:22	all men shall...be judged...according to their **works**.
Alma 34:28	if ye **do** not...these things...your prayer is vain, and
Alma 34:32	this life is the day...to perform their **labors**.
Morm. 9:29	see that ye **do** all things in worthiness, and do it in
Moro. 9:6	if we should cease to **labor**...under condemnation; for
D&C 6:13	if thou wilt do **good**...thou shalt be saved in the
D&C 6:33	fear not to do **good**, my sons, for whatsoever ye sow
D&C 18:38(37-38)	by their...their **works** you shall know them.
D&C 19:3	judging every man according to his **works** and the deeds
D&C 58:27(26-29)	do many **things** of their own free will, and bring to
D&C 64:33(33-34)	be not weary in **well-doing**, for ye are laying the
D&C 76:17(16-17)	they who have done **good** in the resurrection of the
D&C 76:111	they shall be judged according to their **works**, and
D&C 81:4	do the greatest **good**...and wilt promote the glory of
D&C 98:11	forsake all evil and cleave unto all **good**, that ye
D&C 105:24(24-25)	neither boast of faith nor of mighty **works**, but
D&C 112:34	to recompense every man according as his **work** shall
D&C 121:25(24-25)	a time appointed for every man, according...his **works**
A of F 1:13(12-13)	We believe in being honest, true...and in doing **good**
JFS-V 1:59(57-60)	reward according to their **works**, for they are heirs

GOSPEL

Isa. 40:9(9-11)	O Zion, that bringest **good** tidings, get thee up into
Isa. 52:7(7-8)	feet of him that bringeth **good** tidings, that
Isa. 61:1(1-3)	the Lord hath anointed me to preach **good** tidings unto
Matt. 24:14	and this **gospel** of the kingdom shall be preached in
Mark 1:1	the beginning of the **gospel** of Jesus Christ, the Son
Mark 13:10	the **gospel** must first be published among all nations.
Mark 16:15(15-16)	preach the **gospel** to every creature.
Luke 2:10	I bring you **good** tidings of great joy, which shall
Luke 4:18(16-21)	he hath anointed me to preach the **gospel** to the poor
Luke 9:6	preaching the **gospel**, and healing every where.
John 7:16(16-17)	my **doctrine** is not mine, but his that sent me.
John 8:32(31-32)	ye shall know the **truth**, and the truth shall make you
John 12:48	the **word** that I have spoken, the same shall judge him
Acts 4:12	neither is there **salvation** in any other: for there is
Acts 15:7(6-8)	the Gentiles...hear the word of the **gospel**, and
Acts 20:24	to testify the **gospel** of the grace of God.
Rom. 1:16(15-17)	I am not ashamed of the **gospel** of Christ: for it is
Rom. 2:16	God shall judge...according to my **gospel**.
Rom. 10:15(13-15)	that preach the **gospel** of peace, and bring glad
1 Cor. 1:21(18-27)	by...**preaching** to save them that believe.
1 Cor. 4:15(15-16)	I have begotten you through the **gospel**.
1 Cor. 9:14(13-15)	they which preach the **gospel** should live of the gospel
1 Cor. 9:16(16-18)	for though I preach the **gospel**, I have nothing to
1 Cor. 15:1(1-2)	I declare unto you the **gospel** which I preached unto
2 Cor. 11:4(3,4)	if ye receive another spirit...or another **gospel**

GOSPEL cont.

Gal. 1:7(6-9)	there be some that...would pervert the **gospel** of
Gal. 1:8(6-8)	preach any other **gospel** unto you than that which we
Gal. 3:8(6-8)	preached before the **gospel** unto Abraham, saying, in
Eph. 1:13	the word of truth, the **gospel** of your salvation: in
Eph. 4:5(4-6)	one Lord, one **faith**, one baptism
Col. 1:5(5-6)	the word of the truth of the **gospel**
1 Thes. 1:5(5-6)	**gospel** came not unto you in word only, but also in
2 Thes. 1:8(7-10)	that obey not the **gospel** of our Lord Jesus Christ
2 Thes. 2:14(13-17)	he called you by our **gospel**, to the obtaining of the
2 Tim. 2:8	Jesus...raised from the dead according to my **gospel**
Heb. 4:2(2,6)	for unto us was the **gospel** preached, as well as unto
Heb. 5:9(8-9)	author of eternal **salvation** unto all them that obey
1 Pet. 4:6	was the **gospel** preached also to them that are dead
Rev. 14:6(6-7)	having the everlasting **gospel** to preach unto them
1 Ne. 10:14(11,14)	Gentiles had received the fulness of the **gospel**, the
1 Ne. 13:34(34-37)	most plain and precious parts of the **gospel** of the
1 Ne. 15:13(13-14)	fulness of the **gospel** of the Messiah come unto the
1 Ne. 15:24(21-36)	I said unto them that it was the **word** of God; and
Jacob 2:8	the **word** which healeth the wounded soul.
Enos 1:3(3,23)	the **words** which I had often heard my father speak
Mosiah 4:1(1-3)	the **words** which had been delivered...by the angel of
Alma 4:19(18-19)	bearing down in pure **testimony** against them.
Alma 22:17(13-18)	that when Aaron had said these **words**, the king did bow
Alma 26:13	because of the power of his **word** which is in us
Alma 31:5	try the virtue of the **word** of God.
Alma 37:9	and their **words** brought them unto repentance; that
Hel. 3:29(29-30)	whosoever will may lay hold upon the **word** of God
3 Ne. 27:13(13-22)	this is the **gospel** which I have given unto you- that
3 Ne. 27:21(13-22)	I say unto you, this is my **gospel**; and ye know the
3 Ne. 28:23	and did preach the **gospel** of Christ unto all people
4 Ne. 1:38	they who rejected the **gospel** were called Lamanites
Morm. 7:8(8,9)	lay hold upon the **gospel** of Christ, which shall be
Morm. 9:8(7-9)	denieth these things knoweth not the **gospel** of Christ
Ether 4:18(17-19)	believe in my **gospel**, and be baptized in my name; for
D&C 1:23	that the fulness of my **gospel** might be proclaimed by
D&C 10:50(48-50)	believe in this **gospel** in this land might have eternal
D&C 11:24	build upon my rock, which is my **gospel**
D&C 18:28(28,32)	they are called...to preach my **gospel** unto every
D&C 20:9(8-9)	contains...fulness of the **gospel** of Jesus Christ to
D&C 27:13	a dispensation of the **gospel** for the last times; and
D&C 33:12(10-12)	this is my **gospel**; and remember that they shall have
D&C 39:6	and this is my **gospel**- repentance and baptism by water
D&C 42:6	preaching my **gospel**, two by two, in my name, lifting
D&C 42:12(11-12)	in the which is the fulness of the **gospel**.
D&C 45:28	a light shall break forth...fulness of my **gospel**
D&C 76:40(40-42)	and this is the **gospel**, the glad tidings, which the
D&C 76:50(50-70)	this is the testimony of the **gospel** of Christ concern
D&C 76:73	spirits...in prison...the Son...preached the **gospel**
D&C 84:26(26,27)	lesser priesthood...key of...preparatory **gospel**
D&C 110:12	committed the dispensation of the **gospel** of Abraham
D&C 128:18	made perfect without those who have died in the **gospel**
D&C 133:57(57-58)	the Lord sent forth the fulness of his **gospel**, his
Moses 5:58(58-59)	and thus the **gospel** began to be preached, from the beg

GOSPEL cont.

Moses 6:62(58-63)	this is the **plan** of salvation unto all men, through
JFS-V 1:19(18,19,25)	and there he preached to them the everlasting **gospel**
JFS-V 1:57(57-60)	preaching of the **gospel**...among...the dead.

GOSSIP

Ex. 20:16	thou shalt not bear **false-witness** against thy
Lev. 19:16	not go up and down as a **talebearer** among thy people
Ps. 15:3(1-3)	he that **backbiteth** not with his tongue, nor doeth evil
Ps. 31:20(19-20)	keep them...in a pavilion from the **strife** of tongues.
Ps. 34:13	keep thy **tongue** from evil, and thy lips from speaking
Prov. 6:19(16-19)	a false witness that speaketh **lies**, and he that soweth
Prov. 11:13	a **talebearer** revealeth secrets: but he that is of a
Prov. 13:3	he that openeth wide his **lips** shall have destruction.
Prov. 15:2(2-4)	but the mouth of fools poureth out **foolishness**.
Prov. 18:8	the words of a **talebearer** are as wounds, and they go
Prov. 20:19	he that goeth about as a **talebearer** revealeth secrets
Prov. 21:23	whoso keepeth his mouth and his **tongue** keepeth his
Prov. 25:18(18,19)	a man that **beareth** false witness against his neighbour
Prov. 26:20(20-27)	where there is no **talebearer**, the strife ceaseth.
Prov. 26:28	a **lying** tongue hateth those that are afflicted by it
Matt. 7:3(1-5)	why beholdest thou the **mote** that is in thy brother's
Matt. 12:36(36-37)	every idle **word**...they shall give account thereof in
Matt. 15:11	which cometh out of the **mouth**, this defileth a man.
Luke 6:37(36-37)	**condemn** not, and ye shall not be condemned: forgive
Luke 6:45	for of the abundance of the heart his **mouth** speaketh.
Luke 12:3(2-3)	that which ye have **spoken** in the ear in closets shall
John 8:7(2-11)	he that is without sin...let him first cast a **stone**
Eph. 4:29(29-31)	no corrupt **communication**...but that which is...
1 Tim. 5:13(12-15)	tattlers also and **busybodies**, speaking things which
Titus 2:3	women likewise...be...not false **accusers**, not given
James 1:26	if any...bridleth not his **tongue**...this man's religion
James 3:8(2-18)	but the **tongue** can no man tame; it is an unruly evil
James 4:11(11-12)	**speak** not evil one of another, brethren. He that speak
1 Pet. 3:10(9-10)	let him refrain his **tongue** from evil, and his lips
2 Ne. 9:34	wo unto the **liar**, for he shall be thrust down to hell.
Mosiah 4:30(28-30)	watch yourselves, and your thoughts, and your **words**
Alma 1:32	did indulge themselves...in **babblings**, and in envyings
Hel. 16:22	he did go about spreading **rumors** and contentions upon
3 Ne. 14:12	whatsoever ye would that men should **do** to you, do ye
Morm. 8:19(19,20)	the same that **judgeth** rashly shall be judged rashly
D&C 10:25(24-28)	telleth them that it is no sin to **lie** that they may
D&C 20:54(53-54)	see that there is no...**backbiting** nor evil speaking
D&C 42:27	thou shalt not **speak** evil of thy neighbor, nor do him
D&C 88:124	cease to find **fault** one with another; cease to sleep
D&C 136:24(23-24)	let your **words** tend to edifying one another.

GOVERNMENTS

Deut. 17:15(14-20)	**king** over thee, whom the Lord thy God shall choose
Judg. 8:23(22,23)	Gideon said..I will not **rule** over you..the Lord shall
1 Sam. 8:7(5-22)	they...rejected me, that I should not **reign** over them.
1 Sam. 10:25(17-25)	Samuel told the people the manner of the **kingdom**, and
1 Sam. 12:12(12-19)	when the Lord your God was your **king**.
1 Kgs. 12:11(3-11)	I will add to your **yoke**: my father hath chastised you
Ps. 22:28	the kingdom is the Lord's: and he is the **governor**
Prov. 29:2	when the righteous are in **authority**, the people
Eccl. 8:2	I counsel thee to keep the **king's** commandment, and
Isa. 3:12(1-12)	they which **lead** thee cause thee to err, and destroy
Isa. 9:6	the **government** shall be upon his shoulder: and his
Isa. 9:7	increase of his **government** and peace there shall be
Isa. 22:21	I will commit thy **government** into his hand: and he
Isa. 44:28	that saith of **Cyrus**, he is my shepherd, and shall
Isa. 45:1(1-4)	to **Cyrus**, whose right hand I have holden, to subdue
Isa. 45:4(1-4)	I have even **called** thee...though thou hast not known
Dan. 2:37(36-44)	the God of heaven hath given thee a **kingdom**, power
Matt. 12:25(25-29)	every **kingdom** divided against itself is brought to
Matt. 15:14(13-14)	let them alone: they be blind **leaders** of the blind.
Matt. 22:21(19-22)	render therefore unto **Caesar** the things which are
Rom. 13:1(1-14)	let every soul be **subject** unto the higher powers.
Rom. 13:1(1-7)	the **powers** that be are ordained of God.
1 Cor. 12:28	God hath set...helps, **governments**, diversities of
2 Cor. 3:17	where the Spirit of the Lord is, there is **liberty**.
Eph. 6:12(10-12)	against spiritual **wickedness** in high places.
1 Tim. 2:2(1-3)	for **kings**, and for all that are in authority; that we
Titus 3:1	subject to **principalities** and powers, to obey
1 Pet. 2:13(13-17)	submit yourselves to every **ordinance** of man..the king
2 Pet. 2:10(10-12)	them that walk after the flesh..and despise **government**
2 Ne. 19:6	the **government** shall be upon his shoulder; and his
2 Ne. 19:7	of the increase of **government** and peace there is no
Mosiah 23:8(6-14)	just men to be your **kings** it would be well for you to
Mosiah 29:26(16-32)	do your business by the voice of the **people**.
Alma 43:17	Moroni took...the **government** of their wars. And he was
Alma 46:35	that they might maintain a free **government**, he caused
Alma 51:5(5,6)	in a manner to overthrow the free **government** and to
Alma 54:17(17-18)	rob them of their right to the **government** when it
Alma 54:24	and to obtain their rights to the **government**; and I
Alma 58:36(34-36)	there is some faction in the **government**, that they do
Alma 59:13	Moroni was angry with the **government**, because of their
Alma 60:14	even the slothfulness of our **government**, and their
Alma 60:24	yea, even the great head of our **government**.
Hel. 1:18	so much difficulty in the **government**, that they had
Hel. 3:23	those who were at the head of **government**; therefore
Hel. 5:2	their **governments** were established by the voice of the
Hel. 6:39	obtain the sole management of the **government**, insomuch
Hel. 7:4	Gadianton robbers...usurped the **power** and authority
Hel. 7:5	to be held in office at the head of **government**, to
3 Ne. 3:10	my people may recover their rights and **government**, who
3 Ne. 3:19(18-20)	chief **captains**...had the spirit of revelation and also
3 Ne. 7:2	and thus they did destroy the **government** of the land.
3 Ne. 7:6	the regulations of the **government** were destroyed
3 Ne. 7:11	entered into a covenant to destroy the **government**.

GOVERNMENTS cont.

3 Ne. 7:14	their laws, and their manner of **government**, for they
3 Ne. 9:9	did destroy the peace of my people and the **government**
Ether 8:22(20-26)	whatsoever **nation** shall uphold such secret combination
D&C 41:4	I will be your **ruler** when I come; and behold, I come
D&C 58:21(19-22)	laws of God hath no need to break the **laws** of the land
D&C 58:22(21-22)	be **subject** to the powers that be, until he reigns
D&C 63:26(25-27)	render unto **Caesar** the things which are Caesar's.
D&C 88:34(34-39)	that which is **governed** by law is also preserved by law
D&C 98:5(4-7)	law of the land...**constitutional**, supporting that
D&C 98:9(8-10)	when the wicked **rule** the people mourn.
D&C 101:77(76-80)	**constitution** of the people, which I have suffered to
D&C 105:32	let us become **subject** unto her laws.
D&C 109:54(54-56)	have mercy, O Lord, upon all the **nations** of the earth
D&C 134:1(1-4)	We believe that **governments** were instituted of God for
D&C 134:2	secure to...individual the **free** exercise of conscience
D&C 134:5(5,6)	men are bound to sustain and uphold...**governments** in
Abr. 1:25	first **government** of Egypt was established by Pharaoh
Abr. 1:25	the **government** of Ham, which was patriarchal.
Abr. 7:1(1-5)	first in **government**, the last pertaining to the
A of F 1:12	We believe in being **subject** to kings, presidents

GRACE

Gen. 6:8	but Noah found **grace** in the eyes of the Lord.
Gen. 19:19(17-22)	behold now, thy servant hath found **grace** in thy sight
Ex. 22:27	that I will hear; for I am **gracious**.
Ex. 33:13(12-19)	if I have found **grace** in thy sight, shew me now thy
Ex. 34:9(6-9)	if now I have found **grace** in thy sight, O Lord, let
Judg. 6:17(12-24)	and he said unto him, if now I have found **grace** in thy
Ezra 9:8(5-15)	and now for a little space **grace** hath been shewed from
Ps. 84:11(9-11)	the Lord will give **grace** and glory: no good thing will
Prov. 3:34	but he giveth **grace** unto the lowly.
Zech. 12:10(9-14)	I will pour upon the house of David...spirit of **grace**
Luke 2:40	and the **grace** of God was upon him.
John 1:17(14,17)	**grace** and truth came by Jesus Christ.
Acts 4:33	and great **grace** was upon them all.
Acts 14:3(1-7)	which gave testimony unto the word of his **grace**, and
Acts 15:11	through the **grace** of...Jesus Christ we shall be saved
Acts 15:11(7-11)	but we believe that through the **grace** of the Lord
Acts 20:24(18-27)	the ministry...to testify the gospel of the **grace** of
Rom. 1:5(1-7)	by whom we have received **grace** and apostleship, for
Rom. 3:24(21-26)	being justified freely by his **grace** through the
Rom. 4:16(1-18)	it is of faith, that it might be by **grace**; to the end
Rom. 5:17(1-21)	much more they which receive abundance of **grace** and
Rom. 6:15(14-15)	what then? shall we sin, because we are...under **grace**
Rom. 11:6(1-11)	and if by **grace**, then is it no more of works
Rom. 12:6(1-21)	having then gifts differing according to the **grace**
Rom. 15:15(13-22)	I have written the more boldly...because of the **grace**
1 Cor. 3:10(6-15)	according to the **grace** of God which is given unto me
1 Cor. 15:10(1-11)	by the **grace** of God I am what I am: and his grace
2 Cor. 6:1(1-11)	receive not the **grace** of God in vain.
2 Cor. 8:9(1-24)	for ye know the **grace** of our Lord Jesus Christ, that

GRACE cont.

2 Cor. 9:8(7-15)	and God is able to make all **grace** abound toward you
2 Cor. 12:9(7-10)	my **grace** is sufficient for thee...most gladly...will
Gal. 1:15(6-24)	but when it pleased God, who...called me by his **grace**
Gal. 2:9(6-10)	when...perceived the **grace** that was given unto me, the
Gal. 2:21(20-21)	I do not frustrate the **grace** of God: for if
Gal. 5:4	ye are fallen from **grace**.
Eph. 1:7(1-12)	have redemption...according to the riches of his **grace**
Eph. 2:8(8-10)	for by **grace** are ye saved through faith; and that not
Eph. 3:8(1-12)	unto me...is this **grace** given, that I should preach
Eph. 4:7(4-10)	but unto every one of us is given **grace** according to
Philip. 1:7(3-7)	inasmuch as...ye all are partakers of my **grace**.
Col. 1:6(3-8)	since the day ye...knew the **grace** of God in truth
2 Thes. 1:12(11-12)	name..be glorified...according to the **grace** of our God
2 Thes. 2:16(15-17)	now our Lord...hath given us...good hope through **grace**
1 Tim. 1:14(12-17)	and the **grace** of our Lord was exceeding abundant with
2 Tim. 1:9(8-11)	saved us...according to his own purpose and **grace**
Titus 2:11(7-15)	the **grace** of God that bringeth salvation hath appeared
Heb. 2:9(6-13)	he by the **grace** of God should taste death for every
Heb. 4:16	let us therefore come boldly unto the throne of **grace**
Heb. 12:15(14-17)	looking diligently lest any man fail of the **grace** of
James 4:6(5-12)	but he giveth more **grace**. wherefore he saith, God
1 Pet. 1:13(3-16)	hope to the end for the **grace** that is to be brought
1 Pet. 5:10(8-11)	but the God of all **grace**, who hath called us unto his
2 Pet. 3:18	grow in **grace**, and in the knowledge of our Lord and
2 Ne. 2:4	way is prepared...and salvation is **free**.
2 Ne. 2:6(6-8)	the Holy Messiah; for he is full of **grace** and truth.
2 Ne. 9:8(6-15)	O the wisdom of God, his mercy and **grace**! For behold
2 Ne. 9:53(6-53)	because of his greatness, and his **grace** and mercy, he
2 Ne. 10:24	through the **grace** of God that ye are saved.
2 Ne. 11:5(4-7)	yea, my soul delighteth in his **grace**, and in his
2 Ne. 25:23	it is by **grace** that we are saved, after all we can
Jacob 4:7(5-7)	we may know that it is by his **grace**, and his great
Mosiah 18:16(7-16)	baptized...and...filled with the **grace** of God.
Mosiah 18:26(24-26)	for their labor...receive the **grace** of God, that they
Mosiah 27:5(3-7)	doing these things, they did abound in the **grace** of
Alma 5:48(46-58)	Jesus Christ shall come...full of **grace**, and mercy
Alma 7:3(1-6)	ye had continued in the supplicating of his **grace**
Alma 9:26	Only Begotten of the Father, full of **grace**, equity
Alma 13:9(3-13)	the Son...is full of **grace**, equity, and truth. and
Hel. 12:24(7-26)	and may God grant...that men...be restored unto **grace**
Morm. 2:15(10-15)	the day of **grace** was passed with them, both temporally
Ether 12:27(23-28)	my **grace** is sufficient for all men that humble
Ether 12:36	I prayed...that he would give unto the Gentiles **grace**
Ether 12:41(38-41)	that the **grace** of God...may...abide in you forever.
Moro. 7:2(1-4)	it is by the **grace** of God...that I...speak unto you
Moro. 8:3(1-3)	his infinite goodness and **grace**, will keep you through
Moro. 10:32(32-33)	by his **grace** ye may be perfect in Christ; and if by
D&C 17:8(7,8)	my **grace** is sufficient for you, and you shall be
D&C 20:32(30-34)	possibility that man may fall from **grace** and depart
D&C 50:40(40-46)	behold, ye are little children...must grow in **grace**
D&C 76:94(94,95)	having received of his fulness and of his **grace**
D&C 84:99(97-102)	according to the election of **grace**, which was brought
D&C 88:78(78-80)	teach ye diligently and my **grace** shall attend you

GRACE cont.

D&C 93:13(11-14)	but continued from **grace** to grace, until he received
D&C 93:20(19-20)	if you keep my commandments you shall receive...**grace**
D&C 106:8(6-8)	and I will give him **grace** and assurance wherewith he
D&C 109:44(41-44)	say, with thy **grace** assisting them: thy will be done
D&C 109:53	thou art **gracious** and merciful, and wilt turn away thy
Moses 1:6(3-7)	mine Only Begotten is...full of **grace** and truth; but
Moses 1:32(31-33)	by the word of my power...who is full of **grace** and
Moses 5:7(4-9)	Only Begotten of the Father...full of **grace** and truth.
Moses 6:52(47-68)	mine Only Begotten Son, who is full of **grace** and truth
Moses 7:11(10,11)	of the Father, and of the Son, which is full of **grace**
Moses 7:59(55-69)	not of myself, but through thine own **grace**; wherefore
Moses 8:27(23-30)	and thus Noah found **grace** in the eyes of the Lord; for
JFS-V 1:14	resurrection, through the **grace** of God...and...Jesus

GUIDANCE, DIVINE

Gen. 24:27	the Lord **led** me to the house of my master's brethren.
Ex. 13:21	in a pillar of a cloud, to **lead** them the way; and by
1 Kgs. 3:12(9-15)	I have **given** thee a wise and an understanding heart
1 Kgs. 4:29	God **gave** Solomon wisdom and understanding exceeding
Ps. 23:2(1-2)	he **leadeth** me beside the still waters.
Ps. 25:5(4-5)	**lead** me in thy truth, and teach me: for thou art the
Ps. 25:9(8-10)	the meek will he **guide** in judgment: and the meek will
Ps. 27:11	teach me thy way, O Lord, and **lead** me in a plain path
Prov. 3:6	acknowledge him, and he shall **direct** thy paths. I
Isa. 58:11(8-11)	the Lord shall **guide** thee continually, and satisfy thy
Ezek. 3:12	then the **spirit** took me up, and I heard behind me a
Ezek. 11:1	moreover the **spirit** lifted me up, and brought me unto
Amos 3:7	he **revealeth** his secret unto his servants the prophets
Matt. 4:1	then was Jesus **led** up of the Spirit into the
Matt. 28:20	I am **with** you alway, even unto the end of the world.
John 14:26	the **Holy Ghost**...shall teach you all things, and
Gal. 5:16(16-17)	walk in the **Spirit**, and ye shall not fulful the lust
2 Thes. 3:5(3-5)	the Lord **direct** your hearts into the love of God, and
James 1:5(5-6)	if any of you lack **wisdom**, let him ask of God, that
1 Ne. 2:16	I did cry unto the Lord...he did **visit** me, and did
1 Ne. 4:6	I was **led** by the Spirit, not knowing beforehand the
1 Ne. 11:25	rod of iron...which **led** to the fountain of living
1 Ne. 13:12	Spirit of God...**wrought** upon the man; and he went for
1 Ne. 16:30(23-31)	did go...according to the **directions**...upon the ball.
1 Ne. 18:3(1-4)	did pray oft...wherefore...**showed** unto me great things
2 Ne. 5:5	it came to pass that the Lord did **warn** me, that I
Mosiah 3:19	unless he yields to the enticings of the Holy **Spirit**
Mosiah 26:14(13-15)	the **voice** of the Lord came to him, saying
Alma 8:14(14-16)	while...weighed down...an **angel** of the Lord appeared
Alma 48:16(15-16)	God would make it known...whither they should **go** to
Hel. 10:3(3-4)	as he was thus pondering...a **voice** came unto him
Ether 2:5(4-6)	the Lord...gave **directions** whither they should travel.
Moro. 10:4(4-5)	he will manifest the **truth** of it unto you, by the
D&C 6:14(14-16)	as thou hast inquired thou hast received **instruction**
D&C 8:2(2-3)	I will **tell** you in your mind and in your heart, by the
D&C 11:12(12-14)	put your trust in that Spirit which **leadeth** to do good

GUIDANCE, DIVINE cont.

D&C 18:3(2-3)	a commandment...**rely** upon the things which are written
D&C 20:7(5-8)	and gave unto him **commandments** which inspired him
D&C 38:33	I will **lead** them whithersoever I will, and no power
D&C 45:57	they that...have taken the Holy Spirit for their **guide**
D&C 78:18	be of good cheer, for I will **lead** you along. The king
D&C 95:1	with...chastisement I prepare a way for...**deliverance**
D&C 105:36(35-36)	shall be **manifest**...by...Spirit, those that are chosen
D&C 112:10	the Lord thy God shall **lead** thee by the hand, and give
Moses 6:5	it was given...to write by the Spirit of **inspiration**
Moses 6:27(27-34)	and he heard a **voice** from heaven, saying: Enoch, my
Abr. 3:15(14-15)	I **show** these things unto thee before ye go into Egypt
JS-H 1:12(11-14)	if any person needed **wisdom** from God, I did; for how

GUILE

Ex. 21:14	if a man...slay him with **guile**; thou shalt take him
Ps. 28:3	which speak peace...but **mischief** is in their hearts.
Ps. 32:2	blessed is the man...in whose spirit there is no **guile**
Ps. 34:13	keep...thy lips from speaking **guile**.
Ps. 55:11	deceit and **guile** depart not from her streets.
Isa. 53:9	neither was any **deceit** in his mouth.
Matt. 7:15(15-20)	in sheep's clothing, but inwardly ...ravening **wolves**.
Matt. 23:28	appear righteous...but within ye are full of **hypocrisy**
John 1:47	an Israelite indeed, in whom is no **guile**
1 Thes. 2:3	for our exhortation was not of deceit, nor...**guile**
1 Pet. 2:1	wherefore laying aside all malice, and all **guile**, and
1 Pet. 2:22(21,22)	who did no sin, neither was **guile** found in his mouth
1 Pet. 3:10	for he that will love life...speak no **guile**
Rev. 14:5	and in their mouth was found no **guile**: for they are
Mosiah 14:9	neither was any **deceit** in his mouth.
Alma 18:23	thus he was caught with **guile**.
Moro. 7:6(6-11)	except...with real **intent** it profiteth him nothing.
D&C 41:11(9-11)	like unto Nathanael of old, in whom there is no **guile**.
D&C 121:42(41,42)	shall greatly enlarge the soul without ...**guile**
D&C 124:20	my servant George Miller is without **guile**; he may be
D&C 124:97	let him be humble before me, and be without **guile**, and
JS-H 1:6	the seemingly good feelings...were more **pretended** than

GUILT

Gen. 42:21	we are verily **guilty** concerning our brother, in that
Lev. 4:13(13,14)	if the...congregation of Israel sin...and are **guilty**
Lev. 5:2(2-17)	he also shall be unclean, and **guilty**.
Lev. 6:4(2-4)	because he hath sinned, and is **guilty**, that he shall
Num. 35:27	the revenger...shall not be **guilty** of blood
Num. 35:31	take no satisfaction for...a murderer, which is **guilty**
Deut. 19:13	thou shalt put away the **guilt** of innocent blood from
Judg. 21:22	that ye should be **guilty**.
Ezra 10:19	and being **guilty**, they offered a ram of the flock for
Zech. 11:5	slay them, and hold themselves not **guilty**: and they
Matt. 26:66	they answered and said, he is **guilty** of death.

GUILT cont.

Mark 14:64	they all condemned him to be **guilty** of death.
Rom. 3:19	all the world may become **guilty** before God.
1 Cor. 11:27	be **guilty** of the body and blood of the Lord.
James 2:10	yet offend in one point, he is **guilty** of all.
1 Ne. 16:2	the **guilty** taketh the truth to be hard, for it cutteth
2 Ne. 9:14(14,46)	we shall have a perfect knowledge of all our **guilt**
2 Ne. 28:8	if it so be that we are **guilty**, God will beat us with
Jacob 6:9	will bring you to stand with shame and awful **guilt**
Enos 1:6(4,6)	knew that God could not lie...my **guilt** was swept away.
Mosiah 2:38	soul to a lively sense of his own **guilt**, which doth
Mosiah 3:25	consigned to an awful view of their own **guilt** and
Alma 1:12	thou art not only **guilty** of priestcraft, but hast
Alma 5:18	having a remembrance of all your **guilt**, yea, a perfect
Alma 5:23	ye are **guilty** of all manner of wickedness
Alma 11:43	and have a bright recollection of all our **guilt**.
Alma 12:1	tremble under a consciousness of his **guilt**, he opened
Alma 14:7	I am **guilty**, and these men are spotless before God.
Alma 24:10	taken away the **guilt** from our hearts, through the
Alma 30:25	ye say that this people is a **guilty** and a fallen
Alma 36:13(12-18)	remember all my sins...**tormented** with the pains of
Alma 39:7(6,7)	ye had not been **guilty** of so great a crime. I would
Alma 43:46(46,47)	inasmuch as ye are not **guilty** of the first offense
Hel. 7:5	letting the **guilty** and the wicked go unpunished
Hel. 9:34	behold, we know that thou art **guilty**.
3 Ne. 6:29	deliver those who were **guilty** of murder from the grasp
Morm. 9:3	your souls are racked with a consciousness of **guilt**
D&C 38:14	some of you are **guilty** before me, but I will be
D&C 64:22	will not hold any **guilty** that shall go with an open
D&C 68:23	inasmuch as he is found **guilty** before this Presidency
D&C 104:7	that the **guilty** among you may not escape; because I
D&C 134:4(4,6)	should punish **guilt**, but never suppress the freedom
JS-H 1:28	I was **guilty** of levity, and sometimes associated with

HANDS, LAYING ON OF

Gen. 48:17(13-20)	his father laid his right **hand** upon the head of
Ex. 29:10(10,15,19)	his sons shall put their **hands** upon the head of the
Lev. 1:4	and he shall put his **hand** upon the head of the burnt
Lev. 16:21(21-22)	Aaron shall lay both his **hands** upon the head of the
Num. 27:23(18-23)	he laid his **hands** upon him, and gave him a charge, as
Deut. 34:9	Moses had **laid** his hands upon him: and the children
Matt. 9:18(18-19,23-26)	come and lay thy **hand** upon her, and she shall live.
Matt. 19:13(13-15)	brought...children, that he should put his **hands** on
Mark 5:23(22-23,41-42)	come and lay thy **hands** on her, that she may be healed
Mark 6:5	save that he **laid** his hands upon a few sick folk, and
Mark 7:32(31-37)	they beseech him to put his **hand** upon him.
Mark 8:23(22-26)	when he had spit on his eyes, and put his **hands** upon
Mark 16:18(17-18)	they shall lay **hands** on the sick, and they shall
Luke 4:40(40-41)	and he **laid** his hands on every one of them, and healed
Luke 13:13(11-13)	and he **laid** his hands on her: and immediately she was
Acts 6:6(1-6)	they **laid** their hands on them.
Acts 8:17(14-20)	**laid** they their hands on them, and they received the

Acts 9:17(10-18)	putting his **hands** on him said, brother Saul, the Lord
Acts 13:3(1-3)	when they had fasted and prayed, and laid their **hands**
Acts 28:8(8-9)	and prayed, and laid his **hands** on him, and healed him.
1 Tim. 4:14	gift...given...with the laying on of the **hands** of the
1 Tim. 5:22(21-22)	lay **hands** suddenly on no man, neither be partaker of
2 Tim. 1:6	gift of God...in thee by the putting on of my **hands**.
Heb. 6:2(1-2)	of the doctrine of baptisms, and of laying on of **hands**
Alma 6:1	he ordained priests and elders, by laying on his **hands**
Alma 31:36(25-36)	clapped his **hands** upon them, they were filled with the
3 Ne. 18:36(36-37)	he touched with his **hand** the disciples whom he had
Morm. 9:24(22-25)	they shall lay **hands** on the sick and they shall
Moro. 2:2(1-3)	upon whom ye shall lay your **hands**, ye shall give the
Moro. 3:2(1-4)	they **laid** their hands upon them, and said
D&C 20:41(38-43)	laying on of **hands** for the baptism of fire and the
D&C 20:58	teachers nor deacons have authority to...lay on **hands**
D&C 20:68	being confirmed by the laying on of the **hands** of the
D&C 20:70	children...unto the elders...to lay their **hands** upon
D&C 25:8(7-8)	he shall lay his **hands** upon thee, and thou shalt
D&C 33:15(11-15)	confirm in my church, by the laying on of the **hands**
D&C 35:6(5-6)	receive the Holy Ghost by the laying on of the **hands**
D&C 36:2	and I will lay my **hand** upon you by the hand of my
D&C 39:23	lay your **hands**, and they shall receive the...Holy
D&C 42:44(43-44)	shall pray for and **lay** their hands upon them in my
D&C 49:14(13-14)	receive...Holy Ghost, by the laying on of the **hands**
D&C 52:10	the laying on of the **hands** by the water's side.
D&C 53:3	reception of the Holy Spirit by the laying on of **hands**
D&C 55:1(1-3)	reception of the Holy Spirit by the laying on of **hands**
D&C 66:9	lay your **hands** upon the sick, and they shall recover.
D&C 68:21	lineage..by revelation..under the **hands** of..presidency
D&C 68:25(25-27)	gift of the Holy Ghost by the laying on of the **hands**
D&C 76:52(50-53)	receive the Holy Spirit by the laying on of the **hands**
D&C 84:6(6-17)	priesthood which he received under the **hand** of..Jethro
D&C 107:44(42-52)	Enos was ordained...by the **hand** of Adam.
D&C 107:67(65-67)	blessings upon...church, by the laying on of the **hands**
JS-H 1:68(68-71)	having laid his **hands** upon us, he ordained us, saying
A of F 1:4	laying on of **hands** for the gift of the Holy Ghost.
A of F 1:5	must be called of God...by the laying on of **hands**, by

HAPPINESS

Deut. 33:29	**happy** art thou, O Israel: who is like unto thee, O
Job 5:17(17-18)	**happy** is the man whom God correcteth: therefore
Ps. 1:1(1-6)	**blessed** is the man that walketh not in the counsel of
Ps. 127:5(3-5)	**happy** is the man that hath his quiver full of them
Ps. 128:2(1-2)	**happy** shalt thou be, and it shall be well with thee.
Ps. 144:15	**happy** is that people, that is in such a case: yea
Ps. 146:5	**happy** is he that hath the God of Jacob for his help
Prov. 3:13	**happy** is the man that findeth wisdom, and the man that
Prov. 10:1	a wise son maketh a **glad** father: but a foolish son is
Prov. 14:21	he that hath mercy on the poor, **happy** is he.
Prov. 15:13	a **merry** heart maketh a cheerful countenance: but by
Prov. 16:20	whoso trusteth in the Lord, **happy** is he.

HAPPINESS cont.

Prov. 29:18	but he that keepeth the law, **happy** is he.
Eccl. 11:9(9-10)	let thy heart **cheer** thee in the days of thy youth, and
Isa. 32:17	effect of righteousness quietness and **assurance** for
John 10:10	I am come that they might have life...more **abundantly**.
John 13:17(15-17)	if ye know these things, **happy** are ye if ye do them.
John 16:33	but be of good **cheer**; I have overcome the world.
James 5:11(10-11)	we count them **happy** which endure. Ye have heard of the
1 Pet. 3:14	if ye suffer for righteousness' sake, **happy** are ye
1 Pet. 4:14(12-14)	if ye be reproached for the name of Christ, **happy** are
1 Ne. 8:10(10-12)	whose fruit was desirable to make one **happy**.
2 Ne. 2:13(9-13)	if there be no righteousness there be no **happiness**.
Mosiah 2:41	consider...**happy** state of those that keep the
Mosiah 16:11(10-11)	if they be good, to the resurrection of...**happiness**
Alma 3:26	to reap eternal **happiness** or eternal misery, according
Alma 27:18(16-19)	the truly penitent and humble seeker of **happiness**.
Alma 40:12	righteous are received into a state of **happiness**
Alma 41:5(3-5)	the one raised to **happiness** according to his desires
Alma 41:10(10-11)	wickedness never was **happiness**.
Alma 44:5	sacred word of God, to which we owe all our **happiness**
Hel. 12:2(1-3)	doing all things for the...**happiness** of his people
Hel. 13:38(36-38)	sought for **happiness** in doing iniquity...is contrary
4 Ne. 1:16(15-18)	surely there could not be a **happier** people among all
Morm. 2:13	Lord would not...suffer them to take **happiness** in sin.
Morm. 7:7	given unto him to dwell...in a state of **happiness**
D&C 59:18(18-19)	all things...made for...man...to **gladden** the heart
D&C 59:23	reward...**peace** in this world and eternal life in the
D&C 77:2(2-3)	figurative expressions...describing..**happiness** of man
D&C 128:19(19-20)	we hear in the gospel...a voice of **gladness**! A voice
D&C 136:28(28-29)	if thou art **merry**, praise the Lord with singing, with
Abr. 1:2	finding there was greater **happiness**...and rest for me

HARDHEARTEDNESS

Ex. 4:21	I will **harden** his heart, that he shall not let the
Ex. 14:17	I will **harden** the hearts of the Egyptians, and they
Lev. 19:17	thou shalt not hate thy brother in thine **heart**: thou
Deut. 15:7	thou shalt not **harden** thine heart, nor shut thine hand
Deut. 18:16(15-20)	let me not **hear** again the voice of the Lord my God
1 Sam. 6:6	do ye **harden** your hearts, as the Egyptians and Pharaoh
2 Chr. 36:13(11-13)	he stiffened his neck, and **hardened** his heart from
Job 9:4	who hath **hardened** himself against him, and hath
Ps. 95:8(8-11)	**harden** not your heart, as in the provocation, and as
Prov. 6:18(16-19)	an **heart** that deviseth wicked imaginations, feet that
Prov. 21:29	a wicked man **hardeneth** his face: but as for the
Prov. 28:14	he that **hardeneth** his heart shall fall into mischief.
Isa. 6:10(9-10)	make the **heart** of this people fat, and make their ears
Isa. 29:13	have removed their **heart** far from me, and their fear
Isa. 46:12	hearken unto me, ye **stouthearted**, that are far from
Isa. 63:17	**hardened** our heart from thy fear? return for thy
Jer. 7:26(23-28)	they hearkened not unto me...but **hardened** their neck
Ezek. 3:7(4-9)	all the house of Israel are impudent and **hardhearted**.
Dan. 5:20(18-21)	**heart** was lifted up, and his mind hardened in pride

Obad. 1:3(3-4)	pride of thine **heart** hath deceived thee, thou that
Zech. 1:4	but they did not hear, nor **hearken** unto me, saith the
Matt. 13:15(9-17)	this people's **heart** is waxed gross, and their ears are
Matt. 19:8(3-9)	because of the **hardness** of your hearts suffered you
Mark 6:52	considered not the miracle...their heart was **hardened**.
Mark 8:17(14-21)	neither understand? have ye your heart yet **hardened**
John 12:40(37-41)	blinded their eyes, and **hardened** their heart; that the
Acts 28:27(23-28)	for the **heart** of this people is waxed gross, and their
Rom. 2:5	but after thy **hardness** and impenitent heart treasurest
2 Cor. 3:15(7,13-16)	when Moses is read, the vail is upon their **heart**.
Eph. 4:18	ignorance...because of the blindness of their **heart**
Heb. 3:8(7-15)	**harden** not your hearts, as in the provocation, in the
Heb. 4:7	if ye will hear his voice **harden** not your hearts.
1 Jn. 3:17	**shutteth** up his bowels of compassion from him, how
1 Ne. 14:7(2-7)	to the **hardness** of their hearts and the blindness of
1 Ne. 18:20	nothing...could soften their **hearts**; wherefore, when
1 Ne. 22:5(5,18)	against him will they **harden** their hearts; wherefore
2 Ne. 6:10(5-11)	after they have **hardened** their hearts and stiffened
2 Ne. 9:30	their **hearts** are upon their treasures; wherefore, the
2 Ne. 25:10	they **hardened** their hearts; and according to my
2 Ne. 27:25	have removed their **hearts** far from me, and their fear
2 Ne. 28:15(9,15-20)	puffed up in the pride of their **hearts**, and all those
2 Ne. 33:2(1,2)	there are many that **harden** their hearts against the
Jacob 2:13(13-19)	ye are lifted up in the pride of your **hearts**, and wear
Mosiah 3:15	yet they **hardened** their hearts, and understood not
Mosiah 11:29	eyes...blinded; therefore they **hardened** their hearts
Alma 4:8	lifted up in...pride...and to set their **hearts** upon
Alma 12:10(10-18)	he that will **harden** his heart, the same receiveth the
Alma 12:37(33-37)	let us repent, and **harden** not our hearts, that we
Alma 13:4	the **hardness** of their hearts and blindness of their
Alma 24:30	they become more **hardened**, and thus their state become
Alma 34:31	repent and **harden** not your hearts, immediately shall
Hel. 4:12	because of the pride of their **hearts**, because of their
Hel. 6:35	Spirit..withdraw..because of..**hardness** of..hearts.
3 Ne. 11:30	not my doctrine, to stir up the **hearts** of men with
3 Ne. 16:10	lifted up in the pride of their **hearts** above all
3 Ne. 20:28	if they shall **harden** their hearts against me I will
3 Ne. 21:22	repent...hearken...and **harden** not their hearts, I will
4 Ne. 1:28(27-34)	power of Satan who did get hold upon their **hearts**.
Ether 8:25(25,26)	devil...hath **hardened** the hearts of men that they have
Ether 15:19	Satan had full power over the **hearts** of the people
Moro. 9:4(4-10)	when I use no sharpness they **harden** their hearts again
D&C 1:14	they who will not **hear** the voice of the Lord, neither
D&C 5:18	if they **harden** their hearts against them
D&C 10:53(32,53,65)	generation **harden** not their hearts, I will establish
D&C 20:15(14-15)	but those who **harden** their hearts in unbelief, and
D&C 29:7	elect hear my voice and **harden** not their hearts
D&C 38:6(5-6)	not hear my voice but **harden** their hearts, and wo, wo
D&C 42:40	thou shalt not be proud in thy **heart**; let all thy
D&C 45:29(28-33)	they turn their **hearts** from me because of the precepts
D&C 58:15	blindness of **heart**, let him take heed lest he fall.
D&C 78:10	turn their **hearts** away from the truth, that they
D&C 82:21	**hardeneth** his heart against it, shall be dealt with

HARDHEARTEDNESS cont.

D&C 84:24(23-25)	but they **hardened** their hearts and could not endure
D&C 84:76	their evil **hearts** of unbelief, and your brethren in
D&C 121:35	**hearts** are set so much upon the things of this world
Moses 6:27	their hearts have waxed **hard**, and their ears are dull
Abr. 1:6(6,16-17)	for their **hearts** were set to do evil, and were wholly
JS-H 1:19	but their **hearts** are far from me, they teach for

HARVEST

Lev. 19:9(9-10)	when ye reap the **harvest** of your land...not...corners
Job 4:8	they that...**sow** wickedness, reap the same.
Prov. 22:8	he that soweth iniquity shall **reap** vanity: and the rod
Eccl. 11:4(1-6)	he that regardeth the clouds shall not **reap**.
Jer. 51:33(24-37)	Babylon...the time of her **harvest** shall come.
Hosea 10:12(12-15)	sow...in righteousness, **reap** in mercy; break up your
Matt. 9:37(37-38)	the **harvest**...is plenteous, but the labourers are few
Matt. 13:30(24-30)	let both grow together until the **harvest**: and in the
Matt. 13:39(36-43)	the **harvest** is the end of the world; and the reapers
Matt. 25:26(14-30)	I **reap** where I sowed not, and gather where I have not
Mark 4:29(26-29)	putteth in the sickle, because the **harvest** is come.
John 4:38(35-38)	I sent you to **reap** that whereon ye bestowed no labour
2 Cor. 9:6(6-7)	he which soweth sparingly shall **reap** also sparingly
Gal. 6:7(7-10)	whatsoever a man soweth, that shall he also **reap**.
Rev. 14:15(14-20)	reap; for the **harvest** of the earth is ripe.
Mosiah 7:30(29-33)	sow filthiness they shall **reap** the chaff thereof in
Alma 3:26(25-27)	**reap** their rewards according to their works, whether
Alma 9:28(24-30)	all men shall **reap** a reward of their works, according
Alma 17:13(10-17)	they should meet again at the close of their **harvest**
Alma 26:7(4-7)	they are in the hands of the Lord of the **harvest**, and
Alma 32:43(40-43)	ye shall **reap** the rewards of your faith, and your
D&C 4:4	the field is white already to **harvest**; and lo, he that
D&C 6:33(33,34)	whatsoever ye sow, that shall ye also **reap**; therefore
D&C 38:12(7-12)	waiting the great command to **reap** down the earth, to
D&C 45:2(1-2)	the **harvest** ended, and your souls not saved.
D&C 86:5(1-7)	angels are crying...to **reap** down the fields
D&C 101:64(64-65)	gathering...saints...for the time of **harvest** is come

HASTE

Ex. 12:11(11-12)	ye shall eat it in **haste**: it is the Lord's passover.
Ps. 22:19	O Lord: O my strength, **haste** thee to help me.
Ps. 31:22(22-23)	I said in my **haste**, I am cut off from before thine
Prov. 14:29	he that is **hasty** of spirit exalteth folly.
Prov. 19:2	he that **hasteth** with his feet sinneth.
Prov. 21:5	but of every one that is **hasty** only to want.
Prov. 28:20(20-22)	he that maketh **haste** to be rich shall not be innocent.
Prov. 29:20	a man that is **hasty** in his words...hope of a fool than
Eccl. 5:2(1-7)	let not thine heart be **hasty** to utter any thing before
Isa. 16:5	seeking judgment, and **hasting** righteousness.
Isa. 52:12(11,12)	for ye shall not go out with **haste**, nor go by flight
Mark 6:25	with **haste** unto the king, and asked, saying, I will

HASTE cont.

Luke 2:16	they came with **haste**, and found Mary, and Joseph, and
Acts 20:16	for he **hasted**, if it were possible for him, to be at
2 Pet. 3:12	**hasting** unto the coming of the day of God, wherein the
1 Ne. 21:17	thy children shall make **haste** against thy destroyers
2 Ne. 8:14	the captive exile **hasteneth**, that he may be loosed
2 Ne. 15:19(18-19)	**hasten** his work, that we may see it; and let the
3 Ne. 20:42	for ye shall not go out with **haste** nor go by flight
3 Ne. 21:29	and they shall not go out in **haste**, nor go by flight
D&C 58:56(55-56)	let the work of the gathering be not in **haste**, nor by
D&C 88:73	behold, I will **hasten** my work in its time.
D&C 101:68	let not your gathering be in **haste**, nor by flight; but
D&C 101:72	let these things be done in their time...not in **haste**
D&C 133:15	let not your flight be in **haste**, but let all things

HATE

Gen. 24:60	let thy seed possess the gate of those which **hate** them
Ex. 20:5	the third and fourth generation of them that **hate** me
Num. 10:35	let them that **hate** thee flee before thee.
Deut. 5:9	the third and fourth generation of them that **hate** me
Deut. 7:10	he will not be slack to him that **hateth** him, he will
1 Kgs. 22:8	but I **hate** him; for he doth not prophesy good
Job 36:5	God is mighty, and **despiseth** not any: he is mighty in
Ps. 26:5	I have **hated** the congregation of evil doers; and will
Ps. 35:19	neither let them wink with the eye that **hate** me
Ps. 68:1	let them also that **hate** him flee before him.
Ps. 69:4	they that **hate** me without a cause are more than the
Ps. 97:10	ye that love the Lord, **hate** evil: he preserveth the
Prov. 1:22	delight in...scorning, and fools **hate** knowledge
Prov. 6:16(16-19)	these six things doth the Lord **hate**: yea, seven are
Prov. 10:12	**hatred** stirreth up strifes: but love covereth all sins
Prov. 10:18	he that hideth **hatred** with lying lips, and he that
Prov. 13:5	a righteous man **hateth** lying: but a wicked man is
Prov. 26:24(24-28)	he that **hateth** dissembleth with his lips, and layeth
Prov. 29:24	whoso is partner with a thief **hateth** his own soul: he
Eccl. 3:8	a time to love, and a time to **hate**; a time of war, and
Matt. 5:44	do good to them that **hate** you, and pray for them which
Matt. 6:24	two masters...he will **hate** the one, and love the other
Matt. 10:22(21-23)	and ye shall be **hated** of all men for my name's sake
John 3:20	for every one that doeth evil **hateth** the light
John 12:25	he that **hateth** his life in this world shall keep it
John 15:18(18-19)	if the world **hate** you, ye know that it hated me before
John 15:25	this cometh to pass...they **hated** me without a cause.
Eph. 5:29	for no man ever yet **hated** his own flesh; but
1 Jn. 3:15	whosoever **hateth** his brother is a murderer: and ye
1 Jn. 4:20	if a man say, I love God, and **hateth** his brother, he
1 Ne. 19:14	become a hiss and a by-word, and be **hated** among all
2 Ne. 5:14	I knew their **hatred** towards me and my children and
2 Ne. 8:7	neither be ye afraid of their **revilings**.
2 Ne. 9:30	because they are rich they **despise** the poor, and they
2 Ne. 29:5	ye have cursed them, and have **hated** them, and have not
Jacob 4:8	brethren, **despise** not the revelations of God.

HATE cont.

Enos 1:20	labors were vain; their **hatred** was fixed, and they
Mosiah 10:17(11-17)	taught their children that they should **hate** them, and
Mosiah 14:3	he is **despised** and rejected of men; a man of sorrows
Alma 37:29	ye shall teach them to **abhor** such wickedness and
Alma 37:32	teach them an everlasting **hatred** against sin and
Hel. 5:51	lay down their weapons of war, and also their **hatred**
3 Ne. 12:44(43-45)	do good to them that **hate** you, and pray for them who
4 Ne. 1:39	they were taught to **hate** the children of God, even as
Moro. 1:2(2,3)	because of their **hatred** they put to death every
D&C 3:7	set at naught...counsels of God, and **despise** his words
D&C 40:2	the fear of **persecution** and the cares of the world
D&C 43:21	if I...call upon you to repent, and ye **hate** me, what
D&C 88:94	that **persecuteth** the saints of God, that shed their
D&C 98:46(45-46)	upon his children's children of all them that **hate** me
D&C 121:38	to **persecute** the saints, and to fight against God.
D&C 124:50(50,52)	so long as they repent not, and **hate** me, saith the Lord
D&C 127:4	if they **persecute** you, so persecuted they the prophets
Moses 6:31	the people **hate** me; for I am slow of speech; wherefore
Moses 7:8	Canaan, that they were **despised** among all people.
Moses 7:33	without affection, and they **hate** their own blood
JS-M 1:7	ye shall be **hated** of all nations, for my name's sake
JS-H 1:25(22-28)	I was **hated** and persecuted for saying that I had seen
JS-H 1:58(58-74)	**persecution** still followed me, and my wife's father's

HAUGHTINESS

Ex. 9:17(13,17)	as yet **exaltest** thou thyself against my people, that
2 Sam. 22:28	thine eyes are upon the **haughty**, that thou mayest
Ps. 131:1(1-2)	my heart is not **haughty**, nor mine eyes lofty: neither
Prov. 6:17(16-19)	a **proud** look, a lying tongue, and hands that shed
Prov. 16:18(17-19)	and an **haughty** spirit before a fall.
Isa. 2:17(10-17)	the **haughtiness** of men shall be made low: and the Lord
Isa. 3:16(16-26)	the daughters of Zion are **haughty**, and walk with
Isa. 10:33	and the **haughty** shall be humbled.
Isa. 13:11	lay low the **haughtiness** of the terrible.
Zeph. 3:11	thou shalt no more be **haughty** because of my holy mount
Matt. 11:23	thou, Capernaum, which art **exalted** unto heaven, shalt
Matt. 23:12(10-12)	whosoever shall **exalt** himself shall be abased; and he
Luke 14:11(7-11)	for whosoever **exalteth** himself shall be abased; and
Luke 18:14(10-14)	every one that **exalteth** himself shall be abased; and
Rom. 1:30	proud, **boasters**, inventors of evil things, disobedient
1 Ne. 12:18	large and spacious building...**pride** of the children
2 Ne. 12:17(13-17)	the **haughtiness** of men shall be made low; and the Lord
Num. 12:13	unto the Lord, saying, **heal** her now, O God, I beseech
Num. 21:8(6-9)	every one that is bitten..looketh upon it, shall **live**.
2 Kgs. 5:14(1-14)	dipped himself seven times in Jordan...he was **clean**.
2 Kgs. 20:5(1-7)	I have seen thy tears: behold, I will **heal** thee: on
2 Chr. 30:20(18-20)	Lord hearkened to Hezekiah, and **healed** the people.
Ps. 6:2(1-9)	O Lord, **heal** me; for my bones are vexed.
Ps. 30:2(1-4)	I cried unto thee, and thou hast **healed** me.
Matt. 4:23(23-24)	**healing** all manner of sickness and all manner of
Matt. 8:8(5-13)	speak the word only, and my servant shall be **healed**.

HAUGHTINESS cont.

Matt. 8:16(16-17)   with his word, and **healed** all that were sick
Matt. 9:22(20-22)   be of good comfort; thy faith hath made thee **whole**.
Matt. 9:30(27-31)   and their eyes were **opened**; and Jesus straitly charged
Matt. 10:1(1-8)   he gave them power...to **heal** all manner of sickness
Matt. 14:36(34-36)   as many as touched were made perfectly **whole**.
Mark 1:25(21-28)   Jesus **rebuked** him, saying...come out of him.
Mark 1:31(29-31)   took her by the hand, and **lifted** her up; and immediate
Mark 1:34(21-34)   he **healed** many that were sick...and cast out many
Mark 5:8(1-20)   unto him, come out of the man, thou unclean **spirit**.
Mark 5:42(22-43)   and straightway the damsel **arose**, and walked; for she
Mark 9:25(14-29)   he **rebuked** the foul spirit, saying..come out..enter
Mark 16:18(15-18)   shall lay hands on the **sick**, and they shall recover.
Luke 6:19(17-19)   there went virtue out of him, and **healed** them all.
Luke 7:21(19-23)   he **cured** many of their infirmities and plagues, and
Luke 8:47(41-56)   she declared unto him...how she was **healed** immediately
Luke 22:51(47-51)   he touched his ear, and **healed** him.
John 4:50(46-54)   go thy way; thy son **liveth**. And the man believed the
John 5:9(1-9)   and immediately the man was made **whole**, and took up
John 9:14(1-38)   sabbath day...Jesus made the clay, and **opened** his eyes
Acts 3:7(1-8)   took him by the right hand, and **lifted** him up: and
Acts 5:16(12-16)   multitude...bringing sick folds...they were **healed**.
Acts 14:9(8-10)   perceiving that he had faith to be **healed**
1 Cor. 12:9(8-11)   to another the gifts of **healing** by the same spirit
James 5:14(14-16)   any sick among you? let him call for the **elders** of the
1 Ne. 11:31   and they were **healed** by the power of the lamb of God
Mosiah 3:5(5-6)   shall go forth...**healing** the sick, raising the dead
Alma 15:8(3-11)   thou believest..redemption of Christ..canst be **healed**.
3 Ne. 17:9(9-10)   he did **heal** them every one as they were brought forth
3 Ne. 26:15   after having **healed** all their sick, and their lame
4 Ne. 1:5   they did **heal** the sick, and raise the dead, and cause
Moro. 10:11(8-18)   to another, the gifts of **healing** by the same Spirit
D&C 24:13(13-14)   require not miracles, except...**healing** the sick, and
D&C 42:48(43-51)   he that hath faith in me to be **healed**, and is not
D&C 46:20(16-26)   and to others it is given to have faith to **heal**.
D&C 84:68(65-73)   in my name they shall **heal** the sick
A of F 1:7   We believe in...visions, **healing**, interpretation of

HEALTH

Ps. 128:2(1-6)   and it shall be **well** with thee.
Prov. 3:8(7-10)   it shall be **health** to thy navel, and marrow to thy
Isa. 40:31(29-31)   they that wait upon the Lord...renew their **strength**
Isa. 58:8(6-8)   thine **health** shall spring forth speedily: and thy
Jer. 30:17(10-17)   I will restore **health** unto thee, and I will heal thee
Matt. 25:39(36,39)   when saw we thee **sick**...and came unto thee
Acts 27:34(33-36)   for this is for your **health**: for there shall not an
Jacob 2:19(17-19)   administer relief to the **sick** and the afflicted.
Alma 46:40   God had prepared to remove the cause of **diseases**, to
D&C 10:4   do not run faster or **labor** more than you have strength
D&C 42:43   **nourished** with all tenderness, with herbs and mild
D&C 52:40   remember...the poor...needy...**sick** and the afflicted
D&C 59:19(6-20)   to **strengthen** the body and to enliven the soul.

D&C 84:33	sanctified by...Spirit unto...**renewing** of their bodies
D&C 88:124	that your bodies and your minds may be **invigorated**.
D&C 89:18(4-21)	shall receive **health** in their navel and marrow to
D&C 124:23(23-24)	that the weary traveler may find **health** and safety

HEART

Gen. 6:5	every imagination...of his **heart** was only evil
Deut. 6:5(3-7)	thou shalt love the Lord thy God with all thine **heart**
Deut. 11:18	lay up these my words in your **heart** and in your soul
Deut. 30:14(11-15)	the word is very nigh unto thee...in thy **heart**, that
1 Sam. 7:3	prepare your **hearts** unto the Lord, and serve him only
1 Sam. 13:14(13-14)	the Lord hath sought him a man after his own **heart**
1 Sam. 16:7(6-13)	man looketh...appearance...Lord looketh on the **heart**.
1 Kgs. 3:9	give...thy servant an understanding **heart** to judge thy
Ezra 7:10	for Ezra had prepared his **heart** to seek the law of the
Ps. 24:4(3-4)	he that hath clean hands, and a pure **heart**; who hath
Ps. 37:31(30,31)	the law of his God is in his **heart**; none of his steps
Ps. 78:37(36,37)	for their **heart** was not right with him, neither were
Prov. 3:3(1-3)	write them upon the table of thine **heart**
Prov. 3:5(5-6)	trust in the Lord with all thine **heart**; and lean not
Prov. 23:7	for as he thinketh in his **heart**, so is he: eat and
Isa. 29:13(11-14)	but have removed their **heart** far from me, and their
Isa. 51:7	the people in whose **heart** is my law; fear ye not the
Ezek. 18:31(31-32)	and make you a new **heart** and a new spirit: for why
Ezek. 20:16	for their **heart** went after their idols.
Mal. 4:6(5-6)	turn the **heart** of the fathers to the children, and the
Matt. 5:8	blessed are the pure in **heart**: for they shall see God.
Matt. 11:29(28-30)	I am meek and lowly in **heart**: and ye shall find rest
Matt. 22:37(35-40)	thou shalt love the Lord thy God with all thy **heart**
Luke 2:51	but his mother kept all these sayings in her **heart**.
Luke 6:45	for of the abundance of the **heart** his mouth speaketh.
Luke 8:15(4-15)	the good ground are they...in an honest and good **heart**
Luke 24:32(13-35)	did not our **heart** burn within us, while he talked with
Acts 13:22	I have found David...a man after mine own **heart**, which
Rom. 10:10(8-10)	for with the **heart** man believeth unto righteousness
2 Ne. 4:16(15-35)	my **heart** pondereth continually upon the things which
2 Ne. 4:26(26,30)	why should my **heart** weep and my soul linger in the
2 Ne. 4:30	rejoice, O my **heart**, and cry unto the Lord, and say
2 Ne. 31:13(1-21)	follow the Son, with full purpose of **heart**, acting
Mosiah 5:12(1-15)	retain the name written always in your **hearts**, that
Alma 5:14	experienced this mighty change in your **hearts**
Alma 32:28(1-43)	that a seed may be planted in your **heart**, behold, if
Alma 34:27(18-27)	let your **hearts** be full, drawn out in prayer unto him
Hel. 13:8	because of the hardness of the **hearts** of the people
D&C 1:2	there is no...**heart** that shall not be penetrated.
D&C 8:2(1-5)	I will tell you in your mind and in your **heart**, by the
D&C 25:12(12-13)	for my soul delighteth in the song of the **heart**; yea
D&C 29:7(1-11)	mine elect hear my voice and harden not their **hearts**
D&C 59:5	thou shalt love the Lord thy God with all thy **heart**
D&C 64:34(33-34)	the Lord requireth the **heart** and a willing mind; and
D&C 97:21(10-21)	for this is Zion- the pure in **heart**; therefore, let

HEART cont.

D&C 121:4(3-5)   let thine **heart** be softened, and thy bowels moved with

HEATHEN

2 Kgs. 16:3	according to the abominations of the **heathen**, whom the
2 Kgs. 17:8(7-8)	and walked in the statutes of the **heathen**, whom the
2 Chr. 33:9	do worse than the **heathen**, whom the Lord had destroyed
Ezra 6:21	from the filthiness of the **heathen** of the land, to see
Neh. 5:9	the reproach of the **heathen** our enemies
Ps. 2:1(1,8)	why do the **heathen** rage, and the people imagine a vain
Ps. 33:10	bringeth the counsel of the **heathen** to nought: he
Ps. 111:6	give them the heritage of the **heathen**.
Ps. 135:15(15-18)	the idols of the **heathen** are silver and gold, the work
Jer. 9:16	I will scatter them also among the **heathen**, whom
Jer. 10:2	learn not the way of the **heathen**, and be not dismayed
Ezek. 11:12	done after the manners of the **heathen** that are round
Ezek. 25:8	Judah is like unto all the **heathen**
Ezek. 36:19(17-36)	I scattered them among the **heathen**, and they were
Ezek. 37:28	**heathen** shall know that I the Lord do sanctify Israel
Ezek. 39:21(7-23)	I will set my glory among the **heathen**, and all the
Joel 3:12(11,12)	let the **heathen** be wakened, and come up to the valley
Amos 9:12(11,12)	and of all the **heathen**, which are called by my name
Obad. 1:15(1,15,16)	for the day of the Lord is near upon all the **heathen**
Zeph. 2:11	every one...even all the isles of the **heathen**.
Zech. 9:10(9-11)	he shall speak peace unto the **heathen**: and his
Matt. 6:7	use not vain repetitions, as the **heathen** do: for they
2 Cor. 11:26	in perils by the **heathen**, in perils in the city, in
Gal. 1:16(15,16)	that I might preach him among the **heathen**; immediately
Gal. 3:8(7-9)	God would justify the **heathen** through faith, preached
2 Ne. 26:33	he remembereth the **heathen**; and all are alike unto God
3 Ne. 13:7	use not vain repetitions, as the **heathen**, for they
3 Ne. 21:21	fury upon them, even as upon the **heathen**, such as they
D&C 45:54	then shall the **heathen** nations be redeemed, and they
D&C 75:22	more tolerable for the **heathen** in the day of judgment
D&C 90:10	convincing the nations, the **heathen** nations, the house
Abr. 1:5	worshiping of the gods of the **heathen**, utterly refused
Abr. 1:7(5,7)	turned their hearts to the sacrifice of the **heathen**

HEAVEN

Gen. 1:1	in the beginning God created the **heaven** and the earth.
Gen. 1:8(6-8)	and God called the firmament **heaven**. And the evening
Gen. 28:17	the house of God, and this is the gate of **heaven**.
Deut. 10:14	the heaven and the **heaven** of heavens is the Lord's thy
Josh. 2:11	he is God in **heaven** above, and in earth beneath.
1 Kgs. 8:49	in **heaven** thy dwelling place, and maintain their
Job 16:19(16-22)	behold, my witness is in **heaven**, and my record is on
Job 26:13	his spirit he hath garnished the **heavens**; his hand
Job 38:33	knowest thou the ordinances of **heaven**? canst thou set
Ps. 8:3(3-5)	when I consider thy **heavens**, the work of thy fingers
Ps. 11:4	the Lord's throne is in **heaven**: his eyes behold, his

Ps. 19:1	the **heavens** declare the glory of God; and the
Ps. 33:6	by the word of the Lord were the **heavens** made; and all
Ps. 104:2	who stretchest out the **heavens** like a curtain
Isa. 14:12(12-15)	how art thou fallen from **heaven**, O Lucifer, son of the
Isa. 65:17	I create new **heavens** and a new earth: and the former
Ezek. 8:3	spirit lifted me up between the earth and the **heaven**
Joel 2:30(10,30)	I will shew wonders in the **heavens** and in the earth
Matt. 16:1	desired him that he would shew them a sign from **heaven**
Matt. 24:30(29-30)	the sign of the Son of man in **heaven**: and then shall
John 14:2(1-3)	in my Father's **house** are many mansions: if it were not
2 Cor. 12:2(1-4)	such an one caught up to the third **heaven**.
Col. 4:1	knowing that ye also have a master in **heaven**.
2 Pet. 3:13(10-13)	we...look for new **heavens** and a new earth, wherein
Rev. 21:1	I saw a new **heaven** and a new earth: for the first
1 Ne. 1:8	he saw the **heavens** open, and he thought he saw God
Mosiah 2:41	faithful...are received into **heaven**, that thereby they
Alma 5:51(50-52)	repent ye can in nowise inherit the kingdom of **heaven**.
Alma 7:25	their garments are spotless, in the kingdom of **heaven**
Alma 11:37(34-37)	no unclean thing can inherit the kingdom of **heaven**
Alma 18:30(28-32)	the **heavens** is a place where God dwells and all his
Hel. 5:48	they saw the **heavens** open; and angels came down out
3 Ne. 9:15	I am Jesus Christ...I created the **heavens** and the
3 Ne. 12:45	be the children of your Father who is in **heaven**; for
3 Ne. 28:7(4-14)	I shall come in my glory with the powers of **heaven**.
3 Ne. 28:36	three who were caught up into the **heavens**, that I knew
D&C 1:17	spake unto him from **heaven**, and gave him commandments
D&C 38:1(1-4)	all the seraphic hosts of **heaven**, before the world was
D&C 38:11(1,11,12)	in the presence of all the hosts of **heaven**
D&C 45:48	reel to and fro, and the **heavens** also shall shake.
D&C 77:2	used by the revelator, John, in describing **heaven**, the
D&C 88:37(36-39)	and there are many **kingdoms**; for there is no space in
D&C 88:79(78-79)	of things both in **heaven** and in the earth, and under
D&C 93:17	he received all power, both in **heaven** and on earth
D&C 107:19	**heavens** opened unto them, to commune with the general
D&C 110:13	who was taken to **heaven** without tasting death, stood
D&C 121:36(36,37)	inseparably connected with the powers of **heaven**, and
D&C 129:1(1-3)	there are two kinds of beings in **heaven**, namely: angel
D&C 130:20(20,21)	a law, irrevocably decreed in **heaven** before the
D&C 131:1	celestial glory there are three **heavens** or degrees
D&C 132:16	when...out of the world...appointed angels in **heaven**
Moses 1:37(36-39)	**heavens**... they cannot be numbered unto man; but they
Moses 2:1	I reveal unto you concerning this **heaven**, and this
Moses 3:5(5-7)	in **heaven** created I them; and there was not yet flesh
Moses 6:59	born again into the kingdom of **heaven**, of water, and
Moses 6:61	abide in you; the record of **heaven**; the Comforter; the
Moses 7:23(21-23)	Zion was taken up into **heaven**, Enoch beheld, and lo
JS-V 1:1(1-4)	the **heavens** were opened upon us, and I beheld the

HELL

Job 33:18(18-30)	he keepeth back his soul from the **pit**, and his life
Ps. 9:17	the wicked shall be turned into **hell**, and all the
Ps. 16:10	for thou wilt not leave my soul in **hell**; neither wilt
Isa. 14:9(9,10)	**hell** from beneath is moved for thee to meet thee at
Isa. 14:15(12-17)	yet thou shalt be brought down to **hell**, to the sides
Isa. 24:22	and shall be shut up in the **prison**, and after many
Isa. 42:7(6-7)	to bring out the prisoners from the **prison**, and them
Isa. 66:24	neither shall their **fire** be quenched; and they shall
Ezek. 32:21	shall speak to him out of the midst of **hell** with them
Dan. 12:2	awake...some to **shame** and everlasting contempt.
Matt. 5:22(21,22)	shall say, thou fool, shall be in danger of **hell** fire.
Matt. 5:29(29-30)	not that thy whole body should be cast into **hell**.
Matt. 7:13(13-14)	broad is the way, that leadeth to **destruction**, and
Matt. 10:28	fear him...able to destroy both soul and body in **hell**.
Matt. 11:23(20-24)	thou, Capernaum...shalt be brought down to **hell**: for
Matt. 16:18(17-18)	the gates of **hell** shall not prevail against it.
Matt. 25:41	into everlasting **fire**, prepared for the devil and his
Mark 9:43(43-48)	into **hell**, into the fire that never shall be quenched
Luke 16:23(19-31)	and in **hell** he lift up his eyes, being in torments
John 5:29(28-29)	have done evil, unto the resurrection of **damnation**.
John 17:12	none of them is lost, but the son of **perdition**; that
1 Pet. 3:19(18-20)	he went and preached unto the spirits in **prison**
1 Pet. 4:6(5-6)	preached also to them that are **dead**, that they might
2 Pet. 2:4	but cast them down to **hell**, and delivered them into
Rev. 1:18	I am alive for evermore...and have the keys of **hell**
Rev. 17:8(8,11)	the beast that thou sawest...shall...go into **perdition**
Rev. 19:20	cast alive into a **lake** of fire burning with brimstone.
Rev. 20:13(10-15)	death and **hell** delivered up the dead which were in the
Rev. 21:8	lake which burneth...which is the **second** death.
1 Ne. 12:16(16-18)	river...the depths thereof are the depths of **hell**.
1 Ne. 14:3(3-4)	that he might lead away the souls of men down to **hell**
1 Ne. 15:29	that awful **hell**, which...was prepared for the wicked.
1 Ne. 15:35(26-36)	**hell**...devil is the foundation of it; wherefore the
2 Ne. 2:29(28-30)	giveth...the devil power...to bring you down to **hell**
2 Ne. 9:10(10-19,36)	that monster, death and **hell**, which I call the death
2 Ne. 9:16(8-19)	their torment is as a **lake** of fire and brimstone
2 Ne. 9:34(31-36)	wo unto the liar, for he shall be thrust down to **hell**.
2 Ne. 9:39(26-39)	to be carnally-minded is **death**, and to be
2 Ne. 24:9	**hell** from beneath is moved for thee to meet thee at
2 Ne. 28:15	wo be unto them...they shall be thrust down to **hell**
2 Ne. 28:21(19-32)	the devil...leadeth them away carefully down to **hell**.
2 Ne. 33:6	for he hath redeemed my soul from **hell**.
Jacob 3:11	loose yourselves from the pains of **hell** that ye may
Jacob 6:10(8-11)	ye must go away into that **lake** of fire and brimstone
Mosiah 2:38(36-39)	unquenchable **fire**, whose flame ascendeth up forever
Mosiah 3:27(24-27)	and their **torment** is as a lake of fire and brimstone
Alma 5:7(6-10)	encircled...by the bands of death, and..chains of **hell**
Alma 12:11(11-18)	now this is what is meant by the chains of **hell**.
Alma 13:30	may not be bound down by the chains of **hell**, that ye
Alma 26:13(13-15)	thousands...has he loosed from the pains of **hell**; and
Alma 30:60	but doth speedily drag them down to **hell**.
Alma 40:13(11-14)	these shall be cast out into outer **darkness**; there
Alma 40:26	**die** as to things pertaining to things of

HELL cont.

Alma 54:7(6-7)	awful **hell** that awaits to receive such murderers as
Hel. 6:28(26-30)	an entire destruction, and to an everlasting **hell**.
Hel. 14:19(17-19)	to come under condemnation...unto this **second** death.
3 Ne. 11:40(38-40)	the gates of **hell** stand open to receive such when the
3 Ne. 27:11(11-12)	they are hewn down and cast into the **fire**, from whence
Morm. 9:4(3-5)	to dwell with the damned souls in **hell**.
Moro. 8:21(14,20-21)	in danger of death, **hell**, and an endless torment. I
D&C 10:26(20-27)	he draggeth their souls down to **hell**; and thus he
D&C 19:10(10-13)	**punishment** which is given from my hand is endless
D&C 29:28(26-29)	depart...into everlasting **fire**, prepared for the
D&C 29:44(40-45)	they that believe not unto eternal **damnation**; for they
D&C 38:5(5-6)	residue of the wicked have I kept in **chains** of
D&C 43:33	wicked shall go away into unquenchable **fire**, and their
D&C 63:17(17-18)	have their part in that **lake** which burneth with fire
D&C 76:36(31-49)	into the lake of **fire** and brimstone, with the devil
D&C 76:37(25-49)	only ones on whom the second **death** shall have any
D&C 76:84(81-89)	these are they who are thrust down to **hell**.
D&C 76:106(102-106)	these are they who are cast down to **hell** and suffer
D&C 104:18(17,18)	he shall, with the wicked, lift up his eyes in **hell**
D&C 122:1(1,7)	and **hell** shall rage against thee
D&C 123:8(7-10)	they are the...chains...shackles, and fetters of **hell**.
Moses 1:20	he began to fear, he saw the bitterness of **hell**.
Moses 6:29(28,29)	and a **hell** I have prepared for them, if they repent
Moses 7:57(39,55-57)	remainder were reserved in **chains** of darkness until
JFS-V 1:23	redeemer and deliverer from death and...**hell**.

HIGH PRIESTS

Gen. 14:18	and Melchizedek...was the **priest** of the most high God.
Ps. 110:4	thou art a **priest** for ever after the order of
Heb. 3:1	consider the apostle and **high** priest of our profession
Heb. 5:10(5-10)	called of God an **high** priest after the order of Melchi
Heb. 6:20	Jesus, made an **high** priest for ever after the order
Heb. 7:26(11-28)	such an **high** priest became us, who is holy, harmless
Heb. 8:1(1-13)	we have such an **high** priest, who is set on the right
Heb. 9:11(11-24)	Christ being come an **high** priest of good things to come
Heb. 10:21(21-39)	and having an **high** priest over the house of God
Rev. 7:3(3-4)	sealed the **servants** of our God in their foreheads.
Rev. 20:6	**priests** of God and of Christ...reign with him a
2 Ne. 6:2	ordained after the manner of his **holy** order, and
Mosiah 18:24(18-28)	**priests**...should labor with their own hands for their
Alma 4:4	Alma...consecrated the **high** priest over the people of
Alma 4:18(17-20)	he retained the office of **high** priest unto himself
Alma 13:1(1-20)	the Lord God ordained **priests**, after his holy order
D&C 20:67	every...**high** priest, is to be ordained by the
D&C 68:19(14-24)	but, as a **high** priest of the Melchizedek priesthood
D&C 76:57(50-70)	and are **priests** of the most high, after the order of
D&C 77:11	those who are sealed are **high** priests, ordained unto
D&C 84:111	and behold, the **high** priests should travel, and also
D&C 107:10	**high** priests after the order of the Melchizedek priest
D&C 107:53	called Seth, Enos...Enoch...were all **high** priests, wit
D&C 107:66(64-67)	the Presiding **High** Priest over the High Priesthood of

HIGH PRIESTS cont.

D&C 107:91(91-92)	duty of the President...of the **High** Priesthood is to
Abr. 1:2(2-4)	I became a rightful heir, a **High** Priest, holding the
JFS-V 1:41	Shem, the great high **priest**; Abraham, the father of

HOLINESS

Ex. 3:5	the place whereon thou standest is **holy** ground.
Ex. 15:11	who is like thee, glorious in **holiness**, fearful in
Ex. 19:6	be unto me a kingdom of priests, and an **holy** nation.
Ex. 20:8	remember the sabbath day, to keep it **holy**.
Ex. 28:36	like the engravings of a signet, **HOLINESS** TO THE LORD.
Ex. 31:14(13-17)	keep the sabbath therefore; for it is **holy** unto you
Lev. 10:10	put difference between **holy** and unholy, and between
Lev. 19:2(2-37)	ye shall be **holy**: for I the Lord your God am holy.
Lev. 20:26(2-26)	I the Lord am **holy**...severed you from other people
Lev. 21:6(6-15)	they shall be **holy** unto their God, and not profane the
Num. 16:5	Lord will shew who are his, and who is **holy**; and will
Deut. 14:2	for thou art an **holy** people unto the Lord thy God, and
Deut. 28:9	the Lord shall establish thee an **holy** people unto
1 Chr. 16:29	worship the Lord in the beauty of **holiness**.
Ps. 24:3(3-4)	or who shall stand in his **holy** place
Ps. 96:9	O worship the Lord in the beauty of **holiness**: fear
Prov. 9:10	the knowledge of the **holy** is understanding.
Isa. 35:8	an highway shall be there...called the way of **holiness**
Isa. 41:14(14,16,20)	the Lord, and thy redeemer, the **Holy** One of Israel.
Isa. 43:3	I am the Lord thy God, the **Holy** One of Israel, thy
Isa. 63:10(7-13)	they rebelled, and vexed his **holy** Spirit: therefore
Isa. 63:15	behold from the habitation of thy **holiness** and of thy
Dan. 4:18(8-18)	the spirit of the **holy** gods is in thee.
Matt. 7:6	give not that which is **holy** unto the dogs, neither
Mark 1:24	I know thee who thou art, the **Holy** One of God.
Luke 1:75	in **holiness** and righteousness before him, all the days
1 Cor. 3:17(16-17)	the temple of God is **holy**, which temple ye are.
2 Cor. 7:1	perfecting **holiness** in the fear of God.
Eph. 1:4	as he hath chosen us...that we should be **holy** and with
1 Tim. 2:15	if they continue in faith and charity and **holiness**
Heb. 12:10(10-14)	that we might be partakers of his **holiness**.
1 Jn. 2:20	ye have an unction from the **Holy** One, and ye know all
1 Ne. 22:21(5-28)	prophet of whom Moses spake was the **Holy** One of Israel
2 Ne. 2:6	redemption cometh in and through the **Holy** Messiah; for
2 Ne. 2:10	judged of him according to the truth and **holiness**
2 Ne. 9:20	O how great the **holiness** of our God! For he knoweth
Alma 10:9(7-9)	the angel said unto me he is a **holy** man; wherefore I
Alma 13:1(1-11)	the Lord God ordained priests, after his **holy** order
3 Ne. 14:6	give not that which is **holy** unto the dogs, neither
3 Ne. 28:39(36-40)	sanctified in the flesh, that they were **holy**, and that
Morm. 9:5	shall be brought to see...the **holiness** of Jesus Christ
Moro. 10:33(32-33)	through...blood of Christ...become **holy**, without spot.
D&C 20:69	walking in **holiness** before the Lord.
D&C 21:4	give heed unto all his words...walking in all **holiness**
D&C 41:6(5-6)	not meet that...**pearls** to be cast before swine.
D&C 46:7	that which the spirit testifies...do in all **holiness**

HOLINESS cont.

D&C 60:7	lifting up holy hands...for I am able to make you **holy**
D&C 74:7	little children are **holy**...sanctified through the
D&C 101:22	gather together, and stand in **holy** places
D&C 109:13	it is thy house, a place of thy **holiness**.
D&C 110:8	keep my commandments...do not pollute this **holy** house.
D&C 124:44	I will consecrate that spot that it shall be made **holy**
D&C 133:35(34,35)	after their pain shall be sanctified in **holiness**

HOLY GHOST, BAPTISM OF

Matt. 3:11	he shall **baptize** you with the Holy Ghost, and with fir
John 1:13	which were **born**...of God.
John 1:33(29-34)	the same is he which baptizeth with the **Holy** Ghost.
John 3:5	**born** of water and of the Spirit...he cannot enter into
Acts 1:5	ye shall be **baptized** with the Holy Ghost not many days
Acts 2:4(1-4)	and they were all filled with the **Holy** Ghost, and
Acts 2:38(37-39)	and ye shall receive the gift of the **Holy** Ghost.
Acts 10:47(44-48)	be baptized, which have received the **Holy** Ghost as
1 Pet. 1:3	abundant mercy hath **begotten** us again unto a lively
1 Pet. 1:23(22-23)	being **born** again, not of corruptible seed, but of
2 Ne. 31:13(11-17)	then cometh the **baptism** of fire and of the Holy Ghost
Mosiah 4:3(1-3)	filled with joy, having received a **remission** of their
Mosiah 5:7	ye are **born** of him and have become his sons and his
Mosiah 27:25(24-27)	all mankind...must be **born** again; yea, born of God
Alma 5:14(12-28)	have ye spiritually been **born** of God? Have ye receive
Alma 13:12(12-13)	after being sanctified by the **Holy** Ghost, having their
Alma 22:15(15-16)	what shall I do that I may be **born** of God, having this
Alma 36:24(23-28)	be **born** of God, and be filled with the Holy Ghost.
Alma 38:6	if I had not been **born** of God I should not have known
Hel. 5:45(43-49)	the **holy** spirit of God did...enter into their hearts
3 Ne. 9:20	him will I **baptize** with fire and with the Holy Ghost
3 Ne. 11:35(32-36)	he will visit him with fire and with the **Holy** Ghost.
3 Ne. 12:1(1,2)	I will **baptize** you with fire and with the Holy Ghost
3 Ne. 15:23	not manifest myself unto them save...by the **Holy** Ghost
3 Ne. 19:13(9-29)	they were filled with the **Holy** Ghost and with fire.
3 Ne. 27:20(19-20)	sanctified by the reception of the **Holy** Ghost, that
Moro. 8:26(23-26)	the visitation of the **Holy** Ghost, which comforter
D&C 5:16	they shall be **born** of me...of water and of the
D&C 19:31	remission of sins...by fire, yea, even the **Holy** Ghost.
D&C 39:6(1-8)	then cometh the **baptism** of fire and the Holy Ghost
D&C 84:64	remission of sins, shall receive the **holy** ghost.
Moses 5:9	and in that day the **holy** ghost fell upon Adam, which
Moses 6:59	ye must be **born** again into the kingdom of heaven, of
Moses 6:65	he was **born** of the spirit, and became quickened in the
Moses 6:66	**baptized** with fire, and with the holy ghost. this is
JS-H 1:73	we were filled with the **holy** ghost, and rejoiced in

HOLY GHOST, COMFORTER

Isa. 49:13	for the Lord hath **comforted** his people, and will have
John 14:26(16-27)	the **Comforter**, which is the Holy Ghost, whom I will send
John 15:26	but when the **Comforter** is come, whom I will send unto
John 16:7(7,13)	if I go not away, the **Comforter** will not come unto you
Acts 7:55(55,56)	being full of the **Holy** Ghost, looked up stedfastly
Acts 9:31	walking...in the **comfort** of the Holy Ghost, were
Moro. 8:26(25-26)	**Comforter** filleth with hope and perfect love, which
D&C 21:9	words, which are given him through me by the **Comforter**
D&C 24:5	things which shall be given thee by the **Comforter**, and
D&C 28:1	thou shalt teach them by the **Comforter**, concerning the
D&C 31:11	shall be given you by the **Comforter** what you shall do
D&C 36:2	**Comforter**, which shall teach you the peaceable things
D&C 39:6	**Comforter**, which showeth all...teacheth the peaceable
D&C 42:17(13-17)	the **Comforter** knoweth all things, and beareth record
D&C 47:4(3-4)	given him...by the **Comforter**, to write these things.
D&C 50:14(13-14,17)	to preach my gospel by the Spirit, even the **Comforter**
D&C 52:9	that which is taught them by the **Comforter** through the
D&C 75:10(9-10)	**Comforter**, which shall teach them all things that are
D&C 75:27	made known from on high, even by the **Comforter**
D&C 79:2	**Comforter**...shall teach him the truth and the way
D&C 90:11	by the administration of the **Comforter**, shed forth
D&C 90:14(12-14)	by the **Comforter**, receive revelations to unfold the
D&C 124:97	**Comforter**, which shall manifest unto him the truth of
Moses 6:61	it is given to abide in you...the **Comforter**; the peace
JS-H 1:73	were filled with the Holy Ghost, and **rejoiced** in the

HOLY GHOST, DOVE, SIGN OF

Matt. 3:16(16-17)	he saw the Spirit of God descending like a **dove**, and
Mark 1:10	he saw...the Spirit like a **dove** descending upon him
Luke 3:22(21-22)	the Holy Ghost descended...like a **dove** upon him, and
John 1:32(32-33)	I saw the Spirit descending from heaven like a **dove**
1 Ne. 11:27	and abide upon him in the form of a **dove**.
2 Ne. 31:8(5-10)	Holy Ghost descended upon him in the form of a **dove**.
D&C 93:15(11-17)	Holy Ghost descended upon him in the form of a **dove**
Abr. 7:7	sign of the Holy Ghost...in the form of a **dove**.

HOLY GHOST, GIFT OF

1 Sam. 16:13	the **Spirit** of the Lord came upon David from that day
Luke 1:15	he shall be filled with the **Holy** Ghost, even from his
Luke 3:16	he shall **baptize** you with the Holy Ghost and with fire
John 7:39(37-39)	the **Spirit**, which they that believe on him...receive
Acts 1:5	ye shall be **baptized** with the Holy Ghost not many days
Acts 2:38	ye shall receive the **gift** of the Holy Ghost.
Acts 5:32	Holy Ghost, whom God hath **given** to them that obey him.
Acts 9:17(17-18)	that thou mightest...be filled with the **Holy** Ghost.
Acts 10:45(44-45)	on the Gentiles..poured out the **gift** of the Holy Ghost
Acts 11:17(16,17)	God gave them the like **gift** as he did unto us, who
1 Ne. 10:17(17-19)	the Holy Ghost, which is the **gift** of God unto all
1 Ne. 13:37	they shall have the **gift** and...power of the Holy Ghost

HOLY GHOST, GIFT OF cont.

2 Ne. 31:12(12-17)	to him will the Father **give** the Holy Ghost, like unto
Jacob 6:8	will ye...deny...the **gift** of the Holy Ghost, and
Alma 9:21	having...the **gift** of the Holy Ghost, and the gift of
Alma 36:24	be born of God, and be filled with the **Holy** Ghost.
3 Ne. 9:20	**baptized** with fire and with the Holy Ghost, and they
3 Ne. 11:35	he will visit him with fire and with the **Holy** Ghost.
3 Ne. 12:1(1-2)	I will **baptize** you with fire and with the Holy Ghost
D&C 20:26(25-27,41)	spake as...inspired by the **gift** of the Holy Ghost, who
D&C 33:15	I will bestow the **gift** of the Holy Ghost upon them.
D&C 35:6(5-6)	shall receive the **Holy** Ghost by the laying on of the
D&C 39:23	they shall receive the **gift** of the Holy Ghost, and
D&C 49:14	whoso doeth this shall receive the **gift** of the Holy
D&C 68:25	baptism and the **gift** of the Holy Ghost by the laying
D&C 76:116(116-118)	holy **Spirit**, which God bestows on those who love him
D&C 84:64	soul who...is baptized...shall **receive** the Holy Ghost.
D&C 121:26	the unspeakable **gift** of the Holy Ghost, that has not
D&C 130:23	a man may receive the **Holy** Ghost, and it may...not
Moses 5:58	gospel...preached...by the **gift** of the Holy Ghost.
Moses 6:52	ye shall receive the **gift** of the Holy Ghost, asking
A of F 1:4	laying on of hands for the **gift** of the Holy Ghost.
JFS-V 1:33(29-34)	vicarious baptism...the **gift** of the Holy Ghost by the

HOLY GHOST, GIFTS OF

Ex. 31:3(1-6)	filled him with the **spirit** of God, in wisdom, and in
Ex. 36:1(1,2)	in whom the Lord put **wisdom** and understanding to know
Num. 11:25(25-29)	when the spirit rested upon them, they **prophesied**, and
1 Sam. 10:6(5-6)	Spirit...will come upon thee, and thou shalt **prophesy**
Dan. 2:28(20-22,28)	but there is a God in heaven that **revealeth** secrets
Joel 2:28	your sons and your daughters shall **prophesy**, your old
Mark 16:17(17-18)	these **signs** shall follow them that believe; in my name
Luke 1:41(41-44)	babe leaped...Elisabeth was **filled** with the Holy Ghost
Luke 1:67	Zacharias...filled with the Holy Ghost, and **prophesied**
John 14:16	he shall give you another **Comforter**, that he may abide
John 14:26	Holy Ghost...**teach** you all things, and bring all thing
John 16:13(7-13)	he will **guide** you into all truth: for he shall not
Acts 1:8	but ye shall receive **power**, after that the Holy Ghost
Acts 2:4(2-12)	began to speak with other **tongues**, as the Spirit gave
Acts 2:17(17-18)	your sons and your daughters shall **prophesy**, and your
Acts 6:3(2-10)	seven men...full of the Holy Ghost and **wisdom**, whom
Acts 6:5(5,8)	Stephen, a man full of faith and of the **Holy** Ghost
Acts 7:55(55,56)	but he, being full of the **Holy** Ghost, looked up
Acts 8:29	the **Spirit** said unto Philip, go near, and join thyself
Acts 9:31	fear of the Lord, and in the **comfort** of the Holy Ghost
Acts 10:19	the **Spirit** said unto him, behold, three men seek thee.
Acts 10:38	how God anointed Jesus...with the **Holy** Ghost and with
Acts 10:46(45-47)	they heard them speak with **tongues**, and magnify God.
Acts 11:17(16-17)	God gave them the like **gift** as he did unto us, who
Acts 13:2	the **Holy** Ghost said, separate me Barnabas and Saul for
Acts 13:9	Saul...filled with the **Holy** Ghost, set his eyes on him
Rom. 8:26(10,26)	likewise the Spirit also **helpeth** our infirmities: for
Rom. 15:16	being **sanctified** by the Holy Ghost.

HOLY GHOST, GIFTS OF cont.

1 Cor. 7:7	every man hath his proper **gift** of God, one after this
1 Cor. 12:4(4-10)	now there are diversities of **gifts**, but the same
1 Cor. 12:8(8-11)	to another the word of **knowledge** by the same Spirit
1 Cor. 12:31(1-31)	but covet earnestly the best **gifts**: and yet shew I
1 Cor. 14:1	follow after charity, and desire spiritual **gifts**, but
1 Thes. 1:5	gospel came...in **power**, and in the Holy Ghost, and in
1 Thes. 5:19	quench not the **Spirit**.
2 Tim. 1:6	that thou stir up the **gift** of God, which is in thee
Titus 3:5	regeneration, and **renewing** of the Holy Ghost
Heb. 2:4(3-4)	God also bearing them witness, both with **signs** and won
2 Pet. 1:21(20-21)	holy men...spake as they were moved by the **Holy** Ghost.
Rev. 2:7	let him hear what the **Spirit** saith unto the churches
1 Ne. 4:6	I was **led** by the Spirit, not knowing beforehand the
1 Ne. 10:19	**mysteries**...unfolded...by the power of the Holy Ghost
1 Ne. 11:11(2-12)	Spirit...**spake** unto me as a man speaketh with another.
2 Ne. 31:13(13,14)	speak with the **tongue** of angels, and shout praises
2 Ne. 32:5	Holy Ghost...will **show**...all things what ye should do.
2 Ne. 33:1	when a man **speaketh** by the power of the Holy Ghost the
Jacob 7:12	made manifest unto me by the **power** of the Holy Ghost
Alma 9:21(20-22)	**gift** of...tongues...preaching...Holy Ghost...
Alma 12:3(3-7)	thy **thoughts** are made known unto us by his Spirit
Alma 13:28	led by the **Holy** Spirit, becoming humble, meek
Hel. 5:45	Holy Spirit of God did come down...**speak** forth
3 Ne. 19:13(13,20-22)	the **Holy** Ghost did fall upon them, and they were
3 Ne. 27:20	that ye may be **sanctified** by the reception of the Holy
3 Ne. 29:6(5-7)	yea, wo unto him that shall deny...**gifts**, or by tongue
Morm. 9:24(22-25)	these **signs** shall follow them that believe- in my name
Ether 4:18	**signs** shall follow them that believe in my name.
Moro. 6:9	Holy Ghost **led** them whether to preach, or to exhort
Moro. 7:44	**confesses** by the...Holy Ghost that Jesus is the Christ
Moro. 10:5(4-25)	by the..Holy Ghost ye may **know** the truth of all things
Moro. 10:8	deny not the **gifts** of God, for they are many; and the
D&C 6:10(10-13)	thy **gift**...is sacred and cometh from above
D&C 11:12(10-14)	put your trust in that **Spirit** which leadeth to do good
D&C 46:11(7-33)	to every man is given a **gift** by the Spirit of God.
D&C 58:64	gospel...preached...with **signs** following them that
D&C 63:9(7-12)	faith...not by signs, but **signs** follow those that
D&C 84:65(65-73)	and these **signs** shall follow them that believe
D&C 84:88	my **Spirit** shall be in your hearts, and mine angels
D&C 95:4	that I may pour out my **Spirit** upon all flesh
D&C 107:56	Adam...being full of the Holy Ghost, **predicted**
D&C 107:92	a prophet, having all the **gifts** of God which he
D&C 109:36	gift of **tongues** be poured out upon thy people, even
D&C 124:4(4-5)	**written**...by the power of the Holy Ghost, which shall
D&C 124:98(97-101)	these **signs** shall follow him- he shall heal the sick
JS-H 1:73(73-74)	Holy Ghost fell upon him...he stood up and **prophesied**
A of F 1:7	We believe in the **gift** of tongues, prophecy
A of F 1:10	We believe in the literal **gathering** of Israel and in

HOLY GHOST, LOSS OF

Gen. 6:3	my **spirit** shall not always strive with man, for that
Ex. 23:21(20-23)	obey...for he will not **pardon** your transgressions
1 Sam. 16:14(14-23)	the **Spirit** of the Lord departed from Saul, and an evil
Ps. 51:11(10-11)	and take not thy **holy** spirit from me.
Isa. 63:10	**vexed**...holy Spirit...he was turned to be their enemy
Matt. 12:31(31,32)	blasphemy against the Holy Ghost...**not** be forgiven
Rom. 8:9	man have not the **Spirit** of Christ, he is none of his.
1 Cor. 3:17(16-17)	**defile** the temple of God, him shall God destroy; for
Gal. 5:17	flesh lusteth against the **Spirit**, and the Spirit again
1 Thes. 5:19	**quench** not the **Spirit**.
1 Tim. 4:1	**depart** from the faith, giving heed to seducing spirits
Heb. 6:6(4-6)	if they shall **fall** away...crucify...son of God afresh
Jude 1:19(18,19)	sensual, having not the **Spirit**.
1 Ne. 7:14	Spirit of the Lord **ceaseth** soon to strive with them
2 Ne. 26:11	Spirit **ceaseth** to strive with man then cometh speedy
2 Ne. 33:2	harden their hearts against the Holy **Spirit**, that it
Mosiah 2:36(36-38)	**withdraw** yourselves from the Spirit of the Lord, that
Alma 24:30	once enlightened by the Spirit...then have **fallen** away
Alma 34:38	**contend** no more against the Holy Ghost, but that ye
Alma 39:6	**deny** the Holy Ghost...once has had place in you, and
Hel. 4:24	Spirit of the Lord doth not **dwell** in unholy temples
Morm. 1:14	**Holy** Ghost did not come...because of their wickedness
Ether 15:19	the **Spirit** of the Lord had ceased striving with them
Moro. 8:28(28-29)	the Spirit hath **ceased** striving with them; and in this
D&C 1:33	my **Spirit** shall not always strive with man, saith the
D&C 19:20	you have tasted at the time I **withdrew** my Spirit.
D&C 42:23	looketh upon a woman to lust...not have the **Spirit**
D&C 63:16	looketh on a woman to lust...not have the **Spirit**, but
D&C 63:32	I am holding my **Spirit** from the inhabitants of the
D&C 63:55	received not counsel, but **grieved** the Spirit
D&C 64:16	sought evil...I, the Lord, **withheld** my Spirit. They
D&C 70:14	manifestations of the Spirit shall be **withheld**.
D&C 76:35(34-35)	having **denied** the Holy Spirit after having received
D&C 121:37(37-38)	Spirit...is grieved; and when it is **withdrawn**, Amen
D&C 130:23	Holy Ghost...may descend upon him and not **tarry** with

HOLY GHOST, MISSION OF

1 Sam. 16:13(10-13)	the **Spirit** of the Lord came upon David from that day
Neh. 9:30	testifiedst against them by thy **spirit** in thy prophet
Isa. 11:2(1-5)	and the **spirit** of the Lord shall rest upon him, the
Ezek. 11:5(4,5)	and the **Spirit** of the Lord fell upon me, and said unto
Micah 3:8	I am full of power by the **spirit** of the Lord, and of
Matt. 12:18	put my Spirit upon him, and he shall shew **judgment** to
Mark 13:11	it is not ye that speak, but the **Holy** Ghost.
Luke 1:15(15,41,67)	he shall be filled with the **Holy** Ghost, even from his
Luke 4:1	Jesus...was **led** by the Spirit into the wilderness
Luke 12:12(11-12)	Holy Ghost shall **teach** you in the same hour what ye
John 3:5(3-6)	born of water and of the **Spirit**, he cannot enter into
John 14:26(16-18,26)	shall **teach** you..bring all things to your remembrance
John 15:26	Spirit of truth...shall **testify** of me
John 16:8(7-15)	and when he is come, he will **reprove** the world of sin

John 16:13(7-14)	Spirit of truth...will **guide**...shew you things to come
John 16:14(7-15)	he shall **glorify** me: for he shall receive of mine, and
Acts 1:2	through the Holy Ghost...**commandments** unto the apostle
Acts 1:16	Holy Ghost by the mouth of David **spake** before
Acts 2:4(1-4)	filled with the Holy Ghost...speak with other **tongues**
Acts 2:37(37,38,41)	they were **pricked** in their heart, and said unto Peter
Acts 5:32(29-32)	**witnesses** of these things; and so is also the Holy
Acts 19:6(1-6)	Holy Ghost came on them; and they spake with **tongues**
Acts 28:25(25-27)	well **spake** the Holy Ghost by Esaias the prophet unto
Rom. 8:27(26,27)	Spirit...maketh **intercession** for the saints according
1 Cor. 2:13(11-15)	not...man's wisdom...but which the Holy Ghost **teacheth**
1 Cor. 12:3	no man can say...Jesus is the Lord, but by...**Holy**
1 Cor. 12:4(1-11)	there are diversities of **gifts**, but the same Spirit.
Gal. 5:22(22-26)	but the **fruit** of the Spirit is love, joy, peace
Heb. 10:15	Holy Ghost also is a **witness** to us: for after that he
1 Pet. 1:12(10-12)	have **preached** the gospel unto you with the Holy Ghost
2 Pet. 1:21(19-21)	men of God **spake** as they were moved by the Holy Ghost
1 Jn. 4:6	know we the **spirit** of truth, and the spirit of error.
1 Jn. 5:6(5-9)	Spirit...beareth **witness**, because the Spirit is truth.
1 Ne. 10:11(4-11)	make himself **manifest**, by the Holy Ghost, unto the
1 Ne. 13:12(12-15)	Spirit of God...came down and **wrought** upon the man
2 Ne. 26:13	he manifesteth himself..by the power of the **Holy** Ghost.
2 Ne. 31:17(17-21)	cometh a **remission** of your sins...by the Holy Ghost.
2 Ne. 31:18(17-21)	Holy Ghost, which **witnesses** of the Father and the Son
2 Ne. 32:5	**Holy** Ghost, it will show unto you all things what ye
Jacob 4:13	the **Spirit** speaketh the truth and lieth not. Wherefore
Jacob 7:8(6-8)	Lord God poured in his **Spirit** into my soul, insomuch
Mosiah 4:3(2-3)	Spirit of the Lord...**remission** of their sins, and
Mosiah 18:13(12,13)	the **Spirit** of the Lord was upon him, and he said
Alma 5:46(43-46)	they are made known unto me by the Holy **Spirit** of God.
Alma 11:22(21-25)	yea, if it be according to the **Spirit** of the Lord
Alma 12:3(3-7)	thy **thoughts**, and thou seest that thy thoughts are
Alma 30:46	that ye will still resist the **spirit** of the truth
3 Ne. 15:23	manifest myself unto them save...by the **Holy** Ghost.
3 Ne. 20:27	pouring out of the **Holy** Ghost through me upon the
3 Ne. 27:20	**sanctified** by the reception of the Holy Ghost, that
3 Ne. 28:11	Holy Ghost **beareth** record of the Father and me; and
Ether 12:41	Holy Ghost, which **beareth** record of them, may be and
Moro. 8:26	**Comforter** filleth with hope and perfect love, which
Moro. 10:5(3-5)	by the..Holy Ghost ye may **know** the truth of all things
Moro. 10:7(6-19)	ye may know that he is, by the **power** of the Holy Ghost
D&C 6:15(14-16)	thou hast been **enlightened** by the Spirit of truth
D&C 8:2(2-3)	tell you in your mind and...heart, by the **Holy** Ghost
D&C 11:12(12-14)	put your **trust** in that Spirit which leadeth to do
D&C 14:8	Holy Ghost...**giveth** utterance, that...witness of the
D&C 36:2	Comforter, which shall **teach** you the peaceable things
D&C 39:6	Holy Ghost...**showeth** all things, and teacheth the
D&C 42:14(13-17)	receive not the Spirit ye shall not **teach**.
D&C 45:57(56-59)	wise...have taken the Holy Spirit for their **guide**, and
D&C 46:11(11-26)	every man is given a **gift** by the Spirit of God.
D&C 46:30(27-33)	he that **asketh** in the Spirit asketh according to the
D&C 50:17(17-21)	doth he **preach** it by the Spirit of truth or some other
D&C 68:4(1-4)	speak when moved upon by the Holy Ghost...**scripture**

HOLY GHOST, MISSION OF cont.

D&C 72:24(24-26)	**appointed** by the Holy Spirit to go up unto Zion, and
D&C 76:53(50-53)	**sealed** by the Holy Spirit of promise, which the Father
D&C 107:71	having a **knowledge** of them by the Spirit of truth
D&C 121:43(41-45)	reproving betimes...when **moved** upon by the Holy Ghost
D&C 121:46(45-46)	the Holy Ghost shall be thy constant **companion**, and
D&C 130:22(22-23)	Holy Ghost...personage of Spirit...**dwell** in us.
D&C 132:7	**sealed** by the Holy Spirit of promise, of him who is
Moses 1:27	beheld the earth...**discerning** it by the Spirit of God.
Moses 6:5	as called upon God to **write** by the Spirit of
Moses 6:64(64,65)	he was caught away by the **Spirit** of the Lord, and was
Moses 6:65(64,65)	born of the Spirit...became **quickened** in the inner man
Moses 8:24(23,24)	Holy Ghost, that ye may have all things made **manifest**
JS-H 1:73(73,74)	Holy Ghost fell upon him...he stood up and **prophesied**

HOLY GHOST, SOURCE OF TESTIMONY

Neh. 9:20	thou gavest also thy good spirit to **instruct** them, and
John 5:32	there is another that beareth **witness** of me; and I
John 15:26	when the Comforter is come...he shall **testify** of me
Acts 2:37(37,38,41)	they were **pricked** in their heart, and said unto Peter
Acts 5:32	we are his witnesses...and so is also the **Holy** Ghost
1 Cor. 2:11	things of God knoweth no man, but the **Spirit** of God.
1 Cor. 12:3	no man can say...Jesus is the Lord, but by..**Holy** Ghost
1 Thes. 1:5	our gospel came...in power, and in the **Holy** Ghost, and
1 Ne. 10:19	mysteries...unfolded...by the power of the **Holy** Ghost
2 Ne. 31:18(17-21)	Holy Ghost, which **witnesses** of the Father and the Son
Alma 5:46(44-46)	manifest unto me by his **Holy** Spirit...Spirit of
3 Ne. 11:36(32-36)	the **Holy** Ghost will bear record unto him of the Father
3 Ne. 16:6	Holy Ghost, which **witnesses**...of me and of the Father.
Moro. 10:5(3-5)	power of the Holy Ghost ye may **know** the truth of all
Moro. 10:7(6-19)	ye may **know** that he is, by the power of the Holy Ghost
D&C 9:8(7-9)	therefore, you shall **feel** that it is right.
D&C 42:17	the Comforter...**beareth** record of the Father and of
D&C 46:13	given by the **Holy** Ghost to know that Jesus Christ is
D&C 97:1	I speak unto you with my voice...voice of my **Spirit**
D&C 105:36	manifest unto my servant, by the voice of the **Spirit**
Moses 6:61	the **record** of heaven; the Comforter; the peaceable

HOLY GHOST, UNPARDONABLE SIN AGAINST

Matt. 12:31(31-32)	**blasphemy** against the Holy Ghost shall not be forgiven
Mark 3:29(28-30)	he that shall **blaspheme** against the Holy Ghost hath
Luke 12:10(9,10)	**blasphemeth** against the Holy Ghost it shall not be
Heb. 6:6(4-6)	seeing they **crucify** to themselves the Son of God
Heb. 10:26(26-29)	sin **wilfully** after that we have received the knowledge
2 Ne. 31:14	received...Holy Ghost...after this should **deny** me, it
Jacob 6:8(8-10)	**deny** the...the Holy Spirit, and make a mock of the
Jacob 7:19(9-19)	committed the **unpardonable** sin...I have lied unto God
Mosiah 2:37(36-39)	the same cometh out in open **rebellion** against God; the
Alma 39:6	deny the Holy Ghost...is a sin which is **unpardonable**
Moro. 8:28(28,29)	Spirit hath ceased...they are **denying** the Holy Ghost.

D&C 76:35(31-38)	having **denied** the Holy Spirit after having received
D&C 132:27	**blasphemy** against the Holy Ghost, which shall not be

HOME TEACHING

Ps. 142:4(3,4)	refuge failed me; no man **cared** for my soul.
Jer. 3:15(14-15)	and I will give you **pastors** according to mine heart
Ezek. 3:17(17-21)	I have made thee a **watchman** unto the house of Israel
Ezek. 33:7(7-11)	I have set thee a **watchman** unto the house of Israel
Ezek. 34:2	should not the **shepherds** feed the flocks
Luke 22:32(31-32)	when thou art converted, **strengthen** thy brethren.
John 10:11(11-16)	the good **shepherd** giveth his life for the sheep.
John 21:17(15-17)	Jesus saith unto him, **Feed** my sheep.
Eph. 4:12(11-15)	for the **perfecting** of the saints, for the work of the
2 Tim. 2:2	faithful men, who shall be able to **teach** others also.
2 Tim. 2:25(24-26)	in meekness **instructing** those that oppose themselves
Titus 2:1(1-15)	but **speak** thou the things which become sound doctrine
James 1:27	pure religion...to **visit** the fatherless and widows
James 5:14(14-15)	is any sick among you? let him call for the **elders** of
1 Pet. 4:10(7-11)	received the gift, even so **minister** the same one to
2 Ne. 5:26	they should be priests and **teachers** over the land of
Jacob 1:18(18-19)	priests and **teachers** of this people, by the hand of
3 Ne. 18:21(18-21)	**pray** in your families unto the father, always in my
Moro. 6:4(4,5)	to **keep** them continually watchful unto prayer, relying
D&C 20:47(46-51)	and **visit** the house of each member, and exhort them
D&C 20:53(53-55)	the **teacher's** duty is to watch over the church always
D&C 38:23(23,24)	**teach** one another according to the office...appointed
D&C 38:27(25-27)	and if ye are not **one** ye are not mine.
D&C 38:41(40,41)	preaching be the warning **voice**, every man to his
D&C 42:12(12-14)	**teach** the principles of my gospel, which are in the
D&C 44:6	ye must **visit** the poor and the needy and administer
D&C 46:27	ordain to **watch** over the church and to be elders unto
D&C 52:39(39-40)	let...the elders **watch** over the churches, and declare
D&C 82:19	every man seeking the interest of his **neighbor**, and
D&C 84:36(35,36)	for he that receiveth my **servants** receiveth me
D&C 84:106(106,107)	any man..**strong** in the spirit..take..him that is
D&C 84:111	**watch** over the church, to be standing ministers unto
D&C 88:78(74-80)	**teach** ye diligently and my grace shall attend you

HOMOSEXUALITY

Gen. 13:13	the men of Sodom were **wicked** and sinners before the
Gen. 18:20(20-22)	Sodom and Gomorrah ...their **sin** is very grievous
Gen. 19:5(4-9)	bring them out unto us, that we may **know** them.
Lev. 18:22(22-27)	thou shalt not lie with mankind...it is **abomination**.
Lev. 20:13(13,15)	if a man...lie with mankind...committed an **abomination**
Deut. 23:17	there shall be no...**sodomite** of the sons of Israel.
Ezek. 16:50	and they were haughty, and committed **abomination**
Rom. 1:27(24-32)	men...burned in their **lust** one toward another; men
1 Cor. 6:9(9-10)	nor **abusers** of themselves with mankind
1 Tim. 1:10	them that **defile** themselves with mankind, for

Jude 1:7	as Sodom and Gomorrah...going after **strange** flesh, are
2 Ne. 9:40	words of truth are hard against all **uncleanness**; but
2 Ne. 13:9	doth declare their sin to be even as **Sodom**, and they

HONESTY

Ex. 20:16	thou shalt not bear **false** witness against thy
Ex. 23:4	enemy's ox...going astray...**bring** it back to him again
Lev. 19:12	ye shall not swear by my name **falsely**, neither shalt
Lev. 19:16(16-17)	thou shalt not go...as a **talebearer** among thy people
Job 27:4(3-6)	not speak wickedness, nor my tongue utter **deceit**.
Ps. 24:4(3-6)	he that hath...not...sworn **deceitfully**.
Ps. 31:18	let the **lying** lips be put to silence; which speak
Ps. 34:13(13-14)	keep thy tongue from evil...lips from speaking **guile**.
Ps. 101:7	he that telleth **lies** shall not tarry in my sight.
Prov. 6:19(16-19)	a false witness that speaketh **lies**, and he that soweth
Prov. 12:22	they that deal **truly** are his delight.
Prov. 15:4	a wholesome **tongue** is a tree of life: but perverseness
Prov. 16:13	**righteous** lips are the delight of kings; and they love
Prov. 18:8(4-8)	the words of a **talebearer** are as wounds, and they go
Prov. 24:28	and **deceive** not with thy lips.
Eccl. 5:5(4-5)	better...not vow, than...**vow** and not pay.
Isa. 30:10(9-10)	speak unto us smooth things, prophesy **deceits**
Isa. 53:9	no violence, neither was any **deceit** in his mouth.
Ezek. 13:8(2-9)	ye have spoken vanity, and seen **lies**...I am against
Ezek. 22:13	I have smitten mine hand at thy **dishonest** gain which
Jonah 2:8	they that observe **lying** vanities forsake their own
Mal. 2:6(4-8)	law of **truth** was in his mouth...iniquity...not found
Matt. 5:34(33-37)	but I say unto you, **swear** not at all; neither by
Matt. 26:75(69-75)	before the cock crow, thou shalt **deny** me thrice. and
John 8:44(44-46)	the devil...is a **liar**, and the father of it.
Acts 5:3(1-11)	Satan filled thine heart to **lie** to the Holy Ghost, and
Acts 6:3(1-5)	look ye out among you seven men of **honest** report, full
Rom. 12:17	provide things **honest** in the sight of all men.
Rom. 13:13(7-14)	let us walk **honestly**, as in the day; not in rioting
2 Cor. 4:2(1-2)	have renounced the hidden things of **dishonesty**, not
2 Cor. 8:21(16-22)	providing for **honest** things, not only in the sight of
2 Cor. 13:7(6-8)	ye should do that which is **honest**, though we be as
Eph. 4:25	speak every man **truth** with his neighbour: for we are
Philip. 4:8(8-9)	whatsoever things are **honest**, whatsoever things are
Col. 3:9(9,10)	**lie** not one to another, seeing that ye have put off
1 Thes. 4:12(11,12)	walk **honestly** toward them that are without, and that
1 Tim. 2:2(1-3)	lead a quiet and peaceable life in all...**honesty**.
2 Tim. 3:3(1-7)	**trucebreakers**, false accusers, incontinent, fierce
Heb. 13:18(18-19)	in all things willing to live **honestly**.
1 Pet. 2:12(11-12)	having your conversation **honest** among the Gentiles
1 Ne. 4:37(32-37)	Zoram had made an **oath** unto us, our fears did cease
2 Ne. 2:18	the devil, who is the father of all **lies**, wherefore
2 Ne. 9:34	wo unto the **liar**, for he shall be thrust down to hell.
2 Ne. 28:8(7-9)	**lie** a little, take the advantage of one because of
2 Ne. 33:6	I glory in plainness; I glory in **truth**; I glory in my
Jacob 4:13	for the spirit speaketh the **truth** and lieth not.

HONESTY cont.

Jacob 7:19	I fear...for I have **lied** unto God; for I denied the
Mosiah 4:28	should return the thing that he **borroweth**, according
Alma 1:17	they durst not **lie**...for fear of the law, for liars
Alma 7:20(19,20)	neither doth he **vary** from that which he hath said
Alma 27:27(25-30)	they were perfectly **honest** and upright in all things
Alma 41:14(14-15)	deal **justly**, judge righteously, and do good
Alma 53:11(10,11)	had taken an **oath** that they never would shed blood
Alma 53:20(18-21)	they were men who were **true** at all times in whatsoever
Alma 56:8(7,8)	I would not suffer...they should break this **covenant**
3 Ne. 12:37(33-37)	let your communication be **yea**, yea; nay, nay; for what
Ether 3:12(11-12)	thou art a God of **truth**, and canst not lie.
Moro. 10:4	if ye shall ask with a **sincere** heart, with real intent
D&C 8:1	you shall ask in faith, with an **honest** heart
D&C 10:28(24-29)	wo be unto him that **lieth**...because he supposeth that
D&C 11:10	desire of me in faith, with an **honest** heart, believing
D&C 42:21	thou shalt not **lie**; he that lieth and will not repent
D&C 42:86	shall **lie**,...shall be delivered up unto the law of the
D&C 51:9(9-10)	let every man deal **honestly**, and be alike among this
D&C 62:6	I, the Lord, promise the faithful and cannot **lie**.
D&C 63:17(17,18)	all **liars**...shall have their part in...the second
D&C 64:39	**liars** and hypocrites shall be proved by them, and they
D&C 76:103(98-105)	whosoever loves and makes a **lie**.
D&C 93:25(24-26)	more or less than this is the spirit of...**liar** from
D&C 97:8(7-9)	all...who know their hearts are **honest**...are accepted
D&C 98:10(9-10)	**honest** men and wise men should be sought for
D&C 121:37(34-40)	when we undertake to **cover** our sins, or to gratify
D&C 135:7	will touch the hearts of **honest** men among all nations
D&C 136:20	keep all your **pledges** one with another; and covet not
D&C 136:25	if thou **borrowest** of thy neighbor, thou shalt restore
D&C 136:26(25-26)	find that...neighbor has lost..**deliver** it to him again
Moses 4:4(4-6)	the devil, the father of all **lies**, to deceive and to
Moses 4:6(4-11)	Satan...sought also to **beguile** Eve, for he knew not
Moses 5:24	thou shalt be the father of his **lies**; thou shalt be
JS-H 1:25(24-25)	I had seen a vision...and I could not **deny** it, neither
A of F 1:13	we believe in being **honest**, true, chaste, benevolent

HONOR

Ex. 20:12	**honour** thy father and thy mother: that thy days may
1 Sam. 2:30	them that **honour** me I will honour, and they that
Ps. 96:6(1-6)	**honour** and majesty are before him: strength and beauty
Ps. 111:3	his work is **honourable** and glorious: and his righteous
Prov. 3:9(7-10)	**honour** the Lord with thy substance, and with the first
Prov. 15:33	and before **honour** is humility.
Isa. 42:21	he will magnify the law, and make it **honourable**.
Matt. 15:4(4-6)	**honour** thy father and mother: and, he that curseth
John 5:23	that all men should **honour** the Son, even as they
John 5:41	I receive not **honour** from men.
John 8:54	it is my Father that **honoureth** me; of whom ye say
Rom. 13:7	fear to whom fear; **honour** to whom honour.
1 Ne. 17:55	**honor** thy father and thy mother, that thy days may be
2 Ne. 27:25	and with their lips do **honor** me, but have removed the

HONOR cont.

Mosiah 13:20	honor thy father and thy mother, that thy days may be
Alma 1:16	this they did for the sake of riches and honor.
Alma 60:36	I seek not for honor of the world, but for the glory
D&C 29:36	give me thine honor, which is my power; and also a
D&C 75:5	and crowned with honor, and glory, and immortality
D&C 76:5	delight to honor those who serve me in righteousness
D&C 76:75(75-78)	honorable men of the earth...blinded by the craftiness
D&C 84:102	glory...honor...power...might, be ascribed to our God
D&C 97:19	nations of the earth shall honor her, and shall say
D&C 121:35(34-36)	aspire to the honors of men, that they do not learn
D&C 128:12	herein is glory and honor, and immortality and eternal
D&C 136:39	he might be honored and the wicked might be condemned.
A of F 1:12	We believe in...obeying, honoring, and sustaining the

HONORING FATHER AND MOTHER

Ex. 20:12	honour thy father and thy mother: that thy days may
Ex. 21:17(15,17)	he that curseth his father, or his mother, shall
Deut. 5:16	honour thy father and thy mother, as the Lord thy God
Deut. 21:18(18-21)	son, which will not obey the voice of his father, or
Deut. 27:16	cursed be he that setteth light by his father or his
Ezek. 22:7	in thee have they set light by father and mother: in
Mal. 1:6	if then I be a father, where is mine honour? and if
Mal. 4:6(5,6)	he shall turn the heart of the fathers to the children
Matt. 15:4(4-6)	God commanded, saying, honour thy father and mother
Matt. 19:19	honour thy father and thy mother: and, thou shalt love
Mark 7:10(10-13)	whoso curseth father or mother, let him die the death
Mark 10:19	defraud not, honour thy father and mother.
Luke 18:20	honour thy father and thy mother.
John 8:49	I have not a devil; but I honour my Father, and ye do
John 19:27(25-27)	then saith he to the disciple, behold thy mother! and
Eph. 6:2(1-4)	honour thy father and mother; (which is the first
Col. 3:20(20-21)	children, obey your parents in all things: for this
1 Ne. 1:1	I, Nephi, having been born of goodly parents
1 Ne. 2:16	I did believe...my father; wherefore, I did not rebel
Mosiah 13:20	honor thy father and thy mother, that thy days may be
Alma 56:47(47-48)	did think more upon the liberty of their fathers than
Alma 57:21	they did obey...that their mothers had taught them.
3 Ne. 25:6	heart of the children to their fathers, lest I come
D&C 2:2	the hearts of the children...turn to their fathers.
D&C 19:24	I came by the will of the Father, and I do his will.
D&C 27:9	turning...hearts of the children to the fathers, that
JS-H 1:39	the hearts of the children shall turn to their fathers
JS-H 1:50(49,50)	I obeyed; I returned to my father in the field, and

HOPE

Ps. 33:22(18-22)	thy mercy...be upon us, according as we hope in thee.
Ps. 42:11(5,11)	hope thou in God: for I shall yet praise him, who is
Prov. 10:28	the hope of the righteous shall be gladness: but the
Eccl. 9:4	to him that is joined to all the living there is hope

HOPE cont.

Jer. 17:7(5-8)	blessed is the man...whose **hope** the Lord is.
Lam. 3:26(22-26)	**hope** and quietly wait for the salvation of the Lord.
Joel 3:16	the Lord will be the **hope** of his people, and the
Acts 28:20	for the **hope** of Israel I am bound with this chain.
Rom. 4:18	who against hope believed in **hope**, that he might
Rom. 5:5(2-5)	**hope** maketh not ashamed; because the love of God is
Rom. 8:24(23-25)	for we are saved by **hope**: but hope that is seen is not
Rom. 15:4	through patience and...scriptures might have **hope**.
Rom. 15:13	abound in **hope**, through the power of the Holy Ghost.
1 Cor. 13:13(7,13)	and now abideth faith, **hope**, charity, these three; but
1 Cor. 15:19(16-22)	if in this life only we have **hope** in Christ, we are
Col. 1:23(21-23)	be not moved away from the **hope** of the gospel, which
1 Thes. 5:8	and for an helmet, the **hope** of salvation.
Titus 1:2	in **hope** of eternal life, which God, that cannot lie
Heb. 6:18(11-20)	lay hold upon the **hope** set before us
Heb. 11:1	faith is the substance of things **hoped** for, the
1 Pet. 1:3(1-5)	begotten us again unto a lively **hope** by the
1 Pet. 1:21	that your faith and **hope** might be in God.
1 Pet. 3:15	asketh you a reason of the **hope** that is in you with
1 Jn. 3:3(1-3)	this **hope** in him purifieth himself, even as he is pure
2 Ne. 31:20	having a perfect brightness of **hope**, and a love of God
Jacob 2:19	after ye have obtained a **hope** in Christ ye shall
Jacob 4:4(4-11)	not only we ourselves had a **hope** of his glory, but
Alma 7:24	see that ye have faith, **hope**, and charity, and then
Alma 32:21	ye **hope** for things which are not seen, which are true.
Ether 12:4(3-9)	hope for a better world...which **hope** cometh of faith
Ether 12:32	man must **hope**, or he cannot receive an inheritance in
Moro. 7:40	how...can attain unto faith, save ye shall have **hope**
Moro. 7:41(41-44)	have **hope** through the atonement...and...resurrection
Moro. 8:26	which Comforter filleth with **hope** and perfect love
D&C 4:5	faith, **hope**, charity and love...qualify him for the
D&C 18:19	if you have not faith, **hope**, and charity, you can do
D&C 42:45	those that have not **hope** of a glorious resurrection.
D&C 128:21	giving us consolation...confirming our **hope**
A of F 1:13	we **hope** all things, we have endured many things, and

HOSPITALITY

Gen. 18:4(2-8)	wash your feet, and **rest** yourselves under the tree
Gen. 19:3(1-3)	and entered into his house; and he made them a **feast**
Matt. 10:40(40-42)	he that receiveth you **receiveth** me, and he that
Matt. 25:35	I was a **stranger**, and ye took me in
Luke 19:6(1-10)	haste, and came down, and **received** him joyfully.
Acts 28:2	barbarous people shewed us no little **kindness**: for the
Rom. 12:13	to the necessity of saints; given to **hospitality**.
1 Tim. 3:2	a bishop then must be...given to **hospitality**, apt to
2 Tim. 1:16	for he oft **refreshed** me, and was not ashamed of my
Titus 1:8	but a lover of **hospitality**, a lover of good men, sober
Heb. 13:2	be not forgetful to **entertain** strangers: for thereby
1 Pet. 4:9	use **hospitality** one to another without grudging.
Alma 8:21(19-23)	the man **received** him into his house; and the man was
Alma 10:7(7-10)	thou shalt **receive** him into thy house and feed him

HUMILITY

Deut. 8:2	forty years in the wilderness, to **humble** thee, and to
Deut. 8:3(1-3)	and he **humbled** thee, and suffered thee to hunger, and
2 Chr. 7:14	if my people...shall **humble** themselves, and pray, and
Job 22:29	and he shall save the **humble** person.
Ps. 9:12	he forgetteth not the cry of the **humble**.
Ps. 10:12	lift up thine hand: forget not the **humble**.
Prov. 3:6(5-6)	in all thy ways **acknowledge** him, and he shall direct
Prov. 15:33	and before honour is **humility**.
Prov. 22:4	by **humility** and the fear of the Lord are riches, and
Prov. 27:2	let another man **praise** thee, and not thine own mouth
Prov. 29:23	honour shall uphold the **humble** in spirit.
Isa. 2:11	the lofty looks of man shall be **humbled**, and the
Isa. 57:15	him also that is of a contrite and **humble** spirit, to
Micah 6:8	Lord require of thee, but...to walk **humbly** with thy
Matt. 5:3(1-12)	blessed are the **poor** in spirit: for theirs is the king
Matt. 11:29(28-30)	I am **meek** and lowly in heart: and ye shall find rest
Matt. 18:4(1-4)	whosoever...shall **humble** himself as this little child
Matt. 20:27(20-29)	will be chief among you, let him be your **servant**
Matt. 23:12(5-12)	he that shall **humble** himself shall be exalted.
Luke 14:10(7-11)	when thou art bidden, go and sit...**lowest** room; that
Luke 17:10(7-10)	say, we are **unprofitable** servants: we have done that
John 13:14(4-5,12-17)	ye also ought to **wash** one another's feet.
Acts 20:19	serving the Lord with all **humility** of mind, and with
Rom. 12:3(3-4)	not to **think** of himself more highly than he ought to
2 Cor. 12:10	for when I am **weak**, then am I strong.
Philip. 2:3	let each **esteem** other better than themselves.
Philip. 2:8(5-9)	he **humbled** himself, and became obedient unto death
Col. 2:18	in a voluntary **humility** and worshipping of angels
Col. 3:12	as the elect of God...**humbleness** of mind, meekness
James 4:10(6-10)	**humble** yourselves...and he shall lift you up.
1 Pet. 5:5(5-6)	be clothed with **humility**: for God resisteth the proud
2 Ne. 9:42	come down in the depths of **humility**, he will not open
Mosiah 2:21(21-26)	ye would be **unprofitable** servants.
Mosiah 3:19(18-19)	becometh as a child, submissive, meek, **humble**, patient
Mosiah 4:11(11-12)	humble yourselves even in the depths of **humility**, call
Alma 1:26(26,27)	the teacher...the learner...thus they were all **equal**
Alma 5:27(27-28)	die at this time...been sufficiently **humble**? That your
Alma 32:16(12-16)	**humble** themselves without being compelled to be humble
Alma 38:14	rather say: O Lord, forgive my **unworthiness**, and
Alma 48:20(19-20)	people did **humble** themselves because of their words
Hel. 3:35	did wax stronger and stronger in their **humility**, and
Ether 6:12	did **humble** themselves before the Lord, and did shed
Ether 12:27(26,27)	my grace is sufficient for all men that **humble**
Ether 12:39	he told me in plain **humility**, even as a man telleth
Moro. 7:43(42-44)	save he shall be **meek**, and lowly of heart.
D&C 1:28	inasmuch as they were **humble** they might be made strong
D&C 11:12(11-14)	trust in that spirit which leadeth to...walk **humbly**
D&C 12:8	except he shall be **humble** and full of love, having
D&C 29:2	as will hearken to my voice and **humble** themselves
D&C 56:18(16-20)	hearts are broken, and whose spirits are **contrite**, for
D&C 104:79	and it is my will that you shall **humble** yourselves
D&C 112:10	be thou **humble**; and the Lord thy God shall lead thee
D&C 136:32(32-33)	ignorant learn wisdom by **humbling** himself and calling

HUMILITY cont.

Moses 1:10(9-10)   I know that man is **nothing**, which thing I never had

HYPOCRISY

Job 13:16	an **hypocrite** shall not come before him.
Job 15:34(34-35)	the congregation of **hypocrites** shall be desolate, and
Ps. 28:3	speak peace...but **mischief** is in their hearts.
Isa. 1:13(10-15)	bring no more **vain** oblations ...it is iniquity, even
Isa. 9:17	Lord shall have no joy...for every one is an **hypocrite**
Isa. 10:6(5-6)	I will send him against an **hypocritical** nation, and
Isa. 29:13(13-16)	draw near me with their **mouth**...removed their heart
Isa. 32:6(5-7)	vile person will...practise **hypocrisy**, and to utter
Isa. 58:4(3-8)	ye shall not **fast**...to make your voice to be heard on
Jer. 6:20(19-20)	your burnt offerings are not **acceptable**, nor your
Jer. 9:8	speaketh peaceably...but in **heart** he layeth his wait.
Hosea 8:11(11-14)	Ephraim hath made many altars to **sin**, altars shall be
Amos 5:22(21-24)	though ye **offer** me burnt offerings...I will not accept
Matt. 6:2(1-16)	do not sound a trumpet...as the **hypocrites** do in the
Matt. 7:5(3-5)	thou **hypocrite**, first cast out the beam out of thine
Matt. 7:15(15-20)	come to you in sheep's clothing, but **inwardly** ...
Matt. 7:21(21-23)	not every one that **saith** unto me, Lord...but he that
Matt. 15:8(8-9)	**honoureth** me with their lips; but their heart is far
Matt. 16:3	O ye **hypocrites**, ye can discern the face of the sky
Matt. 21:30(28-31)	he answered and said, I go, sir: and **went** not.
Matt. 23:23(1-36)	woe unto you, scribes and Pharisees, **hypocrites**! for
Mark 7:6(6-9)	people **honoureth** me with their lips, but their heart
Luke 11:39(37-44)	clean the outside...but your **inward** part is full of
Luke 12:1	the leaven of the Pharisees, which is **hypocrisy**.
Rom. 2:21(20-23)	thou...teachest another, **teachest** thou not thyself
Rom. 10:14(13,14)	shall they call on him in whom they have not **believed**
2 Cor. 9:7	let him give; not **grudgingly**, or of necessity: for
1 Tim. 4:2(1-3)	speaking lies in **hypocrisy**; having their conscience
Titus 1:16	**profess**...know God; but in works they deny him, being
James 1:22(22-24)	be ye **doers** of the word, and not hearers only
James 3:10(8-10)	out of the same **mouth** proceedeth blessing and cursing.
2 Ne. 31:13	full purpose of heart, acting no **hypocrisy** and no
Alma 31:27(12-27)	they **cry** unto thee..hearts are swallowed up in..pride.
Alma 34:28(26-29)	prayer is vain..ye are as **hypocrites** who do deny the
Alma 38:13(13,14)	they **pray** to be heard of men, and to be praised for
3 Ne. 13:5(1-6)	**hypocrites**...love to pray...that they may be seen of
3 Ne. 13:16(16-18)	**hypocrites**...disfigure their faces that they may
3 Ne. 14:5(1-5)	thou **hypocrite**, first cast the beam out of thine own
Moro. 7:6(6-11)	except...with real **intent** it profiteth him nothing.
D&C 41:5	he that saith he receiveth it and **doeth** it not, the
D&C 50:8(6-9)	the **hypocrites** shall be detected and shall be cut off
D&C 101:90(90,91)	appoint them their portion among **hypocrites**, and
D&C 112:26(24-26)	you...who have **professed** to know my name and have not
D&C 121:37(34-40)	when we undertake to **cover** our sins, or to gratify
JS-H 1:6	seemingly good feelings...were more **pretended** than
JS-H 1:19	draw near...with their lips, but their **hearts** are far

IDLENESS

Prov. 19:15	and an **idle** soul shall suffer hunger.
Prov. 20:4	**sluggard** will not plow...beg in harvest, and have
Prov. 24:30(29-31)	I went by the field of the **slothful**, and by the
Prov. 31:27(10-31)	she...eateth not the bread of **idleness**.
Eccl. 10:18	through **idleness** of the hands the house droppeth
Ezek. 16:49	Sodom, pride...and abundance of **idleness** was in her
2 Thes. 3:10(10,11)	if any would not **work**, neither should he eat.
1 Tim. 5:13(11-15)	and withal they learn to be **idle**, wandering about from
Heb. 6:12(11,12)	that ye be not **slothful**, but followers of them who
1 Ne. 12:23(19-23)	filthy people, full of **idleness** and all manner of
2 Ne. 5:24(17-24)	they did become an **idle** people, full of mischief and
2 Ne. 9:27(26-27)	wo unto him...that **wasteth** the days of his probation
Alma 24:18(17-19)	rather than...**idleness**...labor abundantly with their
Alma 34:33(32-35)	do not **procrastinate** the day of your repentance until
Alma 38:12(10-12)	see that ye refrain from **idleness**.
D&C 42:42	he that is **idle** shall not eat the bread...of the
D&C 56:17(16-19)	wo unto you...who will not **labor** with your own hands
D&C 58:27(26-29)	anxiously **engaged** in a good cause, and do many things
D&C 60:13(12-13)	thou shalt not **idle** away thy time, neither shalt thou
D&C 68:31(30-32)	not well pleased...for there are **idlers** among them
D&C 72:3(3-4)	required...of every steward, to render an **account** of
D&C 75:3(1-5)	neither be **idle** but labor with your might
D&C 75:29(28-29)	the **idler** shall not have place in the church, except
D&C 88:124	cease to be **idle**; cease to be unclean; cease to find
D&C 90:18	keep **slothfulness** and uncleanness far from you.
D&C 107:100(99,100)	he that is **slothful** shall not be counted worthy to

IDOLATRY

Gen. 31:19	Rachel had stolen the **images** that were her father's.
Gen. 35:2	put away the strange **gods** that are among you, and be
Ex. 20:3(3-4)	thou shalt have no other **gods** before me.
Ex. 32:4(1-6)	made it a molten calf...these be thy **gods**, O Israel
Deut. 4:16	ye corrupt yourselves, and make you a graven **image**
Deut. 4:19	seest the sun ...shouldest be driven to **worship** them
Deut. 4:28(27-28)	there ye shall serve **gods**, the work of men's hands
Deut. 7:5(1-5)	destroy their altars, and break down their **images**, and
Deut. 8:19(19-20)	if thou..walk after other **gods**..ye shall surely perish
Deut. 12:2(2-3)	destroy...places, wherein..nations...served their **gods**
Deut. 28:36(36,64)	there shalt thou serve other **gods**, wood and stone.
Deut. 32:16(16,21)	they provoked him to jealousy with strange **gods**, with
Deut. 32:37	and he shall say, where are their **gods**, their rock in
Josh. 24:2	father of Nachor: and they served other **gods**.
Josh. 24:20(19-20)	if ye...serve strange **gods**...he will...do you hurt
Josh. 24:23	put away, said he, the strange **gods** which are among
Judg. 3:7	forgat...their God, and served Baalim and the **groves**.
Judg. 10:14(10-14)	go and cry unto the **gods** which ye have chosen; let the
1 Sam. 7:3	put away the strange **gods** and Ashtaroth from among you
1 Kgs. 12:28(25-33)	thy **gods**, O Israel, which brought thee up out...Egypt.
1 Kgs. 18:25(17-40)	Elijah said...call on the name of your **gods**, but put
2 Kgs. 21:4	and he built **altars** in the house of the Lord, of which
2 Kgs. 21:7	and he set a graven **image** of the grove that he had

201

IDOLATRY cont.

1 Chr. 16:26	all the gods of the people are **idols**: but the Lord
2 Chr. 11:15(13-15)	he ordained him **priests** for the high places, and for
Ps. 96:5(4-5)	for all the gods of the nations are **idols**: but the
Ps. 106:38(34-40)	sons...daughters...sacrificed unto the **idols** of Canaan
Ps. 135:15(15-18)	the **idols** of the heathen are silver and gold, the work
Isa. 2:8	land also is full of **idols**; they worship the work of
Isa. 2:18	and the **idols** he shall utterly abolish.
Isa. 27:9	the groves and **images** shall not stand up.
Isa. 37:19	cast their gods into the fire: for they were no **gods**
Isa. 45:16(12-20)	go to confusion together...makers of **idols**.
Isa. 57:8(7-8)	thou hast discovered thyself to **another** than me, and
Jer. 1:16	forsaken me, and have burned incense unto other **gods**
Jer. 2:11(5-28)	nation changed their **gods**, which are yet no gods? but
Jer. 2:20	upon...high hill...thou wanderest, playing the **harlot**.
Jer. 3:9(2-20)	committed adultery with **stones** and with stocks.
Jer. 5:19	served strange **gods** in your land, so shall ye serve
Jer. 7:31(31,32)	to **burn** their sons and their daughters in the fire
Jer. 8:2	the sun...whom they have **worshipped**: they shall not
Jer. 10:11	the **gods** that have not made the heavens and the earth
Jer. 10:14	every founder is confounded by the graven **image**: for
Jer. 11:13(12-13)	according to the number of thy cities were thy **gods**
Jer. 16:13	there shall ye serve other **gods** day and night; where
Jer. 16:20	man make Gods unto himself, and they are no **gods**
Jer. 17:2	remember their altars and their **groves** by the green
Jer. 19:4(4-5,13)	they have...burned incense in it unto other **gods**, whom
Ezek. 5:11	defiled my sanctuary with all thy **detestable** things
Ezek. 6:13(3-13)	where they did offer sweet savour to all their **idols**.
Ezek. 7:20	they made the **images** of their abominations and of
Ezek. 8:16(5-16)	and they worshipped the **sun** toward the east.
Ezek. 16:17(15-26)	thou...madest to thyself **images** of men, and didst
Ezek. 20:32(7-32)	as the heathen...to serve **wood** and stone.
Ezek. 23:49(1-49)	ye shall bear the sins of your **idols**: and ye shall
Dan. 5:23	thou hast praised the **gods** of silver, and gold, of
Hosea 1:2	for the land hath committed great **whoredom**, departing
Hab. 2:18	what profiteth the graven **image** that the maker thereof
Zech. 13:2	I will cut off the names of the **idols** out of the land
Matt. 6:24	ye cannot serve God and **mammon**.
Acts 17:16	when he saw the city wholly given to **idolatry**.
Acts 17:29(28,29)	not..think..Godhead is like unto **gold**, or silver, or
1 Cor. 8:4(1-13)	eating of...that are offered in sacrifice unto **idols**
1 Cor. 10:14	wherefore, my dearly beloved, flee from **idolatry**.
1 Cor. 12:2	carried away unto these dumb **idols**, even as ye were
Col. 3:5(5,6)	and covetousness, which is **idolatry**
1 Thes. 1:9	ye turned to God from **idols** to serve the living and
1 Pet. 4:3	revellings, banquetings, and abominable **idolatries**
2 Ne. 9:37	wo unto those that worship **idols**, for the devil of all
2 Ne. 12:8	land is also full of **idols**; they worship the work of
Enos 1:20	Lamanites...full of **idolatry** and filthiness; feeding
Mosiah 9:12	they were a lazy and an **idolatrous** people; therefore
Mosiah 11:7(6,7)	became **idolatrous**, because they were deceived by the
Mosiah 12:35(35,36)	thou shalt have no **other** God before me.
Mosiah 13:12(12,13)	not make unto thee any **graven** image, or any likeness
Mosiah 27:8(2-8)	became a very wicked and an **idolatrous** man. And he was

IDOLATRY cont.

Alma 1:32	who did not belong...indulge...in **idolatry** or
Alma 17:15	many of whom did worship **idols**, and the curse of God
Alma 31:1	bow down to dumb **idols**, his heart again began to
Alma 50:21(21,22)	their **idolatry**, their whoredoms, and their abomination
Hel. 6:31	build up unto themselves **idols** of their gold and their
3 Ne. 21:17(14-21)	thy graven **images** I will also cut off, and thy
Morm. 4:14	did offer them up as **sacrifices** unto their idol gods.
Morm. 4:21	children were again sacrificed unto **idols**.
Ether 7:23	wickedness and **idolatry** of the people was bringing a
D&C 1:16	**image** of his own God...in the likeness of the world
D&C 52:39	that there be no **idolatry** nor wickedness practised.

IGNORANCE

Lev. 4:2(1-35)	if a soul shall sin through **ignorance** against any of
Isa. 1:3(2-4)	ox knoweth his owner...but Israel doth not **know**, my
Jer. 5:4(3-5)	they are foolish: for they **know** not the way of the Lord
Hosea 4:6(1,6)	my people are destroyed for lack of **knowledge**: because
John 4:22(7,20-26)	ye worship ye **know** not what: we know what we worship
Acts 17:23(22-31)	the unknown God. whom therefore ye **ignorantly** worship
Eph. 4:18	alienated from the life of God through the **ignorance**
1 Tim. 1:13(12-14)	I obtained mercy, because I did it **ignorantly** in
2 Tim. 3:7	ever learning, and never able...to the **knowledge** of
Titus 1:16(15-16)	they profess that they **know** God; but in works they
1 Pet. 2:15	ye may put to silence the **ignorance** of foolish men
2 Pet. 3:5(3-9)	for this they willingly are **ignorant** of, that by the
2 Ne. 9:26(25-26)	who have not the **law** given...delivered from...death...
Mosiah 1:3(3-7)	we must have suffered in **ignorance**, even at this
Mosiah 3:11	blood atoneth for...those...who have **ignorantly** sinned
Mosiah 5:13(7-13)	how **knoweth** a man the master whom he has not served
Mosiah 15:24(21-26)	died before Christ came, in their **ignorance**, not
Alma 12:11(9-11)	they **know** nothing concerning his mysteries; and then
3 Ne. 6:12	some were **ignorant** because of their poverty, and
3 Ne. 6:18(17-18)	they did not sin **ignorantly**, for they knew the will
D&C 18:25(21-25)	if they **know** not the name by which they are called
D&C 45:54	they that **knew** no law shall have part in the first
D&C 76:72(71-80)	behold, these are they who died without **law**
D&C 93:32(31-32)	spirit receiveth not the **light** is under condemnation.
D&C 131:6(5-6)	it is impossible for a man to be saved in **ignorance**.
D&C 132:22(21-25)	ye receive me not in the world neither do ye **know** me.
D&C 136:32(32-33)	let him that is **ignorant** learn wisdom by humbling

IMMORTALITY

Gen. 2:9	the tree of **life** also in the midst of the garden, and
Job 19:26(25-27)	yet in my **flesh** shall I see God
Ps. 102:12(11-12)	but thou, O Lord, shalt endure for **ever**; and thy
Ps. 145:13	thy kingdom is an **everlasting** kingdom, and thy
Isa. 9:6(6-7)	the mighty God, the **everlasting** Father, the Prince
Isa. 26:19(12-19)	thy dead men shall **live**, together with my dead body
Dan. 12:2(1-4)	some to **everlasting** life..some to..everlasting

IMMORTALITY cont.

Micah 5:2(1-3)	goings forth have been from of old, from **everlasting**.
Mark 16:6(1-11)	he is **risen**; he is not here: behold the place where
Luke 23:43(39-45)	today shalt thou be with me in **paradise**.
John 4:14(11-14)	well of water springing up into **everlasting** life.
John 5:25	and they that hear shall **live**.
Rom. 2:7(1-10)	for glory and honour and **immortality**, eternal life
1 Cor. 15:22(15-26)	even so in Christ shall all be made **alive**.
1 Cor. 15:29	if the dead **rise** not...why...baptized for the dead
1 Cor. 15:54(35-58)	this mortal shall have put on **immortality**, then shall
1 Thes. 4:17(14-18)	and so shall we **ever** be with the Lord.
1 Thes. 5:10(1-11)	we should **live** together with him.
1 Tim. 1:17	now unto the king eternal, **immortal**, invisible, the
1 Tim. 6:16(15-16)	who only hath **immortality**, dwelling in the light which
2 Tim. 1:10(5-11)	hath brought life and **immortality** to light through the
2 Pet. 1:11	the **everlasting** kingdom of our Lord and Saviour Jesus
Rev. 1:18	I am alive for **evermore**, Amen; and have the keys of
Rev. 22:2(1,2)	the tree of **life**, which bare twelve manner of fruits
2 Ne. 9:13(13-16)	and all men become incorruptible, and **immortal**, and
Enos 1:27	day when my mortal shall put on **immortality**, and shall
Mosiah 16:10(6-12)	even this mortal shall put on **immortality**, and this
Alma 11:45(40-45)	mortal body is raised to an **immortal** body, that is
Alma 12:20	changed from this mortal to an **immortal** state that the
Alma 40:2	does not put on **immortality**...until after...Christ.
Alma 41:4(4-6)	mortality raised to **immortality**, corruption to
3 Ne. 28:8	changed...from mortality to **immortality**; and then
3 Ne. 28:36(36-40)	were cleansed from mortality to **immortality**
D&C 19:10(7-13)	for **Endless** is my name. Wherefore
D&C 20:17(13-19)	God...infinite and **eternal**, from everlasting to
D&C 29:26(26-28)	shall all the dead **awake**, for their graves shall be
D&C 29:43(39-45)	he might be raised in **immortality** unto eternal life
D&C 38:2(1-4)	for all things are **present** before mine eyes
D&C 38:20(17-20)	ye shall possess it again in **eternity**, no more to pass
D&C 43:25(23-27)	would have saved you with an **everlasting** salvation
D&C 45:46(39-61)	shall ye come unto me and your souls shall **live**, and
D&C 56:20(14-20)	their generations shall inherit the earth...**forever**
D&C 63:49(49-52)	rise from the dead and shall not **die** after, and shall
D&C 75:5	crowned with honor, and glory, and **immortality**, and
D&C 76:62(1-119)	dwell in the presence of God and his Christ **forever**
D&C 77:1	earth, in its sanctified, **immortal**, and eternal state.
D&C 81:6(5-7)	thou shalt have a crown of **immortality**, and eternal
D&C 88:32(28-32)	they who remain shall also be **quickened**; nevertheless
D&C 88:97(94-98)	and they who have slept...graves shall come **forth**, for
D&C 88:116(110-116)	they shall not any more see **death**.
D&C 103:27(27-28)	whoso layeth down his **life**...shall find it again.
D&C 109:76(68-80)	and reap **eternal** joy for all our sufferings.
D&C 121:46(41-46)	thy dominion shall be an **everlasting** dominion, and
D&C 128:12(10-13)	is glory and honor, and **immortality** and eternal life
D&C 128:23	proclaiming in our ears ...**immortality**, and eternal
D&C 130:9(7-10)	this earth...**immortal** state, will be made like unto
Moses 1:39(7-42)	my work...glory-to bring to pass the **immortality** and
Moses 6:59	eternal life in the world to come, even **immortal** glory
Moses 6:61(60-62)	the Comforter; the peaceable things of **immortal** glory

INDUSTRY

Gen. 2:2(1-3)	he rested...from all his **work** which he had made.
Gen. 3:19(17-19)	in the **sweat** of thy face shalt thou eat bread, till
Gen. 31:42	hath seen mine affliction and the **labour** of my hands
Ex. 20:9(9-11)	six days shalt thou **labour**, and do all thy work
Ex. 35:31(25-35)	in knowledge, and in all manner of **workmanship**
Prov. 13:11	he that gathereth by **labour** shall increase.
Eccl. 5:12	the sleep of a **labouring** man is sweet, whether he eat
Eccl. 5:18(18,19)	enjoy the good of all his **labour** that he taketh under
Eccl. 9:10	whatsoever thy hand findeth...do it with thy **might**
Luke 5:5	Master, we have **toiled** all the night, and have taken
Luke 13:14	there are six days in which men ought to **work**: in them
Col. 3:23	whatsoever ye do, do it **heartily**, as to the Lord, and
1 Thes. 4:11	do your own business, and to **work** with your own hands
2 Thes. 3:10	if any would not **work**, neither should he eat.
2 Ne. 5:17(11-18)	did cause my people to be **industrious**, and to labor
2 Ne. 26:31	but the **laborer** in Zion shall labor for Zion; for if
Mosiah 2:14	have **labored** with mine own hands that I might serve
Mosiah 13:17	six days shalt thou **labor**, and do all thy work
Mosiah 18:24	priests whom he had ordained should **labor** with their
Mosiah 23:5	they were **industrious**, and did labor exceedingly.
Mosiah 27:4	his neighbor as himself, **laboring** with their own hands
Alma 1:26	they all returned again diligently unto their **labors**
Alma 4:6	precious things...they had obtained by their **industry**
Alma 10:4	acquired much riches by the hand of my **industry**.
Alma 23:18	they began to be a very **industrious** people; yea, and
Alma 24:18	rather than spend...days in idleness they would **labor**
Alma 30:34(32-35)	we do not receive anything for our **labors** in the
Alma 32:5	which we have **labored** abundantly to build with our own
Alma 34:32	this life is the day for men to perform their **labors**.
Hel. 6:11	did **work** all kinds of ore and did refine it; and thus
Ether 2:16	go to **work** and build, after the manner of barges which
Ether 10:22(22-27)	they were exceedingly **industrious**, and they did buy
D&C 23:7	you may receive the reward of the **laborer**. Amen.
D&C 26:1	be devoted...to performing your **labors** on the land
D&C 31:5	for the **laborer** is worthy of his hire. Wherefore, your
D&C 38:40	go to with his might, with the **labor** of his hands, to
D&C 42:40	the beauty of the **work** of thine own hands
D&C 52:39	let them **labor** with their own hands that there be no
D&C 58:27(27,28)	men should be **anxiously** engaged in a good cause, and
D&C 68:30	Zion also shall remember their **labors**, inasmuch as the
D&C 75:3	neither be idle but **labor** with your might
D&C 82:18(18-19)	that every man may **improve** upon his talent, that every
D&C 109:78	dedication of this house...the **work** of our hands
D&C 115:10(10-12)	let my people **labor** diligently to build a house unto
D&C 124:121(121-122	recompense of wages for all their **labors** which they
D&C 126:2	I have seen your **labor** and toil in journeyings for my
JS-H 1:23	maintenance by his daily **labor**, should be thought a
JS-H 1:55	under the necessity of **laboring** with our hands, hiring
JS-H 1:58	went to my father's, and **farmed** with him that season.

INGRATITUDE

Gen. 40:23(1-23)	did...the chief butler remember Joseph, but **forgat** him
Ex. 17:3(2,3)	the people **murmured** against Moses, and said
Num. 16:2(1-50)	and they **rose** up before Moses, with certain of the
Deut. 8:14(10-20)	thine heart be lifted up, and thou **forget** the Lord thy
Deut. 32:6(4-6)	do ye thus **requite** the Lord, O foolish people and
Deut. 32:15	then he **forsook** God which made him, and lightly
1 Kgs. 11:6(1-6)	**Solomon** did evil in the sight of the Lord, and went
Hosea 11:7(1-12)	and my people are bent to **backsliding** from me: though
Mal. 3:8(8-10)	**will** a man rob God? yet ye have robbed me. But ye say
Matt. 18:33(23-35)	**shouldest** not thou also have had compassion...as I had
Luke 6:35(32-35)	he is kind unto the **unthankful** and to the evil.
Luke 17:10	we are **unprofitable** servants: we have done that which
Luke 17:17(11-19)	were...not ten cleansed? but where are the **nine**
Rom. 1:21	they glorified him not...neither were **thankful**; but
2 Tim. 3:2	disobedient to parents, **unthankful**, unholy
2 Ne. 29:4(4,5)	and what **thank** they the Jews for the Bible which they
Mosiah 2:19(19-21)	O how you ought to **thank** your heavenly King
Alma 38:14(13-15)	yea, acknowledge your **unworthiness** before God at all
D&C 46:32	and ye must give **thanks** unto God in the Spirit for
D&C 59:21	wrath kindled...those who **confess** not his hand in all

INHERITANCE

Gen. 31:14	is there yet any portion or **inheritance** for us in our
Gen. 48:22	I have given to thee one **portion** above thy brethren
Ex. 34:9	pardon...sin, and take us for thine **inheritance**.
Num. 18:24(20-24)	Levites...shall have no **inheritance**.
Deut. 4:20	to be unto him a people of **inheritance**, as ye are this
Deut. 9:26(25-29)	Lord...destroy not thy people and thine **inheritance**
Deut. 9:29	yet they are thy people and thine **inheritance**, which
Deut. 32:9	Jacob is the lot of his **inheritance**.
Josh. 13:33(15-33)	tribe of Levi...the Lord God...was their **inheritance**
Josh. 19:51	**inheritances** which Eleazar...and Joshua...divided for
1 Kgs. 8:51	for they be thy people, and thine **inheritance**, which
1 Kgs. 21:3(3-4)	give the **inheritance** of my fathers unto thee.
Job 31:2	and what **inheritance** of the Almighty from on high
Ps. 37:18	the upright...their **inheritance** shall be for ever.
Acts 20:32	an **inheritance** among all them which are sanctified.
Gal. 3:18(17,18)	if the **inheritance** be of the law...no more of promise
Eph. 1:18(11,14,18)	riches of the glory of his **inheritance** in the saints
Eph. 5:5	no...unclean person...hath any **inheritance** in the
Col. 3:24(23,24)	ye shall receive the reward of the **inheritance**: for
Heb. 9:15(14,15)	receive the promise of eternal **inheritance**.
2 Ne. 1:9	none...to take away the land of their **inheritance**; and
2 Ne. 10:7(7-8)	shall be restored...unto...lands of their **inheritance**.
Alma 5:58	unto them will I grant an **inheritance** at my right hand
D&C 52:5	be made known unto them the land of your **inheritance**.
D&C 63:20	he that endureth...shall receive an **inheritance** upon
D&C 101:18(6,18)	pure in heart, shall...come to their **inheritances**
D&C 104:24	land...obtained in exchange for his former **inheritance**

INITIATIVE

Ex. 25:2	every man that giveth it **willingly** with his heart ye
Ex. 35:21(5,21,29)	they came...every one whom his spirit made **willing**
Lev. 1:3	offer it of his own **voluntary** will at the door of the
1 Chr. 29:9(6,9,14,17)	with perfect heart they offered **willingly** to the Lord
1 Cor. 9:17(16-18)	for if I do this thing **willingly**, I have a reward: but
1 Pet. 5:2	feed...flock of God...not by constraint, but **willingly**
2 Ne. 2:16	God gave unto man that he should **act** for himself.
2 Ne. 2:27	free to **choose** liberty and eternal life, through the
Mosiah 18:28	impart of their substance of their own free **will** and
Alma 32:16(12-16)	blessed..who humble themselves without being **compelled**
D&C 29:36(36,37)	turned he away from me because of their **agency**
D&C 42:52	have **power** to become my sons; and inasmuch as they
D&C 44:4	shall obtain **power** to organize yourselves according
D&C 50:35(34,35)	**power** to overcome all things which are not ordained
D&C 58:26(26-29)	he that is **compelled** in all things...not a wise
D&C 123:17	let us cheerfully **do** all things that lie in our power

INJUSTICE

Ex. 23:6(6-9)	thou shalt not **wrest** the judgment of thy poor in his
Job 27:13(13-23)	portion of a wicked man...the heritage of **oppressors**
Ps. 94:20(20-23)	iniquity...which frameth **mischief** by a law
Prov. 17:15	he that **justifieth** the wicked, and...condemneth the
Prov. 21:15(12-15)	destruction shall be to the workers of **iniquity**.
Isa. 5:23(20-24)	which **justify** the wicked...and take away the righteous
Isa. 10:1(1-3)	woe unto them that decree **unrighteous** decrees...write
Matt. 23:14	woe unto you..hypocrites! for ye **devour** widows' houses
Luke 18:6(1-8)	the Lord said, hear what the **unjust** judge saith.
Acts 7:26(24-28)	ye are brethren; why do ye **wrong** one to another
1 Cor. 6:8(6-10)	ye do wrong, and **defraud**...your brethren.
Col. 3:25	he that doeth **wrong** shall receive for the wrong which
1 Pet. 3:18(14-18)	Christ...once suffered for sins...just for the **unjust**
2 Ne. 20:1(1-3)	wo unto them that decree **unrighteous** decrees, and that
Mosiah 4:13(11-16)	ye will not have a mind to **injure** one another, but to
Mosiah 10:12(9-17)	believing...they were **wronged** in the wilderness by the
Mosiah 29:32(13,21-32)	desire that this **inequality**...be no more in this land
Alma 10:27	laid by the **unrighteousness** of your lawyers and your
Alma 12:8(8-18)	all shall rise...both the just and the **unjust**, and are
Alma 42:1(1-28)	**injustice** that the sinner...be consigned to...misery.
Alma 54:17(13-18)	your fathers did **wrong** their brethren, insomuch that
Alma 55:19(16-22)	for this cause he might not bring upon him **injustice**
Alma 61:6(6-7)	they are flocking to us daily...to avenge our **wrongs**.
Moro. 7:18(15-19)	see that ye do not judge **wrongfully**; for with that
D&C 76:17(15-17)	they who have done evil...resurrection of the **unjust**
D&C 101:81(76,81-92	the parable of the woman and the **unjust** judge, for men
D&C 101:90(81-92)	cut off those wicked, unfaithful, and **unjust** stewards
D&C 102:15(12-23)	one-half...the council, to prevent insult or **injustice**
D&C 104:7(1-13)	that the innocent...not be condemned with the **unjust**
D&C 105:25(24-25)	execute..justice for us...and redress us of our **wrongs**
D&C 123:2(1-15)	damages...both of character and personal **injuries**, as
D&C 134:11	appeal...for redress of all **wrongs** and grievances
D&C 134:12	such interference we believe to be unlawful and **unjust**

INJUSTICE cont.

JS-H 1:25(24-25)   speaking all manner of evil against me **falsely** for so
JS-H 1:61(60-61)   circulating **falsehoods** about my father's family, and

INSPIRATION

1 Kgs. 19:12(11-13)   and after the fire a still small **voice**.
Job 32:8   **inspiration** of the Almighty giveth them understanding.
Dan. 4:18(8,18)   thou art able; for the **spirit** of the holy gods is in
Dan. 5:11(11,14)   a man...in whom is the **spirit** of the holy gods; and
John 14:26   Comforter...shall **teach** you all things, and bring all
John 16:13   Spirit of truth...will **guide** you into all truth: for
1 Cor. 12:3   say that Jesus is the Lord, but by the **Holy** Ghost.
Gal. 5:22(22,23)   fruit of the **Spirit** is love, joy, peace, longsuffering
2 Tim. 3:16(16-17)   all scripture is given by **inspiration** of God, and is
2 Pet. 1:21(20-21)   holy men...spake as they were **moved** by the Holy Ghost.
1 Ne. 4:6   I was **led** by the Spirit, not knowing beforehand
Enos 1:10(4,5,10)   the voice of the Lord came into my **mind** again, saying
Jarom 1:4   not stiffnecked...have **communion** with the Holy Spirit
3 Ne. 6:20   there began to be men **inspired** from heaven and sent
Moro. 7:13   to do good, and to love God...is **inspired** of God.
D&C 8:2(2-3)   I will tell you in your mind and in your **heart**, by the
D&C 9:8(8-9)   if...right I will cause that your bosom shall **burn**
D&C 11:13(12-14)   Spirit..shall **enlighten** your mind..fill..soul with joy
D&C 20:11(10-11,26)   God does **inspire** men and call them to his holy work
D&C 21:2(2,7)   being **inspired** of the Holy Ghost to lay the foundation
D&C 43:16(15,16)   and ye are to be **taught** from on high. Sanctify
D&C 85:6   still small **voice**...whispereth through and pierceth
Moses 6:5   as many as called upon God to write by...**inspiration**

INTEGRITY

Gen. 6:9   Noah was a just man and **perfect** in his generations
Gen. 17:1   walk before me, and be thou **perfect**.
Gen. 20:5(1-14)   in the **integrity** of my heart and innocency of my hands
Num. 30:2(1-16)   if a man vow a vow...he shall not **break** his word, he
1 Kgs. 9:4(4-5)   walk...in **integrity** of heart, and in uprightness, to
Job 2:3   still he holdeth fast his **integrity**, although thou
Job 27:5(1-10)   till I die I will not remove mine **integrity** from me.
Job 31:6(6-34)   that God may know mine **integrity**.
Prov. 11:3(3,5,6)   the **integrity** of the upright shall guide them: but the
Prov. 20:7   the just man walketh in his **integrity**: his children
James 1:8(6-8)   a **double** minded man is unstable in all his ways.
2 Ne. 31:13   acting no hypocrisy...but with real **intent**, repenting
Alma 24:19(17-19)   were **firm**...suffer even unto death rather than commit
Alma 53:20(10-23)   they were men who were **true** at all times in whatsoever
D&C 108:3(1-3)   more careful henceforth in observing your **vows**, which
D&C 124:15   Lord, love him because of the **integrity** of his heart
D&C 124:20   may be trusted because of the **integrity** of his heart
JS-H 1:25(23-25)   I knew it...God knew it...I could not **deny** it, neither
A of F 1:13   we believe in being **honest**, true, chaste, benevolent

INTELLIGENCE

1 Sam. 2:3	for the Lord is a God of **knowledge,** and by him actions
Prov. 3:5	lean not unto thine own **understanding**.
Isa. 55:8(8-9)	for my **thoughts** are not your thoughts, neither are
John 1:9(6-9)	that was the true **light,** which lighteth every man that
2 Cor. 4:6	to give the **light** of the knowledge of the glory of God
Alma 19:6	the **light** which did light up his mind, which was the
Alma 32:28(28,34)	it beginneth to enlighten my **understanding,** yea, it
D&C 82:3	he who sins against the greater **light** shall receive
D&C 84:46(45-46)	the Spirit giveth **light** to every man that cometh into
D&C 88:40	**intelligence** cleaveth unto intelligence; wisdom
D&C 93:29	**intelligence**...was not created or made, neither
D&C 93:30	all truth is independent...**intelligence** also
D&C 93:36	the glory of God is **intelligence,** or,...light and
D&C 130:18(18-19)	whatever principle of **intelligence** we attain unto in
Abr. 3:19(18-19)	I am the Lord...I am more **intelligent** than they all.
Abr. 3:21	I rule...over all the **intelligences** thine eyes have
Abr. 3:22(21-22)	shown unto me...the **intelligences** that were organized

ISRAEL, BLESSINGS OF

Gen. 12:2(2,3)	I will make of thee a great **nation,** and I will bless
Gen. 13:16(14-17)	I will make thy **seed** as the dust of the earth: so that
Gen. 17:6(1-8)	I will make **nations** of thee, and kings shall come out
Gen. 27:29(26-29)	let people **serve** thee, and nations bow down to thee
Gen. 28:14(12-15)	in thy seed...all the families of the earth be **blessed**
Gen. 35:11(9-12)	a company of **nations** shall be of thee, and kings shall
Gen. 48:17(15-20)	father laid his right hand upon the head of **Ephraim**
Gen. 49:28(1-28)	the twelve tribes..every one according to his **blessing**
Ex. 19:5(5-6)	if ye will obey...ye shall be a...**treasure** unto me
Lev. 26:12(3-13)	I...will be your God, and ye shall be my **people**.
Deut. 4:6(5-8)	this is your **wisdom** and your understanding in the
Deut. 7:6(6-8)	the Lord..hath **chosen** thee to be a special people unto
Deut. 26:19(16-19)	an **holy** people unto the Lord thy God, as he hath
Deut. 28:2(1-14)	all these **blessings** shall come...if thou shalt hearken
Isa. 35:1(1-10)	the desert shall rejoice, and **blossom** as the rose.
Isa. 49:6(5,6)	I will also give thee for a **light** to the Gentiles
Isa. 66:22	so shall your **seed** and your name remain.
Ezek. 34:26(22-30)	there shall be showers of **blessing**.
Zech. 8:13(11-15)	as ye were a curse...ye shall be a **blessing:** fear not
Mal. 3:10	windows of heaven, and pour you out a **blessing,** that
Rom. 9:27(24-29)	**Israel** be as the sand of the sea, a remnant shall be
Rom. 11:2	God hath not cast away his **people** which he foreknew.
Gal. 3:9(7-9)	they which be of faith are **blessed** with...Abraham.
1 Pet. 2:9	a royal priesthood, an **holy** nation, a peculiar people
Rev. 7:4(2-8)	forty and four thousand of...the children of **Israel**.
1 Ne. 20:18(18-19)	then had thy **peace** been as a river, and thy
2 Ne. 8:3(1-3)	the Lord...will make her **wilderness** like Eden, and her
3 Ne. 5:21(21-26)	he hath **blessed** the house of Jacob..merciful unto the
3 Ne. 20:26(26-27)	**bless** you..because ye are the children of the covenant
3 Ne. 22:10(7-10)	my **kindness** shall not depart from thee, neither shall
D&C 3:16(16-20)	**knowledge** of a Savior has come unto the world, through
D&C 35:25	**Israel** shall be saved in mine own due time; and by the

ISRAEL, BLESSINGS OF cont.

D&C 133:34(16-35)	the **blessing** of...God upon the tribes of Israel, and
D&C 133:34(25-35)	this is the **blessing**...upon the tribes of Israel, and
Abr. 2:10(8-11)	I will **bless** them through thy name; for as many as

ISRAEL, BONDAGE OF, IN EGYPT

Gen. 15:13(13-16)	thy seed shall be a **stranger**...four hundred years
Gen. 15:16	but in the **fourth** generation they shall come hither
Gen. 28:15	and will **bring** thee again into this land; for I will
Gen. 46:3(3-7)	fear not to go down into **Egypt**; for I will there make
Gen. 48:21	God shall...**bring** you again unto the land of your
Gen. 50:24(24-25)	God will...**bring** you out of this land unto the land
Ex. 1:14(7-14)	they made their lives bitter with hard **bondage**, in
Ex. 3:7(7-8)	the affliction of my people which are in **Egypt**, and
Ex. 12:40	**sojourning**...in Egypt...four hundred and thirty years
Ex. 20:2	I...brought thee out of...Egypt...the house of
Acts 7:6(6,7)	bring them into **bondage**, and entreat them evil four
Gal. 3:17	covenant...was **four** hundred and thirty years after
1 Ne. 17:25(23-25)	Israel were in **bondage**; and ye know that they were
Alma 36:2(1,2)	captivity of our fathers; for they were in **bondage**
Moses 1:26	thou shalt deliver my people from **bondage**, even Israel

ISRAEL, BONDAGE OF, IN OTHER LANDS

2 Kgs. 15:29(28-29)	king of Assyria...carried them captive to **Assyria**.
2 Kgs. 24:15(10-16)	carried he into **captivity** from Jerusalem to Babylon.
2 Kgs. 25:7	Zedekiah, and bound him...and carried him to **Babylon**.
2 Chr. 36:10(9,10)	Nebuchadnezzar sent, and brought him to **Babylon**, with
2 Chr. 36:20(14-21)	carried he away to **Babylon**; where they were servants
Isa. 48:20	flee ye from the **Chaldeans**, with a voice of singing
Jer. 21:7(3-7)	deliver Zedekiah...into the hand of...king of **Babylon**
Jer. 25:9(8-11)	king of **Babylon**...will bring them against this land
Jer. 32:5	and he shall lead Zedekiah to **Babylon**, and there shall
Jer. 34:3(3-4)	thou shalt not escape...and thou shalt go to **Babylon**.
Jer. 50:8(8,9)	go forth out of the land of the **Chaldeans**, and be as
Jer. 52:11(8-11)	put out the eyes of Zedekiah...carried him to **Babylon**
Ezek. 1:1(1-3)	I was among the **captives** by the river of Chebar, that
Ezek. 12:13	and I will bring him to **Babylon** to the land of the
Ezek. 17:16	with him in the midst of **Babylon** he shall die.
Ezek. 17:20	and I will bring him to **Babylon**, and will plead with
Dan. 1:1(1-2)	third year of the reign of **Jehoiakim**...came
Dan. 9:2(2-27)	seventy years in the **desolations** of Jerusalem.
Matt. 1:11	they were carried away to **Babylon**
Luke 21:24	led away **captive** into all nations: and Jerusalem
1 Ne. 1:4(4,18)	prophesying...**Jerusalem** must be destroyed.
1 Ne. 10:3	and many be carried away **captive** into Babylon
1 Ne. 10:12(12,14)	**branches** should be broken off and should be scattered
1 Ne. 19:14(13,14)	wander in the flesh...**hiss** and a by-word, and be hated
1 Ne. 20:20	flee ye from the **Chaldeans**, with a voice of singing
2 Ne. 6:8	those...at Jerusalem...have been slain and **carried**
2 Ne. 10:6(5,6)	who shall not be destroyed shall be **scattered** among

ISRAEL, BONDAGE OF, IN OTHER LANDS cont.

2 Ne. 25:15(14-17)	the Jews shall be **scattered** among all nations; yea
Jacob 5:14(13,14)	natural **branches** of the tame olive-tree in the
1:15(14-16)	Zedekiah, king...was carried away **captive** into Babylon
D&C 133:26(26-33)	they who are in the **north** countries shall come in

ISRAEL, DELIVERANCE OF

Ex. 3:8	to **deliver** them out of the hand of the Egyptians, and
Ex. 4:31	the Lord had...looked upon their **affliction**, then they
Ex. 14:30(19-30)	thus the Lord **saved** Israel that day out of the hand
Ps. 66:6	he turned the **sea** into dry land: they went through the
Isa. 5:29(28-30)	they shall roar like young **lions**: yea, they shall roar
Isa. 63:11(10-14)	brought them up out of the **sea** with the shepherd of
Ezek. 20:6(5-10)	I lifted up mine hand...to **bring** them forth of the
Micah 5:8(4-15)	remnant...shall be among the Gentiles...as a **lion** among
1 Cor. 10:1(1-4)	all passed through the **sea**
Heb. 11:29	passed through the Red **sea** as by dry land: which the
1 Ne. 14:2(1-2)	Israel shall no more be **confounded**.
1 Ne. 17:26	the waters of the Red **Sea** were divided hither and
Hel. 8:11	waters of the Red **Sea**, and they parted hither and
3 Ne. 20:16(13-19)	remnant...shall be among them as a **lion** among the
D&C 8:3	children of Israel through the Red **Sea** on dry ground.
D&C 35:25	Israel shall be **saved** in mine own due time; and by the
D&C 122:4	more terrible in...thine enemies than the fierce **lion**
Moses 1:26	thou shalt **deliver** my people from bondage, even

ISRAEL, GATHERING OF

Deut. 4:29(27-31)	but if...thou shalt seek the Lord...thou shalt **find**
Deut. 30:3(1-5)	the Lord...will...**gather** thee from all the nations
Isa. 5:26(26-30)	he will lift up an ensign...and...they shall **come** with
Isa. 6:13	yet in it shall be a tenth, and it shall **return**, and
Isa. 10:22(20-22)	yet a remnant of them shall **return**: the consumption
Isa. 11:11(11-12)	**recover** the remnant...from the islands of the sea.
Isa. 27:12(10-13)	shall be **gathered** one by one, O ye children of Israel.
Isa. 35:10(8-10)	the ransomed of the Lord shall **return**, and come to
Isa. 43:5(5-7)	I will **bring** thy seed from the east, and gather thee
Isa. 49:18(18-26)	all these **gather** themselves together, and come to the
Isa. 51:11(9-11)	the redeemed of the Lord shall **return**...unto Zion; and
Isa. 54:7	with great mercies will I **gather** thee.
Isa. 56:8(7-8)	the Lord God which **gathereth** the outcasts of Israel
Jer. 3:17(12-18)	all the nations shall be **gathered** unto...Jerusalem
Jer. 12:15	I will...have compassion...and will **bring** them again
Jer. 16:15(13-18)	**brought**...Israel from the...north, and from all the
Jer. 23:3(1-8)	and I will **gather** the remnant of my flock out of all
Jer. 29:14	I will **gather** you from all the nations, and from all
Jer. 30:3	I will cause them to **return** to the land that I gave
Jer. 31:10(1-14)	he that scattered Israel will **gather** him, and keep him
Jer. 32:37(36-41)	behold, I will **gather** them out of all countries
Jer. 50:4(4-5)	the children of Israel shall **come**, they and the
Jer. 50:19(17-20)	I will **bring** Israel again to his habitation, and he

ISRAEL, GATHERING OF cont.

Ezek. 11:17(16-18)	I will even **gather** you from the people, and assemble
Ezek. 20:41(40-44)	**gather** you out of the countries wherein...scattered
Ezek. 28:25(25-26)	**gathered** the house of Israel from the people among who
Ezek. 34:12(11-16)	as a shepherd...so will I **seek** out my sheep, and will
Ezek. 36:24(24-38)	I will...**gather** you out of all countries, and will
Ezek. 37:12(9-14)	I will...**bring** you into the land of Israel.
Ezek. 37:21(21-28)	will **gather** them on every side, and bring them into
Ezek. 39:27(25-29)	**gathered** them out of their enemies' lands, and am
Hosea 1:11(10-11)	children of Judah and...Israel be **gathered** together
Joel 2:32	the remnant whom the Lord shall **call**.
Amos 9:14(14-15)	will bring again the captivity of my people of **Israel**
Micah 4:6(6-8)	I will **gather** her that is driven out, and her that I
Zeph. 3:19(18-20)	I will...**gather** her that was driven out; and I will
Zech. 10:8(6-12)	I will hiss for them, and **gather** them; for I have
Zech. 12:6(6-7)	Jerusalem shall be **inhabited** again in her own place
Matt. 23:37(37-39)	how often would I have **gathered** thy children together
John 11:52(51-52)	he should **gather**...the children of God that were
Eph. 1:10	dispensation of the fulness of times he might **gather**
1 Ne. 10:14	scattered they should be **gathered** together again; or
1 Ne. 19:16(15-17)	the house of Israel, will I **gather** in, saith the Lord
1 Ne. 21:18(18-26)	all these **gather** themselves together, and they shall
1 Ne. 22:12(10-12)	they shall be **gathered** together to the lands of their
1 Ne. 22:25(24,25)	**gathereth** his children from the four quarters of the
2 Ne. 6:11(6-11)	they shall be **gathered** together again to the lands
2 Ne. 8:11(9-11)	therefore, the redeemed of the Lord shall **return**, and
2 Ne. 9:2	when they shall be **gathered** home to the lands of their
2 Ne. 10:8(7-8)	they shall be **gathered** in...from the isles of the sea
2 Ne. 15:26	they shall **come** with speed swiftly; none shall be
2 Ne. 20:22(21-22)	yet a remnant of them shall **return**; the consumption
2 Ne. 21:12(11-16)	**gather** together the dispersed of Judah from the four
2 Ne. 25:17(10-18)	Lord will set his hand again...to **restore** his people
2 Ne. 29:1(1-2)	I shall...do a marvelous work...to **recover** my people
2 Ne. 30:7(7-8)	Jews...shall begin to **gather** in upon the face of the
Jacob 6:2	the second time to **recover** his people, is the day, yea
3 Ne. 5:24(24-26)	**gather** in...all the remnant of the seed of Jacob, who
3 Ne. 16:5(5-7)	then will I **gather** them in from the four quarters of
3 Ne. 20:13(11-18)	then shall the remnants...be **gathered** in from the east
3 Ne. 20:29(29-35)	I have covenanted...that I would **gather** them together
3 Ne. 21:24(22-29)	assist my people that they may be **gathered** in, who are
D&C 10:65	I will **gather** them as a hen gathereth her chickens
D&C 29:7(7-8)	called to bring to pass the **gathering** of mine elect
D&C 42:9(8-9)	that ye may be **gathered** in one, that ye may be my
D&C 45:9	**standard** for my people, and for the Gentiles to seek
D&C 45:25(24-25)	but they shall be **gathered** again; but they shall
D&C 77:14	little book..a mission..to **gather** the tribes of Israel
D&C 110:11	committed unto us the keys of the **gathering** of Israel
D&C 133:14	go ye out from among the **nations**, even from Babylon
D&C 133:27(23-31)	**highway** shall be cast up in the midst of the great
Moses 7:62(62-63)	to **gather** out mine elect from the four quarters of the
JS-M 1:27(27,37)	mine elect be **gathered** from the four quarters of the
A of F 1:10	we believe in the literal **gathering** of Israel...ten

ISRAEL, JOSEPH, PEOPLE OF

Gen. 30:24(22-24)	and she called his name **Joseph**; and said, the Lord
Gen. 37:3(1-36)	Israel loved **Joseph** more than all his children
Gen. 41:51	Joseph called...the firstborn **Manasseh**: for God, said
Gen. 41:52(50-52)	and the name of the second called he **Ephraim**: for God
Gen. 48:5(1-22)	and now thy two sons, **Ephraim** and Manasseh, which were
Gen. 48:14(14-20)	Israel stretched...right hand...upon **Ephraim's** head
Gen. 48:16(16-19)	bless the lads; and let my **name** be named on them, and
Gen. 48:19(18-20)	his seed shall become a multitude of **nations**.
Gen. 49:26(22-26)	blessings...on the head of **Joseph**, and on the crown
Gen. 50:22(22-26)	and **Joseph** dwelt in Egypt, he, and his father's house
Num. 1:32(32-35)	the children of **Joseph**, namely...of Ephraim, by their
Num. 1:35(34-35)	tribe of **Manasseh**, were thirty and two thousand and
Num. 32:39(39-42)	the children of Machir the son of **Manasseh** went to
Deut. 33:17(13-17)	ten thousands of **Ephraim**...thousands of Manasseh.
Josh. 16:1(1-10)	the lot of the children of **Joseph** fell from Jordan by
2 Kgs. 17:6(6-18)	carried **Israel** away into Assyria, and placed them in
1 Chr. 5:1	Reuben...birthright was given unto the sons of **Joseph**
1 Chr. 7:29(14-29)	in these dwelt the children of **Joseph** the son of
Isa. 7:8(4-9)	shall **Ephraim** be broken, that it be not a people.
Isa. 7:17(16-20)	from the day that **Ephraim** departed from Judah; even
Isa. 17:3(3-7)	the fortress also shall cease from **Ephraim**, and the
Ezek. 37:16(16-21)	take another stick, and write upon it, for **Joseph**, the
John 4:5	ground that Jacob gave to his son **Joseph**.
John 10:16	and other **sheep** I have, which are not of this fold
Acts 7:14(9-14)	then sent **Joseph**, and called his father Jacob to him
Heb. 11:22(21,22)	**Joseph**...gave commandment concerning his bones.
Rev. 7:8	of the tribe of **Joseph** were sealed twelve thousand.
1 Ne. 5:14(14-16)	Lehi...was a descendant of **Joseph**; yea, even that
1 Ne. 13:34	this **remnant** of whom I speak is the seed of thy father
1 Ne. 15:12(12-17)	are we not a **branch** of the house of Israel
2 Ne. 3:5(3-5,18-24)	a **branch** which was to be broken off, nevertheless, to
2 Ne. 19:21	**Ephraim**, Manasseh; they together shall be against
Jacob 2:25	righteous branch from the fruit of the loins of **Joseph**
Alma 10:3	a descendant of Manasseh, who was the son of **Joseph**
Alma 46:23(23-27)	we are a remnant of the seed of **Joseph**, whose coat was
3 Ne. 10:17	are not we a remnant of the seed of **Joseph**? And these
3 Ne. 15:12(12-13)	this people, who are a remnant of the house of **Joseph**.
3 Ne. 20:22	this **people** will I establish in this land, unto the
Ether 13:6(6-10)	New Jerusalem...unto the remnant of the seed of **Joseph**
D&C 3:19(16-20)	promises...be fulfilled, which he made to his **people**
D&C 10:60	other sheep...were a **branch** of the house of Jacob
D&C 27:5	keys of the record of the stick of **Ephraim**
D&C 113:4	descendant of Jesse as well as of **Ephraim**, or of the
D&C 133:32(30-35)	servants of the Lord, even the children of **Ephraim**.

ISRAEL, JUDAH, PEOPLE OF

Gen. 29:35	therefore she called his name **Judah**; and left bearing.
Gen. 49:8(8-10)	**Judah**...thy father's children shall bow down before
Gen. 49:10(8-12)	sceptre shall not depart from **Judah**, nor a lawgiver
Deut. 33:7	this is the blessing of **Judah**: and he said, hear, Lord
2 Sam. 2:11	David was king in Hebron over the house of **Judah** was

2 Kgs. 17:18(18-20)	there was none left but the tribe of **Judah** only.
1 Chr. 5:2(1,2)	**Judah** prevailed above his brethren, and of him came
1 Chr. 6:15	the Lord carried away **Judah** and Jerusalem by the hand
1 Chr. 28:4	he hath chosen **Judah** to be the ruler; and of the house
Isa. 1:1	vision of Isaiah...concerning **Judah** and Jerusalem in
Isa. 7:17	from the day that Ephraim departed from **Judah**; even
Isa. 11:13(12-16)	Ephraim shall not envy **Judah**, and Judah shall not vex
Isa. 40:9	say unto the cities of **Judah**, behold your God
Jer. 29:14	and I will **gather** you from all the nations, and from
Jer. 31:31	I will make a new covenant with the house of **Israel**
Ezek. 37:16(15-17)	one stick...for **Judah**, and for...his companions: then
Zech. 2:12	Lord shall inherit **Judah** his portion in the holy land
Matt. 1:2	Jacob begat **Judas** and his brethren
Matt. 2:6	thou Bethlehem, in the land of **Juda**, art not the least
Luke 3:33	Phares, which was the son of **Juda**
Heb. 7:14	our Lord sprang out of **Juda**; of which tribe Moses
Heb. 8:8(8-12)	new covenant...with the house of **Judah**
Rev. 5:5	behold, the lion of the tribe of **Juda**, the root of
Rev. 7:5	the tribe of **Juda** were sealed twelve thousand. Of the
1 Ne. 10:4(4-11)	Lord God raise up among the **Jews**- even a Messiah, or
1 Ne. 13:25(20-42)	these things go forth from the **Jews** in purity unto the
1 Ne. 14:23	book...proceeded out of the mouth of the **Jew**, or, at
1 Ne. 15:17(13-17)	he shall be rejected of the **Jews**, or...house of Israel
1 Ne. 15:19(13-20)	concerning the restoration of the **Jews** in the latter
2 Ne. 10:3(3-5)	Christ...should come among the **Jews**, among those who
2 Ne. 19:21	Ephraim, Manasseh...together shall be against **Judah**.
2 Ne. 21:13(12,13)	and **Judah** shall not vex Ephraim.
2 Ne. 25:5(5,6)	the **Jews** do understand the things of the prophets, and
2 Ne. 25:15(15-18)	**Jews** shall be scattered among all nations; yea, and
2 Ne. 26:12	the convincing of the **Jews**, that Jesus is the...Christ
2 Ne. 29:4(4-6)	what thank they the **Jews** for the Bible which they
2 Ne. 30:2(1-3)	the **Jews** as will not repent shall be cast off; for the
2 Ne. 30:7(7-8)	**Jews** which are scattered...believe in Christ; and the
2 Ne. 33:10(7-14)	brethren, and...**Jew**...hearken unto these words and
Jacob 4:15(14-18)	by the stumbling of the **Jews** they will reject the
3 Ne. 29:8(8,9)	nor make game of the **Jews**, nor any of the remnant of
Morm. 3:21	that the **Jews**...shall have other witness besides him
Morm. 5:14(12-14)	unto the unbelieving of the **Jews**...that they may be
D&C 45:51	then shall the **Jews** look upon me and say: what are the
D&C 77:15	two prophets...to be raised up to the **Jewish** nation
D&C 98:17	hearts of the **Jews** unto the prophets, and the prophets
D&C 109:64(62-64)	the children of **Judah** may begin to return to the lands
D&C 133:13	let them who be of **Judah** flee unto Jerusalem, unto the
D&C 133:35	tribe of **Judah**, after their pain shall be sanctified
JS-M 1:18(4,18,21)	great tribulation on the **Jews**, and upon the

ISRAEL, LAND OF

Gen. 12:7(6-7)	Abram...unto thy seed will I give this **land**: and there
Gen. 15:18(7-18)	unto thy seed have I given this **land**, from the river
Gen. 17:8	all the **land** of Canaan, for an everlasting possession
Gen. 26:3(2-3)	unto thy seed, I will give all these **countries**, and I

ISRAEL, LAND OF cont.

Gen. 28:15(13-15)	I...will bring thee again into this **land**; for I will
Gen. 35:12	the **land** which I gave Abraham and Isaac, to thee I
Gen. 48:21	God shall...bring you again unto..**land** of your fathers
Ex. 3:17	I will bring you...unto a **land** flowing with milk and
Lev. 18:25	and the **land** is defiled: therefore I do visit the
Num. 13:16(1-33)	names of...men which Moses sent to spy out the **land**.
Num. 33:54(48-55)	ye shall divide the **land** by lot for an inheritance
Num. 34:13(2-29)	this is the **land** which ye shall inherit by lot, which
Deut. 1:8	go in and possess the **land** which the Lord sware unto
Deut. 8:7(7-15)	a good **land**, a land of brooks of water, of fountains
Josh. 1:6	unto this people...divide for an inheritance the **land**
Josh. 21:43	the Lord gave unto Israel all the **land** which he sware
1 Kgs. 9:7(6-7)	then will I cut off Israel out of the **land** which I
2 Kgs. 17:23	so was Israel carried away out of their own **land** to
1 Chr. 16:18(17-20)	unto thee will I give the **land** of Canaan, the lot of
1 Chr. 22:2	gather...the strangers that were in the **land** of Israel
Isa. 14:1	yet choose Israel, and set them in their own **land**
Isa. 62:4	neither shall thy **land** any more be termed desolate
Jer. 4:7	make thy **land** desolate; and thy cities shall be laid
Jer. 11:5	to give them a **land** flowing with milk and honey, as
Jer. 16:15	I will bring them again into their **land** that I gave
Ezek. 11:17(16-17)	saith the Lord...I will give you the **land** of Israel.
Ezek. 20:15	**land** which I had given them...the glory of all lands
Ezek. 20:38	they shall not enter into the **land** of Israel: and ye
Ezek. 21:2(1-32)	and prophesy against the **land** of Israel
Ezek. 27:17	Judah, and the **land** of Israel, they were thy merchants
Ezek. 36:24	of all countries...will bring you into your own **land**.
Matt. 2:20(20-21)	take...child and...mother...go into the **land** of Israel
Acts 13:19	he had destroyed seven nations in the **land** of Canaan
Heb. 11:9	by faith he sojourned in the **land** of promise, as in a
3 Ne. 20:22(21-22)	this people will I establish in this **land**...a New
3 Ne. 20:29	**land** of Jerusalem, which is the promised land unto
3 Ne. 20:33	give unto them Jerusalem for the **land** of their
3 Ne. 21:22(22-25)	remnant of Jacob, unto whom I have given this **land** for
Ether 13:6(6-10)	New **Jerusalem**...unto the remnant of the seed of Joseph
D&C 38:20	for the **land** of your inheritance, and for the
D&C 77:15	built the city of Jerusalem in the **land** of their
D&C 133:24	and the **land** of Jerusalem and the land of Zion shall
Abr. 2:6	Abraham ...a strange **land**...unto thy seed after thee
Abr. 2:18	come into the borders of the **land** of the Canaanites

ISRAEL, MISSION OF

Gen. 12:3(1-3)	in thee shall all **families** of the earth be blessed.
Gen. 17:7(1-8)	establish my **covenant** between me...and thy seed after
Gen. 18:18(16-19)	all the nations of the earth shall be **blessed** in him
Gen. 22:18(15-18)	in thy seed shall all the nations...be **blessed**
Gen. 26:4	in thy seed shall all the **nations** of the earth be
Gen. 28:14(13-15)	in thy seed shall all the families...be **blessed**.
Gen. 49:10	unto him shall the **gathering** of the people be.
Ex. 6:7	and I will take you to me for a **people**, and I will be
Ex. 19:6(3-6)	ye shall be...a kingdom of **priests**, and an holy nation

ISRAEL, MISSION OF cont.

Lev. 26:12	will be your God, and ye shall be my **people**.
Deut. 4:6(5-9)	this is your wisdom...in the sight of the **nations**
Deut. 7:6	the Lord...hath **chosen** thee to be a special people
Deut. 26:18	the Lord hath avouched thee..to be his **peculiar** people
1 Kgs. 8:43(41-43)	that all people of the earth may **know** thy name, to
1 Kgs. 8:60(55-61)	that all the people...**know** that the Lord is God, and
Isa. 2:2(2-5)	and all **nations** shall flow unto it.
Isa. 11:10	to it shall the **Gentiles** seek: and his rest shall be
Isa. 14:1(1-3)	**strangers** shall...cleave to the house of Jacob.
Isa. 19:24(23-25)	in that day shall Israel be...a **blessing** in the midst
Isa. 41:9(8-9)	thou art my **servant**; I have chosen thee, and not cast
Isa. 43:10(9-12)	ye are my **witnesses**, saith the Lord, and my servant
Isa. 44:5(1-8)	one shall say, I am the **Lord's**; and another shall call
Isa. 45:20(20-24)	draw near together, ye that are escaped of the **nations**
Isa. 49:6(1-9)	I will also give thee for a **light** to the Gentiles
Isa. 49:9(1-9)	that thou mayest say to the **prisoners**, go forth; to
Isa. 55:5(4,5)	and **nations** that knew not thee shall run unto thee
Isa. 56:8(3-8)	yet will I gather **others** to him, beside those that
Isa. 60:3(1-22)	and the Gentiles shall come to thy **light**, and kings
Isa. 61:3(3-6)	that they might be called trees of **righteousness**, the
Isa. 66:19(18-20)	they shall **declare** my glory among the Gentiles.
Ezek. 11:20	and they shall be my **people**, and I will be their God.
Ezek. 14:11	but that they may be my **people**, and I may be their God
Ezek. 20:5	in the day when I **chose** Israel, and lifted up mine
Matt. 28:19(19-20)	**teach** all nations, baptizing them in the name of the
Mark 16:15(15-18)	all the world, and **preach** the gospel to every creature
Acts 3:25	in thy seed shall all the kindreds...be **blessed**.
Rom. 11:16(7-32)	if the **root** be holy, so are the branches.
Gal. 3:8	Abraham,...in thee shall all **nations** be blessed.
Gal. 3:14(6-16,27,29)	that the **blessing** of Abraham...come on the Gentiles
1 Pet. 2:9(9-10)	a royal priesthood, an holy nation, a **peculiar** people
1 Ne. 15:18	seed shall all the kindreds of the earth be **blessed**.
1 Ne. 21:22	I will lift up mine hand to the **Gentiles**, and set up
1 Ne. 22:11(7-12)	God...bare his arm in the eyes of all the **nations**, in
Jacob 5:3(1-77)	house of Israel, like unto a tame **olive-tree**, which a
Jacob 5:68(1-77)	that they shall bring forth the natural **fruit**, and the
D&C 1:4(1-4)	the voice of **warning**...by the mouths of my disciples
D&C 84:33(33-45)	faithful unto the obtaining...**magnifying** their calling
D&C 84:62(60-75)	that the **testimony** may go from you into all the world
D&C 128:18(15-18)	neither can they without us be made **perfect**. Neither
D&C 132:31(28-33)	this promise is yours also, because ye are of **Abraham**
D&C 133:34(19-35)	this is the blessing of..God upon the tribes of **Israel**
Abr. 2:11(6-11)	families of the earth be **blessed**...with the...gospel

ISRAEL, ORIGINS OF

Gen. 12:2	and I will make of thee a great **nation**, and I will
Gen. 32:28	thy name shall be called no more Jacob, but **Israel**
Gen. 35:10	thy name shall not be called...more Jacob, but **Israel**
Gen. 46:3	for I will there make of thee a great **nation**
Gen. 46:27	all the souls of the house of **Jacob**, which came into
Ex. 1:5	and all the souls that came out of the loins of **Jacob**

ISRAEL, ORIGINS OF cont.

Deut. 10:22	thy **fathers** went down into Egypt with threescore and
Deut. 26:5	sojourned there with a few, and became there a **nation**
Deut. 33:28	**Israel** then shall dwell in safety alone: the fountain
2 Kgs. 17:34	commanded the children of Jacob, whom he named **Israel**
Acts 7:14	Joseph...called his father **Jacob** to him, and all his
1 Ne. 5:14(14-16)	Lehi...found...a genealogy of his **fathers**; wherefore
1 Ne. 17:40(23-40)	he loved our **fathers**, and he covenanted with them
Mosiah 7:19(19-20)	brought the children of **Israel** out of the land of
D&C 8:3	Moses brought the children of **Israel** through the Red
D&C 10:60(59,60)	that they were a branch of the house of **Jacob**
D&C 27:10	Jacob, and Isaac, and Abraham, your **fathers**, by whom
D&C 98:32	this is the law I gave unto...**Jacob**, and Isaac, and
Abr. 2:9(9-11)	thou shalt be a blessing unto thy **seed** after thee

ISRAEL, REMNANT OF

2 Kgs. 19:4(2-4)	lift up thy prayer for the **remnant** that are left.
2 Kgs. 19:30(30,31)	the **remnant** that is escaped of the house of Judah
Neh. 1:3	the **remnant** that are left of the captivity there in
Isa. 1:9	except the Lord...had left...us a very small **remnant**
Isa. 10:21	the **remnant** shall return, even the remnant of Jacob
Isa. 16:14	Moab...**remnant** shall be very small and feeble.
Isa. 17:6(4-10)	yet **gleaning** grapes shall be left in it, as the
Isa. 19:25(23-25)	blessed be Egypt...and Assyria...and **Israel** mine
Isa. 37:32	for out of Jerusalem shall go forth a **remnant**, and the
Jer. 23:3	I will gather the **remnant** of my flock out of all
Ezek. 6:8(8-10)	yet will I leave a **remnant**, that ye may have some that
Ezek. 12:16	but I will leave a **few** men of them from the sword
Ezek. 14:22	therein shall be left a **remnant** that shall be brought
Joel 2:32	in Jerusalem shall be deliverance...and in the **remnant**
Micah 2:12	I will surely gather the **remnant** of Israel; I will put
Micah 5:8(7-15)	the **remnant** of Jacob shall be among the Gentiles in
Rom. 9:27(27-29)	concerning Israel...a **remnant** shall be saved
1 Ne. 10:14	**remnants** of the house of Israel, should be grafted in
2 Ne. 20:21	the **remnant** shall return, yea, even the remnant of
2 Ne. 28:2	our seed, which is a **remnant** of the house of Israel.
2 Ne. 30:3	words...carry them forth unto the **remnant** of our seed.
Alma 46:23(23-24)	we are a **remnant** of the seed of Joseph, whose coat was
3 Ne. 5:23(22-26)	bring a **remnant**...of Joseph to the knowledge of the
3 Ne. 10:17(15-17)	are not we a **remnant** of the seed of Joseph? And these
3 Ne. 20:16(12-22)	ye, who are a **remnant** of the house of Jacob, go forth
3 Ne. 21:12(11-13)	a **remnant** of Jacob shall be among the Gentiles, yea
Morm. 5:24(9,20,24)	lest a **remnant** of the seed of Jacob shall go forth
Morm. 7:10(9-10)	know that ye are a **remnant** of the seed of Jacob; there
Ether 13:6(3-6)	New Jerusalem...built...unto the **remnant**...of Joseph
D&C 45:43(42-43)	the **remnant** shall be gathered unto this place
D&C 87:5(4-5)	**remnants** who are left...shall vex the Gentiles with a
D&C 109:65	cause that the **remnants** of Jacob, who have been cursed
D&C 113:10(9-10)	scattered **remnants** are exhorted to return to the Lord
JS-M 1:37	gather..the **remainder** of his elect from the four winds

ISRAEL, RESTORATION OF

Deut. 4:30(29-31)	even in the latter days, if thou **turn** to the Lord thy
Deut. 30:2(1-15)	and shalt **return** unto the Lord thy God, and shalt obey
2 Chr. 30:9	if ye **turn** again unto the Lord, your brethren and your
Isa. 4:3(1-6)	he that is **left** in Zion...shall be called holy, even
Isa. 11:11(11-12)	Lord shall set his hand again...to **recover** the remnant
Isa. 40:1(1,2)	**comfort** ye my people, saith your God.
Isa. 44:23(22,23)	the Lord hath **redeemed** Jacob, and glorified himself
Isa. 49:3(1-26)	thou art my **servant**, O Israel, in whom I will be
Isa. 51:11(4-11)	the **redeemed** of the Lord shall return...unto Zion; and
Isa. 52:1(1-3,6)	awake, awake; put on thy **strength**, O Zion; put on thy
Isa. 54:13(1-17)	great shall be the **peace** of thy children.
Isa. 62:4(2-4)	thou shalt no more be termed **forsaken**; neither shall
Isa. 66:13(5-22)	ye shall be **comforted** in Jerusalem.
Jer. 3:12(12-22)	**return**, thou backsliding Israel, saith the Lord; and
Jer. 16:21(16-21)	they shall **know** that my name is the Lord.
Ezek. 37:22(19-28)	I will make them one **nation** ...no more two nations
Rom. 11:26(25-28)	and so all **Israel** shall be saved: as it is written
1 Ne. 15:20(11-20)	the **restoration** of the Jews, or of the house of Israel
1 Ne. 19:15(15-17)	day cometh...that they no more **turn** aside their hearts
1 Ne. 20:20	the Lord hath **redeemed** his servant Jacob.
1 Ne. 22:12(8-12)	they shall be **brought** out of obscurity and out of
2 Ne. 3:24(3-24)	much **restoration** unto the house of Israel, and unto
2 Ne. 6:11(10-18)	they shall come to the **knowledge** of their Redeemer
2 Ne. 8:3	for the Lord shall **comfort** Zion, he will comfort all
2 Ne. 8:9(9,24)	Awake, Awake! Put on **strength**, O arm of the Lord
2 Ne. 9:2(1-2)	they shall be **restored** to the true church and fold
2 Ne. 10:7(5-22)	when...shall believe in me...they shall be **restored**
2 Ne. 25:17(15-17)	to **restore** his people from their lost and fallen state
2 Ne. 29:1(1-2)	set my hand again the second time to **recover** my people
2 Ne. 30:8(3-8)	to bring about the **restoration** of his people upon the
Jacob 5:75(3-77)	ye...have brought unto me again the **natural** fruit
Jacob 6:2(1-7)	set his hand again...second time to **recover** his people
3 Ne. 5:23(21-26)	bring a remnant...of Joseph to the **knowledge** of the
3 Ne. 16:4(4-20)	may be brought to a **knowledge** of me, their Redeemer.
3 Ne. 20:31(11-46)	they shall **believe** in me, that I am Jesus Christ, the
3 Ne. 21:27(1-29)	to prepare the way whereby they may **come** unto me, that
3 Ne. 22:7(1-7)	with great mercies will I **gather** thee.
Morm. 5:14(14-24)	Jews...may be **persuaded** that Jesus is the Christ, the
Ether 13:4(2-12)	Ether..spake concerning a **New** Jerusalem upon this land
Moro. 10:31(31-34)	**awake**, and arise from the dust, O Jerusalem; yea, and
D&C 14:10	fulness of my **gospel** from the Gentiles unto the house
D&C 35:25	**Israel** shall be saved in mine own due time; and by the
D&C 45:17	shall come...the **restoration** of the scattered Israel.
D&C 82:14	Zion must **arise** and put on her beautiful garments.
D&C 84:99	the Lord hath redeemed his people, **Israel**, according
D&C 101:14(12-14)	and all they who have mourned shall be **comforted**.
D&C 101:43(43-67)	know my will concerning the **redemption** of Zion.
D&C 103:15(7-28)	the **redemption** of Zion must needs come by power
D&C 113:8(7,8)	to put on her **strength** is to put on the authority of

ISRAEL, SCATTERING OF

Gen. 49:22(22-26) — Joseph..bough...whose branches **run** over the wall
Lev. 26:33(32,33) — I will **scatter** you among the heathen, and will draw
Deut. 4:27(27-28) — Lord shall **scatter** you among the nations, and ye shall
Deut. 28:64(36-65) — the Lord shall **scatter** thee among all people, from the
1 Kgs. 22:17 — I saw all Israel **scattered**...as sheep that have not a
2 Kgs. 15:29(29-30) — and carried them captive to **Assyria**.
2 Kgs. 17:6(6,16,18) — king of Assyria took Samaria, and **carried** Israel away
2 Kgs. 25:7(1-7) — put out the eyes of Zedekiah...**carried** him to Babylon.
Ps. 44:11 — thou hast...**scattered** us among the heathen.
Isa. 1:7(7-9) — your land, **strangers** devour it in your presence, and
Isa. 36:1(1-22) — king of **Assyria** came up against all the defenced
Jer. 4:29(20,27,29) — every city shall be **forsaken**, and not a man dwell
Jer. 5:19(15,18,19) — shall ye **serve** strangers in a land that is not yours.
Jer. 9:16 — I will **scatter** them also among the heathen, whom
Jer. 14:18(10-18) — go about into a **land** that they know not.
Jer. 16:13(1-4,11-13) — therefore will I **cast** you out of this land into a land
Jer. 17:4 — I will cause thee to **serve** thine enemies in the land
Jer. 29:18(15-19) — to be **removed** to all the kingdoms of the earth, to be
Jer. 30:11 — yet will I not make a full **end** of thee: but I will
Ezek. 5:10 — the whole remnant of thee will I **scatter** into all the
Ezek. 6:8 — when ye shall be **scattered** through the countries.
Ezek. 12:15 — I shall **scatter** them among the nations, and disperse
Ezek. 17:4(1-4) — young twigs, and **carried** it into a land of traffick
Ezek. 17:5(5,6) — and **planted** it in a fruitful field; he placed it by
Ezek. 17:22 — crop off...and will **plant** it upon an high mountain
Ezek. 20:23 — that I would **scatter** them among the heathen, and
Ezek. 22:15 — I will **scatter** thee among the heathen, and disperse
Hosea 9:17(15-17) — they shall be **wanderers** among the nations.
Amos 6:7(7-9,14) — now shall they go **captive** with the first that go
Amos 9:9 — and I will **sift** the house of Israel among all nations
Matt. 15:24(21-28) — I am not sent...the lost sheep of the house of **Israel**.
Matt. 24:16(16-20) — let them which be in Judaea **flee** into the mountains
Luke 21:24 — shall be **led** away captive into all nations: and
John 10:16 — **other** sheep I have, which are not of this fold: them
Rom. 11:20(15-24) — because of unbelief they were **broken** off, and thou
1 Ne. 10:3 — many be carried away **captive** into Babylon, according
1 Ne. 13:14 — they were **scattered** before the Gentiles and were
1 Ne. 22:3(3-5) — will be **scattered** upon all the face of the earth, and
1 Ne. 22:4(3-5) — tribes...are **scattered**...upon the isles of the sea
2 Ne. 3:5 — a branch which was to be **broken** off, nevertheless, to
2 Ne. 10:22(21,22) — the Lord God has **led** away from time to time from the
2 Ne. 10:22(20-22) — the Lord...**led** away...the house of Israel, according
2 Ne. 18:4 — shall be taken away before the king of **Assyria**.
2 Ne. 25:15(14-16) — the Jews shall be **scattered** among all nations; yea
Jacob 5:8(1-9) — I take **away** many of these young and tender branches
1:15(14-15) — people of **Zarahemla** came out from Jerusalem at the
Mosiah 25:2 — the people of Zarahemla, who was a descendant of **Mulek**
Hel. 6:10 — called Mulek, which was after the son of **Zedekiah**; for
Hel. 8:21 — **Mulek**...driven out of the land of Jerusalem? But
3 Ne. 16:8 — come forth...have **scattered** my people who are of the
3 Ne. 20:13 — then shall the remnants, which shall be **scattered**
3 Ne. 28:29(25-32) — they shall minister...the **scattered** tribes of Israel
Ether 13:7(7-11) — the Lord brought a **remnant** of the seed of Joseph out

ISRAEL, SCATTERING OF cont.

D&C 45:19(16-25)   this people shall be...**scattered** among all nations.
D&C 113:10   **scattered** remnants are exhorted to return to the Lord

ISRAEL, TRIBES OF, TEN LOST

Gen. 28:14(10-15)	thou shalt spread abroad to the west...east...**north**
1 Kgs. 11:31(26-35)	he said to Jeroboam...I will...give **ten** tribes to thee
1 Kgs. 12:19(16-20)	**Israel** rebelled against the house of David unto this
1 Kgs. 12:20(16-20)	none...**followed** the house of David, but...Judah only.
1 Kgs. 14:15(10-16)	he shall root up **Israel** out of this good land, which
2 Kgs. 17:6(6-18)	king of Assyria...carried **Israel** away into Assyria
2 Kgs. 17:20(20-23)	Lord **rejected**...Israel...delivered them into the hand
2 Kgs. 17:23	**Israel** carried away out of their own land to Assyria
2 Kgs. 18:11(9-11)	Assyria did carry away **Israel** unto Assyria, and put
Isa. 7:8(4-9)	shall **Ephraim** be broken, that it be not a people.
Isa. 8:4	the spoil of **Samaria** shall be taken away before the
Isa. 11:11(10-12)	his hand again the second time to recover the **remnant**
Isa. 17:3(1-5)	the fortress also shall cease from **Ephraim**, and the
Isa. 42:24	who gave Jacob for a spoil, and **Israel** to the robbers
Isa. 43:6(5-7)	I will say to the **north**, give up; and to the south
Isa. 49:12(5-12)	these shall come from...the **north** and from the west
Isa. 54:7(3-10)	for a small moment have I **forsaken** thee; but with
Jer. 3:12(11-12,18)	proclaim these words toward the **north**...return, thou
Jer. 3:18(12-18)	they shall come together out of the land of the **north**
Jer. 16:15(14-16)	brought up...Israel from the land of the **north**, and
Jer. 23:8(7-8)	which led...Israel out of the **north** country, and from
Jer. 31:8(6-9)	I will bring them from the **north** country, and gather
Jer. 32:44(36-44)	I will cause their **captivity** to return, saith the Lord
Ezek. 22:15	I will **scatter** thee among the heathen, and disperse
Ezek. 28:25(25-26)	I shall have gathered the house of **Israel** from the
Amos 7:17	**Israel** shall surely go into captivity forth of his
Amos 9:9(8-9)	I will sift the house of **Israel** among all nations
Zech. 2:6(6-9)	flee from the land of the **north**, saith the Lord: for
Zech. 7:14(13-14)	I **scattered** them with a whirlwind among all the
Zech. 10:9(7-9)	I will **sow** them among the people: and they shall
Zech. 10:10(10-12)	I will bring them...out of **Assyria**; and I will bring
John 10:16	other **sheep** I have, which are not of this fold: them
1 Ne. 10:14(3,12-14)	after the house of **Israel** should be scattered they
1 Ne. 22:4(3-4)	the more part of all the **tribes** have been led away
2 Ne. 10:22	God has **led** away from time to time from the house of
2 Ne. 29:13(12-14)	shall have the words of the **lost** tribes of Israel; and
3 Ne. 15:15(13-18)	concerning the **other** tribes of the house of Israel
3 Ne. 16:1(1-5)	I have **other sheep** which are not of this land, neither
3 Ne. 17:4	I go...to show myself unto the **lost** tribes of Israel
3 Ne. 21:26(1-29)	work..commence among...the tribes which have been **lost**
Ether 13:11(10-11)	gathered in from...the **north** countries, and are
D&C 35:25	**Israel** shall be saved in mine own due time; and by the
D&C 110:11	leading of the ten tribes from the land of the **north**.
D&C 133:26(20-35)	they who are in the **north** countries shall come in
A of F 1:10	we believe...in the restoration of the **Ten** Tribes

ISRAEL, TRIBES OF, TWELVE

Gen. 35:22(22-26)	the sons of Jacob were **twelve**
Gen. 46:8(8-27)	**names** of the children of Israel, which came into Egypt
Gen. 49:28(1-29)	these are the **twelve** tribes of Israel: and this is it
Ex. 3:10(10-16)	bring...**children** of Israel out of Egypt.
Ex. 19:5(5-6)	ye shall be a **peculiar** treasure unto me above all
Ex. 28:21(9-12,15-21)	stones...twelve...according to the **twelve** tribes.
Num. 1:44(17-46)	the princes of Israel, being **twelve** men: each one was
Num. 34:18(14-27)	one prince of every **tribe**, to divide the land by
Deut. 33:1(1-25)	Moses...blessed the children of **Israel** before his
Jer. 30:3	my people **Israel** and Judah, saith the Lord: and I will
Ezek. 20:40	there shall all the house of **Israel**...serve me: there
Ezek. 39:25	have mercy upon the whole house of **Israel**, and will
Ezek. 45:8	give to the house of Israel according to their **tribes**.
Ezek. 47:13(13,21)	inherit the land according to the twelve **tribes** of
Ezek. 48:1(1-29)	these are the names of the **tribes**. From the north end
Luke 21:24	led away captive into all **nations**: and Jerusalem shall
Acts 26:7(6-7)	which promise our **twelve** tribes, instantly serving God
Rev. 7:4(4-8)	the number...sealed...of all the **tribes** of...Israel.
1 Ne. 10:14(12-14)	the house of **Israel**...gathered together again; or, in
1 Ne. 12:9(9-10)	twelve apostles...shall judge the **twelve** tribes of
1 Ne. 21:6	to raise up the **tribes** of Jacob, and to restore the
Jacob 5:3(2-77)	O house of **Israel**, like unto a tame olive-tree, which
D&C 35:25	**Israel** shall be saved in mine own due time; and by the
D&C 39:11	gospel...sent forth to **recover** my people, which are
D&C 133:34(25-35)	blessing of the everlasting God upon the **tribes** of
Moses 1:26(25-32)	deliver my people from bondage, even **Israel** my chosen.

JEALOUSY

Prov. 6:34(32-35)	for **jealousy** is the rage of a man: therefore he will
Rom. 10:19	provoke you to **jealousy** by them that are no people
Rom. 11:11	the Gentiles, for to provoke them to **jealousy**.
1 Cor. 10:22(21-22)	do we provoke the Lord to **jealousy**? are we stronger
2 Cor. 11:2	I am **jealous** over you with godly jealousy: for I have
Ether 9:7	Akish began to be **jealous** of his son, therefore he
D&C 67:10	inasmuch as you strip yourselves from **jealousies** and

JERUSALEM

Gen. 14:18(18-20)	and Melchizedek king of **Salem** brought forth bread and
2 Kgs. 25:4(2-4)	the **city** was broken up, and all the men of war fled
2 Chr. 36:19(17-20)	and brake down the wall of **Jerusalem**, and burnt all
Isa. 1:26(26-27)	thou shalt be called, the **city** of righteousness, the
Isa. 4:3(2-4)	he that remaineth in **Jerusalem**, shall be called holy
Isa. 48:2	for they call themselves of the **holy** city, and stay
Isa. 52:1	put on thy beautiful garments, O **Jerusalem**, the holy
Jer. 39:1(1-9)	all his army against **Jerusalem**, and they besieged it.
Jer. 52:7(5-7)	then the **city** was broken up, and all the men of war
Ezek. 26:2	said against **Jerusalem**, Aha, she is broken that was
Ezek. 33:21	one...escaped...came...saying, the **city** is smitten.
Joel 2:32	in **Jerusalem** shall be deliverance, as the Lord hath

JERUSALEM cont.

Joel 3:17(16,17)	then shall **Jerusalem** be holy, and there shall no
Micah 4:2	**Zion**, and the word of the Lord from **Jerusalem**.
Zech. 8:3(3-8)	**Jerusalem** shall be called a city of truth; and the
Zech. 12:6	and **Jerusalem** shall be inhabited again in her own
Matt. 23:37(37-39)	**Jerusalem**, thou that killest the prophets, and stonest
Matt. 24:15(1-51)	abomination of desolation ...in the **holy** place, (whoso
Luke 23:28(27-29)	daughters of **Jerusalem**, weep not for me, but weep for
Heb. 7:2(1-2)	also king of **Salem**, which is, king of peace
1 Ne. 1:4(4,13,18)	repent, or the great city **Jerusalem** must be destroyed.
1 Ne. 20:2	they call themselves of the **holy** city, but they do not
2 Ne. 1:4	seen a vision...I know that **Jerusalem** is destroyed
3 Ne. 20:33(29-33)	then will the Father...give unto them **Jerusalem** for
Ether 13:5(4-6)	**Jerusalem**...after it...be destroyed...built up again
D&C 133:13(12-13)	let...Judah flee unto **Jerusalem**, unto the mountains
D&C 133:21(19-21)	he shall speak from **Jerusalem**, and his voice shall
JS-M 1:12(1-55)	concerning the destruction of **Jerusalem**, then you

JERUSALEM, NEW

Isa. 2:2(2-4)	mountain of the Lord's **house** shall be established in
Isa. 40:9	O **Zion**, that bringest good tidings, get thee up into
Micah 4:2(1-7)	law shall go forth of **Zion**...word...from Jerusalem.
Gal. 4:26	**Jerusalem** which is above is free, which is the mother
Rev. 3:12	name of the city of my God, which is **new** Jerusalem
Rev. 21:2(1-27)	I John saw the holy city, new **Jerusalem**, coming down
2 Ne. 12:2(2-4)	mountain of the Lord's **house** shall be established in
3 Ne. 20:22	this people...establish in this land...a New **Jerusalem**
3 Ne. 21:23(20-25)	city, which shall be called the New **Jerusalem**.
Ether 13:3(2-4)	the New **Jerusalem**, which should come down out of
Ether 13:6(5-11)	a New **Jerusalem** should be built upon this land, unto
D&C 42:9	when the city of the New **Jerusalem** shall be prepared
D&C 45:66(66-67)	it shall be called the New **Jerusalem**, a land of peace
D&C 84:2(2-5)	Mount **Zion**, which shall be the city of New **Jerusalem**.
D&C 97:19(19-20)	surely **Zion** is the city of our God, and surely Zion
D&C 133:12(12-13)	let them...who are among the Gentiles flee unto **Zion**.
Moses 7:20(18-21)	surely **Zion** shall dwell in safety forever. But the Lord
Moses 7:62(60-66)	it shall be called Zion, a New **Jerusalem**.

JESUS CHRIST, APPEARANCES, ANTEMORTAL

Gen. 18:1(1-2)	and the Lord **appeared** unto him in the plains of Mamre
Ex. 24:10(9-10)	they **saw** the God of Israel: and there was under his
Ex. 33:11(9-11)	and the Lord **spake** unto Moses face to face, as a man
Ex. 33:20	for there shall no man **see** me, and live.
Num. 12:8(6-8)	the similitude of the Lord shall he **behold**: wherefore
Deut. 5:24	the Lord...hath **shewed** us his glory and his greatness
Deut. 34:10	Moses, whom the Lord knew **face** to face
Isa. 6:1(1,5)	I **saw** also the Lord...high and lifted up, and his
Ezek. 1:26(26-28)	upon...throne...likeness as the **appearance** of a man
John 8:56(56-58)	father Abraham...**see** my day: and he saw it, and was
John 12:41	said Esaias, when he **saw** his glory, and spake of him.

JESUS CHRIST, APPEARANCES, ANTEMORTAL cont.

2 Ne. 2:4(3,4)	and thou hast **beheld** in thy youth his glory; wherefore
2 Ne. 11:2(2-3)	Isaiah...verily **saw** my Redeemer, even as I have seen
2 Ne. 16:5(1,5)	for mine eyes have **seen** the King, the Lord of Hosts.
Alma 19:13	I have **seen** my Redeemer; and he shall come forth, and
3 Ne. 1:12(12,14)	the **voice** of the Lord came unto him, saying
Ether 3:13(6-16)	ye are redeemed...therefore I **show** myself unto you.
Ether 3:20(6-28)	therefore he **saw** Jesus; and he did minister unto him.
Ether 12:39	I have **seen** Jesus, and that he hath talked with me
D&C 107:49(48,49)	he **saw** the Lord, and he walked with him, and was
Moses 1:2(1-41)	he **saw** God face to face, and he talked with him, and
Moses 7:4(2-4)	I **saw** the Lord; and he stood before my face, and he
Moses 7:47(3-69)	Enoch **saw** the day of the coming of the Son of Man
Abr. 1:15(15-16)	he filled me with the **vision** of the Almighty, and the
Abr. 2:6(6-11)	the Lord **appeared** unto me, and said unto me: arise

JESUS CHRIST, APPEARANCES, POSTMORTAL

Matt. 28:9(8-10)	**Jesus** met them, saying, All hail. And they came and
Matt. 28:18(10-20)	and **Jesus** came and spake unto them, saying, all power
Mark 16:9(9,12,14-19)	when Jesus was risen...he **appeared** first to Mary
Luke 24:15(13-35)	**Jesus** himself drew near, and went with them.
Luke 24:34	Lord is risen indeed, and hath **appeared** to Simon.
Luke 24:36(36-50)	as they thus spake, Jesus himself **stood** in the midst
Luke 24:39(36-39)	a spirit hath not **flesh** and bones, as ye see me have.
John 20:14(13-17)	she turned...and **saw** Jesus standing, and knew not that
John 20:19(19-23)	the same day at evening...came Jesus and **stood** in the
John 20:20(11-20)	disciples glad, when they **saw** the Lord.
John 20:29(24-29)	Thomas, because thou hast **seen** me, thou hast believed
John 21:4(4-14)	**Jesus** stood on the shore: but the disciples knew not
John 21:14(1,14-23)	the third time that Jesus **shewed** himself to his
Acts 1:3(1-11)	to whom also he **shewed** himself alive after his passion
Acts 7:55(55-56)	saw...Jesus **standing** on the right hand of **God**
Acts 9:5(1-9)	I am **Jesus** whom thou persecutest: it is hard for thee
Acts 9:10(10-16)	disciple...Ananias...to him said the Lord in a **vision**
Acts 9:27	how he had **seen** the Lord in the way, and that he had
Acts 10:40(39-41)	him God raised up the third day, and **shewed** him openly
Acts 13:31(30-31)	he was **seen** many days of them which came up with him
Acts 18:9(9-10)	then spake the Lord to Paul in the night by a **vision**
Acts 22:18(17-21)	**saw** him saying unto me, make haste, and get thee
Acts 23:11	the night following the Lord **stood** by him, and said
Acts 26:16	I have **appeared** unto thee for this purpose, to make
1 Cor. 15:5(3-8)	and that he was **seen** of Cephas, then of the twelve
1 Cor. 15:6(3-8)	he was **seen** of above five hundred brethren at once
1 Cor. 15:8(5-8)	and last of all he was **seen** of me also, as of one born
Rev. 1:17(10-19)	when I **saw** him, I fell at his feet as dead. And he
3 Ne. 9:15	behold, I am **Jesus** Christ the Son of God. I created
3 Ne. 11:8(1-8)	they **saw** a Man descending out of heaven; and he was
3 Ne. 11:12(8-12)	prophesied...Christ should **show** himself unto them
3 Ne. 11:15(13-17)	did **see** with their eyes and did feel with their hands
3 Ne. 17:4	**show** myself unto the lost tribes of Israel, for they
3 Ne. 17:25	the multitude did **see** and hear and bear record; and
3 Ne. 19:15(15-17)	**Jesus** came and stood in the midst and ministered unto

JESUS CHRIST, APPEARANCES, POSTMORTAL cont.

3 Ne. 27:2(1-2)	Jesus again **showed** himself...Jesus came and stood in
Morm. 1:15	I was **visited** of the Lord, and tasted and knew of the
Ether 12:39(38-39)	I have **seen** Jesus, and that he hath talked with me
D&C 6:37	**behold** the wounds which pierced my side, and also the
D&C 45:52(51-52)	I am he who was lifted up...Jesus that was **crucified**.
D&C 67:10(10-14)	you shall **see** me and know that I am- not with the
D&C 76:23(19-24)	we **saw** him, even on the right hand of God; and we
D&C 93:1	every soul who forsaketh his sins ...shall **see** my face
D&C 110:2(1-10)	we **saw** the Lord standing upon the breastwork of the
D&C 110:8	yea, I will **appear** unto my servants, and speak unto
D&C 130:1	when the Savior shall appear we shall **see** him as he
JS-H 1:17(16-17)	I saw two **Personages**, whose brightness and glory defy
JFS-V 1:18(16-19)	the Son of God **appeared**, declaring liberty to the

JESUS CHRIST, ASCENSION OF

Luke 24:51	he was parted from them, and **carried** up into heaven.
John 3:13	no man hath **ascended** up to heaven, but he that came
John 6:62	if...see the Son of man **ascend** up where he was before
John 14:12(3-12)	I **go** unto my Father.
John 14:28	I said, I **go** unto the Father: for my Father is greater
John 20:17	touch me not; for I am not yet **ascended** to my Father
Acts 1:11(9-11)	this same Jesus, which is **taken** up from you into
Eph. 4:10(8-10)	the same also that **ascended** up far above all heavens
1 Tim. 3:16	believed on in the world, **received** up into glory.
Mosiah 18:2	Christ, and his resurrection and **ascension** into heaven
Alma 40:20	resurrection of Christ, and his **ascension** into heaven.
3 Ne. 11:12	that Christ should show himself...after his **ascension**
3 Ne. 18:39	he departed from them, and **ascended** into heaven.
D&C 20:24	**ascended** into heaven, to sit down on the right hand

JESUS CHRIST, ATONEMENT THROUGH

Lev. 4:31(20-35)	priest shall make an **atonement** for him, and it shall
Lev. 17:11	it is the blood that maketh an **atonement** for the soul.
Isa. 53:6(3-12)	the Lord hath laid on him the **iniquity** of us all.
Isa. 63:9(1-9)	in his pity he **redeemed** them; and he bare them, and
Dan. 9:26(25-26)	shall **Messiah** be cut off, but not for himself: and the
Zech. 9:11(9-11)	by the **blood** of thy covenant...sent forth thy prisoner
Matt. 1:21(20-23)	Jesus: for he shall **save** his people from their sins.
Matt. 8:17	himself took our **infirmities**, and bare our sicknesses.
Matt. 20:28	Son of man came...to give his life a **ransom** for many.
Matt. 26:28(26-30)	my **blood**...shed for many for the remission of sins.
Matt. 26:36(36-46)	cometh Jesus with them unto a place called **Gethsemane**
Luke 22:19(19-46)	this is my **body** which is given for you: this do in
Luke 22:44	his sweat was as it were great drops of **blood** falling
John 1:29(29-36)	Lamb of God, which taketh away the **sin** of the world!
John 3:17(14-18)	that the world through him might be **saved**.
John 6:51(37-40,51)	my flesh, which I will give for the **life** of the world.
John 10:15(15-18)	I lay down my **life** for the sheep.
John 11:25(25-26)	I am the resurrection, and the **life**: he that believeth

John 12:32(27-34)	if I be **lifted** up...will draw all men unto me.
John 17:4(4,19)	I have **finished** the work which thou gavest me to do.
John 17:19	and for their sakes I **sanctify** myself, that they also
John 19:30	he said, it is **finished**: and he bowed his head, and
Acts 4:12(10-12)	none other name under heaven...whereby...must be **saved**
Acts 5:31(30-32)	him hath God exalted...to be a Prince and a **Saviour**
Acts 13:38(38-41)	through this man is preached...**forgiveness** of sins
Rom. 3:25(23-28)	whom God hath set forth to be a **propitiation** through
Rom. 5:9	**justified** by his blood, we shall be saved from wrath
Rom. 5:11(6-21)	Lord Jesus Christ, by whom we have...the **atonement**.
Rom. 8:32	spared not his own **Son**, but delivered him up for us
1 Cor. 15:22(19-22)	even so in Christ shall all be made **alive**.
Eph. 1:7	in whom we have **redemption** through his blood, the
Eph. 2:16(11-18)	**reconcile** both unto God in one body by the cross
Philip. 2:8(6-16)	obedient unto death, even the **death** of the cross.
Col. 1:14(14,21-23)	in whom we have **redemption** through his blood, even the
1 Tim. 1:15	Christ Jesus came into the world to **save** sinners; of
1 Tim. 2:6	who gave himself a **ransom** for all, to be testified in
1 Tim. 4:10	living God, who is the **Saviour** of all men, specially
2 Tim. 1:10(8-11)	Saviour Jesus Christ, who hath abolished **death**, and
Titus 2:14	that he might **redeem** us from all iniquity, and purify
Heb. 2:9	that he...should taste **death** for every man.
Heb. 5:9(5-9)	author of eternal **salvation** unto all them that obey
Heb. 7:27(22,27)	this he did once, when he **offered** up himself.
Heb. 8:6(6-13)	he is the **mediator** of a better covenant, which was
Heb. 9:24(11-25)	now to appear in the **presence** of God for us
Heb. 9:28(11-28)	Christ was once **offered** to bear the sins of many; and
1 Pet. 1:19(18,19)	with the precious **blood** of Christ, as of a lamb
1 Pet. 2:21(20-22)	because Christ also **suffered** for us, leaving us an
1 Pet. 2:24	his own self bare our **sins** in his own body on the tree
1 Pet. 3:18	Christ also hath once **suffered** for sins..bring us to
1 Jn. 1:7(5-7)	blood of Jesus Christ...**cleanseth** us from all sin.
1 Jn. 2:2(1,2)	he is the **propitiation** for our sins: and not for ours
1 Jn. 3:5	he was manifested to take away our **sins**; and in him
1 Jn. 4:10(9-14)	sent his Son to be the **propitiation** for our sins.
1 Ne. 11:33(26-34)	he was lifted up upon the cross and **slain** for the sins
2 Ne. 1:15	Lord hath **redeemed** my soul from hell; I have beheld
2 Ne. 2:7(6-10,26)	he offereth himself a **sacrifice** for sin, to answer the
2 Ne. 9:7(1-53)	wherefore, it must needs be an infinite **atonement**
2 Ne. 10:25(24-25)	from everlasting death by the power of the **atonement**
2 Ne. 11:5(5,6)	the great and eternal plan of **deliverance** from death.
2 Ne. 31:19(17-20)	relying wholly upon...him who is mighty to **save**.
Jacob 4:11	be reconciled unto him through the **atonement** of Christ
Mosiah 3:16(1-18)	the blood of Christ **atoneth** for their sins.
Mosiah 4:6(2-8)	the **atonement** which has been prepared from the
Mosiah 13:28	were it not for the **atonement**, which God himself shall
Mosiah 14:10(1-12)	when thou shalt make his soul an **offering** for sin he
Mosiah 15:8(6-9,18-28)	giving the Son power to make **intercession** for the
Alma 7:11(11-13)	he will take upon him the **pains** and the sicknesses of
Alma 11:40(40-41)	come into the world to **redeem** his people; and he shall
Alma 34:8(8-16)	he shall **atone** for the sins of the world; for the Lord
Alma 42:23(1-31)	the **atonement** bringeth to pass the resurrection of the
Hel. 5:9(9-12)	saved...through the **atoning** blood of Jesus Christ, who

JESUS CHRIST, ATONEMENT THROUGH cont.

3 Ne. 9:21	I have come unto the world to bring **redemption** unto
3 Ne. 11:14(8-15)	have been **slain** for the sins of the world.
3 Ne. 27:15(14-16)	for this cause have I been **lifted** up...draw all men
Morm. 9:12(12-13)	because of Jesus Christ came the **redemption** of man.
Moro. 8:20	setteth at naught the **atonement** of him and the power
Moro. 10:33(32-33)	sanctified..through the shedding of the **blood** of
D&C 18:11(10-13)	he suffered the **pain** of all men, that all men might
D&C 18:23(23-25)	none other name given whereby man can be **saved**
D&C 19:16(15-20)	I, God, have **suffered** these things for all, that they
D&C 29:1(1,42-45)	I Am, whose arm of mercy hath **atoned** for your sins
D&C 38:4	by the virtue of the **blood** which I have spilt, have I
D&C 45:4	behold the **sufferings** and death of him who did no sin
D&C 74:7	little children are holy...through the **atonement** of
D&C 76:69(39-43,69)	Jesus...wrought out this perfect **atonement** through the
D&C 88:14(14-17)	through the **redemption** which is made for you is
Moses 5:7(4-11)	a similitude of the **sacrifice** of the Only Begotten
Moses 6:54(52-59)	the Son of God hath **atoned** for original guilt
A of F 1:3	through the **atonement** of Christ, all mankind may be
JFS-V 1:2(1-23)	the great **atoning** sacrifice that was made by the Son

JESUS CHRIST, AUTHORITY OF

Isa. 9:6(6,7)	the **government** shall be upon his shoulder: and his
Isa. 11:4	but with righteousness shall he **judge** the poor, and
Jer. 23:5(5,6)	**King** shall reign...execute judgment and justice in the
Dan. 7:14(13,14)	given him **dominion**, and glory, and a kingdom, that all
Zech. 14:9(4-9)	the Lord shall be **King** over all the earth: in that day
Matt. 7:29(28,29)	he taught them as one having **authority**, and not as the
Matt. 9:6(4-8)	hath **power** on earth to forgive sins, (then saith he
Matt. 12:18(17,18)	whom I have **chosen**; my beloved, in whom my soul is
Matt. 21:24(23-27)	tell you by what **authority** I do these things.
Mark 1:22(22-27)	he taught them as one that had **authority**, and not as
Mark 1:27	with **authority** commandeth he even the unclean spirits
Mark 3:14(14,15)	and he **ordained** twelve, that they should be with him
Luke 4:32(32-37)	astonished...for his word was with **power**.
Luke 10:22(21,22)	all things are **delivered** to me of my Father: and no
John 1:1(1-5)	and the Word was with God, and the Word was **God**.
John 3:35(34-36)	Father loveth the Son...**given** all things into his hand
John 5:22	but hath **committed** all judgment unto the Son
John 5:27(25-29)	hath given him **authority** to execute judgment also
John 5:43	I am come in my **Father's** name, and ye receive me not
John 7:16(16-18)	my doctrine is not mine, but his that **sent** me.
John 7:29(28,29,33)	but I know him: for I am from him, and he hath **sent**
John 8:29(26,29)	he that **sent** me is with me: the Father hath not left
John 10:18(17-18)	this commandment have I **received** of my Father.
John 12:49(44-50)	but the Father which **sent** me, he gave me a commandment
John 14:31	as the Father gave me **commandment**, even so I do. Arise
John 17:2(1,2)	as thou hast given him **power** over all flesh, that he
John 17:18(11-24)	as thou hast **sent** me into the world, even so have I
John 20:21	as my Father hath **sent** me, even so send I you.
Acts 4:27(24-28)	thy holy child Jesus, whom thou hast **anointed**, both
Acts 10:42	it is he which was **ordained** of God to be the judge of

Acts 17:31	judge the world...by that man whom he hath **ordained**
Rom. 14:9(6-12)	**Lord** both of the dead and living.
1 Tim. 2:5(2-6)	there is one God, and one **mediator** between God and men
Heb. 1:2(1-3)	spoken unto us by his Son, whom he hath **appointed** heir
Heb. 5:9(8-9)	perfect, he became the **author** of eternal salvation
Heb. 5:10(5-6,10)	**called** of God an high priest after the order of
Heb. 7:3(3,11-28)	Son of God; abideth a **priest** continually.
Heb. 7:24(11-28)	this man...hath an unchangeable **priesthood**.
Heb. 8:1(1-7)	an **high** priest...set on the right hand of the throne
Heb. 8:6	by how much also he is the **mediator** of a better
Heb. 9:15(11-26)	he is the **mediator** of the new testament, that by means
Heb. 12:2(1-2)	Jesus the **author** and finisher of our faith; who for
1 Pet. 1:20(18-21)	was **foreordained** before the foundation of the world
1 Jn. 2:1	if any man sin, we have an **advocate** with the Father
1 Jn. 4:10(9,10)	he loved us, and **sent** his Son to be the propitiation
1 Jn. 4:14	the Father **sent** the Son to be the Saviour of the world
Jude 1:15(14,15)	to **execute** judgment upon all, and to convince all that
Rev. 1:18(12-18)	I...have the **keys** of hell and of death.
Rev. 5:12	Worthy is the Lamb that was slain to receive **power**
Rev. 12:10(7-12)	the kingdom of our God, and the **power** of his Christ
Rev. 19:15(11-16)	nations: and he shall **rule** them with a rod of iron
2 Ne. 9:5	that all men might become **subject** unto him.
2 Ne. 10:14	I, the Lord, the **king** of heaven, will be their king
Mosiah 3:5(5-8)	the Lord Omnipotent who **reigneth**, who was, and is from
Mosiah 7:27	that Christ was the **God**, the Father of all things, and
Mosiah 15:1	**God** himself shall come down among the children of men
Alma 5:50	behold the glory of the **King** of all the earth; and
Hel. 14:12	the Son of God, the **Father** of heaven and of earth, the
3 Ne. 9:15	behold, I am Jesus Christ the **Son** of God. I created
3 Ne. 15:5	behold, I am he that **gave** the law, and I am he who
3 Ne. 15:16	this much did the Father **command** me, that I should
3 Ne. 20:14	and the Father hath **commanded** me that I should give
3 Ne. 20:26	Father having raised me up unto you first, and **sent**
3 Ne. 27:13(10-15)	the will of my Father, because my Father **sent** me.
Ether 3:14(11-16)	he who was **prepared** from the foundation of the world
D&C 1:6	this is mine **authority**, and the authority of my
D&C 11:11	and by my **power** I give these words unto thee.
D&C 19:24	I came by the **will** of the Father, and I do his will.
D&C 20:24	**reign** with...power according to the will of the Father
D&C 29:5	in your midst, and am your **advocate** with the Father
D&C 31:13	even Jesus Christ, your Redeemer, by the **will** of the
D&C 32:3	I am their **advocate** with the Father, and nothing shall
D&C 49:5	I...have **sent** mine Only Begotten Son into the world
D&C 62:1	Lord your God, even Jesus Christ, your **advocate**, who
D&C 76:42(41,42)	whom the Father had put into his **power** and made by him
D&C 93:4(3-5)	the Father because he **gave** me of his fulness, and the
D&C 93:17(15-25)	received all **power**, both in heaven and on earth, and
D&C 107:3(1-4)	**priesthood**, after the Order of the Son of God.
D&C 107:19	Jesus the **mediator** of the new covenant.
D&C 110:4	I am he who was slain; I am your **advocate** with the
D&C 124:123	which is after the order of mine **Only** Begotten Son.
D&C 132:59	by mine own voice, and...the voice of him that **sent**
Moses 1:32(32-33)	by the **word** of my power, have I created them, which

JESUS CHRIST, AUTHORITY OF cont.

Moses 4:2(1-2)	which was my Beloved and **Chosen** from the beginning
Moses 5:57	who was **prepared** from before the foundation of the
Moses 6:52(50-52)	Jesus Christ, the only **name**...whereby salvation shall
Abr. 3:27(22-28)	and the Lord said: I will **send** the first.

JESUS CHRIST, BAPTISM OF

Matt. 3:13(13-17)	cometh Jesus from Galilee...unto John, to be **baptized**
Mark 1:9(9-11)	Jesus...was **baptized** of John in Jordan.
Mark 10:38(38-39)	be baptized with the **baptism** that I am baptized with
Luke 3:21(21,22)	Jesus also being **baptized**, and praying, the heaven was
John 1:32(19-34)	I saw the **Spirit** descending...it abode upon him.
1 Ne. 10:9(7-10)	in Bethabara...he should **baptize** with water; even that
1 Ne. 11:27	the Lamb of God went forth and was **baptized** of him
2 Ne. 31:5(4-13)	if the Lamb of God...should have need to be **baptized**

JESUS CHRIST, BETRAYAL OF

Ps. 22:16(13-18)	the assembly of the **wicked** have inclosed me: they
Ps. 41:9	hath lifted up his **heel** against me.
Zech. 11:12(12-13)	they weighed for my price **thirty** pieces of silver.
Zech. 13:6	I was **wounded** in the house of my friends.
Matt. 10:4	and Judas Iscariot, who also **betrayed** him.
Matt. 17:22(22-23)	the Son of man shall be **betrayed** into the hands of men
Matt. 20:18(17-19)	the Son of man shall be **betrayed** unto the chief priest
Matt. 26:2(1-5)	the Son of man is **betrayed** to be crucified.
Matt. 26:16(14-25)	he sought opportunity to **betray** him.
Matt. 26:45(45-56)	the Son of man is **betrayed** into the hands of sinners.
Matt. 27:4(1-10)	I have **betrayed** the innocent blood. And they said
Matt. 27:9	and they took the **thirty** pieces of silver, the price
Matt. 27:18	for he knew that for envy they had **delivered** him.
Mark 11:18(15-19)	the scribes and chief priests...sought how...**destroy**
Mark 14:44(43-52)	he that **betrayed** him had given them a token, saying
Luke 22:48(47-53)	Judas, **betrayest** thou the Son of man with a kiss
John 13:21(18-32)	I say unto you, that one of you shall **betray** me.
1 Ne. 11:32(32-34)	he was **taken** by the people; yea, the Son of the
1 Ne. 19:10	yieldeth himself...into the hands of **wicked** men, to be
2 Ne. 6:9(8-10)	after he should mainifest himself they should **scourge**
D&C 45:53(51-53)	lament because they **persecuted** their king.

JESUS CHRIST, BIRTH OF

Isa. 7:14(10-16)	a **virgin** shall conceive, and bear a son, and shall
Isa. 9:6(6-7)	for unto us a child is **born**...shall be called
Micah 5:2	**Bethlehem**...out of thee shall he come forth unto me
Matt. 1:23(18-25)	a **virgin** shall...bring forth a son...Emmanuel, which
Matt. 2:1	Jesus was **born** in Bethlehem...in the days of Herod the
Luke 1:31(26-35)	bring forth a son, and shalt call his name **Jesus**.
Luke 2:11(1-21)	unto you is **born** this day...a Saviour, which is Christ

JESUS CHRIST, BIRTH OF cont.

John 1:14(3,14)	and the Word was made **flesh**, and dwelt among us, (and
Rom. 1:3	Jesus Christ...made of the **seed** of David according to
Gal. 4:4	God sent..**Son**, made of a woman, made under the law
1 Ne. 10:4	six hundred years...raise up among the Jews..a **Messiah**
1 Ne. 11:18(15-20)	**mother** of the Son of God, after the manner of the
1 Ne. 19:8	he **cometh**..six hundred years from the time..left
2 Ne. 17:14	a **virgin** shall conceive, and shall bear a son, and
2 Ne. 25:19	the **Messiah** cometh in six hundred years from the time
2 Ne. 26:3	shall be signs given unto my people of his **birth**, and
Alma 7:10(7-10)	he shall be **born** of Mary, at Jerusalem which is the
Hel. 14:4(2-12)	it shall be the night before he is **born**.
3 Ne. 1:19(8-21)	the day that the Lord should be **born**, because of the
D&C 19:24	I **came** by the will of the Father, and I do his will.
D&C 20:1	since the **coming** of our Lord...in the flesh, it being
D&C 76:41	that he **came** into the world, even Jesus, to be
D&C 93:4	I...made **flesh** my tabernacle, and dwelt among the sons
Moses 5:57	Son...should **come** in the meridian of time, who was
Moses 6:62(57,62)	**Only Begotten**, who shall come in the meridian of time.

JESUS CHRIST, CONDESCENSION OF

Ps. 113:6(4-6)	who **humbleth** himself to behold...the earth
Isa. 50:6(5,6)	I **gave** my back to the smiters, and my cheeks to them
Isa. 53:2(1-3)	grow...as a root out of a **dry** ground: he hath no form
John 1:14	the Word was made **flesh**, and dwelt among us, (and we
John 3:13(13,16)	he that **came** down from heaven, even the Son of man
John 6:38	I **came** down from heaven, not to do mine own will, but
Rom. 8:3	God sending his...Son in the likeness of sinful **flesh**
Rom. 9:5	fathers...of whom as concerning the **flesh** Christ came
Gal. 4:4	God **sent** forth his Son, made of a woman, made under
1 Tim. 3:16	God was manifest in the **flesh**, justified in the Spirit
Heb. 2:9(9-18)	Jesus, who was made a little **lower** than the angels for
1 Jn. 5:6	he that **came** by water and blood, even Jesus Christ
1 Ne. 11:16(16-33)	knowest thou the **condescension** of God
1 Ne. 11:26(26-28)	look and behold the **condescension** of God
1 Ne. 19:10(10-13)	God of Abraham...**yieldeth** himself...into the hands of
2 Ne. 4:26	if the Lord in his **condescension** unto the children of
Mosiah 15:2(2-7)	because he dwelleth in **flesh** he shall be called the
Alma 7:13(8-13)	Son of God suffereth according to the **flesh** that he
Alma 19:13	my Redeemer...shall...be **born** of a woman, and he shall
3 Ne. 1:13(12-17)	on the morrow **come** I into the world, to show unto the
Ether 3:9(6-9,16,21)	I shall take upon me **flesh** and blood; and never has
D&C 20:26(21,26)	he came in the meridian of time, in the **flesh**, but all
D&C 88:6	as also he **descended** below all things, in that he
D&C 93:4(2-5,11)	the Son because I...made **flesh** my tabernacle, and
Moses 7:47(46-47)	the coming of the Son of Man, even in the **flesh**; and

JESUS CHRIST, CREATOR

Gen. 1:26(26-27)	let **us** make man in our image, after our likeness: and
Gen. 3:22	God said, behold, the man is become as one of **us**, to
2 Kgs. 19:15	O Lord God of Israel...thou hast **made** heaven and earth
Job 10:8(8-12)	thine hands have **made** me and fashioned me together
Job 26:13	by his spirit he hath **garnished** the heavens; his hand
Job 38:4(4-6)	when I **laid** the foundations of the earth? declare, if
Ps. 33:6	by the **word** of the Lord were the heavens made; and all
Isa. 40:28(25-28)	the Lord, the **creator** of the ends of the earth, faint
Isa. 41:20	the Holy One of Israel hath **created** it.
Isa. 42:5	God the Lord, he that **created** the heavens, and
Isa. 44:24	thy Redeemer ...that **maketh** all things; that
Isa. 45:12(12-15)	I have **made** the earth, and created man upon it: I
Isa. 45:18	the Lord that **created** the heavens; God himself that
Isa. 65:17	behold, I **create** new heavens and a new earth: and the
Jer. 51:15(15-16)	he hath **made** the earth by his power, he hath
Amos 4:13	he that **formeth** the mountains, and createth the wind
John 1:3(1-4)	all things were **made** by him; and without him was not
John 1:10	world was **made** by him, and the world knew him not.
Acts 7:50	hath not my hand **made** all these things
Acts 14:15	living God, which **made** heaven, and earth, and the sea
Eph. 3:9	God, who **created** all things by Jesus Christ
Col. 1:16(14-17)	all things were **created** by him, and for him
Col. 3:10(9,10)	after the image of him that **created** him
Heb. 1:2(1-3)	his Son...by whom also he **made** the worlds
Heb. 1:10	thou, Lord...hast laid the **foundation** of the earth
Heb. 11:3	the worlds were framed by the **word** of God, so that
2 Pet. 3:5(5-7)	by the **word** of God the heavens were of old, and the
Rev. 4:11	for thou hast **created** all things, and for thy
1 Ne. 17:36	Lord hath **created** the earth that it should be
2:14	there is a God, and he hath **created** all things, both
2 Ne. 2:15	he had **created** our first parents, and the beasts of
2 Ne. 9:5	the great **Creator** that he suffereth himself to become
2 Ne. 29:7	I, the Lord your God, have **created** all men, and that
Jacob 2:21	him who **created** all flesh? And the one being is as
Jacob 4:9(8-10)	which earth was **created** by the power of his word.
Mosiah 3:8(8-10)	Jesus Christ...the **Creator** of all things from the
Mosiah 4:2	the Son of God, who **created** heaven and earth, and all
Mosiah 4:9	that he **created** all things, both in heaven and in
Mosiah 4:12	the glory of him that **created** you, or in the knowledge
Mosiah 5:15	Lord God Omnipotent...who **created** all things, in
Mosiah 7:27	Christ was the God, the **Father** of all things, and said
Mosiah 26:23	for it is I that hath **created** them; and it is I that
Alma 1:4	for the Lord had **created** all men, and had also
Alma 5:15	in the redemption of him who **created** you? Do you look
Hel. 14:12	Jesus Christ..**Creator** of all things from the beginning
3 Ne. 9:15(15-18)	Jesus Christ...**created** the heavens and the earth, and
Ether 3:16(15-16)	man have I **created** after the body of my spirit; and
Ether 4:7	**Jesus** Christ...Father of the heavens and of the earth
D&C 14:9	Jesus Christ...who **created** the heavens and the earth
D&C 29:31(30-32)	for by the power of my Spirit **created** I them; yea, all
D&C 38:3(1-3)	I am the same which spake, and the world was **made**, and
D&C 45:1	who **made** the heavens and all the hosts thereof, and
D&C 76:24(23-24)	by him...the worlds are and were **created**, and the

JESUS CHRIST, CREATOR cont.

D&C 88:7(5-15)	he is in the sun..and the power...by which it was **made**
D&C 88:13(5-13)	light...which **giveth** life to all things, which is the
D&C 93:9(8-10)	the Redeemer of the world...the world was **made** by him
D&C 104:17(17,18)	yea, I **prepared** all things, and have given unto the
D&C 117:6	have I not **made** the earth? Do I not hold the destinies
Moses 1:33	by the Son I **created** them, which is mine Only Begotten
Moses 2:1	by mine Only Begotten I **created** these things; yea, in
Moses 2:26	mine Only Begotten...Let **us** make man in our image
Moses 2:27(26-27)	I, God, **created** man in mine own image, in the image
Abr. 3:24	**we** will make an earth whereon these may dwell
Abr. 4:1	**Gods**, organized and formed the heavens and the earth.

JESUS CHRIST, CRUCIFIXION OF

Deut. 21:23(22-23)	his body shall not remain all night upon the **tree**, but
Ps. 22:1(1,14-22)	my God, my God, why hast thou **forsaken** me? why art
Ps. 22:16	they **pierced** my hands and my feet.
Isa. 53:12(1-12)	poured out his soul unto **death**...numbered with the
Dan. 9:26(26,27)	shall **Messiah** be cut off, but not for himself: and the
Zech. 12:10	they shall look upon me whom they have **pierced**, and
Zech. 13:6(6-9)	what are these **wounds** in thine hands? then he shall
Matt. 20:19	to mock, and to scourge, and to **crucify** him: and the
Matt. 27:35(26-66)	and they **crucified** him, and parted his garments
Mark 9:12(12,31)	Son of man...must **suffer**...be set at nought.
Mark 15:34	my God, my God, why hast thou **forsaken** me
John 12:32(31-33)	and I, if I be **lifted** up from the earth, will draw all
John 19:31(30-37)	the bodies should not remain upon the **cross** on the
John 19:37	they shall look on him whom they **pierced**.
John 20:25	I shall see in his hands the **print** of the nails, and
Acts 2:23(22-24)	and by wicked hands have **crucified** and slain
Acts 2:36	that same Jesus, whom ye have **crucified**, both Lord and
Acts 5:30	Jesus, whom ye slew and **hanged** on a tree.
1 Cor. 1:23	but we preach Christ **crucified**, unto the Jews a
1 Cor. 2:2	save Jesus Christ, and him **crucified**.
1 Cor. 2:8(7,8)	known it, they would not have **crucified** the Lord of
2 Cor. 13:4	though he was **crucified** through weakness, yet he
Heb. 6:6(4-6)	**crucify** to themselves the Son of God afresh, and put
Rev. 11:8	and Egypt, where also our Lord was **crucified**.
1 Ne. 10:11	after they had **slain** the Messiah, who should come, and
1 Ne. 11:33(32-33)	he was lifted up upon the **cross** and slain for the sins
1 Ne. 19:10(7-14)	yieldeth himself...to be lifted up...and...**crucified**
2 Ne. 6:9(9-11)	they should scourge him and **crucify** him, according to
2 Ne. 10:5(2-8)	they...will stiffen their necks...that he be **crucified**
2 Ne. 25:13(12-14)	they will **crucify** him; and after he is laid in a
Mosiah 3:9(5-12)	they shall...scourge him, and shall **crucify** him.
Mosiah 14:5	he was **wounded** for our transgressions, he was bruised
Mosiah 15:7(5-13)	even so he shall be led, **crucified**, and slain, the
3 Ne. 8:5(5-25)	thirty and fourth year...there arose a great **storm**
3 Ne. 9:16(1-22)	my own **received** me not...scriptures...are fulfilled.
D&C 6:37	the prints of the **nails** in my hands and feet; be
D&C 20:23(21-24)	he was **crucified**, died, and rose again the third day
D&C 21:9(8,9)	Jesus was **crucified** by sinful men for the sins of the

JESUS CHRIST, CRUCIFIXION OF cont.

D&C 35:2	who was **crucified** for the sins of the world, even as
D&C 45:52	I am Jesus that was **crucified**. I am the Son of God.
D&C 46:13	to know...that he was **crucified** for the sins of the
D&C 53:2	who was **crucified** for the sins of the world, give unto
D&C 54:1	who was **crucified** for the sins of the world
D&C 76:41(40-43)	even Jesus, to be **crucified** for the world, and to bear
Moses 7:55(55-57)	beheld the Son of Man lifted up on the **cross**, after
JFS-V 1:27(26-30)	time...between the **crucifixion** and his resurrection
JFS-V 1:35(35-36)	sacrifice of the Son of God upon the **cross**.

JESUS CHRIST, DAVIDIC DESCENT OF

1 Sam. 16:1	**Jesse** the Bethlehemite...a king among his sons.
1 Sam. 17:12	**David** was the son of...Jesse; and he had eight sons
2 Sam. 7:13(12-17)	I will **stablish** the throne of his kingdom for ever.
Ps. 89:4(3,4)	thy seed will I **establish** for ever, and build up thy
Ps. 89:27(22-37)	also I will make him my **firstborn**, higher than the
Ps. 132:11(11-13)	of the **fruit** of thy body will I set upon thy throne.
Ps. 132:17	there will I make the horn of **David** to bud: I have
Isa. 9:7(6,7)	upon the throne of **David**, and upon his kingdom, to
Isa. 11:1(1-10)	a rod out of the stem of **Jesse**, and a Branch shall
Jer. 23:5(5,6)	I will raise unto **David** a righteous Branch, and a King
Jer. 33:15(14-16)	I cause the Branch...to grow up unto **David**; and he
Zech. 3:8(8-9)	behold, I will bring forth my servant the **BRANCH**
Zech. 6:12(9-15)	whose name is The **BRANCH**...he shall grow up out of his
Zech. 12:7(7-12)	the glory of the house of **David** and the glory of the
Matt. 1:1(1-17)	generation of Jesus Christ, the son of **David**, the son
Matt. 12:23	and said, is not this the son of **David**
Matt. 22:42	they say unto him, the son of **David**.
Luke 1:32(26-38)	God shall give...him the throne of his father **David**
Luke 3:23(23-38)	**Jesus**...being (as was supposed) the son of Joseph
John 7:42	Christ cometh of the seed of **David**, and out of the
Acts 2:30(29-31)	of the fruit of his loins...he would raise up **Christ**
Acts 13:23(22,23)	of this man's **seed** hath God...raised...Jesus
Rom. 1:3	Jesus Christ...made of the seed of **David** according to
Rom. 15:12(8-12)	a root of **Jesse**, and he that shall rise to reign over
2 Ne. 21:1(1-10)	and a **branch** shall grow out of his roots.
D&C 113:1(1-6)	who is the **Stem** of Jesse spoken of in the 1st, 2d, 3d

JESUS CHRIST, DEATH OF

Prov. 14:32	the righteous hath hope in his **death**.
Isa. 25:8	he will swallow up **death** in victory; and the Lord God
Isa. 53:9	his grave with the wicked...with the rich in his **death**
Isa. 53:12(7-12)	he hath poured out his soul unto **death**: and he was
Hosea 13:14	O **death**, I will be thy plagues; O grave, I will be thy
Jonah 1:17	in the belly of the fish **three** days and three nights.
Matt. 12:40(39,40)	so shall the Son of man be **three** days and three nights
Matt. 16:4	no sign be given...but the sign of the prophet **Jonas**.
Matt. 20:18	Son of man shall be betrayed...condemn him to **death**
Matt. 26:66(59,66)	they answered and said, he is guilty of **death**.

JESUS CHRIST, DEATH OF cont.

Mark 14:55(55,64)	sought for witness against Jesus to put him to **death**
Luke 9:31	spake of his **decease** which he should accomplish at
John 12:33(31-33)	this he said, signifying what **death** he should die.
Acts 2:24(22-24)	having loosed the pains of **death**: because it was not
Rom. 5:10(1-15)	we were reconciled to God by the **death** of his Son
Rom. 6:4(3-13)	as Christ was raised up from the **dead** by the glory of
Rom. 6:8(3-11)	now if we be **dead** with Christ, we believe that we
1 Cor. 11:26(23-28)	ye do shew the Lord's **death** till he come.
1 Cor. 15:3(3-21)	that Christ **died** for our sins according to the
Philip. 2:8(7-9)	humbled himself, and became obedient unto **death**, even
Col. 1:22(18-22)	the body of his flesh through **death**, to present you
2 Tim. 1:10	who hath abolished **death**, and hath brought life and
Heb. 2:9(9-15)	Jesus...for the suffering of **death**, crowned with glory
Heb. 9:15(14-17)	by means of **death**, for the redemption of the
1 Pet. 3:18(18,19)	being put to **death** in the flesh, but quickened by the
Rev. 1:18	I am he that liveth, and was **dead**; and, behold, I am
1 Ne. 11:33	he was lifted up upon the cross and **slain** for the sins
1 Ne. 19:10	three days of darkness...sign given of his **death** unto
2 Ne. 9:5(5-7)	and **die** for all men, that all men might become subject
2 Ne. 25:14(13,14)	Messiah hath risen from the **dead**, and hath manifested
2 Ne. 26:3	signs given unto my people of his birth...his **death**
Mosiah 14:9	and with the rich in his **death**; because he had done
Mosiah 15:7(6-8)	becoming subject even unto **death**, the will of the Son
Mosiah 16:8(7-9)	the sting of **death** is swallowed up in Christ.
Mosiah 18:2	and sufferings, and **death** of Christ, and his
Alma 7:12(11,12)	and he will take upon him **death**, that he may loose the
Alma 11:42	**death** of Christ shall loose the bands of..temporal
Alma 16:19(18-20)	the Son of God, his sufferings and **death**, and also the
Alma 21:9	save it were through the **death** and sufferings of
Alma 22:14	but the sufferings and **death** of Christ atone for their
Hel. 14:14(14-28)	I give unto you, yea, a sign of his **death**.
3 Ne. 6:20	did testify boldly of his **death** and sufferings.
3 Ne. 8:5(5-25)	thirty and fourth year...there arose a great **storm**
3 Ne. 9:22	for such I have **laid** down my life, and have taken it
3 Ne. 11:2	the sign had been given concerning his **death**.
Morm. 9:13	because the **death** of Christ bringeth to pass the
Moro. 9:25	may his sufferings and **death**, and the showing his body
D&C 18:11(11,12)	your Redeemer suffered **death** in the flesh; wherefore
D&C 20:23	he was crucified, **died**, and rose again the third day
D&C 45:4	behold the sufferings and **death** of him who did no sin

JESUS CHRIST, DIVINE SONSHIP

Ps. 2:7	said unto me, thou art my **Son**; this day have I
Isa. 7:14(14-16)	a virgin shall conceive, and bear a **son**, and shall
Isa. 9:6(6-7)	unto us a **son** is given: and the government shall be
Matt. 3:17(16-17)	this is my beloved **Son**, in whom I am well pleased.
Matt. 16:16(13-17)	thou art the Christ, the **Son** of the living God.
Matt. 17:5(4-9)	this is my beloved **Son**, in whom I am well pleased
Matt. 27:43	for he said, I am the **Son** of God.
Luke 1:32(31-35)	he shall...be called the **Son** of the Highest: and the
John 1:14(1,14)	glory as of the **only** begotten of the Father,) full of

JESUS CHRIST, DIVINE SONSHIP cont.

John 1:18	the **only** begotten Son, which is in the bosom of the
John 3:16(16-18)	for God so loved the world, that he gave his...**Son**
John 3:35	the Father loveth the **Son**, and hath given all things
John 5:26(17-31)	so hath he given to the **Son** to have life in himself
John 10:36	because I said, I am the **Son** of God
John 16:15	all things that the **Father** hath are mine: therefore
John 17:1(1-2)	Father...glorify thy **Son**, that thy Son also may
John 20:21	as my **Father** hath sent me, even so send I you.
Acts 13:33	second psalm, Thou art my **Son**, this day have I
Rom. 15:6	glorify God, even the **Father** of our Lord Jesus Christ.
Col. 1:13(12-19)	translated us into the kingdom of his dear **Son**
Heb. 1:2(1-14)	by his **Son**, whom he hath appointed heir of all things
Heb. 1:5(5-8)	said he at any time, thou art my **Son**, this day have I
Heb. 7:28	the oath...maketh the **Son**, who is consecrated for
1 Ne. 11:21(21,32)	behold the Lamb of God...the **Son** of the Eternal Father
1 Ne. 13:40	the Lamb of God is the **Son** of the Eternal Father, and
2 Ne. 25:12	the **Only** Begotten of the Father, yea, even the Father
2 Ne. 25:19(12,19)	his name shall be Jesus Christ, the **Son** of God.
2 Ne. 31:11(11,13,18)	be baptized in the name of my Beloved **Son**.
Jacob 4:5	a similitude of God and his **Only** Begotten Son.
Jacob 4:11	through the atonement of Christ, his **Only** Begotten Son
Mosiah 15:2(1-2)	be called the **Son** of God, and having subjected the
Mosiah 15:3(1-4)	**conceived** by the power of God; and the Son, because
Alma 5:48(46-48)	Jesus Christ shall come...the **Son**, the Only Begotten
Alma 7:9(9-10)	**Son** of God cometh upon the...earth.
Alma 12:33(33-34)	I have mercy upon you, through mine **Only** Begotten Son
Alma 13:5	through the atonement of the **Only** Begotten Son, who
3 Ne. 9:15	behold, I am Jesus Christ the **Son** of God. I created
3 Ne. 11:7	behold my Beloved **Son**, in whom I am well pleased, in
Morm. 5:14	Jesus is the Christ, the **Son** of the living God; that
D&C 6:21	behold, I am Jesus Christ, the **Son** of God. I am the
D&C 20:21(17-25)	the Almighty God gave his **Only** Begotten Son, as it is
D&C 29:42	through faith on the name of mine **Only** Begotten Son.
D&C 49:5	I am God, and have sent mine **Only** Begotten Son into
D&C 76:25(13,25)	the Only Begotten **Son** whom the Father loved and who
D&C 76:54(50-70)	they are they who are the church of the **Firstborn**
D&C 88:5(4,5)	which glory is that of the church of the **Firstborn**
D&C 93:14(11-21)	called the **Son**...received not of the fulness at the
D&C 93:21	I was...with the Father, and am the **Firstborn**
Moses 1:33(6,21,33)	by the **Son** I created them, which is mine Only Begotten
Moses 2:1	by mine **Only** Begotten I created these things; yea, in
Moses 2:26(26-27)	mine **Only** Begotten, which was with me from the
Moses 3:18	I, the Lord God, said unto mine **Only** Begotten, that
Moses 4:2(1-3)	my Beloved **Son**, which was my Beloved and Chosen from
Moses 5:9	I am the **Only** Begotten of the Father from the
Moses 6:54	that the **Son** of God hath atoned for original guilt
Abr. 3:24(24-27)	stood one among them that was like unto **God**, and he
JS-H 1:17	the other- This is My Beloved **Son**. Hear Him
A of F 1:1	we believe...in His **Son**, Jesus Christ, and in the Holy
JFS-V 1:14	Father and his **Only** Begotten Son, Jesus Christ.

JESUS CHRIST, EXEMPLAR

Isa. 50:6(5-9)	I **hid** not my face from shame and spitting.
Matt. 4:19(19-20)	**follow** me, and I will make you fishers of men.
Mark 8:34	take up his cross, and **follow** me.
Mark 10:21	come, take up the cross, and **follow** me.
Luke 9:23	take up his cross daily, and **follow** me.
John 13:15(13-16)	I have given you an **example**...do as I have done to you
John 21:22(21-22)	what is that to thee? **follow** thou me.
Eph. 5:1	be ye therefore **followers** of God, as dear children
Heb. 4:15(14-16)	but was in all points **tempted** like as we are, yet with
Heb. 5:8(7-9)	yet **learned** he obedience by the things which he
1 Pet. 2:21	Christ...an **example**, that ye should follow his steps
1 Jn. 4:17	because as he **is**, so are we in this world.
2 Ne. 31:16(9-16)	following the **example** of the Son of the living God
3 Ne. 12:48	ye should be **perfect** even as I, or your Father who is
3 Ne. 18:6	this shall ye always observe to **do**, even as I have done
3 Ne. 18:16(15-16)	I have set an **example** for you.
3 Ne. 27:21(21-22)	that which ye have seen me **do** even that shall ye do
3 Ne. 27:27	what **manner** of men ought ye to be?...even as I am.
Moro. 7:48(47-48)	true **followers** of his Son...we shall be like him, for
D&C 35:2	even one in **me** as I am one in the Father, as the
D&C 56:2	take up his cross and **follow** me, and keep my

JESUS CHRIST, FAMILY OF

Matt. 12:46(46-50)	his mother and his **brethren** stood without, desiring
Matt. 13:55(54-56)	his mother called Mary? and his **brethren**, James, and
Mark 3:31(31-35)	there came then his **brethren** and his mother, and
Mark 6:3	son of Mary, the **brother** of James, and Joses, and of
Luke 8:19(19-21)	came to him his mother and his **brethren**, and could not
John 2:12	he, and his mother, and his **brethren**, and his
John 19:27(25-27)	then saith he to the disciple, Behold thy **mother**! And
Acts 1:14	Mary the mother of Jesus, and with his **brethren**.
Gal. 1:19	saw I none, save James the Lord's **brother**.

JESUS CHRIST, FIRSTBORN

Ps. 89:27(27-37)	also I will make him my **firstborn**, higher than the
Isa. 41:4	I the Lord, the **first**, and with the last; I am he.
John 1:1(1-5)	in the **beginning** was the Word, and the Word was with
Rom. 8:29(29-30)	of his Son, that he might be the **firstborn** among many
Col. 1:15(13-15)	invisible God, the **firstborn** of every creature
Col. 1:18	he is...the **firstborn** from the dead; that in all
Heb. 1:6(1-6)	he bringeth in the **firstbegotten** into the world, he
Heb. 12:23	to the general assembly and church of the **firstborn**
Rev. 1:11(8-18)	I am Alpha and Omega, the **first** and the last: and
Rev. 3:14	the Amen...the **beginning** of the creation of God
3 Ne. 9:18	I am **Alpha** and Omega, the beginning and the end.
3 Ne. 20:26	the Father having raised me up unto you **first**, and
D&C 38:1	Alpha and Omega, the **beginning** and the end, the same
D&C 76:54(54-71)	they are they who are the church of the **Firstborn**.
D&C 76:94(92-102)	who dwell in his presence...church of the **Firstborn**

JESUS CHRIST, FIRSTBORN cont.

D&C 77:11	as will come to the church of the **Firstborn**.
D&C 78:21(17-21)	for ye are the church of the **Firstborn**, and he will
D&C 88:5(4-5)	which glory is that of the church of the **Firstborn**
D&C 93:21(21-22)	I was...with the Father, and am the **Firstborn**
D&C 107:19(18-19)	with the general assembly and church of the **Firstborn**
D&C 110:4(1-4)	I am the **first** and the last; I am he who liveth, I am
Moses 2:26	mine Only Begotten...was with me from the **beginning**
Abr. 3:24	**one** among them that was like unto God, and he said
Abr. 3:27(27,28)	Lord said: I will send the **first**.

JESUS CHRIST, FOREORDAINED

Gen. 3:15(14,15)	and her seed; it shall **bruise** thy head, and thou shalt
Job 19:25	**redeemer** liveth, and that he shall stand at the latter
Isa. 25:8	he will swallow up death in **victory**; and the Lord God
Isa. 25:9	this is the Lord; we have **waited** for him, we will be
Isa. 26:19	together with **my** dead body shall they arise. Awake and
Hosea 13:14	I will ransom...I will **redeem** them from death: O death
John 1:1(1-4)	in the **beginning** was the Word, and the Word was with
John 17:5(4,5,24)	glory which I had with thee **before** the world was.
1 Pet. 1:20(19-21)	**foreordained** before the foundation of the world, but
Mosiah 3:5	Lord Omnipotent...who was, and is from all **eternity**
3 Ne. 9:15	I was with the Father from the **beginning**. I am in the
Ether 3:14(11-16)	he who was **prepared** from the foundation of the world
D&C 76:13(12-13)	Son...in the bosom of the Father...from the **beginning**
D&C 93:21(7-11,21)	I was in the **beginning** with the Father, and am the
Moses 4:2(1-2)	which was my Beloved and **Chosen** from the beginning
Abr. 3:27(24-28)	and the Lord said: I will **send** the first.

JESUS CHRIST, GLORY OF

Ex. 33:18(18-23)	and he said, I beseech thee, shew me thy **glory**.
Ex. 40:34(34,35)	the **glory** of the Lord filled the tabernacle.
Isa. 6:3	Lord of hosts: the whole earth is full of his **glory**.
Isa. 40:5	the **glory** of the Lord shall be revealed, and all flesh
Isa. 60:2(1,2)	arise upon thee, and his **glory** shall be seen upon thee
Ezek. 1:28(26-28)	the appearance of the likeness of the **glory** of the Lord
Zech. 2:5	I, saith the Lord...will be the **glory** in the midst of
Matt. 16:27(26-28)	the Son of man shall come in the **glory** of his Father
Matt. 17:2(1-5)	was **transfigured** before them: and his face did shine
Matt. 24:30	see the Son of man coming...with power and great **glory**
John 1:14	we beheld his **glory**, the glory as of the only begotten
John 17:5	glorify thou me...with the **glory** which I had with thee
Acts 7:55	looked up...and saw the **glory** of God, and Jesus
Rev. 1:14(13-17)	and his eyes were as a flame of **fire**
1 Ne. 22:24	the Holy One of Israel must reign in...great **glory**.
2 Ne. 1:15	I have beheld his **glory**, and I am encircled about
2 Ne. 16:3	the whole earth is full of his **glory**.
2 Ne. 33:11	Christ will show unto you, with power and great **glory**
Jacob 4:4	we had a hope of his **glory** many hundred years before
Alma 5:50	the Son of God cometh in his **glory**, in his might

JESUS CHRIST, GLORY OF cont.

Alma 9:26	his glory shall be the **glory** of the Only Begotten of
Alma 13:24(24,25)	his word at the time of his coming in his **glory**.
3 Ne. 26:3	until the time that he should come in his **glory**- yea
D&C 7:3	thou shalt tarry until I come in my **glory**, and shalt
D&C 29:12	being clothed...in **glory** even as I am, to judge the
D&C 45:16(16,17)	in the day when I shall come in my **glory** in the clouds
D&C 45:44	clothed with power and great **glory**; with all the holy
D&C 45:56(56-59)	when I shall come in my **glory**, shall the parable be
D&C 45:67(66,67)	and the **glory** of the Lord shall be there, and the
D&C 49:6	he has taken his power on the right hand of his **glory**
D&C 67:12(11-13)	neither can any natural man abide the **presence** of God
D&C 76:20	and we beheld the **glory** of the Son, on the right hand
D&C 93:6	John saw and bore record of the fulness of my **glory**
D&C 93:11	I beheld his **glory**, as the glory of the Only Begotten
D&C 93:36(36-37)	the **glory** of God is intelligence, or, in other words
D&C 110:3(1-4)	his **countenance** shone above the brightness of the sun
Moses 1:5	behold all my works, except he behold all my **glory**
Moses 1:18(11-18)	his **glory** has been upon me, wherefore I can judge
Moses 1:39(37-39)	this is my work and my **glory**- to bring to pass the
JS-H 1:17	whose brightness and **glory** defy all description

JESUS CHRIST, GOOD SHEPHERD

Gen. 49:24	from thence is the **shepherd**, the stone of Israel
Ps. 23:1	the Lord is my **shepherd**; I shall not want.
Ps. 80:1(1-3)	O **Shepherd** of Israel, thou that leadest Joseph like a
Ps. 95:7(1-11)	we are the people of his pasture...the **sheep** of his
Isa. 40:11(9-11)	he shall feed his flock like a **shepherd**: he shall
Ezek. 34:12(11-19)	so will I seek out my **sheep**, and will deliver them out
Zech. 13:7	smite the **shepherd**, and the sheep shall be scattered
Matt. 9:36(35-38)	were scattered abroad, as sheep having no **shepherd**.
John 10:14(1-30)	I am the good **shepherd**, and know my sheep, and am
Heb. 13:20	our Lord Jesus, that great **shepherd** of the sheep
1 Pet. 2:25	but are now returned unto the **Shepherd** and Bishop of
1 Pet. 5:4	when the chief **Shepherd** shall appear, ye shall receive
1 Ne. 13:41	there is one God and one **Shepherd** over all the earth.
1 Ne. 22:25(23-26)	and he numbereth his **sheep**, and they know him; and
Mosiah 26:21	and he that will hear my voice shall be my **sheep**; and
Alma 5:38(37-60)	good **shepherd** doth call you...in his own name...Christ
Alma 5:57(57-60)	follow the voice of the **good** shepherd, come ye out
Hel. 7:18(18,19)	not hearken unto the voice of the **good** shepherd; yea
Hel. 15:13	knowledge of their Redeemer...great and true **shepherd**
3 Ne. 15:21(16-24)	and there shall be one fold, and one **shepherd**.
3 Ne. 16:3(1-3)	that there may be one fold and one **shepherd**; therefore
3 Ne. 18:31	behold I know my **sheep**, and they are numbered.
Morm. 5:17	and they had Christ for their **shepherd**; yea, they were
D&C 10:59(59,60)	other **sheep** have I which are not of this fold- unto
D&C 50:44(40-46)	I am the good **shepherd**, and the stone of Israel. He

JESUS CHRIST, HEAD OF THE CHURCH

Matt. 16:18(13-20)   upon this rock I will build my **church**; and the gates
Rom. 16:16(1-24)   the **churches** of Christ salute you.
1 Cor. 12:27(18-28)   ye are the body of **Christ**, and members in particular.
Eph. 1:22(15-23)   gave him to be the **head** over all things to the church
Eph. 4:15(11-16)   which is the **head**, even Christ
Eph. 5:23(23-33)   even as Christ is the **head** of the church: and he is
Col. 1:18(9-29)   and he is the **head** of the body, the church: who is the
1 Thes. 1:1(1-10)   unto the **church** of the Thessalonians..in..Jesus Christ
2 Thes. 1:1(1-12)   unto the **church** of the Thessalonians in...Jesus Christ
1 Ne. 14:12(10-14)   I beheld that the **church** of the Lamb, who were the
2 Ne. 25:14(12-20)   wo unto them that fight against God and...his **church**.
Mosiah 18:17   they were called...the **church** of Christ, from that
Mosiah 26:22(14-26)   this is my **church**; whosoever is baptized shall be
Mosiah 27:13(10-17)   for the Lord hath said: this is my **church**, and I will
Alma 1:19(19-26)   **church** of God...had taken upon them the name of Christ
3 Ne. 18:16(5-29)   pray in my **church**, among my people...in my name.
3 Ne. 21:22(20-23)   I will establish my **church** among them, and they shall
3 Ne. 27:8(1-12)   how be it my **church** save it be called in my name? For
3 Ne. 27:21(20-22)   ye must do in my **church**; for the works which ye have
4 Ne. 1:1   the disciples of Jesus had formed a **church** of Christ
4 Ne. 1:29   the true **church** of Christ, because of their humility
Moro. 6:4(1-9)   the **church** of Christ...who was the author and the
Moro. 7:3(1-4)   the **church**...the peaceable followers of Christ, and
D&C 1:1(1,6)   hearken, O ye people of my **church**, saith the voice of
D&C 5:14(9-25)   the coming forth of my **church** out of the wilderness-
D&C 10:67(52-70)   whosoever...cometh unto me, the same is my **church**.
D&C 11:16   you shall have...my **church** ...that you may know of a
D&C 18:5(1-30)   build up my **church**, upon the foundation of my gospel
D&C 30:6(6,7)   for I have given unto him power to build up my **church**
D&C 33:5(5-15)   this **church** have I established and called forth out
D&C 39:13(1-24)   thou art called...to build up my **church**...that it may
D&C 41:3(1-12)   ye may know how to govern my **church** and have all
D&C 42:59(1-93)   thou shalt take...hast received...to govern my **church**
D&C 43:15(1-28)   hearken ye elders of my **church**, whom I have appointed
D&C 45:1   of my **church**, to whom the kingdom has been given;
D&C 58:44   I say concerning...the elders of my **church**, the time
D&C 64:1   thus saith the Lord...O ye elders of my **church**
D&C 69:3(2-4)   continue in writing...history of...my **church**
D&C 84:32(6-42)   many whom I have called...to build up my **church**.
D&C 104:1(1-7)   order which I commanded...for the benefit of my **church**
D&C 115:3(1-4)   my **church** in Zion, for thus it shall be called, and
D&C 117:13(12-14)   let him contend earnestly for...my **church**, saith the
D&C 119:2(1,2)   building of mine house...the Presidency of my **Church**.
D&C 124:41(26-48)   for I deign to reveal unto my **church** things which have
D&C 124:94(91-96)   I appoint...a prophet...unto my **church**, as well as my
D&C 133:4(1-10)   gather ye together, O ye people of my **church**, upon the
D&C 133:16(1-16)   listen, ye elders of my **church** together, and hear the
D&C 136:41   therefore, hearken, O ye people of my **church**; and ye

JESUS CHRIST, JEHOVAH

Gen. 2:4(4-25)	the **Lord** God made the earth and the heavens
Gen. 4:26(25-26)	then began men to call upon the name of the **Lord**.
Gen. 22:14	Abraham called the name of that place **Jehovah-jireh**
Gen. 28:13	I am the **Lord** God of Abraham thy father, and the God
Ex. 3:6	I am the God of thy father, the God of Abraham, the
Ex. 3:14(13-15)	God said unto Moses, I AM THAT I AM: and he said, thus
Ps. 68:4	extol him...by his name **Jah**, and rejoice before him.
Ps. 83:18	thou, whose name alone is **Jehovah**, art the most high
Ps. 96:13	the **Lord**...cometh to judge the earth: he shall judge
Isa. 6:1(1,5)	I saw also the **Lord** sitting upon a throne, high and
Isa. 12:2(1-6)	God is my salvation...the Lord **Jehovah** is my strength
Isa. 26:4(1-4)	in the Lord **Jehovah** is everlasting strength
Isa. 41:4	I the Lord, the **first**, and with the last; I am he.
Isa. 41:14(13,14)	saith the **Lord**, and thy redeemer, the Holy One of
Isa. 43:11(3,11)	the Lord; and beside me there is no **saviour**.
Isa. 43:14	thus saith the Lord, your **redeemer**, the Holy One of
Isa. 44:6	I am the **first**, and I am the last; and beside me there
Isa. 44:24	thus saith the Lord, thy **redeemer**, and he that formed
Isa. 45:17	Israel...saved in the **Lord** with an everlasting
Isa. 45:21(15,21)	a just God and a **Saviour**; there is none beside me.
Isa. 49:26	I the Lord am thy **Saviour**...thy Redeemer, the mighty
Isa. 54:5	the **Lord** of hosts is his name; and thy Redeemer the
Isa. 60:16	know that I the Lord am thy **Saviour** and thy Redeemer
Isa. 63:8(7-14)	surely they are my people...so he was their **Saviour**.
Hosea 13:4	yet I am the Lord thy God...is no **saviour** beside me.
Jonah 1:9	the **Lord**, the God of heaven, which hath made the sea
John 1:1(1-3)	in the beginning was the Word...and the **Word** was God.
John 4:26(25,26)	Jesus saith unto her, **I** that speak unto thee am he.
John 8:58(55-59)	I say unto you, before Abraham was, I am.
1 Cor. 10:4(1-4)	drank of that spiritual Rock...that Rock was **Christ**.
Eph. 3:9	God, who created all things by **Jesus** Christ
1 Tim. 3:16	**God** was manifest in the flesh, justified in the Spirit
Heb. 1:2(1-3)	his **Son**...by whom also he made the worlds
Rev. 1:4	him which **is**, and which was, and which is to come; and
Rev. 21:6(3-7)	I am Alpha and Omega, the beginning and the end. I
1 Ne. 19:10	**God** of Abraham...Isaac...Jacob...to be crucified
1 Ne. 20:12(12,13)	I am the **first**, and I am also the last.
1 Ne. 21:26	I, the Lord, am thy Savior...the **Mighty** One of Jacob.
1 Ne. 22:12	the Lord is their Savior...the **Mighty** One of Israel.
2 Ne. 6:17(17-18)	the **Mighty** God shall deliver his covenant people. For
2 Ne. 11:2	Isaiah...verily saw my **Redeemer**, even as I have seen
Mosiah 3:5(5,17,18)	the **Lord** Omnipotent who reigneth, who was, and is
Mosiah 5:2	the Spirit of the **Lord** Omnipotent, which has wrought
Mosiah 5:15	Christ, the **Lord** God Omnipotent, may seal you his
3 Ne. 15:5	I am he that gave the law, and I am he who covenanted
Moro. 10:34	great **Jehovah**, the eternal judge of both quick and
D&C 19:10(10-12)	for **Endless** is my name. Wherefore
D&C 29:1	voice of Jesus Christ, your Redeemer, the Great I AM
D&C 36:1	thus saith the Lord God, the **Mighty** One of Israel
D&C 38:1(1-3)	Jesus Christ, the Great I AM, Alpha and Omega, the
D&C 39:1	to all eternity, the Great I AM, even Jesus Christ
D&C 93:8(6-17)	therefore, in the beginning the **Word** was, for he was
D&C 109:68	he has covenanted with **Jehovah**...Mighty God of Jacob

JESUS CHRIST, JEHOVAH cont.

D&C 110:3	rushing of great waters, even the voice of **Jehovah**
D&C 128:9	according to the decrees of the great **Jehovah**. This
Moses 1:33(31-33)	by the **Son** I created them, which is mine Only Begotten
Moses 2:1(1-3)	by mine **Only** Begotten I created these things; yea, in
Moses 5:8	call upon God in the name of the **Son** forevermore.
Abr. 1:16	Abraham, behold, my name is **Jehovah**, and I have heard

JESUS CHRIST, JUDGE

Gen. 18:25	shall not the **judge** of all the earth do right
Deut. 32:36	the Lord shall **judge** his people, and repent himself
Judg. 11:27	the Lord the **Judge** be judge this day between the
1 Sam. 2:10(1-10)	the Lord shall **judge** the ends of the earth; and he
1 Chr. 16:33	the Lord, because he cometh to **judge** the earth.
Ps. 7:8(8,11)	the Lord shall **judge** the people: judge me, O Lord
Ps. 9:8	and he shall **judge** the world in righteousness, he
Ps. 50:6	for God is **judge** himself. Selah.
Ps. 58:11	verily he is a God that **judgeth** in the earth.
Ps. 72:2(1-19)	he shall **judge** thy people with righteousness, and thy
Ps. 82:8	arise, O God, **judge** the earth: for thou shalt inherit
Ps. 94:2	lift up thyself, thou **judge** of the earth: render a
Ps. 96:10(10,13)	not be moved: he shall **judge** the people righteously.
Eccl. 3:17	God shall **judge** the righteous and the wicked: for
Eccl. 12:14	for God shall bring every work into **judgment**, with
Isa. 2:4	and he shall **judge** among the nations, and shall rebuke
Isa. 3:14	the Lord will enter into **judgment** with the ancients
Isa. 5:16	the Lord of hosts shall be exalted in **judgment**, and
Isa. 11:4(3-4)	but with righteousness shall he **judge** the poor, and
Isa. 33:22	for the Lord is our **judge**, the Lord is our lawgiver
Isa. 51:5	mine arms shall **judge** the people; the isles shall
Jer. 23:5(2-8)	king...shall execute **judgment** and justice in the earth
Dan. 7:14(13,14)	there was given him **dominion**, and glory, and a kingdom
Joel 3:12	there will I sit to **judge** all the heathen round about.
Matt. 16:27	Son of man...shall **reward** every man according to his
Matt. 25:32(31-46)	he shall **separate** them...as a shepherd divideth his
John 5:27(22-27)	hath given him authority to execute **judgment** also
John 8:16	and yet if I **judge**, my judgment is true: for I am not
John 9:39	for **judgment** I am come into this world, that they
Acts 10:42(40-43)	he which was ordained of God to be the **Judge** of quick
Acts 17:31	**judge** the world...by that man...raised...from the dead
Rom. 2:16	God shall **judge** the secrets of men by Jesus Christ
Rom. 3:6	God forbid: for then how shall God **judge** the world
1 Cor. 4:4	but he that **judgeth** me is the Lord.
2 Cor. 5:10	we must all appear before the **judgment** seat of Christ
2 Tim. 4:1(1,8)	Jesus Christ, who shall **judge** the quick and the dead
2 Tim. 4:8	a crown...which the Lord, the righteous **judge**, shall
Heb. 10:30(28-31)	the Lord shall **judge** his people.
Heb. 12:23	to God the **Judge** of all, and to the spirits of just
Heb. 13:4	but whoremongers and adulterers God will **judge**.
1 Pet. 4:5	him that is ready to **judge** the quick and the dead.
Jude 1:15(14-15)	to execute **judgment** upon all, and to convince all that
Rev. 16:5(5-7)	Lord...thou hast **judged** thus.

JESUS CHRIST, JUDGE cont.

Rev. 18:8	for strong is the Lord God who **judgeth** her.
Rev. 19:2	true and righteous are his **judgments**: for he hath
Rev. 19:11(11-13)	and in righteousness he doth **judge** and make war.
1 Ne. 15:33	stand before God, to be **judged** of their works; and if
1 Ne. 22:21	the Holy One of Israel...shall execute **judgment** in
2 Ne. 2:10	to be **judged** of him according to the truth and
2 Ne. 6:10	behold the **judgments** of the Holy One of Israel shall
2 Ne. 8:5	mine arm shall **judge** the people. The isles shall wait
2 Ne. 12:4	and he shall **judge** among the nations, and shall rebuke
2 Ne. 13:14	the Lord will enter into **judgment** with the ancients
2 Ne. 15:16	the Lord of Hosts shall be exalted in **judgment**, and
2 Ne. 21:4(3-4)	with righteousness shall he **judge** the poor, and
2 Ne. 28:23	stand before the throne of God, and be **judged**
2 Ne. 29:11	out of the books...I will **judge** the world, every man
1:7	the Lord did visit them in great **judgment**
Mosiah 3:10(10,17-18)	he standeth to **judge** the world; and behold, all these
Mosiah 16:10	stand before the bar of God, to be **judged** of him
Mosiah 27:31	all men shall stand to be **judged** of him, then shall
Alma 5:15	to stand before God to be **judged** according to the
Alma 10:20	well doth the Lord **judge** of your iniquities; well doth
Alma 11:44(41-44)	before...Christ the Son...to be **judged** according to
Alma 12:8(8-12)	to stand before God to be **judged** according to their
Alma 33:22	men shall stand before him, to be **judged** at the last
Alma 42:23	restored into his presence, to be **judged** according to
3 Ne. 27:14	to stand before me, to be **judged** of their works
3 Ne. 27:16	that day when I shall stand to **judge** the world.
Morm. 3:20	stand before the **judgment-seat** of Christ, yea, every
Morm. 7:6	man must be raised to stand before his **judgment-seat**.
Morm. 9:14	then cometh the **judgment** of the Holy One upon them
Ether 12:38	until we shall meet before the **judgment-seat** of Christ
Moro. 8:21	they stand against you at the **judgment-seat** of Christ.
Moro. 10:34	great Jehovah, the Eternal **Judge** of both quick and
D&C 1:10(9-12)	Lord shall come to **recompense** unto every man according
D&C 19:3	I shall pass...**judging** every man according to his
D&C 39:18(16-19)	become sanctified, I will stay mine hand in **judgment**.
D&C 43:33(29-33)	shall know, until they come before me in **judgment**.
D&C 50:27	all things are **subject** unto him, both in heaven and
D&C 76:68	heaven, where God and Christ are the **judge** of all.
D&C 77:12	will the Lord God...**judge** all things, and shall redeem
D&C 88:92(92,104)	prepare ye...for the **judgment** of our God is come.
D&C 99:5	behold, and lo, I come quickly to **judgment**, to
D&C 133:2	the Lord who shall come...with a curse to **judgment**
D&C 135:5	until we shall meet before the **judgment-seat** of Christ
Moses 6:57	Son of Man...Jesus Christ, a righteous **Judge**, who

JESUS CHRIST, LAMB OF GOD

Ex. 12:5(3-17)	**lamb**...without blemish, a male of the first year: ye
Isa. 53:7(1-12)	he is brought as a **lamb** to the slaughter, and as a
John 1:29(29,36)	behold the **Lamb** of God, which taketh away the sin of
Acts 8:32(32-35)	led as a sheep to the slaughter; and like a **lamb** dumb
1 Pet. 1:19(18-20)	blood of Christ, as of a **lamb** without blemish and

JESUS CHRIST, LAMB OF GOD cont.

Rev. 5:12(12-13)	Worthy is the **Lamb** that was slain to receive power
Rev. 7:14(13-17)	robes...made them white in the blood of the **Lamb**.
Rev. 13:8	the **Lamb** slain from the foundation of the world.
Rev. 19:7	the marriage of the **Lamb** is come, and his wife hath
Rev. 19:9	blessed...called unto the marriage supper of the **Lamb**.
Rev. 21:23(9-27)	and the **Lamb** is the light thereof.
Rev. 22:3	throne of God and of the **Lamb** shall be in it; and his
1 Ne. 10:10(7-10)	he had baptized the **Lamb** of God, who should take away
1 Ne. 11:21(21-34)	angel said unto me: Behold the **Lamb** of God, yea, even
1 Ne. 12:11(6-11)	made white in the blood of the **Lamb**, because of their
1 Ne. 13:40(26-42)	that the **Lamb** of God is the Son of the Eternal Father
1 Ne. 14:1(1-27)	shall hearken unto the **Lamb** of God in that day that
2 Ne. 31:4(4-6)	baptize the **Lamb** of God, which should take away the
Alma 7:14	the **Lamb** of God, who taketh away the sins of the world
Alma 13:11	washed white through the blood of the **Lamb**.
Morm. 9.6(1-6)	cleansed by the blood of the **Lamb**, at that great and
Ether 13:10(10-11)	garments are white through the blood of the **Lamb**; and
D&C 88:106	the **Lamb** of God hath overcome and trodden the
D&C 109:79	praise, singing Hosanna to God and the **Lamb**
D&C 133:56(52-56)	shall sing the song of the **Lamb**, day and night forever
Moses 7:47	the **Lamb** is slain from the foundation of the world

JESUS CHRIST, LIGHT OF THE WORLD

Ps. 27:1	the Lord is my **light** and my salvation; whom shall I
Isa. 2:5	O house of Jacob...walk in the **light** of the Lord.
Isa. 9:2(2-7)	people that walked in darkness have seen a great **light**
Isa. 60:19	but the Lord shall be unto thee an everlasting **light**
Micah 7:8(8-9)	sit in darkness, the Lord shall be a **light** unto me.
Matt. 4:16(12-16)	the people which sat in darkness saw great **light**; and
Luke 1:79(78-79)	to give **light** to them that sit in darkness and in the
Luke 2:32(21-33)	a **light** to lighten the Gentiles, and the glory of thy
John 1:4(4-9)	in him was life; and the life was the **light** of men.
John 1:9	the true **light**, which lighteth every man that cometh
John 8:12	I am the **light** of the world: he that followeth me
John 9:5	long as I am in the world, I am the **light** of the world
Eph. 5:14(8,14)	and Christ shall give thee **light**.
Rev. 21:23(23,24)	lighten it, and the Lamb is the **light** thereof.
2 Ne. 10:14	I will be a **light** unto them forever, that hear my word
Mosiah 16:9	he is the **light** and the life of the world; yea, a
Alma 38:9	he is the life and the **light** of the world. behold, he
3 Ne. 9:18	I am the **light** and the life of the world. I am Alpha
3 Ne. 11:11(10-11)	I am the **light** and the life of the world; and I have
3 Ne. 15:9	behold, I am the law, and the **light**. Look unto me, and
3 Ne. 18:16	behold I am the **light**; I have set an example for you.
3 Ne. 18:24	I am the **light** which ye shall hold up- that which ye
Ether 4:12(11-13)	I am the **light**, and the life, and the truth of the
D&C 6:21	I am the **light** which shineth in darkness, and the
D&C 10:70	words of him who is the life and **light** of the world
D&C 84:45(45-46)	whatsoever is truth is **light**, and whatsoever is light
D&C 93:9(2,9)	the **light** and the Redeemer of the world; the Spirit

JESUS CHRIST, LORD

Matt. 28:6	come, see the place where the **Lord** lay.
Mark 16:19(19-20)	after the **Lord** had spoken unto them, he was received
Luke 2:11	a Saviour, which is Christ the **Lord**.
Luke 22:61	the **Lord** turned, and looked upon Peter. And Peter
John 11:2	Mary which anointed the **Lord** with ointment, and wiped
John 20:2(2,13)	they have taken away the **Lord** out of the sepulchre
Acts 2:36	that same Jesus, whom ye have crucified, both **Lord** and
1 Cor. 8:6(5-6)	and one **Lord** Jesus Christ, by whom are all things, and
1 Cor. 12:3	say that Jesus is the **Lord**, but by the Holy Ghost.
2 Tim. 4:22	the **Lord** Jesus Christ be with thy spirit. Grace be
James 2:1	the faith of our **Lord** Jesus Christ, the Lord of glory
Rev. 17:14	for he is **Lord** of lords, and King of kings: and they
Rev. 22:21(20-21)	the grace of our **Lord** Jesus Christ be with you all.
2 Ne. 10:7	thus saith the **Lord** God: when the day cometh that they
2 Ne. 28:5	for the **Lord** and the Redeemer hath done his work, and
Mosiah 3:12	repentance and faith on the **Lord** Jesus Christ.
Mosiah 3:17(17-19)	through the name of Christ, the **Lord** Omnipotent.
Mosiah 5:15	that Christ, the **Lord** God Omnipotent, may seal you his
3 Ne. 1:12(12-14)	the voice of the **Lord** came unto him, saying
3 Ne. 11:13(10-13)	and it came to pass that the **Lord** spake unto them
Ether 3:6(6-14)	the **Lord** stretched forth his hand and touched the
D&C 10:70	your Redeemer, your **Lord** and your God. Amen.
D&C 17:9	and I, Jesus Christ, your **Lord** and your God, have
D&C 34:12	I come quickly. I am your **Lord** and your Redeemer.
D&C 35:1(1-2)	listen to the voice of the **Lord** your God, even Alpha
D&C 95:17	even Jesus Christ your **Lord**. Amen.
D&C 110:2(2-4)	we saw the **Lord** standing upon the breastwork of the

JESUS CHRIST, MESSENGER OF THE COVENANT

1 Sam. 3:21	the Lord revealed himself...by the **word** of the Lord.
Isa. 40:8	but the **word** of our God shall stand for ever.
Mal. 3:1	Lord..shall..come...even the **messenger** of the covenant
Matt. 15:24	I am not **sent** but unto the lost sheep of...Israel.
Luke 4:43	I must preach the kingdom...for therefore am I **sent**.
John 1:1	the **Word** was with God, and the Word was God.
John 3:17	God **sent** not his Son...to condemn the world; but that
John 5:36(36-38,43)	works...bear witness...that the Father hath **sent** me.
John 6:57(56-57)	the living Father hath **sent** me...I live by the Father
John 7:16(16-17)	my doctrine is not mine, but his that **sent** me.
John 7:29(28-29)	I know him: for I am from him, and he hath **sent** me.
John 8:42	neither came I of myself, but he **sent** me.
John 10:36	him, whom the Father hath...**sent** into the world, thou
John 11:42	that they may believe that thou hast **sent** me.
John 17:3(3-5,18-25)	know thee...God, and Jesus Christ, whom thou hast **sent**
Heb. 3:1	consider the **Apostle** and High Priest of our profession
1 Jn. 1:1	of the **Word** of life
Rev. 19:13(11-16)	and his name is called the **Word** of God.
3 Ne. 24:1	the Lord...even the **messenger** of the covenant, whom
D&C 93:8(8-10)	he was the Word, even the **messenger** of salvation
Moses 4:2(1-3)	my Beloved Son...**Chosen** from the beginning, said unto
Abr. 3:27	and the Lord said: I will **send** the first.

JESUS CHRIST, MESSIAH

Gen. 49:10	sceptre shall not depart from Judah..until **Shiloh** come
Isa. 10:27	the yoke shall be destroyed because of the **anointing**.
Isa. 11:1(1-5)	a rod out of the **stem** of Jesse, and a Branch shall
Isa. 61:1(1-3)	because the Lord hath **anointed** me to preach good
Dan. 9:26(25-26)	shall **Messiah** be cut off, but not for himself: and the
Matt. 11:27	all **things** are delivered unto me of my Father: and no
Matt. 16:20	should tell no man that he was Jesus the **Christ**.
Matt. 28:18(18-20)	all **power** is given unto me in heaven and in earth.
Mark 8:29	Peter answereth and saith...him, thou art the **Christ**.
Mark 14:61(61-62)	art thou the **Christ**, the Son of the Blessed
Luke 4:18(16-32)	because he hath **anointed** me to preach the gospel to
Luke 4:41	devils...saying, Thou art **Christ** the Son of God.
John 1:41	have found the **Messias**, which is, being interpreted
John 1:49	Son of God; thou art the **King** of Israel.
John 4:25(25-26)	I know that **Messias** cometh, which is called Christ
John 4:42	that this is indeed the **Christ**, the Saviour of the
John 20:31	believe that Jesus is the **Christ**, the Son of God; and
Acts 3:15	killed the **Prince** of life, whom God hath raised from
Acts 4:27(23-30)	thy holy child Jesus, whom thou hast **anointed**, both
Acts 5:31	to be a **Prince** and a Saviour, for to give repentance
Acts 10:38	how God **anointed** Jesus of Nazareth with the Holy Ghost
Acts 18:5	Paul ...testified to the Jews that Jesus was **Christ**.
Eph. 1:22	gave him to be the **head** over all things to the church
Philip. 2:11(9-11)	every tongue should confess that Jesus Christ is **Lord**
Heb. 2:10	the **captain** of their salvation perfect through
Heb. 12:2	looking unto Jesus the **author** and finisher of our
1 Ne. 10:4(4-14)	prophet...among the Jews...a **Messiah**...a Savior of the
1 Ne. 15:13	**Messiah**...manifested in body unto the children of men
2 Ne. 1:10	Holy One of Israel, the true **Messiah**, their Redeemer
2 Ne. 2:6(6-8)	redemption...through the Holy **Messiah**; for he is full
2 Ne. 2:26	the **Messiah** cometh in the fulness of time, that he may
2 Ne. 20:27	the yoke shall be destroyed because of the **anointing**.
2 Ne. 25:14	the **Messiah** hath risen from the dead, and hath
2 Ne. 25:18(17-19)	**Messiah** is...rejected of the Jews.
Mosiah 3:8(7-11)	and he shall be called Jesus **Christ**, the Son of God
D&C 19:1(1-3)	I am...**Christ** the Lord; yea, even I am he, the
D&C 58:22	whose right it is to **reign**, and subdues all enemies
Moses 4:2(1-4)	Beloved Son, which was my Beloved and **Chosen** from the
Moses 6:52	Jesus **Christ**, the only name which shall be given
Moses 7:53	and the Lord said...I am **Messiah**, the King of Zion
Abr. 3:27(22-28)	the Lord said: I will **send** the first.

JESUS CHRIST, MILLENNIAL REIGN

Ps. 89:4(1-4)	will I establish for ever, and build up thy **throne** to
Ps. 132:11(10-11)	David...of...fruit of thy body...set upon thy **throne**.
Isa. 9:6(6-7)	the **government** shall be upon his shoulder: and his
Isa. 11:3(1-9)	he shall not **judge** after the sight of his eyes
Isa. 16:5	in mercy shall the **throne** be established...of David
Isa. 40:11(9-11)	he shall feed his flock like a **shepherd**: he shall
Jer. 23:5(5,6)	a King shall **reign** and prosper, and shall execute
Dan. 2:44	shall the God of heaven set up a **kingdom**, which shall

JESUS CHRIST, MILLENNIAL REIGN cont.

Dan. 7:14(13,14,22,27)	his dominion is an **everlasting** dominion, which shall
Zeph. 3:15	the Lord, is in the **midst** of thee: thou shalt not see
Zech. 2:10	and I will **dwell** in the midst of thee, saith the Lord
Zech. 14:9(4-9)	the Lord shall be **king** over all the earth: in that day
Luke 1:32(30-33)	God shall give unto him the **throne** of his father David
1 Cor. 15:25(24-27)	for he must **reign**, till he hath put all enemies under
Rev. 11:15	he shall **reign** for ever and ever.
Rev. 20:4(1-4)	they lived and **reigned** with Christ a thousand years.
Rev. 20:7(7-15)	when the **thousand** years are expired, Satan shall be
1 Ne. 22:26(24-26)	righteousness, and the Holy One of Israel **reigneth**.
Jacob 5:75(74-76)	**Lord** of the vineyard saw that his fruit was good, and
D&C 1:36	the Lord...shall **reign** in their midst, and shall come
D&C 29:11	I will...dwell in righteousness...a **thousand** years
D&C 43:29	my people shall...**reign** with me on earth.
D&C 58:22	he reigns whose right it is to **reign**, and subdues all
D&C 76:63	come...to **reign** on the earth over his people.
D&C 76:108	sit on the throne...**reign** forever and ever.
A of F 1:10	that Christ will **reign** personally upon the earth; and

JESUS CHRIST, MISSION OF

Deut. 18:15(15-19)	a **Prophet** from the midst of thee, of thy brethren
Isa. 9:6(6-7)	the **government** shall be upon his shoulder: and his
Isa. 25:8	he will swallow up death in **victory**; and the Lord God
Isa. 26:19	together with my dead body shall they **arise**. Awake and
Isa. 53:5(3-12)	he was **wounded** for our transgressions, he was bruised
Isa. 61:1(1-3)	the Lord hath anointed me to **preach** good tidings unto
Zech. 13:6	what are these **wounds** in thine hands? Then he shall
Matt. 1:21(20-21)	he shall **save** his people from their sins.
Matt. 3:15(11-15)	thus it becometh us to fulfil all **righteousness**.
Matt. 18:11	the Son of man is come to **save** that which was lost.
Mark 1:38(38-39)	that I may **preach** there also: for therefore came I
Luke 1:33(30-33)	he shall **reign** over the house of Jacob for ever; and
Luke 4:18(16-21)	he hath sent me to heal the brokenhearted, to **preach**
John 1:3(1-3,14)	all things were **made** by him; and without him was not
John 6:38(38-40)	not to do mine own **will**, but the will of him that sent
John 12:23(23-27)	hour is come, that the Son of man should be **glorified**.
John 17:1(1-26)	glorify thy Son, that thy Son also may **glorify** thee
1 Cor. 15:22(21-22)	as in Adam all die...in Christ shall all be made **alive**
Heb. 5:9	author of eternal **salvation** unto all them that obey
Heb. 9:15(14-17)	he is the **mediator** of the new testament, that by means
2 Ne. 2:9(9-10)	make **intercession** for all the children of men; and
2 Ne. 9:5(5-6,10-11)	he suffereth himself to...**die** for all men, that all
Jacob 4:11(10-11)	**reconciled** unto him through the atonement of Christ
Mosiah 3:9(5-11)	**salvation**...through faith on his name; and even after
Mosiah 12:21	**publisheth** peace; that bringeth good tidings of good
Mosiah 15:1	shall **redeem** his people.
Mosiah 15:9(7-9)	**satisfied** the demands of justice.
Mosiah 18:2	**redemption**...through the...death of Christ, and his
Alma 5:27	Christ...**redeem** his people from their sins
Alma 22:14(13,14)	sufferings and death of Christ **atone** for...sins
Alma 42:15(15-24)	atonement...made...to bring about the plan of **mercy**

3 Ne. 9:17(15-22)	by me **redemption** cometh, and...the law of Moses
3 Ne. 11:11(10-11)	taking upon me the **sins** of the world, in the which I
3 Ne. 15:5(4-5)	I have come to **fulfil** the law; therefore it hath an
3 Ne. 27:13(13-15)	do the **will** of my Father, because my Father sent me.
Ether 3:14	in me shall all mankind have **light**, and that eternally
D&C 19:2(1-3)	that I might **subdue** all things unto myself
D&C 45:52(51-54)	I was **wounded** in the house of my friends. I am he who
D&C 93:9(1-17)	the light and the **Redeemer** of the world; the Spirit
Moses 1:39(38-39)	to bring to pass the **immortality** and eternal life of
Abr. 3:27(24-27)	and the Lord said: I will **send** the first.
JFS-V 1:25(25,26)	Savior spent about three years in his **ministry** among

JESUS CHRIST, POWER OF

Gen. 17:1	I am the **Almighty** God; walk before me, and be thou
Isa. 9:6	his name shall be called...The **mighty** God, The
Matt. 10:1	twelve disciples, he gave them **power** against unclean
Matt. 24:30	coming ...clouds of heaven with **power** and great glory.
Matt. 28:18	all **power** is given unto me in heaven and in earth.
Luke 4:14(14,36)	Jesus returned in the **power** of the Spirit into Galilee
John 1:3(1-4)	all things were **made** by him; and without him was not
John 1:12	to them gave he **power** to become the sons of God, even
John 3:35	hath given all **things** into his hand.
John 13:3	Father had given all **things** into his hands, and that
John 17:2	thou hast given him **power** over all flesh, that he
Acts 2:36	God hath made that same Jesus...both **Lord** and Christ.
Rom. 1:4	declared to be the Son of God with **power**, according
Rom. 1:16	gospel of Christ...the **power** of God unto salvation to
Rom. 1:20	even his eternal **power** and Godhead; so that they are
Rom. 14:9	that he might be **Lord** both of the dead and living.
1 Cor. 8:6	Jesus Christ, by whom are **all** things, and we by him.
1 Cor. 15:24(24-28)	he shall have put down all rule...authority and **power**.
Eph. 1:10(10,21)	gather together in one **all** things in Christ, both
Eph. 1:22(20-22)	and hath put **all** things under his feet, and gave him
Col. 1:11(11-16)	strengthened...according to his glorious **power**, unto
Rev. 5:13(12-13)	**power**, be unto him that sitteth upon the throne, and
Rev. 17:14	he is **Lord** of lords, and King of kings: and they that
Rev. 19:6	the Lord God **omnipotent** reigneth.
2 Ne. 19:6	his name shall be called...The **Mighty** God, The
2 Ne. 28:15	saith the Lord God **Almighty**, for they shall be thrust
Mosiah 3:5	with power, the Lord **Omnipotent**...shall come down from
D&C 19:3(2-3)	retaining all **power**, even to the destroying of Satan
D&C 50:27	for all things are **subject** unto him, both in heaven
D&C 76:10	by my **power** will I make known unto them the secrets
D&C 76:24	by him...and of him, the worlds are and were **created**
D&C 84:20(20-28)	in the ordinances...the **power** of godliness is manifest
D&C 88:7	Christ..light of the sun..power..by which it was made.
D&C 88:13	the **power** of God who sitteth upon his throne, who is
D&C 93:17(16-17)	he received all **power**, both in heaven and on earth
Moses 1:3	I am the Lord God **Almighty**, and Endless is my name
Moses 6:61	hath all **power** according to wisdom, mercy, truth
Abr. 3:17	God shall take in his heart to do...he will **do** it.

JESUS CHRIST, PROPHECIES ABOUT

Gen. 3:15	her seed...shall **bruise** thy head, and thou shalt
Gen. 49:10	from between his feet, until **Shiloh** come; and unto
Gen. 49:24	from thence is the shepherd, the **stone** of Israel
Ex. 12:46	neither shall ye **break** a bone thereof.
Num. 24:17	there shall come a **Star** out of Jacob, and a Sceptre
Deut. 18:15(15-19)	the Lord thy God will raise up unto thee a **Prophet**
Ps. 2:7(6,7,12)	thou art my **Son**; this day have I begotten thee.
Ps. 22:1(1,14-22)	my God, my God, why hast thou **forsaken** me? why art
Ps. 22:16(1-18)	they **pierced** my hands and my feet.
Ps. 24:10	who is this **King** of glory? The Lord of hosts, he is
Ps. 34:20	he keepeth all his bones: not one of them is **broken**.
Ps. 68:18	thou hast led **captivity** captive: thou hast received
Ps. 69:9(8,9)	the **zeal** of thine house hath eaten me up; and the
Ps. 69:20	reproach hath broken my heart...I am full of **heaviness**
Ps. 69:21	in my thirst they gave me **vinegar** to drink.
Ps. 110:4(1-7)	a **priest** for ever after the order of Melchizedek.
Ps. 118:22(22-23)	**stone** which the builders refused is become the head
Ps. 132:17	there will I make the **horn** of David to bud: I have
Isa. 7:14	a **virgin** shall conceive, and bear a son...Immanuel.
Isa. 9:6(1-7)	for unto us a **child** is born, unto us a son is given
Isa. 11:1(1-5)	there shall come...a rod out of the **stem** of Jesse, and
Isa. 22:23(21-23)	I will fasten him as a **nail** in a sure place; and he
Isa. 25:9(8-9)	this is our **God**; we have waited for him, and he will
Isa. 28:16	I lay in Zion for a foundation a **stone**...a sure
Isa. 40:3(3,9,10)	prepare ye the **way** of the Lord, make straight in the
Isa. 42:7(1-7)	to **open** the blind eyes, to bring out the prisoners
Isa. 50:6(5-9)	I gave my **back** to the smiters, and my cheeks to them
Isa. 53:5(1-12)	he was **wounded** for our transgressions, he was bruised
Isa. 55:4(1-4)	I have give him for a **witness** to the people, a leader
Isa. 59:20	the Redeemer shall **come** to Zion, and unto them that
Isa. 61:1(1-3)	**anointed** me to preach good tidings unto the meek; he
Jer. 23:5(1-8)	I will raise unto David a righteous **Branch**, and a King
Jer. 33:15(14-16)	will I cause the Branch...to grow up unto David; and
Ezek. 37:12(1-28)	thus saith the Lord...I will open your **graves**, and
Dan. 9:24(24,25)	end of sins, and to make **reconciliation** for iniquity
Dan. 9:26	shall **Messiah** be cut off, but not for himself: and the
Hosea 11:1	then I loved him, and called my son out of **Egypt**.
Hosea 13:14(4,9,10,14)	I will **redeem** them from death: O death, I will be thy
Jonah 2:6(2-9)	thou **brought** up my life from corruption, O Lord my God
Micah 5:2(1-3)	**Bethlehem**...out of thee shall he come forth unto me
Hab. 3:13(2,13,18)	thou wentest forth for the **salvation** of thy people
Zech. 3:8(8-9)	behold, I will bring forth my servant the **BRANCH**.
Zech. 6:12(9-15)	name is The **BRANCH**; and he shall grow up out of his
Zech. 9:9(9-11)	thy King cometh unto thee...**riding** upon an ass, and
Zech. 11:13(10-14)	I was **prised** at...thirty pieces of silver, and cast
Zech. 13:6(6,7)	I was **wounded** in the house of my friends.
Mal. 3:1	Lord, whom ye seek, shall suddenly **come** to his temple
Matt. 1:21(20-21)	thou shalt call his **name** Jesus: for he shall save his
Matt. 1:23(22,23)	**Emmanuel**, which being interpreted is, God with us.
Matt. 2:6(4-6,15,23)	**Bethlehem**...out of thee shall come a governor, that
Matt. 2:15	prophet, saying, Out of **Egypt** have I called my son.
Matt. 4:16(12-16)	the people which sat in darkness saw great **light**; and
Matt. 11:13	for all the **prophets** and the law prophesied until John

Matt. 21:42(40-43)	stone which the builders rejected...is become the head
Matt. 26:24(24,31,54)	the Son of man goeth as it is **written** of him: but woe
Matt. 27:48(34,48)	took a spunge, and filled it with **vinegar**, and put it
Matt. 27:52(52-53)	**graves** were opened...many bodies of the saints...arose
Mark 9:12(12,31)	**Son** of man...must suffer...be set at nought.
Luke 1:70(68-70)	as he spake by...his holy **prophets**, which have been
Luke 1:79(76-79)	to give **light** to them that sit in darkness and in the
Luke 2:21	Jesus...so **named** of the angel before he was conceived
Luke 4:21(16-21)	this day is this scripture **fulfilled** in your ears.
Luke 24:27	in all the **scriptures** the things concerning himself.
Luke 24:44	that all things must be **fulfilled**, which were written
John 1:45	we have found him, of whom **Moses**...did write, Jesus
John 3:14	as Moses lifted up the **serpent** in the wilderness, even
John 5:46(45-47)	had ye believed Moses...for he **wrote** of me.
John 6:14	this is of a truth that **prophet** that should come into
John 7:42	Christ cometh...out of the town of **Bethlehem**, where
Acts 3:24(19-26)	prophets...have likewise **foretold** of these days.
Acts 7:37(37-40)	Moses...said...A **prophet** shall the Lord your God raise
Rom. 9:33	I lay in Sion a **stumblingstone** and rock of offence
Rom. 16:20	the God of peace shall **bruise** Satan under your feet
1 Ne. 10:11(7-11)	after they had **slain** the Messiah, who should come, and
1 Ne. 11:18(14-34)	**virgin** whom thou seest is the mother of the Son of God
1 Ne. 11:33(32,33)	he was lifted up upon the **cross** and slain for the sins
1 Ne. 19:8(7-13)	he **cometh**...in six hundred years from the time my
1 Ne. 22:12	the Lord is their **Savior**...the Mighty One of Israel.
1 Ne. 22:21(20-21)	this **prophet** of whom Moses spake was the Holy One of
2 Ne. 2:8(6-10)	Holy Messiah, who **layeth** down his life according to
2 Ne. 6:17(17-18)	the Mighty God shall **deliver** his covenant people.
2 Ne. 10:3	Christ...should **come** among the Jews, among those who
2 Ne. 17:14	a **virgin**...shall bear a son...call his name Immanuel.
2 Ne. 18:14(13-17)	he shall be...for a **stone** of stumbling, and for a rock
2 Ne. 25:13(11-19)	he shall **rise** from the dead, with healing in his wings
2 Ne. 25:19	his **name** shall be Jesus Christ, the Son of God.
Jacob 4:15(4,15-17)	Jews...will reject the **stone** upon which they might
Jacob 7:11	none of the **prophets** have written, nor prophesied
Mosiah 3:8(5-10,14-15)	he shall be called **Jesus** Christ...and his mother shall
Mosiah 13:33	even all the prophets who have **prophesied** ever since
Mosiah 15:1(1-11)	**God** himself shall come down among the children of men
Mosiah 16:15(5-15)	**redemption** cometh through Christ the Lord, who is the
Alma 7:10(7-13)	be born of **Mary**, at Jerusalem...she being a virgin, a
Alma 21:9(7-9)	**redemption**...through the death and sufferings of
Hel. 5:9(9-11)	Jesus Christ, who shall come...to **redeem** the world.
Hel. 8:22(14-24)	they have testified of the **coming** of Christ, and have
Hel. 14:2(2-27)	five years more...then **cometh** the Son of God to redeem
3 Ne. 9:16	the **scriptures** concerning my coming are fulfilled.
3 Ne. 20:23(23-26)	I am he of whom Moses spake, saying: A **prophet** shall
Ether 3:14	I am he who was prepared...to **redeem** my people. Behold
D&C 5:19	utterly destroyed by the brightness of my **coming**.
D&C 20:26	prophets...who truly **testified** of him in all things
D&C 29:11(10-13,27)	I will **reveal** myself from heaven with power and great
D&C 33:17	you may be ready at the coming of the **Bridegroom**
D&C 34:7(6-8)	the time is soon at hand that I shall **come** in a cloud
D&C 35:21	shall abide the day of my **coming**; for they shall be

JESUS CHRIST, PROPHECIES ABOUT cont.

D&C 36:8	I will suddenly **come** to my temple. Even so. Amen.
D&C 39:20(20-23)	preparing the way...for the time of my **coming**
D&C 45:16(16,26)	when I shall come in my **glory** in the clouds of heaven
D&C 50:44	I am the good shepherd, and the **stone** of Israel. He
D&C 64:23	he that is **tithed** shall not be burned at his coming.
D&C 84:28	to prepare them for the **coming** of the Lord, in whose
D&C 88:96(92-99)	saints...quickened and be caught up to meet **him**.
D&C 90:2	keys...which **kingdom** is coming forth for the last time
D&C 106:4	the **coming** of the Lord draweth nigh, and it overtaketh
D&C 130:14(14-17)	time of the **coming** of the Son of Man, when I heard a
D&C 133:17	the hour of his **coming** is nigh
Moses 6:57(55-57)	the Son of Man, even **Jesus** Christ, a righteous Judge
Moses 7:55(53-56)	he looked and beheld the **Son** of Man lifted up on the
JS-H 1:40	he said that that **prophet** was Christ; but the day had

JESUS CHRIST, REDEEMER

Job 19:25	for I know that my **redeemer** liveth, and that he shall
Isa. 41:14	the Lord, and thy **redeemer**, the Holy One of Israel.
Isa. 53:4(1-12)	he hath borne our **griefs**, and carried our sorrows: yet
Isa. 54:5	thy **Redeemer** the Holy One of Israel; The God of the
Isa. 63:9(1-9)	in his love and in his pity he **redeemed** them; and he
Hosea 13:4(4,9,10,14)	no god but me: for there is no **saviour** beside me.
Hab. 3:13(2,13,18)	thou wentest forth for the **salvation** of thy people
Matt. 1:21(20-23)	Jesus: for he shall **save** his people from their sins.
Matt. 20:28(20-28)	Son of man came...to give his life a **ransom** for many.
Matt. 26:28(27-28)	blood...which is shed for many for the **remission** of
Luke 1:68(68-79)	the Lord God of Israel...**redeemed** his people
Luke 22:19(19-20)	this is my body which is **given** for you: this do in
John 1:29(29-34)	**Lamb** of God, which taketh away the sin of the world.
John 3:16(16-17)	God so loved the world...he **gave** his only begotten Son
Acts 13:38(38-41)	through this man is preached...**forgiveness** of sins
Rom. 3:24(23-26)	through the **redemption** that is in Christ Jesus
Rom. 5:10(10-11)	we were **reconciled** to God by the death of his Son
1 Cor. 15:3	Christ **died** for our sins according to the scriptures
Gal. 1:4(3-4)	who **gave** himself for our sins, that he might deliver
Eph. 1:7(3,7)	in whom we have **redemption** through his blood, the
1 Tim. 2:6(5-6)	who gave himself a **ransom** for all, to be testified in
Titus 2:14(13-14)	that he might **redeem** us from all iniquity, and purify
Heb. 2:17	to make **reconciliation** for the sins of the people.
Heb. 7:27(26-28)	offer up sacrifice...once, when he **offered** up himself.
Heb. 9:12(11-15)	by his own blood...obtained eternal **redemption** for us.
Heb. 9:28(24-28)	Christ was once **offered** to bear the sins of many; and
1 Pet. 1:18(18-20)	ye were not **redeemed** with corruptible things, as
1 Pet. 2:24	who his own self bare our **sins** in his own body on the
1 Pet. 3:18(18-19)	Christ also hath once **suffered** for sins, the just for
1 Jn. 2:2(1-2)	and he is the **propitiation** for our sins: and not for
1 Jn. 3:5	he was manifested to take away our **sins**; and in him
1 Jn. 4:10	sent his Son to be the **propitiation** for our sins.
Rev. 1:5(5-6)	**washed** us from our sins in his own blood
Rev. 5:9(9-10)	thou wast slain, and hast **redeemed** us to God by thy
2 Ne. 2:6(6-12)	**redemption** cometh in and through the Holy Messiah; for

JESUS CHRIST, REDEEMER cont.

Mosiah 3:11(7,11-12)	his blood **atoneth** for the sins of those who have
Mosiah 13:28	**atonement**, which God himself shall make for the sins
Mosiah 15:10	his soul has been made an **offering** for sin he shall
Mosiah 15:24(21-27)	have eternal life, being **redeemed** by the Lord.
Mosiah 16:15(5-15)	**redemption** cometh through Christ the Lord, who is the
Mosiah 18:2	**redemption**...brought to pass through...death of Christ
Alma 7:13(11-13)	the Son of God **suffereth** according to the flesh that
Alma 9:27(26-27)	he cometh to **redeem** those who will be baptized unto
Alma 11:40(37-41)	he shall come into the world to **redeem** his people; and
Alma 12:33(9-37)	this being the plan of **redemption** which was laid)
Alma 21:9(7-9)	**redemption**...through the death and sufferings of
Alma 22:14(13-14)	the sufferings and death of Christ **atone** for their
Alma 34:8(8-16)	Christ shall...take upon him the **transgressions** of his
Alma 42:15(1-28)	God himself **atoneth** for the sins of the world, to
Hel. 5:9(9-11)	Jesus Christ, who shall come...to **redeem** the world.
3 Ne. 9:17(15-22)	by me **redemption** cometh, and in me is the law of
3 Ne. 11:11(10-14)	glorified the Father in taking upon me the **sins** of the
Morm. 7:7(5-7)	and he hath brought to pass the **redemption** of the
Morm. 9:12(12-14)	because of Jesus Christ came the **redemption** of man.
Ether 3:14	I am he who was prepared...to **redeem** my people. Behold
D&C 18:11(11,12)	the Lord your **Redeemer** suffered death in the flesh
D&C 18:47	I, Jesus Christ...your God, and your **Redeemer**, by the
D&C 19:16(16-20)	I, God, have **suffered** these things for all, that they
D&C 29:46(46-47)	little children are **redeemed**..through mine Only
D&C 34:3(1-3)	who so loved the world that he **gave** his own life, that
D&C 45:4	behold the **sufferings** and death of him who did no sin
D&C 49:5	sent mine...Son...for the **redemption** of the world, and
D&C 77:12	Lord God...shall **redeem** all things, except that which
JFS-V 1:3(1-4)	Father and the Son in the coming of the **Redeemer** into
JFS-V 1:18(16-18,23)	Son of God appeared, declaring **liberty** to the captives

JESUS CHRIST, RELATIONSHIPS WITH THE FATHER

Luke 2:52	Jesus increased...in **favour** with God and man.
Luke 23:35	save himself, if he be Christ, the **chosen** of God.
John 1:1(1-3)	the **Word** was with God, and the Word was God.
John 5:18(17,18)	God was his Father, making himself **equal** with God.
John 8:29(28,29)	Father hath not left me **alone**; for I do always those
John 10:15(14,15)	as the Father knoweth me, even so **know** I the Father
John 14:11(8-11)	that I am in the **Father**, and the Father in me: or else
John 17:7(1-8)	all things whatsoever thou hast **given** me are of thee.
John 17:26(21-26)	that the love wherewith thou hast **loved** me may be in
Acts 7:55(54-56)	saw...Jesus standing on the **right** hand of God
1 Cor. 1:24	Christ the power of God, and the **wisdom** of God.
1 Cor. 11:3	and the **head** of Christ is God.
1 Cor. 15:28(24-28)	then shall the Son also himself be **subject** unto him
2 Cor. 4:6(3-6)	to give...the **glory** of God in the face of Jesus Christ
Philip. 2:6(5-11)	thought it not robbery to be **equal** with God
Col. 1:19(13-19)	pleased the Father that in him should all **fulness**
Col. 2:9	in him dwelleth all the **fulness** of the Godhead bodily.
Heb. 1:2(1-14)	his Son, whom he hath appointed **heir** of all things
1 Jn. 2:1	we have an **advocate** with the Father, Jesus Christ the

JESUS CHRIST, RELATIONSHIPS WITH THE FATHER

Hel. 5:11	hath **power** given unto him from the Father to redeem
3 Ne. 9:15	I am Jesus Christ the **Son** of God...with the Father
3 Ne. 11:32	the Father beareth **record** of me, and the Holy Ghost
3 Ne. 17:15(15-18)	knelt upon the earth; and...**prayed** unto the Father
3 Ne. 19:23(20-34)	now Father, I **pray** unto thee for them, and also for
Moro. 7:28	wherefore he **advocateth** the cause of the children of
Moro. 9:26	Christ, who sitteth on the **right** hand of his power
D&C 29:5	I am in your midst...your **advocate** with the Father
D&C 32:3	and I am their **advocate** with the Father, and nothing
D&C 45:3(3-5)	listen to him who is the **advocate** with the Father, who
D&C 50:43	the Father and I are **one**. I am in the Father and the
D&C 62:1	the Lord your God, even Jesus Christ, your **advocate**
D&C 76:25(23-25)	whom the Father **loved** and who was in the bosom of the
D&C 76:43(41-44)	who **glorifies** the Father, and saves all the works of
D&C 76:107	he shall deliver up the **kingdom**...unto the Father
D&C 88:75	your Father, and your God, and my **God**, that you are
D&C 93:4(3-11)	the Father because he gave me of his **fulness**, and the
D&C 93:21	I was in the **beginning** with the Father, and am the
D&C 110:4	I am your **advocate** with the Father.
JS-M 1:1	he was glorified and **crowned** on the right hand of God.

JESUS CHRIST, RESURRECTION

1 Sam. 2:6	bringeth down to the grave, and **bringeth** up.
Job 19:25(25-27)	that he shall **stand** at the latter day upon the earth
Ps. 16:10(9,10)	neither wilt thou suffer thine **Holy** One to see
Isa. 25:8	he will swallow up death in **victory**; and the Lord God
Isa. 26:19(18,19)	together with my dead body shall they **arise**. Awake and
Hosea 13:14(10-14)	I will **redeem** them from death: O death, I will be thy
Matt. 16:21(21-23)	be killed, and be **raised** again the third day.
Matt. 17:23(22-23)	kill him...third day he shall be **raised** again. And the
Matt. 20:19(17-19)	crucify him: and the third day he shall **rise** again.
Matt. 26:32	after I am **risen** again, I will go...into Galilee.
Matt. 28:6(1-20)	he is not here: for he is **risen**, as he said. Come, see
Mark 9:31(31-32)	after...he is killed, he shall **rise** the third day.
Mark 10:34	and the third day he shall **rise** again.
Mark 16:9(1-20)	when Jesus was **risen** early the first day of the week
Luke 18:33(31-34)	and the third day he shall **rise** again.
Luke 24:6(1-53)	he is not here, but is **risen**: remember how he spake
John 2:19(14-22)	destroy this temple, and in three days I will **raise**
John 10:17(17-18)	I lay down my life, that I might **take** it again.
John 11:25(25-26)	I am the **resurrection**, and the life: he that believeth
John 20:20(1-23)	he shewed unto them his **hands** and his side. Then were
John 21:1(1-25)	Jesus **shewed** himself again...at the sea of Tiberias
Acts 1:3(1-3)	to whom also he **shewed** himself alive after his passion
Acts 1:9(9-11)	he was **taken** up; and a cloud received him out of
Acts 2:32(22-36)	this Jesus hath God **raised** up, whereof we all are
Acts 10:40(40-42)	him God **raised** up the third day, and shewed him openly
Acts 13:37(29-39)	he, whom God **raised** again, saw no corruption.
Acts 26:23(22-23)	the first that should **rise** from the dead, and should
Rom. 6:9(2-11)	Christ being **raised** from the dead dieth no more; death
1 Cor. 15:4(3-8)	that he **rose** again the third day according to the

1 Cor. 15:22(12-26)	in Christ shall all be made **alive**.
Philip. 3:21(20-21)	who shall **change** our vile body, that it may be
Col. 1:18	the **firstborn** from the dead; that in all things he
2 Tim. 2:8	Jesus Christ...was **raised** from the dead according to
Rev. 1:5	Jesus Christ...the **first** begotten of the dead, and the
Rev. 1:18(13-18)	I am he that **liveth**, and was dead; and, behold, I am
1 Ne. 10:11	Messiah...should **rise** from the dead, and should make
2 Ne. 2:8(6-9)	the Holy Messiah...the first that should **rise**.
2 Ne. 9:6(4-9)	there must needs be a power of **resurrection**, and the
2 Ne. 25:13(12-14)	after...three days he shall **rise** from the dead, with
2 Ne. 26:1	after Christ shall have **risen**...show himself unto you
Mosiah 3:10(8-10)	he shall **rise** the third day from the dead; and behold
Mosiah 16:7(6-8)	if Christ had not **risen** from the dead, or have broken
Mosiah 16:8(6-8)	and the **sting** of death is swallowed up in Christ.
Alma 11:42(40-42)	Christ shall loose the **bands** of this temporal death
Alma 33:22	he shall **rise** again from the dead, which shall bring
Alma 40:16(16-21)	down to the **resurrection** of Christ from the dead.
Hel. 14:17(15-17)	the **resurrection** of Christ redeemeth mankind, yea
Hel. 14:20(20-27)	he shall **rise** again from the dead.
3 Ne. 11:8(1-17)	they saw a Man **descending** out of heaven; and he was
Morm. 7:5(5-6)	Jesus Christ...hath gained the **victory** over the grave
D&C 18:12(11,12)	he hath **risen** again from the dead, that he might bring
D&C 20:23(21-24)	he was crucified, died, and **rose** again the third day
D&C 76:22(22-23)	testimony...which we give of him: That he **lives**!
D&C 76:39(39-43)	**triumph** and the glory of the Lamb, who was slain, who
D&C 133:55(52-56)	who were with Christ in his **resurrection**, and the holy
Moses 7:62(54-59,62)	Only Begotten; his **resurrection** from the dead; yea

JESUS CHRIST, SAVIOR

Ex. 15:2	the Lord is...become my **salvation**: he is my God, and
Ps. 27:1	the Lord is my light and my **salvation**; whom shall I
Isa. 43:3(3,11,25)	I am...thy God, the Holy One of Israel, thy **Saviour**
Isa. 45:15	O God of Israel, the **Saviour**.
Joel 2:32(23-32)	whosoever shall call on the...Lord shall be **delivered**
Hab. 3:13(2,13,18)	thou wentest forth for the **salvation** of thy people
Matt. 1:21	he shall **save** his people from their sins.
Luke 1:47	and my spirit hath rejoiced in God my **Saviour**.
Luke 2:11	this day in the city of David a **Saviour**, which is
Acts 2:21(16-21)	whosoever shall call on the...Lord shall be **saved**.
Acts 4:12(10-12)	none other name...whereby we must be **saved**.
Acts 7:35(35-36)	the same did God send to be a ruler and a **deliverer**
Acts 13:23	raised unto Israel a **Saviour**, Jesus
Acts 13:47(46-49)	shouldest be for **salvation** unto the ends of the earth.
Philip. 3:20(20-21)	we look for the **Saviour**, the Lord Jesus Christ
1 Tim. 4:10	we trust in the living God, who is the **Saviour** of all
1 Jn. 2:2(1-2)	he is the **propitiation** for our sins: and not for ours
1 Jn. 4:14	sent the Son to be the **Saviour** of the world.
1 Ne. 13:40	Lamb of God is the Son...the **Savior** of the world; and
1 Ne. 21:26	I, the Lord, am thy **Savior** and thy Redeemer, the
1 Ne. 22:12	the Lord is their **Savior** and their Redeemer, the
2 Ne. 6:17(17-18)	the Mighty God shall **deliver** his covenant people. For

JESUS CHRIST, SAVIOR cont.

2 Ne. 25:20	there is none other name...whereby man can be **saved**.
2 Ne. 31:13	following your Lord and your **Savior** down into the
Mosiah 3:17(12-17)	no other name given...whereby **salvation** can come unto
Mosiah 3:20	the knowledge of the **Savior** shall spread throughout
Mosiah 5:8	no other name given whereby **salvation** cometh
Hel. 14:15(15-19)	he surely must die that **salvation** may come; yea, it
Morm. 3:14	forbidden them by our Lord and **Savior** Jesus Christ
D&C 3:16	the knowledge of a **Savior** come unto my people
D&C 18:23	there is none other name...whereby man can be **saved**
D&C 43:34	I am Jesus Christ, the **Savior** of the world. Treasure
D&C 45:3(3-5)	listen to him who is the **advocate** with the Father, who
D&C 76:1	the Lord is God, and beside him there is no **Savior**.
Moses 1:6	mine Only Begotten is and shall be the **Savior**, for he
Moses 5:15	as many as believed in the Son...should be **saved**; and
Moses 6:52	only name...whereby **salvation** shall come unto...men

JESUS CHRIST, SECOND COMING

Job 19:25	**he** shall stand at the latter day upon the earth
Ps. 24:7(7-10)	lift up...O ye gates...the King of glory shall **come**
Ps. 102:16	Lord shall build up Zion, he shall **appear** in his glory
Isa. 40:3	make straight in the desert a **highway** for our God.
Isa. 40:5(3-5)	and the glory of the Lord shall be **revealed**, and all
Isa. 45:23	every **knee** shall bow, every tongue shall swear.
Isa. 49:11(10-12)	and my **highways** shall be exalted.
Isa. 52:10(7-10)	all...earth shall **see** the salvation of our God.
Isa. 60:2(1-3,19-21)	the Lord shall **arise** upon thee, and his glory shall
Isa. 63:1(1-4)	who is this that **cometh**...with dyed garments from
Ezek. 21:27	until he **come** whose right it is; and I will give it
Dan. 7:13	like the **Son** of man came with the clouds of heaven
Joel 3:16(15-17)	the **Lord** also shall roar out of Zion, and utter his
Micah 1:3(3-4)	the **Lord**...will come down, and tread upon...the earth.
Hag. 2:7(6-7)	the desire of all nations shall **come**: and I will fill
Zech. 12:10(9-14)	shall **look** upon me whom they have pierced, and...mourn
Zech. 13:6	say unto him, what are these **wounds** in thine hands
Zech. 14:4(4-9)	his feet shall **stand** in that day upon the mount of
Mal. 3:2(1-3)	but who may abide the day of his **coming**? and who shall
Matt. 16:27(27-28)	Son of man shall come in the **glory** of his Father with
Matt. 24:30(26-35)	then shall appear the **sign** of the Son of man in heaven
Matt. 24:36(36-51)	of that day and **hour** knoweth no man, no, not the
Matt. 25:31(31-46)	when the Son of man shall come in his **glory**, and all
Matt. 26:64	Son of man...**coming** in the clouds of heaven.
Acts 1:11(9-11)	shall so come in like **manner** as ye have seen him go
Acts 3:20(20-21)	and he shall send **Jesus** Christ, which before was
1 Cor. 15:23	afterward they that are Christ's at his **coming**.
1 Thes. 4:16(15-17)	the Lord himself shall **descend** from heaven with a
2 Thes. 1:7(7,8)	Lord Jesus shall be **revealed** from heaven with his
2 Thes. 2:8(1-2,8)	that wicked...shall destroy..brightness of his **coming**
2 Pet. 3:10	the Lord will **come** as a thief in the night; in the
Jude 1:14(14-15)	Lord **cometh** with ten thousands of his saints
Rev. 1:7	every eye shall **see** him, and they also which pierced
Rev. 6:17(12-17)	for the great **day** of his wrath is come; and who shall

JESUS CHRIST, SECOND COMING cont.

Rev. 8:1(1-13)	when he had opened the **seventh** seal, there was silence
Rev. 19:16(11-16)	on his thigh a name written, **King** Of Kings, And Lord
1 Ne. 21:11	and my **highways** shall be exalted.
Mosiah 12:21	beautiful...feet...good tidings...publisheth **peace**
3 Ne. 20:40(39-42)	feet...bringeth good tidings...publisheth **peace**; that
3 Ne. 24:2(2-3)	he is like a **refiner's** fire, and like fuller's soap.
3 Ne. 27:16	that day when I shall **stand** to judge the world.
D&C 1:12	prepare ye...for the Lord is **nigh**
D&C 29:11(7-11)	for I will **reveal** myself from heaven with power and
D&C 33:18(17,18)	that I **come** quickly. Even so. Amen.
D&C 34:6(6-9,12)	preparing the way of the Lord for his second **coming**.
D&C 35:27(16-27)	the kingdom is yours until I **come**. Behold, I come
D&C 36:8	I will suddenly **come** to my temple. Even so. Amen.
D&C 38:8(8-12)	but the day soon cometh that ye shall **see** me, and know
D&C 39:20(20-24)	preparing the way...time of my **coming**
D&C 41:4	I **come** quickly, and ye shall see that my law is kept.
D&C 43:29(28-31)	for in mine own due time will I **come** upon the earth
D&C 45:39	be looking forth for the great day of the Lord to **come**
D&C 45:51(47-54)	Jews...say: what are these **wounds** in thine hands and
D&C 49:7	but the **hour** and the day no man knoweth, neither the
D&C 49:22	the Son of Man **cometh** not in the form of a woman
D&C 54:10	I **come** quickly, and my reward is with me, and they
D&C 63:34(32-35,53)	I...will **come** down in heaven from the presence of my
D&C 64:23(23-25)	it is called today until the **coming** of the Son of Man
D&C 76:63(62-68)	he shall **come** ...to reign on the earth over his people
D&C 88:95(92-110)	and the **face** of the Lord shall be unveiled
D&C 88:99(95-99)	the redemption of those who are Christ's at his **coming**
D&C 88:104(104-106)	every **knee** shall bow, and every tongue shall confess
D&C 101:32(23-32)	in that day when the Lord shall **come**, he shall reveal
D&C 104:59(58,59)	prepare my people...when I shall **dwell** with them
D&C 110:16(13-16)	the great and dreadful **day** of the Lord is near, even
D&C 128:24	he is like a **refiner's** fire, and like fuller's soap
D&C 130:1(1-2)	when the Savior shall **appear** we shall see him as he
D&C 130:14(14-17)	to know the time of the **coming** of the Son of Man, when
D&C 133:2	the Lord who shall suddenly **come** to his temple; the
D&C 133:20	he shall **stand** upon the mount of Olivet, and upon the
D&C 133:25(23-25)	stand in the midst of his people, and shall **reign** over
D&C 133:46(42-53)	cometh down from God in heaven with dyed **garments**; yea
JS-M 1:4(1-55)	what is the sign of thy **coming**, and of the end of the
JS-M 1:37	for the Son of Man shall **come**, and he shall send his

JESUS CHRIST, SON OF MAN

Dan. 7:13(13-14)	one like the **Son** of man came with the clouds of heaven
Matt. 9:6	know that the **Son** of man hath power on earth to
Matt. 16:27(27-28)	the **Son** of man shall come in the glory of his Father
Matt. 18:11	**Son** of man is come to save that which was lost.
Matt. 24:30(29-31)	see the **Son** of man coming in the clouds of heaven with
Matt. 25:31(31-33)	the **Son** of man shall come in his glory, and all the
Matt. 26:24(2,24)	woe unto that man by whom the **Son** of man is betrayed
Matt. 26:64(63,64)	ye see the **Son** of man sitting on the right hand of
Mark 2:10	the **Son** of man hath power on earth to forgive sins

JESUS CHRIST, SON OF MAN cont.

Mark 2:28	therefore the **Son** of man is Lord also of the sabbath.
Mark 8:38	of him also shall the **Son** of man be ashamed, when he
Mark 9:31(30-32)	the **Son** of man is delivered into the hands of men, and
Mark 10:33(33-34)	the **Son** of man shall be delivered unto the chief
Mark 13:26(26-27)	shall they see the **Son** of man coming in the clouds
Mark 14:62	ye shall see the **Son** of man sitting on the right hand
Luke 9:26	the **Son** of man be ashamed, when he shall come in his
Luke 9:56(54-56)	**Son** of man is not come to destroy men's lives, but to
Luke 22:69	hereafter shall the **Son** of man sit on the right hand
John 3:14	as Moses lifted...so must the **Son** of man be lifted up
John 5:27(26-27)	execute judgment also, because he is the **Son** of man.
John 6:27	everlasting life, which the **Son** of man shall give unto
John 6:53	except ye eat...flesh of the **Son** of man, and drink his
John 6:62	if ye shall see the **Son** of man ascend up where he was
John 13:31	now is the **Son** of man glorified, and God is glorified
Acts 7:56(54-60)	I see...the **Son** of man standing on the right hand of
Rev. 1:13(13-16)	one like unto the **Son** of man, clothed with a garment
Rev. 14:14	upon the cloud one sat like unto the **Son** of man
D&C 45:39	signs of the coming of the **Son** of Man.
D&C 49:6(5-7)	they have done unto the **Son** of Man even as they listed
D&C 76:16(16-17)	those who shall hear the voice of the **Son** of Man, and
D&C 122:8(7-8)	the **Son** of Man hath descended below them all. Art thou

JESUS CHRIST, TAKING THE NAME OF

Matt. 11:29(27-30)	take my **yoke** upon you, and learn of me; for I am meek
Matt. 12:21(16-21)	and in his **name** shall the Gentiles trust.
John 20:31	believing ye might have life through his **name**.
Acts 4:12(10-12)	none other **name** under heaven given among men, whereby
Acts 5:41	rejoicing...worthy to suffer shame for his **name**.
Acts 11:26	disciples were called **Christians** first in Antioch.
1 Cor. 6:11(9-11)	ye are justified in the **name** of the Lord **Jesus**, and
1 Jn. 3:23(23,24)	commandment, that we should believe on the **name** of his
2 Ne. 9:24(20-24)	if they will not repent and believe in his **name**, and
2 Ne. 31:13	to take upon you the **name** of Christ, by baptism- yea
2 Ne. 31:21	none other way nor **name** given under heaven whereby man
Mosiah 1:11(11,12)	I shall give this people a **name**, that thereby they may
Mosiah 5:11(7-11)	this is the **name** that I said I should give unto you
Mosiah 18:10(8-10)	being baptized in the **name** of the Lord, as a witness
Mosiah 25:23	desirous to take upon them the **name** of Christ, or of
Mosiah 26:18	blessed is this people...willing to bear my **name**; for
3 Ne. 27:5(5-10)	ye must take upon you the **name** of Christ, which is my
Ether 4:19(18,19)	blessed is he that is found faithful unto my **name** at
Moro. 4:3	willing to take upon them the **name** of thy Son, and
D&C 18:21(21,22)	take upon you the **name** of Christ, and speak the truth
D&C 18:24(23-25)	all men must take upon them the **name** which is given
D&C 20:37	willing to take upon them the **name** of Jesus Christ
D&C 41:1	hear me not will I curse, that have professed my **name**
D&C 50:4(4-6)	abominations in the church that profess my **name**.
D&C 63:61(61,62)	men beware how they take my **name** in their lips
D&C 109:22(22-26)	and that thy **name** may be upon them, and thy glory be
D&C 112:12(11,12)	be ye faithful before me unto my **name**.

255

JESUS CHRIST, TAKING THE NAME OF cont.

D&C 112:26(24-26)	have professed to know my **name** and have not known me
D&C 132:64	I will magnify my **name** upon all those who receive and

JESUS CHRIST, TEACHING MODE OF

Matt. 7:29(28-29)	for he taught them as one having **authority**, and not
Matt. 12:3(1-8)	have ye not **read** what David did, when he was an
Matt. 13:10(1-23)	why speakest thou unto them in **parables**
Matt. 13:54	astonished, and said, whence hath this man this **wisdom**
Matt. 22:29(23-33)	ye do err, not knowing the **scriptures**, nor the power
Mark 1:14(14-39)	**preaching** the gospel of the kingdom of God
Mark 1:21(21,22)	entered into the synagogue, and **taught**.
Mark 2:2	**preached** the word unto them.
Mark 4:11(2,11)	all these things are done in **parables**
Mark 6:34	he began to **teach** them many things.
Mark 8:31(27-33)	he began to **teach** them, that the Son of man must
Luke 4:32	they were astonished...for his word was with **power**.
Luke 5:22(18-26)	when Jesus **perceived** their thoughts, he answering said
Luke 7:42(36-50)	**tell** me therefore, which of them will love him most
Luke 24:32(13-35)	our heart burn within us, while he **talked** with us by
John 3:34(31-34)	he whom God hath sent **speaketh** the words of God: for
John 7:16(14-18)	my **doctrine** is not mine, but his that sent me.
John 8:6(1-11)	**wrote** on the ground, as though he heard them not.
John 12:50(44-50)	even as the Father said unto me, so I **speak**.
John 13:14(3-17)	if I then...ye also ought to wash one another's **feet**.
John 21:17(14-17)	Jesus saith unto him, **Feed** my sheep.
3 Ne. 11:14(10-17)	that ye may **know** that I am the God of Israel, and the
3 Ne. 11:32(18-41)	and this is my **doctrine**, and it is the doctrine which
3 Ne. 17:2(1-25)	I **perceive** that ye are weak, that ye cannot understand
3 Ne. 23:11(1-14)	how be it that ye have not **written** this thing, that

JESUS CHRIST, TEMPTATION OF

Deut. 6:16	ye shall not **tempt** the Lord your God, as ye tempted
Matt. 4:1(1-11)	then was Jesus led...to be **tempted** of the devil.
Matt. 4:7(5-7)	thou shalt not **tempt** the Lord thy God.
Luke 22:28	they which have continued with me in my **temptations**.
Heb. 2:18	he himself hath suffered being **tempted**, he is able to
Heb. 4:15	was in all points **tempted** like as we are, yet without
Heb. 5:8(2,8)	learned he obedience by the things which he **suffered**
Mosiah 3:7	he shall suffer **temptations**, and pain of body, hunger
Mosiah 15:5	suffereth **temptation**, and yieldeth not to the
Alma 7:11	suffering pains...and **temptations** of every kind; and
D&C 20:22	he suffered **temptations** but gave no heed unto them.

JESUS CHRIST, TRIAL OF

Isa. 53:7(4-12)   he is brought as a **lamb** to the slaughter, and as a she
Matt. 26:57(57-68)   laid hold on Jesus led him away to **Caiaphas** the high
Matt. 27:2(1,2)   bound him...delivered him to **Pontius** Pilate the
Matt. 27:12(11-28)   when he was accused...he answered **nothing**.
Mark 14:64(53-65)   they all **condemned** him to be guilty of death.
Mark 15:2(1-15)   **Pilate** asked him, Art thou the King of the Jews? And
Mark 15:17(16-20)   clothed him with purple, and platted a crown of **thorns**
Luke 18:32   shall be delivered unto the Gentiles, and...**mocked**
Luke 22:63(63-64)   and the men that held Jesus **mocked** him, and smote him.
Luke 22:67(66-70)   art thou the **Christ**? Tell us. And he said unto them
Luke 22:71(54-71)   they said, what need we any further **witness**? For we
Luke 23:4(1-12)   then said Pilate...I find no **fault** in this man.
Luke 23:21(13-26)   but they cried, saying, **crucify** him, crucify him.
John 11:50(49-51)   one man should **die** for the people, and that the whole
John 18:13   and led him away to **Annas** first; for he was father in
John 18:19(12-27)   the high **priest** then asked Jesus of his disciples, and
John 18:29(28-40)   **Pilate** then...said, what accusation bring ye against
John 19:15(1-19)   they cried out, away with him...**crucify** him. Pilate
Acts 8:32(32-35)   a **lamb** dumb before his shearer, so opened he not his
1 Pet. 2:23   when he was **reviled**, reviled not again; when he
Mosiah 14:7   he was afflicted, yet he opened not his **mouth**; he is
Mosiah 15:6   before the shearer is dumb, so he opened not his **mouth**

JESUS CHRIST, TYPES, IN ANTICIPATION

Gen. 4:4(2-7)   Abel...brought of the **firstlings** of his flock and of
Gen. 22:8(1-14)   God will provide himself a **lamb** for a burnt offering
Ex. 12:5(1-13)   your **lamb** shall be without blemish, a male of the
Ex. 12:21(1-30)   take you a lamb...and kill the **passover**.
Ex. 16:15(4,14-15)   **manna**...is the bread which the Lord hath given you to
Ex. 17:6(1-7)   smite the **rock**, and there shall come water out of it
Ex. 24:8(3-8)   behold the **blood** of the covenant, which the Lord hath
Ex. 26:33(31-35)   **vail** shall divide...the holy place and the most holy.
Lev. 16:22(7-10,20-26)   the goat shall bear upon him all their **iniquities** unto
Num. 9:12(11-13)   nor **break** any bone of it: according to all the
Num. 21:9(4-9)   Moses made a **serpent** of brass, and put it upon a pole
Deut. 8:3(1-3)   fed thee with **manna**, which thou knewest not, neither
Ps. 110:4(1-4)   a priest for ever after the order of **Melchizedek**.
Jonah 1:17   in the belly of the fish **three** days and three nights.
Matt. 12:40(38-40)   so shall the Son of man be **three** days and three nights
Matt. 27:51(50-53)   the **veil** of the temple was rent in twain from the top
John 1:29   behold the **Lamb** of God, which taketh away the sin of
John 3:14(14-16)   as Moses lifted up the **serpent** in the wilderness, even
John 6:51(26-58)   I am the living **bread** which came down from heaven: if
John 19:33(31,33)   that he was dead already, they **brake** not his legs
1 Cor. 5:7(6-8)   Christ our **passover** is sacrificed for us
1 Cor. 10:4(1-4)   that **Rock** was Christ.
2 Cor. 3:14(13-16)   which **vail** is done away in Christ.
Gal. 3:24(23-25)   the law was our **schoolmaster** to bring us unto Christ
Col. 2:17(16-17)   which are a **shadow** of things to come; but the body is
Heb. 5:10(1-10)   called...an **high** priest after the order of Melchisedec
Heb. 8:5(1-5)   who serve unto the example and **shadow** of heavenly

Heb. 9:3(1-5)	after the second **veil**, the tabernacle...holiest of all
Heb. 9:9(6-14)	which was a **figure** for the time then present, in which
Heb. 10:1(1-3)	the law having a **shadow** of good things to come, and
Heb. 10:10(1-14)	sanctified through the **offering**...of Jesus Christ once
1 Pet. 1:19(18-19)	blood of Christ, as of a **lamb** without blemish and with
Rev. 2:17	to him that overcometh...to eat of the hidden **manna**
Rev. 5:6(5-10)	midst of the elders, stood a **Lamb** as it had been slain
2 Ne. 2:7	offereth himself a **sacrifice** for sin, to answer the
2 Ne. 11:4	this end hath the law of Moses...the **typifying** of him.
Jacob 4:5	Abraham...offering...Isaac ...a **similitude** of God and
Mosiah 3:15(13-15)	and **types**, and shadows showed he unto them, concerning
Mosiah 13:31(27-33)	all these things were **types** of things to come.
Mosiah 16:14(14-15)	law of Moses...**shadow** of those things which are to come
Mosiah 18:14(8-17)	both Alma and Helam were **buried** in the water; and they
Alma 13:16(1-19)	it being a **type** of his order, or it being his order
Alma 25:15(15-16)	the law of Moses was a **type** of his coming, and
Alma 33:19	behold a **type** was raised up in the wilderness, that
Alma 34:14(9-14)	the law...**pointing** to that great and last sacrifice
Alma 37:45(38-47)	I say, is there not a **type** in this thing? For just as
Hel. 8:14(13-15)	as he lifted up the brazen **serpent** in the wilderness
Moses 5:7(4-8)	a **similitude** of the sacrifice of the Only Begotten
Moses 6:63(59-63)	all things have their **likeness**, and all things are
JFS-V 1:13(11-16)	offered sacrifice in the **similitude** of...Son of God

JESUS CHRIST, TYPES, IN MEMORY

Matt. 26:26(26-28)	Jesus took **bread**...said, take, eat; this is my body.
Mark 14:22(22-25)	Jesus took **bread**...said, take, eat: this is my body.
Mark 16:2(1-8)	**first** day of the week, they came unto the sepulchre
Luke 22:19(13-20)	this do in **remembrance** of me.
John 6:51(26-58)	the **bread** that I will give is my flesh, which I will
Acts 20:7	first **day** of the week...disciples...break bread, Paul
Rom. 6:5(1-6)	been planted together in the **likeness** of his death
1 Cor. 11:24(23-27)	this do in **remembrance** of me.
Col. 2:12	**buried** with him in baptism, wherein also ye are risen
1 Pet. 2:5(1-5)	offer up spiritual **sacrifices**, acceptable to God by
Rev. 1:10	I was in the Spirit on the Lord's **day**, and heard
3 Ne. 9:20(19-22)	**sacrifice** unto me a broken heart and a contrite spirit
3 Ne. 11:26(21-38)	**immerse** them in the water, and come forth again out
3 Ne. 18:3(1-7)	he took of the **bread** and brake and blessed it; and he
3 Ne. 18:8(8-12)	take of the **wine** of the cup and drink of it, and that
D&C 20:40(40,75-79)	bread and wine- the **emblems** of the flesh and blood of
D&C 20:74(72-74)	**immerse** him or her in the water, and come forth again
D&C 27:2(1-4)	**remembering**...my body...and my blood which was shed
D&C 59:8	a **sacrifice**...of a broken heart and a contrite spirit.
D&C 59:12(9-17)	on this, the Lord's **day**, thou shalt offer thine
D&C 128:13(13-14)	the baptismal font was...a **similitude** of the grave

JOY

Deut. 28:47(45-48)	because thou servedst not...thy God with **joyfulness**
Job 20:5(4-7)	the **joy** of the hypocrite but for a moment
Job 38:7(4-7)	all the sons of God shouted for **joy**
Ps. 16:11	in thy presence is fulness of **joy**; at thy right hand
Ps. 30:5	but **joy** cometh in the morning.
Ps. 35:9	my soul shall be **joyful** in the Lord: it shall rejoice
Ps. 37:11(10,11)	meek...**delight** themselves in the abundance of peace.
Ps. 97:12	**rejoice** in the Lord, ye righteous; and give thanks at
Ps. 118:24	Lord hath made; we will **rejoice** and be glad in it.
Ps. 126:5(5-6)	they that sow in tears shall reap in **joy**.
Eccl. 9:9	live **joyfully** with the wife whom thou lovest all the
Isa. 12:3	with **joy**...draw water out of the wells of salvation.
Isa. 29:19(18,19)	the meek also shall increase their **joy** in the Lord
Isa. 32:17(17,18)	effect of righteousness quietness and **assurance** for
Isa. 51:11	and everlasting **joy** shall be upon their head: they
Isa. 55:12(1-3,12-13)	ye shall go out with **joy**, and be led forth with peace
Matt. 5:12(11-12)	**rejoice**...for so persecuted they the prophets which
Matt. 25:21	faithful servant...enter thou into the **joy** of thy Lord
Luke 2:10(9-11)	I bring you good tidings of great **joy**, which shall
Luke 6:23(21-23)	leap for **joy**: for...your reward is great in heaven
Luke 10:20	**rejoice**, because your names are written in heaven.
Luke 15:7(5-7,32)	**joy** shall be in heaven over one sinner that repenteth
John 8:56	your father Abraham **rejoiced** to see my day: and he saw
John 15:11	things have I spoken...that your **joy** might be full.
John 16:20(20-22)	but your sorrow shall be turned into **joy**.
John 16:22(20-22)	rejoice, and your **joy** no man taketh from you.
John 17:13	that they might have my **joy** fulfilled in themselves.
Rom. 14:17	kingdom of God is...**joy** in the Holy Ghost.
2 Cor. 7:4	I am exceeding **joyful** in all our tribulation.
Gal. 5:22	fruit of the spirit is love, **joy**, peace, longsuffering
Col. 1:11	strengthened...unto...longsuffering with **joyfulness**
1 Thes. 5:16	**rejoice** evermore.
Heb. 10:34(32-34)	took **joyfully** the spoiling of your goods, knowing in
3 Jn. 1:4	no greater **joy** than...that my children walk in truth.
1 Ne. 8:12(10-12)	the fruit...filled my soul with exceeding great **joy**
1 Ne. 11:23	saying: yea, and the most **joyous** to the soul.
2 Ne. 2:23	having no **joy**, for they knew no misery; doing no good
2 Ne. 2:25(24-25)	men are, that they might have **joy**.
Mosiah 2:4	taught...commandments...that they might **rejoice** and
Mosiah 2:41	consider...**happy** state of those that keep the
Mosiah 3:3(2-5,13)	I...declare unto you the glad tidings of great **joy**.
Mosiah 4:20(3,20)	caused that your hearts should be filled with **joy**, and
Alma 4:14(13-14)	filled with great **joy** because of the resurrection of
Alma 19:6(6,11-13)	this light had infused such **joy** into his soul, the
Alma 19:14	overpowered with **joy**; and thus they all three had sunk
Alma 22:15	receive his Spirit, that I may be filled with **joy**
Alma 26:11(10-16)	my heart is brim with **joy**, and I will rejoice in my
Alma 26:35(30-37)	my **joy** is carried away, even unto boasting in my God
Alma 27:17(16-19)	**joy** of Ammon was so great...he fell...to the earth.
Alma 29:9(9-10)	bring some soul to repentance...is my **joy**.
Alma 29:16(15-16)	my soul is carried away...so great is my **joy**.
Alma 30:34(34-35)	that we may have rejoicings in the **joy** of our brethren
Alma 36:20(18-22)	soul was filled with **joy** as exceeding as was my pain

JOY cont.

Hel. 5:44(43-45)	filled with that joy which is unspeakable and full of
3 Ne. 17:18(15-18)	so great was the joy of the multitude that they were
3 Ne. 17:20	and now behold, my joy is full.
3 Ne. 27:11(10-11)	they have joy...for a season...and they are hewn down
3 Ne. 27:31	in them I have fulness of joy.
3 Ne. 28:10(9-10)	your joy shall be full...even as I am, and I am even
D&C 11:13	my Spirit...shall fill your soul with joy
D&C 18:16(11-16)	how great will be your joy if you should bring many
D&C 19:39(37-41)	canst thou read this without rejoicing and lifting up
D&C 25:13	wherefore, lift up thy heart and rejoice, and cleave
D&C 27:15	lift up your hearts and rejoice, and gird up your
D&C 35:24	Zion shall rejoice upon the hills and flourish
D&C 42:61	thou shalt receive...knowledge...which bringeth joy
D&C 45:71	come to Zion, singing with songs of everlasting joy.
D&C 50:22	both are edified and rejoice together.
D&C 51:19	a wise steward shall enter into the joy of his Lord
D&C 52:43	crown the faithful with joy and with rejoicing.
D&C 59:13(13-16)	fasting may be perfect, or...that thy joy may be full.
D&C 62:3	angels...rejoice over you, and your sins are forgiven
D&C 93:33(33-34)	spirit and element...receive a fulness of joy
D&C 101:36(36-37)	world your joy is not full, but in me your joy is full
D&C 110:5	your sins are forgiven you...therefore...rejoice.
D&C 128:19(19-23)	what do we hear in the gospel...a voice of gladness
D&C 136:29(28,29)	call on the Lord...that your souls may be joyful.
Moses 5:10(10-11)	because of my transgression...I shall have joy, and
Moses 7:53	shall come forth with songs of everlasting joy.
Moses 7:67	Enoch...received a fulness of joy
JS-H 1:73	filled with the Holy Ghost, and rejoiced in the God
JFS-V 1:17(11-17,23)	that they might receive a fulness of joy.

JUDGMENT

Gen. 18:19	keep the way of the Lord, to do justice and judgment
Ex. 12:12	I will execute judgment: I am the Lord.
Ex. 18:22(19-26)	and let them judge the people at all seasons: and it
Ex. 23:2	thou shalt not...decline after many to wrest judgment
Ex. 23:6	thou shalt not wrest the judgment of thy poor in his
Lev. 18:4	ye shall do my judgments, and keep mine ordinances
Lev. 19:15	ye shall do no unrighteousness in judgment: thou shalt
Deut. 1:17	not respect persons in judgment...judgment is God's
Deut. 4:1	hearken...unto the statutes and unto the judgments
Deut. 16:19	thou shalt not wrest judgment; thou shalt not respect
Deut. 24:17	thou shalt not pervert the judgment of the stranger
1 Sam. 2:25	one man sin against another, the judge shall judge him
1 Sam. 16:7	but the Lord looketh on the heart.
2 Chr. 19:6(6-7)	ye judge...for the Lord, who is with you in...judgment
Ps. 72:2(1-19)	he shall judge thy people with righteousness, and thy
Ps. 89:14	justice and judgment are the habitation of thy throne
Eccl. 5:8	if thou seest the...violent perverting of judgment and
Isa. 1:23	thy princes...judge not the fatherless, neither doth
Isa. 10:2(1-2)	to turn aside the needy from judgment, and to take
Isa. 30:18	Lord is a God of judgment: blessed are all they that

Isa. 61:8	for I the Lord love **judgment**, I hate robbery for burnt
Jer. 5:28	they **judge** not the cause, the cause of the fatherless
Jer. 17:10	I the Lord **search** the heart, I try the reins, even to
Jer. 23:5(2-8)	king...shall execute **judgment** and justice in the earth
Dan. 7:14(13,14)	there was given him **dominion**, and glory, and a kingdom
Dan. 7:22	ancient of days came, and **judgment** was given to the
Mal. 3:5	I will come near to you to **judgment**; and I will be a
Matt. 7:2(1-5)	with what **judgment** ye judge, ye shall be judged: and
Luke 12:48(47-48)	much is given, of him shall be much **required**: and to
John 5:22(22,27,29)	the Father...hath committed all **judgment** unto the Son
John 7:24	**judge** not according to the appearance, but judge
John 8:16	and yet if I judge, my **judgment** is true: for I am not
John 12:48	he that rejecteth me...hath one that **judgeth** him: the
Acts 10:34(34-35)	I perceive that God is no **respecter** of persons
Rom. 2:1(1-29)	wherein thou **judgest** another, thou condemnest thyself
Rom. 8:27	and he that **searcheth** the hearts knoweth what is the
Rom. 14:10	but why dost thou **judge** thy brother? Or why dost thou
Heb. 12:23	to God the **Judge** of all, and to the spirits of just
1 Pet. 4:17(17-18)	**judgment** must begin at the house of God: and if it
Mosiah 4:22(16-23)	if ye **judge** the man who putteth up his petition to you
Mosiah 26:29(19-33)	whosoever transgresseth against me, him shall ye **judge**
Alma 11:41	rise from the dead and...be **judged** according to their
Ether 11:20	God would execute **judgment** against them to their utter
Moro. 7:16(14-18)	I show unto you the way to **judge**; for every thing
D&C 1:36(35-36)	the Lord...shall come down in **judgment** upon Idumea
D&C 38:16	all flesh is mine, and I am no **respecter** of persons.
D&C 42:32	every man shall be made **accountable** unto me, a steward
D&C 63:37	declare...that **desolation** shall come upon the wicked.
D&C 64:11(8-13)	ye ought to say...let God **judge** between me and thee
D&C 64:37(37-38)	my church...like unto a judge...to **judge** the nations.
D&C 76:68	heaven, where God and Christ are the **judge** of all.
D&C 88:35	cannot be sanctified by law...mercy, justice..**judgment**
D&C 88:99(95-99)	the gospel, and be **judged** according to men in the
D&C 102:2(1-34)	**settling** important difficulties...in the church, which
D&C 104:13	the Lord, should make every man **accountable**, as a
D&C 107:72(72,74,78	to sit in **judgment** upon transgressors upon testimony
D&C 121:17	those who cry **transgression**...are the servants of sin
D&C 134:1	he holds men **accountable** for their acts in relation
Moses 6:61	given to abide in you...truth, justice, and **judgment**.
Moses 7:66	looking forth with fear for the **judgments** of the
JS-H 1:45	he informed me of great **judgments** which were coming

JUDGMENT, THE LAST

1 Sam. 2:10(1-10)	the Lord shall **judge** the ends of the earth; and he
Ps. 9:7	he hath prepared his throne for **judgment**.
Ps. 50:4(1-6)	he shall call...that he may **judge** his people.
Eccl. 3:17(16,17)	God shall **judge** the righteous and the wicked: for
Eccl. 11:9(9-10)	for all these things God will bring thee into **judgment**
Eccl. 12:14(13,14)	God shall bring every work into **judgment**, with every
Dan. 7:10(9-14)	the **judgment** was set, and the books were opened.
Dan. 7:26(25-27)	but the **judgment** shall sit, and they shall take away

Matt. 7:23(21-23)	**depart** from me, ye that work iniquity.
Matt. 12:36(36-37)	they shall give account thereof in the day of **judgment**
Matt. 16:27	he shall **reward** every man according to his works.
Matt. 19:28(27-28)	sit upon twelve thrones, **judging** the twelve tribes of
Matt. 25:32(31-46)	and he shall **separate** them one from another, as a she
John 5:22(22-29)	the Father...hath committed all **judgment** unto the Son
John 12:48	the word that I have spoken...shall **judge** him in the
Acts 17:31(29,31)	he will **judge** the world in righteousness by that man
Rom. 2:2(1-16)	the **judgment** of God is according to truth against them
Rom. 2:3(3-8)	that thou shalt escape the **judgment** of God
Rom. 14:10(10-13)	we shall all stand before the **judgment** seat of Christ.
1 Cor. 6:2	ye not know that the saints shall **judge** the world?
2 Pet. 2:4	chains of darkness, to be reserved unto **judgment**
Jude 1:6	under darkness unto the **judgment** of the great day.
Rev. 14:7(6-7)	for the hour of his **judgment** is come: and worship him
Rev. 20:12(4-15)	dead were **judged** out of...things which were written
1 Ne. 12:9(9,10)	twelve apostles...shall **judge** the twelve tribes of
1 Ne. 15:33(26-36)	stand before God, to be **judged** of their works; and if
2 Ne. 9:15(10-19)	must appear before the **judgment-seat** of the Holy One
2 Ne. 9:46(44-46)	justice...administered...even the day of **judgment**
2 Ne. 25:18	which words shall **judge** them at the last day, for the
2 Ne. 33:14(10-15)	these words shall **condemn** you at the last day.
Alma 5:15(15-25)	stand before God to be **judged** according to the deeds
Alma 12:12(11-18)	brought before the bar of God, to be **judged** according
Alma 12:27	after death, they must come to **judgment**, even that
Alma 41:3(1-7)	men should be **judged** according to their works; and if
3 Ne. 26:4(4-5)	stand before God, to be **judged** of their works, whether
3 Ne. 27:16	I shall stand to **judge** the world.
3 Ne. 27:26(23-27)	out of the books...shall the world be **judged**.
Morm. 3:20(18-22)	ye must all stand before the **judgment-seat** of Christ
Morm. 9:14(12-14)	then cometh the **judgment** of the Holy One upon them
D&C 19:3(3-5)	**judging** every man according to his works and the deeds
D&C 29:27(26-28)	righteous shall be gathered on my **right** hand unto
D&C 38:5(5-6)	until the **judgment** of the great day, which shall come
D&C 43:29(25,29,33)	own due time...come upon the earth in **judgment**, and
D&C 77:12	will the Lord God...**judge** all things, and shall redeem
D&C 88:28(25-35)	your **glory**...that glory by which your bodies are
D&C 101:78(65,78)	accountable for his own sins in the day of **judgment**.
D&C 133:2(2,50)	Lord who shall come down...with a curse to **judgment**
Moses 7:66(66,67)	looking forth with fear..**judgments** of..Almighty God
JS-V 1:9(7-10)	the Lord, will **judge** all men according to their works
JFS-V 1:34(33-35)	be **judged** according to men in the flesh, but live

JUSTICE

Ex. 20:5(5,6)	**visiting** the iniquity of the fathers upon..children
Deut. 1:16	**judge** righteously between every man and his brother
Deut. 24:16	every man shall be put to death for his **own** sin.
Deut. 30:19(1-20)	life and death, blessing and cursing: therefore **choose**
Deut. 32:4	God of truth...without iniquity, **just** and right is he.
Job 4:17	shall mortal man be more **just** than God? Shall a man
Ps. 62:12	thou renderest to every man according to his **work**.

Ps. 89:14	justice and judgment are the habitation of thy throne
Prov. 28:10	shall **fall** himself into his own pit: but the upright
Isa. 9:7(6-7)	to establish it with judgment and with **justice** from
Isa. 45:21	a **just** God and a Saviour; there is none beside me.
Isa. 56:1(1-2)	saith the Lord, keep ye judgment, and do **justice**: for
Jer. 17:10	give every man according to his **ways**, and according
Jer. 22:3(2-3)	execute ye **judgment** and righteousness, and deliver the
Jer. 23:5	shall execute judgment and **justice** in the earth.
Jer. 31:30	but every one shall **die** for his own iniquity: every
Jer. 32:19	to give every one according to his **ways**, and according
Ezek. 3:18	the same wicked man shall **die** in his iniquity; but his
Ezek. 18:4(4-30)	the soul that **sinneth**, it shall die.
Ezek. 33:17(17,20)	but as for them, their way is not **equal**.
Ezek. 45:9	execute judgment and **justice**, take away your exactions
Micah 6:8	what...Lord require of thee, but to do **justly**, and to
Zech. 7:9(9,10)	execute true **judgment**, and shew mercy and compassions
Zech. 8:16	execute the **judgment** of truth and peace in your gates
Zech. 9:9	he is **just**, and having salvation; lowly, and riding
Matt. 23:23	omitted the weightier matters of the law, **judgment**
Luke 18:8(1-8)	I tell you that he will **avenge** them speedily.
1 Jn. 1:9	he is faithful and **just** to forgive us our sins, and
Rev. 15:3(3-4)	**just** and true are thy ways, thou King of saints.
1 Ne. 15:30	justice of God did also divide the wicked from the
2 Ne. 1:10	the judgments of him that is **just** shall rest upon them
2 Ne. 1:22(21-22)	may not incur the displeasure of a **just** God upon you
2 Ne. 9:17(16-18)	the greatness and the **justice** of our God! For he
2 Ne. 9:26(25-27)	the atonement satisfieth the demands of his **justice**
2 Ne. 26:7(6-8)	I must cry unto my God: thy ways are **just**.
2 Ne. 26:33(32-33)	he **denieth** none that come unto him, black and white
Jacob 4:10(9-11)	he counseleth in wisdom, and in **justice**, and in great
Jacob 6:10(9-12)	power of justice, for **justice** cannot be denied, ye
1:22(21-22)	according to his judgments, which are **just**; and their
Mosiah 2:38(38-39)	the demands of divine **justice** do awaken his...soul to
Mosiah 3:18(14-19)	he judgeth, and his judgment is **just**; and the infant
Mosiah 4:22(21-23)	if ye **judge** the man who putteth up his petition to you
Mosiah 5:15(13-15)	power, and **justice**, and mercy of him who created all
Mosiah 16:1(1-3)	shall confess before God that his **judgments** are just.
Mosiah 27:31	the judgment of an everlasting punishment is **just** upon
Mosiah 29:12(11-13)	God...just...judgments of man are not always **just**.
Alma 12:15(14-15)	he is **just** in all his works, and that he is merciful
Alma 12:32	works of **justice** could not be destroyed, according to
Alma 14:11(10-11)	in his wrath may be **just**; and the blood of the
Alma 29:4(3-5)	firm decree of a **just** God, for I know that he granteth
Alma 41:3(2-15)	**justice** of God...men...judged according to their works
Alma 42:15(13-15)	atonement...to appease the demands of **justice**, that
Alma 42:25(16-26)	do ye suppose that mercy can rob **justice**? I say unto
Alma 42:30	ye should deny the **justice** of God no more. Do not
Alma 60:13(12-14)	**justice** and judgment may come upon the wicked
3 Ne. 26:5(4-5)	according to the...**justice**...which is in Christ, who
3 Ne. 27:14(13-17)	to be **judged** of their works, whether they be good or
3 Ne. 29:4(3-4)	the sword of his **justice** is in his right hand; and
Morm. 9:4(1-5)	dwell with a holy and **just** God, under a consciousness
D&C 11:12(11-12)	that spirit which leadeth to do good...to do **justly**

JUSTICE cont.

D&C 19:3(3-5)   judging every man according to his works and the deeds
D&C 82:4(3-5)   justice and judgment are the penalty which is affixed
D&C 88:40(34-40)   justice continueth its course and claimeth its own
D&C 107:84   none shall be exempted from the justice and the laws
D&C 109:25   he who diggeth a pit..shall fall into the same himself
JS-V 1:9(7-10)   according to their works, according to the desire of
JFS-V 1:34(33-35)   be judged according to men in the flesh, but live
JFS-V 1:59(57-60)   reward according to their works, for they are heirs

JUSTIFICATION

Ex. 23:7   I will not justify the wicked.
Deut. 25:1   then they shall justify the righteous, and condemn the
Job 13:18   ordered my cause; I know that I shall be justified.
Job 25:4   then can man be justified with God? Or how can he be
Ps. 143:2   in thy sight shall no man living be justified.
Isa. 45:25(24,25)   Lord shall all the seed of Israel be justified, and
Isa. 53:11   my righteous servant justify many; for he shall bear
Acts 13:39(16-43)   justified from all things...not...justified by the law
Rom. 3:28(19-31)   a man is justified by faith without the deeds of the
Rom. 4:25(1-25)   and was raised again for our justification.
Rom. 5:1   justified by faith, we have peace with God through our
Rom. 5:18(11-21)   free gift came upon all men unto justification of life
Gal. 2:16(15-21)   man...not justified by the works...but by the faith
Titus 3:7(4-8)   being justified by his grace, we should be made heirs
James 2:24(14-26)   by works a man is justified, and not by faith only.
2 Ne. 2:5(5-10)   by the law no flesh is justified; or, by the law men
Jacob 2:14(11-19)   do ye suppose that God justifieth you in this thing
Mosiah 4:25(16-25)   if ye say this in your hearts ye remain guiltless
Mosiah 4:26(26-27)   retaining a remission of your sins...walk guiltless
Alma 4:14(10-14)   thus retaining a remission of their sins; being filled
Alma 5:27(26-34)   have ye walked, keeping yourselves blameless before
3 Ne. 27:16(13-22)   him will I hold guiltless before my Father at that day
Morm. 7:7(1-7)   whereby he that is found guiltless before him at the
D&C 20:30(30,31)   we know that justification...is just and true
D&C 88:39(36-40)   abide not in those conditions are not justified.
D&C 98:38(23-48)   this is an ensample...for justification before me.
Moses 6:60(58-60)   by the Spirit ye are justified, and by the blood ye

KINDNESS

Gen. 20:13   this is thy kindness which thou shalt shew unto me
2 Sam. 9:1   that I may shew him kindness for Jonathan's sake
Neh. 9:17   merciful, slow to anger, and of great kindness, and
Ps. 51:1   have mercy upon me...according to thy lovingkindness
Prov. 19:22   the desire of a man is his kindness: and a poor man
Prov. 31:26   and in her tongue is the law of kindness.
Isa. 54:8(8,10)   but with everlasting kindness will I have mercy on the
Isa. 63:7(7-9)   I will mention the lovingkindnesses of the Lord, and
Joel 2:13   he is gracious...slow to anger, and of great kindness
Matt. 7:12   whatsoever ye would that men should do to you, do ye

KINDNESS cont.

Luke 6:38	**give**, and it shall be given unto you; good measure
Luke 10:33(25-37)	a certain Samaritan...had **compassion** on him
2 Cor. 6:6	by pureness...knowledge...longsuffering...**kindness**
Gal. 5:22(22-23)	fruit of the Spirit is love, joy, peace,...**gentleness**
Eph. 4:32(30-32)	and be ye **kind** one to another, tenderhearted
James 5:11(10-12)	the Lord is very pitiful, and of tender **mercy**.
1 Pet. 3:8	having **compassion** one of another, love as brethren
2 Pet. 1:7	to godliness brotherly **kindness**...to brotherly
1 Ne. 19:9	spit...he suffereth it, because of his loving **kindness**
3 Ne. 17:6(6-7)	my bowels are filled with **compassion** towards you.
3 Ne. 22:8(7,8,10)	but with everlasting **kindness** will I have mercy on
Moro. 7:45(44-48)	and charity suffereth long, and is **kind**, and envieth
D&C 4:6	remember faith, virtue...patience, brotherly **kindness**
D&C 107:30	in faith...patience, godliness, brotherly **kindness** and
D&C 121:42	by **kindness**, and pure knowledge, which shall greatly
D&C 133:52	they shall mention the loving **kindness** of their Lord

KINGDOM OF GOD, IN HEAVEN

Ps. 10:16	the Lord is **King** for ever and ever: the heathen are
Ps. 11:4	the Lord's **throne** is in heaven: his eyes behold, his
Ps. 24:8(8,10)	who is this **King** of glory? The Lord strong and mighty
Ps. 29:10	yea, the Lord sitteth **King** for ever.
Ps. 45:6	thy **throne**, O God, is for ever and ever: the sceptre
Ps. 47:8(7-8)	God sitteth upon the **throne** of his holiness.
Ps. 89:18	and the Holy One of Israel is our **king**.
Ps. 95:3	for the Lord is a great God, and a great **King** above
Isa. 6:1(1-8)	Lord sitting upon a **throne**, high and lifted up, and
Isa. 44:6	the Lord the **King** of Israel, and his redeemer the Lord
Isa. 66:1	the heaven is my **throne**, and the earth is my footstool
Jer. 10:10	the living God, and an everlasting **king**: at his wrath
Matt. 3:2	repent ye: for the **kingdom** of heaven is at hand.
Matt. 4:17	repent: for the **kingdom** of heaven is at hand.
Matt. 5:3(3-12)	poor in spirit: for theirs is the **kingdom** of heaven.
Mark 1:15	the **kingdom** of God is at hand: repent ye, and believe
Luke 13:28(24-30)	ye shall see...all the prophets, in the **kingdom** of God
Acts 7:49	heaven is my **throne**, and earth is my footstool: what
Col. 1:13(12-18)	translated us into the **kingdom** of his dear Son
Heb. 1:8	thy **throne**, O God, is for ever and ever: a sceptre of
1 Ne. 13:37	saved in the everlasting **kingdom** of the Lamb; and
Mosiah 2:19	how you ought to thank your heavenly **King**
Alma 11:37(37-41)	no unclean thing can inherit the **kingdom** of heaven
D&C 6:13(3,13)	saved in the **kingdom** of God, which is the greatest of
D&C 6:37	ye shall inherit the **kingdom** of heaven. Amen.
D&C 7:4	thou mightest speedily come unto me in my **kingdom**.
D&C 10:55	for such shall inherit the **kingdom** of heaven.
D&C 15:6	may rest with them in the **kingdom** of my Father. Amen.
D&C 18:16(15,16)	brought unto me into the **kingdom** of my Father, how
D&C 18:25	cannot have place in the **kingdom** of my Father.
D&C 38:21	I will be your **king** and watch over you.
D&C 56:18	they shall see the **kingdom** of God coming in power and
D&C 58:2	same is greater in the **kingdom** of heaven.

265

KINGDOM OF GOD, IN HEAVEN cont.

D&C 65:6(5-6)	**kingdom** of God go...that the kingdom of heaven may
D&C 76:92(92-95)	God...reigns upon his **throne** forever and ever
D&C 84:38(33-41)	receiveth my Father receiveth my Father's **kingdom**; the
D&C 99:3	receiveth you as a little child, receiveth my **kingdom**
D&C 106:3	seeking diligently the **kingdom** of heaven and its
D&C 136:31	chastisement is not worthy of my **kingdom**.
Abr. 3:21	I **rule** in the heavens above, and in the earth beneath
JS-V 1:1(1-10)	the celestial **kingdom** of God, and the glory thereof

KINGDOM OF GOD, ON EARTH

Ps. 89:4(3,4)	and build up thy **throne** to all generations. Selah.
Isa. 2:3(2-4)	out of **Zion** shall go forth the law, and the word of
Isa. 9:7(6-7)	increase of his **government** and peace there shall be
Isa. 11:12	he shall set up an **ensign** for the nations, and shall
Isa. 14:2	they shall **rule** over their oppressors.
Dan. 2:35(34-35)	**stone**...became a..mountain, and filled the whole earth
Dan. 2:44(44-45)	God of heaven set up a **kingdom**, which shall never be
Dan. 4:3	his **kingdom** is an everlasting kingdom, and his
Dan. 7:14(13-27)	there was given him **dominion**...an everlasting dominion
Matt. 3:2	repent ye: for the **kingdom** of heaven is at hand.
Matt. 6:10	thy **kingdom** come. Thy will be done in earth, as it is
Matt. 13:24(24-52)	the **kingdom** of heaven is likened unto a man which
Matt. 16:19(18-19)	I will give unto thee the keys of the **kingdom** of
Matt. 24:14(14-15)	gospel of the **kingdom** shall be preached in all the
Luke 12:32	Father's good pleasure to give you the **kingdom**.
Luke 17:20(20-37)	when the **kingdom** of God should come, he answered them
2 Pet. 1:11	into the everlasting **kingdom** of our Lord and Saviour
Rev. 11:15(15,18)	kingdoms of..world are become the **kingdoms** of our Lord
Rev. 22:5(1-6)	they shall **reign** for ever and ever.
2 Ne. 19:7(6,7)	of the increase of **government** and peace there is no
2 Ne. 24:2	they shall **rule** over their oppressors.
Alma 5:50	the **King** of all the earth; and also the King of heaven
D&C 25:1	are sons and daughters in my **kingdom**.
D&C 29:5	his good will to give you the **kingdom**.
D&C 35:27	the **kingdom** is yours until I come. Behold, I come
D&C 38:9(9,15)	behold, the **kingdom** is yours, and the enemy shall not
D&C 42:69	the **kingdom**, or in other words, the keys of the
D&C 45:59(58,59)	the Lord shall be...their **king** and their lawgiver.
D&C 50:35	the **kingdom** is given you of the Father, and power to
D&C 65:2(2-6)	**gospel** roll forth...until it has filled the whole
D&C 65:2	keys of the **kingdom** of God are committed unto man on
D&C 72:1	to whom the **kingdom** and power have been given.
D&C 76:107	when he shall deliver up the **kingdom**, and present it
D&C 82:24	the **kingdom** is yours, and shall be forever, if you
D&C 97:14	all things pertaining to the **kingdom** of God on the
D&C 99:3	receiveth you as a little child, receiveth my **kingdom**
D&C 105:32(31-32)	kingdom of Zion is...the **kingdom** of our God and his
D&C 115:4(3-6)	thus shall my **church** be called in the last days, even
D&C 133:58	and the little one become a strong **nation**, and two
JFS-V 1:44(44-51)	Daniel, who foresaw...**kingdom** of God in the latter

KINGS, EARTHLY

Gen. 17:6(5,6)	and **kings** shall come out of thee.
Gen. 35:11(10,11)	and **kings** shall come out of thy loins
Deut. 17:15(14-20)	set him **king** over thee, whom the Lord thy God shall
1 Sam. 8:18(4-22)	because of your **king** which ye shall have chosen you
1 Sam. 10:19(17-19)	nay, but set a **king** over us. Now therefore present
1 Sam. 12:17(12-22)	wickedness is great...in asking you a **king**.
2 Sam. 5:3	they anointed David **king** over Israel.
1 Kgs. 12:7(6-7)	if thou wilt be a **servant** unto this people this day
Prov. 20:26	a wise **king** scattereth the wicked, and bringeth the
Prov. 29:14	the **king** that faithfully judgeth the poor, his throne
Eccl. 10:20	curse not the **king**, no not in thy thought; and curse
Isa. 1:23	thy **princes** are rebellious, and companions of thieves
Isa. 32:1	a **king** shall reign in righteousness, and princes shall
Isa. 60:12(9-14)	for the nation and **kingdom** that will not serve thee
Ezek. 22:27	her **princes** in the midst thereof are like wolves raven
Ezek. 45:8	my **princes** shall no more oppress my people; and the
Dan. 7:9(9-14)	I beheld till the **thrones** were cast down, and the
Matt. 4:8(8-10)	sheweth him all the **kingdoms** of the world, and the
Matt. 11:8	they that wear soft clothing are in **kings'** houses.
Matt. 17:25(24-27)	of whom do the **kings** of the earth take custom or
Mark 13:9(9-11)	ye shall be brought before rulers and **kings** for my
Luke 10:24(23,24)	prophets and **kings** have desired to see those things
Luke 22:25(24-27)	the **kings** of the Gentiles exercise lordship over them
Acts 9:15	bear my name before the Gentiles, and **kings**, and the
1 Tim. 2:2(1-3)	for **kings**, and for all that are in authority; that we
1 Pet. 2:17	love the brotherhood. Fear God. Honour the **king**.
Rev. 6:15(12-17)	the **kings** of the earth, and the great men, and the
Rev. 11:15	the **kingdoms** of this world are become the kingdoms of
Rev. 17:10(10-14)	and there are seven **kings**: five are fallen, and one
Rev. 21:24(22-27)	and the **kings** of the earth do bring their glory and
2 Ne. 10:14	he that raiseth up a **king** against me shall perish, for
Mosiah 2:30	my son Mosiah is a **king** and a ruler over you.
Mosiah 7:9	who was made a **king** by the voice of the people.
Mosiah 23:7(7-13)	it is not expedient that we should have a **king**; for
Mosiah 29:13(12-15)	if...could have just men to be your **kings**, who would
Mosiah 29:16(16-20)	not expedient that ye should have a **king** or kings to
Mosiah 29:21(21-23)	ye cannot dethrone an iniquitous **king** save it be
Mosiah 29:23(23-30)	an unrighteous **king** doth pervert the ways of all right
Mosiah 29:35(35-36)	by having an unrighteous **king** to rule over them
Alma 51:5	dethroned from the judgment-seat were called **king-men**
Ether 6:25(22-27)	they should constrain no man to be their **king**.
D&C 1:23	gospel might be proclaimed...before **kings** and rulers.
D&C 38:21	in time ye shall have no **king** nor ruler, for I will
D&C 84:118	I will rend their **kingdoms**; I will not only shake the
D&C 103:7(6-8)	until the **kingdoms** of the world are subdued under my
D&C 124:5(3-5)	**kings** and authorities, even what shall befall them
Moses 8:3	from his loins should spring all the **kingdoms** of the
Abr. 1:20(20,21)	which Pharaoh signifies **king** by royal blood.
A of F 1:12	we believe in being subject to **kings**, presidents, rule

KNOWLEDGE

Gen. 2:9(9,17)	the tree of **knowledge** of good and evil.
Gen. 2:17	tree...**knowledge** of good and evil...shalt not eat of
Gen. 3:5(4-6)	ye shall be as gods, **knowing** good and evil.
Gen. 3:22	man is become as one of us, to **know** good and evil: and
Ex. 31:3(1-5)	I have filled him...spirit of God...in **knowledge**, and
1 Sam. 2:3	the Lord is a God of **knowledge**, and by him actions are
2 Chr. 1:10	give me now wisdom and **knowledge**, that I may go out
Job 37:16	wondrous works of him which is perfect in **knowledge**
Prov. 1:7	the fear of the Lord is the beginning of **knowledge**
Prov. 1:22(22,29)	scorners delight in ...scorning...fools hate **knowledge**
Prov. 2:5(1-10)	then shalt thou...find the **knowledge** of God.
Prov. 12:23	a prudent man concealeth **knowledge**: but the heart of
Prov. 14:18	but the prudent are crowned with **knowledge**.
Prov. 15:14	him that hath understanding seeketh **knowledge**: but the
Prov. 18:15	heart of the prudent getteth **knowledge**; and the ear
Eccl. 1:18	he that increaseth **knowledge** increaseth sorrow.
Isa. 5:13(12,13)	my people...into captivity...they have no **knowledge**
Isa. 11:9	earth shall be full of the **knowledge** of the Lord, as
Isa. 28:9(9-13)	whom shall he teach **knowledge**? And whom shall he make
Isa. 29:14	the **understanding** of their prudent men shall be hid.
Isa. 33:6	wisdom and **knowledge** shall be the stability of thy
Isa. 53:11	by his **knowledge** shall my righteous servant justify
Jer. 3:15(12-16)	pastors...which shall feed you with **knowledge** and
Dan. 2:21	he giveth...**knowledge** to them that know understanding
Hosea 4:6(1-6)	because thou hast rejected **knowledge**, I will also
Hosea 6:6	I desired...the **knowledge** of God more than burnt
Hab. 2:14	earth shall be filled with the **knowledge** of the glory
Matt. 11:27	neither **knoweth** any man the Father, save the Son, and
Rom. 15:14(13,14)	that ye also are...filled with all **knowledge**, able
1 Cor. 2:14(9-16)	neither can he **know** them, because they are spiritually
1 Cor. 3:19(19-21)	for the **wisdom** of this world is foolishness with God.
1 Cor. 12:8	to another the word of **knowledge** by the same Spirit
Col. 1:9(9-17)	that ye might be filled with the **knowledge** of his will
Col. 2:3(1-3)	in whom are hid all the treasures of...**knowledge**.
2 Tim. 3:7(1-7)	never able to come to the **knowledge** of the truth.
2 Pet. 1:5(1-8)	add to your faith virtue; and to virtue **knowledge**
2 Ne. 4:23	given me **knowledge** by visions in the nighttime.
2 Ne. 9:28(28-29)	their **wisdom** is foolishness and it profiteth them not.
2 Ne. 9:42	because of their **learning**, and their wisdom, and their
2 Ne. 15:13	gone into captivity, because they have no **knowledge**
2 Ne. 21:9	earth shall be full of the **knowledge** of the Lord, as
2 Ne. 27:26	and the **understanding** of their prudent shall be hid.
2 Ne. 28:31	or shall hearken unto the **precepts** of men, save their
2 Ne. 32:7	they will not search **knowledge**, nor understand great
Mosiah 18:26(24-26)	having the **knowledge** of God, that they might teach
Mosiah 28:18(17-19)	gave them much **knowledge**, in the which they did
Alma 9:19(18-23)	so much light and so much **knowledge** given unto them
Alma 18:35(34,35)	Spirit dwelleth in me, which giveth me **knowledge**, and
Alma 23:5	brought to the **knowledge** of the Lord, yea, thousands
Alma 26:21(21,22)	there is none that **knoweth** these things, save it be
Alma 32:34(28-42)	your **knowledge** is perfect in that thing, and your
Alma 36:4	I would not that ye think that I **know** of myself- not
Hel. 14:30	God hath given unto you a **knowledge** and he hath made

KNOWLEDGE cont.

Hel. 15:13(12-13)	true **knowledge**, which is knowledge of their Redeemer
3 Ne. 5:20	given...**knowledge** unto the salvation of our souls.
3 Ne. 16:12(10-13)	the **knowledge** of the fulness of my gospel.
Ether 3:19	because of the **knowledge** of this man he could not be
Ether 4:13	the **knowledge** which is hid up because of unbelief.
D&C 1:28	humble they might...receive **knowledge** from time to
D&C 3:16	as the **knowledge** of a Savior has come unto the world
D&C 6:11(10-11)	bring many to the **knowledge** of the truth, yea
D&C 8:1(1,9,11)	you shall receive a **knowledge** concerning the engraving
D&C 9:8(8-9)	you must **study** it out in your mind; then you must ask
D&C 25:4	murmur not because of the **things** which thou hast not
D&C 42:61	ask, thou shalt receive...**knowledge** upon knowledge
D&C 50:40	ye must grow in grace and in the **knowledge** of the
D&C 76:10(5-10)	will I make **known** unto them the secrets of my will
D&C 84:19(19,98)	even the key of the **knowledge** of God.
D&C 88:79(77-80,118	a **knowledge** also of countries and of kingdoms
D&C 89:19	shall find wisdom and great treasures of **knowledge**
D&C 93:24	truth is **knowledge** of things as they are, and as they
D&C 93:53	obtain a **knowledge** of history, and of countries, and
D&C 101:25	that my **knowledge**...may dwell upon all the earth.
D&C 107:71	temporal things...a **knowledge** of them by the Spirit
D&C 109:7	seek **learning** even by study and also by faith
D&C 109:67	may all...Israel...come to a **knowledge** of the truth
D&C 121:33(26-33)	pouring down **knowledge** from heaven upon the heads of
D&C 121:42	pure **knowledge**, which shall greatly enlarge the soul
D&C 128:14	keys of the kingdom...consist in the key of **knowledge**.
D&C 130:19(18,19)	if a person gains more **knowledge** and intelligence in
D&C 131:6	it is impossible for a man to be saved in **ignorance**.
Moses 3:17	tree...**knowledge** of good and evil...shalt not eat of
Moses 4:11	ye shall be as gods, **knowing** good and evil.
Moses 4:28	man is become as one of us to **know** good and evil; and
Moses 7:32	I gave unto them their **knowledge**, in the day I created
JFS-V 1:32(32-37)	preached to those...without a **knowledge** of the truth

LABOR

Ex. 20:9(8,9)	six days shalt thou **labour**, and do all thy work
Ps. 127:1	except the Lord build the house, they **labour** in vain
Prov. 10:16	the **labour** of the righteous tendeth to life: the fruit
Prov. 13:11	he that gathereth by **labour** shall increase.
Prov. 14:23	in all **labour** there is profit: but the talk of the
Prov. 21:25	slothful...his hands refuse to **labour**.
Eccl. 2:24	make his soul enjoy good in his **labour**. This also I
Eccl. 5:12	the sleep of a **labouring** man is sweet, whether he eat
Eccl. 5:19(18-20)	and to rejoice in his **labour**; this is the gift of God.
Isa. 55:2(1-3)	and your **labour** for that which satisfieth not
Isa. 65:23(17-23)	they shall not **labour** in vain, nor bring forth for
Matt. 11:28	come unto me, all ye that **labour** and are heavy laden
Matt. 20:1(1-14)	householder, which went out...to hire **labourers** into
Luke 10:7	the **labourer** is worthy of his hire. Go not from house
John 6:27	**labour** not for the meat which perisheth, but for that
Acts 20:34	these hands have **ministered** unto my necessities, and

LABOR cont.

1 Cor. 4:12	and **labour**, working with our own hands: being reviled
Eph. 4:28	steal no more: but rather let him **labour**, working with
1 Thes. 4:11(11-12)	do your own business, and to **work** with your own hands
2 Thes. 3:10(7-13)	if any would not **work**, neither should he eat.
1 Tim. 4:10	we both **labour** and suffer reproach, because we trust
1 Tim. 5:18	the **labourer** is worthy of his reward.
2 Ne. 5:17(15-17)	Nephi, did cause my people...to **labor** with their hands
Mosiah 2:14	**labored** with mine own hands that I might serve you
Mosiah 18:24(24,26,28)	priests...**labor** with their own hands for their
Mosiah 27:4(4,5)	**laboring** with their own hands for their support.
Alma 1:26	they did all **labor**, every man according to his
Alma 30:32(32-33)	I have **labored**...with mine own hands for my support
D&C 42:42	idle shall not...wear the garments of the **laborer**.
D&C 56:17	wo unto you...who will not **labor** with your own hands
Moses 5:1	and Eve, also, his wife, did **labor** with him.

LANDS OF INHERITANCE

Gen. 12:7	unto thy seed will I give this **land**: and there builded
Gen. 13:15(14,15)	all the **land**...thou seest, to thee will I give it, and
Gen. 49:26(22-26)	unto the **utmost** bound of the everlasting hills: they
Deut. 2:5	for I will not give you of their **land**, no, not so much
Deut. 4:38	land for an **inheritance**, as it is this day.
Deut. 21:23	land...which...thy God giveth thee for an **inheritance**.
Deut. 33:13(13-17)	of Joseph he said, blessed of the Lord be his **land**
Josh. 13:7	divide this land for an **inheritance** unto the nine
Isa. 13:14	they shall...flee every one into his own **land**.
Isa. 57:13	putteth his trust in me...inherit my holy **mountain**
Jer. 50:16	they shall flee every one to his own **land**.
Jer. 51:9(8,9)	let us go every one into his own **country**: for her
Heb. 11:8(8-16)	a place...he should after receive for an **inheritance**
1 Ne. 17:38(36-38)	he leadeth away the righteous into precious **lands**, and
1 Ne. 22:12	gathered together to the lands of their **inheritance**
2 Ne. 6:11	gathered...again to the **lands** of their inheritance.
2 Ne. 9:2(1-2)	gathered home to the **lands** of their inheritance, and
2 Ne. 10:7(7-19)	restored...unto the **lands** of their inheritance.
2 Ne. 23:14	they shall...flee every one into his own **land**.
2 Ne. 25:11(9-11)	be restored again to the **land** of their inheritance.
2 Ne. 29:14	gathered home unto the **lands** of their possessions; and
3 Ne. 20:33(29,33,46)	Jerusalem for the **land** of their inheritance.
3 Ne. 21:22(14-25)	whom I have given this land for their **inheritance**
3 Ne. 29:1	restoration to the **lands** of their inheritance, is
Morm. 5:14	restoring...Israel, to the **land** of their inheritance
Ether 13:8(2-8)	house of Joseph shall be built upon this **land**; and it
D&C 38:20(15-22)	**land** of your inheritance, and for...your children
D&C 45:58	the **earth** shall be given unto them for an inheritance
D&C 52:5(5,42)	made known unto them the **land** of your inheritance.
D&C 56:20	their generations shall inherit the **earth** from
D&C 57:5(5,7)	that they may obtain it for an everlasting **inheritance**
D&C 58:44	time...not yet...for them to receive their **inheritance**
D&C 63:29	**Zion** shall not be obtained but by purchase or by blood
A of F 1:10	Zion will be built upon this the **American** continent

LANGUAGE

Gen. 2:19(19-20)	Adam called every...creature...was the **name** thereof.
Gen. 11:1(1-9)	the whole earth was of one **language**, and of one speech
Gen. 11:9(1-9)	the Lord did there confound the **language** of all the
Deut. 28:49	a nation whose **tongue** thou shalt not understand
Judg. 12:6(5,6)	say now **Shibboleth**: and he said Sibboleth: for he
Neh. 13:24	their children...could not speak in the Jews' **language**
Ps. 19:3	there is no speech nor **language**, where their voice is
Ps. 81:5	of Egypt: where I heard a **language** that I understood
Dan. 3:4(4-7)	you it is commanded, O people, nations, and **languages**
Zeph. 3:9	for then will I turn to the people a pure **language**
Mark 16:17	signs...follow...they shall speak with new **tongues**
Acts 2:6(1-12)	every man heard them speak in his own **language**.
Acts 19:6	they spake with **tongues**, and prophesied.
1 Cor. 12:10	to another the interpretation of **tongues**
1 Cor. 14:19(6-19)	rather **speak** five words with my understanding, that
2 Ne. 31:3	he speaketh unto men according to their **language**, unto
1:17	their **language** had become corrupted; and they had
1:22(22-25)	the Lord confounded the **language** of the people; and
Mosiah 28:17(14-17)	the Lord confounded the **language** of the people and the
Alma 5:61(60-62)	in the **language** of him who hath commanded me, that ye
Alma 29:8	of their own nation and **tongue**, to teach his word, yea
3 Ne. 5:18	according to our **language**, we are not able to write.
Ether 1:33(32-37)	the time the Lord confounded the **language** of the
Ether 1:35	the Lord...did not confound the **language** of Jared; and
Ether 3:22(22-28)	write them in a **language** that they cannot be read.
Ether 12:24(24-25)	not made us mighty in **writing** like unto the brother
Moro. 10:16(15,16)	to another, the interpretation of **languages** and of
D&C 1:24(24-26)	these commandments...given...of their **language**, that
D&C 11:21	obtain my word, and then shall your **tongue** be loosed
D&C 29:33	**speaking** unto you that you may naturally understand
D&C 46:24(24,25)	and again, it is given to some to speak with **tongues**
D&C 90:11	the gospel...in his own **language**, through those who
D&C 90:15(12-15)	become acquainted ...with **languages**, tongues, and
Moses 3:20	Adam gave **names** to all cattle, and to the fowl of the
Moses 6:6(5-6)	having a **language** which was pure and undefiled.
Moses 6:57	for, in the **language** of Adam, Man of Holiness is his
Abr. 5:21(20-21)	Adam gave **names** to all cattle, to the fowl of the air
A of F 1:7	we believe in the gift of **tongues**...interpretation of

LAST DAYS

Gen. 49:1	tell you that which shall befall you in the **last** days.
Deut. 4:30(29-30)	even in the **latter** days, if thou turn to the Lord thy
Isa. 2:2(2-5)	in the **last** days...mountain of the Lord's house shall
Isa. 19:17(11-25)	the land of **Judah** shall be a terror unto Egypt, every
Isa. 24:20	the **earth** shall reel to and fro like a drunkard, and
Isa. 29:18(17,18)	in that **day** shall the deaf hear the words of the book
Ezek. 38:22(1-23)	I will plead against him with **pestilence** and with
Dan. 2:44(31-45)	in the **days** of these kings shall the God of heaven set
Dan. 7:21(8,20-25)	the same horn made **war** with the saints, and prevailed
Dan. 12:1(1-3)	and at that time shall **Michael** stand up, the great
Joel 2:30(28-32)	I will shew **wonders** in the heavens and in the earth

Joel 3:15(9-21)	the **sun** and the moon shall be darkened, and the stars
Joel 3:16	the heavens and the earth shall **shake**: but the Lord
Hag. 2:6(6,7,22)	I will **shake** the heavens, and the earth, and the sea
Zech. 1:16	I am returned to Jerusalem...my **house** shall be built
Zech. 14:2(1-15)	I will gather all nations against Jerusalem to **battle**
Mal. 3:1(1-6)	I will send my **messenger**, and he shall prepare the way
Mal. 4:5(5-6)	I will send you **Elijah** the prophet before the coming
Matt. 24:3(3-51)	sign of thy coming, and of the **end** of the world
Matt. 24:7(6-8)	for **nation** shall rise against nation, and kingdom
Acts 2:17	shall come to pass in the **last** days, saith God,I will
Acts 2:19(19-20)	shew **wonders** in heaven above, and signs in the earth
Eph. 1:10	that in the **dispensation** of the fulness of times he
1 Tim. 4:1(1-3)	in the **latter** times some shall depart from the faith
2 Tim. 3:1(1-7)	this know...in the **last** days perilous times shall come
Heb. 12:26	I **shake** not the earth only, but also heaven.
2 Pet. 3:3(3-10)	there shall come in the **last** days scoffers, walking
Jude 1:18	there should be mockers in the **last** time, who should
Rev. 6:12(12-17)	when he had opened the **sixth** seal, and, lo, there was
Rev. 11:3(3-12)	and I will give power unto my two **witnesses**, and they
Rev. 15:6(5-8)	seven angels...having the seven **plagues**, clothed in
1 Ne. 14:17(10-17)	and when the **day** cometh that the wrath of God is
2 Ne. 6:15(11-18)	they that believe not in him shall be **destroyed**...by
2 Ne. 10:7(5-9)	when the **day** cometh that they shall believe in me
2 Ne. 25:8(7-8)	they are of worth...in the **last** days; for in that day
2 Ne. 25:16(15-18)	and when that **day** shall come that they shall believe
2 Ne. 26:14(14-22)	I prophesy unto you concerning the **last** days
2 Ne. 27:1(1-35)	in the **last** days, or in the days of the Gentiles- yea
2 Ne. 30:10(10-15)	a great **division** among the people, and the wicked will
3 Ne. 20:19(15-20)	I will make thy **horn** iron, and I will make thy hoofs
3 Ne. 21:1(1-29)	a sign, that ye may know the **time** when these things
3 Ne. 25:1	the **day** cometh that shall burn as an oven; and all the
D&C 1:4(1-39)	my disciples, whom I have chosen in these **last** days.
D&C 1:35	the **day** speedily cometh; the hour is not yet, but is
D&C 2:1	Priesthood, by the hand of **Elijah** the prophet, before
D&C 5:19	a desolating **scourge** shall go forth among the
D&C 10:65	I will **gather** them as a hen gathereth her chickens
D&C 29:14(14-16)	before this great **day** shall come the sun shall be
D&C 29:16(15-21)	there shall be a great **hailstorm** sent forth to destroy
D&C 29:21	great and abominable **church**...shall be cast down by
D&C 34:9	the **sun** shall be darkened, and the moon be turned into
D&C 35:16(15-16)	they shall learn the parable of the **fig-tree**, for even
D&C 38:12	angels are waiting...to **gather** the tares that they may
D&C 43:18(17-27)	the heavens shall **shake** and the earth shall tremble
D&C 45:16(16-75)	ye have asked of me concerning the **signs** of my coming
D&C 49:24	and the **Lamanites** shall blossom as the rose.
D&C 61:14(4-15)	in the last days, by...John, I cursed the **waters**.
D&C 65:2(1-6)	gospel roll forth...until it has **filled** the whole
D&C 77:15	two **prophets**...are to be raised up to the Jewish
D&C 84:118	I will not only **shake** the earth, but the starry
D&C 86:4(1-11)	in the **last** days, even now while the Lord is beginning
D&C 87:2(1-8)	**time** will come...war will be poured...upon all nations
D&C 87:4	**slaves** shall rise up against their masters, who shall
D&C 88:85(85-110)	the **desolation** of abomination which awaits the wicked

LAST DAYS cont.

D&C 88:91	men's **hearts** shall fail them; for fear shall come upon
D&C 97:25(25-26)	nevertheless, **Zion** shall escape if she observe to do
D&C 106:4(4,5)	the **coming** of the Lord draweth nigh, and it overtaketh
D&C 110:16(13-16)	that the great and dreadful **day** of the Lord is near
D&C 112:25(24-28)	upon my **house** shall it begin, and from my house shall
D&C 113:6(5,6)	for the gathering of my people in the **last** days.
D&C 115:6	**gathering** together upon the land of Zion, and upon her
D&C 133:37	and this **gospel** shall be preached...every nation
D&C 133:64(63-74)	**day** cometh that shall burn as an oven, and all the
Moses 7:60(60-67)	as I live, even so will I come in the **last** days, in
Moses 7:63(63-64)	the Lord said unto **Enoch**...thy city meet them there
JS-M 1:4(4-55)	what is the **sign** of thy coming, and of the end of the
JS-H 1:37	the **day** cometh that shall burn as an oven, and all the
JS-H 1:41	Joel...not yet fulfilled, but was **soon** to be. And he

LAUGHTER

Gen. 17:17	then Abraham fell upon his face, and **laughed**, and said
Gen. 18:13(13-15)	Lord said...wherefore did Sarah **laugh**, saying, shall
Gen. 21:6	and Sarah said, God hath made me to **laugh**, so that all
2 Kgs. 19:21(20-22)	daughter of Zion hath...**laughed** thee to scorn; the
Neh. 2:19(19,20)	they **laughed** us to scorn, and despised us, and said
Ps. 2:4	he that sitteth in the heavens shall **laugh**: the Lord
Ps. 37:13	the Lord shall **laugh** at him: for he seeth that his day
Ps. 52:6	the righteous...shall **laugh** at him
Prov. 14:13(11-14)	even in **laughter** the heart is sorrowful; and the end
Eccl. 3:4	a time to weep, and a time to **laugh**; a time to mourn
Eccl. 7:6(3-6)	so is the **laughter** of the fool: this also is vanity.
Matt. 9:24(23-26)	the maid is not dead...they **laughed** him to scorn.
Luke 6:21(21-25)	blessed are ye that weep now: for ye shall **laugh**.
Alma 26:23(23,24)	and they **laughed** us to scorn
3 Ne. 9:2	for the devil **laugheth**, and his angels rejoice
D&C 45:49(49,50)	they that have **laughed** shall see their folly.
D&C 59:15	not with much **laughter**, for this is sin, but with a
D&C 88:69(69,121)	cast away...your excess of **laughter** far from you.
Moses 7:26	Satan...looked up and **laughed**, and his angels rejoiced

LAW OF MOSES

Ex. 18:20	thou shalt teach them ordinances and **laws**, and shalt
Ex. 20:1(1-17)	and God **spake** all these words, saying
Ex. 31:18	two **tables**...written with the finger of God.
Ex. 32:16(15-16)	the **tables** were the work of God, and the writing was
Ex. 34:28(1-28)	the words of the covenant, the ten **commandments**.
Deut. 5:22(7-22)	he wrote them in two **tables** of stone, and delivered
Deut. 33:4(2-4)	Moses commanded us a **law**, even the inheritance of the
1 Kgs. 8:9	nothing in the ark save the two **tables** of stone, which
Matt. 5:17(17-20)	think not that I am come to destroy the **law**, or the
Matt. 5:18	one jot...shall in no wise pass...the **law**, till all
Matt. 7:12	do ye...to them: for this is the **law** and the prophets.
Matt. 22:40(35-40)	on these two commandments hang all the **law** and the

LAW OF MOSES cont.

Luke 16:17(16-17)	earth to pass, than one tittle of the **law** to fail.
John 1:17	**law** was given by Moses, but grace and truth came by
Acts 13:39	could not be justified by the **law** of Moses.
Rom. 2:12	as many as have sinned without **law** shall also perish
Rom. 3:20	by the deeds of the **law** there shall no flesh be
Rom. 7:7(6,7)	I had not known sin, but by the **law**: for I had not
Gal. 3:24(10-24)	the **law** was our schoolmaster to bring us unto Christ
Gal. 4:24	the mount Sinai, which gendereth to **bondage**, which is
Gal. 5:1	be not entangled again with the yoke of **bondage.**
Gal. 5:4	justified by the **law**; ye are fallen from grace.
1 Tim. 1:9(8-9)	**law** is not made for a righteous man, but for the
Heb. 2:15	through fear of death were...subject to **bondage.**
Heb. 8:9(5-13)	not according to the **covenant** that I made with their
Heb. 9:1(1-4)	first **covenant** had also ordinances of divine service
1 Ne. 4:16	**law** was engraven upon the plates of brass.
1 Ne. 5:9	offer sacrifice and burnt **offerings** unto the Lord; and
2 Ne. 5:10	all things according to the **law** of Moses.
2 Ne. 11:4	this end hath the law of Moses...the **typifying** of him.
2 Ne. 25:25(24-26)	for, for this end was the **law** given; wherefore the law
Jacob 4:5(5-7)	we keep the **law** of Moses, it pointing our souls to him
Mosiah 3:14(14-16)	he appointed unto them a law, even the **law** of Moses.
Mosiah 12:29(29-37)	if ye teach the **law** of Moses why do ye not keep it
Mosiah 13:30(11-33)	a **law** given them...to keep them in remembrance of God
Mosiah 16:14(14,15)	**law** of Moses...a shadow of...things which are to come
Alma 13:16(3-16)	**ordinances** were given...that...look forward on the Son
Alma 25:15(10-16)	the **law** of Moses was a type of his coming, and
Alma 34:14(11-14)	meaning of the **law**...pointing to that great and last
3 Ne. 1:25(24-25)	the **law** was not yet fulfilled, and that it must be
3 Ne. 9:17(17-22)	and in me is the **law** of Moses fulfilled.
3 Ne. 12:18	one jot nor...tittle hath not passed away from the **law**
3 Ne. 15:5(1-8)	I am he that gave the **law**, and I am he who covenanted
4 Ne. 1:12	they did not walk any more after...**law** of Moses; but
D&C 22:2	cannot enter in at the strait gate by the **law** of Moses
D&C 74:3(2-5)	become subject to the **law** of Moses, which law was
D&C 84:27(23-27)	**law** of carnal commandments, which the Lord in his
JFS-V 1:41	and Moses, the great **law-giver** of Israel

LAZINESS

Judg. 18:9	be not **slothful** to go, and to enter to possess the
Prov. 6:6(6-11)	go to the ant, thou **sluggard**; consider her ways, and
Prov. 10:4	he becometh poor that dealeth with a **slack** hand: but
Prov. 12:24	but the **slothful** shall be under tribute.
Prov. 12:27	the **slothful** man roasteth not that which he took in
Prov. 13:4	the soul of the **sluggard** desireth, and hath nothing
Prov. 15:19	way of the **slothful** man is as an hedge of thorns: but
Prov. 18:9	**slothful**...is brother to him that is great waster.
Prov. 19:15	**slothfulness** casteth into a deep sleep; and an idle
Prov. 19:24	a **slothful** man hideth his hand in his bosom, and will
Prov. 20:13	love not **sleep**, lest thou come to poverty; open thine
Prov. 21:25(25,26)	the desire of the **slothful** killeth him; for his hands
Prov. 24:30(30-34)	I went by the field of the **slothful**, and by the

LAZINESS cont.

Prov. 26:13(13-16)	the **slothful** man saith, there is a lion in the way; a
Eccl. 10:18	by much **slothfulness** the building decayeth; and
Ezek. 16:49	abundance of **idleness** was in her and in her daughters
Matt. 25:26(24-28)	thou wicked and **slothful** servant, thou knewest that I
Col. 3:23	and whatsoever ye do, do it **heartily**, as to the Lord
2 Thes. 3:10	if any would not **work**, neither should he eat.
Heb. 6:12(11-12)	that ye be not **slothful**, but followers of them who
1 Ne. 12:23	full of **idleness** and all manner of abominations.
Mosiah 9:12	they were a **lazy** and an idolatrous people; therefore
Mosiah 11:6	thus they were supported in their **laziness**, and in
Alma 1:32	**idleness**, and in babblings, and in envyings and strife
Alma 17:15(14,15)	they were a very **indolent** people, many of whom did
Alma 33:21	would ye rather harden your hearts...and be **slothful**
Alma 37:41(41-46)	they were **slothful**, and forgot to exercise their faith
Alma 38:12	see that ye refrain from **idleness**.
Alma 47:36	they became more hardened...giving way to **indolence**
Alma 60:14	judgments...upon...people, because of...**slothfulness**
D&C 42:42	he that is **idle** shall not eat the bread nor wear the
D&C 56:17	wo unto you...who will not **labor** with your own hands
D&C 58:26(26-29)	he that is compelled...is a **slothful**...servant
D&C 58:27	men should be **anxiously** engaged in a good cause, and
D&C 60:13	thou shalt not **idle** away thy time, neither shalt thou
D&C 64:33	wherefore, be not **weary** in well-doing, for ye are
D&C 68:30(30,31)	the **idler** shall be had in remembrance before the Lord.
D&C 75:3	neither be **idle** but labor with your might
D&C 75:29	the **idler** shall not have place in the church, except
D&C 88:124	cease to be **idle**; cease to be unclean; cease to find
D&C 90:18	keep **slothfulness** and uncleanness far from you.
D&C 90:31	not be **idle** in her days from thenceforth.
D&C 101:50(49-50)	at variance one with another they became very **slothful**
D&C 107:100(99-100)	he that is **slothful** shall not be counted worthy to

LEADERSHIP

Ex. 18:22(13-27)	they shall bear the **burden** with thee.
Num. 11:17(16-17)	they shall **bear** the burden of the people with thee
Ps. 25:5	**lead** me in thy truth, and teach me: for thou art the
Prov. 4:11	I have taught...I have **led** thee in right paths.
Prov. 29:2	when the wicked beareth **rule**, the people mourn.
Isa. 3:12	they which **lead** thee cause thee to err, and destroy
Isa. 9:16	for the **leaders** of this people cause them to err; and
Isa. 48:17(16-18)	**leadeth** thee by the way that thou shouldest go.
Ezek. 33:7(2-9)	I have set thee a **watchman** unto the house of Israel
Matt. 15:14(13,14)	they be blind **leaders** of the blind. And if the blind
Matt. 20:26(26,27)	whosoever will be **great** among you, let him be your
Matt. 23:11(1-12)	he that is **greatest** among you shall be your servant.
Matt. 25:21(14-30)	I will make thee **ruler** over many things: enter thou
Luke 6:39	can the blind **lead** the blind? shall they not both fall
John 10:12(1-14)	hireling, and not the shepherd...**leaveth** the sheep
John 13:15(4-15)	I have given you an **example**...do as I have done to you
Rom. 8:14	as many as are **led** by the Spirit of God, they are the
1 Cor. 12:21(4-31)	nor again the **head** to the feet, I have no need of you

LEADERSHIP cont.

Eph. 6:9(7-9)	master...neither is there respect of persons with him.
1 Thes. 5:12(11-22)	to know them which **labour** among you, and are over you
Titus 1:7(7-9)	for a **bishop** must be blameless, as the steward of God
Heb. 5:4(1-5,8,9)	no man taketh this **honour** unto himself, but he that
1 Pet. 5:1(1-9)	**elders** which are among you I exhort, who am also an
2 Ne. 9:48(47,48)	as ye are not holy, and ye look upon me as a **teacher**
2 Ne. 13:12	they who **lead** thee cause thee to err and destroy the
2 Ne. 19:16	the **leaders** of this people cause them to err; and they
Jacob 1:19(17-19)	**magnify** our office unto the Lord, taking upon us the
Jarom 1:7	our **leaders** were mighty men in the faith of the Lord
Alma 4:11	began to **lead**...from one piece of iniquity to another
Alma 13:3(1-12)	**called**...on account of their exceeding faith and good
3 Ne. 3:19	chief **captains**...one that had the spirit of revelation
3 Ne. 7:11	their **leaders** did establish their laws, every one
D&C 10:22	that he may **lead** their souls to destruction.
D&C 20:44(39-52)	and to take the **lead** of all meetings.
D&C 20:49(39-52)	and he is to take the **lead** of meetings when there is
D&C 38:42	be ye clean that **bear** the vessels of the Lord. Even
D&C 42:11(11,12)	ordained by some one who has **authority**, and it is
D&C 50:26(13-30)	**ordained** of God...is appointed to be the greatest
D&C 98:9(9,10)	when the wicked **rule** the people mourn.
D&C 101:42	he that **exalteth** himself shall be abased, and he that
D&C 104:13(11-13)	every man **accountable**, as a steward over earthly
D&C 105:7	who are appointed to **lead** my people, who are the first
D&C 107:99(99,100)	let every man **learn** his duty, and to act in the office
D&C 121:39(34-46)	little **authority**...begin to exercise **unrighteous**
D&C 124:45(45,46)	whom I have appointed to **lead** my people, behold
Abr. 1:18	I will **lead** thee by my hand, and I will take thee, to
Abr. 3:23(22-23)	these I will make my **rulers**; for he stood among those

LEARNING

Deut. 31:13(9-13)	that their children...may...**learn** to fear the Lord
Ps. 111:10	the fear of the Lord is the beginning of **wisdom**: a
Ps. 119:71(71,72)	I have been afflicted; that I might **learn** thy statutes
Prov. 1:5(1-7)	a wise man will hear, and will increase **learning**; and
Prov. 4:7	get wisdom: and with all thy getting get **understanding**
Prov. 9:9(9,10)	teach a just man, and he will increase in **learning**.
Isa. 1:17	**learn** to do well; seek judgment, relieve the oppressed
Isa. 29:24	they that murmured shall **learn** doctrine.
Dan. 1:17(4,17)	God gave them knowledge and skill in all **learning** and
Matt. 7:7(7-11)	**knock**, and it shall be opened unto you
Matt. 11:29	**learn** of me...and ye shall find rest unto your souls.
John 5:39	**search** the scriptures; for in them ye think ye have
John 14:26	Holy Ghost...shall **teach** you all things, and bring all
John 16:13(7,13-14)	the Spirit of truth...will **guide** you into all truth
Rom. 1:22	professing themselves to be **wise**, they became fools
1 Cor. 2:14(11-14)	but the **natural** man receiveth not the things of the
1 Cor. 3:18(18-20)	let him become a fool, that he may be **wise**.
Eph. 4:13(11-14)	come in the unity of the faith..of the **knowledge** of
Col. 2:8(6-8)	beware lest any man spoil you through **philosophy** and
2 Tim. 3:7(1-7)	ever **learning**, and never able to come to the knowledge

LEARNING cont.

James 1:5(5-7) — if any of you lack **wisdom**, let him ask of God, that
2 Pet. 1:5(5-9) — add to your faith virtue; and to virtue **knowledge**
1 Ne. 19:23 — **scriptures**...might be for our profit and learning.
2 Ne. 2:14 — I speak...for your profit and **learning**; for there is
2 Ne. 9:29(28-29) — but to be **learned** is good if they hearken unto the
2 Ne. 9:42 — who are puffed up because of their **learning**, and their
2 Ne. 26:20 — preach up...their own wisdom and their own **learning**
Jacob 7:4 — and he was **learned**, that he had a perfect knowledge
Alma 10:15 — now these lawyers were **learned** in all the arts and
Alma 12:10(9-11) — not **harden** his heart...is given the greater portion
Alma 26:22(21-22) — unto such it is given to know the **mysteries** of God
Alma 32:12 — and that ye may **learn** wisdom; for it is necessary that
Alma 37:35 — **learn** wisdom in thy youth; yea, learn in thy youth to
Alma 38:9(9-15) — that ye may **learn** of me that there is no other way or
3 Ne. 6:12 — receive great **learning** because of their riches.
Morm. 9:31 — that ye may **learn** to be more wise than we have been.
Moro. 10:5(3-5) — by the power of the Holy Ghost ye may **know** the truth
Moro. 10:10(8-17) — that he may teach the word of **knowledge** by the same
D&C 19:23 — **learn** of me...and you shall have peace in me.
D&C 42:61 — thou shalt receive...**knowledge** upon knowledge, that
D&C 50:24(17-26) — he that **receiveth** light...continueth...receiveth more
D&C 63:23 — unto him...I will give the **mysteries** of my kingdom
D&C 68:28(25-28) — shall also **teach** their children to pray, and to walk
D&C 75:10(9-11) — Comforter, which shall **teach** them all things that are
D&C 76:7(5-10) — to them will I reveal all **mysteries**, yea, all the
D&C 88:77(77-80) — **teach** one another the doctrine of the kingdom.
D&C 88:118 — seek **learning**, even by study and also by faith.
D&C 90:15 — study and **learn**...books...languages, tongues, and
D&C 93:53 — it is my will that you should...obtain a **knowledge** of
D&C 107:99(99-100) — let every man **learn** his duty, and to act in the office
D&C 121:26 — God shall give unto you **knowledge** by his Holy Spirit
D&C 128:11 — no difficulty in obtaining a **knowledge** of facts in
D&C 130:18(18-21) — **intelligence** we attain unto in this life, it will rise
D&C 131:6 — it is impossible for a man to be saved in **ignorance**.
D&C 136:32(31-33) — let him that is ignorant **learn** wisdom by humbling
JFS-V 1:56(55,56) — their first **lessons** in the world of spirits and were

LEAVEN

Ex. 12:15(15-19) — seven days shall ye eat **unleavened** bread; even the
Ex. 13:7(6,7) — neither shall there be **leaven** seen with thee in all
Ex. 34:25 — not offer the blood of my sacrifice with **leaven**
Lev. 2:11 — no meat offering...shall be made with **leaven**: for ye
Lev. 6:17(16,17) — it shall not be baken with **leaven**. I have given it
Lev. 23:17 — they shall be baken with **leaven**; they are the
Deut. 16:3(3,4) — thou shalt eat no **leavened** bread with it; seven days
Amos 4:5 — and offer a sacrifice of thanksgiving with **leaven**, and
Matt. 13:33 — the kingdom of heaven is like unto **leaven**, which a
Matt. 16:6(6-12) — take heed and beware of the **leaven** of the Pharisees
Luke 12:1(1-2) — the **leaven** of the Pharisees, which is hypocrisy.
1 Cor. 5:8(6-8) — let us keep the feast, not with old **leaven**, neither

LEPROSY

Ex. 4:6	behold, his hand was **leprous** as snow.
Lev. 13:2(2-59)	like the plague of **leprosy**; then he shall be brought
Lev. 14:2(2-57)	this shall be the law of the **leper** in the day of his
Lev. 22:4	what man soever of the seed of Aaron is a **leper**, or
Num. 5:2(2-3)	that they put out of the camp every **leper**, and every
Num. 12:10	Miriam became **leprous**, white as snow: and Aaron looked
Deut. 24:8	take heed in the plague of **leprosy**, that thou observe
2 Kgs. 5:1(1-15)	Naaman...was a **leper**.
2 Kgs. 5:27	the **leprosy** therefore of Naaman shall cleave unto thee
2 Kgs. 15:5	the Lord smote the king, so that he was a **leper** unto
2 Chr. 26:21(21,23)	Uzziah the king was a **leper** unto the day of his death
Matt. 8:2(2-4)	there came a **leper** and worshipped him, saying, Lord
Matt. 10:8	heal the sick, cleanse the **lepers**, raise the dead
Matt. 11:5	the **lepers** are cleansed, and the deaf hear, the dead
Mark 1:40(40-45)	there came a **leper** to him, beseeching him, and
Luke 4:27	and many **lepers** were in Israel in the time of Eliseus
Luke 5:12(12-16)	a man full of **leprosy**: who seeing Jesus fell on his
Luke 17:12(12-14)	ten men that were **lepers**, which stood afar off
3 Ne. 17:7	have ye any that are...**leprous**...afflicted in any

LEVITY

Eccl. 7:6	so is the **laughter** of the fool: this also is vanity.
Eph. 5:4(3-4)	neither...**foolish** talking...which are not convenient
1 Thes. 5:8(5-8)	let us, who are of the day, be **sober**, putting on the
1 Tim. 3:2	a bishop then must be blameless,...**sober**, of good
1 Tim. 3:8(8-11)	likewise must the deacons be **grave**, not doubletongued
Titus 2:12	we should live **soberly**, righteously, and godly, in
1 Pet. 1:13(13-15)	gird up the loins of your mind, be **sober**, and hope to
1 Pet. 5:8	be **sober**, be vigilant; because your adversary the
Jacob 2:2(1-3)	responsibility...to magnify mine office with **soberness**
Mosiah 4:15(14,15)	walk in the ways of truth and **soberness**; ye will teach
Alma 53:21(18-21)	yea, they were men of truth and **soberness**, for they
Morm. 1:15(15-17)	and being somewhat of a **sober** mind, therefore I was
D&C 43:34(34-35)	let the **solemnities** of eternity rest upon your minds.
D&C 84:54(54,55,61)	you have treated **lightly** the things you have
D&C 88:69	cast away your idle thoughts...excess of **laughter** far
D&C 88:121	cease...from all your pride and **light-mindedness**, and
D&C 100:7(5-8)	declare in my name, in **solemnity** of heart, in the
JS-H 1:28	I was guilty of **levity**...associated with jovial

LIBERTY

Ex. 20:2	brought thee...out of the house of **bondage**.
Ex. 21:2(2-11)	in the seventh he shall go out **free** for nothing.
Lev. 25:10	proclaim **liberty** throughout all the land unto all the
Ps. 119:45(44-48)	and I will walk at **liberty**: for I seek thy precepts.
Isa. 58:6(5-7)	to let the oppressed go **free**, and that ye break every
Isa. 61:1	to proclaim **liberty** to the captives, and the opening
Jer. 34:8(8-9)	made a covenant...to proclaim **liberty** unto them
Jer. 34:17(15-17)	I proclaim a **liberty** for you, saith the Lord, to the

278

LIBERTY cont.

Ezek. 46:17	it shall be his to the year of **liberty**; after it shall
Luke 4:18	to set at **liberty** them that are bruised
John 8:32	know the truth, and the truth shall make you **free**.
John 8:36(32-36)	if the Son...make you **free**, ye shall be free indeed.
Rom. 8:21	the glorious **liberty** of the children of God.
1 Cor. 8:9(8-10)	lest...this **liberty** of yours become a stumblingblock
2 Cor. 3:17	where the Spirit of the Lord is, there is **liberty**.
Gal. 2:4(3-5)	our **liberty** which we have in Christ Jesus, that they
Gal. 5:1	stand..in the **liberty** wherewith Christ hath made us
Gal. 5:13(12-14)	ye have been called unto **liberty**; only use not liberty
James 1:25	but whoso looketh into the perfect law of **liberty**, and
James 2:12(11-12)	they that shall be judged by the law of **liberty**.
1 Pet. 2:16(15-18)	not using your **liberty** for a cloke of maliciousness
2 Pet. 2:19(18-20)	they promise them **liberty**, they themselves are the
2 Ne. 1:7	it shall be a land of **liberty** unto them; wherefore
2 Ne. 2:27	men are free...to choose **liberty** and eternal life
2 Ne. 10:11(10-12)	this land shall be a land of **liberty** unto the Gentiles
Mosiah 5:8	no other head whereby ye can be made **free**. There is
Mosiah 23:13	stand fast in this **liberty** wherewith ye have been made
Mosiah 29:32(31-32)	I desire that this land be a land of **liberty**, and
Mosiah 29:39	rejoiced because of the **liberty** which had been granted
Alma 8:17(16-17)	study...that they may destroy the **liberty** of thy
Alma 21:22(21-22)	they might have the **liberty** of worshiping the Lord the
Alma 43:9(8-9)	that they might preserve their...**liberty**, that they
Alma 43:30(29-31)	only desire...their **liberty**, and their church
Alma 43:45	fighting for their homes and their **liberties**, their
Alma 43:49(48-49)	they cried...unto the Lord...for their **liberty** and the
Alma 44:5(2-5)	by that **liberty** which binds us to our lands and our
Alma 46:10(8-17)	to destroy the foundation of **liberty** which God had
Alma 46:24	let us preserve our **liberty** as a remnant of Joseph
Alma 46:28	all...who were desirous to maintain their **liberty**, to
Alma 46:36	he caused the title of **liberty** to be hoisted upon
Alma 48:10(10-11)	he was preparing to support their **liberty**, their lands
Alma 50:32	consequences...lead to the overthrow of their **liberty**.
Alma 51:7	Pahoran and also many of the people of **liberty**, who
Alma 51:13	chief judge, and also with the people of **liberty**, that
Alma 51:17	should take up arms and support the cause of **liberty**.
Alma 51:20(19-20)	yielded to the standard of **liberty**, and were compelled
Alma 53:17(16-18)	they never would give up their **liberty**, but they would
Alma 56:47(46-48)	did think more upon the **liberty** of their fathers than
Alma 58:12(10-12)	our wives...children, and the cause of our **liberty**.
Alma 58:40(37-41)	in that **liberty** wherewith God has made them free; and
Alma 60:36	and the **freedom** and welfare of my country. And thus
Alma 61:6	in the defence of their country and their **freedom**, and
Alma 61:9	my soul standeth fast in that **liberty** in the which God
Alma 61:15	Spirit of God, which is also the Spirit of **freedom**
Alma 62:4	he did raise the standard of **liberty** in whatsoever
Alma 62:37(33-37)	a true friend to **liberty**; and he had suffered very
Hel. 1:8(7-8)	and sought to destroy the **liberty** of the people.
3 Ne. 2:12	of their worship, and their freedom and their **liberty**.
3 Ne. 3:2	in the defence of your **liberty**...property...country
3 Ne. 5:4(3-5)	that they would murder no more were set at **liberty**.
3 Ne. 6:30(29-30)	that the land should no more be at **liberty** but should

LIBERTY cont.

Ether 2:12(11-12)   behold, this is a choice land...**free** from bondage
Ether 8:25   seeketh to overthrow the **freedom** of all lands, nation
D&C 38:22(20-24)   follow me, and you shall be a **free** people, and ye
D&C 88:86   abide ye in the **liberty** wherewith ye are made free
D&C 98:5(4-6)   law of the land...supporting that principle of **freedom**
D&C 98:8   I, the Lord God, make you **free**, therefore ye are free
D&C 101:77(76-79)   laws and Constitution...maintained for the **rights** and
D&C 134:2(1-3)   laws...secure to each...**free** exercise of conscience
D&C 134:5(4-5)   enact...laws...holding sacred the **freedom** of
JFS-V 1:31(31-34,42)   **liberty** to the captives...unto all who would repent

LIFE, SANCTITY OF

Gen. 4:10(9-12)   thy brother's **blood** crieth unto me from the ground.
Gen. 9:6(4-6)   his blood be shed: for in the **image** of God made he man
Ex. 20:13   thou shalt not **kill**.
1 Sam. 26:21(21-24)   because my soul was **precious** in thine eyes this day
Ps. 72:14   **precious** shall their blood be in his sight.
Matt. 18:11   for the Son of man is come to **save** that which was lost
Luke 9:56(54-56)   not come to destroy men's lives, but to **save** them. and
Luke 19:10   Son of man is come to seek and to **save** that which was
John 15:13   greater love...a man lay down his **life** for his friends
1 Cor. 3:16(16-23)   know ye not that ye are the **temple** of God, and that
1 Jn. 3:15   no **murderer** hath eternal life abiding in him.
1 Ne. 4:13   it is better that one man should **perish** than that a
Mosiah 20:22   better...be in bondage than...lose our **lives**
Alma 26:32   they had rather sacrifice their **lives** than even to
Alma 34:12   the law requireth the **life** of him who hath murdered
Alma 39:5(5-6)   above all sins save...shedding of innocent **blood** or
Alma 48:14   never to raise the sword except...to preserve...**lives**.
3 Ne. 12:21   whosoever shall **kill**...in danger of the judgment of
D&C 18:10   remember the **worth** of souls is great in the sight of
D&C 42:18(18-19)   he that **kills** shall not have forgiveness in this world
D&C 49:21   **sheddeth** blood or that wasteth flesh and hath no need.
D&C 109:43(42,43)   their souls are **precious** before thee
D&C 132:19(19,26-27   commit no murder whereby to shed innocent **blood**, and
Moses 3:5(5-7)   created all things..**spiritually**, before..naturally
Moses 3:9   and it became also a **living** soul. For it was spiritual
Moses 5:35(34-37)   thy brother's **blood** cries unto me from the ground.

LIGHT

Gen. 1:3(3-5,14-16)   and God said, let there be **light**: and there was light.
Job 10:22   without any order, and where the **light** is as darkness.
Ps. 27:1   the Lord is my **light** and my salvation; whom shall I
Ps. 36:9   fountain of life: in thy light shall we see **light**.
Ps. 43:3   O send out thy **light** and thy truth: let them lead me
Ps. 112:4   unto the upright there ariseth **light** in the darkness
Ps. 119:105   thy word is a lamp unto my feet...a **light** unto my path
Prov. 4:18   **light**, that shineth more and more unto the perfect day
Eccl. 11:7(6-8)   truly the **light** is sweet, and a pleasant thing it is

LIGHT cont.

Isa. 5:20	put darkness for **light**, and light for darkness; that
Isa. 8:20	this word, it is because there is no **light** in them.
Isa. 9:2	people that walked in darkness have seen a great **light**
Isa. 42:6	a covenant...people, for a **light** of the Gentiles
Isa. 45:7	I form the **light**, and create darkness: I make peace
Isa. 50:10	walketh in darkness, and hath no **light**? let him trust
Isa. 50:11(10,11)	walk in the **light** of your fire, and in the sparks that
Isa. 58:8	then shall thy **light** break forth as the morning, and
Isa. 60:1	arise, shine; for thy **light** is come, and the glory of
Isa. 60:3(3,10-12)	Gentiles shall come to thy **light**, and kings to the
Isa. 60:19(19-20)	the Lord shall be unto thee an everlasting **light**, and
Zech. 14:6(6-7)	the **light** shall not be clear, nor dark
Matt. 5:16(14-16)	let your **light** so shine before men, that they may see
Luke 16:8	in their generation wiser than the children of **light**.
John 1:4(4-9)	in him was life; and the life was the **light** of men.
John 3:19(19-21)	that **light** is come into the world, and men loved
John 5:35	willing for a season to rejoice in his **light**.
John 8:12	I am the **light** of the world: he that followeth me
John 12:35(35-36)	walk while ye have the **light**, lest darkness come upon
Acts 9:3(3-6)	shined round about him a **light** from heaven
Acts 26:18	turn them from darkness to **light**, and from the power
Rom. 13:12	darkness, and let us put on the armour of **light**.
2 Cor. 4:4(4-6)	the **light** of the glorious gospel of Christ, who is the
2 Cor. 6:14	and what communion hath **light** with darkness
Eph. 5:14	arise...dead, and Christ shall give thee **light**.
1 Pet. 2:9	called you out of darkness into his marvellous **light**
1 Jn. 1:5(5-7)	God is **light**, and in him is no darkness at all.
1 Ne. 17:13	I will also be your **light** in the wilderness; and I
2 Ne. 26:10	choose works of darkness rather than **light**, therefore
2 Ne. 26:29	men preach and set themselves up for a **light** unto the
Alma 9:23(23,24)	transgress contrary to the **light** and knowledge which
Alma 19:6	the **light** which did light up his mind, which was the
Alma 32:35	whatsoever is **light**, is good, because it is
Hel. 14:3	shall be great **lights** in heaven, insomuch that in the
Ether 3:4	that we may have **light** while we shall cross the sea.
Ether 6:2	behold, they did give **light** unto the vessels.
D&C 6:21	I am the **light** which shineth in darkness, and the
D&C 11:28	I am the life and the **light** of the world.
D&C 14:9	a **light** which cannot be hid in darkness
D&C 45:28(28-29)	a **light** shall break forth among them that sit in
D&C 50:24	that **light** groweth brighter and brighter until the
D&C 82:3	sins against the greater **light** shall receive the
D&C 84:45(45-46)	whatsoever is truth is **light**, and whatsoever is light
D&C 84:54	your minds in times past have been **darkened** because
D&C 88:7(6-13)	and the **light** of the sun, and the power thereof by
D&C 88:40	**light** cleaveth unto light; mercy hath compassion on
D&C 88:44(44-45)	they give **light** to each other in their times and in
D&C 88:67	bodies shall be filled with **light**, and there shall
D&C 88:87	sun shall hide his face...shall refuse to give **light**
D&C 93:9	the **light** and the Redeemer of the world; the Spirit
D&C 93:29(28-29)	intelligence, or the **light** of truth, was not created
D&C 93:36	intelligence, or, in other words, **light** and truth.
D&C 93:37(36-37)	**light** and truth forsake that evil one.

LIGHT cont.

D&C 103:9	they were set to be a **light** unto the world, and to be
D&C 106:8	faithful witness and a **light** unto the church I have
D&C 115:5	that thy **light** may be a standard for the nations
D&C 124:9	come to the **light** of truth, and the Gentiles to the
D&C 128:20	detecting...devil...he appeared as an angel of **light**
D&C 133:49	the moon shall withhold its **light**, and the stars shall
Moses 2:3	let there be **light**; and there was light.
Moses 2:4	God, divided the **light** from the darkness.
Moses 2:16	greater **light** to rule the day, and the lesser light
JFS-V 1:24(23,24)	countenances **shone**, and the radiance from...the Lord

LIGHT OF CHRIST

Ps. 27:1	the Lord is my **light** and my salvation; whom shall I
Ps. 34:5	they looked unto him, and were **lightened**: and their
Isa. 60:1	arise, shine; for thy **light** is come, and the glory of
Isa. 60:19(1,19)	the Lord shall be unto thee an everlasting **light**, and
John 1:9(4-9)	the true **light**, which lighteth every man that cometh
John 3:19	**light** is come into the world, and men loved darkness
John 8:12	I am the **light** of the world: he that followeth me
John 9:5	I am the **light** of the world.
John 12:35(35,36)	yet a little while is the **light** with you. Walk while
2 Cor. 4:6	to give the **light**...in the face of Jesus Christ.
1 Ne. 17:13	I will also be your **light** in the wilderness; and I
Alma 28:14	joy because of the **light** of Christ unto life.
Moro. 7:18(16-19)	**light** by which ye may judge...is the **light** of Christ
D&C 6:21	I am the **light** which shineth in darkness, and the
D&C 10:70	the life and **light** of the world, your Redeemer, your
D&C 11:13	my Spirit, which shall **enlighten** your mind, which
D&C 14:9	Jesus Christ...a **light** which cannot be hid in darkness
D&C 20:37	they have received of the **Spirit** of Christ unto the
D&C 50:24	that which is of God is **light**; and he that receiveth
D&C 82:3	he who sins against the greater **light** shall receive
D&C 84:46(45-46)	the Spirit giveth **light** to every man that cometh into
D&C 88:7(6-14)	this is the **light** of Christ. As also he is in the sun
D&C 88:12(12-13)	**light** proceedeth forth from the presence of God to
D&C 88:50	that I am the true **light** that is in you, and that you
D&C 93:2(2-10)	I am the true **light** that lighteth every man that
D&C 93:9	the **light** and the Redeemer of the world; the Spirit

LIVING WATER

Isa. 55:1(1-3)	every one that thirsteth, come ye to the **waters**, and
Jer. 2:13	they have forsaken me the fountain of **living** waters
Zech. 14:8	it shall be in that day, that **living** waters shall go
John 4:10(10-15)	asked of him...he would have given thee **living** water.
John 7:37(37-39)	any man thirst, let him come unto me, and **drink**.
Rev. 7:17(15-17)	shall lead them unto living fountains of **waters**: and
Rev. 21:6(6-7)	I will give unto him...of the **water** of life freely.
Rev. 22:17(16-17)	let him take the **water** of life freely.
1 Ne. 11:25(22-25)	fountain of **living** waters, or...the love of God

2 Ne. 9:50(50-52)	my brethren...that thirsteth, come ye to the **waters**
2 Ne. 22:3	with joy...draw **water** out of the wells of salvation.
D&C 10:66(66,67)	they may, and partake of the **waters** of life freely.
D&C 63:23	the same shall be in him a well of living **water**
D&C 133:29	shall come forth pools of **living** water; and the

LOVE

Gen. 22:2	take...thine only son Isaac, whom thou **lovest**, and get
Gen. 29:20	seven years...seemed...a few days, for the **love** he had
Ex. 22:21	thou shalt neither vex a stranger, nor **oppress** him
Lev. 19:18(17,18,34)	thou shalt **love** thy neighbour as thyself: I am the Lord
Lev. 19:34	stranger that dwelleth with you...**love** him as thyself
Lev. 25:14	ye shall not **oppress** one another
Deut. 6:5(4-6)	thou shalt **love** the Lord thy God with all thine heart
Deut. 7:8	because the Lord **loved** you...he...redeemed you
Deut. 30:6	**love** the Lord thy God with all thine heart, and with
Ps. 116:1	I **love** the Lord, because he hath heard my voice and
Prov. 15:17	better is a dinner of herbs where **love** is, than a
Isa. 63:9	in his **love** and in his pity he redeemed them; and he
Jer. 31:3	I have **loved** thee with an everlasting love: therefore
Ezek. 16:8(1-14)	thy time was the time of **love**; and I spread my skirt
Hosea 11:4(1-4)	I drew them...with bands of **love**: and I was to them
Hosea 14:4	I will **love** them freely: for mine anger is turned away
Amos 5:15	**love** the good, and establish judgment in the gate: it
Mal. 1:2	I have **loved** you, saith the Lord. Yet ye say, wherein
Matt. 5:44(43-48)	**love** your enemies, bless them that curse you, do good
Matt. 10:37	he that **loveth** father or mother more than me is not
Matt. 19:19	thou shalt **love** thy neighbour as thyself.
Matt. 22:37(36-40)	thou shalt **love** the Lord thy God with all thy heart
Matt. 22:39(36-40)	second...thou shalt **love** thy neighbour as thyself.
Luke 11:42	ye tithe mint...and pass over...the **love** of God: these
John 3:16	God so **loved** the world, that he gave his Only Begotten
John 5:42(42-43)	I know you, that ye have not the **love** of God in you.
John 13:34(34-35)	a new commandment...that ye **love** one another; as I
John 14:15(15-23)	if ye **love** me, keep my commandments.
John 15:10(9-13,17)	keep my commandments, ye shall abide in my **love**; even
John 15:12(12-14)	commandment, that ye **love** one another, as I have loved
John 15:13(12-13)	greater **love** hath no man than this, that a man lay
Rom. 5:5	the **love** of God is shed abroad in our hearts by the
Rom. 12:10(9-21)	kindly affectioned one to another with brotherly **love**
Rom. 13:8(8-10)	for he that **loveth** another hath fulfilled the law.
1 Cor. 13:13(1-13)	now abideth faith, hope, **charity**...greatest...is
Gal. 5:6	but faith which worketh by **love**.
Gal. 5:14	the law is fulfilled in...this...**love** thy neighbour
Eph. 5:25(25-31)	husbands, **love** your wives, even as Christ also loved
Philip. 2:3(2-3)	let each **esteem** other better than themselves.
1 Thes. 4:9	ye yourselves are taught of God to **love** one another.
2 Tim. 1:7(7-8)	power, and of **love**, and of a sound mind.
Heb. 13:1	let brotherly **love** continue.
James 2:8	thou shalt **love** thy neighbour as thyself, ye do well
1 Pet. 1:22(22-23)	see that ye **love** one another with a pure heart

LOVE cont.

1 Jn. 2:10(10-11)	he that **loveth** his brother abideth in the light, and
1 Jn. 3:14(10-14)	he that **loveth** not his brother abideth in death.
1 Jn. 4:7(7-12)	let us **love** one another: for love is of God; and every
1 Jn. 4:18	no fear in love; but perfect **love** casteth out fear
1 Jn. 4:19	we **love** him, because he first loved us.
1 Jn. 4:21(20-21)	that he who **loveth** God love his brother also.
1 Ne. 11:22(21-23)	the **love** of God, which sheddeth itself abroad in the
2 Ne. 26:30	all men should have charity, which charity is **love**.
2 Ne. 31:20	hope, and a **love** of God and of all men. Wherefore, if
Jacob 2:17	think of your **brethren** like unto yourselves, and be
Jacob 3:2	feast upon his **love**; for ye may, if your minds are
Mosiah 2:4	rejoice...be filled with **love** towards God and all men.
Mosiah 2:17(16-17)	when ye are in the **service** of your fellow beings ye
Mosiah 4:15(11-15)	ye will teach them to **love** one another, and to serve
Mosiah 23:15	every man should **love** his neighbor as himself, that
Mosiah 27:4(3-4)	that every man should **esteem** his neighbor as himself
Alma 13:28	patient, full of **love** and all long-suffering
Alma 38:12	bridle...passions...be filled with **love**; see that ye
3 Ne. 12:44(38-44)	**love** your enemies, bless them that curse you, do good
Ether 12:34	**love**..thou hast had for the children of men is charity
Moro. 7:47(44-48)	charity is the pure **love** of Christ, and it endureth
Moro. 8:16	fear not...man...for perfect **love** casteth out all fear
Moro. 8:17(17-26)	filled with charity, which is everlasting **love**
Moro. 8:26	perfect **love**, which love endureth by diligence unto
D&C 4:5	faith, hope, charity and **love**...qualify him for the
D&C 12:8	no one can assist...except he shall be...full of **love**
D&C 20:19	they should **love** and serve him, the only living and
D&C 34:3	who so **loved** the world that he gave his own life, that
D&C 38:24(24-27)	let every man **esteem** his brother as himself, and
D&C 42:22	thou shalt **love** thy wife with all thy heart, and shalt
D&C 42:29	if thou **lovest** me thou shalt serve me and keep all my
D&C 42:38(37-38)	as ye **do** it unto the least of these, ye do it unto me.
D&C 42:45	thou shalt live together in **love**, insomuch that thou
D&C 59:5	thou shalt **love** the Lord thy God with all thy heart
D&C 59:6	thou shalt **love** thy neighbor as thyself. Thou shalt
D&C 76:116	Holy Spirit, which God bestows on those who **love** him
D&C 88:123	see that ye **love** one another; cease to be covetous
D&C 95:12	if you keep not my commandments, the **love** of the
D&C 121:41(41-43)	by gentleness and meekness, and by **love** unfeigned
D&C 121:45(44-46)	let thy bowels also be full of **charity** towards all men
Moses 7:33(32-33)	commandment, that they should **love** one another, and

LOYALTY

Gen. 18:19(17-19)	and they shall **keep** the way of the Lord, to do justice
Gen. 22:12(2-12)	thou hast not **withheld** thy son, thine only son from
Josh. 24:15(14-24)	but as for me and my house, we will **serve** the Lord.
Judg. 2:7(7-13)	the people **served** the Lord all the days of Joshua, and
Ruth 1:16(16-17)	for whither thou goest, I will **go**; and where thou
Job 19:25(16-27)	for I **know** that my redeemer liveth, and that he shall
Matt. 6:24	**no** man can serve two masters: for either he will hate
Matt. 10:39(37-40)	he that **loseth** his life for my sake shall find it.

LOYALTY cont.

Matt. 16:16(14-16)	thou art the **Christ**, the Son of the living God.
Rom. 1:16(15-16)	for I am not **ashamed** of the gospel of Christ: for it
1 Ne. 2:3(1-3)	he was **obedient** unto the word of the Lord, wherefore
1 Ne. 3:7(6-7)	I will **go** and do the things which the Lord hath
1 Ne. 17:50	if God had commanded me to do all things I **could** do
2 Ne. 4:16	behold, my soul **delighteth** in the things of the Lord
2 Ne. 5:31(29-32)	I, Nephi, to be **obedient** to the commandments of the
2 Ne. 9:49	and my heart **delighteth** in righteousness; and I will
Jacob 1:8	that we could persuade all men **not** to rebel against
Mosiah 5:5(1-5)	to be **obedient** to his commandments in all things that
Mosiah 17:9	I will **not** recall the words which I have spoken unto
Alma 20:26	when he also saw the great **love** he had for his son
Alma 46:15(14-15)	those who did belong to the church were **faithful**; yea
Alma 48:13(11-13)	he had **sworn** with an oath to defend his people, his
Ether 4:19(14-19)	blessed is he that is found **faithful** unto my name at
D&C 64:34(29-34)	the willing and **obedient** shall eat the good of the
D&C 84:33(33-39)	whoso is **faithful** unto the obtaining these two
D&C 134:5(1,3,5)	all men are bound to **sustain**...governments in which
D&C 135:5	thou hast been **faithful**; wherefore thy garments are
Moses 5:6(5-6)	I know not, save the Lord **commanded** me.
JS-H 1:25(24-25)	I had seen a vision...and I could not **deny** it, neither

LUST

Ex. 15:9	my **lust** shall be satisfied upon them; I will draw my
Num. 11:4	mixt multitude...fell a **lusting**: and the children of
Ps. 78:30(30,31)	they were not estranged from their **lust**. But while the
Ps. 81:12	so I gave them up unto their own hearts' **lust**: and the
Ps. 106:14(13,14)	but **lusted** exceedingly in the wilderness, and tempted
Prov. 5:3(3-5)	**lips** of a strange woman...as an honeycomb, and her
Prov. 6:25	**lust** not after her beauty in thine heart; neither let
Prov. 7:10(6-27)	there met him a woman with the attire of an **harlot**
Matt. 5:28(27-30)	looketh on a woman to **lust** after her hath committed
Mark 4:19	the **lusts** of other things entering in, choke the word
John 8:44	the **lusts** of your father ye will do. He was a murderer
Acts 14:15	we also are men of like **passions** with you, and preach
Rom. 1:27(26-27)	burned in their **lust** one toward another; men with men
Rom. 6:12	that ye should obey it in the **lusts** thereof.
Rom. 7:7	for I had not known **lust**, except the law had said
Rom. 13:14	the flesh, to fulfil the **lusts** thereof.
1 Cor. 10:6(6,7)	we should not **lust** after evil things, as they also
Gal. 5:16(16-21)	ye shall not fulfil the **lust** of the flesh.
Eph. 2:3(2,3)	we all had our conversation..in the **lusts** of our flesh
Eph. 4:22	corrupt according to the deceitful **lusts**
1 Thes. 4:5	not in the **lust** of concupiscence, even as the Gentiles
1 Tim. 6:9	many foolish and hurtful **lusts**, which drown men in
2 Tim. 2:22	flee also youthful **lusts**: but follow righteousness
2 Tim. 3:6	women laden with sins, led away with divers **lusts**
2 Tim. 4:3	after their own **lusts**...heap to themselves teachers
Titus 2:12	denying ungodliness and worldly **lusts**, we should live
Titus 3:3	disobedient, deceived, serving divers **lusts** and
James 1:14(13-16)	drawn away of his own **lust**, and enticed.

LUST cont.

James 4:3(1-3)	that ye may consume it upon your **lusts**.
1 Pet. 1:14(14-16)	according to the former **lusts** in your ignorance
1 Pet. 2:11	abstain from fleshly **lusts**, which war against the soul
1 Pet. 4:2(2,3)	no longer...live...in the flesh to the **lusts** of men
2 Pet. 1:4	the corruption that is in the world through **lust**.
2 Pet. 2:10(10,18)	that walk after the flesh in the **lust** of uncleanness
2 Pet. 3:3	scoffers, walking after their own **lusts**
1 Jn. 2:16(15-17)	the **lust** of the flesh, and the lust of the eyes, and
Jude 1:16(16,18)	murmurers, complainers, walking after their own **lusts**
Rev. 18:14	the fruits that thy soul **lusted** after are departed
1 Ne. 3:25	Laban saw our property...did **lust** after it, insomuch
1 Ne. 22:23	those who seek the **lusts** of the flesh and the things
Jacob 3:12	warning them against fornication and **lasciviousness**
Alma 38:12(6-12)	see that ye bridle all your **passions**, that ye may be
Alma 39:9(3-11)	go no more after the **lusts** of your eyes, but cross you
Alma 45:12(11-12)	fall into the works of darkness, and **lasciviousness**
3 Ne. 12:28(27-28)	whosoever looketh on a woman, to **lust** after her, hath
4 Ne. 1:16	nor murders, nor any manner of **lasciviousness**; and
Morm. 9:28	ask not, that ye may consume it on your **lusts**, but ask
D&C 3:4	follows after the dictates of his own...carnal **desires**
D&C 42:23	looketh upon a woman to **lust** after her shall deny the
D&C 63:16	he that looketh on a woman to **lust** after her, or if
D&C 88:121	therefore, cease from all your...**lustful** desires
D&C 101:6	there were...**lustful** and covetous desires among them

LYING

Ex. 20:16	thou shalt not bear **false** witness against thy
Lev. 6:2(2-7)	if a soul sin...and **lie** unto his neighbour in that
Lev. 19:11	ye shall not...deal falsely, neither **lie** one to
Num. 23:19	God is not a man, that he should **lie**; neither the son
Deut. 5:20	neither shalt thou bear **false** witness against thy
Deut. 19:16(16-21)	if a **false** witness rise up against any man to testify
1 Sam. 15:29	the strength of Israel will not **lie** nor repent: for
Ps. 31:18	let the **lying** lips be put to silence; which speak
Ps. 101:7	he that telleth **lies** shall not tarry in my sight.
Prov. 6:19(16-19)	a false witness that speaketh **lies**, and he that soweth
Prov. 12:22	**lying** lips are abomination to the Lord: but they that
Prov. 19:5(5,9)	he that speaketh **lies** shall not escape.
Prov. 19:22	and a poor man is better than a **liar**.
Prov. 24:28	and **deceive** not with thy lips.
Jer. 9:5(3-9)	they have taught their tongue to speak **lies**, and weary
Jer. 20:6	and all thy friends, to whom thou hast prophesied **lies**
Jer. 28:15(15-17)	but thou makest this people to trust in a **lie**.
Ezek. 13:22	with **lies** ye have made the heart of the righteous sad
Hosea 4:2(1-3)	by swearing, and **lying**...they break out, and blood
Zeph. 3:13	the remnant of Israel shall not...speak **lies**; neither
Zech. 8:17(16-17)	love no **false** oath: for all these are things that I
Matt. 24:4(4-5,24)	Jesus...said...take heed that no man **deceive** you.
Mark 14:56(55-59)	many bare **false** witness against him, but their witness
John 8:44(41-47)	when he speaketh a **lie**, he speaketh of his own: for
Acts 5:4(1-10)	thou hast not **lied** unto men, but unto God.

LYING cont.

Eph. 4:25(22-25)	wherefore putting away **lying**, speak every man truth
Col. 3:9(9-10)	**lie** not one to another, seeing that ye have put off
1 Tim. 4:2(1-2)	speaking **lies** in hypocrisy; having their conscience
Titus 1:2	eternal life, which God, that cannot **lie**, promised
1 Jn. 1:8(6-10)	if we say that we have no sin, we **deceive** ourselves
1 Jn. 2:4	I know him...keepeth not his commandments...a **liar**
1 Jn. 4:20	say, I love God, and hateth his brother, he is a **liar**
Rev. 21:8(8,27)	all **liars**, shall have their part in the lake which
Rev. 22:15(14-16)	for without are...whosoever loveth and maketh a **lie**.
2 Ne. 2:18	the devil, who is the father of all **lies**, wherefore
2 Ne. 9:9	to remain with the father of **lies**, in misery, like
2 Ne. 9:34	wo unto the **liar**, for he shall be thrust down to hell.
2 Ne. 28:8(7-9)	yea, **lie** a little, take the advantage of one because
Jacob 7:19(1-2,13-20)	the unpardonable sin, for I have **lied** unto God; for I
Enos 1:6	I, Enos, knew that God could not **lie**; wherefore, my
Alma 1:17	they durst not lie...for **liars** were punished
Alma 12:3(2-5,7-8)	not lied unto men only but thou hast **lied** unto God
Alma 14:6(6-7)	which he had caused among the people by his **lying** word
Alma 30:60(52-60)	the end of him who **perverteth** the ways of the Lord
Ether 3:12	thou art a God of truth, and canst not **lie**.
Ether 8:25	the devil...that same **liar** who beguiled our first pare
D&C 10:25(20-28)	he saith unto them: **deceive** and lie in wait to catch
D&C 42:21	he that **lieth** and will not repent shall be cast out.
D&C 42:86	if...shall **lie**...delivered up unto...law of the land.
D&C 46:8	beware lest ye are **deceived**; and that ye may not be
D&C 52:14(14-15)	a pattern in all things, that ye may not be **deceived**
D&C 63:17(17-18)	whosoever loveth and maketh a **lie**...shall have their
D&C 64:39(37-39)	and **liars** and hypocrites shall be proved by them, and
D&C 76:103(102-106)	these are they who are **liars**, and sorcerers, and
D&C 93:25(24-25)	that wicked one who was a **liar** from the beginning.
D&C 121:18(18-22)	those who swear **falsely** against my servants, that they
D&C 123:7(1-17)	the fathers, who have inherited **lies**, upon the hearts
D&C 129:7	contrary to...heaven for a just man to **deceive**; but
Moses 4:4(3-4)	he became Satan...the devil, the father of all **lies**

MALICE

Lev. 19:18	thou shalt not avenge, nor bear any **grudge** against the
Prov. 1:22	scorners delight in their **scorning**, and fools hate
Prov. 10:12	**hatred** stirreth up strifes: but love covereth all sins
Isa. 53:3(3-5)	he is **despised** and rejected of men; a man of sorrows
Matt. 5:11(10-12)	blessed are ye, when men shall **revile** you, and
Mark 15:32(29-32)	they that were crucified with him **reviled** him.
Rom. 1:29(28-32)	being filled with...**maliciousness**; full of envy
1 Cor. 4:12(9-13)	being **reviled**, we bless; being persecuted, we suffer
1 Cor. 14:20	in **malice** be ye children, but in understanding be men
Eph. 4:31	let all bitterness...be put away...with all **malice**
Col. 3:8	put off all these; anger, wrath, **malice**, blasphemy
Titus 3:3(1-7)	we ourselves were also...living in **malice** and envy
James 5:9	**grudge** not one against another, brethren, lest ye be
1 Pet. 2:1(1-2)	wherefore laying aside all **malice**, and all guile, and
1 Pet. 2:16(13-16)	for a cloke of **maliciousness**, but as the servants of

MALICE cont.

2 Ne. 26:21(20-22)	many churches built up which cause...**malice**.
2 Ne. 26:32(32-33)	Lord God hath commanded...they should not have **malice**
Jacob 7:24(23-26)	they had an eternal **hatred** against us, their brethren.
Mosiah 10:17(11-17)	taught their children that they should **hate** them, and
Mosiah 27:3(1-5)	should be no **persecutions** among them, that there
Alma 1:21(19-24)	there should be no **persecution** among themselves.
4 Ne. 1:39(39,40)	they were taught to **hate** the children of God, even as
D&C 31:9	**revile** not against those that revile. govern your
D&C 98:23(23-27)	ye bear it patiently and **revile** not against them
D&C 101:35(35-37)	and all they who suffer **persecution** for my name, and
D&C 127:4(3,4)	and if they **persecute** you, so persecuted they the
JS-M 1:7(7-10)	ye shall be **hated** of all nations, for my name's sake
JS-H 1:23(22-25)	a spirit of the most bitter **persecution** and reviling.

MAN, A SPIRIT CHILD OF HEAVENLY FATHER

Num. 16:22	the God of the **spirits** of all flesh, shall one man
Job 32:8	but there is a **spirit** in man: and the inspiration of
Job 33:4	the **breath** of the Almighty hath given me life.
Ps. 82:6	ye are Gods...all of you are **children** of the most high
Eccl. 12:7	the spirit shall return unto God who **gave** it.
Isa. 42:5	he that giveth breath...and **spirit** to them that walk
Hosea 1:10	said unto them, ye are the **sons** of the living God.
Luke 23:46	Father, into thy hands I commend my **spirit**: and
Acts 7:59	Stephen, calling upon God...Jesus, receive my **spirit**.
Acts 17:29(28-29)	we are the **offspring** of God, we ought not to think
Rom. 8:16(16-17)	Spirit...beareth witness...we are the **children** of God
Heb. 12:9	be in subjection unto the Father of **spirits**, and live
1 Ne. 17:36	he hath created his **children** that they should possess
Alma 40:11	**spirits**...taken home to that God who gave them life.
D&C 46:26	from God, for the benefit of the **children** of God.
D&C 77:2	the **spirit** of man in the likeness of his person, as
D&C 84:83	for your **Father**, who is in heaven, knoweth that you
D&C 88:15	and the **spirit** and the body are the soul of man.
D&C 88:75	your **Father**, and your God, and my God, that you are
D&C 93:33(33-36)	for man is **spirit**. The elements are eternal, and
Moses 3:5(5-7)	God, had **created** all the children of men; and not yet
Moses 6:51	I made the world, and **men** before they were in the
Abr. 3:22(22-24)	**intelligences** that were organized before the world

MAN, ANTEMORTAL EXISTENCE OF

Num. 16:22	the God of the **spirits** of all flesh, shall one man
Num. 27:16	let the Lord, the God of the **spirits** of all flesh, set
Job 38:7(1-7)	and all the **sons** of God shouted for joy
Eccl. 12:7	the **spirit** shall return unto God who gave it.
Jer. 1:5(4,5)	before I **formed** thee in the belly I knew thee; and
Zech. 12:1	the Lord, which...formeth the **spirit** of man within him
John 1:2(1-2,14)	the same was in the **beginning** with God.
John 8:58(56-58)	I say unto you, **before** Abraham was, I am.
John 9:2(1-2)	who did sin, this **man**, or his parents, that he was

MAN, ANTEMORTAL EXISTENCE OF cont.

John 16:28(27-30) I came forth from the **Father**...am come into the world
John 17:5(3-5,24) glory which I had with thee **before** the world was.
Acts 17:28(26-29) poets have said, for we are also his **offspring**.
Rom. 8:29(28-30) for whom he did **foreknow**...to be conformed to the
Eph. 1:4(3-6) chosen us in him **before** the foundation of the world
Heb. 12:9 subjection unto the Father of **spirits**, and live
Jude 1:6(5-6) the angels which kept not their **first** estate, but left
Rev. 12:7(7-8) **Michael** and his angels fought against the dragon; and
Mosiah 7:27(26,27) **image** after which man was created in the beginning
Alma 13:3(3-9) called and prepared from the **foundation** of the world
Hel. 14:17(16-18) mankind...**back** into the presence of the Lord.
3 Ne. 1:13(13,14) on the **morrow** come I into the world, to show unto the
3 Ne. 26:5(3-5) Christ, who was **before** the world began.
Ether 3:16(14-17) this body...is the body of my **spirit**; and man have I
D&C 29:36(36-38) a third part of the **hosts** of heaven turned he away
D&C 38:1 seraphic hosts of heaven, **before** the world was made
D&C 49:17 man, according to his creation **before** the world was
D&C 93:29(21-23,29) man was also in the **beginning** with God. Intelligence
Moses 3:5(1-7) in heaven **created** I them; and there was not yet flesh
Moses 6:36 and he beheld the **spirits** that God had created; and
Abr. 3:22(22-26) **intelligences** that were organized before the world was
Abr. 3:23(22-28) he stood among those that were **spirits**, and he saw
Abr. 5:7 and took his **spirit** (that is, the man's spirit), and
JFS-V 1:53(53-56) choice **spirits** who were reserved to come forth in the

MAN, NATURAL, NOT SPIRITUALLY REBORN

Gen. 2:17(15-17) in the day that thou eatest...thou shalt surely **die**.
Deut. 1:39 children, which...had no **knowledge** between good and
Isa. 1:4(2-4) Ah **sinful** nation, a people laden with iniquity, a seed
Jonah 4:11(9-11) persons that cannot **discern** between their right hand
Luke 16:15 that which is highly esteemed among men is **abomination**
John 3:7(3-8) I said unto thee, ye must be **born** again.
Rom. 3:10 there is none **righteous**, no, not one
Rom. 3:23 for all have **sinned**, and come short of the glory of
Rom. 5:12 death passed upon all men, for that all have **sinned**
Rom. 7:18 in me...in my **flesh**,) dwelleth no good thing: for to
Rom. 8:6(6-10) for to be **carnally** minded is death; but to be
1 Cor. 1:26(25-27) how that not many wise men after the **flesh**, not many
1 Cor. 2:14(14-15) but the **natural** man receiveth not the things of the
1 Cor. 3:3(1-3) for ye are yet **carnal**: for whereas there is among you
Gal. 4:29 he that was born after the **flesh** persecuted him that
Eph. 2:3 were by **nature** the children of wrath, even as others.
2 Pet. 1:4(3-4) the **corruption** that is in the world through lust.
Mosiah 3:19 the **natural** man is an enemy to God, and has been from
Mosiah 16:3(3,4) all **mankind** becoming carnal, sensual, devilish
Mosiah 16:5 he that persists in his own **carnal** nature, and goes
Mosiah 27:25(24-26) born of God, changed from their carnal and **fallen**
Alma 5:7(6-15) they were encircled about by the bands of **death**, and
Alma 26:21 what **natural** man is there that knoweth these things
Alma 36:4 not of the **temporal** but of the spiritual, not of the
Alma 38:6 if I had not been **born** of God I should not have known

MAN, NATURAL, NOT SPIRITUALLY REBORN cont.

Alma 41:11(11-13)	all men that are in a state of **nature**, or I would say
Alma 42:10(7-10)	carnal, sensual, and devilish, by **nature**, this
D&C 20:20(18-20)	man became sensual and devilish...**fallen** man.
D&C 29:41(41,42)	his transgression, wherein he became **spiritually** dead
D&C 67:12(10-12)	neither can any **natural** man abide the presence of God
D&C 121:39	it is the **nature** and disposition of almost all men
Moses 5:13(13-14)	and men began...to be **carnal**, sensual, and devilish.
Moses 6:49	men have become **carnal**, sensual, and devilish, and are
Moses 6:55	when...begin to grow up, **sin** conceiveth in their heart

MAN, NEW, SPIRITUALLY REBORN

1 Sam. 10:9(9-13)	God gave him another **heart**: and all those signs came
1 Sam. 10:10	the **Spirit** of God came upon him, and he prophesied
Jer. 24:7	I will give them an **heart** to know me, that I am the
Jer. 32:39(39-41)	I will give them one **heart**, and one way, that they may
Ezek. 11:19(19-21)	and I will put a **new** spirit within you; and I will
Ezek. 18:31	make you a new heart and a **new** spirit: for why will
Ezek. 36:26(26-27)	a **new** heart also will I give you, and a new spirit
Matt. 5:48(20-48)	be ye therefore **perfect**, even as your Father which is
John 3:3(3-10)	except a man be **born** again, he cannot see the kingdom
Rom. 6:4(3-11)	even so we also should walk in **newness** of life.
Rom. 12:2(1-2)	be ye transformed by the **renewing** of your mind, that
2 Cor. 5:17(17-18)	if any man be in Christ, he is a **new** creature: old
Eph. 2:15	to make in himself of twain one **new** man, so making
Eph. 4:24(23-24)	that ye put on the **new** man, which after God is created
Col. 3:10(1-23)	have put on the **new** man, which is renewed in knowledge
1 Pet. 1:3(2-5)	hath **begotten** us again unto a lively hope by the
1 Pet. 2:2(1-2)	as **newborn** babes, desire the sincere milk of the word
1 Jn. 2:29	every one that doeth righteousness is **born** of him.
1 Jn. 3:9	whosoever is **born** of God doth not commit sin; for his
1 Jn. 4:7	every one that loveth is **born** of God, and knoweth God.
1 Jn. 5:18	whosoever is **born** of God sinneth not; but he that is
Enos 1:8(1-8)	thy faith hath made thee **whole**.
Mosiah 3:19	putteth off the natural man and becometh a **saint**
Mosiah 4:13(11-16)	ye will not have a **mind** to injure one another, but to
Mosiah 5:2(2-7)	we have no more **disposition** to do evil, but to do good
Mosiah 5:7(2-5,7)	ye are **born** of him and have become his sons and his
Mosiah 27:25(24-29)	all mankind...must be **born** again; yea, born of God
Alma 5:14(7-14,26-28)	have ye spiritually been **born** of God? Have ye received
Alma 5:49	cry unto them that they must repent and be **born** again.
Alma 7:14(14-16)	ye must repent, and be **born** again; for the Spirit
Alma 19:33	their hearts had been **changed**; that they had no more
Alma 22:15(15-16)	what shall I do that I may be **born** of God, having this
Alma 38:6	if I had not been **born** of God I should not have known
3 Ne. 12:48(20-48)	I would that ye should be **perfect** even as I, or your
Moro. 10:32(32-33)	come unto Christ, and be **perfected** in him, and deny
D&C 5:16	they shall be **born** of me, even of water and of the
D&C 50:28(26-30)	possessor of all things except he be **purified** and
D&C 76:69(50-70)	they who are just men made **perfect** through Jesus the
D&C 88:20(17-24)	bodies who are of..celestial kingdom...are..**sanctified**.
D&C 88:68(66-68)	therefore, **sanctify** yourselves that your minds become

290

MAN, NEW, SPIRITUALLY REBORN cont.

D&C 101:5(4,5)	not endure chastening...cannot be **sanctified**.
D&C 105:36(35-37)	those that are chosen; and they shall be **sanctified**
D&C 112:13(12,13)	they shall be converted, and I will **heal** them.
Moses 5:10(10,11)	Adam blessed God and was **filled**, and began to prophesy
Moses 6:59(57-61)	ye must be **born** again into the kingdom of heaven, of
Moses 6:65(64-68)	thus he was **born** of the Spirit, and became quickened

MAN, PHYSICAL CREATION OF

Gen. 1:26(26-28)	God said, let us make **man** in our image, after our
Gen. 2:5(3-7)	and there was not a **man** to till the ground.
Gen. 2:7	the Lord God **formed** man of the dust of the ground, and
Gen. 2:22(18-25)	the rib...taken from man, made he a **woman**, and brought
Gen. 3:19	out of it wast thou taken: for **dust** thou art, and unto
Gen. 5:1(1-3)	in the likeness of God **made** he him
Job 4:19	them that dwell in houses of **clay**...foundation...dust
Job 34:15	and man shall turn again unto **dust**.
Eccl. 12:7	then shall the **dust** return to the earth as it was: and
Isa. 43:7	I have **created** him for my glory, I have formed him
Isa. 45:12	made the earth, and **created** man upon it: I, even my
Mal. 2:10	hath not one God **created** us? why do we deal
Matt. 19:4	he which **made** them at the beginning made them male and
Luke 3:38	the son of Adam, which was the **son** of God.
Acts 17:29(22-31)	we are the **offspring** of God, we ought not to think
Philip. 2:6(5-6)	who, being in the **form** of God, thought it not robbery
Col. 3:10	after the image of him that **created** him
1 Tim. 2:13	for Adam was first **formed**, then Eve.
1 Ne. 2:12	that God who had **created** them.
1 Ne. 17:36	he hath **created** his children that they should possess
2 Ne. 2:15	after he had **created** our first parents, and the beast
2 Ne. 29:7	I, the Lord your God, have **created** all men, and that
Jacob 4:9	by the power of his word **man** came upon the face of the
Mosiah 2:25(20-25)	yet ye were **created** of the dust of the earth; but
Mosiah 4:21(12,21)	and now, if God, who has **created** you, on whom you are
Mosiah 7:27	he said that man was **created** after the image of God
Alma 1:4	the Lord had **created** all men, and had also redeemed
Alma 18:32(32,34)	for by his hand were they all **created** from the
Alma 22:12	how God **created** man after his own image, and that God
4 Ne. 1:16	all the people who had been **created** by the hand of God
Morm. 5:2	without calling upon that Being who **created** them.
Morm. 9:17(12,17)	man was **created** of the dust of the earth; and by the
Ether 3:15(9-16)	all men were **created**...after mine own image.
D&C 20:18	that he **created** man, male and female, after his own
D&C 77:12	**formed** man out of the dust of the earth, even so, in
D&C 93:10(8-11)	the worlds were made by him; men were **made** by him; all
D&C 107:43	his likeness was the express **likeness** of his father
Moses 2:26(26-28)	I, God, said...let us **make** man in our image, after our
Moses 3:5(3-9)	spiritually, before they were **naturally** upon the face
Moses 6:9	in the image of his own body...**created** he them, and
Moses 6:22	Adam, who was the **son** of God, with whom God, himself
Abr. 4:26(26-28)	let us go down and **form** man in our image, after our
Abr. 4:27(26-31)	so the Gods went down to **organize** man in their own

Abr. 5:17(14-19)   flesh of my **flesh**; now she shall be called woman

MAN, POTENTIAL TO BECOME
LIKE HEAVENLY FATHER

Gen. 1:26	let them have **dominion** over the fish of the sea, and
Gen. 3:22	God said...the **man** is become as one of us, to know
Ps. 8:5(4-9)	for thou hast made him a little lower than the **angels**
Ps. 8:6	madest him to have **dominion** over the works of thy hand
Ps. 82:6(1-8)	ye are Gods...all of you are **children** of the most high
Matt. 5:48	be ye therefore **perfect**, even as your Father which is
Luke 24:39(36-39)	for a **spirit** hath not flesh and bones, as ye see me
John 10:34(34-36)	is it not written in your law, I said, ye are **Gods**
Acts 17:29(28,29)	we are the **offspring** of God, we ought not to think
Rom. 8:17(14-21)	heirs of God, and **joint-heirs** with Christ; if so be
2 Cor. 3:18	are changed into the same image from **glory** to glory
Gal. 4:7(1-7)	if a son, then an **heir** of God through Christ.
Eph. 4:13(11-13)	till we all come...unto a **perfect** man, unto the
Heb. 12:9	unto the **Father** of spirits, and live
1 Jn. 3:2(1-3)	when he shall appear, we shall be **like** him; for we
Rev. 3:21	him that overcometh will...sit...in my **throne**, even
1 Ne. 11:11	for I beheld that he was in the **form** of a man; yet
2 Ne. 2:25	and men are, that they might have **joy**.
3 Ne. 9:17	to them have I given to become the **sons** of God; and
3 Ne. 12:48	be **perfect** even as I, or your Father who is in heaven
3 Ne. 27:27	what manner of **men** ought ye to be...even as I am.
3 Ne. 28:10	your **joy** shall be full...shall be even as I am, and I
D&C 14:7	you shall have **eternal** life, which gift is the
D&C 50:24	he...receiveth more light...until the **perfect** day.
D&C 76:58(51-70)	it is written, they are **gods**, even the sons of God
D&C 88:29(28,29)	ye who are quickened by...the celestial **glory** shall
D&C 93:20(1-36)	you shall receive of his fulness, and be **glorified** in
D&C 93:29	man was also in the **beginning** with God. Intelligence
D&C 121:32	every man shall enter into his eternal **presence** and
D&C 129:3	the spirits of just men made **perfect**, they who are not
D&C 130:1	we shall see that he is a **man** like ourselves.
D&C 130:22	the **Father** has a body of flesh and bones as tangible
D&C 131:2(1-4)	and in order to obtain the **highest**, a man must enter
D&C 132:20(1-24)	then shall they be **gods**, because they have all power
D&C 133:57	that men might be made **partakers** of the glories which
Moses 1:39	my glory...the immortality and **eternal** life of man.
Moses 4:28	the **man** is become as one of us to know good and evil
JS-H 1:17	I saw two **Personages**, whose brightness and glory defy

MARRIAGE

Gen. 2:24(22-24)	cleave unto his wife: and they shall be **one** flesh.
Gen. 6:2(1,2)	took them **wives** of all which they chose.
Prov. 31:10(10-31)	who can find a virtuous **woman**? for her price is far
Isa. 4:1	let us be called by thy **name**, to take away our
Mal. 2:14(14-16)	between thee and the **wife** of thy youth, against whom
Matt. 19:5	man leave father and mother...**cleave** to his wife...one

MARRIAGE cont.

Matt. 19:6(3-12)	what...God hath **joined** together, let not man put
Matt. 22:30	neither **marry**, nor are given in marriage, but are as
Mark 10:9(2-12)	what...God hath **joined** together, let not man put
Mark 12:25	they neither **marry**, nor are given in marriage; but are
Luke 20:34(34-35)	children of this world **marry**, and are given in
Rom. 7:2(1-3)	woman which hath an **husband** is bound by the law to her
1 Cor. 6:16	two, saith he, shall be **one** flesh.
1 Cor. 7:2(1-6)	let every man have his own **wife**, and let every woman
1 Tim. 4:3	forbidding to **marry**, and commanding to abstain from
Heb. 13:4	**marriage** is honourable in all, and the bed undefiled
1 Ne. 7:1	should take daughters to **wife**, that they might raise
1 Ne. 16:7	Nephi, took one of the daughters of Ishmael to **wife**
Jacob 2:27(27-32)	shall not any man among you have save it be one **wife**
Jacob 3:7	husbands **love** their wives, and their wives love their
4 Ne. 1:11(10,11)	they were married, and given in **marriage**, and were
D&C 42:22	thou shalt love thy **wife** with all thy heart, and shalt
D&C 49:15(15-17)	for **marriage** is ordained of God unto man.
D&C 74:1	unbelieving **husband** is sanctified by the wife, and the
D&C 132:16(15-20)	they neither marry nor are given in **marriage**; but are
Moses 8:14(14-15)	took them **wives**, even as they chose.

MARRIAGE, CELESTIAL

Gen. 2:18	God said, it is not good that the man should be **alone**
Gen. 2:24(18,23-24)	man...shall cleave unto his wife...shall be **one** flesh.
Eccl. 3:14	whatsoever God doeth, it shall be **for-ever**: nothing
Matt. 16:19	whatsoever thou shalt **bind** on earth shall be bound in
Matt. 19:5(3-6)	a man...shall **cleave** to his wife: and they twain
1 Cor. 11:11	neither is the **man** without the woman, neither the
Eph. 5:31(22-33)	a man...shall be joined unto his wife...be **one** flesh.
1 Pet. 3:7	being **heirs** together of the grace of life; that your
Hel. 10:7	whatsoever ye shall **seal** on earth shall be sealed in
4 Ne. 1:11(10-11)	were **married**, and given in marriage, and were blessed
D&C 49:15(15-16)	**marriage** is ordained of God unto man.
D&C 131:2(1-4)	the new and everlasting covenant of **marriage**
D&C 132:19(1-66)	shall be of full force when they are out of the **world**
Moses 3:24	man...cleave unto his wife...shall be **one** flesh.
Abr. 5:18	man...cleave unto his wife...shall be **one** flesh.

MARRIAGE, CONTINUING COURTSHIP IN

Matt. 7:12	whatsoever ye would that **men** should do to you, do ye
1 Cor. 7:3	husband render unto the wife due **benevolence**: and like
1 Cor. 11:11	neither is the **man** without the woman, neither the
Eph. 5:22(22-24)	**wives**, submit yourselves unto your own husbands, as
Eph. 5:25(25-33)	husbands, love your **wives**, even as Christ also loved
Col. 3:19(18-19)	husbands, **love** your wives, and be not bitter against
1 Pet. 3:7(1-9)	giving **honour** unto the wife, as unto the weaker
Jacob 3:7	behold, their husbands **love** their wives, and their
D&C 25:14(5,13-16)	let thy soul delight in thy **husband**, and the glory
D&C 42:22(22-26)	thou shalt **love** thy wife with all thy heart, and shalt

MARRIAGE, CONTINUING COURTSHIP IN cont.

D&C 42:45 thou shalt live together in **love**, insomuch that thou
D&C 130:2(1-2) same **sociality** which exists among us here will exist

MARRIAGE, FATHERHOOD

Gen. 1:28 be fruitful, and **multiply**, and replenish the earth
Gen. 2:24 shall a man leave his **father** and his mother, and shall
Gen. 9:1(1,7) said unto them, be fruitful, and **multiply**, and
Ex. 20:5 visiting the iniquity of the **fathers** upon the children
Deut. 24:16 **fathers** shall not be put to death for the children
Deut. 25:5(5-10) and perform the duty of an **husband's** brother unto her.
Ps. 44:1(1-3) O God, our **fathers** have told us, what work thou didst
Ps. 127:3(3-5) children are an **heritage** of the Lord: and the fruit
Prov. 3:12 even as a **father** the son in whom he delighteth.
Prov. 10:1 a wise son maketh a glad **father**: but a foolish son is
Prov. 11:29 he that troubleth his own **house** shall inherit the wind
Prov. 17:6 children's children are the **crown** of old men; and the
Prov. 19:13 a foolish son is the calamity of his **father**: and the
Prov. 22:6 **train** up a child in the way he should go: and when he
Lam. 5:7(1-7) our **fathers** have sinned, and are not; and we have born
Mal. 4:6(5,6) turn the heart of the **fathers** to the children, and the
Eph. 6:4(1-4) and, ye **fathers**, provoke not your children to wrath
1 Tim. 3:4(4,5) one that ruleth well his own **house**, having his
Heb. 12:9 had **fathers** of our flesh which corrected us, and we
1 Ne. 1:1 taught somewhat in all the learning of my **father**; and
Mosiah 4:14(14-15) ye will not suffer your **children** that they go hungry
D&C 2:2(1-3) the hearts of the...children...turn to their **fathers**.
D&C 29:48(47-48) great things may be required...of their **fathers**.
D&C 68:25(25-28) and again, inasmuch as **parents** have children in Zion
D&C 75:28 every man...obliged to **provide** for his own family, let
D&C 93:40(40-50) you to bring up your **children** in light and truth.
D&C 93:43(41-44) shall set in order your own **house**, for there are many
D&C 121:43(41-44) **reproving** betimes with sharpness, when moved upon by
D&C 131:4(1-4) end of his kingdom; he cannot have an **increase**.
D&C 132:20(19-23) then shall they be **gods**, because they have all power
Moses 2:28 be fruitful, and **multiply**, and replenish the earth
Moses 5:12 they made all things known unto their **sons** and their
JS-H 1:39(38,39) promises made to the **fathers**, and the hearts of the

MARRIAGE, HUSBANDS

Gen. 2:24 therefore shall a **man** leave his father and his mother
Gen. 3:16 thy desire...to thy **husband**...he shall rule over thee.
Gen. 25:21(20-21) Isaac intreated the Lord for his **wife**, because she was
Gen. 31:4(1-16) **Jacob** sent and called Rachel and Leah to the field
Ex. 20:17 thou shalt not covet thy neighbour's **wife**, nor his
Deut. 24:5 and shall **cheer** up his wife which he hath taken.
Ps. 128:3(1-4) thy **wife** shall be as a fruitful vine by the sides of
Prov. 5:18 and rejoice with the **wife** of thy youth.
Prov. 12:4 a virtuous woman is a crown to her **husband**: but she
Eccl. 9:9 live joyfully with the **wife** whom thou lovest all the

MARRIAGE, HUSBANDS cont.

Mal. 2:15(14-15) — none deal treacherously against the **wife** of his youth.
Mark 10:7(2-11) — **man** leave his father and mother...cleave to his wife
1 Cor. 7:3(2-17) — let the **husband** render unto the wife due benevolence
1 Cor. 7:13(13-16) — the woman which hath an **husband** that believeth not
1 Cor. 11:3 — the **head** of the woman is the man; and the head of
1 Cor. 11:11(3,8-12) — neither is the **man** without the woman...in the Lord.
Eph. 5:23(23-33) — **husband** is the head of the wife, even as Christ is the
Col. 3:19 — **husbands**, love your wives, and be not bitter against
1 Thes. 4:5(1-7) — not in the **lust** of concupiscence, even as the Gentiles
1 Tim. 3:4(1-16) — one that **ruleth** well his own house, having his
1 Tim. 5:8 — if any **provide** not for his own, and specially for
1 Pet. 3:7(1-7) — **husbands**, dwell with them according to knowledge
Jacob 2:27(24-30) — shall not any **man** among you have save it be one wife
Jacob 2:31 — mourning...because of...wickedness...of their **husbands**
Jacob 2:35 — ye have broken the hearts of your tender **wives**, and
Jacob 3:7(6-7) — their **husbands** love their wives, and their wives love
Alma 34:21 — cry unto him...over all your **household**, both morning
3 Ne. 18:21 — **pray** in your families unto the father, always in my
D&C 19:25 — thou shalt not covet thy neighbor's **wife**; nor seek thy
D&C 25:9 — thy **husband** shall support thee in the church; for unto
D&C 42:22(22-26) — thou shalt **love** thy wife with all thy heart, and shalt
D&C 49:16(15-17) — it is lawful that he should have one **wife**, and they
D&C 75:28 — every **man** who is obliged to provide for his own family
D&C 83:2(1-6) — women have claim on their **husbands** for their
D&C 121:41(39-41) — only by **persuasion**, by long-suffering, by gentleness
D&C 121:45(45-46) — let **virtue** garnish thy thoughts unceasingly; then
D&C 132:15(15-27) — therefore, if a **man** marry him a wife in the world, and
Moses 4:22 — thy desire shall be to thy **husband**, and he shall rule

MARRIAGE, INTERFAITH

Gen. 6:2(1-3) — saw the daughters of men...they took them **wives** of all
Gen. 21:21(17-21) — mother took him a **wife** out of the land of Egypt.
Gen. 24:3(1-9) — not take a **wife**...of the daughters of the Canaanites
Gen. 26:34(34-35) — Esau..took to **wife** Judith the daughter of..the Hittite
Gen. 27:46 — I am weary of my life because of the **daughters** of Heth
Gen. 28:9(8,9) — Esau..took..the sister of Nebajoth, to be his **wife**.
Gen. 38:2(1,2) — Judah saw there a **daughter** of a certain Canaanite, who
Ex. 34:16(10-17) — and thou **take** of their daughters unto thy sons, and
Deut. 7:3(3-6) — neither shalt thou make **marriages** with them; thy
Josh. 23:12 — and shall make **marriages** with them, and go in unto the
Judg. 3:6(1-6) — **gave**...daughters to their sons, and served their Gods.
Judg. 14:3(1-3) — to take a **wife** of the uncircumcised Philistines? and
1 Kgs. 11:4(1-4) — his **wives** turned away his heart after other Gods: and
Ezra 9:2(1,2) — they have taken of their **daughters** for themselves, and
Ezra 10:10(10-14) — ye have transgressed, and have taken strange **wives**
Neh. 10:30(28-30) — we would not give our **daughters** unto the people of the
Neh. 13:25(23-27) — not **give** your daughters unto their sons, nor take the
Mal. 2:11(11-13) — loved, and hath **married** the daughter of a strange God.
1 Cor. 7:14(12-16) — unbelieving **husband** is sanctified by the wife, and the
2 Cor. 6:14(14-18) — be ye not unequally **yoked** together with unbelievers
2 Ne. 5:23(20-25) — the seed of him that **mixeth** with their seed; for they

MARRIAGE, INTERFAITH cont.

Mosiah 25:12(11,12)	taken to wife the **daughters** of the Lamanites, were
Alma 3:8(4-19)	that they might not **mix** and believe in incorrect
Alma 5:57	come ye out from the wicked, and be ye **separate**, and
D&C 74:5(1-7)	commandment, not of the Lord...believer...not...**united**
D&C 132:15(8-17)	if a man **marry** him a wife in the world, and he marry
Moses 8:14(13-17)	sons of men...took them **wives**, even as they chose.

MARRIAGE, MOTHERHOOD

Gen. 1:28	**multiply**, and replenish the earth, and subdue it: and
Gen. 3:16	unto the **woman** he said...bring forth children; and thy
Gen. 3:20	Eve; because she was the **mother** of all living.
Gen. 17:16(15-19)	she shall be a **mother** of nations; kings of people
Ex. 20:12	honour thy father and thy **mother**: that thy days may
Judg. 5:7	I Deborah arose, that I arose a **mother** in Israel.
1 Sam. 1:20(1-28)	she bare a **son**..Samuel..because I have asked him of
1 Sam. 1:27(24-28)	for this **child** I prayed; and the Lord hath given me
1 Sam. 2:19(18,19)	**mother** made him a little coat, and brought it to him
2 Kgs. 4:17(8-37)	the **woman** conceived, and bare a son at that season
2 Chr. 22:3(1-3)	his **mother** was his counseller to do wickedly.
Ps. 113:9	to be a joyful **mother** of children. Praise ye the Lord.
Prov. 10:1	a foolish son is the heaviness of his **mother**.
Prov. 15:20	but a foolish man despiseth his **mother**.
Prov. 29:15	child left to himself bringeth his **mother** to shame.
Prov. 31:1(1-31)	king Lemuel, the prophecy that his **mother** taught him.
Isa. 66:13(10-14)	as one whom his **mother** comforteth, so will I comfort
Matt. 12:49(46-50)	behold my **mother** and my brethren
John 16:21	a **woman** when she is in travail hath sorrow, because
John 19:25(25,26)	by the cross of Jesus his **mother**, and his mother's
1 Tim. 2:15	notwithstanding she shall be saved in **childbearing**
1 Ne. 11:18	the **mother** of the Son of God, after the manner of the
1 Ne. 17:55	honor thy father and thy **mother**, that thy days may be
1 Ne. 18:19	grieved because of the afflictions of their **mother**
2 Ne. 2:23(14-30)	would have had no **children**; wherefore they would have
Alma 56:47(47-48)	they had been taught by their **mothers**, that if they
Alma 57:21(18-27)	remember the words...their **mothers** had taught them.
D&C 68:25(25,28)	inasmuch as **parents** have children in Zion, or in any
Moses 5:11	not for...transgression we never should have had **seed**

MARRIAGE, TEMPORAL

Gen. 6:2	they **took** them wives of all which they chose.
Deut. 7:3(3-4)	neither shalt thou make **marriages** with them; thy
Matt. 22:30(23-30)	in the resurrection they neither **marry**, nor are given
Luke 20:34	the children of this world **marry**, and are given in
1 Cor. 7:39	wife is bound by the **law** as long as her husband liveth
2 Cor. 6:14(14-17)	be ye not unequally **yoked** together with unbelievers
1 Tim. 4:3(1-3)	**forbidding** to marry, and commanding to abstain from
Heb. 13:4	**marriage** is honourable in all, and the bed undefiled
2 Ne. 5:21(20-23)	that they might not be **enticing** unto my people the
Alma 3:8(7-10)	that they might not **mix** and believe in incorrect

MARRIAGE, TEMPORAL cont.

D&C 132:15(7,15-18)   covenant and **marriage** are not of force when they are
Moses 8:15(13-17)   the daughters of thy sons have **sold** themselves; for

MARRIAGE, WIVES

Gen. 2:18   I will make him an **helpmeet** for him.
Gen. 2:24   shall cleave unto his **wife**: and they shall be one
Gen. 3:16   thy desire shall be to thy **husband**, and he shall rule
Gen. 3:17   thou hast hearkened unto the voice of thy **wife**, and
Gen. 25:21   Isaac intreated the Lord for his **wife**, because she was
Gen. 28:1   thou shalt not take a **wife** of the daughters of Canaan.
Ex. 20:17   thou shalt not covet thy neighbour's **wife**, nor his
Deut. 24:1(1-2)   when a man hath taken a **wife**...a bill of divorcement
Prov. 12:4   a virtuous **woman** is a crown to her husband: but she
Prov. 18:22   whoso findeth a **wife** findeth a good thing, and
Prov. 31:10(10-31)   a virtuous **woman**...her price is far above rubies.
Eccl. 9:9   live joyfully with the **wife** whom thou lovest all the
Mark 10:7(2-12)   for this cause shall a man...cleave to his **wife**
Rom. 7:2   the **woman** which hath an husband is bound by the law
1 Cor. 7:2(2-4)   let every man have his own **wife**, and let every woman
1 Cor. 7:3   husband render unto the **wife** due benevolence: and like
1 Cor. 7:39(39-40)   **wife** is bound by the law as long as her husband liveth
1 Cor. 11:3(3,7-12)   head of the **woman** is the man; and the head of
1 Cor. 11:11(3,7-12)   neither the **woman** without the man, in the Lord.
Eph. 5:28(22-33)   he that loveth his **wife** loveth himself.
Eph. 5:33(28-33)   and the **wife** see that she reverence her husband.
Col. 3:18   **wives**, submit yourselves unto your own husbands, as
1 Tim. 2:9(9-15)   that **women** adorn themselves in modest apparel, with
1 Tim. 3:11   even so must their **wives** be grave, not slanderers
1 Tim. 5:14(14-15)   I will therefore that the younger **women** marry, bear
Titus 2:4(3-5)   teach the young **women** to be sober, to love their
1 Pet. 3:1(1-6)   ye **wives**, be in subjection to your own husbands; that
1 Pet. 3:7(1-7)   giving honour unto the **wife**, as unto the weaker vessel
1 Ne. 5:8(1-9)   Lord hath commanded my **husband** to flee into the
1 Ne. 18:19   my **wife** with her tears and prayers, and also my child
Jacob 2:27(24-30)   not any man among you have save it be one **wife**; and
Jacob 3:7(5-7)   their **wives** love their husbands; and their husbands
Alma 19:5(1-14)   I would that ye should go in and see my **husband**, for
Alma 46:12(12-13)   in memory of our...**wives**, and our children- and he
Alma 48:10(10-11)   preparing to support their liberty...their **wives**, and
D&C 19:25   thou shalt not covet thy neighbor's **wife**; nor seek thy
D&C 25:5(5,13-15)   thy calling shall be for a comfort...thy **husband**, in
D&C 42:22   thou shalt love thy **wife** with all thy heart, and shalt
D&C 49:16(15-17)   it is lawful that he should have one **wife**, and they
D&C 121:45   let **virtue** garnish thy thoughts unceasingly; then
D&C 132:19(3-28)   if a man marry a **wife** by my word, which is my law, and
Moses 4:22   thy desire shall be to thy **husband**, and he shall rule

MARTYRDOM

Gen. 4:8(3-8)	Cain rose up against Abel his brother, and slew him.
1 Kgs. 18:13(4,13)	Jezebel slew the prophets of the Lord, how I hid
2 Chr. 24:21(20-21)	conspired against him, and stoned him with stones at
Isa. 53:12(7-12)	he hath poured out his soul unto death: and he was
Zech. 13:6(6-7)	with which I was wounded in the house of my friends.
Matt. 10:22(21-22)	and ye shall be hated of all men for my name's sake
Matt. 10:39	loseth his life for my sake shall find it.
Matt. 20:19(17-19)	deliver him to the Gentiles...to crucify him: and the
Matt. 23:31(29-33)	children of them which killed the prophets.
Matt. 23:35(34-35)	all the righteous blood shed upon the earth, from the
Matt. 24:9	deliver you up to be afflicted, and shall kill you
Matt. 26:2	the Son of man is betrayed to be crucified.
Mark 6:25(18-28)	by and by in a charger the head of John the Baptist.
Mark 8:35	whosoever shall lose his life for my sake and the
Luke 11:50(47-51)	the blood of all the prophets, which was shed from the
Luke 14:26	hate not...his own life also, he cannot be my disciple
John 10:15(10-18)	I lay down my life for the sheep.
John 15:13	a man lay down his life for his friends.
Acts 7:59(58-60)	and they stoned Stephen, calling upon God, and saying
Acts 12:2	and he killed James the brother of John with the sword
Acts 20:24	neither count I my life dear unto myself, so that I
Acts 22:20	when the blood of thy martyr Stephen was shed, I also
Acts 26:10	when they were put to death, I gave my voice against
Acts 26:23(22-23)	that Christ should suffer, and that he should be the
Rom. 11:3	they have killed thy prophets, and digged down thine
2 Cor. 4:11(10-11)	delivered unto death for Jesus' sake, that the life
1 Thes. 2:15	who both killed the Lord Jesus, and their own prophets
Heb. 9:16(16-22)	a testament...necessity...death of the testator.
Heb. 11:37(32-40)	they were stoned, they were sawn asunder, were tempted
Rev. 2:10	be thou faithful unto death, and I will give thee a
Rev. 2:13	those days wherein Antipas was my faithful martyr, who
Rev. 6:9(9-11)	souls of them that were slain for the word of God, and
Rev. 11:7(7-12)	the beast...shall overcome them, and kill them.
Rev. 12:11	and they loved not their lives unto the death.
Rev. 16:6	shed the blood of saints and prophets, and thou hast
Rev. 17:6	the blood of the martyrs of Jesus: and when I saw her
Mosiah 17:20(10-20)	Abinadi...sealed the truth of his words by his death.
Alma 14:11(8-11)	the blood of the innocent shall stand as a witness
Alma 25:7(6-9)	put to death...those that believed in these things.
Alma 48:24(23-24)	not suffer...wives and their children...massacred by
Hel. 13:24(24-28)	do slay them, and do all manner of iniquity unto them
3 Ne. 10:15(14-15)	were slain because they testified of these things.
D&C 98:13	whoso layeth down his life in my cause, for my name's
D&C 101:15(11-16)	have given their lives for my name shall be crowned.
D&C 109:49	their blood come up in testimony before thee, and not
D&C 135:6(3-7)	names will be classed among the martyrs of religion
D&C 136:39	seal his testimony with his blood, that he might be
JFS-V 1:40	Abel, the first martyr, was there, and his brother set

MEAT

Gen. 9:3(2-5)	moving thing that liveth shall be **meat** for you; even
Deut. 12:15	thou mayest kill and eat **flesh** in all thy gates
Deut. 14:3(3-21)	thou shalt not **eat** any abominable thing.
Mal. 3:10	that there may be **meat** in mine house, and prove me
1 Ne. 17:2(2,3)	we did live upon raw **meat** in the wilderness, our women
3 Ne. 13:25(25-34)	is not the life more than **meat**, and the body than
3 Ne. 24:10(7-11)	that there may be **meat** in my house; and prove me now
D&C 49:18(18,19)	whoso forbiddeth to abstain from **meats**, that man
D&C 49:21(18-21)	wo be unto man...that wasteth **flesh** and hath no need.
D&C 59:18(16-21)	are made for the **benefit** and the use of man, both to
D&C 89:12(12,13)	**flesh** also of beasts and of the fowls of the air, I

MEDITATION

Gen. 24:63	Isaac went out to **meditate** in the field at the
Josh. 1:8	book of the law...thou shalt **meditate** therein day and
Ps. 1:2	in his law doth he **meditate** day and night.
Ps. 5:1	give ear to my words, O Lord, consider my **meditation**.
Ps. 19:14	let...the **meditation** of my heart, be acceptable in thy
Ps. 63:6	**meditate** on thee in the night watches.
Ps. 77:12(11-13)	I will **meditate** also of all thy work, and talk of thy
Ps. 104:34(33,34)	my **meditation** of him shall be sweet: I will be glad
Ps. 119:15(15,23,78)	I will **meditate** in thy precepts, and have respect unto
Ps. 119:99	thy testimonies are my **meditation**.
Ps. 143:5	I **meditate** on all thy works; I muse on the work of thy
Prov. 4:26(23-27)	**ponder** the path of thy feet, and let all thy ways be
Hag. 1:7(5-7)	thus saith the Lord of hosts; **consider** your ways.
Matt. 6:6(5-8)	pray to thy Father which is in **secret**; and thy Father
Matt. 6:28	**consider** the lilies of the field, how they grow; they
Matt. 7:7(7-11)	ask, and it shall be given you; **seek**, and ye shall
Luke 2:19	Mary kept all these...and **pondered** them in her heart.
Luke 3:15	all men **mused** in their hearts of John, whether he were
Luke 21:14(12-15)	not to **meditate** before what ye shall answer
1 Tim. 4:15(15-16)	**meditate** upon these things; give thyself wholly to the
Heb. 3:1	**consider** the apostle and high priest of our profession
1 Ne. 11:1	I sat **pondering** in mine heart I was caught away in
2 Ne. 4:15(15-16)	delighteth in the scriptures...my heart **pondereth** them
2 Ne. 15:12(12,13)	neither **consider** the operation of his hands.
2 Ne. 32:1(1,8)	why do ye **ponder** these things in your hearts
Enos 1:4(2-4)	and my soul **hungered**; and I kneeled down before my
Mosiah 2:41	**consider** on the blessed and happy state of those that
Alma 17:2(2-3)	had **searched** the scriptures diligently, that they
Alma 34:27(17-28)	let your hearts be **full**, drawn out in prayer unto him
Alma 37:37(36-37)	**counsel** with the Lord in all thy doings, and he will
Hel. 10:2(2,3)	**pondering** upon the things which the Lord had shown
3 Ne. 17:3(2-3)	**ponder** upon the things which I have said, and ask of
Moro. 10:3(3-5)	receive these things, and **ponder** it in your hearts.
D&C 9:8(8-9)	you must **study** it out in your mind; then you must ask
D&C 30:3	**ponder** upon the things which you have received.
D&C 43:34	let the solemnities of eternity **rest** upon your minds.
D&C 46:7	**considering** the end of your salvation, doing all thing
D&C 76:19	while we **meditated** upon these things, the Lord touched

MEDITATION cont.

D&C 84:85	treasure up in your minds continually the words of
D&C 88:62(62-65,71)	leave these sayings with you to **ponder** in your hearts
D&C 95:3	ye have not **considered** the great commandment in all
JS-H 1:47	third visit...I was again left to **ponder** on the
JFS-V 1:1	I sat in my room **pondering** over the scriptures

MEEKNESS

Num. 12:3	(now the man Moses was very **meek**, above all the men
Ps. 34:18(17-22)	saveth such as be of a **contrite** spirit.
Ps. 37:11(7-13)	but the **meek** shall inherit the earth; and shall
Isa. 11:4(1-4)	reprove with equity for the **meek** of the earth: and
Isa. 61:1(1-6)	anointed me to preach good tidings unto the **meek**; he
Matt. 5:5	blessed are the **meek**: for they shall inherit the earth
Matt. 11:29	learn of me; for I am **meek** and lowly in heart: and ye
Matt. 18:4(1-6)	whosoever...shall **humble** himself as this little child
Mark 9:35(33-37)	first...shall be last of all, and **servant** of all.
Mark 10:15	receive the kingdom of God as a little **child**, he shall
Luke 22:27(26-27)	but I am among you as he that **serveth**.
Gal. 5:23(22,23)	**meekness**, temperance: against such there is no law.
Philip. 2:8(5-11)	he **humbled** himself, and became obedient unto death
Col. 3:12	put on therefore...humbleness of mind, **meekness**
2 Tim. 2:25(24-26)	in **meekness** instructing those that oppose themselves
James 1:21	receive with **meekness** the engrafted word, which is
James 3:13	shew out of a good conversation his works with
1 Pet. 3:15	reason of the hope that is in you with **meekness** and
2 Ne. 21:4(1-4)	reprove with equity for the **meek** of the earth; and
2 Ne. 27:30	the **meek** also shall increase, and their joy shall be
2 Ne. 30:9(8-10)	and reprove with equity for the **meek** of the earth. and
Mosiah 3:19	becometh as a child, submissive, **meek**, humble, patient
Alma 13:28	becoming humble, **meek**, submissive, patient, full of
Alma 37:33(33-34)	teach them to humble themselves and to be **meek** and
3 Ne. 12:5	blessed are the **meek**, for they shall inherit the earth
Moro. 7:44(43-44)	none is acceptable before God, save the **meek** and lowly
Moro. 8:26	the remission of sins bringeth **meekness**, and lowliness
D&C 1:19(17-23)	the **weak** things of the world shall come forth and
D&C 19:23	walk in the **meekness** of my Spirit, and you shall have
D&C 35:15	the poor and the **meek** shall have the gospel preached
D&C 56:18(18-20)	blessed are the poor...whose spirits are **contrite**, for
D&C 84:106	that he may be edified in all **meekness**, that he may
D&C 88:17	the poor and the **meek** of the earth shall inherit it.
D&C 112:10	be thou **humble**; and the Lord thy God shall lead thee
D&C 121:41(41,42)	power...by gentleness and **meekness**, and by love
D&C 136:33(32-33)	my Spirit is sent...to enlighten the **humble** and

MEETINGS

Ex. 12:16(1-20)	in the first day there shall be an holy **convocation**
Ex. 19:17	people out of the camp to **meet** with God; and they
Ex. 25:22(21,22)	there I will **meet** with thee, and I will commune with
Lev. 23:3(1-3)	sabbath of rest, an holy **convocation**; ye shall do no

MEETINGS cont.

Lev. 23:7(4-8)	in the first day ye shall have an holy **convocation**
Lev. 23:24(23-25)	shall ye have a sabbath...an holy **convocation**.
Lev. 23:27(26-32)	tenth day of this seventh month...an holy **convocation**
Lev. 23:35(33-44)	on the first day shall be an holy **convocation**: ye
Num. 28:25(24-31)	on the seventh day ye shall have an holy **convocation**
Num. 29:1(1-6)	first day of the month..shall have an holy **convocation**
Deut. 31:11(10-13)	when all Israel is **come** to appear before the Lord thy
Ezek. 44:24	they shall keep my laws...in all mine **assemblies**; and
John 20:19(19,26)	first day of the week...disciples were **assembled** for
Acts 4:31	they were **assembled** together; and they were all
Acts 11:26	they **assembled** themselves with the church, and taught
Acts 20:7	first day...the disciples came **together** to break bread
1 Cor. 11:18(18-20)	when ye come together in the **church**, I hear that there
Heb. 10:25(23-25)	not forsaking the **assembling** of ourselves together
Mosiah 18:25	one day in every week...**gather**...to teach...to worship
3 Ne. 18:22(22-25)	and behold, ye shall **meet** together oft; and ye shall
4 Ne. 1:12	**meeting** together oft both to pray and to hear the word
Moro. 6:6(5,6)	and they did **meet** together oft to partake of bread and
D&C 20:45(38,44-56)	conduct the **meetings** as they are led by the Holy Ghost
D&C 20:61	are to **meet** in conference once in three months, or
D&C 20:75(55,75)	expedient that the church **meet** together often to
D&C 42:89(88-93)	deliver him or her up ...to the elders...in a **meeting**
D&C 43:8	when ye are **assembled** together ye shall instruct and
D&C 46:3(1-6)	never to cast any one out from your public **meetings**
D&C 59:9(9-13)	go to the **house** of prayer...upon my holy day

MERCY

Ex. 34:6(6,7)	the Lord... **merciful** and gracious, longsuffering, and
Deut. 4:31	(for the Lord thy God is a **merciful** God;) he will not
Deut. 5:10(6-21)	shewing **mercy** unto thousands of them that love me and
2 Chr. 30:9	the Lord your God is gracious and **merciful**, and will
Neh. 9:31(17-31)	for thou art a gracious and **merciful** God.
Jonah 4:2	thou art a gracious God, and **merciful**, slow to anger
Micah 6:8	do justly...love **mercy**, and...walk humbly with thy God
Micah 7:18(18-20)	because he delighteth in **mercy**.
Zech. 7:9(9-10)	execute true judgment, and shew **mercy** and compassions
Matt. 5:7	blessed are the **merciful**: for they shall obtain mercy.
Matt. 9:13	I will have **mercy**, and not sacrifice: for I am not
Matt. 18:33(23-35)	shouldest not thou also have had **compassion** on thy
Matt. 23:23	weightier matters of the law, judgment, **mercy**, and
Luke 6:36	be ye therefore **merciful**, as your Father also is
Luke 7:13(12-15)	when the Lord saw her, he had **compassion** on her, and
Luke 15:20(11-24)	his father saw him, and had **compassion**, and ran, and
Luke 23:34	Father, **forgive** them; for they know not what they do.
John 3:16(16-17)	God so **loved** the world, that he gave his...Son, that
John 8:11(3-11)	Jesus said unto her, neither do I **condemn** thee: go
Col. 3:12(12-14)	put on therefore...bowels of **mercies**, kindness, humble
James 2:13	he shall have judgment without **mercy**, that hath shewed
1 Ne. 8:8(8-12)	I began to pray unto the Lord that he would have **mercy**
2 Ne. 19:17	the Lord shall have no...**mercy** on their fatherless and
Mosiah 2:39(38-39)	**mercy** hath no claim on that man; therefore his final

MERCY cont.

Mosiah 3:26(25-26)	mercy could have claim on them no more forever.
Alma 2:30(24-31)	O Lord, have mercy and spare my life, that I may be
Alma 9:11	if it had not been for his...mercy, and his
Alma 12:33(33,34)	then will I have mercy upon you, through mine Only
Alma 15:10(3-12)	have mercy on this man, and heal him according to his
Alma 34:16(8-17)	and thus mercy can satisfy the demands of justice, and
Alma 41:14(1-15)	ye shall have mercy restored unto you again; ye shall
Alma 42:25(13-31)	do ye suppose that mercy can rob justice? I say unto
3 Ne. 29:7	the son of perdition, for whom there was no mercy
Ether 11:8	began to repent...the Lord did have mercy on them.
Moro. 8:19	little children...alive in him because of his mercy.
D&C 1:29	might have power to translate through the mercy of God
D&C 19:16(16-18)	that they might not suffer if they would repent
D&C 29:1	whose arm of mercy hath atoned for your sins
D&C 43:25(23-25)	I called upon you...by the voice of mercy all the day
D&C 54:6(4-6)	they who have kept the covenant...shall obtain mercy.
D&C 88:40(35,40)	mercy hath compassion on mercy and claimeth her own
D&C 97:2(2-6)	I, the Lord, show mercy unto all the meek, and upon
D&C 99:3(2-3)	who receiveth you...shall obtain mercy.
D&C 101:9(1-10)	in the day of wrath I will remember mercy.
D&C 109:50(1,50)	have mercy, O Lord, upon the wicked mob, who have
D&C 110:7	I will manifest myself to my people in mercy in this

MILLENNIUM

Isa. 2:4(2-4)	not lift up sword...neither...learn war any more.
Isa. 11:9(1-9)	the earth shall be full of the knowledge of the Lord
Isa. 35:2(1-10)	they shall see the glory of the Lord, and the
Isa. 65:17(17-25)	I create new heavens and a new earth: and the former..
Ezek. 34:23(23-31)	I will set up one shepherd over them..my servant David
Ezek. 36:35(33-38)	land...was desolate is become like the garden of Eden
Dan. 7:14(9-14)	was given him dominion, and glory, and a kingdom, that
Hosea 2:18	I will...make them to lie down safely.
Joel 3:17(10-18)	I am the Lord your God dwelling in Zion, my holy mount
Micah 4:3(1-7)	they shall beat their swords into plowshares, and
Zech. 2:10(10-12)	I will dwell in the midst of thee, saith the Lord.
Matt. 6:10	thy kingdom come. Thy will be done in earth, as it is
Matt. 16:28	they see the Son of man coming in his kingdom
Matt. 25:31(31-36)	when the Son of man shall come in his glory, and all
2 Pet. 3:13(10-14)	new heavens and a new earth, wherein dwelleth
Rev. 20:4(1-6)	they lived and reigned with Christ a thousand years.
Rev. 21:1(1-7)	I saw a new heaven and a new earth: for the first
1 Ne. 22:26	because of the righteousness...Satan has no power
2 Ne. 21:9(1-9)	the earth shall be full of the knowledge of the Lord
2 Ne. 30:18(11-18)	all things...shall at that day be revealed; and Satan
D&C 1:20	every man might speak in the name of God the Lord
D&C 29:11(9-11)	I will...dwell in righteousness...a thousand years
D&C 29:22(22,23)	when the thousand years are ended, and men again
D&C 43:30(30-33)	great Millennium, of which I have spoken...shall come.
D&C 63:51(50-51)	children shall grow up until they become old; old men
D&C 84:101(96-102)	for he stands in the midst of his people.
D&C 88:101(95-102)	they live not again until the thousand years are ended

MILLENNIUM cont.

D&C 88:110	Satan shall be bound...for...a **thousand** years.
D&C 101:32(24-34)	in that **day** when the Lord shall come, he shall reveal
D&C 101:101	they shall build, and another shall not **inherit** it
D&C 133:25(17-33)	the Lord...shall **reign** over all flesh.
Moses 7:64(50-65)	for the space of a **thousand** years the earth shall rest
JS-M 1:36(26-55)	they shall see the **Son** of Man coming in the clouds of
JS-H 1:38(36-41)	coming of the great and dreadful day of the **Lord**.
A of F 1:10	that Christ will **reign** personally upon the earth; and

MILLENNIUM, PREPARING A PEOPLE FOR

Isa. 2:3(2-4)	let us **go** up to the mountain of the Lord, to the house
Isa. 4:4(2-6)	shall have **purged** the blood of Jerusalem from the
Isa. 5:26(26-30)	he will lift up an **ensign** to the nations from far, and
Isa. 49:22(22,23)	**lift** up mine hand to the Gentiles, and set up my stand
Isa. 52:8(7-12)	when the Lord shall **bring** again Zion.
Jer. 31:34(31-40)	for they shall all **know** me, from the least of them
Ezek. 34:13(11-31)	I will **bring** them out from the people, and gather them
Dan. 2:44(44,45)	**set** up a kingdom, which shall never be destroyed: and
Joel 2:28(28-32)	I will pour out my **spirit** upon all flesh; and your son
Obad. 1:21(17,21)	and **saviours** shall come up on mount Zion to judge the
Mal. 3:1(1-4)	behold, I will send my **messenger**, and he shall prepare
Mal. 4:5(5,6)	I will send you **Elijah** the prophet before the coming
Matt. 24:42(29-51)	**watch**...for ye know not what hour your Lord doth come.
Matt. 25:10(1-13)	they that were **ready** went in with him to the marriage
1 Thes. 5:2(1-6)	the **day** of the Lord so cometh as a thief in the night.
2 Tim. 2:12(10-12)	if we suffer, we shall also **reign** with him: if we deny
1 Ne. 13:34(30-42)	I will be merciful unto the **Gentiles** in that day
1 Ne. 14:1	if the **Gentiles**...hearken unto the Lamb of God in that
1 Ne. 22:20(15-26)	the Lord will surely **prepare** a way for his people
2 Ne. 3:7(5-21)	a choice seer will I **raise** up out of the fruit of thy
2 Ne. 30:8(3-8)	to bring about the **restoration** of his people upon the
Jacob 5:61(61-74)	labor diligently...that we may **prepare** the way, that
Jacob 5:71(70-77)	the last time that I shall **nourish** my vineyard; for
3 Ne. 21:22(2-29)	I will **establish** my church among them, and they shall
Ether 4:19(16-19)	blessed is...**faithful**...for he shall be lifted up to
D&C 1:12(12-16)	**prepare** ye for that which is to come, for the Lord is
D&C 24:19	thou art called to **prune** my vineyard...for the last
D&C 29:8(7-21)	to **prepare** their hearts and be prepared in all things
D&C 38:21(14-42)	in **time** ...I will be your king and watch over you.
D&C 43:14(8-35)	that I may reserve unto myself a pure **people** before
D&C 77:12(1,12)	the **preparing** of the way before the time of his coming
D&C 100:16(13-17)	for I will raise up unto myself a pure **people**, that
D&C 101:23(22-35)	**prepare** for the revelation...when...all flesh shall
D&C 104:59(58-59)	to **prepare** my people for the time when I shall dwell
D&C 136:31(17-32)	my people must be **tried** in all things, that they may
JS-M 1:50(46-50)	**servant**...when he cometh, shall find so doing; and

MIND

Lev. 24:12	that the **mind** of the Lord might be shewed them.
Num. 16:28	for I have not done them of mine own **mind**.
Num. 24:13	to do either good or bad of mine own **mind**; but what
Prov. 29:11	a fool uttereth all his **mind**: but a wise man keepeth
Ezek. 11:5	for I know the things that come into your **mind**, every
Ezek. 38:10	at the same time shall things come into thy **mind**, and
Dan. 5:20	and his **mind** hardened in pride, he was deposed from
Hab. 1:11	then shall his **mind** change, and he shall pass over
Matt. 22:37	love the Lord...with all thy heart...soul...**mind**.
Mark 5:15	sitting, and clothed, and in his right **mind**: and they
Rom. 12:2(2-3)	be ye transformed by the renewing of your **mind**, that
1 Cor. 1:10	perfectly joined together in the same **mind** and in the
2 Cor. 3:14	but their **minds** were blinded: for until this day
2 Cor. 4:4	hath blinded the **minds** of them which believe not, lest
Eph. 4:17(17-24)	walk not as...Gentiles...in the vanity of their **mind**
Philip. 1:27	with one **mind** striving together for the faith of the
Titus 1:15	but even their **mind** and conscience is defiled.
Philem. 1:14	but without thy **mind** would I do nothing; that thy
Heb. 8:10	I will put my laws into their **mind**, and write them in
Heb. 10:16	laws into...hearts...in their **minds** will I write them
Rev. 17:9(9-13)	here is the **mind** which hath wisdom. The seven heads
2 Ne. 9:39(39-47)	to be **spiritually minded** is life eternal.
Jacob 2:9	pierce their souls and wound their delicate **minds**.
Jacob 3:2	feast upon his love; for ye may, if your **minds** are
Enos 1:10	the voice of the Lord came into my **mind** again, saying
Mosiah 2:9	open...your **minds** that the mysteries of God may be
Mosiah 4:13(12-14,30)	ye will not have a **mind** to injure one another, but to
Alma 15:3(3-5)	fever...caused by the great tribulations of his **mind**
Alma 17:5(5-6)	they did suffer much, both in body and in **mind**, such
Alma 19:6	veil of unbelief was being cast away from his **mind**
Alma 31:5	word...had more powerful effect upon the **minds** of the
Alma 32:34(33-36)	your **mind** doth begin to expand.
Alma 36:18(4,12-21)	as my **mind** caught hold upon this thought, I cried with
Alma 57:27(25-27)	their **minds** are firm, and they do put their trust in
Ether 4:15	rend that veil of unbelief...and blindness of **mind**
Moro. 9:25	the hope of his glory...rest in your **mind** forever.
D&C 4:2	serve him with all your heart, might, **mind** and
D&C 6:15(15-23)	inquired of me..I did enlighten thy **mind**..by the
D&C 8:2	I will tell you in your **mind** and in your heart, by the
D&C 9:8(7-9)	you must study it out in your **mind**; then you must ask
D&C 10:2	same time, and your **mind** became darkened.
D&C 11:13(13-21)	my Spirit, which shall enlighten your **mind**, which
D&C 43:34	let the solemnities of eternity rest upon your **minds**.
D&C 46:10	always retain in your **minds** what those gifts are, that
D&C 64:34	the Lord requireth the heart and a willing **mind**; and
D&C 67:10(10-12)	see me..not with the carnal..natural **mind**, but..spirit
D&C 68:4(3,4)	speak...by the Holy Ghost...be the **mind** of the Lord
D&C 84:54	**minds** in times past have been darkened because of
D&C 84:80(61-80)	shall not be weary in **mind**, neither darkened, neither
D&C 84:85	treasure up in your **minds** continually the words of
D&C 88:68(68-69)	sanctify yourselves that your **minds** become single to
D&C 95:13	now here is wisdom, and the **mind** of the Lord- let the
D&C 110:1	the veil was taken from our **minds**, and the eyes of our

MIND cont.

D&C 112:23	gross darkness the **minds** of the people, and all flesh
D&C 121:12	to blind their **minds**, that they may not understand his
D&C 133:61	according to the **mind** and will of the Lord, who ruleth
Moses 4:6	he knew not the **mind** of God, wherefore he sought to
Moses 7:18	Zion, because they were of one heart and one **mind**, and
JS-H 1:42(42-46,74)	the vision was opened to my **mind** that I could see the

MIRACLES

Ex. 3:20	smite Egypt with all my **wonders** which I will do in the
Ex. 7:3	multiply my signs and my **wonders** in the land of Egypt.
Ex. 34:10	I will do **marvels**, such as have not been done in all
Num. 14:22	have seen my glory, and my **miracles**, which I did in
Ps. 77:14	God that doest **wonders**: thou hast declared thy
Ps. 78:12	**marvellous** things did he in the sight of their fathers
Matt. 4:23(23-25)	**healing** all manner of sickness and all manner of
Matt. 8:3(2-4)	and immediately his leprosy was **cleansed**.
Matt. 9:30(27-30)	their eyes were **opened**; and Jesus straitly charged the
Matt. 12:13(10-13)	stretch forth thine hand ...it was **restored** whole
Matt. 12:39(38-39)	an evil and adulterous generation seeketh after a **sign**
Mark 1:34	he **healed** many that were sick...and cast out many
Mark 7:35(32-37)	his ears were **opened**, and the string of his tongue was
Mark 9:39	no man..do a **miracle** in my name..can..speak evil of
Mark 16:17(14-20)	and these **signs** shall follow them that believe; in my
Luke 23:8	hoped to have seen some **miracle** done by him.
John 2:11(1-11)	this beginning of **miracles** did Jesus in Cana of
John 2:23	believed in his name, when they saw the **miracles** which
John 3:2	no man can do these **miracles**...except God be with him.
John 10:25	the **works** that I do in my father's name, they bear
John 12:37	though he had done so many **miracles** before them, yet
Acts 6:8	great wonders and **miracles** among the people.
1 Cor. 12:10(4-11)	to another the working of **miracles**; to another
1 Cor. 12:29	are all apostles...are all workers of **miracles**
Heb. 2:4(3-4)	God also bearing them witness...with signs and **wonders**
Rev. 13:14	deceiveth...by...**miracles** which he had power to do
Rev. 16:14	the spirits of devils, working **miracles**, which go
Rev. 19:20	with him the false prophet that wrought **miracles**
2 Ne. 10:4	should the...**miracles** be wrought among other nations
2 Ne. 26:13	working mighty **miracles**, signs, and wonders, among
Mosiah 3:5	go forth amongst men, working mighty **miracles**, such
Mosiah 8:18	man, through faith, might work mighty **miracles**
Mosiah 15:6	after working many mighty **miracles** among the children
Hel. 16:4	working **miracles** among the people, that they might
3 Ne. 1:4	began to be..greater **miracles** wrought among the people
3 Ne. 17:7	I will **heal** them, for I have compassion upon you; my
3 Ne. 26:15	**opened** the eyes of their blind and unstopped the ears
4 Ne. 1:5	they work **miracles** save it were in the name of Jesus.
Morm. 9:15(7-25)	God has not ceased to be a God of **miracles**.
Morm. 9:24(22-25)	these **signs** shall follow them that believe- in my name
Ether 4:18	**signs** shall follow them that believe in my name.
Ether 12:16(15-18)	all they who wrought **miracles** wrought them by faith
Moro. 7:27	have **miracles** ceased because Christ hath ascended into

MIRACLES cont.

Moro. 7:37(35-37)	for it is by faith that **miracles** are wrought; and it
Moro. 10:12	to another, that he may work mighty **miracles**
D&C 24:13(13,14)	require not **miracles**, except I shall command you
D&C 35:8(8,9)	I will show **miracles**...unto all those who believe on
D&C 45:8	gave I power to do many **miracles**, and to become the
D&C 46:21	and again, to some is given the working of **miracles**
D&C 58:64	gospel...preached...**signs** following them that believe.
D&C 63:9(7-12)	faith...not by signs...**signs** follow those that believe
D&C 84:65(65-73)	and these **signs** shall follow them that believe
D&C 124:98(97-101)	these **signs** shall follow him- he shall heal the sick

MISSION OF EARLY SAINTS

Gen. 12:3(1-3)	in thee shall all families of the earth be **blessed**.
Gen. 22:18(17-18)	in thy seed shall all..nations of the earth be **blessed**
Ps. 145:10(3-12)	O Lord; and thy **saints** shall bless thee.
Eccl. 12:13	for this is the whole **duty** of man.
Matt. 5:14(13-16)	ye are the **light** of the world. A city that is set on
Matt. 5:48	be ye therefore **perfect**, even as your Father which is
Matt. 6:33	but seek ye first the **kingdom** of God, and his
Matt. 28:19(19-20)	go ye therefore, and **teach** all nations, baptizing them
Luke 24:47(46-48)	repentance...should be **preached**...among all nations
John 15:16(15-17)	that ye should go and bring forth **fruit**, and that your
Acts 3:25	children...of the **covenant**...unto Abraham, and in thy
1 Cor. 1:2	called to be **saints**, with all that...call upon...Jesus
Gal. 4:28	we...as Isaac was, are the children of **promise**.
Eph. 4:24(22-32)	and that ye put on the **new** man, which after God is
Philip. 2:15	perverse nation, among whom ye **shine** as lights in the
1 Pet. 2:9(5-9)	a **royal** priesthood, an holy nation, a peculiar people
2 Ne. 25:23	**persuade**...to believe in Christ, and to be reconciled
Jacob 1:19	if we did not **teach** them the word of God with all
Alma 37:33(33,34)	**preach** unto them repentance, and faith on the Lord
Alma 38:10(10-12)	and now, as ye have begun to **teach** the word even so I
3 Ne. 12:13(13-16)	I give unto you to be the **salt** of the earth; but if
3 Ne. 12:48	I would that ye should be **perfect** even as I, or your
3 Ne. 20:25	children...of the **covenant**...unto Abraham: and in thy
Morm. 9:22(22-25)	go ye into all the world, and **preach** the gospel to
D&C 86:2(1-2)	field was the world, and the apostles were the **sowers**
Abr. 2:11(6-11)	in thy seed...all...be blessed...with...the **gospel**

MISSION OF LATTER-DAY SAINTS

Gen. 12:3(1-3)	in thee shall all families of the earth be **blessed**.
Gen. 22:18(17-18)	in thy seed...all the nations of the earth be **blessed**
Isa. 2:3(2-3)	out of Zion shall go forth the **law**, and the word of
Isa. 11:12(10-12)	he shall set up an **ensign** for the nations, and shall
Isa. 52:1(1-2)	awake; put on thy **strength**, O Zion; put on thy
Dan. 2:35(34-35,44)	the **stone**...became a great mountain, and filled the
Obad. 1:21	**saviours** shall come up on mount Zion to judge the
Matt. 28:19(19-20)	**teach** all nations, baptizing them in the name of the
Gal. 3:8(7-9)	in thee shall all nations be **blessed**.

MISSION OF LATTER-DAY SAINTS cont.

1 Pet. 2:9(5-9)	a royal priesthood, an holy nation, a peculiar people
1 Ne. 14:14(13-17)	saints of the church...armed with righteousness and
1 Ne. 15:13(13-18)	gospel..from the Gentiles unto the remnant of our seed
1 Ne. 22:8(4-9)	their being nourished by the Gentiles and being
2 Ne. 9:2(1-2)	gathered home to the lands of their inheritance, and
3 Ne. 16:7(6,7)	truth come unto the Gentiles, that the fulness of the
Ether 13:6(4-8)	and that a New Jerusalem should be built upon this
D&C 1:4(1-34)	and the voice of warning shall be unto all people, by
D&C 6:6	seek to bring forth and establish the cause of Zion
D&C 29:7(7-8)	called to bring to pass the gathering of mine elect
D&C 33:5(3-11)	this church have I established and called forth out
D&C 36:5(4-7)	sent forth to preach the everlasting gospel among the
D&C 42:12(11-17)	teach the principles of my gospel, which are in the
D&C 43:15(15,16)	not sent forth to be taught, but to teach the children
D&C 45:68(63-69)	must needs flee unto Zion for safety.
D&C 57:1(1-5)	Missouri...consecrated for the gathering of the saints
D&C 58:64	the gospel must be preached unto every creature, with
D&C 64:42(41-43)	she shall be an ensign unto the people, and there
D&C 65:2(2-6)	from thence shall the gospel roll forth unto the ends
D&C 82:3	unto whom much is given much is required; and he who
D&C 82:14	Zion must increase in beauty, and in holiness; her
D&C 84:4(2-5)	New Jerusalem shall be built by the gathering of the
D&C 84:58(54-59)	bring forth fruit meet for their Father's kingdom
D&C 86:11(8-11)	a light unto the Gentiles, and through this
D&C 101:22(16-23)	gather together, and stand in holy places
D&C 101:39(39-42)	they are accounted as the salt of the earth and the
D&C 103:15(15-26)	the redemption of Zion must needs come by power
D&C 109:73(72-74)	that thy church may come forth out of the wilderness
D&C 110:12	that in us and our seed all generations...be blessed.
D&C 113:8(7-8)	put on the authority of the priesthood, which she
D&C 115:5(4-5)	arise and shine forth, that thy light may be a
D&C 124:39(36-41)	holy house, which my people are always commanded to
D&C 128:15(14-18)	for their salvation is necessary and essential to our
D&C 128:24	let us present ...the records of our dead, which shall
D&C 133:7(7-16)	gather ye out from among the nations, from the four
D&C 133:32(26-34)	by the hands of the...children of Ephraim.
D&C 133:37(36-39)	and this gospel shall be preached unto every nation
D&C 133:58(57-63)	to prepare the weak for those things which are coming
Abr. 2:9(6-11)	they shall bear this ministry and priesthood unto all
A of F 1:10	that Zion will be built upon this...continent; that
JFS-V 1:30(29-37)	among the righteous...appointed messengers, clothed
JFS-V 1:57(38-60)	faithful elders..when they depart..continue..preaching

MISSIONARY WORK

Gen. 12:3(1-3)	in thee shall all families of the earth be blessed.
Isa. 2:3(2-4)	he will teach us of his ways, and we will walk in his
Isa. 49:6(5-7)	I will also give thee for a light to the Gentiles
Isa. 52:7	beautiful...feet of him...that publisheth salvation
Isa. 61:1(1-3)	Lord hath anointed me to preach good tidings unto the
Jer. 3:14(14-15)	one of..city..two of..family..I will bring you to Zion
Jer. 16:16(14-16)	I will send for many fishers, saith the Lord, and they

MISSIONARY WORK cont.

Ezek. 34:11(11-16)	I, will both **search** my sheep, and seek them out.
Dan. 2:44	break in pieces and **consume** all these kingdoms, and
Jonah 1:2	arise, go to Nineveh...and **cry** against it; for their
Jonah 3:2	**preach** unto it the preaching that I bid thee.
Matt. 4:19(18-20)	follow me, and I will make you **fishers** of men.
Matt. 5:19	whosoever shall do and **teach** them, the same shall be
Matt. 10:6(1-20)	but go rather to the **lost** sheep of the house of Israel
Matt. 11:1	he departed thence to teach and to **preach** in their
Matt. 28:19	go ye therefore, and **teach** all nations, baptizing them
Mark 1:4	**preach** the baptism of repentance for the remission of
Mark 1:17(16-18)	come ye after me, and I will make you...**fishers** of men
Mark 3:14	that he might send them forth to **preach**
Mark 16:15(15-18)	all the world, and preach the gospel to every **creature**
Luke 5:10(2-11)	from henceforth thou shalt **catch** men.
Luke 9:2(1-6)	he sent them to **preach** the kingdom of God, and to heal
Luke 10:1(1-20)	**seventy**...sent them two and two before his face into
Luke 15:7(7-10)	joy shall be in heaven over one **sinner** that repenteth
Luke 22:32(31-32)	when thou art converted, **strengthen** thy brethren.
John 4:35(35-38)	the fields...are white already to **harvest**.
John 15:16	ye should go and bring forth **fruit**...fruit should
John 21:17(15-17)	Jesus saith unto him, **Feed** my sheep.
Acts 5:42	they ceased not to teach and **preach** Jesus Christ.
Acts 8:12(12,13)	they believed Philip **preaching** the things concerning
Acts 10:42(9-48)	he commanded us to **preach** unto the people, and to
Acts 17:2(2-3)	and Paul...**reasoned** with them out of the scriptures
Acts 26:28(1-29)	almost thou **persuadest** me to be a Christian.
Rom. 10:15(13-17)	how shall they **preach**, except they be sent? as it is
1 Cor. 1:23	but we **preach** Christ crucified, unto the Jews a
1 Cor. 9:16(16-23)	woe is unto me, if I **preach** not the gospel
1 Cor. 15:1(1-3)	I **declare** unto you the gospel which I preached unto
2 Cor. 4:5	**preach** not ourselves, but Christ Jesus the Lord; and
2 Tim. 4:2	**preach** the word; be instant in season, out of season
Rev. 14:6(6-7)	gospel to **preach**...to every nation, and kindred, and
Jacob 1:19(18-19)	**teach** them the word of God with all diligence
Mosiah 12:1	go and **prophesy** unto this my people, for they have
Mosiah 15:14(13-19)	these are they...who have **published** salvation; and
Mosiah 18:9	stand as **witnesses** of God at all times ...in all
Alma 17:4(1-17)	success in bringing many to the **knowledge** of the truth
Alma 18:39(1-43)	**expounded** unto them the plan of redemption, which was
Alma 22:23(1-27)	his whole household were **converted** unto the Lord.
Alma 29:8(1-17)	of their own nation and tongue, to **teach** his word, yea
Hel. 5:19(1-19)	there were eight thousand of the Lamanites...**baptized**
Hel. 16:1(1-8)	many who heard the words of **Samuel** ...believed on his
Morm. 9:22(22-25)	go ye into all the **world**, and preach the gospel to Eve
D&C 1:5(1-16)	and they shall **go** forth and none shall stay them, for
D&C 1:23(23-28)	gospel might be **proclaimed** by the weak and the simple
D&C 4:1(1-7)	a marvelous **work** is about to come forth among the
D&C 11:21(21-27)	**declare** my word...first seek to obtain my word, and
D&C 15:6	most worth unto you will be to declare **repentance** unto
D&C 18:15(9-29)	bring, save it be one **soul** unto me, how great shall
D&C 29:7(1-7)	mine elect **hear** my voice and harden not their hearts
D&C 33:8(6-12)	**open** your mouths and they shall be filled, and you
D&C 35:12(12-15)	those who are ready to **receive** the fulness of my

MISSIONARY WORK cont.

D&C 36:5(5-7)	ordained and sent forth to **preach** the everlasting
D&C 39:15(15-23)	from thence men shall go forth into all **nations**.
D&C 42:6(6,7)	and ye shall go forth...**preaching** my gospel, two by
D&C 42:11	go forth to **preach**...except he be ordained by some one
D&C 42:14	if ye receive not the spirit ye shall not **teach**.
D&C 43:15(15-16)	**teach** the children of men the things which I have put
D&C 49:11(11-14)	**go** among this people, and say unto them, like unto
D&C 50:17(13-22)	sent forth to **preach** the word of truth by the
D&C 61:35	journey together, or **two** by two, as seemeth them good
D&C 62:5	**declare** glad tidings unto the inhabitants of the
D&C 63:57(57-58)	those who desire in their hearts, in meekness, to **warn**
D&C 71:1(1-10)	you should open your mouths in **proclaiming** my gospel
D&C 75:4(3-28)	**proclaiming** the truth according to the revelations and
D&C 84:61(60-75)	bearing **testimony** to all the world of those things
D&C 84:87(77-94)	I send you out to **reprove** the world of all their
D&C 88:70(62-74)	the first **laborers** in this last kingdom.
D&C 88:81(81-85)	every man who hath been warned to **warn** his neighbor.
D&C 90:11	every man shall **hear**...the gospel in his own tongue
D&C 100:6(5-8)	it shall be **given** you...what ye shall say.
D&C 107:25	the seventy are also called to **preach** the gospel, and
D&C 112:5(4,5)	let not...inhabitants...slumber, because of...**speech**.
D&C 123:12	kept from the **truth** because they know not where to
D&C 133:8(8,37)	send...elders of my church unto the **nations** which are
D&C 133:38(36-40)	and the **servants** of God shall go forth, saying with a
Moses 8:19(19-20)	go forth and **declare** his gospel unto the children of
Abr. 2:9(6-11)	in their hands they shall bear this **ministry** and

MOCKING

Gen. 19:14	one that **mocked** unto his sons in law.
Judg. 16:10	thou hast **mocked** me, and told me lies: now tell me, I
2 Kgs. 2:23(23-24)	there came forth little children...and **mocked** him, and
2 Chr. 36:16(15,16)	they **mocked** the messengers of God, and despised his
Ps. 35:16(11-17)	with hypocritical **mockers** in feasts, they gnashed upon
Prov. 17:5	whoso **mocketh** the poor reproacheth his maker: and he
Prov. 20:1	wine is a **mocker**, strong drink is raging: and
Lam. 1:7	the adversaries saw her, and did **mock** at her sabbaths.
Matt. 20:19(18-19)	shall deliver him to the Gentiles to **mock**, and to
Matt. 27:29(29-44)	and **mocked** him, saying, hail, king of the Jews
Mark 10:34(32-34)	and they shall **mock** him, and shall scourge him, and
Mark 15:20(17-31)	they had **mocked** him...led him out to crucify him.
Luke 18:32(32-33)	shall be **mocked**, and spitefully entreated, and spitted
Luke 22:63(63-71)	the men that held Jesus **mocked** him, and smote him.
Luke 23:11	Herod with his men of war...**mocked** him, and arrayed
Luke 23:36(36-38)	the soldiers also **mocked** him, coming to him, and offer
Acts 17:32	heard of the resurrection of the dead, some **mocked**
Gal. 6:7	be not deceived; God is not **mocked**: for whatsoever
Heb. 11:36	others had trial of cruel **mockings** and scourgings, yea
Jude 1:18(18-20)	told you there should be **mockers** in the last time, who
1 Ne. 8:27	attitude of **mocking** and pointing their fingers towards
Ether 12:26	fools **mock**, but they shall mourn; and my grace is
Moro. 8:9(9,23)	solemn **mockery** before God...baptize little children.

MOCKING cont.

D&C 45:50	calamity shall cover the **mocker**, and the scorner shall
D&C 63:58	I, the Lord, am not to be **mocked** in the last days.
D&C 104:6(4-7)	for I, the Lord, am not to be **mocked** in these things
D&C 124:71	the Lord...cannot be **mocked** in any of these things.

MODESTY

Gen. 3:7(7-21)	they sewed fig leaves together,...made...**aprons**.
Isa. 3:16(16-26)	because the **daughters** of Zion are haughty, and walk
Philip. 4:5(5,6)	let your **moderation** be known unto all men. The Lord
1 Tim. 2:9(9-10)	that women adorn themselves in **modest** apparel, with
Titus 2:5(2-8)	to be discreet, **chaste**, keepers at home, good
1 Pet. 2:9	but ye are...a **peculiar** people; that ye should shew
1 Pet. 3:3(1-6)	let it not be that outward **adorning** of plaiting the
Jacob 2:13	lifted up in the **pride** of your hearts, and wear stiff
Jacob 2:28	the Lord God, delight in the **chastity** of women.
Moro. 9:9	precious above all things...chastity and **virtue**
D&C 42:40	let all thy **garments** be plain, and their beauty the
D&C 46:33	practise **virtue** and holiness before me continually.
D&C 88:121	cease...**lustful** desires...your wicked doings.
D&C 121:45	let **virtue** garnish thy thoughts unceasingly; then
Moses 4:27(13-27)	make coats of skins, and **clothed** them.
Moses 6:57(56,57)	repent...inherit the kingdom of God...no **unclean** thing
A of F 1:13	if there is anything **virtuous**, lovely, or of good

MORTALITY

Gen. 2:17	in the day...thereof thou shalt surely **die**.
Gen. 3:19(17-19)	for **dust** thou art, and unto dust shalt thou return.
Lev. 17:11	for the life of the **flesh** is in the blood: and I have
Deut. 4:40	that thou mayest prolong thy **days** upon the earth
Job 2:4	all that a man hath will he give for his **life**.
Job 19:26	after my skin worms destroy this **body**, yet in my flesh
Job 21:26(22-26)	they shall lie down alike in the **dust**, and the worms
Ps. 8:4(3-5)	what is **man**, that thou art mindful of him? and the son
Ps. 78:39(35-39)	for he remembered that they were but **flesh**; a wind
Ps. 103:14(13-19)	knoweth our frame; he remembereth that we are **dust**.
Eccl. 12:7(1-7)	the **dust** return to the earth as it was: and the spirit
Isa. 40:6(5-8)	all **flesh** is grass, and all the goodliness thereof
Matt. 4:4	man shall not **live** by bread alone, but by every word
Matt. 16:26(25-26)	shall gain the whole world, and lose his own **soul**? or
Luke 9:56	not come to destroy men's **lives**, but to save them.
Rom. 6:12	let not sin therefore reign in your **mortal** body, that
Rom. 8:11(11-14)	shall also quicken your **mortal** bodies by his spirit
1 Cor. 15:53(50-54)	this **mortal** must put on immortality.
2 Cor. 4:11(10-12)	life...might be made manifest in our **mortal** flesh.
2 Cor. 5:4(1-10)	that **mortality** might be swallowed up of life.
James 1:10(9-12)	as the flower of the **grass** he shall pass away.
1 Pet. 1:24(21-25)	for all **flesh** is as grass, and all the glory of man
2 Ne. 2:11	needs be, that there is an **opposition** in all things.
2 Ne. 2:21(19-21)	their state became a state of **probation**, and their

310

MORTALITY cont.

2 Ne. 2:25(22-26)	Adam fell that men might be; and men **are**, that they
2 Ne. 2:27(27-29)	men are free according to the **flesh**; and all things
Enos 1:27	the day when my **mortal** shall put on immortality, and
Mosiah 3:19	the natural **man** is an enemy to God, and has been from
Mosiah 16:4(3-5)	thus all **mankind** were lost; and behold, they would
Mosiah 16:10	this **mortal** shall put on immortality, and this corrupt
Alma 12:12	being raised from this **mortality** to a state of
Alma 12:24(20-24)	this **life** became a probationary state; a time to
Alma 34:32(30-33)	this **life** is the time for men to prepare to meet God
Alma 41:4(3-4)	**mortality** raised to immortality, corruption to
Alma 42:10(2-13)	**probationary** state became a state for them to prepare
Hel. 12:1	we can behold...the unsteadiness...of **men**; yea, we
3 Ne. 28:8	changed in the twinkling of an eye from **mortality** to
3 Ne. 28:36(36-40)	they were cleansed from **mortality** to immortality
Moro. 7:16(16-18)	the Spirit of Christ is given to every **man**, that he
D&C 29:43(42,43)	appoint unto man the days of his **probation-** that by
D&C 50:5	whether in **life** or in death, for they shall inherit
D&C 63:51(50-52)	old men shall **die**; but...not sleep in the dust, but
D&C 67:12(10-12)	neither can any natural **man** abide the presence of God
D&C 101:36(36-37)	fear not even unto death; for in this **world** your joy
Moses 1:10(7-10)	for this cause I know that **man** is nothing, which
Moses 3:17(15-17)	in the day thou eatest thereof thou shalt surely **die**.
Moses 4:25(17-31)	by the **sweat** of thy face shalt thou eat bread, until
Moses 5:11(9-11)	were it not for our **transgression** we never...had seed
Moses 6:48(48-49)	by his fall came **death**; and we are made partakers of
Abr. 3:26(24-26)	they who keep their second **estate** shall have glory
A of F 1:3(2-3)	all **mankind** may be saved, by obedience to the laws

MOTIVATIONS

Gen. 6:5	every imagination of the **thoughts** of his heart was
Prov. 16:3	commit thy works unto the Lord...thy **thoughts** shall
Prov. 23:7	as he **thinketh** in his heart, so is he: eat and drink
Isa. 55:8(7-9)	my **thoughts** are not your thoughts, neither are your
Matt. 5:28	whosoever looketh on a woman to **lust** ...adultery with
Matt. 6:1(1-8)	do not your **alms** before men, to be seen of them: other
Matt. 6:18(16-18)	appear not unto men to **fast**, but unto thy Father which
Mark 7:23(20-23)	**evil** things come from within, and defile the man.
Luke 6:45	good man out of the good treasure of his **heart**
Acts 8:22(18-24)	pray God...the **thought** of thine heart may be forgiven
Rom. 13:10(9-10)	**love** worketh no ill to his neighbour: therefore love
Rom. 14:14(13-21)	to him that **esteemeth** any thing to be unclean, to him
1 Cor. 8:9(1-13)	take heed lest by any means this **liberty** of yours
2 Cor. 10:5	bringing into captivity every **thought** to the obedience
Philip. 4:8(8-9)	if there be any praise, **think** on these things.
Heb. 4:12(12-13)	a discerner of the thoughts and **intents** of the heart.
James 1:14(12-15)	drawn away of his own **lust**, and enticed.
1 Pet. 4:9(8-9)	use hospitality one to another without **grudging**.
1 Jn. 3:3(1-3)	every man that hath this **hope** in him purifieth himself
2 Ne. 9:9	**stirreth** up the children of men unto secret
2 Ne. 33:4(4,10)	it **persuadeth** them to do good; it maketh known unto
Enos 1:4(1-8)	and my soul **hungered**; and I kneeled down before my

MOTIVATIONS cont.

Enos 1:9(9-12)	began to feel a **desire** for the welfare of my brethren
Mosiah 5:2	we have no more **disposition** to do evil, but to do good
Alma 12:14(12-14)	and our **thoughts** will also condemn us; and in this
Alma 29:4(4-5)	he granteth unto men according to their **desire**
Alma 37:36	let thy **thoughts** be directed unto the Lord; yea, let
Alma 41:5(5-6)	raised to happiness according to..**desires** of happiness
Moro. 7:6(5-11)	except he shall do it with real **intent** it profiteth
Moro. 7:28	they who have faith in him will **cleave** unto every good
D&C 3:6(6-7)	have gone on in the **persuasions** of men.
D&C 4:5	eye single to the **glory** of God, qualify him for the
D&C 6:16	God...knowest thy thoughts and the **intents** of thy
D&C 6:36	look unto me in every **thought**; doubt not, fear not.
D&C 18:38	by their **desires** and their works you shall know them.
D&C 45:57	taken the Holy Spirit for their **guide**, and have not
D&C 46:7(7-9)	that ye may not be **seduced** by evil spirits, or
D&C 58:27(26-29)	should...do many things of their own **free** will, and
D&C 82:19	all things with an eye **single** to the glory of God.
D&C 84:85(84-85)	treasure up in your **minds** continually the words of
D&C 88:67(67-69)	if your eye be **single** to my glory...filled with light
D&C 107:100(99,100)	he that is **slothful** shall not be counted worthy to
D&C 121:35(34-40)	set..upon..this world, and **aspire** to the honors of men
D&C 121:45	let **virtue** garnish thy thoughts unceasingly; then
JS-V 1:8(7-10)	who **would** have received it with all their hearts

MOURNING

Gen. 37:35	for I will go down into the grave unto my son **mourning**
Lev. 19:28	not make any **cuttings** in your flesh for the dead, nor
Deut. 34:8	the days of weeping and **mourning** for Moses were ended.
Neh. 8:9	this day is holy unto the Lord your God; **mourn** not
Job 5:11	those which **mourn** may be exalted to safety.
Ps. 43:2	why go I **mourning** because of the oppression of the
Eccl. 3:4	and a time to laugh; a time to **mourn**, and a time to
Eccl. 7:2	it is better to go to the house of **mourning**, than to
Isa. 22:4	look away from me; I will **weep** bitterly, labour not
Isa. 24:4	the earth **mourneth** and fadeth away, the world languish
Isa. 51:11	and sorrow and **mourning** shall flee away.
Isa. 60:20	the days of thy **mourning** shall be ended.
Isa. 61:2	vengeance of our God; to comfort all that **mourn**
Jer. 9:1	Oh that...mine eyes a fountain of **tears**, that I might
Jer. 16:4(4-6)	they shall not be **lamented**; neither shall they be
Jer. 25:33	they shall not be **lamented**, neither gathered, nor
Jer. 31:13	I will turn their **mourning** into joy, and will comfort
Lam. 2:5(5-11)	hath increased in the daughter of Judah **mourning** and
Lam. 3:48	mine eye runneth down with **rivers** of water for the
Ezek. 7:11	neither shall there be **wailing** for them.
Ezek. 7:16	all of them **mourning**, every one for his iniquity.
Amos 8:10	all your songs into **lamentation**; and I will bring up
Zech. 12:11(10-14)	in that day shall there be a great **mourning** in
Matt. 2:18	great **mourning**, Rachel weeping for her children, and
Matt. 5:4	blessed are they that **mourn**: for they shall be
Luke 7:32(31-35)	we have **mourned** to you, and ye have not wept.

MOURNING cont.

Acts 8:2	made great **lamentation** over him.
Acts 20:38(36-38)	**sorrowing** most of all for the words which he spake
2 Cor. 5:4(2-4)	we...**groan**, being burdened: not for that we would be
2 Cor. 6:10	as **sorrowful**, yet alway rejoicing; as poor, yet making
2 Cor. 7:10(9-11)	for godly **sorrow** worketh repentance to salvation not
1 Thes. 4:13(13-16)	that ye **sorrow** not, even as others which have no hope.
James 4:9(8-10)	let your laughter be turned to **mourning**, and your joy
James 5:1(1-7)	ye rich men, **weep** and howl for your miseries that
Rev. 21:4	no more death, neither **sorrow**, nor crying, neither
2 Ne. 8:11	sorrow and **mourning** shall flee away.
2 Ne. 32:7	I am left to **mourn** because of the unbelief, and the
Jacob 7:26	wherefore, we did **mourn** out our days.
Mosiah 18:9	yea, and are willing to **mourn** with those that mourn
Mosiah 21:9	great **mourning** and lamentation among the people of
Alma 28:4(4-6)	great **mourning** and lamentation heard throughout all
Alma 30:2	after the days of fasting, and **mourning**, and prayer
Hel. 6:33	the great sorrow and **lamentation** of the righteous.
Hel. 7:11	great **mourning** for the wickedness of the people.
Hel. 7:15(14-15)	because of my **mourning** and lamentation ye have
Hel. 9:10	to **mourn** and to fast, at the burial of the great chief
3 Ne. 8:23	there was great **mourning** and howling and weeping among
3 Ne. 10:10	the **mourning**, and the weeping, and the wailing of the
3 Ne. 12:4	and again, blessed are all they that **mourn**, for they
Morm. 2:12(11-13)	saw their lamentation and their **mourning** and their
Morm. 6:16(16-22)	and my soul was rent with **anguish**, because of the
Ether 11:13	and the prophets **mourned** and withdrew from among the
Ether 12:26	fools mock, but they shall **mourn**; and my grace is
Ether 15:3	his soul **mourned** and refused to be comforted.
Ether 15:16(11-17)	a **lamentation** for the loss of the slain of their
D&C 42:45	thou shalt **weep** for the loss of them that die, and
D&C 56:16	be your **lamentation** in the day of visitation, and of
D&C 87:6	inhabitants of the earth shall **mourn**; and with famine
D&C 95:7	your fastings and your **mourning** might come up into the
D&C 97:21(18-28)	let Zion rejoice, while all the wicked shall **mourn**.
D&C 98:9	nevertheless, when the wicked rule the people **mourn**.
D&C 101:14	and all they who have **mourned** shall be comforted.
D&C 112:24	a day of desolation, of weeping, of **mourning**, and of
Moses 5:27	Adam and his wife **mourned** before the Lord, because of
Moses 7:49	when Enoch heard the earth **mourn**, he wept, and cried
JS-M 1:36	then shall all the tribes of the earth **mourn**; and they

MURDER

Gen. 4:8(8-11)	Cain rose up against Abel...and **slew** him.
Gen. 9:6(5-6)	whoso **sheddeth** man's blood, by man shall his blood be
Ex. 20:13	thou shalt not **kill**.
Ex. 21:12(12,14)	he that **smiteth** a man...shall be surely put to death.
Lev. 24:17(17-21)	he that **killeth** any man shall surely be put to death.
Num. 35:30(30-31)	the **murderer** shall be put to death by the mouth of
Deut. 5:17	thou shalt not **kill**.
Jer. 7:9	will ye steal, **murder**, and commit adultery, and swear
Matt. 5:21(21-29)	by them of old time, thou shalt not **kill**; and

MURDER cont.

Matt. 15:19	out of the heart proceed evil thoughts, **murders**
Matt. 19:18	Jesus said, thou shalt do no **murder**, thou shalt not
Mark 10:19	commandments, do not commit adultery, do not **kill**, do
John 8:44	he was a **murderer** from the beginning, and abode not
1 Jn. 3:15(12,15)	no **murderer** hath eternal life abiding in him.
Rev. 9:21	neither repented they of their **murders**, nor of their
Rev. 21:8	**murderers**...shall have their part in the lake which
Rev. 22:15	for without are...**murderers**, and idolaters, and
Mosiah 13:21	thou shalt not **kill**.
Alma 1:13(12-15)	thou hast **shed** the blood of a righteous man, yea, a
Alma 1:18	he that **murdered** was punished unto death.
Alma 30:10	but if he **murdered** he was punished unto death; and if
Alma 34:12(11-12)	the law requireth the life of him who hath **murdered**
Alma 42:19	law given- if a man **murdered** he should die- would he
3 Ne. 30:2	turn...from...your **murders**, and your priestcrafts, and
D&C 42:18(18-19)	not kill; and he that **kills** shall not have forgiveness
D&C 42:79	if any..shall **kill** they shall be delivered up and
D&C 59:6	thou shalt not...**kill**, nor do anything like unto it.
D&C 132:19	that he shall commit no **murder** whereby to shed
D&C 132:27(19,26-27	is in that ye commit **murder** wherein ye shed innocent
Moses 5:31(29-57)	Cain said...I am Mahan...that I may **murder** and get

MURMURING

Ex. 15:24	and the people **murmured** against Moses, saying, what
Ex. 16:2	whole congregation...of Israel **murmured** against Moses
Ex. 17:3	the people thirsted there for water; and...**murmured**
Num. 14:2	children of Israel **murmured** against Moses and...Aaron
Num. 16:41	all...Israel **murmured** against Moses and against Aaron
Deut. 1:27	and ye **murmured** in your tents, and said, because the
Josh. 9:18(18-19)	all the congregation **murmured** against the princes.
Ps. 106:25(24-25)	but **murmured** in their tents, and hearkened not unto
John 6:43(41-43)	Jesus...said unto them, **murmur** not among yourselves.
1 Cor. 10:10	neither **murmur** ye, as some of them also murmured, and
Jude 1:16(16-19)	these are **murmurers**, complainers, walking after their
1 Ne. 2:11(11-12)	they did **murmur** in many things against their father
1 Ne. 3:6(4-6)	favored of the Lord, because thou hast not **murmured**.
1 Ne. 3:31	again began to **murmur**, saying: how is it possible that
1 Ne. 16:20(20-25)	also my father began to **murmur** against the Lord his
1 Ne. 17:17(17-18)	they began to **murmur**...saying: our brother is a fool
1 Ne. 17:49	Nephi, said unto them that they should **murmur** no more
D&C 9:6	do not **murmur**, my son, for it is wisdom in me that I
D&C 25:4	**murmur** not because of the things which thou hast not

MYSTERIES OF GODLINESS

Deut. 29:29	the **secret** things belong unto the Lord our God: but
Ps. 25:14(12-14)	the **secret** of the Lord is with them that fear him; and
Dan. 2:28(14-47)	there is a God in heaven that revealeth **secrets**, and
Matt. 13:11	it is given unto you to know the **mysteries** of the
Mark 4:11	unto you...is given to know the **mystery** of the kingdom

MYSTERIES OF GODLINESS cont.

1 Cor. 2:7(7-16)   we speak the wisdom of God in a **mystery**, even the
1 Cor. 4:1   ministers of Christ...stewards of the **mysteries** of God
1 Cor. 13:2   understand all **mysteries**...and have not charity, I am
Eph. 3:9(1-10)   make all men see what is the fellowship of the **mystery**
Eph. 5:32   this is a great **mystery**: but I speak concerning Christ
Eph. 6:19   to make known the **mystery** of the gospel
Col. 1:26(25-27)   even the **mystery** which hath been hid from ages and
1 Tim. 3:16(9,15-16)   great is the **mystery** of godliness: God was manifest
Rev. 10:7   the **mystery** of God should be finished, as he hath
1 Ne. 2:16   having great desires to know of the **mysteries** of God
1 Ne. 10:19(17-19)   **mysteries** of God shall be unfolded...by...Holy Ghost
2 Ne. 27:22   until I shall see fit...to **reveal** all things unto the
Jacob 4:8   unsearchable are the depths of the **mysteries** of him
Mosiah 1:5(3,5)   that we might read and understand of his **mysteries**
Mosiah 2:9   that the **mysteries** of God may be unfolded to your view
Mosiah 8:19   interpreters...prepared...unfolding all such **mysteries**
Alma 10:5   I have seen much of his **mysteries** and his marvelous
Alma 12:9(9-11)   it is given unto many to know the **mysteries** of God
Alma 26:22   unto such it is given to know the **mysteries** of God
Alma 37:4(3-4)   every nation, kindred...shall know of the **mysteries**
Alma 40:3   many **mysteries**...no one knoweth them save God himself.
D&C 28:7   I have given him the keys of the **mysteries**, and the
D&C 42:61(61,65)   that thou mayest know the **mysteries** and peaceable
D&C 76:7(5-7,114)   to them will I reveal all **mysteries**... all the hidden
D&C 77:6   book which John saw...contains the revealed..**mysteries**
D&C 84:19   greater priesthood...holdeth the key of the **mysteries**
D&C 93:28(26-28)   keepeth his commandments...**knoweth** all things.
D&C 101:33(22-35)   **hidden** things which no man knew, things of the earth
D&C 121:26(26-31)   God shall give unto you **knowledge**...that has not been
JS-H 1:74   intention of their more **mysterious** passages revealed

NATIONS

Gen. 9:19(18-27)   sons of Noah...of them was the whole **earth** overspread.
Gen. 10:5   divided in their **lands**; every one after his tongue
Gen. 10:32(25,32)   the **nations** divided in the earth after the flood.
Gen. 17:4(3-6)   thou shalt be a father of many **nations**.
Gen. 18:18   become a great and mighty **nation**, and all the nations
Deut. 32:8(7-14)   most High divided...**nations**...according to...Israel.
Isa. 2:2(2-4)   Lord's house...all **nations** shall flow unto it.
Isa. 14:12   O Lucifer...which didst weaken the **nations**
Isa. 40:15(15-17)   the **nations** are as a drop of a bucket, and are counted
Isa. 49:6   a light to the **Gentiles**...unto the end of the earth.
Jer. 3:17   Jerusalem...all the **nations** shall be gathered unto it
Dan. 2:44(31-45)   and in the days of these **kings** shall the God of heaven
Matt. 21:43   and given to a **nation** bringing forth the fruits
Matt. 24:7(7,14)   for **nation** shall rise against nation, and kingdom
Matt. 25:32   and before him shall be gathered all **nations**: and he
Matt. 28:19   teach all **nations**, baptizing them in the name of the
Acts 10:35(34-35)   but in every **nation** he that feareth him, and worketh
Acts 17:26(24-27)   hath made of one blood all **nations** of men for to dwell
Rom. 4:18(17,18)   that he might become the father of many **nations**

315

NATIONS cont.

1 Pet. 2:9	a royal priesthood, an holy **nation**, a peculiar people
Rev. 14:6	to every **nation**, and kindred, and tongue, and people
Rev. 20:3	he should deceive the **nations** no more, till the
1 Ne. 13:2(1-6)	I said: I behold many **nations** and kingdoms
1 Ne. 13:42	that he shall manifest himself unto all **nations**, both
1 Ne. 14:13	among all the **nations** of the Gentiles, to fight
1 Ne. 22:5(3,5,28)	shall be scattered among all **nations** and shall be
2 Ne. 1:8	this land should be kept...from...other **nations**; for
2 Ne. 12:12	day of the Lord of hosts soon cometh upon all **nations**
2 Ne. 15:26	and he will lift up an ensign to the **nations** from far
2 Ne. 29:7	know ye not that there are more **nations** than one? Know
Alma 13:22	voice of the Lord...doth declare it unto all **nations**
Alma 29:8	the Lord doth grant unto all **nations**, of their own
Ether 8:25(24-25)	overthrow the freedom of all lands, **nations**, and count
D&C 35:13	to thrash the **nations** by the power of my Spirit
D&C 42:58	for they shall be taught unto all **nations**, kindreds
D&C 52:14	Satan...goeth forth deceiving the **nations**
D&C 58:9(8-12)	supper...unto which all **nations** shall be invited.
D&C 87:2(2,6)	war will be poured out upon all **nations**, beginning at
D&C 88:79	the wars and the perplexities of the **nations**, and the
D&C 97:19	and the **nations** of the earth shall honor her, and
D&C 109:54(54-56)	have mercy, O Lord, upon all the **nations** of the earth
D&C 115:5	thy light may be a standard for the **nations**
D&C 133:8(7-10)	elders of my church unto the **nations** which are afar
Abr. 1:2	father of many **nations**, a prince of peace, and
Abr. 2:9(8-11)	bear this ministry and Priesthood unto all **nations**
JS-M 1:31	preached in...world, for a witness unto all **nations**

NATURE

Gen. 1:1(1-31)	in the beginning God created the heaven and the **earth**.
Gen. 2:5(1-20)	every **plant** of the field before it was in the earth
Gen. 7:12(4-24)	and the **rain** was upon the earth forty days and forty
Ex. 14:21(21,22)	the Lord caused the **sea** to go back by a strong east
Deut. 32:2	my doctrine shall drop as the **rain**, my speech shall
Job 12:10(7-10)	in whose hand is the soul of every **living** thing, and
Job 37:6(5-7)	he saith to the **snow**, be thou on the earth; likewise
Job 38:4(4-41)	when I laid the foundations of the **earth**? declare, if
Job 39:1(1-30)	knowest thou...when the wild **goats** of the rock bring
Ps. 19:1	the **heavens** declare the glory of God; and the
Ps. 24:1(1-2)	the **earth** is the Lord's, and the fulness thereof; the
Ps. 29:3(1-11)	voice of the Lord is upon the **waters**: the God of glory
Ps. 74:17(16,17)	thou hast made **summer** and winter.
Ps. 104:10(8-22)	he sendeth the **springs** into the valleys, which run
Ps. 147:8(7-18)	who maketh **grass** to grow upon the mountains.
Ps. 148:8(7-13)	fire...hail...snow...vapour...**wind** fulfilling his word
Song. 2:12(11-13)	the **flowers** appear...the singing of birds is come, and
Isa. 11:6(6-9)	the **wolf** also shall dwell with the lamb, and the
Isa. 55:10(10-13)	**rain**...snow from heaven...watereth the earth, and make
Jer. 29:5	plant **gardens**, and eat the fruit of them
Matt. 10:31(28-31)	ye are of more value than many **sparrows**.
Matt. 13:32(31-32)	becometh a tree...**birds** of the air come and lodge in

316

NATURE cont.

Mark 4:28(26-29)	for the earth bringeth forth **fruit** of herself; first
Luke 8:25(22-25)	even the **winds** and water, and they obey him.
Luke 12:27(27-30)	consider the **lilies** how they grow: they toil not, they
Alma 30:44(44,45)	the **earth**, and all things that are upon the face of
3 Ne. 8:17(1-25)	**earth** became deformed, because of the tempests, and
3 Ne. 13:28(28-32)	consider the **lilies** of the field how they grow; they
D&C 29:16	there shall be a great **hailstorm** sent forth to destroy
D&C 43:25	called upon you...by the voice of **thunderings**, and by
D&C 84:82(82-83)	consider the **lilies** of the field, how they grow, they
D&C 88:7(7-13)	the light of the **sun**, and the power thereof by which
D&C 88:42(42-47)	all things...in their **times** and their seasons
D&C 89:10(1-21)	all wholesome **herbs** God hath ordained for the
D&C 104:17	the **earth** is full, and there is enough and to spare

NEIGHBOR

Ex. 20:16	shalt not bear false witness against thy **neighbour**.
Lev. 19:13(13-17)	thou shalt not defraud thy **neighbour**, neither rob him
Lev. 19:18	thou shalt love thy **neighbour** as thyself: I am the
Ps. 15:3	nor doeth evil to his **neighbour**, nor taketh up a
Prov. 27:10	for better is a **neighbour** that is near than a brother
Matt. 5:43	it hath been said, thou shalt love thy **neighbour**, and
Matt. 19:19	thou shalt love thy **neighbour** as thyself.
Matt. 25:40(31-46)	one of the **least** of these my brethren, ye have done
Luke 10:29(29-37)	said unto Jesus, and who is my **neighbour**
Rom. 13:9(8-10)	thou shalt love thy **neighbour** as thyself.
Rom. 15:2	please his **neighbour** for his good to edification.
James 2:8	thou shalt love thy **neighbour** as thyself, ye do well
2 Ne. 28:8	dig a pit for thy **neighbor**; there is no harm in this
Mosiah 2:17	service of your **fellow** beings...service of your God.
Mosiah 4:28	**neighbor** should **return** the thing that he borroweth
Mosiah 13:23(23-24)	shalt not bear false witness against thy **neighbor**.
Mosiah 18:8(7-9)	willing to bear one **another's** burdens, that they may
Mosiah 23:15	every man should love his **neighbor** as himself, that
Mosiah 26:31	he that forgiveth not his **neighbor's** trespasses when
Mosiah 27:4(3-5)	every man should esteem his **neighbor** as himself, labor
D&C 19:25	that thou shalt not covet thy **neighbor's** wife; nor see
D&C 38:41	warning voice, every man to his **neighbor**, in mildness
D&C 42:27	thou shalt not speak evil of thy **neighbor**, nor do him
D&C 45:68	not take his sword against his **neighbor** must needs
D&C 59:6(5-16)	thou shalt love thy **neighbor** as thyself. Thou shalt
D&C 82:19	every man seeking the interest of his **neighbor**, and
D&C 88:81	every man who hath been warned to warn his **neighbor**.
D&C 136:25(25-26)	if thou borrowest of thy **neighbor**, thou shalt restore

NEW AND EVERLASTING COVENANT

Gen. 9:16(9-17)	that I may remember the **everlasting** covenant between
Gen. 17:7(1-19)	I will establish my **covenant** between me and thee and
Num. 25:13	even the **covenant** of an everlasting priesthood
Isa. 24:5	changed the ordinance, broken the **everlasting** covenant

NEW AND EVERLASTING COVENANT cont.

Isa. 55:3   I will make an everlasting **covenant** with you, even the
Jer. 31:31(31-34)   I will make a **new** covenant with the house of Israel
Jer. 32:40(37-40)   and I will make an **everlasting** covenant with them
Ezek. 37:26   it shall be an **everlasting** covenant with them: and I
Heb. 8:13(6-13)   a **new** covenant, he hath made the first old. Now that
Heb. 12:24   Jesus the mediator of the **new** covenant, and to the
Heb. 13:20   through the blood of the **everlasting** covenant
D&C 1:15(15,22-23)   they have...broken mine **everlasting** covenant
D&C 22:1(1-4)   this is a new and an **everlasting** covenant, even that
D&C 45:9   I have sent mine **everlasting** covenant into the world
D&C 49:9   I have sent unto you mine **everlasting** covenant, even
D&C 66:2   **everlasting** covenant, even the fulness of my gospel
D&C 76:69   Jesus the mediator of the new **covenant**, who wrought
D&C 76:101   received not...the **everlasting** covenant.
D&C 101:39(39-40)   called unto mine **everlasting** gospel, and covenant with
D&C 131:2(1-3)   meaning the new and **everlasting** covenant of marriage
D&C 132:6(6,7)   and as pertaining to the new and **everlasting** covenant
D&C 132:19(15-27)   marry a wife by...new and **everlasting** covenant, and

OATHS

Gen. 24:3(1-3)   I will make thee **swear** by the Lord, the God of heaven
Gen. 50:25(24-26)   Joseph took an **oath** of the children of Israel, saying
Num. 30:2(1-2)   if a man...swear an **oath** to bind his soul with a bond
Deut. 7:8   he would keep the **oath** which he had sworn unto your
Deut. 29:12(10-15)   covenant with the Lord thy God, and into his **oath**
Ps. 110:4   the Lord hath **sworn**, and will not repent, thou art a
Matt. 5:33(33-37)   but shalt perform unto the Lord thine **oaths**
Luke 1:73(67-75)   the **oath** which he sware to our father Abraham
Acts 2:30(29-32)   God had sworn with an **oath** to him, that of the fruit
Heb. 6:16(13-20)   an **oath** for confirmation is to them an end of all
Heb. 7:20(20-21,28)   inasmuch as not without an **oath** he was made priest
Heb. 7:28(21-28)   but the word of the **oath**, which was since the law
James 5:12   swear not...by any other **oath**: but let your yea be yea
1 Ne. 4:37(32-37)   when Zoram had made an **oath**...our fears did cease
Alma 44:8(1-8)   we will not suffer ourselves to take an **oath** unto you
Alma 50:39   with an **oath** and sacred ordinance to judge righteously
Alma 53:11(11-15)   taken an **oath** that they never would shed blood more
Alma 53:14(11-15)   for they were about to break the **oath** which they had
Hel. 6:25(25,26)   secret **oaths** and covenants which Alma commanded his
Hel. 6:30   their plots, and their **oaths**, and their covenants, and
3 Ne. 12:33(33-37)   but shalt perform unto the Lord thine **oaths**
Ether 9:5   sworn by the **oath** of the ancients, and they obtained
D&C 84:39(33-41)   according to the **oath** and covenant which belongeth to
D&C 124:47   I will not perform the **oath** which I make unto you
D&C 132:7   all covenants, contracts, bonds, obligations, **oaths**
Moses 5:50(49-50)   getting gain, but he slew him for the **oath's** sake.

OBEDIENCE

Gen. 6:22	thus **did** Noah; according to all that God commanded him
Gen. 22:18	because thou hast **obeyed** my voice.
Gen. 26:5	because that Abraham **obeyed** my voice, and kept my
Ex. 15:26	if thou wilt diligently **hearken** to the voice of the
Ex. 19:5(5-6)	if ye will **obey** my voice indeed, and keep my covenant
Ex. 24:7	all...the Lord hath said will we do, and be **obedient**.
Lev. 18:26(26-28)	ye shall...**keep** my statutes and my judgments, and
Lev. 26:3(3,12)	if ye **walk** in my statutes, and keep my commandments
Lev. 26:21(21-46)	if ye walk **contrary** unto me...I will bring...plagues
Deut. 4:23(23-30)	lest ye forget the **covenant** of the Lord your God
Deut. 4:40	thou shalt **keep**...his statutes, and his commandments
Deut. 5:27(27-33)	we will hear it, and **do** it.
Deut. 6:3	hear therefore, O Israel, and **observe** to do it; that
Deut. 7:12(12-16)	if ye **hearken** to these judgments, and keep, and do the
Deut. 28:1(1-14)	if thou shalt **hearken** diligently unto the voice of the
Deut. 28:58(58-68)	if thou wilt not **observe**...all the words of this law
Deut. 30:20(15-20)	love the Lord...**obey** his voice...for he is thy life
1 Sam. 15:22(22-23)	behold, to **obey** is better than sacrifice, and to
2 Kgs. 22:13(11-20)	to **do** according unto all that which is written
Eccl. 12:13(13,14)	fear God, and **keep** his commandments: for this is the
Isa. 1:19(19-20)	if ye be willing and **obedient**, ye shall eat the good
Jer. 6:17(17-19)	I set watchmen over you, saying, **hearken**...we will not
Jer. 7:23(23-24)	**obey** my voice, and I will be your God, and ye shall
Jer. 11:4	saying, **obey** my voice, and do them, according to all
Zech. 6:15	if ye will diligently **obey** the voice of the Lord your
Matt. 7:21(21-23)	not every one...but he that **doeth** the will of my
Matt. 7:24(24-27)	whosoever heareth these sayings of mine, and **doeth** the
Matt. 26:39	nevertheless not as I will, but as thou **wilt**.
Luke 11:28	blessed are they that hear the word...and **keep** it.
John 7:17	if any man will **do** his will, he shall know of the
John 8:29	I **do** always those things that please him.
John 14:15	if ye love me, **keep** my commandments.
John 14:21	he that hath my commandments, and **keepeth** them, he it
John 15:10	if ye **keep** my commandments, ye shall abide in my love
Rom. 1:5	for **obedience** to the faith among all nations, for his
Rom. 5:19	by the **obedience** of one shall many be made righteous.
Rom. 6:16(14-18)	his servants ye are to whom ye **obey**; whether of sin
Rom. 16:26(25,26)	made known to all nations for the **obedience** of faith
1 Cor. 14:34	they are commanded to be under **obedience**, as also
2 Cor. 7:15	he remembereth the **obedience** of you all, how with
2 Cor. 10:5	bringing into captivity every thought to...**obedience**
Heb. 5:8(8-9)	learned he **obedience** by the things which he suffered
Heb. 11:8(7-8)	by faith Abraham, when he was called...**obeyed**; and he
James 2:17(14-20)	faith, if it hath not **works**, is dead, being alone.
James 4:17	knoweth to do good, and **doeth** it not, to him it is sin
1 Pet. 1:2	unto **obedience** and sprinkling of the blood of Jesus
1 Jn. 2:5(3-5)	but whoso **keepeth** his word, in him verily is the love
Rev. 22:14(12-14)	blessed are they that **do** his commandments, that they
1 Ne. 3:7	I will go and **do** the things which the Lord hath
2 Ne. 1:9	if..**keep** his commandments they shall be blessed upon
2 Ne. 31:7	he would be **obedient** unto him in keeping his
2 Ne. 33:15	the Lord commanded me, and I must **obey**. Amen.
3 Ne. 27:17(13-22)	he that **endureth** not unto the end, the same is he that

OBEDIENCE cont.

D&C 1:38	mine own **voice** or...of my servants, it is the same.
D&C 5:22	be firm in **keeping** the commandments wherewith I have
D&C 11:20	this is your work, to **keep** my commandments, yea, with
D&C 20:19(19-20)	commandments that they should love and **serve** him, the
D&C 20:77(77-79)	and keep his **commandments** which he has given them
D&C 42:29	if thou lovest me thou shalt...**keep** all my commandment
D&C 56:3	I, the Lord, command..he that will not **obey** shall be
D&C 58:2	blessed is he that **keepeth** my commandments, whether
D&C 63:5	the Lord, utter my voice, and it shall be **obeyed**.
D&C 64:34	the willing and **obedient** shall eat the good of the
D&C 82:10	bound when ye **do** what I say; but when ye do not what
D&C 93:1	**obeyeth** my voice, and keepeth my commandments, shall
D&C 93:28(20,27,28)	he that **keepeth** his commandments receiveth truth and
D&C 98:22	if ye observe to **do** whatsoever I command you, I, the
D&C 103:7	and by hearkening to **observe** all the words which I
D&C 105:6	people must...be chastened until...learn **obedience**
D&C 130:21(18-21)	by **obedience** to that law upon which it is predicated.
Moses 5:5(5-8)	Adam was **obedient** unto the commandments of the Lord.
Moses 8:13	Noah and his sons hearkened unto the Lord...gave **heed**
Abr. 3:25(24-25)	to see if they will **do** all things whatsoever the Lord
A of F 1:3	saved, by **obedience** to the laws and ordinances of the
A of F 1:12	We believe in...**obeying**, honoring, and sustaining the
JFS-V 1:4	and by **obedience** to the principles of the gospel

OBJECTIVES

Josh. 24:15(14,15)	but as for me and my house, we will **serve** the Lord.
Ps. 40:8	I delight to **do** thy will...thy law is within my heart.
Prov. 16:16(16,17)	much better...to get **wisdom** than gold! and to get
Matt. 5:48	be ye therefore **perfect**, even as your Father which is
Matt. 6:33	seek ye first the **kingdom** of God, and his
Matt. 7:7(7,8)	**seek**, and ye shall find; knock, and it shall be opened
Luke 20:35(34-36)	worthy to obtain that world, and the **resurrection** from
John 6:27	**labour**...for that meat which endureth unto everlasting
John 17:3	life eternal, that they might **know** thee the only true
Philip. 3:14(13,14)	I press toward the mark for the **prize** of the high call
1 Ne. 7:13	if...faithful...we shall obtain the land of **promise**
1 Ne. 8:21(21,24,30)	they might obtain the **path** which led unto the tree by
1 Ne. 10:19(17-19)	he that diligently **seeketh** shall find; and the
2 Ne. 9:42(41-43)	and whoso **knocketh**, to him will he open; and the wise
2 Ne. 31:20(17-21)	if ye shall press forward...ye shall have eternal **life**
Jacob 2:18(18-19)	before ye seek...riches, **seek**...the kingdom of God.
Mosiah 4:27	be diligent, that thereby he might win the **prize**
Alma 27:18	truly penitent and humble seeker of **happiness**.
Alma 32:13(13-16)	if he is compelled to be humble, seeketh **repentance**
3 Ne. 13:33	seek ye first the **kingdom** of God and his righteousness
3 Ne. 14:7(7,8)	**seek**, and ye shall find; knock, and it shall be opened
3 Ne. 27:29(28,29)	**knock**, and it shall be opened unto you; for he that
Moro. 9:6(3-6)	that we may **conquer** the enemy of all righteousness
D&C 4:7	**knock**, and it shall be opened unto you. Amen.
D&C 6:6	seek to bring forth and establish the cause of **Zion**
D&C 11:5(3-7)	if you will **knock** it shall be opened unto you.

OBJECTIVES cont.

D&C 11:21(20-22)   but first seek to obtain my **word**, and then shall your
D&C 14:5(3-6)   if you will **knock** it shall be opened unto you.
D&C 38:39   seek the **riches** which it is the will of the Father to
D&C 46:8(8-9)   seek ye earnestly the best **gifts**, always remembering
D&C 59:23   his reward, even **peace** in this world and eternal life
D&C 78:7(7-8)   a place in the **celestial** world, you must prepare yours
D&C 88:63(62,63)   **seek** me diligently and ye shall find me; ask, and ye
D&C 88:118   yea, seek ye out of the best books words of **wisdom**
D&C 90:24   search **diligently**, pray always, and be believing, and
D&C 97:2(1,2)   blessed are such, for they shall **obtain**; for I, the
D&C 103:36   all **victory**...through your diligence, faithfulness
D&C 104:82(79-83)   as ye are humble...I will give you the **victory**.
D&C 107:99(99,100)   let every man learn his **duty**, and to act in the office
D&C 128:11   consists in obtaining the **powers** of the Holy
D&C 130:19(18-19)   if a person gains...**intelligence**...through his

OFFENSES

2 Chr. 28:13   for whereas we have **offended** against the Lord already
Prov. 18:19   a brother **offended** is harder to be won than a strong
Isa. 8:14(13-17)   a rock of **offence** to both the houses of Israel, for
Isa. 29:21   that make a man an **offender** for a word, and lay a
Matt. 5:29   if thy right eye **offend** thee, pluck it out, and cast
Matt. 13:21(3-9,19-23)   persecution...because...word, by and by he is **offended**
Matt. 13:41   shall gather out of his kingdom all things that **offend**
Matt. 18:6   whoso shall **offend** one of these little ones which
Matt. 18:7   woe unto the world because of **offences**! for it must
Matt. 18:15(15-17)   if thy brother shall **trespass** against thee, go and
Matt. 26:31   all ye shall be **offended** because of me this night: for
Mark 9:42   whosoever shall **offend** one of these little ones that
Luke 17:1(1,2)   **offences** will come: but woe unto him, through whom the
John 6:61   he said unto them, doth this **offend** you
John 16:1   things have I spoken...that ye should not be **offended**.
Rom. 9:33   I lay in Sion a stumblingstone and rock of **offence**
1 Cor. 10:32   give none **offence**, neither to the Jews, nor to the
2 Cor. 6:3   giving no **offence** in any thing, that the ministry be
James 2:10   keep the whole law, and yet **offend** in one point, he
James 3:2   if any man **offend** not in word, the same is a perfect
1 Pet. 2:8   a stone of stumbling, and a rock of **offence**, even to
2 Ne. 27:32(31-32)   they that make a man an **offender** for a word, and lay
Alma 35:15   to be **offended** because of the strictness of the word
Alma 48:14   taught never to give an **offense**, yea, and never to
Ether 12:26   fools **mock**, but they shall mourn; and my grace is
D&C 20:80   any member of the church of Christ **transgressing**, or
D&C 42:88(88-93)   and if thy brother or sister **offend** thee, thou shalt
D&C 54:5   and wo to him by whom this **offense** cometh, for it had
D&C 59:21   nothing doth man **offend** God...save those who confess
D&C 134:8   bringing **offenders** against good laws to punishment.
JS-M 1:8(7-8)   then shall many be **offended**, and shall betray one
JS-H 1:28   temptations, **offensive** in the sight of God. In making

OLD AGE

Gen. 15:15	thou shalt be buried in a good **old** age.
Gen. 18:11(9-14)	Abraham and Sarah were **old** and well stricken in age
Gen. 21:2(1-2)	conceived, and bare Abraham a son in his **old** age, at
Gen. 25:8	and died in a good **old** age, an old man, and full of
Ex. 10:9	we will go with our young and with our **old**, with our
Ruth 4:15(13-15)	he shall be unto thee...a nourisher of thine **old** age
1 Kgs. 12:8(6-8)	but he forsook the counsel of the **old** men, which they
Job 12:12	with the **ancient** is wisdom; and in length of days
Ps. 71:9	cast me not off in the time of **old** age; forsake me not
Ps. 92:14(13-15)	shall still bring forth fruit in **old** age; they shall
Prov. 20:29	the beauty of **old** men is the gray head.
Isa. 46:4	even to your **old** age I am he; and even to hoar hairs
Isa. 65:20	nor an **old** man that hath not filled his days: for the
Joel 2:28(28-32)	your **old** men shall dream dreams, your young men shall
Zech. 8:4(4-5)	there shall yet **old** men and old women dwell in the
Luke 1:36(36-37)	she hath also conceived a son in her **old** age: and this
John 21:18	but when thou shalt be **old**, thou shalt stretch forth
Acts 21:16	an **old** disciple, with whom we should lodge.
Rom. 4:19	when he was about an hundred years **old**, neither yet
1 Tim. 5:9	widow...under threescore years **old**, having been the
Titus 2:2(1,2)	that the **aged** men be sober, grave, temperate, sound
2 Ne. 4:12	my father Lehi...he waxed **old**. And it came to pass
Mosiah 1:9	he waxed **old**, and he saw that he must very soon go the
Mosiah 2:40	O, all ye **old** men, and also ye young men, and you
Mosiah 10:10(9-10)	I, in my **old** age, did go up to battle against the
Mosiah 10:22	and now I, being **old**, did confer the kingdom upon one
Alma 5:49	to preach unto all, both **old** and young, both bond and
Alma 46:41	there were many who died with **old** age; and those who
Ether 10:16	he did live to a good **old** age, and begat sons and
D&C 43:20	repent, both **old** and young, both bond and free
D&C 63:51(50-51)	children shall grow up until they become **old**; old men
D&C 90:20(20,25)	let mine **aged** servant, Joseph Smith, Sen., continue
D&C 101:30	an infant shall not die until he is **old**; and his life
D&C 107:43(42-56)	could be distinguised from him only by his **age**.
D&C 124:19	my **aged** servant Joseph Smith, Sen., who sitteth with

OPPOSITION

Gen. 2:9	tree of life...and..tree of **knowledge** of good and evil
Gen. 3:18(17-19)	**thorns** also and thistles shall it bring forth to thee
Matt. 5:44	love your **enemies**, bless them that curse you, do good
Acts 26:14	hard for thee to kick **against** the pricks.
Rom. 7:19(15-20)	the **good** that I would I do not: but the evil which I
Rom. 8:7	the carnal mind is **enmity** against God: for it is not
Eph. 6:12	for we wrestle not **against** flesh and blood, but
2 Thes. 2:4(3,4)	who **opposeth** and exalteth himself above all that is
2 Tim. 3:8	these also **resist** the truth: men of corrupt minds
James 1:3	that the **trying** of your faith worketh patience.
James 4:4	friendship of the world is **enmity** with God? whosoever
1 Pet. 1:7	the **trial** of your faith, being much more precious than
2 Ne. 2:11(11-13)	must needs be...an **opposition** in all things. If not
2 Ne. 2:15(15-16)	the forbidden fruit in **opposition** to the tree of life

OPPOSITION cont.

2 Ne. 2:27(26,27)	free to **choose** liberty and eternal life, through the
Alma 42:16(16-22)	punishment...affixed **opposite** to the plan of happiness
Ether 12:6(6-7)	receive no witness until after the **trial** of your faith
D&C 29:39(39-40)	devil should **tempt**...men, or they could not be agents
D&C 58:4(2-4)	for after much **tribulation** come the blessings.
D&C 122:7(5-7)	these things shall give thee **experience**, and shall be
D&C 136:31	my people must be **tried** in all things, that they may
Moses 6:55(55,56)	taste the **bitter**, that they may know to prize the

OPPRESSION

Ex. 22:21	neither vex a stranger, nor **oppress** him: for ye were
Lev. 25:17	ye shall not therefore **oppress** one another; but thou
Deut. 26:7	looked on our affliction...and our **oppression**
2 Kgs. 13:4(4,5)	he saw the **oppression** of Israel, because the king of
Job 27:13(13-23)	portion of a wicked man...the heritage of **oppressors**
Ps. 9:9	Lord also will be a refuge for the **oppressed**, a refuge
Ps. 119:134	deliver me from the **oppression** of man: so will I keep
Ps. 146:7(5-9)	which executeth judgment for the **oppressed**: which give
Prov. 3:31	envy thou not the **oppressor**, and choose none of his
Prov. 14:31	he that **oppresseth** the poor reproacheth his maker: but
Prov. 22:16	he that **oppresseth** the poor to increase his riches
Prov. 28:3	a poor man that **oppresseth** the poor is like a sweeping
Eccl. 5:8	if thou seest the **oppression** of the poor, and violent
Isa. 49:26(24-26)	I will feed them that **oppress** thee with their own
Isa. 53:7(7-9)	he was **oppressed**, and he was afflicted, yet he opened
Acts 7:24	and avenged him that was **oppressed**, and smote the
Acts 10:38	Jesus...healing all that were **oppressed** of the devil
James 2:6	do not rich men **oppress** you, and draw you before the
2 Ne. 8:13(12-16)	feared continually...because of..fury of the **oppressor**
2 Ne. 13:5(1-8)	the people shall be **oppressed**, every one by another
2 Ne. 15:7(1-9)	he looked for judgment, and behold, **oppression**; for
2 Ne. 19:4(1-7)	thou hast broken...the rod of his **oppressor**.
2 Ne. 24:2(1-12)	and they shall rule over their **oppressors**.
Mosiah 13:35	he, himself, should be **oppressed** and afflicted
Mosiah 14:7	he was **oppressed**, and he was afflicted, yet he opened
Mosiah 23:12(12-13)	ye have been **oppressed** by king Noah, and have been in
Alma 32:5(1-16)	they are **despised** of all men because of their poverty
Hel. 4:12(11-13)	it was because of their **oppression** to the poor
3 Ne. 24:5(2-6)	those that **oppress** the hireling...widow...fatherless
D&C 109:48(47-51)	they have been greatly **oppressed** and afflicted by
D&C 109:67	be redeemed from **oppression**, and rejoice before thee.
D&C 121:3(1-8)	how long shall they suffer these...unlawful **oppression**
D&C 123:3(1-17)	all persons that have had a hand in their **oppressions**
D&C 124:8(1-9)	appoint the portion of the **oppressor** among hypocrites
D&C 124:53(49-54)	hindered by the hands of their enemies...by **oppression**
D&C 127:3(1-3)	a just recompense...upon...all their **oppressors**.

ORDER

Gen. 1:12(11,12)	seed was in itself, after his **kind**: and God saw that
Gen. 1:14(14-19)	and let them be for signs, and for **seasons**, and for
Gen. 1:24(24-25)	earth bring forth the living creature after his **kind**
Ex. 40:23	set the bread in **order** upon it before the Lord; as the
Lev. 1:7(7-12)	and lay the wood in **order** upon the fire
Lev. 24:3(3-8)	shall Aaron **order** it from the evening unto the morning
1 Chr. 6:32	on their office according to their **order**.
2 Chr. 29:35	service of the house...was set in **order**.
Job 10:22(20-22)	land of darkness...without any **order**, and where the
Acts 17:26	determined the times...and the **bounds** of their
1 Cor. 14:40(37-40)	let all things be done decently and in **order**.
1 Cor. 15:23(21-23)	every man in his own **order**: Christ the firstfruits
Col. 2:5(1-7)	with you in the spirit...beholding your **order**, and the
Titus 1:5	thou shouldest set in **order** the things that are
Mosiah 4:27	see that all these things are done in wisdom and **order**
Alma 41:2(2-4)	restored to their proper **order**. Behold, it is
3 Ne. 6:4(4-5)	years passed...and there was great **order** in the land
Moro. 9:18	depravity...without **order** and without mercy. Behold
D&C 20:68(68-69)	so that all things may be done in **order**.
D&C 28:13	all things must be done in **order**, and by common
D&C 58:55	these things be done in **order**; and let the privileges
D&C 77:3(2,3)	glory of the classes of beings in their destined **order**
D&C 85:7	to set in **order** the house of God, and to arrange by
D&C 88:34(34-39)	that which is **governed** by law is also preserved by law
D&C 88:37(34-39)	no space in the which there is no **kingdom**; and there
D&C 88:42(42-47)	given a **law** unto all things, by which they move in the
D&C 88:60(51-61)	every man in his own **order**, until his hour was
D&C 88:119(117-126)	house of glory, a house of **order**, a house of God
D&C 90:16(15,16)	set in **order** all the affairs of this church and
D&C 90:18	set in **order** your houses; keep slothfulness and
D&C 93:43(43-44)	if you will be delivered...set in **order** your own house
D&C 93:50	hath need to...set in **order** his family, and see that
D&C 107:84	that all things may be done in **order** and in solemnity
D&C 109:8	house of glory, a house of **order**, a house of God
D&C 129:7(6-7)	contrary to the **order** of heaven for a just man to
D&C 132:8(7-14)	mine house is a house of **order**, saith the Lord God
Abr. 1:26	to imitate that **order** established by the fathers in
Abr. 3:9(2-14)	govern...those planets which belong to the same **order**
Abr. 4:18(7-18)	the Gods watched those things...they had **ordered** until

ORDINANCES

Ex. 18:20	teach them **ordinances** and laws, and shalt shew them
Lev. 18:4(3-5)	do my judgments, and keep mine **ordinances**, to walk the
2 Kgs. 17:37(32-41)	and the **ordinances**, and the law, and the commandment
Isa. 24:5(3-6)	they have transgressed the laws, changed the **ordinance**
Isa. 58:2(1,2)	they ask of me the **ordinances** of justice; they take
Jer. 31:36(35,36)	if those **ordinances** depart from before me, saith the
Ezek. 11:20(19-21)	walk in my statutes, and keep mine **ordinances**, and do
Ezek. 43:11(11-12)	keep the whole form thereof, and all the **ordinances**
Mal. 3:7	ye are gone away from mine **ordinances**, and have not
Luke 1:6(5,6)	walking in...commandments and **ordinances** of the Lord

ORDINANCES cont.

1 Cor. 11:2(1-3)	keep the **ordinances,** as I delivered them to you.
Eph. 2:15	commandments contained in **ordinances;** for to make in
Col. 2:20	in the world, are ye subject to **ordinances**
Heb. 9:1	covenant had also **ordinances** of divine service, and a
Heb. 9:10(9-28)	washings, and carnal **ordinances,** imposed on them
2 Ne. 25:30(29,30)	the performances and **ordinances** of God until the law
Mosiah 13:30(27-32)	law of performances and of **ordinances,** a law which
Alma 13:16(8-16)	now these **ordinances** were given after this manner
Alma 25:15	must keep those outward **performances** until the time
Alma 30:3(2,3)	strict in observing the **ordinances** of God, according
Alma 31:10	neither would they observe the **performances** of the
Alma 43:45	for their **rites** of worship and their church.
Alma 44:5	by our religion, and by our **rites** of worship, and by
Alma 50:39	with an oath and sacred **ordinance** to judge righteously
3 Ne. 24:7	ye are gone away from mine **ordinances,** and have not
3 Ne. 24:14	what...profit that we have kept his **ordinances** and
4 Ne. 1:12(10-13)	not walk...after the...**ordinances** of the law of Moses
D&C 1:15	for they have strayed from mine **ordinances,** and have
D&C 52:15(14-16)	same is accepted of me if he obey mine **ordinances.**
D&C 64:5	inasmuch as he obeyeth mine **ordinances.**
D&C 84:20(20-21)	in the **ordinances**...the power of godliness is manifest
D&C 107:20(20-21)	outward **ordinances,** the letter of the gospel, the
D&C 121:19(16-22)	shall be severed from the **ordinances** of mine house.
D&C 124:40(38-40)	that I may reveal mine **ordinances** therein unto my
D&C 128:8	whether they ...have attended to the **ordinances** in the
D&C 136:4(2-4)	our covenant- that we will walk in all the **ordinances**
Moses 5:6(5-8)	why dost thou offer **sacrifices** unto the Lord? And Adam
A of F 1:3	obedience to the laws and **ordinances** of the gospel.
A of F 1:4	the first principles and **ordinances** of the gospel are
JFS-V 1:58(57-60)	obedience to the **ordinances** of the house of God.

PAIN

Job 14:22	but his flesh upon him shall have **pain,** and his soul
Ps. 25:18(16-20)	look upon mine affliction and my **pain;** and forgive all
Ps. 55:4(1-6)	my heart is sore **pained** within me: and the terrors of
Ps. 116:3(1-6)	the **pains** of hell gat hold upon me: I found trouble
Ps. 119:143(143-144)	trouble and **anguish** have taken hold on me: yet thy
Isa. 13:8(6-20)	they shall be in **pain** as a woman that travaileth: they
Jer. 4:19(19-22)	I am **pained** at my very heart; my heart maketh a noise
Jer. 30:23(22-24)	it shall fall with **pain** upon the head of the wicked.
Matt. 13:42(37-43)	there shall be wailing and **gnashing** of teeth.
Matt. 26:38(36-42)	my soul is exceeding **sorrowful,** even unto death: tarry
Luke 22:44(41-46)	being in an **agony** he prayed more earnestly: and his
John 16:20(20-24)	your **sorrow** shall be turned into joy.
Acts 2:24(14-40)	having loosed the **pains** of death: because it was not
Rom. 8:18(14-23)	**sufferings** of this present time are not worthy to be
2 Cor. 11:27(23-28)	in weariness and **painfulness,** in watchings often, in
2 Cor. 12:7(7-9)	there was given to me a **thorn** in the flesh, the
Heb. 5:8(4-10)	learned he obedience by the things which he **suffered**
1 Pet. 3:18(18-21)	Christ also hath once **suffered** for sins, the just for
Rev. 16:11(10,11)	blasphemed the God...because of their **pains** and their

PAIN cont.

Rev. 21:4(1-4)	neither shall there be any more **pain**: for the former
1 Ne. 17:47(41-47)	and my heart is **pained**; I fear lest ye shall be cast
2 Ne. 9:21(21-22)	he suffereth the **pains** of all men, yea, the pains of
2 Ne. 26:7(3-11)	O the **pain**, and the anguish of my soul for the loss
Jacob 3:11(9-11)	loose yourselves from the **pains** of hell that ye may
Mosiah 2:38(36-41)	doth fill his breast with guilt, and **pain**, and
Mosiah 3:7(7-8)	he shall suffer temptations, and **pain** of body, hunger
Mosiah 25:11	filled with **pain** and anguish for the welfare of their
Mosiah 27:29	my soul is **pained** no more.
Alma 7:11(10-16)	shall go forth, suffering **pains** and afflictions and
Alma 7:11(11-12)	suffering **pains** and afflictions and temptations of
Alma 13:27	I wish...even unto **pain**, that ye would hearken unto
Alma 14:6(6-11)	began to be encircled about by the **pains** of hell.
Alma 31:30(30-35)	wickedness among this people doth **pain** my soul.
Alma 36:16(1-21)	I racked, even with the **pains** of a damned soul.
Alma 38:8	I was three days...in the most bitter **pain** and anguish
3 Ne. 28:9(1-40)	ye shall not have **pain** while ye shall dwell in the
D&C 18:11(10-12)	wherefore he suffered the **pain** of all men, that all
D&C 19:18(15-20)	suffering caused myself...to tremble because of **pain**
D&C 45:4(3-5)	behold the **sufferings** and death of him who did no sin
Moses 4:22(22-23)	in **sorrow** thou shalt bring forth children, and thy
Moses 7:48(48-52)	I am **pained**, I am weary, because of the wickedness

PARADISE

Job 3:17(13-19)	troubling; and there the weary be at **rest**.
Isa. 57:2(1,2)	he shall enter into **peace**: they shall rest in their
Dan. 12:13(12,13)	for thou shalt **rest**, and stand in thy lot at the end
Luke 23:43	today shalt thou be with me in **paradise**.
2 Cor. 12:4	that he was caught up into **paradise**, and heard
Rev. 2:7	tree of life...in the...**paradise** of God.
Rev. 6:11(9-11)	that they should **rest** yet for a little season, until
Rev. 14:13	which die in the Lord...may **rest** from their labours
2 Ne. 9:13(13-14)	the **paradise** of God must deliver up the spirits of
Alma 40:12(11-14)	a state of happiness, which is called **paradise**, a
4 Ne. 1:14	had all gone to the **paradise** of God, save it were the
Moro. 10:34	I soon go to rest in the **paradise** of God, until my
D&C 59:2(1,2)	those that die shall **rest** from all their labors, and
D&C 77:2(2,5)	the **paradise** of God, the happiness of man, and of
D&C 124:86(85,86)	die unto me; for they shall **rest** from all their labors
A of F 1:10	earth will be renewed...receive its **paradisiacal** glory
JFS-V 1:16(11-19)	awaiting...the Son of God into the **spirit** world, to
JFS-V 1:36(35-49)	in the world of **spirits**...preparing...the prophets who

PASSOVER

Gen. 22:8(7-13)	God will provide himself a **lamb** for a burnt offering
Ex. 12:5(3-14)	your **lamb** shall be without blemish, a male of the
Ex. 12:17(15-20)	and ye shall observe the **feast** of unleavened bread
Ex. 12:21(1-21)	take you a lamb...and kill the **passover**.
Ex. 12:23(21-28)	Lord will **pass** over the door, and will not suffer the

PASSOVER cont.

Ex. 12:43(30-48)	this is the ordinance of the **passover**: there shall no
Ex. 12:46	neither shall ye break a **bone** thereof.
Ex. 23:15	shalt keep the **feast** of unleavened bread: (thou shalt
Lev. 23:5(5,6)	fourteenth day of the first month..the Lord's **passover**
Lev. 23:12	a he **lamb** without blemish of the first year for a
Num. 9:14(13,14)	and will keep the **passover** unto the Lord; according
Josh. 5:10(10,11)	and kept the **passover** on the fourteenth day of the
2 Chr. 30:13(13-22)	keep the feast of **unleavened** bread in the second
Ezra 6:19(19,20)	children of the captivity kept the **passover** upon the
Matt. 26:2(1-2)	after two days is the feast of the **passover**, and the
Matt. 26:17	where...that we prepare for thee to eat the **passover**
Matt. 27:62	next day, that followed the day of the **preparation**
Mark 14:12	go and prepare that thou mayest eat the **passover**
Mark 14:22(12-22)	Jesus took **bread**, and blessed, and brake it, and gave
Mark 15:42	even was come...**preparation**...day before the sabbath
Luke 22:1	feast of unleavened bread...called the **passover**.
Luke 22:7	day of unleavened bread, when the **passover** must be
Luke 23:54	that day was the **preparation**, and the sabbath drew on.
John 1:29	behold the **Lamb** of God, which taketh away the sin of
John 1:36	looking upon Jesus...he saith, behold the **Lamb** of God
John 2:23(13,23)	in Jerusalem at the **passover**, in the feast day, many
John 5:1	there was a **feast** of the Jews; and Jesus went up to
John 6:4	and the **passover**, a feast of the Jews, was nigh.
John 19:14(14,31)	it was the preparation of the **passover**, and about the
John 19:33(32-36)	he was dead already, they **brake** not his legs
John 19:42	laid...Jesus...because of the Jews' **preparation** day
1 Cor. 5:7(6-8)	even Christ our **passover** is sacrificed for us
1 Pet. 1:19(18-19)	blood of Christ, as of a **lamb** without blemish and with
2 Ne. 11:4	given of God...unto man, are the **typifying** of him.
Mosiah 3:15(14-15)	many signs, and wonders, and **types**, and shadows showed
Mosiah 14:7	as a **lamb** to the slaughter, and as a sheep before her
Moses 7:47(45-47)	the **Lamb** is slain from the foundation of the world

PATIENCE

Gen. 26:22(17-22)	and he **removed** from thence, and digged another well
Job 1:21(13-22)	the Lord gave, and the Lord hath **taken** away; blessed
Job 2:10(9,10)	**good** at the hand of God, and shall we not receive evil
Ps. 37:7(7-11)	rest in the Lord, and wait **patiently** for him: fret not
Prov. 14:29	he that is slow to **wrath** is of great understanding
Prov. 15:1	a **soft** answer turneth away wrath: but grievous words
Eccl. 7:8(8,9)	the **patient** in spirit is better than the proud in
Matt. 5:39(38-47)	whosoever shall smite thee on thy right **cheek**, turn
Matt. 18:22(21-35)	not...seven times: but, until **seventy** times seven.
Luke 21:19	in your **patience** possess ye your souls.
John 16:20(20-22)	but your **sorrow** shall be turned into joy.
Rom. 2:7	**patient** continuance in well doing seek...eternal life
Rom. 5:3(3,4)	knowing that tribulation worketh **patience**
Rom. 15:4(4-7)	through **patience** and comfort of the scriptures might
2 Cor. 6:4(3-6)	ourselves as the ministers of God, in much **patience**
1 Thes. 1:3(2-4)	labour of love, and **patience** of hope in our Lord Jesus
Heb. 6:12(11-15)	followers...through faith and **patience** inherit the

PATIENCE cont.

Heb. 10:36(35-38)	for ye have need of **patience**, that, after ye have done
Heb. 12:1(1-3)	and let us run with **patience** the race that is set
James 1:3(2-4)	that the trying of your faith worketh **patience**.
James 1:19(19,20)	be swift to hear, slow to speak, **slow** to wrath
James 5:8(7,8)	be ye also **patient**; stablish your hearts: for the
1 Pet. 2:20(18-23)	do well, and suffer for it, ye take it **patiently**, this
2 Pet. 1:6(5-9)	to temperance **patience**; and to patience godliness
Rev. 1:9	in the kingdom and **patience** of Jesus Christ, was in
Rev. 13:10	here is the **patience** and the faith of the saints.
Rev. 14:12(12,13)	here is the **patience** of the saints: here are they that
Mosiah 3:19	becometh as a child, submissive, meek, humble, **patient**
Mosiah 23:21(19-24)	yea, he trieth their **patience** and their faith.
Mosiah 24:15(13-16)	did submit...with **patience** to all the will of the Lord
Alma 1:25(24,25)	they bore with **patience** the persecution which was
Alma 7:23	I would that ye should be humble...full of **patience**
Alma 17:11	yet ye shall be **patient** in long-suffering and
Alma 26:27(27-30)	bear with **patience** thine afflictions, and I will give
Alma 32:41(41-43)	but if ye will nourish the word ...with **patience**, look
Alma 34:40(40,41)	I would exhort you to have **patience**, and that ye bear
Alma 38:4(3-5)	thou didst bear all these things with **patience** because
3 Ne. 12:44(38-44)	**bless** them that curse you, do good to them that hate
D&C 4:6	faith, virtue, knowledge, temperance, **patience**
D&C 24:8	be **patient** in afflictions, for thou shalt have many
D&C 31:9	be **patient** in afflictions, revile not against those
D&C 54:10	be **patient** in tribulation until I come; and, behold
D&C 64:33(31-33)	wherefore, be not **weary** in well-doing, for ye are
D&C 67:13	wherefore, continue in **patience** until ye are perfected
D&C 98:2(1-3)	waiting **patiently** on the Lord, for your prayers have
D&C 98:26(23-31)	the third time, and ye bear it **patiently**, your reward
D&C 101:38	seek...the Lord...in **patience** ye may possess your soul
D&C 121:41(41-44)	only by persuasion, by **long-suffering**, by gentleness
D&C 127:4	diligence...perseverance, and **patience**...redoubled

PATRIARCHS

Gen. 25:5(5,6)	and **Abraham** gave all that he had unto Isaac.
Gen. 49:1(1-27)	and Jacob called unto his **sons**, and said, gather yours
Gen. 50:23(22-26)	Joseph saw Ephraim's **children** of the third generation
Acts 2:29(29-32)	freely speak unto you of the **patriarch** David, that he
Acts 7:8(7,8)	Jacob begat the twelve **patriarchs**.
Eph. 4:11(11-14)	some, prophets...**evangelists**...pastors and teachers
Heb. 7:4	even the **patriarch** Abraham gave the tenth of the spoil
2 Ne. 1:1(1-32)	our **father**, Lehi, also spake many things unto them
2 Ne. 2:1(1-30)	and now, **Jacob**, I speak unto you: thou art my
2 Ne. 3:1(1-25)	and now I speak unto you, **Joseph**, my last-born. Thou
2 Ne. 4:3(3-12)	behold, my **sons**, and my daughters, who are the sons
Enos 1:1	**father**...taught me in his language, and also in the
1:3	commandments of my **fathers**; and I conferred them upon
D&C 84:16(6-16)	received the priesthood...by...his **father** Adam, who
D&C 86:10(8-11)	**priesthood** have remained...through you and your
D&C 107:41(39-56)	this **order** was instituted in the days of Adam, and
D&C 124:92(91-96)	he shall hold the keys of the **patriarchal** blessings

PATRIARCHS cont.

D&C 124:124	I give unto you Hyrum Smith to be a **patriarch** unto you
Moses 6:7	now this same **Priesthood**, which was in the beginning
Abr. 1:3(1-4)	it was conferred upon me from the **fathers**; it came
Abr. 2:10(9-11)	shall rise up and bless thee, as their **father**
Abr. 2:11	this right shall continue in thee..thy **seed** after thee
A of F 1:6	prophets, pastors, teachers, **evangelists**, etc.

PEACE

Deut. 20:10(10-12)	fight against it, then proclaim **peace** unto it.
Ps. 28:3	speak **peace** to their neighbours, but mischief is in
Ps. 29:11	Lord will bless his people with **peace**.
Ps. 34:14	do good; seek **peace**, and pursue it.
Ps. 37:37	the perfect man...end of that man is **peace**.
Ps. 46:9(8-9)	he maketh **wars** to cease unto the end of the earth; he
Ps. 119:165	great **peace** have they which love thy law: and nothing
Ps. 122:6(6-8)	pray for the **peace** of Jerusalem: they shall prosper
Prov. 16:7	he maketh even his enemies to be at **peace** with him.
Isa. 2:4(2-4)	neither shall they learn **war** any more.
Isa. 9:6	the everlasting Father, the Prince of **Peace**.
Isa. 11:9(1-9)	they shall not hurt nor **destroy** in all my holy
Isa. 32:17(17-18)	the work of righteousness shall be **peace**; and the
Isa. 48:22	there is no **peace**, saith the Lord, unto the wicked.
Isa. 52:7(7-10)	bringeth good tidings, that publisheth **peace**; that
Isa. 57:21(19-21)	there is no **peace**, saith my God, to the wicked.
Isa. 65:25	the **wolf** and the lamb shall feed together, and the
Jer. 6:14	saying, **peace**, peace; when there is no peace.
Ezek. 13:10(10-16)	seduced..people, saying, **peace**; and there was no peace
Ezek. 13:16	visions of **peace** for her, and there is no peace
Hosea 2:18	I will...make them to lie down **safely**.
Micah 3:5	prophets...that bite with their teeth, and cry, **peace**
Hag. 2:9	in this place will I give **peace**, saith the Lord of
Matt. 5:9	blessed are the **peacemakers**...shall be called the
Matt. 10:34(34-36)	think not that I am come to send **peace** on earth: I
Mark 4:39(37-39)	said unto the sea, **peace**, be still. And the wind cease
Mark 9:50	salt in yourselves, and have **peace** one with another.
Luke 2:14(13-15)	glory to God in the highest, and on earth **peace**, good
John 14:27(26-27)	peace I leave with you, my **peace** I give unto you: not
Rom. 12:18(17-21)	if it be possible...live **peaceably** with all men.
Rom. 14:19(17-19)	follow after the things which make for **peace**, and
1 Cor. 14:33	God is not the author of confusion, but of **peace**, as
2 Cor. 13:11	live in **peace**; and the God of love and peace shall be
Eph. 2:14(12-17)	for he is our **peace**, who hath made both one, and hath
1 Tim. 2:2	lead a quiet and **peaceable** life in all godliness and
2 Tim. 2:22	follow righteousness, faith, charity, **peace**, with them
Heb. 12:11	it yieldeth the **peaceable** fruit of righteousness unto
James 3:18(17-18)	righteousness is sown in **peace** of them that make peace
1 Ne. 13:37	whoso shall publish **peace**, yea, tidings of great joy
1 Ne. 14:7(6-7)	the convincing of them unto **peace** and life eternal
1 Ne. 20:18(17-18)	had thy **peace** been as a river, and thy righteousness
2 Ne. 4:27(27,28)	why..yield to......the evil one...to destroy my **peace**
2 Ne. 19:6	and his name shall be called...the Prince of **Peace**.

PEACE cont.

2 Ne. 26:9	shall have **peace** with him, until three generations
W of M 1:18(16-18)	by laboring..did once more establish **peace** in the land
Mosiah 4:3(2-3)	having **peace** of conscience, because of the exceeding
Mosiah 4:13(11-13)	will not have a mind to injure...but to live **peaceably**
Mosiah 12:21(20-24)	beautiful...feet of him...that publisheth **peace**; that
Mosiah 15:18(13-19)	the founder of **peace**...even the Lord, who has
Mosiah 27:4(3-4)	let no pride nor haughtiness disturb their **peace**; that
Mosiah 29:14	to establish **peace** throughout the land, that there
Alma 24:19	they buried the weapons of war, for **peace**.
Alma 36:19(9-21)	I could remember my **pains** no more; yea, I was harrowed
Alma 38:8	I did cry unto him and I did find **peace** to my soul.
Alma 44:14(14,15,20)	deliver...weapons of war ...with a covenant of **peace**.
Alma 46:12	in memory of our God...and our **peace**, our wives, and
Alma 58:11	he did speak **peace** to our souls, and did grant unto
3 Ne. 12:9	blessed are all the **peacemakers**, for they shall be
4 Ne. 1:4(1-25)	there still continued to be **peace** in the land.
D&C 1:35	when **peace** shall be taken from the earth, and the
D&C 6:23(21-24)	did I not speak **peace** to your mind concerning the
D&C 45:66(66-71)	New Jerusalem, a land of **peace**, a city of refuge, a
D&C 59:23	**peace** in this world and eternal life in the world to
D&C 88:125	charity...which is the bond of perfectness and **peace**.
D&C 98:16	renounce war and proclaim **peace**, and seek diligently
D&C 98:34(33-37)	first lift a standard of **peace** unto that people
D&C 101:26	the **enmity** of all flesh, shall cease from before my
D&C 105:39(38-40)	lift up an ensign of **peace**, and make a proclamation
D&C 134:2	that no government can exist in **peace**, except such law
D&C 134:8	for the public **peace** and tranquility all men should

PEACE OF GOD

Num. 6:26(24-26)	countenance upon thee, and give thee **peace**.
Job 22:21	acquaint now thyself with him, and be at **peace**
Ps. 23:6	surely **goodness** and mercy shall follow me all the days
Ps. 85:8(8-9)	he will speak **peace** unto his people, and to his saints
Ps. 119:165	great **peace** have they which love thy law: and nothing
Prov. 3:2(1-2)	long life, and **peace**, shall they add to thee.
Prov. 16:7	he maketh even his enemies to be at **peace** with him.
Isa. 9:6(6-7)	God, the everlasting Father, the Prince of **Peace**.
Isa. 26:3	thou wilt keep him in perfect **peace**, whose mind is
Isa. 32:17(17-18)	the work of righteousness shall be **peace**; and the
Isa. 48:18	then had thy **peace** been as a river, and thy righteous
Isa. 48:22	there is no **peace**, saith the Lord, unto the wicked.
Isa. 59:8(1-8)	the way of **peace** they know not; and there is no
Hag. 2:9	in this place will I give **peace**, saith the Lord of
Mark 5:34	daughter, thy faith hath made thee whole; go in **peace**
Luke 10:5(5-6)	house ye enter, first say, **peace** be to this house.
John 14:27	**peace** I leave with you, my peace I give unto you: not
John 16:33	that in me ye might have **peace**. In the world ye shall
John 20:19(19-21,26)	saith unto them, **peace** be unto you.
Rom. 2:10(9-10)	glory, honour, and **peace**, to every man that worketh
Rom. 5:1	justified by faith, we have **peace** with God through our
Rom. 8:6(5-9)	to be spiritually minded is life and **peace**.

PEACE OF GOD cont.

Rom. 10:15	preach the gospel of **peace**, and bring glad tidings of
Rom. 14:17(17-19)	but righteousness, and **peace**, and joy in the Holy
Rom. 15:13	God of hope fill you with all joy and **peace** in
1 Cor. 1:3(1-3)	grace be unto you, and **peace**, from God our Father, and
1 Cor. 14:33	not the author of confusion, but of **peace**, as in all
Gal. 5:22(22-23)	fruit of the spirit is love, joy, **peace**, longsuffering
Eph. 2:14(13-17)	for he is our **peace**, who hath made both one, and hath
Eph. 6:15	feet shod with the preparation of the gospel of **peace**
Philip. 4:7(4-7)	and the **peace** of God, which passeth all understanding
Col. 3:15(12-15)	and let the **peace** of God rule in your hearts, to the
Heb. 10:2	purged should have had no more **conscience** of sins.
Heb. 12:14	follow **peace**...without which no man shall see the Lord
James 3:18(17-18)	fruit of righteousness is sown in **peace** of them that
1 Pet. 3:11(10-12)	do good; let him seek **peace**, and ensue it.
Rev. 7:14(13-17)	came **out** of great tribulation, and have washed their
1 Ne. 14:7(6-7)	convincing of them unto **peace** and life eternal, or
1 Ne. 20:22	no **peace**, saith the Lord, unto the wicked.
2 Ne. 4:27	have place in my heart to destroy my **peace** and afflict
Mosiah 4:3(2-3)	having **peace** of conscience, because of the exceeding
Mosiah 12:21(20-24)	beautiful...feet of him that...publisheth **peace**; that
Mosiah 15:18(13-18)	that is the founder of **peace**, yea, even the Lord, who
Mosiah 27:37(34-37)	they did publish **peace**; they did publish good tidings
Alma 38:8(8,15)	and I did find **peace** to my soul.
Alma 40:12	a state of **peace**, where they shall rest from all their
Alma 41:10	I say unto you, wickedness never was **happiness**.
Hel. 5:47(45-48)	**peace**, peace be unto you, because of your faith in my
3 Ne. 20:40	bringeth good tidings...publisheth **peace**; that
D&C 6:23(22-23)	did I not speak **peace** to your mind concerning the
D&C 19:23	you shall have **peace** in me.
D&C 45:46	if ye have slept in **peace** blessed are you; for as you
D&C 59:23	even **peace** in this world and eternal life in the world
D&C 84:102(99-102)	he is full of mercy, justice..grace..and **peace**
D&C 111:8(6-8)	by the **peace**...of my Spirit, that shall flow unto you.
Moses 6:61(60-61)	the **peaceable** things of immortal glory; the truth of
JFS-V 1:22(22-24)	but among the righteous there was **peace**

PEACEMAKERS

Gen. 26:29(27-31)	we have...sent thee away in **peace**: thou art now the
Deut. 20:10(10-12)	thou comest nigh unto a city...proclaim **peace** unto it.
Ps. 34:14(11-16)	depart from evil, and do good; seek **peace**, and pursue
Isa. 32:17	the work of righteousness shall be **peace**; and the
Isa. 52:7	beautiful..are the feet of him..that publisheth **peace**
Zech. 8:16	execute the judgment of truth and **peace** in your gates
Matt. 5:9	blessed are the **peacemakers**: for they shall be called
Rom. 10:15	how beautiful...them that preach the gospel of **peace**
Rom. 12:18(14-21)	as much as lieth in you, live **peaceably** with all men.
Rom. 14:19	follow after the things which make for **peace**, and
1 Cor. 7:11(10,11)	or be **reconciled** to her husband: and let not the
1 Tim. 2:2(1-3)	that we may lead a quiet and **peaceable** life in all
James 3:18(16-18)	is sown in peace of them that make **peace**.
1 Pet. 3:11(8-12)	do good; let him seek **peace**, and ensue it.

PEACEMAKERS cont.

1 Ne. 13:37	whoso shall publish **peace**, yea, tidings of great joy
2 Ne. 3:12	be written...shall grow together...establishing **peace**.
Mosiah 4:13	live **peaceably**...render to every man according to that
Mosiah 15:14(14-18)	these are they who have published **peace**, who have
Mosiah 19:27	Limhi began...to establish **peace** among his people.
Mosiah 29:14	I myself have labored...to establish **peace** throughout
Mosiah 29:40	Mosiah...had established **peace** in the land, and he had
Alma 3:24	they returned again and began to establish **peace** in
Alma 13:18	Melchizedek did establish **peace** ...was called the
Alma 24:19	Lamanites...buried the weapons of war, for **peace**.
Alma 51:1	the judges...established **peace** between the people of
3 Ne. 12:9	blessed are all the **peacemakers**, for they shall be
D&C 88:125(123-125)	bond of charity...the bond of perfectness and **peace**.
D&C 98:16(15,16)	therefore, renounce war and proclaim **peace**, and seek
D&C 98:34(33-37)	first lift a standard of **peace** unto that people
D&C 105:39(38-41)	lift up an ensign of **peace**, and make a proclamation

PECULIAR PEOPLE

Ex. 19:5(5-6)	ye shall be a **peculiar** treasure unto me above all
Lev. 20:26	and ye shall be **holy** unto me: for I the Lord am holy
Deut. 7:6	hath chosen thee to be a **special** people unto himself
Deut. 10:15	he **chose** their seed after them, even you above all
Deut. 14:2(1-2)	a **peculiar** people unto himself, above all the nations
Deut. 26:18(16-19)	to be his **peculiar** people, as he hath promised thee
Ps. 135:4	Lord hath chosen...Israel for his **peculiar** treasure.
Isa. 41:8	Jacob whom I have **chosen**, the seed of Abraham my
Amos 3:2(1-2)	you **only** have I known of all the families of the earth
Titus 2:14(11-15)	purify unto himself a **peculiar** people, zealous of good
1 Pet. 2:9(5-9)	a royal priesthood, an holy nation, a **peculiar** people
2 Ne. 1:19(18,19)	that ye might be a choice and a **favored** people of the
D&C 86:11(8-11)	a **light** unto the Gentiles, and through this
D&C 100:16(15-16)	I will raise up unto myself a **pure** people, that will
D&C 101:39(35-40)	accounted as the **salt** of the earth and the savor of
D&C 115:5(4,5)	shine forth, that thy **light** may be a standard for the

PEER INFLUENCE

Ex. 23:2	thou shalt not **follow** a multitude to do evil; neither
Deut. 13:6(6-11)	if thy brother ...or thy friend...**entice** thee secretly
1 Sam. 15:24	I **feared** the people, and obeyed their voice.
Prov. 29:25	the **fear** of man bringeth a snare: but whoso putteth
Ezek. 2:6	be not **afraid** of them, neither...of their words
Luke 12:4	be not **afraid** of them that kill the body, and after
Gal. 1:10	do I seek to **please** men? for if I yet pleased men, I
1 Thes. 2:4	we speak; not as **pleasing** men, but God, which trieth
1 Ne. 8:28(26-28)	ashamed, because of those that were **scoffing** at them
1 Ne. 8:33	they did point the finger of **scorn** at me and those
1 Ne. 22:23	built up to become **popular** in the eyes of the world
2 Ne. 8:7	**fear** ye not the reproach of men, neither be ye afraid
Mosiah 27:8(8,9)	he **led** many of the people to do after the manner of

PEER INFLUENCE cont.

Alma 39:12(11-13)	children to do good, lest they **lead** away the hearts
Alma 47:36	now these dissenters...drinking in with the **traditions**
Alma 61:4(3-8)	they have **led** away the hearts of many people, which
Hel. 7:21	it is to...be **praised** of men, yea, and that ye might
Hel. 13:27(27,28)	if a man shall come **among** you and shall say: do this
3 Ne. 1:29	**led** away by some who were Zoramites, by their lyings
D&C 3:6(6-7)	have gone on in the **persuasions** of men.
D&C 5:21	command...to yield to the **persuasions** of men no more
D&C 30:1(1,11)	you have **feared** man and have not relied on me for
D&C 60:2	hide the talent...because of the **fear** of man. Wo unto
D&C 122:9	**fear** not what man can do, for God shall be with you

PERFECTION

Gen. 6:9	Noah was a just man and **perfect** in his generations
Gen. 17:1	I am...God; walk before me, and be thou **perfect**.
Deut. 18:13	thou shalt be **perfect** with the Lord thy God.
Deut. 32:4	his work is **perfect**: for all his ways are judgment: a
2 Sam. 22:31	as for God, his way is **perfect**; the word of the Lord
Job 1:1(1,8)	Job; and that man was **perfect** and upright, and one
Job 2:3	my servant Job...a **perfect** and an upright man, one
Ps. 19:7(7-9)	the law of the Lord is **perfect**, converting the soul
Ps. 37:37	mark the **perfect** man, and behold the upright: for the
Ps. 101:6	he that walketh in a **perfect** way, he shall serve me.
Matt. 5:48	be ye therefore **perfect**, even as your Father which is
Matt. 19:21(15-22)	if thou wilt be **perfect**, go and sell that thou hast
Luke 6:40	every one that is **perfect** shall be as his master.
Luke 8:14	choked with cares...and bring no fruit to **perfection**.
Luke 13:32	and the third day I shall be **perfected**.
John 17:23(21-23)	that they may be made **perfect** in one; and that the
1 Cor. 2:6	howbeit we speak wisdom among them that are **perfect**
2 Cor. 13:11	be **perfect**, be of good comfort, be of one mind, live
Eph. 4:13(11-14)	unto a **perfect** man, unto the measure of the stature
Philip. 3:12(12-15)	I had already attained, either were already **perfect**
1 Thes. 3:10(10,11)	and might **perfect** that which is lacking in your faith
2 Tim. 3:17(16,17)	that the man of God may be **perfect**, throughly
Heb. 2:10	to make the captain of their salvation **perfect** through
Heb. 5:9(8-9)	and being made **perfect**, he became the author of
Heb. 6:1(1-2)	let us go on unto **perfection**; not laying again the
Heb. 7:11	if therefore **perfection** were by the Levitical
Heb. 11:40	that they without us should not be made **perfect**.
James 1:4(3,4)	ye may be **perfect** and entire, wanting nothing.
James 2:22(20-22)	by works was faith made **perfect**
James 3:2	the same is a **perfect** man, and able also to bridle
2 Ne. 9:13(12-14,23)	having a **perfect** knowledge like unto us in the flesh
Alma 11:43(40-45)	reunited again in its **perfect** form; both limb and join
Alma 40:23	all things...restored to their proper and **perfect**
Alma 42:15	that God might be a **perfect**, just God, and a merciful
Alma 48:11	Moroni...man of a **perfect** understanding; yea, a man
Alma 50:37	filled the judgment-seat with **perfect** uprightness
Hel. 5:30(28-31)	it was a still voice of **perfect** mildness, as if it had
3 Ne. 12:48	I would that ye should be **perfect** even as I, or your

PERFECTION cont.

3 Ne. 27:19	no **unclean** thing can enter into his kingdom; therefore
Moro. 8:16(16,17)	for **perfect** love casteth out all fear.
Moro. 10:32(32,33)	unto Christ...that by his grace ye may be **perfect** in
Moro. 10:32(32-34)	by his grace ye may be **perfect** in Christ; and if by
D&C 50:24(24-29)	groweth brighter and brighter until the **perfect** day.
D&C 76:69	just men made **perfect** through Jesus the mediator of
D&C 93:13(12-13)	from grace to grace, until he received a **fulness**
D&C 107:43	because he (Seth) was a **perfect** man, and his likeness
D&C 128:15	neither can we without our dead be made **perfect**.
D&C 132:37	Abraham...Isaac...Jacob...are not angels but are **gods**.
D&C 135:4	I have a conscience **void** of offense towards God, and
JFS-V 1:17(16-19)	restored unto its **perfect** frame, bone to his bone, and

PERSECUTION

2 Chr. 36:16	**mocked** the messengers of God, and despised his words
Job 12:4	I am as one **mocked** of his neighbour, who calleth upon
Isa. 53:7	he is brought as a lamb to the **slaughter**, and as a she
Jer. 11:19	I was like a lamb or an ox...brought to the **slaughter**
Lam. 5:5	our necks are under **persecution**: we labour, and have
Matt. 5:10(10-12)	they which are **persecuted** for righteousness' sake: for
Matt. 5:12	for so **persecuted** they the prophets which were before
Matt. 5:44	pray for them which despitefully use...**persecute** you
Matt. 10:22(22-23)	ye shall be **hated** of all men for my name's sake: but
Matt. 10:36(34-38)	a man's **foes** shall be they of his own household.
Matt. 13:21	when...**persecution** ariseth because of the word, by and
Matt. 24:9	**hated** of all nations for my name's sake.
Mark 4:17	afterwards...**persecution** ariseth for the word's sake
Luke 6:22(22-23)	men shall hate you...**separate** you from their company
Luke 13:34(33-34)	Jerusalem, which **killest** the prophets, and stonest the
Luke 21:12	they shall lay their hands on you, and **persecute** you
John 5:16	and therefore did the Jews **persecute** Jesus, and sought
John 15:20(18-21)	if they have **persecuted** me, they will also persecute
John 16:2(1-3)	whosoever **killeth** you will think...he doeth God
Acts 5:41(40-42)	they were counted worthy to **suffer** shame for his name.
Acts 7:59(51-60)	they **stoned** Stephen, calling upon God, and saying, Lord
Acts 8:1(1-4)	there was a great **persecution** against the church
Acts 11:19(19-21)	scattered abroad upon the **persecution** that arose about
Acts 12:19(1-19)	commanded that they should be put to **death**. And he went
Acts 13:50	Jews stirred up...**persecution** against Paul and
Acts 14:19	having **stoned** Paul, drew him out of the city
Rom. 8:17	with Christ; if so be that we **suffer** with him, that
Rom. 8:35	shall...**persecution**, or famine, or nakedness, or
Rom. 12:14	bless them which **persecute** you: bless, and curse not.
1 Cor. 4:12	reviled, we bless; being **persecuted**, we suffer it
2 Cor. 1:7	as ye are partakers of the **sufferings**, so shall ye
2 Cor. 4:17	**affliction**...worketh for us a far more exceeding and
2 Cor. 11:25(24-27)	thrice was I **beaten** with rods, once was I stoned
2 Cor. 12:10	take pleasure...in **persecutions**, in distresses for
Gal. 6:12(11-14)	lest they should suffer **persecution** for the cross of
2 Tim. 2:12	if we **suffer**, we shall also reign with him: if we deny
2 Tim. 3:12	in Christ Jesus shall suffer **persecution**.

PERSECUTION cont.

Heb. 11:36(36-38)   trial of cruel **mockings** and scourgings, yea, moreover
Heb. 12:6(6-7)   whom the Lord loveth he **chasteneth**, and scourgeth ever
1 Pet. 4:13(12-16)   rejoice...**partakers** of Christ's sufferings...be glad
Rev. 6:9(9-11)   souls of them that were **slain** for the word of God, and
1 Ne. 8:33(26,28,33)   they did point the finger of **scorn** at me and those
1 Ne. 18:11(10-15)   they did treat me with much **harshness**; nevertheless
2 Ne. 26:8   steadfastness...notwithstanding all **persecution**
Mosiah 17:10(6-20)   I will **suffer** even until death, and I will not recall
Mosiah 27:2(1-9)   should not any unbeliever **persecute** any...who belonged
Alma 1:21(19-22)   there should be no **persecution** among themselves.
Alma 14:9(9-13)   carried them forth to the place of **martyrdom**, that the
Alma 14:22(22-26)   and thus they did **mock** them for many days. And they
3 Ne. 6:13   while others would receive railing and **persecution** and
3 Ne. 12:10(10-12)   they who are **persecuted** for my name's sake, for theirs
3 Ne. 12:44   pray for them who despitefully use you and **persecute**
4 Ne. 1:29(27-34)   they did **persecute** the true church of Christ, because
D&C 40:2   the fear of **persecution** and the cares of the world
D&C 88:94   that **persecuteth** the saints of God, that shed their
D&C 98:23(23-48)   if men will **smite** you, or your families, once, and
D&C 99:1   proclaim mine...gospel...in the midst of **persecution**
D&C 101:1(1-9)   your brethren who have been afflicted, and **persecuted**
D&C 101:35(35-36)   they who suffer **persecution** for my name, and endure
D&C 121:3(1-25)   they suffer these wrongs and unlawful **oppressions**
D&C 127:2(2-3)   the **perils** which I am called to pass through, they see
D&C 136:34(34-36)   the nation that has **driven** you out
JS-H 1:23(23-25)   a spirit of the most bitter **persecution** and reviling.

PERSEVERANCE

Ex. 15:26(25,26)   if thou wilt **diligently** hearken to the voice of the
Ruth 1:18(16-18)   that she was **stedfastly** minded to go with her, then
Job 2:3(1-3)   still he **holdeth** fast his integrity, although thou
Job 2:9(9,10)   dost thou still **retain** thine integrity? curse God, and
Job 27:5(5,6)   till I die I will not **remove** mine integrity from me.
Hab. 2:4(3,4)   but the just shall live by his **faith**.
Matt. 10:22   but he that **endureth** to the end shall be saved.
Matt. 24:13   he that shall **endure** unto the end...shall be saved.
Luke 18:1(1-7)   men ought **always** to pray, and not to faint
Luke 22:28(28-30)   ye...have **continued** with me in my temptations.
John 8:31(31-32)   if ye **continue** in my word, then are ye my disciples
Rom. 2:7(6-7)   by patient **continuance** in well doing...eternal life
1 Cor. 15:58   be ye **stedfast**, unmoveable, always abounding in the
Eph. 6:18   praying always...with all **perseverance** and
Col. 1:23(21-23)   **continue** in the faith...and be not moved away from the
Heb. 3:14(12-14)   partakers of Christ, if we hold..**stedfast** unto the end
Heb. 6:15(13-15)   after he had patiently **endured**, he obtained the
Heb. 12:1(1-4)   run with **patience** the race that is set before us
James 5:11(10-11)   we count them happy which **endure**. Ye have heard of the
1 Pet. 5:9(8-10)   resist **stedfast** in the faith, knowing that the same
1 Ne. 13:37(35-37)   if they **endure** unto the end they shall be lifted up
2 Ne. 9:24(18-24)   if they will not repent...and **endure** to the end, they
2 Ne. 31:20(19,20)   ye must press forward with a **steadfastness** in Christ

PERSEVERANCE cont.

Jacob 6:3(2,3)	blessed are they who have labored **diligently** in his
Enos 1:4(2-4)	I **cried** unto him in mighty prayer and supplication
Jarom 1:11(9-12)	exhorting with all long-suffering...to **diligence**
Mosiah 4:6(6,7)	and should be **diligent** in keeping his commandments
Mosiah 5:15(11-15)	I would that ye should be **steadfast** and immovable
Mosiah 17:20	because he would not **deny** the commandments of God
Alma 14:26(22-27)	how long shall we **suffer** these great afflictions, O
Hel. 6:1	because of their **firmness** and their steadiness in the
Moro. 8:26(25,26)	love endureth by **diligence** unto prayer, until the end
Moro. 9:6	labor **diligently**; for if we should cease to labor
Moro. 10:32	**deny** yourselves of all ungodliness and love God with
D&C 6:13	if...hold out **faithful** to the end, thou shalt be saved
D&C 10:69	whosoever...**endureth**...him will I establish upon my
D&C 18:22	as many as...**endure** to the end, the same shall be save
D&C 20:25	as many as...**endure** in faith to the end, should be
D&C 20:29	**endure**...to the end, or...cannot be saved in the
D&C 63:47	he that...**endureth** shall overcome the world.
D&C 101:35	all they who...**endure**...shall...partake of...glory.
D&C 121:8(7-9)	if thou **endure** it well, God shall exalt thee on high
A of F 1:13	and hope to be able to **endure** all things. If there is

PLAGUES

Gen. 12:17	Pharaoh and his house with great **plagues** because of
Ex. 7:17(14-25)	waters...shall be turned to **blood**.
Ex. 8:2(1-15)	will smite all thy borders with **frogs**
Ex. 8:16(16-19)	the dust...may become **lice** throughout all the land of
Ex. 8:21(20-32)	I will send swarms of **flies** upon thee, and upon thy
Ex. 9:3(1-7)	thy cattle...there shall be a very grievous **murrain**.
Ex. 9:9(8-12)	and shall be a **boil** breaking forth with blains upon
Ex. 9:18(13-35)	I will cause it to rain a very grievous **hail**, such as
Ex. 10:4(1-20)	I bring the **locusts** into thy coast
Ex. 10:22(21-29)	there was a thick **darkness** in all the land of Egypt
Ex. 11:5(1-6)	and all the **firstborn** in the land of Egypt shall die
Ex. 12:29(29-32)	Lord smote all the **firstborn** in the land of Egypt
Lev. 26:21(21,22)	seven times more **plagues** upon you according to your
Num. 11:33(31-35)	Lord smote the people with a very great **plague**.
Num. 14:37(35-39)	those men...died by the **plague** before the Lord.
Num. 16:46(46-50)	wrath gone out from the Lord; the **plague** is begun.
Deut. 28:15(15-68)	not hearken...all these **curses** shall come upon thee
Deut. 28:59(59-62)	the Lord will make thy **plagues** wonderful, and the
Josh. 24:5	I sent Moses also and Aaron, and I **plagued** Egypt
2 Chr. 21:14(12-15)	with a great **plague** will the Lord smite thy people
Jer. 19:8(6-9)	astonished and hiss because of all the **plagues** thereof
Hosea 13:14	O death, I will be thy **plagues**; O grave, I will be thy
Zech. 14:12(12-19)	the Lord will **smite** all the people that have fought
Rev. 11:6	to smite the earth with all **plagues**, as often as they
Rev. 15:1(1,6,8)	seven angels having the seven last **plagues**; for in the
Rev. 18:8	therefore shall her **plagues** come in one day, death
Rev. 21:9	seven vials full of the seven last **plagues**, and talked
Rev. 22:18	God shall add unto him the **plagues** that are written
2 Ne. 6:15	believe not...destroyed...by **pestilence**, and by famine

PLAGUES cont.

2 Ne. 10:6(5-7)	because of their iniquities...**pestilences**, and
Ether 9:33	Lord did cause the **serpents** that they should pursue
D&C 84:97(96-98)	and **plagues** shall go forth, and they shall not be
D&C 87:6(5-7)	with famine, and **plague**, and earthquake, and the
D&C 97:26	with sore affliction, with pestilence, with **plague**

PLEASURE

Ps. 35:27	which hath **pleasure** in the prosperity of his servant.
Ps. 51:18	do good in thy good **pleasure** unto Zion: build thou the
Ps. 103:21	ye ministers of his, that do his **pleasure**.
Ps. 147:11	the Lord taketh **pleasure** in them that fear him, in
Prov. 21:17	he that loveth **pleasure** shall be a poor man: he that
Eccl. 2:1	enjoy **pleasure**: and, behold, this also is vanity.
Isa. 53:10	the **pleasure** of the Lord shall prosper in his hand.
Isa. 58:3	behold, in the day of your fast ye find **pleasure**, and
Ezek. 18:23(20-23)	have I any **pleasure** at all that the wicked should die
Luke 8:14(11-14)	choked with cares and riches and **pleasures** of this
1 Tim. 5:6	but she that liveth in **pleasure** is dead while she
2 Tim. 3:4(1-7)	traitors, heady, highminded, lovers of **pleasures** more
2 Pet. 2:13(12-15)	as they that count it **pleasure** to riot in the day
1 Ne. 16:38	according to his will and **pleasure**. And after this man
2 Ne. 25:22	shall go according to the will and **pleasure** of God
Enos 1:27	then shall I see his face with **pleasure**, and he will
Mosiah 14:10	the **pleasure** of the Lord shall prosper in his hand.
D&C 29:48	given unto them...according to mine own **pleasure**, that
D&C 63:4	who buildeth up at his own will and **pleasure**; and
D&C 76:7	the good **pleasure** of my will concerning all things

POLLUTION

Gen. 6:11(11-13)	the earth also was **corrupt** before God, and the earth
Lev. 18:25(6-30)	and the land is **defiled**: therefore I do visit the
Num. 18:32	neither shall ye **pollute** the holy things of the
Num. 35:33(33,34)	ye shall not **pollute** the land wherein ye are: for
Jer. 2:7	when ye entered, ye **defiled** my land, and made mine
Jer. 3:1	that land be greatly **polluted**? but thou hast played
Jer. 16:18	because they have **defiled** my land, they have filled
Jer. 34:16(15,16)	but ye turned and **polluted** my name, and caused every
Ezek. 4:14	behold, my soul hath not been **polluted**: for from my
Ezek. 7:22(20-22)	they shall **pollute** my secret place: for the robbers
Ezek. 32:2	thou camest...and **fouledst** their rivers.
Ezek. 34:18	but ye must **foul** the residue with your feet
Ezek. 39:7	I will not let them **pollute** my holy name any more: and
Matt. 15:20(11-20)	these are the things which **defile** a man: but to eat
Acts 15:20	they abstain from **pollutions** of idols, and from
Acts 21:28	Greeks also into the temple, and hath **polluted** this
1 Cor. 3:17(16,17)	if any man **defile** the temple of God, him shall God
Titus 1:15	unto them that are **defiled** and unbelieving is nothing
2 Pet. 2:20	they have escaped the **pollutions** of the world through
Jude 1:8(7,8)	also these filthy dreamers **defile** the flesh, despise

POLLUTION cont.

1 Ne. 20:11	I will not suffer my name to be **polluted**, and I will
Mosiah 25:11	of their sinful and **polluted** state, they were filled
Alma 26:17	snatched us from our awful, sinful, and **polluted** state
Morm. 8:31	there shall be great **pollutions** upon the face of the
Morm. 8:36(36,38)	churches...have become **polluted** because of the pride
D&C 84:59	shall the children of the kingdom **pollute** my holy land
D&C 101:6	by these things they **polluted** their inheritances.
D&C 103:14	**pollute** their inheritances they shall be thrown down
D&C 109:20	no unclean thing...come into thy house to **pollute** it
D&C 110:8	if my people...do not **pollute** this holy house.
D&C 124:46	they **pollute** mine holy grounds, and mine holy

POOR

Ex. 23:11(9-11)	that the **poor** of thy people may eat: and what they
Lev. 14:21(21,22)	if he be **poor**, and cannot get so much; then he shall
Lev. 19:10(9-10)	leave them for the **poor** and stranger: I am the Lord
Lev. 23:22	thou shalt leave them unto the **poor**, and to the
Deut. 15:7(7-11)	thou shalt not...shut thine hand from thy **poor** brother
Deut. 24:19(19-22)	for the fatherless, and for the **widow**: that the Lord
1 Sam. 2:7(7-8)	the Lord maketh **poor**, and maketh rich: he bringeth low
1 Sam. 2:8(7,8)	he raiseth up the **poor** out of the dust, and lifteth
Ps. 41:1(1-3)	blessed is he that considereth the **poor**: the Lord will
Prov. 17:5	whoso mocketh the **poor** reproacheth his maker: and he
Prov. 28:27	he that giveth unto the **poor** shall not lack: but he
Isa. 14:32(30-32)	Zion, and the **poor** of his people shall trust in it.
Isa. 29:19(14,18,19)	**poor** among men shall rejoice in the holy one of
Isa. 58:7(5-10)	bring the **poor** that are cast out to thy house? when
Ezek. 22:29	and have vexed the **poor** and needy: yea, they have
Matt. 5:42	**give** to him that asketh thee, and from him that would
Matt. 6:1(1-4)	do not your **alms** before men, to be seen of them: other
Matt. 19:21(16-21)	if thou wilt be perfect, go...and give to the **poor**
Matt. 25:35(32-40)	I was an **hungred**, and ye gave me meat: I was thirsty
Matt. 25:40(32-40)	unto one of the **least** of these my brethren, ye have
Mark 12:42(41-44)	certain **poor** widow, and she threw in two mites, which
Mark 14:7	ye have the **poor** with you always, and whensoever ye
Luke 4:18	he hath anointed me to preach the gospel to the **poor**
Luke 14:13(12-14)	when thou makest a feast, call the **poor**, the maimed
Luke 16:20(19-25)	there was a certain **beggar** named Lazarus, which was
James 2:2(1-9)	there come in also a **poor** man in vile raiment
James 2:5(1-9)	hath not God chosen the **poor** of this world rich in
2 Ne. 9:30	they despise the **poor**, and they persecute the meek
Mosiah 4:19(16-27)	for behold, are we not all **beggars**? Do we not all
Mosiah 4:26(16-27)	I would that...substance to the **poor**, every man
Alma 1:30(29-31)	they did not send away any who were **naked**, or that
Alma 32:2(2-6)	they began to have success among the **poor** class of
Alma 32:3(2-6)	they were **poor** as to things of the world; and also the
Alma 34:28	if ye turn away the **needy**...your prayer is in vain
Hel. 4:12(11-12)	because of their oppression to the **poor**, withholding
3 Ne. 13:1	do alms unto the **poor**; but take heed that ye do not
Morm. 8:37(35-37,39)	ye do love money...more than ye love the **poor** and the
D&C 42:30(30-31,39)	thou wilt remember the **poor**, and consecrate of thy

POOR cont.

D&C 42:31(30,31,39)	ye impart of your substance unto the **poor**, ye will do
D&C 42:39(30,31,39)	consecrate of the riches...unto the **poor** of my people
D&C 52:40	remember in all things the **poor**...he that doeth not...
D&C 56:16(16-20)	wo...that will not give your substance to the **poor**
D&C 56:18(16-20)	blessed are the **poor** who are pure in heart, whose
D&C 58:8(6-12)	a feast of fat things might be prepared for the **poor**
D&C 58:11(6-12)	**poor**...come in unto the marriage of the Lamb, and part
D&C 84:105(103-105)	if any man shall give...you...cast it unto the **poor**
D&C 88:17(17-22)	the **poor** and the meek of the earth shall inherit it.
D&C 104:16(14-18)	in mine own way...the **poor** shall be exalted, in that
D&C 105:3	evil...not impart of their substance...to the **poor** and

POOR IN SPIRIT

Job 22:29	he shall save the **humble** person.
Ps. 34:18	and saveth such as be of a **contrite** spirit.
Prov. 16:19	better it is to be of an **humble** spirit with the lowly
Isa. 57:15	spirit of the **humble**, and to revive the heart of the
Matt. 5:3(3-5)	blessed are the **poor** in spirit: for theirs is the
2 Cor. 7:9(9-11)	ye were made **sorry** after a godly manner, that ye might
James 4:6(5-7)	but giveth grace unto the **humble**.
1 Pet. 5:5(5-7)	and giveth grace to the **humble**.
2 Ne. 4:17(17-35)	wretched man...my heart **sorroweth** because of my flesh
Mosiah 4:2(1-11)	they had **viewed** themselves in their own carnal state
Alma 26:12(9-12)	I know that I am **nothing**; as to my strength I am weak
Alma 32:3(1-16)	and also they were **poor** in heart.
Alma 32:4(3,4)	were **poor** in heart, because of their poverty as to the
Alma 36:12(8-24)	my soul was **harrowed** up...with all my sins.
Alma 38:14(10-15)	acknowledge your **unworthiness** before God at all times.
Hel. 6:5(1-5)	bringing down many...into the depths of **humility**, to
3 Ne. 9:20(20-22)	sacrifice unto me a broken heart and a contrite **spirit**
3 Ne. 12:3(1-16)	blessed are the **poor** in spirit who come unto me, for
Morm. 2:13(11-15)	their **sorrowing** was not unto repentance, because of
Moro. 6:2(1-9)	save they came forth with a **broken** heart and a
D&C 1:28(24-28)	inasmuch as they were **humble** they might be made strong
D&C 4:6(5,6)	remember...charity, **humility**, diligence.
D&C 20:37	and come forth with broken hearts and **contrite** spirits
D&C 59:8	even that of a broken heart and a **contrite** spirit.

PRAYER

Gen. 4:26	then began men to **call** upon the name of the Lord.
Gen. 12:8	builded an altar...**called** upon the name of the Lord.
Gen. 21:33	**called** there on the name of the Lord, the everlasting
Gen. 25:22(21-23)	she went to **inquire** of the Lord.
Num. 21:7	and Moses **prayed** for the people.
1 Sam. 10:22	therefore they **inquired** of the Lord further, if the
2 Kgs. 19:4(1-7)	lift up thy **prayer** for the remnant that are left.
2 Kgs. 19:20(20-34)	that which thou hast **prayed** to me...I have heard.
2 Chr. 7:14(12-16)	if my people...shall...**pray**, and seek my face, and
Ps. 55:17(16,17)	at noon, will I **pray**, and cry aloud: and he shall hear

PRAYER cont.

Isa. 26:9	I desired thee in the night...I **seek** thee early: for
Isa. 56:7	make them joyful in my house of **prayer**: their burnt
Dan. 6:10	three times a day, and **prayed**, and gave thanks before
Joel 2:32	whosoever shall **call** on...the Lord shall be delivered
Jonah 2:7	my **prayer** came in unto thee, into thine holy temple.
Matt. 5:44	**pray** for them which despitefully use you, and
Matt. 6:6(5-13)	**pray** to thy Father which is in secret; and thy Father
Matt. 6:9(9-13)	after this manner therefore **pray** ye: Our Father which
Matt. 7:7(7-12)	**ask**, and it shall be given you; seek, and ye shall
Matt. 18:19(19,20)	agree...as touching any thing that they shall **ask**, it
Matt. 21:13	my house shall be called the house of **prayer**; but ye
Matt. 21:22	whatsoever ye shall ask in **prayer**, believing, ye shall
Matt. 26:39	**prayed**...nevertheless not as I will, but as thou wilt.
Matt. 26:39(39-44)	fell on his face, and **prayed**, saying, O my father, if
Matt. 26:41	watch and **pray**, that ye enter not into temptation: the
Mark 11:24	when ye **pray**, believe that ye receive them, and ye
Mark 11:25(25-26)	when ye stand **praying**, forgive, if ye have ought again
Mark 13:33	take ye heed, watch and **pray**: for ye know not when the
Luke 11:1(1-4)	Lord, teach us to **pray**, as John also taught his
Luke 18:1(1-8)	men ought always to **pray**, and not to faint
Luke 18:10(10-14)	two men went up into the temple to **pray**...Pharisee
Luke 21:36	watch ye therefore, and **pray** always, that ye may be
Luke 22:32	I have **prayed** for thee, that thy faith fail not: and
John 14:13(13-14)	whatsoever ye shall **ask** in my name, that will I do
John 15:7	ye shall **ask** what ye will, and it shall be done unto
John 16:23(23,24)	whatsoever ye shall **ask** the Father in my name, he will
John 17:9	I **pray** for them: I pray not for the world, but for the
John 17:20(9-21)	neither **pray** I for these alone, but for them also
Rom. 10:13(12,13)	for whosoever shall **call** upon the name of the Lord
Eph. 6:18	**praying** always with all prayer and supplication in the
Philip. 4:6(5-7)	by **prayer**...let your requests be made known unto God.
Col. 3:17	do all in the name of...Jesus, giving **thanks** to God
1 Thes. 5:17	**pray** without ceasing.
James 1:6(5-8)	but let him **ask** in faith, nothing wavering. for he
James 4:3(2,3,7,8)	ye **ask**, and receive not, because ye ask amiss, that
James 5:14(13-18)	let them **pray** over him, anointing him with oil in the
James 5:16(16-18)	the...fervent **prayer** of a righteous man availeth much.
1 Pet. 3:7	honour unto the wife...that your **prayers** be not
1 Pet. 3:12	his ears are open unto their **prayers**: but the face of
1 Jn. 3:22	whatsoever we **ask**, we receive of him, because we keep
1 Jn. 5:15(14,15)	whatsoever we **ask**, we know that we have the petitions
1 Ne. 15:11(7-11)	not harden your hearts...**ask** me in faith, believing
1 Ne. 16:24	he did **inquire** of the Lord, for they had humbled
2 Ne. 4:35(20-35)	my God will give me, if I **ask** not amiss; therefore I
2 Ne. 32:8(8,9)	the Spirit which teacheth a man to **pray** ye would know
Enos 1:4(1-19)	I cried unto him in mighty **prayer**...for mine own soul
1:26	continue in fasting and **praying**, and endure to the end
Mosiah 4:11(11-12)	**calling** on the name of the Lord daily, and standing
Mosiah 24:12(10-13)	pour out their **hearts** to him; and he did know the
Mosiah 27:14(8-37)	Alma...thy father...has **prayed** with much faith
Alma 5:46(43-47)	**prayed** many days that I might know these things of
Alma 10:23(22-23)	is by the **prayers** of the righteous that ye are spared
Alma 13:28(28-29)	watch and **pray** continually, that...not be tempted

PRAYER cont.

they had given themselves to much **prayer**, and fasting
and **call** on his name in faith, believing that ye
I will go and **inquire** of the Lord, and if he say unto
from this stand they did offer up..the selfsame **prayer**
call upon his holy name, that he would have mercy upon
humble yourselves, and continue in **prayer** unto him.
counsel with the Lord in all thy doings, and he will
ye have seen that they **pray** to be heard of men, and
did fast and **pray** oft, and did wax stronger and strong
pray for them who despitefully use you and persecute
when thou **prayest** thou shalt not do as the hypocrites
after this manner therefore **pray** ye: Our Father who
ask, and it shall be given unto you; seek, and ye
he **prayed** unto the Father, and the things which he
watch and **pray** always, lest ye be tempted by the devil
as I have prayed...so shall ye **pray** in my church, among
not multiply many words...given..what they should **pray**
he remembered not to **call** upon the name of the Lord.
if he offereth a gift, or **prayeth** unto God, except he
whatsoever...**ask**...which is good...it shall be done
pray unto the Father with all the energy of heart
which love endureth by diligence unto **prayer**, until
I would exhort you that ye would **ask** God, the Eternal
ask, and ye shall receive; knock, and it shall be open
humble himself in mighty **prayer** and faith, in the
if thou wilt **inquire**, thou shalt know mysteries which
study it out in your mind; then you must **ask** me if it
pray always, that you may come off conqueror; yea
ask the Father in my name, in faith believing that you
thou shalt **pray** vocally as well as in thy heart; yea
pray always, and I will pour out my Spirit upon you
you must **pray** vocally before the world as well as in
the song of the righteous is a **prayer** unto me, and
pray always, lest you enter into temptation and lose
Spirit shall be given unto you by the **prayer** of faith
he that **asketh** in the Spirit asketh according to the
know this, it shall be given you what you shall **ask**
they who have **sought** me early shall find rest to their
go to the house of **prayer** and offer up thy sacraments
they shall also teach their children to **pray**, and to
he that observeth not his **prayers** before the Lord in
the alms of your **prayers** have come up into the ears
whatsoever ye **ask** the Father in my name..shall be
ye shall continue in **prayer** and fasting from this time
establish a house, even a house of **prayer**, a house of
pray always, that ye may not faint, until I come.
for your **prayers** have entered into the ears of the Lord
men ought always to **pray** and not to faint, which saith
establish a house, even a house of **prayer**, a house of
lead thee...and give thee answer to thy **prayers**.
praise the Lord...with a **prayer** of praise and
Moses...**calling** upon God...received strength, and he
thou shalt repent and **call** upon God in the name of the

PRAYER cont.

Moses 6:4(2,3,4)	began these men to **call** upon the name of the Lord, and
JS-H 1:14(14-19)	I had never as yet made the attempt to **pray** vocally.
JS-H 1:29(29-32)	I betook myself to **prayer**...for forgiveness of...sins

PREACHING

Ex. 9:16	my name may be **declared** throughout all the earth.
2 Kgs. 17:13(13-15)	the Lord **testified** against Israel, and against Judah
1 Chr. 16:24(8-36)	**declare** his glory among the heathen; his marvellous
2 Chr. 24:19(18,19)	prophets...**testified** against them: but they would not
Neh. 8:9(4-12)	the Levites that **taught** the people, said unto all the
Ps. 9:11	sing praises to the Lord...**declare** among the people
Ps. 22:31(22-31)	they shall come, and shall **declare** his righteousness
Ps. 105:1(1-15)	give thanks unto the Lord...**make** known his deeds among
Isa. 21:6(5,6)	set a watchman, let him **declare** what he seeth.
Isa. 43:26(25,26)	**declare** thou, that thou mayest be justified.
Isa. 61:1(1-4)	the Lord hath anointed me to **preach** good tidings unto
Jonah 3:2(1-5)	go unto Nineveh...and **preach** unto it the preaching
Matt. 4:17	Jesus began to **preach**, and to say, repent: for the
Mark 6:12(7-13)	and they went out, and **preached** that men should repent
Luke 4:18(16-19)	he hath sent me...to **preach** deliverance to the captive
Luke 4:43(42-44)	I must **preach** the kingdom of God to other cities also
Luke 9:2(1-6)	he sent them to **preach** the kingdom of God, and to heal
John 17:26	I have **declared** unto them thy name, and will declare
Acts 8:12(5-12)	Philip **preaching** the things concerning the kingdom of
Acts 17:23	ye ignorantly worship, him **declare** I unto you.
Rom. 10:15(14-18)	how shall they **preach**, except they be sent? as it is
1 Cor. 9:16	woe is unto me, if I **preach** not the gospel
Col. 1:28(25-29)	whom we **preach**, warning every man, and teaching every
1 Tim. 2:7(1-7)	whereunto I am ordained a **preacher**, and an apostle
2 Tim. 4:2(2-4)	**preach** the word; be instant in season, out of season
1 Pet. 3:19(18-19)	he went and **preached** unto the spirits in prison
Enos 1:23(22-23)	**preaching**...to keep them in the fear of the Lord. I
Mosiah 18:20	should **preach** nothing save it were repentance and
Mosiah 23:17	none received authority to **preach**...except...from God.
Alma 9:21	the gift of **preaching**, and the gift of the Holy Ghost
Alma 29:13	a holy calling, to **preach** the word unto this people
Alma 31:5	the **preaching** of the word had a great tendency to lead
Alma 37:33(32-34)	**preach** unto them repentance, and faith on the Lord
Hel. 5:17	they did **preach** with great power, insomuch that they
Moro. 6:9	the Holy Ghost led them whether to **preach**, or to
D&C 11:15	not suppose..are called to **preach** until you are called
D&C 11:21	seek not to **declare** my word, but first seek to obtain
D&C 19:29(29,31)	and thou shalt **declare** glad tidings, yea, publish it
D&C 38:41	let your **preaching** be the warning voice, every man to
D&C 42:11	it shall not be given to any one to go forth to **preach**
D&C 68:8	all the world, **preach** the gospel to every creature
D&C 107:25	the seventy are also called to **preach** the gospel, and
D&C 133:37	this gospel shall be **preached** unto every nation, and
Moses 5:58(58-59)	the gospel began to be **preached**, from the beginning
Moses 6:23(22-23)	they were **preachers** of righteousness, and spake and
Moses 8:23(23-24)	Noah continued...**preaching**...saying: hearken, and give

JFS-V 1:19(18,19,32)   and there he **preached** to them the everlasting gospel

PRIDE

Lev. 26:19	I will break the **pride** of your power; and I will make
Deut. 8:14	then thine **heart** be lifted up, and thou forget the Lord
Prov. 6:17(16-19)	a **proud** look, a lying tongue, and hands that shed
Prov. 16:18	**pride** goeth before destruction, and an haughty spirit
Isa. 2:12	day of the Lord...upon every one that is **proud** and
Isa. 5:21	woe unto them that are wise in their own **eyes**, and
Isa. 16:6(6-14)	we have heard of the **pride** of Moab; he is very proud
Jer. 13:9	after this manner will I mar the **pride** of Judah, and
Jer. 13:15	give ear; be not **proud**: for the Lord hath spoken.
Jer. 48:29(26-47)	we have heard the **pride** of Moab, (he is exceeding
Ezek. 16:49(44-49)	this was the iniquity of thy sister Sodom, **pride**
Ezek. 28:2(2-5)	because thine **heart** is lifted up, and thou hast said
Mal. 4:1	all the **proud**...shall be stubble: and the day that
Matt. 23:12	whosoever shall **exalt** himself shall be abased; and he
Mark 12:38(38-39)	beware of the **scribes**, which love to go in long
Rom. 1:30(17-32)	haters of God, despiteful, **proud**, boasters, inventors
Rom. 12:16	be not wise in your own **conceits**.
1 Tim. 3:6	lifted up with **pride** he fall into the condemnation of
1 Tim. 6:4(2-4)	he is **proud**, knowing nothing, but doting about
2 Tim. 3:2(1,2)	men shall be lovers of their own selves...**proud**
James 4:6	God resisteth the **proud**, but giveth grace unto the
1 Pet. 5:5	God resisteth the **proud**, and giveth grace to the
1 Jn. 2:16(15-17)	**pride** of life...not of the Father, but is of the world
1 Ne. 11:36	spacious building was the **pride** of the world; and it
1 Ne. 22:15	the **proud** and they who do wickedly shall be as
2 Ne. 9:28(27-29,42)	when they are learned they think they are **wise**, and
2 Ne. 26:20	Gentiles are lifted up in the **pride** of their eyes, and
2 Ne. 28:12	because of **pride**, and because of false teachers, and
2 Ne. 28:15	wise...learned...rich...puffed up in the **pride** of
Jacob 2:16(12-22)	let not this **pride** of your hearts destroy your souls
Alma 1:32(20,32)	being lifted up in the **pride** of their own eyes; lying
Alma 5:28	behold, are ye stripped of **pride**? I say unto you, if
3 Ne. 25:1	all the **proud**, yea, and all that do wickedly, shall
4 Ne. 1:24(24,25)	those who were lifted up in **pride**, such as the wearing
Morm. 8:36(28-36)	churches...polluted because of the **pride** of your heart
Moro. 8:27	the **pride** of this nation...hath proven their
D&C 3:13(12-14)	and **boasted** in his own wisdom.
D&C 23:1	beware of **pride**, lest thou shouldst enter into
D&C 25:14(1-2,14)	continue in the spirit of meekness...beware of **pride**.
D&C 29:9	all the **proud** and they that do wickedly shall be as
D&C 38:39	beware of **pride**, lest ye become as the Nephites of old
D&C 42:40	thou shalt not be **proud** in thy heart; let all thy
D&C 56:8	repent of his **pride**, and of his selfishness, and obey
D&C 64:24	all the **proud** and they that do wickedly shall be as
D&C 88:121(118-126)	cease from all...your **pride** and light-mindedness, and
D&C 90:17	**pride**, for it bringeth a snare upon your souls.
D&C 121:37(34-37)	when we undertake to...gratify our **pride**...heavens
D&C 133:64	all the **proud**, yea, and all that do wickedly, shall

PRIESTCRAFT

Jer. 5:31(30-31)	the **priests** bear rule by their means; and my people
Jer. 6:13(11-13)	prophet even unto the **priest** every one dealeth falsely
Jer. 23:11	both prophet and **priest** are profane; yea, in my house
Micah 2:11(7-11)	a man walking in...**falsehood**...saying, I will prophesy
Micah 3:11	the prophets thereof divine for **money**: yet will they
Matt. 27:20	**priests**..elders persuaded the multitude..destroy Jesus
Luke 22:2	chief **priests** and scribes sought how they might kill
Acts 4:6(6-8)	kindred of the high **priest**, were gathered together at
1 Pet. 5:2(2-3)	feed the flock of God...not for filthy **lucre**, but of
1 Ne. 22:23	all churches which are built up to get **gain**, and all
2 Ne. 10:5(4-6)	because of **priestcrafts** and iniquities, they...stiffen
2 Ne. 26:29(29-31)	**priestcrafts** are that men...may get gain and praise
2 Ne. 27:16(15-16)	because of the glory of the world and to get **gain** will
Alma 1:12(12-16)	first time that **priestcraft** has been introduced among
Hel. 7:5(4-5)	that they might get **gain** and glory of the world, and
3 Ne. 16:10	all manner of hypocrisy, and murders, and **priestcrafts**
3 Ne. 21:19(19-20)	and **priestcrafts**, and whoredoms, shall be done away.
3 Ne. 29:7	wo unto him that shall say at that day, to get **gain**
3 Ne. 30:2	repent of your evil doings...murders...**priestcrafts**
4 Ne. 1:26	to build up churches unto themselves to get **gain**, and
Morm. 8:33(33-40)	why...built up churches unto yourselves to get **gain**
D&C 33:4(3-5)	they err in many instances because of **priestcrafts**

PRIESTHOOD

Ex. 19:6(5,6)	ye shall be unto me a kingdom of **priests**, and an holy
Ex. 40:15(12-15)	anointing shall surely be an everlasting **priesthood**
Num. 25:13	everlasting **priesthood**; because he was zealous for
Matt. 16:19(16-19)	the **keys** of the kingdom of heaven: and whatsoever thou
Mark 3:15(14,15)	to have **power** to heal sicknesses, and to cast out
Acts 6:6(5,6)	they **laid** their hands on them.
Heb. 5:1(1-3)	**ordained** for men in things pertaining to God, that
Heb. 7:24(21-25)	continueth ever, hath an unchangeable **priesthood**.
1 Pet. 2:9(5-9)	but ye are a chosen generation, a royal **priesthood**
Mosiah 18:17(16-18)	baptized by the power and **authority** of God was added
Mosiah 25:19(17-19)	gave him power to **ordain** priests and teachers over
Alma 6:1(1,2)	he **ordained** priests and elders, by laying on his hand
Alma 13:8(6-10)	which calling, and ordinance, and high **priesthood**, is
Alma 13:18(17-19)	according to the **holy** order of God, did preach
Alma 43:2(1-3)	preached after the holy **order** of God by which they
Hel. 8:18(17-19)	even after the **order** of his Son; and this that it
3 Ne. 18:37(36-39)	that he gave them **power** to give the Holy Ghost. And I
Moro. 3:4(1-4)	after this manner did they **ordain** priests and teachers
D&C 84:33(33-38)	faithful unto the obtaining these two **priesthoods** of
D&C 107:1	there are, in the church, two **priesthoods**, namely, the
D&C 121:36(36-37)	that the rights of the **priesthood** are inseparably
D&C 121:41(39-45)	no power or influence...maintained by...**priesthood**
Moses 6:7	now this same **Priesthood**, which was in the beginning
JS-H 1:38	I will reveal unto you the **Priesthood**, by the hand of

PRIESTHOOD, AARONIC

Ex. 28:1(1-3,41)	that he may minister unto me in the **priest's** office
Ex. 29:9(7-9)	the **priest's** office shall be theirs for a perpetual
Ex. 40:15(12-15)	that they may minister unto me in the **priest's** office
Lev. 3:2	**Aaron's** sons the priests shall sprinkle the blood upon
Lev. 8:12(1-36)	anointing oil upon **Aaron's** head, and anointed him, to
Lev. 16:32(32-34)	and the priest, whom he shall **anoint**, and whom he
Lev. 21:10(10-15)	upon whose head the **anointing** oil was poured, and
Num. 3:9(1-51)	thou shalt give the **Levites** unto Aaron and to his sons
Num. 8:19(5-26)	I have given the Levites as a gift to **Aaron** and to his
Num. 16:9(8-10)	separated you...to do the **service** of the tabernacle
Num. 18:6(1-8)	I have taken...the **Levites** from among the children of
Num. 25:13(10-13)	covenant of an everlasting **priesthood**; because he was
Josh. 18:7	**Levites**...the priesthood of the Lord is their
2 Chr. 29:11(1-36)	the Lord hath **chosen** you to stand before him, to serve
Neh. 3:1	then Eliashib the **high** priest rose up with his
Neh. 13:29(29-30)	they have defiled the **priesthood**, and the covenant of
Mal. 3:3	shall purify the sons of **Levi**, and purge them as gold
Luke 1:5	priest named **Zacharias**, of the course of Abia: and
Luke 3:2	Annas and Caiaphas being the **high** priests, the word
John 11:49(47-52)	and one of them, named Caiaphas, being the **high** priest
Heb. 5:4	he that is called of God, as was **Aaron**.
Heb. 7:5	sons of Levi, who receive the **office** of the priesthood
Heb. 7:11(11-12)	if...perfection were by the **Levitical** priesthood, (for
Heb. 7:21	(for those **priests** were made without an oath; but this
Moro. 3:1(1-3)	the elders of the church, ordained **priests** and teacher
D&C 13:1	I confer the Priesthood of **Aaron**, which holds the keys
D&C 20:46(46-65)	the **priest's** duty is to preach, teach, expound, exhort
D&C 27:8	to ordain you unto the first **priesthood** which you have
D&C 68:16(16-21)	literal descendants of **Aaron** they have a legal right
D&C 84:26(18-30)	and the lesser **priesthood** continued, which priesthood
D&C 84:27(26-28)	house of **Aaron**...until John, whom God raised up, being
D&C 107:1	two priesthoods, namely, the Melchizedek and **Aaronic**
D&C 107:6	the other is the **Aaronic** or Levitical Priesthood.
D&C 107:13(13-17)	second priesthood is called the Priesthood of **Aaron**
D&C 107:20	authority of the lesser, or **Aaronic** Priesthood, is to
D&C 132:59	man be called of my Father, as was **Aaron**, by mine own
JS-H 1:69(68-72)	upon you...I confer the Priesthood of **Aaron**, which

PRIESTHOOD, AUTHORITY

Ex. 18:15(13-16)	because the people come unto me to **inquire** of God
Ex. 28:41(1-3,41)	**consecrate** them...that they may minister...in the
Ex. 29:9(4-9)	and thou shalt **consecrate** Aaron and his sons.
Num. 1:50(50-53)	thou shalt appoint the **Levites** over the tabernacle of
Num. 16:5(1-35)	him whom he hath **chosen** will he cause to come near
Num. 17:5(1-11)	the man's rod, whom I shall **choose**, shall blossom: and
Num. 27:23(18-23)	and he laid his hands upon him, and gave him a **charge**
Deut. 34:9(9-10)	for Moses had **laid** his hands upon him: and the
1 Sam. 2:28(27-36)	I **choose** him out of all the tribes of Israel to be my
1 Sam. 3:20(10-21)	Samuel was **established** to be a prophet of the Lord.
1 Sam. 9:9	a man went to inquire of God...let us go to the **seer**
1 Sam. 13:9(8-15)	Saul...**offered** the burnt offering.

345

PRIESTHOOD, AUTHORITY cont.

2 Chr. 26:18(16-23)	the sons of Aaron, that are **consecrated** to burn
2 Chr. 26:18(16-21)	it **appertaineth** not unto thee, Uzziah, to burn incense
Hag. 1:12(12,13)	Lord their God had **sent** him, and the people did fear
Matt. 16:19(13-20)	I will give unto thee the **keys** of the kingdom of
Mark 3:14(14-15)	he **ordained** twelve, that they should be with him, and
Mark 11:28(27-33)	by what **authority** doest thou these things? and who
Luke 9:1(1-2)	gave them power and **authority** over all devils, and
Luke 10:1	the Lord **appointed** other seventy also, and sent them
John 15:16	but I have chosen you, and **ordained** you, that ye
Acts 6:6(1-6)	the apostles...**laid** their hands on them.
Acts 8:18(14-20)	through **laying** on of the apostles' hands the Holy
Acts 10:42	it is he which was **ordained** of God to be the judge of
Acts 13:3(1-3)	had fasted and prayed, and **laid** their hands on them
Acts 19:11(1-12)	and God wrought special **miracles** by the hands of Paul
Gal. 1:1	an **apostle**, (not...by man, but by Jesus Christ, and
1 Tim. 4:14	gift...given thee...with the **laying** on of the hands
Titus 1:5	**ordain** elders in every city, as I had appointed thee
Heb. 5:4	but he that is **called** of God, as was Aaron.
Rev. 1:6(5,6)	and hath made us **kings** and priests unto God and his
2 Ne. 5:26	I, Nephi, did **consecrate** Jacob and Joseph, that they
Mosiah 8:16(16-18)	a man may have great **power** given him from God.
Mosiah 18:18(12-18)	Alma, having **authority** from God, ordained priests
Mosiah 21:33	there was none in the land that had **authority** from God
Mosiah 23:17	none received **authority** to preach...except...from God.
Alma 5:3	I, Alma, having been **consecrated** by my father, Alma
Alma 13:1(1-10)	Lord God **ordained** priests, after his holy order, which
Alma 17:3(2-3)	they taught with power and **authority** of God.
Hel. 10:7(7-10)	whatsoever ye shall **seal** on earth shall be sealed in
3 Ne. 11:21(21-41)	I give unto you **power** that ye shall baptize with
3 Ne. 11:25(24-25)	having **authority** given me of Jesus Christ, I baptize
3 Ne. 18:37(36-37)	he gave them **power** to give the Holy Ghost. And I will
D&C 1:4(4-6)	by the mouths of my disciples, whom I have **chosen** in
D&C 1:38(30,38)	by mine own voice or by the **voice** of my servants, it
D&C 5:17	wait yet a little while, for ye are not yet **ordained**
D&C 11:15	not suppose..are called to preach until you are **called**
D&C 13:1	upon you...I **confer** the priesthood of Aaron, which
D&C 27:12(12-13)	Peter...James, and John...by whom I have **ordained** you
D&C 28:3(1-3)	declare...with power and **authority** unto the church.
D&C 42:11	not be given...to go forth...except he be **ordained** by
D&C 68:8(8-12)	acting in the **authority** which I have given you
D&C 75:21(19-22)	in the day of judgment you shall be **judges** of that
D&C 84:21(20-22)	without...the **authority** of the priesthood, the power
D&C 107:8(1-100)	the Melchizedek Priesthood...has power and **authority**
D&C 113:8(7-8)	her strength is to put on the **authority** of the
D&C 121:36(34-38)	**rights** of the priesthood are inseparably connected wit
D&C 132:7	appointed...Joseph to hold this **power** in the last days
D&C 132:46	whatsoever you **bind** on earth, in my name and by my
Moses 1:25	for they shall obey thy **command** as if thou wert God.
JS-H 1:68(68-73)	a messenger from heaven...**ordained** us, saying
A of F 1:5	a man must be called...by those who are in **authority**

PRIESTHOOD, HISTORY OF

Gen. 5:1(1-32)	this is the book of the **generations** of Adam. In the
Gen. 9:9(8-17)	I establish my **covenant** with you, and with your seed
Gen. 12:3(1-3)	in thee shall all families of the earth be **blessed**.
Gen. 28:14(12-15)	in thy **seed** shall all the families...earth be blessed.
Ex. 19:6(5-6)	ye shall be unto me a kingdom of **priests**, and an holy
Ex. 40:15(12-16)	anointing shall surely be an everlasting **priesthood**
Num. 8:18(5-26)	I have taken the **Levites** for all the firstborn of the
Num. 18:7(1-7)	thou and thy sons with thee shall keep your **priest's**
Num. 27:23(18-23)	he laid his hands upon him, and gave him a **charge**, as
Josh. 18:7	priesthood of the Lord is their **inheritance**: and Gad
1 Chr. 5:2(1,2)	but the **birthright** was Joseph's
Matt. 16:19	I will give unto thee the **keys** of the kingdom of
Mark 3:14(14-15)	he **ordained** twelve, that they should be with him, and
John 15:16(15-16)	I have chosen you, and **ordained** you, that ye should
Acts 14:23	and when they had **ordained** them elders in every church
Eph. 4:11(11-14)	he gave some, **apostles**; and some, prophets; and some
Heb. 5:6(1-14)	a priest for ever after the order of **Melchisedec**.
Heb. 7:12(1-28)	for the **priesthood** being changed, there is made of
Mosiah 18:18(18-26)	Alma, having authority from God, **ordained** priests
Alma 6:1	he **ordained** priests and elders, by laying on his hand
Alma 13:14(1-19)	**Melchizedek**, who was also a high priest after this
3 Ne. 11:21(21-22)	I give unto you **power** that ye shall baptize this
4 Ne. 1:14	there were other disciples **ordained** in their stead
Moro. 3:4(1-4)	after this manner did they **ordain** priests and teachers
D&C 20:38(38-67)	the **duty** of the elders, priests, teachers, deacons
D&C 27:12(12-13)	Peter, and James, and John...by whom I have **ordained**
D&C 84:6(6-32)	received under the hand of his father-in-law, **Jethro**
D&C 84:18	Lord confirmed a **priesthood** also upon Aaron and his
D&C 84:25(19-26)	took Moses out of their midst...Holy **Priesthood** also
D&C 84:26(26-28)	and the lesser priesthood **continued**, which priesthood
D&C 86:8(8-11)	**priesthood** hath continued through the lineage of your
D&C 107:41(40-57)	this **order** was instituted in the days of Adam, and
D&C 110:11(1-16)	**Moses**...committed unto us the keys of the gathering
D&C 110:12	**Elias** appeared, and committed the dispensation...of
D&C 110:16(13-16)	the **keys** of this dispensation are committed into your
D&C 112:32(30-32)	the keys...have **come** down from the fathers, and last
D&C 113:8(7,8)	**priesthood**, which she, Zion, has a right to by lineage
Moses 6:7(1-25)	same **priesthood**, which was in the beginning, shall be
Moses 8:2(1-30)	**Methuselah**...was not taken, that the covenants of the
Abr. 1:2(1-4,31)	a High Priest, holding the **right** belonging to the
Abr. 1:26(21-27)	Noah...cursed him as pertaining to the **Priesthood**.
JS-H 1:68(68-73)	a messenger from heaven...**ordained** us, saying

PRIESTHOOD, KEYS

Ex. 3:10(1-18)	I will **send** thee...that thou mayest bring forth my
Ex. 7:1(1,2)	and Aaron thy brother shall be thy **prophet**.
Isa. 6:8(7-13)	voice of the Lord, saying, whom shall I **send**, and who
Isa. 22:22(22-24)	**key** of the house of David will I lay upon his shoulder
Jer. 1:5(4-10)	I sanctified thee, and I **ordained** thee a prophet unto
Ezek. 2:3(1-10)	son of man, I **send** thee to the children of Israel, to
Amos 7:15(14-16)	the Lord said unto me, **go**, prophesy unto my people

PRIESTHOOD, KEYS cont.

Mal. 1:1(1-5)	**word** of the Lord to Israel by Malachi.
Mal. 4:5(5,6)	I will send you **Elijah** the prophet before the coming
Matt. 16:19(18-19)	I will give unto thee the **keys** of the kingdom of
Matt. 17:3(1-13)	there appeared unto them **Moses** and Elias talking with
Matt. 18:18	whatsoever ye shall **bind** on earth...bound in heaven
John 20:23	sins ye **remit**, they are remitted...ye retain, they are
Rev. 3:7(7,8)	**key** of David, he that openeth, and no man shutteth
Hel. 10:7(1-12)	whatsoever ye shall **seal** on earth shall be sealed in
D&C 1:8	power given to **seal** both on earth and in heaven, the
D&C 2:1(1-3)	reveal unto you the **Priesthood**, by the hand of Elijah
D&C 7:7	unto you three I will give...the **keys** of this ministry
D&C 13:1	Priesthood of Aaron, which holds the **keys** of the
D&C 27:13(5-13)	committed the **keys** of my kingdom, and a dispensation
D&C 28:7	I have given him the **keys** of the mysteries, and the
D&C 35:25	by the **keys** which I have given shall they be led, and
D&C 42:69	the **keys** of the church have been given. Even so. Amen.
D&C 64:5	**keys**...shall not be taken from my servant Joseph Smith
D&C 65:2	**keys** of the kingdom of God are committed unto man on
D&C 68:17	and the **keys** or authority of the same.
D&C 81:2	**keys** of the kingdom...belong...unto...Presidency of
D&C 84:19(19-22)	greater priesthood...holdeth the **key** of the mysteries
D&C 84:26	lesser priesthood...**key** of the ministering of angels
D&C 90:2(2-3)	thou art blessed...that bear the **keys** of the kingdom
D&C 90:3	the keys of this **kingdom** shall never be taken from you
D&C 97:14	the **keys** of which kingdom have been conferred upon you
D&C 107:15	the bishopric...holds the **keys** or authority of the
D&C 107:18(13-20)	is to hold the **keys** of all the spiritual blessings of
D&C 107:76	descendant of Aaron...right...to the **keys** of this
D&C 110:11(11-16)	committed unto us the **keys** of the gathering of Israel
D&C 110:16(1-16)	**keys** of this dispensation are committed into your hand
D&C 112:15	Joseph...and the **keys** which I have given unto him, and
D&C 112:16(16-18)	Thomas...chosen to hold the **keys** of my kingdom, as
D&C 112:32	**keys** of the dispensation...come down from the fathers
D&C 113:6	descendant of Jesse...unto whom...belongs...the **keys**
D&C 115:19(18-19)	unto him have I given the **keys** of this kingdom and
D&C 124:34(33-34)	therein are the **keys** of the holy priesthood ordained
D&C 124:93	**bind** on earth shall be bound in heaven; and whatsoever
D&C 124:123(123-145	my Priesthood, that ye may hold the **keys** thereof, even
D&C 127:7	**bind** on earth, may be bound in heaven; whatsoever you
D&C 128:8(8-11)	whatsoever you **loose** on earth shall be loosed in
D&C 128:14(12-21)	**keys** of the kingdom...consist in the key of knowledge.
D&C 128:20	declaring themselves as possessing the **keys** of the
D&C 128:21	voice...of divers angels...declaring...their **keys**, the
D&C 132:7	never but one...on whom...the **keys** of this priesthood
D&C 132:19(1-24)	I have appointed this power and the **keys** of this
D&C 132:39	the prophets who had the **keys** of this power; and in
D&C 132:45(45-47)	I have conferred upon you the **keys** and power of the
D&C 132:59	I have endowed him with the **keys** of the power of this
JS-H 1:38(37-39)	I will reveal...the **Priesthood**, by the hand of Elijah
JS-H 1:72	Peter, James and John...held the **keys** of the
JS-H 1:72	who held the **keys** of the priesthood of Melchizedek

PRIESTHOOD, MAGNIFYING CALLINGS WITHIN

1 Sam. 2:30(27-36)	them that **honour** me I will honour, and they that
Ps. 132:9	let thy **priests** be clothed with righteousness; and let
Isa. 58:1	lift up thy **voice** like a trumpet, and shew my people
Jer. 1:7(7-8)	thou shalt go to all that I shall **send** thee, and
Ezek. 3:17(17-19)	at my mouth, and give them **warning** from me.
Ezek. 33:9(7-9)	if thou **warn** the wicked of his way to turn from it
Ezek. 34:2(2-6)	should not the shepherds **feed** the flocks
Matt. 6:33(31-33)	but **seek** ye first the kingdom of God, and his
Matt. 10:40(40-42)	he that **receiveth** you receiveth me, and he that
Matt. 20:26(20-28)	great among you, let him be your **minister**
2 Cor. 6:4(3-7)	in all things approving ourselves as the **ministers** of
Eph. 4:12(11-14)	for the **perfecting** of the saints, for the work of the
1 Tim. 4:14(12-16)	**neglect** not the gift that is in thee, which was given
1 Tim. 6:11(11-14,20)	follow after **righteousness**, godliness, faith, love
2 Tim. 1:6(6-8,13,14)	**stir** up the gift of God, which is in thee by the
2 Tim. 2:22(20-26)	flee also youthful lusts: but follow **righteousness**
Heb. 7:26(22-28)	such an high priest...made **higher** than the heavens
1 Pet. 2:5(1-5)	holy priesthood, to offer up **spiritual** sacrifices
1 Pet. 4:10(7-11)	received the gift, even so **minister** the same one to
Jacob 1:19	and we did **magnify** our office unto the Lord, taking
Alma 13:10(1-13)	their exceeding **faith** and repentance, and their
Alma 17:2(2,3)	**searched** the scriptures diligently, that they might
Alma 37:37(35-37)	**counsel** with the Lord in all thy doings, and he will
Alma 38:12(1-15)	**bridle** all your passions, that ye may be filled with
Hel. 10:4(4-11)	thou hast with **unwearyingness** declared the word, which
Moro. 9:6	we have a **labor** to perform whilst in this tabernacle
D&C 1:37(37,38)	**search** these commandments, for they are true and faith
D&C 4:2(1-7)	see that ye **serve** him with all your heart, might
D&C 20:38(38-59)	the **duty** of the elders, priests, teachers, deacons
D&C 21:4(4-6)	thou shalt give **heed** unto all his words and
D&C 36:7	every man which will **embrace** it with singleness of
D&C 38:25(23-25)	let every man **esteem** his brother as himself.
D&C 42:12(12-16)	**teach** the principles of my gospel, which are in the
D&C 50:17(17-22)	sent forth to **preach** the word of truth by the Comfort
D&C 58:27(26-29)	men should be anxiously **engaged** in a good cause, and
D&C 60:13(2,3,13)	thou shalt not **idle** away thy time, neither shalt thou
D&C 84:33(33-44)	priesthoods...**magnifying** their calling, are sanctified
D&C 84:62	that the **testimony** may go from you into all the world
D&C 84:76	to whom..kingdom..given- from you it must be **preached**
D&C 84:109(109-110)	let every man...**labor** in his own calling; and let not
D&C 88:67(67-69)	if your eye be **single** to my glory, your whole bodies
D&C 88:81(80-82)	every man who hath been warned to **warn** his neighbor.
D&C 88:119(118-126)	**organize** yourselves; prepare every needful thing; and
D&C 88:121(121-125)	therefore, **cease** from all your light speeches, from
D&C 107:30(30-32)	decisions of..quorums..to be made in all **righteousness**
D&C 107:99(99-100)	now let every man learn his **duty**, and to act in the
D&C 121:36(34-46)	**controlled**...only upon the principles of righteousness
D&C 121:41(41-46)	**priesthood**, only by persuasion, by long-suffering, by
D&C 121:45(34-46)	let thy bowels also be full of **charity** towards all men

PRIESTHOOD, MELCHIZEDEK

Gen. 14:18	Melchizedek...was the **priest** of the most high God.
Ex. 18:1	**Jethro**, the priest of Midian, Moses' father in law
Num. 16:10(8-11)	and seek ye the **priesthood** also
Ps. 110:4	thou art a **priest** for ever after the order of
John 15:16	I have chosen you, and **ordained** you, that ye should
Heb. 5:6(6-10)	thou art a **priest** for ever after the order of
Heb. 7:1(1-28)	this Melchisedec, king of Salem, **priest** of the most
Heb. 8:6	a better **covenant**, which was established upon better
1 Pet. 2:9(5,9)	ye are a chosen generation, a royal **priesthood**, an
2 Ne. 6:2	ordained after the manner of his holy **order**, and
Alma 13:1(1-19)	the Lord God ordained **priests**, after his holy order
3 Ne. 18:37(36-38)	he gave them **power** to give the Holy Ghost. And I will
Moro. 2:2(1-3)	ye shall have **power**...to...give the Holy Ghost; and
D&C 27:12(12,13)	I have **ordained** you and confirmed you to be apostles
D&C 65:2(1-6)	the **keys** of the kingdom of God are committed unto man
D&C 76:57(56-58)	and are **priests** of the Most High, after the order of
D&C 84:17(17-22)	which **priesthood** continueth in the church of God in
D&C 84:19(6-31)	this greater **priesthood** administereth the gospel and
D&C 84:25	Moses out of their midst, and the Holy **Priesthood** also
D&C 84:40(33-44)	all those who receive the **priesthood**, receive this
D&C 86:10(8-11)	the **priesthood** have remained, and must needs remain
D&C 107:2(2-12)	the first is called the **Melchizedek** Priesthood is
D&C 107:17(17-19)	but as a high priest of the **Melchizedek** Priesthood has
D&C 107:22(21-32)	of the **Melchizedek** Priesthood, three Presiding High
D&C 107:33(33-38)	the Twelve are a Traveling **Presiding** High Council, to
D&C 107:39(39-57)	duty of the Twelve...to ordain **evangelical** ministers
D&C 107:58(58-60)	duty of the Twelve...to ordain..all the other **officers**
D&C 107:65(64-67)	needs be that one be appointed of the High **Priesthood**
D&C 107:69(68-78)	a bishop must be chosen from the High **Priesthood**
D&C 107:79(79-88)	Presidency of the High **Priesthood** and its counselors
D&C 107:89(89-100)	duty of the president over the office of **elders** is to
D&C 110:16(11-16)	the **keys** of this dispensation are committed into your
D&C 113:6	unto whom rightly belongs the **priesthood**, and the keys
D&C 121:21(17-23)	they shall not have right to the **priesthood**, nor their
D&C 124:28(28-42)	restore again ...the fulness of the **priesthood**.
D&C 127:8	about to restore...pertaining to the **priesthood**, saith
D&C 128:20	Peter, James, and John...possessing the **keys** of the
D&C 131:2(1-4)	a man must enter into this order of the **priesthood**
Moses 6:7	same **Priesthood**...in the beginning, shall be in the
Moses 6:67(67,68)	thou art after the **order** of him who was without
Moses 8:19	Lord ordained Noah after his own **order**, and commanded
Abr. 1:2(1-4)	a High **Priest**, holding the right belonging to the
Abr. 2:11	this **right** shall continue in thee, and in thy seed
JS-H 1:38	I will reveal unto you the **Priesthood**, by the hand
JFS-V 1:41	Shem, the great **high** priest; Abraham, the father of

PRIESTHOOD, OATH AND COVENANT

Num. 25:13(10-13)	even the **covenant** of an everlasting priesthood
Neh. 13:29(29-31)	the **covenant** of the priesthood, and of the Levites.
Mal. 2:4(4-8)	my **covenant** might be with Levi, saith the Lord of
Heb. 7:20(20-21)	and inasmuch as not without an **oath** he was made priest

PRIESTHOOD, OATH AND COVENANT cont.

Heb. 7:21(20,21)   but this with an **oath** by him that said unto him, the
Alma 13:8(1-12)   now they were **ordained** after this manner- being called
D&C 84:40(33-41)   receive the priesthood, receive this **oath** and covenant
D&C 107:99   let every man learn his **duty**, and to act in the office
D&C 107:100   he that is slothful shall not be counted **worthy** to
D&C 121:36   **rights** of the priesthood are inseparably connected

PRIESTHOOD, ORDINATION

Ex. 40:15   their **anointing** shall...be an everlasting priesthood
Lev. 8:12(12,13)   he poured of the **anointing** oil upon Aaron's head, and
Num. 27:23(15-23)   he **laid** his hands upon him, and gave him a charge, as
Deut. 34:9   for Moses had **laid** his hands upon him: and the
2 Kgs. 2:15(9-15)   the spirit of Elijah doth **rest** on Elisha. And they
1 Chr. 9:22(22-30)   whom David and Samuel..did **ordain** in their set office.
Isa. 6:8(1-9)   who will go for us? Then said I, Here am I; **send** me.
Jer. 1:5   and I **ordained** thee a prophet unto the nations.
Ezek. 2:3(1-5)   son of man, I **send** thee to the children of Israel, to
Mark 3:14(14,15)   and he **ordained** twelve, that they should be with him
Acts 13:3(1-3)   when they had fasted and prayed, and laid their **hands**
Acts 14:23   when they had **ordained** them elders in every church
1 Tim. 4:14   with the **laying** on of the hands of the presbytery.
Titus 1:5   and **ordain** elders in every city, as I had appointed
Heb. 5:1(1-4)   for every high priest...is **ordained** for men in things
Alma 13:1(1-12)   the Lord God **ordained** priests, after his holy order
D&C 5:17   a little while, for ye are not yet **ordained**
D&C 20:60   he is to be **ordained** by the power of the Holy Ghost
D&C 20:65(65-67)   no person is to be **ordained** to..office...without..vote
D&C 27:12(12,13)   Peter...James, and John...by whom I have **ordained** you
D&C 42:11   except he be **ordained** by some one who has authority
D&C 84:28(26-28)   **ordained** by the angel of God at...eight **days** old unto
Moses 8:19   and the Lord **ordained** Noah after his own **order**, and

PRIESTHOOD, POWER OF

Gen. 32:28(24-30)   as a prince hast thou **power** with God and with men, and
Ex. 15:2   the Lord is my **strength** and song, and he is become my
2 Sam. 22:33(32,33)   God is my strength and **power**: and he maketh my way
Isa. 12:2   the Lord Jehovah is my **strength** and my song; he also
Isa. 49:6(5,6)   that thou mayest be my **salvation** unto the end of the
Isa. 52:1(1-3,6)   Awake, Awake; put on thy **strength**, O Zion; put on thy
Micah 3:8   I am full of **power** by the Spirit of the Lord, and of
Micah 5:4(4,5)   in the **strength** of the Lord, in the majesty of the
Matt. 10:1   he gave them **power** against unclean spirits, to cast
Matt. 28:18   all **power** is given unto me in heaven and in earth.
Mark 3:15(14,15)   and to have **power** to heal sicknesses, and to cast out
Luke 10:19(1-20)   I give unto you **power** to tread on serpents and
Acts 4:7(1-10)   by what **power**...have ye done this
Acts 6:8   Stephen, full of faith and **power**, did great wonders
Acts 8:19(9-24)   give me also this **power**, that on whomsoever I lay hand
Acts 19:11(10-12)   and God wrought special **miracles** by the hands of Paul

PRIESTHOOD, POWER OF cont.

1 Cor. 2:4(1-5)	in demonstration of the Spirit and of **power**
1 Cor. 4:20	for the kingdom of God is not in word, but in **power**.
1 Ne. 2:14(6-14)	father did speak...with **power**...filled with the Spirit
1 Ne. 17:48(48-55)	I am filled with the **power** of God, even unto the
2 Ne. 1:27(25-27)	it must needs be that the **power** of God must be with
Mosiah 13:6(1-9)	he spake with **power** and authority from God; and he
3 Ne. 7:17(15-22)	Nephi did minister with **power** and with great authority
3 Ne. 20:36(36-38)	Awake, Awake again, and put on thy **strength**, O Zion
Moro. 10:31	O Jerusalem...**strengthen** thy stakes and enlarge thy
D&C 45:8(6-8)	unto as many as received me gave I **power** to do many
D&C 50:27(25-30)	he is possessor of all things...Spirit and the **power**
D&C 84:20(20-22)	in the ordinances...**power** of godliness is manifest.
D&C 90:11(10-11)	through those who are ordained unto this **power**, by the
D&C 105:11(10-12)	until mine elders are endowed with **power** from on high.
D&C 112:30(30-32)	unto...the Twelve...**power** of this priesthood given
D&C 113:8(7-8)	who...hold the **power** of priesthood to bring again Zion
D&C 121:36(34-46)	rights..priesthood...connected with...**powers** of heaven
D&C 128:8(8-11)	this ordinance consists in the **power** of the priesthood
D&C 132:7	whom I have appointed on the earth to hold this **power**
Moses 7:13	nations feared...so **powerful** was the word of Enoch
Moses 8:18(18-19)	Lord was with Noah..the **power** of the Lord was upon him
Abr. 1:18	priesthood of thy father...my **power** shall be over thee
JFS-V 1:30(30,31)	organized...and...clothed with **power** and authority

PRIESTHOOD, QUALIFYING FOR

1 Sam. 13:12(8-15)	I **forced** myself therefore, and offered a burnt
2 Chr. 26:18(16-21)	**not** unto thee, Uzziah, to burn incense unto the Lord
Ezra 2:62(61-62)	as polluted, put from the **priesthood**.
Ezra 7:10	for Ezra had **prepared** his heart to seek the law of the
Neh. 7:64(63-65)	as polluted, put from the **priesthood**.
Isa. 52:11	be ye **clean**, that bear the vessels of the Lord.
John 15:16	but I have **chosen** you, and ordained you, that ye
Acts 6:3(1-8)	look ye out among you seven men of **honest** report, full
2 Cor. 4:2(1-10)	but have **renounced**...dishonesty, not walking in
1 Tim. 3:2(1-15)	a bishop then must be **blameless**...vigilant, sober, of
1 Tim. 4:12(12-16)	be thou an **example** of the believers, in word, in
Heb. 5:4(1-6)	but he that is **called** of God, as was Aaron.
Alma 13:3(1-13)	exercising exceeding great **faith**, are called with a
D&C 4:5(1-7)	faith, hope, charity..eye single..**qualify** him for the
D&C 20:6(5-8)	after **repenting**, and humbling himself sincerely
D&C 36:7	every man which will **embrace** it with singleness of
D&C 42:11	except he be **ordained** by some one who has authority
D&C 85:12(11-12)	as unto the children of the **priest**...of Ezra.
Abr. 1:2(1-4)	having been myself a follower of **righteousness**
Abr. 1:27(25-27)	not have the right of **Priesthood**, notwithstanding the
A of F 1:5	We believe that a man must be **called** of God, by

PRIESTS

Ex. 28:4(1-43)	that he may minister unto me in the **priest's** office.
Ex. 29:9(1-9,29)	the **priest's** office shall be theirs for a perpetual
Lev. 13:3(2-3)	**priest** shall look on...plague...pronounce him unclean.
Num. 3:3	sons of Aaron, the **priests** which were anointed, whom
Num. 4:47(23,47)	thirty..unto fifty years old...service of the **ministry**
Num. 8:10(5-10)	children of Israel shall put their hands upon..**Levites**
Num. 18:7	keep your **priest's** office...within the vail; and ye
2 Kgs. 23:4	**priests** of the second order, and the keepers of the
1 Chr. 6:32(16,31-32)	**ministered**...with singing...then...waited on their
2 Chr. 29:34	**priests** were too few...wherefore...Levites did help
2 Chr. 35:11	**priests** sprinkled the blood...Levites flayed them.
Neh. 11:16	**Levites**...oversight of the outward business of the
Ezek. 44:15(11-15)	**priests** the Levites...kept the charge of my sanctuary
Ezek. 44:21(20-24)	neither shall any **priest** drink wine, when they enter
Luke 1:8(5-25)	while he executed the **priest's** office before God in
Acts 6:7	and a great company of the **priests** were obedient to
Heb. 7:5(1-25)	sons of **Levi**...office...take tithes of the people
Heb. 8:4	there are **priests** that offer gifts according to the
Heb. 9:6	the **priests** went always into the first tabernacle
Rev. 1:6	made us kings and **priests** unto God and his Father; to
Rev. 5:10	made us unto our God kings and **priests**: and we shall
Rev. 20:6	they shall be **priests** of God and of Christ, and shall
2 Ne. 5:26	consecrate...that they should be **priests** and teachers
Mosiah 23:17	consecrated all their **priests** and all their teachers
Mosiah 25:19	power to ordain **priests** and teachers over every church
Mosiah 26:7	they were brought before the **priests**, and delivered
Alma 13:1(1-20)	the Lord God ordained **priests**, after his holy order
Moro. 3:1(1-4)	the manner...disciples...ordained **priests** and teachers
Moro. 4:1	**priests** administering the flesh and blood of Christ
D&C 18:32	to ordain **priests** and teachers; to declare my gospel
D&C 20:46(46-52)	**priest's** duty is to preach, teach, expound, exhort
D&C 20:60	**priest**...ordained according to the gifts and callings
D&C 84:111	and also the lesser **priests**; but the deacons and teach
D&C 107:10	**priest** (of the Levitical order), teacher, deacon, and
D&C 107:87(87-88)	president...preside over forty-eight **priests**, and sit

PROBATION

Gen. 3:22(22-24)	the man is become as one of us, to **know** good and evil
Job 1:12(6-12)	all that he hath is in thy **power**; only upon himself
Job 2:6(1-6)	he is in thine **hand**; but save his life.
Job 7:18(17,18)	visit him every morning, and **try** him every moment
Job 36:11(5-12)	if they obey...shall spend their **days** in prosperity
Job 42:9(7-10)	commanded them: the Lord also **accepted** Job.
2 Cor. 8:2	how that in a great **trial** of affliction the abundance
1 Pet. 1:6(6-8)	now for a **season**, if need be, ye are in heaviness
1 Ne. 10:21(20,21)	sought to do wickedly in the days of your **probation**
1 Ne. 15:32(31-32)	works which were done...in their days of **probation**.
2 Ne. 2:21	their state became a state of **probation**, and their
2 Ne. 9:27	that wasteth the days of his **probation**, for awful is
2 Ne. 33:9	continue...path until the end of the day of **probation**.
Alma 12:24	this life became a **probationary** state; a time to

PROBATION cont.

Alma 42:4(4-13)	a **probationary** time, a time to repent and serve God.
Hel. 13:38	but behold, your days of **probation** are past; ye have
Morm. 9:28	be wise in the days of your **probation**; strip
D&C 29:43(42-45)	appoint unto man the days of his **probation-** that by
D&C 58:4	for after much **tribulation** come the blessings.
D&C 103:12	for after much **tribulation**, as I have said unto you
D&C 105:19(6-19)	brought thus far for a **trial** of their faith.
D&C 121:8	if thou **endure** it well, God shall exalt thee on high
Moses 4:28(28,29)	the man is become as one of us to **know** good and evil

PROBLEM-SOLVING

Ps. 49:4(3,4)	I will **open** my dark saying upon the harp.
Prov. 1:7	fools despise wisdom and **instruction**.
Prov. 3:6(5,6)	acknowledge him, and he shall **direct** thy paths. I
Prov. 4:7	with all thy getting get **understanding**.
Prov. 12:15	**fool** is right in his own eyes: but he that hearkeneth
Matt. 7:7(7-11)	**ask**, and it shall be given you; seek, and ye shall
Matt. 11:28(28-30)	**come** unto me, all ye that labour and are heavy laden
Mark 9:29	come forth by nothing, but by prayer and **fasting**.
Luke 14:28(28-29)	sitteth not down first, and counteth the **cost**, whether
John 15:7(4-7)	if ye **abide** in me, and my words abide in you, ye shall
1 Ne. 15:8	I said unto them: have ye **inquired** of the Lord
2 Ne. 32:3	the words of Christ will **tell** you all things what ye
Alma 17:3	they had the spirit of prophecy, and...of **revelation**
Alma 37:37	**counsel** with the Lord in all thy doings, and he will
Moro. 10:5(4-5)	by...the Holy Ghost ye may **know** the truth of all thing
D&C 9:8(7-9)	you must **study** it out in your mind; then you must ask
D&C 46:7	ye are commanded in all things to **ask** of God, who give
D&C 63:47	he that is faithful and **endureth** shall overcome the
D&C 88:124	that your bodies and your **minds** may be invigorated.
D&C 136:19	if any man...seeketh not my **counsel**...have no power

PROCRASTINATION

Josh. 24:15	choose you **this** day whom ye will serve; whether the
Ps. 119:60(57-64)	I made haste, and **delayed** not to keep thy commandments
Prov. 19:15	**slothfulness** casteth into a deep sleep; and an idle
Isa. 22:13(12-14)	let us eat and drink; for **to** morrow we shall die.
Jonah 1:3(1-3)	Jonah rose up to **flee** unto Tarshish from the presence
Matt. 24:44(42-51)	be ye also **ready**: for in such an hour as ye think not
Matt. 25:10(1-13)	they that were **ready** went in with him to the marriage
Mark 13:36(32-37)	lest coming suddenly he find you **sleeping**.
Luke 12:47(37-48)	that servant, which knew...and **prepared** not himself
Luke 21:34(34-36)	so that day come upon you **unawares**.
1 Cor. 15:32	let us eat and drink; for **to** morrow we die.
2 Ne. 28:7(7,8)	eat, drink, and be merry, for **tomorrow** we die; and
Alma 5:29(28,29)	I would that he should prepare **quickly**, for the hour
Alma 5:31	the **time** is at hand that he must repent or he cannot
Alma 10:23	the **time** is soon at hand except ye repent.
Alma 13:21	**now** is the time to repent, for the day of salvation

PROCRASTINATION cont.

Alma 13:27(27-29)	and not **procrastinate** the day of your repentance
Alma 34:33(31-35)	do not **procrastinate** the day of your repentance until
Hel. 13:29(28-30)	how **long** will ye suppose that the Lord will suffer you
Hel. 13:38	ye have **procrastinated** the day of your salvation until
3 Ne. 8:24(24,25)	O that we had repented **before** this great and terrible
3 Ne. 29:4(4,8)	ye need not any **longer** spurn at the doings of the Lord
D&C 6:3	reap while the day **lasts**, that he may treasure up for
D&C 33:17	that you may be **ready** at the coming of the
D&C 50:46	watch, therefore, that ye may be **ready**. Even so. Amen.
D&C 60:13	thou shalt not **idle** away thy time, neither shalt thou
D&C 64:25	ye will labor while it is called **today**.
D&C 88:83	he that seeketh me **early** shall find me, and shall not
D&C 90:18	keep **slothfulness** and uncleanness far from you.
D&C 124:50(49,50)	so **long** as they repent not, and hate me, saith
D&C 133:11	**watch**, therefore, for ye know neither the day nor the
Moses 6:33	choose ye **this** day, to serve the Lord God who made you
JS-M 1:48(46-55)	therefore be ye also **ready**, for in such an hour as ye

PROFANITY

Ex. 20:7	shalt not take the name of the Lord thy God in **vain**
Lev. 19:12	neither shalt thou **profane** the name of thy God: I am
Lev. 20:3	to defile my sanctuary, and to **profane** my holy name.
Lev. 21:6	be holy...and not **profane** the name of their God: for
Lev. 24:11(10-16)	**blasphemed** the name of the Lord, and cursed. And they
Ps. 34:13	keep thy **tongue** from evil, and thy lips from speaking
Prov. 15:4	a wholesome **tongue** is a tree of life: but perverseness
Ezek. 22:26	I am **profaned** among them.
Hosea 4:2	by **swearing**, and lying, and killing, and stealing, and
Mal. 2:10(10,11)	deal treacherously...by **profaning** the covenant of our
Matt. 5:34(33-37)	**swear** not at all; neither by heaven; for it is God's
Matt. 12:36(34-37)	every idle word that men shall **speak**, they shall give
Matt. 15:11(11,18)	that which cometh out of the **mouth**, this defileth a
Acts 19:13	call over them ...the **name** of the Lord Jesus, saying
Eph. 4:29	let no corrupt **communication** proceed out of your mouth
Col. 3:8	put off...filthy **communication** out of your mouth.
James 1:26(19,26)	bridleth not his **tongue**, but deceiveth his own heart
James 3:8(2-12)	but the **tongue** can no man tame; it is an unruly evil
2 Ne. 26:32	not take the name of the Lord their God in **vain**; that
Jarom 1:5	and they **profaned** not; neither did they blaspheme. And
Mosiah 13:15	shalt not take the name of the Lord thy God in **vain**
3 Ne. 12:34(34-37)	**swear** not at all; neither by heaven, for it is God's
Morm. 3:9(9,10)	began to **swear** before the heavens that they would
D&C 20:54	see that there is no...evil **speaking**
D&C 63:61(61-64)	let all men beware how they take my **name** in their lips
D&C 112:26(24-26)	have **blasphemed** against me in the midst of my house
D&C 136:21	from evil to take the **name** of the Lord in vain, for I

PROMISED LAND

Gen. 12:1	unto a **land** that I will shew thee
Gen. 12:7	unto Abram...said, unto thy seed will I give this **land**
Gen. 13:15(14-15,17)	all the **land** which thou seest, to thee will I give it
Gen. 15:18(7,18)	Abram...unto thy seed have I given this **land**, from the
Gen. 17:8(7-8)	I will give unto thee...the **land** wherein thou art a
Gen. 24:7	unto thy seed will I give this **land**; he shall send
Gen. 26:3(1-4)	unto thee, and...seed, I will give all these **countries**
Gen. 28:13(10-16)	the **land** whereon thou liest, to thee will I give it
Gen. 35:12	the **land** which I gave Abraham and Isaac, to thee I
Gen. 48:4(3-4)	will give this **land** to thy seed after thee for an ever
Gen. 48:21	God shall...bring you again unto the **land** of your
Gen. 50:24	the **land** which he sware to Abraham, to Isaac, and to
Ex. 20:12	upon the **land** which the Lord thy God giveth thee.
Ex. 32:13	all this **land**...will I give unto your seed, and they
Num. 27:12	see the **land**...given unto the children of Israel.
Num. 34:2(1-12)	this is the **land** that shall fall unto you for an
Deut. 1:8	possess the **land** which the Lord sware unto your father
Deut. 34:4(1-4)	this is the land which I **sware** unto Abraham, unto
Josh. 21:43	the Lord gave unto Israel all the **land** which he sware
1 Chr. 16:18(16-18)	unto thee will I give the **land** of Canaan, the lot of
Ps. 105:11	unto thee will I give the **land** of Canaan, the lot of
Amos 9:15(14,15)	I will plant them upon their **land**, and they shall no
Acts 7:5(1-7)	yet he **promised** that he would give it to him for a
Heb. 11:9(8-9)	by faith he sojourned in the **land** of promise, as in a
1 Ne. 2:20	ye...shall be led to a **land** of promise; yea, even a
1 Ne. 5:5	I have obtained a **land** of promise, in the which things
1 Ne. 7:13	we shall obtain the **land** of promise; and ye shall
1 Ne. 10:13	should be led...into the **land** of promise, unto the
1 Ne. 12:1	I looked and beheld the **land** of promise; and I beheld
1 Ne. 13:14(14,15)	multitudes of the Gentiles upon the **land** of promise
1 Ne. 13:30	his seed should have for the **land** of their inheritance
1 Ne. 18:23	we did arrive at the promised **land**; and we went forth
2 Ne. 1:5(5-9)	we have obtained a **land** of promise, a land which is
Jacob 2:12	a **land** of promise unto you and to your seed, doth
3 Ne. 20:14(13,14)	I should give unto you this **land**, for your inheritance
Ether 2:7(7-12)	they should come forth even unto the **land** of promise
Ether 6:12	they did land upon the shore of the promised **land**.
Ether 13:8	remnant of..Joseph..it shall be a **land** of their
D&C 38:20(18-22)	ye shall have it for the **land** of your inheritance, and
D&C 103:11	shall return to the **lands** of their inheritances, and
D&C 109:64	Judah may begin to return to the **lands** which thou
Abr. 1:16	into a strange **land** which thou knowest not of
Abr. 2:19	unto thy seed will I give this **land**.

PROMISES

Lev. 26:44(42-45)	I will not...break my **covenant** with them: for I am
Josh. 23:10(9-11)	God...fighteth for you, as he hath **promised** you.
1 Kgs. 8:56	there hath not failed one word of all his good **promise**
Ps. 105:42(7-42)	for he remembered his holy **promise**, and Abraham his
Jer. 33:14(14-16)	I will perform that good thing which I have **promised**
Ezek. 12:25(25-28)	I say the **word**, and will perform it, saith the Lord

PROMISES cont.

Luke 24:49	I send the **promise** of my Father upon you: but tarry
Acts 1:4	wait for the **promise** of the Father, which, saith he
Acts 2:39	for the **promise** is unto you, and to your children, and
Acts 13:23(23-32)	God according to his **promise** raised unto Israel a
Rom. 4:21(16-22)	what he had **promised**, he was able also to perform.
Gal. 3:14(14-28)	that we might receive the **promise** of the Spirit
Eph. 1:13	sealed with that Holy Spirit of **promise**
Heb. 6:12(12-17)	through faith and patience inherit the **promises**.
Heb. 8:6	covenant, which was established upon better **promises**.
Heb. 11:17	he that had received the **promises** offered up his only
Heb. 11:33	obtained **promises**, stopped the mouths of lions
2 Pet. 1:4	given unto us exceeding great and precious **promises**
1 Jn. 2:25	and this is the **promise** that he hath promised us, even
2 Ne. 3:5(5-16)	he obtained a **promise** of the Lord, that out of the
2 Ne. 10:2	**promises** which we have obtained are...according to the
2 Ne. 10:17(2-17)	for I will fulfil my **promises** which I have made unto
Alma 37:17	for he will fulfil all his **promises** which he shall
Alma 50:39	with an **oath** and sacred ordinance to judge righteously
4 Ne. 1:11	blessed according to...**promises** which the Lord had
Morm. 8:22	until all his **promises** shall be fulfilled.
Morm. 9:21	this **promise** is unto all, even unto the ends of the
Ether 12:17	by faith...disciples obtained a **promise** that they
D&C 1:38(37,38)	word...not pass away, but shall all be **fulfilled**
D&C 2:2	plant in the hearts...**promises** made to the fathers
D&C 67:10	a **promise** I give unto you that have been ordained unto
D&C 76:53	sealed by the Holy Spirit of **promise**, which the Father
D&C 82:10	but when ye do not what I say, ye have no **promise**.
D&C 84:40(38-40)	receive this **oath**..of my Father, which he cannot break
D&C 88:75	that I may fulfil this...great and last **promise**, which
D&C 89:3	given for a principle with **promise**, adapted to the
D&C 100:8	and I give unto you this **promise**, that inasmuch as ye
D&C 118:3	a **promise** that I will provide for their families; and
Abr. 2:11	a **promise** that this right shall continue in thee, and

PROPHECY

Ex. 4:12(11,12)	I will be with thy mouth, and **teach** thee what thou
Ex. 4:16(15,16)	he shall be thy **spokesman**...instead of God.
Ex. 7:1	Aaron thy brother shall be thy **prophet**.
Num. 11:29(27-30)	would God that all the Lord's people were **prophets**
2 Sam. 23:2(2,3)	Spirit of the Lord **spake** by me, and his word was in
Jer. 1:9(4-9)	behold, I have put my **words** in thy mouth.
Ezek. 3:27(16-27)	I will open thy **mouth**, and thou shalt say unto them
Amos 3:7	he revealeth his secret unto his servants the **prophets**
Amos 7:15(14-16)	the Lord said unto me, go, **prophesy** unto my people
1 Cor. 12:10	to another **prophecy**; to another discerning of spirits
1 Cor. 13:2(1,2)	and though I have the gift of **prophecy**, and understand
1 Cor. 14:3(1-4)	he that **prophesieth** speaketh unto men to edification
1 Cor. 14:5	I would...rather that ye **prophesied**: for greater is
1 Cor. 14:22	**prophesying** serveth...for them which believe.
1 Tim. 4:14(14-16)	gift that is in thee...given thee by **prophecy**, with
2 Pet. 1:20(19-21)	no **prophecy** of...scripture is of any private

PROPHECY cont.

2 Pet. 1:21	**prophecy** came not in old time by the will of man: but
Rev. 19:10	testimony of Jesus is the spirit of **prophecy**.
1 Ne. 22:2	by...Spirit...all things made known unto the **prophets**
2 Ne. 25:4	words of Isaiah...plain...with the spirit of **prophecy**.
Jacob 4:6	we have many revelations and the spirit of **prophecy**
Alma 45:9	what I **prophesy**...not be made known...until..fulfilled
D&C 1:38(37-39)	whether by mine own **voice** or by the voice of my
D&C 11:25	deny not the spirit...of **prophecy**, for wo unto him
D&C 20:26(26-27)	**prophets**...spake as they were inspired by the...Holy
D&C 21:5(4-5)	for his **word** ye shall receive, as if from mine own
D&C 46:22	and to others it is given to **prophesy**
D&C 131:5	more sure word of **prophecy** means a man's knowing that
A of F 1:5	a man must be called of God, by **prophecy**, and by the
A of F 1:7	We believe in the gift of...**prophecy**, revelation

PROPHETS, MISSION OF

Ex. 4:12(11-16)	I will be with thy mouth, and **teach** thee what thou
Ex. 4:16	and thou shalt be to him **instead** of God.
Ex. 4:30(27-30)	and Aaron **spake** all the words which the Lord had spoke
Ex. 7:1(1-2)	and Aaron thy brother shall be thy **prophet**.
Num. 11:29	would God that all the Lord's people were **prophets**
Num. 12:6	**prophet** among you, I...will make myself known...in a
Deut. 18:18(15-21)	I will raise them up a **prophet** from among their
Deut. 18:22	when a **prophet** speaketh in the name of the Lord, if
1 Sam. 9:9	now called a **prophet** was beforetime called a seer.
2 Kgs. 17:13	Lord testified against Israel...by all the **prophets**
2 Chr. 36:15(15,16)	God of their fathers sent to them by his **messengers**
Neh. 9:30	testifiedst against them by thy spirit in thy **prophets**
Isa. 6:8(8-10)	Lord, saying, whom shall I **send**...who will go for us
Isa. 58:1	cry aloud...**shew** my people their transgression, and
Jer. 1:7	and whatsoever I command thee thou shalt **speak**.
Jer. 1:10(9,10)	to root out, and to pull down...to **build**, and to plant
Jer. 5:14	behold, I will make my words in thy **mouth** fire, and
Jer. 7:25	I have even sent unto you all my servants the **prophets**
Ezek. 2:7	thou shalt **speak** my words unto them, whether they will
Ezek. 3:19(17-21)	if thou **warn** the wicked...thou hast delivered thy soul
Ezek. 3:27(22-27)	thou shalt say unto them, thus **saith** the Lord God; he
Ezek. 33:9(1-16)	if thou **warn** the wicked of his way to turn from it
Amos 3:7	he revealeth his secret unto...the **prophets**.
Amos 7:15(14-17)	Lord said unto me, go, **prophesy** unto my people Israel
Jonah 1:2(1-2)	go to Nineveh, that great city, and **cry** against it
Jonah 3:2(1-4)	Nineveh...**preach** unto it the preaching that I bid thee
Matt. 28:20(19-20)	**teaching** them to observe all things...I have commanded
Luke 1:70(68-70)	as he **spake** by the mouth of his holy prophets, which
Acts 3:21(20-21)	**spoken** by the mouth of all his holy prophets since the
Acts 10:43	to him give all the prophets **witness**, that through his
1 Cor. 12:28(12-28)	God hath set some in the church...apostles...**prophets**
Eph. 2:20(19-22)	built upon...apostles and **prophets**, Jesus Christ
Eph. 3:5	revealed unto his holy apostles and **prophets** by the
Eph. 4:11(11-14)	he gave some, apostles; and some, **prophets**; and some
Heb. 1:1(1-2)	spake in time past unto the fathers by the **prophets**

PROPHETS, MISSION OF cont.

2 Pet. 3:2(1,2)	mindful of the words...spoken...by the holy **prophets**
2 Ne. 3:11	a **seer** will I raise up out of the fruit of thy loins
2 Ne. 3:18(16-22)	and the **spokesman** of thy loins shall declare it.
2 Ne. 9:48(44-48)	expedient that I **teach** you the consequences of sin.
Jacob 1:19(17-19)	by **laboring** with our might their blood might not come
Hel. 5:18(18-19)	they also had what they should **speak** given unto them
D&C 1:38(38,39)	by mine own voice or by the voice of my **servants**, it
D&C 6:9	say nothing but **repentance** unto this generation; keep
D&C 20:26	prophets...who truly **testified** of him in all things
D&C 21:5(4-7)	**receive**, as if from mine own mouth, in all patience
D&C 24:6	be given thee in the very moment what thou shalt **speak**
D&C 43:3(3-4)	none other appointed unto you to receive **commandments**
D&C 52:9	that which the **prophets** and apostles have written, and
D&C 58:18(17,18)	laws of the kingdom...are given by the **prophets** of God
D&C 68:3	they shall **speak** as they are moved upon by the holy
D&C 84:36	he that receiveth my **servants** receiveth me
D&C 90:4	through you shall the **oracles** be given to another, yea
D&C 100:9	a **spokesman** unto my servant Joseph.
D&C 124:45(45,46)	**servants** whom I have appointed to lead my people
D&C 135:3	Joseph Smith, the **Prophet**...has done more...for the
Moses 6:23	spake and **prophesied**, and called upon all men
Moses 6:32	open thy mouth, and it shall be **filled**, and I will
A of F 1:6	apostles, **prophets**, pastors, teachers, evangelists
JFS-V 1:36(36-49)	preparing the faithful spirits of the **prophets** who had

PROPHETS, REJECTION OF

1 Kgs. 17:3(1-16)	**hide** thyself by the brook Cherith, that is before
1 Kgs. 18:17(17-21)	**Ahab** said...art thou he that troubleth Israel
1 Kgs. 19:10(9-14)	I only, am left; and they **seek** my life, to take it
2 Kgs. 17:14(13-15)	notwithstanding they would **not** hear, but hardened
2 Chr. 24:21(19-21)	they conspired against him, and **stoned** him with stones
2 Chr. 36:16(15,16)	but they **mocked** the messengers of God, and despised
Jer. 1:19(17-19)	they shall **fight** against thee; but they shall not
Jer. 11:19	they had **devised** devices against me, saying, let us
Jer. 11:21	the men of Anathoth, that seek thy **life**, saying
Jer. 12:6	even thy **brethren**...have dealt treacherously with thee
Jer. 18:18	let us **devise** devices against Jeremiah; for the law
Jer. 26:8(8-11)	the people took him, saying, thou shalt surely **die**.
Jer. 37:15	wroth with Jeremiah...put him in **prison** in the house
Jer. 44:5(4-6)	they **hearkened** not, nor inclined their ear to turn fro
Ezek. 20:49	they **say** of me, doth he not speak parables
Matt. 13:57	a prophet is not without **honour**, save in his own
Matt. 21:35(33-38)	**beat** one, and killed another, and stoned another.
Matt. 23:31(29-33)	children of them which killed the **prophets**.
Matt. 23:37(34-37)	Jerusalem, thou that **killest** the prophets, and stonest
Luke 4:24(24-26)	no prophet is **accepted** in his own country.
Luke 11:50(47-51)	blood of all the prophets, which was **shed** from the
Luke 13:33	for it cannot be that a **prophet** perish out of
Acts 7:52(51-53)	which of the prophets have not your fathers **persecuted**
1 Thes. 2:15(14,15)	who both **killed** the Lord Jesus, and their own prophets
Heb. 11:37(25-38)	they were **stoned**, they were sawn asunder, were tempted

PROPHETS, REJECTION OF cont.

Rev. 16:6(5,6)	for they have **shed** the blood of saints and prophets
1 Ne. 1:20(19-20)	the Jews...sought his **life**, that they might take it
1 Ne. 3:18(17-20)	they have **rejected** the words of the prophets.
1 Ne. 7:14	they have **rejected** the prophets, and Jeremiah have the
1 Ne. 19:7	they...**hearken** not to the voice of his counsels.
2 Ne. 26:3	they perish because they cast out the **prophets**, and
Mosiah 7:26(25,26)	and a prophet of the Lord have they **slain**; yea, a
Alma 15:16	Amulek...being **rejected** by those who were once his
Alma 37:30(29,30)	they **murdered** all the prophets of the Lord who came
Hel. 13:25(24-26)	we would not have **slain** the prophets; we would not
3 Ne. 28:34(34-35)	whoso **receiveth** not...words of Jesus and the words of
Ether 7:24(23,24)	the people did **revile** against the prophets, and did
Ether 8:25(24-26)	they have **murdered** the prophets, and stoned them, and
Ether 11:2(1,2)	the prophets were **rejected** by the people, and they
Ether 11:22(20-23)	they did **reject** all the words of the prophets, because
D&C 1:14(14-16)	they who will not hear...the voice of his **servants**
D&C 76:101(98-106)	**received** not the gospel...neither the prophets
D&C 90:5	all they who receive the **oracles** of God, let them
D&C 124:46(45-46)	if they will not **hearken**...unto the voice of these men
D&C 133:71	ye **believed** not my servants...received them not.
D&C 136:36(33-37)	for they **killed** the prophets, and them that were sent
JFS-V 1:21(19-21,32)	rebellious who rejected...the ancient **prophets** behold

PROTECTION, DIVINE

Gen. 15:1	I am thy **shield**, and thy exceeding great reward.
Gen. 45:7(1-8)	God sent me before you to **preserve** you a posterity in
Ex. 12:23	will not suffer the **destroyer** to come in unto your
Ex. 13:21(21-22)	Lord went before them...in a pillar of a **cloud**...of
Ex. 14:14	the Lord shall **fight** for you, and ye shall hold your
Num. 14:9	and the Lord is with us: **fear** them not.
Deut. 3:22	not fear...the Lord your God...shall **fight** for you.
Ps. 3:3(1-4)	but thou, O Lord, art a **shield** for me; my glory, and
Ps. 18:2(1-6)	the Lord is my rock, and my **fortress**, and my deliverer
Ps. 31:23	the Lord **preserveth** the faithful, and plentifully
Ps. 145:20	the Lord **preserveth** all them that love him: but all
Isa. 4:5	a **cloud** and smoke by day, and the shining of a flaming
Isa. 29:8(7-10)	so shall...nations be, that **fight** against mount Zion.
Isa. 54:17	no **weapon** that is formed against thee shall prosper
Isa. 66:14(14-16)	the **hand** of the Lord shall be known toward his servant
Jer. 15:20	I am with thee to **save** thee and to deliver thee, saith
Jer. 20:11	persecutors shall stumble, and they shall not **prevail**
Zech. 2:5(2-5)	for I...will be unto her a wall of **fire** round about
Matt. 28:20	I am **with** you alway, even unto the end of the world.
Mark 16:18(17-18)	drink any deadly thing, it shall not **hurt** them; they
Eph. 6:11(11-18)	put on the whole **armour** of God, that ye may be able
1 Ne. 2:2(1,2)	Lord commanded...take his family and **depart** into the
1 Ne. 5:14(14-15)	who was **preserved** by the hand of the Lord, that he
1 Ne. 22:14	all that fight against Zion shall be **destroyed**, and
1 Ne. 22:17	he will **preserve** the righteous by his power, even if
2 Ne. 9:53	our seed...he would **preserve** them; and in future
2 Ne. 10:16(10-16)	he that **fighteth** against Zion...shall perish; for they

PROTECTION, DIVINE cont.

2 Ne. 27:3(1-5)	all the nations that **fight** against Zion, and that
Alma 27:12	people in this generation, for I will **preserve** them.
Hel. 5:24(23-25,43-48)	they were encircled about with a pillar of **fire**, and
3 Ne. 4:30	shall call on the name of their God for **protection**.
D&C 1:36	the Lord shall have **power** over his saints, and shall
D&C 27:15(15-18)	take upon you my whole **armor**, that ye may be able to
D&C 45:66(66-70)	New Jerusalem...a place of **safety** for the saints of
D&C 63:34(32-37)	saints...hardly **escape**...I, the Lord, am with them
D&C 89:21	a promise, that the **destroying** angel shall pass by the
D&C 97:25(25-28)	Zion shall **escape** if she observe to do all things what
D&C 98:37(33-38)	and I, the Lord, would **fight** their battles, and their
D&C 105:14(14-15)	will I fulfil- I will **fight** your battles.
D&C 109:28(25-28)	thou wilt **fight** for thy people as thou didst in the
Moses 7:61	the children of men, but my people will I **preserve**

PROVOKING

Ex. 23:21(20-23)	beware of him, and obey his voice, **provoke** him not
Deut. 31:20	turn unto other gods, and serve them, and **provoke** me
Deut. 32:21(15-22)	they have **provoked** me to anger with their vanities
1 Kgs. 14:15	have made their groves, **provoking** the Lord to anger.
1 Kgs. 14:22	and they **provoked** him to jealousy with their sins
1 Kgs. 16:7(5-7)	in **provoking** him to anger with the work of his hands
Ps. 78:40(40-42)	how oft did they **provoke** him in the wilderness, and
Ps. 95:8(6-11)	harden not your heart, as in the **provocation**, and as
Luke 11:53(52-54)	and to **provoke** him to speak of many things
1 Cor. 13:5(4-7)	seeketh not her own, is not easily **provoked**, thinketh
2 Cor. 9:2(1-2)	and your zeal hath **provoked** very many.
Gal. 5:26	not be desirous of vain glory, **provoking** one another
Eph. 6:4	and, ye fathers, **provoke** not your children to wrath
Col. 3:21(20,21)	fathers, **provoke** not your children to anger, lest they
Heb. 3:15(8,14-18)	harden not your hearts, as in the **provocation**.
Heb. 10:24	and let us consider one another to **provoke** unto love
1 Ne. 16:38	did my brother Laman **stir** up their hearts to anger.
2 Ne. 13:8(7-9)	against the Lord, to **provoke** the eyes of his glory.
Jacob 1:7(6-8)	as in the **provocation** in the days of temptation while
Mosiah 11:28(27,28)	he has said these things that he might **stir** up my
Alma 11:20	they did **stir** up the people to riotings, and all
Alma 12:36(36-37)	your iniquity **provoketh** him that he sendeth down his
Alma 24:1	were **stirred** up by the Amalekites and by the
Alma 25:8	many of their brethren should be **stirred** up to anger
Alma 27:12	who do **stir** up the Lamanites to anger against their
Alma 35:10(9-11)	now this did **stir** up the Zoramites to anger against
Alma 47:1	and did **stir** up the Lamanites to anger against the
Hel. 7:18(17-19)	yea, ye have **provoked** him to anger against you.
Hel. 8:7	they did **stir** up the people to anger against Nephi
Hel. 16:22(21,22)	for Satan did **stir** them up to do iniquity continually
3 Ne. 11:29(28-30)	he **stirreth** up the hearts of men to contend with
Ether 15:6	people of Coriantumr were **stirred** up to anger against
Moro. 7:45	charity suffereth long...is not easily **provoked**, think
D&C 10:63(32,62-64)	Satan doth **stir** up the hearts of the people to content
D&C 56:1	mine anger is **kindled** against the rebellious, and they

PROVOKING cont.

D&C 59:21(20,21)	against none is his wrath **kindled**, save those who
D&C 60:2(1,2)	wo unto such, for mine anger is **kindled** against them.
D&C 60:15(14,15)	lest thou **provoke** them, but in secret; and wash thy
D&C 61:31(30,31)	whose anger is **kindled** against their wickedness, a
D&C 63:2	whose anger is **kindled** against the wicked and
D&C 63:27(26-28)	that they may not be **stirred** up unto anger.
D&C 134:12	to **cause** them to be dissatisfied with their situations

PRUDENCE

1 Sam. 16:18	a son of Jesse...is **prudent** in matters, and a comely
2 Chr. 2:12	a wise son, endued with **prudence** and understanding
Prov. 8:12	I wisdom dwell with **prudence**, and find out knowledge
Prov. 12:16	presently known: but a **prudent** man covereth shame.
Prov. 12:23	a **prudent** man concealeth knowledge: but the heart of
Prov. 13:16	every **prudent** man dealeth with knowledge: but a fool
Prov. 14:15	but the **prudent** man looketh well to his going.
Prov. 14:18	folly: but the **prudent** are crowned with knowledge.
Prov. 16:21(21-23)	the wise in heart shall be called **prudent**: and the
Prov. 18:15	the heart of the **prudent** getteth knowledge; and the
Prov. 19:14	and a **prudent** wife is from the Lord.
Prov. 22:3	a **prudent** man foreseeth the evil, and hideth himself
Isa. 5:21	their own eyes, and **prudent** in their own sight
Isa. 29:14(13-15)	the understanding of their **prudent** men shall be hid.
Isa. 52:13(10-13)	behold, my servant shall deal **prudently**, he shall be
Jer. 49:7	is counsel perished from the **prudent**? is their wisdom
Hosea 14:9	who is...**prudent**, and he shall know them? for the ways
Amos 5:13	therefore the **prudent** shall keep silence in that time
Matt. 11:25	hast hid...from the wise and **prudent**, and hast
Luke 10:21	hid these things from the wise and **prudent**, and hast
Acts 13:7	with the deputy...Sergius Paulus, a **prudent** man; who
1 Cor. 1:19	will bring to nothing the understanding of the **prudent**
Eph. 1:8(3-10)	he hath abounded toward us in all wisdom and **prudence**
2 Ne. 9:43	things of the wise and the **prudent** shall be hid from
2 Ne. 13:2(1,2)	the prophet, and the **prudent**, and the ancient
2 Ne. 15:21	wo unto the wise...and **prudent** in their own sight
2 Ne. 20:13	I have done these things; for I am **prudent**; and I have
2 Ne. 27:26	the understanding of their **prudent** shall be hid.
3 Ne. 20:43	behold, my servant shall deal **prudently**; he shall be
D&C 76:9(7-10)	the understanding of the **prudent** shall come to naught.
D&C 89:11	all these to be used with **prudence** and thanksgiving.

PUNISHMENT

Gen. 4:13(9-24)	Cain said unto the Lord, my **punishment** is greater than
Gen. 9:6	sheddeth man's blood, by man shall his **blood** be shed
Ex. 21:12(12,14)	smiteth a man...that he die, shall be...put to **death**.
Ex. 21:24	**eye** for eye, tooth for tooth, hand for hand, foot for
Lev. 24:17	he that killeth any man shall surely be put to **death**.
Lev. 26:41(40-42)	they then accept of the **punishment** of their iniquity
Deut. 7:10	**repayeth** them that hate him to their face, to destroy

PUNISHMENT cont.

Deut. 24:16 fathers shall not be put to **death** for the children
Deut. 28:27(15-68) the Lord will **smite** thee...with the scab, and with
2 Kgs. 14:6(1-6) but every man shall be put to **death** for his own sin.
2 Chr. 26:20(18-21) hasted...to go out, because the Lord had **smitten** him.
Prov. 19:9 a false witness shall not be **unpunished**, and he that
Isa. 1:20(18-20) if ye refuse and rebel, ye shall be **devoured** with the
Isa. 13:11 and I will **punish** the world for their evil, and the
Isa. 24:21(19-23) the Lord shall **punish** the host of the high ones that
Isa. 59:18 according to their deeds, accordingly he will **repay**
Jer. 8:12(8-12) time of their visitation they shall be **cast** down
Jer. 10:24 O Lord, **correct** me, but with judgment; not in thine
Jer. 11:11 I will bring **evil** upon them, which they shall not be
Ezek. 14:10(6-11) and they shall bear the **punishment** of their iniquity
Ezek. 18:4 the soul that sinneth, it shall **die**.
Ezek. 18:20(19-23) son shall not **bear** the iniquity of the father, neither
Matt. 5:22 angry with his brother...in **danger** of the judgment
Matt. 5:38(38-44) it hath been said, an **eye** for an eye, and a tooth for
Matt. 23:33 ye serpents...how can ye escape the **damnation** of hell
Matt. 25:46 these shall go away into everlasting **punishment**: but
Matt. 26:52 they that take the sword shall **perish** with the sword.
Mark 3:29 blaspheme...Holy Ghost..is in danger of...**damnation**
Luke 12:46(45,46) the Lord of that servant..will appoint him his **portion**
1 Cor. 5:5 deliver...unto Satan for the **destruction** of the flesh
2 Thes. 1:9(8,9) who shall be **punished** with everlasting destruction
Jude 1:7(6,7) suffering the **vengeance** of eternal fire.
1 Ne. 17:33(24-42) **driven** out by our fathers, do ye suppose that they
2 Ne. 2:5 by the spiritual law they...become **miserable** forever.
2 Ne. 2:10 **punishment**...is in opposition to...happiness which is
2 Ne. 9:16(16-26) their **torment** is as a lake of fire and brimstone, who
2 Ne. 9:25 where there is no law given there is no **punishment**
Jacob 7:18 spake of hell...of eternity, and of eternal **punishment**
Mosiah 2:33 he receiveth for his wages an everlasting **punishment**
Mosiah 2:39(38,39) doom is to endure a never-ending **torment**.
Mosiah 4:17 may not suffer, for his **punishments** are just
Mosiah 27:31 the judgment of an everlasting **punishment** is just
Alma 42:1 justice of God in the **punishment** of the sinner; for
Alma 42:16(16-18) come unto men except there were a **punishment**, which
Alma 42:22 there is a law given, and a **punishment** affixed, and a
3 Ne. 12:38(38-44) it is written, an **eye** for an eye, and a tooth for a
D&C 19:6 but it is written endless **torment**.
D&C 19:10(10-13) **punishment**...given from my hand is endless **punishment**
D&C 19:11(10-12) eternal **punishment** is God's punishment.
D&C 19:20(11-20) repent...lest you suffer these **punishments** of which I
D&C 42:28(27-28) he that sinneth and repenteth not shall be **cast** out.
D&C 76:44(43-49) which is eternal **punishment**, to reign with the devil
D&C 82:3 sins against the greater light...greater **condemnation**.
D&C 84:58(49-59) **scourge** and judgment...poured out upon the children
D&C 93:47(47-49) and must needs stand **rebuked** before the Lord
D&C 98:47 if the children...repent...**indignation**...turned away
D&C 101:78 that every man may be **accountable** for his own sins in
D&C 132:39 he hath **fallen** from his exaltation, and received his
Moses 5:38(34-48) Cain said...my **punishment** is greater than I can bear.
Moses 7:43(42-46) upon the residue of the wicked the **floods** came and

PUNISHMENT cont.

A of F 1:2   believe that men will be **punished** for their own sins
JFS-V 1:59(57-59)   after they have paid the **penalty**...heirs of salvation.

PURIFICATION

Gen. 35:2   put away the strange gods...among you, and be **clean**
Ex. 19:10   go unto the people, and **sanctify** them to day and to
Lev. 12:6(2-8)   days of her **purifying** are fulfilled, for a son, or for
Lev. 13:7(6-8)   seen of the priest for his **cleansing**, he shall be seen
Lev. 14:49(44-57)   he shall take to **cleanse** the house two birds, and
Num. 8:7(6-7)   to cleanse them: sprinkle water of **purifying** upon them
Num. 8:21   the Levites were **purified**, and they washed their
Num. 19:17(1-20)   ashes of the burnt heifer of **purification** for sin
2 Kgs. 5:10(1-14)   wash in the Jordan seven times...thou shalt be **clean**.
2 Chr. 30:18(15-20)   not **cleansed** themselves, yet did...eat the passover
Esth. 2:12(2-12)   so were the days of their **purifications** accomplished
Ps. 19:12   **cleanse** thou me from secret faults.
Ps. 51:2   from mine iniquity, and **cleanse** me from my sin.
Ps. 51:10   create in me a **clean** heart, O God; and renew a right
Ps. 119:9   wherewithal shall a young man **cleanse** his way? by
Isa. 1:16(16,17)   wash you, make you **clean**; put away the evil of your
Isa. 1:18   sins...scarlet, they shall be as **white** as snow; though
Jer. 4:14   **wash** thine heart from wickedness, that thou mayest be
Jer. 33:8   I will **cleanse** them from all their iniquity, whereby
Ezek. 37:23   wherein they have sinned, and will **cleanse** them: so
Dan. 12:10   many shall be **purified**, and made white, and tried; but
Mal. 3:3   he shall **purify** the sons of Levi, and purge them as
Matt. 23:26(26-28)   Pharisee, **cleanse** first that which is within the cup
Mark 7:3(3-4)   the Jews, except they **wash** their hands oft, eat not
Luke 2:22   days of her **purification** according to the law of Moses
Luke 11:39(37-41)   ye Pharisees make **clean**...outside..cup and the platter
Luke 17:17(11-19)   were there not ten **cleansed**? but where are the nine
John 2:6   after the manner of the **purifying** of the Jews
John 11:55   many went...up to Jerusalem...to **purify** themselves.
John 13:8(3-17)   Jesus answered him, if I **wash** thee not, thou hast no
Acts 10:15(9-18)   what God hath **cleansed**, that call not thou common.
Acts 11:9(1-18)   what God hath **cleansed**, that call not thou common.
Acts 15:9   no difference...**purifying** their hearts by faith.
Acts 21:26   signify the accomplishment of the days of **purification**
Acts 24:18   certain Jews from Asia found me **purified** in the temple
2 Cor. 7:1   let us **cleanse** ourselves from all filthiness of the
Eph. 5:26(25-27)   sanctify and **cleanse** it with the washing of water by
Titus 2:14   and **purify** unto himself a peculiar people, zealous of
Heb. 9:13(13-14)   ashes...sanctifieth to the **purifying** of the flesh
Heb. 9:14(13-15)   **purge** your conscience from dead works to serve the
James 4:8   cleanse your hands, ye sinners; and **purify** your hearts
1 Pet. 1:22   ye have **purified** your souls in obeying the truth
1 Jn. 1:9(6-9)   to forgive...and to **cleanse** us from all
1 Jn. 3:3   every man that hath this hope in him **purifieth** himself
2 Ne. 25:16   worship the Father...with **pure** hearts and clean hands
Mosiah 4:2   and our hearts may be **purified**; for we believe in
Alma 5:21(19-21,24,27)   his garments must be **purified** until they are cleansed

PURIFICATION cont.

Alma 7:14(14-15)	mighty to save and to **cleanse** from all unrighteousness
Alma 24:15	he imparted his word unto us and has made us **clean** the
Alma 60:23(23,24)	the inward vessel shall be **cleansed** first, and then
Hel. 3:35	**purifying** and the sanctification of their hearts
3 Ne. 8:1	save he were **cleansed** every whit from his iniquity
3 Ne. 19:28	that thou hast **purified** those whom I have chosen
3 Ne. 24:3	**purify** the sons of Levi, and purge them as gold and
3 Ne. 28:36	whether they were **cleansed** from mortality to
Morm. 9:6	having been **cleansed** by the blood of the Lamb, at that
Ether 12:37	thou hast been faithful...garments shall be made **clean**
Moro. 6:4	were...**cleansed** by the power of the Holy Ghost, they
D&C 29:17	my blood shall not **cleanse** them if they hear me not.
D&C 35:21	they shall be **purified**, even as I am pure.
D&C 38:8	he that is not **purified** shall not abide the day.
D&C 38:42	be ye **clean** that bear the vessels of the Lord. even
D&C 42:41	let all things be done in **cleanliness** before me.
D&C 76:41	he came into the world...to **cleanse** it from all
D&C 76:116	those who love him, and **purify** themselves before him
D&C 88:74(74-75)	**purify** your hearts, and cleanse your hands and your
D&C 88:85	garments are not **clean** from the blood of this
D&C 88:86	let your hands be **clean**, until the Lord comes.
D&C 90:36	chasten her until she overcomes and is **clean** before
D&C 109:42	deliver...thy servants...**cleanse** them from their blood
D&C 112:28(28,33)	**purify** your hearts before me; and then go ye into all

PURITY

Ps. 24:4(3-6)	he that hath clean hands, and a **pure** heart; who hath
Ps. 73:1	to Israel, even to such as are of a **clean** heart.
Isa. 1:16(16-19)	wash you, make you **clean**; put away the evil of your
Isa. 52:11	be ye **clean**, that bear the vessels of the Lord.
Jer. 4:14	O Jerusalem, **wash** thine heart from wickedness, that
Matt. 5:8	blessed are the **pure** in heart: for they shall see God.
John 13:10(3-10)	he that is washed...his feet...is **clean** every whit
Acts 15:9(5-12)	put no difference...**purifying** their hearts by faith.
2 Cor. 6:6(1-10)	by **pureness**, by knowledge, by longsuffering, by
Philip. 4:8(4-9)	whatsoever things are **pure**, whatsoever things are love
1 Tim. 4:12(11-16)	in charity, in spirit, in faith, in **purity**.
Titus 1:15	unto the pure all things are **pure**: but unto them that
Titus 2:14(11-15)	and **purify** unto himself a peculiar people, zealous of
James 4:8(1-10)	and **purify** your hearts, ye double minded.
1 Pet. 1:22(17-25)	seeing ye have **purified** your souls in obeying the
1 Jn. 1:9	and to **cleanse** us from all unrighteousness.
1 Jn. 3:3(1-3)	every man that hath this hope in him **purifieth** himself
Rev. 7:14(13-14)	**washed** their robes, and made them white in the blood
1 Ne. 13:25(24-28)	go forth from the Jews in **purity** unto the Gentiles
2 Ne. 9:14(13-14)	their righteousness, being clothed with **purity**, yea
Mosiah 4:2(1-2)	receive forgiveness...and our hearts may be **purified**
Alma 5:21(19-21)	his garments must be **purified** until they are cleansed
Alma 13:12(10-13)	garments made white, being **pure** and spotless before
Alma 16:21	the word of God being preached in its **purity** in all
Hel. 3:35(33-35)	to the **purifying** and the sanctification of their heart

PURITY cont.

3 Ne. 12:8 — blessed are all the **pure** in heart, for they shall see
3 Ne. 19:28(26-29) — be **purified** in me, through faith on their words, even
Moro. 7:48(47-48) — that we may be **purified** even as he is pure. Amen.
D&C 39:10(7-10) — arise and be baptized, and **wash** away your sins
D&C 43:14(8-14) — that I may reserve unto myself a **pure** people before
D&C 50:28(26-29) — no man is possessor of all things except...**purified**
D&C 67:10(10-14) — **strip** yourselves from jealousies and fears, and humble
D&C 76:116(113-118) — those who love him, and **purify** themselves before him
D&C 88:74 — **purify** your hearts...that I may make you clean
D&C 97:16(15-16) — all the **pure** in heart...shall see God.
D&C 97:21 — let Zion rejoice, for this is Zion- the **pure** in heart
D&C 100:16 — for I will raise up unto myself a **pure** people, that
D&C 101:18(17-18) — they that remain, and are **pure** in heart, shall return
D&C 112:28 — but **purify** your hearts before me; and then go ye into
D&C 124:54 — I...will save all those...who have been **pure** in heart
D&C 136:37 — marvel not at these things, for ye are not yet **pure**

RASHNESS

Num. 20:10(1-12) — must **we** fetch you water out of this rock
Num. 22:29(1-35) — were a sword in mine hand, for now would I **kill** thee.
Job 31:5(5,6) — or if my foot hath **hasted** to deceit
Ps. 31:22(21-23) — I said in my **haste**, I am cut off from before thine eye
Ps. 116:11(10-12) — I said in my **haste**, all men are liars.
Prov. 2:11(11,12) — **discretion** shall preserve thee, understanding shall
Prov. 14:29 — but he that is **hasty** of spirit exalteth folly.
Prov. 18:13 — **answereth** a matter before he heareth it, it is folly
Prov. 19:11 — the **discretion** of a man deferreth his anger; and it
Prov. 29:20 — **hasty** in his words? there is more hope of a fool than
Eccl. 5:2(1-5) — be not **rash** with thy mouth, and let not thine heart
Eccl. 7:9 — be not **hasty** in thy spirit to be angry: for anger rest
Isa. 59:7(2-8) — make **haste** to shed innocent blood: their thoughts are
Dan. 2:15(14-18) — why is the decree so **hasty** from the king? then Arioch
Matt. 5:22(21-22) — whosoever is **angry**...without a cause shall be in
John 18:10(1-11) — and **cut** off his right ear. The servant's name was
Acts 19:36 — ought to be quiet, and to do nothing **rashly**.
James 3:5(1-13) — tongue is a little member, and **boasteth** great things.
Mosiah 13:29 — they were...**quick** to do iniquity, and slow to
Alma 51:10(8-10) — his promise which he made was **rash**; nevertheless, he
Hel. 12:5(4,5) — **quick** to be lifted up in pride; yea, how quick to
3 Ne. 20:42 — ye shall not go out with **haste** nor go by flight; for
Morm. 8:19(12-19) — the same that judgeth **rashly** shall be judged rashly
D&C 29:36 — he **rebelled** against me, saying, give me thine honor
D&C 58:56 — let the work of the gathering be not in **haste**, nor by
D&C 60:14 — proclaiming my word...not in **haste**, neither in wrath
D&C 101:72 — done in their time, but not in **haste**; and observe to

REBELLION

Ex. 4:1	they will not **believe** me, nor hearken unto my voice
Ex. 16:2(1-3)	**murmured** against Moses and Aaron in the wilderness
Num. 14:9(1-9)	only **rebel** not ye against the Lord, neither fear ye
Num. 20:24	ye **rebelled** against my word at the water of Meribah.
Deut. 1:26(26,27,43)	ye...**rebelled** against the commandment of the Lord your
Deut. 9:24(23-24)	ye have been **rebellious** against the Lord from the day
Deut. 31:27	I know thy **rebellion**, and thy stiff neck: behold
Josh. 1:18	whosoever...doth **rebel**...shall be put to death: only
1 Sam. 12:14(14-15)	not **rebel** against the commandment of the Lord, then
1 Sam. 15:23	for **rebellion** is as the sin of witchcraft, and
1 Kgs. 12:19	so Israel **rebelled** against the house of David unto
Neh. 9:26(23-27)	disobedient, and **rebelled** against thee, and cast thy
Ps. 68:6	but the **rebellious** dwell in a dry land.
Ps. 107:11(10-12)	they **rebelled** against the words of God, and contemned
Prov. 17:11	an evil man seeketh only **rebellion**: therefore a cruel
Isa. 1:5(5-6)	ye will **revolt** more and more: the whole head is sick
Isa. 1:20(19,20)	but if ye refuse and **rebel**, ye shall be devoured with
Isa. 5:12	they **regard** not the work of the Lord, neither consider
Isa. 9:13	for the people **turneth** not unto him that smiteth them
Isa. 30:1	woe to the **rebellious** children, saith the Lord, that
Ezek. 2:3	I send thee to...Israel...a **rebellious** nation that
Ezek. 20:21	notwithstanding the children **rebelled** against me: they
Ezek. 20:38	I will purge out from among you the **rebels**, and them
Dan. 9:9(5-10)	though we have **rebelled** against him
Hosea 7:10(9-10)	they do not **return** to the Lord their God, nor seek
Matt. 23:37	would I have gathered thy children...and ye **would** not
Acts 7:51(51-54)	ye do always **resist** the Holy Ghost: as your fathers
Rom. 13:2(1-4)	they that **resist** shall receive to themselves damnation
2 Tim. 3:4(1-8)	**traitors**, heady, highminded, lovers of pleasures more
Rev. 12:7(7-10)	there was **war** in heaven: Michael and his angels fought
1 Ne. 17:30	**reviled** against Moses and against the true and living
2 Ne. 15:12	they **regard** not the work of the Lord, neither consider
Jacob 1:8	**rebel** against God, to provoke him to anger, but that
Mosiah 2:37(36-38)	the same cometh out in open **rebellion** against God
Mosiah 3:12(11-12)	wo unto him who knoweth that he **rebelleth** against God
Mosiah 15:26	the Lord redeemeth none such that **rebel** against him
Mosiah 27:11(8-12)	as they were going about **rebelling** against God, behold
Alma 3:18	they had come out in open **rebellion** against God
3 Ne. 6:18(17,18)	they did wilfully **rebel** against God.
4 Ne. 1:38	did wilfully **rebel** against the gospel of Christ; and
Morm. 1:16	they had wilfully **rebelled** against their God; and the
Morm. 2:15	thousands...hewn down in open **rebellion** against their
Ether 11:15	there arose a **rebellion**...because of that secret
D&C 1:3	the **rebellious** shall be pierced with much sorrow; for
D&C 1:8	power given to seal...the unbelieving and **rebellious**
D&C 43:24	often would I have gathered you...but ye **would** not
D&C 56:4(1-4)	answered upon the heads of the **rebellious**, saith the
D&C 63:2	anger is kindled against the wicked and **rebellious**
D&C 63:6	let the **rebellious** fear and tremble; and let the
D&C 64:35(35-38)	**rebellious** shall be cut off out of the land of Zion
D&C 76:25(25-28)	an angel of God...who **rebelled** against the Only
D&C 88:35(34-36)	that which breaketh a law, and **abideth** not by law, but
D&C 134:5	sedition and **rebellion** are unbecoming every citizen

REBELLION cont.

Moses 4:3
Moses 6:28(28-29)
JFS-V 1:21(20-22)

Satan **rebelled** against me, and sought to destroy the
have they gone astray, and have **denied** me, and have
neither did the **rebellious**...look upon his face.

RECONCILIATION

Ex. 23:5(4-5)
Lev. 8:15
1 Sam. 24:17(1-22)
1 Sam. 29:4(4-5)
2 Chr. 29:24(23-24)
Ezek. 33:15(14-16)
Ezek. 45:20(14-20)
Dan. 9:24
Matt. 5:24(23-25)
Luke 6:27(27-36)
Rom. 5:10(8-12)
Rom. 10:1(1-4)
Rom. 11:15
1 Cor. 7:11(10-11)
2 Cor. 5:18(17-20)
2 Cor. 5:19
Eph. 5:21(21-23)
Col. 1:20(20-22)
Heb. 2:17
James 4:7(7-8)
2 Ne. 10:24
2 Ne. 25:23
2 Ne. 33:9
Jacob 4:11
Mosiah 26:31(29-31)
3 Ne. 12:24(24-25)
D&C 42:88
D&C 46:4
D&C 64:9(8-14)

him that hateth thee...thou shalt surely **help** with him
he slew it...and sanctified it, to make **reconciliation**
thou hast rewarded me **good**, whereas I have rewarded
wherewith should he **reconcile** himself unto his master
they made **reconciliation** with their blood upon the
if the wicked **restore** the pledge, give again that he
seventh day of the month..shall ye **reconcile** the house
to make **reconciliation** for iniquity, and to bring in
first be **reconciled** to thy brother...then...offer thy
but I say...**love** your enemies, do good to them which
we were **reconciled** to God by the death of his Son
prayer...for Israel...that they might be **saved**.
casting away of them be the **reconciling** of the world
remain unmarried, or be **reconciled** to her husband: and
who hath **reconciled** us to himself by Jesus Christ, and
God was in Christ, **reconciling** the world unto himself
submitting yourselves one to another in the fear of
made peace...to **reconcile** all things unto himself; by
to make **reconciliation** for the sins of the people.
submit yourselves therefore to God. Resist the devil
reconcile yourselves to the will of God, and not to
to believe in Christ, and to be **reconciled** to God; for
be **reconciled** unto Christ, and enter into the narrow
be **reconciled** unto him through the atonement of Christ
ye shall also **forgive** one another your trespasses; for
first be **reconciled** to thy brother...then come unto
offend thee...if...confess thou shalt be **reconciled**.
let him not partake until he makes **reconciliation**.
ye ought to **forgive** one another; for he that forgiveth

RECORD KEEPING

Ex. 24:4(3-7)
Ex. 25:21
Ex. 32:33(31-35)
Deut. 31:9(9-11,24-26)
1 Chr. 16:4
Ezra 4:15
Ps. 69:28
Isa. 4:3
Jer. 22:30
Ezek. 13:9
Dan. 12:1
John 1:45
1 Jn. 5:13

and Moses **wrote** all the words of the Lord, and rose
in the ark thou shalt put the **testimony** that I shall
whosoever hath sinned...will I blot out of my **book**.
and Moses **wrote** this law, and delivered it unto the
appointed certain of the Levites...to **record**, and to
be made in the **book** of the records of thy fathers: so
let them be blotted out of the **book** of the living, and
every one that is **written** among the living in
write ye this man childless, a man that shall not
be written in the **writing** of the house of Israel
delivered, every one...found written in the **book**.
we have found him, of whom Moses ...did **write**, Jesus
these things have I **written** unto you that believe on

RECORD KEEPING cont.

Rev. 1:19(11,19)	write the things which thou hast seen, and the things
Rev. 3:5	I will not blot out his name out of the **book** of life
1 Ne. 1:1(1,2)	therefore I make a **record** of my proceedings in my days
1 Ne. 3:19	obtain these **records**...preserve...language of our
1 Ne. 5:16(10-16)	he and his fathers had kept the **records**.
1 Ne. 13:41	words of the Lamb shall be made known in the **records**
2 Ne. 5:29	I, Nephi, had kept the **records** upon my plates, which
1:9	after this manner we keep the **records**, for it is
Alma 37:2(1,2)	command you that ye keep a **record** of this people
3 Ne. 23:13(7-13)	Jesus commanded that it should be **written**; therefore
3 Ne. 27:23(23-26)	**write** the things which ye have seen and heard, save
Morm. 6:6	hid up in the hill Cumorah all the **records** which had
Morm. 8:1(1-5)	I, Moroni, do finish the **record** of my father, Mormon.
Ether 4:1(1-5)	brother of Jared...**write** the things which he had seen
Ether 13:1	I, Moroni...finish my **record** concerning the
D&C 6:26	there are **records** which contain much of my gospel
D&C 20:9(8-10)	which contains a **record** of a fallen people, and the
D&C 20:83	names may be blotted out of the general church **record**
D&C 21:1	there shall be a **record** kept among you; and in it thou
D&C 27:5	the **record** of the stick of Ephraim
D&C 47:3	appointed unto him to keep the church **record** and
D&C 62:3	testimony which ye have borne is **recorded** in heaven
D&C 72:6	these things shall be had on **record**, to be handed over
D&C 76:80	the Lord commanded us to **write** while we were yet in
D&C 85:1	keep a history, and a general church **record** of all
D&C 88:2	your prayers...are **recorded** in the book of the names
D&C 90:32	ye shall **write** this commandment, and say unto your
D&C 127:9(6-9)	let all the **records** be had in order, that they may be
D&C 128:8(1-9)	you **record** on earth shall be recorded in heaven, and
Moses 1:23	because of **wickedness** it is not had among...men.
Moses 2:1	**write** the words which I speak. I am the beginning and
Moses 6:5(5-6)	book of remembrance was kept, in...which was **recorded**
Abr. 1:31	but the **records** of the fathers, even the patriarchs

REDEMPTION

Gen. 3:15(14,15)	and her seed; it shall **bruise** thy head, and thou shalt
Ex. 24:8	**blood** of the covenant, which the Lord hath made with
Ruth 2:20(19-23)	near of kin unto us, one of our next **kinsmen**.
Ruth 4:4(1-11)	if thou wilt **redeem** it, redeem it: but if thou wilt
Ps. 72:14(1-20)	he shall **redeem** their soul from deceit and violence
Ps. 103:4(1-5)	who **redeemeth** thy life from destruction; who crowneth
Isa. 43:1	I have **redeemed** thee, I have called thee by thy name
Isa. 43:14(11-15)	the Lord, your **redeemer**, the Holy One of Israel; for
Isa. 49:26	I the Lord am thy Saviour and thy **Redeemer**, the mighty
Isa. 53:5(1-12)	but he was wounded for our **transgressions**, he was
Zech. 9:11	by the **blood** of thy covenant...prisoners out of the
Matt. 1:21(20-23)	his name Jesus: for he shall **save** his people from the
Matt. 20:28	Son of man came...to give his life a **ransom** for many.
John 1:29(29-34)	Lamb of God, which taketh away the **sin** of the world.
Rom. 3:25(23-26)	whom God hath set forth to be a **propitiation** through
Rom. 5:11(6-19)	Jesus Christ, by whom we...received the **atonement**.

REDEMPTION cont.

Rom. 16:20	the God of peace shall **bruise** Satan under your feet
Gal. 1:4(3-4)	that he might **deliver** us from this present evil world
Eph. 1:7	in whom we have **redemption** through his blood, the
Col. 1:14(12-14)	in whom we have **redemption** through his blood, even the
Titus 2:14(13-14)	that he might **redeem** us from all iniquity, and purify
Heb. 2:14(14-16)	destroy him that had the power of **death**, that is, the
Heb. 9:12(8-28)	by his own blood he...obtained eternal **redemption** for
1 Pet. 2:21(21-24)	because Christ also **suffered** for us, leaving us an
1 Pet. 3:18(18-19)	for Christ also hath once **suffered** for sins, the just
1 Jn. 2:2(1-2)	and he is the **propitiation** for our sins: and not for
Rev. 5:9(9-10)	thou wast slain, and hast **redeemed** us to God by thy
2 Ne. 2:6(6-10)	**redemption** cometh in and through the Holy Messiah; for
2 Ne. 2:26	they are **redeemed**...become free forever, knowing good
2 Ne. 9:21(21-27)	he **suffereth** the pains of all men, yea, the pains of
Mosiah 3:11(7,11-12)	his blood **atoneth** for the sins of those who have
Mosiah 13:28	**salvation** doth not come by the law alone; and were it
Mosiah 15:23(21-27)	raised to dwell with God who has **redeemed** them; thus
Mosiah 16:6(6-9)	if Christ had not come...could have been no **redemption**
Mosiah 18:2	**redemption** of the people, which was to be brought to
Alma 7:13(11-13)	that he might blot out their **transgressions** according
Alma 9:27(26-27)	he cometh to **redeem** those who will be baptized unto
Alma 11:40(37-41)	he shall come into the world to **redeem** his people; and
Alma 12:25(9-37)	but there was a plan of **redemption** laid, which shall
Alma 22:13(13-14)	the plan of **redemption**, which was prepared from the
Alma 34:16(8-16)	brought about the great and eternal plan of **redemption**
Alma 42:13(6-28)	the plan of **redemption** could not be brought about
Hel. 5:10(9-11)	he should...come...to **redeem** them from their sins.
Hel. 14:17(15-18)	the resurrection of Christ **redeemeth** mankind, yea
3 Ne. 9:17(16-18)	by me **redemption** cometh, and in me is the law of Moses
3 Ne. 9:21(15-22)	I have come...to bring **redemption** unto the world, to
Morm. 7:7(5-7)	he hath brought to pass the **redemption** of the world
Morm. 9:12(12-14)	because of Jesus Christ came the **redemption** of man.
Moro. 8:22	for the power of **redemption** cometh on all them that
D&C 18:11(11-12)	wherefore he **suffered** the pain of all men, that all
D&C 19:16(16-19)	I, God, have **suffered** these things for all, that they
D&C 29:42(42-44)	declare unto them repentance and **redemption**, through
D&C 29:46(46-47)	little children are **redeemed** from the foundation of
D&C 49:5	have sent mine...Son...for the **redemption** of the world
D&C 76:41(40-43)	he came into...world...to **cleanse** it from all
D&C 88:14(14-17)	through the **redemption** which is made for you is
D&C 93:38	and God having **redeemed** man from the fall, men became
D&C 128:22	ordained, before the world was, that...to **redeem** them
D&C 132:26	delivered unto...Satan unto the day of **redemption**
Moses 4:1(1-4)	send me...I will **redeem** all mankind, that one soul
Moses 5:9(9-11)	as thou hast fallen thou mayest be **redeemed**, and all
JFS-V 1:2(1-60)	made by the Son of God, for the **redemption** of the
JFS-V 1:16(11-18,23)	awaiting...Son of God...to declare their **redemption**

REFUGE

Num. 35:6(6-15)	there shall be six cities for **refuge**, which ye shall
Deut. 4:42(41-43)	that fleeing unto one of these cities he might **live**
Deut. 33:27	the eternal God is thy **refuge**, and underneath are the
Josh. 20:2	appoint out for you cities of **refuge**, whereof I spake
2 Sam. 22:3	God...my **refuge**, my saviour; thou savest me from
Ps. 9:9	the Lord also will be a **refuge** for the oppressed, a
Ps. 46:1	God is our **refuge** and strength, a very present help
Ps. 62:7	my strength, and my **refuge**, is in God.
Isa. 4:6	there shall be a tabernacle...for a place of **refuge**
Isa. 25:4	thou hast been...a **refuge** from the storm, a shadow
Isa. 28:15	we have made lies our **refuge**, and under falsehood have
Ezek. 11:16	I be to them as a little **sanctuary** in the countries
John 17:15(11-15)	but that thou shouldest **keep** them from the evil.
1 Thes. 5:3	when they shall say, peace and **safety**; then sudden
Heb. 6:18(18,19)	who have fled for **refuge** to lay hold upon the hope set
1 Pet. 4:19(16-19)	commit the **keeping** of their souls to him in well
Rev. 3:10(10,11)	I also will **keep** thee from the hour of temptation
2 Ne. 14:6	there shall be a tabernacle for...a place of **refuge**
Hel. 15:2	attempt to flee and there shall be no place for **refuge**
Hel. 15:12	in the latter times...having no place for **refuge**, the
D&C 45:66	New Jerusalem, a land of peace, a city of **refuge**, a
D&C 88:137	school of the prophets, that it may become a **sanctuary**
D&C 115:6	land of Zion...for a **refuge** from the storm and upon
D&C 124:36	those places...appointed for **refuge**, shall be the

REMISSION OF SINS

Ps. 32:1(1-5)	blessed is he whose transgression is **forgiven**, whose
Ps. 34:18(18-22)	and **saveth** such as be of a contrite spirit.
Isa. 43:25(25-27)	I, am he that **blotteth** out thy transgressions for mine
Isa. 45:21(20-23)	a just God and a **Saviour**; there is none beside me.
Isa. 53:5(3-5)	and with his stripes we are **healed**.
Isa. 53:8	for the **transgression** of my people was he stricken.
Ezek. 16:9	I throughly **washed** away thy blood from thee, and I
Hab. 3:13(1,13,18)	thou wentest forth for the **salvation** of thy people
Matt. 26:28(26-30)	my blood...shed for many for the **remission** of sins.
Mark 1:4	John...preach the baptism...for the **remission** of sins.
Luke 1:77	salvation...by the **remission** of their sins
Luke 3:3	the baptism of repentance for the **remission** of sins
Luke 4:18	to preach **deliverance** to the captives, and recovering
Luke 5:21	who can **forgive** sins, but God alone
Luke 5:24(23,24)	son of man hath power...to **forgive** sins, (he said unto
Luke 7:49(47-49)	who is this that **forgiveth** sins also
Luke 24:47	repentance and **remission** of sins should be preached
John 20:23	whose soever sins ye **remit**, they are remitted unto the
Acts 2:38	repent, and be baptized...for the **remission** of sins
Acts 10:43	believeth in him shall receive **remission** of sins.
Acts 13:38(38-41)	through this man is preached...**forgiveness** of sins
Rom. 3:25(23-26)	his righteousness for the **remission** of sins that are
Rom. 6:18	being then made **free** from sin, ye became the servants
Col. 1:14	in whom we have...even the **forgiveness** of sins
Heb. 9:22	and without shedding of blood is no **remission**.

REMISSION OF SINS cont.

Heb. 9:28(11-28)	Christ was once **offered** to bear the sins of many; and
Heb. 10:2	worshippers once **purged**..had no more conscience of sin
Heb. 10:18(17,18)	where **remission** of these is, there is no more offering
1 Jn. 2:2(1-4)	he is the **propitiation** for our sins: and not for ours
Rev. 3:5	he that overcometh...shall be clothed in **white** raiment
Rev. 7:14	washed their robes, and made them **white** in the blood
2 Ne. 25:26	to what source...look for a **remission** of their sins.
2 Ne. 31:17	a **remission** of your sins by fire and by the Holy Ghost
Enos 1:2(1-5)	wrestle...before I received a **remission** of my sins.
Mosiah 3:13(11-13)	believe that Christ should come...receive **remission**
Mosiah 4:3(2,3)	received a **remission** of their sins, and having peace
Mosiah 4:11	a **remission** of your sins, which causeth...great joy
Mosiah 4:26	retaining a **remission** of your sins from day to day
Mosiah 15:10	his soul has been made an **offering** for sin he shall
Mosiah 15:11	looked forward to that day for a **remission** of their
Alma 12:34	have claim on mercy...unto a **remission** of his sins
Alma 13:16	look forward to him for a **remission** of their sins
Alma 38:8	cry out unto the Lord...receive a **remission** of my sins
Hel. 5:10	the Lord surely should come to **redeem** his people, but
3 Ne. 1:23	there was a great **remission** of sins. And thus the
3 Ne. 7:16	repentance and **remission** of sins through faith on the
3 Ne. 7:25	they had repented and received a **remission** of their
3 Ne. 12:2	and shall receive a **remission** of their sins.
3 Ne. 30:2	that ye may receive a **remission** of your sins, and be
Moro. 3:3	preach repentance and **remission** of sins through Jesus
Moro. 8:11	baptism is unto repentance..unto the **remission** of sins
Moro. 8:25(24-26)	fulfilling the commandments bringeth **remission** of sins
Moro. 10:33	covenant of the father unto the **remission** of your sins
D&C 13:1	baptism by immersion for the **remission** of sins; and
D&C 19:16(16-20)	that they might not suffer if they would **repent**
D&C 19:31	declare repentance...and **remission** of sins by baptism
D&C 20:5(5-7)	that he had received a **remission** of his sins, he was
D&C 20:37	received...Spirit...unto the **remission** of their sins
D&C 27:2	my blood which was shed for the **remission** of your sins
D&C 33:11	be baptized...for a **remission** of your sins; yea, be
D&C 53:3	to preach faith and repentance and **remission** of sins
D&C 55:2(1,2)	**remission** of sins by way of baptism in the name of
D&C 64:7	I, the Lord, **forgive** sins unto those who confess their
D&C 68:27	baptized for the **remission** of their sins when eight
D&C 84:27	gospel is the gospel of repentance...**remission** of sins
D&C 84:64	baptized by water for the **remission** of sins, shall
D&C 84:74	baptized in water...for the **remission** of their sins
D&C 107:20	baptism of repentance for the **remission** of sins, agree
D&C 132:46	whosoever sins you **remit** on earth shall be remitted
JS-H 1:68(68-69)	inqure...respecting baptism for the **remission** of sins
A of F 1:4	baptism by immersion for the **remission** of sins; fourth
JFS-V 1:33(29-33)	vicarious baptism for the **remission** of sins, the gift

REPENTANCE

Ex. 22:1(1,4,7)	if a man shall steal an ox...he shall **restore** five
Lev. 6:4(1-7)	he shall **restore** that which he took violently away
Num. 5:7(6-7)	he shall **recompense** his trespass with the principal
Ezra 10:11	now therefore make **confession** unto the Lord God of you
Neh. 9:2	**confessed** their sins, and the iniquities of their
Ps. 38:18(18-22)	will declare mine iniquity; I will be **sorry** for my sin
Ps. 51:10(7-10)	create in me a **clean** heart...renew a right spirit with
Prov. 28:13	whoso confesseth and **forsaketh** them shall have mercy.
Isa. 1:16(10-20)	put away the evil of your doings...**cease** to do evil
Isa. 55:7(6-7)	let him **return** unto the Lord, and he will have mercy
Jer. 18:8(1-10)	if that nation...**turn** from their evil, I will repent
Jer. 35:15(15-17)	**return** ye now every man from his evil way, and amend
Ezek. 6:9	they shall **lothe** themselves for the evils which they
Ezek. 16:61	remember thy ways, and be **ashamed**, when thou shalt
Ezek. 18:21(19-31)	**turn** from all his sins that he hath committed, and
Ezek. 33:15(11-19)	if the wicked **restore**...he shall surely live, he shall
Jonah 3:10(4-10)	and God saw...they **turned** from their evil way; and God
Zech. 1:3	**turn** ye unto me, saith the Lord of hosts, and I will
Mal. 3:7	**return** unto me, and I will return unto you, saith the
Matt. 3:8(1-12)	bring forth therefore fruits meet for **repentance**
Matt. 4:17	**repent**: for the kingdom of heaven is at hand.
Matt. 9:13(10-13)	come to call...sinners to **repentance**.
Matt. 12:41	men of Nineveh...**repented** at the preaching of Jonas
Mark 1:4	preach the baptism of **repentance** for the remission of
Mark 1:15	**repent** ye, and believe the gospel.
Luke 3:8(1-14)	bring forth therefore fruits worthy of **repentance**, and
Luke 13:3(1-9)	but, except ye **repent**, ye shall all likewise perish.
Luke 15:7(1-10)	joy shall be in heaven over one sinner that **repenteth**
Luke 15:17(11-32)	when he **came** to himself, he said, how many hired
Luke 17:4(3,4)	saying, I **repent**; thou shalt forgive him.
Luke 24:47(45-47)	**repentance** and remission of sins should be preached
Acts 2:38(37-38)	**repent**, and be baptized every one of you in the name
Acts 3:19	**repent** ye therefore, and be converted, that your sins
Acts 11:18	also to the Gentiles granted **repentance** unto life.
Acts 17:30	commandeth all men every where to **repent**
2 Cor. 7:10(8-11)	for godly sorrow worketh **repentance** to salvation not
Heb. 6:1(1-2)	the foundation of **repentance** from dead works, and of
James 4:8(8-10)	**cleanse** your hands, ye sinners; and purify your heart
2 Pet. 3:9(9-10)	Lord is..longsuffering...that all...come to **repentance**
1 Jn. 1:9(7-10)	if we **confess** our sins, he...just to forgive us our
Rev. 2:5	remove thy candlestick...except thou **repent**.
1 Ne. 1:4(4-20)	that they must **repent**, or the great city Jerusalem
1 Ne. 7:20(19-22)	plead with me that I would **forgive** them of the thing
1 Ne. 10:18	that they **repent** and come unto him.
1 Ne. 14:5(5-7)	hast heard that whoso **repenteth** not must perish.
1 Ne. 22:28	dwell safely...if it so be that they will **repent**.
2 Ne. 2:21(19-21)	days...prolonged...that they might **repent** while in the
2 Ne. 9:23(23-24)	commandeth all men that they must **repent**, and be
2 Ne. 26:27	people that they should persuade all men to **repentance**
2 Ne. 30:2	them that **repent** and believe in his Son, who is the
Jacob 3:3(3,4)	except ye **repent** the land is cursed for your sakes
Enos 1:2(2-8)	I will tell you of the **wrestle** which I had before God
Mosiah 2:38(33-41)	if that man **repenteth** not, and remaineth and dieth an

REPENTANCE cont.

Mosiah 4:10(4-23)	ye must **repent** of your sins and forsake them, and
Mosiah 26:29(28-32)	**repenteth** in the sincerity of his heart, him shall ye
Mosiah 27:24(8-36)	I have **repented** of my sins, and have been redeemed of
Alma 5:31(26-36)	he must **repent** or he cannot be saved
Alma 5:49(49-56)	cry unto them that they must **repent** and be born again.
Alma 7:14(13-16)	ye must **repent**, and be born again; for the Spirit
Alma 9:12(12-30)	**repent**, or he will utterly destroy you from off the
Alma 12:24	space granted...in which he might **repent**; therefore
Alma 13:18(17-18)	Melchizedek...did preach **repentance** unto his people.
Alma 26:22	he that **repenteth** and exerciseth faith, and bringeth
Alma 34:33(31-35)	do not procrastinate the day of your **repentance** until
Alma 42:22(22-24)	a punishment affixed, and a **repentance** granted; which
Hel. 5:41(9-52)	you must **repent**...until ye shall have faith in Christ
Hel. 12:23(22-26)	blessed are they who will **repent** and hearken unto the
3 Ne. 9:2	wo unto the inhabitants...except they shall **repent**
3 Ne. 9:22	whoso **repenteth** and cometh unto me as a little child
3 Ne. 11:32(32-34)	the Father commandeth all men...to **repent** and believe
3 Ne. 16:13	if the Gentiles will **repent** and return unto me, saith
3 Ne. 23:5	hearken unto my words and **repenteth** and is baptized
3 Ne. 27:16(16-20)	whoso **repenteth** and is baptized in my name shall be
3 Ne. 30:2(1-2)	**repent** of your evil doings, of your lyings and
Moro. 8:24(24-26)	**repentance** is unto them that are under condemnation
Moro. 9:3(3-6)	they do not **repent**, and Satan stirreth them up
D&C 1:27	they might be chastened, that they might **repent**
D&C 1:32(31-33)	he that **repents** and does the commandments of the Lord
D&C 5:19(19-20)	if they **repent** not, until the earth is empty, and the
D&C 6:9	say nothing but **repentance** unto this generation; keep
D&C 11:9	say nothing but **repentance** unto this generation. keep
D&C 13:1	the gospel of **repentance**, and of baptism by immersion
D&C 14:8	that you may declare **repentance** unto this generation.
D&C 16:6	most worth...will be to declare **repentance** unto this
D&C 18:13(9-22)	how great is his joy in the soul that **repenteth**
D&C 18:41	you must **repent** and be baptized, in the name of Jesus
D&C 19:4(4-20)	surely every man must **repent** or suffer, for I, God
D&C 20:29(29-37)	all men must **repent** and believe on the name of Jesus
D&C 20:71(71-72)	accountability before God, and...capable of **repentance**
D&C 29:42(42-45)	angels to declare unto them **repentance** and redemption
D&C 29:49	whoso having knowledge, have I not commanded to **repent**
D&C 33:11(9-12)	**repent** and be baptized, every one of you, for a
D&C 42:28(24-28)	he that sinneth and **repenteth** not shall be cast out.
D&C 49:13(11-14)	**repent** and be baptized in the name of Jesus Christ
D&C 58:42(42-43)	he who has **repented** of his sins, the same is forgiven
D&C 64:12(3-13)	him that **repenteth** not of his sins, and confesseth the
D&C 68:25(25-27)	teach them not to understand...doctrine of **repentance**
D&C 76:116	on those who love him, and **purify** themselves before
D&C 84:27(25-28)	which gospel is the gospel of **repentance** and of
D&C 88:74(74-75)	**purify** your hearts, and cleanse your hands and your
D&C 98:21(19-21)	if they do not **repent** and observe all things
D&C 133:16	he commandeth all men everywhere to **repent**.
Moses 5:8	thou shalt **repent** and call upon God in the name of the
Moses 6:57(52-60)	all men...must **repent**, or they can in nowise inherit
Moses 8:20(20-25)	Noah called...that they should **repent**; but they
A of F 1:4	first principles...first, faith...second, **repentance**

REPENTANCE cont.

JFS-V 1:19(18-20)	from the fall, and...sins on conditions of **repentance**.
JFS-V 1:31(31-33)	proclaim liberty to...all who would **repent** of their
JFS-V 1:58(57-60)	the dead who **repent** will be redeemed, through

REPROACH

Gen. 30:23(22-24)	God hath taken away my **reproach**
Job 16:10(8-12)	they have smitten me upon the cheek **reproachfully**; the
Ps. 22:6(1-8)	but I am a worm, and no man; a **reproach** of men, and
Ps. 44:13(11-18)	thou makest us a **reproach** to our neighbours, a scorn
Ps. 69:9(5-10)	the **reproaches** of them that reproached thee are
Ps. 69:19(19-21)	thou hast known my **reproach**, and my shame, and my dish
Isa. 4:1(1-4)	called by thy name, to take away our **reproach**.
Isa. 51:7(7-8)	fear ye not the **reproach** of men, neither be ye afraid
Isa. 54:4(1-5)	shalt not remember the **reproach** of thy widowhood any
Lam. 3:30(27-36)	that smiteth him: he is filled full with **reproach**.
Dan. 9:16(16-19)	thy people are become a **reproach** to all that are about
Joel 2:17(15-17)	give not thine heritage to **reproach**, that the heathen
Luke 1:25(24-25)	looked on me, to take away my **reproach** among men.
Luke 6:22(22-23)	blessed are ye, when men shall...**reproach** you, and
Luke 11:45(42-49)	thus saying thou **reproachest** us also.
Rom. 15:3(1-4)	the **reproaches** of them that reproached thee fell on
2 Cor. 11:21(20-23)	I speak as concerning **reproach**, as though we had been
1 Tim. 4:10(8-10)	suffer **reproach**, because we trust in the living God
Heb. 11:26(24-26)	esteeming the **reproach** of Christ greater riches than
Heb. 13:13(12-14)	let us go forth...unto him...bearing his **reproach**.
1 Pet. 4:14(12-14)	if ye be **reproached** for the name of Christ, happy are
2 Ne. 8:7(7-8)	fear ye not the **reproach** of men, neither be ye afraid
2 Ne. 14:1(1-4)	called by thy name to take away our **reproach**.
3 Ne. 22:4(1-5)	shalt not remember the **reproach** of thy youth, and
D&C 42:92(88-92)	that the church may not speak **reproachfully** of him or

REPROOF

Prov. 1:30(23-30)	they despised all my **reproof**.
Prov. 10:17	but he that refuseth **reproof** erreth.
Prov. 15:10(10-12)	he that hateth **reproof** shall die.
Prov. 17:10	a **reproof** entereth more into a wise man than an
Prov. 29:15	the rod and **reproof** give wisdom: but a child left to
Eccl. 7:5	better to hear the **rebuke** of the wise...song of fools.
Isa. 11:4(3,4)	**reprove** with equity for the meek of the earth: and
Jer. 2:19	thy backslidings shall **reprove** thee: know therefore
Matt. 18:15(15-17)	if thy brother shall trespass against thee...**tell** him
John 16:8	and when he is come, he will **reprove** the world of sin
Eph. 4:15	but speaking the **truth** in love, may grow up into him
Eph. 5:11(11-13)	unfruitful works of darkness...**reprove** them.
2 Tim. 3:16(16-17)	all scripture...profitable for doctrine, for **reproof**
2 Tim. 4:2	preach the word...**reprove**, rebuke, exhort with all
1 Ne. 17:15	I did **exhort** my brethren to faithfulness and
2 Ne. 21:3(3,4)	neither **reprove** after the hearing of his ears.
Mosiah 11:20(20-25)	except they repent I will **visit** them in mine anger.

REPROOF cont.

Mosiah 14:5	the **chastisement** of our peace was upon him; and with
Alma 9:12(12,13)	except ye repent...he will **visit** you in his anger
Alma 60:2(1-36)	somewhat to say unto them by the way of **condemnation**
Alma 61:9	you have **censured** me, but it mattereth not; I am not
Alma 61:14	let us resist evil ...with our **words**, yea, such as
Ether 2:14	**chastened** him because he remembered not to call upon
D&C 1:27(24-28)	sinned they might be **chastened**, that they might repent
D&C 42:90(84-93)	he or she shall be **chastened** before many.
D&C 84:87(87,117)	I send you out to **reprove** the world of all their
D&C 97:26(25,26)	**visit** her according to all her works, with sore
D&C 98:21(19-22)	I, the Lord, will **chasten** them and will do whatsoever
D&C 101:5(2-5)	those who will not endure **chastening**...cannot be
D&C 101:41(39-41)	therefore they must needs be **chastened**
D&C 121:43	**reproving** betimes with sharpness, when moved upon by

RESPECT

Ex. 20:12	**honour** thy father and thy mother: that thy days may
Lev. 19:32	**honour** the face of the old man, and fear thy God: I
1 Sam. 2:30	them that **honour** me I will honour, and they that
Isa. 53:3	he was despised, and we **esteemed** him not.
Matt. 15:4(3-6)	**honour** thy father and mother: and, he that curseth
John 5:23(22-23)	that all men should **honour** the Son, even as they
John 8:49	but I **honour** my Father, and ye do dishonour me.
Eph. 5:33(31-33)	love his wife...she **reverence** her husband.
Eph. 6:1(1-4)	children, **obey** your parents in the Lord: for this is
Philip. 2:3	let each **esteem** other better than themselves.
1 Thes. 5:13(12-13)	and to **esteem** them very highly in love for their work
1 Tim. 5:1(1-4)	rebuke not an elder, but **intreat** him as a father; and
1 Tim. 5:4(1-4)	let them learn first to shew **piety** at home, and to
1 Pet. 2:17(13-17)	**honour** all men. Love the brotherhood. Fear God. Honour
1 Pet. 5:5(3-6)	likewise, ye younger, **submit** yourselves unto the elder
1 Ne. 17:55(52-55)	**honor** thy father and thy mother, that thy days may be
2 Ne. 27:25(23-26)	with their lips do **honor** me, but have removed their
2 Ne. 33:14(7-15)	**respect** the words of the Jews, and also my words, and
Alma 1:30(28-30)	having no **respect** to persons as to those who stood in
D&C 76:5(5-10)	delight to **honor** those who serve me in righteousness
D&C 107:4(1-4)	but out of **respect** or reverence to the name of the
D&C 122:4(1-4)	thou shalt be had in **honor**; and but for a small moment
D&C 124:55(54,55)	that I may bless you, and crown you with **honor**
D&C 134:6(5,6)	to the laws all men owe **respect** and deference, as with
Moses 5:20(19-23)	and the Lord had **respect** unto Abel, and to his

REST

Gen. 2:2	he **rested** on the seventh day from all his work which
Ex. 23:12	on the seventh day thou shalt **rest**: that thine ox and
Ex. 31:15(15,16)	the seventh is the sabbath of **rest**, holy to the Lord
Ex. 31:17	on the seventh day he **rested**, and was refreshed.
Ex. 33:14	presence...go with thee, and I will give thee **rest**.
Ex. 34:21	but on the seventh day thou shalt **rest**: in earing time

REST cont.

Deut. 12:10(9-10)	when he giveth you **rest** from all your enemies round
Ps. 95:11	sware in my wrath...they should not enter into my **rest**
Isa. 11:10	root of Jesse...an ensign...his **rest** shall be glorious
Jer. 6:16(15-16)	walk therein, and ye shall find **rest** for your souls.
Matt. 11:28(28-30)	come unto me...heavy laden and I will give you **rest**.
Luke 23:56	**rested** the sabbath day according to the commandment.
2 Thes. 1:7	and to you who are troubled **rest** with us, when the Lord
Heb. 3:11(7-19)	so I sware...they shall not enter into my **rest**.
Heb. 4:1(1-11)	a promise being left us of entering into his **rest**, any
Rev. 14:13	that they may **rest** from their labours; and their works
Jacob 1:7	we labored...that they might enter into his **rest**, lest
Enos 1:27	I soon go to the place of my **rest**...with my Redeemer
Alma 12:34(34-37)	whosoever repenteth...shall enter into my **rest**.
Alma 13:6	teach...commandments...that they...enter into his **rest**
Alma 13:29	that ye may be lifted up...and enter into his **rest**.
Alma 37:34(32-34)	meek..lowly in heart..shall find **rest** to their souls.
Alma 40:12	state of happiness...called paradise, a state of **rest**
3 Ne. 27:19	nothing entereth into his **rest** save it be those who
3 Ne. 28:3(1-3)	shall come unto me in my kingdom...with me...find **rest**
Moro. 7:3	by which ye can enter into the **rest** of the Lord, from
Moro. 9:6	that we may...**rest** our souls in the kingdom of God.
Moro. 10:34	I soon go to **rest** in the paradise of God, until my
D&C 15:6	that you may **rest** with them in the kingdom of my
D&C 54:10	they who have sought me early shall find **rest** to their
D&C 59:10(9-14)	**rest** from your labors, and to pay thy devotions unto
D&C 84:24	which **rest** is the fulness of his glory.
D&C 101:31(30-31)	shall be caught up, and his **rest** shall be glorious.
D&C 121:32(28-33)	when every man shall enter into his...immortal **rest**.
Moses 3:2(1-3)	I **rested** on the seventh day from all my work, and all
Moses 7:61	the day shall come that the earth shall **rest**, but
Abr. 1:2	there was greater happiness and peace and **rest** for me
Abr. 5:2(1-3)	we will **rest** on the seventh time from all our work

RESTORATION OF THE GOSPEL

Isa. 2:2(2-5)	Lord's house shall be **established** in the top of the
Isa. 11:11(1-16)	Lord...second time to **recover**...his people, which
Isa. 29:14(1-24)	I will proceed to do a **marvelous** work among this
Jer. 31:31(31-34)	I will make a **new** covenant with the house of Israel
Ezek. 37:26(11-28)	it shall be an everlasting **covenant** with them: and I
Dan. 2:44(26-45)	**kingdom**, which shall never be destroyed: and the
Joel 2:28(28-32)	afterward, that I will **pour** out my spirit upon all
Amos 3:7	revealeth his secret unto his servants the **prophets**.
Mal. 3:1	I will send my **messenger**, and he shall prepare the way
Mal. 4:6(5,6)	**turn** the heart of the fathers to the children, and the
Matt. 17:11	Elias truly shall first come, and **restore** all things.
Matt. 24:14	**gospel** of the kingdom shall be preached in all the
Acts 3:21(20-26)	times of **restitution** of all things, which God hath
Rom. 11:25(16-26)	blindness...until the **fulness** of the Gentiles be come
Eph. 1:10(9-10)	in the **dispensation** of the fulness of times he might
Rev. 14:6(6-7)	I saw another angel fly..having the everlasting **gospel**
1 Ne. 13:34(34-42)	I will bring forth unto them...much of my **gospel**

RESTORATION OF THE GOSPEL cont.

1 Ne. 14:7(1-17)	I will work a great and a **marvelous** work among the
1 Ne. 15:13(7-20)	then shall..fulness of the **gospel**..come unto..Gentiles
1 Ne. 22:8(3-31)	the Lord God will...do a **marvelous** work among the
2 Ne. 3:24(6-25)	bringing to pass much **restoration** unto the house of
2 Ne. 9:2(1-2)	they shall be **restored** to the true church and fold of
2 Ne. 10:2(1-19)	shall be **restored**...true knowledge of their Redeemer.
2 Ne. 25:17(7-8,14-20)	**restore** his people from their lost and fallen state.
2 Ne. 26:14(14-17)	God shall **bring** these things forth unto the children
2 Ne. 27:26(1-35)	I will proceed to do a **marvelous** work among this
2 Ne. 28:2(1-32)	**book** shall be of great worth...the house of Israel.
2 Ne. 29:1(1-14)	that day when I shall proceed to do a **marvelous** work
2 Ne. 30:5(5-8)	shall be **restored** unto the knowledge of their fathers
Alma 37:2(1-5)	a record...upon the **plates**...for a wise purpose that
Hel. 15:11(4-13)	**restoration** of our brethren, the Lamanites, again to
3 Ne. 15:8(1-10)	the **covenant** which I have made...is not all fulfilled
3 Ne. 16:7(4-7)	in the **latter** day shall the truth come unto the
3 Ne. 21:9(1-29)	a great and a **marvelous-work** among them; and there
Morm. 9:36(32-37)	even their **restoration** to the knowledge of Christ, are
D&C 4:1(1-7)	a **marvelous-work** is about to come forth among the
D&C 13:1	upon you...I **confer** the Priesthood of Aaron, which
D&C 27:6	bringing to pass the **restoration** of all things spoken
D&C 65:2	the **keys**...are committed unto man on the earth, and
D&C 77:9(9-10)	to gather...tribes of Israel and **restore** all things.
D&C 77:14	this is Elias, who...must come and **restore** all things.
D&C 77:15	two prophets...last days...the time of the **restoration**
D&C 84:2(1-5)	church, established in the last days for...**restoration**
D&C 86:10(1-11)	priesthood..remain..until the **restoration** of all
D&C 110:16(6-16)	keys of this **dispensation** are committed into your hand
D&C 112:30(1-31)	priesthood given...dispensation of the **fulness** of time
D&C 124:28(25-45)	**restore** again that which was lost...the priesthood.
D&C 127:8(3-9)	I am about to **restore** many things to the earth
D&C 128:17(17-18)	his eye fixed on the **restoration** of the priesthood
D&C 128:21(19-21)	all **declaring** their dispensation, their rights, their
D&C 132:40(28-40)	gave unto thee..an appointment, and **restore** all things
D&C 132:45(45-48)	wherein I **restore** all things, and make known unto you
D&C 133:36(36-40)	sent forth mine angel...having the everlasting **gospel**
D&C 133:57(56-63)	Lord sent forth the fulness of his **gospel**, his
D&C 135:3	has sent the **fulness** of the everlasting gospel, which
JS-H 1:1	rise...of the Church of Jesus Christ of **Latter-day**
JS-H 1:17(15-19)	I saw two **Personages**, whose brightness and glory defy
JS-H 1:34(26-54,59-67)	**fulness** of the everlasting gospel was contained in it
JS-H 1:38(26-67)	I will reveal unto you the **Priesthood**, by...Elijah the
JS-H 1:69(68-73)	I confer the **Priesthood** of Aaron, which holds the keys

RESURRECTION

Deut. 32:39	I kill, and I make **alive**; I wound, and I heal
1 Sam. 2:6	he bringeth down to the grave, and **bringeth** up.
Job 14:14	if a man die, shall he **live** again? all the days of
Job 19:26(25-27)	destroy this body, yet in my **flesh** shall I see God
Ps. 16:9(9-10)	my **flesh** also shall rest in hope.
Ps. 17:15	I shall be satisfied, when I **awake**, with thy likeness.

RESURRECTION cont.

Isa. 25:8	he will swallow up **death** in victory; and the Lord God
Isa. 26:19	together with my dead body shall they **arise**. Awake and
Ezek. 37:12(1-14)	I will open your graves, and cause you to **come** up out
Dan. 12:2(1-3)	them that sleep in the dust of the earth shall **awake**
Hosea 13:14	I will ransom them from the power of the **grave**; I will
Matt. 22:30(28-32)	for in the **resurrection** they neither marry, nor are
Matt. 25:46	but the righteous into **life** eternal.
Matt. 27:52(52-53)	graves were opened...many bodies..which slept **arose**
Matt. 28:6(1-20)	he is not here: for he is **risen**, as he said. Come, see
Mark 12:26(19-27)	and as touching the dead, that they **rise**: have ye not
Luke 14:14	thou shalt be recompensed at the **resurrection** of the
Luke 20:35(35-38)	worthy to obtain that world...**resurrection** from the
Luke 24:39(36-39)	a spirit hath not **flesh** and bones, as ye see me have.
Luke 24:46(1-53)	it behoved Christ...to **rise** from the dead the third
John 2:19(18-22)	destroy this temple..in three days I will **raise** it up.
John 5:21	the Father **raiseth** up the dead, and quickeneth them
John 5:29(28-29)	they that have done good, unto the **resurrection** of
John 6:54(35-54)	I will **raise** him up at the last day.
John 11:25(25-26)	Jesus said...I am the **resurrection**, and the life: he
Acts 1:22(22-26)	be ordained to be a witness...of his **resurrection**.
Acts 2:24	whom God hath **raised** up, having loosed the pains of
Acts 10:40(39-42)	him God **raised** up the third day, and shewed him openly
Acts 24:15(14-15)	a **resurrection** of the dead, both of the just and
Acts 26:8	why...incredible...that God should **raise** the dead
Rom. 4:17	God, who **quickeneth** the dead, and calleth those things
Rom. 6:5(3-5)	we shall be also in the likeness of his **resurrection**
Rom. 8:11	he...shall also **quicken** your mortal bodies by his
1 Cor. 6:14	God...will also **raise** up us by his own power.
1 Cor. 15:21(1-58)	by man came also the **resurrection** of the dead.
1 Cor. 15:23(1-58)	Christ the **firstfruits**; afterward they that are Christ
2 Cor. 1:9	trust...in God which **raiseth** the dead
Eph. 2:5	hath **quickened** us together with Christ, (by grace ye
Philip. 3:21(20-21)	shall change our...**body**...fashioned like unto his
Col. 2:13	you...hath he **quickened** together with him, having
1 Thes. 4:16(13-17)	the dead in Christ shall **rise** first
1 Tim. 6:13	in the sight of God, who **quickeneth** all things, and
1 Jn. 3:2	when he shall appear, we shall be **like** him; for we
Rev. 1:18	I am he that **liveth**, and was dead; and, behold, I am
Rev. 20:6(3-7)	blessed...he that hath part in the first **resurrection**
Rev. 20:12	and I saw the dead, small and great, **stand** before God
1 Ne. 10:11(4-11)	rise from the **dead**, and...manifest, by the Holy Ghost
2 Ne. 2:8(8-10)	that he may bring to pass the **resurrection** of the dead
2 Ne. 9:12(4-22)	bodies...spirits of men will be **restored** one to the
2 Ne. 25:13(11-19)	he shall **rise** from the dead, with healing in his wings
Jacob 4:11	ye may obtain a **resurrection**, according to the power
Mosiah 15:22(8-9,20-27)	therefore, they are the first **resurrection**.
Mosiah 16:8(7-9)	but there is a **resurrection**, therefore the grave hath
Alma 11:41(37-46)	the day cometh that all shall **rise** from the dead and
Alma 33:22	rise again...bring to pass the **resurrection**, that all
Alma 40:3(1-26)	he bringeth to pass the **resurrection** of the dead. but
Alma 41:4(1-15)	all things shall be **restored** to their proper order
Hel. 14:15(15-18,25)	he dieth, to bring to pass the **resurrection** of the
3 Ne. 23:9(9-13)	many saints who should **arise** from the dead, and should

RESURRECTION cont.

Morm. 7:6	he bringeth to pass the **resurrection** of the dead
Morm. 9:13(12-13)	the death of Christ bringeth to pass the **resurrection**
Moro. 10:34	my spirit and body shall again **reunite**, and I am
D&C 20:23(21-24)	he was crucified, died, and **rose** again the third day
D&C 29:26(13,22-28)	then shall all the dead **awake**, for their graves shall
D&C 29:43(42-50)	he might be **raised** in immortality unto eternal life
D&C 43:18	ye saints **arise** and live; ye sinners stay and sleep
D&C 43:32	shall be **changed** in the twinkling of an eye, and the
D&C 45:54	they that knew no law...part in the first **resurrection**
D&C 63:49(49-52)	they shall **rise** from the dead and shall not die after
D&C 76:17(12-119)	good in the **resurrection** of the just...evil in the
D&C 88:14(14-16)	is brought to pass the **resurrection** from the dead.
D&C 88:27	they also shall **rise** again, a spiritual body.
D&C 88:97(96-107)	they who have slept in their graves shall **come** forth
D&C 93:33(33-34)	spirit and element, inseparably **connected**, receive a
D&C 101:31(28-31)	shall be **changed** in the twinkling of an eye, and shall
D&C 129:1(1-2)	**resurrected** personages, having bodies of flesh and
D&C 130:18(18-19)	intelligence...will rise with us in the **resurrection**.
D&C 133:56	the graves of the saints shall be **opened**; and they
Moses 1:39	to bring to pass the **immortality** and eternal life of
Moses 5:10(6-15)	and again in the **flesh** I shall see God.
JFS-V 1:14(11-17)	in the hope of a glorious **resurrection**, through the
JFS-V 1:43(43-51)	dry bones, which were to be **clothed** upon with flesh

RETRIBUTION

Gen. 49:6(5-7)	in their **anger** they slew a man, and in their selfwill
Ex. 21:24	**eye** for eye, tooth for tooth, hand for hand, foot for
Lev. 19:18	thou shalt not **avenge**, nor bear any grudge against the
Deut. 19:19(4-21)	**do** unto him, as he had thought to have done unto his
Deut. 32:35	to me belongeth **vengeance**, and recompence; their foot
Job 21:31	who shall **repay** him what he hath done
Prov. 20:22	say not thou, I will **recompense** evil; but wait on the
Isa. 59:18(16-19)	accordingly he will repay...**recompence** to his enemies
Matt. 5:44(38-47)	love your enemies, **bless** them that curse you, do good
Matt. 16:27	then he shall **reward** every man according to his works.
Matt. 26:52	they that take the sword shall **perish** with the sword.
Luke 6:37(27-38)	**judge** not, and ye shall not be judged: condemn not
Rom. 12:17(9-21)	**recompense** to no man evil for evil. Provide things
Rom. 12:19(17-21)	**avenge** not yourselves, but rather give place unto
Rom. 12:19(17-20)	it is written, **vengeance** is mine; I will repay, saith
Rom. 13:3(3,4)	do...**good**, and thou shalt have praise of the same
1 Cor. 6:7	why do ye not rather take **wrong**? why do ye not rather
1 Thes. 5:15	see that none **render** evil for evil unto any man; but
Heb. 10:30	**vengeance** belongeth unto me, I will recompense, saith
1 Pet. 2:23(22-23)	when he was **reviled**, reviled not again; when he suffer
1 Pet. 3:9	not **rendering** evil for evil, or railing for railing
Rev. 13:10	he that **killeth** with the sword must be killed with the
Rev. 18:6(2-8)	**reward** her even as she rewarded you, and double unto
3 Ne. 12:39(38-44)	but I say unto you, that ye shall not **resist** evil, but
3 Ne. 12:44(38-45)	love your enemies, **bless** them that curse you, do good
Morm. 3:15(9-15)	**vengeance** is mine, and I will repay; and because this

RETRIBUTION cont.

Morm. 8:20	man shall not **smite**, neither shall he judge; for
D&C 19:30	trusting in me, **reviling** not against revilers.
D&C 31:9	be patient...**revile** not against those that revile.
D&C 98:23(23-48)	revile not against them, neither seek **revenge**, ye
D&C 112:24(23-25)	behold, **vengeance** cometh speedily upon the inhabitants

REVELATION

Gen. 18:17	shall I **hide** from Abraham that thing which I do
Gen. 41:39(1-40)	God hath **shewed** thee all this, there is none so
Deut. 8:3	by every **word** that proceedeth out of the mouth of the
Deut. 29:29	things which are **revealed** belong unto us and to our
1 Sam. 3:1(1-10)	in those days; there was no open **vision**.
1 Kgs. 19:12(11-15)	and after the fire a still small **voice**.
Prov. 29:18	where there is no **vision**, the people perish: but he
Lam. 2:9	her prophets also find no **vision** from the Lord.
Dan. 2:29(28-30)	he that **revealeth** secrets maketh known...what shall
Dan. 2:45	the great God hath made **known** to the king what shall
Amos 3:7	he **revealeth** his secret unto his servants the prophets
Matt. 4:4	by every **word** that proceedeth out of the mouth of God.
Matt. 7:7(7-8)	ask, and it shall be **given** you; seek, and ye shall
Matt. 16:17(16-19)	flesh and blood hath not **revealed** it unto thee, but
John 6:46	he which is of God, he hath **seen** the Father.
John 8:26	to the world those things which I have **heard** of him.
John 10:4	the sheep follow him: for they know his **voice**.
John 14:21(19-23)	I will love him, and will **manifest** myself to him.
John 15:15	all things...heard of my Father I have made **known** unto
John 16:13	Spirit of truth...he will **shew** you things to come.
John 17:8	I have given unto them the **words** which thou gavest me
1 Cor. 2:10(9-16)	God hath **revealed** them unto us by his Spirit: for the
1 Cor. 12:3	**say** that Jesus is the Lord, but by the Holy Ghost.
1 Cor. 14:6	I shall speak to you either by **revelation**, or by
1 Cor. 14:10(8-11)	so many kinds of **voices** in the world, and none of them
2 Cor. 12:1(1-4)	I will come to visions and **revelations** of the Lord.
Eph. 1:17(17,18)	God...may give unto you the spirit of...**revelation** in
Eph. 3:5	it is now **revealed** unto his holy apostles and prophets
James 1:5(5,6)	if any...lack wisdom...ask of God, that **giveth** to all
2 Pet. 1:18	and this **voice** which came from heaven we heard, when
Rev. 1:1	the **revelation** of Jesus Christ, which God gave unto
Rev. 4:1	I will **shew** thee things which must be hereafter.
1 Ne. 4:18	therefore I did obey the **voice** of the Spirit, and took
2 Ne. 28:30	I will **give**...children of men line upon line, precept
2 Ne. 29:9(6-12)	because that I have spoken one **word** ye need not
2 Ne. 32:5(1-6)	Holy Ghost...will **show** unto you all things what ye
Jacob 4:8(8-10)	no man knoweth...save it be **revealed** unto him
Enos 1:5	and there came a **voice** unto me, saying: Enos, thy sins
Jarom 1:4(2-4)	have faith, have **communion** with the Holy Spirit, which
1:25	believe in prophesying, and in **revelations**, and in
Alma 5:46	this is the spirit of **revelation** which is in me.
Hel. 5:30	it was a still **voice** of perfect mildness, as if it had
Morm. 9:7(7-9)	I speak unto you who deny the **revelations** of God, and
Ether 3:25(25,26)	he **showed** unto the brother of Jared all the

Ether 3:27(27,28)	I will **show** them in mine own due time unto the
Ether 12:6	ye receive no **witness** until after the trial of your
Moro. 7:37(36-38)	by faith that angels **appear** and minister unto men
Moro. 10:4(3-18)	**manifest** the truth...by the power of the Holy Ghost.
D&C 1:17(11-28)	called upon...Joseph Smith, Jun., and **spake** unto him
D&C 1:38	whether by mine own **voice** or by the voice of my
D&C 3:4	for although a man may have many **revelations**, and have
D&C 8:3(1-3)	now, behold, this is the spirit of **revelation**; behold
D&C 9:8(7-9)	if it is right I will cause that your bosom shall **burn**
D&C 11:25	deny not the spirit of **revelation**, nor...of prophecy
D&C 18:35(34-36)	for it is my **voice** which speaketh them unto you; for
D&C 25:9	that all things might be **revealed** unto them
D&C 27:1	listen to the **voice** of Jesus Christ, your Lord, your
D&C 28:2(2-8)	appointed to receive commandments and **revelations** in
D&C 42:61	if thou shalt ask, thou shalt receive **revelation** upon
D&C 43:2(2-7)	appointed...to receive commandments and **revelations**
D&C 59:4	they shall also be crowned...with **revelations** in their
D&C 67:11(10-12)	no man has **seen** God...except quickened by the Spirit
D&C 68:4	whatsoever...speak...moved upon...**voice** of the Lord
D&C 75:1	I who speak even by the **voice** of my Spirit, even Alpha
D&C 76:7(5-10)	to them will I **reveal** all mysteries, yea, all the
D&C 76:116(116-118)	understood by...**Holy** Spirit, which God bestows on
D&C 82:4(3-4)	ye call upon my name for **revelations**, and I give them
D&C 85:6	still small **voice**, which whispereth through and pierce
D&C 88:49	the day shall come when you shall **comprehend** even God
D&C 88:68(66-68)	you shall see him; for he will **unveil** his face unto
D&C 90:14	receive **revelations** to unfold the mysteries of the
D&C 100:11	and he shall be a **revelator** unto thee, that thou
D&C 101:32(32-34)	when the Lord shall come, he shall **reveal** all things
D&C 102:9	president of the church...is appointed by **revelation**
D&C 102:23	president...obtain the mind of the Lord by **revelation**.
D&C 104:36	made known to him by the **voice** of the Spirit, and
D&C 107:39	they shall be designated unto them by **revelation**
D&C 107:92(91-92)	to be a seer, a **revelator**, a translator, and a prophet
D&C 108:2	resist no more my **voice**.
D&C 121:26(26-31)	shall give...you **knowledge** by his Holy Spirit, yea
D&C 130:3	the Father and the Son...is a personal **appearance**; and
D&C 130:13(13-14)	this a **voice** declared to me, while I was praying
Moses 7:4(3,4)	I will **show** unto thee the world for the space of many
Moses 7:54(54,55)	I pray thee, **show** me these things.
Moses 7:62	**truth** will I send forth out of the earth, to bear
Moses 7:67	the Lord **showed** Enoch all things, even unto the end
JS-H 1:17	when the light rested upon me I saw two **Personages**
JS-H 1:21(21-25)	no such things as visions or **revelations** in these days
A of F 1:7	We believe in...prophecy, **revelation**, visions, healing
A of F 1:9	We believe..God has **revealed**..does now reveal..will
JS-V 1:7(7-9)	thus came the **voice** of the Lord unto me, saying: all
JFS-V 1:11(1-11,29)	eyes of my understanding were **opened**, and the Spirit

382

REVERENCE

Gen. 20:11	surely the **fear** of God is not in this place; and they
Gen. 24:48	and I **bowed** down my head, and worshipped the Lord, and
Gen. 42:18	this do, and live; for I **fear** God
Ex. 3:5	the place whereon thou standest is **holy** ground.
Ex. 18:21	thou shalt provide...able men, such as **fear** God, men
Lev. 19:30	keep my sabbaths, and **reverence** my sanctuary: I am the
Lev. 26:2	keep my sabbaths, and **reverence** my sanctuary: I am the
Deut. 6:24(2,13,24)	to **fear** the Lord our God, for our good always, that
Deut. 10:12(12-13)	but to **fear** the Lord thy God, to walk in all his ways
Josh. 24:14(14-15)	now therefore **fear** the Lord, and serve him in
1 Sam. 12:24	only **fear** the Lord, and serve him in truth with all
Neh. 5:15	so did not I, because of the **fear** of God.
Job 28:28	the **fear** of the Lord, that is wisdom; and to depart
Ps. 2:11	serve the Lord with **fear**, and rejoice with trembling.
Ps. 25:14	the secret of the Lord is with them that **fear** him; and
Ps. 111:9	he sent redemption...holy and **reverend** is his name.
Ps. 112:1(1-3)	blessed is the man that **feareth** the Lord, that delight
Prov. 1:7	the **fear** of the Lord is the beginning of knowledge
Prov. 3:7(7-8)	**fear** the Lord, and depart from evil.
Prov. 8:13	the **fear** of the Lord is to hate evil: pride, and
Prov. 9:10	the **fear** of the Lord is the beginning of wisdom: and
Prov. 10:27	the **fear** of the Lord prolongeth days: but the years
Prov. 14:26(26-27)	in the **fear** of the Lord is strong confidence: and his
Prov. 15:33	the **fear** of the Lord is the instruction of widsom; and
Prov. 19:23	the **fear** of the Lord tendeth to life: and he that hath
Prov. 22:4	by humility and the **fear** of the Lord are riches, and
Prov. 28:14	happy is the man that **feareth** alway: but he that
Eccl. 5:1	**keep** thy foot when thou goest to the house of God, and
Eccl. 8:12(12-13)	it shall be well with them that **fear** God, which fear
Eccl. 12:13(13-14)	**fear** God, and keep his commandments: for this is the
Acts 10:35(34-35)	he that **feareth** him, and worketh righteousness, is
Rom. 11:20(19-21)	be not highminded, but **fear**
Col. 3:22(20-22)	but in singleness of heart, **fearing** God
Heb. 12:9	fathers of our flesh...we gave them **reverence**: shall
Heb. 12:28	serve God acceptably with **reverence** and godly fear
1 Pet. 1:17	pass the time of your sojourning here in **fear**
Rev. 14:7(6-7)	**fear** God, and give glory...worship him that made
Enos 1:4	and I **kneeled** down before my maker, and I cried unto
Mosiah 4:1	fallen to the earth, for the **fear** of the Lord had come
Alma 19:15(14,15)	for the **fear** of the Lord had come upon them also, for
Alma 46:13	he **bowed** himself to the earth, and he prayed mightily
3 Ne. 4:10	did **fear** their God and did supplicate him for
3 Ne. 11:12(11,12)	Jesus...spoken these words the...multitude **fell** to the
D&C 5:24	but if he will **bow** down before me, and humble himself
D&C 76:5	Lord...merciful and gracious unto those who **fear** me
D&C 76:93	before whose throne all things bow in humble **reverence**
D&C 88:104	**fear** God, and give glory to him who sitteth upon the
D&C 107:4	out of respect or **reverence** to the name of the supreme
D&C 109:21	those who shall **reverence** thee in thy house.

REVILING

Ex. 22:28	thou shalt not **revile** the gods, nor curse the ruler
Isa. 51:7	neither be ye afraid of their **revilings**.
Zeph. 2:8	I have heard...the **revilings** of the children of Ammon
Matt. 5:11(10-12)	blessed are ye, when men shall **revile** you, and
Matt. 27:39	they that passed by **reviled** him, wagging their heads
Mark 15:32	they that were crucified with him **reviled** him.
John 9:28	then they **reviled** him, and said, thou art his disciple
Acts 23:4	they that stood by said, **revilest** thou God's high
1 Cor. 4:12(10-13)	being **reviled**, we bless; being persecuted, we suffer
1 Cor. 6:10	thieves, nor covetous, nor drunkards, nor **revilers**
1 Pet. 2:23	who, when he was reviled, **reviled** not again; when he
1 Ne. 17:42	they did **revile** against Moses, and also against God
2 Ne. 9:40	for if ye do, ye will **revile** against the truth; for I
2 Ne. 28:16	wo unto them that...**revile** against that which is good
Jacob 3:9	**revile** no more against them because of the darkness
Alma 30:29(1-60)	they saw that he would **revile** even against God, they
Alma 34:40	do not **revile** against those who do cast you out
Hel. 8:5	why do you suffer this man to **revile** against us?
Hel. 10:15(14,15)	therefore they did **revile** against him, and did seek
3 Ne. 6:13(12-14)	and would not turn and **revile** again, but were humble
3 Ne. 12:11(10-12)	blessed are ye when men shall **revile** you and persecute
Ether 7:24(23-25)	people did **revile** against the prophets, and did mock
D&C 19:30	trusting in me, **reviling** not against revilers.
D&C 20:54	see that there is no iniquity...nor evil **speaking**
D&C 31:9	**revile** not against those that revile. Govern your
D&C 98:23(23-25)	bear it patiently and **revile** not against them, neither
D&C 121:16(10-22)	lift up the **heel** against mine anointed, saith the Lord
JS-H 1:23(23-25)	spirit of the most bitter persecution and **reviling**.

REWARD

1 Sam. 24:19	the Lord **reward** thee good for that thou hast done unto
2 Sam. 3:39	the Lord shall **reward** the doer of evil according to
2 Sam. 22:21	the Lord **rewarded** me according to my righteousness
Job 21:19	he **rewardeth** him, and he shall know it.
Ps. 31:19	**goodness**...thou hast laid up for them that fear thee
Ps. 31:23	and plentifully **rewardeth** the proud doer.
Ps. 58:11	verily there is a **reward** for the righteous: verily he
Ps. 94:2	render a **reward** to the proud.
Ps. 116:12	what shall I **render** unto the Lord for all his benefits
Ps. 127:3	the fruit of the womb is his **reward**.
Prov. 11:18	soweth righteousness shall be a sure **reward**.
Prov. 13:13	he that feareth the commandment shall be **rewarded**.
Prov. 17:13	whoso **rewardeth** evil for good, evil shall not depart
Prov. 25:22(21,22)	and the Lord shall **reward** thee.
Prov. 26:10	both **rewardeth** the fool, and rewardeth transgressors.
Eccl. 4:9	they have a good **reward** for their labour.
Isa. 40:10	behold, his **reward** is with him, and his work before
Isa. 62:11	behold, his **reward** is with him, and his work before
Isa. 64:4	what he hath **prepared** for him that waiteth for him.
Jer. 31:16	thy work shall be **rewarded**, saith the Lord; and they
Jer. 32:19	to **give** every one according to his ways, and according

REWARD cont.

Joel 3:4	if ye **recompence** me, swiftly and speedily will I
Obad. 1:15	thy **reward** shall return upon thine own head.
Matt. 5:12	for great is your **reward** in heaven: for so persecuted
Matt. 6:6(1-6)	thy **Father**...seeth in secret shall **reward** thee openly.
Matt. 6:18(16-18)	Father, which seeth in secret, shall **reward** thee
Matt. 10:41	receiveth a prophet...shall receive a prophet's **reward**
Matt. 16:27	he shall **reward** every man according to his works.
Matt. 25:34	**inherit** the kingdom prepared for you from the
Mark 9:41	he shall not lose his **reward**.
Mark 10:30(29-30)	receive an **hundredfold** now in this time, houses, and
Luke 6:23	behold, your **reward** is great in heaven: for in the
Luke 6:35	your **reward** shall be great, and ye shall be the
Luke 23:41	for we receive the due **reward** of our deeds: but this
1 Cor. 2:9	eye hath not seen...things which God hath **prepared** for
1 Cor. 3:8	every man shall receive his own **reward** according to
1 Cor. 9:17(16-18)	if I do this thing willingly, I have a **reward**: but if
1 Cor. 9:25(24-27)	they...to obtain a corruptible **crown**...we an
Col. 3:24(23-25)	ye shall receive the **reward** of the inheritance: for
2 Tim. 2:5(4-7)	yet is he not **crowned**, except he strive lawfully.
2 Tim. 4:8(7,8)	laid up for me a **crown** of righteousness, which the Lord
Heb. 11:6	he is a **rewarder** of them that diligently seek him.
James 1:12	when he is tried, he shall receive the **crown** of life
1 Pet. 3:12	for the **eyes** of the Lord are over the righteous, and
2 Pet. 2:13	shall receive the **reward** of unrighteousness, as they
Rev. 2:10	be thou faithful...and I will give thee a **crown** of
Rev. 22:12	my **reward** is with me, to give every man according as
Alma 3:26	they might reap their **rewards** according to their works
Alma 9:28	all men shall reap a **reward** of their works, according
Alma 26:5(1-5)	ye did...reap...and behold the number of your **sheaves**
Alma 32:43	ye shall reap the **rewards** of your faith, and your
Alma 41:14	then shall ye receive your **reward**; yea, ye shall have
3 Ne. 12:12	for great shall be your **reward** in heaven; for so
D&C 6:33	sow good ye shall also reap good for your **reward**.
D&C 31:12	pray always, lest you...lose your **reward**.
D&C 42:65	and great shall be thy **reward**; for unto you it is
D&C 54:10	I come quickly, and my **reward** is with me, and they who
D&C 56:19	the Lord shall come...and he shall **reward** every man
D&C 58:2(2-4)	he that is faithful...the **reward** of the same is
D&C 58:28(26-28)	men do good they shall in nowise lose their **reward**.
D&C 58:33	their **reward** lurketh beneath, and not from above.
D&C 59:23	works of righteousness shall receive his **reward**, even
D&C 63:48	his works shall follow him, and also a **reward** in the
D&C 64:11	let God...**reward** thee according to thy deeds.
D&C 98:23(23-31)	if men smite you..and ye bear it..ye shall be **rewarded**
D&C 98:44	until he repent and **reward** thee four-fold in all
D&C 101:65	to **reward** every man according as his work shall be
D&C 127:3	he will mete out a just recompense of **reward** upon the
D&C 127:4	for all this there is a **reward** in heaven.
D&C 135:6	and glory is their eternal **reward**. From age to age
Abr. 3:26(25,26)	shall have **glory** added upon their heads for ever and
JFS-V 1:15(11-15)	I beheld that they were **filled** with joy and gladness
JFS-V 1:59(57-60)	**reward** according to their works, for they are heirs

RIGHTEOUSNESS

Gen. 15:6(1-6)	and he counted it to him for **righteousness**.
Gen. 18:26	if I find in Sodom fifty **righteous**...I will spare all
Lev. 19:15	in **righteousness** shalt thou judge thy neighbour.
Deut. 6:25(24-25)	it shall be our **righteousness**, if we observe to do all
Deut. 9:5(4-6)	not for thy **righteousness**...dost thou go to possess
1 Sam. 26:23	the Lord render to every man his **righteousness** and his
1 Kgs. 8:32	to give him according to his **righteousness**.
2 Chr. 6:23(22-23)	by giving him according to his **righteousness**.
Job 27:6	my **righteousness** I hold fast, and will not let it go
Job 29:14	I put on **righteousness**, and it clothed me: my judgment
Ps. 1:6(1-6)	the Lord knoweth the way of the **righteous**: but the way
Ps. 9:8(7-8)	he shall judge the world in **righteousness**, he shall
Ps. 11:7	for the righteous Lord loveth **righteousness**; his count
Ps. 17:15	I will behold thy face in **righteousness**: I shall be
Ps. 23:3	he leadeth me in the paths of **righteousness** for his
Ps. 33:5	he loveth **righteousness** and judgment: the earth is
Ps. 37:16(16-40)	a little that a **righteous** man hath is better than the
Ps. 45:4(4-7)	ride prosperously because of truth...**righteousness**
Ps. 72:7(1-7)	in his days shall the **righteous** flourish; and
Ps. 128:1(1-4)	blessed is every one that...**walketh** in his ways.
Ps. 132:9	let thy priests be clothed with **righteousness**; and let
Ps. 145:17	the Lord is **righteous** in all his ways, and holy in all
Prov. 4:18	the path of the **just** is as the shining light, that
Prov. 10:2	but **righteousness** delivereth from death.
Prov. 11:18(18-19)	to him that soweth **righteousness** shall be a sure
Prov. 12:28	in the way of **righteousness** is life; and in the
Prov. 14:34	**righteousness** exalteth a nation: but sin is a reproach
Prov. 15:9	Lord...loveth him that followeth after **righteousness**.
Prov. 29:2	when the **righteous** are in authority...people rejoice
Isa. 3:10(10-11)	say ye to the **righteous**, that it shall be well with
Isa. 45:8	let the skies pour down **righteousness**: let the earth
Isa. 60:21(21-22)	thy people also shall be all **righteous**: they shall
Jer. 23:6(5-6)	he shall be called, the Lord our **righteousness**.
Ezek. 3:20(20-21)	when a righteous man doth turn from his **righteousness**
Ezek. 18:20(19-23)	the **righteousness** of the righteous shall be upon him
Ezek. 18:24(24,26)	when the righteous turneth away from his **righteousness**
Ezek. 33:18(18-19)	when the righteous turneth from his **righteousness**, and
Dan. 9:7	**righteousness** belongeth unto thee, but unto us
Dan. 12:3(1-3)	they that turn many to **righteousness** as the stars for
Hosea 10:12	sow to yourselves in **righteousness**, reap in mercy
Amos 5:24(7,24)	let judgment run..and **righteousness** as a mighty stream
Zeph. 2:3	seek **righteousness**, seek meekness: it may be ye shall
Matt. 3:15	thus it becometh us to fulfil all **righteousness**. then
Matt. 5:6	they which do hunger and thirst after **righteousness**
Matt. 5:10	persecuted for **righteousness'** sake: for theirs is the
Matt. 5:20	except your **righteousness** shall exceed the
Matt. 6:33	seek ye first the kingdom of God, and his
Matt. 9:13	I am not come to call the **righteous**, but sinners to
Matt. 13:43	then shall the **righteous** shine forth as the sun in
Matt. 13:49	angels shall...sever the wicked from among the **just**
Matt. 21:32	John came unto you in the way of **righteousness**, and
Matt. 23:35	from the blood of **righteous** Abel unto the blood of
Matt. 25:46	but the **righteous** into life eternal.

Luke 23:47	certainly this was a **righteous** man.
John 16:8(8-10)	reprove the world of sin, and of **righteousness**, and
Acts 10:35	he that...worketh **righteousness**, is accepted with him.
Acts 13:10	child of the devil, thou enemy of all **righteousness**
Rom. 4:3(3-13)	it was counted unto him for **righteousness**.
Rom. 5:18(18-19)	by the **righteousness** of one the free gift came upon
Rom. 5:21	might grace reign through **righteousness** unto eternal
Rom. 6:13(13-20)	your members as instruments of **righteousness** unto God.
Rom. 8:10	but the spirit is life because of **righteousness**.
Rom. 9:30(30-31)	even the **righteousness** which is of faith.
Rom. 10:6(3-10)	**righteousness** which is of faith speaketh on this wise
Rom. 14:17	**righteousness**, and peace, and joy in the Holy Ghost.
2 Cor. 6:7(3-10)	by the armour of **righteousness** on the right hand and
2 Cor. 9:10(8-10)	increase the fruits of your **righteousness**
Gal. 3:6(5-6)	it was accounted to him for **righteousness**.
Eph. 4:24(20-25)	created in **righteousness** and true holiness.
Eph. 6:14(13-18)	having on the breastplate of **righteousness**
Philip. 1:11(9-11)	filled with the fruits of **righteousness**, which are by
Philip. 3:9(8-11)	the **righteousness** which is of God by faith
Philip. 4:8	whatsoever things are **just**, whatsoever things are pure
1 Tim. 6:11	follow after **righteousness**, godliness, faith, love
2 Tim. 3:16(16-17)	for correction, for instruction in **righteousness**
Titus 2:12	we should live soberly, **righteously**, and godly, in
Titus 3:5(4-7)	not by works of **righteousness** which we have done, but
Heb. 1:9(8-9)	thou hast loved **righteousness**, and hated iniquity; the
Heb. 7:2(1-3)	by interpretation king of **righteousness**, and after
Heb. 11:7	Noah...became heir of the **righteousness**...by faith.
James 2:23	imputed unto him for **righteousness**: and he was called
James 3:18	fruit of **righteousness** is sown in peace of them that
1 Pet. 3:12	the eyes of the Lord are over the **righteous**, and his
1 Pet. 3:14	if ye suffer for **righteousness'** sake, happy are ye
1 Pet. 4:18	and if the **righteous** scarcely be saved, where shall
2 Pet. 2:5	Noah...a preacher of **righteousness**, bringing in the
2 Pet. 2:21	not to have known the way of **righteousness**, than
2 Pet. 3:13	a new earth, wherein dwelleth **righteousness**.
1 Jn. 2:29	every one that doeth **righteousness** is born of him.
1 Ne. 14:14	armed with **righteousness** and with the power of God
1 Ne. 17:35(33-38)	he that is **righteous** is favored of God. But behold
1 Ne. 22:17(15-26)	he will preserve the **righteous** by his power, even if
1 Ne. 22:26	because of the **righteousness**...Satan has no power
2 Ne. 1:23(19-23)	put on the armor of **righteousness**. Shake off the
2 Ne. 2:13(11-13)	no **righteousness** nor happiness there be no punishment
2 Ne. 4:33(32-35)	encircle me around in the robe of thy **righteousness**
2 Ne. 9:14(14,49)	shall have a perfect knowledge of..their **righteousness**
2 Ne. 9:18(18,46)	the **righteous**...shall inherit the kingdom of God
2 Ne. 30:11(9-11)	**righteousness** shall be the girdle of his loins, and
2 Ne. 31:5(5-6)	baptized by water, to fulfil all **righteousness**, O then
Jacob 4:5	law of Moses...is sanctified unto us for **righteousness**
Mosiah 2:37	becometh an enemy to all **righteousness**; therefore, the
Mosiah 3:4	the Lord hath...judged of thy **righteousness**, and hath
Mosiah 4:14	evil spirit...he being an enemy to all **righteousness**.
Mosiah 23:18	nourish them with things pertaining to **righteousness**.
Mosiah 27:25	state of **righteousness**, being redeemed of God

Alma 5:42	death, as to things pertaining unto **righteousness**
Alma 7:19	ye are in the paths of **righteousness**; I perceive that
Alma 12:16	shall die as to things pertaining unto **righteousness**.
Alma 26:8	God...doth work **righteousness** forever.
Alma 34:23	the devil, who is an enemy to all **righteousness**.
Alma 34:36	in the hearts of the **righteous** doth he dwell; yea, and
Alma 38:9	Christ...is the word of truth and **righteousness**.
Alma 40:12(11-14,25)	spirits of...**righteous**...received...state of happiness
Alma 41:14	ye shall have a **righteous** judgment restored unto you
Hel. 7:5	comdemning...righteous because of their **righteousness**
Hel. 14:18	cut off again as to things pertaining to **righteousness**
Hel. 14:29	a **righteous** judgment might come upon them; and also
3 Ne. 6:28	the devil, to combine against all **righteousness**.
3 Ne. 7:15	quick return from **righteousness** unto their wickedness
3 Ne. 13:33	seek ye first the kingdom of God...his **righteousness**
3 Ne. 22:14(11-14)	in **righteousness** shalt thou be established; thou shalt
3 Ne. 25:2	Son of **righteousness** arise with healing in his wings
Morm. 9:14	he that is **righteous** shall be righteous still; he that
Ether 8:26	come unto the fountain of all **righteousness** and be
Ether 9:22	he even saw the Son of **righteousness**, and did rejoice
Ether 12:28	bringeth unto me- the fountain of all **righteousness**.
Moro. 9:6	that we may conquer the enemy of all **righteousness**
D&C 11:14	pertaining unto things of **righteousness**, in faith
D&C 13:1	offer again an offering unto the Lord in **rightousness**.
D&C 20:14	work **righteousness**, shall receive a crown of eternal
D&C 25:15	a crown of **righteousness** thou shalt receive.
D&C 27:16	having on the breastplate of **righteousness**, and your
D&C 29:11(11-13)	dwell in **righteousness** with men on earth a thousand
D&C 29:27(26-27)	the **righteous** shall be gathered on my right hand unto
D&C 43:32	liveth in **righteousness** shall be changed in the
D&C 58:27(26-28)	free will, and bring to pass much **righteousness**
D&C 59:8(8-11)	offer a sacrifice...the Lord thy God in **righteousness**
D&C 59:23	he who doeth the works of **righteousness** shall receive
D&C 63:37(36-37)	every man should take **righteousness** in his hands and
D&C 76:5	to honor those who serve me in **righteousness** and in
D&C 88:26(16-26)	and the **righteous** shall inherit it.
D&C 98:30	thou shalt be rewarded for thy **righteousness**; and also
D&C 100:15(15-17)	all things...work together for good...walk **uprightly**
D&C 100:16	a pure people, that will serve me in **righteousness**
D&C 107:30	decisions...are to be made in all **righteousness**, in
D&C 109:76	clothed upon with robes of **righteousness**, with palms
D&C 121:36	handled only upon the principles of **righteousness**.
D&C 121:46	unchanging scepter of **righteousness** and truth; and thy
D&C 128:24	offer unto the Lord an offering in **righteousness**; and
D&C 132:36	it was accounted unto him for **righteousness**.
Moses 6:23	they were preachers of **righteousness**, and spake and
Moses 6:41	a land of **righteousness** unto this day. And my father
Moses 7:18(16-19)	one heart and one mind, and dwelt in **righteousness**
Moses 7:62(62-65)	**righteousness** will I send down out of heaven; and
Abr. 1:2(2-5)	having been myself a follower of **righteousness**
JS-H 1:2	present the various events..in truth and **righteousness**
JS-H 1:69	sons of Levi...an offering...in **righteousness**.

RIOTING AND REVELLING

Ex. 32:17(17-25)	Joshua heard the noise of the people as they **shouted**
Prov. 23:20	be not...among **riotous** eaters of flesh
Prov. 28:7	that is a companion of **riotous** men shameth his father.
Matt. 26:5(4,5)	feast day, lest there be an **uproar** among the people.
Matt. 27:24	Pilate saw...that rather a **tumult** was made, he took
Luke 15:13	there wasted his substance with **riotous** living.
Luke 21:34(34-36)	your hearts be overcharged with **surfeiting**, and
Acts 17:5(5-9)	Jews which believed not..set all the city on an **uproar**
Acts 19:40	danger...called in question for this day's **uproar**, the
Acts 20:1	after the **uproar** was ceased, Paul called unto him the
Acts 21:31	tidings came...that all Jerusalem was in an **uproar**.
Rom. 13:13	let us walk honestly...not in **rioting** and drunkenness
2 Cor. 6:5	in imprisonments, in **tumults**, in labours, in watchings
2 Cor. 12:20	lest there be...whisperings, swellings, **tumults**
Gal. 5:21	**revellings**, and such like...shall not inherit the
1 Pet. 4:3(1-4)	wine, **revellings**, banquetings, and abominable
2 Pet. 2:13	they that count it pleasure to **riot** in the day time.
1 Ne. 18:9	to make themselves merry...dance... with much **rudeness**
Mosiah 11:14	he spent his time in **riotous** living with his wives and
Alma 11:20	they did stir up the people to **riotings**, and all
Alma 45:21	many little dissensions and **disturbances** which had
4 Ne. 1:16	there were no envyings, nor strifes, nor **tumults**, nor
D&C 88:69	cast away your idle thoughts...your **excess** of laughter

ROCK

Gen. 49:24	from thence is the shepherd, the **stone** of Israel
Deut. 32:4(3-4)	he is the **Rock**, his work is perfect: for all his ways
Deut. 32:15(15-31)	lightly esteemed the **Rock** of his salvation.
1 Sam. 2:2	neither is there any **rock** like our God.
2 Sam. 22:2(1-4)	the Lord is my **rock**, and my fortress, and my deliverer
2 Sam. 23:3	the **Rock** of Israel spake to me, he that ruleth over
Ps. 18:2(1-3)	the Lord is my **rock**, and my fortress, and my deliverer
Ps. 18:31	or who is a **rock** save our God
Ps. 18:46(46-50)	my **rock**...the God of my salvation be exalted.
Ps. 61:2	lead me to the **rock** that is higher than I.
Ps. 62:6(1-8)	he only is my **rock** and my salvation: he is my defence
Ps. 118:22	**stone** which the builders refused is become the head
Isa. 8:14(13-15)	and for a **rock** of offence to both the houses of Israel
Isa. 17:10	thou..hast not been mindful of the **rock** of thy
Isa. 51:1(1,2)	the **rock** whence ye are hewn, and to the hole of the
Isa. 54:11(5-14)	I will lay thy **stones**...and lay thy foundations with
Dan. 2:34(31-45)	a **stone** was cut out without hands, which smote the
Matt. 7:25(24-27)	it fell not: for it was founded upon a **rock**.
Matt. 16:18(15-19)	upon this **rock** I will build my church; and the gates
Matt. 21:42(42-44)	the **stone** which the builders rejected...is become the
Luke 20:17(17,18)	the **stone** which the builders rejected, the same is
Acts 4:11(10-11)	this is the **stone** which was set at nought of you build
Rom. 9:33(32-33)	I lay in Sion a stumblingstone and **rock** of offence
1 Cor. 10:4(1-4)	drank of...spiritual **Rock**...and that Rock was Christ.
1 Pet. 2:8(7-8)	a stone of stumbling, and a **rock** of offence, even to
1 Ne. 13:36(34-37)	the Lamb, and my **rock** and my salvation.

ROCK cont.

1 Ne. 15:15	God, their **rock** and their salvation? Yea, at that day
2 Ne. 4:30(30,35)	my God, and the **rock** of my salvation.
2 Ne. 8:1(1,2)	the **rock** from whence ye are hewn, and to the hole of
2 Ne. 9:45(45,46)	God who is the **rock** of your salvation.
2 Ne. 18:14(13-15)	for a stone of stumbling, and for a **rock** of offense
2 Ne. 28:28(27-29)	he that is built upon the **rock** receiveth it with
Jacob 4:15(15-18)	the Jews...will reject the **stone** upon which they might
Jacob 7:25(23-25)	the God and **rock** of their salvation; wherefore, they
Hel. 5:12	upon the **rock** of our Redeemer, who is Christ, the Son
3 Ne. 11:39(39,40)	my doctrine...buildeth upon this buildeth upon my **rock**
3 Ne. 14:24(24-27)	wise man, who built his house upon a **rock**
3 Ne. 18:12(10-14)	for ye are built upon my **rock**.
3 Ne. 22:11(5-14)	I will lay thy **stones** with fair colors, and lay thy
D&C 6:34	if ye are built upon my **rock**, they cannot prevail.
D&C 10:69	him will I establish upon my **rock**, and the gates of
D&C 11:16	you shall have...my **rock**, my church, and my gospel
D&C 11:24	build upon my **rock**, which is my gospel
D&C 18:5(4-5)	upon the foundation of my gospel and my **rock**, the gate
D&C 33:13(11-15)	upon this **rock** I will build my church; yea, upon this
D&C 50:44	he that buildeth upon this **rock** shall never fall.
D&C 65:2(1,2)	**stone** which is cut out of the mountain without hands
Moses 7:53	I am Messiah, the King of Zion, the **Rock** of Heaven
Abr. 2:16	eternity was our covering and our **rock** and our

SABBATH

Gen. 2:3(2,3)	God blessed the **seventh** day, and sanctified it
Ex. 16:23(22-30)	to morrow is the rest of the holy **sabbath** unto the Lord
Ex. 20:8(8-11)	remember the **sabbath** day, to keep it holy.
Ex. 23:12	on the **seventh** day thou shalt rest: that thine ox and
Ex. 31:13(12-18)	my **sabbaths** ye shall keep: for it is a sign between
Ex. 31:17	on the **seventh** day he rested, and was refreshed.
Lev. 23:3	seventh day is the **sabbath** of rest, an holy
Num. 15:32(32-36)	gathered sticks upon the **sabbath** day.
Deut. 5:12(12-15)	keep the **sabbath** day to sanctify it, as the Lord thy
Neh. 9:14(13,14)	and madest known unto them thy holy **sabbath**, and
Neh. 10:31	people..bring...victuals on the **sabbath** day to sell
Neh. 13:15(15-22)	some treading wine presses on the **sabbath**, and
Isa. 56:2(1-8)	that keepeth the **sabbath** from polluting it, and
Isa. 58:13(13-14)	call the **sabbath** a delight, the holy of the Lord
Jer. 17:21(19-27)	bear no burden on the **sabbath** day, nor bring it in
Ezek. 20:12(12,20)	I gave them my **sabbaths**, to be a sign between me and
Ezek. 46:1(1-7)	but on the **sabbath** it shall be opened, and in the day
Hosea 2:11	I will..cause all her mirth to cease..and her **sabbaths**
Amos 8:5(4-7)	and the **sabbath**, that we may set forth wheat, making
Matt. 12:8(1-12)	for the Son of man is Lord even of the **sabbath** day.
Matt. 28:1	end of the **sabbath**, as it began to dawn toward the
Mark 2:27(23-28)	the **sabbath** was made for man, and not man for the
Mark 3:4(1-6)	lawful to do good on the **sabbath** days, or to do evil
Luke 6:5(1-10)	the Son of man is Lord also of the **sabbath**.
Luke 13:16(14-16)	be loosed from this bond on the **sabbath** day
Luke 14:5(1-5)	fallen into a pit...pull him out on the **sabbath** day

SABBATH cont.

John 5:10(8-13)	sabbath day ...not lawful for thee to carry thy bed.
John 7:23(21-24)	man on the sabbath day receive circumcision, that the
John 9:14(13-16)	it was the sabbath day when Jesus made the clay, and
John 20:1(1,19,26)	the first day of the week cometh Mary Magdalene early
Acts 13:42	Gentiles besought...preached to them the next sabbath.
Acts 18:4	and he reasoned in the synagogue every sabbath, and
Acts 20:7	upon the first day of the week...Paul preached unto
1 Cor. 16:2	upon the first day of the week let every one of you
Col. 2:16(16-17)	let no man...judge you...in respect of...sabbath days
Heb. 4:4	spake in a certain place of the seventh day on this
Rev. 1:10	I was in the spirit on the Lord's day, and heard
Rev. 8:1(1-13)	and when he had opened the seventh seal, there was
Jarom 1:5	they observed to keep the law of Moses and the sabbath
Mosiah 13:16(16-19)	remember the sabbath day, to keep it holy.
Mosiah 18:23(23-25)	they should observe the sabbath day, and keep it holy
D&C 59:9(9-13)	thou shalt...offer up thy sacraments upon my holy day
D&C 68:29	inhabitants of Zion shall also observe the sabbath day
D&C 77:12(6-7,12-13)	and on the seventh day he finished his work, and
Moses 3:2(1-3)	I rested on the seventh day from all my work, and all
Abr. 5:2(1-3)	we will rest on the seventh time from all our work

SABBATICAL YEAR

Ex. 21:2(2-6)	six years he shall serve..seventh he shall go out free
Ex. 23:11(10-11)	the seventh year thou shalt let it rest and lie still
Lev. 25:2(1-7)	then shall the land keep a sabbath unto the Lord.
Lev. 25:20(19-22)	what shall we eat the seventh year? behold, we shall
Lev. 26:34(33-35)	then shall the land enjoy her sabbaths, as long as it
Deut. 15:1(1-18)	at the end of every seven years thou shalt make a
2 Chr. 36:21(20,21)	as long as she lay desolate she kept sabbath, to
Neh. 10:31	we would leave the seventh year, and the exaction of
Jer. 34:14(13-17)	at the end of seven years let ye go every man his
D&C 77:12(7,12)	in the beginning of the seventh thousand years will

SACRAMENT

Matt. 26:26(26-28)	Jesus took bread...said, take, eat; this is my body.
Matt. 26:27(26-29)	he took the cup, and gave thanks...drink ye all of it
John 6:54(51-58)	eateth my flesh...drinketh my blood, hath eternal life
Acts 2:42	continued stedfastly...breaking of bread, and in
Acts 20:7	first day...disciples came together to break bread
1 Cor. 11:26(23-26)	for as often as ye eat this bread, and drink this cup
1 Cor. 11:29(27-30)	eateth and drinketh unworthily, eateth and drinketh
3 Ne. 18:7(1-12)	this shall ye do in remembrance of my body, which I
3 Ne. 18:29(28-32)	eateth and drinketh my flesh and blood unworthily
3 Ne. 20:3(3-9)	he brake bread again and blessed it, and gave to the
3 Ne. 26:13	did break bread oft, and bless it, and give it unto
Moro. 4:3(1-3)	we ask thee...to bless and sanctify this bread to the
Moro. 5:2(1-2)	we ask thee...to bless and sanctify this wine to the
Moro. 6:6	bread and wine, in remembrance of the Lord Jesus.
D&C 20:40(40-46)	administer bread and wine- the emblems of the flesh

SACRAMENT cont.

D&C 20:58
D&C 20:68
D&C 20:75(75-79)
D&C 27:2(1-5)
D&C 46:4
D&C 59:9(9-12)
D&C 62:4

neither teachers nor deacons..administer the **sacrament**
previous to their partaking of the **sacrament** and being
partake of bread and wine in the **remembrance** of the
remembering...my **body**...and my blood which was shed
let him not **partake** until he makes reconciliation.
go to the house of prayer and offer up thy **sacraments**
rejoice...and offer a **sacrament** unto the Most High.

SACRED

Gen. 2:3
2 Chr. 7:16
Ezek. 44:23
Matt. 7:6
1 Cor. 3:17(16,17)
1 Ne. 15:36
1 Ne. 19:6(5-7)
Jacob 1:4
Alma 12:9
Alma 13:12(11-12)
Alma 37:2
Alma 37:14(14,15)
Alma 37:47
Alma 44:5
Alma 50:39(38-39)
Alma 63:1
Hel. 4:12(11-12)
3 Ne. 1:2
4 Ne. 1:27
4 Ne. 1:48
Morm. 6:6
Ether 4:5(4-6)
D&C 3:12(12-13)
D&C 6:12(10-12)
D&C 8:11(10-11)
D&C 9:9
D&C 20:11
D&C 25:11
D&C 59:9
D&C 63:64
D&C 94:6(6-9)
D&C 104:66(60-68)
D&C 134:5

God blessed the seventh day, and **sanctified** it
have I...**sanctified** this house, that my name may be
teach...the difference between the **holy** and profane
give not that which is **holy** unto the dogs, neither
the temple of God is **holy**, which temple ye are.
tree of life, whose fruit is most **precious** and most
do not write anything upon plates save it be...**sacred**.
preaching which was **sacred**, or revelation which was
it is given unto many to know the **mysteries** of God
after being **sanctified** by the Holy Ghost, having their
keep all these things **sacred** which I have kept, even
God has entrusted you with...things, which are **sacred**
take care of these **sacred** things, yea, see that ye
by the **sacred** support which we owe to our wives and
their **sacred** privileges to worship the Lord their God
Shiblon took possession of those **sacred** things which
making a mock of that which was **sacred**, denying the
records...had been kept **sacred** from the departure of
did administer that which was **sacred** unto him to whom
did hide up the records which were **sacred**- yea, even
commanded of the Lord...records...which were **sacred**
he commanded me that I should **seal** them up; and he
thou deliveredst up that which was **sacred** into the
trifle not with **sacred** things.
ancient records which have been hid...that are **sacred**
cannot write that which is **sacred** save it be given you
God does inspire men and call them to his **holy** work
given thee...to make a selection of **sacred** hymns, as
go to the house of prayer...upon my **holy** day
that which cometh from above is **sacred**, and must be
it shall be **dedicated** unto the Lord from the
this shall be called the **sacred** treasury of the Lord
holding **sacred** the freedom of conscience.

SACRIFICE

Gen. 4:4(3-7)
Gen. 8:20(20-22)
Gen. 22:9(1-13)
Ex. 12:27(1-27)
Ex. 20:24

the Lord had respect unto Abel and to his **offering**
offered burnt **offerings** on the altar.
bound Isaac his son, and laid him on the **altar** upon
it is the **sacrifice** of the Lord's passover, who passed
thou shalt...**sacrifice**...thy peace offerings, thy

SACRIFICE cont.

Ex. 29:18(1-46)	it is a burnt **offering** unto the Lord: it is a sweet
Lev. 1:3(1-9)	burnt **sacrifice**...offer it of his own voluntary will
Lev. 3:1(1-17)	if his oblation be a **sacrifice** of peace offering, if
Lev. 4:3(1-35)	without blemish unto the Lord for a sin **offering**.
Lev. 6:12(8-13)	and he shall burn...the fat of the peace **offerings**.
Lev. 7:11(11-37)	this is the law of the **sacrifice** of peace offerings
Lev. 14:13(1-32)	he shall kill the sin **offering** and the burnt offering
Lev. 17:5(1-7)	offer them for peace **offerings** unto the Lord.
Lev. 19:5	ye shall **offer** it at your own will.
Lev. 22:19(19,29)	ye shall **offer** at your own will a male without blemish
Num. 6:14(3-21)	one ram without blemish for peace **offerings**
Num. 15:3(1-29)	make an **offering** by fire unto the Lord, a burnt
Num. 28:3(1-31)	this is the **offering** made by fire which ye shall offer
Num. 29:3(1-40)	their meat **offering** shall be of flour mingled with oil
Deut. 15:21(19-23)	if there be any blemish...thou shalt not **sacrifice** it
Deut. 27:7(5-8)	thou shalt offer peace **offerings**, and shalt eat there
1 Sam. 15:22(20-23)	to obey is better than **sacrifice**, and to hearken than
2 Sam. 24:25	David...offered...peace **offerings**. So the Lord was
1 Kgs. 3:15	Solomon...offered peace **offerings**, and made a feast
1 Kgs. 8:63(62-66)	Solomon offered a **sacrifice** of peace offerings, which
1 Kgs. 9:25	three times in a year did Solomon **offer**...peace
Ps. 4:5	offer the **sacrifices** of righteousness, and put your
Ps. 50:5	covenant with me by **sacrifice**.
Prov. 15:8	the **sacrifice** of the wicked is an abomination to the
Isa. 1:11(10-14)	to what purpose is the multitude of your **sacrifices**
Ezek. 43:27	make your burnt **offerings**...and your peace offerings
Ezek. 45:13(13-25)	this is the **oblation** that ye shall offer; the sixth
Ezek. 46:12(2,12)	prince shall prepare a voluntary...peace **offerings**
Hosea 6:6	the knowledge of God more than burnt **offerings**.
Amos 5:22	neither will I regard the peace **offerings** of your
Mal. 1:8	if ye offer the blind for **sacrifice**, is it not evil
Mal. 3:3(1-4)	may offer unto the Lord an **offering** in righteousness.
Matt. 19:21(16-29)	sell that thou hast, and **give** to the poor, and thou
Mark 12:33(32,33)	is more than all whole burnt **offerings** and sacrifices.
Luke 17:33	whosoever shall **lose** his life shall preserve it.
1 Cor. 10:20	the Gentiles...**sacrifice** to devils, and not to God
Heb. 5:1	that he may offer both gifts and **sacrifices** for sins
Heb. 7:27	to offer up **sacrifice**, first for his own sins, and
Heb. 10:3	in those **sacrifices** there is a remembrance...of sins
Heb. 10:12	after he had offered one **sacrifice** for sins for ever
Heb. 11:4	by faith Abel offered...a more excellent **sacrifice**
Heb. 11:17(17-19)	by faith Abraham, when he was tried, **offered** up Isaac
1 Pet. 2:5	offer up spiritual **sacrifices**, acceptable to God by
1 Ne. 2:7	made an **offering** unto the Lord, and gave thanks unto
1 Ne. 5:9	they did rejoice...and did offer **sacrifice** and burnt
2 Ne. 2:7	he offereth himself a **sacrifice** for sin, to answer the
Jacob 4:5	Abraham...**offering** up his son...is a similitude of God
1:26	offer your whole souls as an **offering** unto him, and
Mosiah 2:3	they might offer **sacrifice**...according to the law of
Alma 34:10(10-14)	it must be an infinite and eternal **sacrifice**.
3 Ne. 9:19(19-20)	your **sacrifices** and your burnt offerings.
3 Ne. 24:3(3-4)	offer unto the Lord an **offering** in righteousness.
3 Ne. 24:8	wherein have we robbed thee? In tithes and **offerings**.

SACRIFICE cont.

Morm. 4:14(14-15)	did offer them up as **sacrifices** unto their idol gods.
Morm. 4:21	their children were again **sacrificed** unto idols.
D&C 59:12(8-12)	thou shalt offer thine **oblations** and thy sacraments
D&C 64:23	it is a day of **sacrifice**, and a day for the tithing
D&C 84:31	Aaron shall offer an acceptable offering and **sacrifice**
D&C 97:8(8-12)	willing to observe their covenants by **sacrifice**- yea
D&C 97:12	this is the tithing and the **sacrifice** which I, the Lord
D&C 98:13(13-15)	whoso layeth down his **life**...shall find...life eternal
D&C 124:39(37-39)	your **sacrifices** by the sons of Levi, and for your
D&C 128:24	offer unto the Lord an **offering** in righteousness. Let
D&C 132:9	will I accept of an **offering**...not made in my name
D&C 132:50	I have seen your **sacrifices** in obedience to that which
Moses 5:6(5-8)	why dost thou offer **sacrifices** unto the Lord? And Adam
Moses 5:20(17-21)	the Lord had respect unto Abel, and to his **offering**
Moses 6:3	Seth...offered an acceptable **sacrifice**, like unto his
Abr. 2:18	I offered **sacrifice** there in the plains of Moreh, and
Abr. 6:3(3,4)	priest...attempting to offer up Abraham as a **sacrifice**
Abr. 7:2	revealed from God to Abraham, as he offered **sacrifice**
JFS-V 1:2(1-4)	the great atoning **sacrifice** that was made by the Son
JFS-V 1:13(11-16)	who had offered **sacrifice**...and had suffered

SACRILEGE

Ex. 20:7	not take the name of the Lord thy God in **vain**; for the
Lev. 20:3(1-3)	to **defile** my sanctuary, and to profane my holy name.
1 Sam. 5:2	Philistines took the **ark**...into the house of Dagon
Jer. 7:30(17-31)	set their abominations in the house...to **pollute** it.
Ezek. 5:11(5-11)	because thou hast **defiled** my sanctuary with all thy
Ezek. 23:39(36-39)	they came the same day into my sanctuary to **profane**
Ezek. 44:7(4-14)	brought into my sanctuary strangers...to **pollute** it
Amos 2:7(6-8)	to **profane** my holy name
Zeph. 3:4(1-4)	her priests have **polluted** the sanctuary, they have
Matt. 7:6	give not that which is **holy** unto the dogs, neither
Rom. 2:22	abhorrest idols, dost thou commit **sacrilege**
1 Cor. 3:17(16,17)	if any man **defile** the temple of God, him shall God
Rev. 3:4(4,5)	which have not **defiled** their garments; and they shall
1 Ne. 19:7	very God of Israel do men **trample** under their feet; I
Jacob 6:8(8,9)	make a **mock** of the great plan of redemption, which
Alma 5:53	**trample** the Holy One under your feet; yea, can ye be
Hel. 4:12(12,13)	making a **mock** of that which was sacred, denying the
Hel. 12:2(1,2)	**trample** under their feet the Holy One- yea, and this
D&C 3:12(12,13)	which was **sacred** into the hands of a wicked man
D&C 6:12	**trifle** not with sacred things.
D&C 10:9(1-37)	that which was **sacred**, unto wickedness.
JS-H 1:46	tempt me...to get the plates for...getting **rich**. this

SAINTS

Deut. 33:3(1-3)	all his **saints** are in thy hand: and they sat down at
Ps. 50:5	gather my **saints**...those that have made a covenant
Ps. 89:7	in the assembly of the **saints**, and to be had in

SAINTS cont.

Ps. 149:1	sing unto the Lord...in the congregaion of **saints**.
Dan. 7:18(18,22,27)	**saints** of the most high shall take the kingdom, and
Dan. 8:13	heard one **saint** speaking, and another saint said unto
Zech. 14:5	God shall come, and all the **saints** with thee.
Matt. 27:52(51-53)	many bodies of the **saints** which slept arose
Acts 9:32	he came down also to the **saints** which dwelt at Lydda.
Acts 9:41	when he had called the **saints** and widows, presented
Rom. 1:7	to all...in Rome, beloved of God, called to be **saints**
1 Cor. 1:2	sanctified in Christ Jesus, called to be **saints**, with
1 Cor. 14:33	as in all churches of the **saints**.
Eph. 1:1	to the **saints** which are at Ephesus, and to the
Eph. 2:19(19-21)	no more strangers...but fellowcitizens with the **saints**
Eph. 5:3	let it not be once named among you, as becometh **saints**
1 Thes. 3:13	at the coming of our Lord...with all his **saints**.
2 Thes. 1:10	he shall come to be glorified in his **saints**, and to
Jude 1:14	the Lord cometh with ten thousands of his **saints**
Rev. 13:10	patience and the faith of the **saints**.
Rev. 15:3	just and true are thy ways, thou king of **saints**.
2 Ne. 9:18	the righteous, the **saints** of the Holy One of Israel
Mosiah 3:19	putteth off..natural man..becometh a **saint** through..at
Hel. 14:25	and many **saints** shall appear unto many.
3 Ne. 23:9(9-11)	many **saints** who should arise from the dead, and should
Moro. 8:26	when all the **saints** shall dwell with God.
D&C 1:36	and also the Lord shall have power over his **saints**
D&C 45:45	the **saints** that have slept shall come forth to meet
D&C 63:34(33-34)	the **saints** also shall hardly escape; nevertheless, I
D&C 84:2(2-4)	the gathering of his **saints** to stand upon mount Zion
D&C 88:107	and the **saints** shall be filled with his glory, and
D&C 88:114	devil...shall not have power over the **saints** any more
D&C 89:3(1-3)	weakest of all **saints**, who are or can be called saints
D&C 103:7	and the earth is given unto the **saints**, to possess it
D&C 115:4	even the Church of Jesus Christ of Latter-day **Saints**.
D&C 133:56(53-56)	the graves of the **saints** shall be opened; and they
Moses 7:56	**saints** arose...crowned at the right hand of the Son

SALT

Lev. 2:13	with all thine offerings thou shalt offer **salt**.
Num. 18:19	it is a covenant of **salt** for ever before the Lord unto
2 Chr. 13:5(4-5)	God..gave the kingdom..to David..by a covenant of **salt**
Ezek. 43:24(23-24)	the priests shall cast **salt** upon them, and they shall
Matt. 5:13(13-16)	ye are the **salt** of the earth: but if the salt have
Mark 9:49(49-50)	for every one shall be **salted** with fire, and every
Luke 14:34(34,35)	if the **salt** have lost his savour, wherewith shall it
Col. 4:6	your speech be alway with grace, seasoned with **salt**
3 Ne. 12:13	I give unto you to be the **salt** of the earth; but if
3 Ne. 16:15	they shall be as **salt** that hath lost its savor, which
D&C 101:39(39,40)	when men...covenant...they are accounted as the **salt**
D&C 103:10(9-10)	as they are not...saviors...are as **salt** that has lost

SALVATION

Ps. 3:8	**salvation** belongeth unto the Lord: thy blessing is
Ps. 27:1	Lord is my light and my **salvation**; whom shall I fear
Ps. 35:9	and my soul shall...rejoice in his **salvation**.
Ps. 37:39(39,40)	but the **salvation** of the righteous is of the Lord: he
Ps. 62:2(1,2)	he only is my rock and my **salvation**; he is my defence
Ps. 96:2(1-5)	shew forth his **salvation** from day to day.
Ps. 98:3(1-4)	ends of the earth have seen the **salvation** of our God.
Ps. 118:14(14-15)	Lord is my strength...and is become my **salvation**.
Isa. 12:2(2-3)	Jehovah is my strength...also is become my **salvation**.
Isa. 25:9	we will be glad and rejoice in his **salvation**.
Isa. 45:15	God that hidest thyself, O God of Israel, the **Saviour**.
Isa. 52:10(9-11)	the earth shall see the **salvation** of our God.
Joel 2:32(23-32)	whosoever shall call on the...Lord shall be **delivered**
Jonah 2:9(1-9)	**salvation** is of the Lord.
Hab. 3:13(2,13,18)	thou wentest forth for the **salvation** of thy people
Matt. 1:21	he shall **save** his people from their sins.
Luke 1:47	and my spirit hath rejoiced in God my **Saviour**.
Luke 3:6	and all flesh shall see the **salvation** of God.
Acts 2:21(16-21)	whosoever shall call on the...Lord shall be **saved**.
Acts 2:38(37-38)	**repent**, and be baptized every one of you in the name
Acts 4:12(8-12)	none other name...whereby we must be **saved**.
Acts 7:35(35-36)	the same did God send to be a ruler and a **deliverer**
Acts 13:47(46-49)	shouldest be for **salvation** unto the ends of the earth.
Rom. 1:16	gospel...is the power of God unto **salvation** to every
Rom. 10:10	with the mouth confession is made unto **salvation**.
1 Cor. 15:22(21-22)	even so in Christ shall all be made **alive**.
2 Cor. 6:2	behold, now is the day of **salvation**.
2 Cor. 7:10	godly sorrow worketh repentance to **salvation** not to
Eph. 2:8	for by grace are ye **saved** through faith; and that not
Eph. 6:17	the helmet of **salvation**, and the sword of the Spirit
Philip. 2:12	work out your own **salvation** with fear and trembling.
1 Thes. 5:9(9-11)	to obtain **salvation** by our Lord Jesus Christ
2 Tim. 3:15	able to make thee wise unto **salvation** through faith
Heb. 5:9(8-10)	author of eternal **salvation** unto all them that obey
1 Pet. 1:10(5-10)	of which **salvation** the prophets have inquired and
Rev. 3:5	he that **overcometh**, the same shall be clothed in white
2 Ne. 9:21(18-27)	that he may **save** all men if they will hearken unto his
2 Ne. 10:24(23-25)	it is...through the grace of God that ye are **saved**.
2 Ne. 25:20	none other name...whereby man can be **saved**.
2 Ne. 25:23	by grace that we are **saved**, after all we can do.
2 Ne. 26:27(25-28)	commanded any that they...not partake of his **salvation**
Mosiah 3:18	believe that **salvation** was, and is, and is to come
Mosiah 15:31(28,31)	ends of the earth shall see the **salvation** of our God.
Mosiah 16:1	all shall see the **salvation** of the Lord; when every
Alma 34:15(14-17)	thus he shall bring **salvation** to all those who shall
D&C 6:13	no gift greater than the gift of **salvation**.
D&C 18:17	my gospel before you, and my rock, and my **salvation**.
D&C 18:23	there is none other name...whereby man can be **saved**
D&C 20:29	or they cannot be **saved** in the kingdom of God.
D&C 45:58(57,58)	children shall grow up without sin unto **salvation**.
D&C 68:4	the power of God unto **salvation**.
D&C 76:42(40-48)	that through him all might be **saved** whom the Father
D&C 93:8(8-10)	he was the word, even the messenger of **salvation**

SALVATION cont.

D&C 123:17	then may we stand still...to see the **salvation** of God
D&C 131:6	it is impossible for a man to be **saved** in ignorance.
D&C 133:3(2-5)	ends of the earth shall see the **salvation** of their God
Moses 6:52	the only name...whereby **salvation** shall come unto the
A of F 1:3	through..atonement of Christ, all mankind..be **saved**

SALVATION, FOR THE DEAD

Isa. 24:22	**prison**...after many days shall they be visited.
Isa. 42:7(6-7)	to bring out the **prisoners** from the prison, and them
Isa. 49:9(8-9)	say to the **prisoners**, go forth; to them that are in
Obad. 1:21	**saviours** shall come up on mount Zion to judge the
Zech. 9:11(11,12)	I have sent forth thy **prisoners** out of the pit
Mal. 4:6(5-6)	he shall turn the heart of the **fathers** to the children
Matt. 16:19	whatsoever thou shalt **bind** on earth shall be bound in
Luke 1:17	turn the hearts of the **fathers** to the children, and
Luke 4:18(17-21)	to preach deliverance to the **captives**, and recovering
John 5:25	the **dead** shall hear the voice of the Son of God: and
Rom. 14:9	Lord both of the **dead** and living.
1 Cor. 15:19	if in this **life** only we have hope in Christ, we are
1 Cor. 15:29	why are they then baptized for the **dead**
Heb. 11:40	that they without us should not be made **perfect**.
1 Pet. 3:19(18-20)	he went and preached unto the **spirits** in prison
1 Pet. 4:6	the gospel preached also to them that are **dead**, that
1 Ne. 21:9	**prisoners**: go forth; to them that sit in darkness
3 Ne. 25:6(5,6)	turn the heart of the **fathers** to the children, and the
D&C 2:2(1-3)	plant in the hearts of the children the **promises** made
D&C 76:73(73-74)	spirits...in **prison**...Son visited, and preached the
D&C 76:74	who received not the **testimony** of Jesus in the flesh
D&C 88:99	who have received their part in that **prison** which is
D&C 110:15(13-16)	to turn the **hearts** of the fathers to the children, and
D&C 124:29(29-39)	my saints, may be baptized for those who are **dead**
D&C 127:5(5-8)	a word in relation to the baptism for your **dead**.
D&C 128:5(5,6)	for the **salvation** of the dead who should die without
D&C 128:8(8-10)	whatsoever you **bind** on earth shall be bound in heaven
D&C 128:11	**salvation**...for the dead as for the living.
D&C 128:15(12-22)	neither can we without our **dead** be made perfect.
D&C 128:24	a book containing the records of our **dead**, which shall
Moses 7:38(38-39)	I will shut them up; a **prison** have I prepared for them
Moses 7:57(55-57)	many of the spirits as were in **prison** came forth, and
JS-H 1:39	plant...**hearts** of...children...promises made...fathers
JS-V 1:7(5-10)	who would have received it...shall be **heirs** of the
JFS-V 1:18(6-60)	Son of God appeared, declaring **liberty** to the captives
JFS-V 1:54(16-60)	ordinances therein for the redemption of the **dead**

SALVATION, OF LITTLE CHILDREN

Matt. 18:3(2,3)	except ye...become as little **children**, ye shall not
Matt. 19:14	suffer little **children**...to come unto me: for of such
Mark 9:37(36,37)	whosoever shall receive one of such **children** in my
Mark 10:16(13-16)	put his hands upon them, and **blessed** them.

SALVATION, OF LITTLE CHILDREN cont.

Mosiah 3:16	little children...are **blessed**...Christ atoneth for the
Mosiah 15:25	and little **children** also have eternal life.
Moro. 8:22(5-23)	all little children are **alive** in Christ, and also all
D&C 20:71(70-71)	unless he has arrived unto the years of **accountability**
D&C 29:46(46-48)	**children** are redeemed...through mine Only Begotten
D&C 45:58(58-59)	children shall grow up without sin unto **salvation**.
D&C 68:27(25-28)	children shall be **baptized**...when eight years old, and
D&C 74:7(1,7)	little children are...**sanctified** through the atonement
D&C 93:38	men became again, in their infant state, **innocent**
Moses 6:54	children...are **whole** from the foundation of the world.
JS-V 1:10	all children who die...are **saved** in the celestial

SALVATION, PLAN OF

Ps. 27:1	the Lord is my light and my **salvation**; whom shall I
Isa. 45:17	saved in the Lord with an everlasting **salvation**: ye
Isa. 45:22(21-23)	be ye **saved**, all the ends of the earth: for I am God
Isa. 49:6	that thou mayest be my **salvation** unto the end of the
Isa. 53:5(4-12)	but he was **wounded** for our transgressions, he was
Acts 4:12	none other name under heaven..whereby we must be **saved**
Rom. 5:8(6-21)	while we were yet sinners, **Christ** died for us.
1 Cor. 15:22(20-22)	for as in Adam all die...in **Christ** shall all be made
Eph. 2:8(8-10)	for by grace are ye **saved** through faith; and that not
Titus 1:2(1-3)	**eternal** life, which God...promised before the world
Heb. 5:9(8-9)	he became the author of eternal **salvation** unto all the
1 Pet. 1:20(18-23)	was **foreordained** before the foundation of the world
1 Pet. 4:6	gospel preached also to them that are **dead**, that they
1 Jn. 2:1(1,2)	we have an **advocate** with the Father, Jesus Christ the
Rev. 1:6(5,6)	hath made us **kings** and priests unto God and his Father
Rev. 3:21(20,21)	him that overcometh will...sit with me in my **throne**
2 Ne. 2:26(15-27)	the Messiah cometh...that he may **redeem** the children
2 Ne. 9:6(4-6)	death...to fulfil the merciful **plan** of the great
2 Ne. 9:13(5-7,10-16)	O how great the **plan** of our God! For on the other hand
2 Ne. 10:24	through the grace of God that ye are **saved**.
2 Ne. 25:23	it is by grace that we are **saved**, after all we can
Mosiah 3:17(8-11,17)	no other name given...whereby **salvation** can come unto
Mosiah 13:28(26-35)	**salvation** doth not come by the law alone...atonement
Alma 5:21	can no man be **saved** except his garments are washed
Alma 12:33(25,31-34)	this being the **plan** of redemption which was laid
Alma 22:13(12-14)	**plan** of redemption, which was prepared from the
Alma 34:16(14-16)	faith unto repentance...eternal **plan** of redemption.
Alma 42:13(9-15)	**plan** of redemption could not be brought about, only
Hel. 14:16(12-18)	this death...**redeemeth** all mankind from the first
3 Ne. 11:33(31-41)	whoso believeth in me, and is baptized..shall be **saved**
3 Ne. 27:21(13-22)	I say unto you, this is my **gospel**; and ye know the
Moro. 8:20(20-22)	saith...children need baptism denieth...the **atonement**
Moro. 10:32	then is his **grace** sufficient for you, that by his
D&C 18:23(22-25)	none other name given whereby man can be **saved**
D&C 20:30(21-30)	justification through the **grace** of our Lord and Savior
D&C 33:12(10-13)	this is my **gospel**; and remember that they shall have
D&C 76:40(40-42)	this is the **gospel**, the glad tidings, which the voice
D&C 76:41(24-44)	he came...to **sanctify** the world, and to cleanse it

SALVATION, PLAN OF cont.

D&C 128:15(15-18)	their **salvation** is necessary and essential to our
D&C 128:22	ordained, before the world was...to **redeem** them out
Moses 1:39	my work and my glory...**immortality** and eternal life
Moses 5:9(7-9)	as thou hast fallen thou mayest be **redeemed**, and all
Moses 6:62(52-62)	this is the **plan** of salvation unto all men, through
Abr. 3:24(22-25)	we will make an **earth** whereon these may dwell
Abr. 3:25(22-28)	we will **prove** them herewith, to see if they will do
Abr. 3:26	they who keep their **second** estate shall have glory

SANCTIFICATION

Lev. 11:44	ye shall therefore **sanctify** yourselves, and ye shall
Num. 8:17(17-19)	all the firstborn...I **sanctified** them for myself.
Num. 20:12(12,13)	believed me not, to **sanctify** me in the eyes of the
Jer. 1:5	before thou camest forth out of the womb I **sanctified**
Ezek. 20:12	might know that I am the Lord that **sanctify** them.
Ezek. 20:41	and I will be **sanctified** in you before the heathen.
Ezek. 36:23	when I shall be **sanctified** in you before their eyes.
Ezek. 37:28	the heathen shall know that I the Lord do **sanctify**
Ezek. 38:23	thus will I magnify myself, and **sanctify** myself; and
John 10:36(34-38)	whom the Father hath **sanctified**, and sent into the
John 17:17(17-19)	**sanctify** them through thy truth: thy word is truth.
Rom. 6:22(19-22)	ye have your fruit unto **holiness**, and the end
1 Cor. 1:2	them that are **sanctified** in Christ Jesus, called to
1 Cor. 1:30	ye in Christ Jesus...is made...**sanctification**, and
1 Cor. 6:11	ye are **sanctified**...by the spirit of our God.
1 Cor. 7:14	the unbelieving husband is **sanctified** by the wife, and
Eph. 5:26	**sanctify**...it with the washing of water by the word
1 Thes. 4:4(3,4)	to possess his vessel in **sanctification** and honour
1 Thes. 5:23	God of peace **sanctify** you wholly; and I pray God your
2 Thes. 2:13(13,14)	salvation through **sanctification** of the Spirit and
Heb. 2:11(10,11)	they who are **sanctified** are all of one: for which
Heb. 10:10(10-14)	**sanctified** through the offering of the body of Jesus
Heb. 13:12	that he might **sanctify** the people with his own blood
1 Pet. 1:2	elect...through **sanctification** of the Spirit, unto
Mosiah 5:7(2-13)	your hearts are **changed** through faith on his name; the
Alma 5:14(9-16)	have ye experienced this mighty **change** in your hearts
Alma 5:54	**sanctified** by the Holy Spirit, and they do bring
Alma 13:12(11-13)	**sanctified** by the Holy Ghost, having their garments
Hel. 3:35	**sanctification** cometh...of...yielding..hearts unto God
3 Ne. 27:20(19-21)	be **sanctified** by the reception of the Holy Ghost, that
3 Ne. 28:39	they were **sanctified** in the flesh, that they were holy
Ether 4:7(6-7)	exercise faith in me...may become **sanctified** in me
Moro. 10:33(32-33)	**sanctified**...unto the remission of your sins, that ye
D&C 20:31	**sanctification** through the grace of our Lord and
D&C 20:34(31-34)	and even let those who are **sanctified** take heed also.
D&C 43:9(8-10)	**sanctified**...to act in all holiness before me
D&C 43:16	**sanctify** yourselves and ye shall be endowed with power
D&C 74:1(1-7)	unbelieving husband is **sanctified** by the wife, and the
D&C 76:21	them who are **sanctified** before his throne, worshiping
D&C 76:41	he came...to **sanctify** the world, and to cleanse it
D&C 77:1	it is the earth, in its **sanctified**, immortal, and

SANCTIFICATION cont.

D&C 77:12	beginning..seventh thousand...**sanctify** the earth, and
D&C 84:23	**sanctify**...people that...might behold the face of God
D&C 84:33	**sanctified** by the Spirit unto the renewing of their
D&C 88:2	in the book of the names of the **sanctified**, even them
D&C 88:21(17-26)	**sanctified** through...the law of Christ, must inherit
D&C 88:34(34-35)	that which is governed by law...**sanctified** by the same
D&C 88:68	**sanctify** yourselves that your minds become single to
D&C 88:116	this is the glory of God, and the **sanctified**; and they
D&C 101:5	those who...deny me, cannot be **sanctified**.
D&C 105:31	let my army...be **sanctified** before me, that it may
D&C 105:36	those that are chosen; and they shall be **sanctified**
D&C 133:62	unto him that..**sanctifieth** himself..given eternal life
Moses 6:60(59,60)	by the blood ye are **sanctified**
Moses 7:45	that all they that mourn may be **sanctified** and have

SCRIBES

Ex. 24:4(4-7)	Moses **wrote** all the words of the Lord, and rose up
Ex. 34:27	Moses, **write** thou these words: for after the tenor of
Deut. 31:9	Moses **wrote** this law, and delivered it unto the priest
Judg. 5:14	they that handle the pen of the **writer**.
1 Sam. 10:25	Samuel...**wrote** it in a book, and laid it up before the
2 Sam. 8:17(17,18)	and Seraiah was the **scribe**
1 Kgs. 4:3	the sons of Shisha, **scribes**; Jehoshaphat the son of
2 Kgs. 19:2	and Shebna the **scribe**, and the elders of the priests
1 Chr. 2:55	and the families of the **scribes** which dwelt at Jabez
2 Chr. 26:22	acts of Uzziah...did Isaiah the prophet...**write**
2 Chr. 34:13	and of the Levites there were **scribes**, and officers
Ezra 7:11(6-11)	Ezra...a **scribe** of the words of the commandments of
Neh. 8:1(1-12)	Ezra the **scribe** to bring the book of the law of Moses
Isa. 33:18	where is the **scribe**? where is the receiver? where is
Jer. 36:32	the **scribe**, the son of Neriah; who wrote therein from
Matt. 5:20(19-20)	except your righteousness...exceed...the **scribes** and
Matt. 7:29(28-29)	taught...as one having authority,...not as the **scribes**
Matt. 13:52	every **scribe** which is instructed unto the kingdom of
Matt. 15:1(1-9)	then came to Jesus **scribes** and Pharisees, which were
Matt. 23:2(1-3)	saying, the **scribes** and the Pharisees sit in Moses
Matt. 23:13(13-33)	woe unto you, **scribes** and Pharisees, hypocrites! for
Matt. 23:34(34,35)	I send unto you prophets, and wise men, and **scribes**
Mark 1:22(21,22)	as one that had authority, and not as the **scribes**.
Mark 10:33(32-34)	the Son of man shall be delivered unto...the **scribes**
Mark 12:28(28-34)	and one of the **scribes** came, and having heard them
Mark 14:1(1,2)	and the **scribes** sought how they might take him by
Luke 11:44(37-44)	woe unto you, **scribes** and Pharisees, hypocrites! for
Luke 22:2(1,2)	and **scribes** sought how they might kill him; for they
Luke 23:10(8-11)	chief priests and **scribes** stood and vehemently accused
Acts 4:5(5-8)	that their rulers, and elders, and **scribes**
Acts 23:9(7-10)	and the **scribes** that were of the Pharisees' part arose
1 Cor. 1:20(19,20)	where is the wise? where is the **scribe**? where is the
1 Ne. 1:17(16,17)	I shall make an **account** of my proceedings in my days.
1 Ne. 19:1(1,2)	I did **engraven** the record of my father, and also our
Jacob 1:2(2,3)	gave me, Jacob, a commandment that I should **write** upon

SCRIBES cont.

Jarom 1:1   I, Jarom, **write** a few words according to the
1:1(1-3)   I, Omni, being commanded...**write**...upon these plates
3 Ne. 23:4   **write** the things which I have told you; and according
Morm. 5:9   therefore I **write** a small abridgment, daring not to
Ether 4:1(1-5)   and **write** the things which he had seen; and they were
D&C 9:4   you are called to do is to **write** for my servant Joseph
D&C 24:1   thou wast...chosen to **write** the Book of Mormon, and
D&C 24:6   it shall be given thee...what thou shalt...**write**, and
Moses 2:1   **write** the words which I speak. I am the Beginning and

SCRIPTURES, LOST

Ex. 24:7(4-7)   and he took the book of the **covenant**, and read in the
Num. 21:14   it is said in the **book** of the wars of the Lord, what
Josh. 10:13   is not this written in the book of **Jasher**? so the sun
1 Sam. 10:25   Samuel told the people...and wrote it in a **book**, and
2 Sam. 1:18   it is written in the book of **Jasher**.
1 Kgs. 11:41   are they not written in the **book** of the acts of
1 Chr. 29:29   written in the book of **Samuel** the seer, and in the
2 Chr. 9:29   written in the book of **Nathan** the prophet, and in the
2 Chr. 12:15   written in the book of **Shemaiah** the prophet, and of
2 Chr. 13:22   acts of Abijah...in the story of the prophet **Iddo**.
2 Chr. 20:34   written in the book of **Jehu** the son of Hanani, who is
2 Chr. 33:19   they are written among the **sayings** of the seers.
Matt. 2:23   **spoken** by the prophets, he shall be called a Nazarene.
1 Cor. 5:9   I wrote unto you in an **epistle** not to company with
Eph. 3:3(3-4)   as I **wrote** afore in few words
Col. 4:16   that ye likewise read the **epistle** from Laodicea.
Jude 1:3   when I gave all diligence to **write** unto you of the
Jude 1:14   **Enoch** also...prophesied of these, saying, behold, the
1 Ne. 13:26(23-32) they have **taken** away...many parts which are plain and
1 Ne. 13:34(34-35) I will **bring** forth unto them...much of my gospel
1 Ne. 19:10(10-16) words of Zenock...according to the words of **Neum**, and
2 Ne. 29:12(11-13) I shall...speak unto all nations...they shall **write**
Jacob 5:1(1-77)   do ye not remember...the words of the prophet **Zenos**
Jacob 6:1   the things which this prophet **Zenos** spake, concerning
Alma 33:3(3-17)   what **Zenos**, the prophet of old, has said concerning
Alma 34:7   my brother has called upon the words of **Zenos**, that
Alma 63:12   **parts** which had been commanded...should not go forth.
Hel. 8:20(19-20)   also Zenock, and also **Ezias**, and also Isaiah, and
Hel. 15:11   spoken...by the prophet **Zenos**, and many other
3 Ne. 10:16   **Zenock** spake concerning these things, because they
Ether 1:5(1-5)   I give not the full account, but a **part** of the account
Ether 3:17(17,21) I could not make a **full** account of these things which
Ether 15:33   and the **hundredth** part I have not written) and he hid
D&C 107:57(56-57) these things were all written in the book of **Enoch**
Moses 1:41(40-42) men shall...**take** many of them from the book which thou
Moses 6:5(4-8)   a **book** of remembrance was kept, in the which was

SCRIPTURES, PRESERVATION

Ex. 25:16(16,21,22)	thou shalt put into the ark the **testimony** which I
Ex. 26:34	put...**testimony** in the most holy place.
Deut. 4:2	ye shall not **add** unto the word which I command you
Deut. 12:32	thou shalt not add thereto, nor **diminish** from it.
Deut. 31:26(24-26)	take...**book** of the law...put it in the side of the ark
1 Kgs. 8:9	there was...in the ark...the two **tables** of stone
2 Kgs. 22:8	I have found the **book** of the law in the house of the
2 Chr. 34:15(15,16)	I have found the **book** of the law in the house of the
Prov. 30:6(5,6)	**add** thou not unto his words, lest he reprove thee, and
Isa. 30:8	**write** it...that it may be for the time to come for
Jer. 36:28	**write** in it all the former words that...hath burned.
Jer. 36:32	**added** besides unto them many like words.
Ezek. 37:16(16-20)	take thee one stick, and **write** upon it, for Judah, and
Hab. 2:2(2,3)	**write** the vision, and make it plain upon tables, that
2 Cor. 2:17	we are not as many, which corrupt the **word** of God: but
2 Pet. 3:16(15-17)	unlearned and unstable wrest...**scriptures**, unto their
Rev. 22:18(18-20)	if any man shall **add** unto these things, God shall add
1 Ne. 3:20(19,20)	that we may **preserve** unto them the words which have
1 Ne. 5:21(10-21)	that we could **preserve** the commandments of the Lord
1 Ne. 13:23(23-40)	a **record** of the Jews, which contains the covenants of
1 Ne. 19:5(4-7)	that the more sacred things may be **kept** for the
2 Ne. 3:12(12,18,19)	Judah shall **write**; and...the fruit of thy loins
2 Ne. 26:17(16,17)	they shall be written and **sealed** up in a book, and
2 Ne. 27:11(6-29)	the words...which were **sealed** shall be read upon the
2 Ne. 29:11(10-13)	all men...shall **write** the words which I speak unto the
Jacob 1:3(2-4)	that I should **preserve** these plates and hand them down
Jacob 4:2(2,3)	upon **plates**...which will give our children, and also
Enos 1:15(15-17)	God was able to **preserve** our records, I cried unto him
Mosiah 1:5(3-6)	kept and **preserved** by the hand of God, that we might
Mosiah 28:20	the plates...that he should...**preserve** them, and also
Alma 13:20	**scriptures**...ye will wrest them...to your own
Alma 37:4(1-5)	be kept and **preserved** by the hand of the Lord until
Alma 37:14	which he will keep and **preserve** for a wise purpose in
Alma 37:47	see that ye take **care** of these sacred things, yea, see
Alma 41:1	some have wrested the **scriptures**, and..gone far astray
3 Ne. 16:4	these sayings...shall be **kept** and shall be manifested
4 Ne. 1:48(48,49)	Ammaron...did hide up the **records** which were sacred-
Morm. 5:12(12-14)	they are to be **hid** up unto the Lord that they may come
Morm. 6:6	I...**hid** up in the hill Cumorah all the **records** which
Morm. 8:14(4,14-16)	no one shall have them to get **gain**; but the record the
Ether 3:22(22-28)	write them and shall **seal** them up, that no one can
Ether 4:3(1-6)	I am commanded that I should **hide** them up again in the
Moro. 10:2(2,27)	I **seal** up these records, after I have spoken a few
D&C 3:19(1-20)	for this very purpose are these plates **preserved**
D&C 20:35	neither **adding** to, nor diminishing from the prophecy
D&C 42:56	my scriptures shall be...**preserved** in safety
Abr. 1:31	the records...my God **preserved** in mine own hands
JS-H 1:34	there was a **book** deposited, written upon gold plates
JS-H 1:59(59,60)	I would use all my endeavors to **preserve** them, until

SCRIPTURES, STUDY

Deut. 8:3	man doth not live by bread only, but by every **word**
Deut. 17:19(18-20)	**read** therein all the days of his life: that he may
Deut. 31:11(9-12)	**read** this law before all Israel in their hearing.
Josh. 1:8	thou shalt **meditate** therein day and night, that thou
Josh. 8:34(32-35)	**read** all the words of the law, the blessings and
2 Kgs. 23:2(1-3)	he **read**...all the words of the book of the covenant
Neh. 8:8(1-8)	they read in the book in the **law** of God distinctly
Matt. 22:29	ye do err, not knowing the **scriptures**, nor the power
Luke 16:31(29-31)	if they **hear** not Moses and the prophets, neither will
Luke 24:27	he **expounded** unto them in all the scriptures the thing
John 5:39	**search** the scriptures; for in them ye think ye have
John 5:47(45-47)	if ye believe not his **writings**, how shall ye believe
Acts 17:11	**searched** the scriptures daily, whether those things
Acts 18:28	**shewing** by the scriptures that Jesus was Christ.
Rom. 15:4	through...comfort of the **scriptures** might have hope.
2 Tim. 2:15	**study**...rightly dividing the word of truth.
2 Tim. 3:15(15-17)	**scriptures**, which are able to make thee wise unto
2 Pet. 1:20(19-21)	no prophecy of the **scripture** is of any private
Rev. 1:3	blessed is he that **readeth**...the words of this
1 Ne. 15:25(24-25)	give **heed** unto the word of the Lord; yea, I did exhort
1 Ne. 19:24(22-24)	**hear** ye the words of the prophet, which were written
2 Ne. 4:15	delighteth in the scriptures...my heart **pondereth** them
2 Ne. 6:4	I will **read** you the words of Isaiah. And they are the
Jacob 7:23	they **searched** the scriptures, and hearkened no more
Mosiah 1:7(2-7)	ye should remember to **search** them diligently, that ye
Alma 13:20	scriptures..if ye will **wrest** them..your own
Alma 17:2	they had **searched** the scriptures diligently, that they
3 Ne. 10:14	he that hath the scriptures, let him **search** them, and
3 Ne. 23:1(1-5)	**search** these things diligently; for great are the
3 Ne. 23:14(8-14)	they should **teach** the things which he had expounded
D&C 1:37(37-38)	**search** these commandments, for they are true and faith
D&C 11:22(21-22)	**study** my word which shall come forth among the
D&C 18:4(2-4)	in them are all things **written** concerning the
D&C 21:4(4-5)	give heed unto all his words and **commandments** which
D&C 26:1	time be devoted to the **studying** of the scriptures
D&C 33:16	holy scriptures are given of me for your **instruction**
D&C 84:57	remember...the **Book** of Mormon and the former
D&C 88:118	seek learning, even by **study** and also by faith.
D&C 90:15	**study** and learn, and become acquainted with all good
JS-M 1:37	whoso **treasureth** up my word, shall not be deceived
JFS-V 1:1(1-11)	I sat in my room **pondering** over the scriptures

SCRIPTURES, TO COME FORTH

Isa. 29:11(11-12)	the vision of all...as the words of a **book** that is
Ezek. 37:16(15-20)	take thee one **stick**, and write upon it, for Judah, and
Dan. 12:4	seal the **book**, even to the time of the end: many shall
Amos 3:7	he **revealeth** his secret unto his servants the prophets
2 Tim. 3:16	all **scripture** is given by inspiration of God, and is
1 Ne. 13:39(34-42)	I beheld other **books**, which came forth by the power
2 Ne. 3:11	**bring** forth my word unto the seed of thy loins- and
2 Ne. 29:10(3,6-14)	ye need not suppose that it contains all my **words**

SCRIPTURES, TO COME FORTH cont.

3 Ne. 16:4	ye shall **write** these sayings after I am gone, that if
Morm. 5:12(12-15)	these things are **written**...that they may come forth
Morm. 6:6	and hid up in the hill Cumorah all the **records** which
Morm. 8:16(14-16)	shall be **brought** out of darkness unto light, according
D&C 9:2	other **records** have I, that...you may assist to
D&C 10:45(44-47)	many things engraven upon the **plates** of Nephi which
D&C 43:7	to teach those **revelations** which you have received and
D&C 45:15	I will **speak** unto you and prophesy, as unto men in
D&C 68:4(3-4)	whatsoever they shall speak...shall be **scripture**
D&C 76:7(7-10)	and to them will I **reveal** all mysteries, yea, all the
D&C 93:18(16-18)	you shall receive the **fulness** of the record of John.
D&C 121:26(26-31)	give unto you knowledge ...that has not been **revealed**
D&C 124:41	for I deign to **reveal** unto my church things which have
A of F 1:9(8,9)	we believe that he will yet **reveal** many great and

SCRIPTURES, VALUE

Deut. 17:19(18-20)	**read** therein all the days of his life: that he may
Ps. 19:7(7-11)	the law of the Lord is perfect, **converting** the soul
Isa. 8:20(19-20)	to the **law** and...testimony: if they speak not...no
Luke 16:29(29-31)	they have **Moses** and the prophets; let them hear them.
John 5:39	scriptures...they are they which **testify** of me.
Rom. 15:4	things were written...for our **learning**, that we
2 Tim. 3:16(15-17)	all scripture...for **doctrine** ...reproof...correction
2 Pet. 1:21(20,21)	**prophecy** came not...of man: but holy men of God spake
1 Ne. 5:21(10-22)	records...were desirable...even of great **worth** unto
1 Ne. 13:40	these last records...**establish** the truth of the first
1 Ne. 19:23(23-24)	**liken** all scriptures unto us...for our profit and
2 Ne. 3:15(11,15)	of the Lord shall bring my people unto **salvation**.
2 Ne. 4:15	writeth them for the **learning**...profit of my children.
2 Ne. 25:8(7-30)	they are of **worth** unto the children of men, and he
2 Ne. 33:3(1-3)	I esteem it as of great **worth**, and especially unto my
Mosiah 1:5(1-7)	read and **understand** of his mysteries, and...
Alma 37:8(6-8)	brought them to the **knowledge** of their God unto the
D&C 18:34(34-36)	these **words** are not of men nor of man, but of me
D&C 20:11(8-11)	proving to the world...the holy scriptures are **true**
D&C 33:16(16-17)	holy scriptures are given of me for your **instruction**
D&C 42:12	Bible and the Book of Mormon...**fulness** of the gospel.
D&C 68:4	shall be scripture...the power of God unto **salvation**.
JFS-V 1:11(1-11)	as I pondered...things...**written**...understanding were

SCRIPTURES, WRITING

Gen. 5:1(1-3)	this is the **book** of the generations of Adam. In the
Ex. 24:4	Moses **wrote** all the words of the Lord, and rose up
Ex. 24:12	I will give thee...a law...which I have **written**; that
Ex. 31:18	**written** with the finger of God.
Ex. 32:16	the **writing** was the writing of God, graven upon the
Ex. 34:27	the Lord said unto Moses, **write** thou these words: for
Deut. 4:13	ten commandments...**wrote** them upon two tables of stone
Deut. 5:22	he **wrote** them in two tables of stone, and delivered

Deut. 9:10	two tables of stone **written** with the finger of God
Deut. 10:4(1-5)	**wrote** on the tables, according to the first writing
Deut. 31:9	Moses **wrote** this law, and delivered it unto the priest
Josh. 8:32	he **wrote** there upon the stones a copy of the law of
1 Sam. 10:25	Samuel...**wrote** it in a book, and laid it up before the
2 Sam. 23:2(1-7)	the Spirit of the Lord **spake** by me, and his word was
2 Chr. 26:22	the acts of Uzziah...did Isaiah the prophet...**write**.
Ezra 4:15	in the **book** of the records, and know that this city
Ps. 102:18	this shall be **written** for the generation to come: and
Isa. 8:1	take thee a great roll, and **write** in it with a man's
Isa. 30:8(8-10)	**write** it...and note it in a book, that it may be for
Isa. 38:9	the **writing** of Hezekiah king of Judah, when he had
Jer. 36:4(1-4,23-32)	**wrote** from the mouth of Jeremiah all the words of the
Ezek. 9:2(2-3)	one man...with a **writer's** inkhorn by his side: and the
Ezek. 37:16(15-22)	**write** upon it, for Joseph, the stick of Ephraim, and
Hosea 8:12	I have **written** to him the great things of my law, but
John 21:24	the disciple which testifieth...**wrote** these things
Acts 15:23(20-23)	they **wrote** letters by them after this manner; the
Rom. 15:4(1-4)	things..**written** aforetime were written for our
2 Cor. 1:13	we **write** none other things unto you, than what ye read
2 Cor. 2:9	to this end also did I **write**, that I might know the
Gal. 1:20	now the things which I **write** unto you...I lie not.
2 Tim. 3:16	all **scripture** is given by inspiration of God, and is
2 Pet. 1:21(20-21)	for the **prophecy** came not in old time by the will of
2 Pet. 3:1	this second epistle, beloved, I now **write** unto you
1 Jn. 1:4	these things **write** we unto you, that your joy may be
1 Jn. 2:12(12-14)	I **write** unto you, little children, because your sins
2 Jn. 1:12	I would not **write** with paper and ink: but I trust to
3 Jn. 1:13	I will not with ink and pen **write** unto thee
Rev. 1:11(11,19)	what thou seest, **write** in a book, and send it unto the
Rev. 2:1	the angel of the church of Ephesus **write**; these things
Rev. 21:5	**write**: for these words are true and faithful.
1 Ne. 1:17	behold, I make an **abridgment** of the record of my
1 Ne. 3:3	they are **engraven** upon plates of brass.
1 Ne. 5:12(10-13)	also a **record** of the Jews from the beginning, even
1 Ne. 6:1	neither...upon these plates which I am **writing**; for
1 Ne. 14:26(25-26)	others...hath he shown all things...they have **written**
1 Ne. 19:6(1-7)	do not **write** anything upon plates save it be...sacred.
2 Ne. 3:12(11-12)	thy loins...and...the loins of Judah shall **write**; and
2 Ne. 3:17	but I will **write** unto him my law, by the finger of
2 Ne. 4:15	I **write** the things of my soul, and many of the
2 Ne. 6:3	all things which are **written**, from the creation of the
2 Ne. 25:23	we labor diligently to **write**, to persuade our children
2 Ne. 29:11(11-12)	I command all men...**write** the words which I speak unto
Jacob 1:2(2-4)	Jacob, a commandment that I should **write** upon these
Jarom 1:2	these things are **written** for the intent of the benefit
W of M 1:2(2-7)	survive them, that he may **write**...concerning them, and
Mosiah 28:17	**records**...gave an account of the people who were
Alma 37:3	**records** of the holy scriptures...even from the
3 Ne. 27:26	behold, all things are **written** by the Father
Morm. 6:6	the **records** which had been handed down by our fathers
Ether 3:22	ye shall **write** them and shall seal them up, that no
Ether 4:1	and **write** the things which he had seen; and they were

SCRIPTURES, WRITING cont.

Ether 8:9	is there not an **account** concerning them of old, that
D&C 6:26	there are **records** which contain much of my gospel
D&C 9:4	you are called to do is to **write** for my servant Joseph
D&C 24:1	thou wast called and chosen to **write** the book of
D&C 63:56	his **writing** is not acceptable unto the Lord, and he
D&C 68:4(2-4)	when moved upon by the Holy Ghost shall be **scripture**
D&C 76:80	the Lord commanded us to **write** while we were yet in
D&C 90:32	ye shall **write** this commandment, and say unto your
D&C 94:10	for the work of the **printing** of the translation of my
D&C 104:58	**print** my words, the fulness of my scriptures, the
D&C 107:57	these things were all **written** in the book of Enoch
Moses 2:1	**write** the words which I speak. I am the beginning and
Moses 6:5(5-10)	and a **book** of remembrance was kept, in the which was
Moses 6:46	for a book of remembrance we have **written** among us
Abr. 1:28(28-31)	the **records** have come into my hands, which I hold unto
JS-H 1:67	commenced to translate...he began to **write** for me.

SEALING

Isa. 22:22	the **key** of the house of David will I lay upon his
Matt. 16:19	whatsoever thou shalt **bind** on earth shall be bound
Matt. 18:18	whatsoever ye shall **bind** on earth shall be bound in
John 6:27	the Son of man...hath God the Father **sealed**.
2 Cor. 1:22(21-22)	who hath also **sealed** us, and given the earnest of the
Eph. 1:13(10-14)	ye were **sealed** with that holy Spirit of promise
Eph. 4:30	holy Spirit of God, whereby ye are **sealed** unto the day
Rev. 3:7(7-12)	he that hath the **key** of David, he that openeth, and
D&C 1:8	to them is power given to **seal** both on earth and in
D&C 68:12	to you shall be given power to **seal** them up unto
D&C 76:53(51-60)	overcome by faith, and are **sealed** by the Holy Spirit
D&C 77:8(8,12)	power to shut up the heavens, to **seal** up unto life
D&C 110:16(4-16)	the **keys** of this dispensation are committed into your
D&C 124:93(91-93)	whatsoever he shall **bind** on earth shall be bound in
D&C 124:124	Hyrum Smith...to hold the **sealing** blessings of my
D&C 128:14(8-18)	this...is the **sealing** and binding power...the keys of
D&C 131:5	knowing that he is **sealed** up unto eternal life, by
D&C 132:19(7,15-20)	it is **sealed** unto them by the Holy Spirit of promise
D&C 132:46(45-48)	whatsoever you seal on earth shall be **sealed** in heaven

SEALS

1 Kgs. 21:8	letters in Ahab's name, and sealed...with his **seal**
Esth. 3:12	was it written, and **sealed** with the king's ring.
Isa. 8:16	bind up the testimony, **seal** the law among my disciples
Isa. 29:11	the words of a book that is **sealed**, which men deliver
Jer. 32:44	evidences, and **seal** them, and take witnesses in the
Dan. 6:17	the king **sealed** it with his own signet, and with the
Dan. 12:4	O Daniel, shut up the words, and **seal** the book, even
John 3:33	received his testimony hath set to his **seal** that God
Rev. 5:1(1-4)	I saw...a book written...with seven **seals**.
Rev. 6:1(1-17)	I saw when the Lamb opened one of the **seals**, and I

SEALS cont.

Rev. 7:2(2-9)   angel ascending...having the **seal** of the living God
Rev. 9:4   hurt...only those men which have not the **seal** of God
2 Ne. 27:7(7,22)   and behold the book shall be **sealed**; and in the book
Ether 3:23(22-28)   ye shall **seal** them up also with the things which ye
Moro. 10:2   and I **seal** up these records, after I have spoken a few
D&C 77:7(6-10)   the seven **seals** with which it was sealed? A. We are
D&C 88:84(84-85)   to bind up the law and **seal** up the testimony, and to
D&C 98:2(1-2)   your prayers...are recorded with this **seal** and

SECRET COMBINATIONS

Gen. 4:23(17-24)   Lamech said...I have **slain** a man to my wounding, and
Ps. 64:5(1-6)   they commune of laying snares **privily**; they say, who
John 3:19(19-21)   **darkness** rather than light, because...deeds were evil.
Eph. 6:12(12-13)   against powers, against the rulers of the **darkness** of
2 Thes. 2:7(6-12)   for the **mystery** of iniquity doth already work: only
Rev. 2:6(6-15)   the deeds of the **Nicolaitans**, which I also hate.
Rev. 17:5(5,7)   **Mystery,** Babylon the great, the mother of harlots and
2 Ne. 9:9   stirreth up...**secret** combinations of murder and all
2 Ne. 10:15   I must needs destroy the **secret** works of darkness, and
2 Ne. 26:22(20-25)   secret **combinations**...the combinations of the devil
2 Ne. 27:27   works are in the **dark**; and they say: who seeth us, and
2 Ne. 28:9   hide their counsels from the Lord...works...in...**dark**.
Alma 37:21(21-23)   that the **mysteries** and the works of darkness, and
Alma 37:30(21-32)   judgments of God did come upon...secret **combinations**.
Hel. 2:8(1-13)   murder..gain power..was their secret..**combination)** the
Hel. 6:26(21-30)   **secret** oaths and covenants...put into the heart of
Hel. 16:21   cunning and the **mysterious** arts of the evil one, work
3 Ne. 3:9(2-10)   the **secret** society of Gadianton; which society and
3 Ne. 6:28(27-30)   which **covenant** was given and administered by the devil
3 Ne. 9:5(5,7,8)   to hide their **iniquities**...from before my face, that
4 Ne. 1:42(42-46)   the secret oaths and **combinations** of Gadianton.
Morm. 8:27(26-27,40)   secret **combinations** and the works of darkness.
Ether 8:18(8-26)   a secret **combination**...most abominable and wicked
Ether 10:33(33-34)   old plans, and...**oaths** after the manner of the ancient
Ether 11:15   secret **combination** which was built up to get power and
Ether 11:22   reject...the prophets, because of their **secret** society
D&C 117:11   the Nicolaitane band and...their **secret** abominations
D&C 123:13   bringing to light all the **hidden** things of darkness
Moses 5:51(16-57)   from the days of Cain, there was a secret **combination**
Moses 6:15   Satan had great dominion...because of secret **works**

SEED OF ABRAHAM

Gen. 12:3(2-3)   in thee shall all families of the earth be **blessed**.
Gen. 15:5(1-5)   tell the stars...number them...so shall thy **seed** be.
Gen. 16:10   I will multiply thy **seed** exceedingly, that it shall
Gen. 17:4(1-8)   thou shalt be a **father** of many nations.
Gen. 17:16(15-18)   she shall be a **mother** of nations; kings of people
Gen. 17:19(19-21)   Isaac...I will establish my **covenant** with him for an
Gen. 17:20   **Ishmael**...twelve princes shall he beget...a great

SEED OF ABRAHAM cont.

Gen. 18:10(9-19)	lo, Sarah thy wife shall have a **son**. And Sarah heard
Gen. 21:3(1-5)	Abraham called...**son**...whom Sarah bare...Isaac.
Gen. 21:12	hearken unto her...in Isaac shall thy **seed** be called.
Gen. 21:13(13-21)	of the son of the bondwoman will I make a **nation**
Gen. 21:18	lift up the lad...for I will make him a great **nation**.
Gen. 22:18(17-18)	in thy **seed** shall all the nations of the earth be
Gen. 25:12(12-18)	now these are the **generations** of Ishmael, Abraham's
Gen. 26:4(1-4)	I will make thy **seed** to multiply as the stars of
Gen. 26:24(17-25)	I...will...multiply thy **seed** for my servant Abraham's
Gen. 28:4(1-4)	the blessing of Abraham, to thee, and to thy **seed** with
Gen. 28:14(10-14)	in thee and in thy **seed** shall all...earth be blessed.
Gen. 32:12(9-12)	and make thy **seed** as the sand of the sea, which
Gen. 35:11(9-15)	a nation and a company of **nations** shall be of thee
Gen. 48:4	behold, I will make thee **fruitful**, and multiply thee
Gen. 48:19(5-22)	younger brother...greater..**seed** shall become...nations
Ex. 32:13	I will multiply your **seed** as the stars of heaven, and
Ex. 33:1(1-3)	the land...unto thy **seed** will I give it
Deut. 1:10(6-11)	ye are this day as the stars of heaven for **multitude**.
Josh. 24:3(1-14)	multiplied his **seed**, and gave him Isaac.
2 Chr. 20:7(5-13)	this land...to the **seed** of Abraham thy friend for ever
Ps. 105:43(41-45)	he brought forth his **people** with joy, and his chosen
Luke 1:55	spake...to Abraham, and to his **seed** for ever.
John 8:39(33-39)	if ye were Abraham's **children**, ye would do the works
Acts 3:25	**children**...of the covenant which God made with our
Rom. 4:13(1-25)	promise...to Abraham...**seed**...through the law, but
Rom. 4:18	father of many nations...so shall thy **seed** be.
Rom. 9:7(6-11)	in **Isaac** shall thy seed be called.
Rom. 9:9	at this time will I come, and Sara shall have a **son**.
Gal. 3:29(1-29)	if ye be Christ's, then are ye Abraham's **seed**, and
Gal. 4:28(21-31)	we...as Isaac was, are the children of **promise**.
Heb. 2:16	took on him the **seed** of Abraham.
Heb. 11:12(11-12)	so many as the stars of the sky in **multitude**, and as
Heb. 11:18(17-19)	that in **Isaac** shall thy seed be called
1 Pet. 3:6(1-6)	Sara obeyed Abraham...whose **daughters** ye are, as long
1 Ne. 15:18(12-20)	Abraham...in thy **seed** shall all the kindreds of the
1 Ne. 17:40(40-42)	he **covenanted** with them...did bring them out..of Egypt
1 Ne. 22:9	in thy **seed** shall all the kindreds of the earth be
2 Ne. 29:14	covenanted with Abraham...remember his **seed** forever.
3 Ne. 20:25(25-27)	Abraham...in thy **seed** shall all...earth be blessed.
D&C 84:34(33-41)	they become...the **seed** of Abraham, and the church and
D&C 86:9(8-11)	ye are lawful **heirs**, according to the flesh, and have
D&C 103:17	ye are the children of Israel, and of the **seed** of
D&C 103:17(11-18)	ye are the children of Israel...of the **seed** of Abraham
D&C 124:58	unto Abraham concerning the **kindreds** of the earth
D&C 132:30(29-37)	Abraham received promises concerning his **seed**, and of
Abr. 2:9(9-11)	**seed**...shall bear this ministry and priesthood unto

SEER

1 Sam. 9:9(6-10)	now called a prophet was beforetime called a **seer**.
1 Sam. 9:19(11-19)	Samuel answered Saul, and said, I am the **seer**: go up
2 Sam. 15:27	king said...unto Zadok the priest, art not thou a **seer**

SEER cont.

2 Sam. 24:11	unto the prophet Gad, David's **seer**, saying
2 Kgs. 17:13	Lord testified against Israel...by all the **seers**
1 Chr. 9:22	whom David and Samuel the **seer** did ordain in their
1 Chr. 21:9(9,10)	Lord spake unto Gad, David's **seer**, saying
1 Chr. 25:5	the sons of Heman the king's **seer** in the words of God
1 Chr. 26:28	and all that Samuel the **seer**, and Saul the son of Kish
1 Chr. 29:29	Samuel the **seer**...Gad the seer
2 Chr. 9:29	the visions of Iddo the **seer** against Jeroboam the son
2 Chr. 12:15	of Iddo the **seer** concerning genealogies? and there
2 Chr. 16:7(7-10)	at that time Hanani the **seer** came to Asa king of Judah
2 Chr. 19:2	son of Hanani the **seer** went out to meet him, and said
2 Chr. 29:25	and of Gad the king's **seer**, and Nathan the prophet
2 Chr. 29:30	and of Asaph the **seer**. And they sang praises with glad
2 Chr. 33:18(18,19)	the words of the **seers** that spake to him in the name
2 Chr. 35:15	and Jeduthun the king's **seer**; and the porters waited
Isa. 29:10	the prophets...your rulers, the **seers** hath he covered.
Isa. 30:10(9,10)	which say to the **seers**, see not; and to the prophets
Amos 7:12	Amaziah said unto Amos, O thou **seer**, go, flee thee
2 Ne. 3:6(6-14)	a **seer** shall the Lord my God raise up, who shall be a
2 Ne. 27:5	the **seers** hath he covered because of your iniquity.
Mosiah 8:13(13-18)	whosoever is commanded to look in them..is called **seer**
Mosiah 8:16(13-18)	a **seer** is a revelator and a prophet also; and a gift
Mosiah 8:17(13-18)	a **seer** can know of things which are past, and also of
Mosiah 28:16	whosoever has these things is called **seer**, after the
D&C 21:1	and in it thou shalt be called a **seer**, a translator
D&C 107:92	here is wisdom...to be a **seer**, a revelator, a
D&C 124:94(91-95)	he may be a prophet, and a **seer**...as my servant Joseph
D&C 124:125	to be a translator, a revelator, a **seer**, and prophet.
D&C 127:12	prophet and **seer** of the Church of Jesus Christ of
D&C 135:3	Joseph Smith, the Prophet and **Seer** of the Lord, has
Moses 6:36(35,36)	a **seer** hath the Lord raised up unto his people.

SELF-MASTERY

Ps. 37:8(8,9)	**cease** from anger, and forsake wrath: fret not thyself
Ps. 76:10	remainder of wrath shalt thou **restrain**.
Ps. 119:101	I have **refrained** my feet from every evil way, that I
Prov. 1:15	walk not thou in the way with them; **refrain** thy foot
Prov. 14:29	he that is **slow** to wrath is of great understanding
Prov. 15:1	a **soft** answer turneth away wrath: but grievous words
Prov. 25:28	he that hath no **rule** over his own spirit is like a
Jer. 14:10	they have not **refrained** their feet, therefore the Lord
Matt. 16:24	let him **deny** himself, and take up his cross, and
Matt. 16:25	whosoever will **lose** his life for my sake shall find
Matt. 26:39(36-45)	not as I will, but as thou **wilt**.
Mark 8:34	let him **deny** himself, and take up his cross, and
Mark 9:43(40-43)	and if thy hand offend thee, **cut** it off: it is better
Luke 2:51	came to Nazareth, and was **subject** unto them: but his
Luke 14:26	own life also, he cannot be my **disciple**.
Luke 14:28(25-28)	and **counteth** the cost, whether he have sufficient to
Rom. 12:2(1-3)	be ye **transformed** by the renewing of your mind, that
1 Cor. 9:25	every man that striveth for the **mastery** is temperate

SELF-MASTERY cont.

1 Cor. 13:5(4,5)	seeketh not her own, is not easily **provoked**, thinketh
James 4:7	**resist** the devil, and he will flee from you.
1 Pet. 3:10	let him **refrain** his tongue from evil, and his lips
2 Ne. 4:27(16-35)	why am I **angry** because of mine enemy
Mosiah 3:19	becometh as a child, **submissive**, meek, humble, patient
Alma 34:31	come forth and **harden** not your hearts any longer; for
Alma 34:32	this life is the time for men to **prepare** to meet God
Alma 37:33(32-35)	teach them to **withstand** every temptation of the devil
Alma 38:12(1-15)	**bridle** all your passions, that ye may be filled with
D&C 8:10	do not **ask** for that which you ought not.
D&C 10:5	pray always, that you may come off **conqueror**; yea
D&C 10:63	that there may not be so much **contention**; yea, Satan
D&C 59:9(1-24)	mayest more fully keep thyself **unspotted** from the
D&C 63:61(61-64)	let all men **beware** how they take my name in their lips
D&C 76:53(52-53)	who **overcome** by faith, and are sealed by the Holy
D&C 88:121(121-125)	**cease** from...your wicked doings.
D&C 107:99(99,100)	let every man **learn** his duty, and to act in the office
D&C 121:41(41-46)	persuasion, by **long-suffering**, by gentleness and
D&C 122:9(1-9)	**hold** on thy way...priesthood shall remain with thee
D&C 124:116	clothe himself with charity; and **cease** to do evil, and
D&C 136:21(21-31)	**keep** yourselves from evil to take the name of the Lord

SELF-SACRIFICE

Isa. 53:10	shalt make his soul an **offering** for sin, he shall see
Matt. 6:25(25-34)	take no **thought** for your life, what ye shall eat, or
Matt. 10:39(38-39)	he that loseth his **life** for my sake shall find it.
Matt. 16:25	whosoever will **lose** his life for my sake shall find
Matt. 19:29	every one that hath **forsaken** houses, or brethren, or
Matt. 20:27	whosoever will be chief...let him be your **servant**
Luke 22:27	but I am among you as he that **serveth**.
John 10:17(15-17)	because I **lay** down my life, that I might take it again
Acts 5:41(41,42)	worthy to **suffer** shame for his name.
Acts 9:16	great things he must **suffer** for my name's sake.
Rom. 8:18(17,18)	the **sufferings** of this present time are not worthy to
Rom. 12:1(1-3)	present your bodies a living **sacrifice**, holy
1 Cor. 4:12(10-13)	working with our **own** hands: being reviled, we bless
2 Cor. 8:5(1-5)	but first **gave** their own selves to the Lord, and unto
Gal. 5:13(13,14)	but by love **serve** one another.
Eph. 5:2(1,2)	hath given himself for us an offering and a **sacrifice**
Philip. 3:8	for whom I have **suffered** the loss of all things, and
Philip. 4:12(11-13)	I know both how to be **abased**, and I know how to abound
1 Tim. 2:6(5,6)	who **gave** himself a ransom for all, to be testified in
Titus 2:14(11-15)	who gave **himself** for us, that he might redeem us from
Heb. 9:26(24-28)	put away sin by the **sacrifice** of himself.
Heb. 10:12(7-14)	after he had offered one **sacrifice** for sins for ever
1 Pet. 2:21(21-24)	Christ also **suffered** for us, leaving us an example
1 Pet. 2:24	who his own self **bare** our sins in his own body on the
1 Pet. 3:17(17,18)	better...that ye **suffer** for well doing, than for evil
2 Ne. 2:7(6-9)	he offereth himself a **sacrifice** for sin, to answer the
1:26	**offer** your whole souls as an offering unto him, and
Mosiah 2:14(13-15)	**labored**...that I might serve you, and that ye should

SELF-SACRIFICE cont.

Mosiah 2:17(16-18)	in the **service** of your fellow beings ye are only in
Mosiah 15:9(9-11)	taken upon **himself** their iniquity and their
Mosiah 24:15(15,16)	did **submit** cheerfully and with patience to all the
Alma 24:18(17-19)	they would **give** unto him; and rather than spend their
Alma 26:27(27,28)	**bear** with patience thine afflictions, and I will give
Alma 30:32(32-35)	**labored**...with mine own hands for my support
Alma 53:17(14-18)	protect the land unto the **laying** down of their lives
Hel. 10:4(2-5)	hast not sought thine **own** life, but hast sought my
3 Ne. 9:20(19,20)	offer for a **sacrifice** unto me a broken heart and a
3 Ne. 9:22(21,22)	for such I have laid down my **life**, and have taken it
D&C 18:11(10-12)	he **suffered** the pain of all men, that all men might
D&C 50:26	to be the greatest...is...the **servant** of all.
D&C 59:8(7-9)	offer a **sacrifice** unto the Lord thy God in
D&C 64:33(33,34)	be not weary in **well-doing**, for ye are laying the
D&C 93:46	I called you **servants** for the world's sake, and ye are
D&C 97:8	every **sacrifice** which I, the Lord, shall command- the
D&C 101:35(35-37)	though they are called to lay down their **lives** for my
D&C 103:28(27,28)	whoso is not willing to lay down his **life** for my sake
D&C 117:13(12,13)	his **sacrifice** shall be more sacred unto me than his

SELFISHNESS

Num. 22:7(2-41)	with the **rewards** of divination in their hand; and the
Ruth 4:6(1-8)	I cannot **redeem** it for myself, lest I mar mine own
1 Kgs. 21:15(1-16)	arise, take **possession** of the vineyard of Naboth the
Prov. 1:19(13-19)	the ways of every one that is **greedy** of gain; which
Eccl. 2:1(1-11)	I said in mine heart, go to...enjoy **pleasure**: and
Isa. 14:13(12-15)	I will **exalt** my throne above the stars of God: I will
Isa. 53:6	we have turned every one to his **own** way; and the Lord
Isa. 56:11(10-12)	look to their **own** way, every one for his gain, from
Matt. 16:26	if he shall **gain** the whole world, and lose his own
Acts 5:2(2-3)	**kept** back part of the price, his wife also being privy
Acts 5:3(1-11)	to **keep** back part of the price of the land
Acts 8:19(9-20)	give me also this **power**, that on whomsoever I lay hand
Acts 24:26(24-26)	hoped also that **money** should have been given him of
1 Cor. 6:8(6-8)	nay, ye do wrong, and **defraud**, and that your brethren.
1 Cor. 13:5(1-13)	seeketh not her **own**, is not easily provoked, thinketh
1 Tim. 6:10(7-10)	the love of **money** is the root of all evil: which while
2 Pet. 2:15(15,16)	Balaam...who loved the **wages** of unrighteousness
2 Pet. 3:3	scoffers, walking after their own **lusts**
Mosiah 11:2(1-15)	did walk after the desires of his **own** heart. And he
Mosiah 14:6	we have turned every one to his **own** way; and the Lord
Mosiah 16:5	he that persists in his **own** carnal nature, and goes
Mosiah 19:8(6-8)	not so...concerned about his people as...his **own** life
Alma 11:20	it was for the sole purpose to get **gain**, because they
Alma 31:27(22-28)	while they are **puffed** up, even to greatness, with the
Alma 46:4(3-33)	Amalickiah...lower judges...seeking for **power**.
Hel. 7:21(20-22)	it is to get **gain**, to be praised of men, yea, and that
3 Ne. 6:15	tempting them to seek...power...authority, and **riches**
4 Ne. 1:24(24-26,43)	among them those who were lifted up in **pride**, such as
Ether 14:2	**cleave** unto that which was his own...not borrow
D&C 10:56	build up churches unto themselves to get **gain**, yea

411

SELFISHNESS cont.

D&C 56:8   must repent of his pride, and of his **selfishness**, and
D&C 104:18   abundance...**impart** not his portion, according to the
D&C 121:35(34,35)   hearts are set so much upon the things of this **world**
Moses 4:1(1-4)   wherefore **give** me thine honor.
Moses 5:38(32-38)   Satan tempted me because of my brother's **flocks**.
Moses 6:15   against his own brother...seeking for **power**.

SENSUALITY

Gen. 39:7(7-21)   master's wife cast her **eyes** upon Joseph; and she said
Gen. 49:4(3,4)   wentest up to thy father's bed; then **defiledst** thou
Ex. 20:14   thou shalt not commit **adultery**.
Lev. 18:6(6-24)   to uncover their **nakedness**: I am the Lord.
2 Sam. 11:4(2-4)   she came in unto him, and he **lay** with her; for she
2 Sam. 13:11(1-20)   he **took** hold of her, and said unto her, come lie with
Ezek. 22:9(6-12)   in the midst of thee they commit **lewdness**.
Matt. 5:28(27-29)   whosoever looketh on a woman to **lust** after her hath
James 1:14   he is drawn away of his own **lust**, and enticed.
1 Jn. 2:16(15-17)   the **lust** of the flesh, and the lust of the eyes, and
Jacob 2:33(22-35)   for they shall not commit **whoredoms**, like unto them
Mosiah 16:3   **sensual**, devilish, knowing evil from good, subjecting
Alma 39:3(1-11)   grievous unto me; for thou didst..go..after the **harlot**
Moro. 9:9(7-10)   **depriving** them of...chastity and virtue
D&C 20:20   transgression of these holy laws man became **sensual**
D&C 63:16(14-17)   he that looketh on a woman to **lust** after her, or if
D&C 88:121   from all your **lustful** desires, from all your pride and
D&C 101:6   and **lustful** and covetous desires among them; therefore
Moses 5:13   men began...to be carnal, **sensual**, and devilish.
Moses 6:49   **sensual**, and devilish, and are shut out from the

SEPARATION

Ex. 19:6(5,6)   ye shall be...an holy **nation**. these are the words
Ex. 33:16(16,17)   so shall we be **separated**, I and thy people, from all
Ex. 34:15(11-16)   lest thou make a **covenant**...and...go...after their God
Lev. 19:19   shalt not let thy cattle gender with a **diverse** kind
Lev. 20:26(23-26)   I the Lord am holy...have **severed** you from other
Deut. 7:6(1-6)   the Lord...hath chosen thee to be a **special** people
Ezra 10:11(10-14)   **separate** yourselves from the people of the land, and
Isa. 52:11(11-12)   go ye **out** of the midst of her; be ye clean, that bear
Isa. 59:2(1-2)   your iniquities have **separated**...you and your God, and
Jer. 50:8   **remove** out of the midst of Babylon, and go forth out
Hosea 7:8(8-16)   Ephraim, he hath **mixed** himself among the people
Matt. 25:32(31-46)   he shall **separate** them...as a shepherd divideth his
Luke 16:26   a great **gulf** fixed...they which would pass...cannot
Acts 17:26   determined the times...and the **bounds** of their
2 Cor. 6:17(14-18)   come out from among them, and be ye **separate**, saith
Heb. 7:26   holy, harmless, undefiled, **separate** from sinners, and
Alma 3:8(4-9)   that they might not **mix** and believe in incorrect
Alma 3:14(4-19)   a mark on them that they...may be **separated** from thee
Alma 27:12(1-26)   get this people **out** of this land, that they perish not

SEPARATION cont.

D&C 63:54(53-54)	an entire **separation** of the righteous and the wicked
D&C 76:102(100-107)	they who will not be **gathered** with the saints, to be
D&C 133:14(5-14)	go ye **out** from...Babylon, from the midst of wickedness
D&C 134:9	not believe it just to **mingle** religious influence with
Abr. 2:6(3-6)	take thee away **out** of Haran, and to make of thee a

SERVANTS

1 Sam. 3:10(1-10)	Samuel answered, speak; for thy **servant** heareth.
1 Chr. 6:49	that Moses the **servant** of God had commanded.
Job 1:8(6-12)	unto Satan, hast thou considered my **servant** Job, that
Prov. 17:2	a wise **servant** shall have rule over a son that causeth
Prov. 22:7	and the borrower is **servant** to the lender.
Isa. 42:1(1-4)	behold my **servant**, whom I uphold; mine elect, in whom
Isa. 49:3(1-6)	and said unto me, thou art my **servant**, O Israel, in
Isa. 50:10(4-10)	who is among you...obeyeth the voice of his **servant**
Isa. 52:13	behold, my **servant** shall deal prudently, he shall be
Isa. 53:11(11,12)	shall my righteous **servant** justify many; for he shall
Isa. 54:17	this is the heritage of the **servants** of the Lord, and
Dan. 6:20(18-23)	O Daniel, **servant** of the living God, is thy God, whom
Matt. 18:23(23-35)	certain king, which would take account of his **servants**
Matt. 20:27(25-28)	will be chief among you, let him be your **servant**
Matt. 23:11	he that is greatest among you shall be your **servant**.
Matt. 24:46(42-51)	blessed is that **servant**, whom his Lord when he cometh
Matt. 25:21(14-30)	well done, thou good and faithful **servant**: thou hast
John 8:34(33-38)	whosoever committeth sin is the **servant** of sin.
Rom. 1:1	Paul, a **servant** of Jesus Christ, called to be an
1 Cor. 9:19(18-22)	I made myself **servant** unto all, that I might gain the
Philip. 1:1	Paul and Timotheus, the **servants** of Jesus Christ, to
Titus 1:1(1-4)	Paul, a **servant** of God, and an apostle of Jesus Christ
Heb. 3:5(4-6)	faithful in all his house, as a **servant**, for a
James 1:1	James, a **servant** of God and of the Lord Jesus Christ
1 Pet. 2:16(13-17)	cloke of maliciousness, but as the **servants** of God.
2 Pet. 1:1	Simon Peter, a **servant** and an apostle of Jesus Christ
Jude 1:1	Jude, the **servant** of Jesus Christ, and brother of
Rev. 1:1	to shew unto his **servants** things which must shortly
Rev. 7:3(2,3)	we have sealed the **servants** of our God in their
2 Ne. 9:41	the Holy One of Israel; and he employeth no **servant**
Jacob 5:7(7-70)	he said unto his **servant**: it grieveth me that I should
Hel. 5:29	seek no more to destroy my **servants** whom I have sent
3 Ne. 20:43(41-44)	behold, my **servant** shall deal prudently; he shall be
3 Ne. 21:10(9-11)	the life of my **servant** shall be in my hand; therefore
3 Ne. 22:17(15-17)	heritage of the **servants** of the Lord, and their right
Moro. 7:11	if he follow Christ he cannot be a **servant** of the
D&C 1:17	called upon my **servant** Joseph Smith, Jun., and spake
D&C 1:38	mine own voice or by the voice of my **servants**, it is
D&C 50:26(25-28)	notwithstanding he is the least and the **servant** of all
D&C 76:112(109-113)	and they shall be **servants** of the Most High; but where
D&C 93:46	I called you **servants** for the world's sake, and ye are
D&C 101:52(43-62)	the Lord...called upon his **servants**, and said unto the
D&C 132:16(15-17)	which angels are ministering **servants**, to minister for

SERVICE

Ex. 7:16	that they may **serve** me in the wilderness: and, behold
Ex. 23:5(4,5)	thou shalt surely **help** with him.
Num. 3:8(7,8)	children of Israel, to do the **service** of the
Deut. 6:13	fear the Lord thy God, and **serve** him, and shalt swear
Deut. 10:12	to love him, and to **serve** the Lord thy God with all
Deut. 11:13(13-17)	and to **serve** him with all your heart and with all your
Josh. 24:15(14-16)	choose you this day whom ye will **serve**; whether the
Josh. 24:15	as for me and my house, we will **serve** the Lord.
Josh. 24:21(15-22)	the people said...nay; but we will **serve** the Lord.
Judg. 2:7(6-10)	the people **served** the Lord all the days of Joshua, and
1 Kgs. 12:7(4-16)	if thou wilt be a **servant** unto this people this day
Isa. 41:6(6,7)	they **helped** every one his neighbour; and every one
Matt. 6:24	no man can **serve** two masters: for either he will hate
Matt. 20:27(20-28)	will be chief among you, let him be your **servant**
Rom. 12:1	which is your reasonable **service**.
Eph. 6:7	with good will doing **service**, as to the Lord, and not
1 Tim. 6:2	but rather do them **service**, because they are faithful
Heb. 9:1(1,9)	had also ordinances of divine **service**, and a worldly
Rev. 2:19	I know thy works, and charity, and **service**, and faith
Jacob 2:19(17-19)	administer **relief** to the sick and the afflicted.
Mosiah 2:17(9-27)	when ye are in the **service** of your fellow beings ye
Mosiah 4:15(14-15)	ye will teach them...to **serve** one another.
Mosiah 4:16(16-21)	**succor** those that stand in need of your succor; ye
Mosiah 5:13	knoweth a man the master whom he has not **served**, and
Mosiah 8:18	he becometh a great **benefit** to his fellow beings.
Mosiah 18:8(8-10)	are willing to **bear** one another's burdens, that they
Mosiah 28:3(3-5)	could not bear that any human **soul** should perish; yea
D&C 4:2(2-3)	O ye that embark in the **service** of God, see that ye
D&C 24:7(7-9)	thou shalt devote all thy **service** in Zion; and in this
D&C 42:29(29-31)	if thou lovest me thou shalt **serve** me and keep all my
D&C 50:26	he is the least and the **servant** of all.
D&C 59:5(5,21-23)	in the name of Jesus Christ thou shalt **serve** him.
D&C 81:5	**succor** the weak...and strengthen the feeble knees.

SETTING APART

Num. 6:21(2-21)	this is the law of the Nazarite...for his **separation**
Num. 8:14(6-22)	thus shalt thou **separate** the Levites from among the
Num. 27:19(15-23)	and **set** him before Eleazar the priest, and before all
Deut. 10:8(8,9)	at that time the Lord **separated** the tribe of Levi, to
1 Chr. 23:13(6,12,13)	Aaron was **separated**, that he should sanctify the most
1 Chr. 25:1(1-31)	David and the captains of the host **separated** to the
Ezra 8:24(24-30)	then I **separated** twelve of the chief of the priests
Ps. 4:3(2,3)	know that the Lord hath **set** apart him that is godly
Acts 6:6(1-6)	before the apostles...they laid their **hands** on them.
Acts 13:2(2,3)	**separate** me Barnabas and Saul for the work whereunto
Rom. 1:1	Paul...**separated** unto the gospel of God
1 Tim. 5:22	**lay** hands suddenly on no man, neither be partaker of
Jacob 1:18(17-19)	Jacob, and...Joseph had been **consecrated** priests and
Mosiah 2:4(1-4)	and had **appointed** just men to be their teachers, and
Mosiah 2:11	**consecrated** by my father, and was suffered by the hand
Mosiah 6:3(1-3)	had **appointed** priests to teach the people, that

SETTING APART cont.

Mosiah 6:3	**consecrated** his son Mosiah to be a ruler and a king
Alma 5:3	**consecrated**...to be a high priest over the church of
Alma 45:22(22-24)	they did **appoint** priests and teachers throughout all
D&C 38:23(23,24)	according to the office wherewith I have **appointed** you
D&C 42:31	has appointed and **set** apart for that purpose.
D&C 107:17	called and **set** apart and ordained unto this power by
D&C 107:74	shall be **set** apart unto this ministry, until the

SEVENTY

Ex. 24:1	and **seventy** of the elders of Israel; and worship ye
Ex. 24:9	and **seventy** of the elders of Israel
Num. 11:16(16,24-25)	gather unto me **seventy** men of the elders of Israel
Num. 11:24(24-30)	gathered the **seventy** men of the elders of the people
Ezek. 8:11	**seventy** men of the ancients of the house of Israel
Luke 10:1	the Lord appointed other **seventy** also, and sent them
Luke 10:17	the **seventy** returned again with joy, saying, Lord
D&C 107:25(25-26)	**Seventy** are also called to preach...to be especial
D&C 107:34	the **Seventy** are to act in the name of the Lord, under
D&C 107:97(93-97)	and these **seventy** are to be traveling ministers, unto
D&C 124:138(138-140	I give...you...to preside over the quorum of **seventies**

SEXUAL IMMORALITY

Gen. 19:32(30-38)	we will **lie** with him, that we may preserve seed of
Gen. 35:22	Reuben went and **lay** with Bilhah his father's concubine
Gen. 49:4	because thou wentest up to thy father's **bed**; then
Ex. 20:14	thou shalt not commit **adultery**.
Lev. 18:6(6-30)	none of you shall approach...to uncover their
Lev. 20:10	**adulterer** and the adulteress shall...be put to death.
Num. 25:1	the people began to commit **whoredom** with the daughters
Num. 31:16(13-20)	through the counsel of Balaam, to commit **trespass**
Deut. 22:25(21-30)	the man force her, and **lie** with her: then the man
Josh. 22:17	is the **iniquity** of Peor too little for us, from which
1 Chr. 5:1	defiled his father's **bed**, his birthright was given
Prov. 5:5(3-8)	her feet go down to **death**; her steps take hold on hell
Prov. 6:25(24-33)	**lust** not after her beauty in thine heart; neither let
Prov. 7:10(6-27)	there met him a woman with the attire of an **harlot**
Isa. 57:3(3,4)	the seed of the **adulterer** and the whore.
Hosea 9:10	and their **abominations** were according as they loved.
Mal. 3:5	I will be a swift witness...against the **adulterers**
Mal. 4:1	all that do **wickedly**, shall be stubble: and the day
Matt. 5:28(28,32)	lust after her hath committed **adultery** with her
Matt. 15:19(17-20)	out of the heart proceed...**adulteries**, fornications
Matt. 19:9	shall marry another, committeth **adultery**: and whoso
Acts 15:20(19-21)	abstain...from **fornication**, and from things strangled
1 Cor. 5:1(1-10)	it is reported...that there is **fornication** among you
1 Cor. 6:9(9-11)	not inherit the kingdom of God?...**adulterers**, nor
Eph. 5:3(1-7)	**fornication**...let it not be once named among you, as
Col. 3:5(5,6)	**inordinate** affection, evil concupiscence, and covetous
1 Thes. 4:3(3,4)	that ye should abstain from **fornication**

SEXUAL IMMORALITY cont.

2 Tim. 3:3(2-6)	without natural **affection**, trucebreakers, false
2 Pet. 2:10(10-18)	walk after the flesh in the **lust** of uncleanness, and
Rev. 2:14	Balaam, who taught Balac...to commit **fornication**.
1 Ne. 22:23	seek the **lusts** of the flesh and the things of the
Jacob 2:28	**whoredoms** are an abomination before me; thus saith the
Alma 39:5(3-11)	**abominable** above all sins save it be the shedding of
3 Ne. 12:28(27,28)	**lust** after her, hath committed adultery already in
3 Ne. 12:32(31,32)	shall marry her who is divorced committeth **adultery**.
D&C 42:24(22-26)	he that committeth **adultery**, and repenteth not, shall
D&C 42:74(74-80)	put away their companions for the cause of **fornication**
D&C 63:16	to **lust**...shall commit adultery in their hearts, they
D&C 76:103(103-106)	**adulterers**, and whoremongers, and whosoever loves and

SHAME

Gen. 2:25	and they were both naked...and were not **ashamed**.
2 Sam. 13:13	whither shall I cause my **shame** to go? and as for thee
Job 8:22	they that hate thee shall be clothed with **shame**; and
Ps. 4:2	how long will ye turn my glory into **shame**? how long
Ps. 14:6	ye have **shamed** the counsel of the poor, because the
Ps. 25:2(2,3)	I trust in thee: let me not be **ashamed**, let not mine
Ps. 25:20	O keep my soul...let me not be **ashamed**; for I put my
Ps. 31:1	let me never be **ashamed**: deliver me in thy
Ps. 31:17	let me not be **ashamed**, O Lord; for I have called upon
Ps. 40:15	be desolate for a reward of their **shame** that say unto
Ps. 69:19	thou hast known my reproach, and my **shame**, and my
Ps. 71:24	they are brought unto **shame**, that seek my hurt.
Ps. 89:45	thou hast covered him with **shame**. Selah.
Ps. 119:78	let the proud be **ashamed**; for they dealt perversely
Ps. 132:18	his enemies will I clothe with **shame**: but upon himself
Prov. 3:35	but **shame** shall be the promotion of fools.
Prov. 11:2	when pride cometh, then cometh **shame**: but with the low
Prov. 12:4	but she that maketh **ashamed** is as rottenness in his
Prov. 13:18	**shame** shall be to him that refuseth instruction: but
Prov. 28:7	a companion of riotous men **shameth** his father.
Prov. 29:15	a child left to himself bringeth his mother to **shame**.
Isa. 49:23	for they shall not be **ashamed** that wait for me.
Isa. 50:6	I hid not my face from **shame** and spitting.
Isa. 54:4	for thou shalt forget the **shame** of thy youth, and
Jer. 2:26	the thief is **ashamed** when he is found, so is the house
Jer. 3:25	we lie down in our **shame**, and our confusion covereth
Jer. 46:12	nations have heard of thy **shame**, and thy cry hath
Ezek. 7:18	**shame** shall be upon all faces, and baldness upon all
Ezek. 16:52(52-54)	bear thine own **shame** for thy sins that thou hast
Ezek. 34:29	neither bear the **shame** of the heathen any more.
Ezek. 44:13	shall bear their **shame**, and their abominations which
Dan. 12:2	and some to **shame** and everlasting contempt.
Hosea 2:5	she that conceived them hath done **shamefully**: for she
Hosea 4:7	therefore will I change their glory into **shame**.
Hosea 10:6	Ephraim shall receive **shame**, and Israel shall be
Hab. 2:16	thou art filled with **shame** for glory: drink thou also
Mark 8:38	whosoever therefore shall be **ashamed** of me and of my

SHAME cont.

Luke 14:11(7-11)	whosoever exalteth himself shall be **abased**; and he
Acts 5:41(40-42)	counted worthy to suffer **shame** for his name.
Rom. 1:16	for I am not **ashamed** of the gospel of Christ: for it
1 Cor. 4:14	I write not these things to **shame** you, but as my
1 Cor. 6:5(1-7)	I speak to your **shame**. Is it so, that there is not a
1 Cor. 11:6	but if it be a **shame** for a woman to be shorn or shave
1 Cor. 11:22	despise ye the church...and **shame** them that have not
1 Cor. 15:34	I speak this to your **shame**.
Eph. 5:12	it is a **shame** even to speak of those things which are
Philip. 3:19	whose glory is in their **shame**, who mind earthly
2 Tim. 1:8(7-8)	be not thou therefore **ashamed** of the testimony of our
Heb. 6:6(4-6)	fall away...put him to an open **shame**.
Heb. 12:2(2,3)	Jesus...endured the cross, despising the **shame**, and
1 Ne. 8:25	they did cast their eyes about as if they were **ashamed**
2 Ne. 7:6	I hid not my face from **shame** and spitting.
Jacob 1:8	suffer his cross and bear the **shame** of the world
Jacob 6:9	stand with **shame** and awful guilt before the bar of God
Alma 12:15	to our everlasting **shame** that all his judgments are
Alma 46:21	be **ashamed** to take upon them the name of Christ, the
3 Ne. 22:4	for thou shalt forget the **shame** of thy youth, and
Morm. 8:38	why are ye **ashamed** to take upon you the name of Christ
D&C 42:91	rebuked openly, that he or she may be **ashamed**. And if
D&C 71:7	as ye are faithful their **shame** shall be made manifest.
D&C 76:35	denied the Holy Spirit...and put him to an open **shame**.
D&C 90:17	be not **ashamed**, neither confounded; but be admonished
D&C 109:29	bring to **shame**...all those who have spread lying
D&C 133:49	great shall be the glory...sun shall hide in **shame**
Abr. 5:19	and they were both naked...and were not **ashamed**.

SHEEP

Num. 27:17(15-17)	that the congregation...be not as **sheep** which have no
1 Kgs. 22:17(15-17)	all Israel scattered...as **sheep** that have not a
Ps. 8:7(4-9)	all **sheep** and oxen, yea, and the beasts of the field
Ps. 44:22(20-26)	we are counted as **sheep** for the slaughter.
Ps. 95:7	we are the people...and the **sheep** of his hand. To day
Ps. 100:3	he that hath made us...the **sheep** of his pasture.
Ps. 119:176(174-176)	I have gone astray like a lost **sheep**; seek thy servant
Isa. 40:11	he shall feed his **flock** like a shepherd: he shall
Isa. 53:6(4-7)	all we like **sheep** have gone astray; we have turned
Ezek. 34:6(1-8)	my **sheep** wandered through all the mountains, and upon
Ezek. 34:17(17-24)	and as for you, O my **flock**, thus saith the Lord God
Ezek. 34:31(30,31)	and ye my **flock**, the flock of my pasture, are men, and
Micah 5:8	shall be...as a young lion among the flocks of **sheep**
Zech. 13:7(7-9)	smite the shepherd, and the **sheep** shall be scattered
Matt. 7:15(15,16)	beware of false prophets...in **sheep's** clothing, but
Matt. 9:36(36-38)	they...were scattered...as **sheep** having no shepherd.
Matt. 10:6(5-6)	but go rather to the lost **sheep** of the house of Israel
Matt. 12:12(10-13)	how much then is a man better than a **sheep**? wherefore
Matt. 18:12(10-14)	if a man have an hundred **sheep**, and one of them be
Matt. 25:32(31-46)	as a shepherd divideth his **sheep** from the goats
John 10:2(1-7)	he that entereth in...is the shepherd of the **sheep**.

SHEEP cont.

John 10:16(7-16)	other **sheep** I have, which are not of this fold: them
John 10:27	my **sheep** hear my voice, and I know them, and they
John 21:17(15-17)	Jesus saith unto him, feed my **sheep**.
Rom. 8:36(35-39)	for thy sake...accounted as **sheep** for the slaughter.
1 Pet. 2:25(21-25)	for ye were as **sheep** going astray; but are now
1 Ne. 22:25(24-28)	and he numbereth his **sheep**, and they know him; and
Mosiah 8:21(20,21)	yea, they are as a wild **flock** which fleeth from the
Mosiah 15:6	as Isaiah said, as a **sheep** before the shearer is dumb
Alma 5:37(37-40)	have gone astray, as **sheep** having no shepherd
Alma 5:59(59-60)	what shepherd...having many **sheep** doth not watch over
Alma 25:12(1-12)	as a **sheep** having no shepherd is driven and slain by
Hel. 15:13(12-13)	they shall be...numbered among his **sheep**.
3 Ne. 15:24(11-24)	ye are my **sheep**, and ye are numbered among those whom
D&C 6:34	fear not, little **flock**; do good; let earth and hell
D&C 10:60(57-60)	I will show unto this people that I had other **sheep**
D&C 35:27	fear not, little **flock**, the kingdom is yours until I
D&C 88:72	I will take care of your **flocks**, and will raise up

SHEPHERDS

Gen. 49:24	from thence is the **shepherd**, the stone of Israel
Num. 27:17(15-17)	be not as sheep which have no **shepherd**.
1 Kgs. 22:17(15-17)	all Israel...as sheep that have not a **shepherd**: and
Ps. 23:1	the Lord is my **shepherd**; I shall not want.
Ps. 80:1(1-3)	O **Shepherd** of Israel, thou that leadest Joseph like a
Isa. 40:11	he shall feed his flock like a **shepherd**: he shall
Jer. 2:8	the **pastors** also transgressed against me, and the
Jer. 10:21	for the **pastors** are become brutish, and have not
Jer. 23:4(1-4)	I will set up **shepherds** over them which shall feed the
Ezek. 34:2(1-10)	woe be to the **shepherds** of Israel that do feed
Ezek. 34:12(11-16)	as a **shepherd** seeketh out his flock...so will I seek
Ezek. 34:23(22-24)	I will set up one **shepherd** over them, and he shall
Ezek. 37:24	they all shall have one **shepherd**: they shall also
Zech. 10:2(1-3)	they were troubled, because there was no **shepherd**.
Zech. 13:7(7-9)	smite the **shepherd**, and the sheep shall be scattered
Matt. 9:36(36-38)	they...were scattered...as sheep having no **shepherd**.
Matt. 25:32(31-46)	as a **shepherd** divideth his sheep from the goats
Mark 6:34(32-34)	they were as sheep not having a **shepherd**: and he began
John 10:11(1-16,26-27)	I am the good **shepherd**: the good shepherd giveth his
Heb. 13:20(20,21)	our Lord Jesus, that great **shepherd** of the sheep
1 Pet. 2:25(21-25)	as sheep...returned unto the **Shepherd** and Bishop of
1 Pet. 5:4	the chief **Shepherd** shall appear, ye shall receive a
1 Ne. 13:41(41,42)	one God and one **Shepherd** over all the earth.
1 Ne. 22:25(24-28)	there shall be one fold and one **shepherd**; and he shall
Mosiah 8:21(20,21)	a wild **flock** which fleeth from the **shepherd**, and
Alma 5:37(37-42,55-60)	a **shepherd** hath called after you and is still calling
Alma 25:12(1-12)	as a sheep having no **shepherd** is driven and slain by
Hel. 7:18(17-20)	will not hearken unto the voice of the good **shepherd**
Hel. 15:13(12-13)	their Redeemer...their great and true **shepherd**, and
3 Ne. 15:17(16-24)	there shall be one fold, and one **shepherd**.
Morm. 5:17	they had Christ for their **shepherd**; yea, they were led
D&C 50:44	I am the good **shepherd**, and the stone of Israel. he

SICKNESS

Ex. 23:25(24,25)	I will take **sickness** away from the midst of thee.
Deut. 7:15	the Lord will take away from thee all **sickness**, and
Deut. 28:59(58-61)	and sore **sicknesses**, and of long continuance.
1 Kgs. 8:37(37-39)	whatsoever plague, whatsoever **sickness** there be
1 Kgs. 17:17	and his **sickness** was so sore, that there was no breath
Ps. 6:2	O Lord, **heal** me; for my bones are vexed.
Ps. 35:13(11-14)	when they were **sick**, my clothing was sackcloth: I
Ps. 41:3(1-3)	thou wilt make all his bed in his **sickness**.
Ps. 103:3	thine iniquities; who healeth all thy **diseases**
Ezek. 34:4(2-6)	neither have ye healed that which was **sick**, neither
Ezek. 34:16(15,16)	will strengthen that which was **sick**: but I will
Matt. 4:23	healing all manner of **sickness** and all manner of
Matt. 8:17	himself took our infirmities, and bare our **sicknesses**.
Matt. 10:1	to heal all manner of **sickness** and all manner of
Matt. 14:14	Jesus went forth...and he healed their **sick**.
Mark 3:15	and to have power to heal **sicknesses**, and to cast out
Acts 28:8	the father of Publius lay **sick** of a fever and of a
1 Cor. 11:30(27-30)	many are weak and **sickly** among you, and many sleep.
James 5:14(14-15)	is any **sick** among you? let him call for the elders of
1 Ne. 11:31	I beheld multitudes of people who were **sick**, and who
Mosiah 3:5	mighty miracles, such as healing the **sick**, raising the
Alma 7:11	take upon him the pains and the **sicknesses** of his
Alma 9:22(20-23)	having been saved from famine, and from **sickness**, and
Alma 15:3	Zeezrom lay **sick** at Sidom, with a burning fever, which
Alma 46:40	remove the cause of **diseases**, to which men were
3 Ne. 7:22	healed of their **sicknesses** and their infirmities, did
3 Ne. 17:7(7-10)	have ye any that are **sick** among you? Bring them hither
3 Ne. 26:15	after having healed all their **sick**, and their lame
4 Ne. 1:5	they did heal the **sick**, and raise the dead, and cause
Morm. 9:24	they shall lay hands on the **sick** and they shall
D&C 35:9(8-11)	they shall heal the **sick**; they shall cause the blind
D&C 42:43	**sick**...shall be nourished...with herbs and mild food
D&C 45:31	a desolating **sickness** shall cover the land.
D&C 52:40	remember in all things...the **sick** and the afflicted
D&C 66:9	lay your hands upon the **sick**, and they shall recover.
D&C 84:68	in my name they shall heal the **sick**
D&C 124:87	the **sickness** of the land shall redound to your glory.
D&C 124:98	he shall heal the **sick**, he shall cast out devils, and

SIGHT

Gen. 2:9	every tree that is pleasant to the **sight**, and good for
Ex. 19:11(10,11)	come down in the **sight** of all the people upon mount
Ex. 24:17(16-18)	and the **sight** of the glory of the Lord was like
Eccl. 6:9	better is the **sight** of the eyes than the wandering of
Isa. 11:3(1-5)	and he shall not judge after the **sight** of his eyes
Isa. 29:18	eyes of the **blind** shall see out of obscurity, and out
Isa. 35:5(4-6)	the eyes of the **blind** shall be opened, and the ears
Matt. 11:5(4-5)	the blind receive their **sight**, and the lame walk, the
Matt. 20:34(30-34)	immediately their eyes received **sight**, and they follow
Luke 7:21	and unto many that were blind he gave **sight**.
Luke 18:42(42-43)	and Jesus said unto him, receive thy **sight**: thy faith

SIGHT cont.

John 9:11(8-12)	and I went and washed, and I received **sight**.
Acts 9:18(9-18)	and he received **sight** forthwith, and arose, and was
Acts 22:13(12-15)	brother Saul, receive thy **sight**. and the same hour I
2 Cor. 5:7	(for we walk by faith, not by **sight**
2 Ne. 21:3	he shall not judge after the **sight** of his eyes
Mosiah 3:5	causing...the blind to receive their **sight**, and the
3 Ne. 26:15	having...opened the eyes of their **blind** and unstopped
4 Ne. 1:5	cause...the blind to receive their **sight**, and the deaf
Ether 12:20(20,21)	could not hide it from the **sight** of the brother of
D&C 35:9	they shall cause the blind to receive their **sight**, and
D&C 38:7(7,8)	I am in your midst and ye cannot **see** me
D&C 42:49(48,49)	he who hath faith to **see** shall see.
D&C 67:10(10,11)	you shall **see** me and know that I am- not with the
D&C 84:69	in my name they shall **open** the eyes of the blind, and

SIGN SEEKERS

Ex. 7:9(8-11)	when Pharaoh shall...saying, shew a **miracle** for you
Isa. 5:19	let him...hasten his work, that we may **see** it: and let
Jer. 17:15	where is the word of the Lord? let it **come** now.
Matt. 12:39(38,39)	an evil and adulterous generation seeketh after a **sign**
Matt. 24:24	false prophets...shall shew great **signs** and wonders
Luke 11:16	others, tempting him, sought of him a **sign** from heaven
Luke 11:29	this is an evil generation: they seek a **sign**; and
Luke 23:8(6-11)	he hoped to have seen some **miracle** done by him.
John 2:18(18-22)	what **sign** shewest thou unto us, seeing that thou doest
John 4:48	except ye see **signs** and wonders, ye will not believe.
1 Cor. 1:22(18-25)	for the Jews require a **sign**, and the Greeks seek after
2 Ne. 15:19	let him...hasten his work, that we may **see** it; and let
Jacob 7:13(1-20)	show me a **sign** by this power of the Holy Ghost, in the
Alma 30:43(6-60)	Korihor said unto Alma: if thou wilt show me a **sign**
Alma 32:17(17-19)	many who do say: if thou wilt show unto us a **sign** from
Ether 12:6	ye receive no **witness** until after the trial of your
D&C 24:13(13-14)	require not **miracles**, except I shall command you
D&C 46:9(7-11)	ask and not for a **sign** that they may consume it upon
D&C 63:7(7-11)	he that seeketh **signs** shall see signs, but not unto

SIGNS

Gen. 1:14	lights in the firmament...let them be for **signs**, and
Gen. 9:17(12-17)	**token** of the covenant...between me and all flesh that
Gen. 17:11	circumcise..a **token** of the covenant betwixt me and you
Ex. 4:8(1-8)	they will believe the voice of the latter **sign**.
Deut. 13:1(1-5)	and giveth thee a **sign** or a wonder
Isa. 7:14(13-17)	therefore the Lord himself shall give you a **sign**
Isa. 20:3	for a **sign** and wonder upon Egypt and upon Ethiopia
Ezek. 12:6	I have set thee for a **sign** unto the house of Israel.
Ezek. 12:11	say, I am your **sign**: like as I have done, so shall it
Ezek. 20:20	my sabbaths...they shall be a **sign** between me and you
Matt. 12:39(39-40)	an evil and adulterous generation seeketh after a **sign**
Matt. 24:24	false prophets, and shall shew great **signs** and wonders

SIGNS cont.

Mark 13:4(4-8)	and what shall be the **sign** when all these things shall
Mark 13:22(21,22)	false prophets shall rise, and shall shew **signs** and
Mark 16:17(16-20)	and these **signs** shall follow them that believe; in my
Luke 2:12	**sign**...the babe wrapped in swaddling clothes, lying
John 2:23	many believed...when they saw the **miracles** which he
John 12:37(37-40)	he had done so many **miracles** before them, yet they
John 20:30(30,31)	many other **signs** truly did Jesus in the presence of
Acts 2:19(17-21)	I will shew wonders...and **signs** in the earth beneath
Acts 2:43	many wonders and **signs** were done by the apostles.
Acts 5:12	of the apostles were many **signs** and wonders wrought
Rom. 4:11	**sign** of circumcision, a seal of the righteousness of
1 Cor. 14:22	wherefore tongues are for a **sign**, not to them that
2 Cor. 12:12	the **signs** of an apostle were wrought among you in all
2 Thes. 2:9(9-12)	Satan with all power and **signs** and lying wonders
1 Ne. 11:7	this thing shall be given unto thee for a **sign**, that
1 Ne. 19:10	three days of darkness...**sign** given of his death unto
2 Ne. 17:11(11,14)	ask thee a **sign** of the Lord thy God; ask it either in
2 Ne. 26:3	there shall be **signs** given unto my people of his birth
Alma 32:17(17-19)	if thou wilt show unto us a **sign** from heaven, then we
Alma 37:27	secret...**signs** and their wonders ye shall keep from
Hel. 2:7(3-7)	Kishkumen, and he gave unto him a **sign**; therefore
Hel. 6:22	they did have their...secret **signs**, and their secret
Hel. 14:3(1-7)	this will I give unto you for a **sign**...of his coming
3 Ne. 1:22	not believe in those **signs**...which they had seen; but
3 Ne. 2:1(1-3)	less astonished at a **sign** or a wonder from heaven
3 Ne. 29:7(5-7)	wo unto him..shall say..there can be no **miracle**
Morm. 9:10(7-11)	imagined up...a God who is not God of **miracles**.
Morm. 9:15(15-27)	God has not ceased to be a God of **miracles**.
Morm. 9:24(24-27)	and these **signs** shall follow them that believe- in my
Ether 4:18	and **signs** shall follow them that believe in my name.
Moro. 7:35(35-38)	has the day of **miracles** ceased
D&C 35:8	and I will show miracles, **signs**, and wonders, unto
D&C 45:39(39-42)	he that feareth me shall be looking...for the **signs**
D&C 58:64	with **signs** following them that believe.
D&C 63:7(7-12)	and he that seeketh signs shall see **signs**, but not
D&C 63:9(7-12)	faith cometh not by **signs**, but signs follow those that
D&C 68:10(8-12)	and he that believeth shall be blest with **signs**
D&C 84:65(64-72)	and these **signs** shall follow them that believe
D&C 88:93	there shall appear a great **sign** in heaven, and all

SILENCE

1 Sam. 2:9	the wicked shall be **silent** in darkness; for by
Job 34:29	when he giveth **quietness**, who then can make trouble
Ps. 31:18(17-18)	let the lying lips be put to **silence**; which speak
Ps. 46:10	be **still**, and know that I am God: I will be exalted
Prov. 13:3	he that keepeth his **mouth** keepeth his life: but he
Eccl. 3:7	a time to keep **silence**, and a time to speak
Eccl. 4:6	better is an handful with **quietness**, than both the
Isa. 30:15	in **quietness** and in confidence shall be your strength
Isa. 41:1	keep **silence** before me...let the people renew their
Acts 21:40	there was made a great **silence**, he spake unto them in

1 Cor. 14:28	if there be no interpreter, let him keep **silence** in
1 Tim. 2:11	let the woman learn in **silence** with all subjection.
1 Pet. 2:15	with well doing...put to **silence** the ignorance of
Rev. 8:1	opened the seventh seal, there was **silence** in heaven
3 Ne. 10:1	there was **silence** in the land for the space of many
D&C 38:12	which causeth **silence** to reign, and all eternity is
D&C 88:95	there shall be **silence** in heaven for the space of half

SIN

Gen. 4:7(3-7)	if thou doest not well, **sin** lieth at the door.
Ex. 20:5	visiting the **iniquity** of the fathers upon the children
Lev. 18:27(26-28)	all these **abominations** have the men of the land done
Num. 5:6(5-8)	**sin**...against the Lord, and that person be guilty
Deut. 9:4(4-5)	for the **wickedness** of these nations the Lord doth
Deut. 24:16	every man shall be put to death for his own **sin**.
2 Sam. 12:13(7-14)	David said unto Nathan, I have **sinned** against the Lord
1 Kgs. 8:46	for there is no man that **sinneth** not,) and thou be
2 Kgs. 14:6(5-9)	every man shall be put to death for his own **sin**.
2 Kgs. 21:2(1-9)	he did...**evil**...after the abominations of the heathen
Ezra 9:13	thou...punished us less than our **iniquities** deserve
Ps. 6:8	depart from me, all ye workers of **iniquity**; for the
Ps. 32:1(1-11)	blessed is he whose **transgression** is forgiven, whose
Ps. 51:1	according to...thy..mercies blot out my **transgressions**
Ps. 51:3(1-3)	my transgressions: and my **sin** is ever before me.
Eccl. 7:20	not a just man upon earth, that...**sinneth** not.
Isa. 1:18	though your **sins** be as scarlet, they shall be as
Isa. 53:6	the Lord hath laid on him the **iniquity** of us all.
Jer. 31:34	for I will forgive their **iniquity**, and I will remember
Ezek. 3:18(17-21)	wicked man shall die in his **iniquity**; but his blood
Ezek. 18:4	the soul that **sinneth**, it shall die.
Ezek. 18:20(19-20)	the soul that **sinneth**, it shall die. the son shall not
Matt. 5:19	whosoever...shall **break** one of these least
Matt. 7:23(21-23)	depart from me, ye that work **iniquity**.
Matt. 18:7	woe unto the world because of **offences**! for it must
Luke 17:2	that he should **offend** one of these little ones.
John 1:29	Jesus...taketh away the **sin** of the world.
John 5:29	have done **evil**, unto the resurrection of damnation.
John 8:21	shall die in your **sins**: whither I go, ye cannot come.
John 8:34	whosoever committeth **sin** is the servant of sin.
John 9:41	ye say, we see; therefore your **sin** remaineth.
John 16:9	of **sin**, because they believe not on me
Rom. 3:23	for all have **sinned**, and come short of the glory of
Rom. 5:12	**sin** entered into the world, and death by sin; and so
Rom. 5:13(13,15)	**sin** is not imputed when there is no law.
Rom. 6:18(16-20)	being then made free from **sin**, ye became the servants
Rom. 6:23	for the wages of **sin** is death; but the gift of God is
Rom. 14:23	for whatsoever is not of faith is **sin**.
2 Thes. 2:3	that man of **sin** be revealed, the son of perdition
Heb. 4:15(14-15)	in all points tempted like as we are, yet without **sin**.
Heb. 6:6(4-6)	if they shall **fall** away, to renew them again unto
Heb. 10:26	**sin** wilfully after that we have received the knowledge

SIN cont.

Heb. 12:1	lay aside...the sin which doth so easily beset us, and
James 1:15	when lust hath conceived, it bringeth forth sin: and
James 2:10	whosoever...offend in one point, he is guilty of all.
James 4:17	knoweth to do good, and doeth it not, to him it is sin
1 Pet. 2:22(21-22)	who did no sin, neither was guile found in his mouth
1 Pet. 4:1	hath suffered in the flesh hath ceased from sin
2 Pet. 2:19	they themselves are the servants of corruption: for
1 Jn. 1:8(7-10)	if we say that we have no sin, we deceive ourselves
1 Jn. 3:4	sin is the transgression of the law.
1 Jn. 3:6	whosoever abideth in him sinneth not: whosoever
1 Jn. 3:8(8-12)	he that committeth sin is of the devil; for the devil
1 Jn. 5:17(16-18)	all unrighteousness is sin: and there is a sin not
1 Ne. 17:35(33-35)	people...rejected..word of God...were ripe in iniquity
2 Ne. 2:13	say there is no law...also say...no sin. If ye shall
2 Ne. 2:23	doing no good, for they knew no sin.
2 Ne. 2:29(27-29)	will of the flesh and the evil which is therein
2 Ne. 4:31(17-31)	make me that I may shake at the appearance of sin
2 Ne. 9:38	wo unto all those who die in their sins; for they
Jacob 7:19(15-20)	unpardonable sin, for I have lied unto God; for I
Mosiah 4:14	the devil, who is the master of sin, or who is the
Mosiah 4:29(29-30)	sin...so many that I cannot number them.
Mosiah 13:28	atonement...make for the sins and iniquities of his
Mosiah 27:13	nothing shall overthrow it, save...transgression of
Mosiah 27:29	my soul hath been redeemed from...bonds of iniquity.
Alma 11:37	he cannot save them in their sins; for I cannot deny
Alma 42:17	how could he sin if there was no law? How could there
Alma 45:16	for the Lord cannot look upon sin with the least
Hel. 6:30	behold, it is he who is the author of all sin.
Moro. 7:12	inviteth and enticeth to sin, and to do that which is
Moro. 7:17(17-18)	evil...doth the devil work, for he persuadeth no man
Moro. 8:8	little children...are not capable of commiting sin
D&C 1:31(31-32)	for I the Lord cannot look upon sin with the least
D&C 3:18	unbelief because of the iniquity of their fathers, who
D&C 10:20	stirreth them up to iniquity against that which is
D&C 21:9	Jesus was crucified by sinful men for the sins of the
D&C 29:47(46-48)	they cannot sin ...until they begin to become
D&C 43:11	purge ye out the iniquity which is among you; sanctify
D&C 45:4	the sufferings and death of him who did no sin, in
D&C 45:58	their children shall grow up without sin unto
D&C 49:20	the world lieth in sin.
D&C 50:29(28-30)	if ye are purified and cleansed from all sin, ye shall
D&C 58:42	sins...I, the Lord, remember them no more.
D&C 59:15	not with much laughter, for this is sin, but with a
D&C 82:3(2,3)	sins against the greater light...greater condemnation.
D&C 82:7	unto...soul who sinneth shall the former sins return
D&C 84:51(49-51)	whoso cometh not unto me is under the bondage of sin.
D&C 88:86	entangle not yourselves in sin, but let your hands
D&C 109:34	as all men sin forgive the transgressions of thy
D&C 121:17	cry transgression...because they are...servants of sin
D&C 121:37	when we undertake to cover our sins, or to gratify
D&C 132:27	the blasphemy against the Holy Ghost, which shall not
D&C 132:39(38-39)	David...in none of these things did he sin..save..

SINCERITY

Gen. 20:5(5,6)	in the **integrity** of my heart and innocency of my hands
Josh. 24:14	fear the Lord, and serve him in **sincerity** and in truth
Job 27:5(2-5)	I will not remove mine **integrity** from me.
Ps. 32:2	in whose spirit there is no **guile**.
Ps. 34:13(12-14)	keep...thy lips from speaking **guile**.
Ps. 55:11(9-11)	deceit and **guile** depart not from her streets.
Ps. 78:72	according to the **integrity** of his heart; and guided
Matt. 7:21(21-22)	not every one that **saith** unto me, Lord, Lord, shall
1 Cor. 5:8	the unleavened bread of **sincerity** and truth.
2 Cor. 2:17	as of **sincerity**...in the sight of God speak we in
2 Cor. 8:8	and to prove the **sincerity** of your love.
Eph. 6:24	them that love our Lord Jesus Christ in **sincerity**.
Col. 3:22	but in **singleness** of heart, fearing God
Titus 2:7	in doctrine shewing uncorruptness, gravity, **sincerity**
1 Pet. 2:22(21-22)	who did no sin, neither was **guile** found in his mouth
2 Ne. 31:13	with real **intent**, repenting of your sins, witnessing
Mosiah 4:10	ask in **sincerity** of heart that he would forgive you
Alma 26:31	we can witness of their **sincerity**, because of their
Alma 33:11	thou didst hear me because of mine...**sincerity**; and
Hel. 3:27	in the **sincerity** of their hearts, call upon his holy
3 Ne. 17:21(20-21)	and when he had said these words, he **wept**, and the
Moro. 6:8	sought forgiveness, with real **intent**, they were
Moro. 7:6(6,7)	except he shall do it with real **intent** it profiteth
Moro. 7:9	pray and not with real **intent** of heart; yea, and it
Moro. 10:4	ask with a **sincere** heart, with real intent, having
D&C 5:24	humble himself...in the **sincerity** of his heart, then
D&C 6:16(15,16)	knowest thy thoughts and the **intents** of thy heart.
D&C 33:1	discerner of the thoughts and **intents** of the heart.
D&C 36:7(5-7)	embrace it with **singleness** of heart may be ordained
D&C 121:42(42,43)	which shall greatly enlarge the soul...without **guile**
D&C 124:15	because of the **integrity** of his heart, and because he
D&C 124:20	my servant George Miller is without **guile**; he may be
D&C 124:97	be humble before me, and be without **guile**, and he

SINGING

Ex. 15:1(1-19)	then **sang** Moses and the children of Israel this song
Ex. 15:21	and Miriam answered them, **sing** ye to the Lord, for he
Deut. 31:21(19-30)	this **song** shall testify against them as a witness; for
Deut. 32:44(1-44)	Moses...spake all the words of this **song** in the ears
Judg. 5:1(1-31)	then **sang** Deborah and Barak the son of Abinoam on that
1 Sam. 2:1(1-10)	and Hannah **prayed**, and said, my heart rejoiceth in the
1 Sam. 21:11	did they not **sing** one to another of him in dances, say
2 Sam. 22:1(1-50)	and David spake...the words of this **song** in the day
Job 38:7	when the morning stars **sang** together, and all the sons
Ps. 40:3	he hath put a new **song** in my mouth, even praise unto
Ps. 98:1	O **sing** unto the Lord a new song; for he hath done
Ps. 100:2(1-2)	come before his presence with **singing**.
Ps. 138:5	yea, they shall **sing** in the ways of the Lord: for
Ps. 144:9	I will **sing** a new song unto thee, O God: upon a
Ps. 149:5	let them **sing** aloud upon their beds.
Isa. 12:5(1-6)	**sing** unto the Lord; for he hath done excellent things

SINGING cont.

Isa. 35:6	the tongue of the dumb **sing**: for in the wilderness
Isa. 35:10	**songs** and everlasting joy upon their heads: they
Isa. 42:10	**sing** unto the Lord a new song, and his praise from the
Isa. 44:23	break forth into **singing**, ye mountains, O forest, and
Matt. 26:30	when they had sung an **hymn**, they went out into the
Luke 1:46(46-55)	and Mary **said**, my soul doth magnify the Lord
Acts 16:25	Paul and Silas prayed, and **sang** praises unto God: and
Eph. 5:19	speaking to yourselves in psalms and **hymns** and
Col. 3:16	admonishing one another in psalms and **hymns** and spirit
Rev. 5:9	they **sung** a new song, saying, thou art worthy to take
Rev. 14:3(2-3)	and they sung as it were a new **song** before the throne
Rev. 15:3	and they **sing** the song of Moses the servant of God
1 Ne. 1:8	concourses of angels in the attitude of **singing** and
1 Ne. 21:13	**sing**, O heavens; and be joyful, O earth; for the feet
2 Ne. 4:17(16-35)	my heart **exclaimeth**: O wretched man that I am! Yea
2 Ne. 22:2	Jehovah is my strength and my **song**; he also has become
Mosiah 2:28	join the choirs above in **singing** the praises of a
Mosiah 12:22(22-23)	with the voice together shall they **sing**; for they
Mosiah 18:30	for they shall **sing** to his praise forever.
Mosiah 20:1	did gather themselves together to **sing**, and to dance
Alma 5:26	have felt to **sing** the song of redeeming love, I would
3 Ne. 22:1	break forth into **singing**, and cry aloud, thou that did
Morm. 7:7	to **sing** ceaseless praises with the choirs above, unto
Ether 6:9	the brother of Jared did **sing** praises unto the Lord
Moro. 6:9	the Holy Ghost led them...to **sing**, even so it was done
D&C 25:12(11-12)	the **song** of the righteous is a prayer unto me, and
D&C 66:11	with **songs** of everlasting joy upon their heads.
D&C 84:98(98-102)	with the voice together **sing** this new song, saying
D&C 101:18	with **songs** of everlasting joy, to build up the waste
D&C 109:39	with **songs** of everlasting joy
D&C 128:22	let the earth break forth into **singing**. Let the dead
D&C 133:33	and they shall be filled with **songs** of everlasting joy
D&C 133:56	they shall **sing** the song of the Lamb, day and night
D&C 136:28	praise the Lord with **singing**, with music, with dancing
Moses 7:53	they shall come forth with **songs** of everlasting joy.

SKILLS

Gen. 4:22	an instructer of every **artificer** in brass and iron
Ex. 31:5(1-6)	and in **cutting** of stones, to set them, and in carving
Ex. 36:8(8-38)	**made** ten curtains of fine twined linen, and blue, and
Ex. 37:1(1-29)	and Bezaleel **made** the ark of Shittim wood: two cubits
Ex. 38:1(1-31)	and he **made** the altar of burnt offering of Shittim
Ex. 39:1(1-43)	they **made** cloths of service, to do service in the holy
1 Kgs. 6:1(1-38)	he began to **build** the house of the Lord.
1 Kgs. 7:14(1-51)	widow's son...came...and **wrought** all his work.
Matt. 4:18	Simon...and Andrew...they were **fishers**.
Acts 18:3(1-3)	by their occupation they were **tentmakers**.
1 Thes. 4:11	do your own business, and to **work** with your own hands
1 Ne. 9:3(1-4)	that I should **make** these plates, for the special
1 Ne. 16:18(18-23)	bow, which was **made** of fine steel; and after I did
1 Ne. 17:16(16,17)	did **make** tools of the ore which I did molten out of

425

SKILLS cont.

2 Ne. 5:15(15-17)	I did teach my people to **build** buildings, and to work
Jarom 1:8	in buildings, and in **machinery**, and also in iron and
Alma 43:19(16-19)	**prepared** his people with breastplates and with
Alma 48:8(7-9)	erecting small forts...**building** walls of stone to
Alma 63:5(5-7)	Hagoth...**built** him an exceedingly large ship, on the
Hel. 3:7	exceeding **expert** in the working of cement; therefore
Ether 2:6(6,16,17)	and did **build** barges, in which they did cross many
Ether 3:1(1,4-6)	did **molten** out of a rock sixteen small stones; and the
Ether 10:23(23-28)	they did **work** in all manner of ore, and they did make
D&C 95:14(11-17)	**built** after the manner which I shall show unto three
D&C 109:4	the **workmanship** of the hands of us, thy servants
D&C 109:8	organize yourselves; **prepare** every needful thing, and

SLANDER

Ex. 20:16	thou shalt not bear **false** witness against thy
Ex. 23:1	not raise a **false** report: put not thine hand...to be
Neh. 6:13(12-14)	that they might have matter for an **evil** report, that
Ps. 31:13(11-13)	heard the **slander**...fear was on every side: while they
Ps. 35:11(11-14)	**false** witnesses did rise up; they laid to my charge
Ps. 50:20(19-21)	thy brother; thou **slanderest** thine own mother's son.
Ps. 101:5	whoso privily **slandereth** his neighbour, him will I cut
Prov. 6:19(16-19)	a **false** witness that speaketh lies, and he that soweth
Prov. 10:18	he that hideth hatred...and...uttereth a **slander**, is
Isa. 32:7	wicked devices to destroy the poor with **lying** words
Jer. 6:28	are all grievous revolters, walking with **slanders**: the
Jer. 9:4	every neighbour will walk with **slanders**.
Matt. 5:11	blessed...when men...say all manner of **evil** against
Matt. 26:59	sought false **witness** against Jesus, to put him to
Acts 6:13(11-13)	set up **false** witnesses, which said, this man ceaseth
Eph. 4:31	bitterness...evil **speaking**, be put away from you
1 Tim. 3:11(8-11)	must their wives be grave, not **slanderers**, sober
Titus 3:2	**speak** evil of no man, to be no brawlers, but gentle
1 Pet. 2:1	laying aside...all evil **speakings**
1 Pet. 3:10	let him refrain his **tongue** from evil, and his lips
Alma 12:4(2-6)	to **deceive** this people that thou mightest set them
Hel. 7:21(20,21)	bear **false** witness against your neighbor, and do all
D&C 20:54	neither lying, backbiting, nor **evil** speaking
D&C 42:27	thou shalt not **speak** evil of thy neighbor, nor do him
D&C 124:116	and lay aside all his hard **speeches**

SLAVERY

Rev. 18:13	horses, and chariots, and **slaves**, and souls of men.
1 Ne. 17:25(23-25)	children of Israel were in **bondage**; and ye know that
Mosiah 7:15	we will be their **slaves**; for it is better that we be
Mosiah 23:23(21-23)	they were brought into **bondage**, and none could deliver
Mosiah 24:9(8,9)	Amulon...put **task-masters** over them.
3 Ne. 3:7	not our **slaves**, but our brethren and partners of all
D&C 29:40(40-45)	became **subject** to the will of the devil, because he
D&C 98:8	God, make you **free**...the law also maketh you free.

SLAVERY cont.

D&C 101:79(79,80)	not right...any man...in **bondage** one to another.
D&C 134:12	government allowing human beings...held in **servitude**.

SLEEP

Ps. 127:2	to sit up late...for so he giveth his beloved **sleep**.
Prov. 6:9(9-11)	how long wilt thou **sleep**, O sluggard? when wilt thou
Prov. 24:33	yet a little **sleep**, a little slumber, a little folding
Eccl. 5:12	the **sleep** of a labouring man is sweet, whether he eat
Matt. 25:5(1-13)	while the bridegroom tarried, they all...**slept**.
Matt. 26:40(36-45)	disciples, and findeth them **asleep**, and saith unto
Mark 13:36(35-37)	lest coming suddenly he find you **sleeping**.
Rom. 13:11(11-13)	now it is high time to awake out of **sleep**: for now is
1 Thes. 5:6(6-8)	let us not **sleep**, as do others; but let us watch and
2 Ne. 1:13(13,14)	awake...even from the **sleep** of hell, and shake off
2 Ne. 27:5(4,5)	poured out upon you the spirit of deep **sleep**. For
Alma 5:7	he awakened them out of a deep **sleep**, and they awoke
Alma 37:37	the Lord, that he...watch over you in your **sleep**; and
Morm. 9:13	redemption from an endless **sleep**, from which sleep
D&C 88:124	cease to **sleep** longer than is needful; retire to thy

SOLEMN ASSEMBLY

Lev. 23:36	an holy convocation unto you..it is a **solemn** assembly
Num. 29:35	on the eighth day ye shall have a **solemn** assembly: ye
Deut. 16:8	on the seventh day shall be a **solemn** assembly to the
2 Kgs. 10:20	Jehu said, proclaim a **solemn** assembly for Baal.
2 Chr. 7:9	and in the eighth day they made a **solemn** assembly: for
Neh. 8:18	on the eighth day was a **solemn** assembly, according
Isa. 1:13(10-14)	incense is an abomination...even the **solemn** meeting.
Ezek. 45:17	give...offerings...in all **solemnities** of the house of
Ezek. 46:11	in the feast and in the **solemnities** the meat offering
Joel 1:14	sanctify ye a fast, call a **solemn** assembly, gather the
Joel 2:15(15-17)	sanctify a fast, call a **solemn** assembly
Amos 5:21	I will not smell in your **solemn** assemblies.
D&C 88:70(70-82)	call a **solemn** assembly, even of those who are the
D&C 95:7	commandment that you should call your **solemn** assembly
D&C 108:4	wait patiently until the **solemn** assembly shall be
D&C 109:6(6-10)	call your **solemn** assembly, as I have commanded you
D&C 124:39	and your **solemn** assemblies, and your memorials for you
D&C 133:6	call your **solemn** assemblies, and speak often one to

SONS AND DAUGHTERS OF GOD

Gen. 6:2(1-4)	the **sons** of God saw the daughters of men that they
Deut. 14:1	ye are the **children** of the Lord your God: ye shall not
Job 1:6	when the **sons** of God came to present themselves before
Job 38:7(1-7)	and all the **sons** of God shouted for joy
Ps. 82:6(1,6)	Gods; and all of you are **children** of the most High.

SONS AND DAUGHTERS OF GOD cont.

Isa. 45:11	saith the Lord...ask me...concerning my **sons**, and
Isa. 53:10	soul an offering for sin, he shall see his **seed**, he
Hosea 1:10(10-11)	ye are the **sons** of the living God.
Matt. 5:9	for they shall be called the **children** of God.
Matt. 5:45	that ye may be the **children** of your Father which is
Luke 20:36(34-36)	and are the **children** of God, being the children of the
John 1:12(10-13)	gave he power to become the **sons** of God, even to them
John 10:34(34-36)	is it not written in your law, I said, ye are **Gods**
John 11:52(49-52)	together in one the **children** of God that were
Acts 17:29	then as we are the **offspring** of God, we ought not to
Rom. 8:14(14-21)	led by the Spirit of God, they are the **sons** of God.
Rom. 9:4(4-8)	who are Israelites; to whom pertaineth the **adoption**
Rom. 9:8	these are not the **children** of God: but the children
Rom. 9:26(20-26)	they be called the **children** of the living God.
2 Cor. 6:18(17-18)	ye shall be my **sons** and daughters, saith the Lord
Gal. 3:26(26-29)	ye are all the **children** of God by faith in Christ
Gal. 4:7(4-7)	thou art no more a servant, but a **son**; and if a son
Eph. 1:5	having predestinated us unto the **adoption** of children
Eph. 2:19(12,19)	no more strangers...but...of the **household** of God
Philip. 2:15	blameless and harmless, the **sons** of God, without
Heb. 12:7(5-9)	God dealeth with you as with **sons**; for what son is he
1 Jn. 3:2(1-2)	now are we the **sons** of God, and it doth not yet appear
1 Jn. 5:2	we love the **children** of God, when we love God, and
Rev. 21:7	I will be his God, and he shall be my **son**.
Mosiah 5:7(7-9)	ye shall be called the **children** of Christ, his sons
Mosiah 15:13(10-13)	I say unto you that they are his **seed**.
Mosiah 27:25	being redeemed of God, becoming his **sons** and daughters
3 Ne. 9:17	to them have I given to become the **sons** of God; and
Ether 3:14	they shall become my **sons** and my daughters.
Moro. 7:19(19,48)	ye certainly will be a **child** of Christ.
Moro. 7:26(26,48)	they become the **sons** of God. And as sure as Christ
D&C 11:30(28-30)	to them will I give power to become the **sons** of God
D&C 25:1	all those who receive my gospel are **sons** and daughters
D&C 34:3	as many as would believe might become the **sons** of God.
D&C 35:2	become the **sons** of God, even one in me as I am one in
D&C 39:4(1-6)	gave I power to become my **sons**; and even so will I
D&C 42:52	they who...believe in me, have power to become my **sons**
D&C 45:8(8,9)	power...to become the **sons** of God; and even unto them
D&C 46:26	gifts...from God, for...benefit of the **children** of God
D&C 50:41(40-46)	fear not, little **children**, for you are mine, and I
D&C 58:17(17,51)	divide..lands of the heritage of God unto his **children**
D&C 76:24(23-24)	thereof are begotten **sons** and daughters unto God.
D&C 76:58(54-62)	written, they are gods, even the **sons** of God
D&C 128:23	let all the **sons** of God shout for joy! And let the
Moses 1:13(1-13)	I am a **son** of God, in the similitude of his Only
Moses 6:8	a genealogy was kept of the **children** of God. And this
Moses 6:22(22,27)	sons of Adam, who was the **son** of God, with whom God
Moses 6:68(64-68)	and thus may all become my **sons**. Amen.
Moses 7:1	many have believed and become the **sons** of God, and man
Moses 8:13(13-21)	gave heed, and they were called the **sons** of God.
JFS-V 1:39	glorious mother Eve, with...faithful **daughters** who had

428

SONS OF PERDITION

2 Thes. 1:9(8-10)	punished with everlasting **destruction** from the
Heb. 10:39	not of them who draw back unto **perdition**; but of them
2 Pet. 3:7	day of judgment and **perdition** of ungodly men.
Jude 1:6	the **angels** which kept not their first estate, but left
Rev. 12:4(3-4,7-8)	his tail drew the **third** part of the stars of heaven
2 Ne. 2:17(17-18)	an angel of God...had **fallen** from heaven...became a
2 Ne. 2:29(28-29)	to bring you down to **hell**, that he may reign over you
Jacob 6:10(8-10)	ye must go away into that lake of **fire** and brimstone
Jacob 7:19(14-19)	I fear lest I have committed the **unpardonable** sin, for
Mosiah 2:39(36-39)	final doom is to endure a never-ending **torment**.
Mosiah 16:5(2-7)	he is as though there was no **redemption** made, being
Alma 11:41	wicked remain as though there had been no **redemption**
Moro. 8:28	they are **denying** the Holy Ghost.
D&C 76:26	and was called **Perdition**, for the heavens wept over
D&C 76:43	except those sons of **perdition** who deny the Son after
D&C 84:41(41,42)	shall not have **forgiveness** of sins in this world nor
D&C 132:27	shall not be **forgiven** in the world nor out of the
Moses 4:3(1-4)	because...**Satan** rebelled...I caused...be cast down
Moses 5:24(23-24)	thou shalt be called **Perdition**; for thou wast also
Abr. 3:28(26-28)	second was angry, and kept not his first **estate**; and

SORCERY

Gen. 41:8(1-32)	**magicians** of Egypt, and all the wise men thereof: and
Ex. 7:11(8-12)	Pharaoh also called...the **sorcerers**: now the magicians
Ex. 22:18(16-20)	thou shalt not suffer a **witch** to live.
Lev. 19:31(26,31)	regard not them that have familiar **spirits**, neither
Lev. 20:6(6,27)	soul that turneth after such as have familiar **spirits**
Deut. 18:10(9-14)	there shall not be found among you...an **enchanter**, or
Josh. 13:22	the **soothsayer**, did the children of Israel slay with
1 Sam. 28:3(3-19)	Saul had put away those that had **familiar** spirits, and
2 Kgs. 17:17(16-18)	used **divination** and enchantments, and sold themselves
2 Kgs. 23:24	workers with **familiar** spirits...did Josiah put away
Isa. 2:6	because they...are **soothsayers** like the Philistines
Isa. 8:19(19-20)	shall say...seek unto them that have **familiar** spirits
Isa. 19:3	they shall seek...to them that have **familiar** spirits
Isa. 47:13(9-15)	let now the **astrologers**, the stargazers...save thee
Jer. 27:9(9-10)	hearken not..to your enchanters, nor to your **sorcerers**
Ezek. 12:24	there shall be no more...flattering **divination** within
Ezek. 13:23	ye shall see no more vanity, nor...**divinations**: for I
Dan. 1:20(17-20)	ten times better than all the **magicians** and astrologers
Dan. 2:27(2-28)	the secret...cannot...the **astrologers**, the magicians
Dan. 4:7	came in the **magicians**, the astrologers, the Chaldeans
Dan. 5:7(7-11)	bring in the **astrologers**, the Chaldeans, and the
Dan. 5:15(13-16)	**astrologers**...could not shew the interpretation of the
Micah 5:12	thou shalt have no more **soothsayers**
Mal. 3:5	I will be a swift witness against the **sorcerers**, and
Acts 8:9(9-24)	Simon...used **sorcery**, and bewitched the people of
Acts 13:6(6-11)	they found a certain **sorcerer**, a false prophet, a Jew
Acts 16:16(16-18)	brought her masters much gain by **soothsaying**
Acts 19:13(13-15)	**exorcists**, took upon them to call over them which had
Acts 19:19(18-20)	many...used curious **arts** brought their books together

SORCERY cont.

Rev. 9:21	neither repented they of their...**sorceries**, nor of the
Rev. 18:23	by thy **sorceries** were all nations deceived.
Rev. 21:8	**sorcerers**...shall have their part in the lake which
Rev. 22:15(14-16)	for without are dogs, and **sorcerers**, and whoremongers
2 Ne. 12:6	unto **soothsayers** like the Philistines, and they please
2 Ne. 18:19(19,20)	shall say...seek unto them that have **familiar** spirits
Alma 1:32	did indulge themselves in **sorceries**, and in idolatry
3 Ne. 21:16	and I will cut off **witchcrafts** out of thy land, and
3 Ne. 24:5	I will be a swift witness against the **sorcerers**, and
Morm. 1:19(14,19)	there were **sorceries**, and witchcrafts, and magics; and
D&C 28:11(11-13)	those things...from that **stone** are not of me, and that
D&C 46:7(7-9)	not be seduced by evil **spirits**, or doctrines of devils
D&C 50:1(1-46)	the **spirits** which have gone abroad in the earth.
D&C 63:17	**sorcerer**, shall have their part in that lake which
D&C 76:103(102-106)	liars, and **sorcerers**, and adulterers, and whoremongers

SORROW

Gen. 3:16(16-17)	I will greatly multiply thy **sorrow** and thy conception
Deut. 28:65	Lord shall give thee...**sorrow** of mind
Prov. 15:13	by **sorrow** of the heart the spirit is broken.
Eccl. 1:18	increaseth knowledge increaseth **sorrow**.
Isa. 29:2(1-4)	there shall be heaviness and **sorrow**: and it shall be
Isa. 35:10(7-10)	**sorrow** and sighing shall flee away.
Isa. 50:11	walk in the light of your fire...lie down in **sorrow**.
Isa. 53:3(3-4)	a man of **sorrows**, and acquainted with grief: and we
Isa. 57:18	restore comforts unto him and to his **mourners**.
Isa. 61:2(2,3)	to comfort all that **mourn**
Jer. 20:18	came I forth out of the womb to see labour and **sorrow**
Jer. 31:12	they shall not **sorrow** any more at all.
Jer. 49:24	anguish and **sorrows** have taken her, as a woman in
Hosea 13:13	the **sorrows** of a travailing woman shall come upon him
Matt. 5:4	blessed are they that **mourn**: for they shall be
Matt. 24:8(7-8)	all these are the beginning of **sorrows**.
Matt. 26:38	my soul is exceeding **sorrowful**, even unto death: tarry
John 14:27(1,27)	let not your heart be **troubled**, neither let it be
John 16:22(6,22)	ye now...have **sorrow**: but I will see you again, and
Rom. 2:9	tribulation and **anguish**, upon every soul of man that
Rom. 7:24(15-25)	O **wretched** man that I am! who shall deliver me from
2 Cor. 7:10(6-16)	for godly **sorrow** worketh repentance to salvation not
1 Thes. 4:13	**sorrow** not, even as others which have no hope.
1 Tim. 6:10	erred...pierced themselves through with many **sorrows**.
Rev. 21:4	there shall be no more death, neither **sorrow**, nor
1 Ne. 17:47	behold, my soul is rent with **anguish** because of you
2 Ne. 4:17(16-28)	my heart **sorroweth** because of my flesh; my soul
2 Ne. 26:7	O the pain, and the **anguish** of my soul for the loss
Mosiah 2:38(36-41)	fill his breast with guilt, and pain, and **anguish**
Mosiah 3:7(5-8)	so great shall be his **anguish** for the wickedness and
Mosiah 25:11	they were filled with pain and **anguish** for the welfare
Mosiah 27:29(23-32)	my soul was racked with eternal **torment**; but I am
Alma 8:14(13-16)	being weighed down with **sorrow**, wading through much
Alma 38:8	most bitter pain and **anguish** of soul; and never, until

SORROW cont.

Alma 40:12(11-14)	from all their troubles and from all care, and **sorrow**.
3 Ne. 12:4	blessed are all they that **mourn**, for they shall be
3 Ne. 28:9(6-10)	neither **sorrow** save it be for the sins of the world
Morm. 2:13(13,14)	it was rather the **sorrowing** of the damned, because the
Morm. 5:11(9-11)	they will **sorrow** for the destruction of this people
Morm. 6:16(13-16)	my soul was rent with **anguish**, because of the slain
D&C 1:3	rebellious shall be pierced with much **sorrow**; for
D&C 101:29(22-38)	there shall be no **sorrow** because there is no death.
D&C 109:48(45-51)	our hearts flow out with **sorrow** because of their
D&C 122:5(5-9)	if thou art called to pass through **tribulation**; if
D&C 123:7(1-7)	bow down with grief, **sorrow**, and care, under the most
D&C 124:52	judgment, wrath, and indignation, wailing, and **anguish**
D&C 133:70	have of my hand- ye shall lie down in **sorrow**.
D&C 136:29	if thou art **sorrowful**, call on the Lord thy God with
D&C 136:35(34-36)	their **sorrow** shall be great unless they...repent, yea
Moses 4:22(22-23)	I will greatly multiply thy **sorrow** and thy conception.

SOUL

Gen. 2:7	God formed man of the dust...man became a living **soul**.
Ps. 22:29	and none can keep alive his own **soul**.
Isa. 55:3	hear, and your **soul** shall live; and I will make an
Matt. 10:28	fear him which is able to destroy both **soul** and body
Matt. 16:26	gain the whole world, and lose his own **soul**? or what
Luke 12:20(15-21)	this night thy **soul** shall be required of thee: then
1 Pet. 1:22	ye have purified your **souls** in obeying the truth
1 Ne. 15:35	the final state of the **souls** of men is to dwell in the
Alma 40:7(7-23)	what becometh of the **souls** of men from this time of
Alma 40:11	state of the **soul** between death and the resurrection
Alma 40:23(22-24)	**soul** shall be restored to the body, and the body to
D&C 4:4	but bringeth salvation to his **soul**
D&C 15:6	declare repentance...that you may bring **souls** unto me
D&C 18:10	the worth of **souls** is great in the sight of God
D&C 18:16(14-16)	great...joy if you should bring many **souls** unto me
D&C 41:12	words...to be answered upon your **souls** in the day of
D&C 56:16	your riches will canker your **souls**; and this shall be
D&C 84:64	every **soul** who believeth on your words, and is
D&C 88:15	and the spirit and the body are the **soul** of man.
D&C 101:37	care for the **soul**, and for the life of the soul.
D&C 121:42(41-45)	which shall greatly enlarge the **soul** without hypocrisy
Moses 3:7(7-9)	man became a living **soul**, the first flesh upon the
Moses 6:9	they were created and became living **souls** in the land
Abr. 5:7	and man became a living **soul**.

SPIRIT BODY

Num. 16:22	God of the **spirits** of all flesh, shall one man sin
Num. 27:16	God of the **spirits** of all flesh, set a man over the
1 Kgs. 17:21(21-23)	let this child's **soul** come into him again.
Job 32:8	there is a **spirit** in man: and the inspiration of the
Eccl. 12:7	the **spirit** shall return unto God who gave it.

SPIRIT BODY cont.

Heb. 12:9	subjection unto the Father of **spirits**, and live
James 2:26	the body without the **spirit** is dead, so faith without
1 Pet. 3:19(19,20)	also he went and preached unto the **spirits** in prison
1 Ne. 11:11	**form** of a man...it was the Spirit of the Lord; and he
2 Ne. 9:12	the bodies and the **spirits** of men will be restored one
Mosiah 2:28	my immortal **spirit** may join the choirs above in
Alma 11:45(43,45)	their **spirits** uniting with their bodies, never to be
Alma 40:11	**spirits** of all men, as soon as they are departed from
Ether 3:16(14-17)	which ye now behold, is the **body** of my spirit; and man
Moro. 10:34	until my **spirit** and body shall again reunite, and I
D&C 45:17	the long absence of your **spirits** from your bodies to
D&C 76:73	**spirits** of men kept in prison, whom the Son visited
D&C 77:2	the **spirit** of man in the likeness of his person, as
D&C 88:15	and the **spirit** and the body are the soul of man.
D&C 88:28	celestial **spirit** shall receive the same body which was
D&C 88:100	**spirits** of men who are to be judged, and are found
D&C 93:33	**spirit** and element, inseparably connected, receive a
D&C 93:38	every **spirit** of man was innocent in the beginning; and
D&C 129:3(1-9)	**spirits** of just men made perfect...not resurrected
D&C 130:22	Holy Ghost...is a personage of **spirit**. Were it not so
D&C 131:7(7-8)	all **spirit** is matter, but it is more fine or pure
Moses 6:36(35,36)	he beheld the **spirits** that God had created; and he
Abr. 3:18	**spirits**...have no beginning; they existed before, they
Abr. 5:7	and took his **spirit** (that is, the man's spirit), and

SPIRIT CREATION

Gen. 2:5(4-5)	every plant of the field **before** it was in the earth
Num. 16:22	God of the **spirits** of all flesh, shall one man sin
Job 32:8	but there is a **spirit** in man: and the inspiration of
Ps. 82:6	all of you are **children** of the most High.
Eccl. 12:7	and the **spirit** shall return unto God who gave it.
Isa. 42:5	and **spirit** to them that walk therein
Hosea 1:10	ye are the **sons** of the living God.
Acts 17:29(28,29)	we are the **offspring** of God, we ought not to think
Rom. 8:16(16,17)	our **spirit**, that we are the children of God
Heb. 12:9	in subjection unto the Father of **spirits**, and live
Alma 40:11	the **spirits** of all men, as soon as they are departed
D&C 29:32(31-33)	first **spiritual**, secondly temporal, which is the
D&C 77:2	temporal in the likeness of that which is **spiritual**
D&C 88:15	the **spirit** and the body are the soul of man.
D&C 93:33(33-36)	for man is **spirit**. The elements are eternal, and
D&C 131:7	all **spirit** is matter, but it is more fine or pure
Moses 3:5(5,7,9)	created all things...**spiritually**, before...naturally
Moses 6:36(35,36)	he beheld the **spirits** that God had created; and he
Moses 6:51	I made...world, and men **before** they were in the flesh.
Abr. 3:18(18-19)	**spirits**...have no beginning; they existed before, they
Abr. 3:22(22-24)	the **intelligences** that were organized before the world
Abr. 3:23(22-24)	for he stood among those that were **spirits**, and he saw
Abr. 5:5(1-5)	every plant of the field before it was in the **earth**

SPIRITS, DISEMBODIED

Gen. 49:33	he...yielded up the **ghost**, and was gathered unto his
Ps. 142:7	bring my **soul** out of prison, that I may praise thy
Eccl. 12:7	the **spirit** shall return unto God who gave it.
Mark 15:37	Jesus cried with a loud voice, and gave up the **ghost**.
Luke 20:38	he is not a God of the **dead**, but of the living: for
Luke 23:43(39-43)	to day shalt thou be with me in **paradise**.
Luke 24:39(36-39)	a **spirit** hath not flesh and bones, as ye see me have.
John 5:25(25-26)	**dead** shall hear the voice of the Son...and...live.
Acts 7:59	Stephen, calling upon God...saying...receive my **spirit**
Heb. 12:23	and to the **spirits** of just men made perfect
James 2:26	the body without the **spirit** is dead, so faith without
1 Pet. 3:19(18-19)	also he went and preached unto the **spirits** in prison
1 Pet. 4:6	the gospel preached also to them that are **dead**, that
Rev. 14:13	the **dead** which die in the Lord...may rest from their
Rev. 20:5(4-5)	**dead** lived not again until the thousand years were
2 Ne. 9:12(12-13)	hell must deliver up its captive **spirits**, and the
Alma 40:11(11,13,15)	the state of the **soul** between death and the
D&C 45:17	absence of your **spirits** from your bodies...a bondage
D&C 76:73(71-73)	the **spirits** of men kept in prison, whom the Son
D&C 88:101	the **dead**...live not again until the thousand years are
D&C 93:34(33-34)	**separated**, man cannot receive a fulness of joy.
D&C 129:3(1-8)	the **spirits** of just men made perfect, they who are not
Moses 7:38(38,39)	these...shall perish...a **prison** have I prepared for
Moses 7:57	as many of the **spirits** as were in prison came forth
JFS-V 1:11(11-60)	I saw the hosts of the **dead**, both small and great.
JFS-V 1:50(11-60)	long absence of their **spirits** from their bodies as a

SPIRITS, EVIL, UNCLEAN

Lev. 19:31	regard not them that have **familiar** spirits, neither
Lev. 20:6	soul that turneth after...**familiar** spirits, and after
Lev. 20:27	hath a **familiar** spirit...shall surely be put to death
Deut. 18:11(10-13)	or a charmer, or a consulter with **familiar** spirits
1 Sam. 16:23(14-23)	the **evil** spirit from God was upon Saul, that David too
1 Sam. 28:7(3-14)	said Saul..seek me a woman that hath a **familiar** spirit
2 Kgs. 21:6(1-6)	dealt with **familiar** spirits and wizards: he wrought
2 Kgs. 23:24	workers with **familiar** spirits...did Josiah put away
1 Chr. 10:13(13,14)	Saul died...asking counsel of...a **familiar** spirit, to
2 Chr. 33:6(1-6)	and dealt with a **familiar** spirit, and with wizards
Ps. 78:49	and trouble, by sending **evil** angels among them.
Isa. 8:19	seek unto them that have **familiar** spirits, and unto
Matt. 8:16(16,17)	he cast out the **spirits** with his word, and healed all
Matt. 8:28(28-33)	there met him two possessed with **devils**, coming out
Matt. 10:1	he gave them power against **unclean** spirits, to cast
Matt. 12:26(22-30)	if **Satan** cast out Satan, he is divided against himself
Matt. 12:45(43-45)	seven other **spirits** more wicked than himself, and they
Mark 1:23(23-27)	a man with an **unclean** spirit; and he cried out
Mark 1:34(32-34)	cast out many **devils**; and suffered not the devils to
Mark 3:11	**unclean** spirits, when they saw him, fell down before
Mark 5:8(2-13)	come out of the man, thou **unclean** spirit.
Mark 9:25(17-29)	he rebuked the **foul** spirit, saying unto him, thou
Mark 16:17	in my name shall they cast out **devils**; they shall

SPIRITS, EVIL, UNCLEAN cont.

Luke 6:18	vexed with **unclean** spirits: and they were healed.
Luke 9:55	ye know not what manner of **spirit** ye are of.
Acts 8:7	**unclean** spirits, crying with loud voice, came out of
Acts 16:18(16-18)	said to the **spirit**, I command thee in the name of
Acts 19:15(11-17)	the **evil** spirit answered and said, Jesus I know, and
1 Tim. 4:1(1-3)	giving heed to **seducing** spirits, and doctrines of
2 Pet. 2:4	God spared not the **angels** that sinned, but cast them
1 Jn. 4:1(1-3)	try the **spirits** whether they are of God: because many
Jude 1:6	the **angels** which kept not their first estate, but left
1 Ne. 11:31	diseases, and with devils and **unclean** spirits; and the
2 Ne. 32:8	for the **evil** spirit teacheth not a man to pray, but
Mosiah 2:37(32,37)	open rebellion...he listeth to obey the **evil** spirit
Mosiah 3:6	the **evil** spirits which dwell in the hearts of the
Mosiah 4:14	who is the **evil** spirit which hath been spoken of by
Alma 3:26(26,27)	the **spirit** which they listed to obey, whether it be
3 Ne. 7:19(17-19)	in the name of Jesus did he cast out...**unclean** spirits
D&C 46:7(7-9)	may not be seduced by evil **spirits**, or doctrines of
D&C 50:2(1-8)	there are many spirits which are false **spirits**, which
D&C 50:31(31-33)	a **spirit** manifested that you cannot understand, and
D&C 129:8(1-9)	**devil** as an angel of light, when you ask him to shake
Moses 1:21(12-24)	name of the Only Begotten, depart hence, **Satan**.

SPIRITS IN PRISON

Ps. 16:10	for thou wilt not leave my soul in **hell**; neither wilt
Isa. 14:15(9-17)	yet thou shalt be brought down to **hell**, to the sides
Isa. 24:22(17-23)	as **prisoners** are gathered in the pit, and shall be
Isa. 49:9	that thou mayest say to the **prisoners**, go forth; to
Isa. 61:1(1,2)	the opening of the **prison** to them that are bound
Ezek. 32:18(18-32)	cast them down...unto the **nether** parts of the earth
Luke 4:18(18-21)	to preach deliverance to the **captives**, and recovering
Luke 16:23(19-31)	in **hell** he lift up his eyes, being in torments, and
1 Pet. 3:19(18-20)	he went and preached unto the **spirits** in prison
1 Pet. 4:6(5,6)	gospel preached also to them that are **dead**, that they
Rev. 20:13	death and **hell** delivered up the dead which were in the
1 Ne. 21:9	that thou mayest say to the **prisoners**: go forth; to
2 Ne. 9:12(10-16)	hell must deliver up its **captive** spirits, and the
2 Ne. 9:26(25,26)	have not the law...delivered from...**hell**, and the
Alma 40:13(11-14)	**spirits**...shall be cast out into outer darkness; there
Alma 40:14(11-14)	the state of the **souls** of the wicked, yea, in darkness
D&C 38:5(5,6)	residue of the wicked...kept in **chains** of darkness
D&C 76:73(71-79)	the **spirits** of men kept in prison, whom the Son
D&C 88:100(99-101)	**spirits** of men...are found under condemnation
D&C 128:22	redeem them out of their **prison**; for the prisoners
Moses 7:38(38-40)	I will shut them up; a **prison** have I prepared for them
Moses 7:57	spirits...in **prison** came forth, and stood on the right
JFS-V 1:20(20-22)	but unto the **wicked** he did not go, and among the
JFS-V 1:28	said...Son of God preached unto...**spirits** in prison
JFS-V 1:29(29-37)	Lord went not in person among the **wicked** and the
JFS-V 1:42	and the opening of the **prison** to them that were bound
JFS-V 1:57(57-60)	among those who are in darkness...world of...**spirits**

SPIRITUAL BLINDNESS

Deut. 16:19(18-20)	for a gift doth **blind** the eyes of the wise, and
Ps. 69:23	let their eyes be darkened, that they **see** not; and
Isa. 6:10(9-10)	make their ears heavy, and **shut** their eyes; lest they
Isa. 29:10(9-10)	Lord hath...closed your **eyes**: the prophets and your
Isa. 42:20(13-23)	**seeing** many things, but thou observest not; opening
Ezek. 12:2	which have eyes to see, and **see** not; they have ears
Matt. 13:15(13-16)	ears are dull of hearing...their **eyes** they have closed
Matt. 15:14(12-14)	they be **blind** leaders of the blind. And if the blind
Matt. 23:16(1-33)	ye **blind** guides, which say, whosoever shall swear by
Mark 4:12(11-12)	that seeing they may see, and not **perceive**; and
John 9:41(31-41)	if ye were **blind**, ye should have no sin: but now ye
John 12:40(29-41)	he hath **blinded** their eyes, and hardened their heart
Acts 28:27(25-27)	ears are dull of hearing...their **eyes** have they closed
2 Cor. 3:14(12-14)	their minds were **blinded**: for until this day remaineth
2 Cor. 4:4(3,4)	the God of this world hath **blinded** the minds of them
Eph. 4:18(17-29)	ignorance...because of the **blindness** of their heart
1 Tim. 4:2(1-2)	having their **conscience** seared with a hot iron
2 Ne. 9:32(28-32)	wo unto the **blind** that will not see...shall perish
2 Ne. 27:5(4-5)	for behold, ye have closed your **eyes**, and ye have
2 Ne. 30:6(4-7)	**scales** of darkness shall begin to fall from their eyes
2 Ne. 33:2(1-2)	many that harden their **hearts** against the Holy Spirit
Jacob 4:14(13,14)	**blindness** came by looking beyond the mark, they must
Alma 13:4(4-5)	hardness of their hearts and **blindness** of their minds
Alma 30:15(12-53)	ye cannot know of things which ye do not **see**
D&C 38:8(5-12)	ye shall see me...**veil** of darkness shall soon be rent
D&C 76:75(71-80)	honorable men...were **blinded** by the craftiness of men.
D&C 78:10	hearts away from the truth, that they become **blinded**
D&C 123:12	**blinded** by the subtle craftiness of men, whereby they
Moses 5:13(12-13)	Satan came...saying: **believe** it not; and they believed

SPIRITUALITY

Job 32:8	the **inspiration** of the Almighty giveth them
Isa. 55:9(8,9)	my **ways** higher than your ways, and my thoughts than
Ezek. 11:19(19-21)	and I will put a new **spirit** within you; and I will
Ezek. 36:26(24-28)	a new **spirit** will I put within you: and I will take
Rom. 7:22(12-23)	for I **delight** in the law of God after the inward man
Rom. 8:6	death; but to be **spiritually** minded is life and peace.
1 Cor. 2:14(9-14)	because they are **spiritually** discerned.
Gal. 5:22(18-23)	the fruit of the **Spirit** is love, joy, peace
Eph. 1:3	who hath blessed us with all **spiritual** blessings in
1 Pet. 2:5	ye...are built up a **spiritual** house...offer...
2 Ne. 4:16(16-35)	behold, my **soul** delighteth in the things of the Lord
2 Ne. 9:39	death, and to be **spiritually-minded** is life eternal.
Mosiah 3:19	putteth off the natural man and becometh a **saint**
Mosiah 4:11(9-12)	if ye have **known** of his goodness and have tasted of
Mosiah 5:7(2-9)	ye say that your hearts are **changed** through faith on
Mosiah 18:10	may pour out his **spirit** more abundantly upon you
Alma 5:14(14-33)	have ye **spiritually** been born of God? Have ye receive
Alma 13:10	ordained...on account of their...**repentance**, and their
3 Ne. 12:6(3,6)	they shall be **filled** with the Holy Ghost.
3 Ne. 18:7	always remember me ye shall have my **Spirit** to be with

SPIRITUALITY cont.

3 Ne. 27:27	therefore, what **manner** of men ought ye to be? Verily
Moro. 5:2	always remember him, that they may have his **Spirit** to
D&C 20:37	manifest by...works that they...received of the **Spirit**
D&C 88:67	eye..single...whole bodies shall be filled with **light**
D&C 121:46(45-46)	the Holy Ghost shall be thy constant **companion**, and
Moses 7:18	one heart and one mind, and dwelt in **righteousness**

STAKES

Isa. 33:20	not one of the **stakes** thereof shall ever be removed
Isa. 54:2	lengthen thy cords, and strengthen thy **stakes**
3 Ne. 22:2	lengthen thy cords and strengthen thy **stakes**
Moro. 10:31	strengthen thy **stakes** and enlarge thy borders forever
D&C 68:25(25-26)	or in any of her **stakes** which are organized, that
D&C 82:14(13-14)	her borders must be enlarged; her **stakes** must be
D&C 101:21(17-21)	called **stakes**, for the curtains or the strength of
D&C 115:6(5-6)	the land of Zion, and upon her **stakes**, may be for a
D&C 115:18	other places should be appointed for **stakes** in the
D&C 124:134	presidents or servants over different **stakes** scattered
D&C 133:9	that her **stakes** may be strengthened, and that Zion may

STEADFASTNESS

Ruth 1:18(16-18)	she was **stedfastly** minded to go with her, then she
Job 2:9(7-10)	dost thou still retain thine **integrity**? curse God, and
Job 27:5(3-6)	I will not remove mine **integrity** from me.
Ps. 78:37	neither were they **stedfast** in his covenant.
Dan. 6:26	for he is the living God, and **stedfast** for ever, and
Matt. 10:22	he that **endureth** to the end shall be saved.
Matt. 24:13	but he that shall **endure** unto the end...shall be saved
John 8:31(31-32)	if ye **continue** in my word, then are ye my disciples
Acts 2:42(37-42)	and they continued **stedfastly** in the apostles
1 Cor. 15:58	brethren, be ye **stedfast**, unmoveable, always abounding
Gal. 6:9	let us not be **weary** in well doing: for in due season
Philip. 3:14(13-14)	I **press** toward the mark for the prize of the high call
Heb. 3:14	if we hold...our confidence **stedfast** unto the end
Heb. 12:7(5-11)	if ye **endure** chastening, God dealeth with you as with
James 1:12	blessed is the man that **endureth** temptation: for when
James 5:11(10-11)	we count them happy which **endure**. Ye have heard of the
1 Pet. 1:23(23-25)	word of God, which liveth and **abideth** for ever.
1 Pet. 5:9(8-10)	whom resist **stedfast** in the faith, knowing that the
2 Pet. 3:17	beware lest ye...fall from your own **stedfastness**.
1 Ne. 13:37	if they **endure** unto the end they shall be lifted up
2 Ne. 26:8	look forward unto Christ with **steadfastness** for the
2 Ne. 31:20(19-20)	ye must press forward with a **steadfastness** in Christ
Mosiah 4:11	standing **steadfastly** in the faith of that which is to
Mosiah 4:30	and **continue** in the faith of what ye have heard
Mosiah 5:15	I would that ye should be **steadfast** and immovable
Alma 1:25(24,25)	they were **steadfast**...in keeping the commandments of
Alma 5:48	who **steadfastly** believeth on his name.
Alma 34:40(39-41)	I would exhort you to have **patience**, and that ye bear

STEADFASTNESS cont.

Alma 48:15(15-20)	and this was their **faith**, that by so doing God would
Hel. 10:4(4,5)	thou hast with **unwearyingness** declared the word, which
Hel. 15:10(8-10)	because of their **steadfastness** when they do believe
3 Ne. 27:16(16-17)	if he **endureth** to the end...him will I hold guiltless
D&C 6:13	do good, yea, and hold out **faithful** to the end, thou
D&C 14:7	keep my commandments and **endure** to the end you shall
D&C 18:22	as many as...**endure** to the end, the same shall be
D&C 24:8(7-8)	**endure** them, for, lo, I am with thee, even unto the
D&C 31:9	govern your house in meekness, and be **steadfast**.
D&C 31:13(12-13)	be **faithful** unto the end, and lo, I am with you. These
D&C 58:2(2-4)	he that is **faithful** in tribulation, the reward of the
D&C 59:4(3-4)	they that are **faithful** and diligent before me.
D&C 63:20	he that **endureth** in faith and doeth my will, the same
D&C 81:6	if thou art **faithful** unto the end thou shalt have a
D&C 84:61	remain **steadfast** in your minds in solemnity and the
D&C 103:36	all victory and glory is...through your...**faithfulness**
D&C 107:99(99,100)	act in the office ...in all **diligence**.
A of F 1:13	and hope to be able to **endure** all things. If there is

STEALING

Ex. 20:15	thou shalt not **steal**.
Ex. 21:16	and he that **stealeth** a man, and selleth him, or if he
Ex. 22:1(1-5)	if a man shall **steal** an ox...he shall restore five
Lev. 19:11	ye shall not **steal**, neither deal falsely, neither lie
Deut. 5:19	neither shalt thou **steal**.
Deut. 24:7	if a man be found **stealing**...that thief shall die; and
Prov. 6:30(30,31)	men do not despise a thief, if he **steal** to satisfy his
Hosea 4:2(1-3)	by swearing, and lying, and killing, and **stealing**, and
Zech. 5:3	every one that **stealeth** shall be cut off as on this
Mal. 3:8	will a man **rob** God? yet ye have robbed me. But ye say
Matt. 6:20(19,20)	where thieves do not break through nor **steal**
Matt. 19:18	thou shalt not **steal**, thou shalt not bear false
Mark 7:22(21-22)	**thefts**, covetousness, wickedness, deceit
Mark 10:19	do not **steal**, do not bear false witness, defraud not
John 10:10	the thief cometh not, but for to **steal**, and to kill
Rom. 2:21(20-24)	thou that preachest a man should not **steal**, dost thou
Rom. 13:9(8-10)	thou shalt not **steal**, thou shalt not bear false
1 Cor. 6:10(9,10)	nor **thieves**...shall inherit the kingdom of God.
Eph. 4:28	let him that stole **steal** no more: but rather let him
Titus 2:10(9,10)	not **purloining**, but shewing all good fidelity; that
2 Ne. 26:32	that they should not lie...should not **steal**; that they
Mosiah 2:13	nor that ye should...plunder, or **steal**, or commit
Mosiah 13:22	not commit adultery. thou shalt not **steal**.
Mosiah 29:14(14,36)	there should be...no **stealing**, nor plundering, nor
Alma 1:18	they durst not **steal**, for fear of the law, for such
Alma 16:18	did preach against all...revilings, and **stealing**
Alma 23:3	ought not to murder, nor to plunder, nor to **steal**, nor
Hel. 4:12	lying, **stealing**, committing adultery, rising up in
Hel. 6:21(21-23)	should not suffer for their murders, and...**stealings**.
Hel. 7:5	might the more easily commit adultery, and **steal**, and
3 Ne. 13:19(19,20)	corrupt, and thieves break through and **steal**

STEALING cont.

3 Ne. 27:32	which thieves can break through and **steal**. And in
D&C 42:20	he that **stealeth** and will not repent shall be cast out
D&C 42:85	and if he or she shall **steal**, he or she shall be
D&C 59:6	thou shalt not **steal**; neither commit adultery, nor
JS-H 1:60	exertions were used to **get** them from me. Every

STEWARDSHIP

Gen. 26:5(4,5)	Abraham...kept my **charge**, my commandments, my statutes
Ex. 6:13(10-13)	Lord spake unto Moses...Aaron...gave...**charge** unto the
Num. 4:4(1-49)	this shall be the **service** of the sons of Kohath in the
Num. 27:23(18-23)	laid his hands upon him, and gave him a **charge**, as the
Ps. 50:12(10-12)	for the **world** is mine, and the fulness thereof.
Matt. 18:23	king, which would take **account** of his servants.
Matt. 21:33(33-41)	let it out to **husbandmen**, and went into a far country
Matt. 24:45(43-47)	who then is a faithful and wise **servant**, whom his Lord
Matt. 25:21(14-30)	I will make thee **ruler** over many things: enter thou
Luke 12:42(41-48)	who then is that faithful and wise **steward**, whom his
Luke 12:48	unto whomsoever much is **given**, of him shall be much
Luke 16:2(1-8)	give an account of thy **stewardship**; for thou mayest
Luke 19:17(12-26)	thou hast been **faithful** in a very little, have thou
1 Cor. 4:2(1-2)	it is required in **stewards**, that a man be found
1 Tim. 4:14	neglect not the **gift**...given thee by prophecy, with
Titus 1:7(7-9)	bishop must be blameless, as the **steward** of God; not
1 Pet. 4:10	minister the same one to another, as good **stewards** of
Jacob 1:19(17-19)	taking upon us the **responsibility**, answering the sins
Jacob 2:2	the **responsibility** which I am under to God, to
Alma 35:16	give unto them every one his **charge**, separately
D&C 42:32(32-34)	every man shall be...a **steward** over his own property
D&C 42:70	the priests and teachers shall have their **stewardships**
D&C 51:19	a wise **steward** shall enter into the joy of his Lord
D&C 64:40	if...not faithful in their **stewardships** shall be
D&C 69:5	servants...send...the accounts of their **stewardships**
D&C 70:4(3,4)	account of this **stewardship** will I require of them in
D&C 70:9(7-12)	what the Lord requires of every man in his **stewardship**
D&C 72:3(1-4,16-26)	is required...to render an account of his **stewardship**
D&C 78:22	faithful and wise **steward** shall inherit all things.
D&C 82:3	unto whom much is **given** much is required; and he who
D&C 82:11(11-20)	judgment...follow, in your several **stewardships**
D&C 101:55(55-62)	Lord of the vineyard said unto one of his **servants**
D&C 101:90	cut off...wicked, unfaithful, and unjust **stewards**, and
D&C 104:11(11-86)	organize yourselves..appoint every man his **stewardship**
D&C 124:14	his **stewardship** will I require at his hands.
D&C 136:27	be diligent...that thou mayest be a wise **steward**; for

STIFFNECKEDNESS

Ex. 32:9	behold, it is a **stiffnecked** people
Ex. 33:5(3,5)	ye are a **stiffnecked** people: I will come up into the
Ex. 34:9	for it is a **stiffnecked** people; and pardon our
Num. 22:32(31-34)	because thy way is **perverse** before me

STIFFNECKEDNESS cont.

Deut. 9:6(6,13)	for thou art a **stiffnecked** people.
Deut. 10:16	circumcise...your heart, and be no more **stiffnecked**.
Deut. 31:27(24-30)	for I know thy rebellion, and thy **stiff** neck: behold
1 Sam. 15:23(22-23)	**stubbornness** is as iniquity and idolatry. Because
2 Chr. 30:8(8-9)	now be ye not **stiffnecked**, as your fathers were, but
2 Chr. 36:13(11-13)	but he **stiffened** his neck, and hardened his heart from
Ps. 75:5(4-6)	speak not with a **stiff** neck.
Isa. 30:1(1-3)	woe to the **rebellious** children, saith the Lord, that
Isa. 48:4(1-5)	thou art obstinate, and thy **neck** is an iron sinew, and
Jer. 17:23	made their neck **stiff**, that they might not hear, nor
Ezek. 2:4(3-5)	they are impudent children and **stiffhearted**. I do send
Mark 16:14	their unbelief and **hardness** of heart, because they
Acts 7:51(51-54)	ye **stiffnecked** and uncircumcised in heart and ears
Rom. 2:5(1-5)	thy **hardness** and impenitent heart treasurest up unto
Heb. 3:12	an evil heart of **unbelief**, in departing from the
Rev. 21:8	but the fearful, and **unbelieving**, and the abominable
1 Ne. 2:11(9-14)	he spake because of the **stiffneckedness** of Laman and
2 Ne. 6:10(8-11)	after they have...**stiffened** their necks against the
2 Ne. 10:5(3-6)	they at Jerusalem will **stiffen** their necks against him
2 Ne. 25:28(12,28,29)	my people, ye are a **stiffnecked** people; wherefore, I
2 Ne. 28:14	they wear **stiff** necks and high heads; yea, and because
2 Ne. 32:7	mourn because of the ...**stiffneckedness** of men; for
Jacob 2:13	wear **stiff** necks and high heads because of the
Jacob 4:14(13-14)	the Jews were a **stiffnecked** people; and they despised
Jacob 6:4	they are a **stiffnecked** and a gainsaying people; but
Enos 1:22(22-23)	the people were a **stiffnecked** people, hard to
Jarom 1:4(3-4)	not **stiffnecked**...have faith, have communion with the
W of M 1:17	use much sharpness because of the **stiffneckedness** of
Mosiah 3:14(14,15)	God saw that his people were a **stiffnecked** people, and
Mosiah 13:29	for they were a **stiffnecked** people, quick to do
Alma 9:5(5,31)	they were a hard-hearted and a **stiffnecked** people.
Alma 15:15	remained a hard-hearted and a **stiffnecked** people; and
Alma 20:30	a more hardened and a more **stiffnecked** people
Alma 26:24	as **stiffnecked** a people as they are; whose hearts
Alma 37:10	our **stiffnecked** brethren, the Nephites, who are now
Hel. 4:21	they saw that they had been a **stiffnecked** people, and
Hel. 5:3(1-3)	they were a **stiffnecked** people, insomuch that they
Hel. 9:21	ye blind, and ye **stiffnecked** people, do ye know how
Hel. 13:29	ye hardened and ye **stiffnecked** people, how long will
3 Ne. 15:18(16-19)	because of **stiffneckedness** and unbelief they
Morm. 8:33	**stiffnecked** people, why have ye built up churches unto
D&C 5:8	Oh, this unbelieving and **stiffnecked** generation- mine
D&C 56:6(3-7)	the **stiffneckedness** of my people which are in Thompson
D&C 112:13(12-15)	if they...**stiffen** not their necks against me, they

STRANGERS

Gen. 15:13	thy seed shall be a **stranger** in a land that is not the
Gen. 17:8	the land wherein thou art a **stranger**, all the land of
Gen. 23:4(3,4)	I am a **stranger** and a sojourner with you: give me a
Gen. 37:1	Jacob dwelt...wherein his father was a **stranger**, in
Ex. 2:22(21,22)	he said, I have been a **stranger** in a strange land.

STRANGERS cont.

Ex. 12:43(19,43)	passover: there shall no **stranger** eat thereof
Ex. 20:10	not do any work, thou...nor thy **stranger** that is
Ex. 22:21	thou shalt neither vex a **stranger**, nor oppress him
Lev. 19:34(33-34)	but the **stranger** that dwelleth with you shall be unto
Lev. 25:23	ye are **strangers** and sojourners with me.
Num. 9:14	one ordinance, both for the **stranger**, and for him that
Deut. 10:19	love ye therefore the **stranger**: for ye were strangers
1 Kgs. 8:41(41-43)	concerning a **stranger**, that is not of thy people
1 Chr. 29:15(13-15)	we are **strangers** before thee, and sojourners, as were
2 Chr. 2:17	Solomon numbered all the **strangers** that were in the
Ps. 39:12	I am a **stranger** with thee, and a sojourner, as all my
Ps. 119:19	I am a **stranger** in the earth: hide not thy commandment
Isa. 14:1(1-3)	and the **strangers** shall be joined with them, and they
Jer. 5:19	so shall ye serve **strangers** in a land that is not your
Ezek. 22:7	have they dealt by oppression with the **stranger**: in
Hosea 7:9	**strangers** have devoured his strength, and he knoweth
Joel 3:17	Jerusalem...no **strangers** pass through her any more.
Mal. 3:5(4,5)	that turn aside the **stranger** from his right, and fear
Matt. 25:35(35-44)	gave me drink: I was a **stranger**, and ye took me in
Matt. 27:7(3-8)	the potter's field, to bury **strangers** in.
John 10:5(1-5)	they know not the voice of **strangers**.
Acts 13:17	dwelt as **strangers** in the land of Egypt, and with an
Eph. 2:12(11-13)	ye were...**strangers** from the covenants of promise
Eph. 2:19	ye are no more **strangers** and foreigners, but
Heb. 11:13	died in faith...confessed that they were **strangers** and
Heb. 13:2	be not forgetful to entertain **strangers**: for thereby
1 Pet. 1:1	Peter...to the **strangers** scattered throughout Pontus
1 Pet. 2:11(9-12)	I beseech you as **strangers** and pilgrims, abstain from
3 Jn. 1:5(5-7)	whatsoever thou doest to the brethren, and to **stranger**
2 Ne. 24:1	and the **strangers** shall be joined with them, and they
Mosiah 5:13(12,13)	the master...who is a **stranger** unto him, and is far
Mosiah 13:18	not do any work, thou...nor thy **stranger** that is
Alma 26:9	brethren...would also have been **strangers** to God.
3 Ne. 24:5	turn aside the **stranger**, and fear not me, saith the
D&C 45:13(11-14)	confessed they were **strangers** and pilgrims on the
D&C 124:56(23,56)	house...I have commanded you to build for...**strangers**

STRENGTH

Ex. 15:2(1-2)	the Lord is my **strength** and song, and he is become my
1 Sam. 2:9(8-9)	for by **strength** shall no man prevail.
2 Sam. 22:33	God is my **strength** and power: and he maketh my way
Neh. 8:10	for the joy of the Lord is your **strength**.
Job 12:13	with him is wisdom and **strength**, he hath counsel and
Ps. 18:2(1,2)	my God, my **strength**, in whom I will trust; my buckler
Ps. 19:14	O Lord, my **strength**, and my redeemer.
Ps. 27:1	the Lord is the **strength** of my life; of whom shall I
Ps. 29:11	the Lord will give **strength** unto his people; the Lord
Ps. 71:16(15-16)	I will go in the **strength** of the Lord God: I will make
Ps. 73:26	God is the **strength** of my heart, and my portion for
Ps. 84:5	blessed is the man whose **strength** is in thee; in whose
Ps. 118:14	the Lord is my **strength** and song, and is become my

STRENGTH cont.

Prov. 10:29	the way of the Lord is **strength** to the upright: but
Isa. 12:2	the Lord Jehovah is my **strength** and my song; he also
Isa. 26:4	the Lord Jehovah is everlasting **strength**
Isa. 40:31(29-31)	that wait upon the Lord shall renew their **strength**
Isa. 51:9(9-11)	Awake, put on **strength**, O arm of the Lord; awake, as
Isa. 52:1(1,2)	awake; put on thy **strength**, O Zion; put on thy
Hab. 3:19	God is my **strength**, and he will make my feet like
Mark 12:30	love the Lord thy God...with all thy **strength**: this
Rom. 5:6	when we were yet without **strength**...Christ died for
1 Cor. 10:13	temptation...a way to escape, that ye may..**bear** it.
2 Cor. 12:9(7-10)	for my **strength** is made perfect in weakness. Most
Eph. 3:16	to be **strengthened** with might by his Spirit in the inn
Eph. 6:10(10-17)	be **strong** in the Lord, and in the power of his might.
Rev. 12:10	now is come salvation, and **strength**, and the kingdom
1 Ne. 17:3(2-3)	he doth nourish them, and **strengthen** them, and provide
1 Ne. 21:5(4,5)	and my God shall be my **strength**.
2 Ne. 8:24	Awake, Awake, put on thy **strength**, O Zion; put on thy
2 Ne. 22:2	Jehovah is my **strength** and my song; he also has
Mosiah 4:27	not requisite...should run faster than he has **strength**
Mosiah 9:17	in the **strength** of the Lord did we go forth to battle
Mosiah 11:19	they did boast in their own **strength**, saying that
Alma 20:4	in the **strength** of the Lord thou canst do all things.
Alma 26:12(10-12)	I am weak...but...in his **strength** I can do all things
Alma 48:11(11-17)	Moroni was a **strong**...man...of a perfect understanding
Alma 56:56(52-56)	fought as if with the **strength** of God; yea, never were
Hel. 4:13	because of...their boastings...in their own **strength**
3 Ne. 3:12	cry unto the Lord for **strength** against the time that
Ether 12:27(26-27)	then will I make weak things become **strong** unto them.
Moro. 9:18	and I have but the **strength** of a man, and I cannot any
Moro. 10:32	love God with all your might, mind and **strength**, then
D&C 1:23(19,23-24)	gospel might be proclaimed by the **weak** and the simple
D&C 3:4(3-4)	yet if he boasts in his own **strength**, and sets at
D&C 4:2	see that ye serve him with all your...**strength**, that
D&C 10:4	do not run faster or labor more than you have **strength**
D&C 50:16(15-16)	he that is weak...hereafter shall be made **strong**.
D&C 59:3(3-4)	earth, and it shall bring forth in its **strength**.
D&C 89:20(18-20)	and shall **run** and not be weary, and shall walk and not
D&C 98:47	with all their might, mind, and **strength**, and restore
D&C 101:21	stakes, for the curtains or the **strength** of Zion.
D&C 105:16(16-17)	to say unto the **strength** of my house, even my warriors
D&C 113:8(7-8)	Zion...to put on her **strength** is to put on the
Moses 1:20(20,21)	nevertheless, calling upon God, he received **strength**
Moses 5:37(36,37)	the ground it shall not...yield unto thee her **strength**
JS-H 1:20	I had no **strength**; but soon recovering in some degree
JS-H 1:48	I found my **strength** so exhausted as to render me

STRIFE

Gen. 13:8(7-8)	let there be no **strife**, I pray thee, between me and
Num. 20:13	children of Israel **strove** with the Lord, and he was
Num. 27:14	in the **strife** of the congregation, to sanctify me at
Deut. 1:12(12,13)	how can I myself alone bear...your **strife**

STRIFE cont.

Judg. 12:2	my people were at great **strife** with...Ammon; and when
2 Sam. 19:9	the people were at **strife** throughout all the tribes
Ps. 31:20(19,20)	thou shalt keep them...from the **strife** of tongues.
Ps. 55:9	I have seen violence and **strife** in the city.
Ps. 80:6	thou makest us a **strife** unto our neighbours: and our
Ps. 106:32	they angered him also at the waters of **strife**, so that
Prov. 15:18	a wrathful man stirreth up **strife**: but he that is slow
Prov. 16:28	a froward man soweth **strife**: and a whisperer
Prov. 17:1	than an house full of sacrifices with **strife**.
Prov. 20:3	an honour for a man to cease from **strife**: but every
Prov. 22:10	yea, **strife** and reproach shall cease.
Prov. 28:25	a proud heart stirreth up **strife**: but he that putteth
Prov. 29:22	an angry man stirreth up **strife**, and a furious man
Prov. 30:33	so the forcing of wrath bringeth forth **strife**.
Isa. 58:4(3-5)	behold, ye fast for **strife** and debate, and to smite
Jer. 15:10	that thou hast borne me a man of **strife** and a man of
Hosea 4:4	let no man **strive**, nor reprove another: for thy people
Hab. 1:3(2-4)	there are that raise up **strife** and contention.
Luke 22:24(24-26)	there was also a **strife** among them, which of them
1 Cor. 3:3	among you envying, and **strife**, and divisions, are ye
2 Cor. 12:20	lest there be debates, envyings, wraths, **strifes**
Gal. 5:20(19-21)	emulations, wrath, **strife**, seditions, heresies
Philip. 1:15(15-18)	some indeed preach Christ even of envy and **strife**; and
Philip. 2:3	let nothing be done through **strife** or vainglory; but
1 Tim. 6:4(3-5)	knowing nothing, but doting about...**strifes** of words
2 Tim. 2:23(23,24)	unlearned questions avoid...they do gender **strifes**.
Heb. 6:16	confirmation is to them an end of all **strife**.
James 3:14(14-16)	but if ye have bitter envying and **strife** in your heart
2 Ne. 26:21(20,21)	churches built up which cause...**strifes**, and malice.
Alma 1:32	indulge themselves...in envyings and **strife**; wearing
Alma 4:9	judges...there were envyings, and **strife**, and malice
Alma 16:18	did preach against all lyings...and **strifes**, and
Hel. 11:23	seventy and ninth year there began to be much **strife**.
3 Ne. 11:29(28-30)	he that hath the spirit of **contention** is not of me
3 Ne. 21:19	envyings, and **strifes**, and priestcrafts, and whoredom
3 Ne. 30:2	Gentiles...repent of your...**strifes**, and from all your
4 Ne. 1:16	there were no envyings, nor **strifes**, nor tumults, nor
Morm. 8:21	he that shall breathe out wrath and **strifes** against
Morm. 8:36	none save a few...not lift themselves up in...**strifes**
D&C 10:63(62,63)	that there may not be so much **contention**; yea, Satan
D&C 19:30(30-31)	**reviling** not against revilers.
D&C 60:14	not in haste, neither in wrath nor with **strife**.
D&C 101:6	**strifes**...by these...they polluted their inheritances.
D&C 136:23(23,24)	cease to **contend** one with another; cease to speak evil
JS-H 1:6	entirely lost in a **strife** of words and a contest about
JS-H 1:8	great were the confusion and **strife** among the

STUBBORNNESS

Deut. 2:30	made his heart **obstinate**, that he might deliver him
Deut. 9:27(26-29)	look not unto the **stubbornness** of this people, nor
Deut. 21:18(18-21)	if a man have a **stubborn** and rebellious son, which

STUBBORNNESS cont.

Judg. 2:19	ceased not from...from their **stubborn** way.
1 Sam. 15:23(22-23)	and **stubbornness** is as iniquity and idolatry. because
Ps. 78:8(5-8)	as their fathers, a **stubborn** and rebellious generation
Prov. 7:11	(she is loud and **stubborn**; her feet abide not in her
Isa. 48:4(1-8)	because I knew that thou art **obstinate**, and thy neck
Ezek. 2:4(3-6)	they are impudent children and **stiffhearted**. I do send
Ezek. 3:7	the house of Israel are impudent and **hardhearted**.
Matt. 23:37	how often would I have gathered...and ye **would** not.
Alma 32:16(14-17)	and is baptized without **stubborness** of heart, yea
Alma 51:14(13-21)	wroth because of the **stubbornness** of those people whom

STUDY

Neh. 8:13(8,13)	even to **understand** the words of the law.
Prov. 3:13	happy is the man...that getteth **understanding**.
Prov. 15:28	the heart of the righteous **studieth** to answer: but the
Eccl. 12:12(9-12)	much **study** is a weariness of the flesh.
Matt. 7:7(7-11)	**seek**, and ye shall find; knock, and it shall be opened
Luke 2:52(41-52)	and Jesus increased in **wisdom** and stature, and in
John 5:39(31-39)	**search** the scriptures; for in them ye think ye have
1 Cor. 8:2(1-2)	he knoweth nothing yet as he ought to **know**.
Philip. 4:8	whatsoever things are true...**think** on these things.
1 Thes. 5:21	**prove** all things; hold fast that which is good.
1 Tim. 4:13(12-16)	till I come, give attendance to **reading**, to
2 Pet. 1:5(5-6)	add to your faith virtue; and to virtue **knowledge**
1 Ne. 22:2(1-3)	by the Spirit are all things made **known** unto the
2 Ne. 9:42(42-43)	and whoso **knocketh**, to him will he open; and the wise
2 Ne. 32:3(1-4)	**feast** upon the words of Christ; for behold, the words
Mosiah 1:7(3-7)	**search** them diligently, that ye may profit thereby
Mosiah 12:27(25-27)	ye have not **applied** your hearts to understanding
Alma 5:46(45-47)	I have fasted and prayed...I might **know** these things
Alma 13:20	if ye will **wrest** them it shall be to your own
Alma 17:2(2-3)	they had waxed strong in the **knowledge** of the truth
Alma 32:34(27-43)	your **understanding** doth begin to be enlightened, and
3 Ne. 23:1(1-5)	that ye ought to **search** these things. Yea, a
Moro. 10:3(3-5)	receive these things, and **ponder** it in your hearts.
D&C 1:37	**search** these commandments, for they are true and
D&C 6:7	**seek** not for riches but for wisdom, and behold, the
D&C 9:8(1-9)	you must **study** it out in your mind; then you must ask
D&C 11:22(20-22)	**study** my word which shall come forth among the
D&C 26:1	let your time be devoted to the **studying** of the
D&C 38:30	treasure up **wisdom** in your bosoms, lest the
D&C 58:1	**learn** of me what I will concerning you, and also
D&C 84:85	**treasure** up in your minds continually...words of life
D&C 88:118(118-119)	seek learning, even by **study** and also by faith.
D&C 90:15	**study** and learn, and become acquainted with all good
D&C 107:99(99-100)	now let every man **learn** his duty, and to act in the
JS-M 1:37	and whoso **treasureth** up my word, shall not be deceived

SUBMISSIVENESS

Gen. 16:9(7-9)	return to thy mistress...**submit** thyself under her hand
Ex. 10:3	how long wilt thou refuse to **humble** thyself before me
Ps. 81:15	haters of the Lord should have **submitted**...unto him
Rom. 10:3	have not **submitted** themselves unto the righteousness
Eph. 5:22(18-22)	wives, **submit** yourselves unto your own husbands, as
Heb. 12:9	be in **subjection** unto the Father of spirits, and live
Heb. 13:17	obey them that have the rule...**submit** yourselves: for
James 4:7	**submit** yourselves therefore to God. Resist the devil
1 Pet. 2:13(13-14)	**submit**...to every ordinance of man for the Lord's sake
1 Pet. 5:5	ye younger, **submit** yourselves unto the elder. Yea, all
2 Ne. 9:29(28-29)	learned is good if...**hearken** unto the counsels of God.
Mosiah 3:19	willing to **submit** to all things which the Lord seeth
Mosiah 21:13(13-15)	humble themselves...**submitting** themselves to be
Alma 7:23	I would that ye should be humble, and be **submissive**
Hel. 3:35	sanctification cometh because of...**yielding**...unto God
3 Ne. 12:39(38-41)	ye shall not **resist** evil, but whosoever shall smite
D&C 29:2	will hearken to my voice and **humble** themselves before
D&C 58:22(21-22)	be **subject** to the powers that be, until he reigns
D&C 105:32(31-32)	kingdom of Zion...let us become **subject** unto her laws.
Moses 4:22	thy **desire** shall be to thy husband...he shall rule

SUFFERING

Job 1:21(8-22)	the Lord gave, and the Lord hath **taken** away; blessed
Job 2:7(7,8)	and smote Job with **sore** boils from the sole of his
Job 2:10(9,10)	receive good...of God, and shall we not receive **evil**
Job 3:20(20-26)	light given to him that is in **misery**, and life unto
Ps. 13:2(1-6)	having **sorrow** in my heart daily? how long shall mine
Ps. 18:6	in my **distress** I called upon the Lord, and cried unto
Ps. 22:16(1-21)	they **pierced** my hands and my feet.
Isa. 50:6(6,7)	I gave my back to the **smiters**, and my cheeks to them
Jer. 9:1(1-5)	a fountain of tears, that I might **weep** day and night
Jer. 15:15	know that for thy sake I have **suffered** rebuke.
Jer. 20:7(7-9)	in **derision** daily, every one mocketh me.
Zech. 13:9(8,9)	I will...**refine** them as silver is refined, and will
Mal. 3:2(2,3)	he is like a **refiner's** fire, and like fullers' soap
Luke 13:2(1-5)	suppose ye that these Galilaeans were **sinners** above
Acts 5:41(17-42)	counted worthy to **suffer** shame for his name.
Rom. 8:17(16-18)	if so be that we **suffer** with him, that we may be also
1 Cor. 12:26(25-27)	whether one member **suffer**, all the members suffer with
1 Cor. 13:4	charity **suffereth** long, and is kind; charity envieth
2 Cor. 1:5(5-7)	for as the **sufferings** of Christ abound in us, so our
2 Cor. 1:7(7-10)	as ye are partakers of the **sufferings**, so shall ye
2 Cor. 4:17(14-18)	for our light **affliction**, which is but for a moment
Philip. 1:29	to believe on him, but also to **suffer** for his sake
Philip. 3:8(7-12)	Christ...for whom I have **suffered** the loss of all
2 Thes. 1:5(3-5)	worthy of the kingdom of God, for which ye also **suffer**
2 Tim. 2:12(10-12)	if we **suffer**, we shall also reign with him: if we deny
2 Tim. 3:12(11-12)	live godly in Christ Jesus shall **suffer** persecution.
Heb. 5:8(7-8)	learned he obedience by the things which he **suffered**
Heb. 11:25(24-26)	choosing...to **suffer** affliction with the people of God
James 5:10(10-11)	take...the prophets...for an example of **suffering**

SUFFERING cont.

1 Pet. 2:20(8-23)	if, when ye do well, and **suffer** for it, ye take it
1 Pet. 3:14(13-17)	if ye **suffer** for righteousness' sake, happy are ye
1 Pet. 4:13(12-19)	inasmuch as ye are partakers of Christ's **sufferings**
Rev. 2:10	thou shalt **suffer**...I will give thee a crown of life.
1 Ne. 18:17	having **suffered** much grief because of their children
Mosiah 3:7(5-11)	he shall **suffer** temptations, and pain of body, hunger
Alma 20:29	they were patient in all their **sufferings**.
Alma 26:30(26-31)	we have **suffered** all manner of afflictions, and all
Alma 31:38(24-38)	they should **suffer** no manner of afflictions, save it
3 Ne. 28:38	that they might not **suffer** pain nor sorrow save it
D&C 19:18(15-20)	which **suffering** caused myself, even God, the greatest
D&C 101:35(35-38)	all they who **suffer** persecution for my name, and
D&C 105:6	my people must needs be **chastened** until they learn
D&C 109:76(72-77)	reap eternal joy for all our **sufferings**.
D&C 121:6(1-8)	remember thy **suffering** saints, O our God; and thy
D&C 122:8(5-8)	the Son of Man hath **descended** below them all. art thou
Moses 4:23(22-25)	in **sorrow** shalt thou eat of it all the days of thy

SUPERSTITIONS

Gen. 30:14(14-16)	found **mandrakes** in the field, and brought them unto
Gen. 30:39(37-43)	flocks conceived before the **rods**, and brought forth
Lev. 19:31	neither seek after **wizards**, to be defiled by them: I
Lev. 20:2(1-8)	that giveth any of his seed unto **Molech**; he shall sure
Deut. 18:10(9-14)	maketh his son or his daughter...pass through...**fire**
1 Sam. 28:7(3-25)	seek me a woman that hath a **familiar** spirit, that I
2 Kgs. 21:6(1-9)	made his son pass through the **fire**, and observed times
1 Chr. 10:13(13,14)	for asking counsel of one that had a **familiar** spirit
Isa. 8:19(13-22)	and unto **wizards** that peep, and that mutter: should
Isa. 44:19(9-20)	shall I fall down to the **stock** of a tree
Jer. 23:21(9-40)	I have not sent these **prophets**, yet they ran: I have
Ezek. 8:9(1-16)	behold the wicked **abominations** that they do here.
Ezek. 13:6(1-23)	they have seen vanity and lying **divination**, saying
Ezek. 22:28(23-31)	seeing vanity, and **divining** lies unto them, saying
Dan. 1:20(8-21)	ten times better than all the **magicians** and astrologers
Dan. 2:27(27-28)	cannot the wise men, the **astrologers**...shew unto the
Hosea 4:12(12-14)	my people ask **counsel** at their stocks, and their staff
Micah 3:7(5-12)	then shall the seers be ashamed...**diviners** confounded
Acts 8:9(5-20)	Simon..used sorcery, and **bewitched** the people of
1 Cor. 10:20(19-21)	which the Gentiles sacrifice, they **sacrifice** to devils
3 Ne. 21:16(16-19)	I will cut off **witchcrafts** out of thy land, and thou
D&C 28:11(11-14)	things...written from that **stone** are not of me, and

SUSTAINING CHURCH LEADERS

Num. 27:19(18-21)	and **set** him...before all the congregation; and give
Deut. 34:9	Joshua...and the children of Israel **hearkened** unto him
Josh. 24:15(14-28)	as for me and my house, we will **serve** the Lord.
2 Chr. 20:20	**believe** his prophets, so shall ye prosper.
Matt. 10:41(40-42)	he that **receiveth** a prophet in the name of a prophet
Luke 22:32(31,32)	when thou art converted, **strengthen** thy brethren.

SUSTAINING CHURCH LEADERS cont.

Acts 2:42(37-42)	continued **stedfastly** in the apostles' doctrine and
Rom. 1:12(11,12)	that I may be **comforted** together with you by the
1 Thes. 3:7(6-9)	we were **comforted** over you in all our affliction and
Heb. 13:17(17,18)	**obey** them that have the rule over you, and submit your
1 Ne. 3:6(1-6)	shalt be favored...because thou hast **not** murmured.
2 Ne. 7:9(7-10)	they who shall **condemn** me, behold, all they shall wax
D&C 1:38	mine own voice...voice of my servants, it is the **same**.
D&C 20:63(60-67)	receive their licenses...by **vote** of the church to
D&C 21:5(4-7)	his **word**...receive, as if from mine own mouth, in all
D&C 26:2	all things shall be done by common **consent** in the
D&C 38:34(34-36)	men...shall be appointed by the **voice** of the church
D&C 102:9	**acknowledged**...by the voice of the church.
D&C 107:22	**upheld** by the confidence...and prayer of the church
D&C 124:144(123-145	**approve** of those names...at my general conference

SWEARING

Ex. 20:7	not take the name of the Lord thy God in **vain**; for the
Lev. 18:21	neither shalt thou **profane** the name of thy God: I am
Lev. 19:12	ye shall not **swear** by my name falsely, neither shalt
Ps. 24:4(3-4)	hath not...vanity, nor **sworn** deceitfully.
Isa. 48:1	**swear**...but not in truth, nor in righteousness.
Isa. 48:11	how should my **name** be polluted? and I will not give
Jer. 5:2(1-3)	the Lord liveth; surely they **swear** falsely.
Jer. 23:10(9-14)	because of **swearing** the land mourneth; the pleasant
Hosea 4:2(1-3)	by **swearing**, and lying, and killing, and stealing, and
Amos 8:14	they that **swear** by the sin of Samaria, and say, thy
Matt. 5:34(33-37)	I say unto you, **swear** not at all; neither by heaven,
Mark 6:23	and he **sware** unto her, whatsoever thou shalt ask of
James 5:12	**swear** not, neither by heaven, neither by the earth
1 Ne. 20:1	they **swear** not in truth nor in righteousness.
Alma 49:27	**swearing** with an oath that he would drink his blood
3 Ne. 12:33(33-37)	thou shalt not **forswear** thyself, but shalt perform
3 Ne. 24:5	swift witness against ...false **swearers**, and against
Morm. 3:10(9-11)	did **swear** by the heavens, and also by the throne of
Ether 8:14(11-16)	they all **sware** unto him, by the God of heaven, and
D&C 121:18(18-19)	those who **swear** falsely against my servants, that they

SYMBOLISM

Gen. 1:14	let them be for **signs**, and for seasons, and for days
Ex. 37:9	the **cherubims** spread out their wings on high, and
Num. 21:9(4-9)	Moses made a **serpent** of brass, and put it upon a pole
Josh. 4:7(6-8)	these stones shall be for a **memorial** unto the children
2 Kgs. 18:4	brake in pieces the brasen **serpent** that Moses had made
Isa. 6:2	above it stood the **seraphims**: each one had six wings
Isa. 8:18(17-18)	I and the children...are for **signs** and for wonders in
Ezek. 1:5(5-11)	came the likeness of four living **creatures**. And this
Dan. 2:31(31-45)	thou, O king, sawest, and behold a great **image**. This
Dan. 7:3(1-8)	four great **beasts** came up from the sea, diverse one
John 3:14(14-15)	as Moses lifted up the **serpent** in the wilderness, even

SYMBOLISM cont.

Heb. 2:4	God..bearing them witness, both with **signs** and wonders
Heb. 9:23	the **patterns** of things in the heavens should be
Heb. 10:1	the law having a **shadow** of good things to come, and
Rev. 4:6	about the throne, were four **beasts** full of eyes before
Mosiah 3:15(14,15)	and **types**, and shadows showed he unto them, concerning
Mosiah 13:31(29-31)	these things were **types** of things to come.
Alma 33:19(18-20)	a **type** was raised up in the wilderness, that
Hel. 8:14(14-16)	as he lifted up the brazen **serpent** in the wilderness
Ether 13:6(5-8)	for which things there has been a **type**.
D&C 77:2	What are we to understand by the four **beasts**, spoke
D&C 77:4	their wings are a **representation** of power, to move
D&C 128:13(13-14)	that which is earthly conforming to...**heavenly**, as

TALENTS

Gen. 39:6(1-6)	Joseph was a **goodly** person, and well favoured.
Ex. 31:6(2-6)	in the hearts of all...I have put **wisdom**, that they
Ex. 35:35(30-35)	them hath he filled with **wisdom**...to work all manner
1 Sam. 9:2(1,2)	a choice young man, and a **goodly**: and there was not
1 Chr. 25:7(5-7)	in the songs of the Lord, even all that were **cunning**
Matt. 25:15(14-30)	unto one he gave five **talents**, to another two, and to
Luke 12:48(47,48)	for unto whomsoever **much** is given, of him shall be
Luke 19:13(12-26)	ten servants, and delivered them ten **pounds**, and said
1 Tim. 4:14	neglect not the **gift** that is in thee, which was given
2 Ne. 2:27	all things are **given** them which are expedient unto
Ether 12:35	thou wilt prove them, and take away their **talent**, yea
Moro. 10:18(8-18)	every good **gift** cometh of Christ.
Moro. 10:30	lay hold upon every good **gift**, and touch not the evil
D&C 6:11(11-12)	therefore thou shalt exercise thy **gift**, that thou
D&C 46:11(8-12)	every man is given a **gift** by the Spirit of God.
D&C 60:2(1-3,13)	but they hide the **talent** which I have given unto them
D&C 82:3	unto whom **much** is given much is required; and he who
D&C 82:18	that every man may gain other **talents**, yea, even an

TEACHABLE

1 Sam. 12:7(6-7)	stand still, that I may **reason** with you before the Lord
Prov. 1:3(1-5)	to receive the **instruction** of wisdom, justice, and
Prov. 10:17	he is in the way of life that keepeth **instruction**: but
Prov. 12:1	whoso loveth **instruction** loveth knowledge: but he that
Eccl. 4:13	king, who will no more be **admonished**.
Isa. 1:19(16-19)	if ye be **willing** and obedient, ye shall eat the good
Isa. 54:13(13-15)	all thy children shall be **taught** of the Lord; and
Jer. 7:28(21-28)	this is a nation that **obeyeth** not the voice of the
Matt. 5:6(3-6)	blessed are they which do **hunger** and thirst after
Matt. 10:40(40-41)	he that **receiveth** you receiveth me, and he that
Matt. 13:23(3-8,18-23)	seed into the good ground is he that **heareth** the word
Luke 10:8	into whatsoever city ye enter, and they **receive** you
John 1:12(10-12)	as many as **received** him, to them gave he power to
Acts 2:41(37-41)	they that gladly **received** his word were baptized: and
1 Cor. 2:14(9-16)	natural man **receiveth** not the things of the Spirit of

TEACHABLE cont.

Heb. 12:7(5-11)	if ye endure **chastening**, God dealeth with you as with
2 Ne. 9:42(41-42)	save they...come down in...**humility**, he will not open
2 Ne. 28:28(26-31)	he that is built upon the rock **receiveth** it with
Mosiah 2:9	**hearken** unto me, and open your ears that ye may hear
Mosiah 4:11(11-12)	**humble** yourselves...calling on...Lord daily, and stand
Alma 12:10(9-11)	**not** harden..heart, to him is given the greater portion
Alma 16:16(15-17)	to prepare their hearts to **receive** the word which
Hel. 3:35	sanctification cometh...of their **yielding** their hearts
3 Ne. 12:2(2-6)	more blessed are they who shall **believe** in your words
3 Ne. 22:13(13-15)	all thy children shall be **taught** of the Lord; and
Ether 12:27	my grace is sufficient for all men that **humble**
Moro. 10:32(32-33)	yea, **come** unto Christ, and be perfected in him, and
D&C 1:26(24-28)	as they sought wisdom they might be **instructed**
D&C 6:19	and also **receive** admonition of him. Be patient; be
D&C 28:8	inasmuch as they **receive** thy teachings thou shalt
D&C 39:5	he that **receiveth** not my gospel receiveth not me.
D&C 43:16	ye are to be **taught** from on high. Sanctify yourselves
D&C 45:8(8-15)	unto them that **believed** on my name gave I power to
D&C 50:24(21-24)	he that **receiveth** light...continueth...receiveth more
D&C 64:34	the Lord requireth the heart and a **willing** mind; and
D&C 67:10	**humble** yourselves before me, for ye are not
D&C 101:63	as they are **willing** to be guided in a right and proper
D&C 101:75	were the churches...**willing** to hearken to my voice.
D&C 105:10	that my people may be **taught** more perfectly, and have
D&C 112:20	whosoever **receiveth** my word receiveth me, and
D&C 124:97	let him be **humble** before me, and be without guile, and
D&C 136:32(32-33)	learn wisdom by **humbling** himself and calling upon the

TEACHERS

Ex. 18:20(17-22)	and thou shalt **teach** them...the work that they must
Lev. 10:11(8-11)	and that ye may **teach** the children of Israel all the
Deut. 24:8	all that the priests the Levites shall **teach** you: as
2 Chr. 15:3(1-4)	without the true God, and without a **teaching** priest
Prov. 5:13(7-14)	not obeyed the voice of my **teachers**, nor inclined mine
Isa. 30:20(18-21)	but thine eyes shall see thy **teachers**
Mal. 2:7(4-8)	seek the law at his mouth...**messenger** of the Lord of
1 Cor. 12:28(27-31)	first apostles, secondarily prophets, thirdly **teachers**
Eph. 4:11	he gave some,...pastors and **teachers**
2 Tim. 4:3(3-4)	heap to themselves **teachers**, having itching ears
2 Pet. 2:1(1-3)	there shall be false **teachers** among you, who privily
1 Ne. 2:22	thou shalt be made...a **teacher** over thy brethren.
2 Ne. 5:19	I had been their...**teacher**, according to the
2 Ne. 5:26	that they should be priests and **teachers** over the land
Jacob 1:18	consecrated priests and **teachers** of this people, by
Jarom 1:11	the priests, and the **teachers**, did labor diligently
Mosiah 23:17(17-18)	none received authority...to **teach** except...from God.
Mosiah 25:19(18-22)	gave him power to ordain priests and **teachers** over
Alma 4:7	people whom Alma had consecrated to be **teachers**, and
Alma 15:13	Alma...consecrated priests and **teachers** in the land
Alma 45:22(22,23)	that they did appoint priests and **teachers** throughout
Moro. 3:3(1-3)	I ordain you to be a **teacher**, to preach repentance and

TEACHERS cont.

D&C 20:53(53-59)	teacher's duty is to watch over the church always, and
D&C 42:14(13-15)	if ye receive not the Spirit ye shall not **teach**.
D&C 42:70	**teachers** shall have their stewardships, even as the
D&C 84:30	the offices of **teacher** and deacon are necessary
D&C 84:111	**teachers** should be appointed to watch over the church
D&C 107:86	president over the office of the **teachers** is to

TEACHING

Gen. 18:19	he will **command** his children and his household after
Deut. 4:9(9-10)	**teach** them thy sons, and thy sons' sons
Deut. 6:7	thou shalt **teach** them diligently unto thy children
Josh. 4:22(8,20-24)	then ye shall let your children **know**, saying, Israel
Ps. 32:8	I will instruct thee and **teach** thee in the way which
Prov. 9:9	**teach** a just man, and he will increase in learning.
Prov. 22:6	**train** up a child in the way he should go: and when he
Isa. 2:3	and he will **teach** us of his ways, and we will walk in
Isa. 54:13	all thy children shall be **taught** of the Lord; and
Isa. 61:1	the Lord hath anointed me to **preach** good tidings unto
Matt. 10:19(19,20)	it shall be given you...what ye shall **speak**.
Matt. 26:55	I sat daily with you **teaching** in the temple, and ye
Matt. 28:19	go ye therefore, and **teach** all nations, baptizing them
Mark 1:38(37-39)	that I may **preach** there...for therefore came I forth.
Luke 4:18(16-21)	he hath anointed me to **preach** the gospel to the poor
Luke 11:1	disciples said unto him, Lord, **teach** us to pray, as
John 14:26	the Comforter...shall **teach** you all things, and bring
Col. 3:16	**teaching** and admonishing one another in psalms and
1 Tim. 2:12	suffer not a woman to **teach**, nor to usurp authority
2 Tim. 2:2	faithful men, who shall be able to **teach** others also.
2 Ne. 12:3	he will **teach** us of his ways, and we will walk in his
2 Ne. 25:23	we labor diligently to write, to **persuade** our children
2 Ne. 25:28	they are sufficient to **teach** any man the right way
Mosiah 4:15	but ye will **teach** them to walk in the ways of truth
Mosiah 23:14	trust no one to be your **teacher**...except he be a man
Alma 39:12	**command** thy children to do good, lest they lead away
3 Ne. 26:6	Jesus did truly **teach** unto the people
D&C 20:46	the priest's duty is to preach, **teach**, expound, exhort
D&C 36:2	the Comforter, which shall **teach** you the peaceable
D&C 42:14	if ye receive not the Spirit ye shall not **teach**.
D&C 43:15	not sent forth to be **taught**, but to teach the children
D&C 43:16	and ye are to be **taught** from on high. Sanctify
D&C 52:9	that which is **taught** them by the Comforter through the
D&C 63:65	they are **taught** through prayer by the Spirit.
D&C 68:28	**teach** their children to pray, and to walk uprightly
D&C 75:10	the Comforter, which shall **teach** them all things that
D&C 84:48	and the Father **teacheth** him of the covenant which he
D&C 84:85	given you...portion that shall be **meted** unto every man
D&C 88:77(77-80)	you shall **teach** one another the doctrine of the
D&C 88:118	**teach** one another words of wisdom; yea, seek ye out
JFS-V 1:25(25-28,33)	Savior...endeavoring to **teach** them the everlasting
JFS-V 1:51(33-54)	these the Lord **taught**, and gave them power to come

TEACHING WITH THE SPIRIT

Ex. 31:3(1-5)	the **spirit** of God, in wisdom, and in understanding
2 Sam. 23:2(1,2)	the **Spirit** of the Lord spake by me, and his word was
Neh. 9:20	thou gavest also thy good **spirit** to instruct them, and
Isa. 6:8(8,9)	Lord, saying, whom shall I **send**, and who will go for
Jer. 1:7(5-7)	whatsoever I command thee thou shalt **speak**.
Ezek. 2:2	the **spirit** entered into me when he spake unto me, and
Ezek. 3:27(26,27)	I will open thy **mouth**...thus saith the Lord God
Matt. 7:29(28-29)	he taught them as one having **authority**, and not as the
Matt. 10:20(19-20)	it is not ye that speak, but the **Spirit** of your Father
Luke 4:32	they were astonished...for his word was with **power**.
Luke 24:32(13-35)	did not our heart **burn** within us, while he talked with
John 7:46(32-53)	officers answered, never man **spake** like this man.
Acts 4:8	Peter, filled with the **Holy** Ghost, said unto them, ye
1 Cor. 2:4(4,10-16)	my preaching was...of the **Spirit** and of power
1 Pet. 4:11	if any man speak, let him speak as the **oracles** of God
1 Ne. 17:48(47-55)	I am filled with the **power** of God, even unto the
2 Ne. 25:11	this I speak because of the **spirit** which is in me.
Mosiah 13:6(1-9)	he spake with **power** and authority from God; and he
Alma 5:46(44-52)	this is the spirit of **revelation** which is in me.
Alma 17:3(1-4)	they taught with **power** and authority of God.
Alma 18:34(34-35)	I am called by his Holy **Spirit** to teach these things
Hel. 5:17(17-19)	they did preach with great **power**, insomuch that they
Hel. 13:4(1-8)	**prophesied**...whatsoever...the Lord put into his heart.
Moro. 6:9	**power** of the Holy Ghost led them whether to preach
D&C 11:21	tongue be loosed...you shall have my **Spirit** and my
D&C 28:1(1,4)	whatsoever thou shalt teach them by the **Comforter**
D&C 42:14(6,14-17)	if ye receive not the **Spirit** ye shall not teach.
D&C 43:15(15-16)	teach the children of men...by the power of my **Spirit**
D&C 50:14(13-22)	preach my gospel by the **Spirit**, even the Comforter
D&C 52:9	preaching...that which is taught them by the **Comforter**
D&C 84:85	what ye shall say...shall be **given** you in the very
D&C 88:77(77-79)	you shall teach one another the **doctrine** of the
Moses 6:34(31-34,47)	my **Spirit** is upon you...all thy words will I justify

TELESTIAL GLORY

John 14:2	in my father's house are many **mansions**: if it were not
1 Cor. 15:41(40-42)	and another glory of the **stars**: for one star
Rev. 22:15	and **sorcerers**, and whoremongers, and murderers, and
Mosiah 15:26(26-27)	they that have no part in the first **resurrection**.
D&C 76:81(81-113)	and again, we saw the glory of the **telestial**, which
D&C 88:24(21,24)	who cannot abide the law of a **telestial** kingdom cannot
D&C 88:31	who are quickened by a portion of the **telestial** glory
D&C 88:38(36-39)	and unto every **kingdom** is given a law; and unto every

TEMPERANCE

Prov. 20:1	**wine** is a mocker, strong drink is raging: and
Prov. 23:21(20,21)	for the **drunkard** and the glutton shall come to poverty
Prov. 23:30(29-35)	they that tarry long at the **wine**; they that go to seek
Dan. 1:8(8,12-20)	not defile himself with...king's meat, nor...**wine**

TEMPERANCE cont.

Matt. 23:25(23-26)	within they are full of extortion and **excess**.
1 Cor. 9:25	man that striveth for the mastery is **temperate** in all
Gal. 5:23(21-23)	meekness, **temperance**: against such there is no law.
Eph. 5:18(17-21)	be not drunk with wine, wherein is **excess**; but be fill
Philip. 4:5(5,6)	let your **moderation** be known unto all men. The Lord
Titus 1:8(6-9)	lover of hospitality...good men...holy, **temperate**
Titus 2:2(1-3)	men be sober, grave, **temperate**, sound in faith, in
1 Pet. 4:3(1-5)	we walked in lasciviousness, lusts, **excess** of wine
2 Pet. 1:6(5-8)	and to knowledge **temperance**; and to temperance
Alma 7:23(22-24)	being **temperate** in all things; being diligent in
Alma 38:10(10-12)	be diligent and **temperate** in all things.
D&C 4:6	remember faith, virtue, knowledge, **temperance**
D&C 6:19	be patient; be sober; be **temperate**; have patience
D&C 12:8(7-8)	hope, and charity, being **temperate** in all things
D&C 59:20(16-21)	be used, with judgment, not to **excess**, neither by
D&C 88:69(68-69)	cast away your idle thoughts and...**excess** of laughter
D&C 89:5(5-7)	**wine** or strong drink among you, behold it is not good
D&C 89:11(11-12)	all these to be used with **prudence** and thanksgiving.
D&C 89:12(10-13)	nevertheless they are to be used **sparingly**
D&C 107:30	in faith, and virtue, and knowledge, **temperance**

TEMPLE

Ex. 25:8	let them make me a **sanctuary**; that I may dwell among
Ex. 29:43(43,44)	the **tabernacle** shall be sanctified by my glory.
Ex. 40:9	and anoint the **tabernacle**, and all that is therein
Ex. 40:34	the glory of the Lord filled the **tabernacle**.
Josh. 18:1	Israel assembled...Shiloh, and set up the **tabernacle**
Judg. 18:31	all the time that the **house** of God was in Shiloh.
1 Sam. 1:7(3,7-18)	she went up to the **house** of the Lord, so she provoked
2 Sam. 7:5(4-17)	shalt thou build me an **house** for me to dwell in
1 Kgs. 1:39	Zadok...took an horn of oil out of the **tabernacle**, and
1 Kgs. 5:3	David...could not build an **house** unto the name of the
1 Kgs. 7:51(13-51)	all the work that king Solomon made for the **house** of
2 Kgs. 16:18(8-18)	turned he from the **house** of the Lord for the king of
2 Kgs. 25:9(9-17)	and he burnt the **house** of the Lord, and the king's
1 Chr. 22:6(6-10)	called for Solomon...charged him to build an **house** for
1 Chr. 28:6	Solomon thy son, he shall build my **house** and my courts
2 Chr. 1:3(3-6)	there was the **tabernacle** of the congregation of God
2 Chr. 2:1(1-18)	Solomon determined to build an **house** for the name of
2 Chr. 4:2(2-6)	he made a molten **sea** of ten cubits from brim to brim
Ps. 24:3(3-4)	or who shall stand in his **holy** place
Isa. 2:3(2-4)	let us go up to...the **house** of the God of Jacob; and
Isa. 56:7	make them joyful in my **house** of prayer: their burnt
Jer. 7:11(10-16)	this **house**, which is called by my name, become a den
Jer. 52:17	the brasen **sea** that was in the house of the Lord, the
Jer. 52:20	and twelve brasen **bulls** that were under the bases
Ezek. 37:26(26-27)	I will...set my **sanctuary** in the midst of them for
Ezek. 40:5(2-49)	the **house**...measured the breadth of the building, one
Ezek. 43:4(1-6)	the glory of the Lord came into the **house** by the way
Ezek. 43:11(10-12,18)	shew them the form of the **house**, and the fashion
Ezek. 44:11(4,9-31)	they shall be ministers in my **sanctuary**, having charge

TEMPLE cont.

Ezek. 47:1(1-12)	waters came...from under...the ...side of the **house**
Amos 9:11	in that day will I raise up the **tabernacle** of David
Zech. 1:16	returned to Jerusalem...my **house** shall be built in
Mal. 3:1	the Lord...shall suddenly come to this **temple**, even
Matt. 12:6(5,6)	in this place is one greater than the **temple**.
Matt. 21:13	my **house** shall be called the house of prayer; but ye
Matt. 24:1(1-2)	to shew him the buildings of the **temple**.
Luke 2:46(40-49)	they found him in the **temple**, sitting in the midst of
John 2:20	forty and six years was this **temple** in building, and
1 Cor. 3:16(16,17)	know ye not that ye are the **temple** of God, and that
1 Cor. 6:19	your body is the **temple** of the Holy Ghost which is in
2 Cor. 6:16	ye are the **temple** of the living God; as God hath said
Rev. 7:15(13-17)	they...serve him day and night in his **temple**: and he
Rev. 21:22	God...and the Lamb are the **temple** of it.
2 Ne. 5:16	and I, Nephi, did build a **temple**; and I did construct
Jacob 1:17	I taught them in the **temple**, having first obtained
Jacob 2:2	I come up into the **temple** this day that I might
Alma 7:21	he doth not dwell in unholy **temples**; neither can filth
Hel. 4:24	the Lord doth not dwell in unholy **temples**
3 Ne. 11:1	round about the **temple** which was in the land Bountiful
3 Ne. 24:1	the Lord...shall suddenly come to his **temple**, even the
D&C 59:9	thou shalt go to the **house** of prayer and offer up thy
D&C 84:4(4,5,31,32)	which **temple** shall be reared in this generation.
D&C 88:119(119-120)	establish a **house**...a house of God
D&C 93:35	**temple** is defiled, God shall destroy that **temple**.
D&C 97:15(15-17)	build a **house** unto me in the name of the Lord, and do
D&C 109:8(1-23,37)	establish a house, even a **house** of prayer, a house of
D&C 109:16	that this house may be a **house** of prayer, a house of
D&C 110:7(7-8)	I will manifest myself to my people...in this **house**.
D&C 124:27(27-28)	build a **house** to my name, for the Most High to dwell
D&C 124:38(37-38)	I commanded Moses that he should build a **tabernacle**
D&C 124:40(39-41)	let this **house** be built unto my name, that I may
D&C 128:13(12-13)	the baptismal **font** was instituted as a similitude of
JFS-V 1:54(47-54)	building of the **temples**...ordinances...for...dead

TEMPTATION

Gen. 3:13(1-13)	the serpent **beguiled** me, and I did eat.
Deut. 13:6(6-8)	if thy brother...**entice** thee secretly, saying, let us
Prov. 1:10(10-19)	if sinners **entice** thee, consent thou not.
Matt. 4:1(1-11)	wilderness to be **tempted** of the devil.
Matt. 6:13	lead us not into **temptation**, but deliver us from evil
Matt. 26:41	watch and pray, that ye enter not into **temptation**: the
Luke 8:13	these have no root...in time of **temptation** fall away.
Luke 22:40(40-46)	that ye enter not into **temptation**.
1 Cor. 10:13	will with the **temptation** also make a way to escape
2 Cor. 11:3	as the serpent **beguiled** Eve through his subtilty, so
1 Tim. 6:9(9-10)	they that will be rich fall into **temptation** and a
Heb. 4:15(14-16)	high priest...**tempted** like as we are, yet without sin.
James 1:2(2-3)	count it all joy when ye fall into divers **temptations**
James 1:14(12-15)	every man is **tempted**, when he is drawn away of...lust
1 Pet. 1:6	for a season..ye are in heaviness through..**temptations**

TEMPTATION cont.

2 Pet. 2:9	Lord knoweth how to deliver...godly out of **temptations**
Rev. 3:10	I also will keep thee from the hour of **temptation**
1 Ne. 12:17	the mists of darkness are the **temptations** of the devil
1 Ne. 12:19	because of the pride...and the **temptations** of the
1 Ne. 15:24	neither could the **temptations**...overpower them unto
2 Ne. 4:27(18,27)	why should I give way to **temptations**, that the evil
Mosiah 3:7	he shall suffer **temptations**, and pain of body, hunger
Mosiah 15:5	the flesh...suffereth **temptation**, and yieldeth not to
Alma 7:11	he shall go forth, suffering pains and...**temptations**
Alma 11:23	the righteous yieldeth to no such **temptations**
Alma 13:28	may not be **tempted** above that which ye can bear, and
Alma 31:10	supplication..daily, that...not enter into **temptations**
Alma 34:39	prayer...not be led away by the **temptation** of the
Alma 37:33	teach them to withstand every **temptation** of the devil
3 Ne. 6:15	**tempting** them to seek for power, and authority, and
3 Ne. 6:17	carried about by the **temptations** of the devil
3 Ne. 13:12	lead us not into **temptation**, but deliver us from evil.
3 Ne. 18:18	pray always lest ye enter into **temptation**; for Satan
3 Ne. 18:25	breaketh this commandment...be led into **temptation**.
3 Ne. 28:39	a change wrought...that Satan...could not **tempt** them
Morm. 9:28	be wise in...your probation...yield to no **temptation**
D&C 9:13	be faithful, and yield to no **temptation**.
D&C 20:22	he suffered **temptations** but gave no heed unto them.
D&C 20:33	take heed...pray always, lest...fall into **temptation**
D&C 23:1	beware of pride, lest...shouldst enter into **temptation**
D&C 29:39(36-40)	needs be that the devil should **tempt**...children of men
D&C 29:47	power is not given unto Satan to **tempt** little children
D&C 31:12	pray always, lest you enter into **temptation** and lose
D&C 61:39	pray always that you enter not into **temptation**, that
D&C 62:1	who knoweth...how to succor them who are **tempted**.
D&C 64:20	may not be **tempted** above that which he is able to bear
D&C 95:1	I prepare a way for...deliverance...out of **temptation**
D&C 112:13	after their **temptations**...I, the Lord, will feel after
Moses 5:38	Satan **tempted** me because of my brother's flocks.
Moses 6:49	Satan...**tempteth** them to worship him; and men have
JS-H 1:28	I was left to all kinds of **temptations**; and, mingling
JS-H 1:46	telling me that Satan would try to **tempt** me (in

TERRESTRIAL GLORY

1 Cor. 15:40(40-43)	and the glory of the **terrestrial** is another.
D&C 76:71(71-80)	we saw the **terrestrial** world, and behold and lo, these
D&C 76:91	glory of the **terrestrial**...excels in...glory of the
D&C 88:23(21,23)	cannot abide the law of a **terrestrial** kingdom cannot
D&C 88:30	they...quickened by a portion of the **terrestrial** glory
D&C 88:38(36-39)	unto every **kingdom** is given a law; and unto every law

TEST, TRY, PROVE

Gen. 22:1(1-19)	it came to pass...that God did **tempt** Abraham, and said
Ex. 16:4	that I may **prove** them, whether they will walk in my
Ex. 17:2(1-7)	wherefore do ye **tempt** the Lord
Ex. 20:20	God is come to **prove** you, and that his fear may be
Num. 14:22	have **tempted** me now these ten times, and have not
Deut. 4:34	take him a nation...by **temptations**, by signs, and by
Deut. 6:16	ye shall not **tempt** the Lord your God, as ye tempted
Deut. 7:19	the great **temptations** which thine eyes saw, and the
Deut. 8:2	to **prove** thee, to know what was in thine heart
Deut. 8:16	that he might **prove** thee, to do thee good at thy
Deut. 13:3	the Lord...**proveth** you, to know whether ye love the
Deut. 29:3	the great **temptations** which thine eyes have seen, the
Judg. 2:22(20-23)	that through them I may **prove** Israel, whether they
1 Kgs. 10:1	the queen of Sheba...came to **prove** him with hard
1 Chr. 29:17	I know also, my God, that thou **triest** the heart, and
Job 23:10	when he hath **tried** me, I shall come forth as gold.
Ps. 7:9	the righteous God **trieth** the hearts and reins.
Ps. 11:5	the Lord **trieth** the righteous: but the wicked and him
Ps. 17:3	thou has **proved** mine heart; thou hast visited me in
Ps. 26:2	examine me, O Lord, and **prove** me; try my reins and my
Ps. 66:10	thou...hast **proved** us: thou hast tried us, as silver
Ps. 95:8	as in the day of **temptation** in the wilderness
Ps. 95:9(8,9)	when your fathers tempted me, **proved** me, and saw my
Ps. 139:23	know my heart: **try** me, and know my thoughts
Prov. 17:3	furnace for gold: but the Lord **trieth** the hearts.
Isa. 7:12	Ahaz said, I will not...**tempt** the Lord.
Jer. 11:20	that **triest** the reins and the heart, let me see thy
Jer. 20:12	O Lord of hosts, that **triest** the righteous, and seest
Zech. 13:9	will **try** them as gold is tried: they shall call on my
Mal. 3:10	bring ye all the tithes...and **prove** me now herewith
Matt. 4:1(1-11)	Jesus...into the wilderness to be **tempted** of the devil
Matt. 4:7(5-7)	thou shalt not **tempt** the Lord thy God.
Matt. 6:13	and lead us not into **temptation**, but deliver us from
Matt. 13:21(20,21)	when **tribulation** or persecution ariseth because of
Matt. 22:18	Jesus...said, why **tempt** ye me, ye hypocrites
Matt. 22:35	lawyer, asked him a question, **tempting** him, and saying
Mark 12:15	why **tempt** ye me? bring me a penny, that I may see it.
Luke 4:12(9-12)	Jesus...said...thou shalt not **tempt** the Lord thy God.
Luke 22:28	they which have continued with me in my **temptations**.
Luke 22:31(31-32)	Satan hath desired to **have** you, that he may sift you
John 15:2	he **purgeth** it, that it may bring forth more fruit.
John 16:33	in the world ye shall have **tribulation**: but be of good
Acts 5:9	ye have agreed together to **tempt** the Spirit of the Lord
Acts 14:22	we must through much **tribulation** enter into the
Acts 15:10	why **tempt** ye God, to put a yoke upon the neck of the
Acts 20:19	with many tears, and **temptations**, which befell me by
1 Cor. 3:13	the fire shall **try** every man's work of what sort it
1 Cor. 7:5	that Satan **tempt** you not for your incontinency.
1 Cor. 10:9	neither let us **tempt** Christ, as some of them also
1 Cor. 10:13	who will not suffer you to be **tempted** above that ye
2 Cor. 8:2	in a great **trial** of affliction the abundance of their
Gal. 6:4	but let every man **prove** his own work, and then shall
1 Thes. 2:4	God, which **trieth** our hearts.

TEST, TRY, PROVE cont.

1 Thes. 5:21	**prove** all things; hold fast that which is good.
1 Tim. 3:10	let these also first be **proved**; then let them use the
Heb. 2:18	he himself hath suffered being **tempted**, he is able to
Heb. 3:9(8,9)	when your fathers tempted me, **proved** me, and saw my
Heb. 4:15	but was in all points **tempted** like as we are, yet with
Heb. 11:17	by faith Abraham, when he was **tried**, offered up Isaac
James 1:3(2-3)	that the **trying** of your faith worketh patience.
James 1:12(12-13)	when he is **tried**, he shall receive the crown of life
1 Pet. 1:7(6-7)	that the **trial** of your faith...be found unto praise
1 Pet. 4:12	the fiery **trial** which is to try you, as though some
Rev. 2:10	that ye may be **tried**; and ye shall have tribulation
Rev. 3:10	I also will keep thee from the hour of **temptation**
Jacob 7:14(13-14)	what am I that I should **tempt** God to show unto thee a
Alma 11:23	O thou child of hell, why **tempt** ye me? Knowest thou
3 Ne. 28:39	Satan could have no power...could not **tempt** them; and
Ether 12:6	receive no witness until after the **trial** of your faith
D&C 10:15	to get thee to **tempt** the Lord thy God, in asking to
D&C 35:23	call on the holy prophets to **prove** his words, as they
D&C 40:2	received the word...but straightway Satan **tempted** him
D&C 54:10	be patient in **tribulation** until I come; and, behold
D&C 58:2(2-7)	he that is faithful in **tribulation**, the reward of the
D&C 84:79	I send you out to **prove** the world, and the laborer is
D&C 98:14(12-14)	I will **prove** you in all things, whether you will abide
D&C 101:4(4-5)	they must needs be chastened and **tried**, even as
D&C 103:12	after much **tribulation**...cometh the blessing.
D&C 105:19	brought thus far for a **trial** of their faith.
D&C 112:13	after their **temptations**...I will heal them.
D&C 121:12	that he may **prove** them also and take them in their
D&C 122:5(5-8)	if thou art called to pass through **tribulation**; if
D&C 124:55	that you may **prove** yourselves unto me that ye are
D&C 124:113	when he shall **prove** himself faithful in all things
D&C 127:2	I feel, like Paul, to glory in **tribulation**; for to
D&C 132:51	I did it...to **prove** you all, as I did Abraham, and
Abr. 3:25	we will **prove** them herewith, to see if they will do

TESTIMONY

Ex. 31:18	and he gave unto Moses...two tables of **testimony**
Deut. 6:20(20-25)	what mean the **testimonies**, and the statutes, and the
1 Sam. 17:45(41-47)	I come to thee in the **name** of the Lord of hosts, the
Job 19:25(25,26)	for I **know** that my redeemer liveth, and that he shall
Ps. 19:7	the **testimony** of the Lord is sure, making wise the
Ps. 132:12	children will keep my covenant and my **testimony** that
Isa. 6:5	mine eyes have **seen** the King, the Lord of hosts.
Matt. 16:17(13-20)	flesh and blood hath not **revealed** it unto thee, but
Luke 9:20(18-21)	Peter answering said, the **Christ** of God.
John 1:34(7,15,34)	I saw, and bare **record** that this is the Son of God.
John 3:11	we speak that we do know, and **testify** that we have
John 3:32(31-34)	what he hath seen and heard, that he **testifieth**; and
John 5:39	scriptures...are they which **testify** of me.
John 7:17	do his will...shall **know** of the doctrine, whether it
John 8:32(31-32)	and ye shall **know** the truth, and the truth shall make

TESTIMONY cont.

John 17:3 — life eternal, that they might **know** thee the only true
Acts 14:3 — gave **testimony** unto the word of his grace, and granted
1 Cor. 1:6(5-7) — even as the **testimony** of Christ was confirmed in you
1 Cor. 2:1(1-16) — declaring unto you the **testimony** of God.
1 Cor. 12:3 — **say** that Jesus is the Lord, but by the Holy Ghost.
2 Cor. 1:12 — the **testimony** of our conscience, that in simplicity
Gal. 1:12 — received it...by the **revelation** of Jesus Christ.
2 Tim. 1:8 — be not thou...ashamed of the **testimony** of our Lord
Heb. 11:5(5,6) — before his translation he had this **testimony**, that he
1 Jn. 4:15 — whosoever shall **confess** that Jesus is the Son of God
1 Jn. 5:10 — he that believeth...hath the **witness** in himself: he
Rev. 12:11 — they overcame him...by the word of their **testimony**
Rev. 15:5(4-8) — the temple of the tabernacle of the **testimony** in
Rev. 19:10 — for the **testimony** of Jesus is the spirit of prophecy.
2 Ne. 11:2(2-3) — he verily saw my Redeemer, even as I have **seen** him.
2 Ne. 25:28 — which I have spoken shall stand as a **testimony** against
2 Ne. 27:12(12,13) — three witnesses..shall **testify** to the truth of the
2 Ne. 29:8 — **testimony** of two nations is a witness unto you that I
Jacob 4:4(4-8,12) — know that we **knew** of Christ, and we had a hope of his
Mosiah 17:10 — they shall stand as a **testimony** against you. And if
Mosiah 18:9 — stand as **witnesses** of God at all times and in all
Alma 4:20(19,20) — confined himself wholly...to the **testimony** of the word
Alma 5:45(45-56) — I **testify** unto you that I do know that these things
Alma 6:8 — according to the **testimony** of Jesus Christ, the Son
Alma 7:13(13-16) — now behold, this is the **testimony** which is in me.
Alma 30:41 — ye also have all things as a **testimony** unto you that
Alma 32:28 — Spirit...beginneth to enlighten my **understanding**, yea
Hel. 8:9(8,9) — had not been a prophet he could not have **testified**
Morm. 9:25 — whosoever shall believe...unto him will I **confirm** all
Ether 4:11 — because of my Spirit he shall **know**...things are true
Ether 12:6 — no **witness** until after the trial of your faith.
Moro. 7:44 — **confesses** by the power of the Holy Ghost that Jesus
Moro. 10:7(4-7) — **know** that he is, by the power of the Holy Ghost; where
D&C 1:34 — willing to make these things **known** unto all flesh
D&C 3:18(16-18) — this **testimony** shall come to the knowledge of the
D&C 6:31(28-31) — my words...shall be established by the **testimony** which
D&C 8:1(1-3,9-11) — receive a **knowledge** of whatsoever..you shall ask in
D&C 9:8(8-9) — **study** it out...if it is right...burn within you;
D&C 10:33 — thus Satan thinketh to overpower your **testimony** in
D&C 18:36(34-36) — wherefore, you can **testify** that you have heard my
D&C 20:26(25,26) — who truly **testified** of him in all things, should have
D&C 21:9 — Comforter, which **manifesteth** that Jesus was crucified
D&C 42:61 — ask, thou shalt receive revelation...**knowledge** upon
D&C 45:57 — have taken the Holy Spirit for their **guide**, and have
D&C 46:13 — it is given by the Holy Ghost to **know** that Jesus
D&C 58:6(5,6) — that your hearts might be prepared to bear **testimony**
D&C 58:13(13,14) — that the **testimony** might go forth from Zion, yea, from
D&C 62:3 — the **testimony** which ye have borne is recorded in
D&C 67:4 — I, the Lord, give unto you a **testimony** of the truth
D&C 76:10 — by my spirit will I **enlighten** them...make known unto
D&C 76:22(22,23) — this is the **testimony**...which we give of him: that he
D&C 76:50 — this is the **testimony** of the gospel of Christ
D&C 76:74 — received not the **testimony** of Jesus in the flesh, but

TESTIMONY cont.

D&C 76:79	they who are not valiant in the **testimony** of Jesus
D&C 84:62(61,62)	the **testimony** may go from you into all the world unto
D&C 88:81(81-85)	behold, I sent you out to **testify** and warn the people
D&C 88:88(87-90)	after your **testimony** cometh wrath...upon the people.
D&C 89:19	find wisdom and great treasures of **knowledge**, even
D&C 90:11	Comforter, shed forth...for the **revelation** of Jesus
D&C 100:10	I will give unto him power to be mighty in **testimony**.
D&C 109:38(38-41,56	put upon thy servants the **testimony** of the covenant
D&C 109:46	seal up the law, and bind up the **testimony**, that they
D&C 124:20	for the love which he has to my **testimony** I, the Lord
D&C 135:5	testators are now dead...their **testament** is in force.
D&C 136:39	needful...he should seal his **testimony** with his blood
Moses 7:27	Enoch beheld angels...bearing **testimony** of the Father
Moses 7:62	truth...to bear **testimony** of mine Only Begotten
JS-H 1:26	I had found the **testimony** of James to be true- that a
JFS-V 1:12(11-16)	who had been faithful in the **testimony** of Jesus while
JFS-V 1:60	I bear **record**, and...this record is true, through the

THANKSGIVING

Lev. 7:12(12,13,15)	if he offer it for a **thanksgiving**, then he shall offer
Lev. 22:29	when ye will offer a sacrifice of **thanksgiving** unto
1 Sam. 2:1(1-10)	Hannah prayed...said, My heart **rejoiceth** in the Lord
2 Sam. 22:50(1-51)	therefore I will give **thanks** unto thee, O Lord, among
1 Chr. 16:4	Levites...to **thank** and praise the Lord God of Israel
1 Chr. 16:7(7-36)	David delivered first this psalm to **thank** the Lord
1 Chr. 23:30	to stand every morning to **thank** and praise the Lord
1 Chr. 29:13(11-13)	now therefore...we **thank** thee, and praise thy glorious
Ps. 50:14	offer unto God **thanksgiving**; and pay thy vows unto the
Ps. 95:2	let us come before his presence with **thanksgiving**, and
Ps. 100:4	enter into his gates with **thanksgiving**, and into his
Ps. 105:1(1-5)	give **thanks** unto the Lord; call upon his name: make
Ps. 136:1(1-26)	O give **thanks** unto the Lord; for he is good: for his
Ps. 147:7	sing unto the Lord with **thanksgiving**; sing praise upon
Isa. 12:4	**praise** the Lord, call upon his name, declare his doing
Dan. 6:10	Daniel...kneeled...three times a day...and gave **thanks**
Amos 4:5	offer a sacrifice of **thanksgiving** with leaven, and
Mark 14:23(22-25)	when he had given **thanks**, he gave it to them: and they
Luke 1:47(46-55)	my spirit hath **rejoiced** in God my Saviour.
Luke 1:68(68-79)	**blessed** be the Lord God of Israel; for he hath visited
Luke 17:16(11-19)	fell down on his face at his feet, giving him **thanks**
John 11:41	I **thank** thee that thou hast heard me.
Acts 28:15	Paul saw, he **thanked** God, and took courage.
1 Cor. 15:57	but **thanks** be to God, which giveth us the victory
2 Cor. 4:15	grace might through the **thanksgiving** of many redound
2 Cor. 9:11(11-12)	which causeth through us **thanksgiving** to God.
2 Cor. 9:15	**thanks** be unto God for his unspeakable gift.
Eph. 5:20(19-20)	giving **thanks** always for all things unto God and the
Philip. 4:6	with **thanksgiving** let your requests be made known unto
Col. 2:7(6-7)	abounding therein with **thanksgiving**.
Col. 3:15(15-17)	ye are called in one body; and be ye **thankful**.
1 Thes. 2:13	for this cause also **thank** we God without ceasing

THANKSGIVING cont.

1 Thes. 5:18	in every thing give **thanks**: for this is the will of
1 Tim. 4:4(3,4)	nothing...refused, if it be received with **thanksgiving**
1 Ne. 2:7	and gave **thanks** unto the Lord our God.
1 Ne. 5:9	and they gave **thanks** unto the God of Israel.
2 Ne. 4:16(16-35)	my soul **delighteth** in the things of the Lord; and my
2 Ne. 9:52	give **thanks** unto his holy name by night. Let your
2 Ne. 22:4	**praise** the Lord, call upon his name, declare his
2 Ne. 29:4(4-6)	and what **thank** they the Jews for the Bible which they
Mosiah 2:20(19-21)	render all the **thanks** and praise which your whole
Mosiah 8:19	gave **thanks** to God, saying: doubtless a great mystery
Mosiah 24:21(21,22)	they poured out their **thanks** to God because he had
Mosiah 24:22(21,22)	and they gave **thanks** to God, yea, all their men and
Mosiah 26:39	and to give **thanks** in all things.
Alma 7:23	always returning **thanks** unto God for whatsoever things
Alma 26:8	let us give **thanks** to his holy name, for he doth work
Alma 34:38	live in **thanksgiving** daily, for the many mercies and
Alma 37:37	let thy heart be full of **thanks** unto God; and if ye
Morm. 9:31	but rather give **thanks** unto God that he hath made
D&C 46:7	doing all things with prayer and **thanksgiving**, that
D&C 46:32	must give **thanks** unto God in the Spirit for whatsoever
D&C 59:7	thou shalt **thank** the Lord thy God in all things.
D&C 59:15(7-21)	as ye do these things with **thanksgiving**, with cheerful
D&C 62:7	hand of the Lord, with a **thankful** heart in all things.
D&C 78:19	he who receiveth all things with **thankfulness** shall
D&C 89:11(11-12)	to be used with prudence and **thanksgiving**.
D&C 97:13(12-13)	for a place of **thanksgiving** for all saints, and for a
D&C 98:1	rejoice evermore, and in everything give **thanks**
D&C 136:28	praise...Lord with...prayer of praise and **thanksgiving**

TIME

Gen. 1:1	in the **beginning** God created the heaven and the earth.
Gen. 1:5	and God called the light **day**, and the darkness he call
Ex. 21:19	he shall pay for the loss of his **time**, and shall cause
2 Kgs. 20:6(4-6)	and I will add unto thy **days** fifteen years; and I will
Job 14:5(1-6)	seeing his **days** are determined, the number of his
Ps. 89:47	remember how short my **time** is: wherefore hast thou
Ps. 90:4	thousand **years** in thy sight are but as yesterday when
Eccl. 3:1(1-11)	a **time** to every purpose under the heaven
Eccl. 8:5	a wise man's heart discerneth both **time** and judgment.
Matt. 24:22(15-22)	for the elect's sake those **days** shall be shortened.
Mark 1:15	the **time** is fulfilled, and the kingdom of God is at
Acts 17:26	determined the **times** before appointed, and the bounds
Rom. 13:11	it is high **time** to awake out of sleep: for now is our
2 Pet. 3:8	one day is with the Lord as a thousand **years**, and a
Rev. 10:6(5,6)	that there should be **time** no longer
1 Ne. 10:3	according to the own due **time** of the Lord, they should
2 Ne. 2:3	in the fulness of **time** he cometh to bring salvation
2 Ne. 2:21	**days** of the children of men were prolonged, according
Alma 12:24(22-24)	a **time** to prepare to meet God...for that endless state
Alma 34:32(30-34)	this life is the **time** for men to prepare to meet God
Alma 40:8(4-10)	and **time** only is measured unto men.

TIME cont.

Alma 42:4
Hel. 15:4(4,10-11)
D&C 26:1
D&C 41:9
D&C 60:13
D&C 84:100(98-102)
D&C 88:42(42-47)
D&C 88:110
D&C 121:12
D&C 122:9
D&C 130:4(4,5)
Abr. 3:4(4-10)
Abr. 5:13
Abr. 7:1

there was a **time** granted unto man to repent, yea, a
for this intent hath the Lord prolonged their **days**.
let your **time** be devoted to the studying of the
spend all his **time** in the labors of the church
thou shalt not idle away thy **time**, neither shalt thou
Satan is bound and **time** is no longer. The Lord hath
move in their **times** and their seasons
seventh angel...swear...there shall be **time** no longer
God hath set his hand and seal to change the **times** and
thy **days** are known, and thy years shall not be
God's **time**, angel's **time**, prophet's **time**, and man's
this is the reckoning of the Lord's **time**, according
it was after the Lord's **time**, which was after the
which celestial **time** signifies one day to a cubit.

TITHING

Gen. 14:20
Gen. 28:22
Lev. 27:30(30-32)
Num. 18:26(21,24,26)
Deut. 12:6(6,11,17)
Deut. 14:22(22-29)
Deut. 26:12
2 Chr. 31:5(5-6)
Neh. 10:38(37-38)
Neh. 12:44
Neh. 13:12(5,12)
Prov. 3:9(7-10)
Mal. 3:8(8-12)
Matt. 23:23
Luke 18:12
Heb. 7:2(1-4)
Alma 13:15(7,14-19)
3 Ne. 24:8(7-10)
D&C 64:23(23-24)
D&C 85:3
D&C 97:12(11,12)
D&C 119:4(3-6)

and he gave him **tithes** of all.
I will surely give the **tenth** unto thee.
all the **tithe** of the land...it is holy unto the Lord.
for the Lord, even a **tenth** part of the tithe.
your **tithes**, and heave offerings of your hand, and
thou shalt truly **tithe** all the increase of thy seed
tithing all the **tithes** of thine increase the third
the **tithe** of all things brought they in abundantly.
the Levites shall bring up the **tithe** of the tithes
for the **tithes**, to gather into them out of the fields
brought all Judah the **tithe** of the corn and the new
honour the Lord with thy **substance**, and with the first
wherein have we robbed thee? in **tithes** and offerings.
for ye pay **tithe** of mint and anise and cummin, and
I give **tithes** of all that I possess.
to whom also Abraham gave a **tenth** part of all; first
this same Melchizedek to whom Abraham paid **tithes**; yea
wherein have we robbed thee? In **tithes** and offerings.
for he that is **tithed** shall not be burned at his
that he may **tithe** his people, to prepare them against
behold, this is the **tithing** and the sacrifice which
tithed shall pay one-tenth of all their interest

TRADITIONS OF MEN

Lev. 18:30(26-30)
2 Chr. 30:7(6-8)
Isa. 29:13(11-14)
Jer. 10:3(2-5)
Jer. 16:12(11-13)
Ezek. 20:32(30-32)
Matt. 15:3(1-9)
Mark 7:8(1-13)
Gal. 1:14(13,14)

commit not...these abominable **customs**, which were
be not ye like your **fathers**, and like your brethren
fear toward me is taught by the **precept** of men
for the **customs** of the people are vain: for one
ye have done worse than your **fathers**; for, behold, ye
we will be as the **heathen**, as the families of the
transgress the commandment of God by your **tradition**
laying aside..commandment..ye hold the **tradition** of
exceedingly zealous of the **traditions** of my fathers.

TRADITIONS OF MEN cont.

Col. 2:8
2 Thes. 2:15
2 Thes. 3:6
1 Pet. 1:18
Mosiah 10:12(11-12)
Mosiah 26:1
Alma 3:8(6-8)
Alma 3:11
Alma 8:11(10-11)
Alma 9:8
Alma 37:9
Alma 60:32
Hel. 5:51
Hel. 15:4
Hel. 16:20(19-21)
D&C 74:6(1-7)
D&C 93:39(38-40)
D&C 123:7(7-8)

lest any man spoil you...after the **tradition** of men
and hold the **traditions** which ye have been taught
not after the **tradition** which he received of us.
vain conversation received by **tradition** from your
believing in the **tradition** of their fathers, which is
they did not believe the **tradition** of their fathers.
believe in incorrect **traditions** which would prove
in the **tradition** of their fathers, which were correct
we do not believe in such foolish **traditions**.
have ye forgotten the **tradition** of your fathers; yea
convinced...many...of the incorrect **tradition** of their
when it is the **tradition** of their fathers that has
their hatred and the **tradition** of their fathers.
because of the iniquity of the **tradition** of their
we know that this is a wicked **tradition**, which has bee
tradition..which saith that little children are unholy
taketh away light and truth...because of the **tradition**
creeds of the fathers, who have inherited lies, upon

TRANSFIGURATION

Ex. 34:29(29-35)
Matt. 17:2(1-8)
2 Cor. 3:7
Hel. 5:23(22-27)
3 Ne. 17:24(23-25)
3 Ne. 19:14(13-15)
3 Ne. 19:25
3 Ne. 28:15(6-23)
D&C 63:21(20-21)
D&C 67:11(11-12)
D&C 76:12(11-24)
Moses 1:2
Moses 1:11
Moses 7:3(2-4)

the skin of his face **shone** while he talked with him.
transfigured before them: and his face did shine as
Israel could not...behold..face of Moses for the **glory**
encircled about as if by **fire**, even insomuch that the
encircled about with **fire**; and the angels did
encircled about as if it were by **fire**; and it came
they were as **white** as the countenance...of Jesus; and
it did seem unto them like a **transfiguration** of them
when the earth shall be **transfigured**, even according
no man has seen God...except **quickened** by the Spirit
by the power of the **Spirit** our eyes were opened and
the **glory** of God was upon Moses; therefore Moses
his glory was upon me...for I was **transfigured** before
heavens open, and I was clothed upon with **glory**

TRANSGRESSION

Gen. 3:6
Ex. 23:21(20-22)
Lev. 16:16(15-17)
1 Chr. 9:1
1 Chr. 10:13
Ps. 19:13(12-14)
Ps. 32:1
Ps. 32:5
Ps. 39:8
Ps. 89:32(31,32)
Prov. 12:13
Prov. 19:11
Prov. 29:6

she took of the fruit thereof, and did **eat**, and gave
for he will not pardon your **transgressions**: for my
an atonement...because of their **transgressions** in all
carried away to Babylon for their **transgression**.
so Saul died for his **transgression** which he committed
I shall be innocent from the great **transgression**.
blessed is he whose **transgression** is forgiven, whose
I will confess my **transgressions** unto the Lord; and
deliver me from all my **transgressions**: make me not the
then will I visit their **transgression** with the rod
the wicked is snared by the **transgression** of his lips
it is his glory to pass over a **transgression**.
in the **transgression** of an evil man there is a snare

TRANSGRESSION cont.

Isa. 43:25(24-27)   I, am he that blotteth out thy **transgressions** for mine
Isa. 44:22   blotted out, as a thick cloud, thy **transgressions**, and
Isa. 53:5   but he was wounded for our **transgressions**, he was
Isa. 53:8   for the **transgression** of my people was he stricken.
Isa. 58:1   cry aloud...shew my people their **transgression**, and
Ezek. 18:22(21,22)   all his **transgressions** that he hath committed, they
Ezek. 18:30   repent...turn yourselves from all your **transgressions**
Ezek. 39:24(23,24)   according to their **transgressions** have I done unto
Micah 6:7(6,7)   shall I give my firstborn for my **transgression**, the
Rom. 4:15   for where no law is, there is no **transgression**.
Rom. 5:14(12-14)   not sinned after...similitude of Adam's **transgression**
1 Tim. 2:14   but the woman being deceived was in the **transgression**.
Heb. 9:15(14,15)   by means of death...redemption of the **transgressions**
1 Jn. 3:4   whosoever committeth sin **transgresseth** also the law
2 Ne. 9:6   fall came by reason of **transgression**; and because man
2 Ne. 9:39(39-46)   the awfulness in **transgressing** against that holy God
Enos 1:10   their **transgressions** will I bring down with sorrow
Mosiah 1:12   never..blotted out, except it be through **transgression**
Mosiah 1:13   people of the Lord should fall into **transgression**, and
Mosiah 14:5   he was wounded for our **transgressions**, he was bruised
Mosiah 15:9(9-12)   having...taken upon himself...their **transgressions**
Mosiah 27:13(11-13)   nothing..overthrow it, save..**transgression** of my
Alma 7:13   that he might blot out their **transgressions** according
Alma 9:19(12-23)   they could fall into sins and **transgressions**, after
Alma 9:23(22-23)   should fall into **transgression**, it would be far more
Alma 10:19   fall into **transgression**...would be ripe for
Alma 24:30   enlightened...fallen away into sin and **transgression**
Alma 28:13   inequality of man is because of sin and **transgression**
Alma 32:19   he that only believeth..and falleth into **transgression**
Alma 46:18   until we bring it upon us by our own **transgressions**.
D&C 3:6(6-10)   how oft you have **transgressed** the commandments and the
D&C 20:20(16-20)   by the **transgression** of...holy laws man became sensual
D&C 20:20(19-20)   by the **transgression** of these holy laws man became
D&C 29:40   he partook of the forbidden fruit and **transgressed** the
D&C 101:2(1,2)   been afflicted, in consequence of their **transgressions**
D&C 105:2(1,2,9)   were it not for the **transgressions** of my people, speak
Moses 5:10(10-11)   because of my **transgression** my eyes are opened, and
JFS-V 1:32   or in **transgression**, having rejected the prophets.

TRANSLATED BEINGS

Gen. 5:24   **Enoch** walked with God: and...God took him.
Deut. 34:6   but no man knoweth of his **sepulchre** unto this day.
2 Kgs. 2:11(9-11)   **Elijah** went up by a whirlwind into heaven.
Matt. 16:28(27,28)   some standing here, which shall not taste of **death**
Matt. 17:3(1-4)   appeared unto them **Moses** and Elias talking with him.
John 21:22(20-24)   if I will that he **tarry** till I come, what is that to
Heb. 11:5   faith Enoch was **translated** that he should not see
Heb. 13:2   some have entertained **angels** unawares.
Jude 1:9   Michael...devil...disputed about the body of **Moses**
Alma 45:19(18-19)   Lord took Moses unto himself...has also received **Alma**
3 Ne. 28:7(4-26)   ye shall never taste of **death**; but ye shall live to

TRANSLATED BEINGS cont.

3 Ne. 28:38(36-40)	not taste of death there was a **change** wrought upon the
4 Ne. 1:14	save it were the **three** who should tarry; and there
Morm. 8:11(10-11)	behold, my father and I have seen **them**, and they have
D&C 7:3	thou shalt **tarry** until I come in my glory, and shalt
D&C 45:12(11-14)	a **city** reserved until a day of righteousness shall
D&C 107:49(48,49)	four hundred and thirty years old...he was **translated**.
D&C 110:13(13-16)	**Elijah**...was taken to heaven without tasting death
Moses 7:69(20-21,69)	**Enoch** and all his people...Zion...God received it up

TREASURE

Ex. 19:5(4,5)	then ye shall be a peculiar **treasure** unto me above all
Deut. 8:18(17-20)	he that giveth thee power to get **wealth**, that he may
Deut. 28:12	the Lord shall open unto thee his good **treasure**, the
2 Kgs. 20:13	all that was found in his **treasures**: there was nothing
1 Chr. 29:12(10-13)	both **riches** and honour come of thee, and thou reignest
Ps. 37:16(16,17)	little..righteous..better than..**riches** of many wicked.
Ps. 39:6(6,7)	he heapeth up **riches**, and knoweth not who shall gather
Ps. 49:6(6,7)	they that trust in their **wealth**, and boast themselves
Ps. 104:24(24,25)	O Lord...the earth is full of thy **riches**.
Ps. 135:4	for the Lord hath chosen Jacob...his peculiar **treasure**
Prov. 10:2	**treasures** of wickedness profit nothing: but
Prov. 10:22	the blessing of the Lord, it maketh **rich**, and he
Prov. 11:4	**riches** profit not in the day of wrath: but
Prov. 15:6	in the house of the righteous is much **treasure**: but
Prov. 21:6	the getting of **treasures** by a lying tongue is a vanity
Prov. 21:17	loveth pleasure...wine and oil shall not be **rich**.
Prov. 21:20	there is **treasure** to be desired and oil in the
Prov. 22:1(1-4)	a good name is rather to be chosen than great **riches**
Prov. 22:16	oppresseth the poor to increase his **riches**, and he
Prov. 23:4(4,5)	labour not to be **rich**: cease from thine own wisdom.
Prov. 28:20	he that maketh haste to be **rich** shall not be innocent
Prov. 30:8(8-9)	give me neither poverty nor **riches**; feed me with food
Eccl. 5:10(9-16)	he that loveth **silver** shall not be satisfied with
Eccl. 5:19	every man also to whom God hath given **riches** and
Isa. 33:6(5,6)	the fear of the Lord is his **treasure**.
Jer. 9:23	let not the rich man glory in his **riches**
Ezek. 22:25	they have taken the **treasure** and precious things; they
Micah 6:10	are there yet the **treasures** of wickedness in the house
Zech. 11:5(3-5)	blessed be the Lord; for I am **rich**: and their own
Matt. 6:20(19-21)	lay up for yourselves **treasures** in heaven, where
Matt. 6:24	ye cannot serve God and **mammon**.
Matt. 12:35(33-35)	out of the good **treasure** of the heart bringeth forth
Matt. 13:22	the deceitfulness of **riches**, choke the word, and he
Matt. 13:44	kingdom of heaven is like unto **treasure** hid in a field
Matt. 16:26	if he shall **gain** the whole world, and lose his own
Matt. 19:21(16-26)	give to the poor...thou shalt have **treasure** in heaven
Mark 4:19(18-19)	cares of this world, and the deceitfulness of **riches**
Mark 10:24(17-27)	hard...for them that trust in **riches** to enter into the
Mark 12:44(43-44)	did cast in of their **abundance**; but she of her want
Luke 6:24	but woe unto you that are **rich**! for ye have received
Luke 8:14	choked with cares and **riches** and pleasures of this

462

TREASURE cont.

layeth up **treasure** for himself, and is not rich toward
a **treasure** in the heavens...where no thief approacheth
who will commit to your trust the true **riches**
or despisest thou the **riches** of his goodness and
that he might make known the **riches** of his glory on
same Lord over all is **rich** unto all that call upon him
depth of the **riches** both of the wisdom and knowledge
as poor, yet making many **rich**; as having nothing, and
Jesus Christ...ye through his poverty might be **rich**.
forgiveness...according to the **riches** of his grace
riches of the glory of his inheritance in the saints
the exceeding **riches** of his grace in his kindness
I should preach...the unsearchable **riches** of Christ
would grant you, according to the **riches** of his glory
God shall supply...according to his **riches** in glory
God would make known what is the **riches** of the glory
in whom are hid all the **treasures** of wisdom and
they that will be **rich** fall into temptation and a
reproach of Christ greater **riches** than the treasures
your **riches** are corrupted, and your garments are
because thou sayest, I am **rich**, and increased with
their **treasure** is their God...shall perish with them
neither is there any end of their **treasures**; their
but before ye seek for **riches**, seek ye for the kingdom
they began to be exceeding **rich**, having abundance of
did not set their hearts upon **riches**; therefore they
began to wax proud, because of their exceeding **riches**
seek not after **riches**...you cannot carry them with you
lifted up...because of their exceeding great **riches**
pride...because of their exceeding great **riches** and
lay up for yourselves a **treasure** in heaven, yea, which
Lord had blessed them so long with the **riches** of the
set your hearts upon the **riches** and the vain things
instead of laying up for yourselves **treasures** in
in all manner of **precious** things of every kind and art
hide up **treasures** in the earth shall find them again
yea, we have hid up our **treasures** and they have
lay up for yourselves **treasures** in heaven, where
they had become exceeding **rich**, because of their
inhabitants thereof began to hide up their **treasures**
ye shall **treasure** up the things which ye have seen
he may **treasure** up for his soul everlasting salvation
seek...for wisdom...and then shall you be made **rich**.
therefore **treasure** up these words in thy heart. be
a desire to lay up **treasures** for yourself in heaven-
that he may **treasure** up for his soul...salvation in
seek...for wisdom...and then shall you be made **rich**.
more than...**treasures** of earth and corruptibleness to
and the **rich** have I made, and all flesh is mine, and
if ye seek...ye shall have the **riches** of eternity; and
consecrate of the **riches** of those who embrace my
by the voice of glory...and the **riches** of eternal life
treasure these things up in your hearts, and let the

TREASURE cont.

D&C 56:16(16-18)	wo unto you **rich** men, that will not give your
D&C 67:2	and lo...the **riches** of eternity are mine to give.
D&C 68:31	they also seek not earnestly the **riches** of eternity
D&C 78:18	the kingdom...and the **riches** of eternity are yours.
D&C 84:85	**treasure** up in your minds...and it shall be given you
D&C 89:19(18-19)	great **treasures** of knowledge, even hidden treasures
D&C 111:2	I have much **treasure** in this city for you, for the
D&C 133:30	bring...rich **treasures** unto the children of Ephraim
JS-M 1:37	whoso **treasureth** up my word, shall not be deceived

TRIBULATION

Ex. 3:17(16-22)	I will bring you up out of the **affliction** of Egypt
Deut. 4:30(27-31)	when thou art in **tribulation**...if thou turn to the Lord
Judg. 10:14(13,14)	cry unto the gods...in the time of your **tribulation**.
1 Sam. 10:19(17-25)	God...saved you out of all...your **tribulations**; and
1 Sam. 26:24(23-25)	let him deliver me out of all **tribulation**.
Neh. 9:27(26-28)	in the time of their **trouble**, when they cried unto the
Matt. 13:21(18-23)	when **tribulation**...ariseth because of the word, by and
Matt. 24:21	for then shall be great **tribulation**, such as was not
John 16:33	in the world ye shall have **tribulation**: but be of good
Acts 14:22	we must through much **tribulation** enter into the
Rom. 5:3(3-5)	we glory...knowing that **tribulation** worketh patience
Rom. 8:35(35-39)	separate us from the love of Christ? shall **tribulation**
2 Cor. 1:4(3-7)	who comforteth us in all our **tribulation**, that we may
1 Pet. 2:19(19-23)	if a man...endure **grief**, suffering wrongfully.
Rev. 7:14(13,14)	they which came out of great **tribulation**, and have was
Mosiah 23:10(9-10)	after much **tribulation**, the Lord did hear my cries
Mosiah 27:28(25-32)	after...much **tribulations**...I am born of God.
Alma 8:14(8-32)	wading through much **tribulation** and anguish of soul
Alma 15:3(3-12)	**tribulations** of his mind on account of his wickedness
Alma 53:13	**tribulations** which the Nephites bore for them, they
Alma 60:26(25,26)	faith, and their patience in their **tribulations**
D&C 54:10	be patient in **tribulation** until I come; and, behold
D&C 58:4	for after much **tribulation** come the blessings.
D&C 112:13(12-14)	after...much **tribulation**...the Lord, will feel after
D&C 122:5(1-9)	if thou art called to pass through **tribulation**; if
JS-M 1:36	after the **tribulation** of those days, and the powers
JFS-V 1:13(11-16)	suffered **tribulation** in their Redeemer's name.

TRUST IN GOD

2 Sam. 22:3	him will I **trust**: he is my shield, and the horn of my
1 Chr. 5:20(18-20)	because they put their **trust** in him.
2 Chr. 13:18(13-18)	because they **relied** upon the Lord God of their fathers
Job 13:15	though he slay me, yet will I **trust** in him: but I will
Ps. 2:12	blessed are all they that put their **trust** in him.
Ps. 9:10	they that know thy name will put their **trust** in thee
Ps. 16:1	preserve me, O God: for in thee do I put my **trust**.
Ps. 22:4(4-5)	our fathers **trusted** in thee: they trusted, and thou
Ps. 25:2	O my God, I **trust** in thee: let me not be ashamed, let

TRUST IN GOD cont.

Ps. 25:20	O keep my soul...for I put my **trust** in thee.
Ps. 26:1	I have **trusted** also in the Lord; therefore I shall not
Ps. 31:1(1-3)	in thee, O Lord, do I put my **trust**; let me never be
Ps. 32:10	he that **trusteth** in the Lord, mercy shall compass him
Ps. 34:22	none of them that **trust** in him shall be desolate.
Ps. 37:3(3-5)	**trust** in the Lord, and do good; so shalt thou dwell
Ps. 56:4(3,4,11)	in God I have put my **trust**; I will not fear what flesh
Ps. 62:8	**trust** in him at all times; ye people, pour out your
Ps. 64:10	the righteous shall...**trust** in him; and all the
Ps. 78:22	they believed not in God, and **trusted** not in his
Ps. 91:2	my refuge...my fortress: my God; in him will I **trust**.
Ps. 115:9(9-11)	O Israel, **trust** thou in the Lord: he is their help and
Ps. 118:8(8-9)	it is better to **trust** in the Lord than to put
Ps. 125:1	they that **trust** in the Lord...abideth for ever.
Prov. 3:5(5-6)	**trust** in the Lord with all thine heart; and lean not
Prov. 16:20	whoso **trusteth** in the Lord, happy is he.
Prov. 29:25	whoso putteth his **trust** in the Lord shall be safe.
Jer. 17:7(5-8)	blessed is the man that **trusteth** in the Lord, and
1 Tim. 4:10	suffer reproach, because we **trust** in the living God
1 Pet. 3:5	holy women also, who **trusted** in God, adorned
2 Ne. 4:19(16-23)	I know in whom I have **trusted**.
2 Ne. 4:34	I will **trust** in thee forever. I will not put my trust
Mosiah 4:6(5-7)	salvation might come to him that should put his **trust**
Mosiah 7:19	lift up your heads...rejoice...put your **trust** in God
Mosiah 23:22(21-22)	whosoever putteth his **trust** in him..shall be lifted
Mosiah 29:20	arm of mercy towards them that put their **trust** in him.
Alma 5:13(6-21)	they humbled themselves and put their **trust** in...God.
Alma 19:23	Ammon...therefore, Mosiah **trusted** him unto the Lord.
Alma 36:3	whosoever shall...**trust** in God shall be supported in
Alma 58:33(33,37)	we **trust** in our God who has given us victory over
Alma 61:13	we should put our **trust** in him, and he will deliver
Hel. 12:1	bless and prosper those who put their **trust** in him.
Morm. 9:20	know not the God in whom they should **trust**.
D&C 11:12(12-14)	put your **trust** in that Spirit which leadeth to do good
D&C 14:8	ask the Father in my name, in faith **believing**, you
D&C 19:30(29,30)	do it with all humility, **trusting** in me, reviling not
D&C 35:8	wonders, unto all those who **believe** on my name.
D&C 84:116	let him **trust** in me and he shall not be confounded
D&C 121:45(41-45)	**confidence** wax strong in the presence of God; and the

TRUST IN THE ARM OF FLESH

2 Chr. 32:8(7-22)	with him is an arm of **flesh**; but with us is the Lord
Ps. 146:3(3-4)	put not your **trust** in princes, nor in the son of man
Prov. 3:5(5-6)	and lean not unto thine **own** understanding.
Prov. 28:26	he that **trusteth** in his own heart is a fool: but whoso
Isa. 2:8(6-9)	they **worship** the work of their own hands, that which
Isa. 2:22	cease ye from **man**, whose breath is in his nostrils
Isa. 28:15(9-22)	we have made lies our **refuge**, and under falsehood have
Isa. 30:2(1-7)	to strengthen themselves in the strength of **Pharaoh**
Isa. 31:1(1-3)	woe to them that go down to Egypt for **help**; and stay
Isa. 36:6	this broken reed, on **Egypt**; whereon if a man lean, it

TRUST IN THE ARM OF FLESH cont.

Isa. 59:4	they **trust** in vanity, and speak lies; they conceive
Jer. 7:8	behold, ye **trust** in lying words, that cannot profit.
Jer. 17:5	**trusteth** in man, and maketh flesh his arm, and whose
Micah 7:5	**trust** ye not in a friend, put ye not confidence in a
Luke 6:26(22-26)	woe unto you, when all **men** shall speak well of you
Luke 6:39	can the **blind** lead the blind? shall they not both fall
Rom. 8:1(1-9)	walk not after the **flesh**, but after the Spirit.
Philip. 3:3(1-6)	and have no confidence in the **flesh**.
2 Ne. 4:34	I will not put my **trust** in the arm of flesh; for I
2 Ne. 19:16(15-16)	they that are **led** of them are destroyed.
2 Ne. 28:31	cursed is he that putteth his **trust** in man, or maketh
Mosiah 23:14(12-14)	**trust** no one to be your teacher...except..a man of God
D&C 1:19	neither **trust** in the arm of flesh
D&C 3:7(1-8)	you should not have feared **man** more than God. although
D&C 5:21	yield to the persuasions of **men** no more
D&C 76:61	let no man glory in **man**, but rather let him glory in

TRUSTWORTHINESS

Gen. 18:19(17-19)	I know him, that he will ...**keep** the way of the Lord
Gen. 39:8(4-12)	he hath **committed** all that he hath to my hand
Prov. 3:5(5,6)	**trust** in the Lord with all thine heart; and lean not
Prov. 11:28	he that **trusteth** in his riches shall fall: but the
Ezek. 33:13(13-16)	if he **trust** to his own righteousness, and commit
Dan. 3:28(26-30)	and delivered his servants that **trusted** in him, and
Matt. 25:23(14-30)	thou hast been **faithful** over a few things, I will
Luke 12:42(41-48)	who then is that **faithful** and wise steward, whom his
Luke 16:11(9-12)	who will commit to your **trust** the true riches
1 Cor. 4:2	required in stewards, that a man be found **faithful**.
1 Tim. 1:11(11-12)	glorious gospel...which was committed to my **trust**.
1 Tim. 3:11(10-11)	not slanderers, sober, **faithful** in all things.
1 Tim. 6:20	O Timothy, keep that which is committed to thy **trust**
1 Ne. 4:37(31-38)	made an oath unto us, our **fears** did cease concerning
2 Ne. 4:34(34,35)	I have **trusted** in thee, and I will trust in thee
Mosiah 23:14(13-14)	**trust** no one to be your teacher...except..a man of God
Alma 18:10(8-10)	there has not been any...so **faithful** as this man; for
Alma 52:10	be **faithful** in maintaining that quarter of the land
Alma 57:21(20-22)	they did **obey** and observe to perform every word of
Alma 58:40(39-40)	they **stand** fast in that liberty wherewith God has made
Morm. 1:2(2-4)	I perceive that thou art a **sober** child, and art quick
D&C 1:37(37-39)	search these commandments, for they are...**faithful**
D&C 42:53(53-55)	thou shalt **stand** in the place of thy stewardship.
D&C 51:19	found a **faithful**, a just, and a wise steward shall
D&C 103:36	through your diligence, **faithfulness**, and prayers of
JS-M 1:49(49,50)	who, then, is a **faithful** and wise servant, whom his
JS-H 1:59	I should be **responsible** for them; that if I should

TRUTH

Ps. 19:9(7-9)	the judgments of the Lord are **true** and righteous
Ps. 85:11(9-11)	**truth** shall spring out of the earth; and righteousness
Prov. 3:3(3-5)	let not mercy and **truth** forsake thee: bind them about
Prov. 8:7(4-11)	for my mouth shall speak **truth**; and wickedness is an
Prov. 23:23	buy the **truth**, and sell it not; also wisdom, and
Hosea 4:1	there is no **truth**, nor mercy, nor knowledge of God in
Zech. 8:16	speak ye every man the **truth** to his neighbour; execute
John 1:17(16,17)	grace and **truth** came by Jesus Christ.
John 3:21	he that doeth **truth** cometh to the light, that his deed
John 4:24(23,24)	worship him must worship him in Spirit and in **truth**.
John 7:17(16,17)	he shall **know** of the doctrine, whether it be of God
John 7:28(28,29)	he that sent me is **true**, whom ye know not.
John 8:32(31-32)	ye shall know the **truth**, and the truth shall make you
John 8:44(44-47)	devil...abode not in the **truth**...no truth in him.
John 14:6	I am the way, the **truth**, and the life: no man cometh
John 16:13	he will guide you into all **truth**: for he shall not
John 17:17(3,17)	sanctify them through thy truth: thy word is **truth**.
John 18:37(37-38)	that I should bear witness unto the **truth**. Every one
1 Cor. 13:6	rejoiceth not in iniquity, but rejoiceth in the **truth**
Gal. 4:16(12-16)	am I...your enemy, because I tell you the **truth**
Eph. 4:25	speak every man **truth** with his neighbour: for we are
Eph. 6:14	stand...having your loins girt about with **truth**, and
Philip. 4:8(7-9)	whatsoever things are **true**, whatsoever things are
1 Tim. 3:15	the church...the pillar and ground of the **truth**.
2 Tim. 3:7(1-7)	never able to come to the knowledge of the **truth**.
2 Tim. 4:4(3-4)	they shall turn away their ears from the **truth**...unto
2 Pet. 2:2(1-3)	the way of **truth** shall be evil spoken of.
1 Ne. 16:2(2-3)	guilty taketh the **truth** to be hard, for it cutteth the
2 Ne. 9:40	words of **truth** are hard against all uncleanness; but
3 Ne. 16:7	in the latter day shall the **truth** come unto the
Ether 3:12	thou art a God of **truth**, and canst not lie.
Moro. 10:4(4-5)	he will manifest the **truth** of it unto you, by the
D&C 1:39(37-39)	and the **truth** abideth forever and ever. Amen.
D&C 19:26	Book of Mormon...contains the **truth** and the word of
D&C 27:16(15-18)	stand...having your loins girt about with **truth**
D&C 45:57	they that are wise and have received the **truth**, and
D&C 50:40	ye must grow in grace and in...knowledge of the **truth**.
D&C 84:45	whatsoever is **truth** is light, and whatsoever is light
D&C 88:6(4-7)	he might be in all...the light of **truth**
D&C 88:40	**truth** embraceth truth; virtue loveth virtue; light
D&C 88:66	**truth** abideth and hath no end; and if it be in you it
D&C 93:24	and **truth** is knowledge of things as they are, and as
D&C 93:28(26-28)	he that keepeth his commandments receiveth **truth** and
D&C 93:29	intelligence, or the light of **truth**, was not created
D&C 93:30	all **truth** is independent in that sphere in which God
D&C 93:36	glory of God is intelligence, or...light and **truth**.
D&C 93:39(37,39,40)	wicked one cometh and taketh away light and **truth**
D&C 109:56(54-58)	their prejudices may give way before the **truth**, and
D&C 123:12(12,13)	kept from the **truth** because they know not where to
JS-H 1:10(10-20)	if any one of them be **right**, which is it, and how

TYRANNY

Judg. 9:4(1-57)	Abimelech **hired** vain and light persons, which followed
1 Sam. 8:9(5-22)	the manner of the king that shall **reign** over them.
1 Kgs. 21:10(5-29)	and set two men...to bear witness **against** him, saying
2 Kgs. 21:9(1-18)	Manasseh seduced them to do more **evil** than did the
Esth. 3:6(6-10)	Haman sought to **destroy** all the Jews that were through
Prov. 29:2(1,2)	the wicked beareth **rule**, the people mourn.
Dan. 3:6(1-30)	whoso falleth not down...**cast** into...fiery furnace.
Dan. 6:7(4-24)	ask a petition of any God...**cast** into the den of lions
Matt. 2:16(16-19)	Herod...**slew** all the children that were in Bethlehem
Matt. 14:10(1-12)	and he sent, and **beheaded** John in the prison.
Acts 12:2(1,2)	and he **killed** James the brother of John with the sword
Mosiah 11:2(1-15)	and he did **cause** his people to commit sin, and do
Mosiah 29:17(11-24)	how much **iniquity** doth one wicked king cause to be
Alma 46:10	to **destroy** the foundation of liberty which God had
Alma 47:35(35,36)	by his **fraud**...he obtained the kingdom; yea, he was
Alma 48:4(2-4)	to **overpower** the Nephites and to bring them into
Alma 51:8(1-21)	of high birth, and they sought to be **kings**; and they
Alma 61:8(2-8)	they have appointed a **king** over them, and he hath writ
3 Ne. 6:30(29-30)	at defiance the law...to establish a **king** over the
Ether 9:11(4-12)	Akish was desirous for **power**; wherefore, the sons of
Ether 10:6(5-8)	whoso refused to labor he did **cause** to be put to death
D&C 98:9(6-10)	nevertheless, when the wicked **rule** the people mourn.

UNBELIEF, UNBELIEVERS

Num. 20:12	Moses and Aaron, because ye **believed** me not, to
Deut. 1:32	in this thing ye did not **believe** the Lord your God
2 Kgs. 17:14(6-18)	like...their fathers, that did not **believe** in the Lord
Ps. 106:24	they despised the...land, they **believed** not his word
Isa. 6:9(9-10)	understand not; and see ye indeed, but **perceive** not.
Ezek. 23:35(29-35)	because thou hast **forgotten** me, and cast me behind thy
Mal. 2:11(11,12)	hath married the daughter of a **strange** god.
Matt. 13:15(10-17)	their eyes they have **closed**; lest at any time they
Matt. 17:17	O **faithless** and perverse generation, how long shall I
Matt. 21:32	ye **believed** him not: but the publicans and the harlot
Luke 16:31(27-31)	if they **hear** not Moses and the prophets, neither will
John 3:18	he that **believeth** not is condemned already, because
John 5:38	whom he hath sent, him ye **believe** not.
John 10:25(25-26)	I told you, and ye **believed** not: the works that I do
John 20:27	and be not faithless, but **believing**.
Acts 28:24(24,26-27)	some believed...were spoken, and some **believed** not.
Rom. 11:20	because of **unbelief** they were broken off, and thou
2 Cor. 4:4(3-4)	God of this world hath blinded..which **believe** not
2 Thes. 2:12	all might be damned who **believed** not the truth, but
Heb. 3:19(18-19)	they could not enter in because of **unbelief**.
Heb. 4:11(6,11)	lest any man fall after the same example of **unbelief**.
Jude 1:5	afterward destroyed them that **believed** not.
1 Ne. 17:18	neither would they **believe** that I was instructed of
2 Ne. 1:10	time cometh that they shall dwindle in **unbelief**, after
2 Ne. 26:17	those who have dwindled in **unbelief** shall not have
Mosiah 26:3(1-4)	because of...**unbelief** they could not understand...word
Mosiah 27:8(1-8)	sons of Mosiah were numbered among the **unbelievers**

UNBELIEF, UNBELIEVERS cont.

Alma 4:8(8-10)	they began to persecute those that did not **believe**
Alma 19:6	dark veil of **unbelief** was being cast away from his
Alma 30:42(29-56)	thou **believest**, but thou art possessed with a lying
Alma 33:21	would ye rather harden your hearts in **unbelief**, and
Hel. 4:25(23-26)	fallen into a state of **unbelief** and awful wickedness
3 Ne. 1:9	there was a day set apart by the **unbelievers**, that all
3 Ne. 1:18(16-18)	fear because of their iniquity and their **unbelief**.
3 Ne. 15:18(17,18)	because of...**unbelief** they understood not my word; the
3 Ne. 16:4(4-8)	remnant..shall be scattered..because of their **unbelief**
3 Ne. 19:35(35,36)	I could not show..great miracles, because of..**unbelief**
4 Ne. 1:38	they did not dwindle in **unbelief**, but they did
Morm. 1:14	Holy Ghost did not come upon any because of...**unbelief**
Morm. 5:14	they shall go unto the **unbelieving** of the Jews; and
Morm. 8:28(25-28)	in a day when the power of God shall be **denied**, and
Morm. 9:6	O then ye **unbelieving**, turn ye unto the Lord; cry
Morm. 9:20	they dwindle in **unbelief**, and depart from the right
Ether 4:13(13-18)	greater...knowledge...is hid up because of **unbelief**
Moro. 7:37(35-38)	if these things have ceased..it is because of **unbelief**
Moro. 10:24(24,25)	it shall be because of **unbelief**.
D&C 5:8(6-8)	this **unbelieving** and stiffnecked generation- mine
D&C 20:15	but those who harden their hearts in **unbelief**, and
D&C 63:17	the **unbelieving**...shall have their part in that lake
D&C 74:5	a believer should not be united to an **unbeliever**
D&C 84:54(54-56)	your minds...have been darkened because of **unbelief**
D&C 85:9	portion shall be appointed them among **unbelievers**
D&C 101:90	appoint them their portion among...**unbelievers**
Moses 5:13(13-15)	they **believed** it not, and they loved Satan more than
Moses 5:57(55-57)	they would not hearken...nor **believe** on his Only

UNCLEANNESS

Lev. 5:2(1-7)	if a soul touch any **unclean** thing, whether it be a
Lev. 10:10(8-11)	difference between holy and unholy..**unclean** and clean
Lev. 11:47(1-47)	to make a difference between the **unclean** and the clean
Judg. 13:4	eat not any **unclean** thing
Job 14:4	who can bring a clean thing out of an **unclean**? not one
Isa. 6:5(5-7)	I am a man of **unclean** lips, and I dwell in the midst
Isa. 64:6(5,6)	but we are all as an **unclean** thing, and all our
Ezek. 39:24(23-24)	according to their **uncleanness**...have I done unto them
Ezek. 44:23	teach...discern between the **unclean** and the clean.
Matt. 10:1	gave them power against **unclean** spirits, to cast them
Matt. 12:43	when the **unclean** spirit is gone out of a man, he
Luke 6:18(17,18)	and they that were vexed with **unclean** spirits: and the
Acts 10:28	I should not call any man common or **unclean**.
Acts 11:9(7-9)	what God hath **cleansed**, that call not thou common.
Rom. 1:24(21-25)	God also gave them up to **uncleanness** through the lusts
Rom. 14:14(13-14)	there is nothing **unclean** of itself: but to him that
1 Cor. 3:17(16-17)	if any man **defile** the temple of God, him shall God
2 Cor. 6:17	touch not the **unclean** thing; and I will receive you
Gal. 5:19(19-21)	the works of the flesh...are these...**uncleanness**
Eph. 5:5(3-5)	nor **unclean** person...hath any inheritance in the
1 Thes. 4:7	God hath not called us unto **uncleanness**, but unto

UNCLEANNESS cont.

2 Pet. 2:10(9,10)	them that walk...in the lust of **uncleanness**, and
1 Ne. 10:21	no **unclean** thing can dwell with God; wherefore, ye
1 Ne. 15:34	there cannot any **unclean** thing enter into the kingdom
2 Ne. 9:14	we shall have a perfect knowledge of...our **uncleanness**
2 Ne. 9:40	words of truth are hard against all **uncleanness**; but
Alma 7:21	neither can...**unclean** be received into the kingdom of
Alma 11:37	no **unclean** thing can inherit the kingdom of heaven
Alma 40:26	no **unclean** thing can inherit the kingdom of God; but
3 Ne. 20:41(40-41)	touch not that which is **unclean**; go ye out of the
3 Ne. 27:19	no **unclean** thing can enter into his kingdom; therefore
Morm. 9:28	strip yourselves of all **uncleanness**; ask not, that ye
Moro. 10:30	touch not the evil gift, nor the **unclean** thing.
D&C 88:124	cease to be **unclean**; cease to find fault one with
D&C 90:18	keep slothfulness and **uncleanness** far from you.
D&C 94:8(1-9)	shall not suffer any **unclean** thing to come in unto it
D&C 97:15	do not suffer any **unclean** thing to come into it, that
Moses 6:57	for no **unclean** thing can dwell there, or dwell in his

UNDERSTANDING

Deut. 4:6(5,6)	this is your wisdom and your **understanding** in the
1 Kgs. 3:9(5,9-12)	give...thy servant an **understanding** heart to judge thy
1 Kgs. 4:29	God gave Solomon wisdom and **understanding** exceeding
Job 28:28	to depart from evil is **understanding**.
Job 32:8	inspiration of the Almighty giveth them **understanding**.
Ps. 111:10	a good **understanding** have all they that do his
Ps. 119:34(33-34)	give me **understanding**, and I shall keep thy law; yea
Ps. 119:99(97-104)	I have more **understanding** than all my teachers: for
Ps. 119:130	thy words...giveth **understanding** unto the simple.
Ps. 119:169	Lord: give me **understanding** according to thy word.
Ps. 147:5	of great power: his **understanding** is infinite.
Prov. 2:6(1-11)	out of his mouth cometh knowledge and **understanding**.
Prov. 3:5(1-6)	lean not unto thine own **understanding**.
Prov. 3:13(13-20)	happy is the man...that getteth **understanding**.
Prov. 3:19(19,20)	by **understanding** hath he established the heavens.
Prov. 4:7(5-9)	and with all thy getting get **understanding**.
Prov. 7:4(1-4)	and call **understanding** thy kinswoman
Prov. 9:10	the knowledge of the holy is **understanding**.
Prov. 14:29	he that is slow to wrath is of great **understanding**
Prov. 15:14	the heart of him that hath **understanding** seeketh
Prov. 15:21	a man of **understanding** walketh uprightly.
Prov. 15:32	he that heareth reproof getteth **understanding**.
Prov. 16:16	to get **understanding** rather to be chosen than silver
Prov. 17:27(27-28)	a man of **understanding** is of an excellent spirit.
Prov. 19:8	he that keepeth **understanding** shall find good.
Prov. 21:30	there is no...**understanding**...against the Lord.
Isa. 11:2(2-3)	the spirit of wisdom and **understanding**, the spirit
Isa. 27:11	a people of no **understanding**: therefore he that made
Isa. 29:14	the **understanding** of their prudent men shall be hid.
Jer. 51:15	hath stretched out the heaven by his **understanding**.
Luke 2:47	were astonished at his **understanding** and answers.
Luke 24:45	then opened he their **understanding**, that they might

UNDERSTANDING cont.

Rom. 1:31(28-32)	without **understanding**, covenantbreakers, without
Rom. 15:4	were written aforetime were written for our **learning**
1 Cor. 1:19	will bring to nothing the **understanding** of the prudent
1 Cor. 14:20(13-20)	be not children in **understanding**: howbeit in malice
Eph. 1:18	the eyes of your **understanding** being enlightened; that
Eph. 4:18(17-18)	having the **understanding** darkened, being alienated
Philip. 4:7(6-7)	peace of God, which passeth all **understanding**, shall
Col. 1:9(9-10)	of his will in all wisdom and spiritual **understanding**
Col. 2:2(1-2)	unto all riches of the full assurance of **understanding**
2 Tim. 3:15(15-17)	which are able to make thee **wise** unto salvation
1 Ne. 13:29(25-29)	plain unto the **understanding** of the children of men
1 Ne. 14:23(18-23)	precious and easy to the **understanding** of all men.
1 Ne. 16:29(26-29)	new writing...which did give us **understanding**
2 Ne. 31:3	the Lord God giveth light unto the **understanding**; for
W of M 1:9	I make it according to...the **understanding** which God
Mosiah 1:2	become men of **understanding**; and that they might know
Mosiah 12:27(26-27)	ye have not applied your hearts to **understanding**
Mosiah 26:3	because of their unbelief they could not **understand**
Alma 17:2(1-3)	they were men of a sound **understanding** and they had
Alma 26:35(34,35)	God...has all power, all wisdom, and all **understanding**
Alma 32:28(28-34)	it beginneth to enlighten my **understanding**, yea, it
Alma 48:11(11-13)	Moroni...was a man of a perfect **understanding**; yea, a
D&C 1:24(19-24)	commandments given...that..might come to **understanding**
D&C 20:68(68,69)	expound all things...to their **understanding**, previous
D&C 29:50	he that hath no **understanding**, it remaineth in me to
D&C 32:4(4,5)	that I may unfold the same to their **understanding**.
D&C 71:5	whoso readeth, let him **understand** and receive also
D&C 76:9(5-9)	their **understanding** reach to heaven; and before them
D&C 76:12(10-12)	our **understandings** were enlightened, so as to see and
D&C 88:11	same light that quickeneth your **understandings**
D&C 91:4	whoso readeth it, let him **understand**, For the spirit
D&C 97:14(10-15)	be perfected in the **understanding** of their ministry
D&C 110:1(1-8)	the eyes of our **understanding** were opened.
JFS-V 1:11	as I pondered...the eyes of my **understanding** were open

UNITY

Gen. 2:24(22-24)	and they shall be **one** flesh.
Num. 15:15(13-16)	**one** ordinance...both for...congregation, and...strange
Ps. 133:1	how good...for brethren to dwell together in **unity**
Ezek. 37:22(19-22)	I will make them **one** nation in the land upon the mount
Amos 3:3	can two walk together, except they be **agreed**
Zeph. 3:9	to serve him with one **consent**.
Mal. 2:15(14-16)	and did not he make **one**? yet had he the residue of the
Matt. 18:20	for where two or three are gathered **together** in my
John 10:30	I and my Father are **one**.
John 17:11(11,21-23)	that they may be **one**, as we are.
Acts 1:14(13-14)	these all continued with **one** accord in prayer and
Acts 4:32(31,32)	multitude...were of **one** heart and of one soul: neither
Rom. 12:5(4,5)	so we, being many, are **one** body in Christ, and every
2 Cor. 13:11	be perfect...be of **one** mind, live in peace; and the
Gal. 3:28(28,29)	for ye are all **one** in Christ Jesus.

UNITY cont.

Eph. 4:3(3-6,13)	the **unity** of the Spirit in the bond of peace.
Eph. 5:31(23-31)	and they two shall be **one** flesh.
Philip. 1:27	one spirit, with **one** mind striving together for the
Philip. 2:2	being of **one** accord, of one mind.
Heb. 2:11	they who are sanctified are all of **one**: for which
1 Pet. 3:8	finally, be ye all of **one** mind, having compassion one
1 Jn. 5:7	father...word...holy ghost...these three are **one**.
2 Ne. 31:21	the Father...Son, and...Holy Ghost, which is **one** God
Alma 11:44	Son...Father...Holy Spirit, which is **one** eternal God
3 Ne. 11:36(27,36)	the Father, and I, and the Holy Ghost are **one**.
D&C 6:32	gathered together in my name, as touching **one** thing
D&C 20:28	Father, Son, and Holy Ghost are **one** God, infinite and
D&C 35:2	even **one** in me as I am one in the Father, as the
D&C 38:27(24-27)	be one; and if ye are not **one** ye are not mine.
D&C 41:2(2,3)	assemble yourselves together to **agree** upon my word
D&C 50:43	the Father and I are **one**. I am in the Father and the
D&C 51:9	that ye may be **one**, even as I have commanded you.
D&C 105:4(2-5)	**union** required by the law of the celestial kingdom
D&C 107:27(27-32)	every decision made...must be by the **unanimous** voice
Moses 7:18	they were of **one** heart and one mind, and dwelt in

UNRIGHTEOUS DOMINION

1 Sam. 13:9(8-14)	**Saul**...offered the burnt offering.
1 Kgs. 14:9(6-11)	but hast done **evil** above all that were before thee
1 Kgs. 15:26(25,26)	and he did **evil** in the sight of the Lord, and walked
1 Kgs. 15:34(33,34)	and he did **evil** in the sight of the Lord, and walked
1 Kgs. 16:13(12,13)	sinned, and by which they **made** Israel to sin, in
1 Kgs. 16:25(25-28)	but Omri wrought **evil** in the eyes of the Lord, and did
1 Kgs. 16:30(29-33)	and Ahab...did **evil**...above all that were before him.
Matt. 7:22(21-23)	Lord, have we not **prophesied** in thy name? and in thy
Acts 8:19(18-24)	give me also this **power**, that on whomsoever I lay hand
Acts 19:13(1-16)	we **adjure** you by Jesus whom Paul preacheth.
Rom. 1:18(18-21)	men, who hold the truth in **unrighteousness**
3 Jn. 1:9(9-10)	Diotrephes, who loveth to have the **preeminence** among
2 Ne. 26:29	men preach and set **themselves** up for a light unto the
Mosiah 11:1(1-15)	Noah began to **reign** in his stead; and he did not walk
Mosiah 23:12(7-14)	**oppressed** by king...been in bondage to him and his
Alma 1:6(2-15)	he...began to **establish** a church after the manner of
Alma 2:9(1-31)	they...did **consecrate** Amlici to be their king.
Alma 51:5(2-21)	**king-men**...desirous that the law should be altered in
D&C 58:20	let no man think he is **ruler**; but let God rule him
D&C 121:39(34-40)	will immediately begin to exercise **unrighteous**
Abr. 1:27	priesthood...Pharaohs would fain **claim** it from Noah

URIM AND THUMMIM

Ex. 28:15(5-29)	make the **breastplate** of judgment with cunning work
Ex. 28:30	put in the breastplate...the **Urim** and the Thummim; and
Lev. 8:8	also he put in the breastplate the **Urim** and the
Num. 27:21(19-21)	ask counsel for him after the judgment of **Urim** before

URIM AND THUMMIM cont.

Deut. 33:8	let thy Thummim and thy **Urim** be with thy holy one, who
1 Sam. 28:6	Lord answered him not, neither by...**Urim**, nor by
Ezra 2:63	till there stood up a priest with **Urim** and with
Neh. 7:65	till there stood up a priest with **Urim** and Thummim.
Rev. 2:17	a white **stone**, and in the stone a new name written
1:20(20,21)	he did **interpret** the engravings by the gift and power
Mosiah 8:13(7-19)	the things are called **interpreters**, and no man can
Mosiah 28:20	all the records, and also the **interpreters**, and confer
Alma 37:21	and that ye preserve these **interpreters**.
Alma 37:24(23-24)	these **interpreters** were prepared that the word of God
Ether 3:23(21-28)	behold, these two **stones** will I give unto thee, and
Ether 4:5(5-6)	sealed up the **interpreters**, according to the
D&C 10:1	translate by the means of the **Urim** and Thummim, into
D&C 17:1	**Urim** and Thummim...were given to the brother of Jared
D&C 130:9(8,9)	this earth...will be a **Urim** and Thummim to the inhabit
D&C 130:10(10-11)	the white **stone**...will become a Urim and Thummim to
Abr. 3:1(1-4)	Abraham, had the **Urim** and Thummim, which the Lord my
JS-H 1:35	stones...breastplate...called the **Urim** and Thummim
JS-H 1:52(52,59)	did I behold...the **Urim** and Thummim, and the
JS-H 1:62	by means of the **Urim** and Thummim I translated some of

USURY

Ex. 22:25	neither shalt thou lay upon him **usury**.
Lev. 25:36(35-37)	take thou no **usury** of him, or increase: but fear thy
Deut. 23:19(19-20)	thou shalt not lend upon **usury** to thy brother; usury
Neh. 5:7(7,10)	ye exact **usury**, every one of his brother. And I set a
Ps. 15:5(1-5)	putteth not out his money to **usury**, nor taketh reward
Prov. 28:8	he that by **usury** and unjust gain increaseth his
Isa. 24:2(1-3)	as with the taker of **usury**, so with the giver of usury
Jer. 15:10	I have neither lent on **usury**, nor men have lent to me
Ezek. 18:8(8-17)	he that hath not given forth upon **usury**, neither hath
Ezek. 22:12	thou hast taken **usury** and increase, and thou hast
Matt. 25:27(24-29)	my coming I should have received...with **usury**.
Luke 19:23	I might have required mine own with **usury**

VANITY

Job 15:31	let not him that is deceived trust in **vanity**: for
Job 15:35	they conceive mischief, and bring forth **vanity**, and
Ps. 4:2	how long will ye love **vanity**, and seek after leasing
Ps. 24:4	hath not lifted up his soul unto **vanity**, nor sworn
Ps. 39:11	consume away like a moth: surely every man is **vanity**.
Ps. 62:9	balance, they are altogether lighter than **vanity**.
Ps. 78:33	their days did he consume in **vanity**, and their years
Ps. 94:11	Lord knoweth the thoughts of man, that they are **vanity**
Ps. 119:37	turn away mine eyes from beholding **vanity**; and quicken
Ps. 144:4	man is like to **vanity**: his days are as a shadow that
Ps. 144:11	strange children, whose mouth speaketh **vanity**, and the
Prov. 13:11	wealth gotten by **vanity** shall be diminished: but he
Prov. 21:6	getting of treasures by a lying tongue is a **vanity**

VANITY cont.

Prov. 30:8   remove far from me **vanity** and lies: give me neither
Eccl. 1:2   **vanity** of vanities, saith the preacher, vanity of
Eccl. 1:14   behold, all is **vanity** and vexation of spirit.
Eccl. 2:21   this also is **vanity** and a great evil.
Eccl. 4:7(7-8)   then I returned, and I saw **vanity** under the sun.
Eccl. 5:7   in the...dreams and many words...are...**vanities**: but
Eccl. 5:10   loveth silver...not...satisfied...is also **vanity**.
Eccl. 6:9   wandering of the desire: this is also **vanity** and
Eccl. 6:11   there be many things that increase **vanity**, what is man
Eccl. 7:6   the laughter of the fool: this also is **vanity**.
Eccl. 7:15   all things have I seen in the days of my **vanity**: there
Eccl. 8:14   there is a **vanity** which is done upon the earth; that
Eccl. 9:9   all the days of the life of thy **vanity**, which he hath
Eccl. 11:8   they shall be many. All that cometh is **vanity**.
Eccl. 11:10   for childhood and youth are **vanity**.
Isa. 3:16(16-26)   because the daughters of Zion are **haughty**, and walk
Isa. 5:18   that draw iniquity with cords of **vanity**, and sin as
Isa. 30:28   sift the nations with the sieve of **vanity**: and there
Isa. 32:9(9-11)   ye **careless** daughters; give ear unto my speech.
Isa. 40:17   all nations...counted...less than nothing, and **vanity**.
Isa. 41:29   they are all **vanity**; their works are nothing: their
Hab. 2:13   the people shall weary themselves for very **vanity**
Acts 14:15   turn from these **vanities** unto the living God, which
Rom. 8:20   the creature was made subject to **vanity**, not willingly
Eph. 4:17   other Gentiles walk, in the **vanity** of their mind
2 Pet. 2:18   they speak great swelling words of **vanity**, they allure
2 Ne. 9:28   O the **vainness**, and the frailties, and the foolishness
2 Ne. 15:18   them that draw iniquity with cords of **vanity**, and sin
Jacob 2:13   high heads because of the costliness of your **apparel**
Alma 1:27(27-32)   they did not wear costly **apparel**, yet...were neat and
Alma 4:8   set their hearts...upon the **vain** things of the world
Morm. 8:36(36-37)   pride...unto the wearing of very fine **apparel**, unto
D&C 20:5   he was entangled again in the **vanities** of the world
D&C 84:55(54-55)   which **vanity** and unbelief have brought the whole
D&C 106:7   notwithstanding the **vanity** of his heart, I will lift

VEIL

Ex. 26:33(31-37)   the **vail** shall divide...the holy place and the most
Ex. 27:21(20-21)   in the tabernacle of the congregation without the **vail**
Ex. 34:33(29-35)   speaking with them, he put a **vail** on his face.
Ex. 36:35   and he made a **vail** of blue, and purple, and scarlet
Ex. 40:3(3,21,22)   cover the ark with the **vail**.
Lev. 16:2   the holy place within the **vail** before the mercy seat
Lev. 21:23(16-24)   only he shall not go in unto the **vail**, nor come nigh
Num. 18:7(2-7)   keep your priest's office...within the **vail**; and ye
Eccl. 1:11   there is no **remembrance** of former things; neither
Isa. 25:7(6-8)   the **vail** that is spread over all nations.
Matt. 27:51(50-53)   the **veil** of the temple was rent in twain from the top
1 Cor. 13:12(9-12)   now we see through a **glass**, darkly; but then face to
2 Cor. 3:14(13-16)   minds were blinded...which **vail** is done away in Christ
Eph. 2:14(13-16)   hath broken down the middle **wall** of partition between

VEIL cont.

Heb. 6:19(17-20)	which hope...entereth into that within the **veil**
Heb. 9:3(1-5)	and after the second **veil**, the tabernacle which is
Heb. 10:20(1,20)	he hath consecrated for us, through the **veil**, that is
Alma 19:6(4-6)	the dark **veil** of unbelief was being cast away from his
Ether 3:19(1-28)	could not be kept from beholding within the **veil**; and
Ether 4:15	when ye shall rend that **veil** of unbelief which doth
Ether 12:19(19-21)	many...who could not be kept from within the **veil**, but
D&C 38:8(5-9)	the **veil** of darkness shall soon be rent, and he that
D&C 67:10(10-14)	the **veil** shall be rent and you shall see me and know
D&C 101:23	**veil** of the covering of my temple...shall be taken off
D&C 110:1(1-4)	the **veil** was taken from our minds, and the eyes of our
Moses 7:26	it **veiled** the whole face of the earth with darkness
Moses 7:56	and the heavens were **veiled**; and all the creations of
Moses 7:61	a **veil** of darkness shall cover the earth; and the

VENGEANCE

Deut. 32:35	to me belongeth **vengeance**, and recompence; their foot
Ps. 94:1	O Lord God, to whom **vengeance** belongeth; shew thyself.
Isa. 63:4(2-4)	the day of **vengeance** is in mine heart, and the year
Alma 1:13	his blood would come upon us for **vengeance**.
3 Ne. 21:21	I will execute **vengeance** and fury upon them, even as
Morm. 3:15	**vengeance** is mine, and I will repay; and because this
Morm. 8:20(19-21,41)	**vengeance** is mine also, and I will repay.
Ether 8:22(22-24)	cry unto him from the ground for **vengeance** upon them
D&C 3:4	incur the **vengeance** of a just God upon him.
D&C 29:17	I will take **vengeance** upon the wicked, for they will
D&C 97:22	**vengeance** cometh speedily upon the ungodly as the

VINEYARD OF THE LORD

Gen. 49:22	Joseph is a fruitful **bough**, even a fruitful bough by
Judg. 9:12(1-20)	then said the trees unto the **vine**...reign over us.
Ps. 80:8(7-16)	thou hast brought a **vine** out of Egypt: thou hast cast
Isa. 1:8	daughter of Zion is left as a cottage in a **vineyard**
Isa. 5:7(1-7)	**vineyard** of the Lord of hosts is the house of Israel
Isa. 27:6(2-6)	Israel shall...fill the face of the world with **fruit**.
Isa. 60:21(14,21,22)	inherit the land for ever, the **branch** of my planting
Isa. 61:3(1-3)	**trees** of righteousness, the planting of the Lord
Jer. 2:21(20-22)	I had planted thee a noble **vine**, wholly a right seed
Jer. 11:16(16,17)	Lord called thy name, a green **olive** tree, fair, and
Ezek. 15:6(6-8)	as the **vine** tree among the trees of the forest, which
Ezek. 17:6(1-24)	became a spreading **vine** of low stature, whose branches
Ezek. 19:10(10-14)	thy mother is like a **vine**...planted by the waters: she
Hosea 10:1	Israel is an empty **vine**, he bringeth forth fruit unto
Hosea 14:6(4-7)	his branches shall spread...beauty...as the **olive** tree
Mal. 4:1	it shall leave them neither root nor **branch**.
Matt. 15:13	every **plant**...father hath not planted, shall be rooted
Matt. 20:2(1-8)	agreed...a penny a day, he sent them into his **vineyard**
Matt. 21:19(19-21)	fig tree...let no **fruit** grow on thee henceforward for
Matt. 21:41(33-43)	let out his **vineyard** unto other husbandmen, which

VINEYARD OF THE LORD cont.

Mark 12:9(1-12)	and will give the **vineyard** unto others.
Luke 13:6(6-9)	man had a fig tree planted in his **vineyard**; and he
Luke 20:9(9-19)	man planted a **vineyard**, and let it forth to
John 15:5(1-8)	I am the **vine**, ye are the branches: he that abideth
Rom. 11:17(16-24)	thou, being a wild olive **tree**, wert graffed in among
Rev. 14:18(17-20)	gather the clusters of the **vine** of the earth; for her
1 Ne. 10:12(12-14)	Israel...compared like unto an **olive-tree**, whose
1 Ne. 15:12(7-20)	Israel was compared unto an **olive-tree**, by the Spirit
2 Ne. 3:5	righteous **branch**...to be broken off...remembered in
2 Ne. 9:53	shall become a righteous **branch** unto the house of
2 Ne. 15:7(1-30)	**vineyard** of the Lord of hosts is the house of Israel
Jacob 5:3(3-77)	Israel, like unto a tame **olive-tree**, which a man took
Jacob 6:2(1-13)	servants of the Lord shall...prune his **vineyard**; and
Alma 16:17(15-17)	as a branch be grafted into the true **vine**, that they
D&C 10:60	other sheep...were a **branch** of the house of Jacob
D&C 33:4(3,4)	and my **vineyard** has become corrupted every whit; and
D&C 101:56(44-62)	redeem my **vineyard**; for it is mine; I have bought it
D&C 103:21(15-26)	the servant to whom the Lord of the **vineyard** spake in

VIRTUE

Lev. 18:24(6-25)	**defile** not ye yourselves in any of these things: for
Ps. 24:4(1-4)	he that hath clean hands, and a **pure** heart; who hath
Prov. 12:4	a **virtuous** woman is a crown to her husband: but she
Prov. 31:10(10-31)	a **virtuous** woman?...her price is far above rubies.
Philip. 4:8	if there be any **virtue**...think on these things.
1 Tim. 4:12	be thou an example...in faith, in **purity**.
2 Pet. 1:3	him that hath called us to glory and **virtue**
2 Pet. 1:5(5-9)	add to your faith **virtue**; and to virtue knowledge
Alma 31:5	should try the **virtue** of the word of God.
Moro. 9:9	dear and precious above all...chastity and **virtue**
D&C 4:6	remember faith, **virtue**, knowledge, temperance
D&C 25:2	walk in the paths of **virtue** before me, I will preserve
D&C 38:24	practise **virtue** and holiness before me.
D&C 46:33	ye must practise **virtue** and holiness before me
D&C 88:40	**virtue** loveth virtue; light cleaveth unto light; mercy
D&C 107:30	decisions of these quorums...to be made in...**virtue**
D&C 121:45	let **virtue** garnish thy thoughts unceasingly; then
D&C 132:52	who are **virtuous** and pure before me; and those who are
A of F 1:13	We believe in being..**virtuous**...if...anything virtuous

VISIONS

Gen. 15:1(1-17)	word of the Lord came unto Abram in a **vision**, saying
Gen. 46:2	God spake unto Israel in the **visions** of the night, and
Num. 12:6	I the Lord will make myself known unto him in a **vision**
Num. 24:4	which saw the **vision** of the Almighty, falling into a
1 Sam. 3:1	word of the Lord was precious...was no open **vision**.
Prov. 29:18	where there is no **vision**, the people perish: but he
Isa. 1:1	the **vision** of Isaiah the son of Amoz, which he saw
Jer. 1:11(11-14)	word of the Lord...saying...what **seest** thou? and I

VISIONS cont.

Jer. 14:14(11-16)	I sent them not...they prophesy...you a false **vision**
Dan. 1:17	Daniel had understanding in all **visions** and dreams.
Joel 2:28	old men...dream dreams...young men shall see **visions**
Matt. 17:9(1-9)	tell the **vision** to no man, until the Son of man be
Acts 10:3(1-7)	he saw in a **vision** evidently about the ninth hour of
Acts 16:9	and a **vision** appeared to Paul in the night; there
Acts 18:9	then spake the Lord to Paul in the night by a **vision**
Acts 22:6(6-11)	shone from heaven a great **light** round about me.
Acts 23:11	the night following the **Lord** stood by him, and said
Acts 26:19	I was not disobedient unto the heavenly **vision**
Acts 27:23(23-24)	stood by me this night the **angel** of God, whose I am
1 Ne. 1:8(8,16)	he was carried away in a **vision**, even that he saw the
1 Ne. 5:4	if I had not seen the things of God in a **vision** I
1 Ne. 8:2(2,36)	dreamed a dream; or...I have seen a **vision**.
1 Ne. 10:17	the things which he saw in **vision**, and also the things
2 Ne. 1:4	I have seen a **vision**, in which I know that Jerusalem
2 Ne. 4:23	heard my cry...and...hath given me knowledge by **vision**
Alma 8:20	the man whom an angel said in a **vision**: thou shalt
Alma 19:16	on account of a remarkable **vision** of her father
Alma 38:7	I have **seen** an angel face to face, and he spake with
D&C 76:14(14,28,30)	saw and with whom we conversed in the heavenly **vision**.
D&C 76:47	I, the Lord, show it by **vision** unto many, but straight
D&C 76:50(50-70,92)	we bear record- for we **saw** and heard, and this is the
D&C 76:80(71-80)	end of the **vision** which we saw of the terrestrial
D&C 76:81(81-90)	we **saw** the glory of the telestial, which glory is that
D&C 110:11	after this **vision** closed, the heavens were again
Moses 1:2(1-11)	he saw God face to face, and he talked with him, and
Moses 1:27(24-31)	Moses...**beheld** the earth, yea, even all of it; and
Moses 7:23(23-69)	Enoch **beheld**...all the nations of the earth were
JS-H 1:17(11-20)	I **saw** two Personages...standing above me in the air.
JS-H 1:24(24,25)	nevertheless a fact that I had beheld a **vision**. I have
JS-H 1:33(29-47)	he was a **messenger** sent from the presence of God to
JS-H 1:72(68-72)	the **messenger** who visited us on this occasion and
A of F 1:7	We believe in...prophecy, revelation, **visions**, healing

VOWS

Gen. 28:20	and Jacob vowed a **vow**, saying, if God will be with me
Gen. 31:13	thou vowedst a **vow** unto me: now arise, get thee out
Num. 6:2(2-5)	man or woman shall separate themselves to vow a **vow**
Num. 21:2	Israel vowed a **vow** unto the Lord, and said, if thou
Num. 30:2(1-16)	vow a **vow** unto the Lord...he shall not break his word
Deut. 23:21(21-23)	when thou shalt **vow** a vow unto the Lord...not slack
1 Sam. 1:11	and she vowed a **vow**, and said, O Lord of hosts, if
Job 22:27	hear thee, and thou shalt pay thy **vows**.
Ps. 50:14	and pay thy **vows** unto the most High
Ps. 56:12	thy **vows** are upon me, O God: I will render praises
Ps. 61:5	thou, O God, hast heard my **vows**: thou hast given me
Ps. 76:11	**vow**, and pay unto the Lord your God: let all that be
Ps. 132:2	how he sware unto the Lord, and **vowed** unto the mighty
Isa. 19:21	they shall vow a **vow** unto the Lord, and perform it.
Jonah 2:9	I will pay that that I have **vowed**. Salvation is of

VOWS cont.

Matt. 14:7(7-9)	he **promised** with an oath to give her whatsoever she
Mark 6:26(14-29)	yet for his **oath's** sake, and for their sakes which sat
Luke 1:73(72,73)	the **oath** which he sware to our father Abraham
Acts 18:18	Paul...having shorn his head...for he had a **vow**.
Acts 21:23(23,24)	four men which have a **vow** on them
Acts 23:21	themselves with an **oath**, that they will neither eat
Heb. 6:17(16,17)	God...**confirmed** it by an oath
1 Ne. 3:7	I **will** go and do the things which the Lord hath
1 Ne. 4:37(31-37)	when Zoram had made an **oath** unto us, our fears did
2 Ne. 1:5	God hath **covenanted** with me should be a land for the
Mosiah 18:13	entered into a **covenant** to serve him until you are
Alma 50:39	with an **oath** and sacred ordinance to judge righteously
Alma 53:11(11,14)	taken an **oath** that they never would shed blood more
Alma 56:8	not suffer more because of the fulfilling the **oath**
Morm. 5:1	I...did repent of the **oath** which I had made that I
D&C 59:11	nevertheless thy **vows** shall be offered up in righteous
D&C 108:3	careful henceforth in observing your **vows**, which you
D&C 132:7	all covenants...oaths, **vows**...not made and entered

WAGES

Lev. 19:13	thou shalt not defraud...the **wages** of him that is hire
Prov. 11:18	soweth righteousness shall be a sure **reward**.
Isa. 23:18	and her merchandise and her **hire** shall be holiness to
Jer. 22:13	woe unto him that...useth...service without **wages**, and
Hag. 1:6	earneth **wages** to put it into a bag with holes.
Mal. 3:5	against those that oppress the hireling in his **wages**
Matt. 20:8(1-16)	call the labourers, and give them their **hire**
Luke 3:14	and be content with your **wages**.
Luke 10:7	for the labourer is worthy of his **hire**. Go not from
John 4:36	he that reapeth receiveth **wages**, and gathereth fruit
John 10:13(11-16)	the **hireling** fleeth, because he is an hireling, and
Rom. 6:23	for the **wages** of sin is death; but the gift of God is
1 Cor. 3:8	every man shall receive his own **reward** according to
2 Cor. 11:8	I robbed other churches, taking **wages** of them, to do
1 Tim. 5:18	and, the labourer is worthy of his **reward**.
James 5:4	the **hire** of the labourers...you kept back by fraud
2 Pet. 2:15(10-17)	son of Bosor, who loved the **wages** of unrighteousness
2 Ne. 26:31(30,31)	if they labor for **money** they shall perish.
Mosiah 18:24	the priests...should labor...for their **support**.
Alma 3:27	man receiveth **wages** of him whom he listeth to obey
Alma 5:42(4-42)	for his **wages** he receiveth death, as to things pertain
Alma 11:1	receive **wages** according to the time which they labored
D&C 29:45	they receive their **wages** of whom they list to obey.
D&C 31:5	for the laborer is worthy of his **hire**. Wherefore, your
D&C 70:8(6-8)	**benefits**...consecrated unto the inhabitants of Zion
D&C 82:17(17-19)	equal claims on the **properties**, for the benefit of
D&C 84:79	the laborer is worthy of his **hire**.
D&C 84:89(88-90)	receiveth you receiveth me...and give you **money**.
D&C 106:3	for the laborer is worthy of his **hire**.

WALKING IN DARKNESS

Lev. 18:3	neither shall ye **walk** in their ordinances.
Lev. 20:23	ye shall not **walk** in the manners of the nation, which
Deut. 8:19	**walk** after other gods, and serve them, and worship
1 Sam. 8:5	thy sons **walk** not in thy ways: now make us a king to
2 Kgs. 10:31	Jehu took no heed to **walk** in the law of the Lord God
Ps. 82:5	they **walk** on in darkness: all the foundations of the
Prov. 2:13(12-13)	leave...uprightness, to **walk** in the ways of darkness
Isa. 3:16	**walk** with stretched forth necks and wanton eyes, walk
Isa. 42:24	they would not **walk** in his ways, neither were they
Isa. 59:9	obscurity; for brightness, but we **walk** in darkness.
Jer. 7:9	burn incense unto Baal, and **walk** after other gods whom
Jer. 13:10	**walk** after other gods, to serve them, and to worship
Jer. 18:12	we will **walk** after our own devices, and we will every
Dan. 4:37	those that **walk** in pride he is able to abase.
John 8:12	he that followeth me shall not **walk** in darkness, but
John 12:35(35,36)	he that walketh in **darkness** knoweth not whither he
Acts 14:16	past suffered all nations to **walk** in their own ways.
Acts 26:18	to turn them from **darkness** to light, and from the
1 Pet. 2:9	called you out of **darkness** into his marvellous light
2 Pet. 2:10	them that **walk** after the flesh in the lust of
1 Jn. 1:5(5-7)	and in him is no **darkness** at all.
1 Jn. 1:6	say...have fellowship with him, and **walk** in darkness
1 Jn. 2:11(8-11)	he that hateth his brother...walketh in **darkness**, and
Jude 1:18	mockers...who should **walk** after their own ungodly lust
2 Ne. 7:10(10-11)	servant, that **walketh** in darkness and hath no light
2 Ne. 9:28(28,29)	they **hearken** not unto the counsel of God, for they
2 Ne. 13:16	the daughters of Zion...**walk** with stretched-forth neck
2 Ne. 19:2	the people that **walked** in darkness have seen a great
Mosiah 11:1	he did not **walk** in the ways of his father.
Alma 45:24	would not give heed...to **walk** uprightly before God.
Hel. 12:5	how slow to **walk** in wisdom's paths
Hel. 13:27(27-29)	**walk** after the pride of your eyes, and do whatsoever
Morm. 8:36	I know that ye do **walk** in the pride of your hearts
D&C 1:16	every man **walketh** in his own way, and after the image
D&C 95:6	they are **walking** in darkness at noon-day.
D&C 95:12	keep not my commandments...you shall **walk** in darkness.

WALKING WITH GOD

Gen. 5:24	Enoch **walked** with God: and he was not; for God took
Gen. 6:9	and Noah **walked** with God.
Gen. 17:1	I am...God; **walk** before me, and be thou perfect.
Gen. 24:40	the Lord, before whom I **walk**, will send his angel with
Gen. 48:15	God, before whom my fathers Abraham and Isaac did **walk**
Ex. 3:12(7-12)	I will be **with** thee; and this shall be a token unto
Ex. 16:4	prove them, whether they will **walk** in my law, or no.
Ex. 18:20	shew them the way wherein they must **walk**, and the work
Lev. 18:4	do my judgments..keep mine ordinances, to **walk** therein
Lev. 26:3(3-28)	if ye **walk** in my statutes, and keep my commandments
Lev. 26:12	and I will **walk** among you, and will be your God, and
Deut. 5:33	**walk** in all the ways which the Lord...commanded you
Deut. 8:6	keep the commandments of...God, to **walk** in his ways

WALKING WITH GOD cont.

Deut. 11:22(12,22)	to love the Lord your God, to **walk** in all his ways
Deut. 13:4(4-5)	ye shall **walk** after the Lord your God, and fear him
Deut. 19:9	to love the Lord thy God, and to **walk** ever in his ways
Josh. 22:5	to **walk** in all his ways, and to keep his commandments
Judg. 2:22	they will keep the way of the Lord to **walk** therein
1 Sam. 2:30	thy house...should **walk** before me for ever: but now
1 Kgs. 2:3	the charge of the Lord thy God, to **walk** in his ways
1 Kgs. 8:23(22-61)	thy servants that **walk** before thee with all their hear
1 Kgs. 11:38	if thou wilt...**walk** in my ways, and do that is right
2 Kgs. 23:3	made a covenant...to **walk** after the Lord, and to keep
2 Chr. 6:14(14-31)	thy servants, that **walk** before thee with all their
2 Chr. 7:17	if thou wilt **walk** before me, as David thy father
2 Chr. 34:31	made a covenant...to **walk** after the Lord, and to keep
Neh. 5:9	ought ye not to **walk** in the fear of our God because
Ps. 15:2	he that **walketh** uprightly, and worketh righteousness
Ps. 23:4	though I **walk** through the valley of the shadow of
Ps. 56:13	that I may **walk** before God in the light of the living
Ps. 84:11	no good thing...withhold from them that **walk** uprightly
Ps. 101:6	he that **walketh** in a perfect way, he shall serve me.
Prov. 2:7	he is a buckler to them that **walk** uprightly.
Prov. 3:6(5-6)	acknowledge him, and he shall direct thy **paths**. I
Prov. 10:9	he that **walketh** uprightly walketh surely: but he that
Prov. 14:2	he that **walketh** in his uprightness feareth the Lord
Prov. 20:7	the just man **walketh** in his integrity: his children
Prov. 28:18	whoso **walketh** uprightly shall be saved: but he that
Isa. 2:5(3-5)	house of Jacob, come...**walk** in the light of the Lord.
Isa. 30:21	this is the way, **walk** ye in it, when ye turn to the
Isa. 33:15	he that **walketh** righteously, and speaketh uprightly
Isa. 42:5	he that giveth...Spirit to them that **walk** therein
Jer. 6:16	where is the good way...**walk** therein, and ye shall
Jer. 26:4	**walk** in my law, which I have set before you
Ezek. 11:20	**walk** in my statutes, and keep mine ordinances, and do
Dan. 9:10	**walk** in his laws, which he set before us by his
Hosea 11:10	they shall **walk** after the Lord: he shall roar like a
Hosea 14:9	ways of the Lord are right...just shall **walk** in them
Micah 4:2	we will **walk** in his paths: for the law shall go forth
Micah 6:8	the Lord require...to **walk** humbly with thy God
Zech. 3:7	if thou wilt **walk** in my ways, and if thou wilt keep
John 11:9(9-11)	if any man **walk** in the day, he stumbleth not, because
Rom. 4:12	who also **walk** in the steps of that faith of our father
Rom. 6:4	even so we also should **walk** in newness of life.
Rom. 8:1(1-4)	who **walk** not after the flesh, but after the Spirit.
Gal. 5:16	**walk** in the Spirit, and ye shall not fulful the lust
Eph. 2:10	good works...God..ordained that we should **walk** in them
Eph. 5:2	**walk** in love, as Christ also hath loved us, and hath
Col. 1:10	**walk** worthy of the Lord unto all pleasing, being fruit
Col. 2:6	as ye have...received Christ Jesus...so **walk** ye in him
Col. 4:5	**walk** in wisdom toward them that are without, redeeming
1 Thes. 2:12	that ye would **walk** worthy of God, who hath called you
1 Thes. 4:1	how ye ought to **walk** and to please God, so ye would
1 Jn. 1:7	if we **walk** in the light, as he is in the light, we
2 Jn. 1:6	this is love, that we **walk** after his commandments.
3 Jn. 1:4	no greater joy...hear that my children **walk** in truth.

WALKING WITH GOD cont.

Rev. 3:4	they shall **walk** with me in white: for they are worthy.
Rev. 21:24	nations of them which are saved shall **walk** in the
1 Ne. 16:3(3,5)	that ye might **walk** uprightly before God, then ye would
2 Ne. 4:32	that I may **walk** in the path of the low valley, that I
2 Ne. 12:3(3,5)	we will **walk** in his paths; for out of Zion shall go
2 Ne. 31:20(20-21)	ye must press forward with a **steadfastness** in Christ
2 Ne. 33:9	**walk** in the straight path which leads to life, and
Mosiah 2:27	served you, **walking** with a clear conscience before God
Mosiah 4:15	teach them to **walk** in the ways of truth and soberness
Mosiah 4:26	that ye may **walk** guiltless before God- I would that
Mosiah 6:6	king Mosiah did **walk** in the ways of the Lord, and did
Mosiah 18:29	they did **walk** uprightly before God, imparting to one
Mosiah 23:14	be a man of God, **walking** in his ways and keeping his
Mosiah 26:38	**walking** in all diligence, teaching the word of God
Mosiah 29:43	Alma did **walk** in the ways of the Lord, and he did keep
Alma 5:27	have ye **walked**, keeping yourselves blameless before
Alma 5:54	humble themselves...**walk** after the holy order of God
Alma 7:9(9-22)	repent ye...and **walk** in his paths, which are straight
Alma 25:14	they did **walk** in the ways of the Lord, and did observe
Alma 41:8	whosoever will may **walk** therein and be saved.
Alma 53:21	keep...commandments of God...**walk** uprightly before him
Hel. 12:5	how slow to **walk** in wisdom's paths
Hel. 15:5	they do **walk** circumspectly before God, and they do
4 Ne. 1:12	they did **walk** after the commandments which they had
Ether 6:17	they were taught to **walk** humbly before the Lord; and
D&C 90:24	if ye **walk** uprightly and remember the covenant
D&C 100:15	work together for good to them that **walk** uprightly
D&C 107:49(48-49)	he saw the Lord, and he **walked** with him, and was
D&C 136:4	we will **walk** in all the ordinances of the Lord.
Moses 1:26	I am **with** thee, even unto the end of thy days; for
Moses 6:34	abide in me, and I in you; therefore **walk** with me.
Moses 6:39	all them that heard him; for he **walked** with God.
Moses 7:69	and Enoch and all his people **walked** with God, and he
Moses 8:27	Noah...**walked** with God, as did also his three sons

WAR

Gen. 6:13(12-13)	the earth is filled with **violence** through them; and
Ex. 15:3	the Lord is a man of **war**: the Lord is his name.
Deut. 20:10(10-12)	comest nigh unto a city to **fight** against it, then
2 Sam. 1:27	the mighty fallen, and the weapons of **war** perished
Neh. 4:14	**fight** for your brethren...sons...daughters...wives
Ps. 120:7	I am for peace: but when I speak, they are for **war**.
Isa. 2:4	neither shall they learn **war** any more.
Isa. 13:4(4-13)	the Lord of hosts mustereth the host of the **battle**.
Isa. 66:16(15-16)	by his **sword** will the Lord plead with all flesh: and
Dan. 7:21(19-22)	the same horn made **war** with the saints, and prevailed
Joel 3:9(9-16)	proclaim...among the Gentiles; prepare **war**, wake up
Micah 4:3	rebuke..nations..neither shall they learn **war** any more
Matt. 24:6(6-7)	ye shall hear of **wars** and rumours of wars: see that
2 Cor. 10:3(3,4)	walk in the flesh, we do not **war** after the flesh
James 4:1(1-2)	from whence come **wars** and fightings among you? come

WAR cont.

1 Pet. 2:11	abstain from fleshly lusts, which **war** against the soul
Rev. 12:7	there was **war** in heaven: Michael and his angels fought
Rev. 19:11	in righteousness he doth judge and make **war**.
1 Ne. 14:16	**wars**...among all the nations which belonged to the
1 Ne. 22:13(13-14)	for they shall **war** among themselves, and the sword of
2 Ne. 21:9	shall not hurt nor **destroy** in all my holy mountain
2 Ne. 25:12(11,12)	they shall have **wars**, and rumors of wars; and when the
Alma 43:47(26-54)	ye shall **defend** your families even unto bloodshed. the
Alma 44:6(1-7)	deliver up your weapons of **war** unto us, and we will
Alma 48:14(10-17)	never to raise the **sword** except...preserve their lives
Alma 50:21	quarrelings...brought upon them their **wars** and their
Alma 55:3(1-3)	seek **death** among them until they shall sue for peace.
Alma 56:2	in the tribulations of our **warfare**; behold, my beloved
Alma 60:13(12-14)	not suppose that the righteous are lost because..**slain**
Alma 61:15(10-15)	give unto them power to conduct the **war** in that part
Morm. 6:8	came to **battle** against us, and every soul was filled
Morm. 6:22	repented before this great **destruction** had come upon
Morm. 8:30	heard of **wars**, rumors of wars, and earthquakes in
Ether 15:19	Satan had full power...went again to **battle**.
D&C 27:15(15-16)	take upon you my whole **armor**, that ye may be able to
D&C 38:29(28-30)	ye hear of **wars** in far countries, and you say that the
D&C 45:69(63-71)	the only people that shall not be at **war** one with
D&C 60:4	I, the Lord, rule...among the **armies** of the earth; and
D&C 63:33(32-34)	I have...decreed **wars** upon the face of the earth, and
D&C 76:29	he maketh **war** with the saints of God, and encompasseth
D&C 87:6(6-8)	with the sword and by **bloodshed** the inhabitants of the
D&C 98:16(13-16)	renounce **war** and proclaim peace, and seek diligently
D&C 98:34(33-38)	should proclaim **war** against them, they should first
D&C 130:12(12,13)	the difficulties which will cause much **bloodshed**
D&C 134:11	all men are justified in **defending** themselves, their
Moses 6:15	and from thenceforth came **wars** and bloodshed; and a

WARNINGS

2 Chr. 19:10(4-10)	**warn** them that they trespass not against the Lord, and
Ps. 19:11(9-11)	by them is thy servant **warned**: and in keeping of them
Eccl. 4:13	who will no more be **admonished**.
Jer. 6:10	to whom shall I...give **warning**, that they may hear
Ezek. 3:19(16-21)	**warn** the wicked, and he turn not...delivered thy soul.
Ezek. 33:3(1-9)	seeth the **sword**..blow the trumpet, and **warn** the people
Amos 3:7	God will do nothing, but he **revealeth** his secret unto
Matt. 3:7	who hath **warned** you to flee from the wrath to come
Acts 10:22	was **warned** from God by an holy angel to send for thee
Acts 20:31	I ceased not to **warn** every one night and day with
Rom. 15:14	able also to **admonish** one another.
1 Cor. 4:14	but as my beloved sons I **warn** you.
1 Cor. 10:11	now all these things...are written for our **admonition**
Col. 1:28	whom we preach, **warning** every man, and teaching every
1 Thes. 5:14	brethren, **warn** them that are unruly, comfort the
2 Thes. 3:15(13-15)	not as an enemy, but **admonish** him as a brother.
Heb. 11:7	by faith Noah, being **warned** of God of things not seen
2 Ne. 1:3	**warning** us that we should flee out of the land of

WARNINGS cont.

2 Ne. 5:6	those who believed in the **warnings** and the revelations
Jacob 2:9(5-10)	strict commandment...to **admonish** you according to your
Jacob 3:12	**warning** them against fornication and lasciviousness
1:12(12,13)	he being **warned** of the Lord that he should flee out
Mosiah 16:12(10-13)	they being **warned** of their iniquities and yet they
Mosiah 23:1(1-4)	now Alma, having been **warned** of the Lord that the
Mosiah 26:6(5-7)	who committed sin...should be **admonished** by the church
Mosiah 26:39(38,39)	were also **admonished**, every one by the word of God
Ether 9:3(2-4)	the Lord **warned** Omer in a dream that he should depart
D&C 1:4	the voice of **warning** shall be unto all people, by the
D&C 38:41(40-42)	let your preaching be the **warning** voice, every man to
D&C 63:58(57-58)	this is a day of **warning**, and not a day of many words.
D&C 88:71	ponder the **warning** in their hearts which they have
D&C 88:81	every man who hath been warned to **warn** his neighbor.
D&C 89:4	I have **warned** you, and forewarn you, by giving unto
D&C 98:28	ye **warn** him in my name, that he come no more upon you

WASHING

Gen. 18:4(1-4)	**wash** your feet, and rest yourselves under the tree
Gen. 19:2	tarry all night, and **wash** your feet, and ye shall rise
Gen. 24:32	and water to **wash** his feet, and the men's feet that
Gen. 43:24	and they **washed** their feet; and he gave their asses
Lev. 13:58(54-58)	then it shall be **washed** the second time, and shall be
Num. 19:7(7-21)	the priest shall **wash** his clothes, and he shall bathe
2 Kgs. 5:10(10-13)	go and **wash** in the Jordan seven times, and thy flesh
2 Chr. 4:6(2-6)	he made also ten lavers...to **wash** in them: such
Ps. 26:6	I will **wash** mine hands in innocency: so will I compass
Ps. 73:13	heart in vain, and **washed** my hands in innocency.
Jer. 2:22(20-23)	though thou **wash** thee with nitre, and take thee much
Matt. 23:26(23-28)	**cleanse** first that which is within the cup and platter
Matt. 27:24	Pilate...**washed** his hands before the multitude, saying
Mark 7:5(1-23)	but eat bread with **unwashen** hands
John 13:5(4-17)	began to **wash** the disciples' feet, and to wipe them
Acts 22:16	arise, and be baptized, and **wash** away thy sins
1 Cor. 6:11	but ye are **washed**, but ye are sanctified, but ye are
1 Tim. 5:10	**washed** the saints' feet, if she have relieved the
Heb. 9:10(1-14)	stood only in meats and drinks, and divers **washings**
2 Pet. 2:22(20-22)	the sow that was **washed** to her wallowing in the mire.
Rev. 7:14(9-17)	and have **washed** their robes, and made them white in
2 Ne. 14:4(1-5)	**washed** away the filth of the daughters of Zion, and
Alma 5:21(20-26)	no man be saved except his garments are **washed** white
Alma 7:14	be baptized...that ye may be **washed** from your sins
Alma 13:11(10-12)	garments were **washed** white through the blood of the
3 Ne. 13:17(16-18)	when thou fastest, anoint thy head, and **wash** thy face
Ether 13:11(10-11)	they have been **washed** in the blood of the Lamb; and
D&C 60:15(13-16)	**wash** thy feet, as a testimony against them in the day
D&C 84:92(89-96)	**cleanse** your feet even with water, pure water, whether
D&C 88:74(74-75)	**cleanse** your hands and your feet before me, that I may
D&C 88:139(135-141)	be received by the ordinance of the **washing** of feet
D&C 99:4(1-4)	**cleanse** your feet in the secret places by the way for
D&C 124:37(36-39)	how shall your **washings** be acceptable unto me, except

WASTE

Lev. 26:20(14-20)	and your strength shall be **spent** in vain: for your
Prov. 18:9	slothful...is brother to him that is great **waster**.
Prov. 21:20	treasure...and oil...but a foolish man **spendeth** it up.
Isa. 54:16	I have created the **waster** to destroy.
Isa. 55:2(1-3)	wherefore do ye **spend** money for that which is not
Hag. 1:6(5-11)	wages...into a bag with **holes**.
Matt. 26:8(6-13)	to what purpose is this **waste**
Luke 15:13(11-17)	and there **wasted** his substance with riotous living.
Luke 16:1(1,2)	accused unto him that he had **wasted** his goods.
John 6:12	gather up the fragments that remain...nothing be **lost**.
Acts 17:21(16-23)	**spent** their time in nothing else, but either to tell
2 Ne. 9:27	wo unto him...that **wasteth** the days of his probation
Mosiah 12:29(29-31)	commit whoredoms and **spend** your strength with harlots
Alma 24:18(17-19)	rather than **spend** their days in idleness they would
Alma 34:33(33,34)	if we do not **improve** our time while in this life, the
D&C 49:21	wo be unto man...that **wasteth** flesh and hath no need.
D&C 60:13	thou shalt not **idle** away thy time, neither shalt thou

WATCHFULNESS

Gen. 31:49	the Lord **watch** between me and thee, when we are absent
Deut. 6:25	and it shall be our righteousness, if we **observe** to
Prov. 23:26	me thine heart, and let thine eyes **observe** my ways.
Isa. 29:20	all that **watch** for iniquity are cut off
Jer. 5:21	which have eyes, and **see** not; which have ears, and
Jer. 31:28	so will I **watch** over them, to build, and to plant
Ezek. 3:18(17-18)	and thou givest him not **warning**, nor speakest to warn
Ezek. 12:2	have eyes to see, and **see** not; they have ears to hear
Nahum 2:1	**watch** the way, make thy loins strong, fortify thy
Matt. 24:42(42-44)	**watch**...for ye know not what hour your Lord doth come.
Matt. 25:13	**watch** therefore, for ye know neither the day nor the
Matt. 26:41(38-41)	**watch** and pray, that ye enter not into temptation: the
Mark 13:33(33-37)	take ye heed, **watch** and pray: for ye know not when the
Mark 14:38	**watch** ye and pray, lest ye enter into temptation.
Luke 12:37(37-40)	blessed are...servants...Lord...shall find **watching**
Luke 21:36	**watch** ye therefore, and pray always, that ye may be
1 Cor. 16:13	**watch** ye, stand fast in the faith, quit you like men
Eph. 6:11(11,13-18)	put on the whole **armour** of God, that ye may be able
1 Thes. 5:6	not sleep, as do others; but let us **watch** and be sober
2 Tim. 4:5	but **watch** thou in all things, endure afflictions, do
1 Pet. 4:7(7-8)	be ye therefore sober, and **watch** unto prayer.
1 Pet. 5:8(7-8)	be sober, be **vigilant**; because your adversary the
Rev. 3:3	if therefore thou shalt not **watch**, I will come on thee
Rev. 16:15	I come as a thief. Blessed is he that **watcheth**, and
Mosiah 4:30	that if ye do not **watch** yourselves, and your thoughts
Alma 6:1	to preside and **watch** over the church.
Alma 13:28(27-30)	**watch** and pray continually, that ye may not be tempted
Alma 15:17	**watching** and praying continually, that they might be
Alma 34:39	that ye be **watchful** unto prayer continually, that ye
3 Ne. 1:8	they did **watch** steadfastly for that day and that night
3 Ne. 18:15(15,18)	ye must **watch** and pray always, lest ye be tempted by
Moro. 6:4	to keep them continually **watchful** unto prayer, relying

WATCHFULNESS cont.

D&C 42:76(74-77)	ye shall be **watchful** and careful, with all inquiry
D&C 50:46(45-46)	**watch**, therefore, that ye may be ready. Even so. Amen.
D&C 61:38(38-39)	gird up your loins and be **watchful** and be sober
D&C 82:5	**watch**, for the adversary spreadeth his dominions, and
D&C 84:111	deacons and teachers...to **watch** over the church, to
D&C 133:11(10-11)	**watch**..for ye know neither the day nor the hour.
JS-M 1:46(46-48)	**watch**...for you know not at what hour your Lord doth

WATCHMEN

Isa. 52:8(6-10)	thy **watchmen** shall lift up the voice...together shall
Isa. 56:10(10-12)	his **watchmen** are blind: they are all ignorant, they
Isa. 62:6	I have set **watchmen** upon thy walls, O Jerusalem, which
Jer. 6:17	also I set **watchmen** over you, saying, hearken to the
Jer. 31:6(4-13)	the **watchmen** upon the mount Ephraim shall cry, arise
Ezek. 3:17(17-21)	I have made thee a **watchman** unto the house of Israel
Ezek. 33:7(1-9)	son of man, I have set thee a **watchman** unto the house
Matt. 21:33(33-41)	built a tower, and let it out to **husbandmen**, and went
Mosiah 12:22(21-24)	thy **watchmen** shall lift up the voice; with the voice
Mosiah 15:29	thy **watchmen** shall lift up their voice; with the voice
Alma 6:1	priests and elders...to preside and **watch** over the
3 Ne. 16:18(17-20)	thy **watchmen** shall lift up the voice; with the voice
3 Ne. 20:32(29-40)	then shall their **watchmen** lift up their voice...sing
D&C 88:81(81,82)	behold, I sent you out to testify and **warn** the people
D&C 101:45(43-67)	and set **watchmen** round about them, and build a tower
D&C 105:16	throw down...mine enemies, and scatter their **watchmen**
D&C 124:61	those whom I have set...as **watchmen** upon her walls.

WELFARE

Gen. 41:36(33-57)	that food shall be for **store** to the land against the
Gen. 47:15(13-26)	Egyptians came unto Joseph, and said, give us **bread**
Ex. 23:11(9-11)	that the **poor** of thy people may eat: and what they
Lev. 19:10(9-10)	thou shalt leave them for the **poor** and stranger: I am
Lev. 23:22	thou shalt leave them unto the **poor**, and to the
Deut. 15:7(7-11)	nor shut thine hand from thy **poor** brother
Deut. 24:19(19-22)	for the fatherless, and for the **widow**: that the Lord
Prov. 28:27	he that giveth unto the **poor** shall not lack: but he
Isa. 58:7(6-8)	bring the **poor** that are cast out to thy house? when
Mal. 3:10(10-11)	bring...tithes...there may be **meat** in mine house, and
Matt. 6:4(1-4)	that thine **alms** may be in secret: and thy Father which
Matt. 25:40(35-40)	unto one of the least of these my **brethren**...unto me.
Luke 10:34(30-35)	brought him to an inn, and took **care** of him.
Acts 4:35(32-37)	distribution...unto every man according as he had **need**
Acts 5:2(1-11)	brought a certain **part**...laid it at the apostles' feet
Acts 6:1(1-3)	their widows were **neglected** in the daily ministration.
Acts 11:29(28-29)	send **relief** unto the brethren which dwelt in Judaea
Rom. 15:26(25-28)	**contribution** for the poor saints which are at
1 Cor. 13:3(3-13)	bestow all my goods to feed the **poor**..have not charity
1 Tim. 5:16(8-16)	any...that believeth have widows, let them **relieve** the
James 1:27	to **visit** the fatherless and widows in their affliction

WELFARE cont.

1 Pet. 3:8(8-9)	having **compassion** one of another, love as brethren
Jacob 2:17(17-19)	free with your **substance**, that they may be rich like
Mosiah 4:16(16-18,26)	**administer** of your substance unto him that standeth
Mosiah 18:29(27-29)	imparting to one another...**temporally** and spiritually
Alma 34:27(27-29)	prayer...for your **welfare**...those who are around you.
Alma 34:28(27-29)	and impart of your **substance**, if ye have, to those who
Alma 48:12(11-12)	man who did labor...for the **welfare**...of his people.
4 Ne. 1:3	they had all things **common** among them; therefore there
D&C 38:35(24-35)	they shall...administer to their **relief** that they
D&C 42:30(30-34)	consecrate of thy properties for their **support** that
D&C 42:42	**idle** shall not eat the bread nor wear the garments of
D&C 44:6	visit the poor and the **needy** and administer to their
D&C 51:13	let the bishop appoint a **storehouse** unto this church
D&C 52:40	remember in all things the poor and the **needy**, the
D&C 56:17(17-18)	who will not **labor** with your own hands
D&C 72:10(9-16)	to keep the Lord's **storehouse**; to receive the funds
D&C 83:5	after that, they have claim upon...Lord's **storehouse**
D&C 104:16(14-18)	it must needs be done in mine own **way**; and behold this
Moses 7:18	Zion...of one heart and one mind...no **poor** among them.

WHOREDOM

Lev. 19:29	land fall to **whoredom**, and...become full of wickedness
Lev. 21:7(7,14)	shall not take a wife that is a **whore**, or profane
Num. 25:1(1-9)	Israel...began to commit **whoredom** with the daughters
Prov. 7:27(6-27)	her **house** is the way to hell, going down to the
Hosea 1:2	the land hath committed great **whoredom**, departing
Hosea 4:11(1-14)	**whoredom** and wine and new wine take away the heart.
Hosea 4:12	the spirit of **whoredoms** hath caused them to err, and
Eph. 5:5	no **whoremonger**, nor unclean person, nor covetous man
1 Thes. 4:3	will of God...should abstain from **fornication**
1 Tim. 1:10(8-11)	for **whoremongers**, for them that defile themselves with
Heb. 13:4	but **whoremongers** and adulterers God will judge.
James 4:4	**adulterers** and adulteresses, know ye not that the
Rev. 22:15(11-15)	without are...sorcerers, and **whoremongers**, and
1 Ne. 14:10(10-12)	she is the **whore** of all the earth.
1 Ne. 22:13	church, which is the **whore** of all the earth, shall
2 Ne. 9:36	them who commit **whoredoms**...shall be thrust down to
2 Ne. 10:16	they are they who are the **whore** of all the earth; for
2 Ne. 26:32(32-33)	God hath commanded...not commit **whoredoms**; and that
2 Ne. 28:14(14,15)	because of...**whoredoms**, they have all gone astray save
2 Ne. 28:18	the **whore**...must tumble to the earth, and great must
Jacob 2:23(23-33)	excuse themselves in committing **whoredoms**, because of
Jacob 2:28(23-29)	**whoredoms** are an abomination before me; thus saith
Mosiah 11:6(6-15)	they were supported...in their **whoredoms**, by the taxes
Mosiah 11:14(1-29)	spent...their time with **harlots**.
Alma 30:18(12-18)	leading away...many...to commit **whoredoms**- telling the
Hel. 6:23(22-30)	might...commit **whoredoms** and all manner of wickedness
3 Ne. 16:10(10-12)	Gentiles...shall be filled with...**whoredoms**, and of
3 Ne. 21:19(19,20)	strifes, and priestcrafts, and **whoredoms**, shall be
3 Ne. 30:2(1,2)	turn...ye Gentiles, from your wicked ways...**whoredoms**
Morm. 8:31(26-35)	great pollutions upon...face of the earth...**whoredoms**

WHOREDOM cont.

Ether 10:11(5-11)	**whoredoms**; wherefore he was cut off from the presence
D&C 29:21	**whore** of all the earth, shall be cast down by
D&C 63:17	**whoremonger**...shall have...part in that lake which
D&C 76:103(98-112)	liars, and sorcerers, and adulterers, and **whoremongers**
D&C 86:3(1-3)	persecutor of the church...the **whore**, even Babylon

WICKEDNESS

Gen. 18:23(23-25)	wilt thou also destroy the righteous with the **wicked**
1 Sam. 24:13	**wickedness** proceedeth from the wicked: but mine hand
Ps. 125:3	rod of the **wicked** shall not rest upon the lot of the
Prov. 10:7	but the name of the **wicked** shall rot.
Prov. 29:2	when the **wicked** beareth rule, the people mourn.
Isa. 14:5	broken the staff of the **wicked**, and the sceptre of the
Isa. 14:20(19-23)	the seed of **evildoers** shall never be renowned.
Isa. 57:20	but the **wicked** are like the troubled sea, when it
Isa. 59:8	they have made them **crooked** paths: whosoever goeth the
Jer. 5:6(1-6)	their **transgressions** are many, and their backslidings
Jer. 5:26(25-29)	among my people are found **wicked** men: they lay wait
Jer. 6:7	so she casteth out her **wickedness**: violence and spoil
Jer. 12:1	wherefore doth the way of the **wicked** prosper
Ezek. 7:19	because it is the stumblingblock of their **iniquity**.
Ezek. 14:3(3-8)	put the stumblingblock of their **iniquity** before their
Ezek. 22:18(18-22,29)	the house of Israel is to me become **dross**: all they
Hosea 10:13(12-13)	ye have plowed **wickedness**, ye have reaped iniquity
Mark 7:22(20-23)	thefts, covetousness, **wickedness**, deceit
Luke 11:39	inward part is full of ravening and **wickedness**.
Acts 8:22	repent therefore of this thy **wickedness**, and pray God
Acts 25:5	accuse this man, if there be any **wickedness** in him.
Rom. 1:29(29-32)	filled with all unrighteousness...**wickedness**
Eph. 6:12	against spiritual **wickedness** in high places.
1 Jn. 5:19	and the whole world lieth in **wickedness**.
2 Ne. 24:5	broken the staff of the **wicked**, the scepters of the
2 Ne. 24:20(19-23)	the seed of **evil-doers** shall never be renowned.
Hel. 6:24(22-30)	be tried...according to the laws of their **wickedness**
D&C 6:26	records...kept back because of the **wickedness** of the
D&C 10:21	hearts are corrupt, and full of **wickedness** and
D&C 29:17	I will take vengeance upon the **wicked**, for they will
D&C 38:5(5,6)	residue of the **wicked**...kept in chains of darkness
D&C 61:8	that you might not perish in **wickedness**
D&C 68:31	their children are also growing up in **wickedness**; they
D&C 84:96	to scourge them for their **wickedness**.
D&C 88:85(84,85)	the desolation of abomination which awaits the **wicked**
D&C 98:9	nevertheless, when the **wicked** rule the people mourn.
D&C 133:14	the midst of **wickedness**, which is spiritual Babylon.
D&C 133:64(64-74)	all that do **wickedly**, shall be stubble; and the day
JFS-V 1:20(18-22)	but unto the **wicked** he did not go, and among the

WIDOWS

Gen. 38:8(8-10)	go in unto thy brother's **wife**, and marry her, and
Ex. 22:22	ye shall not afflict any **widow**, or fatherless child.
Deut. 25:5(5,6)	the **wife** of the dead shall not marry without unto a
Ruth 4:5(5-10)	Ruth the Moabitess, the **wife** of the dead, to raise up
Isa. 1:17	judge the fatherless, plead for the **widow**.
Jer. 49:11	preserve them alive; and let thy **widows** trust in me.
Luke 4:25	many **widows** were in Israel in the days of Elias, when
Acts 6:1	their **widows** were neglected in the daily ministration.
1 Cor. 7:8(8-9)	I say therefore to the unmarried and **widows**, it is
1 Tim. 5:3(3-16)	honour **widows** that are widows indeed.
James 1:27	to visit the fatherless and **widows** in their affliction
2 Ne. 19:17	neither shall have mercy on their fatherless...**widows**
2 Ne. 20:2	that **widows** may be their prey, and that they may rob
Mosiah 21:10(10,17)	now there were a great many **widows** in the land, and
Alma 28:5	yea, the cry of **widows** mourning for their husbands
Morm. 8:40	secret abominations..cause that **widows** should mourn
Moro. 9:16	there are many **widows** and their daughters who remain
D&C 83:6	**widows** and orphans shall be provided for, as also the
D&C 123:9	duty that we owe..to the **widows** and fatherless, whose
D&C 136:8	dividend of their property...the poor, the **widows**, the

WISDOM

Gen. 41:39	Pharaoh..unto Joseph...there is none so...**wise** as thou
Ex. 28:3	whom I have filled with the spirit of **wisdom**, that the
Ex. 31:3	filled him with the spirit of God, in **wisdom**, and in
Ex. 35:31	filled him with the spirit of God, in **wisdom**, in
Ex. 36:4(1-4)	**wise** men, that wrought all the work of the sanctuary
Deut. 4:6(5,6)	keep...and do them; for this is your **wisdom** and your
Job 28:28	the fear of the Lord, that is **wisdom**; and to depart
Job 32:8	inspiration of the Almighty giveth them **understanding**.
Ps. 19:7	testimony of the Lord is sure, making **wise** the simple.
Ps. 111:10	the fear of the Lord is the beginning of **wisdom**: a
Prov. 1:7	but fools despise **wisdom** and instruction.
Prov. 2:6(1-11)	for the Lord giveth **wisdom**: out of his mouth cometh
Prov. 3:13(13-20)	happy is the man that findeth **wisdom**, and
Prov. 3:35	the **wise** shall inherit glory: but shame shall be the
Prov. 4:7(1-13)	**wisdom** is the principal thing; therefore get wisdom
Prov. 8:11(1-36)	for **wisdom** is better than rubies; and all the things
Prov. 9:10	the fear of the Lord is the beginning of **wisdom**: and
Isa. 5:21(20-21)	woe unto them that are **wise** in their own eyes, and
Isa. 11:2	the spirit of the Lord...the spirit of **wisdom** and
Isa. 29:14	the **wisdom** of their wise men shall perish, and he
Dan. 2:21(20-21)	he giveth **wisdom** unto the wise, and knowledge to them
Dan. 12:3	and they that be **wise** shall shine as the brightness
Matt. 7:24(24-27)	whosoever heareth...doeth...liken him unto a **wise** man
Luke 21:15	for I will give you a mouth and **wisdom**, which all your
Rom. 16:19	I would have you **wise** unto that which is good, and
1 Cor. 1:17(17-31)	preach the gospel: not with **wisdom** of words, lest the
1 Cor. 2:7(4-7)	but we speak the **wisdom** of God in a mystery, even the
1 Cor. 3:19(18-21)	for the **wisdom** of this world is foolishness with God.
1 Cor. 12:8(7-11)	to one is given by the Spirit the word of **wisdom**; to

WISDOM cont.

Eph. 1:17	may give unto you the spirit of **wisdom** and revelation
Eph. 5:17	wherefore be ye not **unwise**, but understanding what the
Col. 4:5	walk in **wisdom** toward them that are without, redeeming
James 1:5(5-6)	if any of you lack **wisdom**, let him ask of God, that
James 3:17(13-18)	but the **wisdom** that is from above is first pure, then
2 Ne. 9:28(28-29)	when they are learned they think they are **wise**, and
2 Ne. 9:42(41-43)	the **wise**...who are puffed up because of their learning
2 Ne. 27:26	for the **wisdom** of their wise and learned shall perish
2 Ne. 28:30	they shall learn **wisdom**; for unto him that receiveth
Jacob 6:12	O be **wise**; what can I say more
Mosiah 2:17	I tell you these things that ye may learn **wisdom**; that
Alma 37:35	learn **wisdom** in thy youth; yea, learn in thy youth to
D&C 1:26(24-28)	as they sought **wisdom** they might be instructed
D&C 6:7	seek not for riches but for **wisdom**, and behold, the
D&C 10:43	my **wisdom** is greater than the cunning of the devil.
D&C 38:30	wherefore, treasure up **wisdom** in your bosoms, lest
D&C 52:17	bring forth fruits of praise and **wisdom**, according to
D&C 76:9(5-10)	and their **wisdom** shall be great, and their
D&C 78:2(1-2)	shall speak...the words of **wisdom**, that salvation may
D&C 88:40(36-40)	**wisdom** receiveth wisdom; truth embraceth truth
D&C 88:118	seek...and teach one another words of **wisdom**; yea
D&C 89:19	shall find **wisdom** and great treasures of knowledge
D&C 97:1(1-2)	many...are seeking diligently to learn **wisdom** and to
D&C 124:1	show forth my **wisdom** through the weak things of the
D&C 136:32(32-33)	learn **wisdom** by humbling himself..calling upon the Lord

WITNESS OF THE FATHER

Isa. 42:1	behold my **servant**, whom I uphold; mine elect, in whom
Matt. 3:17(16,17)	this is my **beloved** Son, in whom I am well pleased.
Matt. 12:18	my **beloved**, in whom my soul is well pleased: I will
Matt. 17:5	this is my **beloved** Son, in whom I am well pleased
John 5:37	the Father himself...hath borne **witness** of me. Ye have
John 6:45(44-46)	man..that..hath learned of the **Father**, cometh unto me.
John 8:18(16-19)	the Father that sent me beareth **witness** of me.
John 12:28(28-30)	a **voice** from heaven, saying, I have both glorified it
2 Pet. 1:17(17,18)	this is my **beloved** Son, in whom I am well pleased.
2 Pet. 1:18(16-18)	this **voice** which came from heaven we heard, when we
1 Jn. 5:9	**witness** of God which he hath testified of his Son.
Jacob 4:13(12,13)	God also **spake** them unto prophets of old.
3 Ne. 11:7(3-8)	behold my **Beloved** Son, in whom I am well pleased, in
3 Ne. 21:3(1-4)	made **known** unto them of the Father, and shall come
D&C 93:15(14-17)	this is my **beloved** Son.
Moses 4:2	behold, my Beloved **Son**, which was my Beloved and
JS-H 1:17	This is My **Beloved** Son. Hear Him

WITNESSES

Num. 35:30	put to death by the mouth of **witnesses**: but one
Deut. 17:6(6,7)	at the mouth of two **witnesses**, or three witnesses
Matt. 10:32(32,33)	whosoever...**confess** me before men, him will I confess

WITNESSES cont.

Matt. 16:17(15-19)	flesh and blood hath not **revealed** it unto thee, but
Matt. 18:16	mouth of two or three **witnesses** every word may be
Luke 24:48(39-48)	and ye are **witnesses** of these things.
John 5:32(31-46)	I know that the **witness** which he witnesseth of me is
John 8:17(12-19)	that the **testimony** of two men is true.
John 15:27	ye also shall bear **witness**, because ye have been with
Acts 1:22	ordained to be a **witness** with us of his resurrection.
Acts 2:32	Jesus hath God raised up, whereof we all are **witnesses**
Acts 3:15	God hath raised from the dead...we are **witnesses**.
Acts 4:20(19,20)	we cannot but speak...which we have **seen** and heard.
Acts 4:33	apostles **witness** of the resurrection of the Lord Jesus
Acts 5:32(29-33)	we are his **witnesses**...so is also the Holy Ghost
Acts 10:39(39-44)	and we are **witnesses** of all things which he did both
Rom. 8:16	the Spirit itself beareth **witness** with our spirit
2 Cor. 13:1	in the mouth of two or three **witnesses** shall every
Heb. 9:17(16-17)	for a **testament** is of force after men are dead
Heb. 10:15	the Holy Ghost also is a **witness** to us: for after that
2 Pet. 1:16(16-19)	we...were **eyewitnesses** of his majesty.
1 Jn. 1:3(1-3)	that which we have **seen** and heard declare we unto you
1 Jn. 4:14	we have seen and do **testify** that the Father sent the
1 Jn. 5:9	the witness of men, the **witness** of God is greater: for
Rev. 11:3	and I will give power unto my two **witnesses**, and they
2 Ne. 11:3	God sendeth more **witnesses**, and he proveth all his
2 Ne. 18:2(1,2)	I took unto me faithful **witnesses** to record, Uriah the
2 Ne. 27:14(12-14)	as many **witnesses** as seemeth him good will he
2 Ne. 27:22(22,23)	obtained the **witnesses** which I have promised unto thee
Jacob 4:6(3-6)	having all these **witnesses** we obtain a hope, and our
Mosiah 2:14(14-17)	ye yourselves are **witnesses** this day.
Mosiah 7:21(20-22)	ye all are **witnesses** this day, that Zeniff, who was
Mosiah 18:9(9-16)	to stand as **witnesses** of God at all times and in all
Mosiah 24:14(12-16)	that ye may stand as **witnesses** for me hereafter, and
Mosiah 26:9(7-11)	there were many **witnesses** against them; yea, the
Alma 14:11	blood of the innocent shall stand as a **witness** against
Alma 30:45(43-45)	yet will ye deny against all these **witnesses**? And he
Alma 34:8	I will **testify** unto you of myself that these things
Alma 34:30	after ye have **received** so many witnesses, seeing that
Alma 34:33(31-36)	as ye have had so many **witnesses**, therefore, I beseech
Alma 47:33(32,33)	that he should bring **witnesses** with him to testify
Ether 5:4(1-6)	in the mouth of three **witnesses** shall these things be
Moro. 6:7(6-9)	and three **witnesses** of the church did condemn them
D&C 14:8	stand as a **witness** of the things of which you shall
D&C 17:3	with your eyes, you shall **testify** of them, by the
D&C 27:12	apostles...especial **witnesses** of my name, and bear the
D&C 42:80	two **witnesses** of the church, and not of the enemy; but
D&C 76:22(22,23)	this is the **testimony**, last of all, which we give of
D&C 107:23(23,25)	special **witnesses** of the name of Christ in all the
D&C 128:3(1-5)	in the mouth of two or three **witnesses** every word may

WOMAN

God created man...male and **female** created he them.
woman, because she was taken out of man.
thou shalt not uncover the nakedness of a **woman** and
if a man...lie with mankind, as he lieth with a **woman**
if a **woman** also vow a vow unto the Lord, and bind hers
Deborah, a **prophetess**...judged Israel at that time.
blessed above **women** shall Jael the wife of Heber the
but king Solomon loved many strange **women**, together
Shunem, where was a great **woman**; and she constrained
upon them there, and pain, as of a **woman** in travail.
to keep thee from the evil **woman**, from the flattery
a foolish **woman** is clamourous: she is simple, and
a gracious **woman** retaineth honour: and strong men
a virtuous **woman** is a crown to her husband: but she
every wise **woman** buildeth her house: but the foolish
give not thy strength unto **women**, nor thy ways to that
who can find a virtuous **woman**? for her price is far
bitter than death the **woman**, whose heart is snares and
as for my people...**women** rule over them. O my people
rise up, ye **women** that are at ease; hear my voice, ye
can a **woman** forget her sucking child, that she should
called thee as a **woman** forsaken and grieved in spirit
call for the mourning **women**, that they may come; and
hands of..pitiful **women** have sodden their own children
whosoever looketh on a **woman** to lust after her hath
them that are born of **women** there hath not risen a
many **women** were there beholding afar off, which
the Lord is with thee: blessed art thou among **women**.
blessed art thou among **women**, and blessed is the
there was one Anna, a **prophetess**, the daughter of
a **woman**...brought an alabaster box of ointment
Jesus saith...**woman**, what have I to do with thee? mine
brought unto him a **woman** taken in adultery; and when
he saith unto his mother, **woman**, behold thy son
Dorcas: this **woman** was full of good works and
women did change the natural use into that which is
head of the **woman** is the man; and the head of Christ
let your **women** keep silence in the churches: for it
his Son, made of a **woman**, made under the law
women adorn themselves in modest apparel, with
the younger **women** marry, bear children, guide the
lead captive silly **women** laden with sins, led away
holy **women**...who trusted in God, adorned themselves
husbands...**wife**...being heirs together of the grace
were not defiled with **women**; for they are virgins
our **women** did bear children in the wilderness.
and our **women** have toiled, being big with child; and
for can a **woman** forget her sucking child, that she
Lord God, delight in the chastity of **women**.
women should spin, and toil, and work, and work all
woman, there has not been such great faith among all
the **woman** servant who had caused the multitude to be
there was not a **woman** nor a child among all the

491

WOMAN cont.

WORD OF WISDOM

WORK, VALUE OF

WORK, VALUE OF cont.

Rom. 2:10 — glory, honour...to every man that **worketh** good, to the
Eph. 4:28 — steal no more: but rather let him **labour**, working with
1 Thes. 2:9 — **labouring**...because we would not be chargeable unto
1 Thes. 4:11(11-12) — to **work** with your own hands, as we commanded you
2 Thes. 3:8 — wrought with **labour**...that we might not be chargeable
2 Ne. 5:17 — I, Nephi, did cause my people to be **industrious**, and
2 Ne. 9:51 — do not spend..your **labor** for that which cannot
Jacob 1:19 — by **laboring** with our might their blood might not come
Mosiah 2:14(14-18) — I, myself, have **labored** with mine own hands that I
Mosiah 10:5(1-5) — spin, and toil, and **work**...and thus did we prosper in
Mosiah 23:5(1-5) — they were **industrious**, and did labor exceedingly.
Mosiah 27:5 — priests and teachers should **labor**...for their support
Alma 10:4 — also acquired much riches by the hand of my **industry**.
Alma 36:25(24,25) — exceeding great joy in the fruit of my **labors**
D&C 42:42 — idle shall not eat the bread...of the **laborer**.
D&C 58:27(26-29) — men should be anxiously **engaged** in a good cause, and
D&C 68:30(30-32) — shall remember their **labors**...in all faithfulness; for
D&C 72:17(17-19) — received as a wise steward and as a faithful **laborer**
D&C 82:18 — that every man may **gain** other talents, yea, even an
Moses 1:39 — this is my **work** and my glory- to bring to pass the
JS-H 1:55 — by continuous **labor**...enabled to get a comfortable

WORLD

Ps. 22:27 — all the ends of the **world** shall remember and turn unto
Ps. 98:9(7-9) — with righteousness shall he judge the **world**, and the
Isa. 13:11(9-13) — I will punish the **world** for their evil, and the wicked
Isa. 62:11 — proclaimed unto the end of the **world**, say ye to the
John 1:10 — he was in the **world**, and the world was made by him
John 3:16(16,17) — for God so loved the **world**, that he gave his Only
John 8:23 — ye are of this **world**; I am not of this world.
John 15:19(18,19) — if ye were of the **world**, the world would love his own
John 16:33 — in the **world** ye shall have tribulation: but be of
John 17:15(13-18) — I pray not that thou...take them out of the **world**, but
John 18:36(36,37) — Jesus answered, my kingdom is not of this **world**: if
Rom. 12:2(1-2) — be not conformed to this **world**: but be ye transformed
1 Cor. 3:19(18-23) — for the wisdom of this **world** is foolishness with God.
1 Cor. 6:2 — saints shall judge the **world**? and if the world shall
Heb. 6:5(4-6) — and have tasted...the powers of the **world** to come
James 4:4 — friendship of the **world** is enmity with God? whosoever
1 Jn. 2:15(15,16) — love not the **world**, neither the things that are in the
1 Jn. 3:1 — **world** knoweth us not, because it knew him not.
2 Ne. 9:30 — who are rich as to the things of the **world**.
2 Ne. 27:10 — from the foundation of the **world** unto the end thereof.
2 Ne. 27:23 — I will show unto the **world** that I am the same
Jacob 6:3 — and the **world** shall be burned with fire.
Mosiah 16:9(8,9) — he is the light and the life of the **world**; yea, a
Alma 5:57 — come ye out from the **wicked**, and be ye separate, and
Alma 11:40 — he shall come into the **world** to redeem his people; and
Hel. 5:9 — Christ...cometh to redeem the **world**.
3 Ne. 27:16(13-18) — that day when I shall stand to judge the **world**.
Morm. 7:7 — brought to pass the redemption of the **world**, whereby

WORLD cont.

Morm. 9:22	go ye into all the **world**, and preach the gospel to
Ether 4:12	the light, and the life, and the truth of the **world**.
Ether 4:14	laid up for you, from the foundation of the **world**; and
Ether 8:7	set his heart...upon the glory of the **world**.
D&C 4:4	behold the **field** is white already to harvest; and lo
D&C 10:70	him who is the life and light of the **world**, your
D&C 18:6	behold, the **world** is ripening in iniquity; and it must
D&C 19:1(1-3)	I am...the Redeemer of the **world**.
D&C 21:9	crucified...for the sins of the **world**, yea, for the
D&C 25:10	thou shalt lay aside the things of this **world**, and see
D&C 49:20	the **world** lieth in sin.
D&C 53:2	a commandment that you shall forsake the **world**.
D&C 84:53	the whole **world** groaneth under sin and darkness even
D&C 84:75	revelation...in force... upon all the **world**, and the
D&C 95:13	not...live after the manner of the **world**
D&C 101:36	in this **world** your joy is not full, but in me your joy
D&C 121:32	that which was ordained...before this **world** was, that
D&C 127:11	the prince of this **world** cometh, but he hath nothing
Moses 1:33(33-35)	and **worlds** without number have I created; and I also

WORLD, END OF

Ps. 50:3(3-6)	our God shall come...a **fire** shall devour before him
Isa. 4:4(3-4)	Lord shall have washed...purged...by **burning**.
Isa. 5:30	the **light** is darkened in the heavens thereof.
Isa. 10:22(22-23)	the **consumption** decreed shall overflow with
Isa. 13:9(9-13)	he shall **destroy** the sinners thereof out of it.
Isa. 28:22	a **consumption**, even determined upon the whole earth.
Isa. 34:5(1-5)	my sword...shall come down upon **Idumea**, and upon the
Isa. 65:17	a new earth: and the **former** shall not be remembered
Ezek. 35:15	shalt be desolate...all **Idumea**, even all of it: and
Ezek. 38:22(16-22)	rain, and great hailstones, **fire**, and brimstone,
Joel 2:30(28-32)	wonders in...heavens...earth, blood, and **fire**, and
Joel 3:15	the **sun** and the moon shall be darkened, and the stars
Zeph. 1:15(14-18)	a day of wasteness and **desolation**, a day of darkness
Zeph. 2:3(1-3)	be hid in the **day** of the Lord's anger.
Zeph. 3:8(6-9)	the **earth** shall be devoured with the fire of my
Mal. 3:2	he is like a refiner's **fire**, and like fullers' soap
Mal. 4:1(1-3)	the day cometh, that shall **burn** as an oven; and all
Matt. 13:40(38-43)	fire; so shall it be in the **end** of this world.
Matt. 13:49(49,50)	at the **end** of the world...sever the wicked from among
Matt. 24:3(3-51)	sign of thy coming, and of the **end** of the world
Matt. 28:20(19-20)	I am with you alway, even unto the **end** of the world.
Mark 13:25(24-37)	**stars** of heaven shall fall, and the powers that are
2 Thes. 1:8(7,8)	in flaming **fire** taking vengeance on them that know not
2 Pet. 3:10(10-13)	the **elements** shall melt with fervent heat, the earth
1 Jn. 2:17(15-17)	the world **passeth** away, and the lust thereof: but he
Rev. 6:12(12-13)	**sun** became black...moon became as blood
Rev. 21:1	the first heaven and the first **earth** were passed away
2 Ne. 20:22	the **consumption** decreed shall overflow with
2 Ne. 23:10(9-13)	stars...not give light...**sun**...be darkened...moon...no
2 Ne. 27:7	from the beginning of the world to the **ending** thereof.

WORLD, END OF cont.

Jacob 5:77   my vineyard will I cause to be **burned** with fire.
Jacob 6:3(2-3)   and the world shall be burned with **fire**.
3 Ne. 26:3(3-4)   even until the elements should **melt** with fervent heat
Morm. 9:2   the **earth** shall be rolled together as a scroll, and
D&C 1:36(36,38)   come down in judgment upon **Idumea**, or the world.
D&C 19:3(2-3)   destroying of Satan..his works at the **end** of the world
D&C 29:14(8-24)   before this great day...**signs** in heaven above and in
D&C 29:23(8-24)   the heaven and the **earth** shall be consumed and pass
D&C 43:31(26-33)   little season, and then cometh the **end** of the earth.
D&C 45:22(22,23)   ye say that ye know that the **end** of the world cometh
D&C 63:21(20-21)   the earth shall be **transfigured**, even according to the
D&C 64:24(23-24)   after today cometh the **burning**- this is speaking after
D&C 87:6   consumption decreed hath made a full **end** of all
D&C 88:26(17-26)   notwithstanding it shall **die**, it shall be quickened
D&C 97:23(22-26)   the Lord's **scourge** shall pass over by night and by day
D&C 101:25(23-25)   fervent **heat**; and all things shall become new, that
JS-M 1:4   sign...of the **end** of the world, or the destruction of
JS-M 1:55   the **end** of the earth is not yet, but by and by.
JS-H 1:37(37-39)   the day cometh that shall **burn** as an oven, and all the

WORLDLINESS

Job 21:7(7-17)   wherefore do the wicked live...are **mighty** in power
Ps. 37:1(1,7,35,36)   neither be thou **envious** against the workers of
Ps. 73:12(2-12)   these are the ungodly, who prosper in the **world**; they
Jer. 5:27(27,28)   they are become **great**, and waxen rich.
Mal. 3:15   they that work **wickedness** are set up; yea, they that
Matt. 6:24(19-33)   two masters...ye cannot serve God and **mammon**.
Matt. 13:22   and the care of this **world**...choke the word, and he
Matt. 16:26   is a man profited, if he shall gain the whole **world**
Matt. 24:38   before the **flood** they were eating and drinking
Luke 8:14   choked with **cares** and riches and pleasures of this
Luke 21:34   lest...hearts be overcharged with...**cares** of this life
John 14:30   prince of this **world** cometh, and hath nothing in me.
John 15:19(17-19)   if ye were of the **world**, the world would love his own
John 16:33   in the **world** ye shall have tribulation: but be of
John 17:16(9-18)   they are not of the **world**, even as I am not of the
Rom. 12:2   and be not conformed to this **world**: but be ye
1 Cor. 1:20(20-21)   God made foolish the wisdom of this **world**
1 Cor. 3:19(18-19)   the wisdom of this **world** is foolishness with God.
1 Cor. 7:31   the fashion of this **world** passeth away.
2 Cor. 4:4   God of this **world** hath blinded the minds of them which
Eph. 2:2   ye walked according to the course of this **world**
Col. 2:8   man spoil you...after the rudiments of the **world**, and
Col. 3:2   affection on things above, not...on the **earth**.
2 Tim. 4:10   Demas...having loved this present **world**, and is
Titus 2:12   denying ungodliness and **worldly** lusts, we should live
James 1:27   keep himself unspotted from the **world**.
James 4:4   the friendship of the **world** is enmity with God?
1 Jn. 2:15(15-17)   love not...the things that are in the **world**. If any
1 Jn. 4:5(3-6)   they are of the **world**: therefore speak they of the
2 Ne. 9:28(28-30)   when they are **learned** they think they are wise, and

WORLDLINESS cont.

2 Ne. 9:42(42-43)	wise...who are puffed up because of their **learning**
2 Ne. 28:8(8,11-16)	eat, drink, and be **merry**; nevertheless, fear God- he
Jacob 2:18(18,19)	but before ye seek for **riches**, seek ye for the kingdom
Mosiah 3:19	for the **natural** man is an enemy to God, and has been
Alma 4:8(6-9)	set their hearts...upon the vain things of the **world**
Alma 5:37	O ye workers of iniquity; ye that are **puffed** up in the
Alma 5:57	come ye out from the **wicked**, and be ye separate, and
Alma 31:27(24-28)	puffed up...with the vain things of the **world**.
D&C 1:16(15-16)	they seek not the Lord...and shall perish in **Babylon**
D&C 6:7	seek not for **riches** but for wisdom, and behold, the
D&C 25:10	lay aside the things of this **world**, and seek for the
D&C 53:2	a commandment that you shall forsake the **world**.
D&C 121:35(34-37)	their hearts are set...upon the things of this **world**
D&C 133:5(5-7,14)	go ye out from **Babylon**. Be ye clean that bear the

WORSHIP

Gen. 22:5(5-13)	Abraham said..I and the lad will go yonder and **worship**
Ex. 20:3(3-5)	thou shalt have no other **gods** before me.
Ex. 32:31(1-8,19-35)	this people have sinned...have made them **gods** of gold.
Deut. 6:13(13,14)	thou shalt **fear** the Lord thy God, and serve him, and
Deut. 10:12(12,13,20)	to **serve** the Lord thy God with all thy heart and with
Ps. 95:6(6,7)	let us **worship** and bow down: let us kneel before the
Ps. 99:9	exalt the Lord our God, and **worship** at his holy hill
Ps. 138:2(1,2)	I will **worship** toward thy holy temple, and praise thy
Isa. 2:8(8,18-22)	they **worship** the work of their own hands, that which
Isa. 29:13(13-14)	this people...have removed their **heart** far from me
Isa. 46:6(5-11)	they fall down, yea, they **worship**.
Matt. 2:2(1-10)	have seen his star...come to **worship** him.
Matt. 4:10(1-11)	it is written, thou shalt **worship** the Lord thy God
Luke 4:8(3-8)	thou shalt **worship** the Lord thy God, and him only
John 4:23(20-24)	**worship** the Father in Spirit and in truth: for the
Acts 17:25(22-25)	neither is **worshipped** with men's hands, as though he
Philip. 3:3	which **worship** God in the Spirit, and rejoice in Christ
Heb. 1:6(5-7)	and let all the angels of God **worship** him.
Rev. 3:9(7-9)	I will make them to come and **worship** before thy feet
Rev. 13:4(3-4)	they **worshipped** the beast, saying, who is like unto
Rev. 14:7(6-7)	**worship** him that made heaven, and earth, and the sea
Rev. 19:10	I fell at his feet to **worship** him. And he said unto
1 Ne. 17:55(53-55)	**worship** the Lord thy God, and honor thy father and thy
1 Ne. 21:7	kings shall...arise, princes also shall **worship**
2 Ne. 9:37	wo unto those that **worship** idols, for the devil of all
2 Ne. 25:29	**worship** him with all your might, mind, and strength
Jacob 4:5(4,5)	they believed in Christ and **worshiped** the Father in
Alma 15:17(16-18)	assemble...at their sanctuaries to **worship** God before
Alma 31:12(12-24)	did **worship** after a manner which Alma...had never
Alma 32:5(5,10-12)	we have no place to **worship** our God; and behold, wha
Alma 33:3(3-11)	prophet of old, has said concerning prayer or **worship**
Alma 34:38	**worship** God, in whatsoever place ye may be in, in
Alma 43:10(9-10)	whosoever should **worship** God in Spirit and in truth
Alma 50:39(39,40)	grant...them their sacred privileges to **worship** the
3 Ne. 11:17	fall down at the feet of Jesus, and did **worship** him.

WORSHIP cont.

D&C 18:40	you shall fall down and **worship** the Father in my name.
D&C 20:19(17-19,29)	he should be the only being whom they should **worship**.
D&C 42:35(34,35)	and building houses of **worship**, and building up of the
D&C 59:5	in the name of Jesus Christ thou shalt **serve** him.
D&C 59:10(8-12)	day appointed..to pay thy **devotions** unto the Most High
D&C 76:21(20,21)	who **worship** him forever and ever.
D&C 93:19(1-19)	know how to **worship**, and know what you worship, that
D&C 115:8	command...to build a house...that they may **worship** me.
D&C 133:39(38-39)	**worship** him that made heaven, and earth, and the sea
D&C 134:4(4,6)	human law...interfere in prescribing rules of **worship**
Moses 1:15	**worship** God, for him only shalt thou serve.
Moses 5:5	them commandments, that they should **worship** the Lord
Moses 6:49	Satan...tempteth them to **worship** him; and men have
Abr. 1:17(5-17)	because they have turned their **hearts** away from me
A of F 1:11	let them **worship** how, where, or what they may.
JFS-V 1:24(23,24)	they **sang** praises unto his holy name.
JFS-V 1:39(38,39)	who had...**worshiped** the true and living God.

WORTH OF SOULS

Gen. 18:24(24-33)	**spare** the place for the fifty righteous...therein
Ps. 8:5(4-6)	thou hast made him a little lower than the **angels**, and
Ps. 49:8	(for the redemption of their **soul** is precious, and it
Isa. 13:12	I will make a man more **precious** than fine gold; even
Jonah 4:11(9-11)	should not I spare...**persons** that cannot discern
Matt. 18:11(11-13)	the Son of man is come to **save** that which was lost.
Luke 9:56(54-56)	not come to destroy men's lives, but to **save** them.
Luke 15:10(7-32)	there is joy...over one **sinner** that repenteth.
John 3:16	for God so **loved** the world, that he gave his Only
Mosiah 25:11	filled with pain...for the welfare of their **souls**.
Mosiah 28:3	they could not bear that any human **soul** should perish
Alma 24:14	he loveth our **souls** as well as he loveth our children
Alma 31:35	their **souls** are precious, and many of them are our
Alma 39:17	is not a **soul** at this time as precious unto God as a
D&C 7:4(2-5)	he desired of me that he might bring **souls** unto me
D&C 15:6	of the most worth...that you may bring **souls** unto me
D&C 18:10(10-13)	remember the **worth** of souls is great in the sight of
D&C 18:13	how great is his joy in the **soul** that repenteth
D&C 18:15	one **soul** unto me, how great shall be your joy with him
D&C 101:37	care not for the body...but care for the **soul**, and for
D&C 109:43	their **souls** are precious before thee

WORTHINESS

Gen. 32:10(9,10)	I am not **worthy** of the least of all the mercies, and
Ezra 2:62(61-62)	were they, as **polluted**, put from the priesthood.
Neh. 7:64(63-65)	were they, as **polluted**, put from the priesthood.
Ps. 18:3(1-3)	I will call upon the Lord, who is **worthy** to be praised
Ps. 25:3	let none that wait on thee be **ashamed**: let them be
Matt. 3:11	mightier than I, whose shoes I am not **worthy** to bear
Matt. 10:38(34-39)	he that taketh not his cross...is not **worthy** of me.

WORTHINESS cont.

Luke 3:8(7,8)	bring forth therefore fruits **worthy** of repentance, and
Luke 15:21(11-32)	I have sinned...am no more **worthy** to be called thy son
Luke 21:36(34-36)	pray always, that ye may be accounted **worthy** to escape
1 Cor. 6:9(9-10)	the **unrighteous** shall not inherit the kingdom of God
Eph. 4:1(1-3)	walk **worthy** of the vocation wherewith ye are called
Eph. 5:5	nor unclean person...hath any **inheritance** in the
Col. 1:10(7-14)	that ye might walk **worthy** of the Lord unto all
2 Thes. 1:11(7-12)	that our God would count you **worthy** of this calling
1 Pet. 5:10(8-10)	make you **perfect**, stablish, strengthen, settle you.
Rev. 3:4(2-5)	they shall walk with me in white: for they are **worthy**.
Rev. 5:2	who is **worthy** to open the book, and to loose the seal
Mosiah 4:29(29-30)	I cannot tell...all....whereby ye may commit **sin**; for
Alma 36:5(1-5)	not of any **worthiness** of myself.
Morm. 9:29(27-29)	do all things in **worthiness**, and do it in the name of
Moro. 6:1(1-3)	forth fruit meet that they were **worthy** of it.
Moro. 7:59	are not **fit** to be numbered among the people of his
Moro. 10:32	be **perfected** in him, and deny yourselves of all
D&C 38:8	he that is not **purified** shall not abide the day.
D&C 59:4(1-4)	they that are **faithful** and diligent before me.
D&C 76:116(114-118)	God bestows on those who...**purify** themselves before
D&C 84:33	whoso is **faithful**...are sanctified by the Spirit unto
D&C 85:11(11-12)	to have been **cut** off from the church, as well as the
D&C 88:86	let your hands be **clean**, until the Lord comes.
D&C 93:1	who forsaketh his **sins**...shall see my face and know
D&C 95:5(5-6)	whom I have called but few of them are **chosen**.
D&C 105:35	and let those be chosen that are **worthy**.
D&C 107:100(99-100)	slothful shall not be counted **worthy** to stand, and he

ZEAL

Num. 25:13(10-13)	he was **zealous** for his God, and made an atonement for
2 Kgs. 19:31(30,31)	the **zeal** of the Lord of hosts shall do this.
Ps. 69:9(8-9)	the **zeal** of thine house hath eaten me up; and the
Ps. 119:139(137-139)	my **zeal** hath consumed me, because mine enemies have
Isa. 9:7(6-7)	the **zeal** of the Lord of hosts will perform this.
Isa. 37:32(31-32)	the **zeal** of the Lord of hosts shall do this.
John 2:17(13-17)	the **zeal** of thine house hath eaten me up.
Acts 18:25(24-25)	this man was...**fervent** in the spirit, he spake and
Acts 21:20(17-20)	Jews...which believe...they are all **zealous** of the law
Acts 22:3	I...was **zealous** toward God, as ye all are this day.
Rom. 10:2(1-4)	they have a **zeal** of God, but not according to
Rom. 12:11(10-11)	not slothful in business; **fervent** in spirit; serving
Gal. 1:14(13-17)	exceedingly **zealous** of the traditions of my fathers.
Gal. 4:18(17-18)	good to be **zealously** affected always in a good thing
Col. 4:13(12-13)	he hath a great **zeal** for you, and them that are in
Titus 2:14(13-14)	purify...a peculiar people, **zealous** of good works.
Heb. 2:1	we ought to give the more **earnest** heed to the things
Jude 1:3	ye should **earnestly** contend for the faith which was
Mosiah 27:35(34-35)	**zealously** striving to repair all the injuries which
Alma 21:23	they were **zealous** for keeping the commandments of God.
Alma 27:27(26-30)	they were...distinguished for their **zeal** towards God
D&C 58:27(26-29)	men should be **anxiously** engaged in a good cause, and

ZEAL cont.

ZION

ZION cont.

2 Ne. 28:21(2-26)	all is well in **Zion**; yea, Zion prospereth, all is well
3 Ne. 21:1(1-29)	I shall...establish again among them my **Zion**
3 Ne. 21:23(20-26)	build a city, which shall be called the **New** Jerusalem.
4 Ne. 1:17(15-18)	but they were in **one**, the children of Christ, and heir
Ether 13:4(2-11)	Ether..spake concerning a **New** Jerusalem upon this land
Moro. 10:31(31-33)	daughter of **Zion**; and strengthen thy stakes and
D&C 6:6(6-9)	keep my commandments ...establish the cause of **Zion**
D&C 11:6(6-9)	seek to bring forth and establish the cause of **Zion**.
D&C 38:4	I...have taken the **Zion** of Enoch into mine own bosom
D&C 42:35(34-36,62)	and building up of the **New** Jerusalem which is
D&C 45:12(11-14)	a **city** reserved until a day of righteousness shall
D&C 45:66(64-67)	**New** Jerusalem...a place of safety for the saints of
D&C 45:68(68-71)	every man that will not take his sword..flee unto **Zion**
D&C 52:42(42-43)	land of **Missouri**, which is the land of your
D&C 57:2(1-3)	land of promise, and the place for the city of **Zion**.
D&C 58:7(6-14)	the land upon which the **Zion** of God shall stand
D&C 58:49(49-57)	an agent...to receive moneys to purchase lands in **Zion**
D&C 63:25(24-31)	land of **Zion**- I, the Lord, hold it in mine own hands
D&C 64:41(41-43)	**Zion** shall flourish, and the glory of the Lord shall
D&C 76:66(62-70)	these are they who are come unto mount **Zion**, and unto
D&C 78:5(3-12)	that you may be **equal** in the bonds of heavenly things
D&C 84:2(2-4)	mount **Zion**, which shall be the city of New Jerusalem.
D&C 90:36(34-37)	I, the Lord, will contend with **Zion**, and plead with
D&C 97:21	for this is **Zion**- the pure in heart; therefore, let
D&C 97:25(22-28)	**Zion** shall escape if she observe to do all things what
D&C 100:13	**Zion** shall be redeemed, although she is chastened for
D&C 101:17(1-101)	**Zion** shall not be moved out of her place
D&C 103:18(16-34)	as your fathers were led...redemption of **Zion** be.
D&C 105:5(5,32)	**Zion** cannot be built up unless it is by the principles
D&C 105:32(9-34)	kingdom of **Zion** is in very deed the kingdom of our God
D&C 107:49(48-49)	and he saw the Lord, and he **walked** with him, and was
D&C 109:51	thou didst appoint a **Zion** unto thy people.
D&C 113:8(7-10)	the power of priesthood to bring again **Zion**, and the
D&C 115:6(5-8)	gathering together upon the land of **Zion**, and upon her
D&C 133:9(2-59)	that **Zion** may go forth unto the regions round about.
D&C 133:13	unto the **mountains** of the Lord's house.
D&C 133:24	Jerusalem...**Zion** shall be turned back into...own place
D&C 133:32(25-34)	fall down and be crowned with glory, even in **Zion**, by
D&C 133:56	he shall stand upon mount **Zion**, and upon the holy city
D&C 136:31	prepared to receive...the glory of **Zion**; and he that
Moses 7:18(17-31)	Lord called his people **Zion**...they were of one heart
Moses 7:21(17-31)	**Zion**, in process of time, was taken up into heaven.
Moses 7:62(62-64)	and it shall be called **Zion**, a New Jerusalem.
A of F 1:10	**Zion** will be built upon this the American continent